# HUMAN GEOGRAPHY

11TH EDITION

## PEOPLE, PLACE, AND CULTURE

Erin H. Fouberg

Northern State University

Alexander B. Murphy

University of Oregon

H. J. de Blij

Michigan State University

WILEY

| | |
|---|---|
| Vice President & Publisher | Petra Recter |
| Executive Editor | Ryan Flahive |
| Assistant Editor | Julia Nollen |
| Editorial Assistant | Kathryn Hancox |
| Senior Content Manager | Kevin Holm |
| Senior Production Editors | Jackie Henry |
| Marketing Manager | Suzanne Bochet |
| Senior Photo Editor | Billy Ray |
| Production Services | Aptara |
| Cover & Interior Designer | Wendy Lai |
| Front Cover Photo | Alexander B. Murphy |
| Back Cover Photo | Left: Sam W Stearman/Moment/Getty Images |
| | Right: © Dori Moreno/Gallo Images/Getty Images |
| Market Development Manager | Robert Johnston |

This book was set in Jansen by Aptara, Inc., and printed and bound by Courier/Kendallville. The cover was printed by Courier/Kendallville.

This book is printed on acid-free paper. ∞

AP® is a trademark registered and/or owned by the College Board, which was not involved in the production of, and does not endorse, this product.

Founded in 1807, John Wiley & Sons, Inc. has been a valued source of knowledge and understanding for more than 200 years, helping people around the world meet their needs and fulfill their aspirations. Our company is built on a foundation of principles that include responsibility to the communities we serve and where we live and work. In 2008, we launched a Corporate Citizenship Initiative, a global effort to address the environmental, social, economic, and ethical challenges we face in our business. Among the issues we are addressing are carbon impact, paper specifications and procurement, ethical conduct within our business and among our vendors, and community and charitable support. For more information, please visit our website: www.wiley.com/go/citizenship.

AP Edition ISBN   978-1-119-04314-0

Printed in the United States of America

10 9 8 7 6 5 4 3 2

The noted geographer Yi-Fu Tuan once said, "People make places." People create cultures, values, aesthetics, politics, economics, and more, and each of these affects and shapes places. Places do not exist in a vacuum, as places are constantly being changed from within and in the context of the broader world. The study of human geography constantly reminds us of how people shape their world and of how people and places vary across space.

People build homes and buildings, establish economic and political systems, interact with one other, construct cultures, and shape physical environments. In the process they create and transform places. On the front cover, the floating village on the shores of Southeast Asia's largest freshwater lake, the Tonlé Sap in Cambodia, represents an extraordinary human adaption to a lake that rises and falls by as much as eight meters (26 feet) between the wet and dry seasons. For more than a thousand years, people have lived in floating villages and in homes built on stilts, drawing their living by fishing in the lake.

Just a short drive north, more than 1.5 million tourists visit the temple of Angkor Wat each year. Built by the Khmer Empire as a Hindu temple in the tenth century, designs on walls in the temple complex show people fishing in the Tonlé Sap. A later emperor converted to Buddhism and transformed Angkor Wat into a Buddhist temple. Empires shifted again, and the site of Angkor Wat was covered by forests by early 1500. When Europeans came to Southeast Asia in the centuries after 1500, some heard about the massive temple complex and followed local guides through the dense forest to the site.

In the 1990s Cambodia emerged from a period of great political and social upheaval, and the country was opened to tourists who began to flock to see Angkor Wat. The nearby city of Siem Reap now houses more than 170 hotels. The 30 most luxurious are in particularly high demand as Westerners, Japanese, South Koreans, and a growing number of Chinese tour the region. Every morning, tourists come in droves to witness the remarkable sunrise at Angkor Wat, each trying to capture the perfect photo, as the back cover illustrates. After visiting the temple, some choose to journey south to the shores of Tonlé Sap, where they now find children in floating villages selling trinkets and holding snakes in the hope of being photographed for money.

Tourism is an aspect of globalization that is changing places in dramatic ways. In the Eleventh Edition of *Human Geography: People, Place, and Culture*, students will learn to appreciate the pace of change unfolding in the wake of globalization and to expand their understanding of the causes and consequences of the deepening interconnections among places.

Through this course in human geography, and with the help of this book, students will learn to appreciate the types of changes taking place and to think critically about what they see, read, and hear about their world. Globalization factors heavily into the many ways people influence places. Globalization is a set of processes that flow and pulsate across and through country boundaries with varying outcomes in different places and across scales. Improvements in transportation and communication allow ideas and people to move quickly, creating an environment suitable for change.

Our goals in writing the Eleventh Edition of *Human Geography: People, Place, and Culture* were, first, to help students appreciate the diversity of the planet and the role people play in shaping that diversity; second, to provide context for the issues we address so that students can better understand their world; third, to give students the tools to grapple with the complexities of globalization; and fourth, to help students think geographically and critically about their world.

Sadly, Harm de Blij, the book's originator, died shortly before we began work on this edition. We experienced a great sense of loss in planning, researching, and writing without him, but we were buoyed by the extensive collaborations we had with Harm through the years. One of us (Erin) studied with Harm as an undergraduate and became a co-author of this book beginning with the Eighth Edition. The other of us (Alec) became a co-author on the Sixth Edition and worked with Harm on a variety of professional matters. We both had the opportunity to soak up Harm's extraordinary passion for geography, and we continue to draw inspiration from someone who was truly a master of his craft. We dedicate this edition to Harm.

## THE ADVANCED PLACEMENT® EDITION OF THE BOOK

In the late 1990s, co-author Alexander B. Murphy led the campaign to add human geography to the College Board's Advanced Placement® (AP®) Program. *Human Geography: People, Place and Culture* and John Wiley & Sons have supported students and instructors in AP® Human Geography since the very beginning by offering high-quality content and pedagogy that help teachers teach and students learn the concepts, ideas, and terms that they need to perform at the college level. With the Eleventh Edition of *Human Geography*, we continue that legacy of support by offering a special AP® version of the book, along with a revised AP® Student Study Guide and new student resources on the student companion website.

Students who are taking AP® Human Geography can use the "Thinking Geographically" questions found at the end of each section in each chapter as practice for the Free Response Questions (FRQs) on the AP® exam. The 2013 AP® Human Geography exam asked students to compare and contrast Rostow and Wallerstein's theories, which was the second "Thinking Geographically" question in Chapter 10 in the Tenth Edition of *Human Geography: People, Place, and Culture*. Use the "Thinking Geographically" questions to test whether you can define key concepts and models, compare and contrast related concepts and similar models, and use specific examples or case studies to demonstrate the concepts and models. We wrote more detailed captions for maps and photographs in the Eleventh Edition to help students learn to see patterns on maps and recognize geographic concepts in photographs. Several of the captions ask readers to compare and contrast maps, which will help prepare students for FRQs and multiple-choice questions (MCQs) on the AP® exam. Key geographic concepts are defined and explained with examples and context throughout the book, which will help students understand rather than simply memorize geographic concepts that appear in the MCQs.

With the needs of AP® instructors and teachers in mind, we have highlighted a few key issues that are often emphasized on AP® exams. We expanded our coverage of basic concepts such as central place theory. We developed boxes setting forth classic geographic approaches to understanding the political organization of space and the spatial organization of cities, and we evaluate the relevance of these approaches today. We brought in new material on subjects that receive attention in AP® Human Geography outlines, including human trafficking and refugees, threats to human health, biotechnology, genetically modified organisms, impacts of new extractive industries, fair trade movement, development of the galactic city, role of social networks and opinion leaders in the diffusion of popular culture, global sourcing and flexible production of goods, location theory, first mover advantages in new technologies, and interface areas in religion (including a case study on Boko Haram in Nigeria). We also included new graphics that help illustrate core geographic concepts and ideas. Our 3-D models of the spatial organization of cities in in Southeast Asia, Latin America, and Subsaharan Africa will help students quickly grasp the types of urban arrangements that are characteristic of different world regions. Our maps and case studies of Ikea and Nike in the production and distribution of goods will help students better understand theories in economic geography.

## NEW IN THE ELEVENTH EDITION

In writing the Eleventh Edition of *Human Geography: People, Place, and Culture*, we developed a new layout in an effort to promote the book's visual appeal and to facilitate the integration of text, photos, and illustrations. Our goals are to help students understand the role people play in shaping the world, to provide geographic context to the issues we discuss, to teach students to think geographically and critically, and to explain how the complexities of globalization are changing the planet. As in past editions, we drew from our own field experiences as well as the research and fieldwork of hundreds of others in an effort to enrich the text.

The Eleventh Edition of *Human Geography* includes significant revision to and reorganization of the material on population (Chapter 2), popular culture (Chapter 4), political geography (Chapter 8), urban geography (Chapter 9), agriculture (Chapter 11), industry and services (Chapter 12), and the humanized environment (Chapter 13). We also updated examples throughout the book to relate to the existing body of knowledge many college students have before taking human geography. Drawing from current research in human geography, we expanded the number of terms and concepts covered to include the young and old-age dependency ratios, the proto-Eurasiatic linguistic hypothesis, galactic cities, urbicide, economies of scale, first mover advantage, location theory, global sourcing, flexible production, global social networks, and opinion leaders.

The field notes in the Eleventh Edition provide context and help the reader learn to think geographically. As in the past, each chapter in this edition starts with an *opening field note*, written by one of us, which describes an experience from the field and pulls the reader into the chapter. Several of the opening field notes in the Eleventh Edition are new.

Each chapter also includes one or more *author field notes*, in addition to the opening field note. The author field notes serve as models of how to think geographically. We took a significant majority of the approximately 200 photographs in this edition. In addition to the author field notes, we include a number of *guest field notes* written by geographers who have spent time in the field, researching a place that they profile. All guest field notes include a photograph and a paragraph focusing on how the guest field note author's observations in the field influenced his or her research.

In the Eleventh Edition, we continue to offer "Key Questions" and "Thinking Geographically" prompts to promote learning. The Key Questions are listed after the opening field note of each chapter and serve as the outline for the chapter. After each Key Question is answered in the chapter, the reader will find a Thinking Geographically prompt. These prompts ask the reader to apply a geographic concept to a real-life example. Readers who complete the Thinking Geographically prompts will learn to think geographically and to think critically. Instructors can also use the Thinking Geographically prompts as lecture launchers and as the basis for class discussions.

## THE TEACHING AND LEARNING PACKAGE

The Eleventh Edition of *Human Geography: People, Place, and Culture* is supported by a comprehensive supplements package that includes an extensive selection of print, visual, and electronic materials.

AP® is a trademark registered and/or owned by the College Board, which was not involved in the production of, and does not endorse, this product.

## Resources That Help Teachers Teach

**Geography On-Location Videos.** Because of their enduring popularity, we have digitized many of the videos from the original series. This rich collection of original and relevant footage was taken during H. J. de Blij's travels. The videos cover a wide range of themes and are available on the companion websites.

**The *Human Geography: People, Place, and Culture* Instructor Companion Website.** This comprehensive website includes numerous resources to help you enhance your current presentations, create new presentations, and employ our premade PowerPoint presentations. Resources include the following:

- **Image Gallery.** We provide online electronic files for the line illustrations and maps in the book, which the instructor can customize for presenting in class.

- A complete collection of **PowerPoint presentations.** These presentations are available in beautifully rendered, four-color format, and images are sized and edited for maximum effectiveness in large lecture halls. The high-resolution photos, maps, and figures provide a set of strong, clear images that are ready to be projected in the classroom.

- A comprehensive **Test Bank** includes multiple-choice, fill-in-the-blank, matching, and essay questions. The Test Bank is available on the secure Instructor's website as electronic files and can be saved into all major word-processing programs.

- A comprehensive collection of **animations and videos.**

- **ConceptCaching.com** is an online collection of photographs that explores places, regions, people, and their activities. Photographs, GPS coordinates, and explanations of core geographic concepts are "cached" for viewing by professors and students alike. Professors can access the images or submit their own by visiting the website.

**Wiley Faculty Network.** This peer-to-peer network of faculty is ready to support your use of online course management tools and discipline-specific software/learning systems in the classroom. The Wiley Faculty Network will help you apply innovative classroom techniques, implement software packages, and tailor the technology experience to the needs of each individual class, and will provide you with virtual training sessions led by faculty for faculty.

**Course Management.** Online course management assets are available to accompany the Eleventh Edition of *Human Geography: People, Place, and Culture.*

## Resources That Help Students Learn

**Student Companion Website.** The easy-to-use and student-focused website helps reinforce and illustrate key geographic concepts. It also provides interactive media content to prepare for tests. This website provides additional resources to complement the book and enhance student understanding of geography:

- **Videos** provide a first-hand look at life in other parts of the world.

- **Map Quizzes** help students master the place-names that are building blocks for their success in this course. Three game-formatted place-name activities are provided for each chapter.

- **Chapter Review Quizzes** provide immediate feedback to true/false, multiple-choice, and short-answer questions.

- **Annotated Web Links** put useful electronic resources into context.

- **Area and Demographic Data** are provided for every country and world region.

- **ConceptCaching.com** is an online collection of photographs that explores places, regions, people, and their activities. Photographs, GPS coordinates, and explanations of core geographic concepts are "cached" for viewing by professors and students alike. Professors can access the images or submit their own by visiting the website.

**AP® Study Guide** to Accompany Human Geography: People, Place, and Culture, 11th Edition. Written by Greg Sherwin and Paul Gray, this study guide introduces students to the AP® Human Geography Course, provides them with reading strategies, activities and study tools along with a practice AP® exam.

To learn more about resources accompanying the AP® Edition of *Human Geography: People, Place and Culture 11th Edition*, please contact your Wiley High School Solutions representative at WileyHSAP@Wiley.com or 1-855-827-4630.

## ACKNOWLEDGMENTS

In preparing the Eleventh Edition of *Human Geography*, we benefited immensely from the advice and assistance of many of our colleagues in geography. We thank AP® Human Geography teachers, professors, instructors, and students from around the country who emailed us questions and gave us suggestions. Some told us of their experiences using other editions, and others provided insightful comments on individual chapters. The list that follows acknowledges their support, but it cannot begin to measure our gratitude for all of the ways they helped shape this book:

| | |
|---|---|
| Ian Ackroyd-Kelly | *East Stroudsburg University* |
| Frank Ainsley | *University of North Carolina, Wilmington* |
| Jennifer Altenhofel | *California State University, Bakersfield* |
| Charles Amissah | *Hampton University* |
| Alan Arbogast | *Michigan State University* |
| James Ashley | *University of Toledo* |
| Scharmaistha Bagchi-Sen | *SUNY Buffalo* |
| Nancy Bain | *Ohio University* |

| | |
|---|---|
| Brad Bays | Oklahoma State University |
| Sarah W. Bednarz | Texas A&M University |
| Sari Bennett | University of Maryland, Baltimore County |
| J. Best | Frostburg State University |
| Brian Blouet | College of William & Mary |
| Mark Bockenhauer | St. Norbert College |
| Margaret Boorstein | C.W. Post College of Long Island University |
| Patricia Boudinot | George Mason University |
| Michael Broadway | Northern Michigan University |
| Michaele Ann Buell | Northwest Arkansas Community College |
| Scott Carlin | Long Island University |
| Fiona M. Davidson | University of Arkansas |
| L. Scott Deaner | Owens Community College |
| Evan Denney | University of Montana |
| Ramesha Dhussa | Drake University |
| Dimitar Dimitrov | Virginia Commonwealth University |
| Dawn Drake | University of Tennessee, Knoxville |
| Steve Driever | University of Missouri, Kansas City |
| Anna Dvorak | West Los Angeles College |
| James Dyer | Mount St. Mary's College |
| Adrian X. Esparza | University of Arizona |
| Stephen Frenkel | University of Washington, Seattle |
| Juanita Gaston | Florida A&M University |
| Matthew J. Gerike | Kansas State University |
| Lay James Gibson | University of Arizona |
| Sarah Goggin | Santa Ana College |
| Abe Goldman | University of Florida |
| Richard Grant | University of Miami |
| Alyson Greiner | Oklahoma State University |
| Jeffrey A. Gritzner | University of Montana |
| Qian Guo | Northern Michigan University |
| John Heppen | University of Wisconsin, River Falls |
| John Hickey | Inver Hills Community College |
| Miriam Helen Hill | Jacksonville State University |
| Peter R. Hoffmann | Loyola Marymount University |
| Peter Hugill | Texas A&M University |
| Francis Hutchins | Bellarmine University |
| Jay Johnson | University of Nebraska, Lincoln |
| Tarek A. Joseph | Central Michigan University |
| Melinda Kashuba | Shasta College |
| Artimus Keiffer | Wittenberg University |
| Les King | McMaster University |
| Paul Kingsbury | Miami University, Ohio |
| Frances Kostarelos | Governors State University |
| Darrell P. Kruger | Illinois State University |
| Paul Larson | Southern Utah University |
| Jess A. Le Vine | Brookdale Community College |
| Ann Legreid | Central Missouri State University |
| Jose Lopez | Minnesota State University |
| David Lyons | University of Minnesota, Duluth |
| Patricia Matthews-Salazar | Borough of Manhattan Community College |
| Darrell McDonald | Stephen F. Austin State University |
| Wayne McKim | Towson University |
| Ian MacLachlan | University of Lethbridge |
| Glenn Miller | Bridgewater State College |
| Katharyne Mitchell | University of Washington, Seattle |
| John M. Morris | University of Texas, San Antonio |
| Garth A. Myers | University of Kansas |
| Darrell Norris | SUNY Geneseo |
| Ann Oberhauser | West Virginia University |
| Kenji Oshiro | Wright State University |
| Bimal K. Paul | Kansas State University |
| Gene Paull | University of Texas at Brownsville |
| Daniel R. Pavese | Wor-Wic Community College |
| Walter Peace | McMaster University |
| Sonja Porter | Central Oregon Community College |
| Virginia Ragan | Maple Woods Community College |
| Jeffrey Richetto | University of Alabama |
| Rob Ritchie | Liberty University |
| Mika Roinila | State University of New York, New Paltz |
| Karl Ryavec | University of Wisconsin |
| James Saku | Frostburg State University |
| Richard Alan Sambrook | Eastern Kentucky University |
| Joseph E. Schwartzberg | University of Minnesota |
| Allen Scott | University of California Los Angeles |
| Gary W. Shannon | University of Kentucky |
| Betty Shimshak | Towson University |
| Nancy Shirley | Southern Connecticut State University |
| Susan Slowey | Blinn College |
| Andrew Sluyter | Pennsylvania State University |
| Janet Smith | Shippensberg University |
| Herschel Stern | Mira Costa College |
| Neva Duncan Tabb | University of South Florida |
| Thomas Terich | Western Washington University |
| Donald Thieme | Georgia Southern University |
| James A. Tyner | University of Southern California |
| David Unterman | Sierra and Yuba Community Colleges |
| Barry Wauldron | University of Michigan, Dearborn |
| David Wishart | University of Nebraska, Lincoln |

| George W. White | South Dakota State University |
| Leon Yacher | Southern Connecticut State University |
| Donald Zeigler | Old Dominion University |
| Robert C. Ziegenfus | Kutztown University |

In the Eleventh Edition, several of our colleagues in geography provided guest field notes. The stories these colleagues tell and the brilliant photos they provide will help students better appreciate the role of fieldwork in geographic research:

| Jonathan Leib | Old Dominion University |
| Korine Kolivras | Virginia Tech |
| Elsbeth Robson | Keele University |
| Jason Dittmer | University College London |
| Steven M. Schnell | Kutztown University of Pennsylvania |
| Richard Francaviglia | Geo. Graphic Designs |
| Ines Miyares | Hunter College of the City University of New York |
| Sarah Halvorson | University of Montana |
| Derek Alderman | University of Tennessee |
| Mary Lee Nolan | Oregon State University |
| Paul Gray | Russellville High School |
| George White | South Dakota State University |
| Johnathan Walker | James Madison University |
| Rachel Silvey | University of Toronto |
| Judith Carney | University of California, Los Angeles |
| Fiona M. Davidson | University of Arkansas |
| William Moseley | Macalester College |
| Kenneth E. Foote | University of Connecticut |

On a day-to-day basis, many people in the extended John Wiley & Sons family provided support and guidance. We thank Vice President and Publisher Petra Recter for her guidance with this edition of *Human Geography*. Ryan Flahive, Executive Editor for Geography, is a champion of geography, and we are fortunate to work with such a knowledgeable and involved editor. In 2014, the National Council for Geographic Education recognized Ryan Flahive with a well-deserved Presidential Award for his contributions to geography. Kathryn Hancox, Editorial Assistant, organized reviews and oversaw the art manuscripts, which helped us meet several deadlines along the way. Darnell Sessoms, Permissions Editor, tracked down sources around the world to obtain permissions for the Tenth Edition, and he continued his work on permissions with the Eleventh Edition, enabling us to create several new maps and diagrams for this edition. Julia Nollen, Assistant Editor, also organized reviews and helped get the revisions started for this edition. Billy Ray, Photo Editor, gleaned from our sometimes cryptic descriptions the visions we had for several new photos, and his ability to find beautiful images to meet our specifications directly benefits students, as each picture demonstrates geographic concepts and patterns

to a T. Don Larson, Terry Bush, and Beth Robertson from Mapping Specialists are outstanding cartographers who used their design aesthetic and skills in cartography and GIS to update or create more than 60 maps and figures in this edition. We owe a special debt of gratitude to Paula Robbins at Mapping Specialists who researched and hand-drew three-dimensional models of cities for Chapter 9. Her painstaking attention to detail makes the Latin American, Subsaharan African, and Southeast Asian city models come to life. We benefited from two exceptional Production Editors on this edition. Janet Foxman gracefully kept us on track with a tight schedule. Jackie Henry juggled the production of two titles simultaneously and was indispensable to Erin in keeping the book on schedule. Betty Pessagno, Copy Editor, gave careful attention to each word in the book and thoughtful feedback. Katrina Avery, Copy Editor, demonstrated incredible attention to detail, which benefited every chapter of the book. Kim Johnson researched and provided data for dozens of new and revised maps and figures. Marketing Manager Suzanne Bochet worked with the author team to translate our vision for *Human Geography: People, Place, and Culture* into an effective marketing message.

We thank Erin's writing mentor, David Wishart of the University of Nebraska-Lincoln, whose suggestions are found in many new topics discussed in the Eleventh Edition. We thank Paul Gray and Greg Sherwin, both AP Human Geography teachers, whose constructive reviews and feedback helped us plan portions of the content and the mapping program for this edition. Erin appreciates the support and ideas shared by geography educators at the National Council for Geographic Education Conference, as their passion for teaching students and their excitement for the field of human geography inspired her to find new ways to explain several complicated geographic concepts in the Eleventh Edition. Erin also thanks Tino Mendez for his unwavering support and encouragement and Julie Backous for her organizational skills and willingness to help. This edition also benefited greatly from research assistance and editorial input provided by Anna Moore, a doctoral student in geography at the University of Oregon, and by Richard Murphy, Alec's older son.

We are grateful to our family and friends who supported us faithfully through this edition. Special thanks from Erin to Maggie and Henry for tolerating the constant presence of her laptop, giving feedback on photo options and captions, and reading edits to explain what they took from different passages. As always, our greatest thanks go to our spouses, Robert Fouberg and Susan Gary, who through their support, understanding, and patience make us better people and better authors.

**Erin H. Fouberg**
Aberdeen, South Dakota

**Alexander B. Murphy**
Eugene, Oregon

# ABOUT THE AUTHORS

**ERIN HOGAN FOUBERG** grew up in eastern South Dakota. She moved to Washington, D.C., to attend Georgetown University's School of Foreign Service, where she took a class in Human Geography from Harm de Blij. At Georgetown, Erin found her International Relations classes lacking in context and discovered a keen interest in political geography. She earned her master's and Ph.D. at the University of Nebraska-Lincoln (1997). After graduating, Dr. Fouberg taught for several years at the University of Mary Washington in Fredericksburg, Virginia, where the graduating class of 2001 bestowed on her the Mary Pinschmidt Award, given to the faculty member who made the biggest impact on their lives.

Dr. Fouberg is Professor of Geography and Director of the Honors Program at Northern State University in Aberdeen, South Dakota, where she won the Outstanding Faculty Award in 2011. Her research and publications focus on the governance and sovereignty of American Indian tribes, geography education, and the geography of elections. Professor Fouberg served as Vice President of Publications and Products of the National Council for Geographic Education. Dr. Fouberg co-authors *Understanding World Regional Geography* with William G. Moseley, also published by Wiley. She is active in her community, serving leadership roles on the soccer board, PTA, and fundraising campaigns for children's charities. She enjoys traveling, reading, golfing, and watching athletic and theater events at Northern State.

**ALEC MURPHY** grew up in the western United States, but he spent several of his early years in Europe and Japan. He obtained his undergraduate degree at Yale University, studied law at the Columbia University School of Law, practiced law for a short time in Chicago, and then pursued a doctoral degree in geography (Ph.D. University of Chicago, 1987). After graduating, Dr. Murphy joined the faculty of the University of Oregon, where he is now Professor of Geography and holder of the James F. and Shirley K. Rippey Chair in Liberal Arts and Sciences. Professor Murphy is a widely published scholar in the fields of political, cultural, and environmental geography. His work has been supported by the National Science Foundation, the National Endowment for the Humanities, the Rockefeller Foundation, and the Fulbright-Hays foreign fellowship program.

Professor Murphy served as the President of the Association of American Geographers in 2003–2004. He is currently Senior Vice President of the American Geographical Society. In the late 1990s, he led the effort to add geography to the College Board's Advanced Placement Program. He recently chaired a National Academy of Sciences study charged with identifying strategic directions for the geographical sciences. In 2014 he received the Association of American Geographers' highest honor, its Lifetime Achievement Award. His interests include hiking, skiing, camping, music, and of course exploring the diverse places that make up our planet.

**HARM DE BLIJ** received his early schooling in Europe, his college education in Africa, and his higher degrees in the United States (Ph.D. Northwestern, 1959). He published more than 30 books and over 100 articles, and received five honorary degrees. Several of his books were translated into foreign languages.

Dr. de Blij held the position of John A. Hannah Professor of Geography at Michigan State University. He also held the George Landegger Chair at Georgetown University's School of Foreign Service, the John Deaver Drinko Chair of Geography at Marshall University, and faculty positions at the Colorado School of Mines and the University of Miami. He served as the Geography Editor on ABC-TV's "Good Morning America" program for seven years and later served as Geography Analyst for NBC News. He was for more than 20 years a member of the National Geographic Society's Committee for Research and Exploration and was the founding editor of its scholarly journal, *National Geographic Research*. In recognition of his service, he became an honorary lifetime member of the Society.

Professor de Blij was a renaissance man. He was a soccer fan, an avid wine collector, an amateur violinist, and an inveterate traveler.

We dedicate this book to

Harm de Blij:

colleague, friend, mentor,

and indefatigable

champion of geography

# BRIEF CONTENTS

# CONTENTS

# HUMAN GEOGRAPHY: People, Places, and Culture— Fouberg 11E AP® Edition Correlated to the AP® Human Geography Topic Outline

| | page reference |
|---|---|

## I. Geography: Its Nature and Perspectives

A. Geography as a field of inquiry — Ch. 1 pp. 1–28

B. Major geographical concepts underlying the geographical perspective: location, space, place, scale, pattern, nature, and society, regionalization, globalization, and gender issues — Ch. 1 pp. 5–10 and Ch. 14 pp. 119–142

C. Key geographical skills — Ch. 1 p. 11–13, pp. 18–22

  1. How to use and think about maps and geospatial data

  2. How to understand and interpret the implications of associations among phenomena in places

  3. How to recognize and interpret at different scales the relationships among patterns and processes

  4. How to define regions and evaluate the regionalization process

  5. How to characterize and analyze changing interconnections among places

D. Use of geospatial technologies, such as GIS, remote sensing, global positioning systems (GPS), and online maps — Ch. 1 pp. 13–17

E. Sources of geographical information and ideas: the field, census data, online data, aerial photography, and satellite imagery — Figures throughout the book (photos, charts, graphs and maps)

F. Identification of major world regions — See map available on the Student Companion Site

## II. Population & Migration

A. Geographical analysis of population — Ch. 2, pp. 36–77

  1. Density, distribution, and scale

  2. Implications of various densities and distributions

  3. Composition: age, sex, income, education, and ethnicity

  4. Patterns of fertility, mortality, and health

B. Population growth and decline over time and space — Ch. 2, pp. 37–59

  1. Historical trends and projections for the future

  2. Theories of population growth and decline, including the Demographic Transition Model

  3. Regional variations of demographic transition

  4. Effects of national population policies: promoting population growth in some countries or reducing fertility rates in others

  5. Environmental impacts of population change on water use, food supplies, biodiversity, the atmosphere, and climate

  6. Population and natural hazards: impacts on policy, economy, and society

C. Migration — Ch. 3, pp. 60–89

  1. Types of migration: transnational, internal, chain, step, seasonal agriculture (e.g., transhumance), and rural to urban

  2. Major historical migrations

  3. Push and pull factors, and migration in relation to employment and quality of life

  4. Refugees, asylum seekers, and internally displaced persons

  5. Consequences of migration: socioeconomic, cultural, environmental, and political; Immigration policies; remittances

## V. Agriculture, Food Production, and Rural Land Use

A. Development and diffusion of agriculture
   1. Neolithic Agricultural Revolution
   2. Second Agricultural Revolution
   3. Green Revolution
   4. Large-scale commercial agriculture and agribusiness

B. Major agricultural production regions
   1. Agricultural systems associated with major bioclimatic zones
   2. Variations within major zones and effects of markets
   3. Interdependence among regions of food production and consumption

C. Rural land use and settlement patterns
   1. Models of agricultural land use, including von Thünen's model
   2. Settlement patterns associated with major agriculture types: subsistence, cash cropping, Plantation, mixed farming, monoculture, pastoralism, ranching, forestry, fishing and aquaculture
   3. Land use/land cover change: irrigation, desertification, deforestation, wetland destruction, conservation efforts to protect or restore natural land cover, and global impacts
   4. Roles of women in agricultural production and farming communities

D. Issues in contemporary commercial agriculture
   1. Biotechnology, including genetically modified organisms (GMO)
   2. Spatial organization of industrial agriculture, including the transition in land use to large-scale commercial farming and factors affecting the location of processing facilities
   3. Environmental issues: soil degradation, overgrazing, river and aquifer depletion, animal wastes, and extensive fertilizer and pesticide use
   4. Organic farming, crop rotation, value-added specialty foods, regional appellations, fair trade, and eat-local-food movements
   5. Global food distribution, malnutrition, and famine

## VI. Industrialization and Economic Development

A. Growth and diffusion of industrialization
   1. The changing roles of energy and technology
   2. Industrial Revolution
   3. Models of economic development: Rostow's Stages of Economic Growth and Wallerstein's World Systems Theory
   4. Geographic critiques of models of industrial location: bid rent, Weber's comparative costs of transportation and industrial location in relation to resources, location of retailing and service industries, and local economic development within competitive global systems of corporations and finance

B. Social and economic measures of development
   1. Gross domestic product and GDP per capita
   2. Human Development Index
   3. Gender Inequality Index
   4. Income disparity and the Gini coefficient
   5. Changes in fertility and mortality
   6. Access to health care, education, utilities, and sanitation

C. Contemporary patterns and impacts of industrialization and development
   1. Spatial organization of the world economy
   2. Variations in levels of development (uneven development)
   3. Deindustrialization, economic restructuring, and the rise of service and high technology economies

4. Globalization, manufacturing in newly industrialized countries( NICs), and the international division of labor

5. Natural resource depletion, pollution, and climate change

6. Sustainable development

7. Government development initiatives: local, regional, and national policies

8. Women in development and gender equity in the workforce

## VII. Cities and Urban Land Use

A. Development and character of cities          Ch. 9, pp. 245–286

1. Origin of cities; site and situation characteristics

2. Forces driving urbanization

3. Borchert's epochs of urban transportation development

4. World cities and megacities

5. Suburbanization processes

B. Models of urban hierarchies; reasons for the distribution and size of cities    Ch. 9, pp. 260–261 and Ch. 3, pp. 69

1. Gravity model

2. Christaller's central place theory

3. Rank-size rule

4. Primate cities

C. Models of internal city structure and urban development: strengths and limitations of models    Ch. 9, pp. 262–269

1. Burgess concentric zone model

2. Hoyt sector model

3. Harris and Ullman multiple nuclei model

4. Galactic city model

5. Models of cities in Latin America, North Africa and the Middle East, Sub-Saharan Africa, East Asia and South Asia

D. Built environment and social space          Ch. 9, pp. 269–287

1. Types of residential buildings

2. Transportation and utility infrastructure

3. Political organization of urban areas

4. Urban planning and design (e.g., gated communities, New Urbanism, and smart-growth policies)

5. Census data on urban ethnicity, gender, migration, and socioeconomic status

6. Characteristics and types of edge cities: boomburgs, greenfields, uptowns

E. Contemporary urban issues          Ch. 9, pp. 269–287

1. Housing and insurance discrimination, and access to food stores

2. Changing demographic, employment, and social structures

3. Uneven development, zones of abandonment, disamenity, and gentrification

4. Suburban sprawl and urban sustainability problems: land and energy use, cost of expanding public education services, home financing and debt crises

5. Urban environmental issues: transportation, sanitation, air and water quality, remediation or brownfields, and farmland protection

*Source:* AP® Human Geography Course and Exam Descriptions, Effective Fall 2013.

Copyright © 2013 The College Board.

Reproduced with permission.  http://apcentral.collegeboard.com.

# INTRODUCTION TO HUMAN GEOGRAPHY

## Awakening to World Hunger

**D**ragging myself out of bed for a 9:00 A.M. lecture, I decide I need to make a stop at Starbucks. "Grande coffee of the day, please, and leave room for cream." I rub my eyes and look at the sign to see where my coffee was grown. Kenya. Ironically, I am about to lecture on Kenya's coffee plantations. Just the wake-up call I need.

When I visited Kenya in eastern Africa, I drove from Masai Mara to Kericho and I noticed that nearly all of the agricultural fields I could see were planted with coffee or tea (Fig. 1.1). I also saw the poor of Kenya, clearly hungry, living in substandard housing. I questioned, "Why do farmers in Kenya grow coffee and tea when they could grow food to feed the hungry?" Trying to answer such a question sheds light on the complexities of globalization. In a globalized world, connections are many and simple answers are few.

© H. J. de Blij

**■ Figure 1.1**
**Kericho, Kenya.** Tea plantations established by British colonists in western Kenya. The impact of colonialism was pervasive—not just on the political institutions and social relations, but on the landscape as well.

On its face, such a huge problem might seem easy to solve. Take the total annual food production in the world, divide it by the world's population, and we have plenty of food for everyone. Yet one-seventh of the world's population is seriously malnourished. The vast majority of the 1 billion malnourished people on Earth are women and children, who have little money and even less power.

Figure 1.2 shows how food consumption is currently distributed—unevenly. Comparing Figure 1.2 with Figure 1.3 shows that the wealthier countries also are the best fed and that Subsaharan Africa (the part of Africa south of the Sahara Desert) is currently in the worst position, with numerous countries in the highest categories of hunger and malnourishment.

The major causes of malnourishment are poverty (inability to pay for food), the failure of food distribution systems, and cultural and political practices that favor some groups over others. Where food does reach the needy, its price may be unaffordable. Two billion people subsist

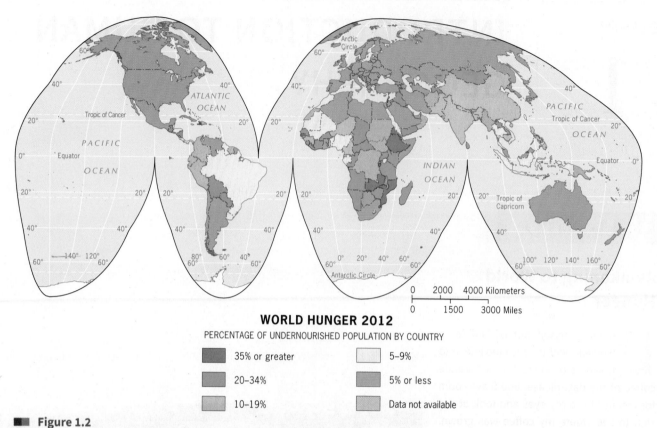

**■ Figure 1.2**

**World Food Program Hunger Map, 2012.**    Classifications designate the proportion of the population malnourished. The World Food Program estimates that just under one billion people worldwide are malnourished.    *Data from*: United Nations World Food Program 2012.

on the equivalent of two dollars a day, and many in the vast shantytowns encircling some of the world's largest cities must pay rent to landlords who own the plots on which their shacks are built. Too little is left for food, and it is the children who suffer most.

Is solving hunger as simple as each country growing enough food to feed its people? Do the best-fed countries have the most arable (farmable) land? Only 4 percent of Norway is arable land, and more than 70 percent of Bangladesh is arable land (Fig. 1.4). Despite this disparity, Norway is wealthy and well fed, whereas Bangladesh is poor and malnourished. Norway overcomes its inadequate food production by importing food. Bangladesh depends on rice as its staple crop, and the monsoon rains that flood two-thirds of the country each year during monsoon season are good for rice production, but they make survival a daily challenge for some.

If a poor country has a small proportion of arable land, does that destine its population to a lifetime of malnourishment? It depends on the place. Of all the land classified as arable, some is much more productive than others. For example, only 8 percent of Kenya's land is arable, but areas in the western highlands are some of the most productive agricultural land in the world. Do the Kenyans simply not produce enough food on their lands? Is that what accounts for their malnutrition rate of over 30 percent? No, hunger in Kenya depends much more on what it produces, who owns the land, and how Kenya is tied into the global economy.

Kenya's most productive lands, those in the western highlands, are owned by foreign coffee and tea corporations. Driving through the open, luxury-crop-covered slopes, I saw mostly Kenyan women working the plantations. The lowland plains are dotted by small farms, many of which have been subdivided to the point of making the land unviable. Here, an even higher proportion of the people working the lands are women, but the lands are registered to their husbands or sons because, by law, they cannot own them.

As I drove through the contrasting landscapes, I continued to question whether it would be better for the fertile highlands to carry food crops that could be consumed by the people in

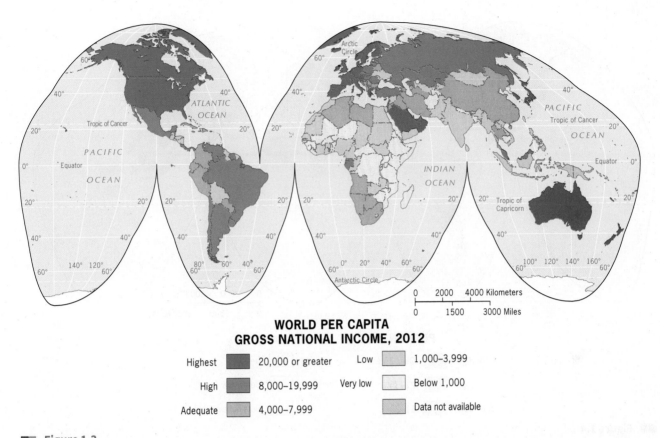

**WORLD PER CAPITA GROSS NATIONAL INCOME, 2012**

| | | | |
|---|---|---|---|
| Highest | 20,000 or greater | Low | 1,000–3,999 |
| High | 8,000–19,999 | Very low | Below 1,000 |
| Adequate | 4,000–7,999 | | Data not available |

**Figure 1.3**

**Per Capita Gross National Income (in U.S. Dollars) (GNI), 2012.**   From a socioeconomic standpoint, we live in an unequal world, but this map only shows the formal economy because the GNI per capita does not estimate the informal economy. Maps, like this, that shade each country a different color report data by country and tell us nothing about the variation within countries.   *Data from*: World Bank, World Development Indicators, 2012.

Kenya. I drove to the tea processing center and talked to the manager, a member of the Kikuyu ethnic group, and asked him my question. He said that his country needed foreign income and that apart from tourism, exporting coffee and tea was the main opportunity for foreign income.

As part of an increasingly globalized economy, Kenya suffers from the complexities of globalization. With foreign corporations owning Kenya's best lands, a globalized economy that thrives on foreign income, tiny farms that are unproductive, and a gendered legal system that disenfranchises the agricultural labor force and disempowers the caregivers of the country's children, Kenya has multiple factors contributing to poverty and malnutrition in the country. In addition to these structural concerns, Kenyan agro-pastoralists, especially in the northeast, have suffered higher rates of famine since a drought began in the region in 2006. Agro-pastoralists raise crops and have livestock; therefore, they struggle against drought as well as livestock diseases and political conflict.

To solve one of the structural problems in Kenya raises another. If Kenyans converted the richest lands to cash crop production, how would the poor people be able to afford the crops? What would happen to the rest of Kenya's economy and the government itself if it lost the export revenue from tea and coffee? If Kenya lost its export revenue, how could the country pay loans it owes to global financial and development institutions?

Answering each of these questions requires geographic inquiry because the answers are rooted in the characteristics of places and the connections those places have to other places. Moreover, geographic **fieldwork** can provide tremendous insights into such questions. Geographers have a long tradition of fieldwork. They go out in the field and see what people are doing, they observe how people's actions and reactions vary across space, and they develop maps and other visualizations that help them situate and analyze what they see. We, the authors,

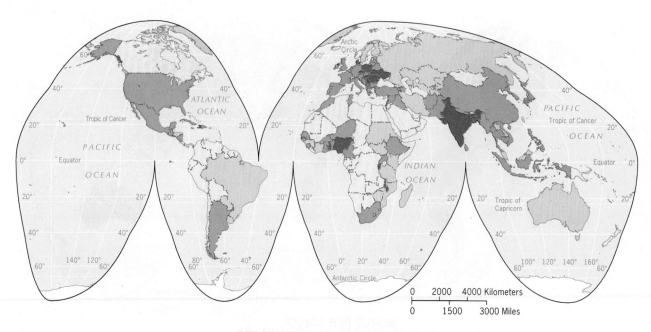

### PERCENTAGE OF ARABLE LAND

| | | | | |
|---|---|---|---|---|
| Very High | Over 35% | Low | 5–10% |
| High | 21–35% | Very low | Below 5% |
| Adequate | 11–20% | | Data not available |

■■ **Figure 1.4**

**Percent of Land that is Arable (Farmable), 2008.**   Arable land is an important resource for countries, but in our globalized world, many countries with limited land suitable for agriculture are able to import the food they need to feed their population.   *Data from*: United Nations Food and Agriculture Organization, 2011.

have countless field experiences, and we share many with you to help you understand the diversity of Earth's surface and show how global processes have unique outcomes in different places.

Solving major global problems such as hunger or HIV-AIDS is complicated in our interconnected world. Each solution has its own ramifications not only in one place, but also across regions, nations, and the world. Our goals in this book are to help you see the multitude of interconnections in our world, enable you to recognize the patterns of human geographic phenomena that shape the world, give you an appreciation for the uniqueness of place, and teach you to ask and answer your own geographic questions about this world we call home.

# Key Questions FOR CHAPTER 1

1. What is human geography?
2. What are geographic questions?
3. Why do geographers use maps, and what do maps tell us?
4. Why are geographers concerned with scale and connectedness?
5. What are geographic concepts, and how are they used in answering geographic questions?

## WHAT IS HUMAN GEOGRAPHY?

Human geographers study people and places. The field of **human geography** focuses on how people make places, how we organize space and society, how we interact with each other in places and across space, and how we make sense of others and ourselves in our localities, regions, and the world.

Advances in communication and transportation technologies are making places and people more interconnected. Only 100 years ago the fastest modes of transportation were the steamship, the railroad, and the horse and buggy. Today, people can cross the globe in a matter of days, with easy access to automobiles, high-speed railroads, airplanes, and ships.

Economic globalization and the rapid diffusion of elements of popular culture, including fashion and architecture, are making many people and places look more alike. Despite the push toward homogeneity, our world still encompasses a multitude of ways in which people identify themselves and others. The world consists of nearly 200 countries, a diversity of religions, thousands of languages, and a wide variety of settlement types, ranging from small villages to enormous global cities. All of these attributes come together in different ways around the globe to create a world of endlessly diverse places and people. Understanding and explaining this diversity is the mission of human geography.

Places all over the world are fundamentally affected by globalization. **Globalization** is a set of processes that are increasing interactions, deepening relationships, and accelerating interdependence across national borders. Globalization is also a set of outcomes that are felt from these global processes—outcomes that are unevenly distributed and differently manifested across the world.

All too often, discussions of globalization focus on the pull between the global, seen as a blanket covering the world, and the local, seen as a continuation of the traditional despite the blanket of globalization. Geographers are well placed to recognize globalization as something significantly more complex. Geographers employ the concept of "scale" to understand individual, local, regional, national, and global interrelationships. What happens at the global scale affects the local, but it also affects the individual, regional, and national, and similarly the processes at these scales influence the global. Reducing the world to "local" and "global" risks losing sight of the complexity that characterizes modern life. In this book, we study globalization, and as geographers we are sensitive to the fact that the same globalized process has different impacts in different places because no two places are the same. Moreover, whenever we look at something at one scale, we always try to think about how processes that exist at other scales may affect what we are looking at, and vice versa (see the discussion of scale later in this chapter).

Globalizing processes occur at the world scale; these processes bypass country borders and include global financial markets and global environmental change. However, the processes of globalization do not magically appear at the global scale: What happens at other scales (individual, local, regional, national) helps create the processes of globalization and shape the outcomes of globalization.

Some argue that the impacts of globalization are exaggerated, but as geographers Ron Johnston, Peter Taylor, and Michael Watts (2002) explain, "Whatever your opinion may be, any intellectual engagement with social change in the twenty-first century has to address this concept seriously, and assess its capacity to explain the world we currently inhabit." We integrate the concept of globalization into this textbook because processes at the global scale, processes that are not confined to local places or national borders, are clearly changing the human geography of the planet. At the same time, as we travel the world and continue to engage in fieldwork and research, we are constantly reminded of how different places and people are from one another—processes at the individual, local, regional, and national scales continue to change human geography and shape globalization.

No place on Earth is untouched by people. As people explore, travel, migrate, interact, play, live, and work, they make places. People organize themselves into communities, nations, and broader societal networks, establishing political, economic, religious, linguistic, and cultural systems that enable them to function in space. People adapt to, alter, manipulate, and cope with their physical geographic environment. No environment stands apart from human action. Each place we see is affected by and created by people, and each place reflects the culture of the people in that place over time.

Imagine and describe the most remote place on Earth you can think of 100 years ago. Now, describe how globalization has changed that place and how the people there continue to shape it and make it the place it is today.

## WHAT ARE GEOGRAPHIC QUESTIONS?

Geographers study human phenomena, including language, religion, and identity, as well as physical phenomena, including landforms, climate, and environmental change. Geographers also examine the interactions between humans and environment. Human geography is the study of the spatial and material characteristics of the human-made places and people, and **physical geography** is the study of spatial and material characteristics of physical environment. Human and physical geographers adopt a similar perspective but focus on different phenomena.

Geographer Marvin Mikesell once gave a shorthand definition of geography as the "why of where." Why and how do things come together in certain places to produce particular outcomes? Why are some things found in certain places but not in others? How do the characteristics of particular places shape what happens? To what extent do things in one place influence those in other places? To these questions, we add "so what?" Why do differences across geographic space matter? What role does a place play in its region and in the world, and what does that mean for people there and elsewhere? Questions like these are at the core of geographic inquiry—whether human or physical—and they are of critical importance in any effort to make sense of our world.

If geography deals with so many aspects of our world, ranging from people and places to coastlines and climates, what do the various facets of this wide-ranging discipline have in common? The answer lies in a perspective that both human and physical geographers bring to their studies: a spatial perspective. Whether they are human geographers or physical geographers, virtually all geographers are interested in the **spatial** arrangement of places and phenomena, how they are laid out, organized, and arranged on Earth, and how they appear on the landscape.

Mapping the **spatial distribution** of a phenomenon can be the first step to understanding it. By looking at a map of how something is distributed across space, a geographer can raise questions about how the arrangement came about, what processes create and sustain the particular distributions or **patterns**, and what relationships exist among different places and things.

## Maps in the Time of Cholera Pandemics

In **medical geography**, mapping the distribution of a disease is the first step to finding its cause. In 1854, Dr. John Snow, a noted anesthesiologist in London, mapped cases of cholera in London's Soho District.

Cholera is an ancient disease associated with diarrhea and dehydration. It was confined to India until the beginning of the nineteenth century. In 1816 it spread to China, Japan, East Africa, and Mediterranean Europe in the first of several **pandemics**, that is, worldwide outbreaks of the disease. This initial wave abated by 1823, but by then cholera was feared throughout the world, for it had killed people everywhere by the hundreds, even thousands. Death was horribly convulsive and would come in a matter of days, perhaps a week, and no one knew what caused the disease or how to avoid it.

Soon a second cholera pandemic struck. It lasted from 1826 to 1837, when cholera crossed the Atlantic and attacked North America. During the third pandemic, from 1842 to 1862, England was severely hit, and cholera again spread into North America.

When the pandemic that began in 1842 reached England in the 1850s, cholera swept through the Soho District of London. Dr. Snow mapped the Soho District, marking all the area's water pumps—from which people got their water supply for home use—with a P and marking the residence of each person who died from cholera with a dot (Fig. 1.5). Approximately 500 deaths occurred in Soho, and as the map took shape, Snow noticed that an especially large number of those deaths clustered around the water pump on Broad Street. At the doctor's request, city authorities removed the handle from the Broad Street pump, making it impossible to get water from it. The result was dramatic: Almost immediately the number of reported new cases fell to nearly zero, confirming Snow's theory about the role of water in the spread of cholera.

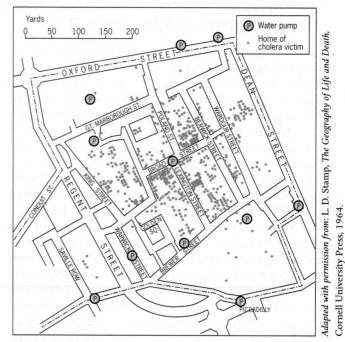

*Adapted with permission from: L. D. Stamp, The Geography of Life and Death, Cornell University Press, 1964.*

■ **Figure 1.5**

**Deaths from Cholera in the Soho District of London, England, 1854.** Dr. Snow mapped the deaths caused by cholera in the Soho neighborhood of London along with the locations of the water pumps and noticed a spatial correlation. Most of the deaths were clustered around a single water pump. As Dr. Snow's experience showed, maps are not just attractive or interesting representations of the world; they also help us understand and confront problems.

Dr. Snow and his colleagues advised people to boil their water, but it would be a long time before his advice reached all those who might be affected, and in any case many people simply did not have the ability to boil water or wash hands with soap.

Cholera has not been defeated completely, and in some ways the risks have been rising in recent years rather than falling (Fig. 1.6). People contract cholera by eating food or water contaminated with cholera bacteria. Cholera bacteria diffuse to broader areas because once one person has cholera it can be spread via his or her feces. In an impoverished area with no sanitary sewer system, the person's feces can easily contaminate the water supply. Even in places with sanitary sewer systems, cholera contamination occurs when rivers, which are typically the water supply, flood the sanitary sewer system.

We expect to find cholera in places that lack sanitary sewer systems and in places that are flood prone. In many of the teeming shantytowns of the growing cities of the developing world, and in some of the refugee camps of Africa and Asia, cholera remains a threat. Until the 1990s, major outbreaks remained few and limited. After remaining cholera-free for a half century, Europe had its first reappearance of cholera in Naples in 1972. In 2006, a cholera outbreak in Angola, in southern Africa, spread quickly throughout the country. When heavy rains came to West Africa in 2010, an outbreak of cholera killed 1500 people in Nigeria alone.

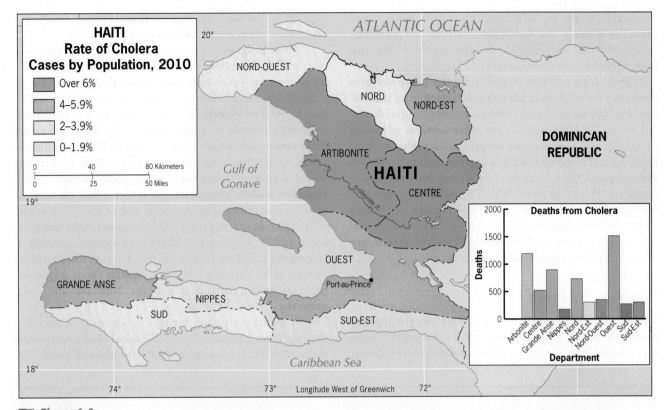

**■ Figure 1.6**

**Cholera in Haiti, 2010.** Artibonite and Centre departments were hit hard by a cholera outbreak in Haiti just after the 2010 earthquake, in part because the Artibonite River is contaminated by cholera bacteria and also because a large number of Haitians displaced from Port-au-Prince fled to camps in Artibonite and Centre. *Data from*: Centers for Disease Control, 2011. http://www.bt.cdc.gov/situationawareness/haiticholera/map_1.asp.

A cholera outbreak in the slums of Lima, Peru, in January 1991 became a fast-spreading **epidemic** (regional outbreak of a disease) that touched every country in the Americas, infected more than 1 million people, and killed over 10,000 in the region. The outbreak in Peru began when ocean waters warmed off the coast. Cholera bacteria live on plankton in the ocean, and the warming of the ocean allowed both the plankton and cholera to multiply. Fish ate the plankton, and people ate raw fish, thus bringing cholera to Peru.

In the slums of Peru, the disease diffused quickly. The slums are densely populated and lack a sanitary sewer system large enough to handle the waste of the population. An estimated 14 million Peruvians were infected with cholera, 350,000 were hospitalized, and 3500 Peruvians died during the outbreak in the 1990s. Peruvians who accessed health care received clean water, salts, and antibiotics, which combat the disease.

In January 2010, an earthquake that registered 7.0 on the Richter scale hit Haiti, near the capital of Port au Prince. Months later there was a cholera outbreak in the Artibonite region of Haiti (Fig. 1.6). Health officials are not certain exactly how cholera reached Haiti, but the disease diffused quickly through refugee camps and by October 2010 reached the capital city of Port au Prince. Scientists worry that the cholera outbreak in Haiti will be long lasting because the bacteria have contaminated the Artibonite River, which is the water supply for a large region. Although purifying water through boiling and thoroughly washing hands prevents the spread of cholera,

water contaminated with cholera and a lack of access to soap abound in many neighborhoods of world cities. A vaccine exists, but its effectiveness is limited, and it is costly. Dr. Snow achieved a victory through the application of geographical reasoning, but the war against cholera is not yet won.

The fruits of geographical inquiry were lifesaving in Snow's case, and the example illustrates the general advantage that comes from looking at the geographic context of events and circumstances. Geographers want to understand how and why places are similar or different, why people do different things in different places, and how the relationship between people and the physical world varies across space.

## The Spatial Perspective

Geographic literacy involves much more than memorizing places on a map. Place locations are to geography what dates are to history. History is not merely about memorizing dates. To understand history is to appreciate how events, circumstances, and ideas came together at particular times to produce certain outcomes. Knowledge of how events have developed over time is thought to be critical to understanding who we are and where we are going.

Understanding change across space is equally important to understanding change over time. The great German philosopher Immanuel Kant argued that we need disciplines focused not only on particular phenomena (such as economics and sociology), but also on the perspectives of time (history) and space (geography). The disciplines of history and geography have intellectual cores defined by these perspectives rather than being confined to a subject matter.

Human geographers employ a **spatial perspective** as they study a multitude of phenomena ranging from political elections and urban shantytowns to gay neighborhoods and folk music. To bring together the many subfields of human geography and to explain to nongeographers what geographers do, four major geographical organizations in the United States formed the Geography Educational National Implementation Project in the 1980s. The National Geographic Society published their findings in 1986, introducing the **five themes** of geography: location, human–environment interactions, region, place, and movement. The five themes are derived from geography's spatial concerns.

## THE FIVE THEMES

The first theme, **location**, highlights how the geographical position of people and things on Earth's surface affects what happens and why. A concern with location underlies almost all geographical work, for location helps to establish the context within which events and processes are situated.

Some geographers develop elaborate (often quantitative) models describing the locational properties of particular phenomena—even predicting where things are likely to occur. Such undertakings have fostered an interest in **location theory**, an element of contemporary human geography that seeks answers to a wide range of questions, some of them theoretical, others highly practical: Why are villages, towns, and cities spaced the way they are? A geographer versed in location theory might assess whether a SuperTarget should be built downtown or in a suburb, given the characteristics of existing neighborhoods and new developments, the median income of people, the locations of other shopping areas, and the existing and future road system. Similarly, a geographer could determine the best location for a wildlife refuge, given existing wildlife habitats and migration patterns, human settlement patterns, land use, and road networks.

A spatial perspective invites consideration of the relationship among phenomena in individual places—including the relationship between humans and the physical world. The

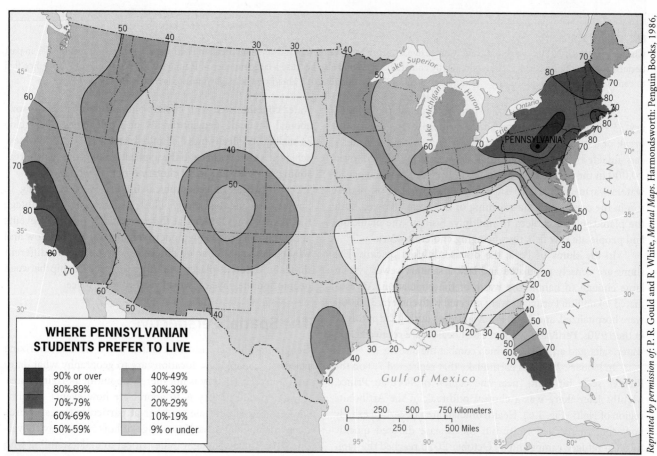

Reprinted by permission of: P. R. Gould and R. White, Mental Maps. Harmondsworth: Penguin Books, 1986, pp. 55 and 58.

**WHERE PENNSYLVANIAN STUDENTS PREFER TO LIVE**

| | |
|---|---|
| 90% or over | 40%–49% |
| 80%–89% | 30%–39% |
| 70%–79% | 20%–29% |
| 60%–69% | 10%–19% |
| 50%–59% | 9% or under |

### ■ Figure 1.7

**Desirable Places to Live.**   Where Pennsylvanian and Californian college students would prefer to live, based on questionnaires completed by college students. Proximity affects the impressions students have of other places—but so do stereotypes about certain parts of the country. How would this map look if we took a survey of Pennsylvanian and Californian college students now? Would the South be more desirable with the growth of Atlanta and other cities in the region? Would the availability of jobs in North Dakota's oil region make it a more desirable place to live?

second of the five themes concerns **human–environment interactions**. Why did the Army Corps of Engineers alter Florida's physical environment so drastically when it drained part of the Everglades? Have the changes in Florida's environment created an easier path of destruction for hurricanes? Why is the Army Corps of Engineers again changing the course of the Kissimmee River, and what does that mean for farmers around the river and residential developments in the south of Florida? Asking locational questions often means looking at the reciprocal relationship between humans and environments.

The third theme of geography is the **region**. Phenomena are not evenly distributed on Earth's surface. Instead, features tend to be concentrated in particular areas, which we call regions. Geographers use fieldwork and both quantitative and qualitative methods to develop insightful descriptions of different regions of the world. Novelist James Michener once wrote that whenever he started writing a new book, he first prepared himself by turning to books written by regional geographers about the area where the action was to occur. Understanding the regional geography of a place allows us to make sense of much of the information we have about places and digest new place-based information as well.

The fourth theme is represented by the seemingly simple word **place**. All places on the surface of Earth have unique human and physical characteristics, and one of the purposes of geography is to study the special character and meaning of places. People develop a **sense of place** by infusing a place with meaning and emotion, by remembering important events that occurred in a place, or by labeling a place with a certain character. Because we experience and give meaning to places, we can have a feeling of "home" when we are in a certain place.

We also develop **perceptions of places** where we have never been through books, movies, stories, and pictures. Geographers Peter Gould and Rodney White asked college students in California and Pennsylvania: "If you could move to any place of your choice, without any of the usual financial and other obstacles, where would you like to live?" Their responses showed a strong bias for their home region and revealed that students from both regions had negative perceptions of the South, Appalachia, the Great Plains, and Utah (Fig. 1.7). What we know shapes our perceptions of places.

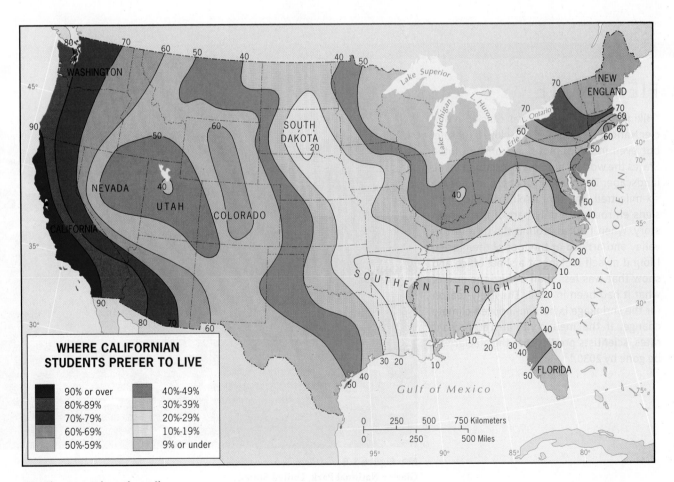

**WHERE CALIFORNIAN STUDENTS PREFER TO LIVE**

- 90% or over
- 80%-89%
- 70%-79%
- 60%-69%
- 50%-59%
- 40%-49%
- 30%-39%
- 20%-29%
- 10%-19%
- 9% or under

■ Figure 1.7 (continued)

The fifth theme, **movement**, refers to the mobility of people, goods, and ideas. Movement is an expression of the interconnectedness of places. **Spatial interaction** between places depends on the **distances** (the measured physical space between two places) among places, the **accessibility** (the ease of reaching one location from another) of places, and the transportation and communication **connectivity** (the degree of linkage between locations in a network) among places. Interactions of many kinds shape human geography.

## CULTURAL LANDSCAPE

In addition to the five themes—location, human–environment, region, place, and movement—**landscape** is a core element of geography. Geographers use the term *landscape* to refer to the material character of a place, the complex of natural features, human structures, and other tangible objects that give a place a particular form.

Human geographers are particularly concerned with the **cultural landscape**, the visible imprint of human activity on the landscape. The geographer whose name is most closely identified with this concept is former University of California at Berkeley professor Carl Sauer. In Sauer's words, cultural landscapes are comprised of the "forms superimposed on the physical landscape" by human activity.

No place on Earth is in a "pristine" condition; humans have made an imprint on every place on the planet (Fig. 1.8). The cultural landscape is the visible imprint of human activity and culture on the landscape. We can see the cultural landscape in the layers of buildings, roads, memorials, churches, fields, and homes that human activities over time have stamped on the landscape.

Cultural landscapes have layers of impressions from compounded years of human activity. As each group of people arrives and occupies a place, they carry their own technological and cultural traditions and transform the landscape accordingly. Imprints made by a sequence of occupants, whose impacts are layered one on top of the other, were described as a cultural landscape of **sequent occupance** in 1929 by Derwent Whittlesey. The Tanzanian city of Dar es Salaam provides an interesting urban example of sequent occupance. Arabs from Zanzibar first chose the African site in 1866 as a summer retreat. Next, German

## FIELD NOTE

"Hiking to the famed Grinnell Glacier in Glacier National Park brings one close to nature, but even in this remote part of the United States the work of humans is inscribed in the landscape. The parking lot at the start of the six-mile trail, the trail itself, and the small signs en route are only part of the human story. When I hiked around the turn in this valley and arrived at the foot of the glacier, I found myself looking at a sheet of ice and snow that was less than a third the size of what it had been in 1850. The likely reason for the shrinkage is human-induced climate change. If the melt continues at present rates, scientists predict that the glacier will be gone by 2030."

© Alexander B. Murphy.

■ **Figure 1.8**
**Glacier National Park, United States.**

■■ **Figure 1.9 A and B**

**Mumbai, India (A) and Dar-es-Salaam, Tanzania (B).**    Apartment buildings throughout Mumbai (formerly Bombay), India, are typically four stories with balconies. In Dar-es-Salaam, Tanzania, this four-story walkup with balconies (right) stands where single-family African dwellings once stood, reflecting the sequent occupance of the city, as migrants from India have arrived in Dar-es-Salaam.

colonizers imprinted a new layout and architectural style (wood-beamed Teutonic) when they chose the city as the center of their East African colonies in 1891. After World War I, when the Germans were ousted, a British administration took over the city and began yet another period of transformation. The British encouraged immigration from their colony in India to Tanzania. The new migrant Asian population created a zone of three- and four-story apartment houses, which look as if they were transplanted from Bombay (now Mumbai), India (Fig. 1.9 A and B). Then, in the early 1960s, Dar es Salaam became the capital of newly independent Tanzania. Thus, the city experienced four stages of cultural dominance in less than one century, and each stage of the sequence remains imprinted on the cultural landscape.

A cultural landscape can be seen as a kind of book offering clues into each chapter of the cultural practices, values, and priorities of its various occupiers. As geographer Peirce Lewis explained in *Axioms for Reading the Landscape* (1979), "Our human landscape is our unwitting autobiography, reflecting our tastes, our values, our aspirations, and even our fears, in tangible, visible form." Like Whittlesey, Lewis recommended looking for layers of history and cultural practice in cultural landscapes, adding that most major changes in the cultural landscape occur after a major event, such as a war, an invention, or an economic depression.

 Geographers who practice fieldwork keep their eyes open to the world around them and through practice become adept at reading cultural landscapes. Take a walk around your campus or town and try reading the cultural landscape. Choose one thing in the landscape and ask yourself, "What is that and why is it there?" Take the time to find out the answers!

## WHY DO GEOGRAPHERS USE MAPS, AND WHAT DO MAPS TELL US?

Maps are incredibly powerful tools in geography, and **cartography**, which is the art and science of making maps, is as old as geography itself. (For details on cartography, see Appendix A on the Wiley website.) Maps are used for countless purposes, including waging war, promoting political positions, solving medical problems, locating shopping centers, bringing relief to refugees, and warning of natural hazards. **Reference maps** show locations of places and geographic features. **Thematic maps** tell stories, typically showing the degree of some attribute or the movement of a geographic phenomenon.

Reference maps accurately show the **absolute locations** of places, using a coordinate system that allows for the precise plotting of where on Earth something is. Imagine taking an orange, drawing a dot on it with a marker, and then trying to describe the exact location of that dot to someone who is holding another orange so she can mark the same spot on her orange. If you draw and number the same coordinate system on both oranges, the task of drawing the absolute location on each orange is not only doable but simple. The coordinate system most frequently used on maps is based on latitude and longitude. For example, the absolute location of Chicago is 41 degrees, 53 minutes north latitude and 87 degrees, 38 minutes west longitude. Using these coordinates, you can plot Chicago on any globe or map that is marked with latitude and longitude lines.

Establishment of the satellite-based **global positioning system** (GPS) allows us to locate features on Earth with extraordinary accuracy. Researchers collect data quickly and easily in the field, and low-priced units encourage fishers, hunters, runners, and hikers to use GPS in their activities. New cars are equipped with GPS units, and dashboard map displays help commuters navigate traffic and travelers find their way. **Geocaching** is a popular hobby based on the use of GPS. Geocachers use their GPS units to play a treasure hunt game all over the world. People leave the treasures ("caches") somewhere, mark the coordinates on their GPS, and post clues on the Internet. If you find the cache, you take the treasure and leave a new one. Smartphones are equipped with GPS units, helping spread the use of GPS even further.

**Relative location** describes the location of a place in relation to other human and physical features. Descriptors such as "Chicago is on Lake Michigan, south of Milwaukee" or "Chicago is located where the cross-country railroads met in the 1800s" or "Chicago is the hub of the corn and soybean markets in the Midwest" are all descriptors of Chicago relative to other features. In the southern Wisconsin, northern Illinois, and western Indiana region, all major roads lead to Chicago (Fig. 1.10). Within this region, people define much of their lives relative to Chicago because of the tight interconnectedness between Chicago and the region. Northwest Indiana is so connected to Chicago that it has a time zone separate from the rest of Indiana, allowing people in northwestern Indiana to stay in the same time zone as Chicago.

Absolute locations do not change, but relative locations are constantly modified and change over time. Fredericksburg, Virginia, is located halfway between Washington, D.C., and Richmond, Virginia. Today, it is a suburb of Washington, D.C., with commuter trains, van pools, buses, and cars moving commuters between their homes in Fredericksburg and their workplaces in metropolitan Washington. During the Civil War, several bloody battles took place in Fredericksburg as the North and South fought halfway between their wartime capitals. The absolute location of Fredericksburg has not changed, but its place in the world around it, its relative location, certainly has.

## Mental Maps

We all carry maps in our minds of places we have been and places we have merely heard of; these are called **mental maps**. Even if you have never been to the Great Plains of the United States, you may have studied wall maps and atlases or come across the region in books, magazines, and newspapers frequently enough to envision the states of the region (North Dakota, South Dakota, Nebraska, Kansas, Oklahoma, and

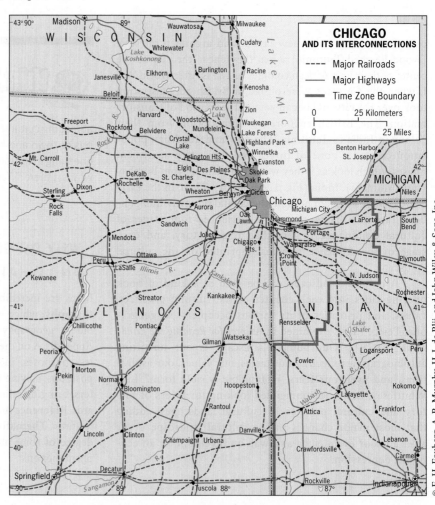

■ **Figure 1.10**
**All Major Roads Lead to Chicago.** The network of Midwestern roads that lead to Chicago reflects the dominance of the city in the region.

Texas) in your mind. Even if your mental map is not accurate, you still use it to process information about the Great Plains. If you hear on the news that a tornado destroyed a town in Oklahoma, you use your mental map of the Great Plains region and Oklahoma to make sense of where the tornado occurred and who was affected by it.

Our mental maps of the places within our **activity spaces**, the places we travel to routinely in our rounds of daily activity, are more accurate and detailed than our mental maps of places where we have never been. If your friend calls and asks you to meet her at the movie theater you go to frequently, your mental map will engage automatically. You will envision the hallway, the front door, the walk to your car, the lane to choose in order to be prepared for the left turn you must make, where you will park your car, and your path into the theater and up to the popcorn stand.

Geographers who study human-environment behavior have made extensive studies of how people develop mental maps. The earliest humans, who were nomadic, had incredibly accurate mental maps of where to find food and seek shelter. Today, people need mental maps to find their way through the concrete jungles of cities and suburbs.

Geographers have studied the mental map formation of children, the blind, new residents to cities, men, and women, all of whom exhibit differences in the formation of mental maps. To learn new places, women, for example, tend to use landmarks, whereas men tend to use paths. Activity spaces vary by age, and the extent of peoples' mental maps depends in part on their ages. Mental maps include **terra incognita**, unknown lands that are off-limits. If your path to the movie theater includes driving past a school that you do not attend, your map on paper may label the school, but no details will be shown regarding the place. However, if you have access to the school and you are instead drawing a mental map of how to get to the school's cafeteria, your mental map of the school will be quite detailed. Thus, mental maps reflect a person's activity space, including what is accessible to the person in his or her rounds of daily activity and what is not.

## Generalization in Maps

All maps simplify the world. A reference map of the world cannot show every place in the world, and a thematic map of hurricane tracks in the Atlantic Ocean cannot pinpoint the precise path of every hurricane for the last 50 years. When mapping data, whether human or physical, cartographers, the geographers who make maps, generalize the information they present on maps. Many of the maps in this book are thematic maps of the world. Shadings show how much or how little of a phenomenon is present, and symbols show where specific phenomena are located.

**Generalized maps** help us see general trends, but we cannot see all cases of a given phenomenon. The map of world precipitation (Fig. 1.11) is a generalized map of mean annual precipitation received around the world. The areas shaded in burgundy, dark blue, and vibrant green are places

that receive the most rain, and those shaded in orange receive the least rain on average. Take a pen and trace along the equator on the map. Notice how many of the high-precipitation areas on the map are along the equator. The consistent heating of the equator over the course of the year brings precipitation to the equatorial region. At the scale of the world, we can see general trends in precipitation, such as this, but it is difficult to see the microscale climates of intense precipitation areas that are found throughout the world.

## Remote Sensing and GIS

Geographic studies include both long- and short-term environmental change. Geographers monitor Earth from a distance, using **remote sensing** technology. Remotely sensed data are collected by satellites and aircraft and are often almost instantaneously available.

After a major weather or hazard event, such as the 2011 floods in the Mississippi River Valley, the unprecedented hurricane season in the Gulf of Mexico in 2005 (which included Hurricane Katrina), or the 2010 earthquakes in Haiti and Chile, remotely sensed data show us the major areas of impact (Fig. 1.12). A remotely sensed image surveys the damage of the earthquake, and photos taken on the ground show the impact and destruction (Fig. 1.13).

In states that restrict foreign access or that do not reliably allow foreign aid to enter the country, remote sensing can help geographers understand the physical and human geography of the place. ArcGIS Online is a free, web-based user-friendly GIS. You can create a map in ArcGIS Online and set the background to world imagery, which is composed of satellite and aerial images from a variety of sources. The images are accurate to .3 meters in the continental United States and western Europe and to 1 meter in the rest of the world.

Remotely sensed images can be incorporated in a map, and absolute locations can be studied by plotting change in remotely sensed imagery over time. Advances in computer technology and data storage, increasing accessibility to locationally based data and GPS technology, and software corporations that tailor products to specific uses have all driven incredible advances in geographic analysis based on **geographic information systems** (GIS) over the last two decades. Geographers use GIS to compare a variety of spatial data by creating digitized representations of the environment (Fig. 1.14), combining layers of spatial data, and creating maps in which patterns and processes are superimposed. Geographers also use GIS to analyze data, which can give us new insights into geographic patterns and relationships.

Geographers use GIS in both human and physical geographic research. For example, political geographers use GIS to map layers showing voters, party registration, race and ethnicity, likelihood of voting, and income in order to determine how to draw voting districts in congressional and state legislative elections. In this case, a geographer can draw a line around a group of people and ask the computer program to tally how

that recover the most rain, and these shoreline areas have

[text partially obscured left column]

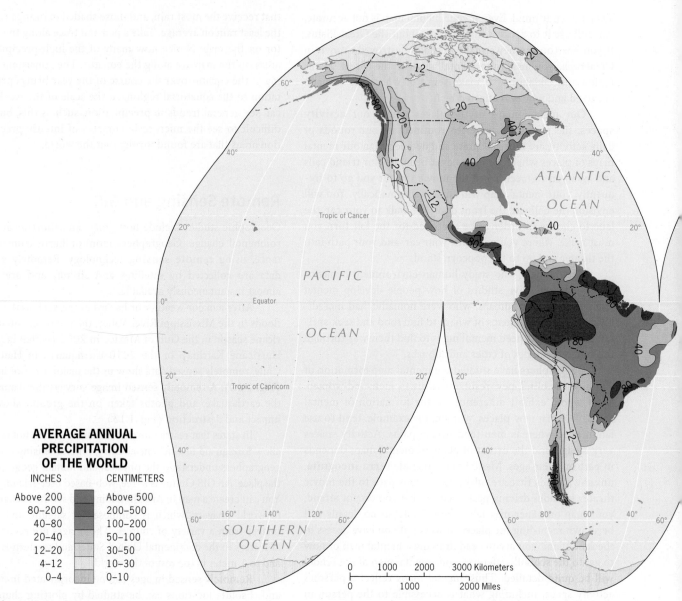

**Figure 1.11**

**Average Annual Precipitation of the World.**    A generalized map of the mean annual precipitation received around the world. The pattern on the map shows high precipitation along the equator, where consistent heating from the sun over the year means more incoming solar radiation is absorbed and released as warm air. When warm, moist air rises and reaches its dew point, condensation and precipitation follow. The rainforest climates are found along the equator. Locations that receive little precipitation are deserts, which are found in areas of Earth dominated by high-pressure cells. In a high-pressure cell, air descends from aloft to the ground and then goes outward, making it impossible for warm air to rise. Deserts receive rain when storms pass through them, not from the solar radiation they receive each day.

many voters are inside the region, determine the racial composition of the district, and show how many of the current political representatives live within the new district's boundaries.

Geographers trained in GIS employ the technology in countless undertakings. Students who earn undergraduate degrees in geography are employed by software companies, government agencies, and businesses to use GIS to survey wildlife, map soils, analyze natural disasters, track diseases, assist first responders, plan cities, plot transportation improvements, and follow weather systems. For example, a group of

geographers working for one GIS company tailors the GIS software to serve the branches of the military and the defense intelligence community. The vast amounts of intelligence data gathered by the various intelligence agencies can be integrated into a GIS and then analyzed spatially. Geographers working in the defense intelligence community can use GIS to query a vast amount of intelligence, interpret spatial data, and make recommendations on issues of security and defense.

The amount of data digestible in a GIS, the power of the location analysis that can be undertaken on a computer

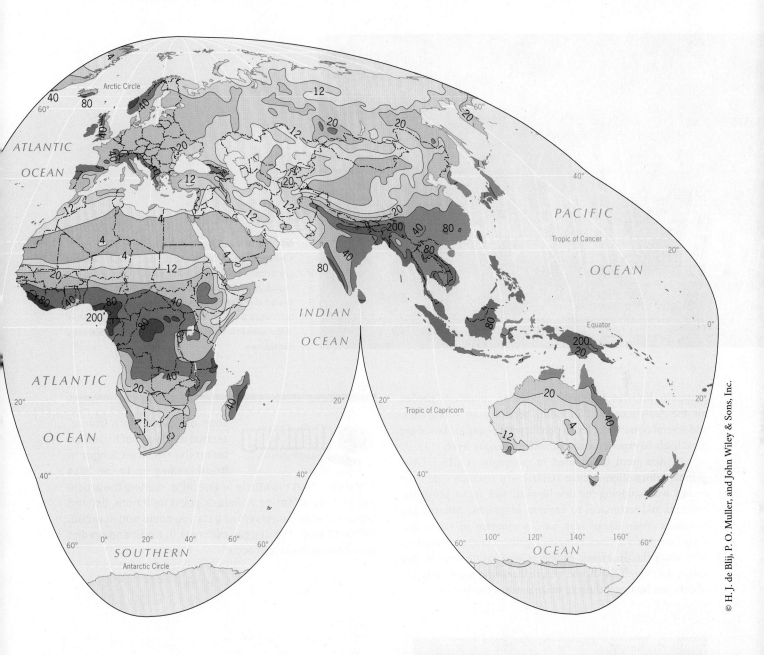

© H. J. de Blij, P. O. Muller, and John Wiley & Sons, Inc.

platform, and the ease of analysis that is possible using GIS software applications allow geographers to answer complicated questions. For example, geographer Korine Kolivras analyzed the probability of dengue fever outbreaks in Hawaii using GIS (Fig. 1.15). The maps Kolivras produced may look as simple and straightforward as the cholera maps produced by Dr. John Snow in the 1800s, but the amount of data that went into Kolivras's analysis is staggering in comparison. Dengue fever is carried by a particular kind of mosquito called the *Aedes*

© NASA/Science Source/Photo Researchers, Inc.

■ **Figure 1.12**

**Concepción, Chile.** Satellite image of the cities of Concepción and Hualpén, Chile, hours after an 8.8 magnitude earthquake occurred in 2010. The damage to the city is not noticeable in this satellite image except for the smoke plume from an oil refinery in the lower left corner.

■ **Figure 1.13**
**Concepción, Chile.** Chile has broadly adopted engineering and architecture practices that lessen the impact of earthquakes. Although the 2010 earthquake caused over $30 billion worth of damage, it could have been much worse without these building practices. Most of the damage in Concepción was to residential buildings like this one.

mosquito. Kolivras analyzed the breeding conditions needed for the *Aedes* mosquito, including precipitation, topography, and several other variables, to predict what places in Hawaii are most likely to experience an outbreak of dengue fever.

A new term of art used in geography is GISci. Geographic information science (GISci) is a research field concerned with studying the development and use of geospatial concepts and techniques to examine geographic patterns and processes. Your school may have a program in GISci that draws across disciplines, bringing together computer scientists who write the programs, engineers who create sensors that gather data about Earth, and geographers who combine layers of data and interpret them to make sense of our world.

**thinking** *geographically*    Look at "Learn More Online" section at the end of this chapter for the article on dengue in Brazil leading up to the 2014 World Cup. Find the article online. After reading the article and looking at Korine Kolivras's guest field note, list and explain at least five layers of data you could add in ArcGIS Online to study the dengue outbreak in Brazil and predict where an outbreak will occur.

A

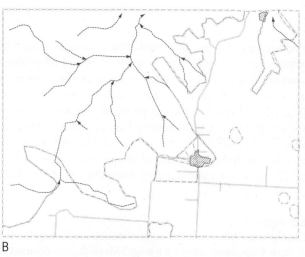

B

■ **Figure 1.14**
**Two Representations of St. Francis, South Dakota.**    1.14A is a panchromatic raster satellite image collected in 2002 at 10 m resolution during a grassland wildfire; 1.14B displays vector data—rivers, roads, cities, and land use/land cover—digitalized from the image 1.14A.

# GUEST FIELD NOTE

The diffusion of diseases carried by vectors, such as the *Aedes* mosquito that transmits dengue, is not solely a result of the environmental factors in a place. I use disease ecology to understand the ways in which environmental, social, and cultural factors interact to produce disease in a place. Through a combination of fieldwork and geographic information systems (GIS) modeling, I studied the environmental habitat of the *Aedes* mosquito in Hawaii and the social and cultural factors that stimulated the outbreak of dengue in Hawaii.

When I went into the field in Hawaii, I observed the diversity of the physical geography of Hawaii, from deserts to rainforests. I saw the specific local environments of the dengue outbreak area, and I examined the puddles in streams (Fig. 1.15A) in which the mosquitoes likely bred during the 2001–2002 dengue outbreak. I talked to public health officials who worked so hard to control the dengue outbreak so that I better understood the local environmental factors contributing to the disease. I visited a family that had been heavily affected by dengue, and I saw their home, which, by their choice, lacked walls or screens on all sides. In talking with the family, I came to understand the social and cultural factors that affected the outbreak of dengue in Hawaii.

I created a GIS model of mosquito habitat that considered not only total precipitation in Hawaii (Fig. 1.15B), but also seasonal variations in precipitation (Fig. 1.15C) and temperature (Fig. 1.15D), to help explain where the *Aedes* mosquito

■ **Figure 1.15 A**

**Maui, Hawaii.** *Aedes* mosquitoes breed in artificial and natural water containers, including standing puddles left behind when streams dry up during a drought as shown in this photograph along the northeast coast of Maui.

is able to breed and survive on the islands. I also studied seasonal fluctuations in streams and population distributions in creating my model of dengue potential areas (Fig. 1.15E).

The GIS model I created can now be altered by public officials in Hawaii to reflect precipitation and temperature variations each year or to incorporate new layers of environmental, social, and cultural data. Officials will be able to better predict locations of dengue outbreaks so they can focus their efforts to combat the spread of the disease.

*Credit: Korine N. Kolivras, Virginia Tech*

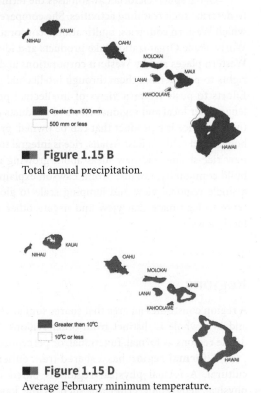

■ **Figure 1.15 B**
Total annual precipitation.

■ **Figure 1.15 C**
Average June precipitation.

■ **Figure 1.15 D**
Average February minimum temperature.

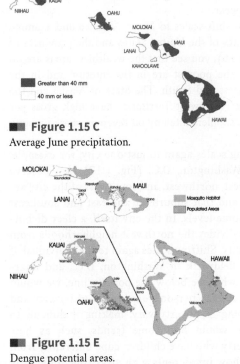

■ **Figure 1.15 E**
Dengue potential areas.

Korine N. Kolivras, Virginia Tech

# WHY ARE GEOGRAPHERS CONCERNED WITH SCALE AND CONNECTEDNESS?

Geographers study places and patterns across scales, including local, regional, national, and global. Scale has two meanings in geography: the first is the distance on a map compared to the distance on Earth, and the second is the spatial extent of something. When we refer to scale we are using the second of these definitions. Geographers' interest in this type of scale derives from the fact that phenomena found at one scale are usually influenced by what is happening at other scales. Explaining a geographic pattern or process requires looking across scales. Moreover, the scale of our research or analysis matters because we can make different observations at different scales. We can study a single phenomenon across different scales in order to see how what is happening at the global scale affects localities and how what is happening at a local scale affects the globe. Or we can study a phenomenon at a particular scale and then ask how processes at other scales affect what we are studying.

The scale at which we study a geographic phenomenon tells us what level of detail we can expect to see. We also see different patterns at different scales. For example, when we study the distribution of material wealth at the scale of the globe (see Fig. 1.3), we see that the countries in western Europe, Canada, the United States, Japan, and Australia are the wealthiest, and the countries of Subsaharan Africa and Southeast Asia are the poorest. Does that mean everyone in the United States is wealthy and everyone in Indonesia is poor? Certainly not, but on a global-scale map of states, that is how the data appear.

When you shift scales to North America and examine the data for States of the United States and the provinces of Canada (Fig. 1.16), you see that the wealthiest areas are on the coasts and the poorest are in the interior and in the extreme Northeast and South. The State of Alaska and the province of the Northwest Territories have high gross per capita incomes, supplemented by oil revenues shared among the residents.

By shifting scales again to just one city, for example, metropolitan Washington, D.C. (Fig. 1.17), you observe that suburbs west, northwest, and southwest of the city are the wealthiest and that suburbs to the east and southeast have lower income levels. In the city itself, a clear dichotomy of wealth divides the northwest neighborhoods from the rest of the city. Shifting scales again to the individual, if we conducted fieldwork in Washington, D.C., and interviewed people who live below the poverty line, we would quickly find that each person's experience of poverty and reasons for being in poverty vary, making it difficult to generalize. We would find some trends, such as how women in poverty who have children cope differently from single men or how immigrants with visas cope differently

from paperless immigrants, but no two individual cases are exactly the same.

Because the level of detail and the patterns observed change as the scale changes, geographers must be sensitive to their scale of analysis and also be wary of researchers who make generalizations about a people or a place at a particular scale without considering other scales of analysis.

Geographers study how processes operating at different scales influence one another. If you want to understand the conflict between the Tutsi and the Hutu people in Rwanda, for example, you cannot look solely at this African country. Developments at a variety of different scales, including patterns of migration and interaction in Central Africa, the economic and political relations between Rwanda and parts of Europe, and the variable impacts of globalization—economic, political, and cultural—all influenced Rwanda and help to explain the context of the conflict.

Geographers are also interested in how people use scale politically. Locally based political movements, like the Zapatistas in southern Mexico, have learned to **rescale** their actions to involve players at other scales and create a global outcry of support for their position. By taking their political campaign from the local scale to the national scale through protests against the North American Free Trade Agreement (NAFTA), and then effectively using the Internet to wage a global campaign, the Zapatistas gained attention from the world media, a feat relatively few local political movements achieve.

Geographer Victoria Lawson uses the term *jumping scale* to describe such rescaling activities. She compares the ways in which Western countries, multinational corporations, and the World Trade Organization take products and ideas created in Western places and by Western corporations and globalize all rights to profits from them through intellectual property law. Efforts to push Western views of intellectual property challenge other local and regional views of products and ideas. To the West, rice is a product that can be owned, privatized, and bought and sold. To East Asians, rice is integral to culture, and new rice strains and new ideas about growing rice can help build community, not just profit. Lawson explains that taking a single regional view and jumping scale to globalize it can serve to legitimate that view and negate other regional and local views.

## Regions

A region constitutes an area that shares similar characteristics and as a whole is distinct from other regions. Geographers define regions as formal, functional, or perceptual.

A **formal region** has a shared trait, either physical or cultural. A formal physical region is based on a shared physical geographic criterion, such as the karst region of

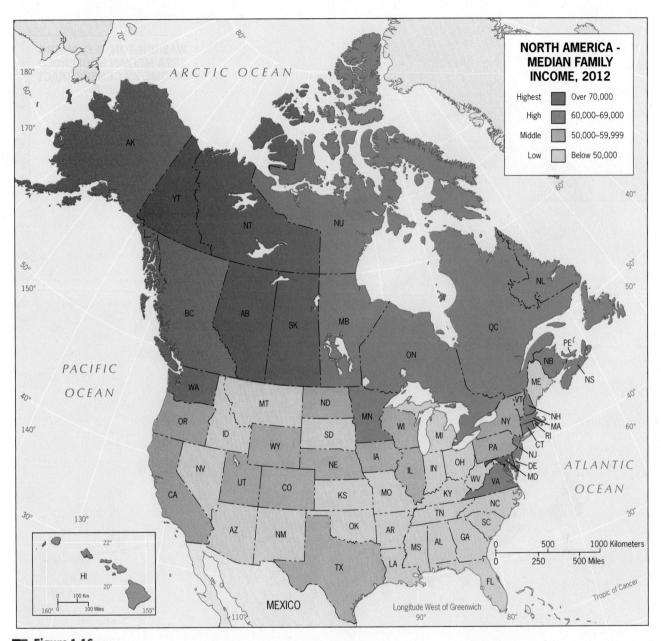

**■■ Figure 1.16**

**Median Family Income (in U.S. Dollars), 2011.** The relatively greater wealth of the East Coast, from New Hampshire through Virginia, stands out. *Data from*: United States Census Bureau and Census Canada, 2010.

China (Fig. 1.18). In a formal cultural region, people share one or more cultural traits. For example, the region of Europe where French is spoken by a majority of the people can be thought of as a French-speaking region. Whether physical or cultural, when the scale of analysis shifts, the formal region changes. If we shift scales to the world, the karst region expands to lands that were previously underwater and are now covered in limestone, and the French-speaking formal region expands beyond France into former French colonies of Africa and into the overseas departments that are still under French jurisdiction.

A **functional region** is defined by a particular set of activities or interactions that occur within it. Places (also called nodes) that are part of the same functional region interact to create connections. Functional regions have a shared political, social, or economic purpose. For example, a city has a surrounding region within which workers commute, either to the downtown area or to office parks in suburbs. That entire urban area, defined by people moving toward and within it, is a functional region. A functional region is a spatial connection among nodes, and the extent of the connections defines the boundaries of the region.

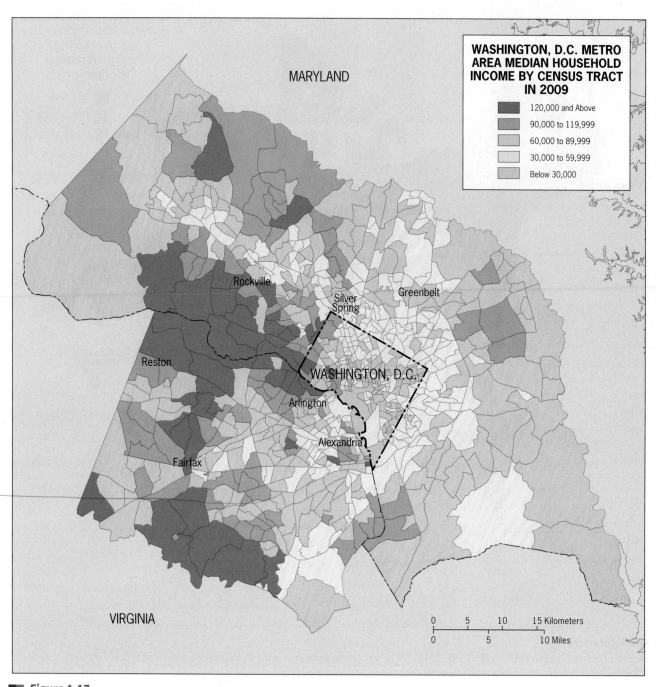

WASHINGTON, D.C. METRO
AREA MEDIAN HOUSEHOLD
INCOME BY CENSUS TRACT
IN 2009

120,000 and Above

90,000 to 119,999

60,000 to 89,999

30,000 to 59,999

Below 30,000

MARYLAND

Rockville

Silver
Spring

Greenbelt

Reston

WASHINGTON, D.C.

Arlington

Alexandria

Fairfax

VIRGINIA

0   5   10   15 Kilometers

0   5   10 Miles

■■ **Figure 1.17**
**Median Family Income (in U.S. Dollars), 2009.**   Notice the sharp contrast between the western and eastern parts of the nation's capital, which shows up clearly on a map at this scale.   *Data from:* United States Census Bureau, 2010.

Functional regions are not necessarily culturally homogeneous; instead, the people within the region function together politically, socially, or economically. The City of Chicago is a functional region and is itself part of hundreds of functional regions—from the State of Illinois to the seventh Federal Reserve district.

Regions may be perceptual, intellectual constructs that help people order their knowledge and understanding of the world. Each person carries **perceptual regions** in their

mind based on accumulated knowledge of regions and cultures (Fig. 1.19). Perceptual regions can include people and their cultural traits (dress, food, language, and religion), places and their physical traits (mountains, plains, or coasts), and built environments (windmills, barns, skyscrapers, or beach houses).

Major news events help us create our perceptual regions by defining certain countries or areas of countries as part of a region. Before September 11, 2001, most Americans thought

© Alexander B. Murphy.

■■ **Figure 1.18**
**Guilin, China.** The South China Karst region, bisected here by the Li River outside Guilin, is a UNESCO World Heritage Site. The landforms of the region clearly distinguish it from surrounding areas.

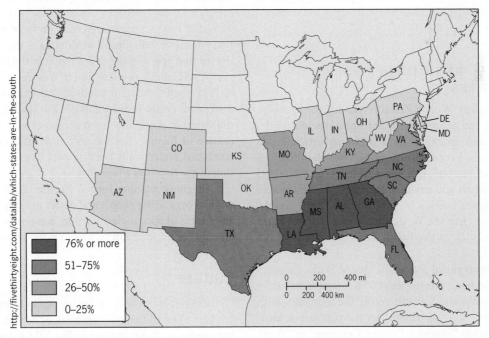

http://fivethirtyeight.com/datalab/which-states-are-in-the-south.

| | |
|---|---|
| ■ | 76% or more |
| ■ | 51–75% |
| ■ | 26–50% |
| ■ | 0–25% |

■■ **Figure 1.19**
**The South.** The boundaries of perceptual regions are difficult to define precisely. Nate Silver's blog FiveThirtyEight (owned by ESPN) teamed up with SurveyMonkey to poll people on the web who identified themselves as a Midwesterner or Southerner "a lot" or "some" and generated maps of the perceptual regions of those who identify with the regions. Lifestyle Editor Walt Hickey analyzed the data and found Midwesterners have less agreement on what states are in the region (Illinois was chosen most frequently, with 80 percent agreeing it's part of the Midwest), whereas Southerners have a clearer idea of the states definitively in the South (about 90 percent agreed Georgia and Alabama are in the South and more than 80 percent put Louisiana and Mississippi in the South).

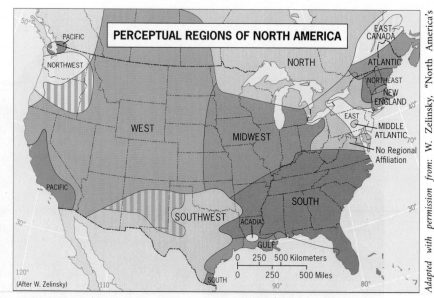

■ **Figure 1.20**
**Perceptual Regions of North America.** This map represents a composite of many people's ideas as to what constitute major cultural-geographic regions in the United States and southern Canada.

the Middle East region included Iraq and Iran but stretched no farther east. As the hunt for Osama bin Laden began and the media focused attention on the harsh rule of the Taliban in Afghanistan, regional perceptions of the Middle East changed; for many, the region now stretched to encompass Afghanistan and Pakistan. Scholars who specialize in this part of the globe had long studied the relationship between parts of Southwest Asia and the traditional "Middle East," but the connections between Afghanistan and Pakistan and the rest of the Middle East had been almost invisible to the American population.

## PERCEPTUAL REGIONS IN THE UNITED STATES

Cultural geographer Wilbur Zelinsky tackled the complex task of defining and delimiting the perceptual regions of the United States and southern Canada. In an article titled "North America's Vernacular Regions," he identified 12 major perceptual regions on a series of maps (summarized in Fig. 1.20). When you examine the map, you will notice some of the regions overlap in certain places. For example, the more general term the West actually incorporates more specific regions, such as the Pacific Region and part of the Northwest.

To make his regional map of the United States, Zelinsky analyzed the telephone directories of 276 metropolitan areas in the United States and Canada, noting the frequency with which businesses and other enterprises use regional or locational terms (such as "Southern Printing Company" or "Western Printing") in their listings. The resulting maps show a close similarity between these perceptual regions and culture regions identified by geographers.

The perceptual region of the South, shown in both Figures 1.19 and 1.20, has changed markedly since the civil rights movement of the 1960s (Fig. 1.21). A "New South"

has emerged, forged by Hispanic immigration, urbanization, movement of people from other parts of the United States to the South, and other processes. At the same time, the South continues to carry imprints of a culture with deep historical roots through language, religion, music, food preferences, and other traditions and customs.

If you drive southward from, say, Pittsburgh or Detroit, you will not pass a specific place where you enter this perceptual region. You will note features in the cultural landscape that you perceive to be associated with the South (such as Waffle House restaurants), and at some stage of the trip these features will begin to dominate the area to such a degree that you will say, "I am really in the South now." This may result from a combination of features in the culture: the style of houses and their porches, items on a roadside restaurant menu (grits, for example), a local radio station's music, the sound of accents that you perceive to be Southern, a succession of Baptist churches in a town along the way. These combined impressions become part of your overall perception of the South as a region.

Regions, whether formal, functional, or perceptual, are ways of organizing people and places geographically. Regions are a form of spatial classification, a means of handling large amounts of information so we can make sense of it.

## Culture

**Culture** refers not only to the music, literature, and arts of a society but to all the other features of its way of life: prevailing modes of dress; routine living habits; food preferences; the architecture of houses and public buildings; the layout of fields and farms; and systems of education, government, and law. Culture is an all-encompassing term that identifies not only the whole tangible lifestyle of peoples, but also their prevailing values and beliefs. Culture lies at the heart of human geography.

# GUEST FIELD NOTE

## Montgomery, Alabama

Located in a predominately African American neighborhood in Montgomery, Alabama, the street intersection of Jeff Davis and Rosa Parks is symbolic of the debates and disputes in the American South over how the past is to be commemorated on the region's landscape. The Civil War and civil rights movement are the two most important events in the history of the region. The street names commemorate Montgomery's central role in both eras, and they do so in the same public space. Montgomery was the site of the first capital of the Confederacy in 1861 while Jefferson Davis was president. The Alabama capital was also the site of the 1955–1956 Montgomery bus boycott that launched the civil rights movement. The boycott was sparked by Rosa Parks's arrest after she refused to give up her seat on a city bus when ordered to do so by a white person. Most of my research examines the politics of how the region's white and African Americans portray these separate heroic eras within the region's public spaces, ranging from support for and against

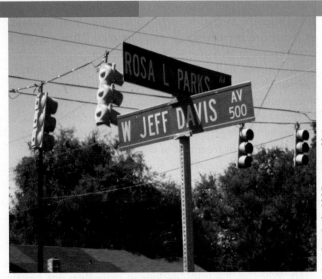

Jonathan Leib, Old Dominion University

■■  **Figure 1.21**

flying the Confederate flag to disputes over placing statues and murals honoring the Civil War and the civil rights movement on the South's landscape.

*Credit: Jonathan Leib, Old Dominion University*

---

Academics, from human geographers to anthropologists, have sought to define culture. Some have stressed the contributions of humans to the environment, whereas others have emphasized learned behaviors and ways of thinking. Several decades ago the noted anthropologist E. Adamson Hoebel defined culture as:

> [the] *integrated system of learned behavior patterns which are characteristic of the members of a society and which are not the result of biological inheritance . . . culture is not genetically predetermined; it is noninstinctive . . . [Culture] is wholly the result of social invention and is transmitted and maintained solely through communication and learning.*

Hoebel's emphasis on communication and learning anticipated the current view of culture as a system of meaning, not just a set of acts, customs, or material products. Clifford Geertz advanced this view in his classic work, *The Interpretation of Cultures* (1973), which has influenced much recent work in human geography. Human geographers are interested not just in the different patterns and landscapes associated with different culture groups, but in the ways in which cultural understandings affect both the creation and significance of those patterns and landscapes.

Cultural geographers identify a single attribute of a culture as a **culture trait**. For example, wearing a turban is a culture trait in certain societies. Many men in the semiarid and desert areas of North Africa, Southwest Asia, and South Asia wore turbans before the birth of Islam. The turbans

protected the wearers from sunlight and also helped distinguish tribes. Not all Muslim men wear turbans, but in some Muslim countries, including Afghanistan, wearing turbans is popular because either religious or political leaders prescribe it for men. Today, turbans often distinguish a man's status in society or are worn as a sign of faithfulness to God. In some Muslim countries, including Egypt and Turkey, men rarely wear turbans. When men in other Muslim countries do wear turbans, the appearance of the turban varies a great deal. For instance, in Yemen men who cover their heads typically wear kalansuwa, which are caps wrapped in fabric. In Palestine, Jordan, and Saudi Arabia, men who cover their heads typically wear kaffiyeh, which are rectangular pieces of cloth draped and secured on the head.

Wearing turbans is not a cultural trait limited to Muslims. In the United States, most men who cover their heads with a turban are Sikhs, which is a different religion from Islam. In the Sikh religion, men are required to keep their hair uncut. The common practice is to twist the hair and knot it on top of one's head and then cover it with a turban. The Sikh religion began in the 1500s, and in the late 1600s, the tenth guru of the religion taught that wearing a turban was a way to demonstrate one's faithfulness to God.

As the turban example exhibits, a culture trait is not always confined to a single culture. More than one culture may exhibit a particular culture trait, like turbans. A distinct combination of cultural traits is a **culture complex**. Herding of cattle is a cultural trait shared by many cultures. Across cultures, cattle are regarded and used in different ways.

The Maasai of East Africa, for example, follow their herds along seasonal migration paths, consuming blood and milk as important ingredients of a unique diet. Cattle occupy a central place in Maasai existence; they are the essence of survival, security, and prestige. Although the Maasai culture complex is only one of many cattle-keeping complexes, no other culture complex exhibits exactly the same combination of traits. In Europe, cattle are milked, and dairy products, such as butter, yogurt, and cheese, are consumed as part of a diet very different from that of the Maasai.

A **cultural hearth** is an area where cultural traits develop and from which cultural traits diffuse. Culture traits, for example the religion of Islam, can be traced to a single place and time. Muhammad founded Islam in the 600s C.E. (common era) in and around the cities of Mecca and Medina on the Arabian Peninsula. Other culture traits, such as agriculture, can be traced to several hearths thousands of years apart. When such a trait develops in more than one hearth without being influenced by its development elsewhere, each hearth operates as a case of **independent invention**.

## Connectedness Through Diffusion

Historians believe the innovation of agriculture began independently in hearths in Europe, Africa, and Asia. Drawing from archaeological evidence, geographer Carl Sauer established that Mesoamerica was also a hearth for agriculture, another case of independent invention. From these hearths of agriculture, the ideas of purposefully planting and caring for seeds and feeding and raising livestock spread throughout the world in a process called diffusion.

In 1970, Swedish geographer Torsten Hägerstrand published pioneering research on the role of time in diffusion. Hägerstrand's research revealed how time, as well as distance, affects individual human behavior and the dissemination of people and ideas. Sauer and Hägerstrand's fascinating research attracted many geographers to the study of **diffusion**.

Geographers are still using principles of diffusion to create models of movement in GIS.

Whether a cultural trait diffuses to a place depends, in part, on the time and distance from the hearth. The farther a place is from the hearth, the less likely an innovation will be adopted. Similarly, the acceptance of an innovation becomes less likely the longer it takes to reach its potential adopters. In combination, time and distance cause **time–distance decay** in the diffusion process.

Not all cultural traits or innovations diffuse. Prevailing attitudes or cultural taboos can mean that certain innovations, ideas, or practices are not acceptable or adoptable in particular cultures. Religious teachings may prohibit certain practices or ideas, such as divorce, abortion, or contraceptive use, on the grounds of theology or morality. Some cultures or religions prohibit consumption of alcoholic beverages, and others prohibit consuming certain kinds of meat or other foods. Prescriptions cultures make about behavior act as **cultural barriers** and can pose powerful obstacles to the spread of ideas or innovations.

### EXPANSION DIFFUSION

When a culture trait, such as a religion, spreads, it does so from a hearth. Islam's hearth was on the Arabian Peninsula, and from there, Islam diffused to Egypt and North Africa, through Southwest Asia, and into West Africa. This is a case of expansion diffusion, when an innovation or idea develops in a hearth and remains strong there while also spreading outward. Geographers classify diffusion into two broad categories: expansion diffusion and relocation diffusion. In the case of **expansion diffusion**, an innovation or idea develops in a hearth and remains strong there while also spreading outward (Fig. 1.22).

When a trend or innovation diffuses quickly, it seems to come out of nowhere and then can "explode" and be seen virtually everywhere you look. In 1996, Kevin Plank, a recent graduate of the University of Maryland who played football as

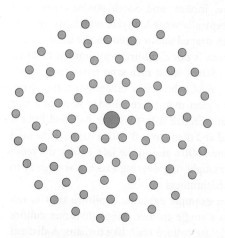

A. Contagious Diffusion

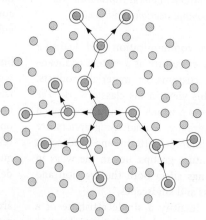
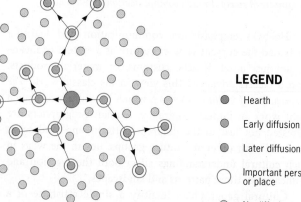

B. Hierarchical Diffusion

**LEGEND**

- Hearth
- Early diffusion
- Later diffusion
- Important person or place
- No diffusion

■■ **Figure 1.22**
**Contagious and Hierarchical Diffusion.**

a walk-on for the Terrapins, invented a heat gear shirt that would wick sweat away and be a cooling layer under football gear. Plank called his new body-hugging gear Under Armour. He gave samples of polyester heat gear Under Armour shirts to his friends at the University of Maryland and to friends at other football teams in the East Coast Conference. The first "knowers" of the new Under Armour brand were football players connected to Kevin Plank or to college teams on the east coast.

The spread of Under Armour heat gear is a case of **hierarchical diffusion**, a pattern in which the main channel of diffusion is some segment of those who are susceptible to (or are already adopting) what is being diffused. Under Armour diffused from college and professional football players who were trying to stay cool and keep their clothing light while practicing in the hot sun twice a day, to lacrosse players and other athletes who were friends of the football players, then to young athletes around the United States who, as fans, took note of the Under Armour logo on their favorite players' sportswear and wanted to wear what their idols were wearing, and finally to those who saw people they knew wearing Under Armour clothing and bought the gear as a fashion trend. The hierarchy of football players, other athletes, and then the **contagious diffusion** among school-age children that followed helps explain the rapid growth of the Under Armour brand, which had revenues of $200 million in 2004 and $2 billion in 2013.

Plank started giving away Under Armour heat gear, sold the shirts out of the trunk of his car from a base at his grandmother's home in Washington, D.C., and then set up headquarters for the company in Baltimore, Maryland. As is the case in expansion diffusion, the hearth of Under Armour has remained strong. The University of Maryland has close ties to Under Armour, which designed an innovative (some thought it was cool and some thought it was garish) new football uniform in 2011 (Fig. 1.23). In 2014, the University of Maryland signed a ten-year sponsorship agreement with Under Armour, one of 19 sponsorships Under Armour has with universities.

College and professional athletes whose teams had contracts with Nike or Adidas wanted to wear heat gear clothing, and some wore Under Armour beneath their Nike and Adidas uniforms. This prompted Nike, Adidas, and other athletic companies to offer their own performance gear, including compression shirts, compression shorts, and sports bras bearing their logo. Under Armour acted as a stimulus to Nike's Pro Performance line and Adidas's Clima Ultimate line. Under Armour's performance line prompted **stimulus diffusion** or local experimentation and change in the Nike and Adidas brands. The performance apparel market alone was expected to reach $7.6 billion by 2014, and Forbes estimates the entire global sports apparel market will reach $178 billion by 2019. According to Forbes, 70 percent of Under Armour's stock revenue in 2014 was generated by sales of performance apparel, and Under Armour captured 14.7 percent of the global sports apparel market, second to Nike with 27 percent of the market.

Culture traits, rather than economics, can prohibit contagious diffusion and encourage stimulus diffusion as well. Not all ideas can be readily and directly adopted by a receiving population; some are simply too vague, too unattainable, too different, or too impractical for immediate adoption. Yet, these ideas can still have an impact. They may indirectly promote local experimentation and eventual changes in ways of doing things. For example, the diffusion of fast, mass-produced food in the late twentieth century led to the introduction of the hamburger to India. Yet the Hindu religion in India prohibits consumption of beef, which is a major cultural obstacle to adoption of the hamburger (Fig. 1.24). Instead, retailers began selling burgers made of vegetable products. The diffusion of the hamburger took on a new form in the cultural context of India. With expansion diffusion, whether contagious or hierarchical, the people stay in place and the innovation, idea, trait, or disease does the moving.

■ **Figure 1.23**
**College Park, Maryland.** Under Armour designed controversial football uniforms for their flagship university partner, the University of Maryland. The State of Maryland's red, black, gold, and white flag is incorporated throughout the uniforms from helmets to jerseys to football gloves. Maryland's flag is divided into four quarters with the upper left and lower right gold and black checkers representing the family crest of the founder of Maryland, Lord Baltimore, and the upper right and lower left red and white cross representing the family crest of George Calvert, who is also credited with founding the State of Maryland.

Rob Carr/Getty Images

© Douglas E. Gurran/AFP/Getty Images

© Alexander B. Murphy

**Figure 1.24 A and B**

**New Delhi, India (A) and Jodhpur, India (B).**   Hindus believe cows are holy, and in India, evidence of that can be seen everywhere from cows roaming the streets to the menu at McDonald's. In 1996, the first McDonald's restaurant opened in New Delhi, India, serving Maharaja Macs and Vegetable Burgers with Cheese. In Indian towns, such as Jodhpur, cows are protected and share the streets with pedestrians, bicyclists, and motorists.

## RELOCATION DIFFUSION

Relocation diffusion occurs most frequently through migration. When migrants move from their homeland, they take their culture traits with them. Developing an ethnic neighborhood in a new country helps immigrants maintain their culture in the midst of an unfamiliar one. **Relocation diffusion** involves the actual movement of individuals who have already adopted the idea or innovation, and who carry it to a new, perhaps distant, locale, where they proceed to disseminate it (Fig. 1.22). If the homeland of the immigrants loses enough of its population, the cultural customs may fade in the hearth while gaining strength in the ethnic neighborhoods abroad.

Knowing that any good, idea, or disease can diffuse in more than one way, look in your closet for a brand of clothing, a genre of music, or a religious symbol and then research and describe how it diffused from its hearth across the globe, using at least three different types of diffusion in your answer.

## WHAT ARE GEOGRAPHIC CONCEPTS, AND HOW ARE THEY USED IN ANSWERING GEOGRAPHIC QUESTIONS?

To think geographically, start by asking a geographic question, one with a spatial or landscape component. Then choose the scale(s) of analysis for your research and apply one or more geographic concepts to answer the question. **Geographic concepts** give us insight and help us understand people, place, space, location, and landscape.

Geographers use fieldwork, remote sensing, GIS, GPS, and qualitative and quantitative techniques to explore linkages among people and places and to explain differences across people, places, scales, and times. Research in human geography today stems from a variety of theories and philosophies and incorporates a broad range of geographic concepts.

## Rejection of Environmental Determinism

To understand what geographers do and how they do it, it is easiest to start by defining what geography is not. The ancient Greeks noticed that some of the peoples subjugated by their expanding empire were relatively docile while others were rebellious; they attributed such differences to variations in climate. Over 2000 years ago, Aristotle described northern European people as "full of spirit . . . but incapable of ruling others," and he characterized Asian people (by which he meant the inhabitants of modern-day Turkey) as "intelligent and inventive . . . [but] always in a state of subjection and slavery." Aristotle attributed peoples' response to being taken over by an outside power to the respective climates of the regions. In his mind, the cold northern European environment encouraged people to rebel and the warmer climate of Southwest Asia forced people to become enslaved.

Aristotle's views on this topic were long-lasting. As recently as the first half of the twentieth century, similar notions still had strong support. In 1940, in the *Principles of*

*Human Geography*, Ellsworth Huntington and C. W. Cushing wrote:

> *The well-known contrast between the energetic people of the most progressive parts of the temperate zone and the inert inhabitants of the tropics and even of intermediate regions, such as Persia, is largely due to climate . . . the people of the cyclonic regions rank so far above those of the other parts of the world that they are the natural leaders.*

Huntington and Cushing claim climate is the critical factor in how humans behave. Yet what constitutes an "ideal" climate lies in the eyes of the beholder. For Aristotle, it was the Mediterranean climate of Greece. Through the eyes of more recent commentators from western Europe and North America, the climates most suited to progress and productiveness in culture, politics, and technology are (you guessed it) those of western Europe and the northeastern United States. Each of these theories can be classified as **environmental determinism**, which holds that human behavior, individually and collectively, is strongly affected by, even controlled or determined by, the physical environment.

Environmentally deterministic theories that explain Europe as "superior" to the rest of the world because of the climate and location of the region ignore the fact that for thousands of years, the most technologically advanced civilizations were not in Europe. The hearths of the agricultural and urban revolutions and the hearths of all of the world's major religions were in North Africa, Southwest Asia, Southeast Asia, and East Asia, not Europe.

Chipping away at deterministic explanations helped move the geographic study of the relationships between human society and the environment in different directions. Everyone agrees that the natural environment affects human activity in some ways, but people are the decision makers and the modifiers—not just the slaves of environmental forces. People, motivated primarily by cultural traits, economics, and politics, shape environments, constantly altering the landscape and impacting environmental systems.

## Possibilism

In response to environmental determinism, geographers argued that the natural environment merely serves to limit the range of choices available to a culture. The choices that a society makes depend on what its members need and on what technology is available to them. Geographers called this doctrine **possibilism**.

Even possibilism, however, has its limitations, partly because it encourages a line of inquiry that starts with the physical environment and asks what it allows. Human cultures, however, frequently push the boundaries of what is "environmentally possible" through their own ideas and ingenuity, and advances in technology. In the interconnected, technologically dependent world, it is possible to transcend many of the limitations imposed by the natural environment.

Today, much research in human geography focuses on how and why humans have altered their environment, and on the sustainability of their practices. In the process, the interest in **cultural ecology**, an area of inquiry concerned with culture as a system of adaptation to and alteration of environment, has been supplemented by interest in **political ecology**, an area of inquiry fundamentally concerned with the environmental consequences of dominant political-economic arrangements and understandings (see Chapter 13). The fundamental point is that human societies are diverse and the human will is too powerful to be determined by environment.

## Today's Human Geography

Human geography today seeks to make sense of the spatial organization of humanity and human institutions on Earth, the character of the places and regions created by people, and the relationships between humans and the physical environment. Human geography encompasses many subdisciplines, including political geography, economic geography, population geography, and urban geography. Human geography also encompasses cultural geography, which incorporates a concern with culture traits such as religion, language, and ethnicity.

Cultural geography is both part of human geography and also its own approach to all aspects of human geography. Cultural geography looks at the ways culture is implicated in the full spectrum of topics addressed in human geography. As such, cultural geography can be seen as a perspective on human geography as much as a component of it.

To appreciate more fully the vast topics researched by human geographers, we can examine the multitude of careers human geographers pursue. Human geographers have varying titles: location analyst, urban planner, diplomat, remote sensing analyst, geographic information scientist, area specialist, travel consultant, political analyst, intelligence officer, cartographer, educator, soil scientist, transportation planner, park ranger, and environmental consultant. All of these careers and more are open to geographers because each of these fields is grounded in the understanding of places and is advanced through spatial analysis.

 Choose a geographic concept introduced in this chapter. Think about something that is of personal interest to you (music, literature, politics, science, sports), and consider how your chosen field could be studied from a geographical perspective. Think about space, landscape, and place. Write a geographic question that could be the foundation for a geographic study of the subject you have chosen.

# Summary

Our study of human geography will analyze people and places and explain how they interact across space and time to create our world. Chapters 2 and 3 lay the basis for our study of human geography by looking at where people live. Chapters 4–7 focus on aspects of culture and how people use culture and identity to make sense of themselves in their world. The remaining chapters examine how people have created a world in which they function economically, politically, and socially, and how their activities in those realms recreate themselves and their world.

# Geographic Concepts

human geography
globalization
physical geography
spatial
spatial distribution
pattern
medical geography
pandemic
epidemic
spatial perspective
five themes
location
location theory
human-environment
region
place
sense of place
perception of place
movement
spatial interaction
distance

accessibility
connectivity
landscape
cultural landscape
sequent occupance
cartography
reference maps
thematic maps
absolute location
global positioning system
geocaching
relative location
mental map
activity space
terra incognita
generalized maps
remote sensing
geographic information
    systems
rescale
formal region

functional region
perceptual region
culture
culture trait
culture complex
cultural hearth
independent invention
diffusion
time-distance decay
cultural barrier
expansion diffusion
hierarchical diffusion
contagious diffusion
stimulus diffusion
relocation diffusion
geographic concept
environmental
    determinism
possibilism
cultural ecology
political ecology

# Learn More Online

About Careers in Geography
www.aag.org/cs/careerswww.bls.gov/opub/ooq/2005/spring/
art01.pdf

About Geocaching
www.geocaching.org

About Globalization and Geography
www.lut.ac.uk/gawc/rb/rb40.html

About John Snow and His Work on Cholera
http://www.ph.ucla.edu/epi/snow.html

About the State of Food Insecurity in the World
www.fao.org

About World Hunger
www.wfp.org

About Dengue in Brazil and the World Cup
www.elsevier.com/connect/scientists-predict-dengue-fever-
risk-during-world-cup-in-brazil

# Watch It Online

About Globalization
www.learner.org/resources/series180.html#program_descriptions
click on Video On Demand for "One Earth, Many Scales"

# CHAPTER 2

# POPULATION AND HEALTH

## FIELD NOTE

### Basic Infrastructure

The words wafted in the air as my colleague and I took a minute to process them. We were in Shanghai, China, visiting with a Chinese student who had spent a semester at our small college in a town of 26,000 in rural South Dakota. My colleague had asked the student what he missed most about our small town of Aberdeen. He replied without hesitating, "Basic infrastructure."

I thought about brand-new subway lines in Shanghai and Beijing, new airports throughout China, and high-speed trains being built to connect China's cities. I visualized the miles of gleaming new concrete we had driven on that afternoon on the ring highway on the outskirts of Shanghai (Fig. 2.1) and the empty fields where houses or other buildings had been leveled to make room for new high-density housing, more concrete, and more infrastructure. Shanghai's metro system only dates to 1995. Shanghai now has the most extensive metro system on Earth—a system capable of transporting 5 million people a day. I

© Erin H. Fouberg

■ **Figure 2.1**

**Shanghai, China.** Air pollution fills the sky above a new transit center and highway interchange. The U.S. Department of State collects its own data and has its own air quality measurement system to inform Americans living in China about unhealthy air quality in major Chinese cities.

thought about the lack of public transportation in my small town. I remembered that in 2010, China made a commitment to spend an additional $1 trillion on urban infrastructure by 2015. I considered the words United States President Barack Obama used as he described, enviously, the infrastructure in China, "their ports, their train systems their airports are all vastly superior to us now."

I looked at the student and said, "Basic infrastructure? But you have better subway lines, high-speed railroads, roads, and airports than we do in the States." "Yes," he said, "But I don't have hot water." He also doesn't have clean drinking water coming from the tap.

A 2010 report in *Foreign Policy* agreed: "China's biggest urban challenge may be water; already, it has little to spare. Some 70 percent of water use today traces back to agriculture, but

29

demand from urban consumers and commercial enterprise is on the rise. Even if the sheer amount of water isn't the problem, location will be; the country will need to spend more than $120 billion on water systems in the coming years to transport, store, and manage supplies." A graduate student in Beijing also pointed out the water problem in China's cities. Her dormitory houses about 1000 students, but they all must leave the building and walk to a central facility to shower, and she reported that they are only allowed to shower between 2 and 4 PM or between 9 and 11 PM.

China's population of 1.36 billion people has been migrating to cities in droves since economic reforms began in 1978. In 2011, the population of the world hit 7 billion people, with rising populations in China and India accounting for 40 percent of the population growth. China has undergone incredibly rapid expansion in its mining and manufacturing sectors, resulting in economic growth rates that have approached 10 percent in some years. But rapid economic growth took its toll on water quality in China, exacerbating water shortages in the country.

Providing services for 1.36 billion people is no small feat. Even though demographers now predict China's population will stabilize at 1.4 billion by 2025 and begin to decline after that, shifts in the composition of the population will continue to challenge the provision of basic infrastructure to the country's people.

Southern, coastal China has a moist climate, much like the southeastern United States, but the climate in northern China is drier. With only 7 percent of the world's fresh water supply, China faces an uphill battle in its efforts to provide water resources for its expanding population. This challenge is compounded by the fact that southern China has 80 percent of the country's water (*Foreign Policy*, 2011). To remedy the imbalance, China is now building a $60 billion canal system called the South–North Water Transfer Project that will include three different routes to divert water from the Yangtze River in southern China to the cities in the north (Fig. 2.2).

In this chapter, we examine the distribution of the world's population at several scales in order to understand where people live and why they live where they do. We also look at global population growth rates, noting that they vary widely across our planet. Even as population growth rates in wealthier parts of the world often fall below zero, the population of poorer regions continues to expand, in some countries at rates far above the global average. No discussion of population would be complete without considering the social conditions prevailing across the world: Health, well-being, and population growth tend to be closely related. Governments play a role in shaping these factors—an issue we explore at the end of the chapter.

Frederic J. Brown/AFP/Getty Images

**■■ Figure 2.2**
**Yixian, China.** This canal is part of the South–North Water Transfer Project. The $60 billion project will divert water from southern China to northern China along three different routes.

# Key Questions FOR CHAPTER 2

1. Where in the world do people live and why?
2. Why do populations rise or fall in particular places?
3. Why does population composition matter?
4. How does the geography of health influence population dynamics?
5. How do governments affect population change?

## WHERE IN THE WORLD DO PEOPLE LIVE AND WHY?

When geographers study population, they focus on the variability of demographic features and factors across space. *Demography* is the study of population in general perspective. Population geographers work in tandem with demographers, seeking answers to the problems posed by these variations. The concept of scale is crucial to studies of population because population dynamics that are evident at small scales (cities, intrastate regions) cannot necessarily be seen when one looks at the country or world regional scale. The reverse is true as well.

Demographers report the **population density** of a country as a measure of total population relative to land size (Fig. 2.3). Population density assumes an even distribution of people over the land. The United States, for example, with a territory of 5,692,815 square miles or 9,161,966 square kilometers (excluding the surfaces of lakes and ponds and coastal waters up to three nautical miles from shore) had a population of 316 million in 2013. This yields an average population density for the United States of just over 83 per square mile (33 per sq km). This density figure is also known as the country's **arithmetic population density**, and in a very general way it emphasizes the contrasts between the United States and such countries as Bangladesh (2817 per sq mi or 1087 per sq km), the Netherlands (1046 per sq mi or 404 per sq km), and Japan (872 per sq mi or 337 per sq km).

No country has an evenly distributed population, and arithmetic population figures do not reflect the emptiness of most of Alaska and the sparseness of population in much of

## FIELD NOTE

"An overpass across one of Yangon's busy streets provides a good perspective on the press of humanity in lowland Southeast Asia. Whether in urban areas or on small back roads in the countryside, people are everywhere—young and old, fit and infirm. When population densities are high in areas of poverty and unsophisticated infrastructure, vulnerabilities to natural hazards can be particularly great. This phenomenon became stunningly evident in 2008 when a tropical cyclone devastated a significant swath of the Irrawaddy Delta south of Yangon, killing some 100,000 people and leaving millions homeless."

© Alexander B. Murphy

■ **Figure 2.3**
**Yangon, Myanmar (Burma).**

# FIELD NOTE

"The contrasting character of the Egyptian landscape could not be more striking. Along the Nile River, the landscape is one of green fields, scattered trees, and modest houses, as along this stretch of the river's west bank near Luxor (Fig. 2.4A). But anytime I wander away from the river, brown, wind-sculpted sand dominates the scene as far as the eye can see (Fig. 2.4B). Where people live and what they do is not just a product of culture; it is shaped by the physical environment as well."

■ **Figure 2.4A**
**Luxor, Egypt.**

© Alexander B. Murphy

■ **Figure 2.4B**
**Luxor, Egypt.**

© Alexander B. Murphy

the West. In other cases, it is actually quite misleading. Egypt, with a population of 84.7 million in 2013, has a seemingly moderate arithmetic population density of 85 per square kilometer (220 per sq mi). Egypt's territory of 995,450 square kilometers (384,345 sq mi) however, is mostly desert, and the vast majority of the population is crowded into the valley and delta of the Nile River. An estimated 98 percent of all Egyptians live on just 3 percent of the country's land, so the arithmetic population density figure is meaningless in this case (Fig. 2.4A, B).

## Physiologic Population Density

A more insightful index of population density relates the total population of a country or region to the area of *arable* (farmable) land it contains. This approach yields a **physiologic population density figure**, which specifies the number of people per unit area of agriculturally productive land. Take again the case of Egypt. Although millions of people live in its great cities (Cairo and Alexandria) and smaller urban centers, the irrigated farmland is densely peopled as well. When we measure the entire population of Egypt relative to the arable land in the country, the resulting physiologic density figure for Egypt in the year 2013 is 2628 per square kilometer (6808 per sq mi). This number is far more reflective of Egypt's population pressure, and it continues to rise rapidly despite Egypt's efforts to expand its irrigated farmlands.

Appendix B (available at www.wiley.com/college/fouberg) provides complete data on both arithmetic and physiologic population densities, and some of the data stand out markedly. Mountainous Switzerland's physiologic density is 10 times as high as its arithmetic density because only 1 out of every 10 acres in Switzerland is arable. Ukraine's population is 45,500,000 and its arithmetic density (population per sq km) is 75 (195 per sq mi). Ukraine has vast farmlands, which make its physiologic density 145 people per square kilometer of arable land (368 per sq mi). The difference in arithmetic density and physiologic density for a single country reveals the proportion of arable land to all land. In the case of Ukraine, the physiologic density is 1.68 times as high as the arithmetic density because 1 out of every 1.68 acres of land in Ukraine is arable.

In Appendix B, the countries and territories of Middle America and the Caribbean stand out as having high physiologic densities compared to the moderate physiologic densities for South America. India's physiologic density is the lowest in South Asia despite its huge population. Both China and India have populations well over 1 billion, but according to the physiologic density, India has much more arable land per person than China.

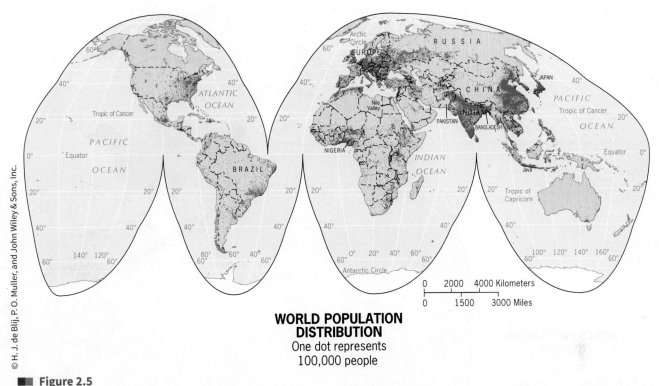

**WORLD POPULATION
DISTRIBUTION**
One dot represents
100,000 people

■ **Figure 2.5**

**World Population Distribution.** Practice reading a thematic map by asking where people are most concentrated. The largest clusters of people globally are in East Asia, South Asia, and Europe. Throughout the world, people are concentrated along coastlines, major rivers, and in cities.

## Population Distribution

People are not distributed evenly across the world or within a country. One-third of the world's population lives in China and India. Yet, each country has large expanses of land (the Himalayas in India and a vast interior desert in China) where people are absent or sparsely distributed. In addition to studying population densities, geographers study **population distributions**—the arrangement of people on the Earth's surface. Geographers often represent population distributions using **dot maps**, with each dot representing a certain number of people. At the local scale, a dot map of population can show each individual farm in a sparsely populated rural area. At the global scale, the data are much more generalized (e.g., Fig. 2.5). In the following section of this chapter, we study world population distribution and density.

## World Population Distribution and Density

From humanity's beginnings, people have been unevenly distributed across the land. Today, contrasts between crowded countrysides and bustling cities on the one hand and empty areas on the other hand have only intensified. Historically, people tended to congregate in places where they could grow food—making for a high correlation between arable land and population density. Cities generally began in agricultural areas, and for most of history, people lived closest to the most agriculturally productive areas. In recent times, advances in agricultural technology and in the transportation of agricultural goods have begun to change this pattern.

At the global scale, where one dot on a map represents 100,000 people, three major clusters of population jump out (Fig. 2.5). Each of the three largest population clusters is on the Eurasian (Europe and Asia combined) landmass. The fourth largest is in North America.

### EAST ASIA

Although the distribution map (Fig. 2.5) requires no color contrasts, Figure 2.6 depicts population density through shading: The darker the color, the larger the number of people per unit area. The most extensive area of dark shading lies in East Asia, primarily in China but also in Korea and Japan. Almost one-quarter of the world's population is concentrated here—over 1.36 billion people in China alone.

In addition to high population density in China's large cities, ribbons of high population density extend into the interior along the Yangtze and Yellow River valleys. Farmers along China's major river valleys produce crops of wheat and rice to feed not only themselves, but also the population of major Chinese cities such as Shanghai and Beijing.

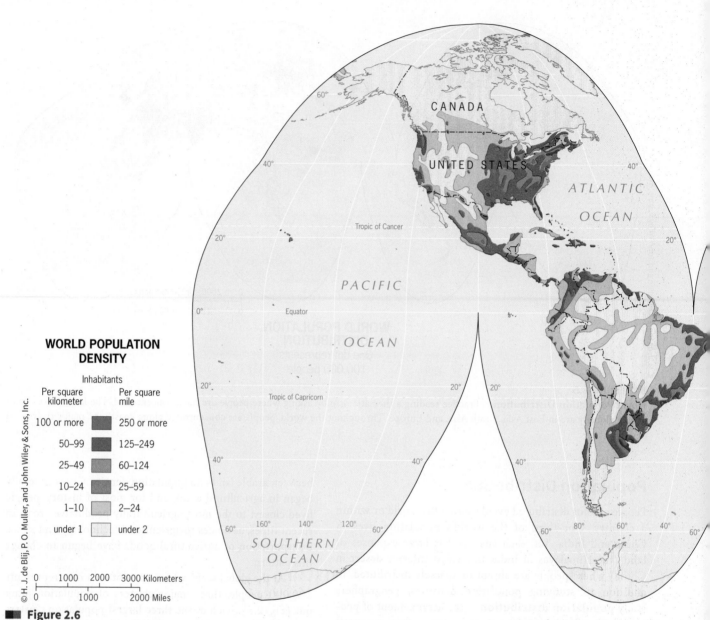

## WORLD POPULATION DENSITY

Inhabitants

| Per square kilometer | Per square mile |
|---|---|
| 100 or more | 250 or more |
| 50–99 | 125–249 |
| 25–49 | 60–124 |
| 10–24 | 25–59 |
| 1–10 | 2–24 |
| under 1 | under 2 |

0   1000   2000   3000 Kilometers

0          1000          2000 Miles

© H. J. de Blij, P. O. Muller, and John Wiley & Sons, Inc.

■ **Figure 2.6**

**World Population Density.**   Classifying population density into levels and using colors to represent levels of density, this map allows comparison between areas. The common color among East Asia, South Asia, and Europe shows these regions have similar population densities. The density level of the east coast of the United States is similar to France and other areas in blue on the map. The sparse density of much of Canada is similar to interior Australia, western China, the interior of South America, and the Sahara in Africa.

## SOUTH ASIA

The second major population concentration also lies in Asia and is similar in many ways to that of East Asia. At the heart of this cluster of more than 1.5 billion people lies India. The concentration extends into Pakistan and Bangladesh and onto the island of Sri Lanka. Here, people again cluster in major cities, on the coasts, and in major river basins, such as those created by the Ganges and Indus. The South Asia population cluster is growing more rapidly than the others as a result of China's declining total fertility rate (TFR). Demographers predict that by 2030, 1 out of 6 people in the world will live in India.

Two physical geography barriers create the boundaries of the South Asia population cluster: the Himalaya Mountains to the north and the mountains west of the Indus River Valley in Pakistan. This is a confined region with a rapidly growing population. As in East Asia, the overwhelming majority of the people here are farmers, but in South Asia the pressure on the land is even greater. In Bangladesh, over 156 million people, almost all of them farmers, are crowded into an area about the size of Iowa. Over large parts of Bangladesh the rural population density is between 3000 and 5000 people per square mile. By comparison, in 2010 the population of Iowa was just

about 3 million people, and the rural population density was 53 people per square mile.

## EUROPE

An axis of dense population extends from Ireland and the United Kingdom into Russia and includes large parts of Germany, Poland, Ukraine, and Belarus. It also includes the Netherlands and Belgium, parts of France, and northern Italy. This European cluster contains over 715 million inhabitants, less than half the population of the South Asia cluster. A comparison of the population and physical maps indicates that in Europe terrain and environment are not as closely related to population distribution as they are in East and South Asia. For example, note the lengthy extension in Figure 2.5, which protrudes far into Russia. Unlike the Asian extensions, which reflect fertile river valleys, the European extension reflects the

orientation of Europe's coal fields. If you look closely at the physical map, you will note that comparatively dense population occurs even in mountainous, rugged country, such as the boundary zone between Poland and its neighbors to the south. A much greater correspondence exists between coastal and river lowlands and high population density in Asia than in Europe generally.

Another contrast can be seen in the number of Europeans who live in cities and towns. The European population cluster includes numerous cities and towns, many of which developed as a result of the Industrial Revolution. In Germany, 73 percent of the people live in urban places; in the United Kingdom, 80 percent; and in France, 78 percent. With so many people concentrated in the cities, the rural countryside is more open and sparsely populated than in East and South Asia (where only about 45 percent of the people reside in cities and towns).

The three major population concentrations we have discussed—East Asia, South Asia, and Europe—account for over 4 billion of the total world population of 7 billion people. Nowhere else on the globe is there a population cluster even half as great as any of these. The populations of South America and Africa combined barely exceed the population of India alone.

## NORTH AMERICA

North America has one quite densely populated region, stretching along the urban areas of the East Coast, from Washington, D.C., in the south to Boston, Massachusetts, in the north. As shown in Figure 2.5, the cities in this region agglomerate into one large urban area that includes Washington, D.C., Baltimore, Philadelphia, New York City, and Boston. Urban geographers use the term **megalopolis** to refer to such huge urban agglomerations. The cities of megalopolis account for more than 20 percent of the U.S. population.

Look at the global-scale map in Figure 2.6 and notice that the dense population concentration of megalopolis is stretched west into the nearby Canadian cities of Toronto, Ottawa, Montreal, and Quebec City. Adding these Canadian cities to the population of megalopolis creates a population cluster that is about one quarter the size of Europe's population cluster. If you have lived or traveled in megalopolis, you can think about traffic and comprehend what dense population means. However, recognize that the total population of megalopolis is 2.8 percent of the East Asian population cluster and that the 10,725 people per square kilometer density of New York City (27,778 per sq mi) does not rival the density in world cities such as Mumbai, India, with a population density of 28,701 per square kilometer (77,609 per sq mi) or Jakarta, Indonesia, with a population density of 15,398 per square kilometer (39,859 per sq mi).

## Reliability of Population Data

When the United States planned and conducted its 2010 population **census**, the government ran advertisements on television and sent mailings encouraging every person in the country to be counted. State and city governments also recognized the importance of having their citizens counted in order to gain more federal dollars in per capita outlays because much federal government funding depends on population data. If the population of a disadvantaged group is undercounted, it translates into a loss of dollars for city governments that rely on federal government funding to pay for social services to disadvantaged groups. As a result, advocates for disadvantaged groups encourage people to fill out their census forms; they are concerned that the people already in disadvantaged groups suffer when they are undercounted in the census. Being undercounted also translates into less government representation because the number of congressional seats allotted to each state is based on the census counts.

In 2000 and again in 2010, advocacy groups urged the Census Bureau to sample the population and derive population statistics from the samples. They argued that this approach would more accurately reflect the number of people in the United States. However, the United States Census Bureau continued to conduct its census as it always has, trying to count each individual in its borders.

If a prosperous country such as the United States has problems conducting an accurate census, imagine the difficulties that must be overcome in less well-off countries. The cost, organization, and reporting of a census go beyond what many countries can afford or handle.

Several agencies collect data on world population. The United Nations records official statistics that national governments assemble and report. The World Bank and the Population Reference Bureau also gather and generate data and report on the population of the world and of individual countries.

If you compare the population data reported by each of these sources, you will find inconsistencies in the data. Data on population, growth rates, food availability, health conditions, and incomes are often informed estimates rather than actual counts.

**thinking** *geographically*   As we discussed in the field note at the beginning of this chapter, the populations of China and India account for 40 percent of the world currently, and India is predicted to outpace China's population in the 2030s. How will Figure 2.5 look different 50 years from now? If you were updating this textbook in 50 years, where would the largest population clusters in the world be?

## WHY DO POPULATIONS RISE OR FALL IN PARTICULAR PLACES?

In the late 1960s, alarms sounded throughout the world with the publication of Paul Ehrlich's *The Population Bomb*. Ehrlich and others warned that the world's population was increasing too quickly—and was outpacing our food production! We can trace alarms over the burgeoning world population back to 1798, when British economist Thomas Malthus published *An Essay on the Principles of Population*. In this work Malthus warned that the world's population was increasing faster than the food supplies needed to sustain it. His reasoning was that food supplies grew *linearly*, adding acreage and crops incrementally by year, whereas population grew *exponentially*, compounding on the year before. From 1803 to 1826, Malthus issued revised editions of his essay and responded vigorously to a barrage of criticism.

Malthus's predictions assumed that food production is confined spatially, that what people can eat within a country depends on what is grown in the country. We now know his assumption does not hold true; countries are not closed systems. Malthus did not foresee how globalization would aid the exchange of agricultural goods across the world. Mercantilism, colonialism, and capitalism brought interaction among the Americas, Europe, Africa, Asia, and the Pacific. Through global interaction, new agricultural methods developed, and commodities and livestock diffused across oceans. In the 1700s, farmers in Ireland grew dependent on a South American crop that was well suited for its rocky soils: the potato. Today, wealthier countries that lack arable land, such as Norway, can import the majority of their food, circumventing the limitations on food production there.

Malthus also assumed that the growth of food production was linear, but food production has grown exponentially as the acreage under cultivation expands, mechanization of agricultural production diffuses, improved strains of seed are developed, and more fertilizers are used. In the twenty-first century, bioengineering continues to bring new hybrids, genetically modified organisms, and countless herbicides and pesticides that enable exponential growth in food production.

Because of the environmental costs of modern farming techniques, serious questions have arisen about future limitations on the exponential expansion of agriculture. However, that is not why Malthus's ideas continue to attract followers. Instead, most neo-Malthusians focus on the continuing rise in

the world's population, which they see as a direct cause of human suffering. Although many demographers predict the world's population will stabilize later in the twenty-first century, neo-Malthusians argue that overpopulation is a real problem that must be addressed now.

## Population Growth at World, Regional, National, and Local Scales

Population change in one place is often affected by developments in neighboring places, but to understand the population picture, it is useful to start by looking at the demographic characteristics of individual places. One basic demographic indicator is the **natural increase** of the population in a given place—calculated by subtracting the total number of deaths from the total number of births. Focusing solely on natural increase, however, misses two other key pieces of the demographic picture: immigration, which along with births adds to the total population, and emigration (outmigration), which along with deaths reduces the total population. Using these four components, we can calculate demographic change within a territory.

Figure 2.7 shows natural increase rates by country but does not take into account emigration and immigration. Other maps and tables of population growth you may see

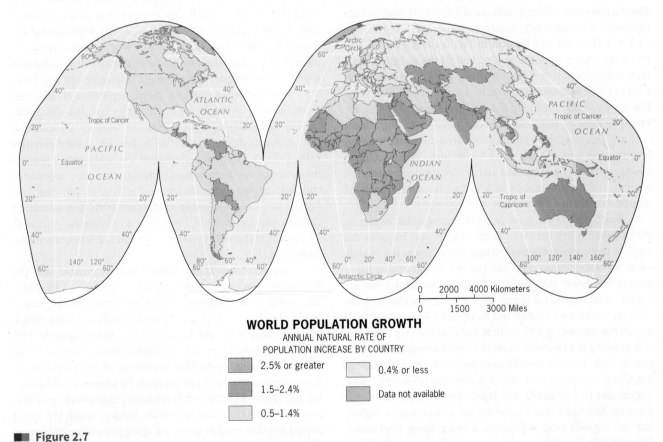

**WORLD POPULATION GROWTH**
ANNUAL NATURAL RATE OF
POPULATION INCREASE BY COUNTRY

- 2.5% or greater
- 1.5–2.4%
- 0.5–1.4%
- 0.4% or less
- Data not available

■ **Figure 2.7**
**World Population Growth, 2012.**   Annual natural rate of population increase by country. Population growth rates in Subsaharan Africa remain relatively high, and population growth rates in Europe and Russia remain relatively low.   *Data from:* Population Reference Bureau, 2012.

consider emigration and immigration. Statistics for each population trait can be calculated globally, by region, by country, or even by smaller locale—each telling a somewhat different story. When studying population data across scales and across the world, we must constantly remind ourselves of exactly what is being calculated and what places are being represented. Otherwise, many of the statistics we read will appear to be contradictory.

## POPULATION GROWTH AT THE REGIONAL AND NATIONAL SCALES

The world map of population growth rates (Fig. 2.7), displayed by country, confirms the wide range of natural increases in different geographic regions. These variations have existed as long as records have been kept: Countries and regions go through stages of expansion and decline at varying times. In the mid-twentieth century, the population of the former Soviet Union was growing vigorously. Thirty years ago, India's population was growing at nearly 3.0 percent, more than most African countries; then India's growth rate fell below that of Subsaharan Africa. Today, Africa's rate of natural increase still is higher than India's (2.6 percent to 1.5 percent), but parts of Subsaharan Africa are still reeling from the impact of the AIDS epidemic, which killed millions, orphaned children, reduced life expectancies, and curtailed growth rates.

The map also reveals continuing high growth rates in Muslim countries of North Africa and Southwest Asia, including Sudan (2.6 percent), Yemen (2.7 percent), Afghanistan (2.8 percent) and the Palestinian territories (2.9 percent). For some time during the second half of the twentieth century, countries in this region saw their growth rates increase even as those in most of the rest of the world were declining. But more recently several of the fast-growing populations, for example, those of Iran and Morocco, have shown significant declines. Demographers point to the correlation between high growth rates and opportunities for women: Where cultural traditions restrict educational and professional prospects for women, and men dominate as a matter of custom, rates of natural increase tend to be high.

South Asia is the most important geographic region in the population growth rate picture. The region includes the country that appears destined to overtake China as the world's most populous: India. Only one country in this region has a growth rate lower than the world average: Sri Lanka. But Sri Lanka's total population is only 20.8 million, whereas the fast-growing countries, Pakistan and Bangladesh, have a combined population exceeding 347 million. India, as the map shows, is still growing at a rate well above the world average. The situation in East Asia, the world's most populous region, is different. China's official rate of natural growth has fallen well below 1.0 percent (0.5 in 2010), and Japan's population is no longer growing. Southeast Asia's natural growth rates remain higher, but this region's total population is much lower than either East or South Asia; key countries, such as Indonesia, Thailand, and Vietnam, have declining growth rates.

South America, whose natural population growth rates were alarmingly high just a generation ago, is experiencing significant reductions in their growth rates. The region as a whole is still growing at 1.1 percent, but Brazil's population growth rate, for example, has declined from 2.9 percent in the mid-1960s to 0.9 percent today. And the populations of Argentina, Chile, and Uruguay are growing at rates well below the world average.

As Figure 2.7 shows, the slowest growing countries—including those with declining rates of natural population increase—lie in the economically wealthier areas of the world extending from the United States and Canada across Europe and Japan. In the Southern Hemisphere, Australia, New Zealand, and Uruguay are in this category. Wealth is not the only reason for negative population growth rates. Russia's population is declining because of the social dislocation that took place in the wake of the collapse of the Soviet Union: Deteriorating health conditions, high rates of alcoholism and drug use, and economic problems combined to shorten life expectancies (especially among males) and to lower birth rates. In recent years, Russia's economy has improved, but its birth rate has remained low. Similar problems afflict Ukraine and Kazakhstan, two of Russia's neighbors, which also show slow or negative growth.

Between 1900 and 2000, the world's population rose from 1.6 billion people to 6.1 billion, and in 2011, it reached 7 billion. This growth is not simply a result of women having more children. Instead, the last century of population growth saw greatly expanded life expectancies. In 1900, global life expectancy was 30 years; by 2000, it was 65 years. Demographers now predict that world population may well stabilize at around 10 billion people somewhere between 2050 and 2100.

Predictions of a stabilized global population are based on a combination of longer life expectancies coupled with lower fertility rates. Demographers measure whether a population can replace its deaths with births by looking at **total fertility rates** (TFRs). To reach replacement levels—to keep a population stable over time without immigration—the women of childbearing age in a country need a TFR of 2.1. The TFR reports the average number of children born to a woman of childbearing age. In 2000, more than 60 countries, containing 45 percent of the world's population, had fallen below replacement level (Fig. 2.8).

Demographers at the United Nations predict that the TFR of the combined world will fall to around 2.2 by 2050. The world TFR combines regions including Europe, where fertility levels are low (Fig. 2.8), and regions including Africa, where fertility levels are high. In 2013, the worldwide TFR was 2.5, ranging from 1.2 in Bosnia-Herzegovina to 7.6 in Niger. Predicting population growth is difficult because so much depends on the decisions made by women of childbearing age. Demographers and population geographers agree that two major current trends will influence how much the world population continues to grow: the aging population of Europe, China, and Japan, and the declining fertility rate in many developing countries, including Brazil and Iran.

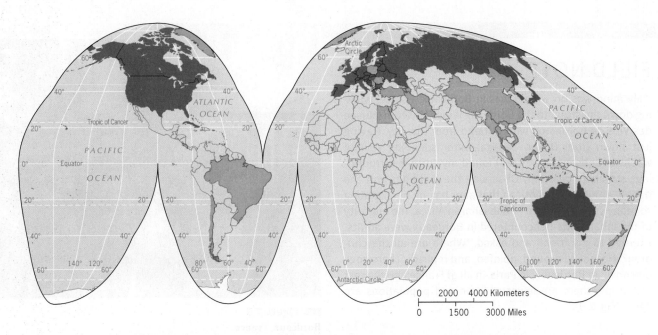

## COUNTRIES WITH TOTAL FERTILITY RATE BELOW REPLACEMENT LEVEL

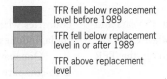

TFR fell below replacement level before 1989

TFR fell below replacement level in or after 1989

TFR above replacement level

**■ Figure 2.8**

**Year That Total Fertility Rate (TFR) Among Women Fell Below Replacement Levels.** The wealthiest parts of the world were the first to see TFRs fall below replacement levels. *Data from*: World Bank, World Development Indicators, 2012.

Both the aging population of developed countries and the declining fertility rates in developing countries lead to predictions that the global population will continue to grow but at a lower rate. In wealthier countries, more women are choosing to stay in school, work on their careers, and marry later, delaying childbirth. The impact of the aging population of Europe can be seen in its **old-age dependency ratio**, which reports the relationship between the number of people over the age of 65 and the working-age population between 15 and 64. Europe had 24 old-age dependents for every 100 working-age people in 2010, and that figure is expected to rise to 47 by 2050. The old-age dependency ratio for Africa, by contrast, was 6 in 2010. For that continent, the challenge is a high **child dependency ratio** (74 in 2010 compared to just 23 in Europe).

An aging population requires substantial social adjustments. Older people retire and eventually suffer health problems, so they need pensions and medical care. The younger workers in the population must work in order to provide the tax revenues that enable the state to pay for these services. As the proportion of older people in a country increases, the proportion of younger people decreases. Thus, fewer young workers are providing tax revenues to support programs for more retired people. To change the age distribution of an aging country and provide more taxpayers, the only answer

is immigration: influxes of younger workers to do the work locals are unable or unwilling to do.

What will happen when a country resists immigration despite an aging population? Over the next half-century, Japan will be an interesting case study. Japan's population is no longer growing, and it is projected that the Japanese population will decline as it ages. The population fell from a peak of 127.84 million in 2004 to 127.3 million in 2013. Japan predicts its population will fall to around 100 million by 2050, a loss of 20 percent of its current population. Japan was a closed society for hundreds of years, and even today the Japanese government discourages immigration. More than 98 percent of the country's population is Japanese, according to government statistics. In August 1999, the British newspaper *The Guardian* reported that the Japanese government's efforts to maintain the homogeneity of the population are often "lauded domestically as a reason for the country's low crime rate" and strong industrial economy. In developing countries, a combination of government and nongovernment organizational programs encourage women to have fewer children. Some women are also choosing to have fewer children because of economic and social uncertainty. Today, TFRs are falling almost everywhere on Earth, in large part because of family planning. In some countries, fertility rates are declining dramatically. Kenya's TFR is now

# FIELD NOTE

"My mind was on wine. I was in Bordeaux, France, walking down the street to the Bordeaux Wines Museum (Musée des Vins de Bordeaux) with a friend from the city. Having just flown from Dakar, Senegal, after spending several weeks in Subsaharan Africa, I found my current surroundings strikingly different. Observing the buildings and the people around me, I noticed that after having been among so many young children in Subsaharan Africa, the majority of the inhabitants I encountered in Bordeaux were adults. I turned to my friend and asked, 'Where are all the children?' He looked around, pointed, and replied, 'There goes one now!' In Bordeaux, in Paris, in all of France and the rest of Europe, there are fewer children and populations are aging (Fig. 2.9)."

© H. J. de Blij

**Figure 2.9**
**Bordeaux, France.**

down to 4.5; China's fell from 6.1 to 1.75 in just 35 years and in 2010 dropped to 1.5, which it maintains today. Once the government of Iran began to allow family planning, the TFR fell from 6.8 in 1980 to 1.9 in 2013.

At one time a low TFR seemed to be a desirable national objective, something that all governments would surely want. However, long-term economic implications and demographic projections gave many governments pause. Countries need a young, vigorous, working-age population who work and pay taxes to support the long-term needs of an aging population. When governments saw their population growth rates decline sharply, many took countermeasures. China softened its one-child only policy; Sweden, Russia, and other European countries provided financial incentives like long maternity leaves and state-paid daycare to prospective mothers; and even the Japanese found themselves in a national debate over family size and immigration. Still, such programs and debates have so far had limited success in encouraging sustained population growth.

How can the worldwide population continue to increase when so many countries are experiencing low TFRs and population decline? Despite declining population growth rates and even negative growth rates (growth rates below 0.0) in a number of the world's countries, the global population continues to rise. The worldwide TFR was 2.5 in 2013, above the replacement level of 2.1. Although the population bomb Ehrlich warned of is no longer ticking at the same rapid pace, the worldwide population continues to grow. The low TFRs and low population growth rates enumerated in this chapter are dwarfed by continued additions to the population in

countries where growth rates are still relatively high, such as India, Indonesia, Bangladesh, Pakistan, and Nigeria.

One way to explain the growth rate in world population is to compare the population's rate of growth to its doubling time. Every rate of growth has a **doubling time**; for example, if you invested $100 at 10 percent, compounded annually

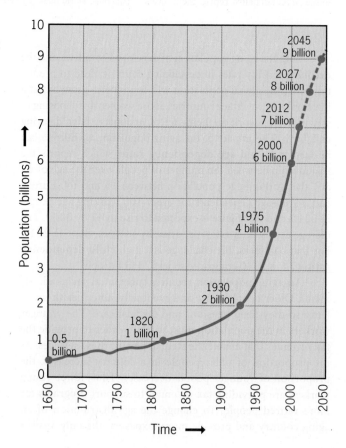

**Figure 2.10**

**Population Growth, 1650 to 2050.** The dashed line indicates one estimate of global population growth until 2050. *Data from:* United States Census Bureau, International Data Base, 2011.

(exponentially), it would take about seven years to double to $200, and then another seven years to become $400, and then another seven years to become $800. Therefore, when the growth rate is 10 percent, the doubling time is around seven years.

Two thousand years ago, the world's population was an estimated 250 million. More than 16 centuries passed before this total had doubled to 500 million, the estimated population in 1650. Just 170 years later, in 1820 (when Malthus was still writing), the population had doubled again, to 1 billion (Fig. 2.10). And barely more than a century after this, in 1930, it reached 2 billion. The doubling time was down to 100 years and dropping fast; the **population explosion** was in full gear. Only 45 years elapsed for the next doubling to take place, to 4 billion (1975). In the mid-1980s, doubling time was only 39 years. Since then, population policies designed to slow growth, including China's One Child Policy, have lengthened the word population's doubling time to 54 years.

For demographers and population geographers who study global population growth today, the concept of doubling time is losing much of its punch. With populations falling in many places, fears of global population doubling quickly are subsiding. Many indicators, such as the slowing of the doubling time, suggest that the worst may be over, that the explosive population growth of the twentieth century will be followed by a marked and accelerating slowdown during the twenty-first century. The global growth rate is now down to 1.4 percent, perhaps slightly lower. But today the world's population is 7 billion, yielding an increase in world population that still exceeds 80 million annually at this growth rate.

As a result of falling TFRs in both the developing and developed world, demographers no longer caution about doubling time. With women having fewer children, many demographers are predicting the world may reach **zero population growth** in the next 50 years. In fact, current predictions point to zero population growth globally by the end of the century, with population rising to 9.3 billion by 2050 and then leveling off to around 10 billion people.

No single factor can explain the variations shown in Figure 2.7. Economic prosperity as well as social dislocation reduce natural population growth rates. Economic well-being, associated with urbanization, higher levels of education, later marriage, family planning, and other factors, lowers population growth. In the table presented in Appendix B, compare the indices for natural population increase and the percentage of the population that is urbanized. In general, the higher the population's level of urbanization, the lower its natural increase. Cultural traditions also influence rates of population growth. Religion, for example, has a powerful impact on family planning and thus on growth rates, not only in Islamic countries but also in traditional Christian societies (such as the Philippines) and in Hindu-dominated communities (such as India).

## POPULATION GROWTH WITHIN COUNTRIES

The information provided in Figure 2.7 is based on countrywide statistics. Significant demographic variations also occur *within* countries. Political geographers call countries states. Governments partition their countries into administrative units called States (United States), provinces (Canada), departments (France) or the like. In India, for example, States in the north record population growth rates far above the national average (Fig. 2.11).

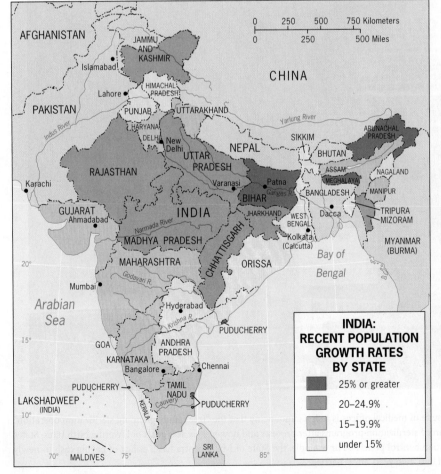

**■ Figure 2.11**

**Population Growth Rates in India, 2001–2011.** The agriculturally rich Ganges plain in northern India, the most densely populated part of the country, continues to have the highest growth rates. Population growth rates are lower in southern India, where women have higher literacy rates, better access to health care and birth control, and higher land ownership rates than in northern India. *Data from*: India Census Bureau, 2011.

But other States, in the west and southwest region, have populations that are growing much more slowly. Women in southern India have higher literacy rates, greater land ownership rates, better access to health care, and more access to birth control methods. All of these factors keep the growth rates lower in the south than the north of India.

In the 1950s, India became the first country in the world to institute a population planning program, before the fear of worldwide overpopulation and a global population bomb spread. In the 1960s, when census numbers revealed the extreme growth rates in the north, the Indian government instituted a national population planning program, encouraging States to join.

Despite the federal effort, rapid population growth continues, especially in the northern and eastern States. India is a federation of 28 States and 7 union territories, and the individual States differ greatly both culturally and politically. Social problems arose in some of the States where governments pursued the population planning campaign vigorously. During the 1970s, the Indian government began a policy of forced sterilization of any man with three or more children. The State of Maharashtra sterilized 3.7 million people before public opposition led to rioting, and the government abandoned the program (Fig. 2.12). Other States also engaged in compulsory sterilization programs, with heavy social and political costs. Eventually, 22.5 million people were sterilized.

Federal sterilization programs have ended in India, but States are free to pursue their own family planning programs, including sterilization. In 2004, three districts in the State of Uttar Pradesh (India's most populous State with over 204 million people) instituted a policy of exchanging gun licenses for sterilization. The policy allowed for a shotgun license in exchange for the sterilization of two people and a revolver license in exchange for the sterilization of five people. Abuse began almost immediately, with wealthy landowners sterilizing their laborers in exchange for gun licenses. Uttar Pradesh now encourages sterilization with incentives including housing and food. Far more women than men have been sterilized. A 2008 survey of households found 19.5 percent of women had been sterilized by tubal ligations and only .3 percent of men had been sterilized by vasectomies in Uttar Pradesh.

Today, most Indian State governments are using advertising and persuasion to encourage families to have fewer children. Posters urging people to have small families are everywhere, and the government supports a network of

**Figure 2.12**

**Maharashtra, India.**   Above the entrance to a suite of medical offices is a sign announcing that the "free family planning sterilization operation" closed in 1996. The Indian government ended forced sterilization programs after protests and now simply sets goals of lowering birth rates. States in India are at liberty to create their own population control policies. For example, the State of Maharashtra has a policy of paying cash to newly married couples who delay having their first child until two years after marriage.

family planning clinics even in the remotest villages. The southern States continue to report the lowest growth rates, correlating with higher wealth and higher education levels as well as higher literacy rates of females in these States. The eastern and northern States, the poorer regions of India, continue to report the highest growth rates.

Our world map of growth rates is a global overview, a mere introduction to the complexities of the geography of population. The example of India demonstrates that what we see at the scale of a world map does not give us the complete story of what is happening within each country or region of the world. Both India and China have over 1 billion people, but as a result of the higher growth rates in India (1.64) and declining growth rates in China (.5), demographers predict India will become the most populated country in the world in 2030.

## The Demographic Transition

The high population growth rates now occurring in many poorer countries are not necessarily permanent. In Europe, population growth has changed dramatically during the last three centuries. Demographers have used data on baptisms and funerals from churches in Great Britain to study changes in birth and death rates of the population. They calculated the **crude birth rate** (CBR)—the number of live births per year per thousand people in the population (Fig. 2.13)—and the

**crude death rate** (CDR)—the number of deaths per year per thousand people (Fig. 2.14). The difference between these two yields the rate of natural increase of a population.

The church data revealed that before the Industrial Revolution began in Great Britain in the 1750s, the country experienced high birth rates and high death rates, with small differences between the two. The result was low population growth. After industrialization began, the death rates in Great Britain began to fall as a result of better and more stable access to food and improved access to increasingly effective medicines. With a rapidly falling death rate and a birth rate that remained high, Britain's population explosion took place. From the late 1800s through two world wars in the 1900s, death rates continued to fall and birth rates began to fall, but stayed higher than death rates, resulting in continued population growth but at a slower rate. Finally, in recent history, both the birth rate and the death rate in Great Britain declined to low levels, resulting in slow or stabilized population growth.

Demographers call the shift in population growth the **demographic transition**. The transition is typically modeled as shown in Figure 2.15. The model is based on the kind of shift that Britain experienced, but other places either have gone through a similar shift or are in the process of doing so. The initial low-growth phase, which in all places endured for most of human history, is marked by high birth rates and

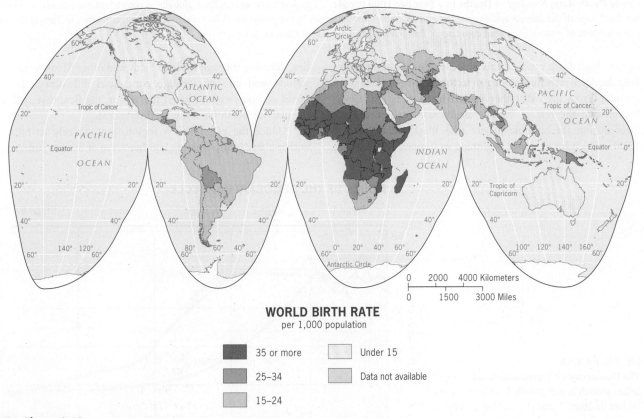

**WORLD BIRTH RATE**
per 1,000 population

- 35 or more
- 25–34
- 15–24
- Under 15
- Data not available

■ ■ **Figure 2.13**
**Crude Birth Rate. Number of Births in a Year per 1000 People.**    A fairly distinct north–south pattern is evident, as northern countries have lower crude birth rates than southern countries. The global south has a few clear outliers with low crude birth rates, notably Australia, New Zealand, Chile, and Uruguay.    *Data from*: Population Reference Bureau 2013.

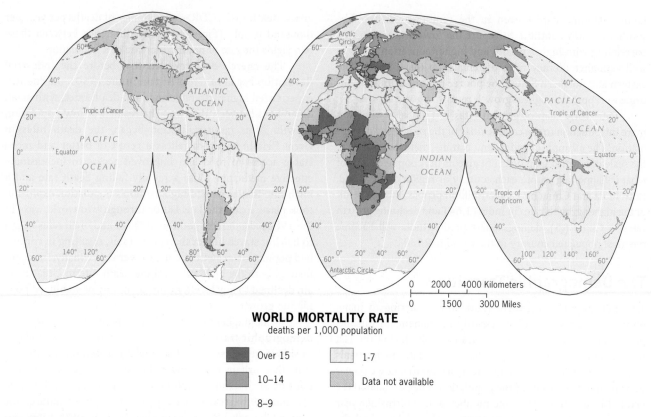

**WORLD MORTALITY RATE**
deaths per 1,000 population

| | |
|---|---|
| Over 15 | 1-7 |
| 10–14 | Data not available |
| 8–9 | |

■ **Figure 2.14**

**Crude Death Rate: Number of Deaths in a Year per 1000 People.**    The death rate has declined globally as countries have transitioned into the third stage of the demographic transition and beyond. A few countries in the global north have relatively high death rates, including Russia and a number of eastern European countries.    *Data from*: Population Reference Bureau, 2013.

equally high death rates. In this phase, epidemics and plagues keep the death rates high among all sectors of the population—in some cases so high that they exceed birth rates. For Great Britain and the rest of Europe, death rates exceeded birth rates during the bubonic plague (the Black Death) of the 1300s, which hit in waves beginning in Crimea on the Black

Sea, diffusing through trade to Sicily and other Mediterranean islands, and moving through contagious diffusion and the travel of rats (which hosted the vector, the flea, that spread the plague) north from the Mediterranean.

Once the plague hit a region, it was likely to return within a few years, creating another wave of human suffering.

**MODEL OF THE DEMOGRAPHIC CYCLE**

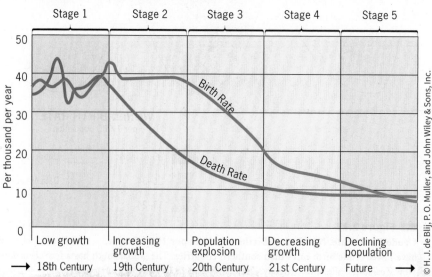

■ **Figure 2.15**

**The Demographic Transition Model.**    Population growth is particularly high between the middle of stage 2 and the middle of stage 4, when death rates have declined due to better food supply and access to medicine but birth rates have stayed relatively high before later declining.

Estimates of plague deaths vary between one-quarter and one-half of the population, with the highest death rates recorded in the West (where trade among regions was the greatest) and the lowest in the East (where cooler climates and less connected populations delayed diffusion). Across Europe, many cities and towns were left decimated. Historians estimate the population of Great Britain fell from nearly 4 million when the plague began to just over 2 million when it ended.

Famines also limited population growth. A famine in Europe just prior to the plague likely facilitated the diffusion of the disease by weakening the people. Records of famines in India and China during the eighteenth and nineteenth centuries document millions of people perishing. At other times, destructive wars largely wiped out population gains. Charts of world population growth show an increase in the world's population from 250 million people 2000 years ago to 500 million people in 1650 and 1 billion people in 1820. However, the lines connecting these points in time should not trend steadily upward. Rather, they turn up and down frequently, reflecting the impacts of disease, crop failures, and wars.

The beginning of the Industrial Revolution ushered in a period of accelerating population growth in Europe. Before workers could move from farms to factories, a revolution in agriculture had to occur. The eighteenth century marked the Second Agricultural Revolution, so named because the first occurred thousands of years earlier (see Chapter 11). During the Second Agricultural Revolution, farmers improved seed selection, practiced new methods of crop rotation, selectively bred livestock to increase production and quality, employed new technology such as the seed drill, expanded storage capacities, and consolidated landholdings for greater efficiencies. With more efficient farming methods, the number of people needed in farming decreased and the food supply increased, thereby supporting a higher population overall.

In the 1800s, as the Industrial Revolution diffused through continental Europe, other advances also helped lower death rates. Sanitation facilities made towns and cities safer from epidemics, soap came to be more widely used, and modern medical practices began to take hold. Disease prevention through vaccination introduced a new era in public health in the twentieth century. The combined improvements in food supply and medical practice resulted in a drastic reduction in death rates. Before 1750, death rates in Europe probably averaged 35 per 1000 (birth rates averaged under 40), but by 1850 the death rate was down to about 16 per 1000.

Birth rates fell at a slower rate, leading to a population explosion. The increase in the rate of population growth in Europe spurred waves of migration. Millions of people left the squalid, crowded industrial cities (and farms as well) to emigrate to other parts of the world. They were not the first to make this journey. Adventurers, explorers, merchants, and colonists had gone before them. In a major wave of colonization from 1500 through the 1700s, European migrants decimated native populations through conquest, slavery, and the introduction of diseases against which the local people had no natural immunity.

When a second wave of European colonization began in Africa and Asia during the late 1800s, the Europeans brought with them their newfound methods of sanitation and medical techniques, but these had the opposite effect. By the mid-1900s, declining death rates in Africa, India, and South America brought rapid population increases to these regions. At this point, new alarms and cautions of worldwide overpopulation rang.

Although the global alarms continued to ring, they subsided for populations in Europe and North America when population growth rates began to decline in the first half of the 1900s. The cause was a significant decline in birth rates. Populations continued to grow but at a much slower rate. Many countries in Central and South America and in Asia experienced falling birth rates later in the twentieth century, which helped slow the global population growth rate.

Why have birth rates declined? Throughout the 1900s, lower birth rates occurred first in countries with greater urbanization, wealth, and medical advances. As more and more people moved to cities, both the economics and the culture of large families changed. Instead of lending a hand on the family farm, children in urban areas became a drain on the family finances. At the same time, new opportunities—especially for women—were not always compatible with large families. Hence, many women delayed marriage and childbearing. Medical advances lowered infant and child mortality rates, lessening the sense that multiple children were necessary to sustain a family. In recent history, the diffusion of contraceptives, the accessibility of abortions, and conscious decisions by many women to have fewer or no children or to start having children at a later age have all lowered birth rates within a country.

In some parts of the world, countries are now experiencing exceptionally low TFRs. Low birth rates along with low death rates put the countries in a position of negligible, or even negative, population growth. Birth rates are lowest in the countries where women are the most educated and most involved in the labor force.

## Future Population Growth

It may be unwise to assume that the demographic cycles of all countries will follow the sequence that occurred in industrializing Europe or to believe that the still-significant population growth currently taking place in Bangladesh, Mexico, and numerous other countries will simply subside. Nonetheless, many agencies monitoring global population suggest that the populations of most (if not all) countries will stop growing at some time during the twenty-first century, reaching a so-called **stationary population level** (SPL).

Such predictions require frequent revision, however, and anticipated dates for population stabilization are often moved back. Only a few years ago, the United Nations predicted world population would stabilize at 10 billion in 200 years. The United Nations changed its predictions based on lower fertility rates in many countries. All agencies reporting population predictions have to revise their predictions periodically. In the late 1980s, for example, the World Bank predicted that the United States would reach SPL in 2035 with 276 million inhabitants. Brazil's population would stabilize at 353 million in 2070, Mexico's at 254 million in 2075, and China's at 1.4 billion in 2090. India, destined to become the world's most populous country, would reach SPL at 1.6 billion in 2150.

These figures have proven unrealistic. China's population passed the 1.2 billion mark in 1994, and India's reached 1 billion in 1998. If we were to project an optimistic decline in growth rates for both countries, China's population would "stabilize" at 1.4 billion in 2025 and India's at 1.7 billion in 2060, according to a 2011 United Nations report. But population increase is a cyclical phenomenon, and overall declines mask lags and spurts as well as regional disparities.

Examine Appendix B at www.wiley.com/college/fouberg. Study the growth rate column. Which countries have the highest growth rates? Determine what stage of the demographic transition these countries are in, and hypothesize what may lead them to the next stage.

## WHY DOES POPULATION COMPOSITION MATTER?

Maps showing the regional distribution and density of populations tell us about the number of people in countries or regions, but they cannot reveal other aspects of those populations: the number of men and women and their ages. These aspects of population, the **population composition**, are important because a populous country in which half the population is very young has quite different problems from a populous country in which a large proportion of the population is elderly. When geographers study populations, they are concerned not only with spatial distribution and growth rates but also with composition: the structure of a population in terms of age, sex, and other properties such as marital status and education. Age and sex are key indicators of population composition, and demographers and geographers use **population pyramids** to represent these traits visually (Fig. 2.16).

Population pyramids are used to display the percentages of each age group in a total population (normally five-year increments) by a horizontal bar whose length represents its share. Males in the group are to the left of the center line, females to the right.

A population pyramid can instantly convey the demographic situation in a country. In poorer countries, where birth and death rates generally remain high, the pyramid looks like an evergreen tree, with wide branches at the base and short ones near the top. The youngest age groups have the largest share of the population. In the pyramid for all poorer countries, the three groups up to age 14 account for more than 40 percent of the population. Older people, in the three highest age groups, represent less than 10 percent of the total. Slight variations of this pyramidal shape mark the population structure of such countries as Pakistan, Yemen, Guatemala, The Congo, and Laos. From age group 15 to 19 upward, each group is smaller than the one below it.

Wealthy countries have population pyramids that do not look like pyramids at all. Families become smaller, children fewer. The "pyramid" looks like a slightly lopsided vase, with the largest components of the population not at the bottom

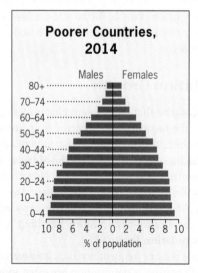

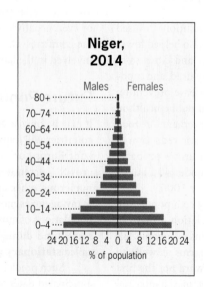

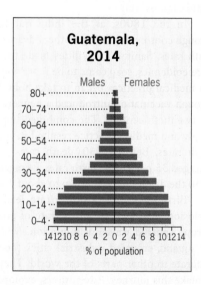

■ **Figure 2.16**

**Age–Sex Population Pyramids for Countries with High Population Growth Rates.**   Countries with high total fertility rates, high infant mortality rates, and low life expectancies will have population pyramids with wide bases and narrow tops.   *Data from*: United States Census Bureau, International Data Base, 2014.

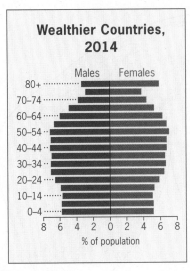

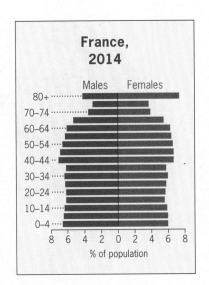

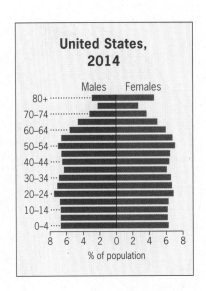

■ **Figure 2.17**

**Age–Sex Population Pyramids for Countries with Low Population Growth Rates.**    Countries with lower total fertility rates and longer life expectancies have population pyramids shaped more uniformly throughout.    *Data from*: United States Census Bureau, International Data Base, 2014.

but in the middle. The middle-age bulge is moving upward, reflecting the aging of the population (Fig. 2.17) and the declining TFR. Countries with low TFR and high wealth, such as Italy, France, and Sweden, fit into this pyramid model.

# HOW DOES THE GEOGRAPHY OF HEALTH INFLUENCE POPULATION DYNAMICS?

The condition of a country's population requires much more than simply knowing the total population or growth rate. Also of significance is the welfare of the country's people across regions, ethnicities, or social classes. Among the most important influences on population dynamics are geographical differences in sanitation, the prevalence of diseases, and the availability of health care. These factors are influenced in significant part by levels of socioeconomic development—an issue we will consider in Chapter 10. Health plays such a central role in population dynamics, however, that we will consider some basic aspects of the health picture here.

## Infant Mortality

One of the leading measures of the condition of a country's population is the **infant mortality rate** (IMR). Infant mortality is recorded as a baby's death during the first year following its birth (unlike child mortality, which records death between ages 1 and 5). Infant mortality is normally given as the number of cases per thousand live births.

Infant and child mortality reflect the overall health of a society. High infant mortality has a variety of causes, the

physical health of the mother being a key factor. In societies where most women bear a large number of babies, the women also tend to be inadequately nourished, exhausted from overwork, suffering from disease, and poorly educated. Often, infants die because they are improperly weaned. Many children die because of diarrhea. This condition, together with malnutrition, is the leading killer of children throughout the world. Poor sanitation is yet another major threat to infants and children. More than one-fifth of the world's population is estimated to lack ready access to clean drinking water or hygienic human waste-disposal facilities.

The lowest infant mortality rate among larger populations has long been reported by Japan, with 2.2 deaths per 1000 live births in a country of over 127 million people. Some less populated countries show even lower IMRs. Singapore has over 5.4 million people and an incredibly low IMR of 1.8, and Sweden's 9.6 million people record an IMR of 2.6.

In 2013, four countries still reported an IMR of 100 or more—Sierra Leone, Central African Republic, Chad, and Democratic Republic of the Congo. Sierra Leone's IMR of 128, the highest in the world, reflects one death or more among every eight newborns. Dreadful as these figures are, they are a substantial improvement over the situation just five years ago, when 22 countries reported IMRs of 100 or more. Globally, infant mortality has been declining, even in the poverty-stricken regions of the world. Afghanistan's IMR, for example, declined from 165 in 2008, the highest in the world at the time, to 71 in 2013.

Each of these observations about infant mortality rates considers what is happening, on average, in a country. The IMR varies within countries and gives us a lens into variations in access to health care and health education depending on region, ethnicity, social class, or other criteria. The IMR of South Africa is 48 per 1000, an average of all the people within the country's borders. The IMR for South African

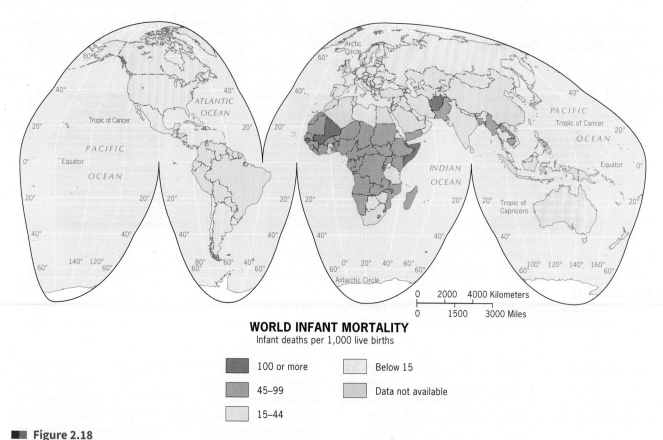

## WORLD INFANT MORTALITY
Infant deaths per 1,000 live births

- 100 or more
- 45–99
- 15–44
- Below 15
- Data not available

■ **Figure 2.18**

**Infant Mortality Rate, 2014.**   The map shows infant mortality patterns at five levels ranging from 100 or more per thousand (one death for every eight live births) to fewer than 15. Compare this map to that of overall crude death rate (CDR) in Figure 2.14, and the correlation between high infant mortality rates and high death rates is evident.   *Data from*: CIA World Fact Book, 2014 estimate.

whites is near the European average; for black Africans it is nearer the African average; and for the Coloured and Asian population sectors it lies between these two figures. The reported average for South Africa does not reflect ethnic and class differences within South Africa.

In the United States, in 2010, the IMR for African Americans was 11.5, above the countrywide average of 6.1 and the IMR of 5.2 for non-Hispanic whites. The risk factors that lead to a high IMR afflict African Americans at a much higher rate than non-Hispanic whites in the United States. According to the Centers for Disease Control, in 2010, 85.7 percent of non-Hispanic whites but only 80.9 percent of African Americans received prenatal care starting in the first trimester of their pregnancy. Lower education levels for African American women also contributed to the higher IMR. However, one risk factor that contributes to high IMR, smoking during pregnancy, was higher for non-Hispanic whites. The Centers for Disease Control found that 22 percent of non-Hispanic whites smoked cigarettes during pregnancy in 2004, and 6.9 percent of African American women smoked during pregnancy.

The IMR in the United States also varies by region, with the highest IMR in the South and the lowest in the Northeast (Fig. 2.19). Race, ethnicity, social class, education levels, and access to health care also vary by region in the United States;

these correlations are found for many health problems ranging from diabetes to heart disease.

According to the Office of Minority Health and Health Disparities at the Department of Health and Human Services in the United States, "The leading causes of infant death include congenital abnormalities, pre-term/low birth weight, Sudden Infant Death Syndrome (SIDS), problems related to complications of pregnancy, and respiratory distress syndrome. SIDS deaths among American Indian and Alaska Natives is 2.3 times the rate for non-Hispanic white mothers."

Another measurement of children's health early in life is the newborn death rate—a measurement of the number of children who die in the first month of life out of every 1000 live births. Save the Children's annual State of the World's Mothers report explains that the high newborn death rate in the United States and in other wealthy countries is typically from premature births and low-birth-weight babies. In the poorer countries of the world, diarrhea and infections cause half of newborn deaths.

Figure 2.20 maps the Mothers' Index from the State of the World's Mothers report. The Mothers' Index measures barometers of well-being for mothers and children. Although the United States has a high newborn death rate, its position on the Mothers' Index is high. The overwhelmingly low measurements

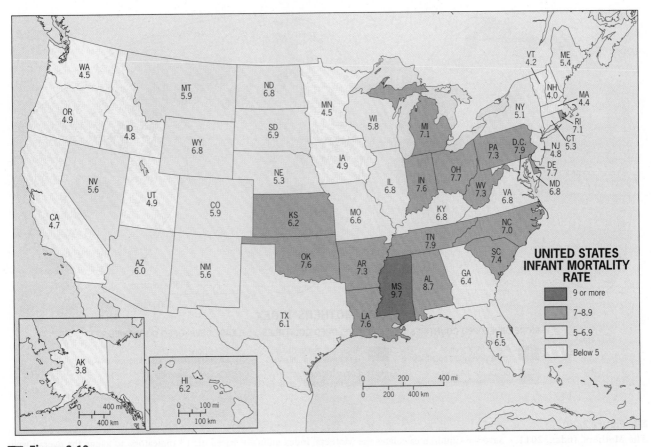

**■ Figure 2.19**

**Infant Mortality Rate in the United States.**   Infant deaths per 1000 live births. In Figure 2.18, the entire United States is in the lowest class on the map. Shifting scales to States within the United States, the infant mortality rate shows variation, with high infant mortality rates in the South and low infant mortality rates in Washington and Massachusetts.   *Data from*: Centers for Disease Control, National Vital Statistics Reports, 2010.

for Subsaharan Africa on the Mothers' Index confirms that poverty is a major factor in the health of women and children. Specifically, 99 percent of newborn deaths and 98 percent of maternal deaths (deaths from giving birth) occur in the poorer countries of the world.

In the countries in the world experiencing violent conflict, the Mothers' Index plunges, and the chances of newborn survival fall. Examine Figure 2.20 again and note the position of countries that have violent conflict or a recent history of conflict: Iraq, Afghanistan, Liberia, Sierra Leone, and Angola.

## Child Mortality

Infants who survive their first year of life still do not have a long life expectancy in the poorer areas of the world. The **child mortality rate**, which records the deaths of children between the ages of 1 and 5, remains staggeringly high in much of Africa and Asia, notably in the protein-deficient tropical and subtropical zones. *Kwashiorkor* (also known as protein malnutrition), a malady resulting from a lack of protein early in life, afflicts millions of children; *marasmus*, a condition that results from inadequate protein and insufficient calories, causes the deaths of millions more. In some countries, more

than one in five children still die between their first and fifth birthdays, a terrible record in the twenty-first century.

## Life Expectancy

Yet another indicator of a society's well-being lies in the **life expectancy** of its members at birth, that is, the number of years, on average, someone may expect to remain alive. Figure 2.21 shows the average life expectancies of populations by country and thus does not take into account gender differences. Women outlive men by about four years in Europe and East Asia, by three years in Subsaharan Africa, by six years in North America, and by seven years in South America. In Russia today, the difference is approximately 12 years.

The map does reveal huge regional contrasts. At the start of the century, world average life expectancy was 68 for women and 64 for men. Not only are these levels exceeded in the wealthy countries of the Western world, but great progress has also been made in East Asia, where Japan's life expectancies are the highest in the world. With its low infant and child mortality rates and low fertility rates, Japan's life expectancy is predicted to rise to 106 by the year 2300. By contrast, tropical Subsaharan African countries have the lowest life expectancies. In Subsaharan Africa, the spread of AIDS

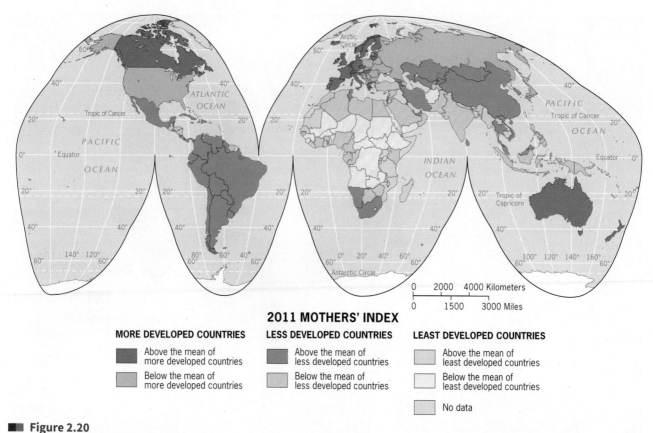

**2011 MOTHERS' INDEX**

| MORE DEVELOPED COUNTRIES | LESS DEVELOPED COUNTRIES | LEAST DEVELOPED COUNTRIES |
|---|---|---|
| Above the mean of more developed countries | Above the mean of less developed countries | Above the mean of least developed countries |
| Below the mean of more developed countries | Below the mean of less developed countries | Below the mean of least developed countries |
| | | No data |

■ **Figure 2.20**

**The Mothers' Index, 2011.**   Save the Children calculates the Mothers' Index annually, based on 13 indicators, to gauge the overall well-being of mothers and their children by country.   *Data from*: Save the Children.

over the past three decades lowered life expectancies in some countries below age 40. Today, the lowest life expectancies are closer to 50 due to access to antiretroviral treatments and programs to prevent mother-to-child transmission.

Life expectancies can change in relatively short order. For example, in South Africa, one of the countries hardest hit by the AIDS epidemic, the life expectancy rose from 56.6 to 60 years between 2009 and 2011 as a result of treatment and education programs. In the former Soviet Union, and especially in Russia, the life expectancies of males dropped quite precipitously following the collapse of communism, from 68 to 62 years. In 2010, the United Nations estimated the life expectancy for males in Russia was 63. In 2014, the BBC, reporting on an article in a medical journal, stated 25 percent "of Russian men die before they are 55" and that most of the deaths are due to alcohol. In 2013, the Population Reference Bureau estimated Russia's life expectancy for females was 76, twelve years longer than the life expectancy of Russian men.

Life expectancy figures do not mean everyone lives to a certain age. The figure is an average that takes account of the children who die young and the people who survive well beyond the average. The dramatically lower figures for the world's poorer countries primarily reflect high infant mortality. A person who has survived beyond childhood can survive

well beyond the recorded life expectancy. The low life expectancy figures for the malnourished countries remind us again how hard hit children are in poorer parts of the world.

## Disease

As we have seen, health is fundamentally influenced by local sanitation conditions. The availability of clean water plays a particularly critical role. Human-driven environmental pollution is also a factor; polluted water and air, and degraded lands, undermine health and well-being. Disease also has a great impact on human health. It is impossible to understand diseases without some understanding of geography because where people live affects what types of diseases they may contract, and where they move affects disease transmission. People who live in Iceland (where mosquitoes are rare) do not need to worry about contracting malaria, unless they travel to parts of the tropics where malaria prevails. Those who live in close proximity to animals, including livestock, run a greater risk of contracting certain diseases than those who live in cities. The importance of "where" questions to the study of disease has given rise to an important geographic subdiscipline known as medical geography.

Medical geographers study diseases, and they also use locational analysis to predict diffusion and to prescribe

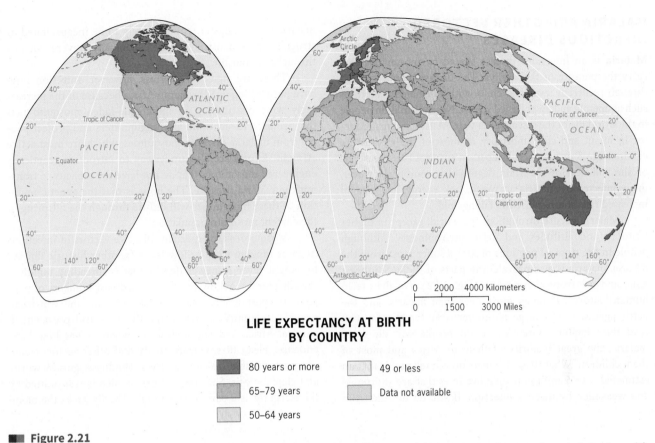

**LIFE EXPECTANCY AT BIRTH BY COUNTRY**

- 80 years or more
- 65–79 years
- 50–64 years
- 49 or less
- Data not available

■ **Figure 2.21**

**Life Expectancy at Birth in Years, 2013.**    This map highlights global inequalities in life expectancies. Someone born in Japan has a life expectancy that is three decades longer than someone born in Afghanistan or Angola.    *Data from*: Population Reference Bureau, 2013.

prevention strategies. A medical geographer can answer questions such as: Where is the bird flu most likely to diffuse and under what time line if an outbreak occurs in New York City? If a country receives enough funding to build 25 clinics for people in rural areas, what locations will allow a maximum of patients to be able to reach them?

Diseases can be grouped into categories to make it easier to understand the risks they pose. Some 65 percent of all diseases are known as **infectious diseases**, resulting from an invasion of parasites and their multiplication in the body. Malaria is an infectious disease. The remainder can be divided into the **chronic** or **degenerative diseases**, the maladies of longevity and old age such as heart disease, and the **genetic** or **inherited diseases** we can trace to our ancestry, that is, the chromosomes and genes that define our makeup. Sickle-cell anemia, hemophilia, and lactose intolerance are among these genetic diseases. These can be of special geographic interest because they tend to appear in certain areas and in particular populations, suggesting the need for special, local treatment.

Three geographic terms are used to describe the spatial extent of a disease. A disease is **endemic** when it prevails over a small area. A disease is **epidemic** when it spreads over a large region. A **pandemic** disease is global in scope.

## Infectious Diseases

Infectious diseases continue to sicken and kill millions of people annually. Malaria, an old tropical disease, alone still takes more than a million lives annually and infects about 300 million people today. HIV/AIDS, an affliction that erupted in Africa just a few decades ago, has killed about 25 million people since that time. These two maladies illustrate two kinds of infectious disease: *vectored* and *nonvectored*.

A vectored infectious disease such as malaria is transmitted by an intermediary *vector*—in malaria's case a mosquito. What happens is that the mosquito stings an already-infected person or animal, called a *host*, and sucks up some blood carrying the parasites. These parasites then reproduce and multiply in the mosquito's body and reach its saliva. The next time that mosquito stings someone, some of the parasites are injected into that person's bloodstream. Now that person develops malaria as the parasites multiply in his or her body, and he or she is a host.

Nonvectored infectious diseases are transmitted by direct contact between host and victim. A kiss, a handshake, or even contact with someone's breath can transmit influenza, a cold, or some other familiar malady. HIV/AIDS is a nonvectored infectious disease that is transmitted primarily through sexual contact and secondarily through needle sharing.

## MALARIA AND OTHER VECTORED INFECTIOUS DISEASES

**Malaria** is an infectious disease spread by mosquitoes that carry the parasite in their saliva. The disease manifests itself through recurrent fever and chills, with associated symptoms such as anemia and an enlarged spleen. Nearly 1 million people in the world die of the disease each year. Malaria is a major factor in infant and child mortality, as most of the victims are children age 5 or younger. If a person survives the disease, he or she will develop a certain degree of immunity. However, many infected by malaria are weak, lack energy, and face an increased risk of other diseases taking hold.

Malaria occurs throughout the world, except in higher latitudes and altitudes and drier environments. Although people in the tropical portions of Africa suffer most from the disease, malaria is also prevalent in parts of India, Southeast Asia, and the tropical Americas (Fig. 2.22). No disease in human history has taken more lives than malaria, and the battle against this scourge is not yet won. On the day you read this chapter, more than 2700 people will die from malaria, the great majority of them in Africa and most of them children. What these numbers do not tell you is that an estimated 3 to 5 million people live lives that are shortened and weakened by malaria infection. If you do not die from

malaria as a youngster, you are likely to be incapacitated or struggle in exhaustion with chronically severe anemia throughout your life.

There are signs of progress, however. Infection rates have been falling in Subsaharan Africa because of the increasingly wide distribution of insecticide-laden mosquito nets that are used to surround sleeping quarters and protect people from malaria-carrying mosquitoes, which are most active at night. Efforts are also underway to introduce genetically engineered mosquitoes that do not have the capacity to transmit the malaria parasite. The hope is that the genetic mutation of these mosquitoes will diffuse through the offspring of the current mosquito population.

Mosquitoes are especially effective vectors of infectious diseases ranging from yellow fever (another historic illness) to dengue fever (a newer disease that is spreading rapidly—see Chapter 1). Yellow fever has killed vast numbers of people in the past. It is being driven back by a vaccine, which can provide immunity for ten years. But it is still prevalent in tropical Africa and South America where it has long been endemic, Fleas, flies, worms, snails, and other vectors transmit such terrible diseases as river blindness, guinea worm, and elephantiasis. Sleeping sickness, which is transmitted by the tsetse fly, is a particular scourge. The fly sucks the blood

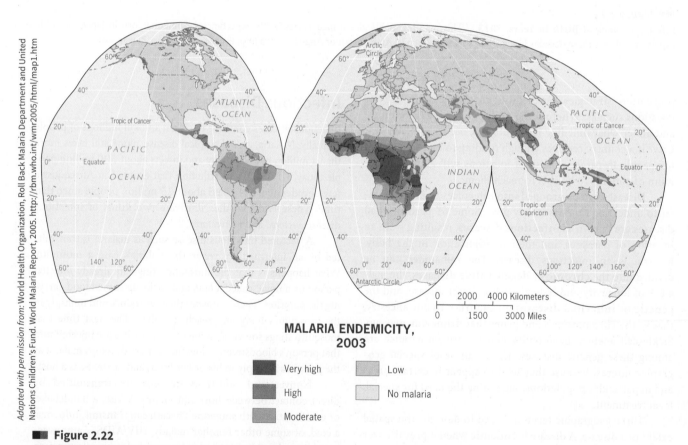

*Adapted with permission from: World Health Organization, Roll Back Malaria Department and United Nations Children's Fund. World Malaria Report, 2005. http://rbm.who.int/wmr2005/html/map1.htm*

**MALARIA ENDEMICITY, 2003**

- Very high
- High
- Moderate
- Low
- No malaria

■■ **Figure 2.22**

**Global Distribution of Malaria Transmission Risk, 2003.**  Malaria was once more widespread, but it is now concentrated primarily in the Tropics where moisture allows higher breeding rates for mosquitos.

from an infected animal or individual and then infects others with its bite. Sleeping sickness began around 1400 in West Africa, but it spread throughout much of Subsaharan Africa in the succeeding centuries. Both people and animals infected by the disease come down with a fever, followed by the swelling of lymph nodes and inflammation of the brain. Death is not uncommon. Progress has been made in combatting the disease through tsetse-fly eradication campaigns, but much of Subsaharan Africa is still affected. Tropical climates, where warm, moist conditions allow vectors to thrive, are the worst-afflicted areas of the world, but vectored infectious diseases are a global phenomenon.

## HIV/AIDS AND OTHER NONVECTORED DISEASES

Low life expectancies in some parts of the world are caused by the ravages of **AIDS** (Acquired Immune Deficiency Syndrome)—a disease identified in Africa in the early 1980s. Undoubtedly, AIDS had taken hold in Africa years earlier, perhaps decades earlier. But its rapid diffusion worldwide began in the 1980s, creating one of the greatest health catastrophes of the past century. Nowhere has its impact been greater than in Africa itself.

Medical geographers estimate that in 1980 about 200,000 people were infected with HIV (Human Immunodeficiency Virus, which causes AIDS), all of them Africans. By 2012, the number worldwide exceeded 75 million, according to the United Nations AIDS Program, with 70 percent (25 million) of all cases in Subsaharan Africa! The infection rate worldwide has fallen 33 percent since 2001 and is continuing to slow, but eastern Europe and Central Asia have recently seen a surge in HIV infection.

The impact of the scourge of AIDS on Subsaharan Africa is striking. In 2013, some 23 percent of people aged 15 to 49 were infected in Botswana, 15.2 percent in Zimbabwe, almost 16 percent in South Africa, and 12.5 percent in Zambia. These are the official data; medical geographers estimate that as much as 20 percent of the entire population of several tropical African countries may be infected. The United Nations AIDS program reports that more than 1.6 million people died of AIDS in Subsaharan Africa in 2012 alone. Geographer Peter Gould, in his book *The Slow Plague* (1993), called Africa a "continent in catastrophe," and the demographic statistics support his viewpoint. In a continent already ravaged by other diseases, AIDS is still the leading cause of death for adults. It has reshaped the population structure of the countries hardest hit by the disease. Demographers look at the projected population pyramids for countries with high rates of infection and no longer see population pyramids; they see population chimneys—reflecting the major impact of AIDS on the younger population in the country (Fig. 2.23).

Over the past three decades, the AIDS pandemic has reached virtually all parts of the world. China is reporting at least 650,000 infected, with 70,000 new cases in 2013 alone, and the number in India may well exceed 5 million. Estimates of the number of cases in the United States surpass

1 million; in Middle and South America, nearly 2 million are infected. Southeast Asia now has as many as 6 million cases. People infected by HIV do not immediately display visible symptoms of the disease; they can carry the virus for years without being aware of it, and during that period they can unwittingly transmit it to others. Add to this the social stigma many people attach to this malady, and it is evident that official statistics on AIDS do not give a full picture of the toll the disease takes.

Fieldwork conducted by geographers is shedding light on the human toll of AIDS locally and within families. Geographer Elsbeth Robson has studied the impact of AIDS in hard-hit Zimbabwe. She found that the diffusion of AIDS and reductions in spending on health care (often mandated by structural adjustment programs) "shape young people's home lives and structure their wider experiences." In Subsaharan Africa, the number of children orphaned when parents die from AIDS is growing rapidly (Fig. 2.24). In 2004, UNICEF reported that in just two years, between 2001 and 2003, the number of global AIDS orphans (children who have lost a parent to AIDS) rose from 11.5 million to 15 million. Robson found that in addition to the rising number of AIDS orphans, many young children, especially

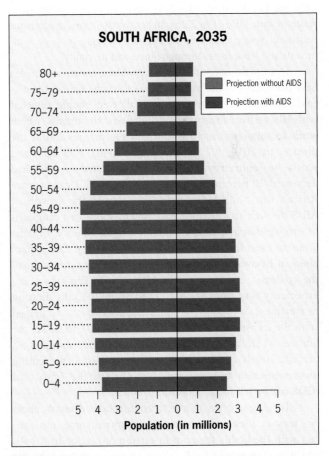

■ **Figure 2.23**

**Effect of AIDS on the Total Population Pyramid for South Africa, Predicted 2035.** Estimated population, male and female, with AIDS and without AIDS. *Data from*: United States Census Bureau, 2005.

# FIELD NOTE

"The day was so beautiful and the children's faces so expressive I could hardly believe I was visiting an AIDS hospice village set up for children. The Sparrow Rainbow Village on the edges of Johannesburg, South Africa, is the product of an internationally funded effort to provide children with HIV/AIDS the opportunity to live in a clean, safe environment. Playing with the children brought home the fragility of human life and the extraordinary impacts of a modern plague that has spread relentlessly across significant parts of Subsaharan Africa."

**■ Figure 2.24**
**Johannesburg, South Africa.**

girls, are taken out of school to serve as caregivers for their relatives with AIDS (Fig. 2.25). In her words, "more children are becoming young carers as households struggle to cope with income and labor losses through illness and mortality."

Despite the magnitude of the problem, enormous strides have been made in the past decade in the fight against the disease. Medical advancements have allowed people infected with HIV to live longer with antiretroviral treatments, which work to suppress the virus and halt the progression of the disease. In 2012, 9.7 million people living with HIV had access to antiretrovirals, and AIDS-related deaths had decreased 30 percent from their peak in 2005. Uganda, once Africa's worst-afflicted country, has slowed the growth of AIDS through an intensive, government-sponsored campaign of propaganda and action—notably the distribution of condoms in even the remotest part of the country. Life expectancy in Botswana and Swaziland, at 34 during the worst of the epidemic, has risen to the high 40s. In Zimbabwe, life expectancy rose from 36 in 2007 to 56 in 2013. In addition to treatment, reproductive education programs have helped stem the transmission of the virus. From 2001 to 2012, the number of children with HIV/AIDS worldwide dropped 52 percent, largely as a result of programs aimed at preventing mother-to-child transmission. Nonetheless, the impact of AIDS will be felt for generations to come.

Turning to other nonvectored infectious diseases, ebola is a serious disease that starts when humans come into contact with the bodily fluids of infected monkeys or fruit bats, and it is then spread from person to person through bodily fluids. Outbreaks in Subsaharan Africa are deadly, as the outbreak in West Africa in 2014 killed more than 3,000 people. The international health community mobilized to help stop the spread of ebola in West Africa. The origin of Middle East respiratory syndrome (MERS) is suggested by the name. A more recent disease, and less deadly than ebola, MERS has spread well beyond its source region, with cases appearing as far away as the United States by 2014.

Every year millions of people succumb to influenza—the "flu"—making it the most common nonvectored infectious disease. Most infected individuals recover, but hundreds of thousands do not. Influenza epidemics often start when humans come into contact with infected pigs, which in turn contract the virus from birds and waterfowl. Southern China is a particularly common source region. In some years the spread of the virus reaches pandemic proportions. The most famous pandemic occurred in 1918–1919, leading to some 50–100 million deaths around the world. More recent pandemics have been less serious, but approximately 500,000 people succumbed to one in 2009–2010 (the so-called swine flu pandemic). Vaccines have served to slow the spread of influenza, but staying ahead of virus mutations is an ongoing challenge.

## Chronic and Genetic Diseases

Chronic diseases (also called degenerative diseases) are the afflictions of middle and old age, reflecting higher life expectancies. Among the chronic diseases, heart disease, cancers, and strokes rank as the leading diseases in this category, but pneumonia, diabetes, and liver diseases also take their toll. In the United States 100 years ago, tuberculosis, pneumonia, diarrheal diseases, and heart diseases (in that order) were the chief killers. Today, heart disease and cancer head the list, with stroke (cerebral hemorrhage) next and accidents also high on the list (Table 2.1). In the early 1900s, tuberculosis

# GUEST FIELD NOTE

## Marich Village, Kenya

"This drawing was done by a Pokot boy in a remote primary school in northwestern Kenya. He agreed to take part in my fieldwork some years after I had started researching young carers in Subsaharan Africa. Since those early interviews in Zimbabwe, I have been acutely aware of young carers' invisibility—you can't tell who are young carers just by looking at them. Indeed, invisibility is a characteristic of many aspects of the social impacts of HIV/AIDS. This young person drew himself working in the fields and taking care of cattle. African young people help with farming and herding for many reasons, but for young caregivers, assisting their sick family members in this way is especially important."

*Elsbeth Robson, Keele University*

■ **Figure 2.25**

and pneumonia caused 20 percent of all deaths; today, they cause fewer than 5 percent. The diarrheal diseases, which were so high on the old list, are now primarily children's maladies. Today, the diarrheal diseases are not even on the list of the 10 leading causes of death.

At the global scale, infectious diseases such as tuberculosis and pneumonia are less serious threats than they once were, but cancer and heart disease take a high toll. Recent decades have brought new lifestyles, new pressures, new consumption patterns, and exposure to new chemicals, and we do not yet know how these are affecting our health. The health impacts of the preservatives that are added to many foods are not fully understood. We substitute artificial flavoring for sugar and other calorie-rich substances, but some of those substitutes have been proven to be dangerous. Moreover, obesity plagues a significant percentage of the U.S. population, bringing with it heart disease and diabetes. Even the treatment of drinking water with chemicals is rather recent in the scheme of global population change, and we do not know its long-term effects. Future chronic diseases may come from practices we now take for granted.

Genetic diseases are of particular interest to medical geographers because they are disorders that tend to be transferred from one generation to the next and display clustering that raises questions about the environment and long-term adaptation. Prominent among these are metabolic

**TABLE 2.1**

**Leading Causes of Death in the United States, 2010.**

| LEADING CAUSES OF DEATH IN THE UNTED STATES, 2010 | |
|---|---|
| Cause | Percent |
| 1. Heart Disease | 25% |
| 2. Cancer | 23% |
| 3. Stroke | 6% |
| 4. Chronic Lower Respiratory Disease | 5% |
| 5. Accidents | 5% |
| 6. Diabetes | 3% |
| 7. Alzheimer's Disease | 3% |

*Data from*: Centers for Disease Control, National Center for Health Statistics, 2010 and U.S. Census Statistical Abstract 2011.

diseases—the body's inability to process all elements of the diet—in which enzymes play a key role. If the body fails to produce enough (or any) of a particular enzyme, the result can be serious metabolic malfunction. For example, some people suffer from a malady called primary lactose intolerance. If you suffer from this disorder, you do not have an adequate supply of one (or a set) of enzymes that you need to break down the milk sugar lactose.

## Geographic Influences on Health

Looking at health questions through a geographic lens means understanding some of the general spatial aspects of health indicators and disease outbreaks discussed above—what places are more or less advantaged or threatened, where diseases are found, and where and how diseases spread. But geographical analysis can contribute to an understanding of health and disease issues in other ways as well. Humans are constantly altering Earth's surface in ways that have the potential to influence health and the spread of diseases. There is growing evidence, for example, that climate-change-induced increases in precipitation and flooding, along with rising temperatures, are expanding the geographic reach of diseases that are transmitted by mosquitoes. Addressing this problem requires geographic studies that look at the impacts of ecosystem changes on health issues in particular places.

Critical social geographic factors also affect health. Medical geographers are increasingly studying not just disease patterns, but issues such as access to medical care and the ways in which place-based social norms affect disease transmission. For many people, access to medical care is fundamentally a geographic matter because access is a function of distance to medical facilities and available transportation infrastructure. As such, understanding geographical inequalities in the distribution of health-care facilities or the ways in which infrastructure impedes or facilitates access to such facilities are matters of great importance. On the social norms front, the transmission of HIV/AIDS is not just influenced by distance and population numbers; it is also a product of attitudes toward the use of condoms, mobility patterns, socioeconomic status, and other place-specific social variables. Understanding the role of such factors requires looking at the geographic context within which health challenges are situated.

**thinking** *geographically*

Study Figure 2.19, the infant mortality rate (IMR) by State in the United States. Hypothesize why the IMR is low in some regions of the country and high in others. Shift scales in your mind, and choose one State to consider: How do you think IMR varies within this State? What other factors involved at this scale and this level of generalization explain the pattern of IMRs? Use the population Internet sites available at www.wiley.com/college/fouberg to determine whether your hypotheses are correct.

## HOW DO GOVERNMENTS IMPACT POPULATION CHANGE?

Over the past century, many of the world's governments have instituted policies designed to influence the overall growth rate or ethnic ratios within the population. Certain policies directly affect the birth rate via laws ranging from subsidized abortions to forced sterilization. Others influence family size through taxation or subvention. These policies fall into three groups: expansive, eugenic, and restrictive.

The former Soviet Union and China under Mao Zedong led other communist societies in **expansive population policies**, which encourage large families and raise the rate of natural increase. Although such policies have been abandoned in China, some countries are again pursuing expansive population policies—because their populations are aging and declining. The aging population in Europe has encouraged some countries to embark on policies to encourage families (through tax incentives and the expansion of family-friendly social services) to have more children.

As noted earlier, birth rates in Russia plummeted after the 1991 collapse of the Soviet Union. The TFR in Russia, which was 2.04 in 1980, had fallen to 1.34 by the mid-2000s, though it has now rebounded somewhat to 1.7. Then Prime Minister of Russia Vladimir Putin called the demographic crisis Russia's greatest problem. The Russian government began to offer cash subsidies of $10,000 to women who give birth to a second or third child.

In response to concerns over Russia's aging population, the government of Ulyanovsk Province has held a National Day of Conception each September 12 since 2005. In 2007, government and businesses in Ulyanovsk offered the afternoon off for people to participate in the National Day of Conception. The government planned to award a free car to the proud parents of one of the children born 9 months later, on June 12— the Russian National Day. On June 12, 2008, eighty-seven children were born in the province, about 4 times its average daily birth rate. Between 2005 and 2011, the number of births in the province rose by 19.5 percent. Although Russia's birth rate has rebounded, its ability to sustain a high TFR will depend on many factors, including alleviating social problems, stabilizing incomes, and continued government support.

In the past, some governments engaged in **eugenic population policies**, which were designed to favor one racial or cultural sector of the population over others. Nazi Germany was a drastic case in point, but other countries also have pursued eugenic strategies, though in more subtle ways. Until the time of the civil rights movement in the 1960s, some observers accused the United States of pursuing social policies tinged with eugenics that worked against the interests of African Americans. Many countries have a history of forced sterilization of lesbian, gay, transgender, and bisexual individuals; some even maintain those policies today despite the efforts of some organizations to label such programs as human rights abuse. Eugenic population policies can be practiced covertly through discriminatory taxation, biased allocation of resources, and other forms of racial favoritism.

Today many of the world's governments seek to reduce the rate of natural increase through various forms of **restrictive population policies**. These policies range from toleration of officially unapproved means of birth control to outright prohibition of large families. China's **one-child policy**, instituted after the end of the Maoist period in the 1970s, drastically reduced China's growth rate from one of the world's fastest to one of the world's slowest (Fig. 2.26). Under the one-child policy, families that had more than one child were penalized financially, and educational opportunities and housing privileges were kept from families who broke the one-child mandate.

Population growth rates in China fell quickly under the one-child policy. In the 1970s, China's growth rate was 3 percent; in the mid-1980s, it was 1.2 percent; and today it is 0.5 percent (Fig. 2.27). The main goal of the one-child policy was achieved, but the policy had several unintended consequences, including an increased abortion rate, an increase in female infanticide, and a high rate of abandoned girls (many of whom were adopted in the United States and Canada).

During the 1990s, under pressure to improve its human rights records and also with the realization that the population was quickly becoming gender and age imbalanced, China

© H. J. de Blij

■ **Figure 2.26**

**Chengdu, China.** A large billboard warning readers to follow China's one-child policy.

relaxed its one-child policy. Several exemptions now allow families to have more than one child. For example, if you live in a rural area and your first child is a girl, you can have a second child, and if both parents of the child are only children, they can have a second child. In late 2013, China's top legislature officially amended the one-child policy to allow all couples to have two children provided both parents are only children. With these changes, the National Bureau of Statistics of China now estimates that the population growth rate in China will climb again over the next 10 years. Although the one-child policy has begun to ease, China could see its impact for decades to come. The program has been blamed for what some older Chinese see as a generation of self-centered, financially dependent adults. The members of the so-called

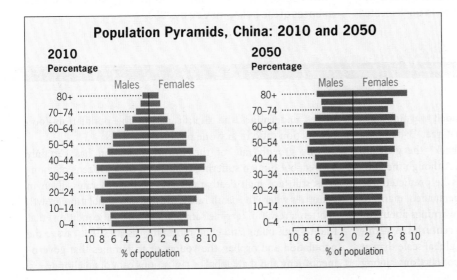

■ **Figure 2.27**

**Population Pyramids, China: 2010 and 2050.** The 2050 pyramid assumes present growth rates continue into the future. A continued relaxation of the one-child policy might change what the 2050 pyramid will look like. *Data from:* Population Reference Bureau, 2010.

me generation are quick to marry, have staggeringly high divorce rates, and often prefer to have only one child.

## Limitations

Population policies are not independent of circumstances that can influence growth and decline. In the 1980s, the government of Sweden adopted family-friendly policies designed to promote gender equality and boost fertility rates. The programs focused on alleviating much of the cost of having and raising children. In Sweden, couples that work and have small children receive cash payments, tax incentives, job leaves, and work flexibility that last up to eight years after the birth of a child. The policies led to a mini-birth-rate-boom by the early 1990s.

When the Swedish economy slowed shortly thereafter, however, so did the birth rate. The children born in 1991 made up a class of 130,000 students in the Swedish education system. But the children born three years later, in 1994, made up a class of only 75,000 students. The government had to build new classrooms for the temporary population boom, but then faced excess capacity when the boom subsided. The birth rate fell to 1.5 children by the end of the 1990s, and the country had to think anew about how to support families and promote fertility. One imaginative approach was suggested by a spokeswoman for the Christian Democrat Party, who urged Swedish television to show racier programming at night in hopes of returning the population to a higher birth rate! Over the last 15 years, increases in child allowances and parental benefits helped to produce a natural rate of increase that is a little higher than that in many other European countries and a TFR of 1.9, the third highest in Europe behind Iceland and the United Kingdom. And in 2013, the population saw its largest annual increase in 70 years, a result of family-friendly policies but also record-high immigration.

Similarly, Singapore implemented restrictive policies only to see its population fall too rapidly. The small country's "economic miracle" in the 1960s contributed to a population boom, illustrated by a TFR of 3.5 in 1965. The population increase was seen as unsustainable, and Singapore's government implemented measures designed to decrease family size. Today Singapore's TFR of 1.3 is troubling, and the government is working to increase the birth rate among citizens while also encouraging immigration and intermarriage.

## Contradictions

Some areas of the world with low population growth rates (Fig. 2.9) are in the very heart of the Roman Catholic world. Roman Catholic doctrine opposes birth control and abortion. Adherence to this doctrine appears to be stronger in areas remote from the Vatican (headquarters of the Catholic Church). For example, the Philippines, thousands of miles from the Vatican, is Asia's only Roman Catholic-majority country. The Church and the Philippine state agree on abortion, as the Philippine constitution prohibits abortion. However, the Philippine government disagrees with the Church on the issue of artificial contraceptives: The government supports birth control in order to stem population growth.

Among Islamic countries, the geographic pattern is the opposite. Saudi Arabia, home to Mecca—the hearth of Islam—has a relatively high population growth rate, with the population increasing at 1.8 percent each year. But in Indonesia, thousands of miles from Mecca, the government began a nationwide family planning program in 1970 when the population growth rate was 2.6 percent. Fundamentalist Muslim leaders objected, but the government used a combination of coercion and inducement to continue their program. By 2000, Indonesia's family planning program had lowered the growth rate to 1.6 percent, and in 2012 it stood at 1.2 percent.

When studying government policies on population, one of the most important things to remember is unintended consequences. Choose a government population policy discussed in this section of the chapter and predict what the consequences of the policy may be by 2050.

## Summary

In the late 1700s, Thomas Malthus sounded warning bells about the rapidly growing population in Great Britain. He feared a massive famine would soon "check" the growing population, bringing widespread suffering. Although the famine in Great Britain did not take place as he predicted, the rapidly growing worldwide population persuaded many to embrace Malthusian ideas, issuing similar warnings about the population explosion of the preceding two centuries. A stronger case can be made for these ideas at the global scale than at smaller scales, however, because the interconnections among places undermines the significance of the population–food production ratio in any one place.

The growth rate of the world population has certainly slowed, but human suffering is far from over. Dozens of countries still face high death rates and high birth rates. Even in countries where the death rate is low, slowed population growth is often a result of terrible sanitary and medical conditions that lead to high infant and child mortality, diseases that ravage the population and orphan the young, or to famines that governments deny and that global organizations cannot ameliorate.

Population pyramids illustrate that as wealthier countries worry about supporting their aging populations, poorer countries have problems of their own. A high birth rate in a poor country does not necessarily mean overpopulation; some of the highest population densities in the world are found in wealthy countries. Even poor countries that have lowered their birth rates and their death rates are constantly negotiating what is morally acceptable to their people and their cultures.

Geography offers much to the study of population. Through geography we can see differences in population problems across space; we can also see how what happens at one scale affects developments at other scales, and how different cultures and countries approach population questions.

## Geographic Concepts

population density
arithmetic population density
physiological population density
population distribution
dot map
megalopolis
census
total fertility rate (TFR)
old-age dependency ratio
child dependency ratio
doubling time
population explosion

zero population growth
crude birth rate
crude death rate
natural increase
demographic transition
stationary population level (SPL)
population composition
population pyramids
infant mortality rate
child mortality rate
life expectancy
infectious diseases

chronic or degenerative diseases
genetic or inherited diseases
endemic
epidemic
pandemic
malaria
AIDS
expansive population policies
eugenic population policies
restrictive population policies
one-child policy

## Learn More Online

About China's South–North Water Transfer Project
news.bbc.co.uk/2/hi/programmes/from_our_own_
correspondent/9132843.stm

About Population Growth in the World
www.prb.org
www.pbs.org/wgbh/nova/earth/global-population-growth.html

About the Composition of the Population of the United States
www.census.gov

About the Global AIDS Crisis
www.unaids.org/en/
www.npr.org/healthscience/aids2004/

About International Population Programs
www.unfpa.org

## Watch It Online

About the Population Transition in Italy
www.learner.org/resources/series85.html#program_descriptions

# CHAPTER 3

# MIGRATION

## Expanding Slums

From the top of a building in the heart of one of India's great cities—Mumbai—I look down on a massive slum settlement nestled amidst modern high rises. In almost every direction I can see other slums—and even larger ones were in evidence as I drove in from the airport.

More than 60 percent of the people in Mumbai live in slums or shanties like the one shown in Figure 3.1. The settlements are concrete manifestations of one of the great human geographic changes to have occurred in India since the 1970s: massive migration of people from rural areas to cities. The 1971 Indian census reported 5.9 million people living in the city limits of Mumbai. By 2011, the population in the city more than doubled to 12.5 million, and the larger urban area has a population of more than 20 million.

Starting in the 1970s, Indians left rural areas and migrated to urban areas in large numbers because in rural areas landholdings are often too small to support growing families and employment opportunities outside the agricultural sector are few. Cities offer at least the possibility of improved job prospects and a better life.

The Indian government did little to dissuade rural residents from migrating to cities. Rakshar Kumar described the development of slum-shanties in Mumbai in the *New York Times* (2011): "Amid unchecked migration, Mumbai's slums often began as clusters of illegal dwellings on public property, including parks, roads and pavements. Local and state governments, seeing potential votes in the slums, helped to make them permanent by providing them with electricity and drinking water." As population rose and the number of shanties built in Mumbai's slums grew, politicians gave shanty owners papers saying they owned their shanties, in hopes of garnering more votes. At times, governments have extended electrical lines to the slums, but access to utilities, including electric and sewer, is limited.

With the population of the Mumbai urban area now topping 20 million, the city is experiencing a dramatic housing shortage. The value of shanties in Mumbai has increased, particularly for those located close to the city center or close to major transportation routes.

© Alexander B. Murphy

**Figure 3.1**

**Mumbai, India.** A view from the top of a high-rise building in the central city, looking down on one of the slums found throughout the city. The 2011 census of India reported that 60 percent of Mumbai's population live in slums.

By 2025, more than 40 percent of India's population (expected to be 1.45 billion by then) will live in cities—a stark testament to the importance of migration to the human geographic story.

At the global scale, rural-to-urban migration represents one of the most dramatic shifts in the human geography of the planet over the last century. In 1900, only 13 percent of the world's people lived in cities; now the figure exceeds 50 percent, and it is on the rise. Other types of migration are increasingly important as well. Across the world, hundreds of thousands of people have fled their homelands in recent decades for opportunities in North America, Australia, China, and Europe. Immigrants are sometimes welcomed and sometimes turned away. In the 1940s, the U.S. government encouraged Mexicans to come work in the United States as contract laborers (the **Bracero Program**). Several decades later, U.S. authorities were hard at work building a fence along the country's southern border in an effort to stem the inflow of migrants. This shift shows the important influence of government policy and public opinion on migration. Migration is sometimes a choice, but for many people it is a survival strategy. The "Lost Boys of Sudan" fled their homelands between the ages of 7 and 17 in the face of a devastating civil war in the closing decades of the twentieth century. They walked tremendous distances seeking refuge from the conflict. Many lost their lives along the way; others ended up in **refugee camps** in Kenya, Uganda, and the more stable parts of Sudan. More recently, millions of Syrians have sought refuge from the civil war wracking their homeland—settling in camps in Turkey, Lebanon, Jordan, and elsewhere.

It is hard to generalize about migration because it has so many causes and consequences. In some cases people want to leave a troubled place; in other cases they are forced to leave; and in yet others they are enticed by what another place might have to offer. Moreover, migration flows vary along gender, socioeconomic class, age, race, and ethnic lines. The Lost Boys of Sudan principally came from two ethnic groups that were caught up in the fighting. Not infrequently, labor migration is either heavily male or female, depending on particular job requirements and associated assumptions about gender roles. Geographers who study migration seek to understand who migrates, where they come from, when they migrate, and where they go.

In 2007, the number of undocumented migrants in the United States peaked at 12 million. In 2010, the number fell to 11.2 million as a result of the economic recession in the United States, but it is on the rise again with 11.7 undocumented migrants in 2013. The goal of most undocumented migrants is to work in the United States and send money home to their families. Monies migrants send home are called **remittances**. Haitians living in the United States, Canada, and the Caribbean sent home over $1.9 billion in remittances in 2012, a figure equivalent to 30 percent of Haiti's gross domestic product and far outpacing the value of Haitian exports. It is estimated that one in ten Haitians resides abroad, with some 500,000 Haitians in the United State alone. Thirty-six percent of Haiti's population is under 15 and, among the working-age population, the unemployment rate in 2010 was estimated at 40.6 percent. In addition, the country's gross national income per capita is $1240, far lower than the regional average of $10,870. One of five Haitian households receives remittances from abroad.

The economies of many poorer countries in the Caribbean, Africa, Central and South America, and parts of Eurasia depend on remittances sent to their citizens. In 2011, Ghanaian immigrants sent an estimated $119 million home, largely from the United States, the United Kingdom, Italy, and Nigeria. Ghana's government, in an effort to make it easier for remittances to flow into the country, established a Diaspora Support Unit within the Ministry of Foreign Affairs.

The downturn in the U.S. economy after 2007 generated a new flow of money called **reverse remittances**: money flowing from Mexico to the U.S. Mexican immigrants sent nearly $24 billion home in 2007 but only $22 billion in 2013. Remittances to Mexico make up 19 percent of household incomes in urban areas and 27 percent of household incomes in rural areas of Mexico. Unemployed, undocumented migrants in the United States have asked families in Mexico for financial support.

Not all immigrants are undocumented. Of the estimated 41.7 million immigrants in the United States today, 30 million are documented immigrants (Fig. 3.2). Countries recognize the

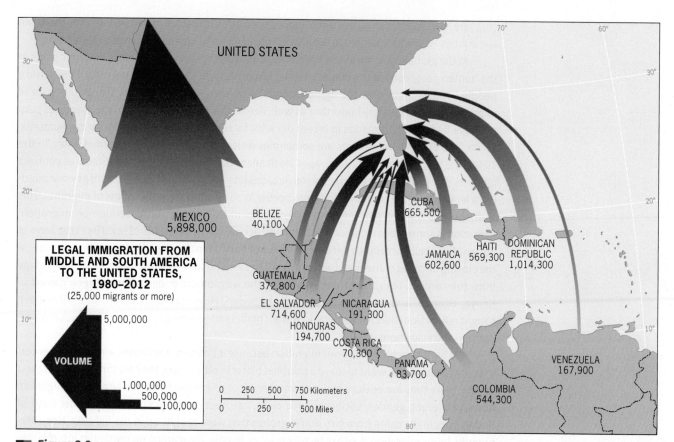

**Figure 3.2**

**Documented Immigration from Middle and South America to the United States, 1980–2012.** *Data from*: United States Department of Homeland Security, Yearbook of Immigration Statistics, 2012.

need for immigrant labor, and many have policies allowing, indeed encouraging, legal immigrants to work under temporary visas to fill a need. Thousands of people who work in the United States and Canada are there on temporary visas to fill seasonal jobs in agriculture and forestry. In the United States, over 45,000 agricultural laborers enter the country each year under a formally sanctioned program that allows unskilled laborers into the country as long as no Americans want the jobs. Canada began to allow agricultural laborers into the country in 1966. In both Canada and the United States, the vast majority of documented agricultural laborers come from Mexico. Canadian companies travel to Mexico to recruit agricultural laborers from rural Mexico and laborers for the hotel industry from urban areas of Mexico.

After September 11, 2001, many countries tightened up border security. In recent years, the United States has earmarked significant sums for building fences along its border with Mexico, hiring additional border patrol agents and installing new technology to intercept undocumented migrants. In the process, the cultural landscape of the border region is changing. The government is erecting specially designed fences that are difficult to climb, though there are openings in the fences where people across the border can speak with one another. The new fences and security south of San Diego, California, are pushing those seeking to cross the border without documentation farther east into the desert. The fences there are marked by empty water bottles and memorials to Mexicans who have died trying to cross the border (Fig. 3.3).

Even though globalization has promoted a freer flow of goods across the world, and the North American Free Trade Agreement (NAFTA) was designed to facilitate trade among Mexico, the United States, and Canada, the free flow of people is far from realized. It is not unusual to wait in line for two or more hours when crossing the border from Canada or Mexico into the United States. The flow of undocumented migrants has slowed in recent years, but that may well have more to do

ASSOCIATED PRESS

■ **Figure 3.3**
**Tijuana, Mexico.** Tijuana and San Diego, California, are separated by a highly guarded border infrastructure that in this section includes two walls to discourage crossing by those who do not have visas. Human rights activists placed crosses on the wall to memorialize people who died while attempting to cross into the United States.

with changing economic circumstances than with walls and fences. Undocumented immigrants go to great lengths to find their way into the United States; similarly, the U.S. government goes to great lengths to deter the influx of undocumented migrants. In this chapter, we examine various types of migration and ask why migrants choose to leave a particular place and why they go to another. We also examine the barriers governments erect to slow human migration, questioning why government policies shift and how policies affect migration flows. By looking at human migration through a geographic lens, we seek to shed light on the nature and meaning of migration flows and to gain an appreciation for why people migrate, where they migrate, and how people, places, and landscapes change as a result of the movement of people.

# Key Questions FOR CHAPTER 3

1. What is migration?
2. Why do people migrate?
3. Where do people migrate?
4. How do governments affect migration?

## WHAT IS MIGRATION?

Movement is inherently geographical because it affects the distribution of peoples and alters the character of the places from which migrants come and to which they go. Movement also changes people, as well as the way they see themselves in the world. Human movement speeds the diffusion of ideas and innovations; it intensifies spatial interaction and transforms regions.

The movement of humans takes several forms. Mobility occurs at scales ranging from the local to the global—from the daily to once in a lifetime. **Emigration** refers to the movement of people away from a place; **immigration** is the reverse—the movement of people to a place.

Geographers recognize three basic types of movement. **Cyclic movement** involves shorter, regular trips away from home for defined amounts of time. **Periodic movement** involves longer periods away from home undertaken from time to time. Actual **migration** carries with it a degree of permanence that is not characteristic of the other two forms of movement: The mover may never return "home."

## Cyclic Movement

Cyclic movement describes a regular journey that begins at a home base and returns to the exact same place. The great majority of people have a daily routine that takes them through a regular sequence of short moves within a local area. These moves create what geographers call **activity spaces**. The scale of activity space varies across societies. You may go to classes every weekday and perhaps to a job as well, creating a relatively confined and stable activity space, diversified by shopping trips and social activities.

*Commuting* is also a cyclic movement. Commuting—the journey from home to work and home again—takes from minutes to hours and can involve several modes of transportation. The average North American commuter travels a greater distance each day than the average Chinese villager does in a year. Advances in transportation technology have expanded daily activity spaces. Cars and vast infrastructure enable people to commute over long distances. In Washington, D.C., commuters combine use of their cars, commuter trains, and the metro to travel upwards of 100 miles each way, each day, commuting not only from the surrounding suburbs but also from Delaware, West Virginia, and central Virginia. By airplane, commuters arrive at work in Washington, D.C., from New York City. Others, such as members of Congress, commute from their home State, keeping houses there and apartments in the Washington, D.C., area.

Another form of cyclic movement is seasonal movement. Every autumn, hundreds of thousands of people leave their homes in Canada and the northern parts of the United States and seek the winter sun in Florida and other "Sun Belt" States, returning in the spring. This seasonal transfer has huge economic consequences (and electoral significance) in depopulated northern towns and burgeoning tourist centers in the South.

This kind of seasonal movement is a luxury. Another type of cyclic movement, **nomadism**, is a matter of survival, culture, and tradition. Nomadism is dwindling across the world, but it can still be found in parts of Asia and Africa. Westerners often envision nomadism as an aimless wandering across steppe and desert by small groups of rootless roamers, people who claim no territory. In reality, nomads need to know their territory well in order to find water, food, and shelter in their cyclic movements. Nomadic movement is purposeful and takes place along long-familiar routes, repeated time and again. The nomads move their animals to visit water sources and pastures that have served their ancestors for centuries. Weather conditions may affect the timing of their route, but barring obstacles such as fenced international borders or the privatization of long-used open country, nomads engage in cyclic movement.

## Periodic Movement

Periodic movement does not necessarily involve returning to the same places, and sometimes it takes place at irregular intervals. Periodic movement involves *a longer period of time* away from the home base than cyclic movement. Some migrant laborers are involved in periodic movement—for example, millions of workers in the United States and tens of millions worldwide move periodically to take advantage of employment opportunities. The need for migrant labor in the farm fields of California, Florida, and other parts of the United States creates a large flow of cross-border movers, many of whom eventually become immigrants.

A specialized form of periodic movement is **transhumance**, which is a system of pastoral farming in which ranchers move livestock according to the seasonal availability of pastures. This is a periodic form of movement because, unlike classic nomadism, it involves a substantial period of residential relocation in a different place. In Switzerland, for example, farmers drive cattle up mountain slopes to high, fresh pastures during the summer, and farm families follow the herds, taking up residence in cottages that are abandoned during the cold winter. In the "Horn" of Northeast Africa, hundreds of thousands of people follow their livestock from highland to lowland and back in search of pastures renewed by seasonal rainfall.

Periodic movement takes on other forms as well. If you leave home to attend a college far away, you are living away from home for four (or more) years. Although you may retain a home address in your place of origin, you now spend the majority of your time in your new abode (traveling home at irregular times), and your mobility cannot be categorized as cyclic.

Military service is another form of periodic movement. In a given year, several million U.S. citizens, including military personnel and their families, are moved to new locations where they will spend tours of duty that can last several years. Someone in the service moving from military base to military base would be engaged in periodic movement because they are not returning to the same place.

## Migration

When movement results in permanent relocation across significant distances, it is classified as *migration*. The process of migration involves the long-term relocation of an individual, a household, or larger group to a new locale outside the community of origin.

**International migration**, movement across country borders, is also called transnational migration. When a migrant leaves the home country, he or she is classified as an

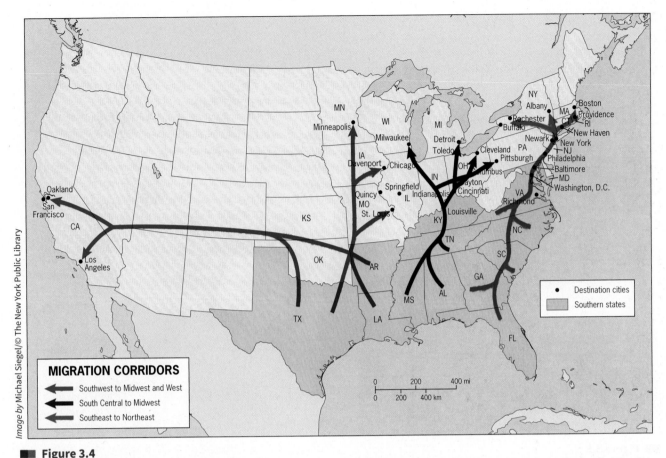

*Image by Michael Siegel/© The New York Public Library*

**MIGRATION CORRIDORS**

← Southwest to Midwest and West

← South Central to Midwest

← Southeast to Northeast

■ **Figure 3.4**

**Migration Patterns of African Americans in the United States in the Early Twentieth Century.** In a movement now called the Great Migration, African Americans left the South and moved along three migration paths into cities of the North and in California. Migrants had the promise of jobs, as expanding industrial sectors in northern cities, including Detroit, Chicago, and Baltimore needed more laborers.

emigrant (one who migrates out) of the home country. When the same migrant enters a new country, he or she is classified as an immigrant (one who migrates in) to the new country. Emigration subtracts from the total population of a country, and immigration adds to it.

Countries also experience **internal migration**—migration that occurs within a single country's borders. Mapping internal migration routes reveals patterns of well-defined streams of migrants that change over time. Early in the twentieth century, a major migration stream took tens of thousands of African American families from the South of the United States to the industrializing cities of the Northeast and Midwest (Fig. 3.4). The advent and diffusion of mechanical cotton pickers resulted in fewer employment opportunities in the South. Southern States, where slavery was legal before the Civil War, enacted Jim Crow laws separating blacks and whites in schools, hospitals, public spaces, public transportation, and even cemeteries. It is estimated that 5 million to 8 million African Americans migrated from the South to industrialized northern cities between 1900 and 1970. African Americans fled the segregated South and headed north to the growing industrial cities of Chicago, Detroit, and Baltimore.

More recently, economic opportunities in the South have begun to reverse the Great Migration. A growing number of middle-class, college-educated African Americans are moving to southern cities such as Atlanta, Dallas, and Charlotte. Other internal migration trends are significant as well: migrants moving to the economically dynamic regions of the Sun Belt and Far West (Fig. 3.5); people escaping from large cities and rural areas to move to medium-sized cities for retirement or family-friendly lifestyles; and wealthy individuals seeking solace and space moving into environmentally attractive rural areas, trying to keep the area "rural" while pushing out farmers.

Mobility within the United States depends on the country's economy. After decades of increasing levels of mobility, the U.S. population had what William Frey of the Brookings Institute called the "least mobile period in postwar American society" following the downturn in the economy between 2007 and 2008. The mortgage crisis and higher unemployment rates led to a pronounced reduction in the long-distance moves, according to a study by the Brookings Institute. Would-be movers "were unable to find financing to buy a new home, buyers for their existing homes, or a new job in more desirable areas" (Frey 2009).

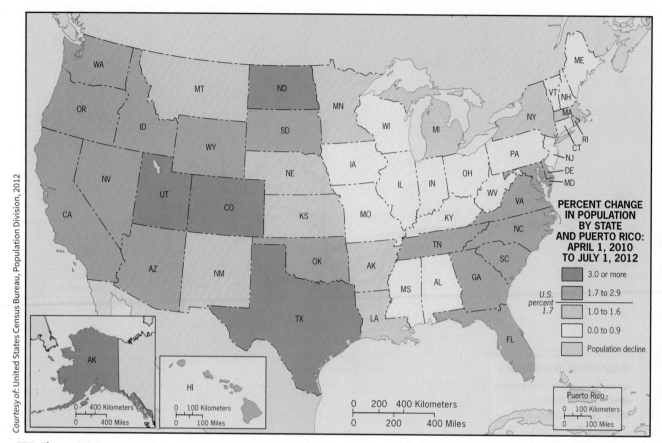

*Courtesy of:* United States Census Bureau, Population Division, 2012

**PERCENT CHANGE IN POPULATION BY STATE AND PUERTO RICO: APRIL 1, 2010 TO JULY 1, 2012**

| | |
|---|---|
| | 3.0 or more |
| U.S. percent 1.7 | 1.7 to 2.9 |
| | 1.0 to 1.6 |
| | 0.0 to 0.9 |
| | Population decline |

■ **Figure 3.5**

**Population Change 2010–2012 by State.** States with growing economies, including North Dakota, which is experiencing an oil boom, grew in population between 2010 and 2012. Midwestern States from Iowa along the Great Lakes to Pennsylvania grew at a much slower rate (with the population of Michigan actually declining), as the manufacturing sector remained weak in the Midwest.

International migrants also frequently move within their destination countries. Since the 1940s, millions of people from Latin America have migrated to the American Southwest and Florida. Most migrants have stayed in these same basic regions, perhaps migrating part of the year to work in agricultural fields. In 1986, the U.S. government passed the Immigration Reform and Control Act (IRCA), legislation that gave amnesty and permanent residence to 2.6 million migrants who had been living in the United States for a long period of time. The newly legal migrants under IRCA could move anywhere, and during the 1990s, many moved to the Great Plains and Midwest as well as to the South (Fig. 3.5). Migrants found the South attractive for the same reasons other Americans did.

In Peru, which has a less mobile society than the United States, the pattern of internal migration is generally from rural to urban. Migrants have left rural areas and moved to Lima, the capital. Global and national investment capital is concentrated in Lima. The capital represents the major focus of economic opportunity for the rural population. Lima receives the vast majority of Peru's migrants, regardless of age, gender, or marital status.

**thinking** *geographically*

Choose one type of cyclic or periodic movement and then think of a specific example of the kind of movement you chose. Now, determine how this movement changes the home, the destination, and the lives of the migrants.

## WHY DO PEOPLE MIGRATE?

Migration can be the result of a voluntary action, a conscious decision to move from one place to the next. It can also be the result of an involuntary action, a forced movement imposed on a group of people. **Forced migration** involves the imposition of authority or power, producing involuntary movements that cannot be understood based on theories of choice. **Voluntary migration** occurs after a migrant weighs options and choices, even if somewhat desperately or not so rationally.

The distinction between forced and voluntary migration is not always clear-cut. The enormous European migration to the United States during the nineteenth and early twentieth centuries is often cited as a prime example of voluntary migration. However, some European migration can be construed as forced. The British treatment of the Irish during their colonial rule over Ireland can be seen as political persecution, which led to forced migration. The British took control of nearly all Irish Catholic lands and discouraged the operation of the Catholic Church in Ireland. Until 1829, the British enforced penal laws preventing Irish Catholics from buying land, voting, or carrying weapons. The mass exodus of migrants from Ireland to North America in the mid-1800s can be seen as forced, both because of the British treatment of the Irish and because of the collapse of the agricultural economy due to the so-called Potato Famine from 1845 to 1852. But it can also be seen as voluntary in that although some Irish had other options, they chose to go to North America.

At the scale of an individual region or country, we can question whether a decision to migrate is forced or voluntary. At the scale of the household, the decision to migrate is all the more complex. For certain members of a migrating household, the move may be under duress; for others the move may be a preferred choice. The neutral title "migrant" veils the complexities of decision making at the household scale. Geographic studies of gender in migration demonstrate that at the household scale, power relationships, divisions of labor, and gender identities all factor into migration flows. At the household scale, decisions are made, in geographer Victoria Lawson's terms, in a "cooperative conflict bargaining process." Who has a say in this process and how much of a say each individual has depend on gendered power relationships and responsibilities in the household.

Studies of gender and migration find that, in many regions, men are more mobile than women and men migrate farther than women. Generally, men have more choices of employment than women, and women earn less than men in the jobs they find at the destination locations. One study of migration in Mexican households found that strongly patriarchal households tend to shield young women from migrating, sending young men out to work instead. Mexican households without a strong patriarchy more commonly send young, unmarried women to the city or another country to gain employment.

Ultimately, the decision or directive to migrate happens to an individual migrant within a household, place, country, region, and world, each of which has its own dynamics. The key difference between voluntary and forced migration, however, is that voluntary migrants have an option—at the very least, where to go or what to do once there; forced migrants do not.

## Forced Migration

The largest and most devastating forced migration in the history of humanity was the Atlantic slave trade during the European colonial period, which carried tens of millions of Africans from their homes to South America, the Caribbean, and North America. The number of Africans sold into slavery will never be known, but estimates range from 12 million to 30 million. Many lost their lives in transit to the Western Hemisphere. Figure 3.6 shows an approximation of the numbers who survived the journey, as well as the destinations of the trans-Atlantic African deportees.

Because slavery plays a major role in U.S. history, many students in the United States assume that the vast majority of African slaves were taken to the southeastern United States. However, as the map shows, a considerable majority of Africans were forced across the Atlantic to the Caribbean region, to coastal Central America, and to Brazil.

The Atlantic slave trade began early in the sixteenth century, when Spain and Portugal brought Africans to the Caribbean. In the early decades of the seventeenth century, African slaves arrived in small numbers on plantations in coastal eastern North America. Wealth promised through plantation agriculture from the southeastern United States to Brazil created a demand for slaves by plantation owners, who paid European shippers for slaves. Those shippers, in turn, paid African raiders for slaves.

Of all crops produced on plantations in the Americas and Caribbean during the 1700s, sugar was the most important economically. Figure 3.6 reflects the scramble for sugar islands in the Caribbean, as the map names Spanish, British, Danish, French, and Dutch colonies in the Caribbean as destinations for slaves. Add the coffee, fruit, and sugar plantations in Brazil and the cotton plantations of the southeastern United States, and the destinations of slaves on the map make sense.

The terror and destruction of slave raiding afflicted large areas of Africa. Europeans and African raiders exploited much of West Africa from Liberia to Nigeria and inland to the margins of the Sahara. So many Africans were taken from the area that is now Benin in West Africa to Bahia in Brazil that significant elements of the local culture remained intact in the transition. Today Bahia and Benin have strong ties, and cultural exchanges are growing stronger. The entire Equatorial African coastal region fell victim to the slave trade as well, when Portuguese slave traders raided the Portuguese domains of Angola and Mozambique. Arab slave raiders were active in East Africa and the Horn of Africa (present-day Somalia), penetrating Equatorial Africa and often cooperating with Europeans. Zanzibar, off the coast of mainland Tanzania, long was a major slave market.

We know proportionately where slaves ended up, but we can never gauge the full impact of this horrific period. In *A Colonizer's Model of the World*, geographer James Blaut discussed the sheer loss to African civilizations that occurred when Europeans and African raiders enslaved significant populations. The Atlantic slave trade also changed the Caribbean, where the vast majority of people on many of its islands are of African-Caribbean descent, and few, if any, indigenous peoples remain. In combination, the slave trade inflicted incalculable damage on African societies and communities, and changed the cultural and ethnic geography of both source and destination regions.

Although no forced migration in human history compares in magnitude to the Atlantic slave trade, other forced

Adapted with permission from: Philip D. Curtin, *The Atlantic Slave Trade*. University of Wisconsin Press, 1969, p. 57 and Donald K. Fellows, *Geography*. John Wiley & Sons, Inc., 1967, p. 121

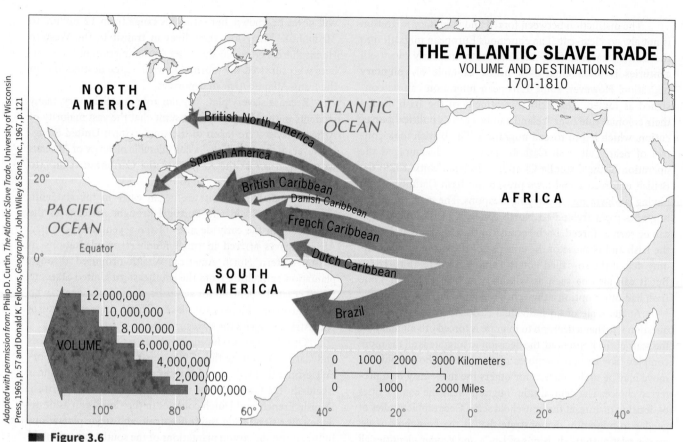

**■ Figure 3.6**

**The Atlantic Slave Trade.**   For every African brought to the United States, eight or more were brought to the Caribbean and Central and South America. Demand for sugar increased between 1701 and 1810, encouraging the intensive production of the crop in the Caribbean. Europeans purchased enslaved people to labor on the sugar plantations. As a result, the majority of enslaved people brought from Africa to the Americas landed in the Caribbean.

migrations have shaped the contemporary demographic map of the world. For 50 years beginning in 1788, Great Britain shipped tens of thousands of convicts from Britain to Australia, where they had a lasting impact on the continent's population geography. In the 1800s, the U.S. government took lands from thousands of Native Americans and forcibly moved tribes to other areas of the country, many far from their traditional homelands. In the Soviet Union during Stalin's ruthless rule between the late 1920s and 1953, the government forcibly moved millions of non-Russians from their homes to remote parts of Central Asia and Siberia for political reasons. During the 1930s in Germany, the Nazis were responsible for a significant forced migration of Jews from portions of western Europe that fell under their control.

Forced migration still happens today. It continues to occur, for example, in the form of countermigration, in which governments detain migrants who enter or attempt to enter their countries illegally and return the migrants to their home countries. It also occurs in the wake of armed conflicts and environmental disasters such as those discussed below.

**Human trafficking** is another ongoing example of forced migration and an issue of concern in the international community. Sex trafficking, child sex trafficking, forced labor, bonded or debt bondage labor, involuntary domestic servitude, forced child labor, and the recruitment of child soldiers all fall within the broad umbrella of human trafficking. This modern form of slavery likely affects millions worldwide at any given time, though data are notoriously unreliable due to the informal and illegal nature of these practices, the stigma surrounding human trafficking, and the reluctance of some governments to act. The U.S. Department of State's annual Trafficking-in-Persons (TIP) report identified 40,000 victims in 2013, far fewer than many nongovernmental organizations and social scientists believe exist. The Congressionally mandated TIP report has become an important feature of U.S. foreign policy. The report places countries on a series of tiers, depending on how well they have reported on and combatted human trafficking within their borders. If they rate poorly, they are placed on a watch list. If countries are placed on or fall to the lowest tier, they may face economic sanctions or the cessation of aid. The conditions of human trafficking are profoundly unsettling and detail the extent to which forced migration continues to shape human experiences, cultural landscapes, and migration patterns.

## Push and Pull Factors in Voluntary Migration

Why do people choose to migrate? Researchers have been intrigued by this question for more than a century. Studies of voluntary migration flows indicate that the intensity of a migration flow varies with factors such as similarities between the source and the destination, the effectiveness of the flow of information from the destination back to the source, and the physical distance between the source and the destination.

Over a century ago, British demographer Ernst Ravenstein sought an answer to the question of why people voluntarily migrate. He studied internal migration in England, and on the basis of his data he proposed several **laws of migration**, many of which are still relevant today, including:

1. Every migration flow generates a return or counter-migration.
2. The majority of migrants move a short distance.
3. Migrants who move longer distances tend to choose big-city destinations.
4. Urban residents are less migratory than inhabitants of rural areas.
5. Families are less likely to make international moves than young adults.

Ravenstein also posited an inverse relationship between the volume of migration and the distance between source and destination; that is, the number of migrants to a destination declines as the distance they must travel increases. Ravenstein's idea is an early observation of the **gravity model**, which predicts interaction between places on the basis of their population size and distance between them. The gravity model assumes that spatial interaction (such as migration) increases as the size and importance of places becomes greater, and decreases as the distance between them grows. The balance between population size and distance predicts the likelihood of migration. In mathematical terms, the model holds that migration potential can be calculated by multiplying the size of the populations of two places, and then dividing the product by the distance between them. That calculation had more meaning in an age before airplane travel and the Internet, when physical distance meant something different from what it means today. But even now more migrants move shorter rather than longer distances, suggesting the model still has some relevance.

Although the gravity model gives us a guide to expected migration, migration is not as simple as a mathematical equation. When an individual, family, or group of people makes a voluntary decision to migrate, push and pull factors come into play. **Push factors** are the conditions and perceptions that help the migrant decide to leave a place. **Pull factors** are the circumstances that effectively attract the migrant to certain locales from other places, the decision of where to go. A migrant's decision to emigrate from the home country and migrate to a new country results from a combination of push and pull factors, and these factors play out differently depending on the circumstance and scale of the migration. Because a migrant is likely to be more familiar with his or her place of residence (source) than with the locale to which he or she is moving (destination), a migrant will likely perceive push factors more accurately than pull factors. Push factors include individual considerations such as work or retirement conditions, cost of living, personal safety and security, and, for many, environmental catastrophes or even issues such as weather and climate. Pull factors tend to be vaguer and may depend solely on perceptions construed from things heard and read rather than on experiences in the destination place. Often, migrants move on the basis of unrealistically positive images and expectations regarding their destinations.

When considering pull factors, the principle of **distance decay** comes into play (Fig. 3.7). Prospective migrants are likely to have more complete perceptions of nearer places than of farther ones, which confirms the notion that the intensity of human activity, process, or function declines as distance from its source increases. Since interaction with faraway places generally decreases as distance increases, prospective migrants are likely to feel much less certain about distant destinations than about nearer ones. This prompts many migrants to move to a locale closer to home than they originally contemplated.

Migration streams may appear on maps as long, unbroken routes, but in fact they often consist of a series of stages, a phenomenon known as **step migration**. A peasant family in rural Brazil, for example, is likely to move first to a village, then to a nearby town, later to a city, and finally to a metropolis such as São Paulo or Rio de Janeiro. At each stage a new set of pull factors comes into play.

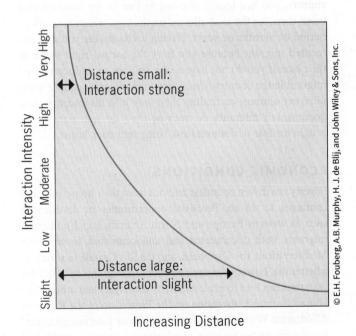

**■ Figure 3.7**

**Distance Decay.**  The farther from the hearth in time and distance, the less likely a trait or innovation will diffuse.

Not all migrants from one place follow the same steps. When 1000 people leave a village and migrate to a town in a given year, most, if not all, of them may dream of making it to, and in, the "big city." But only about 500 may actually move from town to city, and of these, only 200 eventually reach the metropolis that impelled them to move in the first place. Along the way the majority are captured by **intervening opportunity**. This happened during the Great Migration when African Americans by the tens of thousands migrated northward after World War I to seek work in growing cities such as Chicago and Cleveland. Many found employment in St. Louis and Cincinnati; that is, they encountered intervening opportunities along their northbound routes.

## Types of Push and Pull Factors

What specific factors impel people to pull up stakes and leave the familiar for the uncertain? What factors help migrants choose a destination? Research has shown that typically a combination of factors, not just one, leads to deciding it is time to move and deciding where to go. Any single factor can be either a push for the migrant to leave the home country or a pull to the new country. Which factor matters most depends on the migrant and the circumstances surrounding the decision to migrate.

### LEGAL STATUS

Migrants can arrive in a country with or without the formal consent of the host country. Each country around the world determines who is allowed to enter and under what circumstances. If you apply for and receive a work visa from another country, you are legally allowed to live in the country and work there for the time allotted on the visa, which is usually a period of months or years. Having a visa makes you a documented migrant because you have the formal right to be in the place. If you do not have a visa, you are an undocumented migrant in the country. Undocumented migrants choose quite different options for finding their way into the country than documented migrants do because they do not want to be caught for fear of **deportation**, being sent back home.

### ECONOMIC CONDITIONS

Poverty has driven countless millions from their homelands and continues to do so. Perceived opportunities in destinations such as western Europe and North America impel numerous migrants, both documented and undocumented, to cross the Mediterranean, the Caribbean, and the Rio Grande in search of a better life. Lower economic positions of migrants in their host countries can lead to exploitation by employers and others. The United Nations Convention on the Protection of the Rights of All Migrant Workers and Members of Their Families, recognizing the precarious position of migrant workers, has established standards of treatment for migrant workers. Fifty-eight states, most of which are countries that send more migrants than they receive, have ratified or signed the convention. Even though no

member of the European Union and only 4 of 19 states in the G-20 states have signed it (the 20 largest economies in the world including the European Union, which primarily receive migrants), the convention's statements on human trafficking and the right of migrant workers to equal wages influence the migration policies of many nonsignatory states.

The global recession of 2008 dramatically altered internal migration patterns in the United States. During economic downturns, populations tend to be less mobile. At the turn of the second decade of the twenty-first century, the lack of economic opportunities for would-be migrants and the inability of Americans to sell their homes slowed internal migration dramatically. Florida, a State that previously received large numbers of internal migrants, recorded a net loss in migration for the first time since the 1940s. Other previously booming States such as Arizona and Nevada recorded similarly low numbers. At the same time, typical sending States—Massachusetts, California, and New York—saw 90 percent fewer migrants leave between 2008 and 2010 than had left earlier in the decade.

### POWER RELATIONSHIPS

Gender, ethnicity, race, and money are all factors in the decision to migrate. Power relationships already embedded in society enable the flow of migrants around the world. Employers who hire migrant workers often know what kinds of migrants would work best for them.

Women in the Middle East hire Southeast Asian women to work as domestic servants, housekeepers, and nannies. Geographer Paul Boyle points out that by hiring women from abroad, the female head of household establishes a relationship in which the employee's "ethnicity and citizenship status differentiates them from their female employer and this influences the power relationships that underpin the working arrangements." In their study of placement agencies that help people hire domestic workers, Stiell and England found that in Toronto, Canada, placement agencies portrayed certain ethnicities according to scripted stereotypes. For instance, workers from the Caribbean went from being portrayed as "docile, jolly and good with children" to being depicted as "difficult, aggressive and selfish." Soon after, employers sought to hire women from the Philippines whom, at the time, placement agencies portrayed as "'naturally' docile, subservient, hardworking, good natured, domesticated, and willing to endure long hours of housework and child-care with little complaint."

Race is also a factor in the hiring of migrant workers. For example, carpet companies in Dalton, Georgia, the carpet capital of the world, began hiring Mexican workers after the 1986 passage of IRCA because they saw them as hard workers who were loyal to one company. In the same time frame, North and South Carolina also experienced surges in the Mexican migrant population. Geographer Jamie Winders cites the work of several researchers in the South whose research "raises the issue of displacement of black workers by Mexican migration—a topic hinted at by many studies but addressed by few." Issues of race and migrant status in hiring can spill over into neighborhoods, as they did recently in Raleigh, North Carolina. In the last 10 years conflicts have arisen over affordable housing between the African Americans who lived in Raleigh's neighborhoods and Mexican migrants who moved into the neighborhoods for the same affordable housing.

Geographer Paul Boyle also cites power relationships based on money in the growing migration industry, whereby migration flows are contractually arranged in order to fill labor needs for particular economic sectors throughout the world. Contractors give migrants advances on their earnings, help them migrate to the new country or region within a country, and then take migrants' wages in order to pay for advances and other needs the contractor supplies to the migrants.

## Political Circumstances

Throughout history, oppressive regimes have engendered migration streams. Desperate migrants fled Vietnam and Cambodia by the hundreds of thousands as new regimes came to power in the wake of the Vietnam War. In 1972 Uganda's dictator, Idi Amin, expelled 50,000 Asians and Ugandans of Asian descent from his country. The Cuban communist dictatorship expelled more than 125,000 Cubans in 1980 in the "Mariel Boatlift." Politically driven migration flows are marked by both escape and expulsion.

## Armed Conflict and Civil War

The dreadful conflict that engulfed the former Yugoslavia during the 1990s drove as many as 3 million people from their homes, mostly into western Europe. Many people became permanent emigrants, unable to return home. During the mid-1990s, a civil war engulfed Rwanda in Equatorial Africa, a conflict that pitted militant Hutu against the minority Tutsi and "moderate" Hutu. The carnage claimed an estimated 800,000 to 1 million lives and produced huge migration flows into neighboring Zaïre (now Congo) and Tanzania. More than 2 million Rwandans fled their homeland.

As we discuss in more detail below, for more than 30 years people from Afghanistan have left the country in search of safety first from a succession of upheavals. Well over 10 million Afghans have been refugees since 1979, fleeing mainly to Pakistan and Iran. More recently, the ongoing civil war in Syria has contributed to a significant percentage of worldwide refugees and internally displaced peoples. Recent and longstanding conflicts in Subsaharan Africa, particularly Sudan, South Sudan, the Democratic People's Republic of the Congo, Somalia, and Mali, represent another large percentage of what the United Nations Refugee Agency calls their "population of concern," an estimated 40 million refugees, internally displaced peoples, asylum seekers, and stateless peoples.

## Environmental Conditions

Environmental crises including earthquakes, hurricanes, volcanic eruptions, and tsunamis also stimulate migrations. Because many migrants return, the net outflow generated by such momentary crises is often temporary, but this is not always the case. Between the 2000 and 2010 censuses, the population of New Orleans fell by 11 percent as a result of the devastation of Hurricane Katrina in 2005 and the economic recession since. The proportion of children in New Orleans' population also fell, from 27 percent in 2000 to 23 percent in 2007. Mapping where children live in New Orleans reflects another trend in post-Katrina New Orleans: Families with children in the New Orleans region are moving out of the city center and close-in suburbs and into the farther suburbs and exurbs, including Belle Chasse (Fig. 3.8).

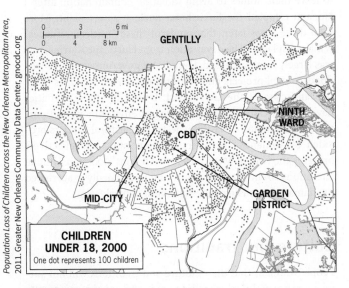

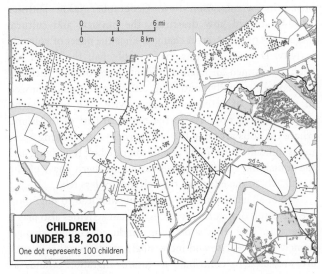

■■ **Figure 3.8**

**Population Density of Children Under Age 18 in New Orleans, 2000 and 2010.**   Families with children were less likely to return to New Orleans to reside after Hurricane Katrina. A dramatic drop in the number of young people in the city, especially in Mid-city, Gentilly, the Garden District, and the Ninth ward, has led to the need for fewer schools and has changed the vibe of neighborhoods.

## GUEST FIELD NOTE

### Plymouth, Montserrat

This photo shows the damage caused by the 1995 eruption of the Sourfriere Hills volcano on the Caribbean Island of Montserrat. In the foreground you can see the gray volcanic ash clogging the roadbed, and in the background is the abandoned capital city of Plymouth. Many buildings cannot even be entered because the ash has buried their first floors or caved in their ceilings. This scene illustrated for me the complexities of migration in the face of natural disasters. Many Montserratians fled to the United States when Plymouth was destroyed and were given "temporary protected" immigration status. The U.S. government told Montserratian refugees to leave in 2005—not because the volcanic crisis was over or because the housing crisis caused by the volcano was solved. Rather, the U.S. government expected the volcanic crisis to last at least 10 more years; so, the Monsterratians no longer qualified as "temporary" refugees.

*Credit: Jason Dittmer, University College London*

Jason Dittmer, University College London

■■ **Figure 3.9**

Some environmental crises, such as volcanic eruptions, bring long-term environmental changes to the landscape, making return migration difficult, if not impossible. For example, the Caribbean island of Montserrat had a small population of about 10,000 prior to a volcanic eruption that began in 1995. The volcano has been active since then, prompting a migration flow. Geographer Jason Dittmer (2004) studied how drastically the physical and cultural landscapes of Montserrat changed since the onset of volcanic activity. Dittmer explains that roughly half the island has been proclaimed an Exclusion Zone, a region that includes the capital city of Plymouth (Fig. 3.9). People are not allowed in this zone of active volcanic activity. The people who remained must now live in the northern part of the island where the soils are thin, the land is rocky, and making a living is difficult. Over 7000 people migrated off the island, and the remaining 3000 migrated to the northern coast of the island, where the effects of the volcano are less felt.

Not all environmental conditions that lead to migration are the result of natural processes; human activities also play a large role. The effects of human-induced climate change, namely sea-level rise and increasingly erratic weather events, are projected to contribute to future migration strands as "climate refugees" from low-lying areas seek refuge elsewhere. One report suggests that the world will see as many as 150 million climate refugees from 40 countries by 2050. In 2009, the president of the Maldives held a cabinet meeting underwater to draw attention to the plight of his country, where all 400,000 Maldivians are likely to become refugees due to sea-level rise in the near future. Similarly, nuclear accidents and other industrial disasters have contributed to migration flows. In 2011, as many as 83,000 Japanese were forced to leave their homes to avoid radiation contamination after a tsunami crippled the Fukushima nuclear power plant. More than three years later, thousands of these "nuclear refugees" remain displaced. The devastation from Hurricane Katrina, too, was largely human-caused. Decades of government-sponsored flood-control projects and resource extraction activities mark the landscape of the Gulf Coast. Over time these activities have dramatically altered the physical environment and particularly Louisiana's coastline, destroying natural barriers provided by wetlands, increasing erosion rates, and effectively bringing the Gulf of Mexico to New Orleans' doorstep. Human alterations to the physical environment decidedly exacerbated the damage from Hurricane Katrina, a natural event.

## Culture and Traditions

People who fear that their culture and traditions will not survive a major political transition, and who are able to migrate to places they perceive as safer, will often do so. When the British partitioned South Asia into a mainly Hindu India and an almost exclusively Muslim Pakistan in 1947, millions of

Muslim residents of India migrated across the border to the new Islamic state, and millions of Hindus migrated from Pakistan to secular India—an estimated 8 million in all. In the 1990s after decades of Soviet obstruction, more than 2 million Jews left the former Soviet Union for Israel and other destinations. The decline in minority white power and uncertain political conditions in South Africa during the mid-1990s impelled many whites to emigrate to Australia, Europe, and North America.

## Technological Advances

For some migrants, emigration is no longer the difficult and hazardous journey it used to be. Although most migrants, especially refugees, still move by foot, some use modern forms of transportation and communication, the availability of which can itself encourage migration.

Gone is the time when would-be emigrants waited months, even years, for information about distant places. News today travels faster than ever, including news of job opportunities and ways to reach desired destinations. Television, radio, cellular phone, and telephone stimulate millions of people to migrate by relaying information about relatives, opportunities, and already established communities in destination lands. Advances in communication technology strengthen the role of **kinship links** as push or pull factors. When deciding where to go, a migrant is often pulled to places where family and friends have already found success. Thus, Turks quickly heard about Germany's need for migrant labor after World War II, and Algerians knew where the most favorable destinations were in France in the same time period.

When a migrant chooses a destination and writes, calls, or communicates through others to tell family and friends at home about the new place, the migrant helps create a positive perception of the destination for family and friends, and may promise help with migration by providing housing and assistance obtaining a job. Geographers call flows along and through kinship links **chain migration**. When a migrant reassures family and friends that a new community has been formed, a place where they can feel home, further migration often occurs along the same chain. Chains of migration built upon each other create **immigration waves** or swells in migration from one origin to the same destination.

Think about a migration flow within your family, whether internal, international, voluntary, or forced. The flow can be one you experienced or one you only heard about through family. List the push and pull factors. Then, write a letter in the first person (if you were not involved, pretend you were your grandmother or whoever) to another family member at "home" describing how you came to migrate to the destination and the circumstances you encountered when you arrived.

## WHERE DO PEOPLE MIGRATE?

Several major global-scale migration flows have occurred over the past 500 years—flows characterized by the movement of hundreds of thousands of people migrating along the same general path. Important population shifts have taken place at the regional and national scales as well. In this section of the chapter, we focus on the destinations of these major migration flows. Looking at migration flows at the global, regional, and national scales provides only a generalized picture of human movement, however. At the local and household scales, each individual or family migration reflects life-altering decisions, and those decisions collectively foster global change.

## Global Migration Flows

Before 1500, long-distance migration occurred haphazardly, typically in pursuit of spices, fame, or exploration. Things changed in the age of European **colonization**. Colonization is a physical process whereby the colonizing entity takes over another place, putting its own government in charge and either moving its own people into the place or bringing in indentured outsiders to gain control of the people and the land. First, Europeans colonized the Americas and the coasts of Africa and parts of Asia from the 1500s to the 1800s. Then, starting in the late 1800s and into the 1900s, Europeans colonized interior Africa and Asia.

The major flows of global migration from 1500 on are shown in Figure 3.10. The migration flows include movements from Europe to North America (1); from southern Europe to South and Central America (2); from Britain and Ireland to Africa and Australia (3); from Africa to the Americas during the period of slavery (4); and from India to eastern Africa, Southeast Asia, and Caribbean America (5).

Among the greatest human migrations in recent centuries was the flow from Europe to the Americas. Emigration from Europe (1 and 2 in Fig. 3.10) began slowly. Before the 1830s, perhaps 2.75 million Europeans left to settle overseas. The British went to North America, Australia, New Zealand, and South Africa (3). From Spain and Portugal, many hundreds of thousands of Europeans emigrated to Middle and South America. Early European colonial settlements grew, even in coastal areas of present-day Angola, Kenya, and Indonesia. The rate of European emigration increased sharply between 1835 and 1935, with perhaps as many as 75 million departing for colonies in Africa and Asia and for economic opportunities in the Americas. Although millions of Europeans eventually returned to their homelands, the net outflow from Europe was enormous, as evidenced by the sheer number of Canadians and Americans who identify themselves as being of European ancestry.

As already discussed, the Americas were the destination of another mass of immigrants: African slaves. African slaves were among the early non-American Indian settlers in this country (4). Although this migration is mapped as just one of the eight major

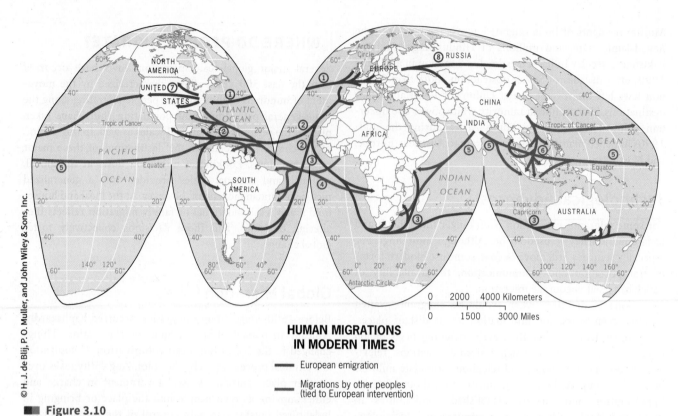

© H. J. de Blij, P. O. Muller, and John Wiley & Sons, Inc.

**HUMAN MIGRATIONS
IN MODERN TIMES**

— European emigration

— Migrations by other peoples
(tied to European intervention)

■ **Figure 3.10**

**Major Routes of Human Migration Between 1500 and 1950.**   1. Europeans moving to North America during and after the colonial period. 2. Movement of southern Europeans to South and Central America during the colonial period. 3. Movement of British and Irish to Africa and Australia during the colonial period. 4. Africans transported to the Western Hemisphere as slaves. 5. Indians brought to other British colonies to serve administrative and commercial roles. 6. Chinese migrants to Southeast Asia and the Americas in the nineteenth and twentieth centuries. 7. Westward migration in the United States. 8. Eastward migration of Russians across Siberia and into Central Asia.

migration streams, its immense and lasting impact on both sides of the Atlantic sets it apart from all the others.

Even as the Atlantic slave trade was in progress, European colonialism generated major migrations in other places in the world. The British, who took control over South Asia, transported tens of thousands of "indentured" workers from present-day India, Pakistan, and Sri Lanka to East and South Africa (see symbol (5) in Fig. 3.10). Today, people of South Asian ancestry are substantial minorities in South Africa, Kenya, and Tanzania. South Asian immigrants in eastern and southern Africa became business leaders in the region. South Asians control a disproportionate share of commerce and hold significant wealth in the region, fueling ethnic friction.

Long before the British arrived in India, Hindu influences radiated into Southeast Asia, reaching the Indonesian islands of Java and Bali. Later, the British renewed the Indian migration stream, bringing South Asians to the Malay Peninsula (including Singapore) and to their Pacific holdings, including Fiji (Fig. 3.10).

The British were also instrumental in relocating Asians, mainly from India, to such Caribbean countries as Trinidad and Tobago and Guyana, the trans-Pacific stream labeled 5 in Fig. 3.10. The Dutch were pivotal in the migration of many Javanese from what is today Indonesia to the former Dutch dependency of Suriname along the same route.

## Guest Workers

Significant global migration flows in recent decades have come in response to governmental efforts to promote immigration to fill labor needs. The countries of Europe that were major participants in World War II lost millions of young men in the long conflict. After the war, European countries, rebuilding their economies with the help of the U.S.-sponsored Marshall Plan, found themselves in need of laborers. Two flows of migration into Western European countries began: first within the European region, as workers from poorer European countries and regions migrated to economically growing areas; and second from outside of Europe, as millions of foreign workers immigrated from North Africa (the majority to France) and Turkey (mostly to Germany) as well as from the Caribbean region, India, and Africa (many to the United Kingdom).

Western European governments called the labor migrants **guest workers**—a term that is now used to describe migrant labor in other places as well. The laws allowing guest workers into Europe assumed the workers would fill the void left by those who died during World War II, and then they would return to their home countries. Instead, most guest workers stayed both because they wanted to and because they were needed. Two to three generations of Turks have now been born in Germany, making them far more than "guests." The German government, which had for decades defined German citizens as those of German descent, allowed Turks to become citizens of the country in 2005.

Not only in Germany, but in countries around the world, millions of guest workers live outside of their home country and send remittances from their jobs home. Guest workers often work as agricultural laborers or in service industries, including hotels, restaurants, and tourist attractions. The home states of these workers are fully aware that their citizens have visas and are working abroad. In many instances, the economies of the home countries come to rely on the remittances, and the home governments work with destination countries and with the international labor organization to protect the rights of the guest workers.

Despite the legal status of guest workers and the work of governments and international organizations to protect them, many employers abuse them because guest workers are often unaware of their rights. Long hours and low pay are common, but guest workers continue to work because the money is better than they would ordinarily receive and because they are supporting families at home.

When the need for labor declines, destination governments can squeeze out guest workers. At the same time, the government of the home country can pull out its guest workers, bringing them home when conditions in the destination region become perilous. For example, over 30,000 Indonesians were working in the Middle East before the 2003 Iraq War; the Indonesian government decided to pull its workers home just before the war began.

Guest workers are documented migrants who have work visas, usually short term. Often the destination governments extend the visas if certain sectors of the economy still need laborers. Whether short or long term, the international flow of guest workers changes the ethnic, linguistic, and religious mosaic of the places where they go. In Europe, for example, guest workers from Turkey, North Africa, South Asia, and other former colonial holdings have altered the cultural landscape of the region. New temples, mosques, restaurants, grocery stores, shops, and service industries geared toward migrants have taken root in Europe's cultural landscape.

## Regional Migration Flows

The huge flows of migrants mapped in Figure 3.10 were unprecedented and meet few rivals in terms of sheer numbers today. Although some global migration flows already discussed

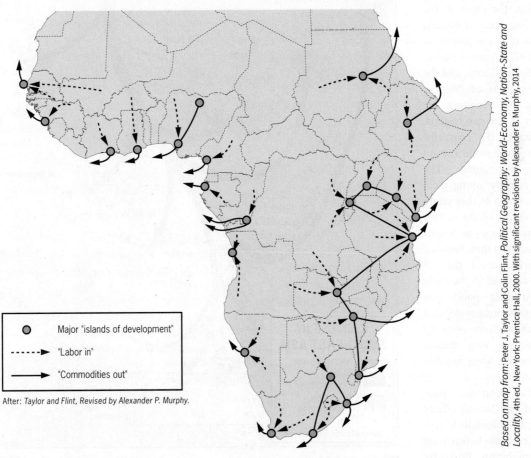

*Based on map from: Peter J. Taylor and Colin Flint, Political Geography: World-Economy, Nation-State and Locality, 4th ed., New York: Prentice Hall, 2000. With significant revisions by Alexander B. Murphy, 2014*

Major "islands of development"

- - - ▶ "Labor in"

———▶ "Commodities out"

After: *Taylor and Flint, Revised by Alexander P. Murphy.*

■ **Figure 3.11**

**Islands of Development in Subsaharan Africa.** Islands of development are cities that receive foreign and domestic investment. Migrants from rural areas and neighboring countries are pulled toward these cities to find work. Commodities produced in islands of development are typically exported.

were forced and some were voluntary, each occurred at a global scale and across major world regions. Migration also occurs at a regional scale, with migrants going to a neighboring country to take advantage of short-term economic opportunities, to reconnect with their cultural group across borders, or to flee political conflict or war.

## ECONOMIC OPPORTUNITIES

To understand migration flows from one poor country to another, it is not sufficient to analyze the flow at the global scale. We need to understand where the region fits into the global interaction picture and to see how different locations within the region fit into interaction patterns at both global and regional scales. Cities in the developing world are typically where most foreign investment goes, where the vast majority of paying jobs are located, and where infra-structure is concentrated. These port cities become so-called **islands of development** within larger less-developed regions (Fig. 3.11).

Within the region of West Africa, the cities in the oil-producing areas of Nigeria are islands of development. In the mid-1970s, poorer people in Togo, Benin, Ghana, and the northern regions of Nigeria, perceiving that economic life was better in coastal Nigeria, were lured to the coast for short-term jobs while the oil economy was good. The migrants, usually young men, worked as much as they could and sent almost all the money they earned home as remittances to support their families. They worked until the oil economy declined in the early 1980s. At that point, the Nigerian government decided the foreign workers were no longer needed. Two million foreign workers were forcibly pushed out.

Global economic processes and the lasting effects of European colonialism certainly played a role in this West African migration flow. By looking at migration flows at the regional scale, we can see regional economic influences and the pull of islands of development in places such as Nigeria.

European colonialism also had an impact on regional migration flows in Southeast Asia. Europe's colonial occupation of Southeast Asia presented economic opportunities for the Chinese. During the late 1800s and early 1900s, millions of Chinese laborers fled famine and political strife in southern China to work as contract laborers in Southeast Asia (Fig. 3.12). Many remained, and today their descendants constitute a Chinese minority in Southeast Asian countries that accounts for substantial portions of the population: 14 percent in Thailand, 23 percent in Malaysia, and 74 percent in Singapore. The Chinese minority in Indonesia accounts for only about 3 percent of the total population, but Indonesia has more than 200 million people, so its Chinese minority is one of Southeast Asia's largest clusters. Over time, the

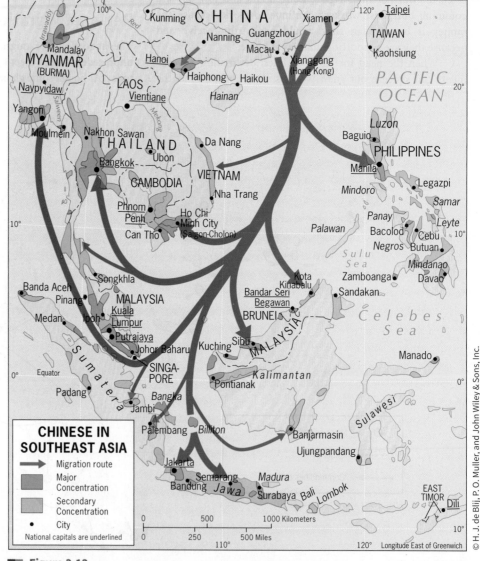

**CHINESE IN SOUTHEAST ASIA**
→ Migration route
Major Concentration
Secondary Concentration
• City
National capitals are underlined

■ **Figure 3.12**
**Chinese in Southeast Asia.** The great majority of Chinese who live in Southeast Asia migrated from southeastern China.

overseas Chinese in Southeast Asia became leaders in trade, commerce, and finance in the region, taking an economic position much like that of Southern Asians in Eastern and Southern Africa. The presence of overseas Chinese migrants has sometimes led to significant discord in receiving countries. In May 2014, longstanding Sino-Vietnamese tensions erupted into violent protests after China announced plans to build an oil rig in an area in the South China Sea that is also claimed by Vietnam. Rioters attacked Chinese migrants, 21 of whom died, and set fire to Chinese businesses (many of which were actually owned by Taiwanese migrants).

A significant recent example of regional migration is the movement of peoples from Mexico and countries farther south into the United States. That migration rapidly accelerated in the 1970s and 1980s—peaking around the year 2000 with close to 1 million immigrants arriving each year. The number of migrants fell off sharply after the economic downturn of 2008, but the imprint of this decades-long migration is still very much in evidence. Mexican immigrants alone now comprise close to 4 percent of the U.S. population, and they play a fundamentally important economic role in many States and locales.

## RECONNECTION OF CULTURAL GROUPS

Regional migration flows also center on reconnecting cultural groups across borders. A migration stream with enormous consequences is the flow of Jewish immigrants to Israel. At the turn of the twentieth century, fewer than 50,000 Jewish residents lived in what was then Palestine. From 1919 to 1948, the United Kingdom of Great Britain and Northern Ireland held control over Palestine, and Britain encouraged Jews, whose ancestors had fled more than a thousand years earlier from the Middle East to Europe, to return to the region. By 1948, as many as 750,000 Jews resided in Palestine, when the United Nations intervened to partition the area and establish the independent state of Israel. The original boundaries of the new state are shown in orange in Figure 3.13. Following the division of the land between the newly created Israeli state and the state of Palestine, another migration stream began when 600,000 Palestinian Arabs fled or were pushed out of Israeli territories. Palestinians sought refuge in neighboring Jordan, Egypt, Syria, and beyond.

Through a series of wars, Israel expanded its area of territorial control (Fig. 3.13) and actively built settlements for new Jewish immigrants in Palestinian territories (Fig. 3.14). Jewish immigrants from the Eurasian region continue to migrate to Israel. Following the collapse of the Soviet Union in the early 1990s, thousands of Jews who had been unable to practice their religion in the Soviet Union migrated to Israel. Today Israel's population of 7.8 million, including almost 2 million Arab Israelis, continues to grow through immigration as well as substantial natural increase.

## CONFLICT AND WAR

At the end of World War II, as many as 15 million Germans migrated westward from their homes in Eastern Europe, either voluntarily or because they were forced to leave. Before the East German government built the Berlin Wall and the Iron Curtain divided Western and Eastern Europe, several million Germans fled Soviet-controlled East Germany into what was then West Germany. And millions of migrants left Europe altogether to go to the United States (1.8 million), Canada (1.1 million), Australia (1 million), Israel (750,000), Argentina (750,000), Brazil (500,000), Venezuela (500,000),

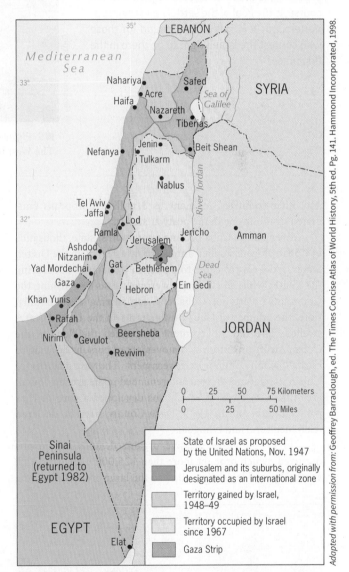

*Adapted with permission from: Geoffrey Barraclough, ed. The Times Concise Atlas of World History, 5th ed. Pg. 141. Hammond Incorporated, 1998.*

■ **Figure 3.13**

**Changing Boundaries of Israel.** The areas in green on the map along with the areas in yellow were the territory of Palestine under the 1947 United Nations plan. After partition, Palestine quickly lost the areas in green to Israel. Israel returned the Gaza Strip to Palestine in 2005. The areas in yellow on the map are the "Occupied Territories," including the West Bank, to the west of the River Jordan and the Golan Heights, west of Syria.

# FIELD NOTE

"Just a few miles into the West Bank, not far from Jerusalem, the expanding Israeli presence could not be missed. New settlements dot the landscape, often occupying strategic sites that are also easily defensible. These 'facts on the ground' will certainly complicate the effort to carve out a stable territorial order in this much-contested region. That, of course, is the goal of the settlers and their supporters, but it is salt on the wound for those who contest the Israeli right to be there in the first place."

© Alexander B. Murphy

■■ **Figure 3.14**
**The West Bank, Outside Jerusalem, Israel.**

and other countries. As many as 8 million Europeans emigrated from Europe in the postwar stream.

Even before Cuba became a communist state, thousands of Cuban citizens applied annually for residency in the United States. Fidel Castro came to power in Cuba in 1959. During the 1960s, while the Cuban government was establishing the Communist Party of Cuba and formalizing a communist state, the number of Cuban immigrants in the United States swelled. The U.S. government formalized the flow as the Cuban Airlift, an authorized movement of persons desiring to escape from a communist government. The vast majority of Cuban immigrants arrived and remained in the greater Miami area. In southern Florida, Cubans developed a core of Hispanic culture, and in 1973, Dade County, Florida, declared itself bicultural and bilingual.

In 1980 another massive, organized exodus of Cubans occurred, which brought more than 125,000 Cubans to U.S. shores. Special legislation allowed the large group to become

naturalized citizens over time. The Cuban influx persisted throughout the 1980s, and then in 1994 over 30,000 Cubans fled for the United States. By that point, the Soviet Union had collapsed, and its financial support for the Cuban government was cut substantially. The 1994 exodus pushed diplomats in both the United States and Cuba to come to an agreement on Cuban migration. In 1995, the U.S. government established a new policy designed to stem the flow of Cuban migrants to the United States.

## National Migration Flows

National migration flows can also be thought of as internal migration flows. Internal migration can be quite significant. In the United States, a massive two-centuries-long migration stream has carried the center of population west and more recently also south, as Figure 3.15 shows. As the American populace migrates westward, it is also shifting from north to

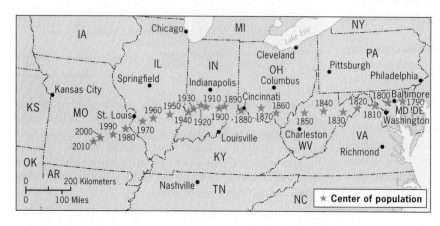

■■ **Figure 3.15**
**Changing Center of Population.** The steady march west has been unrelenting, with the slight southward trend reflecting increased migration to the Southwest over the past few decades. *Data from*: United States Census Bureau, *Statistical Abstract*, 2011.

south, to reflect migration flows from south to north and back again. After the American Civil War, and gaining momentum during World War I, millions of African Americans migrated north to work in the industrial Northeast and Midwest. This internal migration flow continued during the 1920s, declined during the depression years of the 1930s, and then resumed its upward climb.

In the 1970s, the trend began to reverse itself: African Americans began leaving the North and returning to the South. The reversal had several causes. Although the civil rights movement in the 1960s did not change conditions in the South overnight, it undoubtedly played a role in the reverse migration. Disillusionment with deteriorating living conditions in the Rustbelt of the urban North and West, coupled with growing economic opportunities in southern cities, also drew African Americans southward. African Americans who lived in northern cities migrated to southern cities, not to rural areas, as the urban economies of the Sun Belt began to grow.

Russia also experienced a major internal migration, but in Russia people migrated east, from the heartland of the Russian state (near Moscow and St. Petersburg) to the shores of the Pacific. This eastward migration significantly altered the cultural mosaic of Eurasia, and understanding this migration flow helps us understand the modern map of Eurasia. During the tsarist (1800s–1910s) and communist (1920s–1980s) periods, Russian and Soviet rulers tried to occupy and consolidate the country's far eastern frontier, moving industries eastward, building railroads and feeder lines, and establishing Vladivostok on the Pacific Coast as one of the world's best equipped naval bases. As Russia and then the Soviet Union expanded outward and to the east, the country incorporated numerous ethnic minorities.

During the communist period, the Soviet government also employed a policy of **Russification**, which sought to assimilate all the people in the Soviet territory into the Russian culture. One way the Soviets pushed for Russification was by encouraging people of Russian heritage to move out of Moscow and St. Petersburg and fill in the country. By 1980, as many as 30 million Russians had moved out toward the borders. After the collapse of the Soviet Union in 1991, some people moved back to their original homelands, but the map will long carry the impact of Russia's eastward expansion.

Mexico offers a more recent example of significant internal migration driven by international migration. Northern Mexico was the most important source-region for the Mexican migration to the United States described above. By 2005, an estimated one out of every two people born in the northern Mexican State of Zacatecas lived in the United States. As a result, the northern areas of Mexico experienced a labor shortage. In response, Mexican workers from areas farther south in the country migrated northward, taking jobs especially in Mexico's agricultural sector. Many such migrants were Huichol Indians, one of Mexico's indigenous populations. Ironically, the Huichol in northern Mexico are experiencing the same kind of substandard living conditions, lack of acceptance by locals, and exploitation by employers that many Mexicans from the north experienced once they arrived in the United States.

## The Special Case of Refugees

You may have seen a story on the televised news showing thousands upon thousands of poor people fleeing a crisis in their home region or country by walking. They put their few earthly possessions and their babies on their backs and walk. They walk to another town. They walk beyond their country's border. They walk to a refugee camp without adequate food, water, or amenities. International agencies try to mount emergency relief efforts while disease spreads, dooming infants and children and emaciating adults. As they walk, they remember all they are leaving behind: the only life they have known. But in the midst of war and persecution, it is too hard to hold onto this life. So, they walk.

The vast majority of refugees do not make it far from home. The Office of the United Nations High Commissioner for Refugees (UNHCR) estimates that 83 percent of refugees flee to a country in the same region as their home country. The world's refugee population has grown steadily since the founding of the Refugee Convention in 1951, which established an international law specifying who is a refugee and what legal rights they have. The main goal of the 1951 Refugee Convention was to help European refugees following the end of World War II. The UNHCR helped to repatriate most of the refugees from World War II.

In 1970, the United Nations reported that 2.9 million persons were refugees; the majority were Palestinian Arabs dislocated by the creation of the state of Israel and the armed conflicts that followed. In 1980, the global refugee total had nearly tripled, to over 8 million. By 2013, the UNHCR reported 11.1 million refugees fleeing from their homes and across country borders (Fig. 3.16).

The United Nations agency that monitors the refugee problem is the key organization supporting refugees. It organizes and funds international relief efforts and negotiates with governments and regimes on behalf of the refugees. But UNHCR is not alone in tracking this global problem; other offices often contradict UNHCR's data, arguing that the situation is even worse than the United Nations suggests.

The 1951 Refugee Convention defines a **refugee** as "a person who has a well-founded fear of being persecuted for reasons of race, religion, nationality, membership of a particular social group, or political opinion." Countries interpret this definition in different ways, especially since the phrase "well founded" leaves much room for judgment.

Perhaps the biggest problem with the UN definition has to do with internally displaced persons (called IDPs, sometimes called internal refugees). **Internally displaced persons** are people who have been displaced within their own countries, such as the victims of Hurricane Katrina, but they do not cross international borders as they flee. IDPs tend to remain undercounted, if not almost invisible. In 2013, UNHCR estimated that 20.8 million people (in addition to the 11.1 million

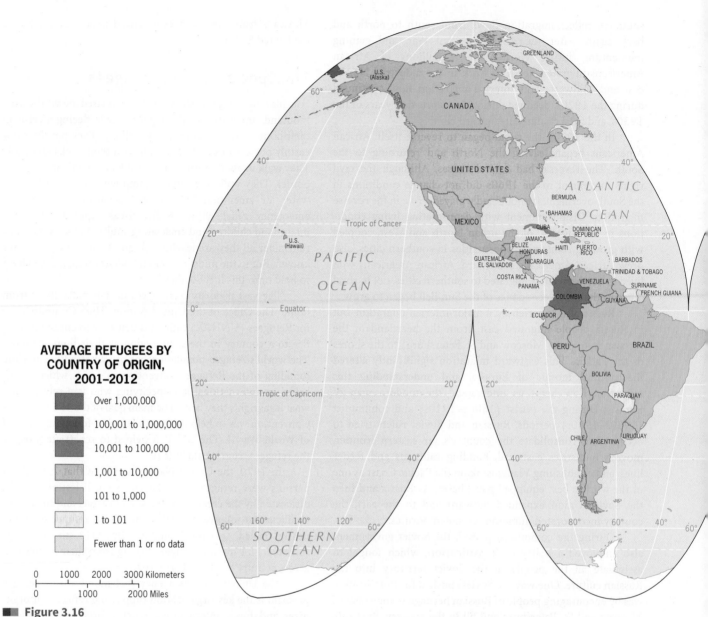

**■ Figure 3.16**

**Average Number of Refugees by Country of Origin from 2001 to 2012.**    This map highlights the home countries of the world's refugees. Afghanistan and Iraq had the highest average number of refugees between 2001 and 2012. The war in Afghanistan generated more than twice as many refugees as the war in Iraq. Civil war in Sudan and continuing strife in Somalia also caused millions to leave their home countries and be classified as refugees. The data are reported through 2012; so, refugees generated by civil war in Syria are not as evident as the protests against Assad and ensuing full scale civil war began in 2011.    *Data from: World Bank, 2014.*

international refugees) were IDPs—forced to abandon their homes. The United Nations and international law distinguish between *refugees*, who have crossed one or more international borders during their move and encamped in a country other than their own, and *internally displaced persons*, who abandon their homes but remain in their own countries.

Because the status of a refugee is internationally defined and recognized and comes with legal rights, the UN Refugee Agency and the world's states must distinguish between refugees and migrants who may be just as poor or desperate but who do not qualify for refugee status. When a refugee meets the official criteria, he or she becomes eligible for assistance,

including possible **asylum**, which is the right to protection in the first country in which the refugee arrives. Other migrants do not have the right to asylum. Refugee status can extend over decades and become the very basis for a way of life, as has happened in the Middle East. In Jordan, Palestinian refugees have become so integrated into the host country's national life that they are regarded as permanent refugees, but in Lebanon other Palestinians wait in refugee camps for resettlement and still qualify as temporary refugees.

The United Nations helps ensure that refugees and internally displaced persons are not forcibly returned to a homeland where persecution is still continuing. Once the violence subsides

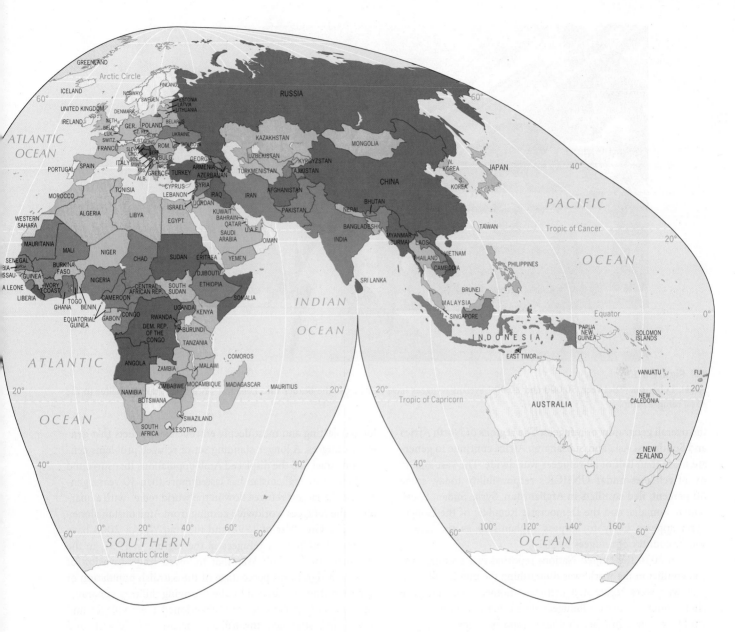

in a place and the conditions improve, the UNHCR helps return refugees to their homelands, a process called **repatriation**.

In the 1990s, hostilities broke out between the Hutu and Tutsi ethnic groups in Rwanda that led to a genocide killing hundreds of thousands and a disastrous exodus of more than one million refugees who fled to neighboring Democratic Republic of the Congo (then called Zaire), Tanzania, and Uganda. The Tutsi–Hutu strife in Rwanda spread to neighboring Burundi and dislocated tens of thousands. After the civil war in Rwanda calmed down in 1996, the UNHCR and the World Health Organization watched and aided as 500,000 Rwandans returned from across the border in the Democratic Republic of Congo.

In addition, some 9 million Syrians have been uprooted since the outbreak of civil war in 2011. Most refugees fled to neighboring Turkey, Lebanon, Jordan, and Iraq, which already had substantial refugee populations from other regional conflicts. In 2012, UNHCR built the temporary Zaatari refugee camp in Jordan near the Syrian border. The camp, only 7.8 square kilometers (3 sq mi), has become a more permanent living space for over 100,000 refugees from the conflict who live in harsh conditions and cramped quarters. Another 50,000 to 80,000 Syrian refugees have fled across the border to the tiny town of Arsal, Lebanon. The refugees now outnumber the local population in Arsal, and the "town's electrical grid, waste management system and water supply are struggling to serve a population almost three times its original size" (Gebeily and Haines-Young 2014) (Fig. 3.17). In addition, 6 million Syrians remain internally displaced, and an estimated 100,000 have been resettled in Europe and elsewhere.

## REGIONS OF DISLOCATION

The refugee situation changes frequently as some refugees return home, conditions permitting, and as other new streams suddenly form. Yet we can make certain generalizations about

Ratib Al Safadi/Anadolu Agency/Getty Images

■ **Figure 3.17**

**Arsal, Lebanon.** Between 50,000 and 80,000 Syrians refugees have fled across the border into Lebanon since 2011, taking shelter in the Arsal refugee camp.

the overall geography of refugees. The regions of North Africa and Southwest Asia and Subsaharan Africa continue to generate more than half of all refugees worldwide. The vast majority of refugees under UNHCR's responsibility today, some 60 percent, fled conflicts in Afghanistan, Syria, Sudan, South Sudan, Somalia, and the Democratic Republic of the Congo. Syria appears likely to surpass Afghanistan as the largest source country of refugees in 2014.

In 2010 the United Nations reported that festering war and conflict in the world was diminishing the number of refugees who were repatriated (returned home) each year. The High Commissioner on Refugees stated that a majority of the world's refugees had been refugees (and not repatriated) for more than five years. Most refugees move without any more goods than they can carry with them. When the United States and its allies began their retaliatory bombing in Afghanistan following the terrorist attack on New York and Washington in September 2001, tens of thousands of Afghan refugees climbed across mountain passes to reach the relative safety of Pakistan, able only to bring a few personal belongings. Most refugees make their first "step" on foot, by bicycle, wagon, open boat, or crowded caravan (Fig. 3.18). Refugees are suddenly displaced, limiting their options, and most have few resources to invest in their journey. As a result, the vast majority of the world's refugees come from relatively poor countries and they travel to neighboring countries that are also poor. The impact of refugee flows is certainly felt most in the poorest countries of the world.

## North Africa and Southwest Asia

This geographic region extending from Morocco in the west to Afghanistan in the east contains some of the world's

longest-lasting and most deeply entrenched conflicts that generate refugees. A longer-standing set of refugee problems centers on Israel and the displaced Arab populations that surround it. Conflict in Afghanistan has lasted more than 30 years, generating the largest refugee flow in the world today, with a quarter of the refugees worldwide coming from Afghanistan alone.

The Gulf War of 1991 and the Iraq War of 2003 have generated millions of refugees in the region. In 1991, in the aftermath of the Gulf War that followed Iraq's invasion of Kuwait, a significant percentage of the Kurdish population of northern Iraq, threatened by the surviving military apparatus and under Baghdad's control, abandoned their villages and towns and streamed toward and across the Turkish and Iranian borders. The refugee movement of Iraq's Kurds involved as many as 1.85 million people and riveted world attention on the plight of people who are condemned to such status through the actions of others. It led the United States and its allies to create a secure zone for Kurds in northern Iraq in the hope of persuading displaced Kurds in Turkey and Iran to return to their country. But this effort was only partially successful. The events surrounding the Gulf War severely dislocated the Kurdish people of Iraq, as Figure 3.18 shows; many remain refugees in Turkey as well as Iran. The war in Iraq generated over 2 million refugees, most of whom are living in neighboring Syria and Jordan, and 2.8 million IDPs. Following the outbreak of civil war in Syria in 2011, hundreds of thousands of Kurds, some of whom had sought refuge in Syria only a few years earlier, were forced to flee. Some 200,000 Syrian Kurds became refugees in Iraq. In contrast to the tensions that have arisen following the influx of Syrian refugees into Lebanon, Jordan, and Turkey, Iraqis have

ASSOCIATED PRESS

■■ **Figure 3.18**

**Pakistan.** Refugees from Afghanistan pour across the border into Pakistan in crowded caravans after the U.S. military action began in Afghanistan in 2001.

been more welcoming, perhaps because many have been displaced themselves. To make matters even more complex, there is still a sizable population of Iranian refugees in Iraq stemming from the Iran–Iraq conflict over three decades ago, including members of the exiled People's Mujahedin of Iran, or MEK, that remain in a camp and are vulnerable to attack.

During the 1980s, Afghanistan was caught in the Soviets' last imperialist campaign and paid an enormous price for it. The Soviet invasion of Afghanistan at the end of 1979, in support of a puppet regime, as well as Afghan resistance, generated a double migration stream that carried millions westward into Iran and eastward into Pakistan. At the height of the exodus, 2.5 million Afghans were estimated to be living in camps in Iran, and some 3.7 million gathered in tent camps in Pakistan's northwestern province and in southern Baluchistan. The Soviet invasion seemed destined to succeed quickly, but the Russian generals underestimated the strength of Afghan opposition. U.S. support for the Muslim forces in the form of weapons supplies helped produce a stalemate and eventual Soviet withdrawal, but this was followed by a power struggle among Afghan factions. As a result, most of the more than 6 million refugees in Iran and Pakistan, about one-quarter of the country's population, stayed where they were.

In 1996, the Taliban, an Islamic fundamentalist movement that began in northwest Pakistan, emerged in Afghanistan and took control of most of the country, imposing strict Islamic rule and suppressing the factional conflicts that had prevailed since the Soviet withdrawal. Although several hundred thousand refugees moved back to Afghanistan from Pakistan, the harsh Taliban rule created a countermigration and led to further refugee movement into neighboring Iran, where their number reached 2.5 million. Eventually, Afghanistan became a base for anti-Western terrorist operations, which reached a climax in the attack on the United States on September 11, 2001. Even before the inevitable military retaliation began, and despite efforts by both Pakistan and Iran to close their borders, tens of thousands of Afghan refugees flooded across, intensifying a refugee crisis that is now more than a quarter-century old.

Amidst the crises in Israel/Palestine, Iraq, Syria, and Afghanistan, nearly every country in Southwest Asia is currently experiencing the impact of refugees.

## Africa

During the last decade of the twentieth century and the first years of the twenty-first, several of the world's largest refugee crises occurred in Subsaharan Africa. In the 1990s and early 2000s, refugee flows in West, Central, and East Africa combined to put Subsaharan Africa at the head of the world's refugee flows. Today, however, there are fewer refugees in Subsaharan Africa than in North Africa and Southwest Asia.

Despite ongoing problems with political instability in the region, the refugee situation has improved in some parts of Subsaharan Africa in recent years. In 1997, civil wars in Liberia and Sierra Leone sent columns of hundreds of thousands of refugees streaming into Guinea and the Ivory Coast. The UNHCR reported more than 1.5 million refugees in West Africa in 1997. In 2013, the number of refugees in West

Africa declined to under 270,000 as a result of improved political stability and repatriation. The largest refugee flows in Subsaharan Africa now come out of Central and East Africa, including the Democratic Republic of the Congo, Sudan, and Somalia.

Sudan, which began a second civil war in 1983, demonstrates the complexities of refugee crises in Subsaharan Africa today. The conflict in Sudan was originally between the north, which is largely Arab and Muslim, and the south, which is majority black African and Christian or animist. Sudan, a country whose borders exist because of European colonialism, was home to traditional religions in the south, Christianity brought by Western missionaries in the south, and Islam brought by North African traders in the north.

The government in Khartoum, located in the largely Muslim north, waged a campaign of genocide aimed at ethnic groups in the Christian and animist south during the north–south civil war, which lasted from 1983 to 2005. The government of Sudan funded the Janjaweed militia, which practiced a scorched-earth campaign, burning villages throughout the south.

The civil war between north and south in Sudan caused immense damage. Over 2.2 million people died in the fighting or starved as a result of the war. More than 5 million people were displaced, with over 1.6 million fleeing to neighboring Uganda alone. Both sides of the Sudanese civil war interfered with the efforts of international agencies to help the refugees.

In 1999, Sudan began exporting oil, which is extracted from southern Sudan. Global attention to the humanitarian crisis of the Sudanese civil war prompted the northern government to agree to a compromise. In 2002, the north and

south brokered a temporary peace deal, but shortly thereafter, violence began in the Darfur region in western Sudan. The entire north of Sudan is largely Muslim, but only two-thirds of the northerners speak Arabic as their native language. The other one-third are Muslim but are not ethnically Arab. The non-Arab Muslims are part of at least 30 different ethnic groups in the Darfur region of western Sudan. The Arab Muslim government (located in the north) began a campaign of genocide against the non-Arab Muslims in Darfur. The Janjaweed has waged a genocide campaign against the non-Arab, Muslim, darker-skinned Africans in Darfur—a campaign that includes killing over 400,000 people, raping women and girls, taking lands and homes from Africans, and displacing 2.5 million people (Fig. 3.19).

In 2004, U.S. Secretary of State Colin Powell labeled the Janjaweed's actions in Darfur a **genocide**. The 1948 Convention on Genocide defines genocide as "acts committed with intent to destroy, in whole or in part, a national, ethnical, racial, or religious group." The international community is trying to negotiate an end to the government-backed campaign in Darfur, with mixed success. In the meantime, South Sudan in 2011 voted to secede from Sudan. Ironically, the new border, which was created as a solution to a civil war and refugee crisis, has already generated new refugee flows in the region. Many people living in the borderlands between Sudan and South Sudan are unhappy with the placement of the international boundary. In 2012 the countries fought a six-month-long border war, displacing thousands. Violence in South Sudan has resumed as different groups vie for power. In a country of 12 million, recent violence has displaced 1.3 million people, with over

■ **Figure 3.19**

**Bredjing, Chad.** Refugees from the Darfur region of Sudan bake bread near their tent in Chad's largest refugee camp.

300,000 South Sudanese fleeing across the border. The long-lasting refugee and IDP crisis in Sudan and South Sudan help us understand the complexity of political conflict and migration flows in Subsaharan Africa. The Muslim against Muslim conflict in Darfur demonstrates that political conflict is not just religious; it is also ethnic and political.

Regionally, neighboring countries have not helped create stability for the country. Since 1998, just under 6 million people have died in violence in neighboring Democratic Republic of the Congo. Violence in the Democratic Republic of the Congo was partially spurred by the instability created as a result of refugee flows from the 1994 war in neighboring Rwanda. In 2009, attacks by the rebel group Lord's Resistance Army in the northeastern portion of the Democratic Republic of the Congo generated over 1 million refugees.

## South Asia

In terms of refugee numbers, South Asia is the third-ranking geographic realm, mainly because of Pakistan's role in accommodating Afghanistan's refugees. During the Soviet intrusion in the 1980s, the UNHCR counted more than 3 million refugees; during the 1990s, the total averaged between 1.2 and 1.5 million. That number rose when U.S.-led forces began retaliating against terrorist bases in October 2001. Today, Afghanistan has an enormous refugee crisis with more than 2 million refugees living outside of Afghanistan, mostly in Pakistan and Iran.

The other major refugee problem in South Asia stems from a civil war in Sri Lanka. This conflict, which formally ended in 2009, arose from demands by minority Tamils for an independent state on the Sinhalese-dominated and -controlled island. The conflict cost tens of thousands of lives and severely damaged the economy. The United Nations reports that about 200,000 people are internally displaced. The United Nations, the European Union, and the Canadian government are working to repatriate the IDPs, particularly in the northern provinces of Sri Lanka. An estimated 90,000 internally displaced persons are uprooted in Sri Lanka today.

Climate change will likely have a significant impact on the refugee picture in South Asia in the decades to come. While the effects of climate change will be felt worldwide, scientists believe Bangladesh will be "ground zero" for climate refugees. The country's 156.6 million citizens live in a river delta one-fifth the size of France, most of which is no more than 6.1 meters (20 ft) above sea level and through which 230 major rivers and streams flow. The country is thus unusually vulnerable to flooding and typhoons. The situation is made worse by human alterations of the environment; extensive groundwater pumping is causing cities to sink, and mangrove deforestation has increased erosion rates and removed natural barriers against storm surges. By 2050, 17 percent of the country may well be inundated. For years, so-called environmental refugees have been moving from Bangladesh into neighboring India, but India is building a border wall to ward off further migration. In a country

already facing significant demographic challenges, climate change puts Bangladesh in an even more precarious position.

## Southeast Asia

Southeast Asia is a reminder that refugee problems can change quickly. Indochina was the scene of one of the twentieth century's most desperate refugee crises when a stream of between 1 and 2 million people fled Vietnam in the aftermath of the long war that ended in 1975. In the early 1990s, Cambodia produced an exodus of 300,000 refugees escaping from their country's seemingly endless cycle of violence, ending up in refugee camps on the Thailand side of the border. Today, the largest camps in this realm are for IDPs in Myanmar (formerly Burma). Victims of the 2004 tsunami, the 2008 cyclone, and the repressive rule of generals who are seeking to subjugate the country's minorities seek refuge in the camps.

## Europe

In the 1990s, the collapse of Yugoslavia and its associated conflicts created the largest refugee crisis in Europe since the end of World War II. In 1995, the UNHCR reported the staggering total of 6,056,600 refugees, a number that some observers felt was inflated by the Europeans' unusually liberal interpretations of the United Nations' rules for refugee recognition. Nevertheless, even after the cessation of armed conflict and the implementation of a peace agreement known as the Dayton Accords, the UNHCR still reports over 100,000 IDPs in the area.

## Other Regions

The number of refugees and internally displaced persons in other geographic realms is much smaller. In the Western Hemisphere, only Colombia has a serious internally displaced person problem, numbering around 5.7 million people, caused by the country's protracted political violence coupled with its struggle against narcotics. Colombia's IDP numbers were the largest in the world until 2013, when Syria's civil war generated two million more IDPs than Colombia. Significant areas of Colombia's countryside are vulnerable to armed attack by "narcoterrorists" and paramilitary units; these rural areas are essentially beyond government control, and thousands of villagers have died in the crossfire. Hundreds of thousands more have left their homes to seek protection. Elsewhere in the Western Hemisphere recent earthquakes have displaced millions. A 2010 earthquake in Chile killed hundreds and displaced 2 million Chileans. Six weeks before the Chilean quake, an earthquake in Haiti killed 200,000 people and displaced 1.5 million. Four years later 280,000 Haitian IDPs are still in camps, according to UNHCR. Another 200,000 of the displaced Haitians are living with host families.

People who abandon their familiar surroundings because conditions have become unlivable perform an ultimate act of desperation. In the process, they often face unimaginable challenges and hardships. Refugee and internally displaced person populations are a barometer of the world's future.

Imagine you are from an extremely poor country, and you earn less than $1 a day. Choose a country to be from, and look for it on a map. Assume you are a potential migrant facing a desperate situation. You look at your access to transportation and the opportunities you have to go elsewhere. Be realistic, and describe how you determine where you will go, how you will get there, and what you will do once you get there.

## HOW DO GOVERNMENTS AFFECT MIGRATION?

The control of immigration, legal and illegal, the granting of asylum to asylum-seeking refugees, and the fate of cross-border refugees, permanent and temporary, have become hot issues around the world. In Europe, right-wing political parties whip up anti-immigrant sentiment. In California, the state government demands federal monies to provide services for hundreds of thousands of illegal immigrants; if the federal government cannot control its borders, they argue, states should not have to foot the bill. And in the United States today, the federal government faces reproach both from those who want to stop the flow of migration from Mexico and those who argue for opening the United States' doors for migrants from humanitarian crises, including Haiti. In, or at the western edge of, the West Bank, a security barrier is being built in an effort to control the flow of Palestinians into Israel (Fig. 3.20).

Efforts to restrict migration flows are nothing new. Media coverage, political debates, and political wrangling only make it seem so. In the fourteenth century, China built the Great Wall in part as a defensive measure but also as a barrier to emigration (by Chinese beyond the sphere of their authority) and immigration (mainly by Mongol "barbarians" from the northern plains). The Berlin Wall, the Korean DMZ (demilitarized zone), the fences along the Rio Grande—all are evidence of governments' desire to control the movement of people across their borders.

## Legal Restrictions

Typically, the obstacles placed in the way of potential immigrants are legal, not physical. In the United States, restrictive legislation on immigration can be traced to 1882, when Congress approved the Oriental Exclusion Acts (1882–1907). Congress designed **immigration laws** to prevent the immigration of Chinese people to California. In 1901, the Australian government approved the Immigration Restriction Act, which ended all nonwhite immigration into the newly united country. The Australian government was particularly

■ **Figure 3.20**

**Security Barrier Near Jerusalem.**   In the wake of decades of conflict, controlling the movement of people has become an increasingly prominent policy response on the part of the Israeli government.

targeting Japanese, Chinese, and South Asian immigrants. The act also prohibited immigration by South Pacific Islanders who worked on Australia's large sugar plantations. The Australian government furthered action against the plantation workers (the Kanakas) by deporting the South Pacific Islanders by the end of 1906. These immigration policies created what is known as the *White Australia Policy*, which remained in effect until the 1970s.

## Waves of Immigration in the United States

Changes in a country's migration policies are reflected in the number of people entering the country and the origin of the immigrants (see Fig. 3.21). The United States experienced two major waves of immigration before 1930 and another great wave in recent decades. Major changes in the government's migration policies are reflected in this graph. Push factors are also reflected in Figure 3.21, as people in different regions found reasons to leave their home and migrate to the United States.

During the 1800s, the United States opened its doors to immigration. Most of the immigrants arrived from Europe, especially Northern Europe (Scandinavia) and western Europe (including Ireland, Great Britain, Germany, and France). In the later part of the 1800s, a greater proportion of Europeans who immigrated to the United States came from southern and eastern Europe (including Italy, Spain, Portugal, Russia, and Poland).

Following World War I, political tides in the United States turned toward *isolationism*—a policy that favors staying out of entanglements abroad. In addition, at that time, Congress feared the growing migration from eastern and southern Europe. Many whites in the United States at the time saw migrants from this area of the world as darker skinned and therefore inferior. In this context, Congress passed restrictive legislation in 1921, deterring immigration from southern and eastern Europe. Congress set immigration quotas limiting immigration to the United States to 3 percent of the number of a given European country's nationals living in the United States in 1910. In 1910, the greatest proportion of immigrants in the United States came from Northern and western

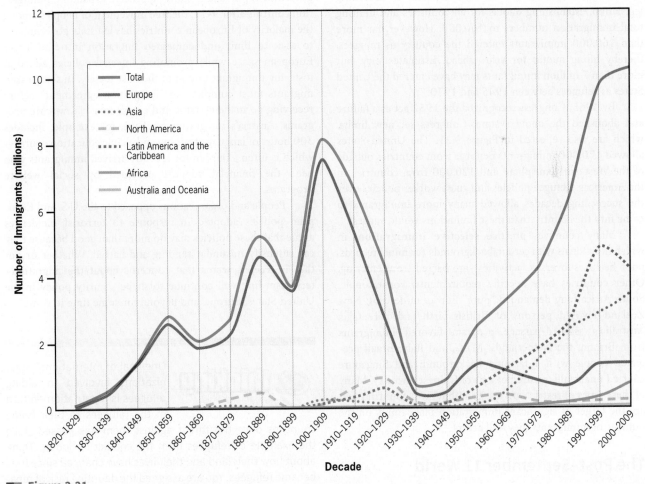

**Figure 3.21**

**Immigration to the United States by Region, 1820 to 2010.** During the first wave of migration to the United States, from 1820 to 1930, the vast majority of migrants to the United States came from Europe. During the second wave of migration, from 1930 to the present, a shift occurred and migrants to the United States mainly come from Latin America and Asia. *Data from*: United States Census Bureau, 2012.

Europe; thus the quotas meant that migration from Northern and western Europe greatly outpaced immigration from southern and eastern Europe (Fig. 3.21).

In 1924, Congress altered the Immigration Act by lowering the quota to 2 percent and making 1890 the base year, further reducing the annual total to 150,000 immigrants and further discouraging eastern and southern European migration.

The rapid fall in total immigration to the United States is clearly shown in Figure 3.21. Just prior to the Great Depression, Congress passed the National Origins Law in 1929, which limited immigration to 150,000 persons per year. Congress also tied immigration quotas to the national origins of the U.S. population in 1920. As a result, Congress in effect prevented substantial immigration from Asia. With these laws in effect and the Great Depression in full swing, immigration slowed to a trickle during the 1930s.

After 1940, Congress modified the restrictions on immigration. In 1943, Congress gave China equal status to that of European countries and in 1952 granted Japan a similar status. In 1952, immigration began to rise again (Fig. 3.21) after Congress passed a new Immigration and Nationality Act. Congress designed the act to incorporate all preceding legislation, establishing quotas for all countries and limiting total immigration numbers to 160,000. However, far more than 160,000 immigrants entered the country as refugees, thereby filling quotas for years ahead. Estimates vary, but more than 7 million immigrants may have entered the United States as refugees between 1945 and 1970.

By 1965, Congress recognized the 1952 act as a failure and abolished the quota system. Congress set new limits, which are also reflected in Figure 3.21. The United States allowed 170,000 immigrants per year from countries outside of the Western Hemisphere and 120,000 from countries in the Americas. Refugee policies and guest worker policies over the succeeding decades allowed many more immigrants to come into the country than these limitations would suggest.

Many countries practice **selective immigration**, in which individuals with certain backgrounds (criminal records, poor health, subversive activities) are barred from entering. Other countries have specific requirements. For example, South Africa long demanded "pure" European descent; New Zealand favored persons of British birth and parentage; Australia's assisted-passage program favored immigrants from Britain, the Netherlands, Malta, and Italy; Brazil preferred people with a farming background; and Singapore courted financially secure persons of Chinese ancestry. Many of these types of restrictions are gone, but most countries that are the target of significant immigration place limits on the number of immigrants they will accept.

## The Post–September 11 World

Since September 11, 2001, U.S. government immigration policies have incorporated security concerns. Prior to that date, the U.S. border patrol was concerned primarily with drug trafficking and human smuggling. The new government policies affect asylum-seekers and both documented and undocumented immigrants.

After September 11, the U.S. government designated 33 countries as places where al-Qaeda or other terrorist groups operate, and the government automatically detained anyone from one of these 33 countries who entered the United States looking for asylum under a policy called "Operation Liberty Shield." On March 25, 2003, Human Rights Watch criticized the policy, contending that it created "a blanket suspicion of links to terrorism based on nationality alone." On April 17, 2003, the Department of Homeland Security quietly terminated "Operation Liberty Shield." Nonetheless, controls along the U.S. border are much tighter than they were prior to 9-11, with implications not just for the flow of immigrants, but for business and commerce in border regions as well.

In the wake of terrorist attacks in Europe—including major bombings in Madrid in 2004 and London in 2005—European state governments have also focused more attention on immigration matters. Whereas the United States government pursued a "hard" approach, expanding immigration controls after 9-11, the free movement of peoples among the majority of European countries has led state governments to seek to limit undocumented migration into the larger European space while promoting internal policies aimed at fostering immigrant buy-in to the host society. In some cases, migrants must complete an "integration agreement" before receiving permanent status and access to social welfare programs. Austria's integration package, for example, includes 300 hours of language training and a civic education course—which is often a burden for recently arrived immigrants who need the financial support provided by social welfare programs.

People and organizations opposed to the U.S. and European policies adopted in response to terrorist incidences argue that these policies may do more than good because they can intensify misunderstanding and hatred. Whether or not that is true, it seems that concerns about the migration–terrorism link will continue to shape security policy in the United States, Europe, and beyond for some time to come.

One goal of international organizations involved in aiding refugees is repatriation—return of the refugees to their home countries once the threat against them has passed. Take the example of refugees from the conflict in Sudan. Think about how their land and their lives have changed since they became refugees. You are assigned the daunting task of repatriating refugees. What steps would you have to take to rediscover a home for these refugees?

# Summary

In the last 500 years, humans have traveled the globe, mapped it, connected it, and migrated across it. In this chapter, we discussed major global, regional, national, and local migration flows. Migration can occur as a result of a conscious decision, resulting in a voluntary migration flow, or migration can occur under duress, resulting in forced migration. Both kinds of migration have left an indelible mark on the world and on its cultural landscapes. Governments attempt to strike a balance among the need for migrant labor, the desire to help people in desperate circumstances, and the desire to stem the tide of migration.

As the world's population mushrooms, the volume of migrants will likely continue to expand. In an increasingly open and interconnected world, neither physical barriers nor politically motivated legislation will hold back tides that are as old as human history. Migrations will also further complicate an already complex global cultural mosaic—raising questions about identity, race, ethnicity, language, and religion, the topics we turn to in the next four chapters.

# Geographic Concepts

Bracero Program
refugee camps
remittances
reverse remittances
cyclic movement
periodic movement
migration
activity spaces
nomadism
transhumance
international migration
emigration
immigration
internal migration

forced migration
voluntary migration
human trafficking
laws of migration
gravity model
push factors
pull factors
distance decay
step migration
intervening opportunity
deportation
kinship links
chain migration
immigration wave

colonization
guest workers
regional scale
migration
islands of development
Russification
refugees
internally displaced persons
asylum
repatriation
genocide
immigration laws
selective immigration

# Learn More Online

About Immigration to the United States
www.uscis.gov

About Refugees
www.unhcr.org

About Geographic Mobility and Movement in the United States
www.census.gov/hhes/migration/

About the Origin of the World's Migrants Interactive map from Pew Research
http://www.pewglobal.org/2014/09/02/global-migrant-stocks/

# Watch It Online

About Migration and Identity
www.learner.org/resources/series85.html#program_descriptions
click on Video On Demand for "A Migrant's Heart"

About the United States–Mexico Border Region
www.learner.org/resources/series180.html#program_descriptions
click on Video On Demand for "Boundaries and Borderlands"

# LOCAL CULTURE, POPULAR CULTURE, AND CULTURAL LANDSCAPES

## Preserving Culture

This used to be an Italian restaurant. Not anymore, the young man with a thick New York accent said to me, offering a few expletives to describe the Chinese moving into the neighborhood, as well as a prediction: "It's probably gonna be a Chinese restaurant next."

Positano stood, along with dozens of other Italian restaurants on Mulberry Street, at the heart of Little Italy, an ethnic neighborhood in New York City that dates to 1880 (Figure 4.1). By 1900, upwards of 10,000 Italian immigrants clustered in Little Italy, which at its greatest extent covered 50 square blocks of Manhattan.

Young Chinese men left work on the railroads in California and settled in New York, establishing Chinatown south of Little Italy in the late 1800s. In the 1910s, Chinese immigrants established a business association, and in the 1920s a Chinese food industry took root in the neighborhood.

After World War II, second and third generations of Italians were moving to other parts of the city. The *New York Times* reported that in 1950, 50 percent of the residents of Little Italy identified as Italian-American, but that by 2010 only 5 percent identified as Italian-American.

The United States overturned constraints on Chinese immigration in 1965, and after that Chinese immigrants moved into Chinatown in droves. Chinatown expanded into Little Italy, and today only 3 blocks on Mulberry Street constitute the heart of Little Italy. "Of the 8600 residents counted by the census's American Community Survey in the heart of Little Italy in 2009, nearly 4400 were foreign-born. Of those, 89 percent were born in Asia" (Roberts 2011). Many of the Asians in Chinatown today are from Southeast Asia, especially Vietnam and Malaysia.

The closing of Italian restaurants including Positano is not only the result of a declining Italian population in the neighborhood. Little Italy is also pressured from the west by

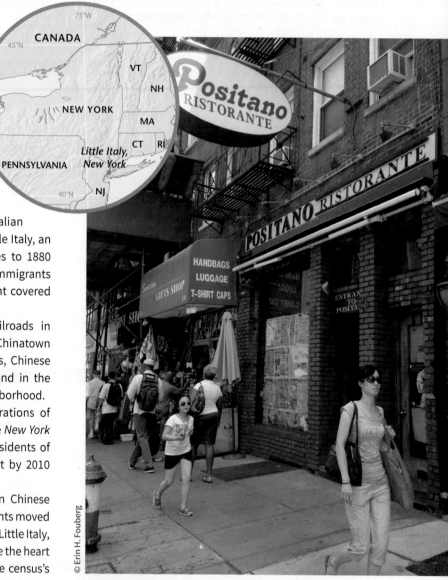

© Erin H. Fouberg

■ **Figure 4.1**

**New York, New York.** An Asian woman and child walk past the closed Italian eatery Positano in Little Italy. The restaurant, windows now lined by newspaper, closed in January 2014. The *New York Post* reported eight Italian eateries closed within a year's time, as new landlords have doubled rents. Down the block, a former restaurant now houses a year-round Christmas store, and the owners pay $50,000 a month in rent.

the upscale SoHo neighborhood. New landlords are purchasing buildings and raising the rent on retail spaces in Little Italy. Positano closed after the rent jumped, and the New York Post reported in 2014 that "Eight eateries have shut down in the past year" as rents have doubled.

Immigrant groups establish ethnic neighborhoods in cities, imprinting the place with cultural traits from their homeland, from eateries to specialty shops to churches. Having a place where people with a shared identity belong helps sustain a local culture. In this chapter, we examine what local cultures are and how they make an imprint on the landscape in both cities and rural areas. We consider how innovations in popular culture are created and diffused; and, we study how cultural landscapes are shaped and changed overtime by popular and local cultures.

# Key Questions FOR CHAPTER 4

1. What are local and popular cultures?
2. How are local cultures sustained?
3. How is popular culture diffused?
4. How can local and popular cultures be seen in the cultural landscape?

## WHAT ARE LOCAL AND POPULAR CULTURES?

A culture is a group of belief systems, norms, and values practiced by a people. Although this definition of culture sounds simple, the concept of culture is actually quite complex. A group of people who share common beliefs can be recognized as a culture in one of two ways: (1) the people may call themselves a culture or (2) other people (including academics) can label a certain group of people as a culture. Traditionally, academics label cultural groups as either folk cultures or as part of popular culture. The idea is that a **folk culture** is small, incorporates a homogeneous population, is typically rural, and is cohesive in cultural traits, whereas **popular culture** is large, incorporates heterogeneous populations, is typically urban, and experiences quickly changing cultural traits. Instead of using this polarity of folk and popular cultures, some academics now see folk and popular cultures as ends of a continuum, defining most cultures as fitting somewhere between folk and popular.

We find folk culture to be a limiting concept because it requires us to create a list of characteristics and look for cultures that meet the list. This methodology of defining folk cultures leaves much to be desired. Once we have our list of characteristics, we must ask ourselves, are the Amish a folk culture? Are the Navajo a folk culture? And it is in this very process that we get frustrated with the concept of folk culture. It is not how we academics define a culture that matters; it is how the people define themselves that counts.

We are interested in questions such as: do the Amish have a group identity, and what cultural practices do they share? How do the Amish navigate through popular culture and defend their local customs? Why do a group of Americans in a small town identify themselves as Swedish Americans and hold festivals to commemorate important Swedish holidays, while other Swedish Americans in other parts of the country function completely unaware of the Swedish holidays? Why do certain ethnic holidays such as St. Patrick's Day transcend ethnicity to be celebrated as a part of popular culture?

In this chapter, we chose to use the concept of local culture rather than folk culture. A **local culture** is a group of people in a particular place who see themselves as a collective or a community, who share experiences, customs, and traits, and who work to preserve those traits and customs in order to claim uniqueness and to distinguish themselves from others.

Local and popular cultures are not ends of a continuum. Both cultures exist in the same places and spaces, manifest in different ways, and are constantly being refined. In an era of globalization, popular culture diffuses around the globe, being embraced by some and rejected by others, all the while infiltrating every corner of the globe. Local cultures persist, and in many places the communities thrive, but they face constant pressure from larger cultural groups and from the enveloping popular culture. The variety of ways people choose to accept, reject, or alter the diffusion of popular cultural practices is remarkable. Some local cultures rely primarily on religion to maintain their belief systems; others rely on community celebrations or on family structures; and still others rely on a lack of interaction with other cultures.

Local cultures are constantly redefining or refining themselves based on interactions with other cultures (local and popular) and diffusion of cultural practices (local and popular). Local cultures also affect places by establishing neighborhoods, building churches or community centers to celebrate important days, and by expressing their material and nonmaterial cultures in certain ways.

The **material culture** of a group of people includes things they construct, such as art, houses, clothing, sports, dance, and foods. **Nonmaterial culture** includes beliefs, practices, aesthetics (what is seen as attractive), and values of a group of people. What members of a local culture produce in their material culture reflects the beliefs and values of their nonmaterial culture.

Unlike local cultures, which are found in relatively small areas, popular culture is ubiquitous and can change in a matter of days or hours. Popular culture is practiced by a heterogeneous group of people: people across identities and across the world. Like local culture, popular culture encompasses music, dance, clothing, food preferences, religious practices, and aesthetic values. The main paths of diffusion of popular culture are the transportation, marketing, and communication networks (including social networks) that interlink vast parts of the world.

Fashions diffuse incredibly quickly today. When Kate Middleton, Duchess of Cambridge, graced Westminster Abbey in a lace wedding gown designed by Sarah Burton for the House of Alexander McQueen at an estimated cost of $65,000, dress designers around the world interpreted or copied the gown within hours (Fig. 4.2). Fewer than ten hours after the wedding aired at 5:30 A.M. Eastern Time, dress designers at Kleinfeld Bridal Salon in New York had replicated Middleton's dress, and they started selling it for $3500 within 48 hours.

In popular culture, fashion trends spread very quickly through the interconnected world; it is a classic case of **hierarchical diffusion**. Hierarchical diffusion can occur through a hierarchy of places. The hierarchy in the fashion world typically begins with the runways of major fashion houses in world cities, including London, Milan, Paris, and New York, which act as the **hearth**, the point of origin. The next tier of places includes flagship stores for the fashion house and editorial headquarters of fashion magazines, also located in global cities. Department store brands interpret the runway fashions for consumption by a larger audience, and the suburban mall receives the innovation. Hierarchical diffusion can also occur through a hierarchy of people. In this case, a designer is the hearth, models are the next tier, celebrities and editors and writers of major magazines follow, and subscribers to fashion magazines follow in close order. Finally, anyone walking through a shopping mall can become a "knower" in the diffusion of a fashion innovation.

We do not see local and popular cultures as being ends of a continuum; rather, we see both operating on the same plane, affecting people and places in different ways across different scales. For example, you may go to a major department

Samir Hussein/WireImage/Getty Images, Inc.

■ **Figure 4.2**

**London, United Kingdom.** Catherine Middleton, Duchess of Cambridge, enters Westminster Abbey in a wedding gown reminiscent of Grace Kelly's. Sarah Burton of the House of Alexander McQueen, located in London, designed the lace gown. Members of the Royal School of Needlework hand cut and sewed the intricate lace. The Official Royal Wedding website reported that each sewer washed his or her hands every 30 minutes and replaced the needles every three hours to keep the dress pristine and the work exact.

store such as Target or Wal-Mart and see Hutterites or Mennonites dressed in distinctive local clothing in the midst of the ultimate in popular culture: a major international department store. Traditions such as painting henna on one's hands or practicing mystical Kabbalah beliefs are carried from centuries-old customs of local cultures to the global popular culture through a popular culture icon or through the corporations (such as marketing firms) that work to construct popular culture (Fig. 4.3).

Both local cultures and popular cultures are constantly navigating through a barrage of customs diffused from each other and across scales, through a complex of political and economic forces that shape and limit their practices, and through global communications and transportation networks that intricately link certain parts of the world and distance others.

Josiah Kamau/BuzzFoto/FilmMagic

■ **Figure 4.3**
**New York.** In a truly global fashion, New York City tattoo artist Keith McCurdy flew to the Dominican Republic to ink a design based on traditional Indian henna over an existing tattoo based on a traditional New Zealand design on the hand of Barbados-born singer Rihanna.

In this chapter, we focus on how local cultures are sustained despite the onslaught of popular culture, how popular culture diffuses and is practiced in unique ways in localities of the world, and how local and popular cultures are imprinted on the cultural landscape.

Employing the concept of hierarchical diffusion, describe how you became a "knower" of your favorite kind of music—where is its hearth, and how did it reach you?

## HOW ARE LOCAL CULTURES SUSTAINED?

During the 1800s and into the 1900s, the U.S. government had an official policy of **assimilation**. The federal government wanted to assimilate indigenous peoples into the dominant culture in order to make American Indians into "Americans" rather than "Indians." Canadians, Australians, Russians, and other colonial powers adopted similar policies toward indigenous peoples, using schools, churches, and government agents to discourage native practices. In the United States, the federal government forced tribal members to settle in one place and to farm rather than hunt or fish. Public and missionary school teachers punished tribal members for using their native language.

Government agents rewarded the Indians they deemed most "American" with citizenship and paid jobs. The federal government even employed East Coast women from 1888 until 1938 to live on reservations and show the native women how to be "good housewives" by teaching them Victorian ways of cooking, cleaning, and sewing.

Today, several churches and governments have apologized for assimilation policies. In 2008, the governments of Australia and Canada each officially apologized to their indigenous populations: Aboriginals in Australia and First Nations and Inuit in Canada.

The Australian Parliament unanimously passed a motion stating: "We apologize for the laws and policies of successive parliaments and governments that have inflicted profound grief, suffering and loss on these our fellow Australians." Former Australian Prime Minister Kevin Rudd apologized specifically for the government's policy of taking Aboriginal children from their homes and placing them in residential schools—a policy that lasted from the 1800s until the late 1960s.

Canadian Prime Minister Stephen Harper likewise cited the disastrous outcomes of the assimilation policies in his apology to Canada's 1.3 million indigenous people. Prime Minister Harper apologized for the abuse and the lasting negative effects of Canada's residential schools, stating: "We now recognize that it was wrong to separate children from rich and vibrant cultures and traditions, that it created a void in many lives and communities, and we apologize for having done this. We now recognize that, in separating children from their families, we undermined the ability of many to adequately parent their own children and sowed the seeds for generations to follow." Speaking to the indigenous people seated in the House of Commons, he continued, "Not only did you suffer these abuses as children, but as you became parents, you were powerless to protect your own children from suffering the same experience, and for this we are sorry."

The United States government has not formally apologized to American Indians for the policy of assimilation. American Indians in the United States are working to push back assimilation and popular culture by reviving the customs of their local cultures. Many tribes are teaching younger generations their language, reviving their traditional religion, and eating the foods and herbs of their lands, the foods and herbs on which their ancestors depended.

Local cultures are sustained through **customs**. A custom is a practice that a group of people routinely follows. People have customs regarding all parts of their lives, from eating and drinking to dancing and sports. To sustain a local culture, the people must retain their customs. The customs change in small ways over time, but they are maintained despite the onslaught of popular culture.

Researcher Simon Harrison recognizes that local cultural groups purposefully and often fervently define themselves as unique, creating boundaries around their culture and distinguishing themselves from other local cultures. In the age of globalization, where popular culture changes quickly and diffuses rapidly, Harrison finds that local cultures typically have two goals: keeping other cultures out and keeping their own culture in.

For example, a local culture can create a boundary around itself and try to keep other cultures out in order to avoid "contamination and extinction." Harrison uses the example of the Notting Hill carnival in London to describe how Londoners from the West Indies (the Caribbean) claimed the festival as their own, in conjunction with an increasing sense of collective West Indies cultural identity. The festival did not begin as a West Indies celebration. As people from the West Indies shared experiences of "unemployment, police harassment and poor housing conditions" during the 1970s, they began to define themselves as a local culture and redefined the festival as a West Indian celebration.

A local culture can also work to avoid **cultural appropriation**, the process by which other cultures adopt customs and knowledge and use them for their own benefit. Harrison explains that cultural appropriation is a major concern for local cultures because people outside the local culture often privatize the cultural knowledge of a local culture, including natural pharmaceuticals or musical expression, to accumulate wealth or prestige. Local cultures can thus work to keep their customs and knowledge to themselves, to avoid cultural appropriation.

Around the world, local cultures desire to keep popular culture out, keep their culture intact, and maintain control over customs and knowledge. Geographers also recognize that through these actions, places become increasingly important. When defining a place (a town or neighborhood) or a space for a short amount of time (an annual festival) as quintessentially representing the local culture's values, members of a local culture reinforce their culture and their beliefs.

## Rural Local Cultures

Members of local cultures in rural areas often have an easier time maintaining their cultures because of their isolation. By living together in a rural area, members of a local culture can more easily keep external influences on the outside. It is no accident that we find Anabaptist groups, such as the Hutterites, the Amish, and the Mennonites, living in rural areas of South Dakota, Pennsylvania, and Virginia, respectively.

For the past five centuries, Anabaptist groups have migrated to rural areas beyond these three states (often fleeing persecution) with the expressed purpose of living apart and staying together. During the Protestant Reformation, Anabaptists broke from both the Catholic Church and the new Protestant churches. Followers of the new religion were called Anabaptists, meaning baptized again, because of their belief in adult baptism, despite having been baptized as infants in the Catholic or Protestant churches.

Anabaptists broke from the state as well as the church; they stressed pacifism and soon suffered persecution. As a consequence, Anabaptists migrated east to Moravia and Austria, and then to Russia and the Ukraine. Continually moving to rural areas to live apart, alone, and avoid persecution, a group of Anabaptists called the Hutterites, named for leader Jacob Hutter, eventually migrated to North America in the second half of the 1800s.

Old Order Anabaptist groups are often shown in stereotypical ways in the popular media, but major differences exist across Old Order Amish, Mennonites, Hutterites, and Brethren. Hutterites are the only Anabaptist group who live communally (Fig. 4.4). Rather than living with immediate family on a farmstead, Hutterites live in colonies of about 100 people, with individuals ranging in ages from infant to elderly. More than 425 colonies are located in Minnesota, South

© Erin H. Fouberg

■ **Figure 4.4**

**Stratford, South Dakota.** A Hutterite boy who lives in the Hutterville Farm colony near Stratford, South Dakota. Distinctive modes of dress and ways of living help to sustain group identity.

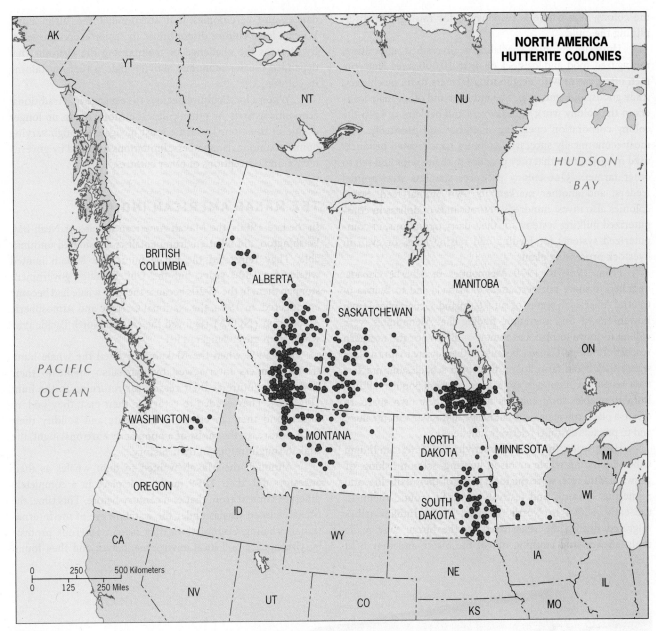

**Figure 4.5**
**Hutterite Colonies in North America.**   *Data from*: www.hutterites.org, last accessed July 10, 2014.

Dakota, North Dakota, Saskatchewan, Montana, and Alberta (Fig. 4.5). In their book *On the Backroad to Heaven*, Donald Kraybill and Carl Bowman explain that the lynchpin of each colony is the Hutterite religion. Members of the colony join together for a 30-minute service every night as well as on Sundays. The most prominent position in a colony is held by the minister, who speaks in archaic German, reading sermons written in the sixteenth century.

Unlike the Amish, Hutterites readily accept technologies that help them in their agricultural pursuits. Hutterite colonies were generally slow to accept technologies such as cameras and cell phones out of concern that they would encourage individualistic behaviors or undermine the Hutterite religion. Today, it is common for young adult Hutterites to

use cell phones and Internet dating sites to find suitable marriage partners in colonies in other states or countries.

Colonies assign separate jobs and tasks to men and women, which reinforces a patriarchal social structure. Kraybill and Bowman explain that marriages happen across colonies, and women move to their husband's colony after marrying. If a Hutterite woman from Alberta meets a Hutterite man from North Dakota through an Internet dating site, and they eventually decide to marry, the Canadian woman will move to the United States. As a result, a single colony is usually composed of only one or two surnames. Moving to their husband's colony perpetuates women's weaker political position in the colony. Women are expected to rear many children, averaging five or six currently, but the colony as a whole is responsible for raising and disciplining the child.

Hutterite colonies specialize in diversified agriculture, raising feed, food, and livestock on up to 10,000 acres. Hutterite men often barter with neighboring farmers to fix machinery, trade goods, and lend help. The minister and other male leaders in the colony work with lawyers and bankers to keep the colony corporation operating smoothly and profitably. The most economically successful colonies have created products used in agriculture that they produce in their shops and sell to other farmers. One colony produces stainless steel animal feeders, and another markets its own animal feed. Some colonies also invest hundreds of thousands of dollars in computerized milking systems for their dairy operations, in computerized systems for feeding and raising hogs, or even in livestock processing plants.

From 1950 to 1970 Mennonites in Alberta, Canada, migrated to more northern areas of Canada and to Bolivia in Central America in search of rural farmland. Geographer Dawn Bowen traced this migration, finding that Mennonites were willing to move to places as remote as Bolivia or the northern reaches of Alberta, Canada, because of their desire to find a place where they could farm, found their own schools, and practice their religion without pervasive pressures from popular culture. Rurality enables local cultures to define their own space, to create a place, town, or rural landscape that reflects their values, and to practice customs relatively unfettered.

Historically, the economic activities of American Indian tribes, including whale or bison hunting, salmon fishing, or growing wild rice, were the focal point of their daily life, and numerous customs and festivals revolved around them. In the early 1800s in North America, Plains Indians tribes migrated during the year based on the bison; they made tools, shelter, and clothing out of the bison; and they held dances and ceremonies that surrounded the bison hunt. When a local culture discontinues its major economic activity, it faces the challenge of maintaining the customs that depended on the economic activity and, in turn, sustaining its culture.

When a local culture decides to reengage in a traditional economic activity or other cultural custom, it can no longer decide in isolation. The tribe must navigate through varying opinions among its members, limitations imposed by governments, and perceptions of other cultures.

## THE MAKAH AMERICAN INDIANS

In the late 1990s, the Makah American Indians of Neah Bay, Washington, did what environmentalists considered unthinkable: They reinstated the whale hunt. The Makah hunted whales for 1500 years, but the United States government stopped them in the 1920s because the gray whale had become endangered. In 1994, the National Oceanic and Atmospheric Association (NOAA) removed the eastern North Pacific gray whale from the endangered list.

In 1999, when the Makah reinstated the whale hunt, tribal members interviewed by journalists spoke to their traditional culture as their reason for returning to the hunt (Fig. 4.6). They needed to return to their past, they said, to understand their ancestors, to re-create and solidify their local culture. In the midst of a popular culture onslaught, the Makah sought refuge in their history.

Although the Makah wanted to hunt whales as their ancestors did, their 1999 hunts took place in a completely different context from that of a century before. This time, the Makah hunted whales under the watchful eye of the International Whaling Commission; they faced numerous protests by Greenpeace and local environmentalists; and they found

■ **Figure 4.6**
**Neah Bay, Washington.** The whale hunt is a traditional Makah practice. Support for maintaining it is a way of resisting the forces of assimilation.

themselves in federal court with the George W. Bush administration on their side supporting the reinstatement of the whale hunt.

The Makah wanted to hunt with their traditional canoes and harpoons because they wanted to hunt as the tribe's elders and ancestors did. However, in the context of the twentieth and twenty-first centuries, the choice of tools for the Makah's hunt was not up to them alone. Actors at the regional, national, and global scale influenced not only whether the Makah could hunt whales but also the methods they used in their hunt. The International Whaling Commission dictated that the Makah hunt gray whales with a .50 caliber rifle, arguing the rifle would kill the whale more quickly and humanely than the harpoons their ancestors used. In May 1999 the Makah hunted and killed a gray whale, using a .50 caliber rifle.

The Makah hunt ended up in court in the United States and under consideration by the International Whaling Commission. In July 2012, the International Whaling Commission extended the license for subsistence hunting of gray whale by the Makah until 2018.

American Indians are not the only Americans looking to the customs of their ancestors to reinvigorate their local cultures. Throughout the rural United States, small towns were built by immigrants from Europe, and many local cultures have defined entire small towns as places to maintain their culture and to teach others about their customs and beliefs.

### Little Sweden, U.S.A.

The residents of Lindsborg, Kansas, proclaim their town Little Sweden, U.S.A. Geographer Steven Schnell asked why a town of 3300, which a few decades ago had little or no sign of Swedishness on its landscape, transformed itself into a place where Swedish culture is celebrated every day in gift stores on Main Street and in buffets in restaurants (Fig. 4.7).

## GUEST FIELD NOTE

### Lindsborg, Kansas

Lindsborg, Kansas, founded by Swedish Lutherans in 1869, has remade itself in recent decades as "Little Sweden, U.S.A." Swedish gift shops, restaurants, and ethnic festivals, along with faux-Swedish storefronts, all attract visitors interested in the Swedish American heritage. Here you see a Dala horse, a traditional Swedish folk craft that has been adopted as the town symbol. Note, too, the Swedish and American flags flying in the background. Most visitors to the town assume one of two things: Either the town is an island of nineteenth-century culture passed on unchanged for generations, or it is a crock of Disneyesque fakery cooked up to draw in gullible tourists. The fascination of fieldwork is that it undermines any such simplifications. I found ethnicity here to be complex, quirky, ever-changing, and very much a part of the people's lives. Swedishness in Lindsborg has been invented and reinvented time and time again through the decades, as people constantly look for answers to that most basic of questions: Who am I?

*Credit: Steven M. Schnell, Kutztown University of Pennsylvania*

Courtesy of Steven Schnell

■ **Figure 4.7**

Cynics would argue the reason is purely economic, but there is more to it than that. Certainly, Lindsborg benefits economically from tourists who flock to buy Swedish trinkets and celebrate Swedish festivals. Nonetheless, as Schnell found, on a daily basis the people of Lindsborg benefit from promoting a sense of a shared history and a common place in this world. In the 1930s, the townspeople shared stories about the roles of Swedes in American history and the importance of their Swedishness to Lindsborg. From that base, the townspeople began to celebrate their Swedish heritage in the 1950s, highlighting the "everyday existence" (the local culture) of the Swedes who immigrated to Lindsborg. During festivals today, the townspeople, whether Swedish or not, dress up in peasant clothes modeled after those worn by Swedish immigrants in the 1800s. Geographer James Shortridge (1996) refers to this as **neolocalism**, seeking out the regional culture and reinvigorating it in response to the uncertainty of the modern world.

The Makah, the Hutterites, and the people of Lindsborg have something in common: Each is inundated with a pulsating popular culture that challenges their place in the world. Each has chosen to maintain or reconnect with its local culture. For the Hutterites, the goal is to maintain what they have, to adopt only those technologies that advance their agricultural pursuits, and to limit those that challenge their religion. Central concerns for the Makah include thinking in their own language, embracing their history, and coming to know who they are despite what others have done to subvert their identity. The people of Lindsborg seek to celebrate the Swedish immigrants who made the place unique and connect with others around them.

## Urban Local Cultures

Some local cultures have successfully built a world apart, a place to practice their customs, within a major city by constructing tight-knit **ethnic neighborhoods**. Hasidic Jews in Brooklyn, New York, and Italian Americans in the North End of Boston, Massachusetts, maintain their distinct local cultures in urban environments.

Runners of the New York City Marathon can see the ethnic neighborhoods of New York City's boroughs firsthand. Running through Brooklyn, they pass through a predominantly Mexican neighborhood full of Mexican flags and mariachi bands, followed in sharp contrast by a Hasidic Jewish neighborhood with streets lined with men and boys on one side and women and girls on another, all dressed in clothes modeled after eighteenth-century Russian and Polish fashions (Fig. 4.8).

In the North End of Boston, the Italian community still celebrates the feast days of Italian saints. Twelve religious societies, each focusing on an Italian saint, hold festivals between June and September. Members of the society march through the North End holding a statue of their saint, collecting money and adorning the saint with it. The Romaband, an Italian band that has been in existence since 1919, leads each

society through the streets of the North End. Each march ends with a street celebration, including vendors selling everything from fried calamari to hot dogs.

Having their own ethnic neighborhood enables members of a local culture in an urban area to set themselves apart and practice their customs. Schools, houses of worship, food stores, and clothing stores all support the aesthetics and desires of members of the local culture. The greatest challenge to local cultures in cities is the migration of members of other local cultures or ethnic groups into the neighborhood. Local cultures in Brooklyn and the North End work to maintain their culture and customs as young artists and professionals move into their respective neighborhoods. Rents and housing costs are climbing in each neighborhood, and the cultural landscapes are starting to reflect the neighborhood's new residents. A new arts community is inundating the traditionally Hasidic neighborhood of Brooklyn called Williamsburg. Today, you will find art galleries, artistically painted old warehouses converted into residences, and even a new brewery. In Boston, young professionals are taking advantage of the North End neighborhood's favorable location, choosing apartments there so they can walk to their jobs in the city center. Today, you will find apartments in the North End being renovated to appeal to the area's newest residents.

## Local Cultures and Cultural Appropriation

Local cultures, whether rural or urban, often find themselves trying to keep their customs for themselves, to prevent others from appropriating their customs for economic benefit. Anthropologists and geographers have studied how others are using local cultural knowledge, customs, and even names. For example, the estate of Crazy Horse (a Lakota Indian leader) sued a brewery that produced Crazy Horse beer.

The process through which something (a name, a good, an idea, or even a person) that previously was not regarded as an object to be bought or sold becomes an object that can be bought, sold, and traded in the world market is called **commodification**. Commodification affects local cultures in numerous ways. First, their material culture, their jewelry and clothing, their food and games, can be commodified by themselves or by nonmembers. Similarly, their nonmaterial culture, their religion, language, and beliefs, can be commodified, often by nonmembers selling local spiritual and herbal cures for ailments. Local cultures may also be commodified as a whole—think of tourist buses "observing" the Amish culture of Lancaster, Pennsylvania, or travel agencies offering trekking trips with "traditional" Nepalese guides on spiritual journeys through the Himalayas.

When commodification occurs, the question of **authenticity** follows. When local cultures or customs are commodified, usually one image or experience is typecast as the "authentic" image or experience of that culture, and it is that image or

# FIELD NOTE

"One of the most amazing aspects of running the New York City marathon is seeing the residents of New York's many ethnic neighborhoods lining the streets of the race. Running through the Hasidic Jewish neighborhood in Williamsburg, Brooklyn was striking: even before noticing the traditional dress of the neighborhood's residents, I noticed the crowd was much quieter—the people were not yelling, they were clapping and quietly cheering."

Spencer Platt/Getty Images

**Figure 4.8**
**Williamsburg, Brooklyn, New York.**

experience that the tourist or buyer desires. However, local cultures are dynamic, and places and people change over time. To gain an "authentic" sense of place, people need to experience the complexity of a place directly rather than the stereotype of a place. An "authentic" local culture does not fit into a single experience or image; rather, an "authentic" local culture is one that is complex and not stereotyped.

The act of stereotyping local culture is quite confusing for the members of the local culture because rarely is there consensus that all things must be done in one traditional way. Tourists in Lancaster County, for example, may be disappointed to see some Amish driving tractors across their fields. European, Canadian, American, or Australian trekkers in Nepal desire the same "authentic" experience that a travel website promotes in the Himalayas.

## Authenticity of Places

During the process of colonization, Europeans tagged the cultures they encountered as either savage or mystic. "Authentic" tourist destinations are often designed to exploit the mystical in local cultures. A South African theme park, The Lost City (built on the site of the resort Sun City), capitalizes on *mystical images of Africa described in a legend*, thereby "freezing" the continent to a time that never existed (Fig. 4.9).

**■ Figure 4.9**
**Sun City, South Africa.** The Lost City resort in Sun City evokes the mystical images of Africa described in a legend. Landscapes such as this blur what is "authentic" and what is not.

A local culture need not be "mystical" in order to create an authentic place. The city of Branson, Missouri, is capitalizing on a local culture in the Ozarks, melding a number of people and perceptions in one place for tourists to consume. Geographer Johnathan Bascom studied the processes by which the city of Branson has effectively tapped its local customs, such as food preferences, history, and music, to create an "authentic" identity for Branson that sets it apart from neighboring towns. Branson becomes "authentic," and surrounding towns that try to capitalize on their rural, country heritage become "copies."

## GUINNESS AND THE IRISH PUB COMPANY

Theme parks and entertainment venues overtly choose a stereotype and perpetuate it, but a discerning tourist or consumer may be aware of what is occurring. The act of corporations commodifying the mystique of local cultures to drive profits can, however, be less obvious to the consumer. The Guinness Brewing Company of Dublin, Ireland, created a business plan in 1991 aimed at capitalizing on the global mystique of the traditional Irish pub. Guinness saw the sales of its stout beer declining in Ireland and the United Kingdom and decided to go global.

Guinness formed a partnership with the Irish Pub Company, which has offices in Dublin, Atlanta, the United Arab Emirates, and Australia. The Irish Pub Company studied traditional Irish pubs and created five Irish pub prototypes—shop, country, Victorian, Celtic, and brewery. A hotel owner in Naples, Florida, or a businessperson in Dubai, United Arab Emirates (Fig. 4.10), to cite two examples, might work with

the Irish Pub Company to choose a good site and to choose the pub type. The specifications are sent to Ireland, and the pub itself is built in Ireland and shipped abroad. Along with the pub, the Irish Pub Company provides food recommendations, training, music suggestions, and notably, Irish bartenders trained in their Dublin "pub school." The Irish Pub Company also sells bric-a-brac (Irish antiques and reproductions) to give the place the feel of an Irish pub. Of course, every pub has Guinness on tap. All of these components create what the Irish Pub Company refers to as ambience that leads to craic (an Irish term for fun).

Guinness and the Irish Pub Company have built over 1000 pubs in 40 countries around the world (Fig. 4.11).

**■ Figure 4.10**
**Dubai, United Arab Emirates.**    An old Irish truck marks the entrance to an Irish Pub Company pub in Dubai.

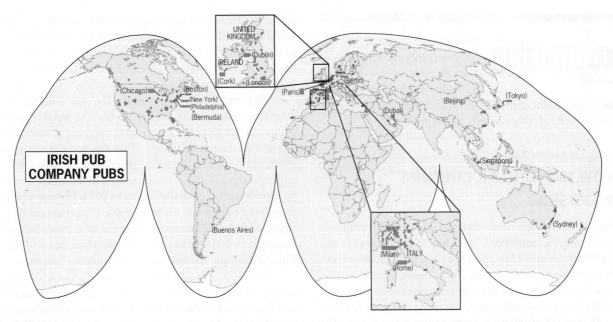

**Figure 4.11**

**Irish Pubs Designed by the Irish Pub Company.** The distance decay principle is evident here, with the greatest number of pubs located in Europe and North America, as is the Irish Pub Company. The map also highlights the diffusion of popular culture to world cities, including Buenos Aires and Singapore. *Data from*: Irish Pub Company, by e-mail and http://www.irishpubcompany.com/pubsworldwide.asp, last accessed July 2011.

Remarkably, dozens of the pubs are in Ireland proper. The most enigmatic of the pubs is in Las Vegas, Nevada. The Irish Pub Company designed and built a pub called Nine Fine Irishmen that spans 9000 square feet in the New York-New York Hotel and Casino and spills an additional 20,000 square feet onto Las Vegas Boulevard. The "authentic" Irish pub in "authentic" New York in the "Disneyfied" Las Vegas is one mashup we can chew on for a while.

The commodification of local customs freezes customs in place and time for consumption, with claims of "authenticity"

abounding. The search for "authentic" local cultures implies an effort to identify peoples who are seemingly untouched by change or external influence. However, all local cultures (rural and urban) are dynamic, and all have been touched by external influences throughout their existence (Fig. 4.12). The search for an "authentic" local culture merely perpetuates myths about local cultures. Members of local cultures are constantly renegotiating their place in this world and making sense of who they are in the midst of the popular culture onslaught.

## FIELD NOTE

"The Dingle Peninsula in Ireland was long one of the more remote parts of the country, and even its largest town, Dingle, was primarily an agricultural village just a few decades ago. As I walked through the streets of town, I noticed the colorful inns and houses of the older town. The 'Little Bridge Pub' on the corner of this intersection in the older town is an 'authentic' pub, the kind that the Irish Pub Company works to replicate."

© Alexander B. Murphy

**Figure 4.12**
**Dingle, Ireland**

What is the last place you went to or the last product you purchased that claimed to be "authentic?" What are the challenges of defending the authenticity of this place or product while refuting the authenticity of other similar places or products?

## HOW IS POPULAR CULTURE DIFFUSED?

Extraordinary changes have occurred since 1900 in the time it takes for people, innovations, and ideas to diffuse around the globe. The innovation of agriculture took nearly 10,000 years to diffuse around the world. In much more recent times, the diffusion of developments such as the printing press or the Industrial Revolution was measured over the course of 100 years or more.

During the twentieth century, however, the pace of diffusion shrank to months, weeks, days, and in some cases even hours. Simultaneously, the spatial extent of diffusion has expanded, so that more and more parts of Earth's surface are affected by ideas and innovations from faraway places. For example, the social networking site Facebook, which Mark

Zuckerberg launched in 2004, passed 500 million subscribers worldwide in 2010 and reported 1.23 billion monthly users at the end of 2013. In 2013, Facebook released data on the number of daily users, reporting that one-third of the U.S. and UK populations access Facebook at least once a day.

The map of Facebook users (Fig. 4.13) highlights the interconnectedness of individuals around the world, and it also points out the lack of interconnection between individuals in China with the rest of the world via this social media tool. In 2009, China banned Facebook, Twitter, and Google. Over 500 million of the 618 million Chinese with Internet access reached the internet through mobile devices in 2014. Chinese who want to use Facebook have to use proxy servers to get around the government's ban. Chinese social networks have grown in place of Facebook. In 2014, the social network Qzone had 644 million Chinese users and Renren boasted 210 million Chinese users.

In 2005, the Chinese company Tencent established Qzone, a blogging cite where users can post photos and their thoughts. Tencent, established in 1998 by Chinese entrepreneur Huateng Ma, is an internet service provider that also owns QQ, an instant messaging application. As of March 2014, Tencent was the "fifth largest Internet company in the world—currently valued at over $140 bn" (Gittleson 2014).

QQ is more than an instant messaging service. Users link their accounts to bank cards and "use the platform to do

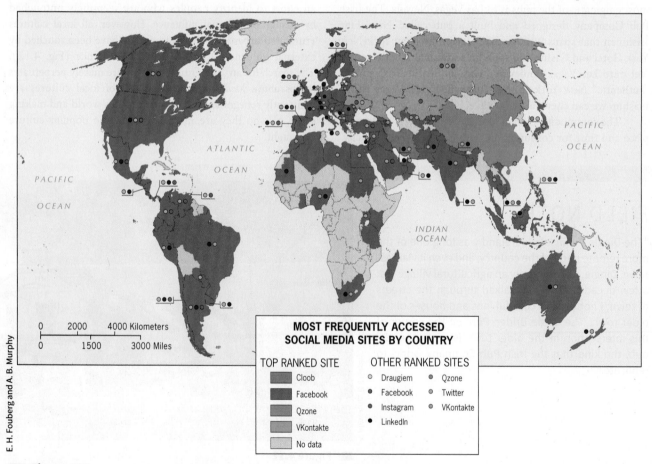

MOST FREQUENTLY ACCESSED
SOCIAL MEDIA SITES BY COUNTRY

TOP RANKED SITE
- Cloob
- Facebook
- Qzone
- VKontakte
- No data

OTHER RANKED SITES
- Draugiem
- Facebook
- Instagram
- LinkedIn
- Qzone
- Twitter
- VKontakte

E. H. Fouberg and A. B. Murphy

■ **Figure 4.13**

**Social Networks Worldwide.** The most popular social networks vary across the world, with Facebook having the largest imprint. *Data from:* Alexa.com, September 2014.

**■ Figure 4.14**
**Beijing, China.** Renren, the Facebook of China, is a popular social network among college students. It now has over 210 million registered users. Wang Xing, who launched and sold Renren, has since launched Chinese versions of Twitter and Groupon.

everything from book a table at a restaurant to order a taxi" (Gittleson 2014). During the Chinese New Year, money is often exchanged as gifts. QQ tapped into that market and offered a service to send gifts of money through its platform during the holiday. According to the BBC, "more than 200 million users signed up for the service in 15 days."

Chinese entrepreneur Wang Xing launched the Chinese social network Xiaonei ("on campus"), which copied Facebook down to its color scheme, in 2005 and 2006. Now known as Renren, which means "everybody" (Fig. 4.14), the site functions as a Chinese Facebook. China allows Renren and its competitor, Kaixin001, to operate because they have agreed to the political censorship mandated by the Chinese government. For example, according to a report in business magazine *Fast Company*, Renren censors "a range of sensitive keywords, including terms related to the Dalai Lama, the 1989 Tiananmen Square massacre, and Chinese dissidents including 2010 Nobel Peace laureate Liu Xiaobo" (Rabkin 2011). Renren users report that they receive a warning message when they update their status or post a comment that is censored by Renren.

Controlling information flow is increasingly difficult in China, and many argue that despite being censored, Renren and its competitors allow for freer flow of ideas than previously was possible in communist China.

Transportation and communication technologies have altered **distance decay**. No longer does a map with a bull's-eye surrounding the hearth of an innovation describe how quickly the innovation will diffuse to areas around it (Fig. 4.15a). Rather, what geographer David Harvey called **time–space compression** explains how quickly innovations diffuse and refers to how interlinked two places are through transportation and communication technologies (Fig. 4.15b).

In the past few decades, major world cities have become much closer to one another as a result of modern technologies, including airplanes, high-speed trains, expressways, wireless connections, fax machines, e-mail, and telephone. Places that lack transportation and communications technologies are now more removed from interconnected places than ever. All of the new technologies create the infrastructure through which innovations diffuse. Because the technologies link some places more closely than others, ideas diffuse through interconnected places rapidly rather than diffusing at constant rates across similar distances.

## Hearths of Popular Culture

Popular culture diffuses hierarchically in the context of time–space compression, with diffusion happening most rapidly across the most compressed spaces. As we saw in the last section, even local customs practiced for centuries in one place can be swept up into popular culture. How does a custom, idea, song, or object become part of popular culture? It is relatively easy to follow the communications, transportation, and marketing networks that account for the diffusion of popular culture, but how do we find the hearths of popular culture, and how do certain places establish themselves as the hearths of popular culture?

### ESTABLISHING A HEARTH

All aspects of popular culture—music, sports, television, and dance—have a hearth, a place of origin. Typically, a hearth begins with contagious diffusion: Developers of an idea or innovation may find they have followers who dress as they do or listen to the music they play. A multitude of American musical groups (REM, Hootie and the Blowfish, MGMT) began as college bands or in college towns. They play a few sets in a

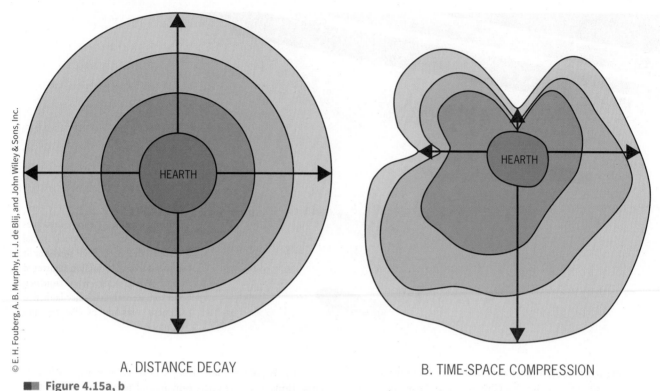

A. DISTANCE DECAY                    B. TIME-SPACE COMPRESSION

■■ **Figure 4.15a, b**

**Distance Decay and Time–Space Compression.**   With distance decay, the likelihood of diffusion decreases as time and distance from the hearth increases. With time–space compression, the likelihood of diffusion depends on the connectedness (in communications and transportation technologies) among places.

campus bar or at a campus party and gain followers. The group starts to play to bars and campuses in nearby college towns, and soon they produce their own music and sell it at their concerts.

Bands that begin on college campuses or in college towns and build from their base typically establish a hearth for their sound's diffusion first through contagious diffusion and then through hierarchical diffusion. College towns including Athens, Georgia; Burlington, Vermont; and Charlottesville, Virginia, are the perfect nesting spaces for new bands. The Dave Matthews Band created and perfected their sound in Charlottesville, Virginia, in the early 1990s. Lead singer and guitarist Dave Matthews was born in South Africa and landed in Charlottesville as a young adult after living in Johannesburg, New York, and London (Fig. 4.16).

Matthews was a bartender in Charlottesville when he met Ross Hoffman, a local songwriter who mentored Matthews in song writing. The Dave Matthews Band was formed when Matthews invited Carter Beuford (drums), LeRoi Moore (saxophone, who died in 2008), Stefan Lessard (bass), and Boyd Tinsley (violin) to join him in creating a demo of some of his songs. The Dave Matthews Band's first live show was in Charlottesville on Earth Day in April 1991. The band played bars throughout the Charlottesville area from 1991 through 1993. Manager Coran Capshaw followed the path of diffusion carved by the Grateful Dead and Phish, through a grassroots campaign of word of mouth (contagious diffusion).

■■ **Figure 4.16**

**Detroit Lakes, Minnesota.**   Dave Matthews of the Dave Matthews Band performs at the 10,000 Lakes Music Festival in 2009.

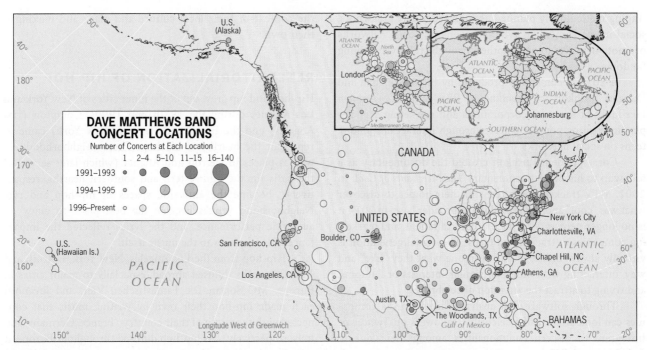

**Figure 4.17**

**World Distribution of Dave Matthews Band concerts.**   The earliest Dave Matthews Band concerts, noted by red circles on the map, were in college towns in North America. After 1996, as noted by the light yellow circles on the map, when Dave Matthews Band concerts diffused beyond North America and Europe, the band connected first with the lead singer's home country of South Africa.   *Data from*: http://www. bmbalmanac.com, last accessed June 2014. Compiled by Kim Johnson, Liz Sydnor, and Lennea Mueller.

Hierarchical diffusion of the band soon followed, through the hierarchy of college towns in the United States (Fig. 4.17). The Dave Matthews Band played 200 nights a year in fraternities, sororities, bars, and clubs throughout the American South, following the same circuit as college band Hootie and the Blowfish. The band encouraged fans to record their music and send it to friends; this helped to establish audiences for the band in college towns far removed from Charlottesville.

Their first album, released in 1993, was on the band's independent label. It hit the college charts, and a union with RCA soon followed with their second album, Under the Table and Dreaming, released in 1994. As *Entertainment Weekly* explained in 1995, "By playing nearly 200 gigs a year and releasing their own CDs, they built up such a zealous following that when Under the Table entered the album chart at No. 34, neither MTV nor most of America had even heard of them." The band's first video was not released until three months after their first single, "What Would You Say," hit the Billboard charts.

The Dave Matthews Band became broadly popular after 1995 and began playing large arenas throughout the United States and in Australia. The band continues to rely on its fan base for support. Manager Capshaw and the Dave Matthews Band were early adopters of using the Internet to stay connected with fans. Today, the official Dave Matthews Band fan club has over 80,000 online members, each of whom pays $35 a year to belong.

The music of groups including the Dave Matthews Band, Phish, Grateful Dead, and Jimmy Buffet also diffuses relocationally, as fans follow the musicians along their concert routes, living in their cars and selling tie-dyed shirts and beaded necklaces out of the backs of their vehicles in the parking lots of concert venues.

The action of following the bands for years (an estimated 500 to 1000 fans traveled to every Grateful Dead concert) led fans to create their own customs and culture. As with other acts of pilgrimage (see Chapter 7 on religion), environmental effects can be grave. Prior to their final concert, Phish (breaking up for the second time) used their website to beg their fans to leave their beloved rural Vermont as they found it. Founded in 2004, Reverb, a nonprofit organization, helps bands, including the Dave Matthews Band, create environmentally conscious concerts by having bands purchase carbon offset credits for each of their concerts, supporting recycling, selling eco-friendly merchandise, and setting up Reverb Eco-Villages at concert venues to encourage eco-friendly behaviors among fans.

## MANUFACTURING A HEARTH

The question of whether a college band "makes it" depends greatly on the choices and actions of record producers and corporate music media giants. Marketing companies, such as the Audience, founded by Oliver Luckett, Sean Parker, and Ari Emanuel, generate and produce popular culture by waging meticulously planned, though seemingly grassroots, social-media campaigns whereby teens on social networks promote new acts to one another through crossovers among fandoms.

A 2014 documentary produced by Frank Koughan and Douglas Rushkoff for *Frontline* on PBS entitled *Generation Like* looks at the roles corporations and marketing agencies play in creating popular culture through interactions among teens on social networks.

Correspondent Rushkoff created the documentary as a followup to his 2001 documentary *The Merchants of Cool.* In 2001, MTV tracked down teens in their homes to discover what was "cool" and then resell it to a broader base. In 2014 it is no longer necessary for media, entertainment, and marketing companies to track down teens. The digital generation is virtually always online telling everyone what they "like" and why, interacting with others of similar interests or fandoms, and trying to attract the attention of celebrities.

Through software that analyzes "likes," media companies can look at a list of a celebrity's followers on Twitter or Instagram to discern commonalities among their fans in order to carefully plan marketing campaigns for new products, movies, and music. Everyday people like Tyler Oakley—who as of July 2014 had 4 million YouTube subscribers, 2 million followers on Instagram, and more than 2.6 million followers on Twitter—can use their large fan base or fandom to leverage corporate sponsors and advertising opportunities. This "fame" is, according to Rushkoff, an online currency that is used in media campaigns to create what is "cool" in popular culture.

Social networks create opportunities for constant contagious and hierarchical diffusion. Teens become "knowers" of new trends both contagiously—by reading posts from friends (although they may have been fed the information through a celebrity post)—and hierarchically by **opinion leaders** with large fan bases like Tyler Oakley. In 2013, Oakley promoted products from Pepsi and Taco Bell through YouTube videos and social networks. He strategically invites fans to interact with him during his videos and interjects fan comments into his videos and through retweets. While local news and other media companies are trying to mimic Oakley's success in interacting with fans, often in an awkward way, Oakley and other opinion leaders have mastered the art, which has given them social currency to pair up with major corporations and help create and shape popular culture.

With this kind of infrastructure behind the production of popular culture, we might expect popular culture to act as a blanket, evenly covering the globe. But even as popular culture has diffused throughout the world, it has not blanketed it, hiding all existing local cultures underneath it. Rather, one aspect of popular culture (such as music or food) will take on new forms when it encounters a new locality and the people and local culture in that place. Geographers and anthropologists call this the **reterritorialization** of popular culture: a term referring to a process in which people start to produce an aspect of popular culture themselves, doing so in

the context of their local culture and place and making it their own.

## RETERRITORIALIZATION OF HIP HOP

Hip-hop and rap grew out of the inner cities of New York and Los Angeles during the 1980s and 1990s. Compton (Los Angeles) and the Bronx and Harlem (New York) came to represent the hearths of hip-hop. These neighborhoods, as well as places in Detroit and Atlanta (which later served as the basis for the midwestern and southern hearths, respectively), became the authentic spaces of hip-hop and rap. Neighborhood venues became the best place to enjoy an authentic performance, and the lyrics reflected the importance of local places to the music itself.

Hip-hop from the Los Angeles, New York, Detroit, and Atlanta hearths diffused abroad, especially to major cities in Europe. MC Solaar, Die Fantastischen Vier, and Jovanotti each made hip-hop their own by writing music that connected with the youth of their country (France, Germany, and Italy, respectively). As hip-hop diffused throughout Europe, it mixed with existing local cultures, experiences, and places, reterritorializing the music to each locale.

In Southeast Asia, Indonesia serves as a good example of the process of reterritorialization. Imported hip-hop diffused first to a small group of people in Indonesia; then, Indonesians began to create hip-hop music themselves. Through the creation of their own music, Indonesian hip-hop artists integrated their local culture with the practices of the "foreign" hip-hop hearth to create a hybrid that was no longer foreign.

As hip-hop has diffused and grown, artists have addressed the major concerns of their local cultures in their lyrics. Hip-hop artists in the United States wrote about social issues in the 1980s and 1990s, and some wrote about violence, crime, and surviving urban life in the gangsta rap of the 1990s. Other artists write more about having fun and partying. In France and Germany, American hip-hop music diffused first to immigrants living in major cities. In France, for example, some of the first hip-hop artists were African, Arab, and Spanish immigrants writing about the racism they experienced in France.

The results of reterritorialization are seen in the ways hip-hop artists around the world compose lyrics about the real problems surrounding them and sample music from their local cultures in their music. In 2005, the U.S. State Department launched Rhythm Road, sending hip-hop artists to Muslim countries as part of diplomatic efforts in the "War on Terror." The program is credited both with inspiring revolutionary democracy and inciting radicalization against the U.S. During the Arab Spring in 2011, Tunisian hip-hop artist El Général (Fig. 4.18) helped spur massive political change by posting his song "Mr. President" on Facebook. The words he rapped about government corruption spoke to Tunisians and Egyptians, inspiring revolutionaries in both countries.

FETHI BELAID/AFP/Getty Images

■■ **Figure 4.18**
**Tunis, Tunisia.** Tunisian hip-hop artist El Général helped spark the Arab Spring with his anthem "Mr. President."

## Replacing Old Hearths with New: Beating Out the Big Three in Popular Sports

Baseball, football, and basketball are historically the big three sports in the United States. During the 1800s and 1900s, they all benefited from advances in transportation technology, communication technology, and institutionalization. First, the railroad connected cities across the country, allowing baseball teams to compete and baseball to diffuse. The telegraph enabled newspapers to report baseball scores, which added to the sport's following. In the late 1880s, electric lighting made basketball a nighttime spectator sport, played inside gymnasiums. The founding of the National Football League in 1920 helped institutionalize the sport of football (by creating institutions to support it, formalize it, and regulate it), with rules for the game remaining relatively unchanged since then.

During much of the twentieth century, the big three dominated sports popular culture. Figures including Mark McGwire, Michael Jordan, and Brett Favre found their ways onto Wheaties boxes and reached icon status. In the last decades of the twentieth century, advertising contracts and corporate sponsorship padded and eventually surpassed the salaries of the biggest sports heroes.

While the big three continued to draw millions of fans and huge crowds to their venues, a growing number of alternative sports captured the imagination of young sports fans. Popular films (including *Endless Summer*) of the 1960s immortalized the freedom of surfing. In the 1970s, sidewalk surfing, now known as skateboarding, diffused from its hearth in Southern California. In the 1980s, snowboarding found a following but initially met strong resistance on ski slopes in the United States.

The debut of ESPN's X Games in 1995 and the proliferation of video games involving extreme sports propelled previously alternative sports into popular culture. Snowboarding debuted as a winter Olympic sport in 1998. Video games sparked interest in such sports, even among kids who had never tried them before. Tony Hawk, the famous skateboarder, worked with Activision to create several versions of Tony Hawk's Pro Skater, with average annual sales of $180 million. In 2001, sales relating to video games were higher than the movie industry's box office receipts. That same year, baseball took a back seat to skateboarding, with more children under the age of 18 skateboarding than playing baseball.

Extreme sports greats, like Tony Hawk, gain corporate sponsors, create their own brands, and sign lucrative advertising deals. Hawk, who retired from competitive skate boarding in 1999, reportedly generates more than $200 million a year in revenue through sponsorships, skate tours, and sales of his skateboards, clothing lines, and video games. Hawk combined popular sports with popular music, creating his Boom Boom Huck Jam tour that features famous skateboarders, BMX bike riders, and motorcycle stunt drivers, neatly choreographed and enhanced by alternative live music. Tony Hawk, Inc., employs 24 full-time employees to oversee Hawk's branded products.

**Figure 4.19**

**Sochi, Russia.** Olympic gold medal winner Sage Kotsenburg celebrates at the end of the Men's Snowboard Slopestyle Final at the Sochi Winter Olympics in 2014.

Advertisers who court the 12–34 age demographic, fans looking for athletes who are outside of major league sports, and fans who desire a sport that is different from their parents' sport drove the expansion of extreme sports into mainstream popular culture. Rising stars in extreme sports look to Tony Hawk and see the business side of professional snowboarding and skating. Sage Kotsenburg, who won a gold medal at the 2014 Sochi Olympics (Figure 4.19), reportedly read "every book he could find about finance and money management" before becoming a professional snowboarder (Kragthorpe 2014).

Like new music or other forms of popular culture, extreme sports have become more popular, mainstream, and commodified. Once that happens, the fan base turns its attention to a new extreme sport, and the corporate sponsors begin

to tap into the new popular sport, helping it follow the same path to popular, mainstream, and commodified status.

One of the best known recent examples of this trend is the popularization of ultimate fighting. In the early 1990s, advertising executives and sports promoters drew from a long history of mixed martial arts fights in Brazil to produce a series of fights in the United States among different martial arts and boxing experts to see who was the best fighter. The new fights, called mixed martial arts, grew a fan base through live matches and pay per view on cable television. Early mixed martial arts fights had just a few rules, including no head-butting and no weight classes.

The fan base grew quickly, and by 1993, the Ultimate Fighting Championship (UFC) formed to serve as a professional organization for mixed martial arts (Fig. 4.20). The

**Figure 4.20**

**Toronto, Canada.** Light Heavyweight Jon "Bones" Jones won his fight with Alexander Gustafsson in September 2013.

sport continued to grow during the 1990s, with the establishment of rules over time allotments for matches, the institutionalization of promotions and marketing, and the growth in popularity of ultimate fighting reality television shows. The rules of the UFC, including seven weight classes and specifications for the fighting arena called "the Octagon" or "the Cage," have been institutionalized as the basis for ultimate fighting worldwide. References to ultimate fighting and ultimate fighters (such as Chuck Liddell's appearance on HBO's *Entourage*) are diffusing into other aspects of popular culture, spreading both the commodification and the popularization of the sport.

Identity and the desire to remain outside of popular culture will continue to spur the creation of extreme sports to rival the big three. In discussing the production of popular culture, geographer Clayton Rosati explained that the foundation of industrial capitalism is not simply "meeting the existing needs of the public." Rather, industrial capitalism demands that corporations continue to produce goods that "become socially desirable." The need for corporations to create the "new" so that they have something to sell that is "socially desirable" applies to all markets, whether music, entertainment, or athletics. Skateboarding and ultimate fighting will be followed by the next extreme sport and the next, as long as corporations can spur the consumption of the new.

## Stemming the Tide of Popular Culture—Losing the Local?

Assimilation policies practiced by American, Canadian, Russian, Australian, and New Zealand governments were official policies designed for the express purpose of disrupting and changing indigenous, local cultures. Western, democratic governments no longer have official policies of assimilation. Yet, for people in many local cultures and in regions that are not hearths of popular culture, popular culture itself can feel like a policy of assimilation.

Popular media such as music, television, and film from the United States and the United Kingdom diffuse quickly. American and British products can now be seen and heard around the world. If you turn on the television in Harare, Zimbabwe, you can easily find reruns of a 10-year-old American television show or a contemporary CNN broadcast. If you go to a cinema in Seoul, South Korea, you can choose among several just-released American films shown in English with Korean subtitles.

The influence of Europe, the United States, Japan, and South Korea in global popular culture makes many people feel threatened by cultural homogenization. At the global scale, North America, western Europe, Japan, India, and South Korea exert the greatest influence on popular culture at present. Each region acts as a major hearth for certain aspects of popular culture. North American influences are seen mainly in movies, television, music, sports, and fast food; Japan's influences are primarily in children's television programs, electronic games, and new entertainment technologies; western Europe's in fashion, television, art, and philosophy; South Korea's in television dramas, movies, and popular music; and India's mainly in movies.

South Korea has made a mark on popular culture from television to popular music. In 1995, Chinese television stations began broadcasting South Korean television dramas. The South Korean dramas typically aired late at night, often after midnight, but they quickly gained a large following in China. The Chinese government changed a law that restricted Korean content on television to 15 percent of air time, and in response South Korean popular television dramas took off in China. An entire wave of South Korean popular culture, including television shows, movies, fashions, and music diffused throughout China, Japan, and Southeast Asia. Hallyu (also called Hanryu) are waves of South Korean popular culture that move quickly through Asia and have resulted in significant growth in the South Korean entertainment and tourism industries (Fig. 4.21).

Beginning with television dramas and movies, Hallyu expanded to music in the early part of this century. South Korean popular music, known as K-pop, has followed the same path of diffusion. The Chinese government allowed Korean band H.O.T. to play in a stadium in Beijing in 2002. Today, K-pop bands, including Super Junior (called SuJu) and Girls Generation; K-pop recording artists, including Psy, Rain, and BoA; and Korean movie stars, including Bae Yong Joon, have fans throughout East Asia, Southeast Asia, and increasingly in the Middle East.

Ironically, South Korea was quite protective of its entertainment industry in the post-World War II era, for fear that Japan, which formerly colonized South Korea, would export its entertainment industry to South Korea and overpower South Korea's entertainment industry. But Hallyu has diffused not only to China but also to Japan. In turn, millions of Japanese and Chinese are taking Korean language classes, traveling and studying abroad in South Korea, and adopting South Korean fashions.

A 2009 article in *Tourism Geographies* describes the diffusion and proliferation of Hallyu in Asia:

> Having first penetrated the Chinese mainland, the Korean cultural phenomenon of Hallyu, in particular Korean television, has spread throughout the East and South-east of Asia, including Japan, Hong Kong, Taiwan, Singapore, Malaysia, Thailand, Vietnam, Philippines and later even to the Middle East and East Europe. The infatuation with Korean popular culture and celebrities has not stopped at popular media consumption but has also led to more general interest in popular music, computer games, Korean language, food, fashion, make-up and appearance, and even plastic surgery (Kim et al. 2009).

When popular culture displaces or replaces local culture, it will usually be met with resistance. In response to an influx of American and British films, the French government

# FIELD NOTE

"Just days before the Japanese tsunami in 2011, I walked out of the enormous Lotte department store in Seoul, South Korea, and asked a local where to find a marketplace with hand-crafted goods. She pointed me in the direction of the Insa-dong traditional market street. When I noticed a Starbucks sign written in Korean instead of English, I knew I must be getting close to the traditional market. A block later, I arrived on Insa-dong. I found quaint tea shops and boutiques with handcrafted goods, but the market still sold plenty of bulk-made goods, including souvenirs like Korean drums, chopsticks, and items sporting Hallyu stars. Posters, mugs, and even socks adorned with the faces of members of Super Junior smiled at the shoppers along Insa-dong."

© Erin H. Fouberg

■ **Figure 4.21**
**Seoul, South Korea.**

heavily subsidizes its domestic film industry. French television stations, for example, must turn over 3 percent of their revenues to the French cinema. The French government also stemmed the tide of American and British music on the radio by setting a policy in the 1990s requiring that 40 percent of on-air time be in French. Of the 40 percent, half must be new artists. These policies directly benefited the French hip-hop industry. By performing in French, the new artists received quite a bit of air time on French radio.

Through policies and funding, the French government has helped maintain its cultural industries, but in countless other cases, governments and cultural institutions lack the means or the will to promote local cultural productions.

Concern over the loss of local distinctiveness and identity is not limited to particular cultural or socioeconomic settings. We find such concern among the dominant societies of wealthier countries, where it is reflected in everything from the rise of religious fundamentalism to the establishment of semiautonomous communes in remote locations. We find this concern among minorities (and their supporters) in wealthier countries, where it can be seen in efforts to promote local languages, religions, and customs by constructing barriers to the influx of cultural influences from the dominant society. We find it among political elites in poorer countries seeking to promote a nationalist

ideology that is explicitly opposed to cultural globalization. And we find it among social and ethnic minorities in poorer countries that seek greater autonomy from regimes promoting acculturation or assimilation to a single national cultural norm.

Geographers realize that local cultures will interpret, choose, and reshape the influx of popular culture. People interpret individual cultural productions in very different ways, depending on the cultural context in which they view them. What people choose to adopt from popular culture, how they reterritorialize it, and what they reject help shape the character and culture of people, places, and landscapes.

Read about the U.S. government effort to use hip-hop in the War on Terror in "America's Hip-Hop Foreign Policy" in the *Atlantic* (theatlantic.com/international/archive/2014/03/americas-hip-hop-foreign-policy/284522/). Determine whether and how the U.S. could use social networks to help make hip-hop diplomacy more successful.

# HOW CAN LOCAL AND POPULAR CULTURES BE SEEN IN THE CULTURAL LANDSCAPE?

The tension between globalized popular culture and local culture can be seen in **cultural landscapes**, the visible imprint of human activity on the landscape. Human imprint includes everything from how people have changed and shaped the environment to the buildings, signs, fences, and statues people erect. Cultural landscapes reflect the values, norms, and aesthetics of a culture. On major roadways in North American towns and suburbs, the landscape is a series of big box stores, gas stations, and restaurants that reflect popular culture (Fig. 4.22). As you drive down one of these roadways, one place looks like the next. You drive past TGI Fridays, Applebee's, Wal-Mart, Target, and McDonald's. Then, several miles down the road, you pass another conglomeration (clustering) of the same stores. Geographer Edward Relph coined the word **placelessness** to describe the loss of uniqueness of place in the cultural landscape to the point that one place looks like the next.

Globalization and cultural diffusion have led to the convergence of cultural landscapes worldwide. Three developments are at the heart of this convergence: (1) particular architectural forms and planning ideas have diffused around the world; (2) individual businesses and products have become so widespread that they now leave a distinctive landscape stamp on far-flung places; and (3) the wholesale borrowing of idealized landscape images has promoted a blurring of place distinctiveness, if not actual convergence.

The global diffusion of the skyscraper provides a clear illustration of the first point—particular architectural forms and planning ideas have diffused around the world (Fig. 4.23). In the second half of the 1800s, with advancements in steel production and improved costs and efficiencies of steel use, architects and engineers created the first skyscrapers. The fundamental difference between a skyscraper and another building is that the outside walls of the skyscraper do not bear the major load or weight of the building; rather, the internal steel structure or skeleton of the building bears most of the load. The Home Insurance Building of Chicago is typically credited as the first building to meet these specifications.

From Singapore to Johannesburg and from Caracas to Toronto, the commercial centers of major cities are dominated by tall buildings, many of which were designed by the same architects and engineering firms. With the diffusion of the skyscraper around the world, the cultural landscape of cities has been profoundly impacted. Skyscrapers require substantial land clearing in the vicinity of individual buildings, the construction of wide, straight streets to promote access, and the reworking of transportation systems around a highly centralized model. Skyscrapers are only one example of the globalization of a particular landscape form. The proliferation of skyscrapers in Taiwan, Malaysia, and China in the 1990s marked the integration of these economies into the major players in the world economy (Fig. 4.24). Today, the growth of skyscrapers in Dubai, United Arab Emirates, signals Dubai's world city status.

Reading signs is an easy way to see the second dimension of cultural landscape convergence: the far-flung stamp of global businesses on the landscape. Walking down the streets of Rome, you will see signs for Pizza Hut and Subway. The main tourist shopping street in Prague hosts Dunkin' Donuts and McDonald's. A tourist in Munich, Germany, will wind through streets looking for the city's famed beer garden dating from 1589, the Hofbräuhaus and will happen upon the Hard Rock Café, right

© Bridget Hogan Hoye

■ **Figure 4.22**
**Roseville, Minnesota.** A series of signs advertising national chains creates a nondescript landscape on Snelling Avenue in this St. Paul suburb. Across the street from where this photo was taken is the site of T-1, the first Target store ever built, which was recently torn down and replaced with the largest Target store in the world.

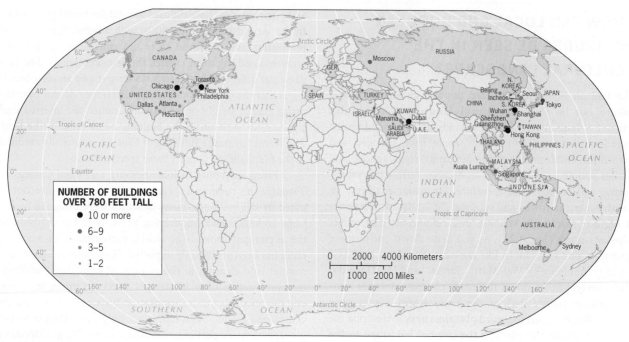

**Figure 4.23**

**World Distribution of Skyscrapers.**   The map shows the number of skyscrapers that are taller than 700 feet. The map reflects the growing importance of East Asia as a business center—particularly China. But Dubai stands out as well, a city that has staked its future on its role as an international commercial node.   *Data from*: Emporis, Inc., 2005.

**Figure 4.24**

**Kuala Lampur, Malaysia.**  The Petronas Towers. When the Pretronas were completed in 1998, they were the tallest buildings in the world. They were overtaken by Taipei 101 in 2004, which in turn was dwarfed by the Burj Khalifa in Dubai in 2010.

next door (Fig. 4.25). If the tourist had recently traveled to Las Vegas, he might have déjà vu. The Hofbräuhaus Las Vegas, built in 2003, stands across the street from the Hard Rock Hotel and Casino. The storefronts in Seoul, South Korea, are filled with Starbucks, Dunkin' Donuts, and Outback Steakhouses. China is home to more than 3,200 KFC restaurants; KFC's parent company, Yum!, controls 40 percent of the fast-food market in China.

Marked landscape similarities like these can be found everywhere from international airports to shopping centers. Global corporations that develop spaces of commerce have wide-reaching impacts on the cultural landscape. Architectural firms often specialize in building one kind of space— performing arts centers, stadiums, medical laboratories, or international airports. Property management companies have worldwide holdings and encourage Gap, The Cheesecake Factory, Barnes and Noble, and other companies to lease space in all of their holdings. Facilities such as airports and college food courts begin to look the same even though they are separated by thousands of miles.

The third dimension of cultural landscape convergence is the wholesale borrowing of idealized landscape images across the world. As you study the cultural landscape, you may notice landscape features transplanted from one place to another— regardless of whether the landscape feature even "fits."

The strip in Las Vegas, Nevada, represents an extreme case of the tendency toward convergence, with various structures designed to evoke different parts of the planet. The popular Venetian Hotel and Casino in Las Vegas replicates the Italian city of Venice, including canals. The Las Vegas Sands

Figure 4.25

**Munich, Germany.** In modern-day Munich, the famed Hofbräuhaus shares a street corner with the Hard Rock Café. The juxtaposition of different cultural-commercial traditions is increasingly common.

Corporation, a casino developer and owner, built the Venetian Hotel and Casino across the Pacific from Las Vegas in Macao in 2007. The port city of Macao was once a colony of Portugal but reverted to Chinese control in 1999. The Venetian Macao Resort cost $2.4 billion and is three times the size of the largest casino in Las Vegas (Fig. 4.26b). Gambling is illegal in mainland China, but Macao's recent incorporation into China and its special status allow gambling to flourish on the small island.

The borrowing of landscape is not confined to grand-scale projects like the Venetian. A more common borrowed landscape in North America is the town center. Town centers popping up in suburbia in North America have a similar look— one that is familiar if you have walked on Main Street, U.S.A. at Disneyland or Disney World, or if you have visited the centers of any number of "quaint" historic towns on the eastern seaboard. Each town center is designed to make you think of all things American and to feel immediately "home" in the place.

In less obvious ways, cultural borrowing and mixing are happening all around the world. This idea is behind the **global–local continuum** concept. This notion emphasizes that what happens at one scale is not independent of what happens at other scales. Human geography is not simply about documenting the differences between places; it is also about understanding the processes unfolding at different scales that produce those differences. What happens in an individual place is the

Figure 4.26a

**Venice, Italy. UNESCO World Heritage Site.** Designation as a World Heritage Site is reserved for sites with great cultural-historical significance. But as the two photos below suggest, knockoffs of such sites are not uncommon—eroding the distinctiveness of places.

Figure 4.26b

**The Venetian Hotel and Casino in Las Vegas, Nevada.**

Figure 4.26c

**The Venetian Hotel and Casino in Macau, China.**

product of interaction across scales. People in a local place mediate and alter regional, national, and global processes, in a process called **glocalization**. The character of place ultimately comes out of a multitude of dynamic interactions among local distinctiveness and wider-scaled events and influences.

## Cultural Landscapes of Local Cultures

What makes travel interesting for most people is the presence of variety in the cultural landscape. Travel beyond the tourist sites and the main roads, and one will easily find landscapes of local cultures, even in wealthy countries such as the United States and Canada. By studying cultural landscapes, you can gain insight into the social structures of local cultures. In everything from the houses to the schools to the churches to the cemeteries, a local cultural landscape reveals its foundation.

Founders and early followers of the Church of Jesus Christ of Latter-day Saints created the Mormon landscape of the American West as they migrated westward under persecution

and in search of a place where they could practice their religion freely. The Mormon Church began in New York, and then Joseph Smith and his followers moved westward to Independence, Missouri. From there, Mormons migrated farther west to present-day Salt Lake City, Utah. The easiest place to see the foundations of the Mormon cultural landscape are in the small towns established by Mormons throughout Utah and stretching into Arizona, Nevada, and Idaho (Fig. 4.27).

Geographers, including Donald Meinig, Richard Francaviglia, and Allen Noble, have studied the Mormon landscape and found the roots of the Mormon culture inscribed in the local landscape. If you drove from Chicago west to Las Vegas and traveled through the rural areas of Nebraska and Utah on your path, you would immediately notice one fundamental difference in the landscape: farmsteads in the plains replaced by farming villages in the west. In the Great Plains, the Homestead Act encouraged farmers to establish single farmsteads where a farm family lived alone on their 160 acres and the nearest neighbor was down the dirt road. In the rural Mormon

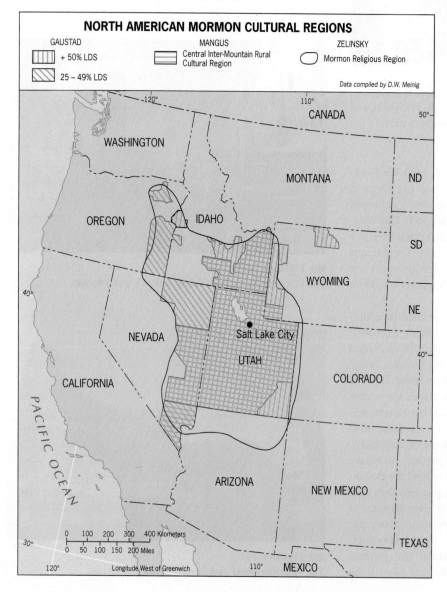

■ **Figure 4.27**

**The Mormon Cultural Region.** The Mormon culture region surrounds Salt Lake City, Utah where Mormon migrants established farms and farming communities. The religion diffused both through migration and missionary work to solidify a Mormon cultural region in North America. From this base, Mormon missionaries have diffused the religion to widespread parts of the world. *Adapted with permission from:* D.W. Meinig, "The Mormon Culture Region: Strategies and Patterns in the Geography of the American west, 1847–1964," *Annals of the Association of American Geographers,* 55, 2 (1965), p. 196.

# GUEST FIELD NOTE

## Paragonah, Utah

I took this photograph in the village of Paragonah, Utah, in 1969, and it still reminds me that fieldwork is both an art and a science. People who know the American West well may immediately recognize this as a scene from "Mormon Country," but their recognition is based primarily on their impressions of the place. "It is something about the way the scene looks," they may say, or "it feels like a Mormon village because of the way the barn and the house sit at the base of those arid bluffs." These are general impressions, but how can one prove that it is a Mormon scene? That is where the science of fieldwork comes into play. Much like a detective investigating a crime scene or a journalist writing an accurate story, the geographer looks for proof. In this scene, we can spot several of the ten elements that comprise the Mormon landscape. First, this farmstead is not separate from the village, but part of it—just a block off of Main Street, in fact.

Next we can spot that central-hall home made out of brick; then there is that simple, unpainted gabled-roof barn; and lastly the weedy edge of a very wide street says Mormon Country. Those are just four clues suggesting that pragmatic Mormons created this cultural landscape, and other field-work soon confirmed that all ten elements were present here in Paragonah. Like this 40-year-old photo, which shows some

Richard Francaviglia

■ **Figure 4.28**
**Paragonah, Utah.** Photo taken in 1969.

signs of age, the scene here did not remain unchanged. In Paragonah and other Mormon villages, many old buildings have been torn down, streets paved, and the landscape "cleaned up"—a reminder that time and place (which is to say history and geography) are inseparable.

*Credit: Richard Francaviglia, Geo.Graphic Designs, Salem, Oregon*

landscape, early settlers established farming villages where houses clustered together and croplands surrounded the outskirts of the village (Fig. 4.28). Clustering houses together in a farming village allowed Mormons to protect each other, a paramount concern because the religion's followers were experiencing persecution in the East and because the settlers' fears were raised by stories of Indians attacking villages in the West. Equally importantly, through clustering they sought to join together for services in each village's chapel.

Geographer Richard Francaviglia offers several factors that delimit the Mormon landscape in the western United States and Canada, including symmetrical brick houses that look more similar to houses on the East Coast than to other pioneer houses, wide streets that run due north–south and east–west, ditches for irrigation, poplar trees for shade, bishop's storehouses for storing food and necessities for the poor, and unpainted fences. Because the early Mormons were farmers and were clustered together in villages, each block in the town was quite large, allowing for one-acre city lots where a farmer could keep livestock and other farming supplies in town. The streets were wide so that farmers could easily turn a cart and horses on them.

The morphology (that is, the size and shape of a place's buildings, streets, and infrastructure) of a Mormon village tells us a lot, and so too can the shape and size of a local

culture's housing. In Malaysia, the Iban, an indigenous people, live along the Sarawak River in the Borneo region of the country in longhouses. Each longhouse is home to an extended family of up to 200 people. The family and the longhouse function as a community, sharing the rice farmed by the family, supporting each other through frequent flooding of the river (the houses are built on stilts), and working together on the porch that stretches the length of the house. The rice paddies surrounding each longhouse are a familiar shape and form throughout Southeast Asia, but the Iban longhouse tells you that you are experiencing a different kind of place—one that reflects a unique local culture.

Focus on the cultural landscape of your college campus. Think about the concept of placelessness. Determine whether your campus is a "placeless place" or whether the cultural landscape of your college reflects the unique identity of the place. Imagine you are hired to build a new student union on your campus. How could you design the building to reflect the uniqueness of your college?

# Summary

Advances in transportation and communications technology help popular culture diffuse at record speeds around the world today. Popular culture changes quickly, offering new music, foods, fashions, and sports. Popular culture envelops and infiltrates local cultures, presenting constant challenges to members of local cultures. Some members of local cultures have accepted popular culture, others have rejected it, and still others have forged a balance between the two.

Customs from local cultures are often commodified, propelling them into popular culture. The search for an "authentic" local culture custom generally ends up promoting a stereotyped local culture or glorifying a single aspect of that local culture. Local culture, like popular culture, is dynamic, and the pursuit of authenticity disregards the complexity and fluidity of cultures.

# Geographic Concepts

| | | |
|---|---|---|
| culture | assimilation | time–space compression |
| folk culture | custom | opinion leaders |
| popular culture | cultural appropriation | reterritorialization |
| local culture | neolocalism | cultural landscape |
| material culture | ethnic neighborhood | placelessness |
| nonmaterial culture | commodification | global-local continuum |
| hierarchical diffusion | authenticity | glocalization |
| hearth | distance decay | |

# Learn More Online

About the Irish Pub Company
www.irishpubcompany.com

About the Makah Tribe
www.makah.com

About the City of Lindsborg
www.lindsborgcity.org/

About the Hutterites
www.hutterites.org

# Watch It Online

Generation Like
www.pbs.org/wgbh/pages/frontline/generation-like/

Merchants of Cool
www.pbs.org/wgbh/pages/frontline/shows/cool/

The Way the Music Died
www.pbs.org/wgbh/pages/frontline/shows/music/

# IDENTITY: RACE, ETHNICITY, GENDER, AND SEXUALITY

## Building Walls

Traveling on the Indonesian island of Bali, I saw a brick-making facility and stopped to visit. Boys and women were building bricks by hand, in the hot sun. I watched young boys scoop wet mud from a quarry by a creek into their wheelbarrows. They poured the mud into wooden forms. Once the bricks began to dry and harden in the sun, someone had to turn the bricks repeatedly to prevent them from cracking. The woman in Figure 5.1 worked ten hours a day, six days a week, turning, stacking, and restacking bricks to prevent them from cracking.

More than a century ago, bricks were made this way in the United States. Today, the brick-making industry in the United States makes use of a great deal of technology and robotics to manufacture bricks. Instead of using the sun to bake the bricks, brick-making factories in the United States employ enormous tunnel-shaped kilns. The *Mississippi Business Journal* described how bricks are made in one factory: "Clay and water go in one end of the new 590 foot tunnel kiln and brick pallets will roll out the other end as robots and employees work side by side."

What hit me harder than the difference in technology between the two countries is the difference in labor. In Bali, women and boys make bricks. In the United States, the vast majority of brick-makers are men, aided by machines. One company estimated that 98 percent of its operations' employees in the factory are men. What makes brick-making a job for women and boys in Bali and a job for men and robots in the United States? *Does being a brick-maker mean different things in each of these places?*

Throughout the world, different cultures and societies have different ideas about what jobs are appropriate for men

© H. J. de Blij

■ **Figure 5.1**

**Bedugul, Indonesia.** A woman turns bricks at a brick-making facility in the village of Bedugul on the Indonesian island of Bali. She works in the formal economy for low wages and long hours.

and for women. Geographers, especially those who study gender, realize that people create divisions of labor that are *gendered*. Geographers Mona Domosh and Joni Seager define **gender** as "a culture's assumptions about the differences between men and women: their 'characters,' the roles they play in society, what they represent." Divisions of labor are one of the clearest ways in which societies are gendered.

In Bali, brick-making is still done by hand by boys and women. The industry is not technologically sophisticated, and bricks are made one by one. Even beyond brick-making facilities, most of the factory jobs in Indonesia and in poorer countries of the world go to women instead of men. Factory managers often hire women over men because they see women as an expendable labor pool. Researcher Peter Hancock (2000) studied gender relations and women's work in factories in Indonesia and reported, "Research in different global contexts suggests that factory managers employ young women because they are more easily exploited, less likely to strike or form membership organizations, are comparatively free from family responsibilities, and more adept at doing repetitive and delicate tasks associated with assembly line work."

In many societies in poorer countries, young women are seen as the financial supporters of their families. Women migrate from rural areas and travel to cities or central industrial locales (such as export production zones—EPZs) to produce and earn a wage that is then sent home to support the schooling of their brothers and younger sisters (until these girls are also old enough to leave home and work).

In Indonesia and in neighboring Malaysia and the Philippines, many women temporarily migrate to the Middle East to work as domestics, cooking, cleaning, and providing childcare in order to send money home to support the family. In the United States, rarely does an oldest daughter migrate to the city to labor in a factory so that she can pay for her younger brothers' schooling.

Although public education in the United States is free and open to boys and girls, American society still has gendered divisions of labor. The few women who work in brick-manufacturing facilities in the United States are typically assigned to tasks that require little lifting—such as gluing pieces of the various types of brick to boards so that salespeople can use them as samples. A long-standing assumption in American society is that work requiring heavy lifting needs to be completed by men and that good-paying, unionized jobs need to go to men because men are the "heads of the household." Times are changing and gendered work is being increasingly challenged, but assumptions about gender still have an impact on the labor market.

Society creates boxes in which we put people and expect them to live. These boxes are in a sense stereotypes embodying assumptions we make about what is *expected from* or *assumed about* women, men, members of certain races or ethnic groups, and people with various sexual preferences. By creating these boxes, society can assign entire professions or tasks to members of certain categories—for example, "women's work"—thereby gendering the division of labor. Places, notably the kitchen of a home or a store in the mall, can also be gendered. People are constantly negotiating their personal identities, finding their ways through all the expectations placed on them by the boxes society puts around them, and modifying and reinforcing the social relations that create the places where they work and live.

Rarely do the social relations that create gendered divisions of labor focus only on gender. The social relations in a place also create boxes for other identities. In this chapter, we focus on gender, race, ethnicity, and sexuality. We examine how people and society construct identities, how place factors into identity, and how geography reflects and shapes power relationships among different groups of people.

# Key Questions FOR CHAPTER 5

1. What is identity, and how are identities constructed?
2. How do places affect identity, and how can we see identities in places?
3. How does geography reflect and shape power relationships among groups?

## WHAT IS IDENTITY, AND HOW ARE IDENTITIES CONSTRUCTED?

A man gets off the airplane, walks to the baggage carousel to find his suitcase, and is greeted by dozens of black suitcases. He walks to the parking garage to find his car and sees a sea of black cars that all look the same. The narrator intones, "Maintain your identity. Drive a Saab."

Identities are marketed through cars, clothing, club memberships, jewelry, and houses. Advertisements often convey the impression that we can purchase our identity. Yet, identity is much more personal than what we drive, wear, belong to, or where we live. Geographer Gillian Rose (1995) defines **identity** as "how we make sense of ourselves." How do we each define ourselves? We construct our own identities through experiences, emotions, connections, and rejections. We work through derivations and delineations to find an identity that meshes with who and where we are at any given time. An identity is a snapshot, an image of who we are at that moment. Identities are fluid, constantly changing, shifting, and becoming. Place and space are integral to our identities because our experiences in places and our perceptions of places help us make sense of who we are.

In addition to defining ourselves, we define others and others define us. One of the most powerful ways to construct an identity is by **identifying against** other people. To identify against, we first define the "Other," and then we define ourselves in opposing terms. Edward Said wrote thoughtfully about how Europeans, over time, constructed an image of regions that are now commonly called the Middle East and Asia. He described the circumstances that led Europeans to define this area as the "Orient," a place with supposedly mystical characteristics that were depicted and repeated in European art and literature. In a similar vein, geographer James Blaut wrote eloquently about how Europeans came to define Africans and Native Americans as "savage" and "mystical." Through these images of the "Other," which developed during periods of European exploration and colonialism, Europeans defined themselves as "not mystical" or "not savage" and, therefore, as "civilized." These ideas are still part of our vernacular speech even today, as seen in references to "the civilized world" or a time "before civilization." Phrases like these invariably carry with them a sense of superiority in opposition to an "Other."

One of the most powerful foci of identity in the modern world is the state. State nationalism has been such a powerful force that in many contexts people think of themselves first and foremost as French, Japanese, American, or the like. Nationalist identities are a product of the modern state system, so we defer consideration of this form of identity to the chapter that focuses on the rise of the state system (Chapter 8). But nationalist identities coexist with all sorts of other identities that divide humanity—identities that can trump state nationalism in certain contexts and certain scales of interaction. Language and religion can function as foci of identity, and we will turn to these in the next two chapters. This chapter takes up several other important foundations of identity—those based on race, gender, ethnicity, and sexuality. We look at issues of identity construction, place, and scale by way of an analysis of race. We examine ethnicity and sexuality as identities that are shaped by and that in turn shape place. Our concluding discussion in this chapter looks at power relationships through the lenses of gender and ethnicity.

## Race

**Race** provides an excellent example of how a change in geographic context shapes definitions of identity. The various "races" people identify are tied to physical attributes of humans that have developed over time as modern humans spread around the world. Closer to the poles, humans developed lighter skin pigment so that skin could absorb sunlight that bodies could convert into vitamin D during the half of the year when the region received sunlight. Closer to the equator, humans developed darker skin pigment with higher amounts of melanin, which protects the skin from ultraviolet radiation emitted by the sun.

In precolonial Africa, societies had lines of division that sometimes reflected differences in skin tones. In colonial Africa, however, all of the different shades of "black" in Africa came to be viewed as one by European colonizers. The clumping of various societies and peoples into a few racial categories based on skin pigment still occurs in the modern world. Think of how often we are asked to complete applications, census forms, product warranty information, surveys, and medical forms that ask us to check a box identifying ourselves by race,

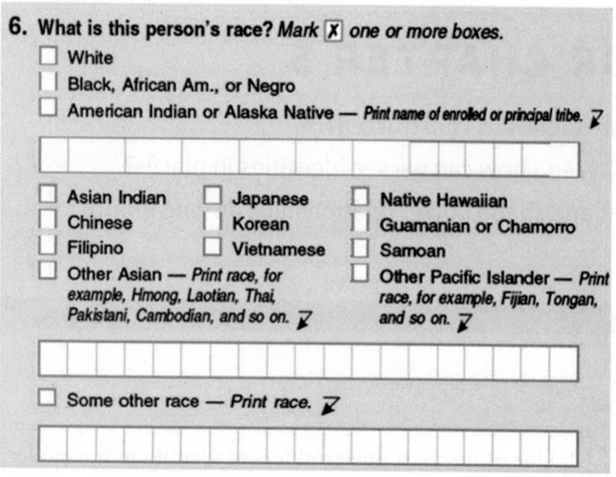

**6. What is this person's race?** Mark ☒ one or more boxes.

☐ White
☐ Black, African Am., or Negro
☐ American Indian or Alaska Native — *Print name of enrolled or principal tribe.* ↘

[ write-in boxes ]

☐ Asian Indian    ☐ Japanese    ☐ Native Hawaiian
☐ Chinese    ☐ Korean    ☐ Guamanian or Chamorro
☐ Filipino    ☐ Vietnamese    ☐ Samoan
☐ Other Asian — *Print race, for example, Hmong, Laotian, Thai, Pakistani, Cambodian, and so on.* ↘    ☐ Other Pacific Islander — *Print race, for example, Fijian, Tongan, and so on.* ↘

[ write-in boxes ]

☐ Some other race — *Print race.* ↘

[ write-in boxes ]

© U.S. Census Bureau

■ **Figure 5.2**

**United States.** Although biologically there is only one human race, we are often asked to choose race boxes for ourselves. This page of the 2010 United States Census asks the individual, "What is this person's race?" and directs the individual to "Mark one or more races to indicate what you consider yourself to be." The 2010 Census listed 14 racial categories, as well as a place to write in a specific race not listed on the form. Since 2000, the Census has allowed individuals to choose more than one race as their identity.

for example, "white," "black," "Asian" (Fig. 5.2). Such practices institutionalize and reinforce modern ways of viewing race. With each box we check, we learn to think the categories of race on the census are natural, fixed, mutually exclusive, and comprehensive. The more social scientists study race, the more we recognize racial categories are constructed, fluid, overlapping, and incomplete.

Where did society get the idea that humans fall into different, seemingly unchangeable categories of race? Throughout history, societies in different parts of the world have drawn distinctions among peoples based on their physical characteristics, but many of societies' modern assumptions about race grew out of the period of European exploration and colonialism since 1500. Benedict Anderson notes that even before 1500, before the Age of Exploration and colonialism, wealthy Europeans defined themselves as superior to those living elsewhere, suggesting that socioeconomic differences can fuel the sense of superiority attached to race known as **racism**. With the onset of the colonial era, what changed in Europe is that even poorer Europeans came to define themselves as superior to the people in the colonies. Anderson (1982) explains:

*Colonial racism was a major element in that conception of "Empire" which attempted to weld dynastic legitimacy and national community. It did so by generalizing a principle of innate, inherited superiority on which its own domestic position was (however shakily) based to the vastness of the overseas possessions, covertly (or not so covertly) conveying the idea that if, say, English lords were naturally superior to other Englishmen, no matter: these other Englishmen were no less superior to the subjected natives.*

The stories the commoners heard about the "mystical" and "savage" "Others" fostered feelings of superiority. One of the easiest ways to define the "Other" is through skin color because it is visible. Differences in the color of skin, then, became the basis for a fundamental social divide.

What society typically calls a "race" is in fact a combination of physical attributes in a population. Differences in skin, eye, and hair color likely result from a long history of adaptation to different environments. Sunlight stimulates the production of melanin, which protects skin from damaging ultraviolet rays; the more melanin that is present, the darker the skin will be. Biologists explain that this helps to explain why, over the millennia, humans living in low latitudes (closer to the equator, from tropical Africa through southern India to Australia) had darker skins. Over the millennia, natural selection in higher latitudes, closer to the North and South Poles, favored those with the least amount of pigmentation. People with less pigmentation could more easily absorb ultraviolet rays, which, in the higher latitudes, are sparse in winter months when the amount of sunlight is lower and less direct. When humans absorb ultraviolet light, their bodies in turn produce vitamin D, which is a necessary nutrient for survival.

Although melanin varies by latitude, skin color is not a reliable indicator of genetic closeness. The indigenous peoples of southern India, New Guinea, and Australia, for example, are about as dark-skinned as native Africans, but native Africans, southern Indians, and Aboriginal Australians are not closely related genetically (Fig. 5.3). No biological basis exists for dividing the human species into four or five groups based on skin color. Instead, those racial categories are the product of how particular cultures have dominantly viewed skin color.

The racial distinctions found in places today are the product of cultural history, power relationships, and local political developments over the past few centuries. Geographer Benjamin Forest (2001) gives us a global overview of racial distinctions:

*In Britain, the term "black" refers not only to Afro-Caribbeans and Africans, but also to individuals from the Indian subcontinent. In Russia, the term "black" is used to describe "Caucasians," that is, people such as Chechens from the Caucasus region. In many parts of Latin America, particularly Brazil, "racial" classification is really a kind of class placement, in which members of the wealthy upper class are generally considered as "white," members of the middle class as mixed race or Mestizo, and members of the lower class as "black." Indeed, because racial classifications are based on class standing and physical appearance rather than ancestry, "the designation of one's racial identity need not be the same as that of the parents, and siblings are often classified differently than one another."*

In each of these cases, and in countless others, people have constructed racial categories to justify power, economic exploitation, and cultural oppression.

## FIELD NOTE

"We were traveling in Darwin, Australia, in 1994 and decided to walk away from the modern downtown for a few hours. Darwin is a multicultural city in the midst of a region of Australia that is largely populated by Aboriginals. At the bus stops on the outskirts of the city, Aboriginals reached Darwin to work in the city or to obtain social services only offered in the city. With a language barrier between us, we used hand gestures to ask the man in the white shirt and his son if we could take their picture. Gesturing back to us, they agreed to the picture. Our continued attempts at sign language soon led to much laughter among the people waiting for the next bus."

© H. J. de Blij

■ **Figure 5.3**
**Darwin, Australia.**

## Race and Ethnicity in the United States

Unlike a local culture or ethnicity to which we may choose to belong, race is an identity that is more often assigned. In the words of geographer Benjamin Forest (2001): "In many respects, racial identity is not a self-consciously constructed collection of characteristics, but a condition which is imposed by a set of external social and historical constraints." In the United States, racial categories are reinforced through residential segregation, racialized divisions of labor, and the categories of races recorded by the United States Census Bureau and other government and nongovernmental agencies.

Definitions of race in the United States historically focused on dividing the country into "white" and "nonwhite." Our understanding of race has changed over time, but those in the public eye, whether golfer Tiger Woods or President Barack Obama, are still asked to explain their racial identity (Figure 5.4). Governments have also determined racial identities, especially during the 20th century

William Thomas Cain/Getty Images

■ **Figure 5.4**
**President Barack Obama.** In March 2008, running for his first term as president, Obama addressed the issue of his racial identity by explaining, "I am the son of a black man from Kenya and a white woman from Kansas.... I am married to a black American who carries within her the blood of slaves and slaveowners—an inheritance we pass on to our two precious daughters." He described his far-flung family as being made of "every hue" and "scattered across three continents."

when several countries limited immigration to those who were "white." In the early 1900s, immigration to the United States shifted from northern and western Europe to southern and eastern Europe and the United States government redefined what constituted "white" so that people with olive-colored skin from the Mediterranean would count as "white."

As a result of immigration and differences in fertility rates, the United States is becoming increasingly racially diverse (Table 5.1). At the same time, how Americans define "race" is changing. Before 2000, the United States Census classified "Hispanic" as a race. This categorization was chosen because people in Latin America, as in North America, represent different races. Before the 2000 census, a white person from Venezuela, a black person from Brazil, and a native person from Bolivia were all classified as "Hispanic." This example demonstrates the arbitrary nature of racial and ethnic classifications. In this example, coming from Latin America "trumped" all other identities, and the person was defined as "Hispanic." In 2000, the Census recognized that Hispanic is not a race and that it is better defined as an ethnicity. However, the word "Hispanic" means coming from a country where Spanish is the predominant language, including Spain, Mexico, and many countries in Central and South America and the Caribbean. In our example above, the black person from Brazil who was classified as "Hispanic" should not have been under this definition. The predominant language in Brazil is Portuguese, not Spanish.

Because of the redesignation of "Hispanic" as an ethnicity, in the boxes provided by the United States Census Bureau a person can now be "White, non-Hispanic," "White, Hispanic," "Black, non-Hispanic," "Black, Hispanic," and so forth.

In 2010, the United States Census recognized that "Hispanic" excludes people from Latin America who are not native Spanish speakers. The Census also recognized that some people, including United States Supreme Court Justice Sonia Sotomayor, prefer the term *Latina* or *Latino* to *Hispanic*. In 2010, the United States Census Bureau described the Hispanic ethnicity as "Hispanic, Latino, or Spanish origin," and continued to list Hispanic as an ethnicity and not a race.

With the evolution in understanding of race and ethnicity, it is sometimes difficult to choose the right term to describe an individual or group of people. In this chapter and in the rest of the textbook, we use the most precise

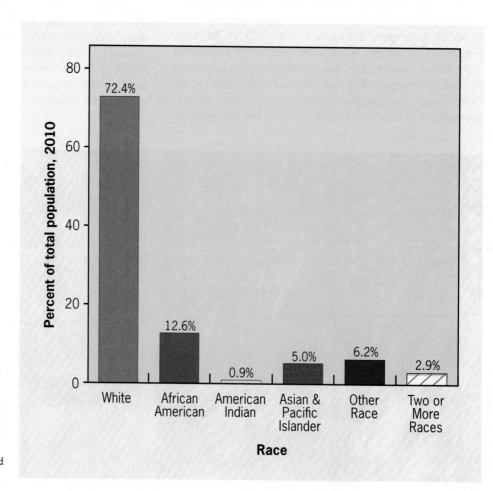

**TABLE 5.1**

**Population of the United States by Race, 2010.**   In 2000 and in 2010, the United States Census Bureau, for the first time, allowed Americans to categorize themselves as one race or more than one race. The "two or more races" self-designation is projected to grow in the decades ahead.   *Data from*: United States Census Bureau, 2010.

description possible. Instead of a generic term like *Hispanic*, if we are talking about a group of immigrants from Bolivia, we call them immigrants from Bolivia. If we discuss a study about Cree Indians in Canada, we describe the Cree tribe, not a generic term such as First Nations. In general references, we use the term *Hispanic* instead of *Latino* or *Latina* in accordance with the results of a 2013 Pew Research survey. This survey of Americans who defined themselves as Hispanic or Latino reported that "half (50%) say they have no preference for either term. But among those who *do* have a preference, 'Hispanic' is preferred over 'Latino' by a ratio of about 2 to 1."

In the United States, 64 percent of the Hispanic population is of Mexican origin, and 9 percent of people who define themselves as Hispanic are of Puerto Rican descent. In the 2000 and 2010 censuses, all persons who defined themselves as Hispanic also defined themselves by a racial category. By combining race and ethnicity boxes, statisticians can still separate the American population into "White, non-Hispanic" and "everyone else." According to the data projections provided after the 2010 Census, the population of "everyone else" will surpass (in numbers) the "White, non-Hispanic" population around 2042 (Table 5.2).

## Residential Segregation

Racism has affected the distribution of African Americans, American Indians, and others throughout the history of the United States. During the past century, some of the most dramatic geographic impacts of racism could be found at the neighborhood scale. Historically, states, cities, and towns passed laws that promoted residential segregation by disallowing the migration of certain racial groups into particular neighborhoods. Laws passed during and after the civil rights movement of the 1960s in the United States made it illegal to legislate residential segregation. Despite these changes, many cities in the United States remain strongly segregated along racial lines.

Geographers Douglas Massey and Nancy Denton defined **residential segregation** as the "degree to which two or more groups live separately from one another, in different parts of the urban environment." Massey and Denton defined different kinds of residential segregation in a 1988 article, explaining that residential segregation is complex because:

*groups may live apart from one another and be "segregated" in a variety of ways. Minority members may be distributed*

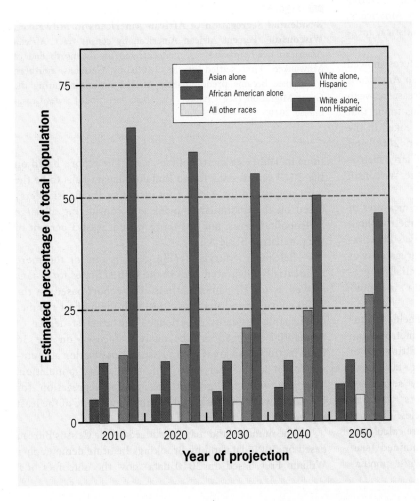

**TABLE 5.2**

**Estimated Percentage of United States Population by Race and Ethnicity Until 2050.** In 2000, the United States Census Bureau began to calculate race and Hispanic origin separately, allowing people to place themselves in one or more race categories plus one of two Hispanic origin categories (Hispanic or Non-Hispanic). According to the race categories provided in the 2010 census estimates, starting in 2042, the "White, non-Hispanic" population will no longer be the majority population in the United States. *Data from:* United States Census, 2010.

*so that they are overrepresented in some areas and under-represented in others, varying on the characteristic of even-ness. They may be distributed so that their exposure to majority members is limited by virtue of rarely sharing a neighborhood with them. They may be spatially* concen-trated *within a very small area, occupying less physical space than majority members. They may be spatially* cen-tralized, *congregating around the urban core, and occupy-ing a more central location than the majority. Finally, areas of minority settlement may be tightly* clustered *to form one large contiguous enclave, or be scattered widely around the urban area.*

A special report issued by the United States Census Bureau in 2002 statistically analyzed, charted, and mapped residential segregation in metropolitan areas of the country, using the following five statistical measurements of segrega-tion: evenness, exposure, concentrated, centralized, and clus-tered. These five measurements directly correspond to the five types of segregation outlined by Massey and Denton.

In the 2002 Census Bureau report, the authors reported on the levels of residential segregation in metropolitan areas of the United States between 1980 and 2000. They found that overall residential segregation by race/ethnicity is on the decline. For each of the four identities they researched—American Indians and Alaska Natives; Asians, Native Hawaiians, and Pacific Islanders; Black/African Americans; and Hispanics/Latinos—they calculated five statistical mea-sures of residential segregation.

The researchers reported that all five measures showed a decrease in residential segregation for African Americans between 1980 and 1990 and another such decrease between 1990 and 2000. A report after the 2010 census found that residential segregation for African Americans peaked in the 1960s and 1970s and declined again between 2000 and 2010. In 2010, the most residentially segregated large metro-politan area for African Americans was Milwaukee, Wisconsin (Fig. 5.5).

In 2000, when using an average of all five measures of segregation, the most residentially segregated metropolitan area for American Indians and Alaska Natives was Phoenix-Mesa, Arizona, and the least residentially segregated was Oklahoma City. In 2000, the four least residentially segre-gated metropolitan areas (with at least 3 percent of the popu-lation American Indian) were all in Oklahoma.

Grouping Asians, Native Hawaiians, and Pacific Island-ers, researchers of the 2000 report found 30 metropolitan areas with at least 3 percent of the population fitting one of these identities. Based on calculations for all five statistics of residential segregation, the most residentially segregated metropolitan area for Asians/Pacific Islanders was San Francisco, followed by New York and Los Angeles. The data and maps change depending on how statistics are calculated. A report that appeared after the 2010 census examined Asian segregation using a dissimilarity index with white popula-

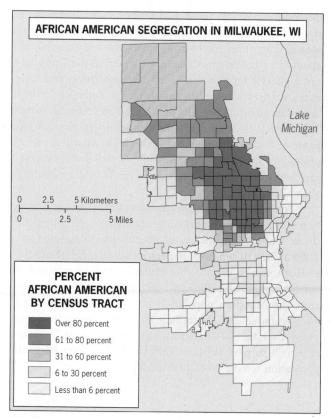

**■ Figure 5.5**

**Residential Segregation of African Americans in Milwaukee, Wisconsin.**   Percent African American by census tract. African American neighborhoods are concentrated on the north end of Milwaukee. First settled in the 1800s by Germans, northern Milwaukee became predominantly African American during the Great Migration (see Chapter 3).   *Data from:* United States Census Bureau, 2010.

tions in 102 large metropolitan areas. The report, based on the 2010 census data, found Buffalo/Niagara Falls to be the most segregated for Asians (not including Pacific Islanders) based on the dissimilarity index and considering all large metropolitan areas, not just those with at least 3 percent of the population being Asian.

Baltimore, Maryland (Fig. 5.6) is one of the more residentially integrated cites in the United States for Asians as well as for Hispanics/Latinos. The report based on the 2000 census found that the cities with the highest number of Hispanic residents experienced the greatest degree of residential segregation. The analysis focused on the 36 large metropolitan areas with a Hispanic population account-ing for at least 3 percent of the total urban population. The city with the greatest residential segregation for Hispanics was New York, and Baltimore was one of the least segregated.

The numbers and maps produced by the Census Bureau based on 2000 data and by Brookings Institute demographer William Frey based on 2010 data show the outcomes of a

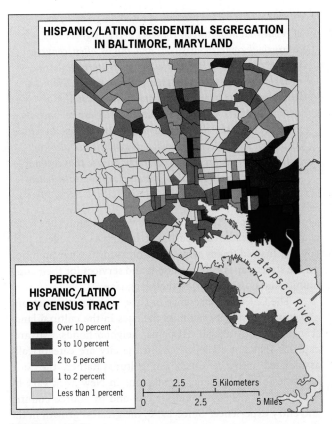

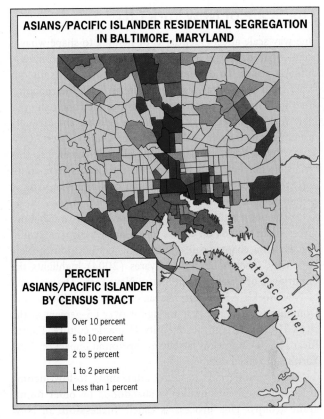

**■ Figure 5.6**
**Residential Segregation of Latinos and Asians/Pacific Islanders in Baltimore, Maryland.**   Baltimore, Maryland, is one of the least segregated cities for Hispanics and Asians/Pacific Islanders. The Hispanic population is distributed throughout the city with some neighborhoods standing out as strongly Hispanic. The City of Baltimore began encouraging immigrants to settle in the city in 2012 in hopes to grow the population by 10,000 families. If the program is successful, by the 2020 census, the proportion of Hispanics in the city will increase, and the pattern and neighborhood concentration may change.   *Data from:* United States Census Bureau, 2010.

variety of stories, but they do not tell us the stories that created these patterns. Why does residential segregation persist in some places and not in others? In some of the most segregated cities, people know where the "Other" lives and will purposely choose to live in neighborhoods with people like themselves. Real estate agents and community leaders may consciously or subconsciously direct people to their "own" neighborhoods (blockbusting and redlining are discussed in Chapter 9). In almost all cities, race is related to class, making it difficult to afford a higher-class neighborhood that is also populated by another race. In other cities, residents may choose to live in a blighted neighborhood because it is their neighborhood, one they have helped create and that reflects their culture.

## Identities Across Scales

The way we make sense of ourselves in an increasingly globalized world is complex. We have different identities at different scales: individual, local, regional, national, and global.

At the individual scale, we may see ourselves as a daughter, a sister, a golfer, or a student. At the local scale, we may see ourselves as members of a community, leaders of a campus organization, or residents of a neighborhood. At the regional scale, we may see ourselves as Southerners, as north Georgians, as Atlantans, as Yankees living in the South, or as migrants from another region of the world. At the national scale, we may see ourselves as American, as college students, or as members of a national political party. At the global scale, we may see ourselves as Western, as educated, as relatively wealthy, or as free.

One way to view an individual's various identities is to treat them as nested, one inside of the other; the appropriate identity is revealed at the appropriate scale. In this vein, each larger territorial extent of geographic space has its own corresponding set of identities. Today, more geographers see identities as fluid, intertwined, and context dependent rather than as neatly nested. Identities affect each other in and across scales, and the ways places and peoples interact across scales simultaneously affect identities within and across scales.

## The Scale of New York City

One way scale affects identity is by helping to shape what is seen—what identity is apparent to others and to ourselves at different scales. To demonstrate this idea, we can shift our focus from residential segregation in all large metropolitan areas in North America to one enormous metropolitan area, New York City. New York has a greater number and diversity of immigrants than any other city in the United States. At the scale of New York, we can see how identities change so that we are no longer simply Hispanic (as the Census enumerates us); we are Puerto Rican or Mexican or Dominican from a certain neighborhood.

The point is that the people in New York are much more diverse than the box on census forms labeled Hispanic would suggest. In a chapter called "Changing Latinization of New York City," geographer Inés Miyares (2004) highlights the importance of Caribbean culture to New York. The majority of New York's 2.3 million Hispanics are Puerto Ricans and Dominicans (together accounting for over 65 percent of the city's Hispanics). As the majority Hispanic culture, Puerto Ricans and Dominicans have had a profound impact on New York's cultural landscape.

New immigrants to a city often move to low-income areas that are being gradually abandoned by older immigrant groups. This process is called **succession**. In New York, Puerto Ricans moved into the immigrant Jewish neighborhood of East Harlem in the early twentieth century, successively assuming a dominant presence in the neighborhood. With the influx of Puerto Ricans, new names for the neighborhood developed, and today it is frequently called Spanish Harlem or El Barrio (meaning "neighborhood" in Spanish). As the Puerto Rican population grew, new storefronts appeared, catering to the Puerto Rican population, including travel agencies (specializing in flights to Puerto Rico), specialty grocery stores, and dance and music studios.

Similar to the immigrant flow from Puerto Rico, the large-scale immigrant flow from the Dominican Republic that began in 1965 resulted in a distinct neighborhood and cultural landscape. Dominican immigrants landed in the Washington Heights/Inwood neighborhood of upper Manhattan, a neighborhood previously occupied by immigrant Jews, African Americans, Puerto Ricans, and Cubans. Miyares reports that although a Jewish cultural landscape persists, including a Jewish university, synagogues, and Jewish delicatessens, the cultural landscape of Washington Heights is clearly Dominican—from store signs in Spanish to the presence of the colors of the Dominican flag (Fig. 5.7).

New York is unique because of the sheer number and diversity of its immigrant population. The city's cultural landscape reflects its unique population. As Miyares explains:

*Since the overwhelming majority of New York City's population lives in apartments as opposed to houses, it is often difficult to discern the presence of an ethnic group by looking at residential housescapes. However every neighborhood has a principal commercial street, and this is often converted into an ethnic main street. It is commonly through business signs that immigrants make their presence known. Names of businesses reflect place names from the home country or key cultural artifacts. Colors of the national flag are common in store awnings, and the flags themselves and national crests abound in store décor. Key religious symbols are also common. Immigrants are so prevalent and diverse that coethnic proprietors use many kinds of visual clues to attract potential customers.*

Throughout the process, new immigrants need not change the facades of apartment buildings to reflect their culture. Instead, many new immigrants focus their attention on the streetscapes, offering goods and services for their community and posting signs in their language.

The Caribbean presence in New York City is so strong a visitor or resident may miss the cues in the cultural landscape that distinguish Hispanic neighborhoods. Miyares explains that not all Hispanics in the city are categorically assimilated into the Caribbean culture. Rather, the local identities of the Hispanic populations in New York vary by "borough, by neighborhood, by era, and by source country and entry experience." Since 1990, the greatest growth in the Hispanic population of New York has been Mexican. Mexican migrants have settled in a variety of ethnic neighborhoods, living alongside new Chinese immigrants in Brooklyn and Puerto Ricans in East Harlem. The process of succession continues in New York, with Mexican immigrants moving into and succeeding other Hispanic neighborhoods, sometimes producing tensions between and among the local cultures.

In New York and in specific neighborhoods like East Harlem, the word "Hispanic" does little to explain the diversity of the city. At these scales, different identities are claimed and assigned, identities that reflect local cultures and neighborhoods. The overarching category "Hispanic" tells us even less about diversity when one moves up the scale to the United States, but as long as that category persists in the Census, people will be encouraged to think about it as a meaningful basis for understanding social differences.

 Recall the last time you were asked to check a box for your race. Does that box factor into how you make sense of yourself individually, locally, regionally, nationally, and globally? What impact might it have on how other people view you?

# GUEST FIELD NOTE

## Washington Heights, New York

It is a warm, humid September morning, and the shops along Juan Pablo Duarte Boulevard are already bustling with customers. The Dominican flag waves proudly from each corner's traffic signal. Calypso and salsa music ring through the air, as do the voices of Dominican grandmothers negotiating for the best prices on fresh mangos and papayas. The scents of fresh *empanadas de yuca* and *pastelitos de pollo* waft from street vendor carts. The signage, the music, the language of the street are all in Spanish and call out to this Dominican community. I am not in Santo Domingo but in Washington Heights in upper Manhattan in New York City.

Whenever I exit the "A" train at 181st Street and walk toward St. Nicholas Avenue, renamed here Juan Pablo Duarte Boulevard for the founding father of the Dominican Republic, it is as if I have boarded a plane to the island. Although there are Dominicans living in most neighborhoods of New York's five boroughs, Washington Heights serves as the heart and soul of the community. Dominicans began settling in Washington Heights in 1965, replacing previous Jewish, African American, and Cuban residents through processes of invasion and succession. Over the past 40 years they have established a vibrant social and economic enclave that is replenished daily by transnational connections to the residents' homeland. These transnational links are pervasive on the landscape, and include travel agencies advertising daily flights to Santo Domingo and Puerto Plata and stores

Courtesy of Inés Miyares, Hunter College of the City University of New York

■ **Figure 5.7**

handling *cargas, envios,* and *remesas* (material and financial remittances) found on every block, as well as *farmacias* (pharmacies) selling traditional medicines and *botanicas* selling candles, statues, and other elements needed by practitioners of Santería, a syncretistic blending of Catholicism and Yoruba beliefs practiced by many in the Spanish Caribbean.

*Credit: Inés Miyares, Hunter College of the City University of New York.*

## HOW DO PLACES AFFECT IDENTITY, AND HOW CAN WE SEE IDENTITIES IN PLACES?

The processes of constructing identities and identifying against an "Other," just like any other social or cultural process, differ from place to place and are rooted in places. When we construct identities, part of what we do is infuse place with meaning by attaching memories and experiences to it. This process of infusing a place "with meaning and feeling" is what Gillian Rose and countless other geographers refer to as "developing a sense of place." Like identity, our **sense of place** is fluid; it changes as the place changes and as we change.

Of particular interest to geographers is how people define themselves through places. Our sense of place becomes part of our identity, and our identity affects the ways we define and experience place. Rose (1995) explains:

*One way in which identity is connected to a particular place is by a feeling that you belong to that place. It's a place in which you feel comfortable, or at home, because part of how you define yourself is symbolized by certain qualities of that place. The geographer Relph, for example, has even gone so far as to claim that "to be human is to live in a world that is filled with significant places: to be human is to have to know your place."*

The uniqueness of a place can become a part of who we are.

■ **Figure 5.8**
**New Glarus, Wisconsin.** Immigrants from Switzerland established the town of New Glarus in 1845. The Swiss American town takes pride in its history and culture, as the flags at the New Glarus Hotel Restaurant demonstrate.

© Don Smetzer/Alamy

## Ethnicity and Place

Ethnicity offers a good example of how identities affect places and how places affect identities. The idea of **ethnicity** as an identity stems from the notion that people are closely bounded, even related, in a certain place over time. The word "ethnic" comes from the ancient Greek word *ethnos*, meaning "people" or "nation." Geographer Stuart Hall (1995) explains, "Where people share not only a culture but an ethnos, their belongingness or binding into group and place, and their sense of cultural identity, are very strongly defined." Hall makes clear that ethnic identity is "historically constructed like all cultural identities" and is often considered natural because it implies ancient relations among a people over time.

This definition may sound simple, but the concept of ethnicity is not. In the United States, for example, a group of people may define their ethnicity as Swiss American. Switzerland is a state in Europe. The people in Switzerland speak four major languages and other minor ones. The strongest identities in Switzerland are most often at the canton level—a small geographically defined area that distinguishes cultural groups within the state. So, which Swiss are Swiss Americans? The way Swiss Americans see Switzerland as part of who they are may not exist in Switzerland proper (Fig. 5.8). Ethnicity sways and shifts across scales, across places, and across time. A map showing all recognizable ethnic areas would look like a three-dimensional jigsaw puzzle with thousands of often-overlapping pieces—some no larger than a neighborhood, others as large as entire countries.

Ethnic identity is greatly affected by scale and place. In 2002, the *Washington Post* reported on the thriving South Asian community in Fairfax County, Virginia, a suburb of Washington, D.C. In South Asia, the countries of Pakistan and India have a history of animosity, and people identify themselves by country within the region of South Asia and by areas within each country. However, in Fairfax County, Virginia, a world apart from India and Pakistan, many South Asians identify with each other. A South Asian video rental store rents both Pakistani and Indian movies. South Asian grocery stores carry foods from both countries and areas within the countries. The geographical context of suburban Washington, D.C., fosters a collective South Asian identity.

Cultural groups often invoke ethnicity when race cannot explain differences and antagonism between groups. Just as "racial conflicts" are rooted in perceptions of distinctiveness based on differences in economics, power, language, religion, lifestyle, or historical experience, so too are "ethnic conflicts." A conflict is often called ethnic when a racial distinction cannot easily be made. For example, using physical appearance and skin color, an observer cannot distinguish the ethnic groups in many of the conflicts around the world. The adversaries in post–World War II conflicts in Northern Ireland, Spain, the former Yugoslavia, Sri Lanka, Ivory Coast, or Rwanda cannot be identified racially; thus "ethnicity" becomes the marker of difference.

In some instances, the term *ethnicity* is reserved for a small, cohesive, culturally linked group of people who stand apart from the surrounding culture (often as a result of migration). Like other aspects of culture, ethnicity is a dynamic phenomenon that must be understood in terms of the geographic context and scales in which it is situated.

### CHINATOWN IN MEXICALI

The border region between the United States and Mexico is generally seen as a cultural meeting point between Mexicans and Anglo Americans. Yet the ethnic composition of people in the border region is more varied than Mexican and Anglo.

Through migration, people from Germany, Russia, India, China, Japan, and many other places also live in the cities and rural areas of the United States–Mexico border region. Over time some of the migrants to this region have blended into the larger community, and others have created distinct patterns of settlement and ethnically imprinted cultural landscapes.

The town of Mexicali is the capital of the State of Baja California (located in Mexico, just south of the State of California in the United States). Not far from the central business district of Mexicali lies one of the largest Chinatowns in Mexico. A 1995 study of the Mexicali Chinatown by geographer James R. Curtis showed that it has been the crucible of Chinese ethnicity in the Mexicali Valley throughout much of the twentieth century. Chinese began arriving in 1902, brought there by the Colorado River Land Company, which started growing cotton in Mexicali when diversion of the Colorado River brought water to irrigate fields in the area. Chinese settled the town of Mexicali, and by 1919 more than 11,000 Chinese were either permanent or temporary residents of the valley. They established a thriving Chinatown in the heart of Mexicali that served as the uncontested center of Chinese life in the region for decades (Fig. 5.9).

Mexicans migrated into Mexicali over time, but the Chinese of Mexicali remained prominent players in the social and economic life of the city during the twentieth century. Chinese owned and operated restaurants, bars, retail trade establishments, commercial land developments, currency exchanges, and more. By 1989, Chinese owned nearly 500 commercial or service properties. In an effort to sustain their cultural traditions and add to the cultural life of the city, they established the China Association, which plays an active role in Mexicali's social and civic life.

Mexicali's Chinatown is experiencing a transformation, as Chinese residents have dispersed to the edges of the city and beyond (many because they can afford to move out of town now). Relatively few Chinese continue to live in the city's Chinatown; some have even moved across the border to Calexico (a city of 27,000 on the California side of the border), while retaining business interests in Mexicali. Yet Mexicali's Chinatown continues to play an important symbolic and functional role for individuals of Chinese ancestry in the area, who are still shaping the region's social and economic geography. Even if the ethnic population in a region is small, ethnic-group identity and consciousness can have a lasting effect on the cultural landscape.

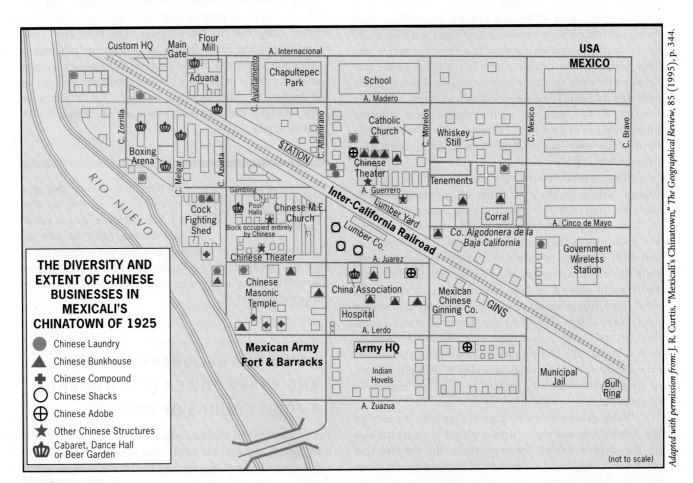

Adapted with permission from: J. R. Curtis, "Mexicali's Chinatown," *The Geographical Review*, 85 (1995), p. 344.

◼ **Figure 5.9**

**Chinatown in Mexicali, Mexico.**   The diversity and extent of Chinese businesses in Mexicali's Chinatown of 1925 is shown in this map. The city still has over 100 Chinese restaurants today.

## Identity and Space

One way of thinking about place is to consider it as a cross section of space. Doreen Massey and Pat Jess (1995) define **space** as "social relations stretched out" and **place** as "particular articulations of those social relations as they have come together, over time, in that particular location." Part of the social relations of a place are the embedded assumptions about ethnicity, gender, and sexuality, regarding what certain groups "should" and "should not" do socially, economically, politically, even domestically. Geographers who study identities, gender, ethnicity, race, and sexuality, realize that when people make places, they do so in the context of surrounding social relationships. We can, for example, create places that are **gendered**—places seen as being appropriate for women or for men. A building can be constructed with the goal of creating gendered spaces within it, or a building can become gendered by the way people make use of it.

### SEXUALITY AND SPACE

Sexuality is part of humanity. Just as gender roles are culturally constructed, so too do cultures decide sexual norms. In their installment on "Sexuality and Space" in *Geography in America at the Dawn of the 21st Century*, geographers Glen Elder, Lawrence Knopp, and Heidi Nast argue that most social science across disciplines is written in a heteronormative way. This means that the default subject in the minds of the academics who write studies is heterosexual—and usually white and male as well. These geographers and many others are working to find out how heternormative ideas influence understandings of places and cultures, and how the practices of peoples who do not conform to these ideas influence the development of places.

Geographers' initial forays into the study of sexuality focused largely on the same kinds of questions posed by those who first took up the study of race, gender, and ethnicity. Geographers ask where people with shared identity live and gather, what they do to create a space for themselves, and what kinds of problems they confront. For example, early studies examining gay neighborhoods in San Francisco and London focused on how gay men created spaces and what those spaces meant to gay identities. Specific studies have looked at the role of gay pride parades in creating communities and the political struggle for access to other parades such as St. Patrick's Day parades in some cities. Other studies examine the role gays and lesbians play in the gentrification of neighborhoods in city centers (a topic we explore in Chapter 9).

Today, geographers studying sexuality focus not only on the distributions and experiences of people in places but also on the theories behind the experiences, the theories that explain and inform our understanding of sexuality and space. Many of the geographers who study sexuality are employing queer theory in their studies. By using the term **queer theory**, Elder, Knopp, and Nast explain that social scientists (in geography and other disciplines) are appropriating a commonly used word with negative connotations and turning it in a way that "highlights the contextual nature" of opposition to the heteronormative and focuses on the political engagement of queers with the heteronormative. Geographers also concentrate on extending fieldwork on sexuality and space beyond the Western world of North America and Europe to the rest of the world, exploring and explaining the local contexts of political engagement.

In 2000, the United States Census Bureau began counting the number of same-sex households in the United States. In 2010, the Census added same-sex marriage to their counts. These data, by census tract—a small area in cities and a larger area in rural America—made it possible for Gary Gates and Jason Ost to publish *The Gay and Lesbian Atlas*. Their detailed maps of major cities in the United States show concentrations of same-sex households in certain neighborhoods of cities (Fig. 5.10), such as Adams-Morgan and DuPont Circle in Washington, D.C., and the West Village and Chelsea in Manhattan (Fig. 5.11).

Demographer Gary Gates analyzed the geography of same-sex couples in the United States after the 2010 Census. He found a changing pattern, as cities with well-established gay and lesbian neighborhoods fell in the rankings of the proportion of same-sex couples, and retirement communities and smaller cities rose in the rankings. The *New York Times* reported that San Francisco fell to 28th in the rankings of communities with the top proportions of same-sex couples. Same-sex couples in the baby boomer generation are retiring and moving to cities including Rehoboth Beach, Delaware, Palm Springs, California, and Provincetown, Massachusetts (ranked number 1).

**thinking** *geographically*   In the 2010 census, the government tallied the number of *households* where a same-sex couple (with or without children) lived. Study the map of same-sex households in New York by census tract in Figure 5.10. How would the map change if sexuality were one of the "boxes" *every* person filled out on the census?

## HOW DOES GEOGRAPHY REFLECT AND SHAPE POWER RELATIONSHIPS AMONG GROUPS OF PEOPLE?

Power relationships are assumptions and structures about who is in control and who has power over others. Power relationships affect identities directly, and the nature of those effects depends on the geographical context in which they are situated. Power relationships also affect cultural landscapes by determining what is seen and what is not. Massey and Jess (1995)

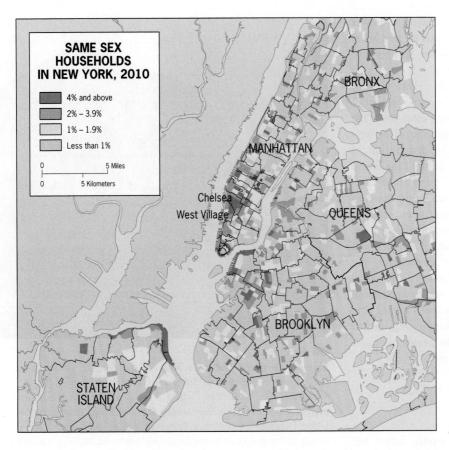

SAME SEX
HOUSEHOLDS
IN NEW YORK, 2010

- 4% and above
- 2% – 3.9%
- 1% – 1.9%
- Less than 1%

0 ——— 5 Miles
0 ——— 5 Kilometers

**▉▉ Figure 5.10**
**Same-Sex Households in New York, 2010.**
The map shows the concentrations of same-sex households in New York, by census tract. Chelsea and West Village, both on the west side of lower Manhattan, stand out as having a large concentration of same sex households.  *Data from*: United States Census Bureau, 2010.

# FIELD NOTE

"It's July 26, 2011, and I happen to be in New York City the weekend just after the State of New York legalized same-sex marriages. I cut it close getting to the airport so I could catch the first part of the annual Gay Pride parade. The parade, which started on the edge of the Chelsea neighborhood at 36th Street, traveled down 5th Avenue toward where I took this photograph near Union Square, and ended in the West Village. Always a boisterous, celebratory event, the parade has a special feel this year as celebrants cheer what many describe as one of the great civil rights victories of the current era."

© Alexander B. Murphy

**▉▉ Figure 5.11**
**New York, New York.**

contend that power is central to the study of place, as power controls "the contest over how the place should be seen, what meaning to give it" and power constructs the "imaginative geography, the identities of place and culture."

Power relationships do much more than shape the cultural landscape. Power relationships can also subjugate entire groups of people, enabling society to enforce ideas about the ways people should behave or where people should be welcomed or turned away—thus altering the distribution of peoples. Policies created by governments can limit the access of certain groups. Jim Crow laws in the United States once separated "black" spaces from "white" spaces, right down to public drinking fountains. Even without government support, people create places where they limit the access of other peoples. For example, in Belfast, Northern Ireland, Catholics and Protestants defined certain neighborhoods as excluding the "other" through painting murals, hanging bunting, and painting curbs (Fig. 5.12). In major cities in the United States, local governments do not create or enforce laws defining certain spaces as belonging to members of a certain gang, but the people themselves create these spaces, as the people of Belfast do, through graffiti, murals, and building colors.

## Just Who Counts?

The statistics governments collect and report reflect the power relationships involved in defining what is valued and what is not. Think back to the Constitution of the United States prior to the Fourteenth Amendment, when the government enumerated a black person as three-fifths of a white person. Until 1924, the U.S. government did not recognize the right of all American Indians to vote even though the Fifteenth Amendment guaranteed the right to vote regardless of race in 1870. The U.S. government separated American Indians into those who were "civilized" enough to be citizens and those who were not ("Indians not taxed") until 1924, when it recognized the citizenship of all American Indians born in the United States. In 1920, enough states finally ratified the Nineteenth Amendment to the Constitution, which extended voting rights regardless of sex, to allow women to vote. Despite progress in counting people of all races, ethnicities, and sex, some charge that the United States Census Bureau continues to undercount minority populations (see Chapter 2).

Throughout the world, the work of women is often undervalued and uncounted. When the United States and other state governments began to count the value of goods and services produced within state borders, they did so with the assumption that the work of the household is reserved for women and that this work does not contribute to the productivity of the state's economy. The most commonly used statistic on productivity, the gross national income (the monetary worth of what is produced within a country plus income received from investments outside the country), does not include work in the home. The gross national income (GNI) includes neither the unpaid labor of women

© Erin H. Fouberg

**■ Figure 5.12**
**Belfast, Northern Ireland.**   Signs of the conflict in Northern Ireland mark the cultural landscape throughout Belfast. In the Shankhill area of Belfast, where Protestants are the majority population, a mural commemorating Steve McKeag, member of the Ulster Defence Association, a Protestant paramilitary organization, stands in the middle of a residential neighborhood. McKeag is called "Top Gun" for killing 12 Catholics, most of whom were ordinary citizens, in the 1990s. He died in his home of a drug overdose in 2000 at the age of 30.

in the household nor, usually, the work done by rural women in less wealthy countries. GNI counts only the formal economy (what is reported to and taxed by government), not the informal economy (economic activities not counted or taxed by government).

Scholars estimate that if women's productivity in the household alone were given a dollar value by calculating what it would cost to hire people to perform these tasks, the gross national income (GNI) for all countries of the world combined would grow by about one-third. In poorer countries, women produce more than half of all the food; they also build homes, dig wells, plant and harvest crops, make clothes, and do many other things that are not recorded in official statistics as being economically productive because they are in the informal economy (Fig. 5.13).

Despite these conditions, the number of women in the "official" labor force is rising while the proportion of men in the labor force globally declined between 1990 and 2010. In *The World's Women 2010: Trends and Statistics*, the United Nations reported that "women are predominantly and increasingly employed in the services sector" of the formal economy. Combining paid work with work in the informal economy and unpaid domestic work, "women work longer hours than men do." The proportion of women in the labor force grew in all

© Alexander B. Murphy

■ **Figure 5.13**
**South Korea.**   The women in this photo sit near one of the ancient temples in southern Korea, selling the modest output from their own market gardens. This activity is one part of the informal economy, the "uncounted" economy in which women play a large role.

regions reported by the United Nations except Asia and eastern Europe. In South America, for example, the percent of women in the labor force rose from 38 in 1990 to 59 in 2010. In North Africa, the participation of women in the labor force increased from 23 percent in 1990 to 29 percent in 2010, while over the same time period in Subsaharan Africa, women accounted for 60 percent of the labor force.

Even though women are in the official labor force in greater proportions than ever before, they continue to be paid less and have less access to food and education than men in nearly all cultures and places around the world. A 2010 report from the United Nations stated that two-thirds of the 774 million illiterate adults in the world are women and that women account for 60 percent of the world's poorest citizens. The United Nations Development Program reports that "75 percent of the world's women cannot get bank loans because they have unpaid or insecure jobs and are not entitled to property ownership." As a result, women worldwide only own "one percent of the world's wealth."

*The World's Women 2010* reported regional variations in agriculture employment for women. In Africa, for example, the proportion of women employed in agriculture ranges from a low of 19 percent in countries in southern Africa to a high of 68 percent in countries in eastern, middle, and western Africa. In Northern Africa, 42 percent of women are employed in agriculture and 41 percent of women are employed in services. In Asia, employment of women in agriculture ranges from 11 percent in eastern Asia, where 76 percent of women are employed in the service sector, to South Asia, with 55 percent of women working in agriculture and 28 percent in the service sector.

Although the number of women working in industries globally is small relative to the proportion of men, it is rising.

Employment of women in the industrial sector was slowed by the global economic downturn of the 2008, as well as by mechanization, which leads to job reductions and hence to layoffs of women workers. In the maquiladoras of northern Mexico (see Chapter 10), for example, many women workers lost their jobs when labor markets contracted between 2001 and 2002, and then again between 2008 and 2010.

As the foregoing discussion has highlighted, many women engage in informal economic activity—that is, private, often home-based activities, including tailoring, beer brewing, food preparation, and soap making. Women who seek to move beyond subsistence activities but cannot enter the formal economic sector often turn to such work. In the migrant slums on the fringes of many cities, informal economic activity is the mainstay of communities.

Statistics showing how much women produce and how little their work is valued are undoubtedly interesting. Yet, the work geographers who study gender have done goes far beyond the accumulation of data. Since the 1980s, geographers have asked why society talks about women and their roles in certain ways and how these ideas, heard and represented throughout our lives, affect geographic circumstances and how we understand them. For example, Ann Oberhauser (2003) and her co-authors explained that people in the West tend to think that women are employed in the textile and jewelry-making fields in poorer countries because the women in these regions are "more docile, submissive, and tradition bound" than women in more prosperous parts of the world. A geographer studying gender asks where these ideas about women come from and how they influence women's work possibilities and social positions in different places—key elements in making places what they are.

## GUEST FIELD NOTE

One of the leading causes of mortality and morbidity among children under the age of five in developing countries is waterborne disease. My research has focused on building an understanding of the factors that contribute to the vulnerability of young children to this significant public health problem. I have conducted my research in communities located in the relatively remote Karakoram Range of northern Pakistan. Of interest to me is the microenvironment of water-related disease risk, and in particular, the factors at the household and local scale that influence the prevalence and severity of childhood illness. One of the primary methodological strategies that I employ in this research involves household microstudies, which entail in-depth interviews with family members (primarily mothers who are the principal child health providers), child health histories, and structured observations. One of the most important findings of this research in these mountain communities, in my opinion, is that the education, social networks, and empowerment of women are all critical to breaking the cycle of disease impacts and to ensuring long-term child survival.

*Credit: Sarah J. Halvorson, University of Montana*

Sarah J. Halvorson

■ **Figure 5.14**

## Vulnerable Populations

Power relations can have a fundamental impact on which populations or areas are particularly vulnerable to disease, death, injury, or famine. Geographers use mapping and spatial analysis to predict and explain what populations or people will be affected most by natural hazards, including earthquakes, volcanoes, hurricanes, and tsunamis, or by environmental policies. The study of vulnerability requires thinking geographically because social, political, economic, or environmental change does not affect all people and places in the same way. Rather, vulnerability is fundamentally influenced by geographically specific social and environmental circumstances.

Fieldwork is often the best way to understand how power structures in society create vulnerable groups at the local scale and how those vulnerable groups might be affected by particular developments. Through fieldwork and interviews, geographers can see differences in vulnerability within groups of people.

Geographer Sarah Halvorson (2004) studied differences in the vulnerabilities of children in northern Pakistan. She examined the vulnerability of children to diarrheal diseases by paying attention to "constructions of gender, household politics, and gendered relationships that perpetuate inherent inequalities and differences between men and women and within and between social groups."

Halvorson studied 30 families, 15 of whom had a low frequency of diarrhea and dysentery and 15 of whom had a high frequency of these diseases. Through her fieldwork, Halvorson came to understand that several tangible resources, including income and housing, and several intangible resources, such as social status and position within the family structure, all influenced the vulnerability of children to diarrheal diseases in northern Pakistan. Halvorson found that people with higher incomes generally had lower disease rates, but that income was not the only relevant factor (Fig. 5.14). The least vulnerable children and women were those who had higher incomes and an established social network of support. In cases where income was low, if a woman had a strong social network, her children were more likely to be in the low-disease group.

Geographer Joseph Oppong recognized that the spatial analysis of a disease can reveal what populations are most vulnerable in a country. In North America and Europe, HIV/AIDS is much more prevalent among homosexual and bisexual men than among heterosexual men and women. In Subsaharan Africa, women have much higher rates of HIV/AIDS than men. As Oppong (1998) explains, "AIDS as a global problem has unique local expressions that reflect the spatial distribution and social networks of vulnerable social groups."

According to Oppong, in most of Subsaharan Africa, HIV/AIDS rates are highest for women in urban areas and for women who work as sex workers. However, in Ghana, HIV/AIDS rates were lower for women in the urban area of Accra.

Oppong postulates that women in Accra have lower HIV/AIDS rates because they have greater access to health care than women in rural areas. Women in rural areas who were not treated for malaria had higher incidences of HIV/AIDS, according to his research. Oppong also found that women in polygamous relationships in the Muslim part of northern Ghana had lower HIV/AIDS rates. Oppong offers two theories to explain why Muslim women in polygamous relationships had lower HIV/AIDS rates: First, as a matter of cultural practice, most Muslims tend to avoid sexual promiscuity, and second, Muslims in Ghana practice circumcision, which helps lower the rate of HIV/AIDS transmission in that part of the country.

Fieldwork helps geographers apply vulnerability theory to understand how existing spatial structures, power relationships, and social networks affect the susceptibility of people to diseases and other hazards around the world.

## Women in Subsaharan Africa

Migration flows, birth rates, and child mortality rates affect the gender composition of cities, states, and regions. Some regions of the world have become male-dominated, whereas other regions have become female-dominated—at least numerically.

Much of Subsaharan Africa, especially rural areas, is dominated numerically by women. In this region of the world, most rural-to-urban migrants are men. Domosh and Seager (2001) point out that men leave rural areas to work in heavy industry and mines in the cities, "while women are left behind to tend the farms and manage the household economy. Indeed parts of rural South Africa and Zimbabwe have become feminized zones virtually depopulated of men."

In the large region of Subsaharan Africa, women outnumber men in many rural areas. Women in Subsaharan Africa have heavy responsibilities, coupled in many places with few rights and little say (Fig. 5.15). Women produce an estimated 70 percent of the region's food, almost all of it without the aid of modern technology. Their backbreaking hand cultivation of corn and other staples is an endless task. As water supplies decrease, the exhausting walk to the nearest pump gets longer. Firewood is being cut at ever-greater distances from the village, and the task of hauling it home becomes more difficult every year. As men leave for the towns, sometimes to marry other wives and have other children, the women left in the villages often struggle for survival.

Even though a woman in this position becomes the head of a household, if she goes to a bank for a loan she may well be refused; traditional banks throughout much of Africa do not lend money to rural women. Not having heard from her husband for years and having reared her children, she might wish to apply for title to the land she has occupied and farmed for decades, but in many places land titles are not awarded to women.

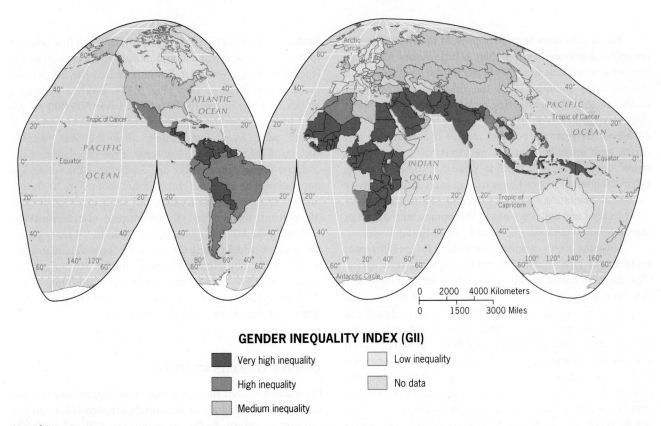

### GENDER INEQUALITY INDEX (GII)

- Very high inequality
- High inequality
- Medium inequality
- Low inequality
- No data

■ **Figure 5.15**

**Gender Inequality Index (GII) 2013.** The GII measures inequality in labor-market participation, access to reproductive health, and empowerment. The GII measures how much achievement is lost by women as a result of inequalities in these three areas. *Data from*: United Nations Development Program, Human Development Report 2013.

# FIELD NOTE

"I am filled with admiration for the women and girls carrying water on their heads up the bank from the Niger River. Other women are at the water's edge, filling their buckets. These women are performing a daily ritual requiring incredible endurance and strength. Once they carry their buckets to their dwellings, they will likely turn to preparing the evening meal."

© Alexander B. Murphy

■■ **Figure 5.16**
**Along the banks of the Niger River just outside Mopti, Mali.**

Young girls soon become trapped in the cycle of female poverty and overwork. Often there is little money for school fees; what is available first goes to pay for the boys. As soon as she can carry anything at all, the girl child goes with her mother to weed the fields, bring back firewood, or fetch water (Fig. 5.16). She will do so for 12 hours a day, 7 days a week, during all the years she remains capable of working. In east Africa, cash crops such as tea are sometimes called "men's crops" because the men trade in what the women produce. When the government of Kenya tried to increase productivity on the tea plantations in the 1970s and 1980s, the government handed out bonuses—not to the women who did all of the work but to the men who owned title to the land!

Since the 1990s, women have lobbied for greater representation in governments in southern and eastern Africa. Uganda was a leader in affirmative action for women by setting up a quota or guarantee that women must hold at least 20 percent of the legislative seats. In South Africa, Apartheid, the systematic oppression of the majority black population by the minority white population, ended in 1994. The South African government established a constitution with universal suffrage (voting rights) in 1997. The constitution does not include an affirmative action policy for women's representation in the parliament. Instead, major political parties, starting with the African National Congress (ANC), reserved a certain percentage of their seats won for women.

Today, the country where women hold the highest proportion of legislative seats is neither Uganda nor South Africa.

Rather, another African country, Rwanda, is the first country in the world where women hold more than 50 percent of the legislative seats. Women in Rwanda passed the 50 percent mark in the 2008 election (Fig. 5.17). Rwanda suffered a bloody civil war in the 1990s in which over 800,000 people died (one-tenth of the population at the time), a majority of whom were men. Immediately after the war, women accounted for more than 70 percent of the population of the country. Today, women make up 55 percent of the voting-age population. The Rwandan constitution, adopted in 2003, recognizes the equality of women and set a quota of at least 30 percent women in all government decision-making bodies. Of the 80 legislative seats in Rwanda, 24 are reserved for women, and in these 24 seats, the only candidates are women and only women can vote. In the 2013 elections, women won 26 seats in the legislature in addition to the 24 seats reserved for women, and now women hold 62.5 percent of the seats in the Rwanda legislature.

## Dowry Deaths in India

On a 2004 *Oprah!* show, the talk show hostess interviewed journalist Lisa Ling about her travels through India and her reports on dowry deaths in India. The Chicago audience looked stunned to discover that thousands of girls in India are still betrothed through arranged marriages and that in some extreme cases, disputes over the dowry, which is the price to be paid by the bride's family to the groom's father, have led to the death of the bride. The bride may be brutally punished, often burned, or killed for her father's failure to fulfill a marriage agreement. Only a small fraction of India's girls are involved in **dowry deaths,** but the practice is not declining. According to the Indian government, in 1985, the number was 999; in 1987, 1786 women died at the hands of vengeful husbands or in-laws; in 1989, 2436 perished; in 2001, more than 7000 women died; and in 2012, it was reported that 8233 women died from dowry deaths. These figures report only confirmed dowry deaths; many more are believed to occur but are reported as suicides, kitchen accidents, or other fatal domestic incidents.

The power relationships that place women below men in India cannot simply be legislated away. Government entities in India (federal as well as State) have set up legal aid offices to help women who fear dowry death and seek assistance. In 1984, the national legislature passed the Family Courts Act, creating a network of "family courts" to hear domestic cases, including dowry disputes. But the judges tend to be older males, and their chief objective, according to women's support groups, is to hold the family together—that is, to force the threatened or battered woman back into the household. Hindu culture attaches great importance to the family structure, and the family courts tend to operate on this principle.

Recognizing that movement away from arranged marriages and dowries among the Indian population is slow in coming, Ling and Oprah took the issue of dowry deaths to the global scale—to generate activism in the West and create change at the local scale in India. Ling explained that the place of women in India has changed little. She described women as a financial burden on the bride's family, who must save for a sizable dowry to marry her off. Ling describes the dowry as a financial transaction; through marriage the burden of the woman moves from the bride's family to her husband's family. Yet Oprah and Ling interviewed a woman in India to show that global change can help make local change possible. Nisha Sharma was to marry in front of 1500 guests in a town just outside of the capital of New Delhi. On her wedding day, the groom's family demanded $25,000 in addition to the numerous luxury items they had already received as dowry (including washing machines, a flat-screen TV, and a car). Nisha's father refused to pay, the man's family became violent, and Nisha called the police on her cell phone. She has become a local hero. Her story also serves as an example of how global technology (in this case a cell phone) can help combat the practice of dowry deaths.

India is starting to see the impact on marriage of its booming economy and growing proportion of educated young women and men in well-paid jobs. The number of love marriages is on the rise (Fig. 5.18), and many couples in love marriages in India are meeting online. The number of divorces is also on the rise, with 1 in 1000 marriages ending in divorce in India today. Although this is one of the lowest divorce rates in the world, it is also double the country's divorce rate five years ago. These changes will not necessarily result in fewer dowry deaths in the short run in India. An article in *The Times of India* in 2010 explained that in the city of Chennai, where the information technology boom is in full swing, police reported a rise in dowry deaths. This rise was likely a result of increasing materialism among the middle class and an accompanying feeling of desperation for more goods and cash, coupled with the fact that many men in less powerful positions have begun to act out violently.

Understanding shifting gender relations and power structures in India is very difficult. Just as some statistics point to an improving place of women in Indian society, other statistics confirm that India still gives preference to males overall. India's 2011 census reported a sex ratio of 940 girls for every 1000 boys, which seems to be an improvement over the 2001 sex ratio of 933 girls for every 1000 boys. However, the sex ratio for children 0 to 6 years in India was at a record low of 914 girls for every 1000 boys in 2011. The 2011 census data surprised many because between 2001 and 2011, while India gained unprecedented economic growth, the number of girls ages 0 to 6 dropped from 927 in 2001 to 914 in 2011. Many pregnant women in India, especially in northern states, undergo gender-determining tests (ultrasound and amniocentesis) and elect to have abortions when the fetus is a girl. Girls who make it to birth may suffer female infanticide as many parents fear the cost of dowries and place little social value on girls.

In India and elsewhere, directing the attention of people in far-flung places to social ills—moving the issues up in scale—has the potential to create change. Yet problems cannot really be solved unless power relations shift at the family, local, regional, and national scales. As the number of women and men in the middle class in urban India continues to rise, love marriages will continue to rise as well. The number of dowry deaths, arranged marriages, and divorces in the country will continue to fluctuate as power relations shift across gender and scales.

## Shifting Power Relations Among Ethnic Groups

In Chapter 4, we discussed local cultures that define themselves ethnically. The presence of local ethnic cultures can be seen in the cultural landscapes of places we discussed in Chapter 4: "Little Sweden" in Kansas and the Italian North End in Boston. In many places, more than one ethnic group lives in a place, creating unique cultural landscapes and revealing how power relations factor into the ways ethnicities are constructed, revised, and solidified, where ethnic groups live, and who is subjugating whom.

Three urban geographers—John Frazier, Florence Margai, and Eugene Tettey-Fio—tracked the flow of people and shifts in power relations among the multiple ethnic groups that have lived in Alameda County, California, in their book *Race and Place: Equity Issues in Urban America*. Alameda County borders San Francisco and includes the cities of

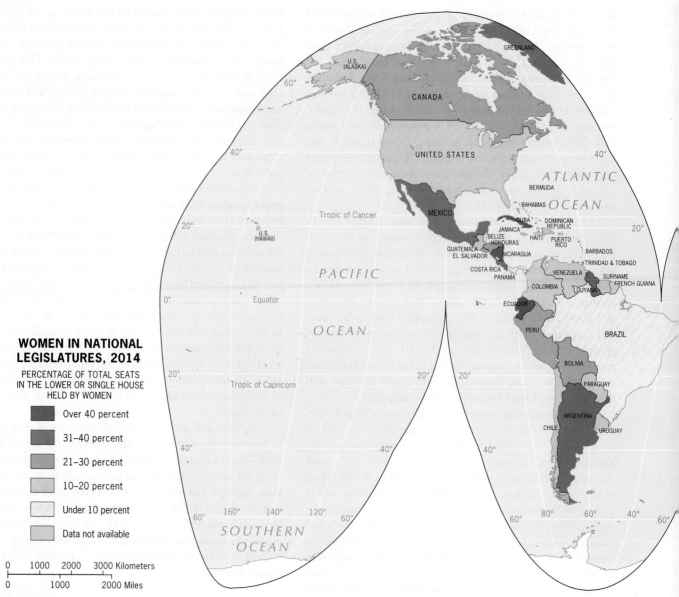

WOMEN IN NATIONAL
LEGISLATURES, 2014

PERCENTAGE OF TOTAL SEATS
IN THE LOWER OR SINGLE HOUSE
HELD BY WOMEN

Over 40 percent

31–40 percent

21–30 percent

10–20 percent

Under 10 percent

Data not available

0    1000    2000    3000 Kilometers

0         1000         2000 Miles

**■  Figure 5.17**

**Women in National Legislatures, 2014.**    Compare and contrast the pattern of the Gender Inequality Index (GII) in Figure 5.15 with this map of Women in National Legislatures. Several countries in Subsaharan Africa are high on the GII but have a large proportion of women in the national legislatures. Countries such as the United States and Australia have low gender inequality, but they do much less well when it comes to female representation in legislative bodies.    *Data from:* www.ipu.org/wmn-e/classif.htm.

Berkeley and Oakland. Latinos populated the region prior to the Gold Rush. After 1850, migrants from China came to the county. The first Asian migrants to the county were widely dispersed, but the first African Americans lived in a segregated section of the county.

Areas with multiple ethnicities often experience an ebb and flow of acceptance over time. When the economy is booming, residents are generally more accepting of each other. When the economy takes a downturn, residents often begin to resent each other and can blame the "Other" for their economic hardship. In Alameda County, much of the population resented Chinese migrants when the economy took a

downturn in the 1870s. The United States government passed the first Chinese Exclusion Act, which prohibited immigration of Chinese in 1882. Chinese exclusion efforts persisted for decades afterward in Alameda County and resulted in the city of Oakland moving Chinatown several times.

During the 1910s, the economy of the region grew again, but the city of Oakland limited the Chinese residents to Chinatown, using ethnic segregation to keep them apart from the rest of the population. Frazier, Margai, and Tettey-Fio (2003) described how the location and homogeneity of Oakland's Chinatown were dictated by law and not matters of choice for the Chinese:

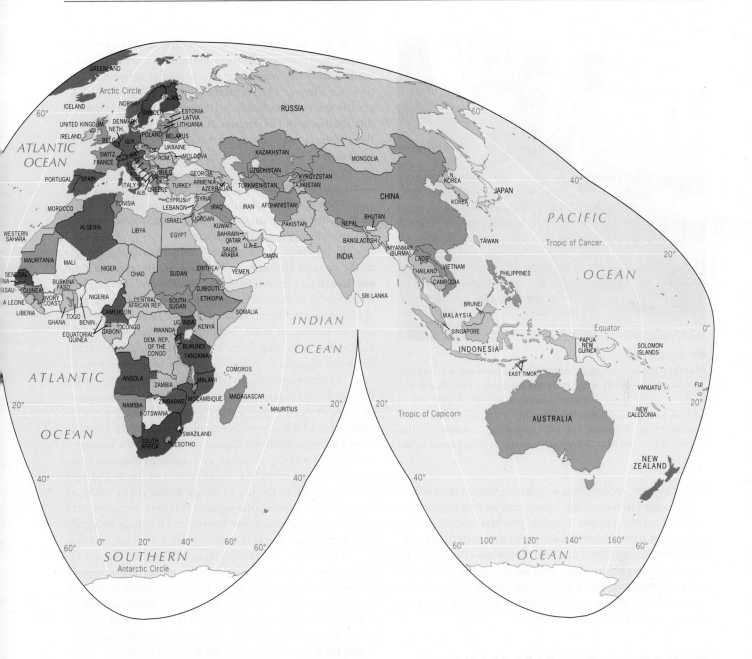

*At a time when the Chinese were benefiting from a better economy, the "whites only" specifications of local zoning and neighborhood regulations forced separatism that segregated the Oakland Chinese into the city's Chinatown. What today is sometimes presented as an example of Chinese unity and choice was, in fact, place dictated by law.*

Chinese were segregated from the rest of Oakland's population until World War II. When the war began, residents of Alameda County, like much of the rest of the United States, focused on the Japanese population in the county, segregating, blaming, and interning them in relocation centers.

After World War II, the ethnic population of Asians in Alameda County became more complex. The Asian population alone doubled in the decade between 1980 and 1990 and diversified to include not only Chinese and Japanese but also Koreans, Vietnamese, Cambodians, and Laotians. In Alameda County today, as in much of the rest of the United States, the first wave of immigrants from Asia (mainly from China, India, and Korea), who came to the region already educated, are not residentially segregated from the white population. However, the newer immigrants from Asia (mainly Southeast Asia—during and following the Vietnam War) are segregated from whites residentially, mixing much more with the African American population in inner-city neighborhoods. Here, Asians experience a high rate of poverty, much as the Hispanic and African American populations in the same regions of the county do.

In California and in much of the rest of the United States, the "Asian" box is drawn around a stereotype of what some call the "model minority." Frazier and his colleagues explain the myth of the model minority: The myth "paints

**◼ Figure 5.18**
**Mumbai, India.**   Arranged marriages were the norm not long ago in India, and the family of the bride was expected to provide a dowry to the groom's family. Arranged marriages are still widespread in parts of rural India, but in urban areas they are rapidly giving way to love marriages following romantic courtships. Evidence of this cultural shift is not hard to find on the streets of India's major cities.

Asians as good, hardworking people who, despite their suffering through discrimination, harassment, and exclusion, have found ways to prosper through peaceful means." Other researchers have debunked the myth by demonstrating statistically the different levels of economic success experienced by various Asian peoples, with most success going to the first wave of migrants and lower-paying jobs going to newer migrants. Both groups are burdened by the myth that stereotypes them as the "model minority."

## POWER RELATIONS IN LOS ANGELES

Over the last four decades, the greatest migration flow into California and the southwestern United States has come from Latin America and the Caribbean, especially Mexico. The 2010 census reported a 43 percent increase in the Hispanic or Latino population of the country. The city of Los Angeles had over 3.79 million people, 48.48 percent of whom were Hispanic. The Hispanic population in the city grew from 39.32 percent of the population in 1990 to 48.48 percent by 2010.

The area of southeastern Los Angeles County is today "home to one of the largest and highest concentrations of Latinos in Southern California," according to a study by geographer James Curtis. Four decades ago, this area of Los Angeles was populated by working-class whites who were segregated from the African American and Hispanic populations through discriminatory policies and practices. Until the 1960s, southeastern Los Angeles was home to corporations

such as General Motors, Bethlehem Steel, and Weiser Lock. During the 1970s and 1980s, corporations began to close as the United States went through a period of deindustrialization (see Chapter 11). As plants shut down and white laborers left the neighborhoods, a Hispanic population migrated into southeastern Los Angeles. A housing crunch followed in the 1980s, as more and more Hispanic migrants headed to southeastern Los Angeles. With a cheap labor supply now readily available in the region again, companies returned to southeastern Los Angeles, this time focusing on smaller-scale production of textiles, pharmaceuticals, furniture, and toys. In addition, the region attracted industrial toxic-waste disposal and petrochemical refining facilities.

In his study of the region, Curtis records the changes to the cultural landscape in the process. He uses the term **barrioization** (derived from the Spanish word for neighborhood, *barrio*) to describe a change that saw the Hispanic population of a neighborhood jump from 4 percent in 1960 to over 90 percent in 2000. With the ethnic succession of the neighborhood moving from white to Hispanic, the cultural landscape changed to reflect the culture of the new population. The structure of the streets and the layout of the housing remained largely the same, giving the Hispanic population access to designated parks, schools, libraries, and community centers built by the previous residents and rarely found in other barrios in Southern California. However, the buildings, signage, and landscape changed as "traditional Hispanic houseescape elements, including the placement of fences and yard shrines as well as the use of bright house colors" diffused through the barrios. Curtis explains that these elements were added to existing structures, houses, and buildings originally built by the white working class of southeastern Los Angeles.

The influx of new ethnic groups into a region, the replacement of one ethnic group by another within neighborhoods, changes to the cultural landscape, the persistence of myths such as the "model minority" myth about Asian Americans, and an economic downturn can create a great deal of volatility in a city.

On April 29–30, 1992, Los Angeles became engulfed in one of the worst incidents of civil unrest in United States history. During two days of rioting 43 people died, 2383 were injured, and 16,291 arrested. Property damage was estimated at approximately $1 billion, and over 22,700 law enforcement personnel were deployed to quell the unrest. According to the media, the main catalyst for the mass upheaval was the announcement of a "not guilty verdict in the trial of four white police officers accused of using excessive force in the arrest of Rodney King, a black motorist." (Johnson et al. 1992, 356). To the general public, the Los Angeles riots became yet another symbol for the sorry state of race relations between blacks and whites in the United States. Yet, a geographic perspective on the Los Angeles riots helps us understand that they were not simply the product of localized reactions to police brutality, but reflected sweeping economic, political, and ethnic changes unfolding at regional and even global scales.

The riots took place in South Central Los Angeles. Like the region of southeast Los Angeles described above, the

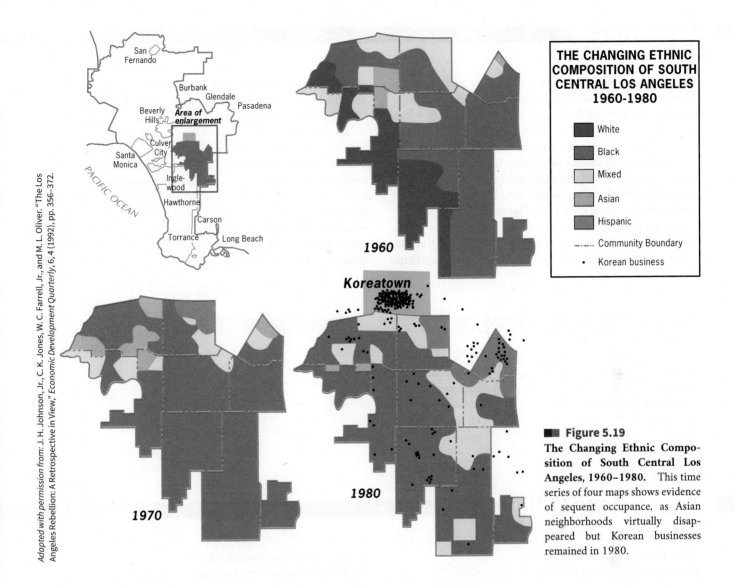

Adapted with permission from: J. H. Johnson, Jr., C. K. Jones, W. C. Farrell, Jr., and M. L. Oliver. "The Los Angeles Rebellion: A Retrospective in View," *Economic Development Quarterly*, 6, 4 (1992), pp. 356–372.

**THE CHANGING ETHNIC COMPOSITION OF SOUTH CENTRAL LOS ANGELES 1960-1980**

- White
- Black
- Mixed
- Asian
- Hispanic
- – – – Community Boundary
- • Korean business

1960

Koreatown

1970

1980

■ **Figure 5.19**
**The Changing Ethnic Composition of South Central Los Angeles, 1960–1980.** This time series of four maps shows evidence of sequent occupance, as Asian neighborhoods virtually disappeared but Korean businesses remained in 1980.

South Central area was once a thriving industrial region with dependable, unionized jobs employing the resident population. By the 1960s, however, the population of South Central Los Angeles was working-class African American, and the population of southeastern Los Angeles was working-class white. After 1970, South Central Los Angeles experienced a substantial decrease in the availability of high-paying, unionized manufacturing jobs when plants closed and relocated outside of the city and even outside the country. The people of South Central Los Angeles lost over 70,000 manufacturing jobs between 1978 and 1982 alone!

Geographer James Johnson and his colleagues explored the impact of economic loss on the ethnic and social geography of South Central Los Angeles. They found that the population of the area was over 90 percent African American in 1970, but by 1990, the population was evenly split between African Americans and Hispanics. This change in population composition was accompanied by a steady influx of Korean residents and small-business owners seeking a niche in the rapidly changing urban area (Fig. 5.19).

Johnson and his colleagues argued that the Los Angeles riots were more than a spontaneous reaction to a verdict. They were rooted in the growing despair and frustration of different ethnic groups competing for a decreasing number of jobs in an environment of declining housing conditions and scarce public resources. At a time when significant unemployment is affecting communities all over the United States, Johnson et al.'s work shows the importance of looking beyond the immediate catalysts of particular news events to the local, national, and global geographical contexts in which they unfold.

**thinking** *geographically*

Geographers who study race, ethnicity, gender, or sexuality are interested in the power relations embedded in a place from which assumptions about "others" are formed or reinforced. Consider your own place, your campus, or your locality. What power relations are embedded in this place?

# Summary

Identity is a powerful concept. The way we make sense of ourselves is a personal journey that is mediated and influenced by the political, social, and cultural contexts in which we live and work. Group identities such as gender, ethnicity, race, and sexuality are constructed, both by self-realization and by identifying against and across scales. When learning about new places and different people, humans are often tempted to put places and people into boxes, into myths or stereotypes that make them easily digestible.

The geographer, especially one who spends time in the field, recognizes that how people shape and create places varies across time and space and that time, space, and place shape people, both individually and in groups. James Curtis ably described the work of a geographer who studies places: "But like the popular images and stereotypical portrayals of all places—whether positive or negative, historical or contemporary—these mask a reality on the ground that is decidedly more complex and dynamic, from both the economic and social perspectives." What Curtis says about places is true about people as well. What we may think to be positive identities, such as the myths of "Orientalism" or of the "model minority," and what we know are negative social ills, such as racism and dowry deaths, are all decidedly more complex and dynamic than they first seem.

# Geographic Concepts

| | | |
|---|---|---|
| gender | residential segregation | place |
| identity | succession | gendered |
| identifying against | sense of place | queer theory |
| race | ethnicity | dowry deaths |
| racism | space | barrioization |

# Learn More Online

About the Gay and Lesbian Atlas
www.urban.org/pubs/gayatlas/

About Racial and Ethnic Segregation in the United States, 1980–2000
www.census.gov/hhes/www/housing/resseg/papertoc.html

About the Murals in Northern Ireland
http://cain.ulst.ac.uk/mccormick/intro.htm

About Society Constructing Gender
www.bbc.com/news/world-europe-24767225

About Gender Composition in India
http://censusmp.gov.in/censusmp/All-PDF/5Gender Composition21.pdf

# Watch It Online

About Ethnicity and the City
www.learner.org/resources/series180.html#program_descriptions
click on Video On Demand for "Boston: Ethnic Mosaic"

About Ethnic Fragmentation in Canada
www.learner.org/resources/series180.html#program_descriptions

click on Video On Demand for "Vancouver: Hong Kong East" and "Montreal: An Island of French"

About Migration and Identity
www.learner.org/resources/series85.html#program_descriptions
click on Video on Demand for "A Migrant's Heart"

# LANGUAGE

## What Should I Say?

In stores throughout Brussels, Belgium, you can see the capital city's bilingualism all around you—literally. From McDonald's to health insurance offices (Fig. 6.1) to the metro, signs in Brussels are posted in duplicate, with one in Flemish (a variant of Dutch) and one in French.

Walking into a travel agency in Brussels one afternoon, I immediately noticed the signs in duplicate: Two signs towered over the woman behind the counter; two signs advertised a new budget airline carrier that would be serving the Brussels airport; two signs labeled the restrooms; and two signs announced the travel agency's hours of operation.

I debated for a minute whether to speak to the person behind the counter in French or Flemish. She was speaking Flemish with the person in front of me, but I decided to use French since my knowledge of that language is better. The student from Italy who stood behind me in line apparently had no such debate. She stepped up to the counter, asked her question in English, and received a reply in excellent English.

© Erin H. Fouberg

■ **Figure 6.1**
**Brussels, Belgium.** A health insurance office in the bilingual capital city of Brussels displays duplicates of each of their posters, one in French and one in Flemish.

Many geographers are initially drawn to the discipline through maps. However, maps, especially at the world or continental scale, generalize so much information that they hide the complexities of everyday life. Once you become a geographer, you begin to question every map you examine. Look at the European map of languages (Fig. 6.2), and zero in on Belgium. The map shows a neat line dividing Flemish speakers (a Germanic language) in the northern region of Flanders from French speakers (a Romance language) in the southern region of Wallonia.

Behind this neat line on the language map is a complicated, at times contentious, linguistic transition zone. To understand language patterns in Belgium, we must also study the issue at the local scale. Although the bilingual capital of Brussels is located in the Flemish-speaking north (Flanders), for upwards of 80 percent of the locals, French is the mother tongue (Fig. 6.3).

**LANGUAGES OF EUROPE**

0 200 400 600 Kilometers
0 100 200 300 Miles

Icelandic

Arctic Circle

*Norwegian Sea*

Saami

Saami

Samoyedic

Karelian

Finnish

Faeroese

ATLANTIC

OCEAN

Scots Gaelic

English

*North Sea*

Norwegian

Swedish

*Baltic Sea*

SWEDISH

Estonian 22

Latvian 22

Lithuanian 22

Russian

Irish Gaelic

English

Welsh

English

Danish

Frisian

Dutch

German

Belarusian 22

Polish

Ukrainian 22

22

22

Breton 14

Alsatian

Czech 37

Slovak 37

37

Hungarian 37

Romanian 42 42

22

French

Provençal

Slovene

16

37

2

26

37

Serbo-Croatian 37

37

Bulgarian 37

*Black Sea*

Galician 11

10

Basque 11

Catalan 11

Catalan

Macedonian

Albanian

Greek

Turkish

Portuguese

Spanish

37

*Mediterranean Sea*

Italian

**Major Indo-European Branches**

Germanic group

WESTERN GERMANIC
1 Dutch
2 German
3 Frisian
4 English

NORTHERN GERMANIC
5 Danish
6 Swedish
7 Norwegian
8 Icelandic
9 Faeroses

Romance group
10 Portuguese
11 Spanish
12 Catalan
13 Provençal
14 French
15 Italian
16 Rhaeto-Romance
17 Romanian

Slavic group

WEST SLAVONIC
18 Polish
19 Slovak
20 Czech
21 Sorbian

EAST SLAVONIC
22 Russian
23 Ukrainian
24 Belarusian

SOUTH SLAVONIC
25 Slovene
26 Serbo-Croatian
27 Macedonian
28 Bulgarian

**Other Indo-European Branches**

Celtic group

BRITTANIC
29 Breton
30 Welsh

GAULISH
31 Irish Gaelic
32 Scots Gaelic

Baltic group
33 Latvian      34 Lithuanian

Hellenic
35 Greek

Thracian/Illyrian group
36 Albanian

Thracian/Illyrian group
37 Romani

**Uralic Language Family**

Finno-Ugric group
38 Ginnish      41 Estonian
39 Karelian     42 Hungarian
40 Saami

Samoyedic group
44 Samoyedic

**Altaic Language Family**

Turkic group
45 Turkish

**Other Languages**

Basque
46 Basque

Areas with significant concentrations of other languages (usually adjacent national languages).

Boundary between languages.

Boundary between Indo-European and non-Indo-European languages.

Adapted with permission from: A. B. Murphy, "European Languages," in T. Unwin, ed., A European Geography. London: Longman, 1998, p. 38.

**■ Figure 6.2**

**Languages of Europe.** Language families and sub-families are regionally concentrated in Europe. Within the Indo-European language family, Germanic languages are in the north, Romance languages are in the south, and Slavic languages are in the east. Celtic languages are found in the far west, more remote areas of the region.

Adapted with permission from: A. B. Murphy, "Belgium's Regional Divergence Along the Road to Federation," in G. Smith, ed., *Federalism: The Multiethnic Challenge*. London: Longman, 1995, p. 82.

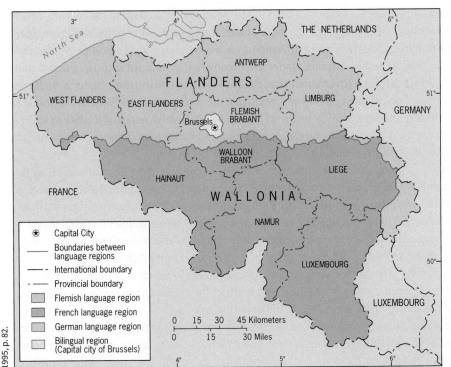

**Figure 6.3**

**Divided Belgium.** Flemish, French, and German dominate the different administrative areas in Belgium. Basing administrative units on language means that disagreements among the units, even on noncultural issues, tend to reinforce tensions among the language communities.

In Belgium, economic differences between linguistic groups have been a divisive issue for generations. During the nineteenth century, French speakers controlled the industrial economy and government of the country. The concentration of industry in southern Belgium strengthened their position. The French-speaking elite in Brussels and other Flemish cities began a process of "Frenchification." They promoted French and used it when interacting with their counterparts in other countries. By the twentieth century, a majority of the people in Brussels spoke French, although people in the areas surrounding Brussels continued to speak Flemish.

Many people in northern Belgium (surrounding Brussels) opposed the growing Frenchification of Flanders. The leaders of the Flemish movement initially sought linguistic rights, specifically the right of Flemish speakers to use their language in public affairs, court proceedings, and schools. Yet they were constantly frustrated by the opposition of French speakers to their demands. By the 1920s, the Flemish leadership began calling for the country to be partitioned along linguistic lines so that those living in northern Belgium could control their own affairs.

By the 1960s, a fixed partition scheme was established, which divided the country into Flemish-speaking Flanders in the north and French-speaking Wallonia in the south. The government recognizes Brussels as a distinct region, a bilingual capital, but places strict limits on the use of French in the rest of northern Belgium.

The partitioning process produced upheavals throughout the country. The experience helped strengthen the sense of Flemish identity and fueled a countermovement among the French Walloons. With language-group identity on the rise, conflicts between linguistic "communities" became a central feature of Belgian political life. After the 1960s, Belgian heavy industry became less competitive, and the country's economy shifted to high technology, light industry, and services, with much of the new economy concentrating in Flemish-speaking Flanders. As a result, the economic power in Belgium flipped, with the French-speaking industrial south taking a back seat to the Flemish-speaking north. Today, Wallonia has an unemployment rate of almost 17 percent, and economists consider unemployment in Wallonia to be structural, making it difficult for the economy or job market to bounce back. Flanders, on the other hand, has an unemployment rate below 9 percent, one of the lower unemployment rates in Europe.

The vast majority of power and decision making rests with the individual governments of Flanders and Wallonia rather than with a centralized government in Brussels. With their newfound wealth, many in Flanders wanted to see greater federalization of the country, which would give each of the two regions even more power. Today, no political party in Belgium operates at the national scale. Wallonia and Flanders each have their own political parties that vie for power in their respective regions. Under the circumstances, it is not surprising that it took Belgium 589 days to form a government after the 2010 elections. In those elections, a moderate separatist party won the most parliamentary seats in the more prosperous Flanders region. The *New York Times* quoted the political leader of the separatist Flemish nationalist party as saying, "We do not want a revolution. We do not want to declare Flanders independent overnight. But we do believe in a gradual evolution."

Brussels is going in another direction entirely, serving as the principal capital of the European Union (EU). Brussels is home to the EU Council and Commission. Moreover, much of the committee work done by the European Parliament takes place in Brussels (the formal home of the Parliament is in Strasbourg, France). The role Brussels serves as the EU capital may prevent Belgium from splitting into two countries. Both Flanders and Wallonia have vested interests in Brussels, so neither would abandon it lightly. And the French-speaking majority in Brussels has little interest in casting its lot with the region in which it is situated—Flanders. Some have proposed making Brussels a capital district for the European Union, much like the District of Columbia (Washington, D.C.) in the United States.

The example of Belgium gives us a multitude of insights into language. Language questions are often politicized. Language frequently is tied to other identity issues, and socioeconomic divisions can exacerbate tensions between language groups. At the same time, the role of English continues to expand as the dominant language of global commerce, electronic communication, and popular culture.

In this chapter, we question what languages are and examine the roles they play in cultures. We study the spatial distribution of the world's languages and learn how they diffuse, change, rise to dominance, and even become extinct. Finally, we examine how language contributes to making places unique.

# Key Questions FOR CHAPTER 6

1. What are languages, and what role do languages play in cultures?
2. Why are languages distributed the way they are?
3. How did certain languages become dominant?
4. What role does language play in making places?

## WHAT ARE LANGUAGES, AND WHAT ROLE DO LANGUAGES PLAY IN CULTURES?

A scene in Quentin Tarantino's cult classic movie *Pulp Fiction* shows Vincent and Jules in the front seat of a car talking about France. Vincent, trying to demonstrate his knowledge of French culture, turns to Jules and says, "You know what they call a....a....a quarter pounder with cheese in Paris?" Jules replies, "They don't call it a quarter pounder with cheese?" Vincent, ever the expert, explains in a few choice words that France uses the metric system and that the French would not know what a quarter pounder is. Then, he explains, "They call it a 'royale' with cheese." Jules, surprised, asks, "What do they call a Big Mac?" Vincent explains, "Well a Big Mac is a Big Mac, but they call it 'Le Big Mac.'"

This humorous exchange shows the juxtaposition of two opposing forces in our globalized world: globalization of culture and preservation of local and national culture. Are the two contradictory, or can we have globalized restaurants, food, music, and culture while preserving local languages?

Language is a fundamental element of local and national culture. The French government has worked diligently, even aggressively, to protect the French language, dating back to 1635 and the creation of the Académie Française, an institution charged with standardizing and protecting the French language. Since the 1970s, diffusion of globalized terms (linguists calls these loanwords or borrowed words) into France has posed an enormous challenge for the Académie Française.

With the support of many French people, the French government passed a law in 1975 banning the use of foreign words in advertisements, television, and radio broadcasts, as well as official documents, unless no French equivalent could be found. In 1992, France amended its constitution to make French the official language. In 1994, the French government passed another law to stop the use of foreign (mainly English) words in France, with a hefty fine imposed for violators. The law mandates French translations for globalized words, requiring the use of official French terms in official communications rather than le meeting, le weekend, le drugstore, or le hamburger. The Internet, where 50 percent of Internet users browse in English or Chinese (Fig. 6.4), has posed another set of challenges for the Académie Française. Many of the translations the Académie requires are somewhat cumbersome. For example, the official translation of e-mail was "courrier electronique," but the Académie shortened it to "courriel."

In addition to demonstrating the conflicting forces of globalized language and local or national language, the example of France reveals that language is much more than a way of communicating. A **language** is a set of sounds and symbols that is used for communication. But language is also an integral part of culture, reflecting and shaping it.

## Language and Culture

Language is one of the cornerstones of culture; it shapes our very thoughts. We can use vast vocabularies to describe new experiences, ideas, and feelings, or we can create new words to represent these things. Who we are as a culture, as a people, is reinforced and redefined moment by moment through shared language. Language reflects where a culture has been, what a culture values, even how people in a culture think, describe, and experience events. Perhaps the easiest way to understand the role of language in culture is to examine people who have experienced the loss of language under pressure from others. During the colonial period, both abroad and within countries, colonizers commonly forced the subjugated peoples to speak the language of the colonizer. These language practices continued in many places until recently and were enforced primarily through public (government) and church (mission) schools.

American, Canadian, Australian, Russian, and New Zealand governments each had policies of forced assimilation during the twentieth century, including not allowing indigenous peoples to speak native languages. For example, the United States forced American Indians to learn and speak English. Both mission schools and government schools

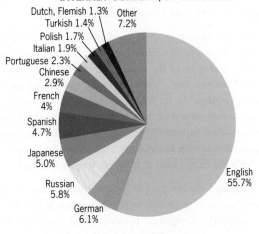

INTERNET CONTENT, BY LANGUAGE

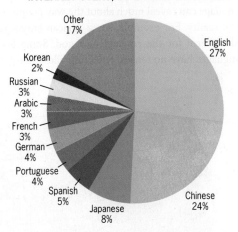

INTERNET USERS, BY LANGUAGE SPOKEN

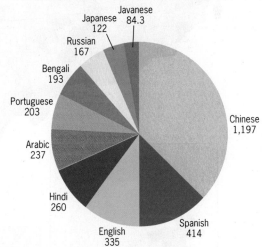

TOP 10 LANGUAGES, BY MILLIONS OF SPEAKERS

■ **Figure 6.4**
**Languages Used on the Internet.** The disproportionate impact of English is evident. *Data from*: Red Line, 2014; W3Techs.com, 2014; and Ethnologue, 2014.

enforced English-only policies in hopes of assimilating American Indians into the dominant culture. In an interview with the producers of an educational video, Clare Swan, an elder in the Kenaitze band of the Dena'ina Indians in Alaska, eloquently described the role of language in culture:

> No one was allowed to speak the language—the Dena'ina language. They [the American government] didn't allow it in schools, and a lot of the women had married non-native men, and the men said, "You're American now so you can't speak the language." So, we became invisible in the community. Invisible to each other. And, then, because we couldn't speak the language—what happens when you can't speak your own language is you have to think with someone else's words, and that's a dreadful kind of isolation [emphasis added].

Shared language makes people in a culture visible to each other and to the rest of the world. Language helps cement cultural identity. Language is also quite personal. Our thoughts, expressions, and dreams are articulated in our language; to lose that ability is to lose a lot.

Language can reveal much about the way people and cultures view reality. For example, some African languages have no word or term for the concept of a god. Some Southeast Asian languages have no tenses, reflecting a less sharp cultural

distinction between then and now. Given the American culture's preoccupation with dating and timing, it is difficult for many in the United States to understand how speakers of these languages perceive the world.

Language is so closely tied to culture that people use it as a weapon in cultural conflict and political strife. In the United States, where the Spanish-speaking population is growing (Fig. 6.5), some Spanish speakers and their advocates are promoting the use of Spanish in the public arena. In turn, people opposed to the use of Spanish in the United States are leading counter movements to promote "Official English" policies. Of course, Spanish is one of many non-English languages spoken in the United States, but it overshadows all others in terms of number of speakers and is therefore the focus of the official English movement (Table 6.1). During the 1980s, over 30 different States considered passing laws declaring English the State's official language. Some 30 States today have declared English the official language of the State either by statute or by amending the State constitution (one law was subsequently overturned by the courts). A few States have passed English-plus laws,

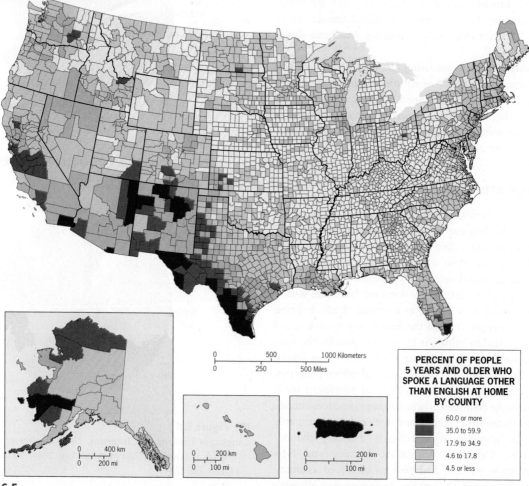

PERCENT OF PEOPLE 5 YEARS AND OLDER WHO SPOKE A LANGUAGE OTHER THAN ENGLISH AT HOME BY COUNTY

- 60.0 or more
- 35.0 to 59.9
- 17.9 to 34.9
- 4.6 to 17.8
- 4.5 or less

■■ Figure 6.5

**Percent of People 5 Years and Older Who Speak a Language Other than English at Home in the United States.** The data presented include all non-English languages by county. Latino migration in the Southwest, parts of California, and southern Florida is particularly evident. *Data from:* United States Census Bureau, 2010.

**TABLE 6.1**

**Top Ten Non-English Languages Spoken at Home by People over the Age of 5 in the United States, 2014.**

| TOP TEN LANGUAGES SPOKEN AT HOME BY NON-ENGLISH SPEAKERS | | |
|---|---|---|
| **Language** | **Total** | **Percent** |
| 1. Spanish | 35,468,501 | 12.4 |
| 2. Chinese | 2,600,150 | 0.9 |
| 3. Tagalog | 1,513,734 | 0.5 |
| 4. French | 1,305,503 | 0.5 |
| 5. Vietnamese | 1,251,468 | 0.4 |
| 6. German | 1,109,216 | 0.4 |
| 7. Korean | 1,039,021 | 0.4 |
| 8. Russian | 881,723 | 0.3 |
| 9. Arabic | 845,396 | 0.3 |
| 10. Italian | 753,992 | 0.3 |

*Data from*: United States Census Bureau Statistical Abstract, 2014.

encouraging bilingualism for non-English speakers, and a few other States are officially bilingual, including Hawai'i (Hawai'ian and English), or have bilingual education, including New Mexico (Spanish and English).

In Quebec, Canada, the focus is on passing laws that promote the use of the province's distinct version of the French language. Canada is officially bilingual, a reflection of the colonial division of the country between France and Great Britain. Government documents and even scholarly journals are printed in both English and French. Most of the country's French speakers live in the province of Quebec. The majority of people in Quebec speak French at home.

Since the 1970s, the Québécois (the people of Quebec) have periodically called for more independence for their province within Canada, even voting on secession at times. Although a majority has never voted for secession, the provincial government has passed several laws requiring and promoting the use of French in the province. In 1977, the Quebec government compelled all businesses in the province to demonstrate that they functioned in French. Upon passage of this law, many businesses and individuals moved out of the province of Quebec into neighboring Ontario. In 1993, the Quebec government passed a law requiring the use of French in advertising (Fig. 6.6). The Quebec law allows the inclusion of both French and English (or another language) translations on signage, as long as the French letters are twice the size of the other language's letters. In 2013, the province's strict language policies made international news when an Italian restaurant was asked to provide French-language translations for menu items, including pasta. The outrage over Pastagate, as the scandal became known, led the provincial government to promise to respond to language compliance complaints in a

■ **Figure 6.6**

**Quebec Province, Quebec.** The imprint of the French Canadian culture is evident in the cultural landscape of Rue Saint-Louis in Quebec. Here, the architecture and store signs confirm that this region is not simply Canadian; it is French Canadian.

more "balanced" and "measured" manner, recognizing that menus and bank statements cannot be held to the same standard as educational materials and signage.

Not all of Quebec's residents identify with the French language. Within the province, a small proportion of people speak English at home, others speak indigenous languages, and still others speak another language altogether—one associated with their country of origin. When the Quebec Parliament passed several laws promoting French during the 1980s and 1990s, members of Canada's First Nations, including the Cree and Mohawk, who live in Quebec, expressed a desire to remain part of Canada should Quebec secede from the country. During the same period, Quebec has experienced a flow of international migrants, many of whom seek residence in Quebec as a way to enter Canada and North America at large. These new immigrants must learn French under Quebec law.

Quebec, like any other place, is susceptible to change. Calls for independence in Quebec are waning since the separatist political party has captured fewer seats in recent parliamentary elections for the province. Nonetheless, the Québécois still feel a connection to France. The province even has a presence in Paris in the *Maison Quebec* (House of Quebec), an embassy-like entity of the province. As people, ideas, and power flow through the province, change will continue. Yet the province's laws, programs, presence in France, and the desire of the Québécois to remain loyal to their French language will keep the language alive as the province continues to experience change.

## What Is a Language?

Many geography textbooks differentiate languages based on a criterion of mutual intelligibility. **Mutual intelligibility** means that two people can understand each other when speaking. The argument goes that if two of us are speaking two different languages, say Spanish and Portuguese, we will not be able to understand each other, but if we are speaking two dialects of one language, we will achieve mutual understanding. Yet linguists have rejected the criterion of mutual intelligibility as strongly as geographers have rejected environmental determinism.

First, mutual intelligibility is almost impossible to measure. Even if we used mutual intelligibility as a criterion, many languages would fail the test. Famous linguist Max Weinreich once said that "a language is a dialect with an army." Think about it. How could we possibly see Mandarin Chinese and Cantonese Chinese as dialects of the same language, when two people speaking the language to each other cannot understand what each other is saying? Both can read the standard form of Chinese that has been built up by a strongly centralized Chinese government. But the spoken dialects are not mutually intelligible. Yet, we see Chinese as one language because of the weight of political and social institutions that lie behind it.

A further complication with the mutual intelligibility test is revealed in Scandinavia, where, for example, a Danish speaker and a Norwegian speaker (at least one from Oslo) will be able to understand what each other is saying. Yet we think of Danish and Norwegian as distinct languages. Having

a Norwegian language helps Norwegians identify themselves as Norwegians rather than as Danes or Scandinavians. Other languages that are recognized as separate but are mutually intelligible in many (or nearly all) aspects are Serbian and Croatian, Hindi and Urdu, and Navajo and Apache.

Given the complexities of distinguishing languages from dialects, the actual number of languages in use in the world remains a matter of considerable debate. The most conservative calculation puts the number at about 3000. However, most linguists and linguistic geographers today recognize between 5000 and 7000 languages, including more than 600 in India and over 2000 in Africa.

## Standardized Language

Language is dynamic: New discoveries, technologies, and ideas require new words. Technologically advanced societies are likely to have a **standard language**, one that is published, widely distributed, and purposely taught. In some countries, the government sustains the standard language through official state examinations for teachers and civil servants. Ireland promotes the use of the Irish (Celtic) language by requiring all government employees to pass an Irish-language examination before they can be hired. The phrase "the King's English" is a popular reference to the fact that the English spoken by well-educated people in London and its environs is regarded as British Received Pronunciation (BRP) English—that is, the standard.

Who decides what the standard language will be? Not surprisingly, the answer has to do with influence and power. In France, the Académie Française chose the French spoken in and around Paris as the official, standard language during the sixteenth century. In China, the government chose the Northern Mandarin Chinese heard in and around the capital, Beijing, as the official standard language. Although this is China's official standard language, the linguistic term *Chinese* actually incorporates many variants. The distinction between the standard language and variations of it is not unique to China; it is found in all but the smallest societies. The Italian of Sicily is quite different from the Italian spoken north of Venice, and both tongues differ from the standard Italian spoken in Florence and Tuscany, the region where many leaders of the Italian Renaissance wrote and published in what became the standard Italian language.

## Dialects

Variants of a standard language along regional or ethnic lines are called **dialects**. Differences in vocabulary, syntax (the way words are put together to form phrases), pronunciation, cadence (the rhythm of speech), and even the pace of speech all mark a speaker's dialect. Even if the written form of a statement adheres to the standard language, an accent can reveal the regional home of a person who reads the statement aloud. In the United States, the words "horse" and "oil" are written the same way in New England and in the South, but to the Southerner, the New Englander may be saying "hahse," and to the New Englander, the Southerner seems to be saying "all."

Linguists think about dialects in terms of **dialect chains** distributed across space. Dialects nearest to each other geographically will be the most similar (greater spatial interaction), but as you travel across the space, the dialects become less intelligible to each other because less interaction occurs. If all of these dialects are part of one language, which one of the dialects is *the language*? This question points to another challenge in defining languages. Is one of the many English dialects in the world the one, true English? Language is actually an umbrella for a collection of dialects, and we tend to see one of these dialects as the "true" language only because it is the one we speak or because it is the one a government claims as the standard.

Frequently, dialects are marked by actual differences in vocabulary. A single word or group of words can reveal the source area of the dialect. Linguistic geographers map the extent of particular words, marking their limits as isoglosses. An **isogloss** is a geographic boundary within which a particular linguistic feature occurs, but such a boundary is rarely a simple line. Usually, outlying areas of usage extend beyond the isogloss. Fuzzy isoglosses may signify that the dialect has expanded or contracted. Linguists who study dialects examine pronunciations, vocabularies, use of colloquial phrases, and syntax to determine isoglosses.

Linguistic geographer Hans Kurath published atlases of dialects in the United States, defining northern, southern, and midland dialect in the eastern part of the country. In the mid-1900s, Kurath drew distinct isoglosses among the three dialects, based on pronunciation of certain sounds and words. A more recent study of American dialects by linguist Bert Vaux used a 122-question online survey to map dialects in the United States. Maps of the soda, pop, and coke question (Fig. 6.7) and the hero, sub, poor-boy question reveal the prominent dialects of New England and the deep South, the fuzzy border between the two regions (Kurath's Midland dialect), the mixture of dialects in much of the rest of the country, and a few scattered areas outside the dialect regions where one or the other dialect dominates.

Linguist Bert Vaux's study of dialects in American English points to the differences in words for common things such as soft drinks and sandwiches. Describe a time when you said something and a speaker of another dialect did not understand the word you used. Where did the person with whom you were speaking come from? Was the word a term for a common thing? Why do you think dialects have different words for common things, things found across dialects, such as soft drinks and sandwiches?

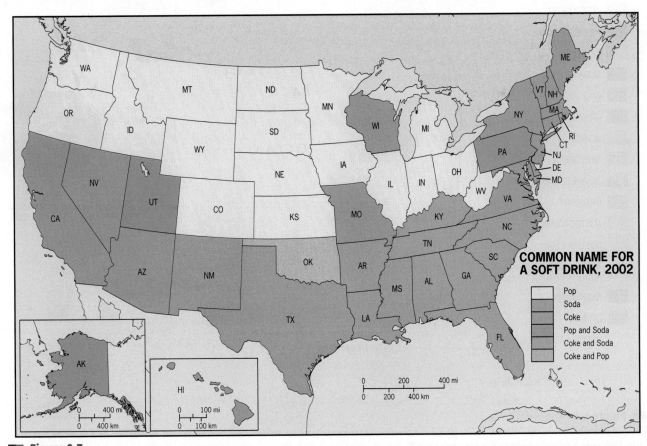

**■ Figure 6.7**
**Common Name for a Soft Drink in the United States, by State, 2002.** *Data from*: Bert Vaux, Harvard Survey of North American Dialects. http://cfprod01.imt.uwm.edu/Dept/FLL/linguistics/dialect/, accessed September 2005.

## WHY ARE LANGUAGES DISTRIBUTED THE WAY THEY ARE?

The first step in mapping the distribution of world languages is to classify languages. Linguists and linguistic geographers classify languages in terms that are also used in biology and for the same reasons: like species, some languages are more closely related to one another than others. At the global scale, we classify languages into **language families**. Each family encompasses multiple languages that have a shared but fairly distant origin. We break language families into **subfamilies** (divisions within a language family), where the commonalities are more definite and their origin is more recent. The spatial extent of subfamilies is smaller than language families, and every individual language has its dialects, whose territorial extent is smaller still.

## Definition and Debate

Although language families and subfamilies seem to be a logical way to classify languages, the classification of languages is subject to intense debate. Defining a language family is a daunting challenge: Some linguists argue that there are not just a few, but many dozens of language families. So when you study Figure 6.8, be aware that this is only one depiction of the world's geography of languages today. This map shows the distribution of some 20 language families, among which

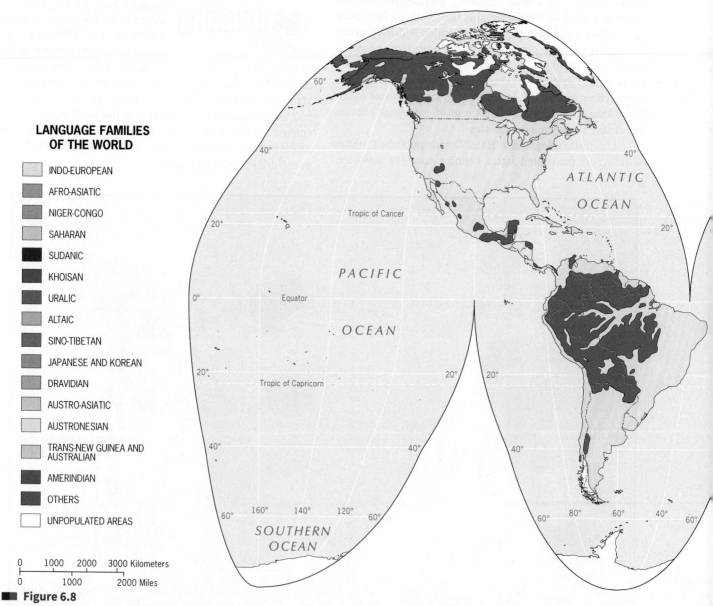

**LANGUAGE FAMILIES OF THE WORLD**

- INDO-EUROPEAN
- AFRO-ASIATIC
- NIGER-CONGO
- SAHARAN
- SUDANIC
- KHOISAN
- URALIC
- ALTAIC
- SINO-TIBETAN
- JAPANESE AND KOREAN
- DRAVIDIAN
- AUSTRO-ASIATIC
- AUSTRONESIAN
- TRANS-NEW GUINEA AND AUSTRALIAN
- AMERINDIAN
- OTHERS
- UNPOPULATED AREAS

0    1000    2000    3000 Kilometers
0        1000        2000 Miles

■■ **Figure 6.8**

**Language Families of the World.** The global distribution of language families reflects centuries of spatial interaction and flows of migrants. Indo-European languages came to the Americas from Europe through relocation diffusion after 1500 during the European colonial era. Languages in China and Southeast Asia are connected in the Sino-Tibetan language family as a result of centuries of spatial interaction. *Adapted with permission from:* Hammond, Inc., 1977.

the Indo-European language family has the widest distribution and claims the largest number of speakers. What you see here, of course, results from a combination of contiguous as well as relocation diffusion: Indo-European languages spread from a western source in all directions into Eurasia, but colonialism also transplanted Indo-European languages to the Americas, Africa, and Australia.

Even when it comes to individual languages, complicated issues arise. English is the most widely spoken Indo-European language; its speakers encircle the world with more than 350 million in North America, 60 million in Britain and Ireland, 205 million in Australia and New Zealand, and tens of millions more in South Africa, India, and elsewhere in the postcolonial world. Hundreds of millions of people speak

versions of English as a second or third language. Our map does not reflect this complexity, but the Indo-European family has actually diffused even more than Figure 6.8 suggests.

Sometimes you will see Chinese listed as the language with more speakers than any other, but herein lies still another complication. Although Figure 6.8 shows China and neighboring areas to be the heartland of the Sino-Tibetan language family, "Mandarin" Chinese, called *Putonghua* in China, is in common use by less than half of China's population of 1.36 billion. China has more than 1400 dialects, many of them mutually incomprehensible. What unites the "People of Han" is not their ability to understand each other's spoken word, but their ability to read the characters in which Chinese is written. When you watch television in China, you will see

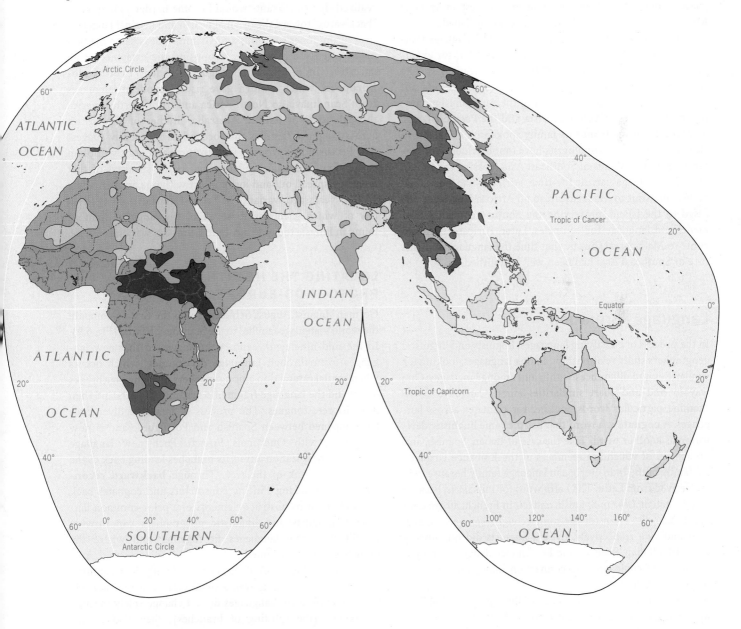

news reports and other programs subtitled by Chinese characters so that speakers of many different dialects can read and understand what is being said. But this does not mean that a billion Chinese speak Mandarin.

At the other end of the scale, the world map of languages shows several language families spoken by dwindling, often marginally located or isolated groups. The Indo-European languages of European colonizers surround the language families of Southeast Asia. Languages in the Austro-Asiatic language family survive in the interior of eastern India and in Cambodia and Laos. Languages in the Austronesian family are numerous and quite diverse, and many of the individual languages are spoken by fewer than 10 million people. Remoteness helps account for the remaining languages in the Amerindian language family. These languages remain strongest in areas of Middle America, the high Andes, and northern Canada.

If we look carefully at the map of world language families, some interesting questions arise. Consider, for example, the island of Madagascar off the East African coast. The primary languages people in Madagascar speak belong not to an African language family but to the Austronesian family, the languages of Southeast Asia and the Pacific Islands. Why is a language from this family spoken on an island so close to Africa? Anthropologists have found evidence of seafarers from the islands of Southeast Asia crossing the Indian Ocean to Madagascar. At the time, Africans had not sailed across the strait to Madagascar, so no African languages diffused to the island, preserving the Southeast Asian settlements and language for centuries. Later, Africans began to come to Madagascar, but by that time the language and culture of Southeast Asia had been well established.

## Language Formation

In the process of classifying languages, linguists and linguistic geographers study relationships among languages, looking for similarities and differences within and among languages. One way to find and chart similarities among languages is to examine particular words, looking for cognates across languages. A **cognate** is a word that has the same linguistic derivation as another word. Take the case of Italian, Spanish, and French, all of which are members of the Romance language subfamily of the Indo-European language family because they are derived from Latin. The Latin word for milk, *lacte*, became *latta* in Italian, *leche* in Spanish, and *lait* in French; all are cognates. Also, the Latin for the number eight, *oto*, became *otto*, *ocho*, and *huit*, respectively. Even if linguists did not already know that Italian, Spanish, and French were languages rooted in Latin, they could deduce a connection among the languages through such cognates.

More than two centuries ago William Jones, an Englishman living in South Asia, undertook a study of Sanskrit, the language in which ancient Indian religious and literary texts were written. Jones discovered that the vocabulary and grammatical forms of Sanskrit bore a striking resemblance to the ancient Greek and Latin he learned while in college. "No philologer [student of words] could examine all three," Jones wrote, "without believing them to have sprung from some common source, which, perhaps, no longer exists." His idea was a revolutionary notion in the 1700s.

During the nineteenth century Jakob Grimm, a scholar and a writer of fairy tales, suggested that cognates might prove the relationships between languages in a scientific manner. He explained that related languages have similar, but not identical, consonants. He believed these consonants would change over time in a predictable way. Hard consonants, such as the *v* and *t* in the German word *vater*, softened into *vader* (Dutch) and *father* (English). Using Grimm's theory that consonants became softer as time passed, linguists realized that consonants would become harder as they went "backwards" toward the original hearth and original language.

From Jones's notions and Grimm's ideas came the first major linguistic hypothesis, proposing the existence of an ancestral Indo-European language called **Proto-Indo-European**, which in turn gave rise to modern languages from Scandinavia to North Africa and from North America through parts of Asia to Australia. Studies of similarities across language families that occur less frequently suggest that Proto-Indo-European was, in turn, an outgrowth of an earlier **Proto-Eurasiatic** language. As the speakers of that language spread out and lost contact with one another some 15,000 years ago, variants of Proto-Eurasiatic emerged—a few of which gave rise to seven of the language families found in Eurasia today. Proto-Indo-European was one of these.

## LOCATING THE HEARTH OF PROTO-INDO-EUROPEAN

German linguist August Schleicher was the first to compare the world's language families to the branches of a tree (Fig. 6.9). In the mid-nineteenth century, he suggested that new languages form through **language divergence**, which occurs when spatial interaction among speakers of a language breaks down and the language fragments first into dialects and then into discrete tongues. The process of language divergence has happened between Spanish and Portuguese and is now happening with Québécois French. Each new language becomes a new leaf on a tree, its branches leading back to the hearth, the trunk of the tree. Through **backward reconstruction** (tracking shifting consonants and cognates back in an effort to reconstruct elements of a prior common language), linguists and linguistic geographers can provide insight into how languages fit together and where the branches were once joined.

Finding the trunk of a language family is a daunting task, for reconstructing even a small branch of the language tree is complicated. Languages do not change solely through divergence (the splitting of branches); they also change through convergence and extinction. If peoples with different languages have consistent spatial interaction, **language convergence** can take place, collapsing two languages into

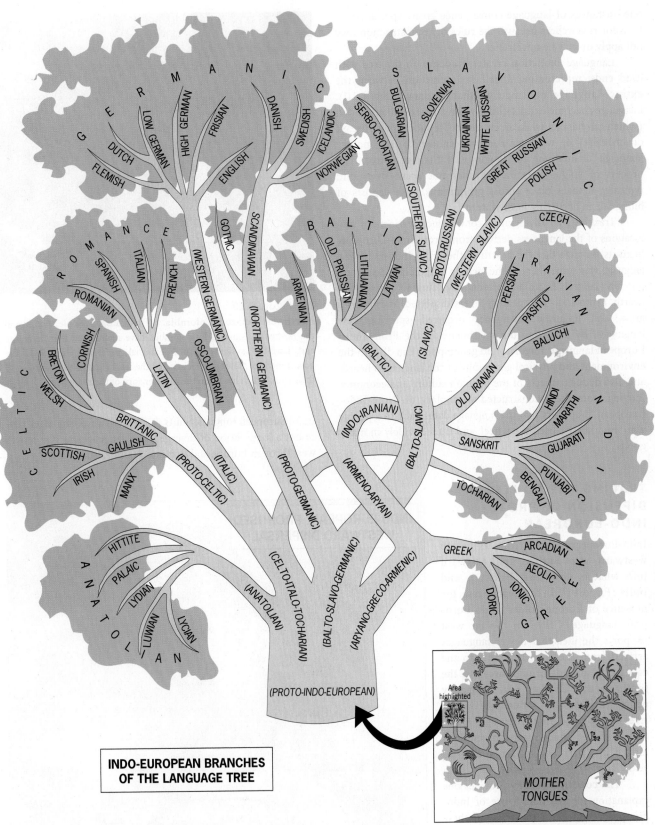

Adapted with permission from: T. V. Gamkrelidze and V. V. Ivanov. "The Early History of Indo-European Languages," *Scientific American*, March 1990, p. 111.

INDO-EUROPEAN BRANCHES
OF THE LANGUAGE TREE

MOTHER
TONGUES

Area
highlighted

■ **Figure 6.9**
**Indo-European Branches of the Language Tree.**    The inset shows all of the languages of the world in a massive tree. The Indo-European language family makes up just one part of that massive tree and is highlighted in this figure. Compare this figure to the map of the Indo-European languages in Europe (Figure 6.2) and notice how the language groups in Europe are related on this tree and where the languages on this tree are geographically located in Europe.

one. Instances of language convergence create special problems for researchers because the rules of reconstruction may not apply or may be unreliable.

Language extinction creates branches on the tree with dead ends, representing a halt in interaction between the **extinct language** and languages that continued (Fig. 6.10). Languages become extinct either when all descendants perish (which can happen when an entire people succumb to disease or invaders) or when descendants choose to use another language, abandoning the language of their ancestors. The process of language extinction does not occur overnight; typically, it takes place across generations, with degrees of bilingualism occurring in the interim.

Tracking the divergence, convergence, extinction, and locations of the languages derived from Proto-Indo-European, linguists theorize that the hearth of the Proto-Indo-European language was somewhere in the vicinity of the Black Sea—very possibly central Anatolia (present-day Turkey). From this hearth, Proto-Indo-European speakers dispersed, vocabularies grew, and linguistic divergence occurred, spurring new languages. By analyzing the vocabulary of the Proto-Indo-European language, linguists and geographers can discern the environment and physical geography of the language's hearth and also deduce aspects of the people's culture and economy. Judging from the reconstructed vocabulary of Proto-Indo-European, it appears that the language dates back to a people who used horses, used the wheel, and traded widely in many goods.

**Figure 6.10**

**Northwest Amazon, Colombia.** The Barasana people, who live in the northwest Amazon in Colombia, have maintained their language and land-use systems despite external pressures. In 1991, the government of Colombia recognized the legal right of the Barasana to their land, which has aided the maintenance of their language.

Indo-European tongues. Shifts in the derivative languages represent a long period of divergence in languages as one moves west through Europe and east into South Asia.

## TRACING THE ROUTES OF DIFFUSION OF PROTO-INDO-EUROPEAN

Indo-European spread from its hearth westward into Europe and eastward into what is now Iran, Pakistan, and India (Fig. 6.11). In the former case, the presence of Europe's oldest Indo-European language, Celtic, in the far west supports the idea that newer languages arrived from the east. Migrants to the east likely moved through areas to the south of the Caspian Sea, ultimately penetrating into the Indus and Ganges river basins some 3500 years ago. A second wave of Indo-European speakers moved into present-day Iran some 700 years later.

The **conquest theory** provides one explanation for the dominance of Indo-European tongues in the wake of these migrations. This theory holds that early speakers of Proto-Indo-European spread from east to west on horseback, overpowering earlier inhabitants and beginning the diffusion and differentiation of

**Figure 6.11**

**Indo-European Language Family: Proposed Westward Dispersal.** Approximate timings and routes for the westward dispersal of the Indo-European languages.

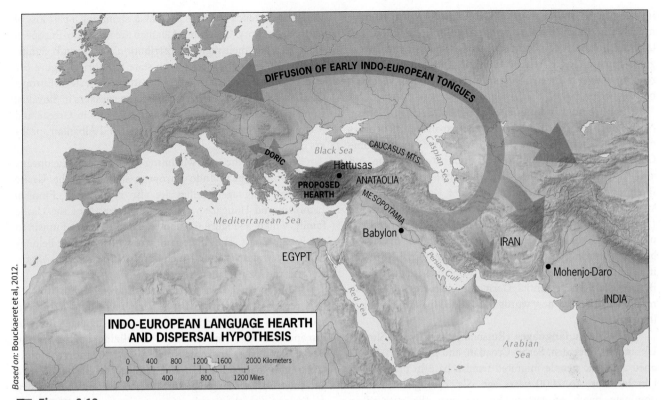

*Based on: Bouckaeret et al, 2012.*

■ **Figure 6.12**

**Indo-European Language Family: Proposed Hearth and Dispersal Hypothesis.**    This theory proposes that the Indo-European language family began in Anatolia and dispersed eastward into South Asia and westward into Europe.

An alternative agricultural theory proposes that Proto-Indo-European spread with the diffusion of agriculture. Citing the archaeological record, Luca Cavalli-Sforza and Albert Ammerman proposed that for every generation (25 years) the agricultural frontier moved approximately 18 kilometers (11 mi). This means farmers would have completely penetrated the European frontier over several thousand years, which is what the archaeological record suggests (Fig. 6.12). With established farming providing a more reliable food supply, population could increase. As a result, a slow but steady wave of farmers dispersed into Europe and mixed with nonfarming peoples. But some of the nonfarming societies in their path held out, and their languages persevered. Thus, Etruscan did not become extinct until Roman times, and Euskera (the Basque language) survives to this day as a probable direct link to Europe's pre-farming era.

## The Languages of Europe

The map of world languages (Fig. 6.8) demonstrates how widely spread the Indo-European language family is across the globe, dominating not just Europe, but significant parts of Asia (including Russia and India), North and South America, Australia, and portions of Southern Africa. About half the world's people speak Indo-European tongues. The Indo-European language family is broken into subfamilies including Romance, Germanic, and Slavic. And each subfamily is broken into individual languages, such as English, German, Danish, and Norwegian within the Germanic subfamily.

The language map of Europe (Fig. 6.2) shows that the Indo-European language family prevails in this region, with pockets of the Uralic family occurring in Hungary (the Ugric subfamily) and in Finland and adjacent areas (the Finnic subfamily), and a major Altaic language, Turkish, dominating Turkey west of the Sea of Marmara.

Celtic people first brought Indo-European tongues into Europe when they spread across the continent over 3000 years ago. Celtic speech survives in the British Isles and northwestern France, but in most places Celtic tongues fell victim to subsequent migrations and empire building. These historical developments led to the creation of a European linguistic pattern characterized by three major subfamilies: Romance, Germanic, and Slavic.

### THE SUBFAMILIES

The **Romance languages** (French, Spanish, Italian, Romanian, and Portuguese) lie in the areas of Europe that were once controlled by the Roman Empire. Over time, local languages mixed with Latin, which the Roman Empire introduced to the region. The Romance languages have much in common because of their Latin connection, but they are not mutually comprehensible. Spanish and Portuguese remain closely related to each other, but even there, reading between the two languages is easier than speaking between them.

The **Germanic languages** (English, German, Danish, Norwegian, and Swedish) reflect the expansion of peoples out of Northern Europe to the west and south. Some Germanic peoples spread into areas dominated by Rome, and at the northern and northeastern edges of the Roman Empire their tongues gained ascendancy. Other Germanic peoples spread into areas that were never part of an ancient empire (present-day Sweden, Norway, Denmark, and the northern part of the Netherlands). The Germanic character of English bears the imprint of a further migration—that of the Normans into England in 1066, bringing a Romance tongue to the British Isles. The essential Germanic character of English remained, but many new words were added that are Romance in origin.

The **Slavic languages** (Russian, Polish, Czech, Slovak, Ukrainian, Slovenian, Serbo-Croatian, and Bulgarian) developed as Slavic people migrated from a base in present-day Ukraine close to 2000 years ago. Slavic tongues came to dominate much of eastern Europe over the succeeding centuries. They, too, overwhelmed Latin-based tongues along much of the eastern part of the old Roman Empire—with the notable exception of an area on the western shores of the Black Sea, where a Latin-based tongue either survived the Slavic invasion or was reintroduced by migrants. That tongue is the ancestor of the modern-day Romance language: Romanian.

## RELATIONSHIP TO THE POLITICAL PATTERN

A comparison of Europe's linguistic and political maps shows a high correlation between the languages spoken and the political organization of space (see Fig. 6.2). The Romance languages, of Romanic-Latin origin, dominate in five countries, including Romania. The eastern boundaries of Germany coincide almost exactly with the transition from Germanic to Slavic tongues. Even at the level of individual languages, boundaries can be seen on the political map: between French and Spanish, between Norwegian and Swedish, and between Bulgarian and Greek.

In some places, however, linguistic and political borders are far from coincident. The French linguistic region extends into Belgium, Switzerland, and Italy, but in France, French coexists with Basque in the southwest, a variant of Dutch in the north, and a Celtic tongue in the northwest. The Celtic languages survive in the western region of France called Brittany (Breton), in the northern and western parts of Wales (Welsh), in western Ireland (Irish Gaelic), and in the western Highlands and islands of Scotland (Scots Gaelic). The use of

Romanian extends well into Moldavia, signifying a past loss of national territory. Greek and Albanian are also Indo-European languages, and their regional distribution corresponds significantly (though not exactly) with state territories. Figure 6.2 underscores the complex cultural pattern of eastern Europe: German speakers in Hungary; Hungarian speakers in Slovakia, Romania, and Yugoslavia; Romanian speakers in Greece and Moldavia; Turkish speakers in Bulgaria; and Albanian speakers in Serbia.

Although the overwhelming majority of Europeans and Russians speak Indo-European languages, the Uralic and Altaic language families are also represented. Finnish, Estonian, and Hungarian are major languages of the Uralic family, which, as Figure 6.8 shows, extends across Eurasia to the Pacific Coast. The Altaic family to which Turkish belongs is equally widespread and includes Turkish, Kazakh, Uigur, Kyrgyz, and Uzbek languages.

One language on the map of Europe stands out for two reasons: First, it covers a very small land area, and second, it is *in no way related to* any other language family in Europe. Did you find it? This tantalizing enigma is the Basque language, Euskera. Isolated in the Andorra Mountain region between Spain and France, the Basque people and their Euskera language survived the tumultuous history of Europe for thousands of years—never blending with another language or diffusing from the Andorra region. (Some recent genetic evidence points to a link between Euskera and an extinct language in the Middle East.) The Basques have a strong identity tied to their language and independent history, an identity that was cemented by repression under fascist dictator Francisco Franco, who ruled Spain during and after World War II. In response, a Basque separatist group began demanding autonomy within Spain—periodically resorting to violence in pursuit of the cause. The Spanish government finally recognized Basque autonomy in its 1979 constitution, granting the Basque region its own parliament, giving the Basque language official status, and transferring some taxation and education powers from the capital to the Basque region. A group of Basque separatists continued to demand more, for a time waging a campaign of violence against Spanish targets and even moderate Basque leaders. The situation has calmed down in recent years, but agitation for greater autonomy for the Basques continues (Fig. 6.13).

## Languages of Subsaharan Africa

The world map of language families masks the extreme fragmentation of languages in parts of the world such as Subsaharan Africa. In Subsaharan Africa, the map of world language families reflects the dominance of the Niger-Congo language family. By including language subfamilies, we can gain a more meaningful picture of Subsaharan Africa's linguistic diversity (Fig. 6.14).

■ **Figure 6.13**

**San Sebastián, Spain.** Graffiti on the wall of this building uses the English language, "Freedom for the Basque Country," to show support for the Basque separatist movement.

Studying language subfamilies helps us understand migration and settlement patterns in Subsaharan Africa. The oldest languages of Subsaharan Africa are the Khoisan languages, which include "click" sounds. Although they once dominated much of the region, Khoisan languages were marginalized by the invasion of speakers of Bantu languages. Studying the languages in the Bantu subfamily, we can see that the languages are still closely related, with similar prefixes and vocabularies. Similarities among the Bantu languages mean that the languages have been in Subsaharan Africa for a shorter time—typically, the longer a language has been in a place, the more likely sounds will have shifted and languages splintered.

Focusing on the country scale reveals the linguistic diversity of Subsaharan Africa. Nigeria encompasses several subfamilies of the Niger-Congo family, and its population includes speakers of two major Subsaharan African language families. Indeed, Nigeria's 173.6 million people speak more

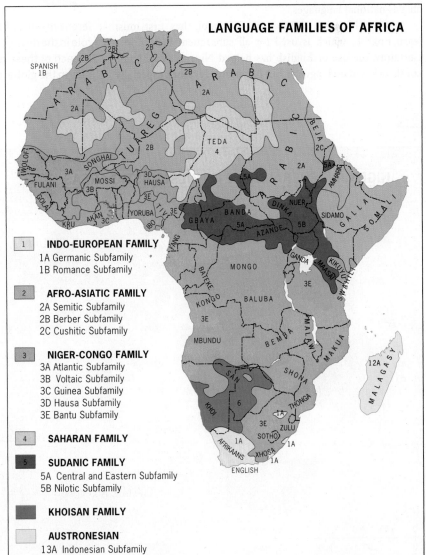

■ **Figure 6.14**

**Language Families of Africa.** The geographical distribution of African language families and their subfamilies show the history of spatial interaction among Africans. For example, in the Niger-Congo family region, the people in the Bantu subfamily area historically interacted with each other, developing connections among and diffusing languages in the Bantu subfamily. What this maps hides is the role that the language of colonists plays in many parts of Africa—serving as a lingua franca among speakers of different languages and dialects.

Adapted with permission from: Hammond, Inc., 1977.

than 500 different languages. The three most prominent languages are distributed regionally: Hausa is in the north and is spoken by some 39 million, Yoruba is in the southwest and is spoken by 22 million, and Ibo is in the southeast and is spoken by more than 24 million people (Fig. 6.15). Of the remaining languages spoken in Nigeria, the vast majority are spoken by fewer than one million people. These minor languages persist because daily survival, community, and culture are tied closely to the local scale in Nigeria. Even people who leave their home towns for work send money back to support the local culture and economy.

Were it not for British colonialism, the country of Nigeria would never have existed. The diverse people of this place have been amalgamated into the Nigerian borders for less than 150 years. As we will see in Chapter 8, European colonists are responsible for the arbitrary borders of most of Africa—borders that ignore cultural divides. When Nigeria gained its independence in 1962, the government decided to adopt English as the "official" language, as the three major regional languages are too politically charged and thus unsuitable as national languages.

When Nigeria's children go to school, they first must learn English, which is used for all subsequent instruction. Certainly, the use of English has helped Nigeria avoid some conflicts based on language, but Nigerian educators, especially in the north, are having second thoughts about the policy. Upon entering school, children who have grown up speaking a local language are suddenly confronted with a new, unfamiliar tongue. The time and energy spent learning English take away from learning other subjects. Moreover, for many students, knowledge of English is irrelevant when they emerge from school (as many do after only six years). Some argue against deference to a language brought by colonists who arbitrarily established their multilinguistic and multiethnic country in the first place. Yet from a communication perspective, English is a common denominator for the country that cannot easily be abandoned.

Education affects the distribution of languages across the globe and within regions and countries. Thinking about different regions of the world, consider how education plays a role in the distribution of English speakers. Who learns English in each of these regions and why? What role does education play in the global distribution of English speakers?

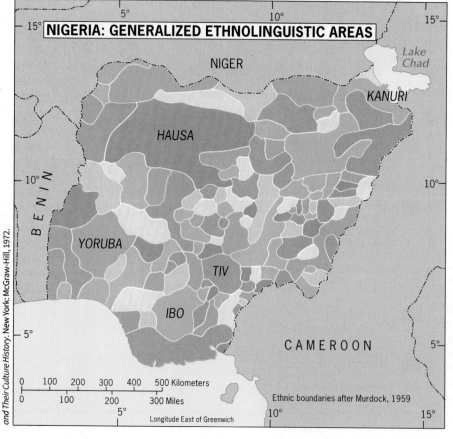

*Data from: Ethnolinguistic area boundaries are based on a map in G. P. Murdock, Africa: Its Peoples and Their Culture History. New York: McGraw-Hill, 1972.*

■ **Figure 6.15**
**Nigeria: Generalized Ethnolinguistic Areas.** This map demonstrates the mosaic of languages in Nigeria by shading each of the country's ethnolinguistic areas. The colors represent diversity; they do not show associations among ethnolinguistic areas.

# HOW DID CERTAIN LANGUAGES BECOME DOMINANT?

Just a few thousand years ago most habitable parts of Earth were characterized by a tremendous diversity of languages. With the rise of empires, of more technologically sophisticated literate societies, some languages began to spread over larger areas. By 2000 years ago, languages such as Chinese and Latin had successfully diffused over large regions. The Han Empire in China and the Roman Empire in Europe and North Africa knit together large swaths of territory, encouraging the diffusion of one language over substantial chunks of territory. The most powerful and wealthiest people were the first to learn Chinese and Latin in these empires, as they had the most to lose by not learning these languages. Local languages and illiteracy continued among the poor in the empires, and some blending of local with regional languages occurred. When the Roman Empire disintegrated, places within the former empire became much more isolated from one another, prompting a round of linguistic divergence.

In the late Middle Ages, the invention of the Gutenberg printing press and the rise of nation-states worked to spread literacy and stabilize certain languages through widely distributed written forms. Johann Gutenberg perfected the printing press, inventing the movable-type printing press, the Gutenberg press, in Germany in 1440. In 1452, Gutenberg printed the first Gutenberg Bible (the sacred text for Christians), which brought the scriptures out of churches and monasteries. The printing press diffused quickly in the century following—throughout Europe and beyond. It allowed for an unprecedented production of written texts in languages besides Latin. The printing press made it possible to print the Bible in vernacular languages, such as French or German, rather than Latin, which in turn gave rise to standardized variants of those languages. The Luther Bible played this role for German, as did the King James Bible for English.

The rise of relatively large independent states was equally important (see Chapter 8), for these political entities had a strong interest in promoting a common culture, often through promotion of a common language (such as French or Dutch). Political elites who were literate and had access to written texts brought peoples together and played a key role in distributing printed texts. Moreover, as the leaders of countries such as England and Spain sought to expand their influence overseas through mercantilism and colonialism, they established networks of communication and interaction, helping to diffuse certain languages over vast portions of Earth's surface.

Since 1500, the world has experienced several waves of globalization ranging from European colonialism to American-led globalization, resulting in widespread cultural, linguistic, political, and economic interaction. Trade and commerce stimulated the formation of new, hybrid languages to facilitate such interaction, but other local languages collapsed under the onslaught of change. Although new languages are created through trade and interaction over time, local languages with few native speakers have increasingly become extinct. Globalization is shrinking the world's linguistic heritage. National Geographic Explorer in Residence Wade Davis estimates that half of "the world's 7000 languages are endangered." Davis argues that most languages are lost because one group dominates another and the dominant language is privileged.

## Lingua Franca

Even before the expansion of trade encouraged the global diffusion of languages such as English and Spanish, regional trade encouraged people speaking different tongues to find ways to communicate with one another. A **lingua franca** is a language used among speakers of different languages for the purposes of trade and commerce. A lingua franca can be a single language, or it can be a mixture of two or more languages. When people speaking two or more languages are in contact and they combine parts of their languages in a simplified structure and vocabulary, we call it a **pidgin language**.

The first widely known lingua franca was a pidgin language. During the 1200s, seaborne commerce in the Mediterranean Sea expanded, and traders from the ports of southern France (the Franks) revitalized the ports of the eastern Mediterranean. But the local traders did not speak the seafarers' language. Thus began a process of convergence in which the tongue of the Franks was mixed with Italian, Greek, Spanish, and Arabic. The mixture came to be known as the Frankish language, or lingua franca, and it served for centuries as the common tongue of Mediterranean commerce.

The term *lingua franca* is still used to denote a common language for trade and commerce that is spoken by peoples with different native tongues. Arabic became a lingua franca during the expansion of Islam, and English did so in many areas during the colonial era. English is the only linguistic common denominator that binds together multilingual India—both in India itself and among those from the subcontinent who have migrated to other areas (Fig. 6.16).

A different sort of a lingua franca in wide use today is Swahili, the lingua franca of East Africa. Through centuries of trade and interaction, Swahili developed from an African Bantu language mixed with Arabic and Persian, encompassing 100 million speakers from southern Somalia to northern Mozambique and from coastal Kenya and Tanzania to Uganda and the East African Great Lakes region. Swahili has a complex vocabulary and structure, and while millions of East Africans communicate in the language, most still learn and speak a local language as their first or primary language. Swahili has gained prominence since 2000 because of its status as the most widely used African language on the Internet. The British Broadcasting Corporation (BBC) has a

© Alexander B. Murphy

■ **Figure 6.16**
**Dubai, United Arab Emirates.** The message on this bench is aimed at Indian migrants living in the United Arab Emirates and is written in English, the lingua franca of virtually all Indian migrants on the Arabian Peninsula.

Swahili language website, and Wikipedia offers pages of its free encyclopedia in Swahili.

Over time a pidgin language may gain native speakers, becoming the first language children learn in the home. When this happens, we call it a creolized or Creole language. A **Creole language** is a pidgin language that has developed a more complex structure and vocabulary and has become the native language of a group of people. The word *Creole* stems from a pidgin language formed in the Caribbean from English, French, and Portuguese languages mixed with the languages of African slaves. The language became more complex and became the first language of people in the region, replacing the African languages.

Pidgin and Creole languages are important unifying forces in a linguistically divided world. They tend to be simple and accessible, and therefore disseminate rapidly. In Southeast Asia a trade language called Bazaar Malay is heard from Myanmar (Burma) to Indonesia and from the Philippines to Malaysia; it has become a lingua franca in the region. A simplified form of Chinese also serves as a language of commerce even beyond the borders of China.

## Multilingualism

In a world of some 200 political entities and several thousand languages, most countries are characterized, to varying degrees, by *multilingualism*—the use of more than one language by sectors of the population. In the United States, the current issue of Spanish as a second language is only the most recent manifestation of a debate that is as old as the country itself. Canada is

officially a bilingual state, but quite a few Canadians speak a language other than English or French at home.

To be sure, a few virtually **monolingual states**—countries where almost everyone speaks the same language—do exist. These include Japan in Asia; Uruguay in South America; Iceland, Denmark, Portugal, and Poland in Europe; and Lesotho in Africa. Even these countries, however, have small numbers of people who speak other languages; for example, more than a half-million Koreans live in Japan. In fact, as a result of migration and diffusion, no country is truly monolingual today. English-speaking Australia has more than 180,000 speakers of Aboriginal languages. Predominantly Portuguese-speaking Brazil has some 1.5 million speakers of Amerindian languages.

Countries in which more than one language is in use are called **multilingual states**. In some of these countries, linguistic fragmentation reflects strong cultural pluralism as well as divisive forces. This is true in former colonial areas where colonizers threw together peoples speaking different languages, as happened in Africa and Asia.

Multilingualism takes several forms. In Canada and Belgium, the two major languages each dominate particular areas of the country. In multilingual India, the country's official languages generally correspond with the country's States (Fig. 6.17). In Peru, centuries of acculturation have not erased the regional identities of the American Indian tongues spoken in the Andean Mountains and the Amazonian interior, and of Spanish, spoken on the coast. In Gabon, 42 recognized languages coexist as part of a complex linguistic mosaic.

## Official Languages

Countries with linguistic fragmentation often adopt an **official language** (or languages) to tie the people together. In former colonies, the official language is often one that ties them to their colonizer, as the colonizer's language invariably is one already used by the educated and politically powerful elite. For Gabon, that language is French, for Angola it is Portuguese, and for Ghana it is English. States adopt an official language in an effort to promote communication and interaction among peoples who speak different local and regional languages.

Designating an official language is not without risks. As we noted earlier in this chapter in the case of Nigeria, the long-term results of using a foreign language may not be positive. In some countries, citizens object to using a language that they associate with colonial repression. Some former colonies have chosen not just one but two official languages: the European colonial language plus one of the country's own major languages. English and Hindi, for example, are official languages of India. Similarly, English and Swahili are official languages of Tanzania. In Mauritania, French and Arabic are official languages. South Africa has perhaps the largest number of official tongues. In a nod to its complex colonial and postcolonial history, South Africa's constitution mandates 11 official languages. But this solution is not always enough. When India gave Hindi official status, riots and disorder broke out in non-Hindi areas of the country. Kenya, which at first made English and Swahili its official languages, decided to drop English in the face of public opposition to rules requiring candidates for public office to pass a test of their ability to use English.

The European Union is not a country, but it recognizes 24 official languages, and the United Nations has 6 official languages: Arabic, Chinese, English, French, Russian, and Spanish. In each of these cases, the international organization offers simultaneous translation among the official languages to any member of the parliament (European Union) or the general assembly (United Nations) who requests it. Each international organization also maintains its website in all official languages. The European Union only produces legislation and policy documents of "major public importance" in all of its official languages; other documents are translated only into the languages relevant to each document. All United Nations documents must be translated into all the official languages (and sometimes German as well) prior to being published.

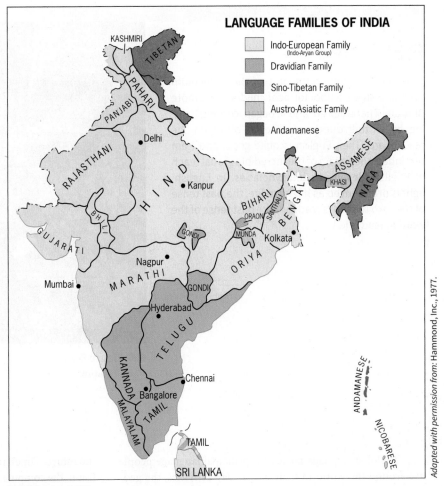

### Figure 6.17

**Language Families of India.** The language map of India reflects the history of spatial interaction in the region. Southern India, where Dravidian languages are spoken, was not incorporated in every empire that ruled northern India over the last 2,500 years. The presence of Indo-European languages in northern India demonstrates the region's historical connectedness to areas to the west, including Central Asia, where Indo-European languages are also found.

*Adapted with permission from: Hammond, Inc., 1977.*

## The Prospect of a Global Language

What will the global language map look like 50 years from now? More and more people are using English in a variety of contexts. English is now the standard language of international business and travel (the lingua franca), much of contemporary popular culture bears the imprint of English, and the computer and telecommunications revolution relies heavily on the use of English terminology. Does this mean that English is on its way to becoming a global language?

# FIELD NOTE

"English is an important part of the curriculum even at a small school for deaf children in remote Bhutan. The children and I began communicating by writing questions to each other on the blackboard. Their English is quite good, and I am reminded once again of the incredible global reach of English, despite its idiosyncrasies. In English, light is pronounced as if it were lite, the past tense of the verb to read is read, but the past tense of the word to lead is led."

■ **Figure 6.18**
**Paro, Bhutan.**

If global language means the principal language people use around the world in their day-to-day activities, the geographical processes we have examined so far do not point to the emergence of English as a global tongue. Population growth rates are generally lower in English-speaking areas than they are in other areas, and little evidence shows people in non-English speaking areas willing to abandon their local language in favor of English. Indeed, since language embodies deeply held cultural views and is a basic feature of cultural identity, many people actively resist switching to English.

Yet if **global language** means a common language of trade and commerce used around the world, the picture looks rather different. Although not always welcomed, the trend throughout much of the world is to use English as a language of cross-cultural communication—especially in the areas of science, technology, travel, business, and education (Fig. 6.18). Korean scholars are likely to communicate with their Russian counterparts in English; Japanese scientific journals are increasingly published in English; Danish tourists visiting Italy commonly use English to get around; and the meetings of most international financial and governmental institutions are dominated by English. Under these circumstances, the role of English as an international language of commerce will likely grow.

We must be careful in this conclusion, however. Anyone looking at the world 200 years ago would have predicted French as the principal language of cross-cultural communication in the future. Times are different now, of course. The role of English in the computer revolution alone makes it hard to imagine a fundamental shift away from the dominance of English in international affairs. Yet, economic and political influences on language use are always in flux, and nothing is inevitable.

Choose a country in the world. Imagine you become a strong leader of a centralized government in the country. Pick a language used in the country other than the tongue spoken by the majority. Determine what policies you could put in place to make the minority language an official language of the country. What reactions would your initiative generate? Who would support it and who would not?

## WHAT ROLE DOES LANGUAGE PLAY IN MAKING PLACES?

The cultural geographer Yi-Fu Tuan has studied the role and function of language in the shaping of places. He researched the way people use language as a tool to give perceptual meaning to areas on Earth's surface, large and small. Each

**place** has a unique location and constitutes a reflection of human activities, ideas, and tangible, durable creations. Tuan argued that by simply naming a place, people in effect call that place into being, and thereby impart a certain character to it.

Geographers call place-names **toponyms**. Such names often refer to the social processes going on in a particular area, and these may determine whether a toponym is passed down or changed, how the people will interpret the history of a place, and how the people will see a place. Tuan contrasts the examples of "Mount Prospect" and "Mount Misery" to help us understand that a name alone can color the character of a place and even the experiences of people in a place. If you planned to travel to "Mount Prospect," your expectations and even your experiences might well be quite different than they would be if you took a trip to "Mount Misery."

## The Ten Toponyms

A toponym can give us a quick glimpse into the history of a place. Simply by knowing who named the place and how the name was chosen helps us understand the uniqueness of that place. In his book, *Names on the Land: A Historical Account of Place-Naming in the United States* (1982), English professor George Stewart recognized that certain themes dominate American toponyms. Stewart developed a classification scheme focused on ten basic types of place-names, including: *descriptive* (Rocky Mountains), *commendatory* (Paradise Valley, Arizona), and *possession* (Johnson City, Texas) (Table 6.2). Stewart explains that some of the most interesting toponyms are *manufactured*, such as Truth or Consequences, New Mexico, which voted to change its name in response to an incentive offered by a 1950s-era radio game show. Stewart's final category of toponyms is *shift names*. Shift names include relocated names, examples of relocation diffusion and typically found in migrant communities (Lancaster, England to Lancaster, Pennsylvania).

Knowing Stewart's ten categories of toponyms at the very least helps us understand that a story lies behind every toponym. The stories of toponyms quite often have their roots in migration, movement, and interaction among people. When languages diffuse through migration, so too do toponyms. Studying the toponyms in a place can tell us much about the historical migration of peoples. George Stewart's classic book on toponyms reveals many clusters of migrants and corresponding toponyms. Often the toponyms remain long after the migrants moved on. Clusters of Welsh toponyms in Pennsylvania, French toponyms in Louisiana, and Dutch toponyms in Michigan reveal migration flows and can also provide insight into language change and the evolution of dialects.

## Toponyms and Globalization

Brazil provides an interesting case study of migration flows and toponyms. Most Brazilian toponyms are Portuguese, reflecting the Portuguese colonization of the land. Amid the Portuguese toponyms sits a cluster of German toponyms in the southern state of Santa Catarina. The map of the state is marked by the place-naming activities of German immigrants. For example, the German word for flower is "Blume," and several last names in German begin with "Blum." The German immigrants had a fondness for the tropical flowers they saw in Brazil: southern Brazil is therefore dotted with towns named Blumenau, Blumberg, Blumenhof, Blumenort, Blumenthal, and Blumenstein. Brazilian toponyms also reveal the enormous flow of forced migration from West Africa to Brazil during the slave trade. The Brazilian State of Bahia has a number of toponyms that originated in West Africa, especially Benin and Nigeria.

The toponyms we see on a map depend in large part on who produced the map. Some embattled locales have more than one name at the same time. Argentineans refer to a small cluster (archipelago) of islands off the southeast coast of South America as the Malvinas, but the British call the same cluster of islands the Falkland Islands. In 1982, Argentina invaded the Malvinas, but the British forces fought back, and the islands remain under British control. British, American, and other allies call and map the islands as the Falklands, but Argentineans continue to call and map the islands as the Malvinas. The war ended in a matter of weeks, but the underlying dispute lingers, and so do both names.

## Changing Toponyms

Tuan explained that when people *change the toponym* of a place, they have the power to "wipe out the past and call forth the new." For example, people in a small town in Wales feared the loss of the Welsh language and despised the role the English had played in diminishing the use of the Welsh language. They also wanted to boost their local economy by attracting tourists to their town. A century ago, the people renamed their town with a Welsh word unpronounceable by others: Llanfairpwllgwyngyllgogerychwyrndrobwllllantysiliogogogoch (Fig. 6.19).

**TABLE 6.2**
**Toponym Classification Scheme Designed by George Stewart.**

| Type of Toponym | Example |
| --- | --- |
| Descriptive | Rocky Mountains |
| Associative | Mill Valley, California |
| Commemorative | San Francisco, California |
| Commendatory | Paradise Valley, Arizona |
| Incidents | Battle Creek, Michigan |
| Possession | Johnson City, Texas |
| Folk | Plains, Georgia |
| Manufactured | Truth or Consequences, New Mexico |
| Mistakes | Lasker, North Carolina |
| Shift | Lancaster, Pennsylvania |

© Alexander B. Murphy

■ **Figure 6.19**

**Llanfairpwllgwyngyllgogerychwyrndrobwllllantysiliogogogoch, Wales.**    The town with the self-proclaimed longest name in the world attracts hordes of tourists each year to a place whose claim to fame is largely its name.

The name accurately describes the geographical context within which the town in northern Wales is situated: "The Church of St. Mary in the hollow of white hazel near the rapid whirlpool by the church of St. Tysilio of the red cave." Since 1988, Wales has had an official policy of teaching both Welsh and English in the schools in order to preserve and boost usage of the Welsh language. Saying the name of this town correctly is now a benchmark for students learning Welsh, and the residents of the town take pride in their ability to pronounce it.

Toponyms are part of the cultural landscape. Changes in place-names give us an idea of the layers of history, the layers of cultural landscape in a place. For example, on the Kenai Peninsula in Alaska, where Clare Swan (whom we cited earlier in this chapter) is from, the changing place-names give us insight into identity questions in the place. Natives in one town on the Kenai Peninsula called their home Nanwalek in the early 1800s; when the Russians came in and took over the peninsula, they changed the name to Alexandrof. Americans mapped Alaska and then made it a State, and in the process, they changed the name to English Bay. In 1991, the townspeople changed the name of their home back to Nanwalek. When you arrive in Nanwalek, you will see native people, see signs of the Russian Orthodox religion, hear them speak English, and then talk with the native people who are reviving their native language and culture. The changes in the place-name provide insight into the cultural landscape.

## POSTCOLONIAL TOPONYMS

The question of changing toponyms often arises when power changes hands in a place. When African colonies became independent countries, many of the new governments immediately changed the toponyms of places named after colonial figures. The new governments renamed several countries: Upper Volta to Burkina Faso, Gold Coast to Ghana, Nyasaland to Malawi, and Northern and Southern Rhodesia to Zambia and Zimbabwe, respectively. Countries in Asia also chose new toponyms to mark their independence and separate themselves from their past: East Pakistan became Bangladesh, and the Netherlands East Indies became Indonesia.

Newly independent countries also changed the names of cities, towns, and geographic features to reflect their independence. Thus, Leopoldville (named after a Belgian king) became Kinshasa, capital of the Congo; Salisbury, Zimbabwe, named after a British leader, became Harare; and Lourenço Marques, Mozambique, commemorating a Portuguese naval hero, became Maputo. However, newly independent countries did not wipe all colonial names and references from their maps. Etoile (the Congo), Colleen Bawn (Zimbabwe), and Cabo Delgado (Mozambique) remain on the postcolonial map.

Sometimes the push to rename a toponym from one that reflects a colonial heritage occurs long after independence. In India, the large port city of Bombay was renamed Mumbai in 1995, despite the fact that India became independent from Britain some 50 years earlier. In this case, a nationalist party won local elections and implemented a long sought-after name change. The party renamed the city Mumbai, a toponym that both reinforces the city's Marathi identity and celebrates its patron Hindu goddess, Mumbadevi. Not everyone embraced the change, however; many locals continue to use Bombay—particularly those who are not Marathis.

Similarly, in 1996 the southern Indian city of Madras officially changed its name to Chennai. This change reflects the efforts of local leaders to honor the influence of Tamil language and culture in the southern State of Tamil Nadu. In another example, a Canadian bay named after British explorer Frobisher is now called Iqaluit Bay, reverting back to its indigenous Inuit name. But efforts to rename colonial-era cities have faced resistance as well. Often the local non-indigenous community is most resistant, arguing that the name change would erase their history. By and large, however, the push to change colonial-era names has been successful. These shifts have also led to confusion in the global arena, illustrated by embarrassing public gaffes when former colonial-era names have been used erroneously by political leaders in speeches and policy documents. In 2005 the United Nations published two manuals to standardize and keep up with changing toponyms in an increasingly globalized world.

## POSTREVOLUTION TOPONYMS

Independence prompts name changes, and so too do changes in power through coups and revolutions. During his reign, authoritarian dictator General Mobutu Sese Seko changed the name of the Belgian Congo in Subsaharan Africa to Zaïre. At first, other governments and international agencies did not take this move seriously, but eventually they recognized Mobutu's Zaïre. Governments and companies changed their maps and atlases to reflect Mobutu's decision. The government of Zaïre changed the name of their money from the franc to the zaïre, and they even changed the name of the Congo River to the Zaïre.

In 1997, the revolutionary leader Laurent Kabila ousted Mobutu and established his regime in the capital, Kinshasa. Almost immediately, he renamed the country. Zaïre became the Democratic Republic of the Congo (reflecting the colonial name). Again, governments and companies reacted, changing their maps and atlases to reflect Kabila's decision.

Recent revolutions in power in Russia and South Africa have led to many changes in toponyms in these countries. When the Soviet Union began, the communist government changed many places named for tsars who were in power before them, replacing them (of course) with Soviet names. Once the Soviet Union collapsed, a new round of name changes occurred, often going back to Tsarist-era names. In the new Russia, Leningrad reverted to St. Petersburg, Sverdlovsk went back to Yekaterinburg (its name under the tsars), and Stalingrad was renamed Volgograd (for the river). These

changes reverberated across the entire former Soviet sphere, with many cities in Central Asia abandoning Russified toponyms. Reformers, nationalists, and lingering communists argued bitterly over the toponym changes, and many people continued to address their mail according to their city's former name.

In the same time frame, South Africa experienced a major revolution that also resulted in a fundamental change in governance. The government of South Africa wrestled with pressures for and against toponym changes. The government restructured the country's administrative framework, creating nine provinces out of four and giving some of the new provinces African names (Mpumalanga for the new Eastern Transvaal, Gauteng for a new central province). One of the old provinces, Natal, has become Kwazulu-Natal. The government also changed some names of towns and villages, but South Africa's map still includes many names from the Boer-British and Apartheid periods. A push to change the name of the capital from Pretoria to the more indigenous Tshwane has been challenged by white South Africans who say the city was named Pretoria when it was founded and that the current name is therefore uniquely South African. Name changes can evoke strong reactions from people, and the South African government is trying to move slowly and carefully to avoid arousing emotions in their still-divided country.

## MEMORIAL TOPONYMS

People can choose to change a toponym to memorialize an important person or event. Hundreds of parks in the United States are named Memorial Park to commemorate a person or event. Towns or government agencies can vote to change the name of a school, a library, or a public building to memorialize people who have played a role in shaping the place or who have had an enormous influence on people in the place.

Certain events such as decolonization or a political revolution can spur changes in toponyms, and so too can revolutions in thought and behavior. The civil rights movement of the 1960s in the United States left many lasting impressions of people and events, especially in the South, where many protests, sit-ins, and marches occurred. Geographer Derek Alderman explains that, in recent decades, African Americans in the South have "taken a particularly active role in reconstructing commemorative landscapes—from calling for the removal of Confederate symbols from public places to the building of memorials and museums honoring the civil rights movement." Streets are often the focal point of commemoration in the cultural landscape because so many people travel along them daily, serving as a constant reminder of the person or event being memorialized.

Alderman studied the practice of changing street names to memorialize Martin Luther King Jr. (MLK), the major African American leader of the civil rights movement.

Although streets named after MLK are found throughout the United States, the greatest concentration of memorial streets are in the South, especially in Georgia (King's home state) and Mississippi (Fig. 6.20). Alderman studied the distribution of MLK streets in the South, comparing their locations with census data on race and socioeconomics. He found that although MLK streets are found in both cities and rural areas, "MLK streets are located—whether by choice or by force—in census areas that are generally poorer and with more African Americans than citywide averages" (Fig. 6.21). Alderman tempers this finding with a caution that not all MLK streets are located in poorer areas of cities. Even when MLK streets are located in depressed areas, the African American population may have purposely chosen a street because it runs through an African American neighborhood. Alderman's subsequent studies explore the scale of the city and the contested views of what kinds of streets should be named for MLK—be they residential, commercial, major thoroughfares (perhaps those that connect white and African American neighborhoods), or residential streets in largely African American neighborhoods.

The presence of streets named for civil rights leaders in the cultural landscapes of the American South creates a significant counterbalance to the numerous places of commemoration named for leaders of the Confederacy during the Civil War (see Chapter 1).

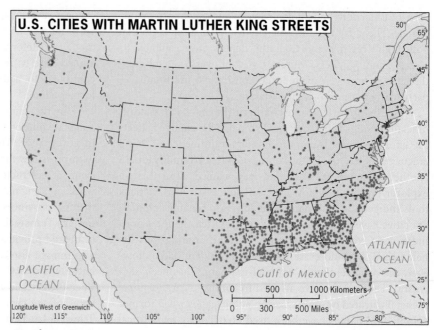

**■ Figure 6.20**

**Cities in the United States with a Street Named for Martin Luther King Jr.**   Commemorating Martin Luther King through street naming displays a strong concentration in the southeastern United States (almost 70% of all MLK-named roads) even as it is a national trend. King hailed from Georgia and the South was an early battleground in the Civil Rights Movement. Moreover, African Americans still make up a significant proportion of the southern population across varying sizes of cities involved in the naming process.   Data drawn from several sources by Derek Alderman, Janna Caspersen, Matthew Mitchelson, and Chris McPhilamy, 2014.

# GUEST FIELD NOTE

## Greenville, North Carolina

Greenville, North Carolina, changed West Fifth Street to Martin Luther King Jr. Drive in 1999. Originally, African American leaders wanted all of Fifth Street renamed—not just part of it—but residents and business owners on the eastern end strongly opposed the proposal. After driving and walking down the street, I quickly realized that King Drive marked an area that was predominantly black with limited commercial development, whereas East Fifth was mostly white and more upscale. When I interviewed members of Greenville's African American community, they expressed deep frustration over the marginalization of the civil rights leader. In the words of one elected official, "The accomplishments of Dr. King were important to all Americans. A whole man deserves a whole street!" Naming streets for King is a controversial process for many cities, often exposing continued racial tensions and the

**■ Figure 6.21**

potential for toponyms to function as contested social boundaries within places.

*Credit: Derek Alderman, University of Tennessee*

Patrick Pease and Derek Alderman

## COMMODIFICATION OF TOPONYMS

The practice of commodifying (buying, selling, and trading) toponyms is growing. International media corporations that reach across the globe bring known names to new places, drawing consumers to the place based on what they have heard or experienced elsewhere. For example, the Disney Corporation opened Tokyo Disneyland in 1983 and Disneyland Paris in 1990, both places that capitalize on the success of Disneyland and Disneyworld in the United States. As corporations spread their names and logos to other places, they seek to "brand" places, creating or re-creating places that consumers associate with places of the same brand.

In recent years, the activities of corporations with a global reach have been stamped on the landscape. Stadiums are especially susceptible to this form of commodification: FedEx Field, Verizon Center, TD Bank Garden, CenturyLink Field, and Coors Field are perfect examples. In 2004, the cash-strapped Metropolitan Transit Authority (MTA) in New York City proposed renaming the metro stops, bridges, and tunnels after corporate sponsors. The plan was approved in 2013, and metro riders have been assured the name changes will not elicit confusion. Corporate sponsors are only eligible to buy naming rights provided they have "a unique or iconic geographic, historic or other connection" to a particular MTA facility "that would readily be apparent to typical MTA customers."

*This place was first named by Gabrielino Indians. In 1769, Spanish Franciscan priests renamed the place. In 1850, English speakers renamed the place.* Do not use the Internet to help you. Use only maps in this book or in atlases to help you deduce what this place is. Maps of European exploration and colonialism will help you the most. Look at the end of the chapter summary for the answer.

## Summary

The global mosaic of languages reflects centuries of divergence, convergence, extinction, and diffusion. Linguists and linguistic geographers have the interesting work of uncovering, through deep reconstruction, the hearths of the world's language families. Some languages, such as Basque, are not easily explained. Other languages are the foci of countless studies, many of which come to differing conclusions about their ancient origins.

As certain languages, such as English and Chinese, gain speakers and become global languages, other languages become extinct. Some languages come to serve as the lingua franca of a region or place. Governments choose official languages, and through public schools, educators entrench an official language in a place. Some countries, faced with the global diffusion of the English language, defend and promote their national language. Whether mandating that signs be written a certain way or requiring a television station to broadcast some proportion of programming in the national language, governments can preserve language, choose a certain dialect as the standard, or repel the diffusion of other languages.

Regardless of the place, people, or language used, language continues to define, shape, and maintain culture. How a person thinks about the world is reflected in the words used to describe and define it.

Answer to Final Thinking Geographically Question: Los Angeles, California.

## Geographic Concepts

language
mutual intelligibility
standard language
dialects
dialect chains
isogloss
language families
subfamilies
cognate
Proto-Indo-European

Proto-Eurasiatic
language divergence
backward reconstruction
language convergence
extinct language
conquest theory
Romance languages
Germanic languages
Slavic languages
lingua franca

pidgin language
Creole language
monolingual states
multilingual states
official language
global language
place
toponym

# Learn More Online

**About Learning Foreign Languages Online:**
www.bbc.co.uk/languages

**About Maps of Dialect Differences in the United States**
www4.uwm.edu/FLL/linguistics/dialect/maps.html

**About the most recent Pop vs. Soda Map**
www.tekstlab.uio.no/cambridge_survey/

**About Careers as a Language Professional:**
careers.un.org/lbw/home.aspx?viewtype=LE
ec.europa.eu/dgs/translation/translating/index_en.htm

# Watch It Online

**About the Loss of Native Languages in Alaska**
www.learner.org/resources/series85.html#program_descriptions
click on Video On Demand for "Alaska: The Last Frontier?"

**About the Impact of Technology on Language Development:**
www.pbs.org/wgbh/pages/frontline/digitalnation/learning/literacy/hey-prof-i-just-txtd-u-my-paper.html

# RELIGION

## Peace Walls

I felt uneasy as I stood in the Clonnard Martyrs Memorial Garden. Built to honor Catholics who had fallen during the Troubles between Catholics and Protestants, the gardens were more of a brick patio with brick walls than a garden. A 40-foot-tall peace wall towered behind the gardens, and next to the garden stretching along the wall was a row of houses settled by Catholics. On the other side of the peace wall was the Protestant Shankhill neighborhood, where I had been 10 minutes earlier. My sense of unease came from a sound that I typically find comforting, children laughing.

I looked over the brick wall of the memorial garden to see the children. It was a scene I could see in my backyard on a summer evening, kids jumping on a trampoline (Fig. 7.1), but I did not see trees, grass, swing sets, barbeques, or the other familiarities of backyards in my neighborhood. The peace wall loomed behind the trampoline, and on the other side was the child's home. The back side of his house was shielded by a rather large cage. I looked up at the wall again and realized the cage was there to protect the back door and windows from anything being flung over the wall from the Protestant Shankhill neighborhood into the Catholic Falls neighborhood.

© Erin H. Fouberg

■ **Figure 7.1**

**Belfast, Northern Ireland.** A child jumps on a trampoline in a backyard in the Catholic Falls neighborhood. A 40-foot-tall peace wall stands to the left of the trampoline, dividing this Catholic neighborhood from the Protestant Shankhill neighborhood on the other side.

Built beginning in the 1960s to separate Catholics and Protestants in hopes of suppressing violence, the Belfast peace walls have now stood 20 years longer than the Berlin Wall (1961–1989). This wall, which runs more than 3 miles (5 km) through the city, is the largest of the city's

99 peace walls. The peace wall between Shankhill and Falls has five gates that are open between about 7 A.M. and 7 P.M., Monday through Friday. Otherwise, you have to go all of the way around the wall to get from one neighborhood to the next.

The peace walls are quite visible, but the residents of this area of Belfast also carry invisible lines in their minds of routes that are safe and paths that are not. Geographer Frederick Boal established through extensive field research in 1969 that Protestants and Catholics in Belfast chose to separate themselves in their rounds of daily activity, their **activity spaces**. Boal found that members of each group traveled longer distances to shop in grocery stores tagged as their respective religion, walked further to catch a bus in a neighborhood belonging to their own religion, gave their neighborhood different toponyms, read different newspapers, and cheered for different football (soccer) teams.

In the journal *Children's Geographies*, Madeleine Leonard (2006) studied how teens in Belfast negotiate living in **interface areas** where Catholic and Protestant neighborhoods meet and where violence and trauma occurred. She found that teens identify with the Protestant football team (the Rangers) or the Catholic football team (the Celtics), but they consciously choose not to wear their team's gear when they go into shared spaces such as leisure areas in the city. Likewise, teens who go into a park or shared public space report that they do not call each other by name if their names are commonly Catholic (like Paddy) or Protestant (like Billy).

Children growing up in religious interface areas around the world experience childhood in distinct ways, learning to choose when to share identities, what routes are safe, which door to use to enter a movie theater, which grocery store to shop, and which football team to support. Particularly violent religious interface areas like Palestine/Israel, Iraq, and Sudan appear on the news, but thousands of religious interface areas around the world, like Belfast, receive less global media attention while being a very real part of everyday life for the children, teens, and adults who live there.

In this chapter we study the origins, diffusions, and transformations of the world's great religions, their regional patterns, and their cultural landscapes. As we will find, religion can unite and divide, flourish and stagnate, surge and fade. Understanding the changing map of world religions and the role of religion in culture is essential to appreciating human geography.

# Key Questions FOR CHAPTER 7

1. What is religion, and what role does it play in culture?
2. Where did the world's major religions originate, and how do religions diffuse?
3. How is religion seen in the cultural landscape?
4. What role does religion play in political conflicts?

## WHAT IS RELIGION, AND WHAT ROLE DOES IT PLAY IN CULTURE?

Religion and language lie at the foundation of culture: Both confer and reflect identity. Like languages, religions are constantly changing. Although religious leaders and bureaucracies sometimes attempt to slow the pace of change, religions nevertheless change over time.

Religions diffuse through both contagious and hierarchical forms of expansion diffusion, as well as through relocation diffusion. In any of these cases, leaders or followers of a religion interact with people who do not espouse the religion, and the interactions sometimes lead to conversion. Spatial interaction occurs through migration, missionary efforts, and even conquest. Along these paths, major religions of the world have diffused.

# FIELD NOTE

"Each religion approaches the disposition of the deceased in its own way, and cultural landscapes reflect religious traditions. In largely Christian, Western regions, the deceased are buried in cemeteries. The Hindu faith, which is predominantly found in India, requires cremation of the deceased. When the British colonized both India and Kenya in the late nineteenth and early twentieth centuries, they brought Indians to Kenya as 'bonded laborers' to lay the Kenya-Uganda railroad (Bhowmick 2008). The number of Indians in Kenya peaked at 175,000 in 1962 and is approximately 100,000 today, large enough to need a crematorium, the equivalent of a Hindu funeral home."

■ **Figure 7.2**
**Mombasa, Kenya.**

The cultural landscape is marked by religion—most obviously by church, synagogues, temples, and mosques, cemeteries and shrines, statues and symbols (Fig. 7.2). Other more subtle markers of religion dot the landscape as well. The presence or absence of stores selling alcohol or of signs depicting the human form in particular ways reflects prevailing religious views. Religion is also proclaimed in modes of dress (veils, turbans) and personal habits (beards, ritual scars). The outward display of religious beliefs often reveals the inward structure of a religion. For example, in the Islamic Republic of Pakistan, in 1991, the government proclaimed that possessing a beard would be a condition for the appointment of judges. The beard requirement was an outward display of religion, and it also shows the inward structure of Islam in Pakistan, where women have not been in a place of judicial power.

**Religion** is an extraordinarily difficult concept to define. Geographers Robert Stoddard and Carolyn Prorak define religion as "a system of beliefs and practices that attempts to order life in terms of culturally perceived ultimate priorities" (2004). They explain that the idea of "perceived ultimate priorities" is often expressed in terms of *should*: People explain and justify how they and others should behave based on their religious beliefs. From eating habits to dress codes, religions set standards for how adherents should behave (Fig. 7.3). "Shouldness" goes beyond religion to other belief systems, but in this chapter we focus on formal religions, their distribution, and their role in making and shaping places and cultures. The idea that a "good" life has rewards and that "bad" behavior risks punishment has an enormous influence on cultures, on how people behave, and on how people perceive and evaluate the behavior of others.

Religion is also seen in places and practices that do not involve large buildings or expansive cemeteries. We can see religion in the worship of the souls of ancestors who are thought to inhabit natural objects such as mountains, animals, or trees; in the belief that a certain living person possesses special abilities granted by a supernatural power; and in the belief in a deity or deities, as in the great world religions. In some places, societies are so infused with religion that religious tradition strongly influences behaviors during waking hours through ritual and practice and even during periods of sleep in prescribing what direction a person should face when sleeping.

Across the multitude of religions, some practices such as ritual and prayer are common. Rituals may mark important events in people's lives: birth and death, attainment of adulthood, or marriage. Rituals are typically expressed at regular intervals in a routine manner, as is done on certain days in the Christian and Jewish worlds, certain times of the day in the Muslim world, or according to certain astronomical events in the Jewish, Hindu, Muslim, and Christian worlds. A common ritual is prayer, whether at mealtime, at sunrise and sundown, at night upon retiring, or in the morning when arising (Fig. 7.4).

Although religious beliefs and prescriptions influence many societies, in other places, religion, at least in its organized form, has become less significant in the lives of people. **Secularism** is the indifference to or rejection of formal religion. The most secular countries in the world today are in Europe. A 2009 Pew survey asked people in 56 countries how important religion is in their lives. Among the wealthiest countries surveyed, the United States stood out as the highest, with 55 percent of Americans surveyed saying religion is very important in

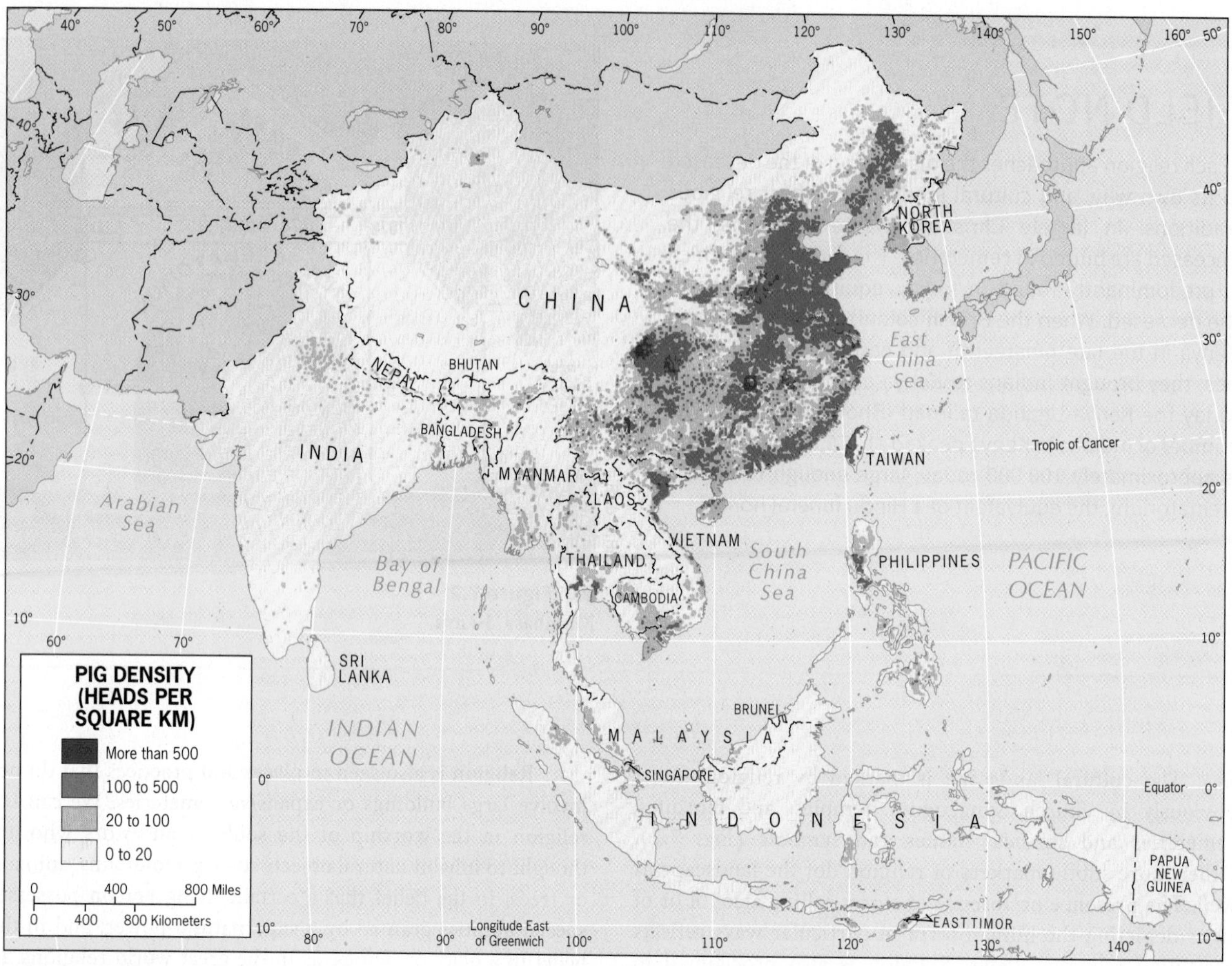

**PIG DENSITY (HEADS PER SQUARE KM)**

- More than 500
- 100 to 500
- 20 to 100
- 0 to 20

0   400   800 Miles
0   400   800 Kilometers

■ **Figure 7.3**

**Pork Production and Religious Prohibitions.**   Pork is the most common meat source in China, but pork production is slim to none in predominantly Muslim countries, including Bangladesh and Indonesia and in the predominantly Hindu country of India, where pork consumption is prohibited for religious reasons.   *Source: Geographical Trends in Livestock Densities and Nutrient Balances, 2011. http://pigtrop.cirad.fr*

STRUNIN ANATOLY/ITAR-TASS/Landov

their lives. Only 13 percent of people surveyed in France, 19 percent in Great Britain, and 7 percent in the Czech Republic agreed that religion is very important in their lives. Regionally, survey respondents in Subsaharan Africa, South Asia, Southwest Asia, and South America more strongly agreed that religion is very important in their lives: 98 percent in Senegal, 97 percent in Bangladesh, 95 percent in Indonesia, and 78 percent in Brazil.

Regardless of Europe's present-day secularism, religion certainly has had a critical role in the history of Europe. During the Middle Ages and into the colonial period, the Christian church was a dominant force politically, economically and culturally in Europe. Because Christianity was a major part of life in Europe for

■ **Figure 7.4**

**New York, United States.**   A Muslim man takes a break from serving food off a vendor cart to pray on a busy Manhattan street.

centuries, much of the region's art, architecture, history, customs, and cultural norms derive from Christian beliefs and teachings. Even in a secular society, and regardless of your religious beliefs, what you eat, when you work, when you shop, and what you are allowed to do are influenced by religion.

Organized religions have had a powerful effect on human societies. Religion has been a major force in combating social ills, sustaining the poor, promoting the arts, educating the deprived, and advancing medical knowledge. However, religion has also blocked scientific study, encouraged the oppression of dissidents, supported colonialism and exploitation, and condemned women to an inferior status in many societies. Religion is, if nothing else, one of the most complex and often controversial aspects of the human condition.

 Compare and contrast the maps of world religions and world language families (Chapter 6). Then consider the map of major global immigration movements (Chapter 3) and how migration has helped religions and languages diffuse through relocation diffusion. Describe how migration, religion, and language affect and change one another to shape cultures.

## WHERE DID THE MAJOR RELIGIONS OF THE WORLD ORIGINATE, AND HOW DO RELIGIONS DIFFUSE?

Despite the wide variety of religions found around the world, they are commonly classified into three categories based on their approaches to the concept of divinity.

Adherents of **monotheistic religions** worship a single deity, a God ('Allah' in Arabic). Believers in **polytheistic religions** worship more than one deity, even thousands. **Animistic religions** are centered on the belief that inanimate objects, such as mountains, boulders, rivers, and trees, possess spirits and should therefore be revered. Throughout much of human history, virtually all religions were either animistic, polytheistic, or both. Somewhere around 3500 years ago, however, a monotheistic religion developed in Southwest Asia called Zoroastrianism. Some believe that the monotheism of late Judaism, Christianity, and Islam can be traced to Zoroastrian influences. Others believe that Judaism itself was the first monotheistic religion. Whichever the case, the eventual diffusion of Christianity and Islam spread monotheistic ideas throughout much of the world and marked a major theological shift away from the long dominance of polytheistic and animist beliefs in most places. The transformation from polytheistic to monotheistic religions happened quite rapidly in Subsaharan Africa. In 1900, neither Islam nor Christianity had many followers in Subsaharan Africa. By 2012, the number of Muslims in Subsaharan Africa had grown from 11 million to 248 million, and the number of Christians had grown from 7 million to 517 million.

By 500 BCE, four major hearths of religion and philosophy had developed in the world (Fig. 7.5). From a hearth in South Asia, along the Indus River Valley, came Hinduism; from a hearth on the eastern Mediterranean came Judaism; from a hearth on the Huang He (Yellow River) Valley in China came Chinese philosophies; and from the northern shores of the Mediterranean Sea came Greek philosophy. These early-established religions and philosophies profoundly impacted other religions, as the arrows in Figure 7.5 demonstrate. Philosophies and religions diffused from their hearths, affecting one another and influencing the ways founders established newer religions. The two religions with the greatest number of

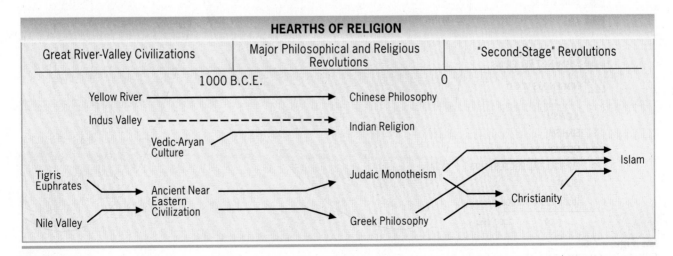

**■ Figure 7.5**

**Hearths of Major World Religions.** © *Adapted with permission from:* Albert M. Craig, William M. Graham, Donald Kagan, Stephen Ozment, and Frank M. Turner. *The Heritage of World Civilizations*, 7th ed., New York: Prentice Hall, 2006.

adherents in the world today, Christianity and Islam, were both influenced by Judaism and Greek philosophy.

## The World Map of Religions Today

The map in Figure 7.6 provides a global overview of the distribution of the world's major religions. Any map of world religions is a generalization, and caution must be used when making observations from the map. First, the shadings on the map show the major religion in an area, thereby masking minority religions, many of which have a significant number of followers. India, for example, is depicted as a Hindu region (except in the northwest), but other religions, including Islam and Sikhism, attract millions of adherents in India. Of the 1.2 billion people in India, 161 million are Muslims,

which makes India the third largest Muslim country in the world behind Indonesia and Pakistan.

Second, some of the regions shown as belonging to a particular religion are places where faiths have penetrated relatively recently and where traditional religious ideas influence the practice of the dominant faith. Many Christian and Muslim Africans, for example, continue to believe in traditional spirits even as they profess a belief in a universalizing religion. A 2010 Pew Research survey of 25,000 people in 19 African countries found that "Large numbers of Africans actively participate in Christianity or Islam yet also believe in witchcraft, evil spirits, sacrifices to ancestors, traditional religious healers, reincarnation and other elements of traditional African religions." The survey found that 25 percent of Christian Africans and 30 percent of Muslim Africans they interviewed believed in the protective

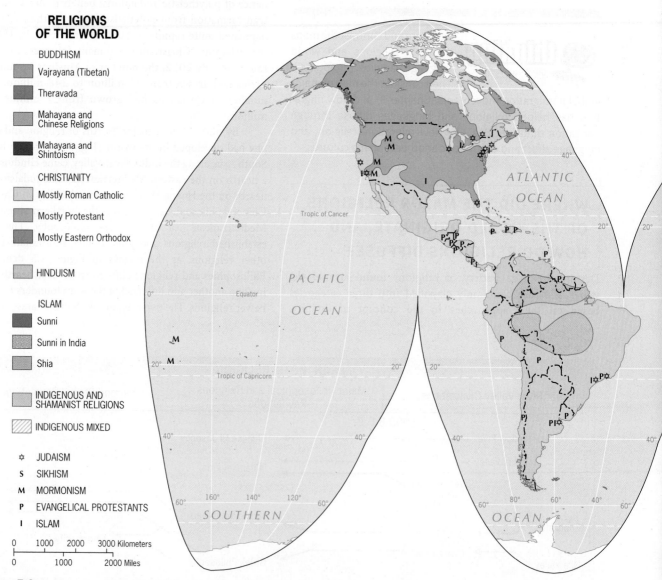

**RELIGIONS OF THE WORLD**

BUDDHISM
- Vajrayana (Tibetan)
- Theravada
- Mahayana and Chinese Religions
- Mahayana and Shintoism

CHRISTIANITY
- Mostly Roman Catholic
- Mostly Protestant
- Mostly Eastern Orthodox

HINDUISM

ISLAM
- Sunni
- Sunni in India
- Shia

INDIGENOUS AND SHAMANIST RELIGIONS

INDIGENOUS MIXED

✡ JUDAISM
S SIKHISM
M MORMONISM
P EVANGELICAL PROTESTANTS
I ISLAM

0   1000   2000   3000 Kilometers
0       1000       2000 Miles

■ **Figure 7.6**

**Religions of the World.** *Data from*: Several sources, including Hammond, Inc., 1977; H. J. de Blij, P. O. Muller, and A. Winkler Prins, *The World Today*, 4e, 2008; State Department Religious Freedom Report, CIA World Factbook, Pew Forum on Religion and Public Life, and author observations. © E. H. Fouberg, A. B. Murphy, H. J. de Blij, and John Wiley & Sons, Inc.

power of sacrifices to spirits or ancestors. The country with the highest percentage of respondents who held this belief was Tanzania with 60 percent, and the lowest was Rwanda with 5 percent.

In Cameroon, 42 percent of those surveyed believed in the protective power of sacrifices to spirits or ancestors. For example, the Bamileke tribe in Cameroon lives in an area colonized by the French, who brought Catholicism to the region. The Bamileke are largely Christian today, but they also continue to practice aspects of their traditional animist religion. Ancestors are still very important in the lives of the Bamileke; many believe ancestors decide everything for them. It is common practice to take the skull of a deceased male member of the tribe and place it in the basement of the home of the family's oldest living male. Birth practices also reflect traditional religious practices. The Bamileke bury the

umbilical cord in the ground outside their home so that the baby remembers where he or she came from. Members of the Bamileke tribe also commonly have two weddings: one in the church and one traditional.

A final limitation of Figure 7.6 is that it does not reflect the rise in secularism in the world, especially in Europe. In a number of areas, many people have moved away from organized religion entirely. Thus, France appears on the map as a Roman Catholic country, yet a large proportion of people in France profess adherence to no particular faith.

Despite the limitations of the map of world religions, it illustrates how far Christian religions have diffused (2.2 billion adherents worldwide), the extent of the diffusion of Islam (1.6 billion), the connection between Hinduism (950 million adherents) and one of the world's major population concentrations, and the continued importance of Buddhism

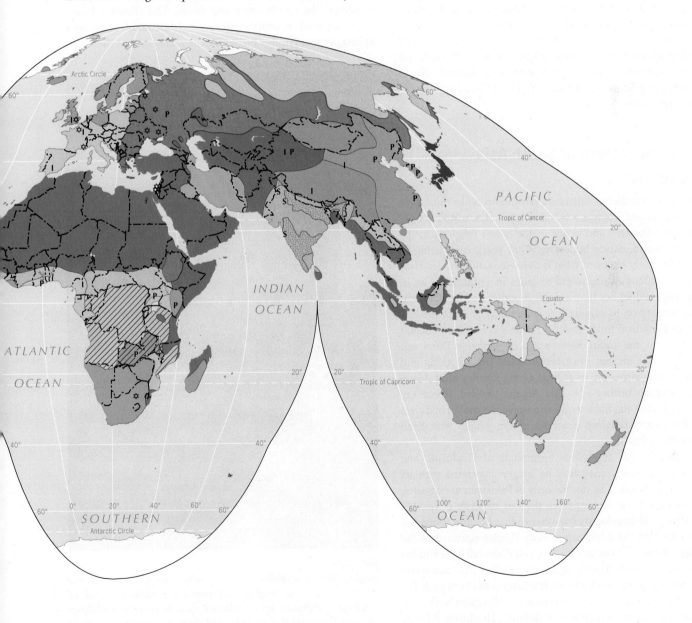

(347 million followers) in parts of Asia. Many factors help explain the distributions shown on the map, but each of the widespread religions shares one characteristic in common: They are all universalizing religions. **Universalizing religions** actively seek converts because they view themselves as offering belief systems of universal appropriateness and appeal. Christianity, Islam, and Buddhism all fall within this category, and their universalizing character helps explain their widespread distribution.

Universalizing religions are relatively few in number and of recent origin. Throughout human history, a greater number of religions have not actively sought converts. Rather, a given religion has been practiced by one particular culture or ethnic group. In an **ethnic religion**, adherents are born into the faith and converts are not actively sought. Ethnic religions (405 million followers) tend to be spatially concentrated—as is the case with traditional religions, which are found primarily in small areas of Asia, the Pacific, Africa, and South America. The principal exception is Judaism (14 million adherents), an ethnic religion whose adherents are widely scattered through Southwest Asia, Europe, North America, and South America as a result of forced and voluntary migrations.

## From the Hearth of South Asia

### HINDUISM

In terms of number of adherents, **Hinduism** ranks third after Christianity and Islam as a world religion. Hinduism has over 1 billion adherents and is one of the oldest religions in the modern world, dating back over 4000 years, originating in the Indus River Valley of what is today part of Pakistan. Hinduism is unique among world religions in a number of ways. The religion does not have a single founder, a single theology, or agreement on its origins. The common account of the history of Hinduism holds that the religion is based on ancient practices in the Indus River cities of Mohenjo-Daro and Harappa. The ancient practices included ritual bathing and belief in reincarnation, or at least a long journey after death. The common history says that Aryans invaded (some say migrated into) the Indus region and gave the name Hinduism to the diverse religious practices of the people who lived along the Indus River.

Despite the ambiguous beginnings of Hinduism, one thing is certain: Hinduism is no longer associated with its hearth in Pakistan. The vast majority of Pakistanis are Muslim, and as Figure 7.6 demonstrates, the vast majority of Indians are Hindu. Archaeologists hypothesize that flooding along the Indus spurred the migration of early Hindus eastward to the Ganges River. The Ganges (*Ganga*, as Indians call it) is Hinduism's sacred river. Hindus regard its ceaseless flow and spiritual healing power as earthly manifestations of the Almighty.

Just as there is no consensus on Hinduism's origins, there is a lack of agreement on defining Hinduism relative to other major world religions. Some define Hinduism as a

polytheistic religion because of the presence of many gods. However, many Hindus define their religion as monotheistic. The one god is Brahman (the universal soul), and the other gods in the religion are various expressions of Brahman. Western academics define Hinduism today as an ethnic religion because Hindus do not actively seek converts. At the same time, historical evidence shows Hindus migrating into Southeast Asia and diffusing their religion, as a universalizing religion would, before the diffusion of Buddhism and Islam into Southeast Asia (Fig. 7.7). Although Hinduism is now more of an ethnic religion, the religion has millions of adherents in the populous region of South Asia, extending beyond India to Bangladesh, Myanmar, Sri Lanka, and Nepal.

The Hindu religion is not centrally organized. The religion does not have an administrative or bureaucratic structure like Christianity and Islam. The Hindu religion does not have a prophet or a single book of scriptures, although most Hindus recognize the sacredness of the *Vedas*,

© Alexander B. Murphy

■ **Figure 7.7**

**Angkor Wat, Cambodia.** The extensive walled structure at the temple complex in Angkor Wat marks the earliest period of Hinduism's diffusion into Southeast Asia. Eventually, Buddhism replaced Hinduism in Cambodia, and many Hindu temples such as this one were abandoned.

four ancient collections of texts that have particular sacred status.

Hinduism is a conglomeration of beliefs characterized by a great diversity of institutional forms and practices. The fundamental doctrine is *karma*, which has to do with the transferability of the soul. According to Hindu doctrine, all beings have souls and are arranged in a hierarchy. The ideal is to move upward in the hierarchy and then escape from the eternal cycle of *reincarnation* through union with Brahman (the universal soul). A soul moves upward or downward according to the individual's behavior in the present life. Good deeds and adherence to the faith lead to a higher level in the next life, whereas bad behavior leads to demotion to a lower level. All souls, those of animals as well as humans, participate in this process. The principle of reincarnation is a cornerstone of Hinduism.

Hinduism's doctrines are closely bound to Indian society's caste system, for castes themselves are steps on the universal ladder. The **caste system** locks people into particular social classes and imposes many restrictions, especially in the lowest of the castes and in those considered beneath the caste system, Dalits. Until a generation ago, Dalits could not enter temples, were excluded from certain schools, and were restricted to performing the most unpleasant tasks. The coming of other religions to India, the effects of modernization during the colonial period, the work of Mahatma Gandhi, and affirmative action policies helped loosen the social barriers of the caste system. Today the Indian government's affirmative action policies reserve seats in universities and jobs in government for scheduled castes, scheduled tribes, and Dalits.

## DIFFUSION OF HINDUISM

Hinduism evolved in what is today Pakistan. From there, Hinduism migrated to the Ganges River and diffused throughout South Asia and into Southeast Asia before the advent of Christianity. Hinduism first attached itself to traditional faiths and then slowly replaced them. Later, when Islam and Christianity appeared and were actively spread in Hindu areas, Hindu thinkers attempted to integrate certain new teachings into their own religion. For example, elements of the Sermon on the Mount (Jesus' sermon in which he described God's love for the poor and the peacemakers) now form part of Hindu preaching, and Christian beliefs contributed to the weakening of caste barriers. In other instances, the confrontation between Hinduism and other faiths led to the emergence of a **syncretic** or compromise religion. Islam stimulated the rise of Sikhism, whose followers disapproved of the worship of idols and disliked the caste system but retained the concepts of reincarnation and karma. Given its current character as an ethnic religion, it is not surprising that Hinduism's geographical extent is relatively small. Throughout most of Southeast Asia, Buddhism and Islam overtook the places where Hinduism had diffused during its universalizing period. In overwhelmingly Muslim Indonesia,

the island of Bali remains a Hindu outpost. Bali became a refuge for Hindu holy men, nobles, and intellectuals during the sixteenth century (Fig. 7.8), when Islam engulfed neighboring Java, which now retains only architectural remnants of its Hindu age. Since then, the Balinese have developed a unique faith, still based on Hindu principles but mixed with elements of Buddhism, animism, and ancestor worship. Religion plays an extremely important role in Bali. Temples and shrines dominate the cultural landscape, and participation in worship, festivals, and other ceremonies of the island's unique religion is almost universal. Religion is so much at the heart of Balinese culture that it is sometimes described as a celebration of life.

Outside South Asia and Bali, Hinduism's presence is relatively minor. Over the last two centuries, Hinduism has diffused to small parts of the world through migration. During the British colonial era, the British transported hundreds

© Alexander B. Murphy

■ **Figure 7.8**

**Bali, Indonesia.** The town of Ubud in central Bali is dotted with Hindu temples. Hinduism arrived in Southeast Asia some 2000 years ago. It was gradually replaced by Buddhism, and then Islam came to the southern parts of the region. Bali became a refuge for believers in Hinduism; it is the one place in Indonesia where Hinduism continues to dominate today.

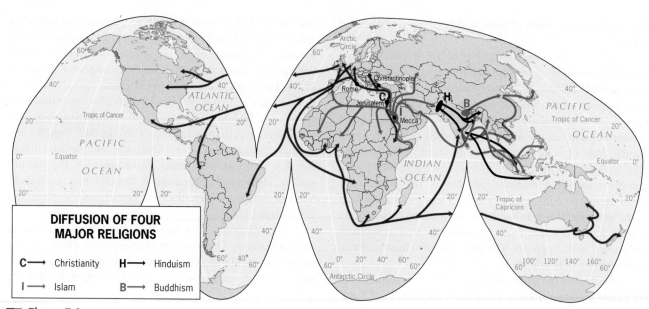

**Diffusion of Four Major World Religions.**   The hearths and major routes of diffusion are shown on this map. It does not show smaller diffusion streams: Islam and Buddhism, for example, are gaining strength in North America, although their numbers are still comparatively small.   © E. H. Fouberg, A. B. Murphy, and H. J. de Blij, John Wiley & Sons, Inc.

of thousands of Hindu adherents as bonded laborers from India to their other colonies in East and South Africa, the Caribbean, northern South America, and the Pacific Islands (see Fig. 7.2). Because Hinduism is not a universalizing religion today, the relocation diffusion produced pockets rather than regions of Hinduism.

## BUDDHISM

**Buddhism** splintered from Hinduism over 2500 years ago. Buddhism and several other religions appeared in India as a reaction to questions about Hinduism's teachings at the time. Reformers questioned Hinduism's strict social hierarchy that protected the privileged and kept millions in poverty. Prince Siddhartha, who was heir to a wealthy kingdom in what is now Nepal, founded Buddhism. Siddhartha was profoundly shaken by the misery he saw around him, which contrasted sharply with the splendor and wealth in which he had been raised. Siddhartha came to be known as Buddha, the enlightened one. He may have been the first prominent Indian religious leader to speak out against Hinduism's caste system. Salvation, he preached, could be attained by anyone, no matter what his or her caste. Enlightenment would come through knowledge, especially self-knowledge; elimination of greed, craving, and desire; complete honesty; and never hurting another person or animal.

After Buddha's death in the fifth century BCE at the age of 80, the faith grew rather slowly until the middle of the third century BCE, when the Emperor Asoka became a convert. Asoka was the leader of a large and powerful Indian empire that extended from the Punjab to Bengal and from the Himalayan foothills to Mysore. He not only set out to

rule his country in accordance with the teachings of Buddha; but also sent missionaries to carry Buddha's teachings to distant peoples (Fig. 7.9). Buddhism spread as far south as Sri Lanka and later advanced westward toward the Mediterranean, north into Tibet, and east into China, Korea, Japan, Vietnam, and Indonesia, over a span of about ten centuries (Fig. 7.8). Although Buddhism diffused to distant lands, it began to decline in its region of origin. During Asoka's rule there may have been more Buddhists than Hindu adherents in India, but after that period Hinduism gained followers in India. Today Buddhism is practiced by relatively few in India, but it thrives in Sri Lanka, Southeast Asia, Nepal, Tibet, and Korea. Along with other faiths, Buddhism is part of Japanese culture.

Like Christianity and Islam, Buddhism changed as it grew and diffused, and now the religion is strongly regional with three major forms. Buddhism's various branches have an estimated 488 million adherents, with Mahayana, Theravada, and Vajrayana (Tibetan) Buddhism claiming the most adherents. Theravada Buddhism translates as "the way of the elders." The hearth of Theravada Buddhism was established first, and it was the first branch of Buddhism to diffuse, spreading to Sri Lanka, Myanmar (Burma), Thailand, Laos, and Cambodia. Theravada Buddhism holds that salvation is a personal matter, achieved through good behavior and religious activities, including periods of service as a monk or nun. Theravada Buddhists tie their teachings back to the historical Buddha and contend that their beliefs are the "true Buddhism."

Mahayana Buddhism was the second form of Buddhism established in northern India, and it diffused into China, Vietnam, Korea, and Japan. Mahayana Buddhism translates as

© H. J. de Blij

■ **Figure 7.10**
**Kyoto, Japan.**   In Japan, both Buddhism and Shintoism make their marks on the cultural landscape. This Shinto shrine, with its orange trim and olive-green glazed tiles, is visible after passing under a torii—a gateway usually formed by two wooden posts topped by two horizontal beams turned up at their ends—which signals that you have left the secular and entered the sacred world.

"the greater vehicle," and the idea is that more people can achieve enlightenment through its teachings than through the strict teachings of Theravada Buddhism. The Buddha is regarded as a divine savior, and other great Buddhists are regarded as bodhisattvas (those who have reached enlightenment) and are worshipped along with the Buddha. Mahayana Buddhists do not serve as monks, but they spend much time in personal meditation and worship, believing that achieving enlightenment helps all beings on Earth. Mahayana Buddhism was influenced by Chinese and Japanese religions, including Taoism and Shintoism.

The third largest branch of Buddhism is Vajrayana (Tibetan), which emphasizes the role of the guru or lama as religious and political leader. Vajrayana Buddhism was the last branch to be established, diffusing north from India into Tibet and Mongolia. Gurus in Vajrayana Buddhism use mantras, tantras, and meditation to help followers achieve enlightenment faster than the bodhisattva approach in Mahayana Buddhism, which can take several lifetimes.

Buddhism has become a global religion over the last two centuries, diffusing to many areas of the world, but not without conflict in its wake. Militant regimes have attacked the religion in Cambodia, Laos, and Vietnam. In Thailand, Buddhism has been under pressure owing to rising political tensions. At the same time, Buddhism has gained adherents in the Western world.

### SHINTOISM

Buddhism is mixed with a local religion in Japan, where **Shintoism** is found. This ethnic religion, which is related to

Buddhism, focuses particularly on nature and ancestor worship (Fig. 7.10). The Japanese emperor made Shintoism the state religion of Japan in the nineteenth century, giving himself the status of divine-right monarch. At the end of World War II, Japan separated Shintoism from the emperor, taking away the state sanctioning of the religion. At the same time, the role of the emperor in Japan was diminished and given a ceremonial status. The number of Shinto adherents in Japan is somewhere between 105 and 118 million, depending on the source. The majority of Japanese observe both Buddhism and Shintoism.

## From the Hearth of the Huang He River Valley

### TAOISM

While the Buddha's teachings were gaining converts in India, a religious revolution of another kind was taking place in China. Two major schools of Chinese philosophy, Taoism and Confucianism, were forming. The beginnings of **Taoism** are unclear, but scholars trace the religion to an older contemporary of Confucius, Lao-Tsu, who published a volume titled *Tao-te-ching*, or "Book of the Way." In his teachings, Lao-Tsu focused on the proper form of political rule and on the oneness of humanity and nature: People, he said, should learn to live in harmony with nature. This idea gave rise to the concept of **Feng Shui**—the art and science of organizing living spaces in order to channel the life forces that exist in nature in favorable ways. According to tradition, nothing should be done to nature without consulting *geomancers*, people who know the desires of the powerful spirits of ancestors, dragons, tigers, and other beings that occupy the natural world and can give advice on how to order things according to Feng Shui.

Among the Taoist virtues are simplicity and spontaneity, tenderness, and tranquility. Competition, possession, and even the pursuit of knowledge are to be avoided. War, punishment, taxation, and ceremonial ostentation are viewed as evils. The best government, according to Lao-Tsu, is the least government. Thousands of people began to follow Taoism. Taoist temples include statues of deities who teach specific lessons, along with the yin-yang symbol to remind followers of the duality of life, and swords to remind adherents that struggle is part of life.

## CONFUCIANISM

Confucius lived from 551 to 479 BCE, and his followers constructed a blueprint for Chinese civilization in almost every field, including philosophy, government, and education. In religion, Confucius addressed the traditional Chinese tenets that included belief in heaven and the existence of the soul, ancestor worship, sacrificial rites, and shamanism. He held that the real meaning of life lay in the present, not in some future abstract existence, and that service to one's fellow humans should supersede service to spirits.

**Confucianism** is mainly a philosophy of life, and like Taoism, it had great and lasting impacts on Chinese life. Appalled at the suffering of ordinary people at the hands of feudal lords, Confucius urged the poor to assert themselves. He was not a prophet who dealt in promises of heaven and threats of hell. He denied the divine ancestry of China's aristocratic rulers, educated the landless and the weak, disliked supernatural mysticism, and argued that human virtues and abilities, not heritage, should determine a person's position and responsibilities in society.

After his death in 479 BCE, Confucius came to be revered as a spiritual leader, and his teachings diffused widely throughout East and Southeast Asia. Followers built temples in his honor all over China. From his writings and sayings emerged the Confucian Classics, a set of 13 texts that were the focus of education in China for 2000 years. Over the centuries, Confucianism (with its Taoist and Buddhist ingredients) became China's state ethic, although the Chinese emperor modified Confucian ideals over time. For example, one emperor made worship of and obedience to the emperor part of Confucianism. In government, law, literature, religion, morality, and many other ways, the Confucian Classics have been the guide for Chinese civilization.

## DIFFUSION OF CHINESE RELIGIONS

Confucianism diffused early into the Korean Peninsula, Japan, and Southeast Asia, where it has long influenced the practice of Buddhism. More recently, Chinese immigrants expanded the influence of the Chinese religions in parts of Southeast Asia and helped to introduce their principles into societies ranging from Europe to North America.

The diffusion of Chinese religions even within China has been tempered by the Chinese government's efforts to suppress religion in the country. The communist government that took control of China in 1949 attempted to ban religion, in this case Confucianism, from public practice. But after guiding all aspects of Chinese education, culture, and society for 2000 years, Confucianism did not fade easily from the Chinese consciousness.

Geomancy is still a powerful force in China today, even in urban areas with large populations. Geographer Elizabeth Teather (1999) studied the rise of cremation and columbaria (resting places for ashes) in Hong Kong, investigating the impact Feng Shui has had on the structures and the continued influence of Chinese religious beliefs on burial practices in the densely populated city of Hong Kong. Traditional Chinese beliefs favor a coffin and burial plot aligned with Feng Shui teachings. However, with the growth of China's population, the government has strongly encouraged cremation over the past few decades. The availability of burial plots in cities like Hong Kong is quite low, and the costs of burial plots have risen in turn.

Teather explains that although cremation is on the rise in Hong Kong, traditional Chinese beliefs are dictating the final resting places of ashes. Most Chinese people, she states, have a "cultural need to keep ancestral remains appropriately stored and in a single place." In North America and Europe, a family often chooses to scatter the ashes of a cremated loved one, but a Chinese family is more likely to keep the ashes together in a single identifiable space so that they can return to visit the ancestor during Gravesweeping Festivals—annual commemorations of ancestors during which people visit and tend the graves of their ancestors. Teather describes how Feng Shui masters are consulted in the building of columbaria and how Feng Shui helps dictate the price placed on the niches for sale in the columbaria, with the lowest prices for the niches near the "grime of the floor."

# From the Hearth of the Eastern Mediterranean

## JUDAISM

**Judaism** grew out of the belief system of the Jews, one of several nomadic Semitic tribes living in Southwest Asia about 4000 years ago. The roots of Jewish religious tradition lie in the teachings of Abraham (from Ur), who is credited with uniting his people to worship only one God. According to Jewish teaching, Abraham and God have a covenant in which the Jews agree to worship only one God, and God agrees to protect his chosen people, the Jews.

The history of the Jews is filled with upheaval. Moses led them from Egypt, where they had been enslaved, to Canaan, where an internal conflict developed and the nation split into two branches, Israel and Judah. Israel was subsequently wiped out by enemies, but Judah survived longer, only to be conquered by the Babylonians and the Assyrians. The Jews regrouped to rebuild their headquarters, Jerusalem,

# FIELD NOTE

"The Orthodox Jewish community in Long Beach, New York, is large enough that the Dunkin Donuts on Beech Street is kosher. Supervised by a Rabbi, kosher-prepared foods follow strict requirements of what foods can be eaten, what can be eaten together, how animals are slaughtered, and how foods are prepared. In addition to the kosher Dunkin Donuts, another sign of the large Orthodox Jewish community in Long Beach is the Eruv, a line encircling the town that distinguishes private space from public space. The Eruv is not noticeable, as it generally follows utility lines and the boardwalk. But the Eruv creates a private space that allows Orthodox Jews to carry keys, foods, and even babies on the Sabbath."

© Erin H. Fouberg

■ **Figure 7.11**
**Long Beach, New York.**

but then fell victim to a series of foreign powers. The Romans destroyed their holy city in 70 CE and drove the Jews away, scattering adherents to the faith to Europe and North Africa. Jews retained only a small presence on the eastern shores of the Mediterranean until the late nineteenth century.

Our map shows that, unlike most other ethnic religions, Judaism is not limited to contiguous territories. Rather, Judaism is distributed throughout parts of Southwest Asia and North Africa, Russia, Ukraine, Europe, and parts of North and South America (Fig. 7.6). According to *The Atlas of Religion*, of all the world's 14 million Jews, 40.5 percent live in the United States, 40.2 percent live in Israel, and then in rank order, less than 5 percent live in France, Canada, the United Kingdom, Russia, and Argentina. Judaism is one of the world's most influential religions, although it claims few adherents compared to Christianity, Islam, and Hinduism.

During the nineteenth century, a Reform movement developed with the objective of adjusting Judaism and its practices to current times. However, many feared that this reform would cause a loss of identity and cohesion, and the Orthodox movement sought to retain the old precepts. Orthodox Jews typically are the strictest followers of Jewish dietary laws requiring the consumption of kosher foods (Fig. 7.11). Between the Reform and Orthodox extremes is a sector that is less strictly orthodox but not as liberal as that of the reformers; it is known as the Conservative movement.

These three branches differ significantly in ideas and practices, but Judaism is united by a strong sense of ethnic distinctiveness.

## DIFFUSION OF JUDAISM

The scattering of Jews after the Roman destruction of Jerusalem is known as the **diaspora**—a term that now signifies the spatial dispersion of members of any ethnic group. The Jews who went north into Central Europe came to be known as *Ashkenazim*, and the Jews who scattered across North Africa and into the Iberian Peninsula (Spain and Portugal) are called *Sephardim*. For centuries, both the Ashkenazim and the Sephardim were persecuted, denied citizenship, driven into ghettos, and massacred.

In the face of constant threats to their existence, Jews were sustained by extraordinary efforts to maintain a sense of community and faith. The idea of a homeland for the Jewish people, which became popular during the nineteenth century, developed into the ideology of **Zionism**. Zionist ideals are rooted in the belief that Jews should not be absorbed into other societies. The horrors of the Nazi campaign against Jews from the 1930s through World War II, when the Nazis established concentration camps and killed some six million Jews, persuaded many Jews to adopt Zionism. Jews from all over the world concluded that their only hope of survival was to establish a strongly defended homeland on the shores of the eastern Mediterranean. Aided by sympathetic members of the international community, the Zionist goal of a Jewish state became a reality in 1948, when a United Nations resolution carved two states, Israel and Palestine, out of the territory of the eastern Mediterranean.

While adherents to Judaism live across the world, many Jews have moved to Israel since its establishment in 1948. The Israeli government passed the Law of Return in 1950, which recognizes the rights of every Jew to immigrate to Israel. In 2012, over 7000 Jews left the former Soviet Union for Israel, along with over 2000 Jews from the United States and Canada and over 2000 from France and the United Kingdom. Since the fall of communism in the former Soviet Union in 1989, more than one million people have migrated from the former Soviet Union to Israel.

## CHRISTIANITY

**Christianity** can be traced back to the same hearth in the Mediterranean as Judaism, and like Judaism, Christianity stems from a single founder—in this case Jesus. Christian teachings hold that Jesus is the son of God, placed on Earth to forgive people of their sins and to teach people how to live according to God's plan. Christianity split from Judaism, and it, too, is a monotheistic religion. Jesus of Nazareth was born in Bethlehem, and during his lifetime, he traveled through the eastern Mediterranean region preaching, performing miracles, and gaining followers. Christians celebrate Easter as the day Jesus rose from the dead after being crucified three days prior (Good Friday). According to Christian teaching, the crucifixion of Jesus fulfilled an ancient prophecy and changed the fate of Jesus' followers by giving them eternal life.

The first split in Christianity, between Roman Catholicism and the **Eastern Orthodox Church**, developed over a number of centuries. At the end of the third century, the Roman Emperor Diocletian attempted to keep the empire together by dividing it for purposes of government. His divisions left a lasting legacy. When the Roman Empire fell and broke apart, the western region, centered on Rome, disintegrated. The eastern region, with Constantinople (now Istanbul in Turkey) at its heart, continued on, and later became known as the Byzantine Empire (Fig. 7.12). Christianity thrived there and radiated into other areas, including the Balkan Peninsula. This split into west and east at the end of the Roman Empire became a cultural fault line over time. It was formally recognized in 1054 CE when the Roman Catholic Church (centered in Rome) and the Eastern Orthodox Christian Church (centered in Constantinople) separated.

The Eastern Orthodox Church suffered blows when the Ottoman Turks defeated the Serbs in Kosovo in 1389, the Turks took Constantinople in 1453, and the Soviet Union suppressed Eastern Orthodox churches in the twentieth century (Fig. 7.13).

The **Roman Catholic Church** claims the most adherents of all Christian denominations (more than 1 billion). Centered in Rome, Catholic theology teaches the infallibility of the pope in interpreting Jesus' teachings and in formulating ways to navigate through the modern world. The power of the Roman Catholic Church peaked in the Middle Ages, when the Church controlled sources of knowledge and worked in conjunction with monarchs to rule much of western Europe.

During the Middle Ages, Roman Catholic authorities often wielded their power in an autocratic manner and distanced themselves from the masses. The widespread diffusion of the Black Death during the 1300s and the deaths that resulted caused many Europeans to question the role of religion in their lives. The Roman Catholic Church itself also experienced divisions within its hierarchy, as evidenced by the Western Schism during the early 1300s, which at one point resulted in three people claiming to be the pope. Reformers to the Church soon followed. During the fifteenth and sixteenth centuries, John Huss, Martin Luther, John Calvin, and others challenged fundamental teachings of Roman Catholicism and opposed the practices of Church leaders—leading to the Protestant Reformation. The Protestant sects of Christianity compose the third major branch of Christianity. Like Buddhism's challenge to Hinduism, the Protestant Reformation affected Roman Catholicism, which answered some of the challenges to its theology in the Counter-Reformation.

Christianity is the largest and globally the most widely dispersed religion. Christian churches claim more than

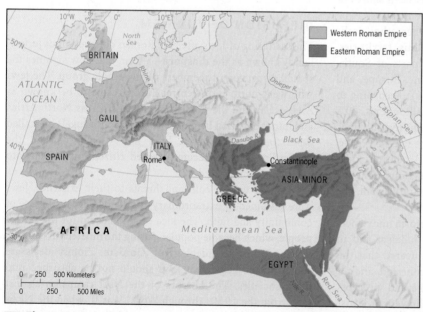

**Figure 7.12**
**The Roman Empire, Divided into West and East.** This map reflects the split in the empire, with the western empire focusing on Rome and the eastern empire focusing on Constantinople.   © H. J. de Blij, A. B. Murphy, and E. H. Fouberg, and John Wiley & Sons, Inc.

**■ Figure 7.13**

**Religions in the Former Yugoslavia.** The split in the Christian Church between Catholic and Eastern Orthodox and the expansion of the Ottoman Turks into southeastern Europe are reflected in the map of ethnic and religious groups in the former Yugoslavia. During much of the twentieth century, seven now independent countries were part of one country, Yugoslavia. After a civil war in the 1990s, they split. Slovenia and Croatia are predominantly Catholic. Serbia, Montenegro, and Macedonia are Eastern Orthodox. Bosnia and Herzegovina is split among Croats, Serbs, and Muslims. Kosovo is Muslim and Eastern Orthodox. Although never physically part of Yugoslavia, Albania, with a predominantly Muslim population, is part of the same religious fault line that cuts through the Balkan Peninsula.

2.2 billion adherents, including some 558 million in Europe and the former Soviet Union; approximately 266 million in North America; about 531 million in Latin America; perhaps 517 million in Africa; and an estimated 286 million in Asia. Christians thus account for 31 percent of the members of the world's major religions. Roman Catholicism, as noted earlier, is the largest segment of Christianity. Figure 7.6 reveals the strength of Roman Catholicism in parts of Europe and North America, and throughout much of Central and South America. Among religious adherents in parts of North America, Australia, New Zealand, and South Africa, Protestant churches prevail. Eastern Orthodox churches have as many as 200 million followers in Europe, Russia and its neighboring states, Africa (where a major cluster exists in Ethiopia), and North America.

## DIFFUSION OF CHRISTIANITY

The dissemination of Christianity occurred as a result of expansion combined with relocation diffusion. In western Europe, Christianity declined during the centuries immediately after the fall of the Roman Empire. Then a form of contagious diffusion took place as the religious ideas that had been kept alive in remote places such as coastal Ireland and Scotland spread throughout western Europe. In the case of the Eastern Orthodox faith, contagious diffusion took place from the religion's hearth in Constantinople to the north and northeast. **Protestantism** began in several parts of western Europe and expanded to some degree through contagious diffusion. Much of its spread in Northern and Central Europe, however, was through hierarchical diffusion, as political leaders would convert—sometimes to escape control from

Rome—and then the population would gradually accept the new state religion.

The worldwide diffusion of Christianity occurred during the era of European colonialism beginning in the sixteenth century. Spain invaded and colonized Central and South America, bringing the Catholic faith to those areas. Protestant refugees who were tired of conflict and oppression in Europe came to North America in large numbers. Western European colonists, aided by missionaries, brought Catholicism to Congo, Angola, Mozambique, and the Philippines. The Christian faith today has over 33,000 denominations. Hundreds of these denominations engage in proselytizing (purposeful spreading of religious teachings) around the world, creating an incredibly complex geographical distribution of Christians within the spaces of the world map that are shaded in "Christian" (Fig. 7.6).

The Christian faith has always been characterized by aggressive and persistent proselytism, and Christian missionaries created an almost worldwide network of conversion during the colonial period that endures and continues to expand today (Fig. 7.14).

## ISLAM

Like Christianity, **Islam**, the youngest of the major religions, can be traced back to a single founder, in this case, Muhammad, who was born in Mecca in 570 CE. According to Muslim belief, Muhammad received the truth directly from Allah in a series of revelations that began in 612 when the Prophet was about 42 years old. During these revelations, Muhammad spoke the verses of the Qu'ran (Koran), the Islamic holy book. Muhammad admired the monotheism of

SAM PANTHAKY/AFP/Getty Images

**■ Figure 7.14**
**Ahmedabad, India.** Catholic nuns from the order of the Missionaries of Charity distribute free rations to impoverished women on the anniversary of the funeral of Mother Teresa, the founder of the religious order. The building in the background is the Shishu Bhavan, an orphanage for discarded babies operated by the same nuns.

Judaism and Christianity; he believed Allah had already revealed himself through other prophets, including Judaism's Abraham and Christianity's Jesus. Muhammad came to be viewed as the one true prophet among Muslims.

After his visions, Muhammad had doubts that he could have been chosen to be a prophet but was convinced by further revelations. He subsequently devoted his life to the fulfillment of the divine commands. In those days the eastern Mediterranean and the Arabian Peninsula were in religious and social disarray, with Christianity and Judaism coexisting with polytheistic religions. Muhammad's opponents began to combat his efforts. The Prophet was forced to flee Mecca, where he had been raised, for Medina, and he continued his work from this new base.

In many ways, the precepts of Islam revised Judaic and Christian beliefs and traditions. The central precept of Islam is that there is but one god, who occasionally reveals himself through the prophets—first and foremost Muhammad, but Abraham and Jesus are regarded as non-divine prophets. Another key precept is that Earthly matters are profane; only Allah is pure. Allah's will is absolute; he is omnipotent and omniscient. Muslims believe that all humans live in a world that was created for their use but only until the final judgment day.

Adherents to Islam are required to observe the "five pillars" of Islam (repeated expressions of the basic creed, frequent prayer, a month of daytime fasting, almsgiving, and, if possible, at least one pilgrimage to Mecca in one's lifetime). The faith dictates behavior in other spheres of life as well. Islam forbids alcohol, smoking, and gambling. In Islamic settlements, the people build mosques to observe the Friday prayer and to serve as social gathering places (Fig. 7.15).

Islam, like all other major religions, is divided—principally between **Sunni** Muslims (the great majority) and the **Shi'ite** or Shiah Muslims (concentrated in Iran). Smaller sects of Islam include Wahhabis, Sufis, Salafists, Alawites, Alevis, and Yazeedis. The religion's main division between Sunni and Shi'ite occurred almost immediately after Muhammad's death, and was caused by a conflict over his succession. Muhammad died in 632 CE, and to some, the rightful heir to the Prophet's caliphate (area of influence) was Muhammad's son-in-law, Ali. Others preferred different

© Alexander B. Murphy

**■ Figure 7.15**
**Kuala Lampur, Malaysia.** The sprawling National Mosque serves as a landscape reminder of Islam's dominant religious role in the country.

candidates who were not necessarily related to Muhammad. The ensuing conflict was marked by murder, warfare, and lasting doctrinal disagreements. The Sunni Muslims eventually prevailed, but the Shi'ite Muslims, the followers of Ali, survived in some areas. Then, early in the sixteenth century, an Iranian (Persian) ruling dynasty made Shi'ite Islam the only legitimate faith of that empire—which extended into what is now southern Azerbaijan, southeastern Iraq, and western Afghanistan and Pakistan. This gave the Shi'ite branch unprecedented strength and created the foundations of its modern-day culture region centered on the state of Iran.

Descendants of Muhammad through his daughter Fatimah and his son-in-law Ali are recognized through titles that honor them, including sayyids, syeds or sharifs. They generate respect from both Sunni and Shi'ites. However, Shi'ites place much more emphasis on lineage. Shi'ite veneration of the descendants of Muhammad has contributed to a much more centralized and hierarchical clergy than that in the Sunni world.

In the Shi'ite branch, imams are religious leaders. Shi'ites treated the early Imams as the sole source of true knowledge, and

their successors continue to have great social and political authority. Sunni Islam is less centralized; an imam is simply a religious leader or scholar. Nonetheless, the Sunni branch has given rise to more doctrinaire offshoots of the religion over the centuries.

## DIFFUSION OF ISLAM

At the time of his death in 632 CE, Muhammad and his followers had converted kings on the Arabian Peninsula to Islam. The kings then used their armies to spread the faith across the Arabian Peninsula through invasion and conquest. Moving west, in waves of invasion and conquest, Islam diffused throughout North Africa. By the early ninth century, the Muslim world included emirates extending from Egypt to Morocco, a caliphate occupying most of Spain and Portugal, and a unified realm encompassing Arabia, the Middle East, Iran, and most of what is today Pakistan. Ultimately, the Arab Empire extended from Morocco to India and from Turkey to Ethiopia. Through trade, Muslims later spread their faith across the Indian Ocean into Southeast Asia (Fig. 7.16). As Muslim traders settled trading ports in Southeast Asia, they

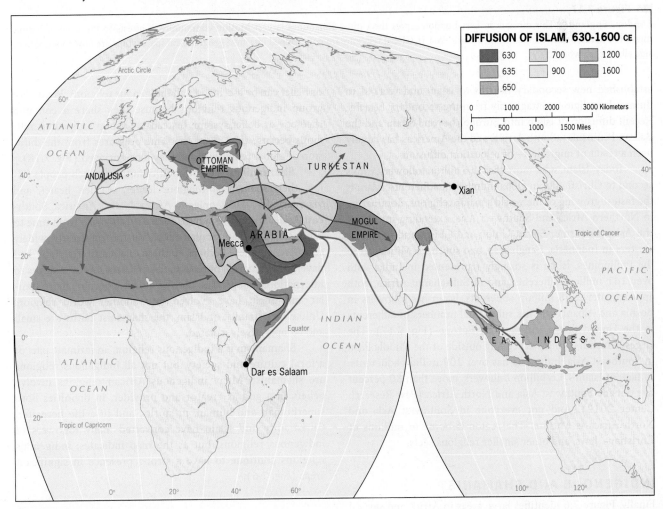

## ■ Figure 7.16

**Diffusion of Islam.** The map shows the diffusion of Islam from 600 CE to 1600 CE. The hearth of Islam is the dark brown area on the map where Islam was established by 630. By 650, Islam diffused through the areas in tan and in orange. As of 700, Islam diffuses through the pink region of the map. By 900, Islam reached the area in light green in Spain, North Africa, and Central Asia. By 1200, Islam reached Indonesia through trade. Islam diffused into Southeast Europe, South Asia, and North Africa by 1600.   © H. J. de Blij, P. O. Muller, and John Wiley & Sons, Inc.

© Alexander B. Murphy

**Figure 7.17**

**London, England.** This mosque in East London serves the United Kingdom's largest Muslim community. It attests to the scale of Islamic migration to the United Kingdom since World War II. Global religions are not grouped into neat geographical spaces; they are now found side by side all over the world.

established new secondary hearths of Islam and worked to diffuse the religion contagiously from the secondary hearths. Recent diffusion of Islam into Europe (beyond Spain and the Balkan Peninsula), South Africa, and the Americas has largely been a result of migration—of relocation diffusion.

Today, Islam, with more than 1.6 billion followers, ranks second to Christianity in global number of adherents. Islam is the fastest growing of the world's major religions, dominating in Northern Africa and Southwest Asia, extending into Central Asia, the former Soviet Union and China, and including clusters in Indonesia, Bangladesh, and southern Mindanao in the Philippines. Islam is strongly represented in India, with over 161 million adherents, and in Subsaharan Africa, with approximately 248 million adherents. Islam has followers in Bosnia and Albania and has substantial numbers of adherents in the United States and western Europe (Fig. 7.17). The largest Muslim country is actually outside of the Middle East, in Southeast Asia. Indonesia has over 209 million adherents. In fact, of Islam's 1.6 billion followers, more than 80 percent live outside Southwest Asia and North Africa (Pew Research Center 2012). And not everyone in Southwest Asia and North Africa is Muslim. The region is home to millions of Christians, Jews, and other smaller religious sects.

## INDIGENOUS AND SHAMANIST

Finally, Figure 7.6 identifies large areas in Africa and several other parts of the world as "Indigenous and Shamanist." **Indigenous religions** are local in scope, usually have a reverence for nature, and are passed down through family units and groups (tribes) of indigenous peoples. No central tenet

or belief can be ascribed to all indigenous religions. We do not group indigenous religions because they share a common theology or belief system. Instead, we group indigenous religions because they share the same pressures from the diffusion of global religions—and they have survived (Fig. 7.18).

**Shamanism** is a community faith in which people follow their shaman—a religious leader, teacher, healer, and visionary. Various peoples in Africa, Native America, Southeast Asia, and East Asia have embraced shamans from time to time, and they had similar effects on the cultures of widely scattered peoples. Perhaps if these shamanist religions had developed elaborate bureaucracies and sent representatives to international congresses, they would have become more similar and might have evolved into another world religion. Unlike Christianity or Islam, the shamanist faiths are small and comparatively isolated.

Shamanism is a indigenous religion, an intimate part of a local culture and society, but not all indigenous religions are shamanist. Many indigenous African religions involve beliefs in a god as creator and provider, in divinities both superhuman and human, in spirits, and in a life hereafter. Christianity and Islam have converted many followers of indigenous religions, but as the map indicates, indigenous religions continue to have a strong presence in significant areas (Fig. 7.6).

## THE RISE OF SECULARISM

The world map of religion might mislead us into assuming that all or even most of the people in areas portrayed as Christian or Buddhist do in fact adhere to these faiths. This is not

## FIELD NOTE

"Arriving at the foot of erosion-carved Uluru just before sunrise, I do not find it surprising that this giant monolith, towering over the Australian desert, is a sacred place to local Aboriginal peoples. Throughout the day, the changing sun angle alters its colors until, toward sunset, it turns a fiery red that yields to a bright orange. At night it looms against the moonlit, starry sky, silent sentinel of the gods. Just two years before this, my first visit in 1987, the Australian government had returned Ayers Rock (named by European settlers after a South Australian political leader) to Aboriginal ownership, and reclaimed its original name, Uluru. Visitors continued to be allowed to climb the 1100 feet (335 m) to the top, from where the view over the desert is awesome.

My day had begun eventfully when a three-foot lizard emerged from under my motel-room bed, but the chain-assisted climb was no minor challenge either. At the base you are warned to be 'in good shape' and some would-be climbers don't make it, but the rewards of persisting are dramatic. Uluru's iron-rich sandstone strata have been sculpted into gullies and caves, the latter containing Aboriginal carvings and paintings, and on the broad summit there are plenty of places where you can sit quietly to contemplate the historic, religious, and cultural significance of a place that mattered thousands of years before globalization reached Australia."

■ **Figure 7.18**
**Uluru, Australia.**

the case. Even the most careful analysis of worldwide church and religious membership produces a total of about 5.8 billion adherents—in a population of over 6.9 billion (Pew Research Center 2012). The figure 5.8 billion adherents is inflated when we start to analyze the difference between those who say they are members of a religion and those who are active followers of a religion. When polled about their church-going activities, fewer than 3 percent of the people in Scandinavia reported frequent attendance, and in France and Great Britain, less than 10 percent reported attending church at least once a month. The lack of members active or otherwise underscores the rise of **secularism**—indifference to or rejection of organized religious affiliations and ideas.

The level of secularism throughout much of the Christian and Buddhist worlds varies from country to country and regionally within countries. A 2009 Pew Research poll asked whether people felt religion was very important to them. Only 24 percent of Italians agreed with this statement, whereas 55 percent of Americans felt religion was very important to them. In France, the government recently banned the wearing of overt religious symbols in public schools. The French government wanted to remove the "disruption" of Muslim girls wearing hijab (head scarves), Jewish boys wearing yarmulke (skullcaps), and Christian students wearing large crosses to school. The French government took the position that banning all religious symbols was the only egalitarian approach.

Looking at polls that ask about the importance of religion for people in a country does not give us the complete picture, however. The 30 percent of Canadians who agreed religion is very important to them would be much, much lower if we removed recent or second-generation immigrants from the tally. Immigrants often hold onto their religion more fervently in part to help them ease into a new place and to link into a community in their new home. Buddhists and Hindus on Canada's west coast and Muslims in the eastern part of Canada have a higher rate of adherence to their religion than many long-term residents of the country.

In some countries, antireligious ideologies are contributing to the decline of organized religion. Church membership in Russia, which dropped drastically during the twentieth century under communist rule, rebounded after the collapse of the Soviet system but to much lower numbers. Maoist China's drive against Confucianism was, in part, an antireligious effort, and China continues to suppress some organized religious practices, as reports of religious persecution continue to emanate from China.

In many areas labeled Christian on the world map of religions, from Canada to Australia and from the United States to western Europe, the decline of organized religion as a cultural force is evident. In the strongly Catholic regions of southern Europe and Latin America, many people are dissatisfied with the papal teachings on birth control, as the desire for larger families wanes in these regions of the world. In Latin America, the Catholic Church is being challenged by rapid social change, the diffusion of Evangelical Protestant denominations into the region, and sexual abuse scandals similar to those that have occurred in the United States and Canada.

Secularism has become more widespread during the past century. People have abandoned organized religion in growing numbers. Even if they continue to be members of a church, their participation in church activities has declined. Traditions have also weakened. For example, there was a time when almost all shops and businesses were closed on Sundays, preserving the day for sermons, rest, and introspection. Today, shopping centers are mostly open as usual, and Sunday is increasingly devoted to business and personal affairs, not to church. To witness the rise of secularism among Christians in America first-hand, explore your town, city, or suburb on a Sunday morning: How many people are wearing casual clothes and hanging out at the coffee shop reading newspapers, and how many people are attending church services?

At the same time that secularism is on the rise in the United States, many people who do follow their religion seem to be doing so more fervently. Religious traditions are stronger in some cultural regions of the United States than in others, and Sunday observance continues at a high level in, for example, the Mormon culture area of the United States. Even though Catholic dioceses are closing churches and declaring bankruptcy in some parts of the Northeast, other Catholic dioceses are building new churches and enormous activity halls in other parts of the country. Moreover, Evangelical and other alternative churches are growing rapidly in some parts of the United States and western Europe. Entire industries, including Christian music and Christian publications, depend on the growing commitment of many Americans and Europeans to their religion.

The division between secularism and fervent adherence is not confined to the Christian world. Secularism is growing in South Korea, where half of the population does not profess adherence to any particular religion. Although major faiths are experiencing an overall decline in adherence, several smaller religions are growing in importance: Baha'i, Cao Dai, Jainism, and the Spiritual Church of Brazil, for example.

Migration plays a large role in the diffusion of religions, both universalizing and ethnic. As Europe becomes more secular, migrants from outside of Europe continue to settle in the region. Imagine Europe 30 years from now. Predict where in Europe secularism will be the most prominent and where religious adherence will strengthen.

## HOW IS RELIGION SEEN IN THE CULTURAL LANDSCAPE?

Religion marks cultural landscapes with houses of worship such as churches, mosques, synagogues, and temples; cemeteries dotted with religious symbols and icons; stores designated for sales of religious goods; and even services provided to religious adherents who travel to sacred sites. When adherents voluntarily travel to a religious site to pay respects or participate in a ritual at the site, the act of travel is called a **pilgrimage**. Geographers who study religion are interested in the act of pilgrimage and its impacts on place, people, religion, culture, and environment.

**Sacred sites** are places or spaces people infuse with religious meaning. Members of a religious group may define a space or place as sacred out of either reverence or fear. If a sacred site is held with reverence, adherents may be encouraged to make a pilgrimage to the sacred site for rejuvenation, reflection, healing, or fulfillment of a religious commitment.

In ancient human history, sacred spaces were typically features in the physical geographic landscape, such as buttes, mountain peaks, or rivers. In more recent history, as universalizing religions diffused across the world, sacred sites were abandoned, usurped, or altered. Geographer Mary Lee Nolan studied Irish sacred sites and observed that many of the remote physical geographic features of the Irish landscape were sacred to the Celtic people (Fig. 7.19). When Roman Catholicism diffused to Ireland, the Catholic Church usurped many of these features, infusing them with Christian meaning. Nolan described the marriage of Celtic sacred sites and Christian meaning:

> The early Celtic Church was a unique institution, more open to syncretism of old and new religious traditions than was the case in many other parts of Europe. Old holy places, often in remote areas, were "baptized" in the new religion or given new meaning through their historical, or more often legendary, association with Celtic saints. Such places were characterized by sacred site features such as heights, insularity, or the presence of holy water sources, trees, or stones.

Nolan contrasted Irish sacred sites with those in continental Europe, where sacred sites were typically built in urban, accessible areas. In continental Europe, Nolan found that the "sacred" (bones of saints or images) was typically brought to a place in order to infuse the place with meaning.

In many societies, certain features in the physical geographic landscape remain sacred to religious groups. Access to and use of physical geographic features are constrained by private ownership, environmental concerns, and the act of designating certain sacred spaces as public recreational or tourist areas. Geographer Kari Forbes-Boyte (1999) studied Bear Butte, a site sacred to members of the Lakota and Cheyenne people in the northern Great Plains of the United States and a site that became a state park in the 1960s. Bear Butte is used today by both Lakota and Cheyenne people in religious

## GUEST FIELD NOTE

At St. Declan's Holy Well in Ireland, I found a barbed wire fence substituting for the more traditional thorn tree as a place to hang scraps of clothing as offerings. This tradition, which died out long ago in most parts of Continental Europe, was one of many aspects of Irish pilgrimage that led me to speculate on 'Galway-to-the-Ganges' survival of very old religious customs on the extreme margins of an ancient Indo-European culture realm. My subsequent fieldwork focused on contemporary European pilgrimage, but my curiosity about the geographical extent of certain ancient pilgrimage themes lingered. While traveling in Asia, I found many similarities among sacred sites across religions. Each religion has formation stories, explanations of how particular sites, whether Buddhist monasteries or Irish wells, were recognized as sacred. Many of these stories have similar elements. And, in 1998, I traveled across Russia from the remote Kamchatka Peninsula to St. Petersburg. Imagine my surprise to find the tradition of hanging rag offerings

**Figure 7.19**
Ardmore, Ireland.

on trees alive and well all the way across the Russian Far East and Siberia, at least as far as Olkon Island in Lake Baikal.

*Credit: Mary Lee Nolan, Oregon State University.*

ceremonies and by tourists who seek access to the recreational site. Nearby Devils Tower, which is a national monument, experiences the same pull between religious use by American Indians and recreational use by tourists.

Places such as Bear Butte and Devils Tower experience contention when one group sees the sites as sacred and another group does not. In many parts of the world, sacred sites are claimed as holy or significant to adherents of more than one religious faith. In India, for example, several sites are considered sacred by Hindus, Buddhists, and Jains. Specifically, Volture Peak in Rajgir in northeastern India is holy to Buddhists because it is the site where Buddha first proclaimed the Heart Sutra, a very important canon of Buddhism. Hindus and Jains also consider the site holy because they hold Buddha to be a god or prophet. The site has created little discord among religious groups. Pilgrims of all faiths peacefully congregate in the place year after year. Other sacred sites are not so fortunate: Some of the most contentious sites are in Jerusalem, a city that three major world religions regard as holy.

## Sacred Sites of Jerusalem

The ancient city of Jerusalem is sacred to Jews, Christians, and Muslims. Jews saw Jerusalem as sacred before the birth of Jesus, but most Jews fled from the city and surrounding area during the diaspora. For Jews, Jerusalem remained sacred even though they did not control it, and when the Zionist movement gained strength, Jews set their sights on controlling the sacred city once again. The most important sacred site for Jews is the Western Wall (also called the Wailing Wall), at the edge of the Temple Mount in Jerusalem (Fig. 7.20). The Temple Mount occupies the top of a modest hill where, according to the Torah (the sacred book of Judaism that is also part of the Old Testament of Christianity's sacred book, the Bible), Abraham almost sacrificed his son Isaac. On this hill, Jews built two temples, each of which was destroyed by invaders. The Western Wall is all that remains of the second temple, and Jews gather in the place to remember the story of Abraham and the destruction of the temples and to offer prayers. The name "Wailing Wall" evokes the sounds of mourning over the temple's demise made by Jewish pilgrims and recognizes the suffering of Jews over time.

For Christians, Jerusalem is sacred both because of the sacrifice Abraham was willing to make of his son at the Temple Mount and because Jesus' crucifixion took place just outside of the city's walls. Jesus was then buried in a tomb that Roman Emperor Constantine later marked with a basilica that is now the Church of the Holy Sepulchre (Fig. 7.21). Christians believe that from that tomb Jesus rose from the dead on Easter. For centuries the Roman, and then the Byzantine, Empire controlled the city and protected the sacred site.

© Alexander B. Murphy

**Jerusalem, Israel.** The Western Wall (foreground, right), which is sacred to Jews, stands right next to the Dome of the Rock (background, left), which is sacred to Muslims.

In the seventh century, Muslim armies took control over the city from the Byzantine Empire. Muslims constructed a mosque called the Dome of the Rock adjacent to the Western Wall to mark the site where Muslims believe Muhammad arrived from Mecca and then ascended into heaven (Fig. 7.20). The site Jews call Temple Mount is called al-Haram al-Sharif (the Noble Sanctuary) by Muslims.

Christians and Muslims fought the Crusades of the Middle Ages over the question of who should control the sacred land of Jerusalem. Between 1095 and 1199, European political and religious leaders organized a series of Crusades to retake the so-called Holy Land. The first Christian crusaders captured Jerusalem in 1099, ruling the city for almost 100 years. As the first crusaders made their way across what is modern-day Turkey on their way to Jerusalem, they also left a series of conquests in their wake—laying claim to the city of Antioch and a number of other strategically important sites. Some of the crusaders returned to western Europe, but many settled, mingled, and intermarried with the local people.

Muslims ultimately retook Jerusalem in 1187, and later Christian crusaders were unable to conquer it again. The Crusades helped cement a commitment by Christians to protect the Church of the Holy Sepulchre. Similarly, the Crusades cemented a commitment by Muslims to protect the Dome of the Rock and later Zionism cemented a commitment by Jews to protect the Western Wall. The commitment by three major

Reuters,/© Corbis

**Jerusalem, Israel.** The Church of the Holy Sepulchre is sacred to Christians who believe it is the site where Jesus Christ rose from the dead. Inside the church, a Christian worshipper lights a candle at Jesus' tomb.

religions to protect and control their sacred sites has led to political turmoil that echoes far beyond Jerusalem, as we will see in the next section of this chapter.

## Landscapes of Hinduism and Buddhism

Traditional Hinduism is more than a faith; it is a way of life. Pilgrimages follow prescribed routes, and rituals are attended by millions of people. Festivals and feasts are frequent, colorful, and noisy. Hindus believe that the erection of a temple, whether modest or elaborate, bestows merit on the builder and will be rewarded. As a result, the Hindu cultural landscape—urban as well as rural—is dotted with countless shrines, ranging from small village temples to structures so large and elaborate that they are virtually holy cities. The location of shrines is important because Hindus prescribe that such holy places should minimally disrupt the natural landscape. Whenever possible, a Hindu temple is located in a "comfortable" position, for example, under a large, shady tree. Hindus also want their temples to be near water because many gods will not venture far from water and because water has a holy function, ritual bathing, in Hinduism (Fig. 7.22). A village temple should face the village from a prominent position, and followers must make offerings frequently. Small offerings of fruit and flowers lie before the sanctuary of the deity honored by the shrine.

The cultural landscape of Hinduism is the cultural landscape of India, its main culture region. As one travels through India, the Hindu faith is a visual as well as an emotional experience. Temples and shrines, holy animals by the tens of millions, distinctively garbed holy men, and the sights and sounds of long processions and rituals all contribute to a unique atmosphere (Fig. 7.23).

When Buddha received enlightenment, he sat under a large tree, the Bodhi (enlightenment) tree at Bodh Gaya in India. The Bodhi tree now growing on the site is believed to be a descendant of the original tree. The Bodhi tree has a thick, banyan-like trunk and a wide canopy of leafy branches. Because of its association with the Buddha, the tree is revered and protected. Buddhists make pilgrimages to Bodh Gaya and other places where Buddha may have taught beneath Bodhi branches. With Buddhism, the Bodhi tree diffused as far as China and Japan, its purposeful planting marking the cultural landscape of numerous villages and towns.

Buddhism's architecture includes some magnificent achievements, especially the famed structures at Borobudur in central Java (Indonesia). Buddhist shrines include stupas, bell-shaped structures that protect burial mounds. Buddhists also construct temples that enshrine an image of Buddha in his familiar cross-legged pose, as well as large monasteries that tower over the local landscape. The pagoda is perhaps Buddhism's most familiar structure. Its shape is derived from the relic (often funeral) mounds of old. Every fragment of its construction is a meaningful representation of Buddhist philosophy (Fig. 7.24).

© Alexander B. Murphy

■■ **Figure 7.22**

**Varanasi, India.**   Hindus perform morning rituals in the Ganges River at one of Hinduism's most sacred places, the city of Varanasi, known as the city of Lord Shiva. For Hindus, the river itself is a sacred site.

# FIELD NOTE

"In the summer of 2007, the newer, Hi-Tec city area of Hyderabad, India, was under construction. Migrant workers built new roads, apartment houses, and office buildings throughout the city. Beautiful homes reflected the wealth accrued by many. In front of the new homes, I saw Hinduism in the cultural landscape where owners built temples for their favorite Hindu god. In the older part of the city, I visited Golconda Fort, built more than 1500 years ago. On the day I was there, Hindu women participated in the Bonalu Festival as an act of honoring Mother Goddess. The women climbed nearly 400 steps to the top of the fort, carrying with them offerings of food. At the top, I was welcomed into the temple. I took off my shoes and took part in a festival that began in the mid-1800s, when Hindu women began the festival to ward off the anger of the gods, as the city stood under the siege of the bubonic plague."

© Erin H. Fouberg

■ **Figure 7.23**
**Hyderabad, India.**

# FIELD NOTE

"To reach the city of Yangon, Myanmar (Burma), we had to transfer to a ferry and sail up the Rangoon River for several hours. One of Southeast Asia's most spectacular Buddhist shrines is the golden Shwedogon Pagoda in the heart of Yangon. The golden dome (or *chedi*) is one of the finest in Southeast Asia, and its religious importance is striking: eight hairs of the Buddha are preserved here. Vast amounts of gold have gone into the creation and preservation of the Shwedogon Pagoda; local rulers often gave the monks their weight in gold—or more. Today, the pagoda is a cornerstone of Buddhism, drawing millions of faithful to the site."

© H. J. de Blij

■ **Figure 7.24**
**Yangon, Myanmar.**

Along with the religious structures such as temples, we can see evidence of religion in the cultural landscapes of the dead. Traditionally, Hindus, and more recently Buddhists, and Shintoists cremate their dead. Thus, wherever a large pocket of Hindus, Buddhists, or Shintoists live, a crematorium will be nearby. The Hindu crematorium in Kenya stands in stark contrast to much of the rest of the cultural landscape and signals the presence of a large Hindu population (see Fig. 7.2).

The cultural landscapes of South Asian religions extend into Southeast Asia, where several religions that began in the South Asian hearth (including Hinduism and Buddhism) diffused into the region. Later, Islam replaced the South Asian religions in many of these places, and even later Christian missionaries gained adherents in Southeast Asia when Christian governments encouraged the migration of their people and their religion to their colonies in these areas. Today, we can stand in Singapore, study the cultural landscape, and see the influences of Christianity, Buddhism, Hinduism, and Islam.

## Landscapes of Christianity

The cultural landscapes of Christianity's branches reflect the changes the faith has undergone over the centuries. In medieval Europe the cathedral, church, or monastery was the focus of life. Other buildings clustered around the tower, steeple, and spire of the church that could be seen (and whose bells could be heard) for miles in the surrounding countryside (Fig. 7.25). In the square or plaza in front of the church, crowds gathered for ceremonies and festivals, and the church was always present—even if the event was not primarily religious. Good harvests, military victories, public announcements, and much else took place in the shadow of the symbol of religious authority. As a result of mercantilism and colonialism, Europeans exported the ornate architecture of European Christian churches wherever they settled (Fig. 7.26).

The Reformation, the rise of secularism, and the decline of organized religion are reflected in the cultural landscape as well. Many of the ornate churches in the town squares of medieval cities now function as museums instead of serving active congregations. Other churches in secular regions are closing their doors or

**Figure 7.25**

**Antwerp, Belgium.**   The cathedral in Antwerp was built beginning in 1352 and still dominates the central part of town.

**Figure 7.26**

**Mombasa, Kenya.**   Built at the end of the nineteenth century, the neo-gothic Holy Ghost Cathedral reflects the European colonial imprint on the city. The sign in the street next to the cathedral serves as a reminder of a more recent external cultural influence—this time from China. The number of Chinese in the city is not large, but Chinese immigrants have found niches in the restaurant business and as purveyors of Chinese traditional medicine.

© Franco Origlia/Getty Images

■■ **Figure 7.27**
**Vatican City.**   Pope Francis waves to pilgrims as he arrives in the Popemobile at St. Peter's Square for his weekly audience. Thousands gather each week to see the pope and hear him greet visitors in multiple languages.

significantly reducing the number of religious services offered. Yet, not all of Europe's sacred sites have become secularized. Famous cathedrals continue to hold services while tourists peruse the interior of the vast churches. And other sacred sites of Christianity, such as churches for specific saints, places where significant events occurred, and Vatican City in Rome, are still major pilgrimage sites in Europe. When in Rome, the leader of the Catholic Church, the pope, holds an outdoor service for pilgrims to Vatican City, attracting thousands of followers to St. Peter's Square each week (Fig. 7.27).

Cities in Europe are also home to centuries-old Christian cemeteries. Traditionally, Christians bury, rather than cremate, their dead, and in cities, the cemeteries are often crowded with tombstones. Outside of European cities and in North America, Christian cemeteries can resemble large parks. These cemeteries often reflect class differences: Some graves are marked by simple tombstones, whereas others are elaborate structures. With rising land-use pressures and the associated costs of burial, however, cremation is becoming increasingly common among Christians—particularly in North America and western Europe.

## RELIGIOUS LANDSCAPES IN THE UNITED STATES

The United States, a predominantly Christian country, demonstrates considerable diversity in its religious cultural landscapes. In *The Cultural Geography* of the United States, geographer Wilbur Zelinsky constructed a map identifying religious regions in the country. Figure 7.28 presents a modified version of Zelinsky's map.

The New England region is strongly Catholic; the South's leading denomination is Baptist; the Upper Midwest has large numbers of Lutherans; and the Southwest is predominantly Spanish Catholic. The broad midland region extending from the Middle Atlantic to the Mormon region (in the western United States) has a mixture of denominations in which no single church dominates; this is also true of the West. As Figure 7.28 shows, some regions represent local clustering, such as the French Catholic area centered in New Orleans and the mixed denominations of Peninsular Florida, where a large Spanish Catholic cluster has emerged in metropolitan Miami.

In a 2008 study, geographers Barney Warf and Mort Winsberg used data on religious adherents by county in the United States to discern what counties and regions of the country have the most and the least religious diversity. Warf and Winsberg defined religious diversity as having a variety of religions within a small spatial unit, in this case a county. One way the authors mapped religious diversity is presented in Figure 7.29, a map showing counties with the least religious diversity in the darkest colors. In counties with the darkest shading, one religion accounts for 64 percent or more of all religious adherents in the county. In comparing Figure 7.29 to Figure 7.28, we can see that the Mormon region in Utah and southern Idaho, the Southern Baptist region in the South, and the Catholic region of the Northeast are some of the least diverse regions in the country. In these regions, you can expect to see the imprint of one major religion throughout the cultural landscape. By contrast, religious regions characterized by many lightly colored counties have a rich religious mix.

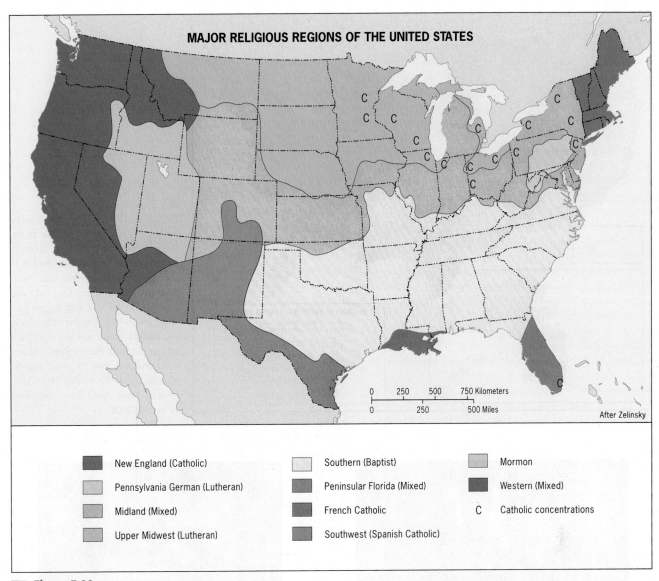

## MAJOR RELIGIOUS REGIONS OF THE UNITED STATES

0   250   500   750 Kilometers
0   250   500 Miles

After Zelinsky

New England (Catholic)

Pennsylvania German (Lutheran)

Midland (Mixed)

Upper Midwest (Lutheran)

Southern (Baptist)

Peninsular Florida (Mixed)

French Catholic

Southwest (Spanish Catholic)

Mormon

Western (Mixed)

C   Catholic concentrations

■ **Figure 7.28**

**Major Religious Regions of the United States.**   A generalized map of the religious regions of the United States shows concentrations of the major religions.   *Adapted with permission from*: W. Zelinsky, *The Cultural Geography of the United States*, rev. ed., Englewood Cliffs, NJ: Prentice Hall, 1992, p. 96.

The plain white churches of the South and Lutheran Upper Midwest coincide with the Protestant Church's pragmatic spending of church money—not on art and architecture as the Catholic Church historically did (Fig. 7.30). Conversely, many Catholic churches in the United States, both in the Northeast and in Chicago, as well as in other immigrant-magnet cities, were built by immigrants who lived in ethnic neighborhoods. Immigrants spent their own money and used their building skills to construct ornate churches and dozens of cathedrals that tied them back to their country of origin and demonstrated their commitment to their faith (Fig. 7.31).

## Landscapes of Islam

Elaborate, sometimes magnificently designed mosques whose balconied **minarets** rise above the townscape dominate Islamic cities, towns, and villages. Often the mosque is the town's most imposing and most carefully maintained building. Five times every day, from the towering minarets, the faithful are called to prayer. The sounds emanating from the minarets fill the streets as the faithful converge on the holy place to pray facing Mecca.

At the height of Islam's expansion into eastern North Africa and southern Europe, Muslim architects incorporated earlier Roman models into their designs. The results included some of the world's greatest architectural masterpieces, such as the Alhambra Palace in Granada and the Great Mosque of Cordoba in Spain. Islam's prohibition against depicting the human form led to the wide use of geometric designs and calligraphy—the intricacy of which is truly astounding (Fig. 7.32). During the eleventh century, Muslim builders began glazing the tiles of domes and roofs.

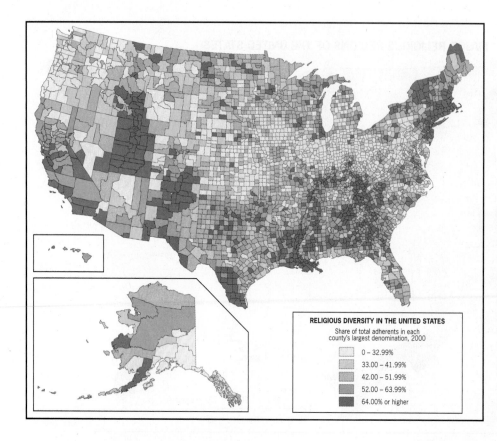

■ **Figure 7.29**
**Religious Diversity in the United States.** The counties shaded in the darkest color have the least diversity in religions. The counties shaded in the lightest color have the most diversity within them. Compare and contrast Figure 7.28 with Figure 7.29 and explain which major religions in the United States are the dominant religions within their region. *Adapted with permission from*: B. Warf and M. Winsberg, "The Geography of Religious Diversity in the United States," *Professional Geographer*, 2008.

■ **Figure 7.30**
**Brown County, South Dakota.** The Scandinavian Lutheran Church was founded by immigrants from northern Europe. The simple architecture of the church is commonly found in Protestant churches in the Great Plains.

■ **Figure 7.31**
**Zell, South Dakota.** St. Mary's Catholic Church was built by nuns in 1875 to serve Catholic immigrants and American Indians. The more ornate architecture and stained glass of St. Mary's Church is commonly found in Catholic churches in the Great Plains.

© Alexander B. Murphy

■■ **Figure 7.32**
**Isfahan, Iran.** The dome of this mosque demonstrates the geometric art evident in Muslim architecture. The towers to the right of the dome are minarets from which the call to prayer is broadcast.

To the beautiful arcades and arched courtyards, they added the exquisite beauty of glass-like, perfectly symmetrical cupolas. Muslim architecture represents the unifying concept of Islamic monotheism: the perfection and vastness of the spirit of Allah.

Islam achieved its greatest artistic expression, its most distinctive visible element, in architecture. Even in the smallest town, the community helps build and maintain its mosque. The mosque symbolizes the power of the faith and its role in the community. Its primacy in the cultural landscape confirms the degree to which, in much of the Muslim world, religion and culture are one.

One of the best-known pilgrimages in the modern world is the Muslim pilgrimage to Mecca, the **hajj**. The hajj is one of the five pillars of Islam. Religious doctrine implores all Muslims (if financially and physically able) to make the pilgrimage to Mecca at least once during their lifetime. Each year, over 1.3 million Muslims from outside of Saudi Arabia and over 1 million from inside the country make the hajj (Fig. 7.33). The pilgrimage requires the faithful to follow certain steps of reverence in a certain order and within a certain time frame. As a result, the pilgrims move from Mecca through the steps of the hajj en masse. In 2004, over 250 pilgrims were trampled to death as hordes of people followed the steps of the pilgrimage, and in 1990 over 1400 pilgrims suffered the same fate. The Saudi government now restricts the number of visas granted each year to Muslims from outside of the country. Yet, the number of pilgrims continues to climb, and the services needed for Muslim pilgrims during the hajj and during the rest of the year now employ four times as many people in Saudi Arabia as the oil industry does. The landscape around Mecca reflects the growing number of pilgrims year round, as towers of apartment buildings and hotels encircle the sacred city.

Geographer Surinder Bhardwaj has studied non-hajj pilgrimages in Islam, which include "visits to sacred shrines of holy men, the graves of saints and Imams, and the tombs of martyrs of the faith" (1998). Although some sects of Islam see non-hajj pilgrimage as non-Islamic, the ziarats (non-hajj pilgrimages) are important to a growing number of Muslims. Bhardwaj points out that the hajj is obligatory but the ziarat is voluntary. He explains that study of the ziarat helps geographers understand the many variations and regional forms of Islam in the world today. For example, Bhardwaj describes how the ziarat in Indonesia (the country with the largest number of Muslims) reflects the continued influence of pre-Islamic ways. Especially in the interior of Indonesia, Islam has mixed with Buddhism and Hinduism, both of which stress the importance of pilgrimage. Similar to Ireland, where the Catholic Church usurped Celtic sacred sites, Bhardwaj found that many sites in Indonesia that were sacred under Hinduism and Buddhism were usurped by Islam, which changed the object of pilgrimage from non-Muslim to Muslim.

©AP/Wide World Photos

**■ Figure 7.33**
**Mecca, Saudi Arabia.**   Pilgrims circle the holy Kaaba in the Grand Mosque in Mecca during the hajj.

  Choose a pilgrimage site, such as Mecca, Vatican City, or the Western Wall, and describe how the act of pilgrimage (in some cases by millions) alters this place's cultural landscape and environment.

## WHAT ROLE DOES RELIGION PLAY IN POLITICAL CONFLICTS?

Religious beliefs and histories can bitterly divide peoples who speak the same language, have the same ethnic background, and make their living in similar ways. Such divisions arise not only between people adhering to different major religions (as with Muslims and Christians in the former Yugoslavia) but also among adherents of the same religion. Some of the most destructive conflicts have pitted Christian against Christian and Muslim against Muslim.

Religious conflicts usually involve more than differences in spiritual practices and beliefs. Religion often functions as a symbol of a wider set of cultural and political differences. The "religious" conflict in Northern Ireland is not just about different views of Christianity, and the conflict between Hindus and Muslims in India has a strong political as well as religious dimension. Nevertheless, in these and other cases religion serves as the principal symbol around which conflict is organized.

## Conflicts Along Religious Borders

A comparison between Figure 7.6 and a political map of the world (see Fig. 8.3) reveals that some countries lie entirely within the realms of individual world religions, whereas other countries straddle **interfaith boundaries**, the boundaries between the world's major faiths. Many countries that lie astride interfaith boundaries are subject to potentially divisive cultural forces—particularly when the people see their religious differences as a source of social division within their country. This is the case in several countries in Africa that straddle the Christian–Muslim interfaith boundary (Fig. 7.34). Other countries with major religious disputes straddle **intrafaith boundaries**, the boundaries within a single major faith. Intrafaith boundaries include divisions between Christian Protestants and Catholics (Northern Ireland), divisions between Muslim Sunni and Shi'ite (Iraq), and the like.

Interface areas, where interfaith and intrafaith boundaries occur, may be peaceful, or they can spur enormously violent political conflict. Israel/Palestine and Nigeria provide

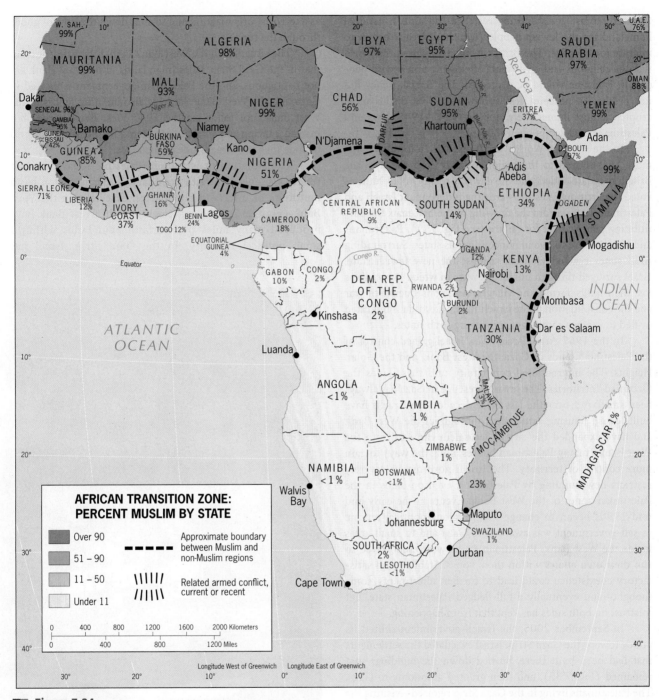

**Figure 7.34**

**African Transition Zone.**   Percent Muslim by Country. The divide shown on the map marks interfaith boundaries between religions. Considerable conflict has occurred in the transition zone.   © H. J. de Blij, P. O. Muller, and John Wiley & Sons, Inc.

examples of interfaith conflicts, and Northern Ireland is an example of an intrafaith conflict. In each case, religious difference is not the only factor, but it certainly plays an important symbolic and perceptual role.

## Israel and Palestine

Earlier in this chapter, we discussed the history of the conflict over the sacred space of Jerusalem. The region of Israel and

Palestine is home to one of the most contentious religious conflicts in the world today. In the aftermath of World War I, European colonialism came to a region that had previously been controlled and fought over by Jews, Romans, Christians, Muslims, and Ottomans. A newly formed League of Nations (a precursor to the United Nations) recognized British control of the land, calling the territorial mandate Palestine. At that point, the vast majority of people living in the land were Muslim Palestinians. The goal of the British government was to meet Zionist goals and to create, in Palestine, a national homeland for the Jewish people (who had already begun to migrate to the area). The British explicitly assured the world that the religious and civil rights of existing non-Jewish peoples in Palestine would be protected. The British policy did not produce a peaceful result, however. Civil disturbances erupted almost immediately, and, by 1947–1948, Jews and Palestinians engaged in open warfare.

In the wake of World War II and the Holocaust, many more Jews moved to the region. Shortly after the war, the British mandate ended, and the newly formed United Nations voted to partition Palestine—creating independent Israeli and Palestinian states. From the drawing of the first map, the partitioning plan was set for failure (see Fig. 3.11). Palestinians and Israelis were to live in noncontiguous states. Surrounding Arab states reacted violently against the new Jewish state. Israel survived through numerous wars in which Palestinians lost their lands, farms, and villages. As a consequence of war and the consolidation of the Israeli state, Palestinians migrated or fled to refugee camps in neighboring Arab states.

In the 1967 Arab–Israeli War, Israel gained control of the Palestinian lands in Gaza, the West Bank, and the Golan Heights. The international community calls these lands the Occupied Territories. The Jewish presence in Gaza has always been small. But over the last three decades, the Israelis have built Jewish housing settlements throughout the West Bank and have expanded the city of Jerusalem eastward into the West Bank (razing Palestinian houses along the way) to gain more control of territory. The Israeli government severely restricts new building by Palestinians, even on lands in the Palestinian zones of the West Bank. Events in the early and mid-1990s began to change this religious-political mosaic as self-government was awarded to Gaza and to small areas inside the West Bank. Palestinian Arabs were empowered to run their own affairs within these zones. Stability and satisfactory coexistence could lead to further adjustments, some thought—and eventually a full-fledged Palestinian state, but mistrust on both sides has kept that from happening.

In September 2005, the Israeli government shifted its policy toward the Gaza Strip. Israel evacuated the settlements that had been built there, burned down the buildings that remained (Fig. 7.35), and then granted autonomy to Gaza. The Palestinians living in the Gaza Strip rejoiced—visiting the beaches that were previously open only to Israeli settlers and traveling across the border into Egypt to purchase goods. Although Palestinians now have a degree of autonomy within the Gaza Strip, they are economically isolated, the standard of living has dropped, and continued conflict with Israel has taken a major toll.

The Israeli government tightly controls the flow of Palestinians and goods into and out of the Gaza Strip. Gaza is surrounded by fences, and in some places a wall—with land mines in certain areas and dust roads to show footprints. Dozens of tunnels between Egypt and Gaza have been used to supply arms, fuel, and goods to the Hamas government in Gaza. In 2014, Egypt agreed with Israel to recognize Hamas as a terrorist organization and to shut down the flow of goods through the tunnels.

The situation in the West Bank is slightly different from that in the Gaza Strip. Palestinian lands in the West Bank are not contiguous, and the Palestinian government is located in Gaza, not the West Bank. Israel is also building fences in the West Bank, not following the 1947 West Bank border but instead carving out Israeli settlements in the West Bank to include them on Israel's side of the fence.

The situation in Israel and Palestine today does not reflect a simple interfaith boundary. The tiny region has a multitude of interfaith boundaries, especially in the West Bank (Fig. 7.36). The settlements in the West Bank have produced many miles of interfaith boundaries within a small political territory. In the Gaza Strip, Israel has

©AP/Wide World Photos

**■ Figure 7.35**

**Erez Crossing, Gaza Strip.** The Israeli Army withdrew from the Gaza Strip in 2005, after occupying the territory for 38 years. Israeli troops demolished the Israeli Army liaison offices on September 9, 2005, in preparation for completing the Israeli retreat from the Gaza Strip on September 11, 2005.

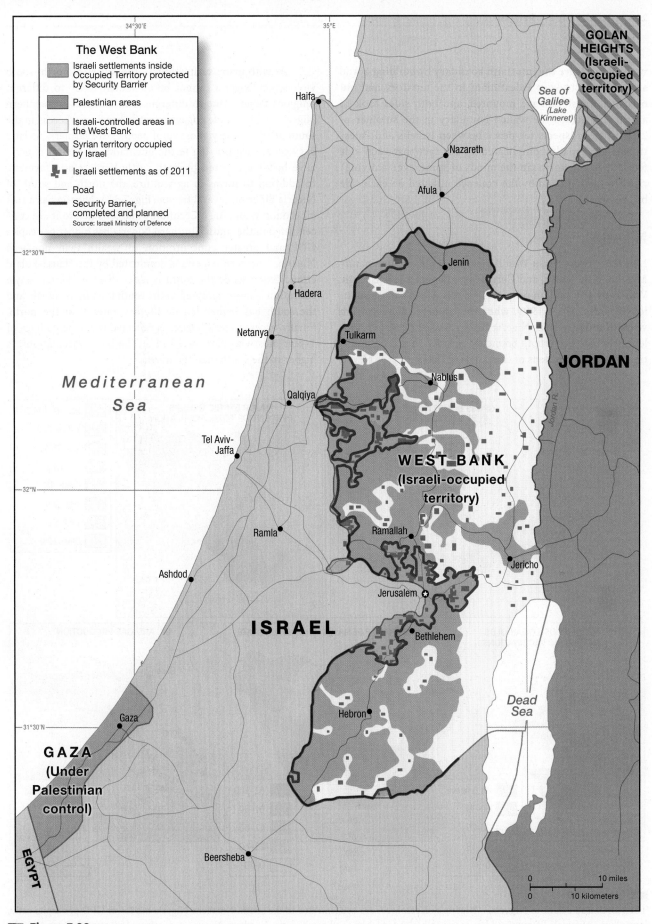

**The West Bank**

Israeli settlements inside Occupied Territory protected by Security Barrier

Palestinian areas

Israeli-controlled areas in the West Bank

Syrian territory occupied by Israel

Israeli settlements as of 2011

Road

Security Barrier, completed and planned
Source: Israeli Ministry of Defence

GOLAN HEIGHTS (Israeli-occupied territory)

*Sea of Galilee (Lake Kinneret)*

Haifa

Nazareth

Afula

Jenin

JORDAN

Hadera

Netanya

Tulkarm

Nablus

Qalqiya

*Mediterranean Sea*

Tel Aviv-Jaffa

WEST BANK (Israeli-occupied territory)

*Jordan R.*

Ramla

Ramallah

Jericho

Ashdod

Jerusalem

ISRAEL

Bethlehem

*Dead Sea*

Gaza

Hebron

GAZA (Under Palestinian control)

Beersheba

EGYPT

0     10 miles
0     10 kilometers

■■ **Figure 7.36**

**The West Bank.**   Palestinian territories in the West Bank are punctuated by Israeli settlements. The security fence surrounds the West Bank, and in several places it juts into the West Bank to separate Israeli settlements from Palestinian areas.   *Adapted with permission from*: C. B. Williams and C. T. Elsworth, *The New York Times,* November 17, 1995, p. A6. © The New York Times.

worked to secure the interfaith boundary by building a wall around Gaza to keep Palestinians in the territory and out of Israel. Tensions have mounted, and both sides took to air attacks across the walled boundary in the summer of 2014. The prospects for peace between Israelis and Palestinians are greatly complicated by the fact that each side feels it has a historic (in the minds of some, even a divine) right to the land and by the violence inflicted on each side by the other.

## Nigeria

Like other countries in West Africa, Nigeria is predominantly Muslim in the north, and Christian and animist in the south. With over 168 million people, Nigeria is Africa's most populous country. Since 1999, when the country emerged from years of military rule, Nigeria has witnessed persistent violence along the interfaith boundary between these communities, which has cost tens of thousands of lives.

As with many such conflicts, the causes of north–south violence in Nigeria cannot be attributed solely to different religious beliefs. Due to differences in climates, in northern Nigeria, many people engage in cattle herding, whereas in the south of the country, most rural peoples are farmers. As land has become scarcer, the fertile grasslands of central Nigeria have become coveted by both cattle herders and farmers. In addition to forms of agriculture, the north and south of Nigeria differ on several fronts (Fig. 7.37). Nigeria has a rich oil economy, and the oil economy and jobs tied to it are concentrated in the south. Southern Nigeria has higher per capita GDP and greater concentration of wealth than northern Nigeria. Northern Nigeria is dominated by the Hausa-Fulani ethnic group while the south is more diverse. Western-style education is more accepted in the south than in the north, and the south has higher female literacy rates than the north. Finally, access to health care, as reflected in the percentage of 1-year-olds who have received all the basic vaccinations, is higher in the south than the north.

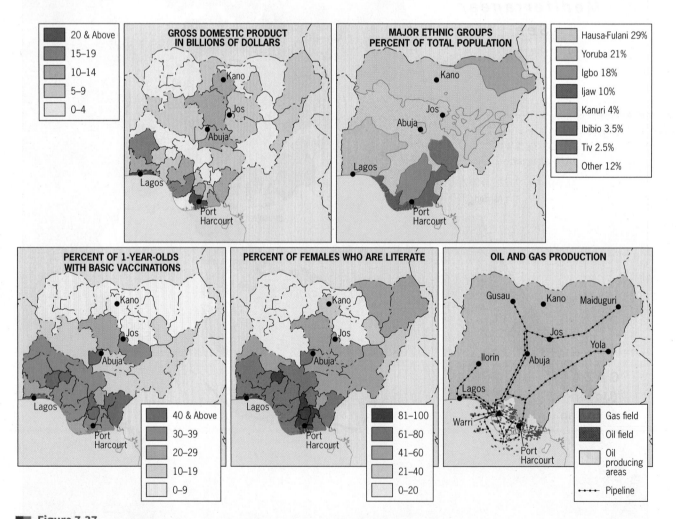

■■ **Figure 7.37**

**The North and South of Nigeria.** Nigeria's oil resources are concentrated in the south. Northern Nigeria has lower GPD per capita rates, lower levels of female literacy, and less access to health care than southern Nigeria. Northern Nigeria is dominated by two ethnic groups, the Hausa-Fulani and Kanuri, both predominantly Muslim, and southern Nigeria has more diverse ethnic groups, whose members are predominantly Christian or animist.    *Data from*: Nigeria Demographic and Health Survey 2008; platts.com; wikipedia.org; africacenter.org; and bbc.com.

Since 2009, the worst violence in Nigeria has taken place in the northern half of the country, along the interfaith boundary and in the northeast where the extremist Muslim group, Boko Haram, operates. Mohammed Yusuf began the organization in 2002 in Maiduguri, Nigeria, with the goal of pushing Western-style education out of northern Nigeria. The words "Boko Haram" roughly translate to "Western education is forbidden" in the Hausa language. Yusuf built an Islamic school, which drew mainly students from the Kanuri ethnic group. Yusuf then used the school to recruit members to Boko Haram. The U.S. State Department reported that Boko Haram "receives the bulk of its funding from bank robberies and related criminal activities, including extortion and kidnapping for ransom" and has received some funds and training from al-Qaeda in the Islamic Maghreb (2014).

In 2009, Nigerian police killed the founder of Boko Haram. In response, members armed themselves, found a new leader, and began issuing attacks in 2011. At first, the group focused attacks on police and military as vengeance for the killing of their leader. In 2012, Boko Haram turned their attention to attacking schools (*New York Times* 2014). In 2014, northern Nigeria made global news when members of the terrorist organization kidnapped 250 teenage girls from their school in Chibok (Fig. 7.38).

The violence may have its roots in the struggle for access to land, political power, and resources, but religion has served as a key marker of difference in the region. Violence along the interfaith Christian–Muslim boundary reinforces the perceptual importance of the boundary and promotes a sense—whether right or wrong—that religious differences represent the most important obstacle to social cohesion in Nigeria.

## Northern Ireland

A number of western European countries, as well as Canada and the United States, have large Catholic communities and large Protestant communities, and often these are reflected in the regional distribution of the population. In most places, the split between these two sects of Christianity along intrafaith lines creates little if any rift today. The most notable exception is Northern Ireland.

Northern Ireland and Great Britain (which includes England, Scotland, and Wales) form the United Kingdom of Great Britain and Northern Ireland (the UK). This was not always the case. For centuries, the island of Ireland was its own entity, marked by a mixture of Celtic religious practices and Roman Catholicism. As early as the 1200s, the English began to infiltrate the island of Ireland, taking control of its agricultural economy. Colonization began in the sixteenth century, and by 1700, Britain controlled the entire island. During the 1800s, the Irish colony produced industrial wealth for Britain in the shipyards of the north. Protestants from the island of Great Britain (primarily Scotland) migrated to Ireland during the 1700s to Northern Ireland to take advantage of the political and economic power granted to them in the colony. During the 1800s, migrants were drawn to northeastern Ireland where industrial jobs and opportunities were greatest. During the colonial period, the British treated the Irish Catholics harshly, taking away their lands, depriving them of their legal right to own property or participate in government, and regarding them as second-class citizens.

In the late 1800s, the Irish began reinvigorating their Celtic and Irish traditions; this strengthening of their identity fortified their resolve against the British. In the early 1900s,

■ **Figure 7.38**
**Abuja, Nigeria.**    Malala Yousafzai, a Pakistani who was attacked by the Taliban while on a school bus in her home country at the age of 15 in 2012, holds a picture of kidnapped schoolgirl Sarah Samuel with her mother Rebecca Samuel, during a visit to Abuja, Nigeria, Sunday July 13, 2014. Malala Yousafzai traveled to Abuja in Nigeria to meet the relatives of 250 schoolgirls who were kidnapped by Boko Haram in northern Nigeria. The hashtag #BringBackOurGirls was used in a social media campaign in spring 2014 in response to the kidnapping of the Nigerian girls.

the Irish rebelled against British colonialism. The rebellion was successful throughout most of the island, which was Catholic dominated, leading to the creation of the Republic of Ireland. But in the 1922 settlement ending the conflict, Britain retained control of six counties in the northeast, which had Protestant majorities. These counties constituted Northern Ireland, which became part of the United Kingdom. The substantial Catholic minority in Northern Ireland, however, did not want to be part of the United Kingdom (Fig. 7.39)—particularly since the Protestant majority, constituting about two-thirds of the total population (about 1.6 million) of Northern Ireland, possessed most of the economic and political advantages.

As time went on, economic stagnation for both populations worsened the situation, and the Catholics in particular felt they were being repressed. Terrorist acts by the Irish Republican Army (IRA), an organization dedicated to ending British control over all of Ireland by violent means if necessary, brought British troops into the area in 1968. Although the Republic of Ireland was sensitive to the plight of Catholics in the North, no official help was extended to those who were engaging in violence.

In the face of worsening conflict, Catholics and Protestants in Northern Ireland increasingly distanced their lives and homes from one another. The cultural landscape marks the religious conflict, as each group clusters in its own neighborhoods and celebrates either important Catholic or Protestant dates (see Fig. 6.11). Irish geographer Frederick Boal wrote a seminal work in 1969 on the Northern Irish in one area of Belfast. Boal used fieldwork to mark Catholic and Protestant neighborhoods on a map, and he interviewed over 400 Protestants and Catholics in their homes. Boal used the concept of **activity space** to demonstrate how Protestants and Catholics had each chosen to separate themselves in their rounds of daily activity.

Although religion is the tag-line by which we refer to "The Troubles" in Northern Ireland, the conflict is much more about nationalism, economics, oppression, access to opportunities, terror, civil rights, and political influence. But religion and religious history are the banners beneath which the opposing sides march, and church and cathedral have become symbols of strife rather than peace.

Belfast now has 99 peace lines, or peace walls, separating Catholic and Protestant neighborhoods. In the 1990s,

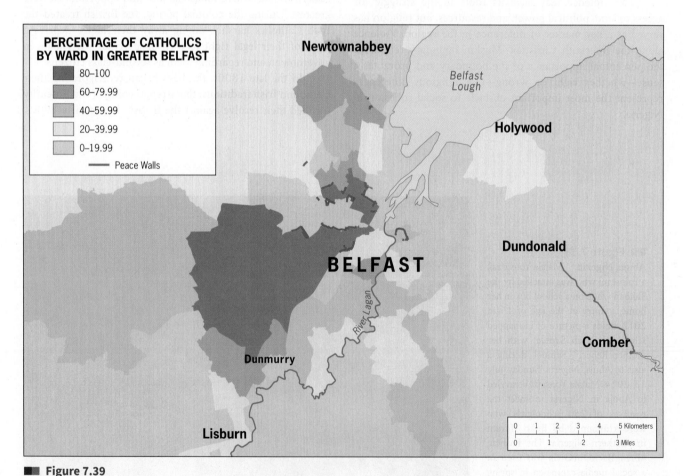

■ **Figure 7.39**

**Religious Affiliation and Peace Lines in Belfast, Northern Ireland.** Catholic neighborhoods are clustered west of the Central Business District and west of the River Lagan. Protestant neighborhoods are separated from Catholic neighborhoods by Peace Walls in West Belfast.

Boal updated his study of Northern Ireland and found hope for a resolution. Boal found that religious identities were actually becoming less intense among the younger generation and among the more educated. He found Catholics and Protestants intermixing in spaces such as downtown clubs, shopping centers, and college campuses.

In April 1998, the parties involved in The Troubles adopted the Anglo-Irish peace agreement known as the Belfast Agreement and Good Friday Agreement, which raised hopes of a new period of peace in Northern Ireland.

In her 2006 study, Leonard found teens that grew up in Catholic or Protestant neighborhoods rarely interacted with the "Other" and that "some children restricted their movements" to local neighborhoods and demonstrated little mobility beyond their respective neighborhood. Belfast, and Northern Ireland more broadly, have made major strides toward reconciliation in recent years. Mixing across Christian faiths is more common among the educated and less common among those living in distinctly Catholic or Protestant neighborhoods. The two sides have made major strides toward reconciliation in recent years, but the conflict has not gone away.

## Religious Fundamentalism and Extremism

The drive toward **religious fundamentalism** is often born out of frustration over the perceived breakdown of society's morals and values, lack of religious authority, failure to achieve economic goals, loss of a sense of local control, failure of a government to protect a religion, or a sense of violation of a religion's core territory. Regardless of the religion, a fundamentalist group holds its religious beliefs as nonnegotiable and uncompromising.

People in one society often fear fundamentalism in other societies without recognizing it in their own. What many call fundamentalism is sometimes better defined as extremism. **Religious extremism** is fundamentalism carried to the point of violence. The attacks on the United States in September 2001 reinforced the tendency of many Americans to equate extremism with Islam. Yet Christian extremism is also a potent force, as witnessed in the United States when religious zealots kill physicians who perform legal abortions. Fundamentalists can be extremists, but by no means are all fundamentalists, whether Christian, Muslim, Jewish, or any other religion, extremists.

Today the forces of globalization affect religions. Education, radio, television, and travel have diffused notions of individual liberties, sexual equality, and freedom of choice—but also consumerism and secularism. In the process, the extent of cultural diffusion and innovation has accelerated. Some churches have managed to change with the times, allowing women to serve as priests and homosexuals to marry, and generally liberalizing their doctrines. Others have gone in the opposite direction, reaffirming fundamental or literalist interpretations of religious texts and trying to block modern influences and external cultural interference.

### CHRISTIANITY

The Roman Catholic Church has long resisted innovations deemed incompatible with the fundamentals of the faith. Among the issues giving rise to disputes are birth control, family planning, and the role of women in the religious bureaucracy. The major religions tend to be male-dominated, and few women have managed to enter the hierarchy. This is true in the Roman Catholic Church, where women are not allowed to serve as priests. The Roman Catholic Church has over 1 billion adherents and has a global diplomatic and political presence, affecting policies in numerous places and on many topics. For example, the Roman Catholic Church preaches against the use of artificial means of birth control as well as abortion. During the September 1994 United Nations Conference on Population and Development, the Roman Catholic Church allied itself with Islamic countries against advocates of population control.

In the United States, certain sects of the Catholic Church continue to hold Mass in Latin and are much more fundamentalist than the rest of the Church. Some of these sects are part of the Catholic Church and continue to operate within the purview of the Church. Others stand apart from the Catholic Church and do not recognize the pope, nor does the Vatican sanction them. For example, actor/director Mel Gibson belongs to the Holy Family Church, which does not recognize the pope, and the Vatican does not recognize that church as part of the Catholic Church. Gibson's church is most associated with the Traditionalist Catholic Movement, a fundamentalist movement that believes the Mass should still be conducted in Latin and that modern popes and clergy are not following the traditional theology and practices of the Church.

In the United States, Christian fundamentalism is also associated with Protestant faiths. Preaching a doctrine of strict adherence to the literal precepts of the Bible, many Protestant Christian fundamentalists believe that the entire character of contemporary society needs to be brought into alignment with biblical principles. Fundamentalist Protestant churches range from tiny churches to enormous warehouse-style churches with thousands of members. Regardless of the size of the congregation, fundamentalist Protestant churches have become increasingly active in political and social arenas—arguing for prayer in public schools, the teaching of creationism in science courses, a strict ban on abortion, and the adoption of laws outlawing gay marriage (Fig. 7.40). In the process, they have gained considerable influence, especially in local politics (school boards and city councils).

### JUDAISM

Like all other major religions, Judaism has fundamentalist sects. The most conservative of the three major sects of Judaism is Orthodox. Yet, the Orthodox sect itself is divided into

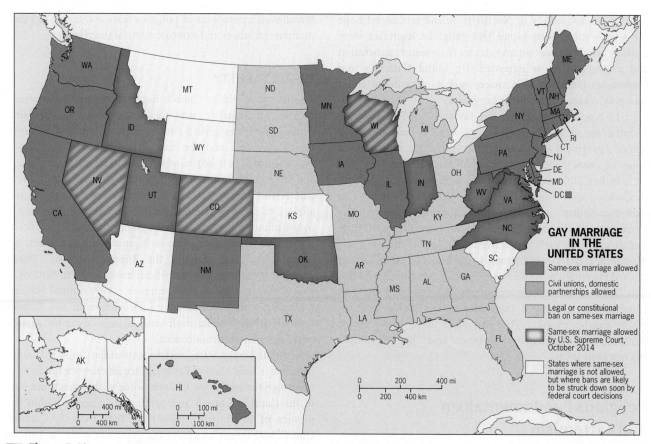

GAY MARRIAGE
IN THE
UNITED STATES

- Same-sex marriage allowed
- Civil unions, domestic partnerships allowed
- Legal or constitutional ban on same-sex marriage
- Same-sex marriage allowed by U.S. Supreme Court, October 2014
- States where same-sex marriage is not allowed, but where bans are likely to be struck down soon by federal court decisions

■ **Figure 7.40**

**Gay Marriage in the United States.**   The map looks much different from what it did just a few years ago—a reflection of a remarkably rapid embrace of gay marriage across the United States. The map will continue to change, as recognition of same-sex marriage is in the courts in Virginia, Colorado, and other states.   *Data from*: *National Journal*, 25 June 2014. http://www.nationaljournal.com/domesticpolicy/same-sex-marriage-decision-in-utah-could-go-all-the-way-to-the-supreme-court-this-fall-20140625.

several different schools of thought, teachings, and synagogues. Much diversity exists among Orthodox Jews, with varying views on Israel, education, and interaction with non-Orthodox Jews. Fundamentalist Jews who have migrated to Israel tend to vote for more conservative candidates in Israeli elections, affecting election outcomes. Similarly, some fundamentalist Jews who remain in Europe or North America send money to certain politicians in Israel in support of policies such as Israeli settlements on the West Bank.

Judaism also has its extremist element—people whom the majority of Jews denounce and whom the government of Israel has even banned from the country. Among the Jewish extremist groups is the Kach and Kahane Chai—followers of the late American-born, Israeli Rabbi Meir Kahane. Rabbi Kahane espoused anti-Arabism in his teachings, and his followers (Kahane Chai) continue to do so. Members of Kach or Kahane Chai are suspected in several terrorist acts in Israel.

## ISLAM

Other major faiths must also confront the pressures of change. Not all Muslim communities, for example, adhere precisely to the rules of the Qu'ran prohibiting the use of alcohol. The laws of Islam, which (like some other religions) are very strict

when interpreted literally, are not applied with equal force throughout the Muslim world.

Prior to September 11, the growth of a fundamentalist movement, the Taliban in Afghanistan, provided a particularly striking example of how quickly a fundamentalist government can use extremism to change a place. The Taliban regime seized control of much of the country during the 1990s and asserted the strictest fundamentalist regime in the contemporary world. The leadership imposed a wide range of religious restrictions, sought to destroy all statues depicting human forms, required followers of Hinduism to wear identifying markers, and forbade women to appear in public with their head exposed.

The Taliban in Afghanistan also provided a haven for the activities of Islamic extremists who sought to promote an Islamic holy war, or **jihad**, against the West in general and the United States in particular. One of the key figures in the Islamic extremist movement of the past decade, Osama bin Laden, helped finance and mastermind a variety of terrorist activities conducted against the United States, including the destruction of the World Trade Towers, the attack on the Pentagon, and the downing of Flight 93 on September 11, 2001. Bin Laden is now dead, but those following in his footsteps are a product of a revolutionary Islamic movement that views the West as a great enemy and that opposes both the westernization and liberalization of the traditionally Islamic realms. These beliefs are certainly not representative of Islam as a whole, but they are religious beliefs. Indeed, they can be traced to a form of Islam, known as Wahhabi Islam, which developed in the eighteenth century in opposition to what was seen as sacrilegious practices on the part of Ottoman rulers. The champions of the opposition movement called for a return to a purportedly pure variant of Islam from centuries earlier. The Saudi Arabian state is the hearth of Wahhabi Islam today, as the Saudi Royal family has championed Wahhabi Islam since the 1800s. Saudis fund Wahhabi Islamic schools, called madrassas, around the world.

A variety of forces have fueled the violent path on which the Wahhabi extremist movement has embarked, but some of these forces are unambiguously geographic. Perhaps the most important is the widely held view among movement followers that "infidels" have invaded the Islamic holy land over the past 80 years. Of particular concern to Islamic extremists are the presence of American military and business interests in the Arabian peninsula, the establishment of the state of Israel, and the support European and American governments have given Israel. A principal goal of the movement is to bring an end to what are seen as improper territorial incursions. A second geographically related concern of Wahhabi extremists is the diffusion of modern culture and technology and its impact on traditional lifestyles and spiritual practices. Ridding the Islamic world of such influences is also a major goal.

Islamic fundamentalists who have resorted to violence in pursuit of their cause (thereby becoming extremists) are relatively small in number. The majority of Muslims in the Middle East do not support Islamic extremism. Pew Research (2014) reported a rise in concerns about Islamic extremism throughout the Middle East. Nigerians were increasingly concerned about Boko Haram; those surveyed in 14 Islamic countries had a majority negative opinion about Al-Qaeda; the majority of people surveyed in Pakistan opposed the Taliban; and Palestinians had majority unfavorable views of Hezbollah and Hamas.

## Summary

Religion is a major force in shaping and changing culture. The major world religions today all stem from an area of Eurasia stretching from the eastern Mediterranean to China. Major world religions are distributed regionally, with Hinduism in India; Buddhism, Taoism, Shintoism, and Chinese philosophies in East and Southeast Asia; Islam reaching across North Africa, through the Middle East and into Southeast Asia; Shamanist religions mainly in Subsaharan Africa; and Christianity in Europe, Western Asia, the Americas, Australia, and New Zealand. Judaism, another major world religion, is not as concentrated. Today, Judaism has a base in Israel and has adherents scattered throughout Europe and the Americas.

As the 2014 Boko Haram kidnapping of 250 teenage girls in Nigeria made clear, religious beliefs can drive people to extremist behaviors. On a day-to-day basis, however, religion more typically drives cultures—shaping how people behave, how people perceive the behaviors of others, and how people across place, scale, and time interact with each other.

## Geographic Concepts

activity spaces
interface areas
religion
secularism
monotheistic religion
polytheistic religion
animistic religion
universalizing religion
ethnic religion
Hinduism
caste system
syncretic
Buddhism
Shintoism
Taoism

Feng Shui
Confucianism
Judaism
diaspora
Zionism
secularism
interfaith
intrafaith
extremism
Christianity
Eastern Orthodox Church
Roman Catholic Church
Protestant
Islam
Sunni

Shi'ite
indigenous religions
Shamanism
pilgrimage
sacred sites
minarets
hajj
interfaith boundaries
intrafaith boundaries
activity space
religious fundamentalism
religious extremism
jihad

# Learn More Online

About Devils Tower
www.nps.gov/deto

About Religions of the World
www.bbc.co.uk/religion/religions

About the Sacred Sites in Jerusalem
http://news.bbc.co.uk/hi/english/static/in_depth/middle_
east/2000/holy_places/default.stm

# Watch It Online

Christianity in European History
Choose among several programs. Click on Video on
Demand.
www.learner.org/resources/series58.html#program_
descriptions

The Confucian Tradition
http://www.learner.org/courses/worldhistory/unit_
video_12-2.html

Sacred Sites in Jerusalem
Choose program 17 "Jerusalem, Capital of Two States."
Click Video on Demand.
www.learner.org/resources/series180.html#program_
descriptions

# POLITICAL GEOGRAPHY

## Challenging the Political-Territorial Order

In the summer of 2012 I found myself at the European Central Bank, looking up at a large sign out front displaying the symbol of the euro, the common currency adopted by many European Union countries (Fig. 8.1). For more than a decade, Europe's common currency has been a visible representation of a project that has reshaped the political map of the continent. The states of the EU have pooled key aspects of their sovereignty, creating a new political-territorial unit that has become an increasingly significant actor in local and global affairs.

A building and a sign representing the European integration project were not all that was on display the day of my visit. In the shadow of both was an encampment of a group of people from the "Occupy Frankfurt" movement. Occupy Frankfurt was one of many "occupy" movements around the world that sprang up to contest growing socioeconomic inequalities and the concentration of economic power in relatively few hands. Their goals were economic, but also political; the occupy protests sought to draw attention to the ways in which political institutions and practices sustain what they regard as unfair economic arrangements.

The juxtaposition of elements that greeted me that day showed how dynamic the world's political geography is. Since the seventeenth century, sovereign states have been the bedrock of the international political order. In 1648, at the end of the Hundred Years' War, western European governments defined the territory of their country and exerted substantial control over their populations. States claimed to represent the people within their borders and organized militaries against external incursions. Europeans diffused the system of sovereign states throughout the world through colonialism and trade. As European states assumed positions of global

© Alexander B. Murphy

■ **Figure 8.1**

**The European Central Bank in Frankfurt, Germany.** The bank has played an important role in Europe's ongoing experiment with integration, but that role is increasingly being challenged.

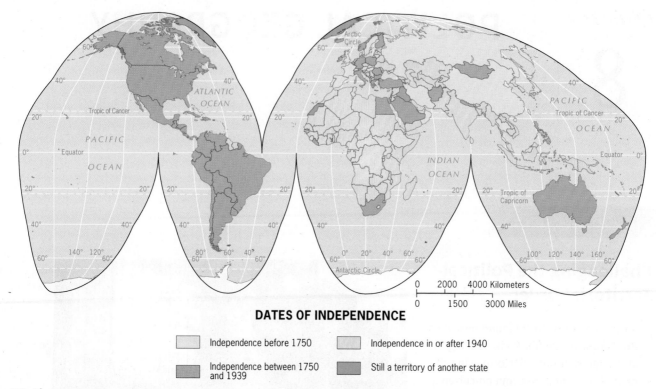

**DATES OF INDEPENDENCE**

| | | | |
|---|---|---|---|
| ☐ | Independence before 1750 | ☐ | Independence in or after 1940 |
| ■ | Independence between 1750 and 1939 | ■ | Still a territory of another state |

■ **Figure 8.2**

**Dates of Independence for States.**   The first major wave of independence movements between 1750 and 1939 occurred mainly in the Americas. The second major wave of independence movements after 1940 occurred mainly in Africa and Asia. South Sudan became the most recently recognized independent state in July, 2011, bringing the total number of member states in the United Nations to 193.   *Data from: United Nations, 2014.*

dominance, breaking empires in other regions of the world into colonies, which eventually became independent states through decolonization of the Americas in the early nineteenth century and Africa in the mid-twentieth century (Fig. 8.2).

Decolonization was fueled by the desire for political and economic independence. Former colonies became states, gaining political independence under international law; and each new country was theoretically sovereign, legally having the ultimate say over what happened within its borders. But the legacies of colonialism were inescapable, ranging from entrenched internal inequalities to external economic dependencies that made it difficult to obtain political and economic stability. Moreover, each new country was comprised of a mixture of peoples, cultures, languages, and religions that had been grouped together during the colonial period.

With globalization in the twentieth century, being economically independent is virtually impossible not only for former colonies but also for the European powers that colonized them. The rise of the EU and the adoption of a common currency represent efforts to create a political and economic unit at a different scale—one that its proponents hope can be a more influential global actor than any individual country could be and that can produce economic and social advantages within its borders. There have clearly been many successes, but that unit finds itself increasingly under attack from a variety of directions. Facilitated by new technologies and heightened global interconnections, movements such as Occupy Frankfurt are representative of a new type of challenge to the way politics is organized geographically.

Political activity is as basic to human culture as language or religion. All individuals, groups, communities, nations, governments, and supranational organizations engage in political activity. Each desires power and influence to achieve personal and public goals. Whether or not we like politics, each of us is caught up in these processes, with effects ranging from the composition of school boards to the conduct of war.

In this chapter, we examine how geographers study politics. Political geographers study the spatial assumptions and structures underlying politics, the ways people organize space, the role territory plays in politics, and the problems that result from changing political and territorial circumstances. The state continues to be an influential political actor, and we thus devote considerable attention to the geographical foundations of the modern state system. We also consider a few of the key large-scale changes that are shaping life in the early twenty-first century.

# Key Questions FOR CHAPTER 8

1. How is space politically organized into states and nations?
2. How do states spatially organize their governments?
3. How are boundaries established, and why do boundary disputes occur?
4. How does the study of geopolitics help us understand the world?
5. What are supranational organizations, and what is the future of the state?

## HOW IS SPACE POLITICALLY ORGANIZED INTO STATES AND NATIONS?

**Political geography** is the study of the political organization of the world. Political geographers study the spatial manifestations of political processes at various scales: how politically meaningful spaces came into being and how these spaces influence outcomes. At the global scale, the most influential political-territorial are individual countries, which are commonly called states. A **state** is a politically organized territory with a permanent population, a defined territory, and a government. To be a state, an entity must be recognized as such by other states.

The present-day division of the world political map into states is a product of endless accommodations and adjustments within and between human societies. The political map of the world is the world map most of us learn first. We study the names of the countries and perhaps each country's capital. It hangs in the front of our classrooms, it is used to organize maps in our textbooks, and it becomes so natural looking to us that *we begin to think it is natural.*

The world map of states is anything but natural. The mosaic of states on the map represents a way of politically organizing space that is less than 400 years old. Just as people create places, imparting character to the landscape and shaping culture, people make states. States and state boundaries are made, shaped, and refined by people, their actions and their interactions. The very idea of dividing the world into

discrete territorially defined units of governance is one created and exported by people.

Central to the state are the concepts of **territory** and territoriality. As geographer Stuart Elden has pointed out, the modern concept of territory arose in early modern Europe as a system of political units came into being with fixed, distinct boundaries and at least quasi-independent governments. **Territoriality** is the process by which such units come into being. Territoriality, however, can take place at different scales. In a book published in 1986, geographer Robert Sack defined territoriality as "the attempt by an individual or group to affect, influence, or control people, phenomena, and relationships, by delimiting and asserting control over a geographic area." Sack sees human territoriality as a key ingredient in the construction of social and political spaces. He calls for a better understanding of the human organization of the planet through a consideration of how and why certain territorial strategies are pursued at different times and in different places.

Today, territoriality is tied to the concept of **sovereignty**. As Sack explained, territorial behavior implies an expression of control over a territory. In international law, the concept of sovereignty is territorially defined. Sovereignty refers to a government's right to control its own territory, both politically and militarily. The state governments of the world have the last say, at least legally, over their respective territories. When the international community recognizes an entity as a state, it also recognizes the entity as being sovereign within its borders. Under international law, states are sovereign, and they have the right to defend their **territorial integrity** against incursion from other states.

# The Modern State Idea

In the 1600s, Europeans were not the only ones who behaved territorially, organized themselves into distinct political units, or claimed sovereignty. Because territoriality manifests itself in different ways, ideas about the relationship between political arrangements and geographical space varied from place to place.

In North America, American Indian tribes behaved territorially but not necessarily exclusively. Plains tribes shared hunting grounds with neighboring tribes that were friendly, and they fought over hunting grounds with neighboring tribes that were unfriendly. Territorial boundaries were usually not delineated on the ground. Plains tribes also held territory communally, so that individual tribal members did not "own" land. Similarly, in Southeast Asia and in Africa, state-like political entities also existed. In all of these places, and in Europe before the mid-1600s, rulers held sway over a people, but there was no collective agreement among them about how territory would be organized or what rulers could do within their respective domains.

The European state idea deserves particular attention because it most influenced the development of the modern state system. We can see traces of this state idea more than two millennia ago near the southeastern shores of the Mediterranean Sea, where distinct kingdoms emerged within discrete territories. The works of Greek philosophers on governance and aspects of ancient Greece and Rome play parts in the modern state idea. The emergence of larger-scale political-territorial units in the western portions of Late Medieval Europe developed as the feudal system broke down. In the case of what are now England and France, a single ruler was able to gradually wrest power and territory from weak feudal arrangements. At the same time, increasingly autonomous cities emerged in northern Italy and northwestern Europe where urban elites sought some degree of independence from the structures of power that dominated elsewhere. Following these developments, Early Modern European scholars advanced new ways of thinking about political space. Aiming to promote peace, great thinkers of the time drew on the concept of property rights as developed in ancient Greece and Rome to presuppose a territorial order whereby entities were free from outside control and rulers had absolute power over their realm.

By the early seventeenth century, a few larger-scale political-territorial units in western Europe (notably England, France, and Spain) coexisted with a complicated patchwork of state-like entities, including the Republic of Venice, Brandenburg, the Papal States of central Italy, the Kingdom of Hungary, and a large number of minor German states—many with poorly defined borders (Fig. 8.3). The emerging political map was accompanied by the development of **mercantilism**,

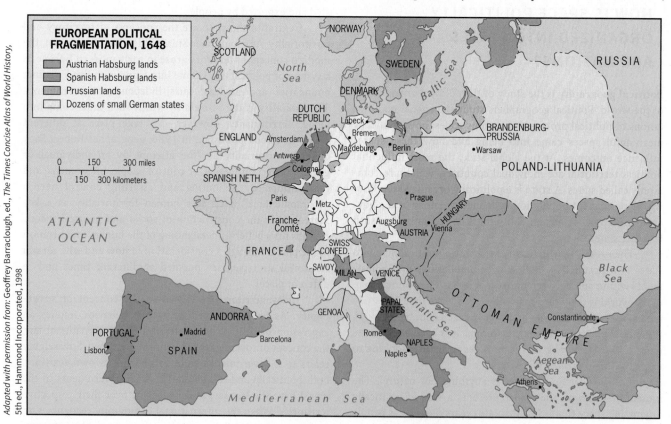

*Adapted with permission from: Geoffrey Barraclough, ed., The Times Concise Atlas of World History, 5th ed., Hammond Incorporated, 1998*

■ **Figure 8.3**

**European Political Fragmentation in 1648.**   At the time the treaty known as the Peace of Westphalia was agreed to in 1648, Europe was divided into a few larger territories and dozens of small principalities. With the treaty, each territory and principality became a sovereign state, with the legal right to have the last say.

which led to the accumulation of wealth through plunder, colonization, and the protection of home industries and foreign markets. Rivalry and competition intensified in Europe as well as abroad. Powerful royal families struggled for dominance in eastern and southern Europe. Instability was the rule, strife occurred frequently, and repressive governments prevailed.

The event in European history that marks the formal beginning of the modern state system is the **Peace of Westphalia**, negotiated in 1648 among the princes of the states making up the Holy Roman Empire, as well as a few neighboring states. The various treaties that constituted this peace put an end to Europe's most destructive internal struggle over religion during the Thirty Years' War. They contained new language recognizing the rights of rulers within defined, demarcated territories. The language of the treaties laid the foundations for a Europe made up of mutually recognized territorial states.

The rise of the Westphalian state system marked a fundamental change in the relationship between people and territory. In previous eras, *where* a society lived constituted its territory; in the Westphalian system it became the *territory* that defined the *society*. Territory is treated as a fixed element of political identification, and states define exclusive, non-overlapping territories.

Even well after the Peace of Westphalia, absolutist rulers controlled most European states. During the later seventeenth and eighteenth centuries, however, the development of an increasingly wealthy middle class and monarchial regimes that were increasingly out of touch with the lives of their subjects proved to be the undoing of absolutism in parts of western Europe. City-based merchants gained money, influence, and prestige, while the power of the nobility was increasingly challenged. The traditional measure of power—land—became less important. The merchants and businessmen demanded political recognition. In the 1780s, a series of upheavals began that changed the sociopolitical face of the continent, most notably the French Revolution of 1789. The revolution, conducted in the name of the French people, ushered in an era in which the foundations for political authority came to be seen as resting with a state's citizenry, not with a hereditary monarch.

## Nations

The popular media and press often use the words *nation, state,* and *country* interchangeably. Political geographers use *state* and *country* interchangeably (often preferring *state*), but the word *nation* is distinct. State is a legal term in international law, and the international political community has some agreement about what this term means. *Nation,* on the other hand, is a culturally defined term, and few people agree on exactly what it means. Some argue that a nation is simply the people within a state's borders, for example, all people who live in Germany. Yet the term is also used to describe peoples who do not have a state (the Kurds, indigenous groups, and the like).

The aforementioned ambiguity reflects the fact that a **nation** was traditionally understood to be a group of people who think of themselves as one based on a sense of shared culture and history, and who seek some degree of political-territorial autonomy. This idea encompasses different kinds of culturally defined nations. Nations variously see themselves as sharing a religion, a language, an ethnicity, or a history. How a nation is defined depends on the people who see themselves as part of the nation. One of the most widely read scholars on nationalism today, Benedict Anderson, defines the nation as an "imagined community": It is imagined because one will never meet all of the people in the nation, and it is a community because individuals nonetheless see themselves as part of the larger national group.

All nations are ultimately mixtures of different peoples. The French are often considered to be the classic example of a nation, but the most French-feeling person in France today is the product of a melding together of a wide variety of cultural groups over time, including Celts, Ancient Romans, Franks, Goths, and many more. If the majority of inhabitants of modern France belong to the French nation, it is because, during the formation of the French territorial state, the people came to think of themselves as French—not because the French nation existed as a primordial group that has always been distinct.

People in a nation tend to look to their past and think, "we have been through much together," and when they look to their future they often think, "whatever happens, we will go through it together." A nation is identified by its own membership; therefore, we cannot simply define a nation as the people within a territory. Indeed, rarely does a nation's extent correspond precisely with a state's borders. Many countries have multiple nations within their borders. For example, in the country of Belgium, two nations, the Flemish and the Walloons, exist within the state's borders.

## Nation-State

Over time the European idea that the map of *states* should look like the map of *nations* became the aspiration of governing elites around the world. A **nation-state** is a politically organized area in which nation and state occupy the same space. Since few (if any) states are nation-states, the importance of the concept of the nation-state lies primarily in the idea behind it. In the effort to form nation-states, some states have chosen to privilege one ethnic group at the expense of others, and other states have outlined a common history and culture. Either way, the state works to temper identities that might challenge the state's territorial integrity.

The goal of creating nation-states dates to the French Revolution, which sought to replace control by a monarchy or colonizer with an imagined cultural-historical community of French people. The Revolution initially promoted **democracy**, the idea that the people are the ultimate sovereign—that is, the people, the *nation,* have the ultimate say over what happens within the state. Each nation, it was argued, should have its own sovereign territory, and only when that is achieved can true democracy and stability exist.

People began to see the idea of the nation-state as the ultimate form of political-territorial organization, the appropriate unit entitled to sovereignty, and the best route to stability. The key problem associated with the idea of the nation-state is that it assumes the presence of reasonably well-defined, stable nations living contiguously within discrete territories. Very few places in the world come close to satisfying this requirement. Nonetheless, in the Europe of the late-eighteenth and nineteenth centuries, many believed the assumption could be met.

The quest to form nation-states in the Europe of the 1800s gave rise to the age of nationalism. We can view nationalism from two vantage points: that of the people and that of the state. When *people* have a strong sense of nationalism, they have a loyalty to and a belief in the nation itself. This loyalty does not necessarily coincide with the borders of the state. A *state*, in contrast, seeks to promote a sense of nationhood that coincides with its own borders. In the name of nationalism, a state with more than one nation within its borders may attempt to build a single national identity out of the divergent people within its borders. In the name of nationalism, a state may also promote conflict with another state that it sees as threatening to its territorial integrity.

Even though the roots of nationalism lie in earlier centuries, the nineteenth century was the true age of nationalism in Europe. In some cases the pursuit of nationalist ambitions produced greater cohesion within long-established states, such as in France or Spain; in other cases nationalism became a rallying cry for bringing together people with some shared historical or cultural elements into a single state, such as in the cases of Italy or Germany. Similarly, people who saw themselves as separate nations within other states or empires launched successful separatist movements. Ireland, Norway, and Poland all serve as examples of this phenomenon.

European state leaders used the tool of nationalism to strengthen the state. The modern map of Europe is still fragmented, but much less so than in the 1600s (Fig. 8.3). In the process of creating nation-states in Europe, states absorbed smaller entities into their borders, resolved conflicts by force as well as by negotiation, and defined their borders more precisely.

To help people within the borders relate to the dominant national ideal, state governments seek to provide security, infrastructure, and goods and services for their citizens. States support education, health care, and a military to preserve the state and to create a connection between the people and the state—to build a nation-state. European states even used the colonization of Africa and Asia in the late 1800s and early 1900s as a way to promote nationalism. People could take pride in their nation's vast colonial empire. People could identify themselves with their nation, be it French, Dutch, or British, by contrasting themselves with the people in the colonies whom they defined as mystical or savage. By defining themselves in relation to an "Other," the state and the people

helped identify the supposed "traits" of their nation; in so doing, they began to build a nation-state.

## Multistate Nations, Multinational States, and Stateless Nations

People with a sense of belonging to a particular nation rarely all reside within a single state's borders. The lack of fit between nation and state therefore creates complications. Such complications might include states containing more than one nation, nations residing in more than one state, and even nations without a state at all.

Nearly every state in the world is a **multinational state**, a state with more than one nation inside its borders. The people living in the former state of Yugoslavia never achieved a strong sense of Yugoslav nationhood. Millions of people who were citizens of Yugoslavia never had a Yugoslav nationality. They identified themselves as Slovenes, Croats, Serbs, or members of other nations or ethnic groups. Yugoslavia was a state that was comprised of more than one nation, and it eventually collapsed.

When a nation stretches across borders and across states, the nation is called a **multistate nation**. Political geographer George White studied the states of Romania and Hungary and their overlapping nations (Fig. 8.4). As he has noted, the territory of Transylvania is currently in the middle of the state of Romania, but it has not always been that way. For two centuries, Hungary's borders stretched far enough east to encompass Transylvania. The Transylvanian region today is populated by Romanians and by Hungarians, and places within Transylvania are seen as pivotal to the histories of both Hungary and Romania. In keeping with the nation-state ideal, it is not surprising that both Romania and Hungary have interests in Transylvania, and some Hungarians continue to look upon the region as a territory that has been illegitimately lost. White explains how important territory is to a nation: "The control and maintenance of territory is as crucial as the control and maintenance of a national language, religion, or a particular way of life. Indeed, a language, religion or way of life is difficult to maintain without control over territory." In the case of Romania and Hungary, as in other similar situations, territory is as important as "language, religion, or way of life." When multiple nations or states claim attachments to the same piece of territory, the potential for conflict is significant.

Another complication that arises from the lack of fit between nations and states is that some nations do not have a state; they are **stateless nations**. The Palestinians are an example of a stateless nation. The Palestinian Arabs have gained control over the Gaza Strip and fragments of the Occupied Territories of the West Bank and Golan Heights. These territories may provide the foundations of a future state. The United Nations agency for Palestinian refugees records 5 million registered Palestinian refugees. Well over half of these registered refugees continue to live in Jordan,

# GUEST FIELD NOTE

## Cluj-Napoca, Romania

To Hungarians, Transylvania is significant because it was an important part of the Hungarian Kingdom for a thousand years. Many of their great leaders were born and buried there, and many of their great churches, colleges, and architectural achievements are located there too. For example, in the city of Cluj-Napoca (Kolozsvár in Hungarian) is St. Michael's Cathedral, and next to it is the statue of King Matthias, one of Hungary's greatest kings. Romanians have long lived in the territory too, tracing their roots back to the Roman Empire. To Romanian nationalists, the existence of Roman ruins in Transylvania is proof of their Roman ancestry and their right to govern Transylvania because their ancestors lived in Transylvania before those of the Hungarians. When archaeologists found Roman ruins around St. Michael's Cathedral and King Matthias's statue, they immediately began excavating them, which in turn aggravated the ethnic Hungarians. Traveling in

Courtesy of Steven Schnell

**■ Figure 8.4**

Transylvania made me very aware of how important places are to peoples and how contested they can be.

*Credit: © George White, Frostburg State University.*

---

Lebanon, Syria, and other Arab states. Over 2 million Palestinians live in the Gaza Strip and West Bank; however, the international community does not universally recognize the Palestinian lands as a state.

A much larger stateless nation is the Kurds, a group comprised of between 25 and 30 million people living in an area called Kurdistan that covers parts of six states (Fig. 8.5). In the aftermath of the 1991 Gulf War, the United Nations established a Kurdish Security Zone north of the 36th parallel in Iraq, and that area continues to have significant autonomy in present-day Iraq. The no-fly zone in the Kurdish region of northern Iraq has created a relatively peaceful place compared to continued violence in southern Iraq. Violent acts still mar the Kurdish north, but prosperity has also come to the region through petrodollars. A recent travel article in the *New York Times* described new theme parks and gated communities that reflect the affluence in the city of Erbil, which is the Kurdish capital city in Iraq. The article also described Erbil's 6000-year-old citadel as a reminder that the city is "one of the oldest continuously inhabited cities in the world."

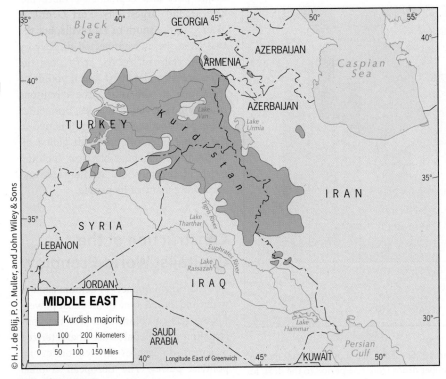

© H. J. de Blij, P. O. Muller, and John Wiley & Sons

**MIDDLE EAST**
Kurdish majority

0    100    200 Kilometers
0    50    100    150 Miles

**■ Figure 8.5**
**Kurdish Region of the Middle East.**

An independent Kurdish state seems unlikely, at least in the near future. In addition to northern Iraq, the Kurds form the largest minority in Turkey, where the city of Diyarbakir is the unofficial Kurdish capital of Turkey. Relations between the 10 million Kurds in Turkey and the Turkish government in Ankara have been volatile, and Turkey regards the Kurdish region as part of the state's core territory. Without the consent of Turkey, establishing a truly independent Kurdish state will be difficult.

## European Colonialism and the Diffusion of the Nation-State Model

Europe exported its concepts of state, sovereignty, and the desire for nation-states to much of the rest of the world through two waves of colonialism (Fig. 8.6). In the sixteenth century, Spain and Portugal took advantage of an increasingly well-consolidated internal political order and newfound wealth to expand their influence to increasingly far-flung realms during the first wave of colonialism. Later joined by Britain, France, the Netherlands, and Belgium, the first wave of colonialism established a far-reaching political and economic system. After independence movements in the Americas during the late 1700s and 1800s, a second wave of colonialism began in the late 1800s. The major colonizers were Britain, France, the Netherlands, Belgium, Germany, and Italy. The colonizing parties met for the Berlin Conference in 1884–1885 and arbitrarily laid out the colonial map of Africa without reference to indigenous cultural or political

arrangements. Driven by motives ranging from economic profit to national pride to the desire to bring Christianity to the rest of the world, colonialism projected European power and a European approach to organizing political space into the non-European world (Fig. 8.7).

With Europe in control of so much of the world, Europeans laid the ground rules for the emerging international state system, and the modern European concept of the nation-state became the model adopted around the world. Europe also established and defined the ground rules of the capitalist world-economy, creating a system of economic interdependence that persists today.

During the heyday of **colonialism**, the imperial powers exercised ruthless control over their domains and organized them for maximum economic exploitation. The capacity to install the infrastructure necessary for such efficient profiteering is itself evidence of the power relationships involved: Entire populations were regimented in the service of the colonial ruler. Colonizers organized the flows of raw materials for their own benefit. The tangible evidence of that organization (plantations, ports, mines, and railroads) are prominent features of the cultural landscape to this day.

The colonial era is now largely behind us, but the political organization of space and associated economic arrangements are still very much with us. Most of the former colonies are now independent states, but their economies are anything but independent. In many cases, raw material flows are as great as they were before the colonial era came to an end. For example, today in Gabon, Africa, the railroad goes from the interior forest, which is logged for plywood, to the major port and capital city, Libreville. The second largest city, Port Gentil, is located to the south of Libreville, but the two cities are not connected directly by road or railroad. As the crow flies, the cities are 90 miles apart, but if you drive from one to the other, the circuitous route will take you 435 miles. Both cities are export focused. Port Gentil is tied to the global oil economy, with global oil corporations responsible for building much of the city and its housing, and employing many of its people.

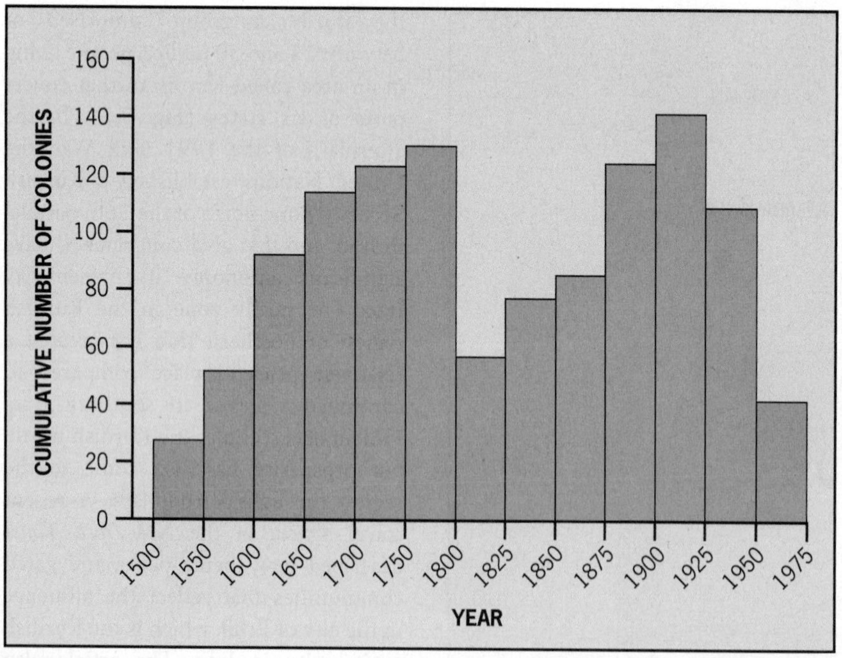

Adapted with permission from: Peter J. Taylor and Colin Flint, *Political Geography: World-Economy, Nation-State and Locality*, 4th edition,, New York: Taylor & Francis, 2000.

■ **Figure 8.6**
**Two Waves of Colonialism Between 1500 and 1975.**    Each bar shows the total number of colonies around the world. When the total number drops from one period to the next, for example from 1950 to 1975, the drop reflects the number of colonies that became independent between those two dates.

## Construction of the Capitalist World-Economy

The long-term impacts of colonialism are many and varied. One of the most powerful impacts of colonialism was the construction of a global order characterized by great differences in economic and political power. The European colonial enterprise gave birth to a globalized economic order in which the European

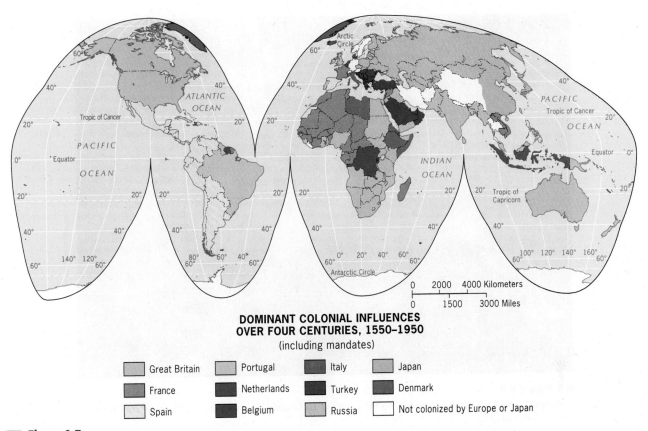

**DOMINANT COLONIAL INFLUENCES
OVER FOUR CENTURIES, 1550–1950**
(including mandates)

| | | | |
|---|---|---|---|
| Great Britain | Portugal | Italy | Japan |
| France | Netherlands | Turkey | Denmark |
| Spain | Belgium | Russia | Not colonized by Europe or Japan |

**Figure 8.7**

**Dominant Colonial Influences, 1550–1950.**  The map shows the *dominant* European or Japanese colonial influence in each country over the four centuries.  © H. J. de Blij, John Wiley & Sons.

states and areas dominated by European migrants emerged as the major centers of economic and political activity. Through colonialism, Europeans extracted wealth from colonies and put colonized peoples in a subservient position.

Of course, not all Europeans profited equally from colonialism. Enormous poverty persisted within even the most powerful European states. Moreover, sustaining control over colonies was costly. In the late seventeenth century, the high cost of maintaining the large Spanish colonial empire was beginning to take a toll on the Spanish economy. Western Europeans were not the only people to profit from colonialism. During the period of European colonialism (1500–1950), Russia and the United States expanded over land instead of overseas, profiting from the taking of territory and the subjugation of indigenous peoples. Japan was a regional colonial power, controlling Korea and other parts of East and Southeast Asia as well as Pacific Islands. But the concentration of wealth that colonialism brought to Europe, and to parts of the world dominated by European settlers, including the United States, Canada, and Australia, is at the heart of the highly uneven global distribution of power that continues today.

The forces of colonialism played a key role in knitting together the economies of widely separated areas, which gave birth to a global economic order—a world-economy. Wealth is unevenly distributed in the world-economy, as can be seen in

statistics on per capita gross national income (GNI): Bangladesh's GNI is only $2070, whereas Norway's GNI is $64,030. But to truly understand why wealth is distributed unevenly, we cannot simply study each country, its resources, and its production of goods. Rather, we need to understand where countries fit in the world-economy. That is, we need to see the big picture.

Think of a pointillist painting. Specifically, envision the magnificent work of nineteenth-century French painter Georges Pierre Seurat, *Sunday Afternoon on the Island of La Grande Jatte* (Fig. 8.8). The painting hangs in the Art Institute of Chicago. If you have the opportunity to see the painting and if you stand close enough, you will see Seurat's post-Impressionist method of painting millions of points or dots— single, tiny brush strokes, each a single color. When you step back again, you can gain a sense of how each dot fits into the picture as a whole.[1] In the last few decades, social scientists have sought to understand how each dot, how each country and each locality, fit into the picture of the world as a whole. If you focus on a single dot or even each dot one at a time, you miss the whole. Even if you study every single dot and add them together, you still miss the whole. You need to step back

---

[1]We give credit to former student Kelsey Lynd, who came up with this metaphor for world-systems theory in a political geography class at the University of Mary Washington in 1999.

© Bridgeman Art Library, London/SuperStock

■ **Figure 8.8**

**Chicago, Illinois.**   Sunday Afternoon on the Island of La Grande Jatte, by Georges Pierre Seurat, hangs in the Art Institute of Chicago.

and see the whole, as well as the individual dots, studying how one affects the other. By now, this should sound familiar: It is one of the ways geographers think about **scale**.

Political geographers took note of one sociologist's theory of the world-economy and added much to it. Building on the work of Immanuel Wallerstein, proponents of **world-systems theory** view the world as much more than the sum total of the world's states. Much like a pointillist painting, world-systems theorists hold that to understand any state, we must also understand its spatial and functional relationships within the world-economy.

Wallerstein's publications number in the hundreds, and the political and economic geography publications tied to world-systems theory number in the thousands. To simplify the research, we can study the three basic tenets of world-systems theory, as Wallerstein defines them:

1. The world-economy has one market and a global division of labor.

2. Although the world has multiple states, almost everything takes place within the context of the world-economy.

3. The world-economy has a three-tier structure.

According to Wallerstein, the development of a world-economy began with capitalist exchange around 1450 and encompassed the globe by 1900. **Capitalism** means that in the world-economy, individuals, corporations, and states own land and produce goods and services that are exchanged for profit. To generate a profit, producers seek the cheapest production and costs. For example, when labor (including salaries and benefits) became the most expensive component of production costs, corporations sought to move production from North Carolina to Mexico and then to China, simply to take advantage of cheaper labor. In addition to the world labor supply, producers gain profit by commodifying whatever they can. **Commodification** is the process of placing a price on a good, service, or idea and then buying, selling, and trading that item. Companies create new products, generate new twists on old products, and create demand for the products through marketing. As children, none of the authors of this book could have imagined buying a bottle of water. Now, the sale of water in bottles is commonplace.

Second, despite the existence of approximately 200 states, most economic interactions take place within the context of the world-economy (and have since 1900). Colonialism played a major role in establishing this system by exporting the European state idea and facilitating the construction of an interdependent global economy. When colonies became independent, gaining the legal status of sovereign states was relatively easy for most colonies. The United Nations Charter even set up a committee to help colonies do so after World War II. But gaining true economic independence is all but impossible. The economies of the world are tied together, generating intended and unintended consequences that fundamentally change places.

Lastly, world-systems theorists see the world-economy as a three-tiered structure comprised of a core, a periphery, and a semiperiphery (an intermediary or transitional

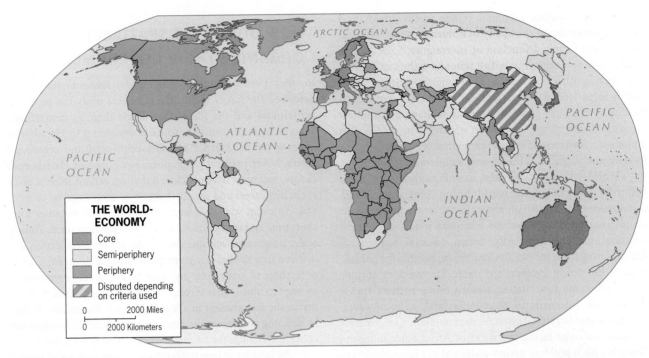

**Figure 8.9**

**The World-Economy.**    One representation of core, periphery, and semiperiphery based on a calculation called World-Economy Centrality, derived by sociologist Paul Prew. The authors took into consideration factors not quantified in Prew's data, including membership in the European Union, in moving some countries from the categories Prew's data recommended to other categories.    *Data from*: Paul Prew, *World-Economy Centrality and Carbon Dioxide Emissions: A New Look at the Position in the Capitalist World-System and Environmental Pollution, American Sociological Association, 12, 2 (2010): 162–191.*

category). The **core** and the periphery are not just places but the sites where particular processes take place. The core is where one is most likely to find higher levels of education, higher salaries, and more technology—core processes that generate more wealth in the world-economy. The **periphery** more commonly has lower levels of education, lower salaries, and less sophisticated technology—peripheral processes associated with a more marginal position in the world-economy.

Figure 8.9 presents one way of dividing up the world in world-systems terms. The map designates some states as part of the **semiperiphery**—places where core and periphery processes are both occurring—places that are exploited by the core but in turn exploit the periphery. The semiperiphery acts as a buffer between the core and periphery, preventing the polarization of the world into two extremes.

Political geographers, economic geographers, and other academics continue to debate world-systems theory. Detractors argue that it overemphasizes economic factors in political development, that it is very state-centric, and that it does not fully account for how places move from one category to another. Nonetheless, Wallerstein's work has encouraged many to see the world political map as a system of interlinking parts that need to be understood in relation to one another and as a whole. As such, the impact of world-systems theory has been considerable in political geography, and it is increasingly commonplace for geographers to refer to the

kinds of core–periphery distinctions suggested by world-systems theory.

World-systems theory helps explain how colonial powers were able to amass and sustain great concentrations of wealth. During the first wave of colonialism, colonizers extracted goods from the Americas and the Caribbean and exploited Africa for slave labor, amassing wealth through sugar, coffee, fruit, and cotton production. During the second wave of colonialism, which happened after the Industrial Revolution, colonizers set their sights on cheap industrial labor, cheap raw materials, and large-scale agricultural plantations.

Not all core countries in the world today were colonial powers, however. Countries including Switzerland, Singapore, and Australia have significant global clout even though they were never classic colonial powers, and that clout is tied in significant part to their positions in the global economy. The countries gained their core positions through access to the networks of production, consumption, and exchange in the wealthiest parts of the world and through their ability to take advantage of that access.

## World-Systems and Political Power

Are economic power and political power one and the same? No, but certainly economic power can bring political power.

In the current system, economic power means wealth, and political power means the ability to influence others. Political power is not simply a function of sovereignty. Each state is theoretically sovereign, but not all states have the same ability to influence others or achieve their political goals. Having wealth helps leaders amass political power. For instance, a wealthy country can establish a mighty military. But political influence is not simply a function of hard power; it is also diplomatic. Switzerland's declared neutrality, combined with its economic might, aids the country's diplomatic efforts.

World-systems theory helps us understand how Europe politically reorganized the world during colonialism. When colonialism ended in Africa and Asia, the newly independent people continued to follow the European model of political organization. The arbitrarily drawn colonial borders of Africa, dating from the Berlin Conference, became the boundaries of the newly independent states. On the map, former colonies became new states; administrative borders transformed into international boundaries; and, in most cases, colonial administrative towns became capitals. The greatest political challenge facing the states of Africa since independence has been building nation-states out of incredibly divergent (sometimes antagonistic) peoples. The leaders of the newly independent states continually work to build nation-states in the hope of quelling division among the people, securing their territory, and developing their economic (as well as other) systems of organization.

## The Enduring Impact of the Nation-State Idea

Major players in international relations still seek solutions to complex political conflicts by trying to redraw the political map in an effort to bring political and national borders into closer correspondence. Faced with the disintegration of the former Yugoslavia or the complex problems of Israel/ Palestine, for example, the tendency is often to propose new state boundaries around nations, with the goal of making the nation and state fit. Drawing neat boundaries of this sort is usually impossible, and the creation of new territories can lead to different ethnonational problems. Regardless of the multitude of problems and lack of simple solutions to nation and state conflicts, the European territorial state idea became the world model, and that idea is still shaping how the world is thought about and governed today.

Imagine you are the leader of a newly independent state in Africa or Asia. Determine what your government can do to build a nation that corresponds with the borders of your state. Consider the roles of education, government, military, and culture in your exercise in nation-building.

## HOW DO STATES SPATIALLY ORGANIZE THEIR GOVERNMENTS?

In the 1950s, political geographer Richard Hartshorne described the forces within the state that unify the people as **centripetal** and the forces that divide them as **centrifugal**. Whether a state continues to exist, according to Hartshorne, depends on the balance between centripetal and centrifugal forces. Many political geographers have debated Hartshorne's theory, and most have concluded that we cannot select a given event or process and simply define it as centrifugal or centripetal. An event such as a war can pull the state together for a short time and then divide the state over the long term. Timing, scale, interaction, and perspective factor into unification and division in a state at any given point. Instead of creating a balance sheet of centripetal and centrifugal forces, governments attempt to unify states through nation-building, through structuring the government in a way that melds the nations within, by defining and defending boundaries, and through expressing control over all of the territory within those boundaries.

By looking at how different governments have attempted to unify the peoples and territories within their domains, we are reminded how important geography is. Governance does not take place in a vacuum. The unique characteristics of places shape whether any possible governmental "solution" solves or exacerbates matters.

## Form of Government

The internal political geographic organization of states can have an impact on state unity. Most states in the world are either unitary or federal states.

Until the end of World War II, many European states, including multinational states, were highly centralized, with the capital city serving as the focus of power. Few states sought to accommodate minorities (such as Bretons in France or Basques in Spain) or outlying regions where identification with the state was weaker. Political geographers call these highly centralized states **unitary** governments. The administrative framework of a unitary government is designed to ensure the central government's authority over all parts of the state. The French government divided the state into more than 90 *départements*, but their representatives came to Paris not just to express regional concerns but to implement central-government decisions back home.

One way of governing a multinational state is to construct a *federal* system, organizing state territory into regions, substates (which we refer to as States), provinces, or cantons. In a strong **federal** system, the regions have much control over government policies and funds, whereas in a weak federal system, the central government retains a significant measure of power. Most federal systems are somewhere in between, with governments at the state scale and at the substate scale each having control over certain revenues and particular policy areas. Giving control over certain policies (especially culturally relative policies) to smaller-scale governments is one strategy for keeping the state as a whole together.

Federalism functions differently depending on the context. In Nigeria, the 36 constituent States choose their own judicial system. In the Muslim north, 12 States have Shari'a laws (legal systems based on traditional Islamic laws), and in the Christian and animist south, the States do not (Fig. 8.10). Shari'a law in the northern states of Nigeria is only applied to Muslims, not to Christians and Animists. The move to Shari'a law in the north came at the same time as democracy swept Nigeria in 2000. Nigerians in the north hoped stricter laws would help root out corruption among politicians, although it has failed to do so. Supporters of the Shari'a tradition also cite the need to curb rampant crime, prostitution, and gambling. Some northerners seek to expand Shari'a law to other States. That idea is a motivating force for the Islamic fundamentalist group Boko Haram, which has resorted to violence in an effort to overthrow the existing government and bring into being an Islamic state. The movement has used bombings, assassinations, and abductions to advance its agenda. The Nigerian government has declared a state of emergency in the country's northeast and has put significant resources toward fighting the militant group, but Nigeria's security forces have been largely unsuccessful in rooting out the organization's leaders and supply networks. Many Nigerians, in the north as well as the south, oppose Boko Haram's tactics, but chronic poverty, widespread corruption, and north–south tensions play into the organization's hands.

In the United States, States take different approaches to matters such as the death penalty, access to alcohol (Fig. 8.11), and the right to carry concealed weapons, but many of the fundamentals of the legal system do not differ among States.

Federalism accommodates regional interests by vesting primary power in provinces, States, or other regional units over all matters except those explicitly given to the central government. The Australian geographer K. W. Robinson described a federation as "the most geographically expressive of all political systems, based as it is on the existence and accommodation of regional differences... federation does not create unity out of diversity; rather, it enables the two to coexist."

Choosing a federal system does not always quell nationalist sentiment. After all, the multinational states of the Soviet Union, Yugoslavia, and Czechoslovakia fell apart, despite their federalist systems, and the future of Belgium and Iraq as single states is in some doubt.

## Devolution

**Devolution** is the movement of power "downwards" from the central government to regional governments within the

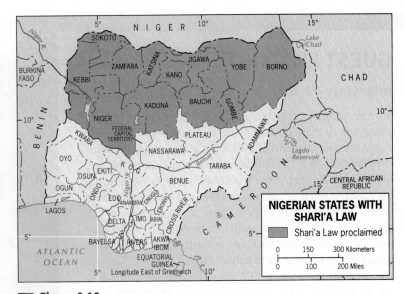

■ **Figure 8.10**

**States in Nigeria with Shari'a Law.** *Data from*: BBC, http://news.bbc.co.uk/2/hi/ africa/1962827.stm#map.

state. Sometimes devolution is achieved by reworking a constitution to establish a federal system that recognizes the status of the regional governments, as Spain has done. In other places, governments devolve power without altering constitutions, almost as an experiment. In the United Kingdom, the Northern Ireland Assembly, a parliamentary body, resulted from devolution, but the British government suspended its activities in 2002 and then reinstated the assembly in 2007. Devolutionary forces can emerge in all kinds of states, old and young, large and small. These forces arise from several sources of internal division: ethnocultural, economic, and territorial.

## ETHNOCULTURAL DEVOLUTIONARY MOVEMENTS

Many of Europe's devolutionary movements came from nations within a state that define themselves as being ethnically, linguistically, or religiously distinct.

The capacity of ethnocultural forces to stimulate devolutionary processes has been evident, for example, in eastern Europe. Parts of the eastern European map have changed quite drastically over the past two decades, and two countries, Czechoslovakia and Yugoslavia, succumbed to devolutionary pressures. In the case of Czechoslovakia, the process was peaceful: Czechs and Slovaks divided their country, creating a new international border in 1992. As Fig. 8.12 shows, however, one of the two new states, Slovakia, is not homogeneous. About 11 percent of Slovakians are Hungarian, and that minority is concentrated along the border between Slovakia and Hungary. The Hungarian minority, concerned about linguistic and cultural discrimination, has at times demanded greater autonomy or self-governance to protect its heritage in the new state of Slovakia.

# GUEST FIELD NOTE

## Interstate 40, Near Blackwell, Arkansas

In most states in the United States, a "dry county" might cause one to think of a place where there is very little rain. But in the southern part of the United States, there are many dry counties—that is, counties with laws forbidding the sale of packaged alcohol. In the late 1800s and early 1900s, keeping counties dry was much easier than it is today. A hundred years ago, it took up to a day to travel to the next town or city on very poor roads. Today, with cars traveling 70 mph on an interstate, the same trip takes a matter of minutes. Why would counties continue to ban alcohol sales today? Many of the reasons are cultural. Of the Arkansas residents who attend church, most are Baptists (see Fig. 7.28) or other Protestant denominations. Many of these churches prohibit consumption of alcoholic beverages. The Arkansas legislature supports dry counties by requiring counties that want to sell packaged liquor to get 38 percent of the voters in the last election to sign a petition. It only takes 10 percent of that voter pool to get any other issue on the ballot. Today, however, many dry counties in Arkansas are known as "damp." Damp counties are those where restaurants, country clubs, and social organizations can apply and receive a license to serve alcohol by the drink. This arrangement seems counterintuitive to the idea of a dry county. But

■ Figure 8.11

business and economic development authorities want damp counties to encourage investment and growth in the local economy.

*Credit: Paul T. Gray, Jr., Russellville High School.*

Compared to the constituent units of the former Yugoslavia (discussed in detail in Chapter 7), other countries shown in Figure 8.13 have dealt with devolutionary pressures more peacefully. Elsewhere in the world, however, ethnocultural fragmentation has produced costly wars. For example, ethnocultural differences were at the heart of the civil war that wracked Sri Lanka (South Asia) between the 1980s and 2009, with the Sinhalese (Buddhist) majority ultimately suppressing the drive by the Tamil (Hindu) minority for an independent state.

Devolutionary forces based on ethnocultural claims are gaining momentum in places that have long looked stable from the outside. The communist government of China has pragmatically, and in many cases relatively successfully, integrated 56 ethnic nations into the state of China. China has acknowledged the precarious place of the minority nations within the larger Han-dominated state by extending rights to minorities, including the right to have two children under the government's one-child policy. Some nations within China continue to challenge the state, however. In China's far west, Tibetan and Uyghur separatist movements have become more visible, but the Chinese government's firm hold and control of the media and Internet makes it difficult, if not impossible, for separatist groups to hold Egyptian-style protests in China. Hence, some resort to terrorist attacks.

Devolution does not *necessarily* fuel greater calls for independence; it can, in fact, help to calm tensions by giving constituent groups within a state a sense of control over their own affairs. That hope led the United Kingdom, in 1997, to allow Scotland to establish its own parliament, which had last met in 1707. The 129 members of the Scottish Parliament swear allegiance to the Queen of England, but they are in a position to dictate how a variety of issues in Scotland will be handled, including education, health, housing, and police. Those concessions were not enough to head off a referendum on independence in September 2014 (ultimately unsuccessful), but they make it more difficult for the champions of independence to paint Scotland as subservient to London. Parliaments were also established in Wales and Northern Ireland in the late 1990s, but their powers were more limited.

## ECONOMIC DEVOLUTIONARY FORCES

Devolutionary pressures often arise from a combination of sources. In Catalonia, ethnocultural differences play a significant role, but economics plays a role as well; with some 8 percent of Spain's territory and just 16 percent of its population, Catalonia produces some 35 percent of all Spanish exports by value and 54 percent of its high-tech exports.

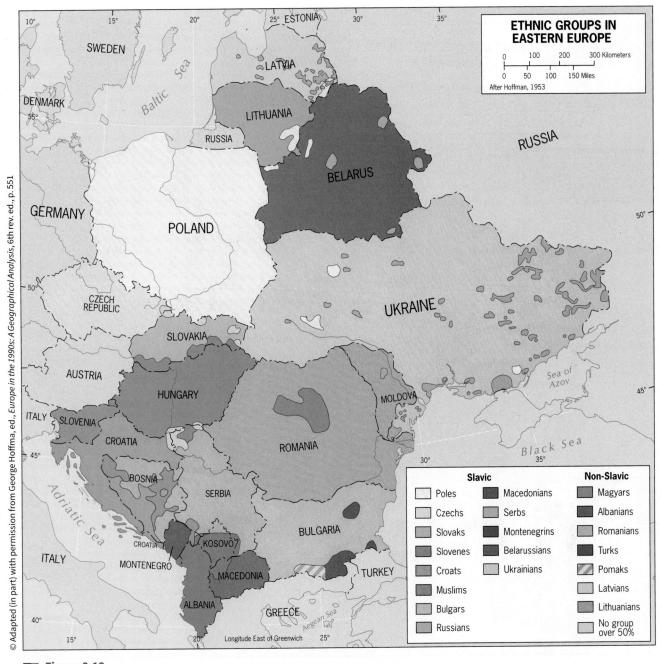

**ETHNIC GROUPS IN EASTERN EUROPE**

| Slavic | | Non-Slavic |
|---|---|---|
| Poles | Macedonians | Magyars |
| Czechs | Serbs | Albanians |
| Slovaks | Montenegrins | Romanians |
| Slovenes | Belarussians | Turks |
| Croats | Ukrainians | Pomaks |
| Muslims | | Latvians |
| Bulgars | | Lithuanians |
| Russians | | No group over 50% |

■ **Figure 8.12**

**Ethnic Mosaic of Eastern Europe.** The ethnic groups in this map are largely based on language. The presence of Russians in Ukraine, Belarus, and Latvia is a result of the Soviet policy of Russification, where Russians were moved throughout the Soviet Union to help spread the Russian culture and establish a Soviet national identity based on Russian culture. The central part of Romania, where there is a concentration of Magyars, is Transylvania, a land important to both Hungarians and Romanians.

What is more, nearly 70 percent of all Spanish exports pass through the region (Fig. 8.14). Pro-independence groups in Catalonia held a referendum in April 2011 seeking a vote for independence. The vote failed, but devolutionary forces continue to argue that Catalonia's economy pays more into the Spanish government than it receives from the state of Spain. In 2013, pro-independence groups announced plans to hold another referendum, prompting the Spanish government to reply that it would block the poll.

Economic forces have also fostered devolutionary pressures in Italy. Demands for autonomy for Sardinia are deeply rooted in the island's economic circumstances, with accusations of neglect by the government in Rome high on the list of grievances. Italy also faces serious devolutionary pressures on its mainland peninsula because of north–south differences. The Mezzogiorno region lies to the south, below the Ancona Line (an imaginary border extending from Rome to the Adriatic coast at Ancona). The wealthier north stands in sharp

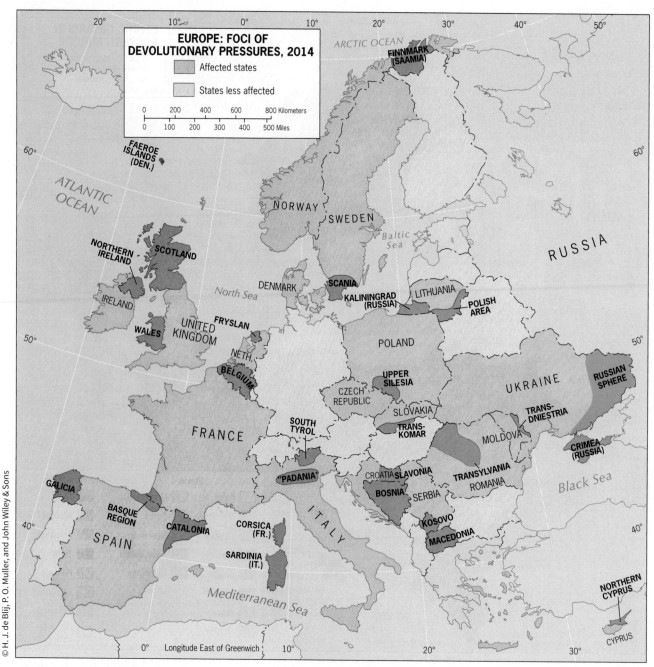

■ **Figure 8.13**

**Europe: Foci of Devolutionary Pressures, 2014.**   Devolutionary movements in Europe are found where a nation with a shared history has the political goal of greater autonomy, unification with the rest of their nation, or independence. In 2014 Scotland voted on whether to secede from the United Kingdom, with 55 percent of the people voting against independence.

contrast to the poorer south. Despite the large subsidies granted to the Mezzogiorno, the development gap between the north, very much a part of the European core, and the south, part of the European periphery, has been widening. Some Italian politicians have exploited widespread impatience with the situation by forming organizations to promote northern interests, including devolution. One of these organizations, the Northern League, has raised the prospect of an independent state called Padania in the northern part of Italy centered on

the Po River. After a surge of enthusiasm, the Padania campaign faltered, but it pushed the Italian government to focus more attention on regional inequalities within the country.

Brazil provides another example of the interconnections between devolutionary movements and economics. As in northern Italy, a separatist movement emerged in the 1990s in a better-off region in the south that includes the three southernmost States of Rio Grande do Sul, Santa Catarina, and Parana. Southerners complained that the

**■ Figure 8.14**

**Barcelona, Spain.** Barcelona's long-standing economic and political significance is indelibly imprinted in the urban landscape. Once the heart of a far-flung Mediterranean empire, Barcelona went on to become a center of commerce and banking as the Iberian Peninsula industrialized. In the process, the city became a center of architectural innovation where major streets are lined with impressive buildings—many with intricate stone façades.

government was misspending their tax money on assistance to Amazonia in northern and interior Brazil. The southerners found a leader, manufactured a flag, and demanded independence for their Republic of the Pampas. The Brazilian government responded by outlawing the separatists' political party, but the economic differences between north and south continue, and devolution pressures will certainly arise again.

### TERRITORIAL INFLUENCES ON DEVOLUTION

We have seen how political decisions and cultural and economic forces can generate devolutionary processes in states. Devolutionary events have at least one feature in common: they most often occur on the margins of states. Note that every one of the devolution-affected areas shown in Figure 8.13 lie on a coast or on a border. Distance, remoteness, and marginal location frequently strengthen devolutionary tendencies (see

Box 8.1). The regions most likely to seek devolution are those far from the national capital. Many are separated by water, desert, or mountains from the center of power and adjoin neighbors that may support separatist objectives.

Note also that many islands are subject to devolutionary processes: Corsica (France), Sardinia (Italy), Taiwan (China), Singapore (Malaysia), Zanzibar (Tanzania), Jolo (Philippines), Puerto Rico (United States), Mayotte (Comoros), and East Timor (Indonesia) are notable examples. As this list indicates, some of these islands became independent states, while others were divided during devolution. Insularity clearly has advantages for separatist movements.

Not surprisingly, the United States faces its most serious devolutionary pressures on the islands of Hawai'i (Fig. 8.15). The year 1993 marked the hundred-year anniversary of the United States' annexation of Hawai'i. In that year, a vocal minority of native Hawai'ians and their sympathizers demanded the return of rights lost during the "occupation." These demands included the right to reestablish an independent state called Hawai'i (before its annexation Hawai'i was a Polynesian kingdom) on several of the smaller islands. Their hope is that ultimately the island of Kauai, or at least a significant part of that island, which is considered ancestral land, will become a component of the independent Hawai'ian state.

At present, the native Hawai'ian separatists do not have the numbers, resources, or influence to achieve their aims. The potential for some form of separation between Hawai'i and the mainland United States does exist, however. The political geographer Saul Cohen has argued that political entities situated in border zones between geopolitical powers may become gateway states, absorbing and assimilating diverse cultures and traditions and emerging as new entities, no longer dominated by one or the other. Hawai'i, he suggests, is a candidate for this status.

Territorial characteristics can play a significant role in starting and sustaining devolutionary processes. Distance can be compounded by differences in physical geography—a feeling of remoteness can be fueled by being isolated in a valley or separated by mountains or a river. Basic physical-geographic and locational factors can thus be key ingredients in the devolutionary process.

## Electoral Geography

The partitioning of state territory into electoral districts represents another key component of a state's internal political geography. Electoral geographers examine how the spatial configuration of electoral districts and the voting patterns that emerge in particular elections reflect and influence social and political affairs. Various countries use different voting systems to elect their governments. For example, in the 1994 South African election, government leaders introduced a system of majority rule while awarding some power to each of nine newly formed regions. The overall effect was to protect, to an extent, the rights of minorities in those regions.

# BOX 8.1

## The Territorial Configuration of States

Classical political geography devoted considerable attention to the ways in which different territorial configurations might influence state stability. The focus of attention was on the potential centrifugal or centripetal impacts of differently shaped states (see figure). Particularly before the advent of modern transportation and communication, it was easier for a central government to knit together the territory of a compact state—one in which the distance from the geometric center to any point on the boundary did not vary greatly—than it was for states lacking this characteristic. Some states are fragmented, consisting of two or more separate pieces; examples include the Philippines and Indonesia. This fragmentation makes certain kinds of interactions more difficult. Other states are elongated (Chile, Vietnam), making integration more difficult. Still others have a protruded or prorupted area—one that extends out from a more compact core; this area sometimes has developed in different ways from the core (e.g., the southern portion of Thailand). Finally, a few states are perforated by another country (e.g., South Africa by Lesotho).

The shape of states no longer receives a great deal of attention because it is increasingly clear that other factors have more influence on the viability and integrity of states. The Côte d'Ivoire (Ivory Coast) is relatively compact, but the country struggles with ethnoregional differences. Norway is elongated and the United States is fragmented, but these are

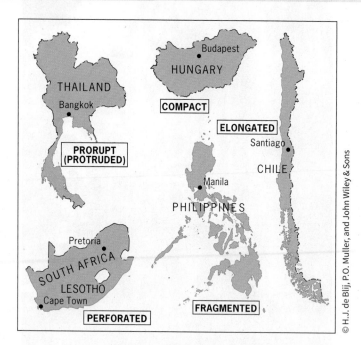

© H.J. de Blij, P.O. Muller, and John Wiley & Sons

comparatively well-integrated states. The point is that the legitimacy and effectiveness of governmental and social institutions, and the position of states in the global economy, tend to be far more significant than shape. But shape is not entirely irrelevant. There is a long-standing north–south divide in Vietnam, and Thailand has struggled to integrate its prorupted south. The key is to view shape as a matter that varies in influence depending on the political, economic, and historical circumstances at play.

# FIELD NOTE

"As I drove along a main road through a Honolulu suburb I noticed that numerous houses had the Hawai'i State flag flying upside down. I knocked on the door of this house and asked the homeowner why he was treating the State flag this way. He invited me in and we talked for more than an hour. 'This is 1993,' he said, 'and we native Hawai'ians are letting the State government and the country know that we haven't forgotten the annexation by the United States of our kingdom. I don't accept it, and we want our territory to plant our flag and keep the traditions alive. Why don't you drive past the royal palace, and you'll see that we mean it.' He was right. The Iolani Palace, where the Hawai'ians' last monarch, Queen Liliuokalani, reigned until she was deposed by a group of American businessmen in 1893, was draped in black for all of Honolulu to see. Here was devolutionary stress on American soil."

© H. J. de Blij

■■ **Figure 8.15**
**Honolulu, Hawai'i.**

In the 1994 election in South Africa, the leading political party, the African National Congress, designated at least 35 percent of its slate of candidates to women, helping South Africa become one of the world leaders in the percent of women who hold seats in a national legislative body (see Fig. 5.17).

The geographic study of voting behavior is especially interesting because it helps us assess whether people's voting tendencies are influenced by their geographic situation. Maps of voting patterns often produce surprises that can be explained by other maps, and geographic information systems have raised this kind of analysis to new levels. Political geographers study church affiliation, income level, ethnic background, education attainment, and numerous other social and economic factors to gain an understanding of why voters in a certain region might vote the way they do.

The domain in which electoral geographers can have the most concrete influence is in the drawing of electoral districts. In a democracy with representatives elected by district, the spatial organization of the districts determines whose voice is heard in a given place—with impacts on who is elected. A voter's most direct contact with government is at the local level. The United States Constitution establishes a system of **territorial representation**. In the Senate, each major territorial unit (State) gets two representatives, and the 435 members of the House of Representatives are elected from territorially defined districts that have similar-sized populations.

The Constitution requires a census every ten years in order to enumerate the population and reapportion the representatives accordingly. **Reapportionment** is the process by which districts are moved according to population shifts, so that each district encompasses approximately the same number of people. For example, after the 2010 census, several States in the so-called Rust Belt, including Pennsylvania, Ohio, and Michigan, lost representatives, whereas the Sun Belt States of Georgia, South Carolina, and Florida, along with the southwestern States of Arizona, Nevada, and Utah gained representatives.

In the United States, once reapportionment is complete, individual States go through the process of redistricting, each following its own system. The criteria involved in redistricting are numerous, but the most important is equal representation, achieved by ensuring that districts have approximately the same populations. In addition, the Supreme Court prefers compact and contiguous districts that keep political units (such as counties) intact. Finally, the courts have repeatedly called for representational equality of racial and linguistic minorities.

Even after the civil rights movement of the 1950s and 1960s in the United States, minorities were refused voting rights in a multitude of districts and States around the country. County registrars would close their doors when African Americans came to register to vote, and intimidation kept many away from voting at the polls. Even in places where minorities were allowed to register and vote, the parties drawing the voting districts or choosing the electoral system would make it nearly impossible for the election of a minority to occur. For example, if a government has to draw ten districts in a State that is 60 percent white, 30 percent African American, and 10 percent Hispanic, it can easily dilute the minority voters by **splitting** them among multiple districts, ensuring that the white population holds the majority in each district.

In 1982, the United States Congress amended the 1965 Voting Rights Act by outlawing districts that have the effect of weakening minority-voting power. In a series of decisions, the courts interpreted this amendment to mean States needed to redistrict in a way that would ensure minority representation. Using this criterion in the redistricting that followed the 1990 census, States increased the number of majority–minority districts in the House of Representatives from 27 to 52. **Majority–minority districts** are packed districts in which a majority of the population is from the minority. In the hypothetical State described above, a redistricting following this criterion could have the goal of creating at least three majority-minority districts and a fourth where minorities had a sizable enough population to influence the outcome of the election.

Ideally, majority–minority districts would be compact and contiguous and follow existing political units. Political geographers Jonathan Leib and Gerald Webster have researched the court cases that have resulted from trying to balance these often-conflicting criteria. To pack minorities who do not live compactly and contiguously, States have drawn bizarrely shaped districts, connecting minority populations with meandering corridors and following Interstates to connect urban areas that have large minority populations (Fig. 8.16).

Strange-looking districts constructed to attain certain political ends are nothing new in American politics. In 1812, Governor Elbridge Gerry of Massachusetts signed into law a district designed to give an advantage to his party—a district that looked so odd to artist Gilbert Stuart that he drew it with a head, wings, and claws. Stuart called it the "salamander district," but a colleague immortalized it by naming it a gerrymander (after the governor). Ever since, the term **gerrymandering** has been used to describe "redistricting for advantage." Certainly, many of the districts now on the United States electoral map may be seen as gerrymanders, but for an important purpose: to provide representation to minorities who, without it, would not be represented as effectively in the House of Representatives. Despite this well-intentioned goal, others argue that the packing of minorities into majority–minority districts simply concentrates minority votes, creating a countrywide government that is less responsive to minority concerns.

The larger point is that the spatial organization of voting districts is a fundamentally geographical phenomenon, and it can have profound impacts on who is represented and who is not—as well as peoples' notions of fairness. And that is only the beginning people's. The voting patterns that emerge from particular elections can help reinforce a sense of regionalism and can shape a government's response to issues in the future. Small wonder, then, that many individuals who have little general understanding of geography at least appreciate the importance of its electoral geography component.

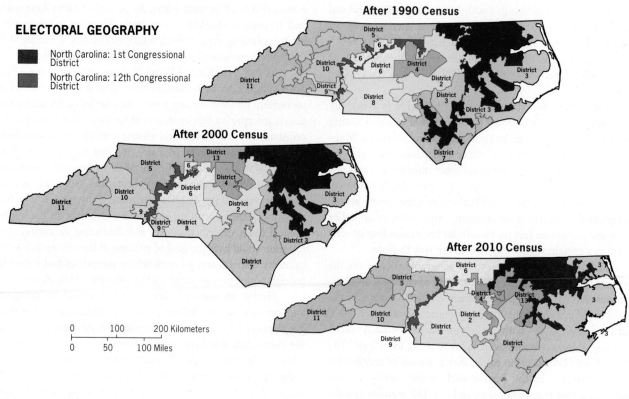

**ELECTORAL GEOGRAPHY**

North Carolina: 1st Congressional District

North Carolina: 12th Congressional District

**After 1990 Census**

**After 2000 Census**

**After 2010 Census**

0      100      200 Kilometers
0    50    100 Miles

■ **Figure 8.16**
**Electoral Geography.** North Carolina's congressional districts in 1992, 2002, and 2012. In 1992, North Carolina concentrated minorities into majority–minority districts. In 2002, North Carolina made its districts more compact and explained they were based on criteria other than race, in accordance with Supreme Court decisions during the 1990s. Using the same criteria, North Carolina redistricted again after the 2010 census, shaping districts that once again prioritized concentrating minorities while trying to achieve compactness and contiguity.    *Data from*: United States Census, 2012.

Choose an example of a devolutionary movement and consider which geographic factors favor, or work against, greater autonomy (self-governance) for the region. Would granting the region autonomy strengthen or weaken the state in which the region is currently located?

## HOW ARE BOUNDARIES ESTABLISHED, AND WHY DO BOUNDARY DISPUTES OCCUR?

The territories of individual states are separated by international boundaries, often referred to as borders. Boundaries may appear on maps as straight lines or may twist and turn to conform to the bends of rivers and the curves of hills and valleys. But a boundary is more than a line, far more than a fence or wall on the ground. A **boundary** between states is actually a vertical plane that cuts through the rocks below (called the

subsoil) and the airspace above, dividing one state from another (Fig. 8.17). Only where the vertical plane intersects Earth's surface (on land or at sea) does it form the line we see on the ground.

Many borders were established on the world map before the extent or significance of subsoil resources was known. As a result, coal seams and aquifers cross boundaries, and oil and gas reserves are split between states. Europe's coal reserves, for example, extend from Belgium underneath the Netherlands and on into the Ruhr area of Germany. Soon after mining began in the mid-nineteenth century, these three neighbors began to accuse each other of mining coal that did not lie directly below their own national territories. The underground surveys available at the time were too inaccurate to pinpoint the ownership of each coal seam.

During the 1950s–1960s, Germany and the Netherlands argued over a gas reserve that lies in the subsoil across their boundary. The Germans claimed that the Dutch were withdrawing so much natural gas that the gas was flowing from beneath German land to the Dutch side of the boundary. The Germans wanted compensation for the gas they felt they lost. A major issue between Iraq and Kuwait, which in part led to Iraq's invasion of Kuwait in 1990, was the oil in the Rumaylah reserve

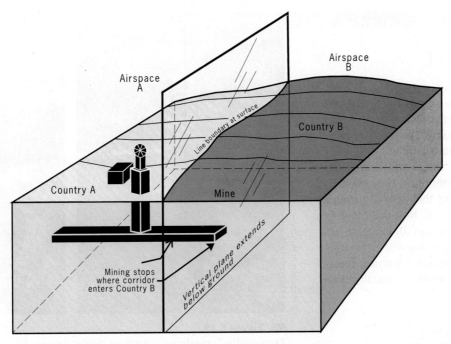

■ **Figure 8.17**
**The Vertical Plane of a Political Boundary.**    © E. H. Fouberg, A. B. Murphy, H. J. de Blij, and John Wiley & Sons, Inc.

that lies underneath the desert and crosses the border between the two states. The Iraqis asserted that the Kuwaitis were drilling too many wells and draining the reserve too quickly; they also alleged that the Kuwaitis were drilling oblique boreholes to penetrate the vertical plane extending downward along the boundary. At the time the Iraq–Kuwait boundary was established, however, no one knew that this giant oil reserve lay in the subsoil or that it would contribute to an international crisis (Fig. 8.18).

Above the ground, too, the interpretation of boundaries as vertical planes has serious implications. A state's "airspace" is defined by the atmosphere above its land area as marked by its boundaries, as well as by what lies beyond, at higher altitudes.

■ **Figure 8.18**
**The International Boundary Between Iraq and Kuwait.** Kuwait's northern boundary was redefined and delimited by a United Nations boundary commission; it was demarcated by a series of concrete pillars 1.24 miles (2 km) apart.

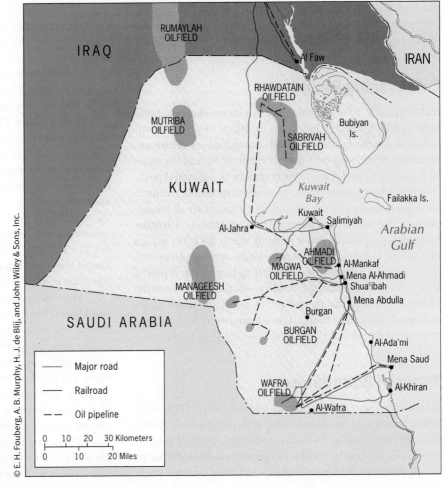

© E. H. Fouberg, A. B. Murphy, H. J. de Blij, and John Wiley & Sons, Inc.

# FIELD NOTE

"Seeing the border between Italy and Slovenia marked by a plaque on the ground reminded me of crossing this border with my family as a teenager. The year was 1973, and after waiting in a long line we finally reached the place where we showed our passports to the authorities. They asked us many questions and they looked through the luggage in our trunk. Now that Slovenia is part of the European Union and has signed the Schengen Agreement eliminating border controls between countries, crossing that same border today is literally like a walk in the park."

© Alexander B. Murphy

■ **Figure 8.19**

**Piazza della Transalpina.** A square divided between the towns of Gorizia, Italy and Nova Gorica, Slovenia.

But how high does the airspace extend? Most states insist on controlling the airline traffic over their territories, but states do not yet control the paths of satellite orbits.

## Establishing Boundaries

States typically *define* the boundary in a treaty-like legal document in which actual points in the landscape or points of latitude and longitude are described. Cartographers *delimit* the boundary by drawing on a map. If either or both of the states so desire, they can *demarcate* the boundary by using steel posts, concrete pillars, fences, walls, or some other visible means to mark the boundary on the ground. By no means are all boundaries on the world map demarcated. Demarcating a lengthy boundary is expensive, and it is hardly worth the effort in high mountains, vast deserts, frigid polar lands, or other places with few permanent settlements. Demarcating boundaries is part of state efforts to *administrate* borders—to determine how the boundaries will be maintained and to determine which goods and people may cross them. How a boundary is administered can change dramatically over time, however (Fig. 8.19).

## Types of Boundaries

Boundaries come into being in variable ways (Box 8.2). When boundaries are drawn using grid systems such as latitude and longitude or township and range, political geographers refer to these boundaries as **geometric boundaries**. In North America, the United States and Canada used a single line of latitude west of the Great Lakes to define their boundary. During the Berlin Conference, colonial powers used arbitrary reference points and drew straight lines to establish the boundaries in much of Africa.

At different times, political geographers and other academics have advocated "natural" boundaries over geometric boundaries because they are visible on the landscape as physical geographic features. **Physical-political boundaries** (also called natural-political boundaries) are boundaries that follow an agreed-upon feature in the natural landscape, such as the center point of a river or the crest of a mountain range. The Rio Grande is an important physical-political boundary between the United States and Mexico. Another physical-political boundary follows the crest lines of the Pyrenees separating Spain and France. Lakes sometimes serve as boundaries as well; for example, four of the five Great Lakes of North America are borders between the United States and Canada, and several of the Great Lakes of East Africa are borders between Congo and its eastern neighbors.

Physical features sometimes make convenient political boundaries, but topographic features are not static. Rivers change course, volcanoes erupt, and slowly, mountains erode. People perceive physical-political boundaries as stable, but many states have entered territorial conflicts over borders based on physical features (notably Chile and Argentina). Similarly, physical boundaries do not necessarily stop the flow of people or goods across boundaries, leading some states to reinforce physical boundaries with human-built obstacles (the United States on the Rio Grande). The stability of boundaries has more to do with local historical and geographical circumstances than with the character of the boundary itself.

# BOX 8.2

## Genetic Political Boundary Types

Leading mid-twentieth-century political geographer Richard Hartshorne (1899–1992) reasoned that how boundaries function is affected by how they came into being. Hartshorne proposed a fourfold genetic classification of boundaries (see figure). An *antecedent boundary* is one that predates the development of large-scale politically organized communities (e.g., the boundary between Malaysia and Indonesia, which passes through sparsely inhabited tropical rainforest). A second category of boundaries evolves as the cultural landscape takes shape. These *subsequent boundaries* are relatively common (e.g., the border between China and Vietnam, which reflects a long-term process of adjustment and modification).

Some boundaries are forcibly drawn by outsiders without reference to cultural patterns. Such *superimposed boundaries* are often contested by groups that straddle the boundary (e.g., the boundary separating Indonesia's West Irian from the country of Papua New Guinea). The fourth, more minor, genetic boundary type is the *relict boundary*— a border that has ceased to function but whose imprints are still evident on the cultural landscape. The boundary between former North Vietnam and South Vietnam is a classic example.

How a boundary came into being does not determine its degree of stability, but it can affect how the boundary is viewed and how it functions. It is one of many ingredients, then, that shapes the landscape of conflict and cooperation in the contemporary world.

## GENETIC POLITICAL BOUNDARY TYPES

**(A) ANTECEDENT**

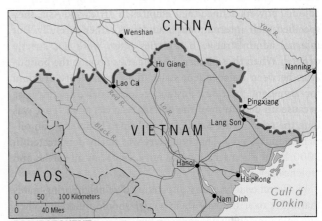

**(B) SUBSEQUENT**

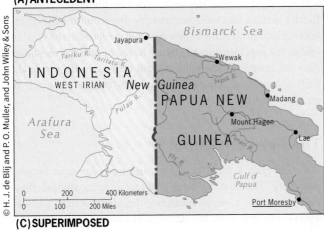

**(C) SUPERIMPOSED**

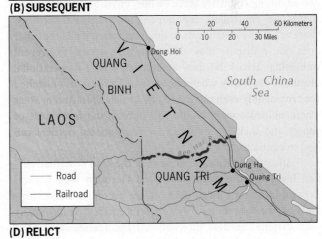

**(D) RELICT**

© H. J. de Blij and P. O. Muller, and John Wiley & Sons

# Boundary Disputes

The boundary we see as a line on a map is the product of a complex series of legal steps that begins with a written description of the boundary. Sometimes that legal description is old and imprecise. Sometimes it was dictated by a stronger power that is now less dominant, giving the weaker neighbor a reason to argue for change. At other times the geography of the borderland has actually changed; the river that marked the boundary may have changed course, or a portion of it has been cut off. Resources lying across a boundary can lead to conflict. In short, states often argue about their boundaries. Boundary disputes take four principal forms: definitional, locational, operational, and allocational.

*Definitional boundary disputes* focus on the legal language of the boundary agreement. For example, a boundary definition may stipulate that the median line of a river will mark the boundary. That would seem clear enough, but the water levels of rivers vary. If the valley is asymmetrical, the median line will move back and forth between low-water and high-water stages of the stream. This may involve hundreds of meters of movement—not very much, it would seem, but enough to cause serious argument, especially if there are resources in the river. The solution is to refine the definition to suit both parties.

*Locational boundary disputes* center on the delimitation and possibly the demarcation of the boundary. The definition is not in dispute, but its interpretation is. Sometimes the language of boundary treaties is vague enough to allow mapmakers to delimit the line in various ways. For example, when the colonial powers defined their empires in Africa and Asia, they specified their international boundaries rather carefully. But internal administrative boundaries often were not strictly defined. When those internal boundaries became the boundaries between independent states, there was plenty of room for argument. In a few instances, locational disputes arise because no definition of the boundary exists at all. That was long the case for the Saudi Arabia–Yemen boundary—an oil-rich boundary area. That boundary was finally demarcated in 2000, but the demarcation was not accepted by all parties and violence persists.

*Operational boundary disputes* involve neighboring states that differ over the way their border should function. When two adjoining countries agree on how cross-border migration should be controlled, the border functions satisfactorily. However, if one state wants to limit migration while the other does not, a dispute may arise. Similarly, efforts to prevent smuggling across borders sometimes lead to operational disputes—especially when one state's efforts are not matched (or are possibly even sabotaged) by its neighbor. And in areas where nomadic ways of life still prevail, the movement of people and their livestock across international borders can lead to conflict.

*Allocational boundary disputes* of the kind described earlier, involving the Netherlands and Germany over natural gas and Iraq and Kuwait over oil, are becoming more common as the search for resources intensifies. Today many such disputes involve international boundaries at sea. Oil reserves under the seafloor below coastal waters sometimes lie in areas where exact boundary delimitation may be difficult or subject to debate. Another growing area of allocational dispute has to do with water supplies: The Tigris, Nile, Colorado, and other rivers are subject to such disputes. When a river crosses an international boundary, the rights of the upstream and downstream users of the river often come into conflict.

 People used to think physical-political boundaries were always more stable than geometric boundaries. Through studies of many places, political geographers have confirmed that this idea is false. Using the concepts of nation and state, explain why physical-political boundaries can create just as much instability as geometric boundaries.

## HOW DOES THE STUDY OF GEOPOLITICS HELP US UNDERSTAND THE WORLD?

Geopolitics is the interplay among geography, power, politics, and international relations on Earth's surface. Political science and international relations tend to focus on governmental institutions, systems, and interactions. Geopolitics brings locational considerations, environmental contexts, territorial ideas and arrangements, and spatial assumptions to the fore. Geopolitics helps us understand the spatial power arrangements that shape international relations.

## Classical Geopolitics

Classical geopolitics was born out of efforts to promote the interests of individual states as the modern state system took root in the late nineteenth and early twentieth centuries. Geopoliticians of the time generally fit into one of two camps: the German school, which sought to explain why and how certain states became powerful, and the British/American school, which sought to offer strategic advice by identifying parts of Earth's surface that were particularly important for the maintenance and projection of power. A few geopoliticians tried to bridge the gap, blending the two schools, but for the most part classical geopoliticians who are still writing today are in the British/American school, offering geostrategic perspectives on the world.

## The German School

Why are certain states powerful, and how do states become powerful? The first political geographer who studied these issues was the German professor Friedrich Ratzel (1844–1904). Influenced by the writings of Charles Darwin, Ratzel postulated that the state resembles a biological organism whose life cycle extends from birth through maturity and, ultimately, decline and death. To prolong its existence, the state requires nourishment, just as an organism needs food. Such nourishment is provided by the acquisition of territories that provide adequate space for the members of the state's dominant nation to thrive, which is what Ratzel called *Lebensraum*. If a state is confined within permanent and static boundaries and deprived of overseas domains, Ratzel argued, it can atrophy. Territory is thus seen as the state's essential, life-giving force.

Ratzel's theory was based on his observations of states in the nineteenth century, including the United States. It was so speculative that it might have been forgotten if some of Ratzel's German followers in the 1930s had not translated his abstract writings into policy recommendations that ultimately were used to justify Nazi expansionism.

## The British/American School

Not long after the publication of Ratzel's initial ideas, other geographers began looking at the overall organization of power in the world, studying the physical geographic map, with a view toward determining the locations of the most strategic places on Earth. Prominent among them was the Oxford University geographer Sir Halford J. Mackinder (1861–1947). In 1904, he published an article titled "The Geographical Pivot of History" in the Royal Geographical Society's *Geographical Journal*. That article became one of the most intensely debated geographic publications of all time.

Mackinder was concerned with power relationships at a time when Britain had acquired a global empire through its strong navy. To many of his contemporaries, the oceans—the paths to colonies and trade—were the key to world domination, but Mackinder disagreed. He concluded that a land-based power, not a sea power, would ultimately rule the world. His famous article contained a lengthy appraisal of the largest and most populous landmass on Earth—Eurasia (Europe and Asia together). At the heart of Eurasia, he argued, lay an impregnable, resource-rich "pivot area" extending from eastern Europe to eastern Siberia (Fig. 8.20). Mackinder issued a warning: If this pivot area became unified, a great empire could be formed.

Mackinder later renamed his pivot area the heartland, and his warning became known as the heartland theory. In his book *Democratic Ideals and Reality* (1919), Mackinder (calling

Eurasia "the World Island") issued a stronger warning to the winners of World War I, stating:

> *Who rules East Europe commands the Heartland*
> *Who rules the Heartland commands the World Island*
> *Who rules the World Island commands the World*

When Mackinder proposed his **heartland theory**, there was little to foretell the rise of a superpower in the heartland. Russia was in disarray, having recently lost a war against Japan (1905), and was facing revolution. Eastern Europe was fractured. Germany, not Russia, was gaining power. But when the Soviet Union emerged and Moscow controlled over much of Eastern Europe at the end of World War II, the heartland theory attracted renewed attention.

In 1943, Mackinder wrote a final paper expressing concern that the Soviet Union, under Stalin, would seek to exert control over the states of Eastern Europe. He offered strategies for keeping the Soviets in check, including avoiding the expansion of the Heartland into the Inner Crescent (Fig. 8.20) and creating an alliance around the North Atlantic to join the forces of land and sea powers against the Heartland. His ideas were not embraced by many at the time, but within ten years of publication, the United States began its containment policy to stop the expansion of the Soviet Union, and the United States, Canada, and Western Europe formed an alliance called the North Atlantic Treaty Organization (NATO). Further proof of the importance of Mackinder's legacy can be seen in the fact that, even after the collapse of the Soviet Union, his theories enjoy widespread currency in Russian foreign policy circles.

## Influence of Geopoliticians on Politics

Ratzel and Mackinder are only two of many geopoliticians who influenced international relations. Their writings, grounded in history, current events, and physical geography, sounded logical and influenced many politicians, and in some ways still do. NATO still exists and has not invited Russia to join the military alliance, but it has extended membership to 28 states since the end of the Cold War, including eastern European states. NATO has a working partnership with former republics of the Soviet Union, though the war between Russia and Georgia in 2008 and Russia's 2014 seizure of Crimea (formerly part of Ukraine), produced a chilling effect on NATO's eastward expansion.

Despite the staying power of geopolitical theories, geopolitics declined as a formal area of study after World War II. Because of the influence Ratzel's theory had on Hitler—as championed by another geopolitician, Karl Haushofer—the term *geopolitics* acquired a negative connotation. For some decades after World War II, the term was in such disrepute that few political geographers, even those studying power relationships, would identify themselves as students of geopolitics. Time, along with more balanced perspectives, has

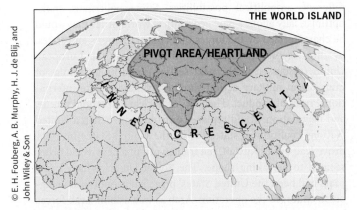

© E. H. Fouberg, A. B. Murphy, H. J. de Blij, and John Wiley & Son

**■ Figure 8.20**

**The Heartland Theory.** The Pivot Area/Heartland, the Inner Crescent/Rimland, and the World Island, following the descriptions of Halford Mackinder.

reinstated geopolitics as a significant field of study, encompassing efforts to understand the spatial and territorial dimensions of power relationships past, present, and future.

## Critical Geopolitics

Rather than focusing on prediction and prescription, many current students of geopolitics focus on revealing and explaining the underlying geographical assumptions and territorial perspectives of international actors. Political geographers Gearoid O'Tuathail and John Agnew refer to those actors in the most powerful states, the core states, as "intellectuals of statecraft." The basic concept behind **critical geopolitics** is that intellectuals of statecraft construct ideas about geographical circumstances and places, these ideas influence and reinforce their political behaviors and policy choices, and those behaviors and choices then affect what happens and how most people interpret what happens.

O'Tuathail has focused particular attention on American geopolitical reasoning—examining speeches and statements by U.S. intellectuals of statecraft. He has drawn attention to how several American leaders often spatialize politics into a world of "us" and "them." Political leaders can shape how their constituents see places and organize international space in their minds. By drawing on American cultural logic and certain representations of America, O'Tuathail argues that presidents have repeatedly defined an "us" that is pro-democracy, independent, self-sufficient, and free and a "them" that is in some way against all of these things.

During the Cold War, President Ronald Reagan coined the term *Evil Empire* for the Soviet Union and represented the United States as "the shining city on a hill." During ensuing presidencies, terrorism replaced the Soviet Union as the "they." Sounding remarkably similar, Democratic President William J. Clinton and Republican President George W. Bush justified military actions against terrorists. In 1998, President Clinton justified American military action in Sudan and Afghanistan as a response to terrorist plans by Osama bin Laden by noting that the terrorists "come from diverse places but share a hatred for democracy, a fanatical glorification of violence, and a horrible distortion of their religion, to justify the murder of innocents. They have made the United States their adversary precisely because of what we stand for and what we stand against." Immediately after September 11, President George W. Bush made a similar claim, arguing that "They [the terrorists] stand against us because we stand in their way." In 2002, President Bush again explained, "I've said in the past that nations are either with us or against us in the war on terror."

Statements such as these are rooted in a particular geopolitical perspective on the world—one that divides the globe into opposing camps. That much may seem obvious, as there are clear ideological fault lines between an organization such as al-Qaeda and a state such as the United States. But critical geopolitics seeks to move beyond such differences to explore the spatial ideas and understandings that undergird particular political perspectives and that shape policy approaches.

One of the most powerful geopolitical ideas since the end of the Cold War in 1989 came from Samuel Huntington (1996), who argued that the world is entering a period when conflicts will increasingly reflect major religious-civilization divides. His emphasis on the importance of the "Islamic World" helped to shape responses to the September 11, 2001 attacks on the United States. The U.S. government, concerned about al-Qaeda's influence, justified military involvement in Iraq and Afghanistan based on the threat of a volatile "Islamic World." That idea was picked up and amplified by countless policy analysts, news commentators, and bloggers.

The critical geopolitics literature does not simply aim to identify geopolitical ideas; it also often critiques them. It is not surprising, then, that commentators began to point out that the "Islamic World" is tremendously diverse, culturally and religiously, and that some of the most intractable conflicts of recent times have been fought within the Islamic World, not between Muslims and others. Belief in the geopolitical significance of a unified "Islamic World" is not any more rational than belief in a geopolitically unified "Judeo-Christian World"—hardly an easy belief to sustain given recent conflicts between Russia and Ukraine. Regardless, if geopolitical ideas are believed, they shape the policies that are pursued and they become the narratives through which we perceive what happens on the ground. An important task for geographers, then, is to understand the ideological roots and implications of geopolitical reasoning by intellectuals of statecraft.

## Geopolitical World Order

Geopolitical world orders are the temporary periods of stability in the way international politics is conducted. For example, during the Cold War, the geopolitical world order was bipolar—the Soviet Union and its Warsaw Pact satellites versus the United States and its close allies in Western Europe.

After the Soviet Union collapsed in 1991, the world entered a transition period, again opening up a variety of different geopolitical possibilities. Some politicians spoke optimistically about a new geopolitical world order that would be characterized by the forces that connect nations and states; by the rise of supranational entities such as the European Union (discussed in the next section); and by a promise of multilateral military action should any state violate international rules of conduct. The risks of nuclear war would recede, and negotiation would replace confrontation. When a United Nations coalition of states led by the United States in 1991 drove Iraq out of Kuwait, the framework of a new world order seemed to be taking shape. The Soviet Union, which a few years had been the United States' principal geopolitical antagonist, endorsed the operation. Arab as well as non-Arab forces helped repel the invaders.

Soon, however, doubts and uncertainties began to cloud hopes for a mutually cooperative geopolitical world order. Despite deepening interconnections crossing state lines, national self-interest still acted as a powerful force. Nations wanted to become states, and many did, as the number of United Nations members increased from 159 in 1990 to 184 by 1993 and 193 as of 2011, when South Sudan seceded from Sudan. At the same time, a variety of organizations not tied to specific territories posed a new challenge to the territorially defined state. The number and power of economic and social networks that extend across state borders increased, and nonstate organizations with political agendas that are not channeled through states came to assume a greater role.

Moreover, not everyone embraced the new geopolitical complexity. Some U.S.-based commentators championed a geopolitical world order based on **unilateralism**, with the United States assuming a position of hard-power dominance—believing that any other course of action would risk global instability. The fact that the U.S. military budget is almost as large as all the military budgets of all other states in the world combined puts it in a position to play a significant international role, but recent events have brought into question whether military dominance can achieve the ends unilateralists hope to achieve. The United States' controversial invasion of Iraq significantly undermined its influence in many parts of the globe. A rift developed across the Atlantic between the United States and some European countries, and anti-Americanism surged around the world. The processes of globalization, the diffusion of nuclear weapons, the emergence of China and India as increasingly significant powers, and the growth of networked groups and organizations, including terrorist groups, also represent challenges to American unilateralism and complicate the geopolitical picture.

Nuclear weapons, for example, give even small states the ability to inflict massive damage on larger and distant adversaries. Combined with missile technology, this may be one of the most serious dangers the world faces, which is why the United Nations insisted on dismantling Iraq's nuclear capacity after the 1991 Gulf War and why concerns over Iran's nuclear program are so great. Some states publicize their nuclear weapons programs, whereas other nuclear states have never formally acknowledged that they possess nuclear weapons. Reports of nuclear proliferation have led to military actions in the last few decades. In 1981, when reports of Iraq's nuclear program reached Israel, the Israelis attacked Iraq. As nuclear weapons have become smaller and "tactical" nuclear arms have been developed, the threat of nuclear weapons sales is of growing concern. It is now possible for a hostile state or group to purchase the power with which to threaten the world.

Russia's new assertiveness, first in Georgia in 2008, and then in Ukraine in 2014, raises the specter of a return to Cold War geopolitical realities. But Russia is no longer widely seen as the champion of a political-economic system with broad appeal, and it is a much less formidable military power than was the Soviet Union at its height. Hence, many believe that a Russian rift with its neighbors to the west will simply be one dimension of a rapidly evolving geopolitical order characterized by several influential powers (such as the United States, Germany, China, India, Brazil, and Russia) seeking to exert political and economic influence over regional or global affairs in an increasingly disaggregated world.

When geopolitical strategists and intellectuals of statecraft predict future geopolitical orders, they often assume that individual states will continue to be the dominant actors in the international arena. Yet as we discuss in the next section, many of the same forces that worked against American unilateralism have undermined some of the traditional powers of the state. The rise of regional blocs could alter the system, with key clusters of states functioning as major geopolitical nodes. Alternatively or simultaneously, as we will discuss in Chapter 9, global cities may gain increasing power over issues typically addressed by states.

 Read a major newspaper (in print or online) and look for a recent statement by a world political leader regarding international politics. Adopting a critical geopolitics perspective, what generalizations can you make about the geopolitical views and priorities of the world leader? How does he or she view and divide up the world spatially?

## WHAT ARE SUPRANATIONAL ORGANIZATIONS, AND WHAT IS THE FUTURE OF THE STATE?

Ours is a world of contradictions. Over the past couple of decades some French Canadians, Québécois, have demanded independence from Canada even as Canada joined the United States and Mexico in NAFTA (the North American Free Trade Agreement). Flemings in northern Belgium have called for autonomy or even independence despite the fact that Brussels, the capital of Belgium (and Flanders), has served as the de facto capital of the European Union. At every turn we are reminded of the interconnectedness of nations, states, and regions; yet, separatism and calls for autonomy are rampant. In the early decades of the twenty-first century, we appear to be caught between the forces of division and unity.

Despite conflicts arising from these contradictory forces, today hardly a country exists that is not involved in some supranational organization. A **supranational organization** is an entity composed of three or more states that forges an association and forms an administrative structure for mutual benefit and in pursuit of shared goals. The twentieth century witnessed the establishment of numerous supranational associations in political, economic, cultural, and military spheres.

Today, states have formed over 60 major supranational organizations (such as NATO and NAFTA), many of which have subsidiaries that bring the total to more than 100 (Fig. 8.21). The more states participate in such multilateral associations, the less likely they are to act alone in pursuit of a

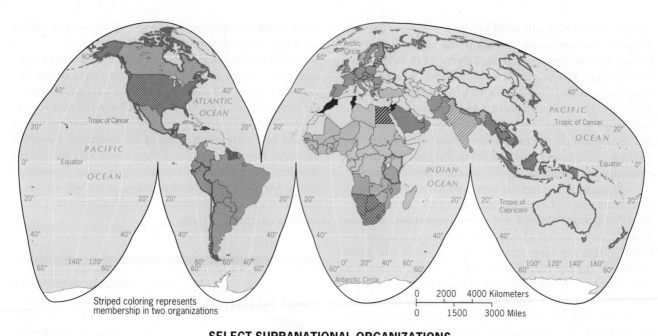

Striped coloring represents
membership in two organizations

0      2000    4000 Kilometers

0      1500    3000 Miles

## SELECT SUPRANATIONAL ORGANIZATIONS

Agadir Agreement

Andean Community

Asia-Pacific Economic
Cooperation

Asia-Pacific Trade Agreement

Association of South East Asian
Nations

Caribbean Community and
Common Market

Central American
Common Market

Central American-Dominican
Free Trade Agreement

Common Market for Eastern
and Southern Africa

Commonwealth of Independent
States

East African Community

Economic and Monetary
Community of Central Africa

Economic Community of
West African States

European Community

European Customs Union
(Andorra, Monaco, San Marino,
and Turkey)

European Free Trade
Association

Gulf Cooperation Council

North American Free Trade
Agreement

South Africa Customs Union

South Africa Development
Community

South Asian Preferential Trade
Arrangement

Southern Common Market

**■ Figure 8.21**

**Select Supranational Organizations.**   *Data from*: Crawford, Jo-Ann and Roberto V. Fiorentino, "Changing Landscape of Regional Trade Agreements,"
World Trade Organization. http://www.wto.org/english/res_e/booksp_e/discussion_papers8_e.pdf.

self-interest that might put them at odds with other association members. And in most cases participation in a supranational entity is advantageous to the partners, while being left out can have serious negative implications.

## From League of Nations to United Nations

The modern beginnings of the supranational movement can be traced to conferences following World War I. Woodrow Wilson, president of the United States, proposed an international organization that would include all the states of the world (fewer than 75 states existed at that point). That idea took on concrete form with the founding of the League of Nations in 1919. Even though it was the idea of an American president, the United States was among the countries that did not join the organization because isolationists in the U.S. Senate opposed membership. In all, 63 states participated in the League, although the total membership at any single time never reached that number. Costa Rica and Brazil left the League before 1930; Germany departed in 1933,

shortly before the Soviet Union joined in 1934. The League later expelled the Soviet Union in 1939 for invading Finland.

The League was born of a worldwide desire to prevent future aggression, but the failure of the United States to join dealt the organization a severe blow. In the mid-1930s, the League had a major opportunity to play a significant international role when Ethiopia's Haile Selassie made a dramatic appeal for help in the face of an invasion by Italy, a member state until 1937. The League failed to take action, and in the chaos of the beginning of World War II the organization collapsed.

Even though the League of Nations ceased functioning, it spawned other supranational organizations. Between World War I and World War II, many states came together to create the Permanent Court of International Justice, which was charged with adjudicating legal issues between states, such as boundary disputes and fishing rights. The League of Nations also initiated international negotiations on maritime boundaries and related aspects of the law of the sea. The conferences organized by the League laid the groundwork for the final resolution of the size of territorial seas decades later.

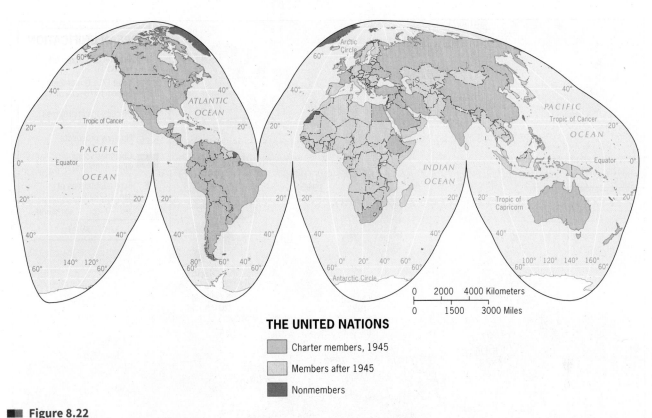

## THE UNITED NATIONS

- Charter members, 1945
- Members after 1945
- Nonmembers

### ◼◼ Figure 8.22

**Member States of the United Nations.**   This map shows charter members, members after 1945 (with dates of entry), and nonmembers of the United Nations.   *Data from*: The United Nations.

After World War II, a new organization was founded in an effort to promote international security and cooperation: the United Nations (UN). Membership in the UN has grown significantly since its inception in 1947 (Fig. 8.22). A handful of states still do not belong to the organization, but with the most recent additions in 2011, it now has 193 member states. Additionally, the organization allows permanent observers, including nonmember states Palestine and the Holy See and several supranational and nongovernmental organizations, to participate in the work of the UN General Assembly. The United Nations organization includes numerous less visible but nonetheless significant subsidiaries, including the FAO (Food and Agriculture Organization), UNESCO (United Nations Educational, Scientific and Cultural Organization), and WHO (World Health Organization). Not all United Nations members participate in every United Nations subsidiary, but many people around the world have benefited from their work.

We can find evidence of the United Nations' work in the "world" section of any major newspaper. UN peacekeeping troops have helped maintain stability in some of the most contentious regions of the world. The United Nations High Commissioner on Refugees is called upon to aid refugees in crises in far-flung places. UN documents on human rights standards, such as the Universal Declaration on Human Rights, the Covenant on Civil and Political Rights, and the Covenant on Economic and Social Rights, set a precedent and

laid the groundwork for countless human rights groups working in the world today.

By participating in the United Nations, states commit to internationally approved standards of behavior. Many states still violate the standards embodied in the United Nations Charter, but such violations can lead to collective action, such as economic sanctions or Security Council-supported military action. The United Nations' aid, refugee, and peacekeeping efforts as well as actions in South Africa (Apartheid) and Iraq (the Gulf War) are examples of UN successes, but the organization has its critics as well. Some argue that the composition of its Security Council reflects the world of 1950 more than the world of today. All five permanent members of the Council—the victors of World War II: the United States, United Kingdom, France, China, and Russia (formerly the Soviet Union)—wield veto power over Council resolutions and use the veto regularly, often making the UN ineffective during times of crisis. The ongoing Syrian civil war has showcased Security Council tensions as Russia and China have forcefully vetoed resolutions aimed at greater UN involvement to curb violence directed at civilians. Those who seek UN reform say the Permanent Five and their veto power destroys UN credibility and reinforces outdated power arrangements. Other UN critics express concern about power being vested in an organization that is not directly responsible to voters and that provides little room for non-state interests. Still others criticize the fact that states such as

■ **Figure 8.23**

**European Supranationalism.**   Members of the European Union and their dates of entry.

China and Cuba currently sit on the organization's Human Rights Council. For all its weaknesses, however, the United Nations represents the only truly international forum for addressing many significant problems confronting the globe.

## Regional Supranational Organizations

The League of Nations and the United Nations are global manifestations of a phenomenon that is expressed even more strongly at the regional level. States organize supranational organizations at the regional scale to position themselves more strongly economically, politically, and even militarily.

Belgium, the Netherlands, and Luxembourg undertook the first major modern experiment in regional economic cooperation. The three countries have much in common culturally and economically. Dutch farm products are sold on Belgian markets, and Belgian industrial goods go to the Netherlands and Luxembourg. During World War II, representatives of the three countries decided to remove tariffs between them and eliminate import licenses and quotas. In 1944, even before the end of the war, the governments of the three states met in London to sign an agreement of cooperation, creating the *Benelux* (*Be*lgium, the *Ne*therlands, and *Lux*embourg) region.

*Data from:* The European Union, www.europa.eu.int ©H. J. de Blij, P. O. Muller, and John Wiley & Sons, Inc.

Following World War II, U.S. Secretary of State George Marshall proposed that the United States finance a European recovery program. A committee representing 16 West European states plus (then) West Germany presented the United States Congress with a joint program for economic rehabilitation, and Congress approved it. From 1948 to 1952, the United States gave Europe some $12 billion under the Marshall Plan, the largest foreign aid program in history. This investment revived European national economies and spurred a movement toward cooperation among European states. That movement was also driven by the rise of an increasingly integrated and potentially threatening Soviet bloc to the east and the desire to create a framework that could help break the pattern of European conflict that had characterized the first half of the twentieth century.

## The European Union

From the European states' involvement in the Marshall Plan came the Organization for European Economic Cooperation (OEEC), a body that in turn gave rise to other cooperative organizations. Soon after Europe established the OEEC, France proposed the creation of a European Coal and Steel Community (ECSC), with the goal of lifting the restrictions and obstacles that impeded the flow of coal, iron ore, and steel among the mainland's six primary producers: France, West Germany, Italy, and the three Benelux countries. The six states entered the ECSC and gradually, through negotiations and agreement, enlarged their sphere of cooperation to include reductions and even eliminations of certain tariffs and a freer flow of labor, capital, and commodities beyond steel. This led, in 1958, to the creation of the European Economic Community (EEC).

The success of the EEC induced other countries to apply for membership. Denmark, Ireland, and the United Kingdom joined in 1973, Greece in 1981, and Spain and Portugal in 1986. The organization became known as the European Community (EC) because it began to address issues beyond economics. By the late 1980s, the EC had 12 members: the three giants (Germany, France, and the United Kingdom); the four southern countries (Italy, Spain, Portugal, and Greece); and five smaller states (the Netherlands, Belgium, Luxembourg, Denmark, and Ireland). These 12 members initiated a program of cooperation and unification that led to the formal establishment of a European Union (EU) in 1992. In the mid-1990s, Austria, Sweden, and Finland joined the EU, bringing the total number of members to 15 (Fig. 8.23).

In the late 1990s, the EU began preparing for the establishment of a single currency—the euro (Fig. 8.24). First, all electronic financial transactions were denominated in euros, and on January 1, 2002, the EU introduced euro coins and notes. Not all EU member states are currently a part of the euro zone, but the euro has emerged as a significant global currency.

The integration of ten eastern European and Mediterranean island states into the European Union in 2004, two

*Alexander B. Murphy*

■ **Figure 8.24**

**Cortina, Italy.**   A market in northern Italy advertises the price of fruit in euros.

more in 2007, and one more in 2014 represents a significant development. Integration is a difficult process and often requires painful adjustments because of the diversity of the states involved. Take the case of agricultural practices and policies. These have long varied widely, but some general policy must govern agriculture throughout the European Union. Individual states have found these adjustments difficult at times, and the EU has had to devise policies to accommodate regional contrasts and delays in implementation. In addition, integration requires significant expenditures. Under the rules of the EU, the richer countries must subsidize (provide financial support to) the poorer ones; therefore, the entry of eastern European states adds to the financial burden on the wealthier western and northern European members. A major economic downturn at the end of the first decade of the twenty-first century, and associated financial crises in Greece, Ireland, Spain, and Portugal, put the union under unprecedented pressure. The citizens of wealthier countries such as Germany began to question why they should foot the bill for countries that have not (at least in German eyes) managed their finances responsibly.

The Union is a patchwork of states with many different ethnic traditions and histories of conflict and competition, and some in Europe express concern over losing local control over economic, social, and political matters. Economic success and growing well-being tend to submerge hesitancy and differences, but in the face of difficult economic or social times, divisive forces can, and have, reasserted themselves. Moreover, as the EU gets bigger, it becomes increasingly difficult for individual states (even powerful ones) to shape the direction of the union. And some citizens in smaller states such as Denmark and Sweden worry about getting lost in the mix. As a result, there are growing challenges to the legitimacy of an increasingly powerful EU.

Another difficult problem involves Turkey. Some western Europeans would like to see Turkey join the EU, thereby widening the organization's reach. The government of Turkey has long sought to join, but many Greeks are hesitant to support Turkish membership because of the long-standing dispute between Greece and Turkey over Cyprus and a number of islands off the Turkish coast. Other EU members have expressed concern over Turkey's human rights record and are worried about adding such a large, yet in some ways different, country to the mix. Behind these claims lies an often-unspoken sense among many Europeans that Turkey is not "European" enough to warrant membership, perhaps rooted in a historical and cultural tendency to define Muslims as the "Other." The debate within the EU about Turkey has alienated many Turkish people, causing them to question their support for EU membership.

## How Does Supranationalism Affect the State?

Supranationalism is a worldwide phenomenon. Other economic associations, such as the North American Free Trade Agreement (NAFTA), the Association of Caribbean States (ACS), the Central American Common Market, the Andean Group, the Southern Cone Community Market (MERCOSUR), the Economic Community of West African States (ECOWAS), the Asia-Pacific Economic Council (APEC), and the Commonwealth of Independent States (CIS), have drawn up treaties to reduce tariffs and import restrictions in order to ease the flow of commerce in their regions. Not all of these alliances are successful, but economic supranationalism is a sign of the times, a grand experiment still in progress.

Yet, when we turn back to the European Union, we see a supranational organization that is unlike any other. It is not a state, nor is it simply an organization of states. The European Union is remarkable in that it has taken on a life of its own—with a multifaceted government structure, three capital cities, and billions of euros flowing through its coffers. The European Union is extending into foreign relations, domestic policies, and military policies, with sovereignty over a variety of issues having been transferred "upward" from states to the European Union. One of the authors of this book has studied the degree to which Europeans in some regions are feeling a greater attachment to their region and to the European Union than to their own state (Fig. 8.25). Identifying with the European Union (over the state) is strong in the Benelux countries (the first members) and in regions where people have been disempowered by their state governments. Even though the EU represents the world's boldest attempt to move beyond a political order dominated by states, the challenges it is facing remind us of the continuing power of the state as an international actor and focus of identity.

Other types of movements, however, are also posing major challenges to the state as we know it, raising questions as to whether the division of the world into territorial states is logical, effective, or even necessary. Among these challenges are the demand of nations within states for independence, economic globalization, and the rise of increasingly powerful

**Figure 8.25**
**Brussels, Belgium.**  A woman with a European Union umbrella shops in the flower market in the Grande Place of Brussels. On their website, the European Union states that the number of stars on the flag has no official meaning and that the circle of stars represents "unity, solidarity and harmony among the peoples of Europe."

nonstate or extrastate groups and actors. These latter developments raise the question of whether we are embarking on an era of **deterritorialization** characterized by a geometry of political power less rooted in the power of the territorial state. There is no denying that states continue to provide the territorial foundation from which producers and consumers still operate, and they continue to exert considerable regulatory powers, but economic globalization makes it ever more difficult for states to control economic relations. States are responding to this situation in a variety of ways, with some giving up traditional regulatory powers and others seeking to insulate themselves from the international economy. Still others are working to build supranational economic blocs that they hope will help them cope with an increasingly globalized world. The impacts of many of these developments are as yet uncertain, but it is increasingly clear that states now compete with a variety of other forces in the international arena.

The state's traditional position is being further eroded by the globalization of social and cultural relations. Networks of interaction are being constructed in ways that do not correspond to the map of states. In 2011, when unrest broke out in Egypt, for example, activists used Facebook to garner support. Scholars and researchers in different countries work together in teams. Increased mobility has brought individuals from far-flung places into much closer contact than before. Paralleling all this change is the spread of popular culture in ways that make national borders virtually meaningless. Pharrell Williams is listened to from Iceland to Australia; fashions developed in northern Italy are hot items among Japanese tourists visiting South Korea; Thai restaurants are found in towns and cities across the United States; Russians hurry home to watch the next episode of soap operas made in Mexico; and movies produced in Hollywood are seen on screens from Mumbai to Santiago.

The rise of fundamentalist religious movements with geopolitical goals represents another global phenomenon with potentially significant implications for a future world order. In Chapter 6, we noted that fundamental religious movements sometimes become extremist by inciting violent acts in the name of their faith. Violence by extremists challenges the state—whether undertaken by individuals at the local scale or by widely diffused groups spread across major world realms. The state's mission to combat religious violence can produce support for

the state in the short term, but its inability to defeat extremist attacks may weaken the state in the long term. Terrorist attacks have been threatened or carried out by religious extremists from a variety of different faiths, but the wave of international terrorism that began in the 1980s in the name of Islam has dominated the international scene over the past several decades. The attacks of September 11, 2001, and the invasions of Iraq and Afghanistan that followed, moved terrorism to the geopolitical center stage. Other high-profile terrorist attacks in Madrid, Moscow, Mombasa, and Mumbai have helped to keep it there. Almost daily, newspapers report on terrorist incidents in cities around the world; the University of Maryland's Global Terrorism Database has tracked some 113,000 terrorist-related bombings, assassinations, and kidnappings from 1970 to 2012.

All of the foregoing processes are suggestive of deterritorialization, but the state is far from disappearing, and nationalism continues to be a fundamental social force in the world today. Indeed, in many instances. the state is moving to solidify control over its territory through a process known as **reterritorialization**. For example, in response to concerns over undocumented immigration, some state borders are becoming more heavily fortified, and moving across those borders is becoming more difficult. However one views the balance between deterritorialization and reterritorialization, the state of the geopolitical order is clearly in flux. We appear to be headed toward a world in which the spatial distribution of power is more complex than the traditional map of states would suggest. Describing that spatial distribution will be a challenge for geographers for generations to come.

 Consider how nation, state, and supranational organization are related. Are nations like Scotland more likely to remain within their states and not vote for independence because they are also part of a supranational organization (in the case of Scotland, the European Union)? Will the growth of supranational organizations lead to a decline in nations calling for statehood or will shifting more decision making from the state to the supranational organization actually increase the call for independence of nations within states?

# Summary

We tend to take the state for granted, but the modern state idea is less than 400 years old. Politically organizing the world into states diffused around the globe through colonialism and trade. Globalization has brought about other ways of politically organizing space, including supranational organizations like the United Nations and the European Union. These new political entities challenge the sovereignty of the state and may help transition the world to a new political organization. In addition to understanding political organization of space, political geographers look at how key international decision makers, intellectuals of statecraft, identify the world and construct narratives about how the world works. Geopolitician Halford Mackinder's Heartland Theory influenced perceptions of politics, place and power during the Cold War, and Samuel Huntington's warning of an "Islamic World" continues to shape the narratives of the post-Cold War world.

# Geographic Concepts

| | | |
|---|---|---|
| political geography | colonialism | reapportionment |
| state | scale | splitting |
| territory | world-systems theory | majority-minority districts |
| territoriality | capitalism | gerrymandering |
| sovereignty | commodification | boundary |
| territorial integrity | core | geometric boundary |
| mercantilism | periphery | physical-political boundary |
| Peace of Westphalia | semiperiphery | heartland theory |
| nation | centripetal | critical geopolitics |
| nation-state | centrifugal | unilateralism |
| democracy | unitary | supranational organization |
| multinational state | federal | deterritorialization |
| multistate nation | devolution | reterritorialization |
| stateless nation | territorial representation | |

# Learn More Online

About Each State in the World
http://news.bbc.co.uk/2/hi/country_profiles/default.stm

About the United Nations
www.un.org/en/

About the European Union
http://europa.eu/index_en.htmAbout Nationalism
www.nationalismproject.org

About Political Geography
www.politicalgeography.org

About the Electoral Geography of the United States
www.washingtonpost.com/blogs/wonkblog/wp/2014/05/15/
americas-most-gerrymandered-congressional-districts/

# Watch It Online

Devolution

Slovakia: New Sovereignty. Click on Video on Demand
www.learner.org/resources/series180.html#program_
descriptions

International Boundaries

Boundaries and Borderlands. Click on Video on Demand
www.learner.org/resources/series180.html#program_
descriptions

Supranationalism and the European Union

Strasbourg: Symbol of a United Europe. Click on Video on
Demand
www.learner.org/resources/series180.html#program_
descriptions

# URBAN GEOGRAPHY

## Ghosts of Detroit?

The semicircular-shaped Grand Circus Park in Detroit, Michigan, is divided by several streets, making it look like the hub and spokes of a bicycle wheel from above. The grouping of buildings along Grand Circus Park (Fig. 9.1) reflects the rise, fall, and revitalization of the **central business district (CBD)** in Detroit. The central business district is a concentration of business and commerce in the city's downtown.

The Kales Building is the tall structure on the far left of the photograph. It was once the headquarters of the Kresge Corporation, which became K-Mart. Abandoned in 1986 and left to deteriorate, the Kales Building was renovated at a cost of $15 million in 2005. It now houses over 100 luxury apartments, and in 2011, it was 100 percent occupied.

The short building to the right of the Kales Building, tucked behind the trees, was the Adams Theater. Closed in 1988, the Adams Theater fell into such a severe state of disrepair that it could no longer be saved. The Downtown Detroit Development Authority required investors to save the façade of the building and allowed them to demolish the rest of it. A new building is slated to go up behind the façade.

Erin H. Fouberg

■ **Figure 9.1**

**Detroit, Michigan.** The buildings along West Adams Street face Grand Park Circus in Detroit, Michigan. From left to right, the Kales Building, Adams Theater, Grand Park Centre, and Fyfe Apartments have experienced the rise, decline, and revitalization of the neighborhood, which is located in the CBD.

To the right of that building is the Grand Park Centre, which underwent a $7 million renovation in 2000. Grand Park Centre is an office building, but downtown Detroit has an abundance of office space. The occupancy rate was at 65 percent when the property was sold in 2013. The 20-storey building and its 9-story annex fetched between $4 and $5.5 million, prompting local commentator Daniel Burnham to write, "Buildings in downtown Detroit continue to be the real estate equivalent of a $19.95 DVD player on Black Friday: Everyone wants at least one of them, even if they don't exactly know why."

The building on the far right houses the Fyfe Apartments, named for Richard H. Fyfe, who built a fortune in the shoe trade in Detroit. The building was converted to apartments in 1960 and has functioned as apartments since that time. By 2011 the Fyfe Apartments were 97 percent occupied.

Buildings in the Grand Circus Park neighborhood have attracted millions in renovation funds because of the neighborhood's close proximity to the revitalized entertainment district in downtown Detroit. Just around the corner from Grand Circus Park are Comerica Park, Fox Theater, and Ford Field. The property manager of the Kales Building indicated that the central business district of Detroit is bouncing back because of the entertainment district. He said it's now tough to find an apartment there, speculating that people are drawn to living downtown because of high gas prices and low crime rates in the CBD. Another real estate developer contended that the main reason rental units are full in Detroit is because so many people lost their houses in the recent mortgage crisis that they are renting now. Across Grand Circus Park, the Broderick Towers are now almost fully leased after a massive renovation, which will bring a new shopping complex and more apartments to this revitalized neighborhood.

■ **Figure 9.2**

**Detroit, Michigan.** The Lafayette Building once housed the offices of the Michigan Supreme Court. This photo from 2008 shows the boarded-up first and second floors and broken windows on the third floor. Urban explorers broke into and photographed abandoned buildings in Detroit (several websites are devoted to their photographs and videos), and vandals painted graffiti on the windows of Lafayette and other so-called ghosts of Detroit.

© Alexander B. Murphy

Other neighborhoods of the city are not bouncing back as well. Abandoned high-rise buildings called the ghosts of Detroit (Fig. 9.2) are joined by empty single-family homes. The population of Detroit rose and fell with the automobile industry. The population peaked at 1.8 million in 1950, but a 2014 U.S. Census Bureau report estimates the city's population falling to below 700,000.

Empty high-rise office buildings, apartments, government buildings, hotels, and train depots stand throughout the city like dead trees in a forest. The Lafayette Building (Fig. 9.2) stood across the street from the Book Cadillac Hotel for nearly a century. Once home to the offices of the Michigan Supreme Court, the Lafayette closed due to financial woes and lack of tenants in 1997. In the first decade of the 2000s, the Book Cadillac Hotel benefited from a $200 million renovation, but the Lafayette fell into a greater state of disrepair after that. I took this photograph in October 2008, the same month that a portion of the Lafayette fell off the building to the street below. In 2009, the Detroit City Council voted to demolish the Lafayette, and in 2010, the city tore down the building.

The Lafayette is not the only Detroit building to face such a prospect. The mayor of Detroit announced a plan in 2010 to demolish 10,000 abandoned buildings and houses in Detroit by 2014. As of 2013, Mayor Bing reported that 8966 structures had been demolished. In 2014, however, a task force convened by the Obama administration on urban blight in Detroit issued the most comprehensive study to date and recommended 40,000 additional dilapidated structures and trash-filled lots for demolition or restoration. The study labeled 30 percent of Detroit's properties as dilapidated or heading that way.

Geographers are leading the study of cities today, focusing on the impacts of developments at different scales on cities, including the ways in which globalization and political-economic shifts are affecting the organization and character of urban areas. Urban geographer Edward Soja urges scholars to think of cities, including Detroit, as integral to the development of societies, not simply as discrete stages on which the human drama plays out. Soja uses the term **synekism** to refer to the "conditions that derive from dwelling together in a particular home place or space" (2003, 273). As a result of people dwelling together in close-knit cities, a set of conditions occur that make change possible. To Soja, cities do not simply reflect changing economies and politics. Rather, cities create the conditions necessary for contemporary economic and political change.

Viewed through the concept of synekism, Grand Circus Park and the Lafayette Building in Detroit are not merely reflections of the changing political economy of Detroit. This block of buildings and the larger city of Detroit created the conditions necessary for industrial production to expand to the global scale and are creating the conditions necessary for portions of Detroit to rebound.

In our study of urban geography in this chapter, we look at the city spatially, examining the forms of cities around the world, the role of people in building and shaping cities, and the changes that cities have undergone over space and time.

# Key Questions FOR CHAPTER 9

1. When and why did people start living in cities?
2. Where are cities located and why?
3. How are cities organized, and how do they function?
4. How do people shape cities?
5. What role do cities play in globalization?

## WHEN AND WHY DID PEOPLE START LIVING IN CITIES?

Worldwide, more people live in urban areas than in rural areas today. China, a traditionally rural country, reached the point where more than 50 percent of its population lived in urban areas in 2010. According to China's census, the country was 36.1 percent urban in 2000. The rapid urbanization of China is due to the migration of millions of people from rural to urban areas since economic liberalization began in 1979.

**Urban** refers to the built-up space of the central city and suburbs. Urban areas include the city and surrounding environment connected to the city. An urban place is distinctively nonrural and nonagricultural. Cities are characterized by occupational specialization, where people work in a wide variety of fields. Cities have governments, and their citizens pay taxes to support public services.

For the vast majority of human history, the world was largely rural. From the beginnings of human society to about 3000 BCE, less than 1 percent of people lived in urban areas. With cities established in Mesopotamia, the Nile River, Mesoamerica, and Asia, the proportion of the world's population living in cities rose only slightly.

After the start of the Industrial Revolution in the mid-1700s in Great Britain, urbanization exploded when the number of urban dwellers in states such as Great Britain and the Netherlands outnumbered their rural counterparts. In western Europe, the United States, Canada, and Japan, four out of five people now live in cities or towns (Fig. 9.3). In China, the figure is five out of ten, and in India, the country's 2011 census reported nearly seven out of ten living in rural areas.

The agglomeration of people, services, and goods in cities affords people the luxury of time to innovate. Cities are centers of political power and industrial might, higher education and technological innovation, artistic achievement, and medical

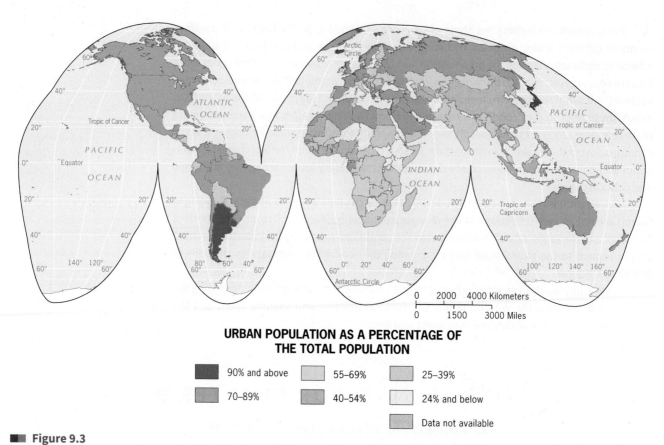

**URBAN POPULATION AS A PERCENTAGE OF THE TOTAL POPULATION**

- 90% and above
- 70–89%
- 55–69%
- 40–54%
- 25–39%
- 24% and below
- Data not available

**Figure 9.3**

**Urban Population as a Percentage of the Total Population, by Country, 2013.**    The regions of Europe, North America, Latin America, Russia, and Southwest Asia and North Africa are the most urbanized.    *Data from*: Population Reference Bureau 2013.

advances. They are the great markets, centers of specialization and interaction, sources of news and information, suppliers of services, and providers of sports and entertainment. Cities are the anchors and instigators of modern culture. A **city** is an agglomeration of people and buildings clustered together to serve as a center of politics, culture, and economics.

In the modern world, urbanization can happen quite quickly. A rural area or a small town can be transformed into a major metropolitan area. During the latter part of the twentieth century, the Chinese government announced a major economic development project in Guangdong, a province in southern China. The Chinese government established a special economic zone (SEZ) in Guangdong Province, and business and industry mushroomed. The small fishing village of Shenzhen in Guangdong Province is adjacent to Hong Kong. Hundreds of industries moved from Hong Kong to Shenzhen to take advantage of lower labor costs. The small fishing village of Shenzhen experienced extraordinary growth as its population, rushing to the area to find work, swelled from 20,000 to 8 million in just three decades. Shenzhen was quickly transformed: Skyscrapers now tower where thatch houses, rice paddies, and duck ponds once stood (Fig. 9.4).

Urbanization that can happen so quickly today took thousands of years to develop originally. The rise of the city is a very recent phenomenon in human history. Human communities have existed for over 100,000 years, but more than

90,000 years passed before people began to cluster in towns. Archaeological evidence indicates that people established the first cities about 8000 years ago. However, only in the last 200 years did cities begin to resemble their modern size and structure.

## The Hearths of Urbanization

The switch from hunting and gathering to agriculture occurred prior to urbanization. Archaeologists have found evidence of early agriculture between 10,000 and 12,000 years ago. Most contend that the first cities came "several millennia" after the origins of agriculture (Smith 2009). Geographers Edward Soja and Peter Taylor, in contrast, argue that the first cities came before agriculture, and as evidence, they cite the 12,000-year-old settlement of Catal Huyuk (Fig. 9.5). Archaeologists usually view Catal Huyuk as an agricultural village, not a city.

Agricultural villages were relatively small in size and in population. Everyone living in an **agricultural village** was involved in agriculture, and the people lived at near-subsistence levels, producing just enough to get by. The dwellings in ancient agricultural villages were about the same size and contained about the same number of possessions, reflecting the egalitarian nature (sharing of goods in common among the people) of the societies living in these early villages. The populations were permanent, reflected in the

■ **Figure 9.4**

**Shenzhen, China.** Shenzhen changed from a fishing village to a major metropolitan area in just 25 years. Everything you see in this photograph is less than 30 years old; all of this stands where duck ponds and paddies lay less than three decades ago.

dwelling units where people built permanent structures. Egalitarian societies persisted long after agriculture began.

Scholars are fairly certain that these descriptors accurately depict the agricultural villages in the first agricultural hearth, the area of Southwest Asia called the Fertile Crescent. Additional archaeological evidence portrays agricultural villages in the later hearths of agricultural innovation, the Indus River Valley and Mesoamerica, as also fitting these descriptors. When people establish cities, however, these descriptors become inaccurate. In cities, people generate personal material wealth, trade over long distances, live in stratified classes that are usually reflected in the housing stock, and engage in a diversity of economic activities—not just agriculture.

■ **Figure 9.5**

**Catal Huyuk.** Dated to 12,000 years ago, the early city of Catal Huyuk was in a western extension of the Fertile Crescent, in present-day Turkey. This image is a reproduction of cave art found in Catal Huyuk. Archaeologists believe the cone structure in the background is a volcano, and the squares in the front are houses. *Altered from:* Meece S (2006) A Bird's Eye View-of a Leopard's Spots: The Çatalhöyük 'Map' and the Development of Cartographic Representation in Prehistory. Anatolian Studies: 1–16.

Two components enabled cities to stabilize and grow: **agricultural surplus** and **social stratification.** Archaeologists, anthropologists, and geographers have studied the remains and records of the first cities, creating numerous theories as to how cities came about. Most agree that some series of events led to the formation of an agricultural surplus and a leadership class; which came first varies by theory. The series of events spurring these two components also varies by theory. One theory maintains that advances in technology such as irrigation generated an agricultural surplus, and a leadership class formed to control the surplus and the technology that produced it. Another theory holds that a king or priest-king centralized political power and then demanded more labor to generate an agricultural surplus, which would help the ruler retain political power.

Regardless of how the leadership class was established, we know that once established, it helped generate the surplus and controlled the distribution of that surplus. The link between the surplus and the leadership class is clear in early cities, where the home of the leaders was often positioned close to the grain storage. The **leadership class**, or urban elite, consisted of a group of decision makers and organizers who controlled the resources, and often the lives, of others. The urban elite controlled the food supply, including its production, storage, and distribution. Generating an agricultural surplus enabled some people to devote their efforts to pursuits other than agriculture. The urban elite, for instance, did not work the fields. Rather, they devoted time to other pursuits such as religion and philosophy. Out of such pursuits came the concepts of writing and record keeping. Writing made possible the codification of laws and the preservation of traditions. Urban elites defended themselves by constructing walls on the outskirts of the city. However, the leadership class collected taxes and tribute from people within their control beyond the city walls.

Some cities grew out of agricultural villages, and others grew in places previously unoccupied by sedentary people. The innovation of the city is called the **first urban revolution**, and it occurred independently in six separate hearths, a case of independent invention[1] (Fig. 9.6). In each of the urban hearths, people became engaged in economic activities

[1]Some scholars argue that there are fewer than six hearths and attribute some early centers of urbanization to diffusion.

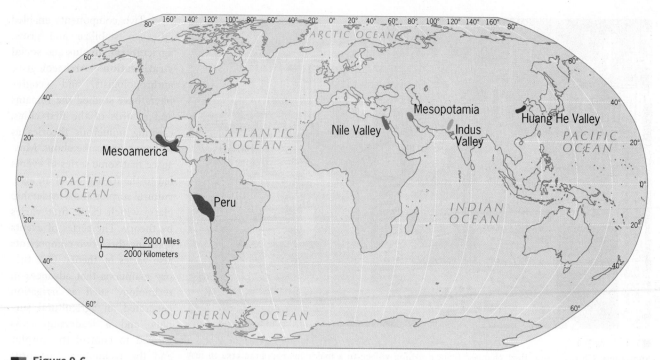

beyond agriculture, including specialty crafts, the military, trade, and government.

The six urban hearths are tied closely to the hearths of agriculture. The first hearth of agriculture, the Fertile Crescent, is the first place archaeologists find evidence of cities, dating to about 3500 BCE. This urban hearth is called **Mesopotamia**, referring to the region of great cities (such as Ur and Babylon) located between the Tigris and Euphrates rivers. Studies of the cultural landscape and urban morphology of Mesopotamian cities have found signs of social inequality in the varying sizes and ornamentation of houses. An urban elite erected palaces, protected themselves with walls, and employed countless artisans to beautify their spaces. They also established a priest-king class and developed a religious-political ideology to support the priest-kings. Rulers in the cities were both priests and kings, and they levied taxes and demanded tribute from the harvest brought by the agricultural laborers.

Archaeologists, often teaming up with anthropologists and geographers, have learned much about the ways ancient Mesopotamian cities functioned by studying their organization and form (urban morphology). The ancient Mesopotamian city was usually protected by a mud wall surrounding the entire community, or sometimes a cluster of temples and shrines at its center. Temples dominated the urban landscape, not only because they were the largest structures in town but also because they were built on artificial mounds, often over 100 feet (30 m) high.

In Mesopotamia, priests and other authorities resided in substantial buildings, many of which might be called palaces. Ordinary citizens lived in mud-walled houses packed closely

together and separated only by narrow lanes. Craftspeople set up their workshops lining the narrow lanes. The informal urban housing of Mesopotamia surrounded well-planned central cities.

The second hearth of urbanization, in the **Nile River Valley**, dates back to 3200 BCE. The interrelationship between urbanization and irrigation in this region distinguishes it from other urban hearths. The might of the rulers of the Nile River Valley is reflected in the great pyramids, tombs, and statues they created. Traditional theories hold that slaves built these feats of engineering, but more recent excavations suggest that ordinary citizens built ancient monuments as part of their tax payment.

The third urban hearth, dating to 2200 BCE, is the **Indus River Valley**, another place where agriculture likely diffused from the Fertile Crescent. Unable to decipher ancient Indus writing, scholars are puzzled by Harappa and Mohenjo-Daro, the first cities of the Indus River Valley (Fig. 9.7). The intricate planning of the cities points to the existence of a leadership class, but the houses continued to be equal in size, with no palaces or monuments appearing in the cities. In addition, all the dwellings in the cities had access to the same infrastructure, including wastewater drains and carefully maintained stone-lined wells. The cities had thick walls, and the discovery of coins from as far away as the Mediterranean points to significant trade over long distances.

The fourth urban hearth arose around the confluence of the **Huang He** (Yellow) and **Wei Valleys** of present-day China, dating to 1500 BCE. The Chinese purposely planned their ancient cities to center on a vertical structure in the middle of the city and then built an inner wall around it. Within the inner wall, the people of this hearth typically placed temples and palaces for the leadership class. The urban elite of the Huang He and Wei region demonstrated their power by building enormous, elaborate structures. Around 200 BCE, the Emperor Qin Xi Huang directed the building of the Great Wall of China. Like the Egyptians, he also had an elaborate mausoleum built for himself. An estimated 700,000 laborers worked for over 40 years to craft the intricate faces and weapons, horses, and chariots of an army of over 7000 terracotta warriors who stand guard over his burial place (Fig. 9.8).

Chronologically, the fifth urban hearth, found in **Mesoamerica**, dates to 1100 BCE. The ancient cities of Mesoamerica were religious centers. The Olmec built cities, including San Lorenzo, on the Gulf Coast of Mexico. The Olmec carved stone monuments, and archaeologists believe they moved the volcanic stones 50 miles from the interior of Mexico to the coast. The Olmec civilization died out, but based on cultural teachings of the Olmec, the Maya built cities in the same region that were also centered on religious temples (including Tikal, Chichén-Itzá, Uxmal, and Copán in Fig. 9.9).

The most recent archaeological evidence establishes **Peru** as the sixth urban

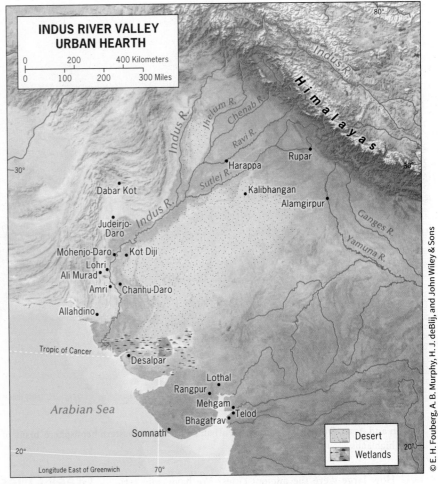

**Figure 9.7**

**Indus River Valley Urban Hearth.** Most cities were sited along rivers and coasts.

**Figure 9.8**

**Terracotta Warriors Guarding the Tomb of the Chinese Emperor Qin Xi Huang.** An estimated 700,000 laborers worked for over 40 years, around 200 BCE, to craft more than 7000 terracotta warriors who stand guard over the emperor's tomb.

hearth chronologically. The Chavín built cities in Peru dating to 900 BCE. The largest settlement, Chavín, was sited at an elevation of 10,530 feet in the Andean highlands.

## The Role of the Ancient City in Society

Ancient cities not only were centers of religion and power, but also served as economic nodes. Cities were the chief marketplaces and bases from which wealthy merchants, land and livestock owners, and traders operated. As educational centers, the cities included teachers and philosophers as residents. The cities also had handicraft industries that attracted the best craftspeople and inventors. In all of these roles, ancient cities were the anchors of culture and society, the focal points of power, authority, and change.

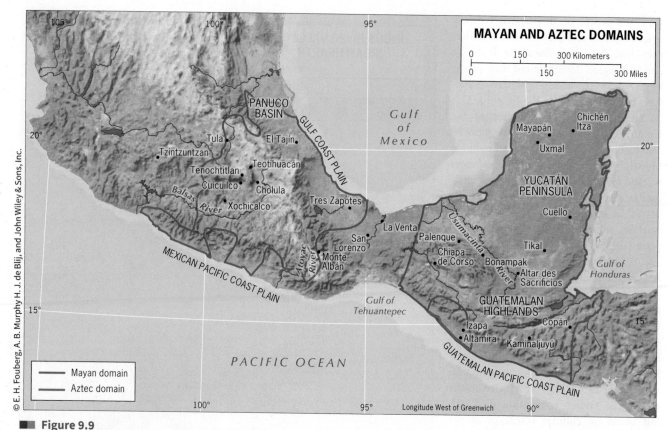

■ **Figure 9.9**

**Mayan and Aztec Domains.**   Unlike the urban hearths of the eastern hemisphere, many of the earliest cities in the Americas were founded in the highlands.

How large were the ancient cities? We have only estimates because it is difficult to judge from excavated ruins the dimensions of a city at its height or the number of people who might have occupied each residential unit. By modern standards, the ancient cities were not large. The cities of Mesopotamia and the Nile Valley may have had between 10,000 and 15,000 inhabitants after nearly 2000 years of growth and development. That, scholars conclude, is about the maximum sustainable size based on existing systems of food production, gathering, distribution, and social organization, These urban places were geographical exceptions in an overwhelmingly rural world. The modern city we know today did not emerge until several thousand years later.

## Diffusion of Urbanization

Urbanization diffused from Mesopotamia in several directions. Populations in Mesopotamia grew as the food supply became more secure and steady. People migrated out from the hearth, diffusing their knowledge of agriculture and urbanization. Diffusion from Mesopotamia happened early, even before agriculture developed independently in some other hearths. In fact, urbanization diffused to the Mediterranean from Mesopotamia (and perhaps the Nile River Valley) more than 3500 years ago, at about the same time cities were developing in the hearth of the Huang He and long before cities originated in Mesoamerica.

## Greek Cities

Greece is not an urban hearth because agriculture and urbanization diffused to Greece from Mesopotamia, rather than being independently innovated in Greece. Greece is more accurately described as a **secondary hearth** of urbanization because the Greek city influenced urban developments in Europe and beyond, as European ideas diffused around the world during the colonial era. Greek cities began more than 3500 years ago, when the city of Knossos on the island of Crete became the cornerstone of a system of towns in the Minoan civilization.

By 500 BCE, Greece had become one of the most urbanized areas on Earth. The urbanization of Ancient Greece ushered in a new stage in the evolution of cities. At its height, Ancient Greece encompassed a network of more than 500 cities and towns, not only on the mainland but also on the many Greek islands. Seafarers connected these urban places with trade routes and carried the notion of urban life throughout the Mediterranean region. Athens and Sparta, often vying with each other for power, soon became Greece's leading cities. Athens may have been the largest city in the world at the time, with an estimated 250,000 inhabitants.

With the hilly topography of Greece, the people had no need to build earthen mounds on which to perch temples; these were provided by nature. Every city had its **acropolis** (acro meaning high point; polis meaning city), on which the

© H. J. de Blij

■ **Figure 9.10**
**Athens, Greece.**   The rocky hilltop of Athens is home to the Acropolis (acro means high point). The Athens Acropolis is still crowned by the great Parthenon, standing after nearly 25 centuries.

people built the most impressive structures—usually religious buildings. The Parthenon of Athens remains the most famous of all, surviving to this day despite nearly 2500 years of wars, earth tremors, vandalism, and environmental impact (Fig. 9.10). Building this magnificent columned structure, designed by the Athenian architect-engineer Phidias, began in 447 BCE, and its rows of tapering columns have inspired architects ever since.

© H. J. de Blij

■ **Figure 9.11**
**Athens, Greece.**   Looking down from the Acropolis, you can see the agora, the ancient trade and market area, which is surrounded by new urban buildings.

Like the older Southwest Asian cities, Greece's cities also had public places. In the Southwest Asian towns, these seem to have been rather cramped, crowded, and bustling with activity, but in Ancient Greece they were open, spacious squares, often in a low part of town with steps leading down to them (Fig. 9.11). On these steps the Greeks debated, lectured, judged each other, planned military campaigns, and socialized. As time went on, this public space, called the **agora** (meaning market), also became the focus of commercial activity.

Greece's cities had excellent theaters. The aristocracy attended plays and listened to philosophical discourses, but for many people life in a Greek city was miserable. Housing was no better than it had been in the Mesopotamian cities thousands of years earlier. Sanitation and health conditions were poor. And much of the grandeur designed by Greece's urban planners was the work of hundreds of thousands of slaves.

Urbanization diffused from Greece to the Roman Empire. Roman urbanization and urban culture diffused throughout western Europe. The city declined in Europe for a time after the fall of the Roman Empire, but Europeans eventually carried Western concepts of city life (drawn from Greece and Rome) around the world through colonialism and capitalism. From Washington, D.C., to Canberra, Australia, the urban landscape shows the imprints of Greco-Roman urban culture.

## Roman Cities

The great majority of Greece's cities and towns were located near the Mediterranean Sea on peninsulas and islands, and were linked by sea routes. When the Romans succeeded the Greeks (and Etruscans) as rulers of the region, their empire incorporated not only the Mediterranean shores but also a large part of interior Europe and North Africa (Fig. 9.12). The Roman urban system was the largest yet—much larger than Greece's domain. The capital, Rome, served as the apex of a hierarchy of settlements ranging from small villages to large cities. The Romans linked these places with an extensive transportation network that included hundreds of miles of roads, well-established sea routes, and trading ports along the roads, sea, and rivers. Roman regional planners displayed a remarkable capacity for choosing favorable sites of cities and for identifying suitable locales for settlements. The **site** of a city is its absolute location, often chosen for its advantages in trade or defense, or as a center for religious practice.

The **situation** of a city refers to its position in relation to the surrounding context.

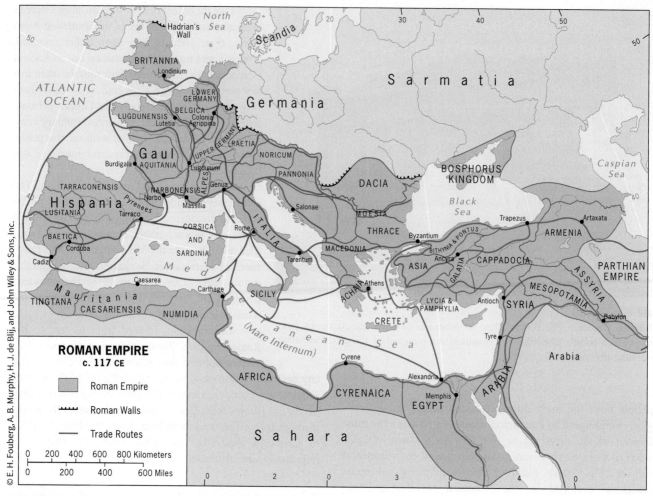

**■ Figure 9.12**

**Roman Empire c. 117 CE.**　The Romans established a system of cities linked by a network of land and sea routes. Many of the Roman cities have grown into modern metropolises.

The site of a city is a function of its absolute location: its precise position on the globe. The situation of a city is its relative location, its place in the region and the world around it. The situation of a city changes over time. For example, Rome was the center of the Roman Empire, but when the Roman Empire dissolved, the situation of Rome changed as well. It developed into the center of the Roman Catholic Church, a role it still plays today. But during the Renaissance when Florence flourished and during the Industrial Revolution when Naples and points north of Rome grew economically, the situation of Rome within Italy as a whole shifted. It no longer was the scientific and economic focal point of the country.

The Romans were greatly influenced by the Greeks, as is evident in Roman mythology and visible in the cultural landscape and **urban morphology** of Roman cities. The urban morphology of a city is the layout of the city, its physical form and structure. Greeks planned their colonial cities in a rectangular grid pattern, and Romans adopted this plan wherever surface conditions made it possible. The Romans took the Greek acropolis (zone of religion and center of power) and agora (zone of public space and the marketplace) and

combined them into one zone: the **Forum**, which served as the focal point of Roman public life (Fig. 9.13).

Throughout the Roman Empire, cities were places of cultural contrast. What still stands in ruins in many places around the Mediterranean are monumental buildings, impressive villas, spacious avenues, ingenious aqueducts and baths, and sewage systems built of stone and pipe (Fig. 9.14). What we can no longer see in the ruins of the empire are the thousands of slaves who built these structures (estimates are that between one-third and two-thirds of the population of the empire was enslaved) and the wretchedly poor who were crammed into overcrowded tenements and lived in filth. The city of the Roman Empire, like the city of today, was home to both rich and poor and reflected both the greatest achievements and the worst failings of civilization.

## Urban Growth After Greece and Rome

After the Roman Empire fell in 476 CE, Europe entered an era historians called the Middle Ages, which spanned from about

## FIELD NOTE

"There can be few spaces of greater significance to the development of Western civilization than the Roman Forum. This was the nerve center of a vast empire that transformed the face of western Europe, Southwest Asia, and North Africa. It was also the place where the decisions were made that carried forward Greek ideas about governance, art, urban design, and technology. The very organization of space found in the Roman Forum is still with us: rectilinear street patterns; distinct buildings for legislative, executive, and judicial functions; and public spaces adorned with statues and fountains."

■ **Figure 9.13**
**Rome, Italy.**

500 to 1300 (or later in parts of Europe). During the first two-thirds of this period, little urban growth occurred in Europe; in some parts of the continent, urbanism went into sharp decline. The urban growth that did take place during this time occurred on sites of oases and resting places along the Silk Route between Europe and Asia. Many of these places grew into towns, and some, such as Bukhara and Samarqand, became major cities. In Asia, Chinese styles of city-building diffused into Korea and Japan, with Seoul becoming a full-fledged city by 1200 and Kyoto, Japan's historic capital, growing rapidly after the turn of the ninth century.

During Europe's Middle Ages, urbanization continued vigorously outside of Europe. In West Africa, trading cities developed along the southern margin of the Sahara. By 1350, Timbuktu (part of Mali today) was a major city: a seat of government, a university town, a market, and a religious center. The Americas also experienced significant urban growth during Europe's Middle Ages, especially within the Mayan and Aztec empires (Fig. 9.15). The largest pre-Columbian

■ **Figure 9.14**
**Nimes, France.** Aqueducts outside of Nimes, France, were built during the Roman Empire, about 2000 years ago. Aqueducts made it possible to bring fresh water to relatively large cities at the time.

■ **Figure 9.15**
**Altun Ha, Belize.** Between 300 and 900 CE, Altun Ha served as a thriving trade and distribution center for the Caribbean merchant canoe traffic. Some of the trails in Altun Ha led all the way to Teotihuacán.

city in the Americas was in the Aztec Empire on the Mexican Plateau. The Aztec capital of Tenochtitlán had nearly 100,000 inhabitants at a time many European cities lay in ruins.

## Site and Situation During European Exploration

Early Eurasian urban areas extended in a crescent-shaped zone across Eurasia from England in the west to Japan in the east, including the cities of London, Paris, Venice, Constantinople (Istanbul today), and Tabriz, Samarqand, Kabul, Lahore, Amra, Jaunpur, Xian, Anyang, Kyoto and Osaka. Before European exploration, most cities in the world were sited on trade routes in the interiors of continents, not just in Eurasia, but also in West Africa and indigenous America. Interior trade routes such as the Silk Route and the caravan routes of West Africa sustained these inland cities and, in many cases, helped them prosper.

The relative importance of the interior trade routes changed, however, when European maritime exploration and overseas colonization ushered in an era of oceanic, worldwide trade. With this shift, the situation of cities like Basle (Switzerland) and Xian (China) changed from being crucial nodes on interior trading routes to being peripheral to ocean-oriented trade.

After European exploration took off during the 1400s, the dominance of interior cities declined. Other cities, sited on coasts, gained prominence as their situations changed. In Asia, coastal cities such as Bombay (now Mumbai, India),

Madras (Chennai, India), Malacca (Malaysia), Batavia (Jakarta, Indonesia), and Tokyo (Japan) came to the fore. Exploration and oceanic trade altered the situations of cities in West Africa as well. Before 1500, urbanization in West Africa was concentrated in a belt extending along the southern margin of the Sahara, including such cities as Timbuktu (Mali), Niani (Guinea), Gao (Mali), Zaria (Nigeria), Kano (Nigeria), and Maiduguri (Nigeria). Here, cross-desert caravan traffic met boat traffic on the River Niger (where "camel met canoe"), and people exchanged goods from northern deserts for goods from coastal forests. Maritime trade disrupted this pattern of trade. Coastal ports became the leading markets and centers of power, and the African cities of the interior began a long decline.

Coastal cities remained crucial after exploration led to colonialism. During the colonial period, key cities in international trade networks included the coastal cities of Cape Town (South Africa), Lima-Callao (Peru), and New York City.

The trade networks European powers commanded (including the slave trade) brought unprecedented riches to Europe's burgeoning medieval cities, such as Amsterdam (the Netherlands), London (England), Lisbon (Portugal), Liverpool (England), and Seville (Spain). Successful merchants built ornate mansions, patronized the arts, participated in city governance, and supported the reconstruction of city centers. As a result, cities such as Antwerp (Belgium), Copenhagen (Denmark), Lisbon (Portugal), and Genoa (Italy) thrived. A central square became the focus of the city, fronted by royal, religious, public, and private buildings evincing wealth and prosperity, power and influence (Fig. 9.16). Streets leading

## FIELD NOTE

"The contemporary landscape of Genoa stands as a reminder of the city's historic importance. Long before Europe became divided up into states, a number of cities in northern Italy freed themselves from the strictures of feudalism and began to function autonomously. Genoa and Venice were two of these, and they became the foci of significant Mediterranean maritime trading empires. In the process, they also became magnificent, wealthy cities. Although most buildings in Genoa's urban core date from a more recent era, the layout of streets and public squares harks back to the city's imperial days. Is it a surprise that the city gave birth to one of the most famous explorers of all time: Christopher Columbus?"

© Alexander B. Murphy

■ **Figure 9.16**
**Genoa, Italy.**

to these central squares formed arteries of commerce, and the beginnings of "downtowns" emerged.

During the sixteenth and seventeenth centuries, European mercantile cities became the nodes of a widening network of national, regional, and global commerce. So wealthy and powerful were the urban merchants that, supported by their rulers, they were able to found and expand settlements in distant lands. Cities such as Dakar (Senegal), Lourenco Marques (now Maputo, Moçambique), and Saigon (now Ho Chi Minh City, Vietnam) were endowed with the ornate trappings of the mercantile cities of Europe, including elaborately inlaid sidewalks, tree-lined avenues, and neo-Gothic architecture.

## The Second Urban Revolution

During the last decades of the eighteenth century, the Industrial Revolution was in full swing in Great Britain. None of Europe's cities was prepared for what lay ahead: an avalanche of changes that ripped the fabric of urban life. Around 1800, western Europe was still overwhelmingly rural. As thousands migrated to the cities with industrialization, cities had to adapt to the mushrooming population, the proliferation of factories and supply facilities, the expansion of transport systems, and the construction of tenements for the growing labor force.

## A Second Agricultural Revolution

Before the second urban revolution could take place, a second revolution in agriculture was necessary. During the late seventeenth century and into the eighteenth century, Europeans made a series of important improvements in agriculture, including invention of the seed drill, hybrid seeds, and improved breeding practices for livestock. The second agricultural revolution also improved organization of production, market collaboration, and storage capacities. Agricultural laborers migrated to cities in hopes of obtaining jobs in the formal economy, which included wages usable in the growing cash-based economies of Europe. Manufacturers tapped into the new labor force and expanded industrial production (for a further discussion of industrialization, see Chapter 12).

Not all mercantile cities turned into industrial cities. Many industrial cities grew from small villages or along canal and river routes. The primary determinant in the location of early industrial cities was proximity to a power source. For textile manufacturing, industrial cities had to be sited near fresh water sources to power the water loom. In Great Britain, industrial cities involved in textile manufacturing were located in the Pennines, where fresh water flowed down the hillsides. Industrial cities involved in iron manufacturing were located around Birmingham and Coalbrookdale, which were easily accessible to Britain's coal and iron ore fields.

When industrialization diffused from Great Britain to the European mainland, the places most ready for industrialization had undergone their own second agricultural revolution, had surplus capital from mercantilism and colonialism, and were located near coal fields (Fig. 9.17).

## The Chaotic Industrial City

With industrialization, cities became unregulated jumbles of activity. Factories engulfed private homes. Open spaces became garbage dumps. Urban dwellers converted elegant housing into overcrowded slums. Sanitation systems failed, and water supplies were inadequate and often polluted. By the late 1800s, the Industrial Revolution had changed transportation significantly. The steam engine, powered by coal, not only pumped water from mines for coal mining but also powered railroads and steamships. The diffusion of the railroad gave cities that were not near coal fields the chance to industrialize. The central parts of cities such as London, Paris, and Amsterdam retained their preindustrial shape. But with the diffusion of the railroad, railroad tracks knifed through long-stable neighborhoods.

Living conditions were dreadful for workers in cities, and working conditions were shocking. Children worked 12-hour shifts in textile mills, typically six days a week. In industrial cities, health conditions were worse than they had been in medieval times; the air was polluted and the water contaminated. The grimy, soot-covered cities of the British Midlands were appropriately deemed the "black towns." Few if any safety mechanisms protected the laborers, and injuries were common.

In the mid-1800s, as Karl Marx and Frederick Engels (writing in Germany, Belgium, and England) encouraged "workers of the world" to unite, conditions in European manufacturing cities gradually improved. Industrialists were forced to recognize workers' rights, and governments intervened by legislating workers' rights and introducing city planning and zoning. Many manufacturing cities in North America never suffered as much as their European predecessors, although living and working conditions for factory workers (and "blue-collar" workers generally) were far from satisfactory. American manufacturing cities did not altogether escape the problems of the European industrial cities. During the late nineteenth and early twentieth centuries, the American manufacturing city grew rapidly, often with inadequate planning and rapid immigration leading to the development of slums and ghettos.

During the second half of the twentieth century, the nature of manufacturing changed, as did its location: cities repositioned many factories away from congested, overcrowded, expensive urban areas. Companies simply abandoned large manufacturing plants, making "rust belts" out of once-thriving industrial districts. Many of these plants still stand today, overgrown by weeds, with broken windows and cracking walls, while others have been turned into parks and green spaces that showcase industrial relics (Fig. 9.18).

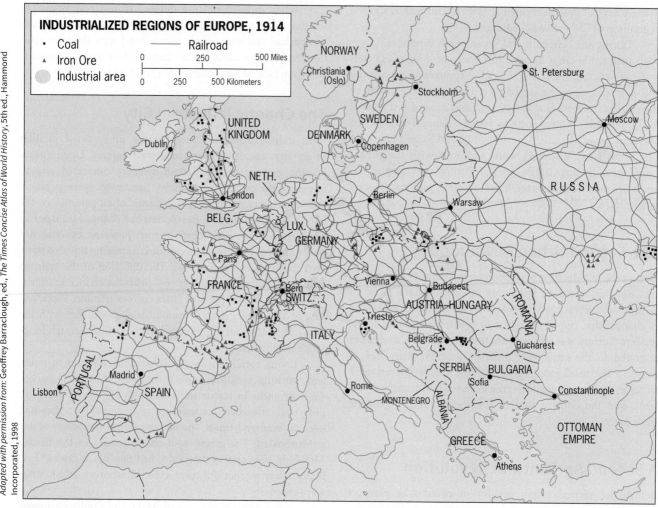

Adapted with permission from: Geoffrey Barraclough, ed., *The Times Concise Atlas of World History*, 5th ed., Hammond Incorporated, 1998

**■ Figure 9.17**

**Industrialized Regions of Europe, 1914.**   Industrial centers were close to coal or iron ore deposits and near water transportation, whether coasts or rivers.

# FIELD NOTE

"The Ruhr Valley long functioned as the incubator of Germany's industrial economy. Largely destroyed during World War II, the Ruhr rose again to help Germany back to recovery. But as declining transportation costs and rising labor costs prompted heavy industries to move their operations to other parts of the world, factories such as this iron and steel mill on the edge of Duisburg fell silent. Unemployment soared, and the area became depressed. In an effort to rebound, local authorities are now trying to turn a few of these relics into tourist destinations. They are unlikely to compete with the great churches or medieval palaces found elsewhere in Germany, but for the geographer they provide fascinating insights into the urban and economic arrangements that made modern Europe what it is today."

© Alexander B. Murphy

**■ Figure 9.18**
**Duisburg, Germany.**

Although factories and factory jobs are not permanent, the urbanization that went along with industrialization is still apparent. Depending on the sometimes variable definition of "urban," western Europe today is more than 75 percent urbanized and urbanization has become a global phenomenon. Worldwide, more people now live in cities than in rural areas.

Archaeologists have found that the houses in Indus River cities, such as Mohenjo-Daro and Harappa, were a uniform size: each house had access to a sewer system, and palaces were absent from the cultural landscape. Derive a theory as to why these conditions were present in these cities that had both a leadership class and a surplus of agricultural goods.

## WHERE ARE CITIES LOCATED AND WHY?

When you look at a map in an atlas of the United States or Canada, or at a road map of a State or province, you see an array of places of different sizes, with varying distances between them. The map looks like a jumble, yet each place is where it is because of some decision, some perception of the site or its situation. Site and situation help explain why certain cities were planned and why cities thrive or fail. To understand why a conglomeration of cities is distributed across space the way it is and why cities are different sizes, it is necessary to examine more than one city at a time and see how those cities fit together, into the region, into the state, and into the globe as a whole.

Urban geographers studied the distribution of cities in Europe and the Americas during the 1900s, using quantitative techniques to determine how many cities and what size cities are needed within a certain space. In studying the size of cities and distances between them, urban geographers explored the **trade areas** of different-size cities. Every city and town has a trade area, an adjacent region within which its influence is dominant. Customers from smaller towns and villages come to the city to shop and to conduct other business. An online survey of approximately 50,000 people helped one armchair geographer create a map of trade areas for the contiguous United States (Fig. 9.19). The city's newspapers are read, and its television stations are watched in the surrounding region (Fig. 9.20).

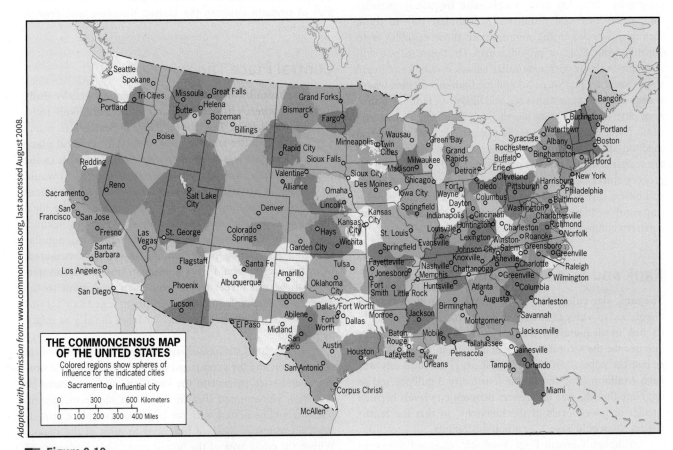

■ **Figure 9.19**

**Regions of Influence for Cities in the Contiguous United States.** This map is based on survey data from over 45,000 voters on commoncensus.org who answered the question, "On the level of North America as a whole, what major city do you feel has the most cultural and economic influence on your area overall?"

**Figure 9.20**

**Monterey, California.** Business names often reflect the trade area where they are located. Many trade areas have a toponym in the local vernacular that those in the region use. When you travel to a new trade area, you may see the toponymn, such as "Bay Area," "Northern Virginia" or "South Florida," on service vehicles, billboards, and business names. Around Santa Cruz, Elkhorn, and Monterey, California, may businesses use the toponym "Monterey Bay" to describe the trade area.

Across the multitude of quantitative studies in urban geography, three key components arise frequently: population, trade area, and distance. The simplest way to think through the relationship among these three variables is to consider your State or province map. On the map, you will see many villages with unfamiliar names, a number of small towns sited on highways, several medium-sized cities where transportation routes converge, and likely one familiar, dominant city. The largest city has the largest trade area, and as a result fewer places rival it as the major trade area: the several medium-sized cities trade in smaller areas of commerce and are scattered apart from the major city, small towns house the grocery stores and other necessities, and finally villages may still have a café or a gas station. The trade areas and population combine to give us a hierarchy of urban places, following a pattern commonly called the rank-size rule.

## Rank and Size in the Urban Matrix

The **rank-size rule** holds that in a model urban hierarchy, the population of a city or town will be inversely proportional to its rank in the hierarchy. Thus, if the largest city has 12 million people, the second largest will have about 6 million (that is, half the population of the largest city); the third city will have 4 million (one-third); the fourth city 3 million; and so on. Note that the size differences between city levels become smaller at lower levels of the hierarchy, so that the tenth-largest city would have 1.2 million inhabitants.

Although German Felix Auerbach suggested the rank-size rule in 1913, linguist George Zipf is credited with establishing the mathematical equation for the rank-size rule in 1941. Since then, scholars across disciplines have tested the

rule and questioned when the rule applies and when it does not. Studies in 1966, 1980, and again in 2002 found that the majority of countries had populations with more even distributions than the rank-size rule would predict. Other recent studies have questioned why the rank-size rule fits the countries where it does fit, and these studies have offered answers including a combination of random growth (chance) and economies of scale (efficiency).

The rank-size rule does not apply in all countries, especially countries with one dominant city. States often focus development in one particular city, such as the capital city, thereby bolstering that city and its population above the rest of the cities in the state. In 1939, geographer Mark Jefferson defined a **primate city** as "a country's leading city, always disproportionately large and exceptionally expressive of national capacity and feeling." He saw the primate city as the largest and most economically influential within the state, with the next largest city in the state being much smaller and much less influential.

Many former colonies have primate cities, as the colonial powers often ruled from a single dominant city, where economic and political activities were concentrated. Examples of primate cities in former colonies include Mexico City, Mexico, and Manila, the Philippines. In the noncolonial context, London and Paris each serve as examples of primate cities in the United Kingdom and France, respectively.

## Central Place Theory

Walter Christaller wrote the classic urban geography study to explain where cities, towns, and villages are likely to be located. In his book *The Central Places in Southern Germany* (1933), Christaller laid the groundwork for **central place theory**. His goal was to predict where central places in the urban hierarchy (hamlets, villages, towns, and cities) would be located. Christaller began his theory of development with a set of assumptions: First, the surface of the ideal region would be flat and have no physical barriers; second, soil fertility would be the same everywhere; third, population and purchasing power would be evenly distributed; next, the region would have a uniform transportation network to permit direct travel from each settlement to the other; and, finally, from any given place, a good or service could be sold in all directions as far from the city as might be profitable.

Through his studies, Christaller posited an ideal central place system and then compared his model to real-world situations and tried to explain the variations and exceptions he observed. He assumed that in the urban hierarchy, central places would be nested, with the largest central place providing the greatest number of functions to most of the region. Within the trade area of the largest central place, a series of substantial towns would provide functions to several smaller places. The smaller places would then provide fewer central functions to a smaller-yet service area.

To determine the locations of each central place, Christaller needed to define the goods and services provided and calculate the distance people would willingly travel to acquire them. Cities, he postulated, would be regularly spaced, with central places where the same product was sold at the same price located a standard distance apart. He reasoned that a person would not be expected to travel 11 miles to one place to buy an item if it were possible to go only 9 miles to purchase it at another place. Central place theory maintains that each central place has a surrounding complementary region, an exclusive trade area within which the town has a monopoly on the sale of certain goods, because it alone can provide such goods at a given price and within a certain range of travel.

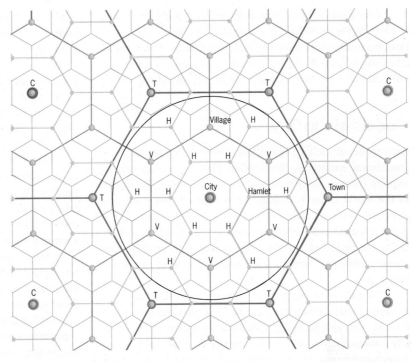

## Hexagonal Hinterlands

From the foregoing description of Christaller's theory, you would expect the shape of each central place's trade area to be circular (a bull's-eye shape surrounding each place). But circles either have to overlap or leave certain areas unserved. Hence, Christaller chose perfectly fitted hexagonal regions as the shape of each trade area (Fig. 9.21).

Urban geographers were divided on the relevance of his model. Some saw hexagonal systems everywhere; others saw none at all. Christaller received support from geographers, who applied his ideas to regions in Europe, North America, and elsewhere. In China, both the North China Plain and the Sichuan Basin display the seemingly uninterrupted flatness assumed by Christaller's model. When G. William Skinner examined the distribution of villages, towns, and cities there in 1964, he found a spatial pattern closely resembling the one predicted by Christaller's model. Studies in the U.S. Midwest suggested that while the square layout of the township-and-range system imposed a different kind of regularity on the landscape, the economic forces at work there tended to confirm Christaller's theory.

Christaller recognized that not all his assumptions would be met in reality; physical barriers, uneven resource distributions, and other factors all modify Christaller's hexagons. Nonetheless, his model yielded a number of practical insights. His studies pointed to a hierarchy of urban places that are spatially balanced and also established that larger cities would be spaced farther from each other than smaller towns or villages. Although Christaller's model of perfectly fit hexagons is not often realized, his studies confirm that the distribution of cities, towns, and villages in a region is not an accident but is tied to trade areas, population size, and distance.

**Figure 9.21**
**Christaller's Hierarchy of Settlements and Their Service Areas.**   In this model: C = city, T = town, V = village, H = hamlet.   © E. H. Fouberg, A. B. Murphy, H. J. deBlij, and John Wiley & Sons.

Sketch a map of your city or town and the cities or towns nearby. Make a list of the kinds of goods and services available in each of these towns. Do the ideas about central places presented in this section of the chapter apply to your region?

## HOW ARE CITIES ORGANIZED, AND HOW DO THEY FUNCTION?

We all know that cities have certain features in common, and we use geographic terms to identify these features, including downtowns, suburbs, industrial districts, and shopping malls. Cities in various regions of the world also have their own, distinct characteristics. Mumbai, India, looks vastly different from Chicago, Illinois. Tokyo, Japan, is distinct from Lagos, Nigeria. Cities in South America tend to be graced by magnificent plazas not commonly seen in Australia or Subsaharan Africa.

One way to conceptualize the layout of cities is through models that illustrate the structures of cities. Since the 1920s, urban geographers have studied, charted, and mapped cities to create models that describe the urban morphology, functional zonation, and overall layout of cities in world regions.

City models reveal how cities are purposely structured to perform the roles they have as centers of commerce, education, transportation, industry, and governance. The form of cities also reflects the historic, spatial, economic, cultural, and political processes that shaped cities in each world region.

## Models of the City

Each model of the city, regardless of the region, is a study in **functional zonation**—the division of the city into certain regions (zones) for certain purposes (functions). Every city in the world is an assemblage of functional zones, orderly designed in some places and jumbled chaos in others. Zones of the city exist and play certain roles in the city's life, whether to house residents, produce goods, educate students, or accommodate government. Each zone or region is part of the larger city.

Globalization has created common cultural landscapes in the financial districts of many world cities. Until little more than 30 years ago, Shanghai, China, was a vast, low-rise Chinese city centered on a colonial-era riverfront with British and French architectural imprints that had endured for more than a century. Today, you might mistake the financial districts in downtown Shanghai for New York City, with its forest of skyscrapers housing international corporations, banks, hotels, and hundreds of thousands of apartment dwellers. You will also see the names of the same corporations and hotels on high-rise buildings in central Mumbai (India), Bangkok (Thailand), Dubai (United Arab Emirates) and Singapore.

With globalization reflected in cultural landscapes around the world, are regional models of cities no longer useful? Quite the opposite: They help us understand the processes that forged cities in the first place and the impact of modern linkages that are now changing cities. In Shanghai, China, for example, the government chose to preserve the unique colonial riverfront architecture and develop around the colonial neighborhood and across the Huangpu River. In South America, cities are protecting historic plazas against modernization through regulations that limit high-rise development to areas outside of the plazas. The city of Paris protects the old city by outlawing high rises. Instead, Paris concentrates skyscraper development in the technology cluster called La Défense, which is located just outside the city proper, a little over 3 miles west of the Arc de Triomphe.

Models of cities give us context for understanding the history and geography of regions and major cities within them. Studying the location and interplay of zones within cities and the changing cultural landscape of cities helps us grasp the interplay of local and global forces that shape urban development.

## Functional Zones

Before examining specific models of urban space, we must define some terms commonly used in referring to parts of the city. The term **zone** is typically preceded by a descriptor that conveys the purpose of that area of the city. Urban models treat zones as areas with a relatively uniform land use, for example, an industrial zone or a residential zone. Most models define the key economic zone of the city (if there is such) as the central business district. The American CBD typically has high land values, tall buildings, busy traffic, converging highways, and mass transit systems.

The term **central city** describes the urban area that is not suburban. In effect, the central city refers to the older city as opposed to the newer suburbs. A **suburb** is an outlying, functionally uniform part of an urban area, and is often (but not always) adjacent to the central city. Most suburbs are residential, but some have other land uses, including schools, shopping malls, and office parks.

**Suburbanization** is the process by which lands that were previously outside of the urban environment become urbanized, as people and businesses from the city move to these spaces. The process of suburbanization holds special interest for human geographers because it involves the transformation of large areas of land from rural to urban uses and affects large numbers of people who can afford to move to larger and more expensive suburban homes. The aesthetic of the suburb reveals the occupants' idealized living patterns because their layout can be planned in response to choice and demand.

In *Contemporary Suburban America* (1981), urban geographer P. O. Muller noted that suburbia "evolved into a self-sufficient urban entity, containing its own major economic and cultural activities, that is no longer an appendage to the central city." Muller found suburban cities ready to compete with the central city for leading urban economic activities such as telecommunications, high-technology industries, and corporate headquarters. In addition to expanding residential zones, the process of suburbanization rapidly creates distinct urban regions complete with industrial, commercial, and educational components.

The overall importance of suburban life in the United States is underscored by the results of the 2000 census, which indicated that no less than 50 percent of the country's population resided in the suburbs (up from 37 percent in 1970); the remaining 50 percent were divided between the central cities (30.3 percent) and nonmetropolitan or rural areas (19.7 percent). Of the population living in metropolitan areas, 62.2 percent resided in the suburbs, which in 2000 had 141 million residents. Thus, the suburbs have become the essence of the modern American city.

Just by using such terms as *residential area* and *central business district*, people acknowledge the existence of a regional structure within cities. When you refer to downtown, or to the airport, or to the city zoo, you are in fact referring to urban regions where certain functions prevail (business activity, transportation, and recreation, in the three just mentioned). All of these urban regions or zones lie near or adjacent to each other and together make up the city. But how are they arranged?

# The Spatial Organization of the Typical European City

In the previous section of this chapter we paid considerable attention to the development of the European city. That history is reflected in the geographical structure of the older cities of Europe. The center of those cities are typically characterized by a dense conglomeration of residential, retail, civic, and religious structures. The low degree of functional zonation in the preindustrial urban core is similar to the medieval city. Since many of these cities developed gradually over time, with no overall planning, there is no particular order to the street pattern. Streets are narrow and winding, but some of the neighborhoods are quite well off—a reflection of the advantages in prior eras of living close to the cultural and civic center.

Surrounding these cores is a preindustrial periphery that, in earlier times, housed more of the poorer people. This part of the city was significantly affected by the coming of railroads and larger manufacturing establishments during the industrial era. Functional zonation is somewhat greater there than in the preindustrial core, but it is still comparatively low because their roots can still be traced to an era before large-scale urban planning. Some parts of the preindustrial periphery became wealthy as nineteenth-century urban redevelopment plans paved the way for the emergence of up-scale retail and residential districts.

Beyond the preindustrial core lies a ring of industrial and postindustrial suburbs. These did not grow substantially until well into the twentieth century, and they often are the product of urban planning. As a result, functional zonation is higher in these suburbs. Some developed as commercial centers with high-rise buildings. Others housed millions of migrants streaming into the cities to take industrial jobs, and some of these are now the poorest sections of European cities. Yet others, usually those farther from the center, became bedroom communities for wealthier people with the time and resources to commute to the city for work.

Many of the ethnic neighborhoods in European cities are the product of migrations from former colonies. Algeria was a colony of France, and now Paris and other French cities have distinct Algerian neighborhoods. Similarly, London (the United Kingdom) has a Jamaican neighborhood, and Madrid (Spain) has a distinct Moroccan neighborhood, reflecting colonial ties with these now sovereign countries. Other European countries cultivated relationships with countries outside of Europe after the colonial era. For example, after World War II, Germany invited young men from Turkey to migrate to Germany as guest workers (see Chapter 3). Cities in Germany, such as Frankfurt, have distinct Turkish neighborhoods. The vast majority of migrants currently coming to Europe end up in cities. And most of the migrants to European cities come from the global periphery or from poorer areas in eastern and southern Europe.

# Modeling the North American City

Recognition of regularities in the organization of cities has prompted urban geographers to construct spatial models of cities in various world regions. Early models of North American cities emphasized the functional organization of activities within cities (Box 9.1). As modern cities became increasingly complex, the construction of explanatory models became almost impossible. Today's larger cities are regions in themselves, and cities-within-cities make earlier models seem simplistic. Earlier models continue to shed light on some of the spatial characteristics of the urban centers, but contemporary urban geographers recognize these centers as only one part of the expansive urban area that functions somewhat autonomously from the central city around which it is located.

Following World War II, the availability of personal automobiles and the construction of ring roads and other arteries around cities led to rapid suburbanization, especially around new transportation corridors. The outer edges of many urban areas grew quickly and became more functionally independent of the central city. Suburban downtowns emerged to serve their new local economies. Often located near key freeway intersections, these suburban downtowns developed mainly around big regional shopping centers and attracted industrial parks, office complexes, hotels, restaurants, entertainment facilities, and even sports stadiums. Tysons Corner, Virginia (outside Washington, D.C.) and Irvine, California (outside Los Angeles) flourished as **edge cities**. They attracted tens of thousands of nearby suburbanites—offering workplaces, shopping, leisure activities, and all the other elements of a complete urban environment—thereby loosening remaining ties not only to the central city but to other suburban areas as well (Fig. 9.22).

As early as 1973, American suburbs surpassed the central cities in total employment. By the mid-1980s, in some metropolises in the Sun Belt, the majority of jobs in the metropolitan area were located outside the urban core. Rapid population dispersal to outer suburbs not only created distant nuclei but also reduced the volume and level of interaction between the central city and these emerging suburban cities. This situation made the new outer cities of the suburban ring more self-sufficient as locational advantages produced an ever-greater range of retailing and employment activity. Regional shopping centers in the suburban zone became the CBDs of the outer nuclei, and new business and industrial parks sprang up outside the central city. In short, a new decentered urban metropolitan area came into being.

Present-day Los Angeles and Toronto are cited as prime examples of what is sometimes called a **galactic city**—a complex urban area in which centrality of functions is no longer significant. Instead, the old downtown plays the role of a festival or recreational area, and widely dispersed industrial parks, shopping centers, high-tech industrial spaces, edge-city downtowns, and industrial suburbs are the new centers of economic activity.

## BOX 9.1

Efforts to model the North American city capture some of the changing characteristics of such cities during the early to mid-twentieth century. The first such model to receive wide attention, the **concentric zone model** (see accompanying figure), resulted from sociologist Ernest Burgess's study of Chicago in the 1920s. Burgess's model divides the city into five concentric zones, defined by their function. As the city grew, land was converted into zones around the outside margins of the city, and the concentric zone model emerged. At the center is the CBD (1), itself subdivided into several subdistricts (financial, retail, theater).

The zone of transition (2) is characterized by residential deterioration and encroachment by business and light manufacturing. Zone 3 is a ring of closely spaced, modest homes occupied by the blue-collar labor force. Zone 4 consists of middle-class residences, and Zone 5 is the suburban ring. Burgess described his model as dynamic: As the city grew, inner zones encroached on outer ones, so that CBD functions invaded Zone 2 and the problems of Zone 2 affected the inner margins of Zone 3.

In the late 1930s, Homer Hoyt published his **sector model**, partly as an answer to the limitations of the Burgess model. Hoyt focused on residential patterns, explaining where the wealthy in a city chose to live. Hoyt argued that the city grows outward from the center, so a low-rent area could extend all the way from the CBD to the city's outer edge, creating zones that are shaped like a piece of pie. Hoyt found that the pie-shaped pieces describe the high-rent residential, intermediate rent residential, low-rent residential, education and recreation, transportation, and industrial sectors.

Researchers studied both theories, and Chauncy Harris and Edward Ullman argued that neither the concentric rings nor the sector model adequately reflected city structure by the mid-twentieth century. In the 1940s, they proposed the **multiple nuclei model**. Their model recognizes that the CBD was losing its dominant position as the single nucleus of the urban area. Several of the urban regions shown in the figure have their own nuclei.

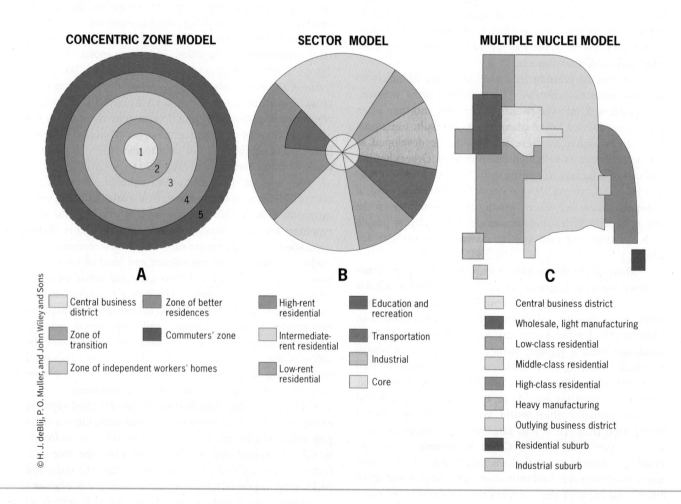

**CONCENTRIC ZONE MODEL**

**SECTOR MODEL**

**MULTIPLE NUCLEI MODEL**

A

B

C

© H. J. deBlij, P. O. Muller, and John Wiley and Sons

Central business district

Zone of better residences

Zone of transition

Commuters' zone

Zone of independent workers' homes

High-rent residential

Intermediate-rent residential

Low-rent residential

Education and recreation

Transportation

Industrial

Core

Central business district

Wholesale, light manufacturing

Low-class residential

Middle-class residential

High-class residential

Heavy manufacturing

Outlying business district

Residential suburb

Industrial suburb

■ **Figure 9.22**
**Tysons Corner, Virginia.**   In the suburbs of Washington, D.C., on Interstate 495 (the Beltway), Tysons Corner has developed as a major edge city, with offices, retail, and commercial services.

*© Rob Crandall/The Image Works*

## Modeling Cities in World Regions

As the number of cities in the world with millions of inhabitants can now be counted in the hundreds, it has become increasingly difficult to model, classify, or typify urban centers. In the 1960s, researchers classified "colonial" cities as urban areas where European transplants dominated the form of the city, laying it out with Western styles. Researchers also drew models of "indigenous" cities that remained remote from globalizing influences and various Western urban forms.

The rapid growth in the population and territorial footprint of **megacities** in the developing world has made it difficult to model many urban areas. Such cities have large populations, a vast territorial extent, and frequently a strained, inadequate infrastructure. For example, Mumbai, India, has more people than the country of Australia. São Paulo, Brazil, covers more land than the country of Belgium. Kinshasa, Democratic Republic of the Congo, is the fastest growing city in Africa. Jakarta, Indonesia, is the largest city in the world without a subway or metro system.

In Middle and South America, Mexico City (Mexico) and São Paulo (Brazil) are now the kinds of megacities that make analysis difficult. Nonetheless, some cities located in South American countries once colonized by Spain have retained a common social-spatial geography. Also, some former colonial cities in Subsaharan Africa have maintained the spatial components lost in megacities such as Lagos (Nigeria) and Kinshasa (Democratic Republic of the Congo).

## The South American City

In 1980, geographers Ernst Griffin and Larry Ford studied South American cities and derived a model of the South American city referred to as the **Griffin–Ford model**. Griffin and Ford found that South American cities blend traditional elements of South American culture with the forces of globalization that are reshaping the urban scene, combining radial sectors and concentric zones.

Anchoring the model is the thriving CBD, which remains the city's primary business, employment, and entertainment focus. The CBD is divided into a traditional market sector and a more modern high-rise sector. Adequate public transit systems and nearby affluent residential areas assure the dominance of the CBD. Emanating outward from the urban core along the city's most prestigious axis is the commercial spine, which is surrounded by the elite residential sector. This widening corridor is essentially an extension of the CBD. It features offices, shopping, high-quality housing for the upper and upper-middle classes, restaurants, theaters, and such amenities as parks, zoos, and golf courses. At the end of the elite spine sector lies an incipient edge city shown as "mall" on the model and flanked by high-priced residences. This development reflects the emergence of suburban nodes from the North American model in South America's cities.

In the Griffin–Ford model, the remaining concentric zones are home to less-well-off residents, who compose the great majority of the urban population. Socioeconomic levels and housing quality decrease markedly with greater distance from the city center (Fig. 9.23). The zone of maturity in the inner city contains the best housing outside the spine sector, attracting middle-class residents who invest sufficiently to keep their solidly built but aging dwellings from deteriorating. The adjacent zone is one of much more modest housing. Interspersed with the more modest areas are densely populated unkempt areas that represent a transition from inner-ring affluence to outer-ring poverty. The outermost zone of peripheral squatter settlements is home to the impoverished and recent migrants who live in shantytowns. **Shantytowns** are unplanned developments of crude dwellings and shelters made mostly of scrap wood, iron, and pieces of cardboard that develop around cities. Although the ring of peripheral squatter settlements consists mainly of teeming, high-density shantytowns, many residents here are surprisingly optimistic about finding work and improving their living conditions.

A structural element common to many South American cities is the **disamenity sector**, the very poorest parts of cities that in extreme cases are not connected to regular city services and are controlled by gangs and drug lords. The

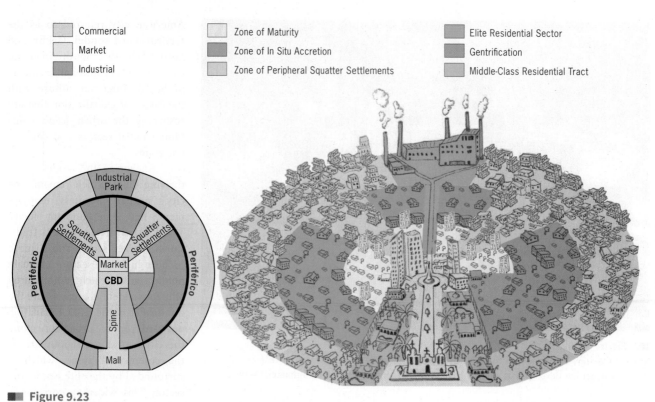

Commercial

Market

Industrial

Zone of Maturity

Zone of In Situ Accretion

Zone of Peripheral Squatter Settlements

Elite Residential Sector

Gentrification

Middle-Class Residential Tract

■ **Figure 9.23**

**Latin American City Model.**   This model includes both the zones created in the original Griffin–Ford model and the new Ford model of the South American city.   *Adapted with permission from*: L. Ford, "A New and Improved Model of Latin American City Structure," *The Geographical Review* 86 (1996), p. 438.

disamenity sectors in South American cities contain relatively unchanging slums known as *barrios* or *favelas*. The worst of these poverty-stricken areas often include large numbers of people who are so poor that they are forced to live in the streets (Fig. 9.24). There is little in the way of regular law enforcement within such communities, and drug lords often run the show—or battle with other drug lords for dominance. Such conditions also prevail in places beyond the ring highway or *periférico*, which is now a feature of most South American cities.

Finally, the Griffin–Ford model displays two smaller sectors: an industrial park, reflecting the ongoing concentration of industrial activity in the city, and a gentrification zone, where historic buildings are preserved. Gentrification remains much less common in South American cities than in North America, but it is an emerging phenomenon.

To what extent is the Griffin–Ford model a realistic portrayal of the South American city? The model reflects the enormous differences between the spaces of privilege and the spaces of abject poverty within the South American city. The model also describes elements of sector development evident in many large South American cities, but the concentricity suggested by the model seems to be breaking down. Figure 9.24 incorporates both the original zones of the Griffin–Ford model and the updates Larry Ford added in a 1996 article.

Larry Ford's updated Griffin–Ford model adds a ring highway (*periférico*) around the outskirts of the city, divides the downtown business district into a CBD and a market, adds a mall near the elite space, and leaves space for suburban industrial parks.

## The African City

At the beginning of this century, Subsaharan Africa included countries with some of the world's lowest levels of urbanization. In the tropical region of Africa, the majority of the people are farmers, and most countries in the tropics remain under 40 percent urbanized. Outside the tropics, the region is about 57 percent urban. Despite the region's comparatively low overall level of urbanization, Africa now has the world's fastest growing cities, followed by those in South Asia and mainland East Asia and South and Middle America. In contrast, the cities of North America, southern South America, and Australia are growing more slowly, and those of western Europe are barely growing at all.

The imprint of European colonialism can still be seen in many African cities. During the colonial period, Europeans laid out prominent urban centers such as Kinshasa (Democratic Republic of the Congo), Nairobi (Kenya), and Harare

## FIELD NOTE

"February 1, 2003. A long-held hope came true today: Thanks to a Brazilian intermediary I was allowed to enter and spend a day in two of Rio de Janeiro's hill-slope *favelas*, an eight-hour walk through one into the other. Here live millions of the city's poor, in areas often ruled by drug lords and their gangs, with minimal or no public services, amid squalor and stench, in discomfort and danger. And yet life in the older *favelas* has become more comfortable as shacks are replaced by more permanent structures, electricity is sometimes available, water supply, however haphazard, is improved, and an informal economy brings goods and services to the residents. I stood in the doorway of a resident's single-room dwelling for this overview of an urban landscape in transition: satellite-television disks symbolize the change going on here. The often blue cisterns catch rainwater; walls are made of rough brick and roofs of corrugated iron or asbestos sheeting. There are no roads or automobile access, so people walk to the nearest road at the bottom of the hill. Locals told me of their hope that they will someday have legal rights to the space they occupy. During his campaign for president of Brazil, former president Lula de Silva suggested that long-term inhabitants should be awarded title, and in 2003 his government approved the notion. It will be complicated: As the photo shows, people live quite literally on top of one another, and mapping the chaos will not be simple (but will be made possible with geographic information systems). This would allow the government to tax

© H. J. de Blij

■ **Figure 9.24**
**Rio de Janeiro, Brazil.**

residents, but it would also allow residents to obtain loans based on the value of their *favela* properties, and bring millions of Brazilians into the formal economy. The hardships I saw on this excursion were often dreadful, but you could sense the hope for and anticipation of a better future. In preparation for the 2014 World Cup, the city of Rio and government of Brazil demolished several favelas and spent millions of dollars working to provide services to remaining favelas in the path of the public eye."

---

(Zimbabwe) in the interior, and Dakar (Senegal), Abidjan (Côte d'Ivoire), Luanda (Angola), Maputo (Mozambique), and other ports along the coast. Africa even has cities that are neither traditional nor colonial. The centers of South Africa's major cities (Johannesburg, Cape Town, and Durban) remain essentially Western, with elements of European as well as American models and a veneer of globalization, including high-rise CBDs and sprawling upper-income suburbs.

As a result of this diversity, it is difficult to formulate a model of the African city. Studies of African cities indicate that the central city often consists of not one but three CBDs (Fig. 9.25): a remnant of the colonial CBD, an informal and sometimes periodic market zone, and a transitional business center where commerce is conducted from curbside, stalls, or storefronts. Vertical development occurs mainly in the former colonial CBD; the traditional business center is usually a zone of single-story buildings with some traditional architecture; and the market zone tends to be open-air, informal, yet still important. Sector development marks the encircling zone of

ethnic and mixed neighborhoods (often characterized by strong ethnic identities as people of ethnic kin tend to cluster together). Since many African cities began as mining towns, such operations still occur in conjunction with this zone in some instances. Manufacturing companies still function here—taking advantage of the proximity to a nearby labor force. Invariably, fast-growing African cities are encircled by vast shantytowns rapidly growing as a result of significant in-migration.

## The Southeast Asian City

Some of the most populated cities in the world are in Southeast Asia. The city of Kuala Lumpur, Malaysia, is a complex of high-rise development, including the 1483-foot-tall Petronas Towers, which until recently was the world's tallest building. The city of Jakarta, Indonesia, called Jabotabek by the locals, is an enormous conurbation of Bogor, Tangerang, and Bekasi.

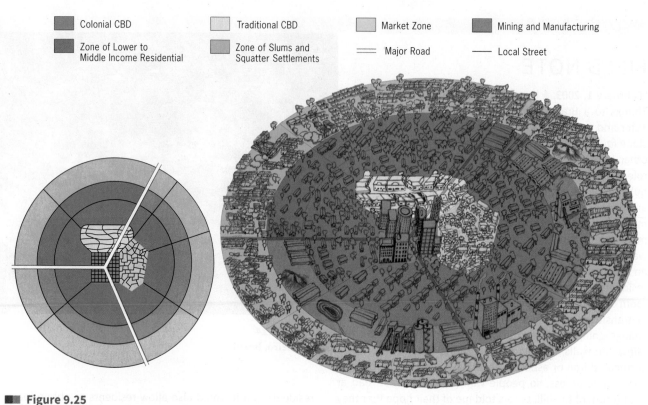

| Colonial CBD | Traditional CBD | Market Zone | Mining and Manufacturing |
|---|---|---|---|
| Zone of Lower to Middle Income Residential | Zone of Slums and Squatter Settlements | Major Road | Local Street |

■ **Figure 9.25**
**Subsaharn Africa City Model.** One model of the African city includes a colonial CBD, a traditional CBD, and a market zone.
© E. H. Fouberg, A. B. Murphy, H. J. de Blij, and John Wiley & Sons, Inc.

In 1967, urban geographer T. G. McGee studied the medium-sized cities of Southeast Asia and found that they exhibit similar land-use patterns, creating a model referred to as the **McGee model** (Fig. 9.26). The focal point of the city is the old colonial port zone combined with the largely commercial district that surrounds it. McGee found no formal CBD; rather, he found the elements of the CBD present as separate clusters surrounding the old colonial port zone: the government zone; the Western commercial zone (practically a CBD by itself); the alien commercial zone, dominated by Chinese merchants whose residences are attached to their places of business; and the mixed land-use zone that contains miscellaneous economic activities, including light industry. The other nonresidential areas are the market-gardening zone at the outskirts of the urban area and, still farther from the city, a recently built industrial park or "estate."

The residential zones in McGee's model are similar to those in the Griffin–Ford model of the South American city. Other similarities between the McGee and Griffin–Ford model are the hybrid structure of sectors and zones, an elite residential sector that includes new suburbs, an inner-city zone of middle-income housing, and peripheral low-income

squatter settlements. One main difference is that the McGee model includes middle-income housing in a suburban zone, reflecting the larger middle class in these cities of the global semiperiphery and the small middle class in South American cities.

Regardless of the region or city, we recognize that models do not explain how or why cities are organized the way they are. A model of a city shows us an end product, whether planned or not, and suggests the forces that created that end product.

Employing the concepts defined in this section of the chapter, compare and contrast the Latin American city model with either the African city or Southeast Asian city model. What is similar—can you see influences of colonialism in each model; are the poorest residential areas located on the outskirts of the city; where are the wealthiest residential areas located relative to manufacturing zones?

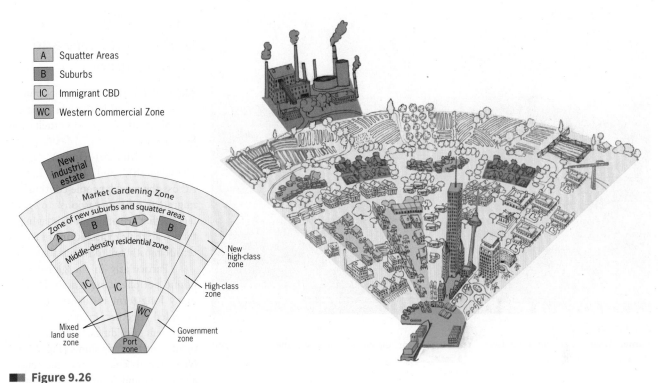

**A** Squatter Areas

**B** Suburbs

**IC** Immigrant CBD

**WC** Western Commercial Zone

New industrial estate

Market Gardening Zone

Zone of new suburbs and squatter areas

A B A B

Middle-density residential zone

IC IC

WC

Mixed land use zone

Port zone

Government zone

High-class zone

New high-class zone

■■ **Figure 9.26**

**Southeast Asian City Model.** A model of land use in the Southeast Asian city includes sectors and zones within each sector. *Adapted with permission from*: T. G. McGee, *The Southeast Asian City*, London: Bell, 1967, p. 128.

## HOW DO PEOPLE SHAPE CITIES?

People and institutions make places, including cities. The roles individual people, governments, corporations, developers, financial lenders, and realtors play in shaping cities vary across the world. Government planning agencies can directly affect the layout of cities by restricting the kinds of development allowed in certain regions or zones of cities.

Through **zoning laws**, cities divide up the city and designate the kinds of development allowed in each zone. Portland, Oregon, is often described as the best planned city in North America because it is built around free transportation in the central city to discourage the use of cars. Portland is a compact city with office buildings and residential zones in close proximity to encourage walking, biking, and public transportation. On the other hand, Houston, Texas, is the only large city that does not have zoning laws on the books. Houstonites voted against the creation of zoning laws three different times (most recently in 1993).

In addition to government planning and zoning laws, people shape cities by choosing to live in certain neighborhoods and by opening stores, houses of worship, and even sporting fields that reflect the values of their culture. If you wander through the neighborhoods of any city and pay close attention, you can see differences in the existence of single-family or multifamily homes, in particular styles of construction and building materials, in the distance between houses, in the nature and style of vegetation around houses, in the distance between the houses and the streets, and even in the amount of space devoted to automobile movement and storage.

Comparing and contrasting the urban cultural landscapes of two cities helps us understand the different social and cultural forces at play. Compare Figure 9.27 with Figure 9.28. Analyze each picture and guess which city is located in a wealthy country in the world and which is located in a poor country. What factors can you consider? You may look at the presence or absence of high-rise buildings, the aesthetics of the buildings, the road, and the distance between houses. After doing so, you might guess that Figure 9.27 is in the wealthy country. Look again. This time, look for whether there are telephone and electrical wires, and note what building materials were used. Figure 9.27 is actually in a poorer country; it is the city of Lomé, Togo, in Subsaharan Africa. Figure 9.28 is part of a suburb of Tokyo, Japan. Japanese houses in this middle-class neighborhood are almost on top of each other because the city is so densely populated that land is at a premium. In Lomé, the high rises are part of the CBD, and some of the houses immediately surrounding them are where the wealthy live. The houses in the foreground are where the poor live. Here the roofs are tin or cardboard, the

**■ Figure 9.27**

**Lomé, Togo.** The city's landscape reflects a clear dichotomy between the "haves" and "have-nots."

# Shaping Cities in the Global Periphery and Semiperiphery

Many of the world's most populous cities are located in the less prosperous parts of the world, including São Paulo (Brazil), Mexico City (Mexico), Mumbai (India), Dhaka (Bangladesh), and Delhi (India). Across the world, people continue to migrate to cities in response to "pull" factors that are often more imaginary than real; their expectations of a better life mostly fail to materialize.

Particularly in the global economic periphery, new arrivals (and many long-term residents, too) are crowded together in overpopulated apartment buildings, dismal tenements, and teeming slums (Fig. 9.29). New arrivals come from other cities and towns and from the rural coun-

houses are makeshift, and utility lines are lacking. Notice that in this picture of Lomé, we see no evidence of a middle class; this is common in cities of the periphery, where there are "haves" and "have-nots," but little in between.

tryside, often as large families; they add to the cities' rate of natural growth. Housing cannot keep up with this massive inflow. Almost overnight huge shantytowns develop around these cities. The overcrowding and dismal conditions do not

**■ Figure 9.28**

**Tokyo, Japan.**    The city's landscape reflects the presence of a large middle class in a densely populated city.

# GUEST FIELD NOTE

## Manila, the Philippines

I passed through cargo shipping piers in Manila, the Philippines, and encountered row after row of hand-built squatter houses. I was struck by the scale of the settlements and the sheer number of people who inhabit them. I was shocked at the level of squalor in people's living conditions. The garbage scavengers in this picture wore cotton gloves and held prods to dig through the trash for items they can use, trade, or sell. The poor and destitute live throughout the city because housing stocks are inadequate, underlying poverty persists, and thousands flock to Manila daily recognizing that petty services and even trash picking often offer more opportunity than life in the rural provinces.

*Credit: Johnathan Walker, James Madison University*

■ **Figure 9.29**

deter additional urban migration; as a result, millions of people spend their entire lives in urban housing of wretched quality.

Cities in poorer parts of the world generally lack enforceable zoning laws. Without zoning laws, cities in the periphery have mixed land use throughout the city. For example, in cities such as Madras, India (and in other cities in India), open space between high-rise buildings is often occupied by squatter settlements (Fig. 9.30). In Bangkok, Thailand, elementary schools and noisy, polluting factories stand side by side. In Nairobi, Kenya, hillside villas overlook some of Africa's worst slums. Over time, such incongruities may disappear, as is happening in many cities in East Asia. Rising land values and greater demand for enforced zoning regulations are transforming the central cities of East Asia. But in South Asia, Subsaharan Africa, Southwest Asia, North Africa, and Middle and South America, unregulated, helter-skelter growth continues.

Across the global periphery, the one trait all major cities display is the stark contrast between the wealthy and the poor. Sharp contrasts between wealthy and poor areas can be found in major cities all over the world—for example, homeless people sleep on heating grates half a block from the White House in Washington, D.C. Yet the intensity and scale of the contrast are greater in cities of the periphery. If you stand in the central area of Cairo, Egypt, you see what appears to be a relatively modern, Mediterranean metropolis (Fig. 9.31). But if you get on a bus and ride it toward the city's outskirts, that impression fades almost immediately as paved streets give way to dusty alleys, apartment buildings to harsh tenements, and sidewalk coffee shops to broken doors and

© Erin H. Fouberg

■ **Figure 9.30**

**Hyderabad, India.** Temporary shelters, built to withstand the summer monsoon, protect the migrants who work to build the new construction in the background.

## FIELD NOTE

"Central Cairo is full of the multistory buildings, transportation arteries, and commercial signs that characterize most contemporary big cities. Outside of a number of mosques, few remnants of the old medieval city remain. The first blow came in the nineteenth century, when a French-educated ruler was determined to recast Cairo as a world-class city. Paris's Baron von Hausman transformed the urban core into a zone of broad, straight streets. In more recent years the forces of modern international capitalism have had the upper hand. There is little sense of an overall vision for central Cairo. Instead, it seems to be a hodge-podge of buildings and streets devoted to commerce, administration, and a variety of producer and consumer services."

**Figure 9.31**
Cairo, Egypt City Center.

windows (Fig. 9.32). Traffic-choked, garbage-strewn, polluted Cairo is home to an estimated 9.1 million people, more than one-fifth of Egypt's population; the city is bursting at the seams. And still people continue to arrive, seeking the better life that pulls countless migrants from the countryside year after year.

## Shaping Cities in the Global Core

The goals people have in establishing cities have changed over time. People constantly remake the cities where they live, reinventing neighborhoods or changing layouts to reflect changing goals and aesthetics. During the segregation era in the United States, realtors, financial lenders, and city

## FIELD NOTE

"Moving out from central Cairo, evidence of the city's rapid growth is all around you. These hastily built housing units are part of the (often losing) effort to keep up with the city's exploding growth. From a city of just one million people in 1930, Cairo's population expanded to six million by 1986. And then high growth rates really kicked in. Although no one knows the exact size of the contemporary city, most estimates suggest that Cairo's population has doubled in the last 20 years. This growth has placed a tremendous strain on city services. Housing has been a particularly critical problem—leading to a landscape outside the urban core dominated by hastily built, minimally functional, and aesthetically nondescript housing projects."

**Figure 9.32**
Cairo, Egypt Residential Area.

governments defined and segregated spaces in urban environments. For example, before the civil rights movement of the 1960s, financial institutions in the business of lending money could engage in a practice known as **redlining**. They would identify what they considered to be risky neighborhoods in cities—often predominantly black neighborhoods—and refuse to offer loans to anyone purchasing a house in the neighborhood encircled by red lines on their maps. This practice, which is now illegal, worked against those living in poorer neighborhoods and helped to precipitate a downward spiral in which poor neighborhoods became increasingly rundown because funds were not available for upkeep or to purchase homes for sale.

Before the civil rights movement, realtors could purposely sell a house in a white neighborhood at a very low price to a black buyer. In a practice called **blockbusting**, realtors would solicit white residents of the neighborhood to sell their homes under the guise that the neighborhood was going downhill because a black person or family had moved in. This produced what urban geographers and sociologists call *white flight*—movement of whites from the city and adjacent neighborhoods to the outlying suburbs. Blockbusting led to significant turnover in housing, which of course benefited real estate agents through the commissions they earned as representatives of buyers and sellers. Blockbusting also prompted landowners to sell their properties at low prices to get out of the neighborhood quickly, which in turn allowed developers to subdivide lots and build tenements. Typically, developers did not maintain tenements well, dropping the property values even further.

Developers and governments are also important actors in shaping cities. In cities of the global core that have experienced high levels of suburbanization, people left the city proper for the suburbs in search of single-family homes, yards, better schools, and safety. With suburbanization, city governments lose tax revenue, as middle- and upper-class taxpayers leave the city and pay taxes in the suburbs instead. In order to counter the suburbanization trend, city governments are encouraging commercialization of the CBD and gentrification of neighborhoods in and around that district.

The plans that city governments develop to revive central cities usually involve cleaning streets, sidewalks, and buildings; tearing down old, abandoned buildings; and building up commercial offerings and residences. City governments have often created programs to encourage **commercialization** of CBDs, which entails transforming the central business district into an area attractive to residents and tourists alike. Several cities, including Miami, New York, and Baltimore, have created waterfront "theme" areas to attract visitors. These areas include festival marketplaces, parks with exotic sculptures and play areas, and amusement zones occupying former industrial sites. Cities including Detroit and Minneapolis commercialize their CBDs by building or using tax incentives to attract professional sports stadiums to the central areas in the city. Ventures have been successful in attracting tourists and in generating business,

but they alone cannot revive downtowns because they cannot attract what the core of the city needs most: permanent residents with a stake in its future. The newly commercialized downtowns often stand apart from the rest of the central city.

Beginning in the 1960s, poor central-city neighborhoods located conveniently close to CBDs began to attract buyers who were willing to move back into the city to rehabilitate rundown houses and live in central-city neighborhoods. A process called **gentrification**—the rehabilitation of deteriorated houses in low-income neighborhoods—took hold in areas near the centers of many cities.

In the United States, gentrification began in cities with a tight housing market and defined central-city neighborhoods, including San Francisco, Portland, and Chicago. Gentrification slowed in the 1990s, but it is growing again as city governments encourage gentrification through beautification programs and significant tax breaks to people who buy up abandoned or dilapidated housing. The growing interest in central-city housing has resulted in part from the changing character of American society: the proportion of childless couples (heterosexual and homosexual) is growing, as is the number of single people in the population. Childless couples and singles often choose to live in cities because the suburbs do not look as attractive to them as they typically do to families with young children. Gentrified central-city neighborhoods attract residents who want to live within walking distance of their workplace and close to cultural, entertainment, and recreational amenities, nightlife, and restaurants (Fig. 9.33).

One consequence of gentrification is increased housing prices in central-city neighborhoods. Gentrification usually displaces lower income residents because property taxes rise as land values rise, and the cost of goods and services in the neighborhood, from parking to restaurants, rises as well. For urbanites displaced by gentrification, the consequences can be serious. Rising housing costs associated with gentrification have played a key role in the growing homelessness problem facing American cities.

The suburb is not immune to gentrification. In suburbs that are close to the city or directly connected by commuter rail, people purchase smaller or older homes with the intention of tearing the house down and building a much larger home. The homes intended for suburban demolition are called **teardowns**. In their place, suburbanites build newer homes that often are supersized and stretch to the outer limits of the lot. New supersized mansions are sometimes called **McMansions** (Fig. 9.34).

Like gentrification in the city, the teardown phenomenon changes the landscape and increases average housing values, tax revenue for the city, and the average household income of the neighborhood. Unlike inner-city gentrification, with teardowns the original houses are destroyed instead of preserved. Also unlike inner-city gentrification, teardowns often occur in middle-class and wealthy suburbs such as Greenwich, Connecticut, and Hinsdale, Illinois.

# FIELD NOTE

"In 2008, downtown Fort Worth, Texas, looked quite different than it did when I first visited in 1997. In that 11-year period, business leaders in the city of Fort Worth gentrified the downtown. The Bass family, who has a great deal of wealth from oil holdings and who now owns about 40 blocks of downtown Fort Worth, was instrumental in the city's gentrification. In the 1970s and 1980s, members of the Bass family looked at empty, stark, downtown Fort Worth and sought a way to revitalize the downtown. They worked with the Tandy family to build and revitalize the spaces of the city, which took off in the late 1990s and into the present century. The crown jewel in the gentrified Fort Worth is the beautiful cultural center called the Bass Performance Hall, named for Nancy Lee and Perry R. Bass, which opened in 1998."

© Erin H. Fouberg

■■ **Figure 9.33**
**Fort Worth, Texas.**

© Erin H. Fouberg

■■ **Figure 9.34**
**Hinsdale, Illinois.**   In this upscale suburb of Chicago, a new McMansion stands in the place where a smaller house (similar in size to the one still standing in the right of the photo) used to stand. In the last 20 years, about 25 percent of Hinsdale's houses have been torn down to make room for much larger houses.

Greenwich, a high-end neighborhood in Fairfield County, Connecticut, just outside of New York City, issued 138 permits for teardowns in 2004 (56 more than it did the year before). The collapse of the housing market brought a decline in the number of teardowns in Fairfield County starting in 2007, but in May 2010 the *Wall Street Journal* reported that teardown permits had begun rising again in Fairfield County. Permits in Greenwich, however, did not rise. As noted in the *Wall Street Journal,* "The most expensive corners of Fairfield County, including Greenwich, haven't seen much of a pickup in teardowns, local brokers say. A surplus of homes priced at more than $2 million, and difficulties in getting financing for these purchases, has kept that activity to a minimum."

In Hinsdale (just outside Chicago), one-third of the suburb's houses have been torn down since 1986. Those in favor of teardowns argue that the phenomenon slows urban sprawl by replacing existing homes with new homes, rather than converting farmland to residential lots. Those opposed to teardowns see the houses as too large for their lots, dwarfing the neighboring houses, and destroying the character of the street by demolishing the older homes on it.

## Urban Sprawl and New Urbanism

As populations have grown in certain areas of the United States, such as the Sun Belt and the West, urban areas have experienced **urban sprawl**—unrestricted growth of housing, commercial developments, and roads over large expanses of land, with little concern for urban planning. Urban sprawl is easy to spot as you drive down major roadways in any urbanized part of the country. You will see strip malls, big box stores, chain restaurants, huge intersections, and numerous housing developments, all spread out over many acres (Fig. 9.35). Sprawl is a phenomenon of the automobile era. Cities that expanded before the automobile typically grew "up" instead of "out." For instance, Boston grew around the marketplace and port, but it grew before the automobile, resulting in development over smaller areas. When you go through the central city of Boston today, you can walk where you need to go or take the T (metro). Places are built up vertically, and curving, narrow streets and commercial developments with a flavor of the old city (Quincy Market) give the city a cozy, intimate feel.

Does population growth explain which cities experience the most urban sprawl? In a study of sprawl from 1960 through the 1990s, Leon Kolankiewicz and Roy Beck (two anti-sprawl writers) used United States Census data on urbanized areas and found that urban sprawl happened even in urban areas without significant population growth. In the

**TABLE 9.1**

**Most Sprawling Metro Areas with a Population Over 1 Million in the United States.**  Smart Growth America created an index to measure urban sprawl based on development density, land use mix, activity centering, and street accessibility. These then major metro areas have the lowest density over a wide space, creating urban sprawl.  *Data from:* Ewing, R., Rolf Pendall and Don Chen. Measuring Sprawl and Its Impact. Volume 1. Smart Growth America. http://www.smartgrowthamerica.org/documents/MeasuringSprawlTechnical.pdf.

| MOST SPRAWLING LARGE METRO AREAS, 2014 | |
|---|---|
| Cities with a population of more than one million | State |
| 1. Atlanta-Sandy Springs/Marietta | GA |
| 2. Nashville/Davidson/Murfreesboro/Franklin | TN |
| 3. Riverside-San Bernardino/Ontario | CA |
| 4. Warren/Troy/Farmington Hills | MI |
| 5. Charlotte/Gastonia-Rock Hill | NC/SC |
| 6. Memphis | TN/MS/AR |
| 7. Birmingham-Hoover | AL |
| 8. Rochester | NY |
| 9. Richmond | VA |
| 10. Houston/Sugar Land/Baytown | TX |

United States, urban sprawl is more common in the Sun Belt of the South (Atlanta) and in the West (Houston) in urban areas whose population is rapidly growing (Table 9.1). Yet, even in cities such as Detroit and Pittsburgh, where urban populations fell between 1960 and 1990—by 7 percent in Detroit and 9 percent in Pittsburgh—urban sprawl increased the urbanized areas of the cities by 28 percent and 30 percent, respectively. When urban sprawl happens, farmlands and old industrial sites are razed, roads are built or widened, strip malls are erected, and housing developments come to monopolize the horizon.

To counter urban sprawl, a group of architects, urban planners, and developers (now numbering over 2000 in more than 20 countries) proposed an urban design vision they call new urbanism. Forming the Congress for the New Urbanism in 1993, the group defines **new urbanism** as development, urban revitalization, and suburban reforms that create walkable neighborhoods with a diversity of housing and jobs. On their website, the Congress for the New Urbanism explains that "New Urbanists support regional planning for open space, appropriate architecture and planning, and the balanced development of jobs and housing. They believe these strategies are the best way to reduce how

Ethan Miller/Getty Images

■ **Figure 9.35**

**Henderson, Nevada.**  Henderson is the largest suburb of Las Vegas, and it was also the fastest-growing urban settlement in the United States between 1990 and 2000. Many of the houses in this photograph are empty today, as Las Vegas had ranked first or second in the number of home and rental vacancies in United States cities in 2009 and 2010.

# FIELD NOTE

"When I visited Celebration, Florida, in 1997, one year after residents moved into the first houses in the community, I felt like I was walking onto a movie or television set. The architecture in the Walt Disney-designed new urbanist development looked like a quintessential American town. Each house has a porch, but on the day I was there, the porches sat empty—waiting to welcome the arrival of their owners at the end of the work day. We walked through town, past the 50s'-style movie marquee, and ate lunch at a 50s'-style diner. At that point, Celebration was still growing. Across the street from the 'Bank of Celebration' stood a sign marking the future home of the 'Church in Celebration.'

In 2013, I returned to Celebration, and I spent the day walking the same streets. The 'Church in Celebration,' a Presbyterian community church, was built, and the main street through the town square was hosting an arts festival focused on dogs. The city had grown to 11,000 residents, suffered its first murder, and was experiencing a higher rate of foreclosures than the rest of Florida. The movie theater still stood but no longer showed movies. A Starbucks took up a main corner in town, standing next door to a Morgan Stanley office and an Irish pub. Disney no longer owns the town, but the influence of the Disney vision still stands, with architectural covenants allowing only certain house styles, a few pastel house colors, and hiding the trash and cars in alleys."

■ **Figure 9.36**
**Celebration, Florida.**

long people spend in traffic, to increase the supply of affordable housing, and to rein in urban sprawl." New urbanists want to create neighborhoods that promote a sense of community and a sense of place.

The most famous new urbanist projects are cities that new urbanists designed from the ground up, including Seaside, Florida (featured in the movie *The Truman Show*), West Laguna, California, and Kentlands, Maryland. When new urbanists build a town, the design is reminiscent of Christaller over a much smaller area. The planners choose the central shopping areas and open spaces and develop the neighborhoods around them, with housing clustered around the central space so that people can walk to the shopping area within five minutes. One goal of new urbanist designs is to build housing more densely, taking up less space. Along with that, making shopping and other amenities walkable decreases

dependency on the automobile, which in the process helps the environment.

Although some see new urbanist designs as manufactured communities and feel disconnected in a new urbanist space, others see these designs as an important antidote to sprawl. Celebration, Florida, is a remarkable new urbanist space: It is adjacent to Walt Disney's theme parks, was envisioned by Walt Disney himself, and was owned by the Disney Company (Fig. 9.36). Built in 1994, Celebration is centered on Market Street, a shopping district with restaurants (including a 1950s-style diner and a pizza place), a town hall, banks, a post office, and a movie theater with a nostalgic marquee (Fig. 9.37). The town includes schools, a health center, a fitness center, and churches. The Disney Company chose certain architectural styles for the houses in Celebration, and builders initially offered homes and townhouses in

■ **Figure 9.37**

**Celebration, Florida.** Opened in 1996 with two screens and operated by AMC, the Celebration Cinema closed in 2010. The spires remain landmarks in the town.

a price range from $300,000 to over $1 million. To meet the new urbanist goal of incorporating diverse people in a community, Celebration includes apartments for rent and condominiums for sale.

For geographers new urbanism marks a redefinition of space in the city. Public spaces, they say, become privatized for the enjoyment of the few (the residents of the neighborhood). Geographers Stuart Aitken, Don Mitchell, and Lynn Staeheli note that as new urbanism strives to turn neighborhoods back in time, "spaces and social functions historically deemed public (such as parks, neighborhood centers, shopping districts)" are privatized. The houses with porches that encourage neighbors to talk and the parks that are within walking distance for the residents create "mythic landscapes that are ingratiating for those who can afford them and exclusionary for those who cannot."

Noted geographer David Harvey offers one of the strongest critiques of new urbanism, explaining first that most new urbanist designs are "greenfield" projects designed for the affluent to make suburban areas more livable. This fact is

evidence, Harvey argues, that the new urbanism movement is a kind of "spatial determinism" that does not recognize that "the fundamental difficulty with modernism was its persistent habit of privileging spatial forms over social processes." Harvey, and others who critique new urbanism, claim that new urbanism does nothing to break down the social conditions that privilege some while disadvantaging others; that new urbanist projects take away much of the grittiness and character of the city; and that the "communities" that new urbanists form through their projects are exclusionary communities that deepen the racial segregation of cities.

Despite the critiques against new urbanism, developments in the new urbanist tradition are attracting a growing number of people, and when they are situated within cities, they can work against urban sprawl.

## Gated Communities

As you drive through urban spaces in the United States, suburban and central city alike, you will note more and more neighborhoods being developed or redesigned to align with new urbanist principles. In your inventory of landscapes, even more overwhelming will be the proliferation of gated communities. **Gated communities** are fenced-in neighborhoods with controlled access gates for people and automobiles. Often, gated communities have security cameras and security forces (privatized police) keeping watch over the community, as the main objective of a gated community is to create a space of safety within the uncertain urban world. A secondary objective is to maintain or increase housing values in the neighborhood through enforcement of the neighborhood association's bylaws that control everything from the color of a house to the character and size of additions.

During the late 1980s and early 1990s, developers in the United States began building gated communities in urban areas around the country. In a 2001 census of housing, the United States government reported that 16 million people, or about 6 percent of Americans, live in gated communities. The urban design of gating communities has diffused around the globe at record speed, with gated communities now found in Europe, Asia, Africa, and Latin America.

In poorer countries, where cities are divided between wealthy and poor, gated communities provide another layer of comfort for the city's wealthy. In the large cities of Latin America and Africa, you commonly see walls around individual houses belonging to wealthy and middle-class families, walling in yards and pools and keeping out crime. These walls often include barbed wire or shards of glass fixed to the top to discourage intruders from scaling the walls. During the last ten years, many neighborhoods in these cities have added gates around the neighborhoods in addition to the walls. Walled houses and gated communities in the wealthy northern suburbs of Johannesburg, South Africa, are threatening the desegregation of the post-Apartheid city. White, wealthy residents fear crime in the city which, along with neighboring

© Alexander B. Murphy

■ **Figure 9.38**
**Guangzhou, China.** This gated housing community just outside the city is much more serene than the teeming metropolis next door.

Pretoria, has a murder rate of 5000 per year (in an area with about 5 million people). In response to their fear of crime, by 2004 people in the suburbs of Johannesburg had blocked off over 2500 streets and posted guards to control access to these streets. Many view the gated communities as a new form of segregation. Since the vast majority of the crimes in the city occur in poor black townships or in the central city, the concern is that these developments only worsen the plight of less well-off segments of society.

Gated communities have taken off in China as well, with communities now crossing socioeconomic classes and assuming a prominent place in the urban landscape (Fig. 9.38). Like the gated communities in Europe and North America, the gated communities of China privatize spaces and exclude outsiders with gates, security cameras, and restricted access. However, China's gated communities are five to ten times more densely populated than Europe's and North America's. Geographer Youqin Huang has found other differences between gated communities in China and those in North America and Europe. China has a long history of gated communities, dating back to the first Chinese cities and persisting since. Huang argues that the "collectivism-oriented culture and tight political control" in China explain why the Chinese government built gated communities during the socialist period and why a proliferation of privately developed gated communities has occurred since China's housing reform in 1998 promoted individual home ownership.

In Europe and North America, gated communities are not only for the wealthy and privileged; the middle and lower classes also have a growing desire to feel safe at home. Some urban planners have encouraged governments to recast low-income housing as small communities, gated from each other, in order to reduce the flowthrough traffic and associated crime. Cities have sometimes torn down enormous high rises, typically ridden with crime and referred to as "the projects," including Cabrini Green in Chicago and Pruitt-Igoe in St. Louis, in an effort to remake the spaces of the poor into "defensible," and more livable, spaces.

Champions of middle-income and low-income neighborhoods seek to create a sense of community and make the spaces "defensible" from undesired activities such as drug dealing and prostitution. One of the best-documented cases of gating a middle-income community is the Five Oaks district of Dayton, Ohio, a neighborhood that is about 50 percent African American and 50 percent white and has a high rate of rentals. Urban planner Oscar Newman encouraged planners in Dayton to divide the 2000 households in the Five Oaks district into ten smaller, gated communities with restricted access. The city turned most of the residential streets in each of these mini-neighborhoods into cul-de-sacs. They have experienced a serious reduction in crime, along with an increase in housing sales and housing values.

## Urban Geopolitics

Geographer Stephen Graham coined the term *urban geopolitics* to draw attention to the impact of global-scale geopolitical developments on the character of cities. Urban areas play a central role in twenty-first-century geopolitics. The existence of globe-circling surveillance networks and advanced weaponry has transformed how war is conducted and planned—prompting militant groups to retreat to urban areas where they can hide and take advantage of the urban infrastructure. The door-to-door urban combat that marked the recent United States campaign in Iraq illustrates these changes. A key theme geographers have identified in their studies of contemporary warscapes is **urbicide**, which Graham defines as the deliberate killing of the city. Urbicide was used to describe the conflict in the Balkans in the 1990s. The Yugoslav National Army intentionally destroyed Bosnia's famous Mostar Bridge in 1992 in a move that has since been interpreted not as strategic, but as rooted in the desire to destroy cultural property (Fig. 9.39). Geographer Sara Fregonese has traced the concept of urbicide to Beirut in the 1970s, where local militias used barricades to take control over parts of the city and restrict movement.

© Alexander B. Murphy

■ **Figure 9.39**
**Mostar, Bosnia and Herzegovina.** Stari Most means Old Bridge, but this photo, taken in 2009, depicts the new bridge that was built in 2004 to replace the one destroyed in 1993. Long considered to be a triumph of Islamic architecture, the new bridge looks exactly like the old one, which long served to connect Islamic and non-Islamic parts of the city.

Terrorism has affected cities in profound ways. In the wake of large-scale terrorist attacks in Beirut, New York, Madrid, London, and Mumbai, geographers and other urban scholars have highlighted changes in everyday urban life, notions of security, and urban technology and defensive infrastructure. Following the attacks, highly visible security apparatuses appeared almost overnight in many cities around the world. In post–9/11 Washington, D.C., concrete barricades, jersey barriers, and bollards now surround government facilities as well as embassies and other high-profile buildings. In some cases, these fixtures close off entire blocks of sidewalks and bike lanes in the name of safety and security. In other cities, local governments have redirected the flow of traffic in the urban core, even closing some streets off to vehicular traffic altogether. London's "ring of steel" was erected as a physical defensive cordon following a spate of small bombings in the 1970s to root out terrorist activities. Surveillance systems, too, have shaped contemporary urban landscapes. Nowhere is this phenomenon more apparent than in London, where highly controversial closed-circuit television (CCTV) cameras are seemingly everywhere, tracking people's movement across public spaces in the name of public safety.

You don't have to look any further than Hollywood to see the ways in which urban violence, security infrastructure, and surveillance technology have transformed urban systems and popular culture. Think about recent espionage and action films, the Jason Bourne, James Bond, and Jack Ryan franchises. Note the extent to which cities are often characters in the plots, providing venues upon which global wars, militant insurgencies, cyber-attacks, bombings, and even entertaining car chases take place. These films often make extensive use of urban surveillance technology as a mechanism to track characters' movements, monitor space, and govern from a distance.

## Immigration and the Changing Ethnic Geography of Cities

Immigration is changing the spatial-cultural geography of cities around the world. As immigrants settle in large numbers in transitional areas, locals frequently move out. Walking from the city center of Paris out through immigrant neighborhoods, one can see the cultural landscape change to reflect the significant number of immigrants from the "Maghreb" of Africa, the region of North Africa around Algeria and Morocco. Maghrebis are by far the most numerous inhabitants in the tough, hardscrabble immigrant neighborhoods around Paris, where unemployment is high, crime is widespread, and resentment festers.

Whether a public housing zone is divided into ethnic neighborhoods depends in large part on government policy. Urban geographers Christian Kesteloot and Cees Cortie studied housing policies and zones in Brussels, Belgium, and Amsterdam, the Netherlands. They found that Brussels has very little public housing and that immigrants live in privately owned rentals throughout the city. Kesteloot and Cortie also found that immigrant groups in Brussels who came from a distinct region of their home country (especially rural regions), such as the Turks in Brussels, tend to cluster in ethnic neighborhoods. In contrast, the researchers reported that immigrants who came from cities, such as the Moroccans in Brussels, chose rental units scattered throughout the city and therefore did not establish ethnic neighborhoods in Brussels.

Amsterdam is quite different from Brussels: Amsterdam has a great deal of public housing and few ethnic neighborhoods within the public housing units. When immigration to Amsterdam from former colonies (Indonesia, Surinam) and noncolonies (Morocco and Turkey) increased in the 1960s, Amsterdammers moved from the transition zone of public housing to neighboring towns such as Almere. The Dutch government then implemented a policy in the public housing zone that slowed the creation of ethnic neighborhoods. The Dutch government allots public housing to legal immigrants by assigning homes on a sequential basis in the city's zone of transition, where some 80 percent of the housing stock is public housing. As a result of government assignment of housing, if you walk through the public housing zone of Amsterdam, you will find a family from Suriname living next to an Indonesian family and a Moroccan family, not just other Surinamese. The housing and neighborhoods are multicultural. The ethnic groups maintain their local cultures through religious and cultural organizations rather than through residential segregation. In Amsterdam, the call to Friday prayer for Muslims rings out all over the immigrant areas, as Muslims from various countries are spread throughout the city.

In many cities in the global economic periphery and semiperiphery, a sea of slum development begins where the permanent buildings end, in some cases engulfing and dwarfing the central city. If you stand on a hill outside Lima (Peru) or overlooking the Cape Flats near Cape Town (South Africa), you see an unchanging panorama of makeshift shacks built of every conceivable material, vying for every foot of space, extending to the horizon. You will notice few, if any, trees, and you will see narrow footpaths leading to a few unpaved streets that go into the central city.

Millions of migrants travel to such environments every year. The total number of people living in these types of slum developments is uncertain because government control is impossible and enumeration impractical. In Rio de Janeiro (Brazil), the migrants build their dwellings on dangerous, landslide-prone slopes; in Port Moresby (Papua New Guinea), the migrants sink stilts in the mud and build out over the water, risking wind and waves. In Kolkata (India), thousands of migrants do not even try to erect shelters: There and in many other cities they live in the streets, under bridges, even in storm drains. City governments do not have the resources to adequately educate, medicate, or police the burgeoning populations, let alone to provide even minimal housing for most.

The people living in most shanty settlements are not really squatters—they pay rent. When the settlements expand outward from the central city, they occupy land owned by previous residents, families who farmed what were once the rural areas beyond the city's edge. Some of the farming families were favored by the former colonial administration; they moved into the cities but continued to own the lands their farms were on. As shanty developments encroached on their lands, the landowners began to charge people rent for living on the dilapidated housing the new residents built on the land. After establishing an owner-tenant relationship, the landowners steadily raise rents, threatening to destroy the flimsy shacks if residents fail to pay. In this way, powerful long-term inhabitants of the city exploit the weaker, more recent arrivals.

The vast slums of cities in poorer parts of the world are typically ethnically delineated, with new arrivals precariously accommodated. For example, Nairobi, Kenya, has a large slum area, one of the worst in Subsaharan Africa in terms of amenities, called Kibera. This settlement houses one million individuals, almost half of Nairobi's approximately 2.5 million slum dwellers, which account for 60 percent of the city's total population. Much of the land where Kibera is located is owned by Nubians, who are of Sudanese descent. The Sudanese Nubians settled in the area of Kibera during the colonial era. Many of the Nubians have become businesspeople in the city of Nairobi. The modern tenants of the shanty settlements in Kibera are largely Luo from western Kenya and Luhya from northwestern Kenya. During the fall of 2001, some of the Kiberian tenants were unable to pay the latest increase in rents. The Nubian landowners came to evict them, and in the fighting that followed, a number of people were killed. Groups of Luo, Luhya, and others even took to fighting among themselves. The government intervened to stabilize the situation. The rent increases were withdrawn, but the fundamental problems—crowding, unemployment, unsanitary conditions, little access to electricity, hunger, and lack of education—remain, and the ethnic groups living in the neighborhoods of Kibera will likely experience fighting again.

## The Enduring Impact of Colonialism

The settlement patterns of cities developed during the colonial period often persist long after independence—with enduring impacts on ethnic relations. In a study of the city of Mombasa, Kenya, during the 1960s, H. J. de Blij found that the central city, in effect the island on which Mombasa was built, was informally partitioned among major ethnic groups. Apart from the Swahili who occupied the Old Town and adjacent historic portions of the built-up area, the spatial pattern of occupancy by ethnic groups in the city of

© Alexander B. Murphy

■ **Figure 9.40**

**Mumbai, India.**   The millions of people who live in shanties in Mumbai assemble their homes with a variety of materials and tap into electricity to power their satellites.

Mombasa mirrored the status of the ethnic groups in the country of Kenya as a whole. The port of Mombasa, the country's largest, was the city's major employer. The Kikuyu, whose historic homeland lies far away from Mombasa to the north of Nairobi, were privileged by the British during colonial times. Because of their important position during the colonial era, Kikuyu workers and their families living in Mombasa resided closest to the port and to the center of economic power. Although the most powerful workers lived closest to the central commercial district, the Asians (often from India and thus referred to as Indians in Mombasa) who controlled the city's commerce were concentrated on the opposite side of the island, away from the port. Another powerful ethnic group, the Kamba, occupied a zone farther outward from the port. The Mijikenda, a less powerful African ethnic group, migrated from off-island villages to work in Mombasa and lived farther from the commercial center.

Today, as the city's population has grown seven times larger than it was in the 1960s, the spatial pattern of Mombasa still reflects the power of ethnic groups. The most recent immigrants, desperate for jobs, crowd the outer zone of the city, off of the island, and in the shanty settlements.

How do the many millions of urban immigrants living in the slum-ridden rings and pockets of the cities of the global periphery and semiperiphery survive? Extended families share and stretch whatever meager sums they can earn; when one member of the family has a salaried job, his or her income saves the day for a dozen or more relatives. When a member of the family (or several members of a larger community) manages to emigrate to a core country or an island of development and makes good money there, part of that income is sent back home and becomes the mainstay for those left behind. Hundreds of millions of dollars are transferred this way every year; *remittances* make a critical difference in the poorer countries of the world (see Chapter 3).

## The Informal Economy

In the vast slums, barrios, and favelas, those who are jobless or unsalaried are not idle. Everywhere you look people are at work, inside or in front of their modest habitats, fixing things, repairing broken items for sale, sorting through small piles of waste for salvageable items, trading and selling goods from makeshift stands (Fig. 9.40). What prevails here is referred to as the **informal economy**—the economy that is not taxed and is not counted toward a country's gross national income. What is generated in the informal economy can add up to a huge total in unrecorded monetary value. The informal economy worries governments because it is essentially a recordless economy and no taxes are paid. Remittances are usually delivered in cash, not via Western Union or a bank. Typically, a trusted community member (who might pay a comparatively small bribe at the airport when passing through immigration) carries remittances to family members.

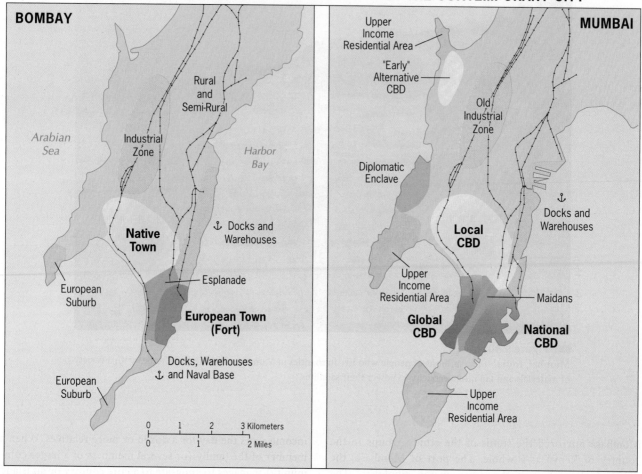

**A. THE COLONIAL CITY**

BOMBAY

Arabian Sea

Rural and Semi-Rural

Industrial Zone

Harbor Bay

⚓ Docks and Warehouses

**Native Town**

Esplanade

European Suburb

**European Town (Fort)**

Docks, Warehouses ⚓ and Naval Base

European Suburb

0   1   2   3 Kilometers
0       1       2 Miles

**B. THE CONTEMPORARY CITY**

MUMBAI

Upper Income Residential Area

"Early" Alternative CBD

Old Industrial Zone

Diplomatic Enclave

**Local CBD**

⚓ Docks and Warehouses

Upper Income Residential Area

Maidans

**Global CBD**

**National CBD**

Upper Income Residential Area

■ **Figure 9.41**

**The Changing Character of Mumbai, India.**    The desire to live near the global business district has made neighborhoods around the coast more attractive in contemporary Mumbai. Developers have expanded the upper income residential areas by filling in land around the two southern peninsulas.    *Adapted with permission from*: Richard Grant and Jan Nijman, "Globalization and the Corporate Geography of Cities in the Less-Developed World," *Annals of the Association of American Geographers*, 92, 2 (2002).

## From Colonial to Global CBD

Even as the informal economy thrives among the millions in the shantytowns, the new era of globalization is making a major impact in the larger cities founded or fostered by the colonial powers. In 2002, geographers Richard Grant and Jan Nijman documented this transformation in former colonial port cities, including Mumbai, India. In this city, colonial rule produced an urban landscape marked by strong segregation of foreign and local activities, commercial as well as residential (Fig. 9.41), and high levels of functional specialization and concentration. Adjacent to the port area was a well-demarcated European business district containing foreign (mostly British) companies. Most economic activities in this European commercial area involved trade, transport, bank-

ing, distribution, and insurance. Zoning and building codes were strictly enforced. Physically separated from this European district were the traditional markets and bazaars of the so-called Native Town, a densely populated mix of commercial and residential land uses.

In this era of globalization, a new spatially demarcated foreign presence has arisen. The city now has a global CBD at the heart of the original colonial city, housing mostly foreign corporations and multinational companies and linked mainly to the global economy. The former European Town has a large presence of big domestic companies and a pronounced orientation toward the national (Indian) economy. And the Native Town now has a high concentration of small domestic company headquarters.

Using the city you sketched in the last "Thinking Geographically" question, consider the concepts and processes introduced in this section of the chapter and explain how people and institutions created this city and the model you sketched.

## WHAT ROLE DO CITIES PLAY IN GLOBALIZATION?

Globalization, as we defined the term in the first chapter, is a set of processes and outcomes that occur on the global scale, circumventing and leaping over state boundaries to affect the world. In the processes of globalization, cities are taking over in ways we barely understand. Most statistics about economic activity at the global scale are gathered and disseminated by states. Nonetheless, many of the most important processes occur among and between cities, not states as a whole, masking the integral role world cities play in globalization. **World cities** function at the global scale, beyond the reach of the state borders, functioning as the service centers of the world economy.

Contending that models of cities and hierarchies of cities within states (such as Christaller's) no longer represent what is happening with the city, Taylor and Lang (2004) maintain that the city has become "something else" than a simple CBD tied into a hierarchy of other cities within the state. The world city is a node in globalization, reflecting processes that have "redrawn the limits on spatial interaction," according to Felsenstein, Schamp, and Shachar (2002). A node is a place through which action and interaction occur. As a node, a world city is connected to other cities, and the forces shaping globalization pulse across these connections and through the cities.

Most lists of world cities provide a hierarchy of the most important nodes, the most important world cities, then the next most important, and so forth. Virtually all agree that New York, London, and Tokyo are the most important world cities, but beyond these three, the definition of what makes a world city and the list of world cities changes depending on the perspective of the researcher. Geographers Jon Beaverstock and Peter J. Taylor and their Globalization and World Cities Study Group and Network have produced over 400 research papers, chapters, and books on the geography of world cities over the past few years. By studying which cities provide producer services (integral to the processes of globalization) in the areas of banking, law, advertising, and accounting, these geographers have produced an inventory of world cities mapped in Figure 9.42. They delineate 10 Alpha, 10 Beta, and 35 Gamma world cities. The Alpha cities (London, Paris, New York, Tokyo, Chicago, Frankfurt, Hong Kong, Los Angeles, Milan, and Singapore) have a global capacity to provide services in the world-economy.

World cities do not exist merely to service players in the global economy. Major world cities such as London and Paris are also capital cities. States concentrate development and encourage interconnectedness between certain cities and the rest of the world. Even though London and Paris are a short distance apart, both function as world cities in part because of the role they play within their respective states: Each became a magnet for economic and political activity within its state, and then the globe.

Some countries such as the United States and Germany have two or more world cities within their borders. They thus do not have a single, distinct primate city. To understand the role of cities in globalization, the services cities provide to places and peoples around the world and the interconnectedness among cities must also be considered. Geographers are now working to uncover the globalized flows and processes occurring across world cities, bringing them closer together.

## Cities as Spaces of Consumption

In addition to being nodes in globalization, cities are also products of globalization. Major changes in cities, such as the redevelopment of New York's Times Square and the remaking of Berlin's Potsdamer Platz, are the result of global processes. Frank Roost has found that "the global media industry is becoming the driving force in the reshaping of cities" such as New York and Berlin, turning city centers into **spaces of consumption**. Global media giants such as Time Warner, Viacom, and Walt Disney use cross promotion to encourage the consumption of their products. It is no accident that characters on television sitcoms produced and aired on ABC (a television channel owned by the Walt Disney Company) visit Disney theme parks or host Disney Princess-themed birthday parties on a given episode. These same media companies are investing heavily in urban centers in order to create entertainment spaces, places where tourists can go to consume their products. Media corporations are helping to transform urban centers into major entertainment districts ("variations on a theme park") where items are *consumed*.

For example, in New York City, government entities began to try to redevelop Times Square in the early 1980s. At that time, this area of the city was known for its neon lights, movie houses showing pornographic films, prostitution, and other illicit economic activities. The city sought to push these businesses out of Times Square and return the business district to a conglomeration of restaurants, hotels, bars, and entertainment spaces (as it had been before World War II). Over the decade of the 1980s, the city closed hundreds of small businesses in Times Square. In 1995, Mayor Rudolph

Giuliani reached a deal with Michael Eisner, CEO of Walt Disney. The mayor promised to remove the remaining sex shops, and Eisner committed to renovating the New Amsterdam Theater, a focal point in Times Square (Fig. 9.43). Secured with a $26 million low-interest loan from the State of New York, Disney set the new course for a family-friendly entertainment district in New York. The restored New Amsterdam Theater hosts Disney musicals such as *The Lion King* and *Aladdin* (both based on Disney movies). The Times Square area is assuredly a space of consumption and a variation on a theme park, including themed restaurants (Hard Rock Café, ESPN Zone), cross-promoting themed stores (Warner Brothers Store, Disney Store), and retail stores that cater to families (an enormous Toys R Us with a Ferris wheel inside).

In 2009, then-New York Mayor Michael Bloomberg closed portions of Broadway in Times Square to traffic and created an urban esplanade with lawn chairs and seating to advance his goal of making the city more livable. New Yorkers and tourists took to the new seating and moved in with laptops in hand. Times Square and the Hi-Line Walkway in New York now have bleacher-style seating as well as chairs to encourage New Yorkers to sit a spell and enjoy the city.

Potsdamer Platz in Berlin is also becoming a new space of consumption in the city center. Prior to the bombing of Berlin during World War II, Potsdamer Platz was a center of entertainment for Berlin's middle class. After the war, little was left of the area. Soon, a 500-yard border zone and the Berlin Wall occupied the formerly vibrant area of the city. After reunification, the city divided Potsdamer Platz and sold the land. The two largest owners are the German company Daimler-Benz and the Japanese company Sony. Sony built a huge entertainment structure called the Sony Center for cross promotion. According to Roost, much of the Daimler-Benz structure, Daimler City, is a space of consumption, with entertainment venues, restaurants, bars, and hotels.

Although the tourist focuses on the theme park atmosphere of these spaces of consumption, the renovations of the districts in both of these cities have also brought spaces of media production to the cities. Sony has placed its European headquarters in Berlin, Warner Brothers moved its offices to Times Square, and new office towers around Times Square house many other media companies.

Think through the challenges to the state presented in Chapter 8 and predict whether and under what circumstances world cities might replace states as the basic and most powerful form of political organization in the world. What arguments can be made for and against this proposition?

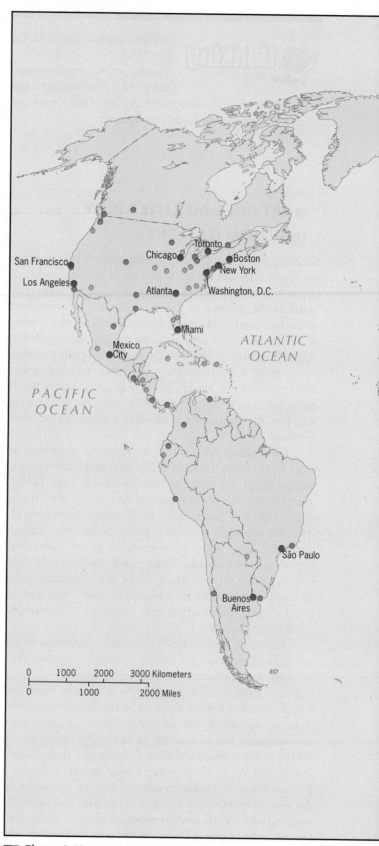

■ **Figure 9.42**

**World Cities: Alpha, Beta, and Gamma.**  *Data from:* "The World According to GaWC 2012," posted 13 January 2014. Globalization and World Cities Research Network, http://www.lboro.ac.uk/gawc/world2012t.html.

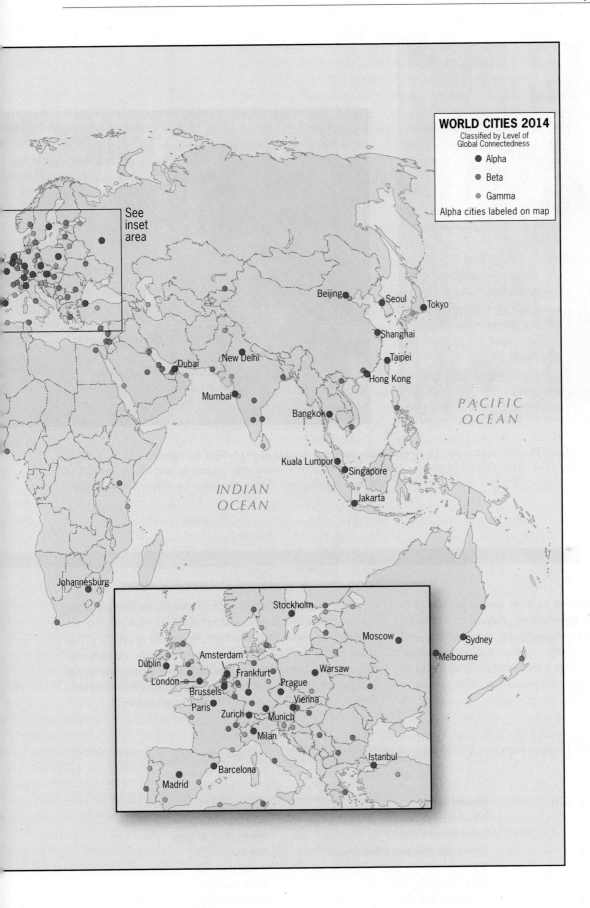

WORLD CITIES 2014
Classified by Level of
Global Connectedness
● Alpha
● Beta
● Gamma
Alpha cities labeled on map

See
inset
area

Beijing
Seoul
Tokyo
Shanghai
Taipei
Dubai
New Delhi
Hong Kong
Mumbai
Bangkok
PACIFIC
OCEAN
Kuala Lumpur
Singapore
INDIAN
OCEAN
Jakarta

Johannesburg

Stockholm
Moscow
Sydney
Melbourne
Dublin
Amsterdam
Frankfurt
Warsaw
London
Brussels
Prague
Paris
Vienna
Zurich
Munich
Milan
Istanbul
Barcelona
Madrid

Richard Levine/Alamy Images

© Corbis.Bettmann

■■ **Figure 9.43**

**New York, New York.**   (Left) The New Amsterdam Theater in Times Square as it stood in 1947. Note the signs around the building advertising arcade games and a flea circus. (Right) During the 1980s and 1990s, Times Square was "cleaned up" and reinvigorated. The Walt Disney Company renovated the New Amsterdam Theater and now shows productions of musicals such as *Aladdin* and *The Lion King*.

## Summary

The city is an ever-changing cultural landscape, its layers reflecting grand plans by governments, impassioned pursuits by individuals, economic decisions by corporations, and processes of political-economic change and globalization. Geographers who study cities have a multitude of topics to examine. From gentrification to teardowns, from favelas to McMansions, from spaces of production to spaces of consumption, from ancient walls to gated communities, cities have so much in common, and yet each has its own pulse, its own feel, its own spatial structure, its own set of realities. The pulse of the city is undoubtedly created by the peoples and cultures who live there. For it is the people, whether working independently or as part of global institutions, who continuously create and recreate the city and its geography.

## Geographic Concepts

central business district (CBD)
synekism
urban
city
agricultural village
agricultural surplus
social stratification
leadership class
first urban revolution

Mesopotamia
Nile River Valley
Indus River Valley
Huang He and Wei River Valleys
Mesoamerica
Peru
secondary hearth
acropolis
agora

site
situation
urban morphology
Forum
trade area
rank-size rule
primate city
central place theory
functional zonation

zone
central city
suburb
suburbanization
edge cities
galactic city
megacities
Griffin–Ford model
shantytowns
disamenity sector

McGee model
zoning laws
redlining
blockbusting
commercialization
gentrification
teardowns
McMansions
urban sprawl
new urbanism

gated communities
urbicide
informal economy
world city
spaces of consumption
concentric zone model
sector model
multiple nuclei model

## Learn More Online

About Celebration, Florida
www.celebration.fl.us

About the Congress for the New Urbanism
www.cnu.org

About the Decline of Detroit
www.nytimes.com/interactive/2014/05/27/us/Defining-Blight-in-Detroit.html?_r=0

About Globalization and World Cities
www.lboro.com/gawc/

About Urban Sprawl
http://environment.nationalgeographic.com/environment/habitats/urban-sprawl/

About Opposition to Urban Sprawl
www.sierraclub.org/sprawl

About Seaside, Florida
www.seasidefl.com

## Watch It Online

About Berlin
www.learner.org/resources/series180.html#program_descriptions

Click on Video On Demand for "Berlin: United We Stand"
www.learner.org/resources/series85.html#program_descriptions

Click on Video On Demand for "Berlin: Changing Center of a Changing Europe"

About Sprawl in Chicago
www.learner.org/resources/series180.html

Click on Video On Demand for "Chicago: Farming on the Edge" Source: Smart Growth.org

# CHAPTER 10

# DEVELOPMENT

## Geography, Trade, and Development

**W**alking down one of the major streets of Timbuktu, Mali (Fig. 10.1), I could hardly believe I was in the renowned intellectual, spiritual, and economic center of the thirteenth to sixteenth centuries. At that time, the place had a great reputation for wealth, which spurred the first European explorations along the African coast. What survives is a relatively impoverished town of some 35,000 people providing central place functions for the surrounding area and seeking to attract some tourist business based on its legendary name.

What happened to Timbuktu? The city's wealth many centuries ago derived from its ability to control the trans-Sahara trade in gold, salt, ivory, kola nuts, and slaves. But when trade patterns shifted with the development of sea trade routes along the west coast of Africa, Timbuktu lost its strategic position and a long period of decline set in.

Timbuktu's story serves as a reminder that where a place is situated in relation to patterns of economic development and exchange can be as important as, or even more important than, the commodities found in that place. Indeed, there are many examples of places where the presence of a valuable commodity does not translate into

© Alexander B. Murphy

■ **Figure 10.1**

**Central Square, Timbuktu, Mali.** Sited along the Niger River on the edge of the Sahara Desert, Timbuktu was once a major trade center. Goods from the north, carried on camels, were traded with goods from the south brought in on boats. The development of sea trade routes on the west coast of Africa in the sixteenth century allowed traders to circumvent Timbuktu. In turn, the city's central trade role declined.

improved economic lives for those living nearby. The people working on the oil booms in Gabon or Nigeria or workers chopping down rare hardwood trees in Thailand or Malaysia, for example, are not the ones who benefit from most of the wealth associated with demand for the goods they help produce. Instead, international corporations or the wealthiest families in a place, those who own the industry, are the principal beneficiaries.

To understand how the production of a good creates wealth for some and not for others, we must understand the concept of a commodity chain and the role of places in the chain of production. A **commodity chain** is a series of links connecting the many places of production and distribution and resulting in a final product that is then bought and sold on the market. The generation of wealth differs along the commodity chain. Each link along the chain adds a certain value to the commodity, producing differing levels of wealth for the place and the people where the steps of production occur.

What Timbuktu had to offer was the ability to coordinate and facilitate trade based on its geographic site where the Niger River turned north at the edge of the Sahara Desert. The river was the last major water source for those crossing the Sahara from south to north across what is now Mali and Algeria. Timbuktu was a **break-of-bulk location**, where goods traded on one mode of transport, camel, were transported to another mode of transport, boat. The points along the chain where materials and goods are traded change over time, directly impacting the situation of places.

Places along a commodity chain do not all benefit equally from the production of a good. The generation of wealth depends on how production occurs at each step. In Chapter 8 we introduced the concepts of core and periphery. Sophisticated technology, high skill levels, extensive research and development, and high salaries tend to be associated with the segment of global commodity chains located in the core. The segments located in the periphery, by contrast, tend to be associated with low technology, less education, little research and development, and lower wages.

Countries pursue development by becoming nodes along commodity chains, transform- ing peripheral processes into core ones, and redirecting the profit generated through core pro- cesses to improve the periphery. As the twenty-first century unfolds, governments, academics, nongovernmental organizations, and international financial institutions offer ideas about how to lift up the poorer parts of the world. The theories, methods, and recommendations vary, but they all focus on the elusive goals of development.

In this chapter, we review how development is defined and measured and some of the theories of development. We also examine how geography affects development, considering the structures of the world economy. We look at the geographical barriers to and costs of devel- opment within countries, and we ask why uneven development occurs not just across the globe but within states.

# Key Questions FOR CHAPTER 10

1. How is development defined and measured?
2. How does geographical context affect development?
3. What are the barriers to and the costs of development?
4. How do political and economic institutions influence uneven development within states?

## HOW IS DEVELOPMENT DEFINED AND MEASURED?

The economic and social geography of the contemporary world is a patchwork of almost inconceivable contrasts. On the fields in equatorial American and African forests, farmers practice shifting cultivation to grow root crops using ancient methods and rudimentary tools. On the Great Plains of North America, in Ukraine, and in eastern Australia, farmers use expensive, modern machines to plow the land, plant seeds, and harvest grains. Toolmakers in the villages of Papua New Guinea still fashion their implements by hand, as they did many centuries ago; whereas factory workers in Japan or South Korea work with robots to produce automobiles by the shipload for distri- bution to markets thousands of miles away. Our perception is that Japan and South Korea are more developed than Papua

New Guinea and shifting cultivators in equatorial America and Africa. Our modern notion of development is related to the Industrial Revolution and the idea that technology can improve the lot of humans. Through advances in technology, people can produce more food, create new products, and accrue material wealth. But these things do not necessarily bring happiness (see Chapter 14), social stability, or environmental sustainability, which makes development a narrow, and sometimes controversial, indicator of the human condition.

In the first section of this chapter, we examine methods of measuring development and assess the advantages and disadvantages of each measurement. We also look at models of development that academics have created to try to help countries develop. Both the measurements and models of development assume that development implies progress, and they generally look at development in terms of improvements in technology, production, and socioeconomic well-being. In the second section of this chapter, we look at the geographic context of development to see why development is uneven globally and within countries. We then consider approaches and barriers to development.

## Gross National Income

Three common ways of measuring development are development in economic welfare, development in technology and production, and development in social welfare. Beginning in the 1960s, the most common way of comparing development in economic welfare was to use the index economists created to compare countries, the gross national product. **Gross national product (GNP)** is a measure of the total value of the officially recorded goods and services produced by the citizens and corporations of a country in a given year. It includes goods and services made both inside and outside the country's territory, and it is therefore broader than **gross domestic product (GDP)**, which encompasses only goods and services produced within a country during a given year.

In recent years, economists have increasingly turned to **gross national income (GNI)**, which calculates the monetary worth of what is produced within a country plus income received from investments outside the country minus income payments to other countries around the world. GNI is seen as a more accurate way of measuring a country's wealth in the context of a global economy because it accounts for wealth generated by investments outside a country's borders.

In order to compare GNI across countries, economists must standardize the data. The most common way to standardize GNI data is to divide it by the population of the country, yielding the **per capita GNI**. In Japan the per capita gross national income in U.S. dollars in 2013 was $46,140. In the United States it was $53,670. In Norway it was $102,610. But in India it was $1570, in Nigeria it was $2760, and in Indonesia, the world's fourth most populous country, it was $3580. This enormous range across the globe in per capita GNI reflects the often-searing contrasts between rich and poor.

Although the map of per capita GNI clearly shows the startling contrasts between rich and poor in the world, the statistic has several shortcomings. GNI is a limited measure because it includes only transactions in the **formal economy**, the legal economy that governments tax and monitor. Quite a few countries have per capita GNI of less than $1000 per year—a figure so low it seems impossible that people could survive. A key component of survival in these countries is the **informal economy**, the uncounted or illegal economy that governments do not tax and keep track of, including everything from a garden plot in a yard to the black market to the illegal drug trade. The informal economy is a significant element in the economies of many countries, but GNI statistics omit the informal economy entirely (Fig. 10.2).

GNI per capita also masks extremes in the distribution of wealth within a country. The Middle Eastern oil countries of Kuwait and the United Arab Emirates (UAE) have per capita GNIs of $44,940 and $34,320, respectively, both ahead of Spain, Israel, and New Zealand In 2011. These figures give us no hint of what proportion of the population participates in the country's economy, the average citizen's material standard of living, or gaps between genders or among regions. Economic production and the wealth it generates are not distributed evenly across the seven emirates that make up the United Arab Emirates. In 2013, the UBS Billionaire Census reported "40 percent of the Middle East's wealth is held by the region's 157 wealthiest billionaires, known by the term ultra-high net worth (UHNW), compared to 28 percent in Europe, 22 percent in North America and 18 percent in Asia" (Kapur 2013). Billionaires in the UAE own a quarter of the economy and number 4.5 billionaires per million people. Abu Dhabi, the emirate that dominates the banking and financial sector and the petroleum industry, generated over half of the country's GDP in 2010. Dubai, the next largest emirate, generated about 30 percent of the GDP, The Sharjah emirate accounted for 5 percent of the GPD, and the Qaywayn emirate generated less than 1 percent of the country's gross GDP.

Another limitation of GNI per capita is that it measures only outputs (i.e., production). It does not take into account the nonmonetary costs of production, which take a toll on the environment through resource depletion and pollution of air and water. Per capita GNI may even treat such externalities as a plus. For example, the sale of cigarettes augments GNI. If cigarette use causes sickness and hospitalization is required, the GNI figure is boosted further. Conversely, quitting smoking improves health and saves lives but reduces money spent on cigarettes and health care, thus reducing the total production and the GNI in a country.

The limitations of GNI have prompted analysts to look for alternative measures of economic development, ways of measuring the roles technology, production, transportation, and communications play in an economy.

To gauge the use of technology, we can look at the number of workers relative to the production in a certain sector. For example, the United States produces twice the amount of corn as China. At the same time, the United States employed

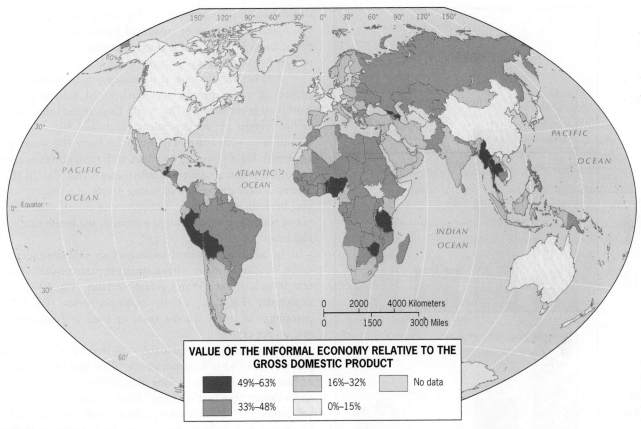

**■■ Figure 10.2**

**Percent of Informal Economy Relative to GDP.**　The World Bank estimates the contribution of the informal economy to each country's overall economy. Panama and Bolivia have the largest informal economies as a proportion of their GDP at 63.5 percent. Of the countries with data, Switzerland and the United States have the two smallest informal economies relative to their GDP at 8.1 and 8.4 percent, respectively. *Data from*: World Bank, 2013.

about 2 percent of its labor force in the agriculture sector, and China employed about 35 percent of its labor force in agriculture. The large proportion of the labor force employed in agriculture demonstrates that China is still producing agriculture in labor-intensive instead of technologically intensive ways. China can move more of its labor force into other sectors of the economy by adopting more technologically intensive agricultural methods.

A high percentage of laborers engaged in the production of agriculture signals a low overall level of development, as conventionally defined, and a high percentage of workers involved in high-tech industries and services signals a high level of development. Productivity per worker is examined by summing production over the course of a year and dividing it by the total number of persons in the labor force. The World Bank reported that agricultural productivity per worker in the United States was $49,817 in 2011, while China's agricultural productivity per worker was $713 the same year. A more productive workforce also suggests a higher level of mechanization in production.

One good measure of access to technology is access to railway, road, airline connections, telephone, radio, television, and so forth on a per capita basis—a statistic that reflects the amount of infrastructure that exists to facilitate economic activity.

Figure 10.3 highlights some of the extraordinary disparities in communications access, including access to the Internet, mobile cellular subscriptions, and telephone landlines around the world. The world average for Internet and mobile access is increasing, while the world average for landline access is declining. Nonprofit and nongovernmental development agencies, including one called the Living Cities, have called the mobile phone "the great equalizer," connecting hopes of giving the poor better access to education and services to diffusing technologies in cities. In a 2014 study, analysts at Pew Research Center surveyed residents of 24 emerging countries, including Turkey, Venezuela, Kenya, Brazil, and Nigeria. They found that while cell phones "are almost omnipresent in many nations," most people "in the 24 nations surveyed are still offline" (Pew 2014). A high correlation between wealth and Internet access (Fig. 10.4) means that instead of mobile phones equalizing Internet access for rich and poor countries, the technology can either reinforce or exacerbate the **digital divide** between rich and poor. The Pew survey data also confirmed that people with college educations are more likely to have smartphones and thus mobile access to the Internet.

Another way to measure development is to compare the size of the working-age population to the number of older or younger people in the society who are not contributing to the

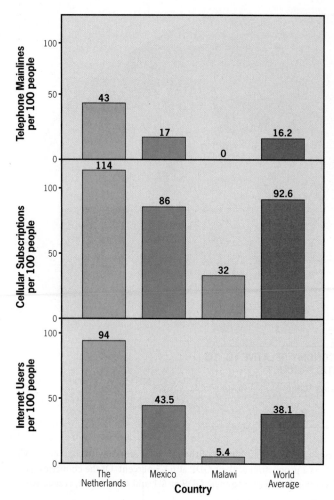

**Figure 10.3**

**Differences in Communications Connectivity, 2013.** *Data from:* World Bank, 2013.

of older adults in society can be a financial strain on the country. Aging populations in Japan and Europe require greater investments in health care, elderly housing, and retirement welfare (similar to Social Security in the U.S.).

Another way to look at dependency is to measure the percent of young people, ages birth to 14, relative to the working-age population. The World Bank reports these data as the younger person dependency ratio, and Niger has the highest ratio, with 106 young people for every 100 working-age adults. Eight of the ten countries with the highest younger person dependency ratio are in Subsaharan Africa (Fig. 10.5b). Having a large proportion of young people in a country can also be a financial strain, if countries invest in child care, public education, immunization programs, and health care for children.

In addition to access to technology and dependency ratios, we can use many other statistics to measure social welfare, including literacy rates, infant mortality (Fig. 2.18), life expectancy (Fig. 2.21), caloric intake per person (Fig. 1.2), percentage of family income spent on food, and amount of savings per capita.

The United Nations calculates the Human Development Index (Fig. 10.6) to incorporate the "three basic dimensions of human development: a long and healthy life, knowledge and a decent standard of living." Several statistics, including per capita GDP, literacy rates, school enrollment rates, and life expectancy at birth, factor into the calculation of the Human Development Index.

In 2000, the United Nations held a high-profile summit, during which 189 world leaders adopted the United Nations Millennium Declaration, with the goal of improving the condition of the people in the countries with the lowest standards of human development. At the summit, world leaders recognized the principal barriers to economic development and

country's economy. The *dependency ratio* measures the proportion of dependents in the population relative to every 100 people of working age.

The overall dependency ratio of young and old relative to the working age population can be divided into an older person dependency ratio, population over the age of 64 relative to the working age population, and a younger person dependency ratio, population ages birth to 14 relative to the working age population. The older person dependency ratio (proportion of the population over age 64) in Japan is 41, meaning that every group of 100 working-age adults (ages 15 to 64) is paying taxes to support 41 people over the age of 64 (Fig. 10.5a). Just behind Japan in the older person dependency ratio are European countries including Italy, Germany, and Sweden. The countries with high older person dependency ratios generally have high per capita GNIs, but the larger proportion

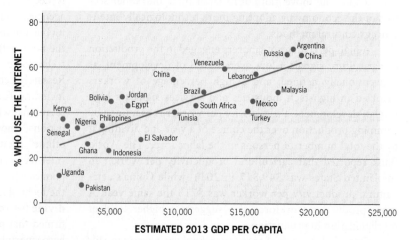

**Correlation Between Internet Users and GDP Per Capita**

**Figure 10.4**

**Correlation Between Wealth and Internet Access, 2014.** The correlation between wealth and Internet access is positive and relatively high, with wealthier countries having greater access to the Internet. *Courtesy of:* Pew Research Global Attitudes Project, 2014.

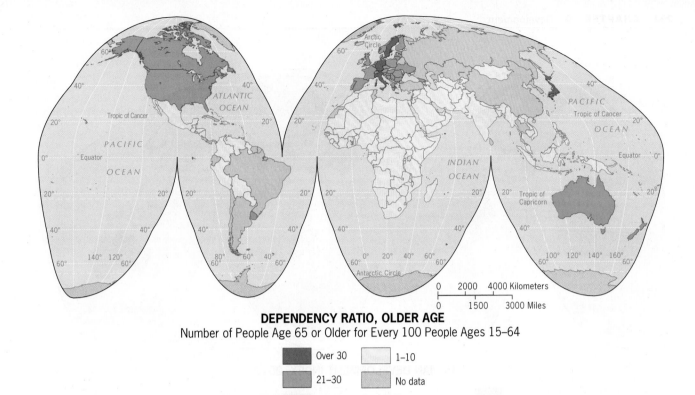

**DEPENDENCY RATIO, OLDER AGE**

Number of People Age 65 or Older for Every 100 People Ages 15–64

- Over 30
- 21–30
- 11–20
- 1–10
- No data

■■ **Figure 10.5a**

**Older Person Dependency Ratio.** The older person dependency ratio is a measure of the number of people 65 and older relative to 100 working-age adults, between 15 and 64. The working-age adults in the formal economy contribute to a country's tax base, thereby supporting the older population of a country. *Data from*: World Bank, 2014.

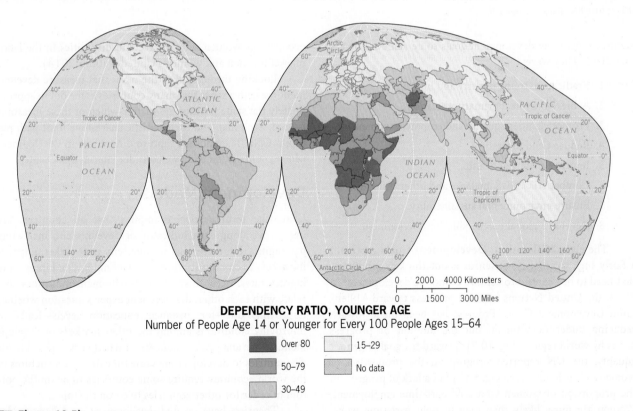

**DEPENDENCY RATIO, YOUNGER AGE**

Number of People Age 14 or Younger for Every 100 People Ages 15–64

- Over 80
- 50–79
- 30–49
- 15–29
- No data

■■ **Figure 10.5b**

**Younger Person Dependency Ratio.** The younger person dependency ratio is a measure of the number of people birth to age 14 relative to 100 working-age adults, between 15 and 64. The working-age adults in the formal economy contribute to a country's tax base, thereby supporting the younger population of a country. *Data from*: World Bank, 2014.

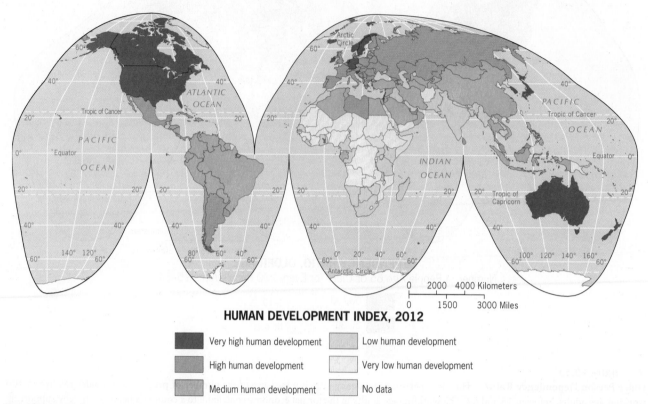

## HUMAN DEVELOPMENT INDEX, 2012

| | |
|---|---|
| ■ Very high human development | ▢ Low human development |
| ▨ High human development | ▢ Very low human development |
| ▨ Medium human development | ▢ No data |

■ **Figure 10.6**

**Human Development Index, 2012.**   The Human Development Index measures development beyond GNI or GDP by taking into account literacy, school enrollment, and other factors that contribute toward quality of life in a country.   *Data from:* http://hdr.undp.org/en/media/HDR_2010_EN_Table1_reprint.pdf.

identified eight key development goals to be achieved by the year 2015. They were:

1. Eradicate extreme poverty and hunger.
2. Achieve universal primary education.
3. Promote gender equality and empower women.
4. Reduce child mortality.
5. Improve maternal health.
6. Combat HIV/AIDS, malaria, and other diseases.
7. Ensure environmental sustainability.
8. Develop a global partnership for development.

The eight **Millennium Development Goals** represent a fairly high degree of consensus about the key conditions that need to be changed to achieve economic development. In 2014, the United Nations assessed progress toward Millennium Development Goals. Progress has been made toward reducing undernourishment, but the amount of progress varies by world region (Fig. 10.7). Toward the goal of gender equality, the UN reported progress in the proportion of women in legislatures (see Fig. 5.17) but a lack of progress in the proportion of women who hold part-time employment. Women are more likely than men to hold part-time work, which reflects "gender inequality in family roles, the absence of adequate and affordable childcare and elderly-care facilities," as well as gendered stereotypes regarding the kinds of occupations women should have and disparities in the labor market for men and women (United Nations 2014).

Looking through all of the maps that measure development, we gain a sense that many countries come out in approximately the same position no matter which of these measures is used. Each map and each statistic shares one limit with per capita GNI: They do not capture differences in development *within* countries, an issue we consider later in this chapter.

## Development Models

Using the term *developing* implies that all countries are improving along each indicator of development, increasing per capita GNI, increasing productivity per worker, improving access to communications and technology, and improving literacy rates. Because so many development indicators correlate with each other, development experts question whether improving one—for instance education levels—leads to improving conditions among the other markers of development. Other analysts are concerned whether it is possible for all countries to develop at the same time or if the structures of the world economy require some countries to be on the bottom in order for other countries to be on the top.

Theorists have created development models as guides for governments, nongovernmental organizations, and international financial institutions (including the World Bank, the World Trade Organization, and the International Monetary

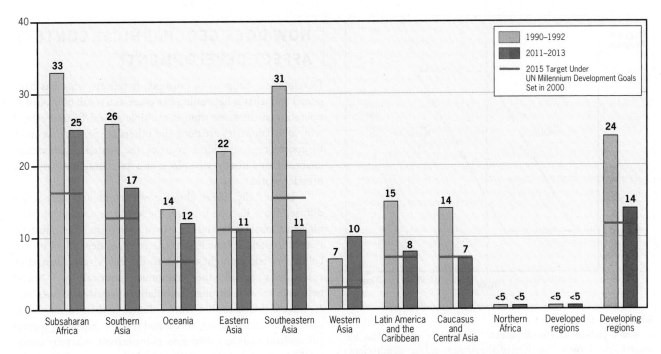

**Percent of People Who Are Undernourished by World Region, 1990–1992 and 2011–2013**

■■ **Figure 10.7**

**Progress in Reducing Undernourishment by Region.** The United Nations Millennium Development Goals sought to reduce undernourishment in each world region. According to these data, these goals were achieved in every region except Western Asia, where undernourishment actually rose between 1991–1992 and 2011–2013.  *Courtesy of:* United Nations Millennial Development Goals, 2014.

Fund) to help countries develop. The fundamental problem with development models is that each suggests a single trajectory through which all countries move. The underlying message of most development models is that countries can develop if they just behave like a country that is already considered developed.

Development models, then, do not take geographical differences very seriously. Just because Japan moved from a rural, agrarian state to an urbanized, industrial one does not mean that Mali will or that it will do so in the same way. Another criticism of development models is that the very idea of development has a Western bias. Critics argue that some of the measures taken in poorer countries that the West views as progress, such as attracting industry and mechanizing agriculture, can lead to worsened social and environmental conditions for many people in the poorer countries. Still others criticize development models because they do not consider the ability of some countries to influence what happens in other countries, or the different positions countries occupy in the world economy. Instead, development models treat countries as autonomous units moving through a process of development at different speeds.

The classic development model, one that is subject to each of these criticisms, is economist Walt Rostow's **modernization model**. Many theories of development grew out of the major decolonization movements of the 1960s. Concerned with how the dozens of newly independent countries in Africa and Asia would survive economically, Rostow looked

to how the countries that were already economically powerful in the 1960s had gotten where they were.

Rostow's model assumes that all countries follow a similar path to development or modernization, advancing through five stages of development. In the first stage, the society is *traditional*, and the dominant activity is subsistence farming. The social structure is rigid, and technology is slow to change. The second stage brings the *preconditions of takeoff*. New leadership moves the country toward greater flexibility, openness, and diversification. These changes, in turn, will lead to the third stage, *takeoff*. Now the country experiences something akin to an industrial revolution, and sustained growth takes hold. Urbanization increases, industrialization proceeds, and technological and mass-production breakthroughs occur. Next, the economy enters the fourth stage, the *drive to maturity*. Technologies diffuse, industrial specialization occurs, and international trade expands. Modernization is evident in key areas of the country, and population growth slows. Finally, some countries reach the final stage in Rostow's model, *high mass consumption*, which is marked by high incomes and widespread production of many goods and services. During this stage, a majority of workers enter the service sector of the economy.

Another name for Rostow's model (and other models derived from it) is the *ladder of development*. Visually, we can see his five stages of development as rungs on a ladder (Fig. 10.8), with each country climbing the ladder one rung at a time. In addition to the general criticisms of development models, the major problem with Rostow's model is that it

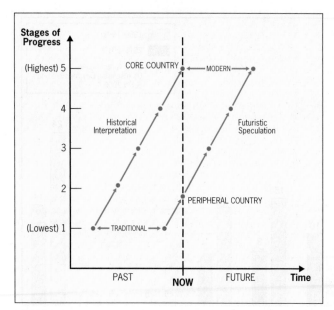

**■ Figure 10.8**

**Rostow's Ladder of Development.** This ladder assumes that all countries can reach the same level of development and that all will follow a similar path. *Adapted with permission from:* P. J. Taylor. "Understanding Global Inequalities: A World-Systems Approach," *Geography,* 77 (1992): 10–21.

provides no larger context to development. Is a climb up the ladder truly dependent on what happens within one country? Or do we need to take into account all of the other countries, their places on the ladder, and how their actions and global forces affect an individual country's movement on the ladder? The theory also misses the particular conditions that can influence development decisions within an individual country, leaving us to wonder where cultural and political differences fit into the picture.

Rostow's model is still influential, despite all of these criticisms. Even the notion of calling wealthy countries "industrialized" and saying poor countries need to "industrialize" implies that economic development can be achieved only by climbing the same ladder of development wealthier countries have already climbed. Yet if a poor country quickly industrialized today through foreign investment, it might not reap much economic benefit, but it could experience severe environmental consequences. The wealthier countries we call "industrial" today are really "postindustrial," as post-Fordist production has moved the manufacturing of goods around the world and many of the wealthiest countries have economies built on the service sector, not the industrial sector (see Chapter 12).

Is the idea of economic development inherently Western? If the West (North America and Europe) were not encouraging the "developing world" to "develop," how would people in the regions of the "developing world" think about their own economies?

## HOW DOES GEOGRAPHICAL CONTEXT AFFECT DEVELOPMENT?

Development happens in **context**: It reflects what has happened and what is happening in a place as a result of processes operating at the same time at multiple scales. To understand why some countries are poor and others are wealthy, we need to consider geographical context: the spatial organization, character, and history of a place, and its interactions with the broader world.

Historically, ideas about government and economics diffused from Europe through the world as a result of colonialism, global trade, and the rise of capitalism. The Industrial Revolution and colonialism made colonies dependent on the colonizers and brought wealth to the colonizers. Even after colonialism ended, the economic, political, and social networks created through colonialism persisted. Goods and capital continued to flow from colonies to their former colonizers. The continuation of colonial relationships after formal colonialism ends is called **neo-colonialism**, whereby major world powers continue to control the economies of the poorer countries, even though the poorer countries are now politically independent states.

Development scholars have produced a number of theories to explain the barriers to development under neo-colonialism; these theories are called structuralist theories. A **structuralist theory** holds that difficult-to-change, large-scale economic arrangements shape what is possible for a country's development in fundamental ways. The world economy has a set of structural circumstances, such as the concentration of wealth in certain areas and unequal relations among places, which make it very difficult for poorer countries to improve their economic situation. Structuralists argue that developing countries face a very different set of development circumstances, a different context, than those faced by the countries of western Europe that Rostow looked to as models when constructing his modernization model.

## Dependency Theory

Structuralists have developed a major body of development theory called **dependency theory**, which holds that the political and economic relationships between countries and regions of the world control and limit the economic development possibilities of poorer areas. Dependency theorists note, for example, that colonialism created political and economic structures that caused the colonies to become dependent on the colonial powers. They further argue that such dependency helps sustain wealth in developed regions and poverty in other areas, even after decolonization occurs.

Dependency theory contends that economic prosperity is extremely difficult to achieve in regions and countries that have traditionally been dominated by external powers because that dependency continues after independence. For example, 14 countries in Central and West Africa have used the CFA franc as their currency since 1945.[1] They tie the value of their currency to the value of the French franc, and now to the value of the European Monetary Union's euro (France changed to the euro in 2000). The economies of these 14 African countries are tied to the economy of the European Union—they rise and fall together. The CFA franc was set up before African countries gained independence starting in the 1950s and 60s, and the former colonies (12 of the 14 were colonies of France) continue to use the CFA franc because their economies are based on the currency and changing is quite difficult. At the same time, the countries are dependent on France because the French treasury and French parliament set policies that directly affect the economies of 14 African countries.

The countries with the CFA franc had their currency set up by their colonizer during colonialism. Although the United States did not colonize Latin America (except in the Caribbean), several countries in Latin America now recognize that their economy is dependent on the United States and explicitly link their economy to the U.S. dollar. *The Economist* reported that in 2011, 66 countries have currencies (including China, Saudi Arabia, and Bangladesh) tied to the U.S. dollar: More than 40 countries peg the value of their currency to the U.S dollar, and 8 countries have abandoned their currency and have completely adopted the U.S. dollar. The process of adopting the U.S. dollar as a country's currency is called **dollarization**.

For the people of El Salvador, dollarization made sense because the economy of El Salvador depends on the economy of the United States (Fig. 10.9). Over 2 million Salvadorians live in the United States, and in 2010, they sent $3.5 billion in remittances to El Salvador. With this flow of American dollars to El Salvador, many transactions occurred in dollars long before the official switch. The United Nations Development Program estimates that 22.3 percent of families in El Salvador receive remittances. In addition, over two-thirds of El Salvador's exports go to the United States. When the Federal Reserve Board in the United States controls the supply of dollars by altering the interest rates or when the U.S. economy enters a recession, the ramifications are felt directly in El Salvador. The greatest disadvantage of dollarization is surrendering the last say over policies that affect your economy to the United States, and the biggest advantage of dollarization is stabilization of the country's currency because the U.S. dollar is a relatively stable currency.

Like modernization theory, dependency theory is based on generalizations about economic change that pay relatively little attention to geographical differences in culture, politics, and society. Not every country is in the same situation at the same time, so they cannot all follow the same path of development, as modernization theory would have it. Likewise, not every country will be affected by a dependent relationship in

AFP/NewsCom

■■ **Figure 10.9**

**San Salvador, El Salvador.**   A woman and young boy use dollars to pay for groceries in El Salvador, a country that underwent dollarization in 2001.

the same way. Pegging a currency to or adopting the currency of a wealthier country may be beneficial for one developing country but not for another. Although both models provide some insights, neither is greatly concerned with the spatial and cultural context of particular places—central elements of geographical analysis.

## Geography and Context

As geographers, economists, and other social scientists came to realize that studying economic development divorced from geographical, historical, and political context did not reflect reality, geographers began to search for a development theory that encompassed geography, scale, place, and culture. Immanuel Wallerstein's **world-systems theory** is attractive to geographers because it incorporates space (geography) and time (history) as well as power relationships (politics) that shape the context in which development takes place. We discussed world-systems theory in Chapter 8, focusing on how the theory provides insights into the political organization

---

[1]The CFA franc is actually two currencies, one in West Africa and one in Central Africa, but they are closely tied, and so we consider them together as encompassing 14 countries.

of space. In this chapter, we focus on how world-systems theory helps us understand the geography of development.

Wallerstein's division of the world into a **three-tier structure**—the core, periphery, and semiperiphery—helps explain the interconnections among places in the global economy. As discussed in more detail in Chapter 8, core processes generate wealth in a place because they require higher levels of education, more sophisticated technologies, and higher wages and benefits. When core processes are embedded in a place (such as the Telecom corridor in Richardson-Plano, Texas), wealth is generated for the people in that place. Peripheral processes, on the other hand, require little education, lower technologies, and lower wages and benefits. Producing agriculture by hand using little technology may generate a stable food supply in a place, but it does not produce capital, as few formal wages, low education, and little research and technology were required to produce the crop in that place.

Core regions are those where core processes are clustered. Core regions have achieved high levels of economic prosperity and are dominant players in the world economy. When peripheral processes are embedded in a place, the processes often generate little wealth for the people in that place. Periphery regions are areas where peripheral processes are concentrated. They are poor regions that are dependent in significant ways on the core and do not have as much control over their own affairs, economically or politically. The semiperiphery exhibits both core and peripheral processes, and semiperipheral places serve as a buffer between the core and periphery in the world-economy. Countries of the semiperiphery exert more power than peripheral regions but remain heavily influenced by core regions.

Dividing the world into cores, semiperipheries, and peripheries might seem to do little more than replace developed, developing, and underdeveloped with a new set of terms. But the core–periphery model is fundamentally different from the modernization model because it holds that not all places can be equally wealthy in the capitalist world-economy. World-systems theory also makes the power relations among places explicit and does not assume that socioeconomic change will occur in the same way in all places. It is thus sensitive to geographical context, at least in economic terms.

Geographer Peter J. Taylor uses the analogy of a school of tadpoles to demonstrate these ideas. He envisions different places in the world as tadpoles and explains that not all tadpoles can survive to develop into toads. Rather, those who dominate survive, and the others perish. World-systems theorists see domination (exploitation) as a function of the capitalist drive for profit in the global economy. Thus, capitalists can move production quickly from one place to another around the globe to enhance profits, but places that lose a production facility can suffer. Moreover, their coping capacity can be small if, as is often the case, they earlier abandoned traditional ways and shifted to an export economy when external investment first arrived.

Another benefit of Wallerstein's three-tier structure is that he focuses on how a good is produced instead of what is produced. Rostow looked at what is produced, arguing that in order to develop a country needed to move from agricultural production to industrial manufacturing. Wallerstein disagreed and recognized that a country can produce agriculture using core processes and gain wealth while another country can produce the very same agricultural product with peripheral processes and gain almost no wealth. Generating wealth along a commodity chain is not determined by *what is produced*; it depends on *how it is produced*. Farmers can grow cotton with rudimentary tools or with $700,000 combines. Using the $700,000 combine produces more wealth because of all that went into the combine: Educated engineers designed it, laborers manufactured it, marketing professionals and salespeople sold it, the John Deere dealership received $700,000 for it, and the educated farmer employs the combine to markedly increase productivity per worker (Fig. 10.2).

Another reason geographers are drawn to world-systems theory is its applicability at multiple scales. For example, Los Angeles can be described as the core of the Southern California region; the Johannesburg area can be described as the core of the South African state; or the central business district can be studied as the core of São Paulo, Brazil.

Compare and contrast Rostow's ladder of development with Wallerstein's three-tier structure of the world-economy as models for understanding development. Choose a product and break down its commodity chain. Which theory, Rostow's or Wallerstein's, better helps you understand where wealth is accumulated along the commodity chain and where it is not?

## WHAT ARE THE BARRIERS TO AND THE COSTS OF DEVELOPMENT?

Regardless of which development theory you find the most persuasive, all the theories agree that structures are built into the world-economy, including the concentration of power in core states and entrenched poverty in peripheral states, that inhibit economic development in the periphery.

Conditions within the periphery, such as high population growth rates (see Chapter 2), lack of education, foreign debt, autocratic (and often corrupt) leadership, political instability, and widespread disease (see Chapter 2) hamper development. It is possible to get into the chicken-or-the-egg debate here: Did the structures of the world-economy create these conditions, or do these conditions help to create the structures of the world-economy? Many think that neither argument can stand alone, but understanding both structures and conditions is important for you to form your own opinion.

## Social Conditions

Across the global periphery, as much as half the population is 15 years old or younger (see Fig. 10.5b), making the supply of adult, taxpaying laborers low relative to the number of dependents. Low life expectancies and high infant and child mortality rates stem from inadequate nutrition. Despite the UN's efforts to achieve the Millennium Development Goals, one in four children worldwide had stunted growth in 2012— that is, they do not receive enough calories to grow as tall as they should be for their age. Underweight and stunted children are at risk for "diminished cognitive and physical development" from undernourishment (UN 2014).

Access to public sewage systems, clean drinking water, and health care are low in peripheral countries, making economic development all the more difficult. According to the United Nations, 748 million people still rely on unsafe drinking water from rivers, ponds, and unprotected wells and springs, and 1 billion people still used "open defecation" in 2012. Open defecation spreads disease and is found most often in South Asia, Oceania, and Subsaharan African (UN 2014).

Lack of access to education is also a major problem in the periphery. The number of children in the periphery enrolled in primary school, both boys and girls, has increased since 2000, thanks to governmental efforts to extend education. The government of Rwanda eliminated fees for primary education in 2003, guaranteeing 6 years of primary and 3 years of secondary school for all children in Rwanda, and two years later started distributing funds to schools based on the number of students they were educating. Rwanda successfully increased the proportion of students attending school through grade 6, reporting a 95 percent enrollment rate (Republic of Rwanda 2014). Growing education so quickly makes it difficult to establish quality education, and the government reported in 2011 that the quality of education in Rwanda is lagging, as only 5 percent of "pupils met or exceeded curricular expectations in reading and that a majority do not meet expectation in numeracy" (UNDP 2014).

Governments have used innovative policies, including cash transfer policies such as Brazil's Bolsa Familia and South Africa's Child Support Grant, to create a financial incentive for families to enroll and send their children to school. Historically, children would drop out of primary school or have low attendance in order to help their family by earning wages or by working on the farm or providing child or elderly care at home. Children in peripheral countries typically have to pay a fee for attending school, and it was common for a girl to drop out of school to earn wages to pay school fees for her brother. Cash transfer policies seek to undermine the financial incentive to drop out by providing a financial incentive to enroll in school and attend regularly. Girls who live in rural areas and are from poor families remain the least likely to attend primary school (United Nations 2014).

Brazil's Bolsa Familia conditional cash transfer program began in the 1990s, and former President Lula da Silva expanded the scope of the program in 2003. Bolsa Familia pays families in cash under the condition that their children enroll and attend school (children cannot miss more than 15 percent of classes) and that they receive medical check-ups. One-fourth of the country, about 50 million people, is enrolled in the program, and Brazil credits the program with bringing "36 million Brazilians out of extreme poverty" (Barnes 2013). Bolsa Familia is held up as a model for economic development, as it gives the poor the ability to choose how to spend their financial assistance instead of living within the constraints of separate programs designed to address different aspects of poverty. Conditional cash transfer programs have the added benefit of increasing school attendance for girls and boys alike.

South Africa's conditional cash transfer program has led to an increase in the number of children receiving primary education. However, the schools are in poor condition, and the quality of education is below par. Data from South Africa's national literacy and numeracy tests reveal that "only 15% of 12 year olds (sixth graders) scored at or above the minimum proficiency on the language test" and in math, only 12% were proficient (*The Economist*, South Africa 2012).On the whole, the country of South Africa needs 25,000 new, qualified teachers each year but only 10,000 teachers meet standards (*The Economist* 2012). The South African economy suffers from having a poor education system because the schools do not produce enough graduates to fill jobs in the South African economy that require an educated workforce.

Lack of education for girls is founded on and compounded by the assumption held not just in the periphery but in most of the world that girls will leave their homes (and communities) when they marry and contribute to their husband's family and not their own. The views that girls are less important than boys and that girls cost a family money and provide little financial support are at the root of human trafficking. Mike Dottridge, a modern antislavery activist, explains that **trafficking** happens when "adults and children fleeing poverty or seeking better prospects are manipulated, deceived, and bullied into working in conditions that they would not choose."

Trafficking is not usually considered slavery because the family does not sell a child; instead, the family sends the child away with a recruiter in the hopes that the child will earn money to send home. Trafficked children are often taken to neighboring or nearby countries that are wealthier and in demand of domestic servants. Others are trafficked across the world, again typically to work as domestic servants. Dottridge explains that the majority of trafficked children are girls and that the majority of girls are "employed as domestic servants or street vendors," although some girls are "trafficked into prostitution" (see Chapter 3).

## Foreign Debt

Shortly after the decolonization wave of the 1960s, international financial institutions (IFIs), including banks, the World Bank, and the International Monetary Fund, began lending large sums of money to the newly independent states in the periphery and semiperiphery—money earmarked for development projects, especially large infrastructure projects like building highways and dams and building government-owned utility companies to provide electricity and telephone service.

Developing countries were generally able to repay their loans until the world economy shifted in the 1970s. The price of oil rose in the late 1970s, and in the early 1980s commodity prices dropped. Rising oil prices make the production of goods more expensive, and falling commodity prices make it difficult to repay loans as the value of exports declines. The Third World Debt Crisis began as export revenue declined, the cost of oil increased, and state-run companies created in the 1960s and 1970s were found to be both inefficient and draining on government funds.

The World Bank and the International Monetary Fund stepped in to lend more money to developing countries to help them out of the Third World Debt Crisis. The IFIs determined that peripheral and semiperipheral countries needed to restructure their governments and economies in order to develop. To secure the loans, countries had to agree to implement economic or governmental reforms, including privatizing government entities, opening the country to foreign trade, reducing tariffs, and encouraging foreign direct investment. These loans are known as **structural adjustment loans**, and the set of policies surrounding them came to be known as the **Washington Consensus** in the 1980s.

Opponents of to the Washington Consensus argue that the policies support and protect core country economies at the expense of peripheral and semiperipheral economies. Countries had limited options to reject structural adjustment loans because the hefty cost of servicing debts (cost of repayments plus interest) often exceeded revenues from the export of goods and services (Fig. 10.10). Developing countries also needed to demonstrate they were repaying their debts and restructuring their economies to attract multinational corporations that could offer employment to their people and investment in their economies.

Structural adjustment loans were part of a larger trend toward **neoliberalism** in the late twentieth century. Neoliberalism derives from the neo-classical economic idea that government intervention into markets is inefficient and undesirable, and should be resisted wherever possible. These ideas were at the heart of the structural adjustment conditions that were attached to loans and refinancing programs. Neoliberal ideas spurred a trend toward transferring economic control from states to the private sector. As a result, the size of the public sector in a number of countries shrunk. Corporate control expanded, and state and regional governments had less control over their economic destinies. High debt obligations and related neoliberal reforms arguably contributed to the economic and political crisis in Argentina at the end of 2001 and beginning of 2002. Argentina privatized government sectors in the 1990s and took out loans,

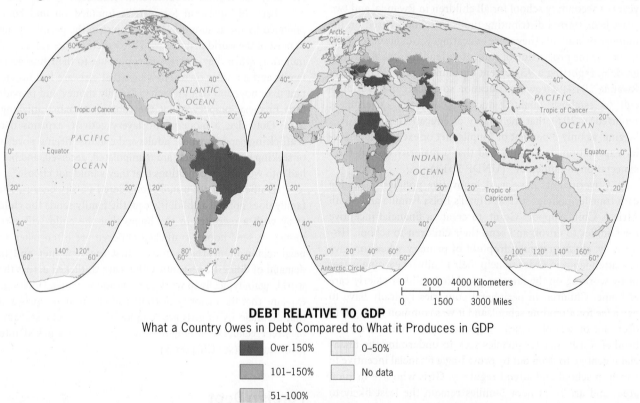

**DEBT RELATIVE TO GDP**
What a Country Owes in Debt Compared to What it Produces in GDP

- Over 150%
- 101–150%
- 51–100%
- 0–50%
- No data

**Figure 10.10**

**External Debt Service as a Percentage of Exports of Goods and Services for Low- and Middle-Income Economies, 2012.** Repaying back loans, let alone paying the interest on the loans, is more difficult for countries with debt much higher than their GDP. *Data from*: World Bank, 2013. http://data.worldbank.org/indicator/DT.DOD.DECT.EX.ZS.

# FIELD NOTE

"Arriving in Argentina during the political and economic upheavals that had begun in 2001, I saw signs of dislocation and trouble everywhere. Beggars pursued pedestrians on the once-fashionable Avenida Florida. Banks had installed protective shutters against angry crowds demanding return of their frozen and devalued deposits. A bus trip on the Patagonian Highway turned into an adventure when masked protesters carrying rocks and burning rags stopped vehicles and threatened their occupants. Newspapers carried reports of starvation in Tucumán Province—in a country capable of producing seven times the food its population needs."

**Figure 10.11**
**Buenos Aires, Argentina.**

leading to short-term economic growth in the 1990s. In 1999, a recession hit Argentina, and by 2000, the country had a debt equal to 50 percent of its GDP (Blustein 2003) (Fig. 10.11). The IMF extended emergency loans in 2000 and again in 2001. Coupled with unchecked government spending and corruption, Argentina's economy experienced a meltdown, and the country defaulted on its debt in 2002. More than half the population of 38 million ended up in poverty (McCarthy 2007).

By 2005, internal economic growth and aid from Venezuela put Argentina in a position to work out a complex debt restructuring plan that has pulled the country back from the brink. Argentina's agricultural economy bounced back in 2010 with the rise of corn and soy prices. Argentina's economy is stabilizing, but in cases where countries are facing imminent economic, political, and social meltdown, the only alternative may be to default on loans. Defaulting countries then find themselves in a severely disadvantaged position when it comes to attracting future external investment. And if a substantial number of countries were to default at the same time, a global economic crisis could ensue that would work to the disadvantage of almost everyone.

## Political Corruption and Instability

Political corruption and instability can greatly impede economic development. In peripheral countries, a wide divide often exists between the very wealthy and the poorest of the poor. In Kenya, for example, the wealthiest 10 percent of the population controls nearly 50 percent of the country's wealth, and the poorest 10 percent control less than 1 percent. The

disenfranchisement of the poor and the competition among the rich for control of the government (and the potential spoils that go along with that) can lead to extreme political instability within a state—as Kenya experienced in 2007–2008. Add to these factors involvement from outside the country, especially by powerful countries, and the political instability can easily escalate, yielding horrid conditions in which military dictators, selfish megalomaniacs, and corrupt governments can come to power.

Countries of the core have established democracies for themselves; since World War II, they have held regularly scheduled democratic elections. But countries in the periphery and semiperiphery have had a much harder time establishing and maintaining democracies. In the process of decolonization, the colonizing countries typically left governments that reflected political and social hierarchies of the colonial period. Some failed, some were overthrown by military coups, and some saw the consolidation of power around a dictatorial strongman. Many countries in the periphery and semiperiphery have alternated repeatedly between quasidemocratic and military governments. Some argue that without considerable wealth, maintaining a liberal democracy is all but impossible.

Opening the homepage of any major newspaper on any given day will reveal a story somewhere in the world that demonstrates the link between economic stability and political stability. In Afghanistan, economic woes represent one of the greatest threats to the stability of the U.S.-supported government in Kabul. More than half of the population is impoverished, and the government lacks the funds to invest in development. Foreign aid—much of it from the United States—has provided some help, but the flow of aid has been variable and its amount insufficient to address the country's searing economic problems. Many analysts see this as a key impediment to achieving stability in Afghanistan. As *The Economist* put it in 2006, "poverty helps the Taliban."

In places where poverty is rampant, politicians often become corrupt, misusing aid and exacerbating the plight of the poor. In Zimbabwe, the year 2002 left many people starving, as poor weather conditions created a meager harvest. The country's ruling party, ZANU-PF, headed by Robert Mugabe, demanded cards from Zimbabweans who registered for the "food for work" program—cards demonstrating membership in the ZANU-PF political party. As conditions worsened in subsequent years, the Mugabe government faced increasing resistance. A potential challenger, Morgan Tsvangirai, emerged in 2008. Members of his opposition party were killed and the challenger was harassed, but after a contested election that many believe Tsvangirai won, a power-sharing agreement came into effect that kept Mugabe as president and made Tsvangirai the prime minister. Some stability returned to the country, but continuing tensions make it difficult to address Zimbabwe's enormous economic problems.

The Zimbabwe case shows that in low-income countries, corrupt leaders can stay in power for decades because the people are afraid to rise up against the leader's extreme power or because those who have risen up have been killed or harmed by the leader's followers. Circumstances and timing need to work together to allow a new government to come to power. When governments become excessively corrupt, other countries and nongovernmental organizations sometimes withdraw development aid to the country. Yet when this happens, everyday people often bear the brunt of hardship. Even when the global community cuts off the corrupt government's aid, core countries and nongovernmental organizations often

try to provide food aid to the people. All too frequently, when this type of aid reaches its intended beneficiaries, it is rarely sufficient to meet basic needs or reverse the trajectory of hardship in the country.

## Costs of Economic Development

Economic development changes a place. To increase productivity, whether industrial or agricultural, people transform the environment. When a country goes through intensification of industrial production, air and surface water are often polluted. Pollution is not confined to industry. With intensification of *agricultural production*, the introduction of pesticides and herbicides can have deleterious impacts on the soil and groundwater. Tourism can be just as difficult on the environment—taxing the existing infrastructure beyond its capacities. The costs of tourism often stretch far beyond the environment, affecting ways of life and fundamentally altering the cultural landscape.

### INDUSTRIALIZATION

In their efforts to attract new industries, the governments of many countries in the global periphery and semiperiphery have set up special manufacturing export zones called **export processing zones (EPZs),** which offer favorable tax, regulatory, and trade arrangements to foreign firms. By 2006, 130 countries had established 3500 EPZs, and many of these had become major manufacturing centers (Engman et al. 2007) (Fig. 10.12). Two of the best known of these zones are the Mexican **maquiladoras** and the **special economic zones** of China (discussed in Chapter 9). Governments locate such zones in places with easy access to export markets. Maquiladora zones in Mexico

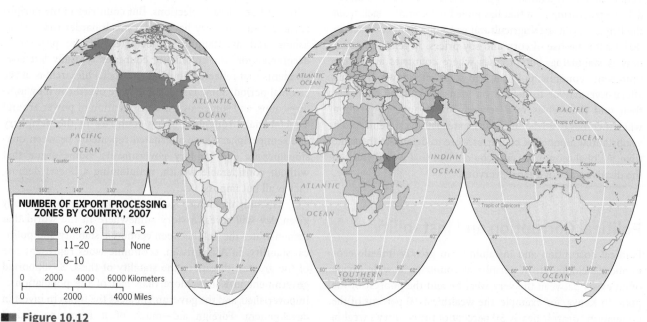

■ **Figure 10.12**

**Export Processing Zones.**　Number of export processing zones by country, 2007.　*Data from:* International Labor Organization.

are mainly sited directly across the border from the United States, and the special economic zones of China are located near major ports. These zones typically attract a mix of manufacturing operations, depending on the skill levels of the labor force and the available infrastructure.

The maquiladora program started in 1965 when the Mexican government designated the region of northern Mexico as a maquiladora district, making it a place where raw materials could be shipped into Mexico, manufactured into goods, and then sent back to the United States free of import tariffs. U.S. corporations relocated manufacturing plants to Mexico to take advantage of the program.

Although the maquiladora phenomenon started in 1965, it did not really take off until the 1980s. During the 1980s, American companies recognized the expanding wage and benefit differences between the U.S. and Mexican worker and began relocating to the maquiladora district in northern Mexico. Competition from other parts of the world has since led to the closing of some plants, but some 3000 maquiladoras continue to function, employing 1 million workers and accounting for 50 percent of Mexico's exports. The maquiladora plants produce goods such as electronic equipment, electrical appliances, automobiles, textiles, plastics, and furniture. The plants are controversial both in Mexico and the United States, as corporations that have relocated there avoid the employment and environmental regulations that are in force just a few miles to the north. Many maquiladora factories hire young women and men for low pay and few if any benefits, putting them to work in repetitive jobs, often in environmentally questionable conditions.

In 1992, the United States, Mexico, and Canada established the **North American Free Trade Agreement (NAFTA)**, which prompted further industrialization of the border region. NAFTA took effect January 1, 1994. In addition to manufacturing plants, NAFTA has facilitated the movement of service industries from the United States to Mexico, including data processing operations. Most of the new plants are located in two districts: Tijuana on the Pacific Coast—linked to San Diego across the border—and Ciudad Juarez on the Rio Grande across from El Paso, Texas. In recent years the socioeconomic and environmental contrasts between cities on either side of the U.S.–Mexico border have become increasingly stark. Violent crime has become a particularly serious problem in Juarez, even as El Paso remains comparatively safe, and the slums of Tijuana are a world apart from much of San Diego. Although NAFTA was designed to foster increased interaction in North America, cross-border disparities have worked together with growing U.S. concerns over illegal immigration and the infiltration of foreign terrorists to make the U.S.–Mexico border more tightly controlled and more difficult to cross than in prior decades.

### AGRICULTURE

In peripheral countries, agriculture typically focuses on personal consumption or on production for a large agricultural conglomerate. Where zones of larger-scale, modernized agriculture have developed in the periphery, foodstuffs are produced for the foreign market and often have minimal impact on the impoverished conditions of the surrounding lands. Little is produced for the local marketplace because distribution systems are poorly organized and because the local population is typically unable to pay for foodstuffs. If the local population owns land, their landholdings are usually fragmented, creating small plots of land that are difficult to farm in a manner that produces much income. Even on larger plots of land, most farmers are equipped with outdated, inefficient tools and equipment. The main crops tend to be grains and roots; farmers produce little protein because high-protein crops typically have lower yields than grain crops. On the farms in the periphery, yields per unit area are low, subsistence modes of life prevail, and many families are constantly in debt.

Impoverished farmers can ill afford such luxuries as fertilizers, and educational levels are typically too low to achieve widespread soil conservation. As a result, soil erosion is commonplace in most peripheral areas. Severe soil erosion in areas with dry or semiarid climates around deserts results in extreme degradation of the land and the spread of the desert into these lands. Although the expansion and contraction of deserts can occur naturally and cyclically, the process of **desertification** is more often exacerbated by humans destroying vegetation and eroding soils through the overuse of lands for livestock grazing or crop production.

Desertification has hit Africa harder than any of the other continents (Fig. 10.13). More than half of Africa is arid or semiarid, and many people farm the marginal, dry lands of the continent. Land ownership patterns, the need for crops and protein sources (both for local consumption and for export), and power differences among groups of people lead some farmers and ranchers to turn marginal, semiarid lands into farm and ranch lands. Lands that are available for farming or ranching may be used more intensively in order to increase agricultural production (see Chapter 13). In semiarid regions, the decision to farm more intensively and increase agricultural production has the unintended consequence of eroding the land, encouraging outmigration, and creating conflict.

In Subsaharan Africa over the last 50 years, more than 270,000 square miles (700,000 km$^2$) of farming and grazing land have become desert, extending the Sahara Desert to the south. Some of the African desertification may be caused by climatic fluctuations, but overgrazing, woodcutting, soil exhaustion, and misuse have undoubtedly accelerated the process.

### TOURISM

All development strategies have pros and cons, as is well illustrated by the case of tourism. Peripheral island countries in the Caribbean region and in Oceania have become leading destinations for millions of tourists from richer states.

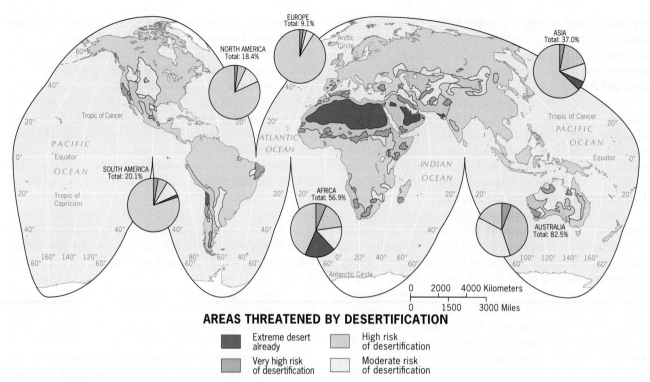

AREAS THREATENED BY DESERTIFICATION

- Extreme desert already
- Very high risk of desertification
- High risk of desertification
- Moderate risk of desertification

■■ **Figure 10.13**

**Areas Threatened by Desertification.** Deserts expand and contract cyclically, but nature's cycles can be distorted by human intervention. This map shows areas threatened or affected by desertification. *Data from*: Several sources, including J. Turk et al., *Environmental Science*, Philadelphia: Saunders, 1984, p. 305.

Tourism is now one of the major industries in the world and has surpassed oil in its overall economic value (see Chapter 12). While tourism can bring employment to peripheral countries, tourism may also have serious negative effects on cultures and environments.

To develop tourism, the "host" country must make substantial investments in infrastructure, including airports, cruise ports, roads, and communication systems. Beautiful hotels, swimming pools, and man-made waterfalls are typically owned by large multinational corporations, not locals. The multinational corporations earn enormous profits, most of which are sent back to owners, shareholders, and executives outside of the country. Tourism can create local jobs, but they are often low-paying and have little job security. In tourist zones, many employees work two or three jobs in order to break even.

Tourism frequently strains the fabric of local communities as well. The invasion of poor communities by wealthier visitors can foster antipathy and resentment. Tourism can also have the effect of altering, and even debasing, local culture (see Chapter 4), which is adapted to suit the visitors' taste. In many instances tourism fosters a "demonstration effect" among locals that encourages them to behave in ways that may please or interest the visitors but that is disdained by the larger local community. Some tourism workers consider employment in the tourist industry dehumanizing because it demands displays of friendliness and servitude that locals find insulting.

A flood of affluent tourists may be appealing to the government of a poor country whose elite may have a financial stake in the hotels where they can share the pleasures of the wealthy. Local entrepreneurs have difficulty tapping into tourist revenues because powerful multinational corporations and national governments often intervene to limit the opportunities of local, small-scale operators in favor of mass, prearranged tourist destinations that isolate the tourist from local society.

Overreliance on tourism can also leave an economy vulnerable if shifting economic circumstances cause a sharp decline in the number of tourists or if natural disasters hit. Because many tourist destinations in poorer countries are beach attractions, natural hazards such as the 2004 tsunami in Southeast Asia can destroy the lynchpin of a country's economy (we discuss the tsunami and other natural hazards in greater detail in Chapter 13). Suffering the loss of thousands of people; dealing with the after-effects of sewage, homelessness, orphans, and the destitute; and coping with rebuilding the tourist destinations must occur while the flow of tourist-related income has stopped.

The cultural landscape of tourism is frequently a study in harsh contrasts: gleaming hotels tower over modest, often poor housing; luxury liners glide past poverty-stricken villages; opulent meals are served in hotels while, down the street, children suffer from malnutrition. If the tourist industry offered real prospects for economic progress in low-income countries, such circumstances might be viewed as temporary, unfortunate by-products. However, the evidence too often points in the other direction.

Think of a trip you have made to a poorer area of the country or a poorer region of the world. Hypothesize how your experience in the place as a tourist was fundamentally different from the everyday lives of the people who live in the place.

## HOW DO POLITICAL AND ECONOMIC INSTITUTIONS INFLUENCE UNEVEN DEVELOPMENT WITHIN STATES?

Poverty is not confined to the periphery. Core countries have regions and peoples that are markedly poorer than others. On the Pine Ridge Indian Reservation in the northern Great Plains of the United States, unemployment hovers at 80 percent, and more than 60 percent of the people live in poverty with a per capita income of just over $6000. Other countries of the core have similar regions where peoples' economic lives do not improve when the country's economy grows. In Europe, areas of isolation and stagnation persist—particularly in the east. At the same time, areas within peripheral countries are experiencing rapid economic growth. In each of these cases, the local conditions in these places differ sharply from those prevailing in surrounding areas. Regional contrasts in wealth are a reminder that per capita GNI does not accurately represent the economic development of an individual country. Any statistic that is derived for an entire country hides the variety of economic situations within. Peripheral countries are notoriously marked by severe regional disparities. In Chapter 9 we discussed the stark contrasts between wealthy and poor within Latin American and African cities. When viewed at the scale of the State, major cities (particularly capitals) and their surroundings often look like islands of prosperity, with modern buildings, factories on the outskirts, and modern farms nearby. In some cases roads and rails lead to a bustling port, where luxury automobiles are unloaded for use by the privileged elite and raw materials or agricultural products from the country are exported to points around the world. In these core areas of countries, the rush of "progress" may be evident. If you travel a few miles into the countryside or into a different neighborhood in the city, however, you will likely see a very different picture. The contrasts between rich and poor areas are not simply the result of differences in the economic endowments of places. Government policy frequently affects development patterns as well. Hence, in this section of the chapter we turn to how governments collaborate with corporations to create islands of development, and consider how people try to generate growth in the periphery of the periphery (the poorest regions of peripheral countries).

## The Role of Governments

The actions of governments influence whether, how, and where wealth is produced. This is because the distribution of wealth is affected by tariffs, trade agreements, taxation structures, land ownership rules, environmental regulations, and many other manifestations of governmental authority. Government policies shape patterns of development within States—between urban and rural areas and also among sectors of the economy. Governments alone do not determine patterns of wealth and poverty, but they are almost always part of the picture. Consider the case of the Ninth Ward in New Orleans, which was devastated by Hurricane Katrina in 2005. On its surface, what happened to the Ninth Ward was the result of a natural disaster. But the flooding of that part of New Orleans was also the result of government decisions decades ago to build levies and settle flood-prone areas. The concentration of people living there was also the product of innumerable policies affecting housing, the construction of businesses, and the like. Once the hurricane hit, many looked to government to rebuild the devastated section of the city. The shortcomings of governmental response are evident in the landscape today (Fig. 10.14).

Every government policy has a geographical expression, meaning that some regions are favored whereas others are disadvantaged as a result of the implementation of that policy. When policies come together to favor some regions over others, uneven development is the result. And uneven development can easily be exacerbated over time as the wealthy grow wealthier.

Consider the contrasting outcomes of U.S. agricultural policy in parts of rural Wisconsin and rural Appalachia. In rural Wisconsin, farmers typically hold college degrees, usually from land-grant universities, in plant and animal sciences and in agribusiness. A farmer may run a highly mechanized dairy farm where he equips each cow with a barcode and keeps a range of data about that particular cow. The data include any medical attention the cow has needed, how much milk the cow is producing, and when the cow last calved. The farmer feeds the cow a diet geared toward improving or maintaining milk production. When the cow ambles over to the trough to feed, a sensor reads the cow's barcode and automatically mixes the correct balance of proteins, carbohydrates, and nutrients for the cow, dispensing them into the trough for the cow to eat. If the cow has already eaten that day, the computer dispenses nothing into the trough, and the cow is left to amble away.

In parts of rural Appalachia, by contrast, hardscrabble farming is the norm. Farmers have limited education, and there is little mechanization. In short, life in some of the poorest parts of rural Appalachia is a world apart from life on a modern Wisconsin dairy farm. Some of those differences can be attributed to geographic situation and economic swings. But others are the product of government policies that influence educational opportunities, provide subsidies for particular agricultural pursuits, and promote the development of

# FIELD NOTE

"As I walked through New Orleans' Lower Ninth Ward more than two years after Hurricane Katrina, it seemed as if the natural disaster had just happened. Street after street of devastated, vacant buildings was all the eye could behold—many still bearing the markings of the emergency crews that had moved through the neighborhood in the wake of the hurricane, showing whether anyone had died inside. It struck me that reconstruction would require a public commitment on the order of what occurred in Europe after World War II, when cities reduced to rubble by bombing were rebuilt almost from scratch. No such commitment ever materialized, but some progress has been made in recent years. Recent census data shows a city that is slightly smaller and slightly richer than the pre-Katrina city, with a somewhat reduced black population, and a modestly expanding number of Hispanics."

© Alexander B. Murphy

■■ **Figure 10.14**
**Destroyed House in the Lower Ninth Ward, New Orleans.**

particular technologies within certain places. The State of Wisconsin supports its $26 billion dairy industry, and the University of Wisconsin receives huge grants and corporate funding to constantly improve dairy farming. Government policy can also help alleviate uneven development. In the case of Appalachia, the U.S. Congress created an Appalachian Regional Commission in 1965 to address poverty in the region. The Commission has orchestrated a program of government investment in roads, schools, health care facilities, and water and sewer systems that has fostered development in parts of the region. Significant parts of Appalachia have benefited from these policies, although pockets of deep poverty remain.

Looking at commodity chains can also help us understand the role of governments in uneven development both within and between states. In her 2005 book *The Travels of a T-Shirt in the Global Economy*, economist Pietra Rivoli described the significant influences governments have on the distribution of wealth between and within states. Rivoli grabs a T-shirt out of a bin at a Walgreens in Florida, buys it, and then traces its production back through the commodity chain to see how it ends up in her hands. The cotton for her T-shirt was grown in West Texas, where the cotton lobby (the political arm of America's cotton producers) has effectively politicked for governmental labor programs and price supports that help the industry grow cotton and sell it at predictable prices.

From West Texas, the cotton bale reaches China by ship. There it is spun into thread and woven into fabric. Women from rural China work in state-owned factories set up in regions that are slated for economic development—cutting and sewing T-shirts and keeping the textile machines in good repair. The women are considered cheap labor at the global scale, earning about $100 per month. Rivoli reports that over 40,000 garment factories operate in China alone.

The T-shirts are then shipped to the United States for sale. In an attempt to protect T-shirts produced in America with higher labor costs from those produced in China, the U.S. government has established quotas on how many items from various clothing categories can be imported into the United States from China and other countries. An unintended consequence of the quota system has been a "quota market" that allows countries to buy and sell their U.S. quota numbers to producers in other countries (an illegal but rampant practice). Instead of trading in quotas, some production facilities have moved to places where quotas and cheap labor are available—places such as Sri Lanka, Poland, and Lesotho. Rivoli describes how one producer of cotton shirts has moved around the world:

*The Esquel Corporation, today the world's largest producer of cotton shirts, started in Hong Kong in the late 1970s, but, unable to obtain quota to sell to the United States, shifted production to mainland China. When the United States tightened Chinese shirt quotas in the early 1980s, Esquel moved production to Malaysia. When Malaysian quota also became difficult to obtain, Esquel moved yet again, this time to Sri Lanka. The globe hopping continued, with the Chinese shirt producer setting up operations in Mauritius and Maldives.*

The point is that quota laws, like other policies made by governments, regional trade organizations, and international political regimes (such as the World Trade Organization and the International Labor Organization), affect whether and how regions can produce and exchange goods on the world market.

## Islands of Development

In both periphery and core, governments often invest in growing the economy of the capital city so that it can act as a showcase for the country. Capital cities are home to government buildings and jobs; they often house universities, museums, heritage centers, convention centers, and the headquarters of large corporations. After gaining independence, many former colonial states spent lavishly on their capitals, not because such spending was essential to political or economic success but because the states wanted to showcase their independence and their futures, and create a national treasure. European colonizers who focused their wealth and treasures on their capital cities, including the United Kingdom's London, France's Paris, and the Netherlands' Amsterdam, served as models for the newly independent states.

In many countries of the global economic periphery and semiperiphery, the capital cities are by far the largest and most economically influential cities in the state (i.e., primate cities, discussed in Chapter 9). Some newly independent states have built new capital cities, away from the colonial headquarters. Their goals in doing so are to separate themselves from their colonizers, to bring together diverse groups into one state with a city built to reflect their common culture, to extend economic development into the interior of the state, or to help establish control over a region with a population whose loyalties might not be to the state.

Nigeria moved its capital from Yoruba-dominated Lagos along the coast to an ethnically neutral territory in the center of the state: Abuja. Malawi moved its capital from Zomba, deep in the south, to more central Lilongwe. Pakistan moved the capital from the colonial headquarters of Karachi to Islamabad in the far north to symbolize the country's reorientation toward its historically important interior and north. Brazil moved its capital from coastal Rio de Janeiro to centrally located Brasília in order to direct attention to the huge, sparsely populated, yet poorly integrated interior. More recently, Kazakhstan moved its capital from Almaty in the south to Astana in the north, partly to be closer to Russia and the center of the possibly restless Russian population. Malaysia has also recently moved its capital from the colonial capital of Kuala Lumpur to a completely new center called Putrajaya, about 25 miles (40 km) to the south. The Malaysian government decided to build a new, ultramodern seat of government to symbolize the country's rapid economic growth (Fig. 10.15).

Corporations can also make cities focal points of development by concentrating corporate activities in a particular place. Often, corporations build up the cities near the resources they are extracting or near manufacturing centers they have built. Multinational oil companies create subsidiaries in countries of the periphery and semiperiphery, creating or expanding cities near oil reserves. For example, in Gabon, Elf and Shell, two oil companies based in Europe, run ElfGabon and ShellGabon in the Central African country. The oil companies took the small colonial town of Port Gentil in Gabon and turned it into a city that the locals call "oil city." The oil companies built housing, roads, and stores, and provide much of the employment in the town (Fig. 10.16).

When a government or corporation builds up and concentrates economic development in a certain city or small region, geographers call that place an **island of development**. In Chapter 3, we identified islands of development in the periphery and semiperiphery and discussed why people migrate to these cities from rural areas and other poorer cities. The hope for a job drives many migrants to move to these islands of comparative prosperity.

■ **Figure 10.15**
**Putrajaya, Malaysia.** Putrajaya is the newly built capital of Malaysia, replacing Kuala Lumpur.

## FIELD NOTE

"Before the 1970s, Gabon's principal exports were manganese, hardwoods, and uranium ores. The discovery of oil off the Gabonese coast changed all that. This oil storage tank at the edge of Port Gentile is but one reminder of a development that has transformed Gabon's major port city—and the economy of the country as a whole. Oil now accounts for 80 percent of Gabon's export earnings, and that figure is climbing as oil prices rise and new discoveries are made. But how much the average citizen of Gabon is benefiting from the oil economy remains an open question. Even as health care and infrastructure needs remain unmet, the French publication *L'Autre Afrique* listed Gabon's recently deceased ruler as the African leader with the largest real estate holdings in Paris."

© Alexander B. Murphy

■ **Figure 10.16**
**Port Gentil, Gabon.**

## Creating Growth in the Periphery of the Periphery

One of the greatest challenges to development is creating development opportunities outside of islands of development. In the most rural, impoverished regions of less prosperous countries, some nongovernmental organizations try to improve the plight of people. **Nongovernmental organizations (NGOs)** are not run by state or local governments. Rather, NGOs operate independently, and the term is usually reserved for entities that operate as nonprofits. Thousands of NGOs operate in the world today, from churches to charities such as Heifer International. Each NGO has its own set of goals, depending on the primary concerns outlined by its founders and financiers (Fig. 10.17).

Some countries have so many NGOs operating within them that they serve as what *The Economist* (1998) calls "a parallel state, financed by foreigners and accountable to nobody." For example, more than 20,000 NGOs operate within the country of Bangladesh at any time, focusing mainly on the rural areas and villages of the state. But the NGO phenomenon can be a bit of a mirage, masking the depth of problems some places face. In the wake of the 2010 earthquake in Haiti, one respected British newspaper, the *Guardian*, reported that there was approximately one NGO per 1000 people in Haiti, but that much of the money funneled through these NGOs was misappropriated.

One particular kind of program by NGOs that has found success in South Asia and South America is the microcredit program. The idea behind a **microcredit program** is simple: Give loans to poor people, particularly women, to encourage development of small businesses. Programs either have women in the village guarantee each other's credit, or they make future lending to others contingent on repayment by the first borrowers. With repayment rates hovering at 98 percent, microcredit programs can finance themselves, and many NGOs offer the programs (Fig. 10.18).

By providing microcredit to women, NGOs can alter the gender balance in a region, giving more fiscal power to women. Some microcredit programs are credited with lowering birth rates in parts of developing countries and altering the social fabric of cultures by diminishing men's positions of power. Successful microcredit programs also help alleviate malnourishment, as women with incomes can feed themselves and their children.

Microcredit programs have been less successful in places with high mortality rates from diseases such as AIDS. If the borrower is unable to work or if the family has medical and funeral bills, the borrower is much more likely to default on the microcredit loan. When people in the periphery of the periphery experience a multitude of challenges, such as disease, corrupt governments, high mortality rates, high fertility rates, and disruptions from natural hazards, the goal of economic development takes a backseat to daily survival.

**thinking** *geographically* Find something in your house (an item of clothing, an electronic device, etc.) and, using the Internet, try to trace the commodity chain of production. What steps did the item and its components go through before reaching you? Consider the types of economic processes that were operating at each step and think of the roles governments and international political regimes played along the way.

# GUEST FIELD NOTE

## Sukabumi, West Java

My own research is based on fieldwork in Indonesia as well as ongoing engagement with students in the United States. The women pictured here collaborated with me on a research/activism project for migrant women workers in Indonesia. The woman on the left ("Rina") had returned from working in Saudi Arabia as a domestic worker for two years. She wanted to return to Saudi Arabia for another contract to earn more money for herself and her family, but she was concerned about her rights and her safety. She had been employed by a person she considered fair and reasonable, but she had heard from friends and neighbors that many migrants had experienced serious abuses while abroad. The woman pictured on the right ("Sorani") is an Indonesian activist who works in support of migrant rights. She discussed with Rina and me her strategies for mobilizing political change, and she helped us to see possibilities for building transnational alliances among American and Indonesian workers, students, and activists. Based on these interviews, as well as many years of working with migrant women working in factories in Indonesia, my own research has increasingly sought to understand the ways in which we in the United States, as scholars, students, workers, and consumers, can better serve global justice.

Rachel Silvey, University of Toronto

■ Figure 10.17

*Credit: Rachel Silvey, University of Toronto.*

© Alexander B. Murphy

■ Figure 10.18

**Bwindi, Uganda.**   Women walk by a microcredit agency that works to facilitate economic development in the town.

# Summary

The idea of economic development is relatively new; it implies a sense of progressively improving a country's economic situation. The idea took hold in the wake of the Industrial Revolution. Geographers focus on the spatial structure of the economy, assessing how that structure influences the ability of states and regions to reach greater levels of economic development. Geographers also recognize that economic development in a single place is based on a multitude of factors, including the situation within the global economy, the link the place plays in commodity chains, the efficacy of government, the presence of disease, the health and well-being of the population, the presence and amount of foreign debt, the success or failure of government policies, and the influence of nongovernmental programs. Geographers also realize that all of these processes are operating concurrently across scales, making a country's journey toward economic development much more complicated than climbing a ladder.

# Geographic Concepts

commodity chain
break-of-bulk location
gross national product (GNP)
gross domestic product (GDP)
gross national income (GNI)
per capita GNI
formal economy
informal economy
digital divide
Millennium Development Goals
modernization model

context
neo-colonialism
structuralist theory
dependency theory
dollarization
world-systems theory
three-tier structure
trafficking
structural adjustment loans
Washington Consensus
neoliberalism

export processing zones (EPZs)
maquiladoras
special economic zones
North American Free Trade Agreement (NAFTA)
desertification
island of development
nongovernmental organizations (NGOs)
microcredit program

# Learn More Online

About Brazil's Bolsa Familia
www.worldbank.org/en/news/opinion/2013/11/04/bolsa-familia-Brazil-quiet-revolution

About Global Poverty
www.worldbank.org/poverty

About Global Economic Development
www.brookings.edu/global.aspx

About United Nations Millennium Goals
www.un.org/millenniumgoals/

# Watch It Online

About Gabon
www.learner.org/resources/series180.html#program_descriptions

Click on Video On Demand for "Gabon: Sustainable Resources?"

# AGRICULTURE AND THE RURAL LANDSCAPE

## Changing Greens

Driving across the semiarid ranchlands of western South Dakota, I noticed the presence of a crop in the landscape that was recently found only in the eastern, moister region of the state: soybeans (Fig. 11.1).

I called a colleague who works in agriculture at South Dakota State University to ask, "When did the cattle ranchers of western South Dakota start growing soybeans?" He replied, "When the soy biodiesel plants started popping up in Nebraska and Kansas and when genetically modified soybeans made it possible to grow the crop here." He explained the development of Roundup Ready soybeans, a particular genetically modified soybean that can grow in more arid regions of the country. First, you plant the soybean; then you use an airplane to spray Roundup, a common weed killer that is manufactured by the company that produces the Roundup Ready soybeans, over the field. The application of Roundup over the entire field saves a lot of time and energy for the farmers because the genetically modified soybeans are resistant to the Roundup, but the weeds are killed. Monsanto, the company that produces Roundup, has developed soybeans, corn, cotton, and other crops that are resistant to Roundup.

© Erin H. Fouberg

■■ **Figure 11.1**
**Presho, South Dakota.** Soybeans growing in the semiarid ranchlands of western South Dakota.

Counter to the genetically modified Roundup Ready crops, **organic agriculture**—the production of crops without the use of synthetic or industrially produced pesticides and fertilizers—is also on the rise in North America. In wealthier parts of the world, the demand for organic products has risen exponentially in recent years. Sales of organic food in the United States, for example, went from under $200 million in 1980 to $1.5 billion by the early 1990s to over $10 billion by 2003 and $31.5 billion in 2013. Organic foods are now just over 4 percent of all food sales in the country. The growth rate is so strong that some predict organic sales will approach 10 percent of total U.S. food sales within a decade. Parts of western Europe are already approaching that figure—notably Denmark, Sweden, Finland, and parts of Germany.

311

Agricultural fields are devoted to organic agriculture in the core, semiperiphery, and periphery. Fields devoted to organic agriculture produce all kinds of foodstuffs, including fruits, vegetables, coffee, tea, grains, nuts, and spices. Compared to all agricultural land, the organic segment is still quite small and relatively scattered, but a farmer who can gain organic certification from a government or an internationally recognized third party is increasingly at a competitive advantage (Fig. 11.2).

Although organic crops are grown everywhere, most organic foods are sold in the global economic core: in the United States, Canada, Japan, Europe, and Australia. The best-selling organic crops in the United States are fruits and vegetables, accounting for 43 percent of organic food sales, followed by dairy at 15 percent and packaged food and nondairy beverages at 15 percent and dairy between 9 and 11 percent. Organic products typically cost more than conventional products in the grocery store. Nonetheless, a 2002 report issued by the United States Department of Agriculture explains that in 2000 organic foods crossed a threshold, moving out of health food stores and into supermarkets: "for the first time, more organic food was purchased in conventional supermarkets than in any other venue." Organic foods are sold in well over half of the conventional grocery stores in the United States, with increasing demands for organic animal products such as meats and dairy.

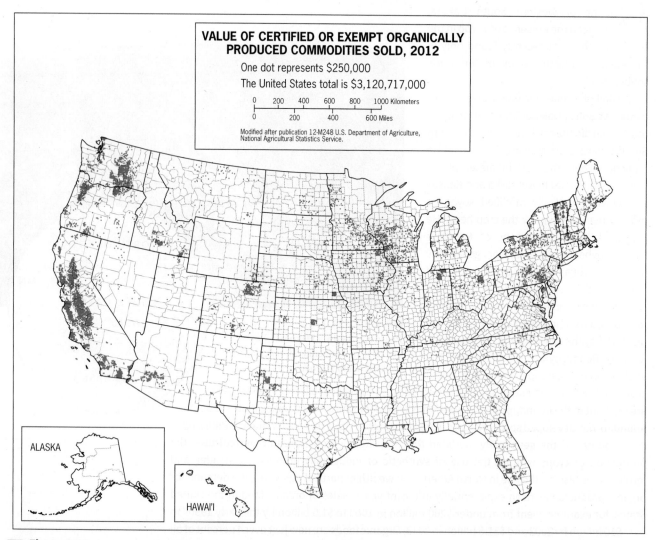

**Figure 11.2**

**Value of Certified Organically Produced Commodities Sold, 2012.**    Farms on the west coast, the Midwest, and the northeast produce the greatest amount of organic commodities based on sales. Northeastern Colorado also has a relatively large area of organic production for sale. This map does not show organically produced crops sold in farmers markets or for self-consumption.

Organic farming has helped some farmers in the core extract themselves to a degree from the control of large, external corporate interests. The role of organic agriculture in the periphery and semiperiphery is similar to that of other major cash crops: Production is almost entirely for export to the global economic core. When organic agriculture bears a fair trade certification, some producers in the periphery and semiperiphery benefit substantially, though they also have to abide by rules established in the core (see the discussion of fair trade coffee in the last section of this chapter).

The organic movement has some clear environmental benefits, particularly in reducing levels of synthetic chemicals in soil and water. The putative health and taste advantages of organic produce help ensure the continued growth of the organic movement. The continually increasing demand for organic products has led the United States Department of Agriculture to certify organic products in the country, giving some degree of standardization to organic agriculture.

In this chapter, we examine the origins of agriculture and trace the geography of changes in the production of food and the raising of livestock from the earliest domestication of plants to such contemporary developments as genetic modification and the turn toward large-scale agribusiness. In the process, we describe the early hearths of agriculture, the geography of technological changes in agriculture, the global pattern of agricultural production, and the imprint of agriculture on the cultural landscape.

# Key Questions FOR CHAPTER 11

1. What is agriculture, and where did agriculture begin?
2. How did agriculture change with industrialization?
3. What imprint does agriculture make on the cultural landscape?
4. How is agriculture currently organized geographically, and how has agribusiness influenced the contemporary geography of agriculture?

## WHAT IS AGRICULTURE, AND WHERE DID AGRICULTURE BEGIN?

**Agriculture** is the deliberate tending of crops and livestock to produce food, feed, fiber, and fuel. When we think about agriculture, we tend to think about the production of foodstuffs for humans. Grain is also used for *feed*, grains fed directly to livestock. Raising livestock for milk, eggs, or meat makes up a large segment of U.S. agriculture. Feed also comes from the remnants of biofuel production; in 2012, around 40 percent of all grain produced in the United States was used to produce fuel for cars, not for human or animal consumption.

A common way of classifying economic activities is to focus on what is being produced. Economic activities that involve the extraction of economically valuable products from the earth, including agriculture, ranching, hunting and gathering, fishing, forestry, mining, and quarrying, are called **primary economic activities**. Both the growing of food or feed and the raising of livestock are considered primary economic activities. Activities that take a primary product and change it into something else such as toys, ships, processed foods, chemicals, and buildings are **secondary economic activities**. Manufacturing is the principal secondary economic activity. **Tertiary economic activities** are those service industries that connect producers to consumers and facilitate commerce and trade or help people meet their needs. People who work as bankers, lawyers, doctors, teachers, nurses, salespeople, clerks, and secretaries belong to the tertiary sector. Some analysts separate specialized services into **quaternary** and **quinary economic activities**, distinguishing between those services concerned with information or the exchange of money or goods (quaternary) and those tied to research or higher education (quinary). In this chapter, however, for simplicity's sake we limit ourselves to three categories: primary, secondary, and a broadly conceived tertiary or service sector.

By classifying economic activities into sectors and analyzing the percentage of the population employed in each sector, we can gain insight into how the production of goods is organized, as well as the employment structures of different societies. As we explained in our discussions of world-systems theory in Chapters 8 and 10, the story of any product (such as wheat or rice) can be better illuminated by focusing on how the good is produced (the kinds of technology, research, wages, and education that go into its production), rather than concentrating simply on what is produced. Examining the proportion of people employed in a given economic sector gives us a basic idea of how the good is produced. For example, in Guatemala the agriculture sector accounts for 26 percent of the country's gross domestic product (GDP), and over 50 percent of the labor force is employed in agriculture. Contrast that with Canada, where the agriculture sector accounts for 2.3 percent of GDP and only 2 percent of the labor force is employed in agriculture. The tertiary sector in Canada accounts for 75 percent of the labor force and over 71 percent of GDP, and the tertiary sector in Guatemala accounts for 35 percent of the labor force and 65 percent of the country's GDP.

These data do not tell us exactly how goods are produced, but they are revealing. The high proportion of the labor force involved in agriculture in Guatemala (relative to the role of agriculture in the GDP) tells us that agriculture is still quite labor dependent in Guatemala, implying a lack of mechanization. In Canada, the United States, and much of the rest of the global economic core, agriculture is produced on a large scale for commercial consumption. When agricultural goods are produced in these ways, the number of people working directly in the field is quite small. In the United States, less than 2 percent of the workforce is involved in agricultural production. Thousands of others participate in supporting agricultural production by working in the tertiary sector as research scientists for universities, seed companies, or chemical (antibiotics, pesticides, and herbicides) producers; as lobbyists for industry groups such as wheat producers or cattle ranchers; as engineers who design farm implements; as the people who sell and repair the implements; and as owners and clerks at retail establishments where farmers buy other farm and nonfarm goods.

In the United States, total agricultural production is at an all-time high, but the proportion of the labor force in agriculture is at an all-time low. Mechanization and efficiencies created by new technologies have led to a significant decrease in the number of workers needed in agricultural production. In 1950, one farmer in the United States produced enough to feed 27 people; today, one farmer in the United States produces enough to feed 144 people. The mechanization of agriculture goes beyond machinery such as combines and harvesters. New technologies include hybrid seeds and genetically engineered crops, pesticides, and herbicides, all of which are designed to increase yields. The drive toward economic efficiency has meant that the average size of farms (acres in production) in the United States has been growing, regardless of the kind of agricultural good produced. The U.S. Department of Agriculture keeps data showing the dollar value of agricultural production. The farms with the highest total production have at least $500,000 in annual production. These high-producing farms accounted for 53.7 percent of agricultural goods produced in 2007 (compared with 28.9 percent in 1989). The number of these high-producing farms increased by 33 percent between 2007 and 2012, while the number of smaller farms fell, resulting in a loss of 95,500 farms. Now the largest 4 percent of U.S. farms produce 66 percent of the country's agricultural sales.

Clearly, agriculture in the United States has changed enormously in the last decade. A recent study by the National Research Council of the U.S. National Academy of Sciences identifies four major issues that affect food security worldwide: "1) varying abilities to balance production and consumption across regions and countries, 2) accelerating conversions of agricultural land to urban uses, 3) increasingly energy-intensive food production methods in a world of shrinking fossil fuel resources, and 4) expanding use of food crops for biofuel production." Agricultural production changes rapidly as farmers worldwide react to price fluctuations in fossil fuels, seeds, fertilizers, crops, and land.

To set the stage for understanding the contemporary agriculture picture, in the next section of the chapter, we discuss how people lived before the origins of agriculture and the circumstances that gave rise to the domestication of plants and animals many millennia ago.

# Hunting, Gathering, and Fishing

Before the advent of agriculture, hunting, gathering, and fishing were the most common means of subsistence throughout the world. Of course, what people hunted or gathered depended on where they lived. North America provides a good example of the diversity of regional specializations among hunter-gatherers. The oak forests of parts of North America provided an abundant harvest of nuts, sometimes enough to last more than a full year; American Indian communities living in and around these forests therefore collected and stored this food source. Other American Indians living near the Pacific Ocean became adept at salmon fishing. The bison herds of the Great Plains provided sustenance, and so bison served as a focal point for many plains cultures. In the colder climates of North America, people followed the migrations of the caribou herds. In the north, in the coastal zone stretching from present-day Alaska to Russia, the Aleut developed specialized techniques for fishing and for sea mammal hunting.

The size of hunting and gathering clans varied according to climate and resource availability. Hunting and gathering communities in areas of abundance could support larger populations. People living on the margins of forests could gather food in the forest when hunting yielded poor results and then return to hunting when circumstances improved.

## Terrain and Tools

Before developing agriculture, hunter-gatherers worked on perfecting tools, controlling fires, and adapting environments to their needs. The first tools used in hunting were simple clubs—tree limbs that were thin at one end and thick and heavy at the other. The use of bone and stone and the development of spears made hunting far more effective. The fashioning of stone into hand axes and, later, handle axes was a crucial innovation that enabled hunters to skin their prey and cut the meat; it also made it possible to cut down trees and build better shelters and tools.

The controlled use of fire was another important early achievement of human communities. The first opportunities to control fire were offered by natural conditions (lightning, spontaneous combustion of surface-heated coal). Archaeological digs of ancient settlement sites suggest that people would capture a fire caused accidentally and would work to keep the fire burning continuously. Later, people learned that fire could be generated by rapid hand rotation of a wooden stick in a small hole surrounded by dry tinder. Fire became the focal point of settlements, and the campfire took on symbolic and functional importance. It was a means of making foods digestible, and it was used to drive animals into traps or over cliffs.

In addition to hunting game on land, humans harvested shellfish, trapped fish by cutting small patches of standing water off from the open sea, and invented tools to catch fish, including harpoons, hooks, and baskets.

Using tools and fire, human communities altered their environments, which helped to establish more reliable food supplies. Along with hunting and gathering, early humans were adept at keeping track of the migration cycles of fish and other animals. American Indians along the Pacific Coast and on Arctic shores, the Ainu of Japan and coastal East Asia, and communities in coastal western Europe caught salmon as they swam up rivers and negotiated rapids and falls. Archaeologists have found huge accumulations of fish bones at prehistoric sites near salmon runs.

Hunter-gatherers migrated to take advantage of cyclical movements of animals and to avoid exhausting the supply of edible plants in any one area. After the summer salmon runs, people hunted deer during the fall and again in the spring, taking advantage of seasonal movements to trap deer where they crossed rivers or in narrow valleys. During the winter, people lived off dried meat and other stored foods.

## The First Agricultural Revolution

Out of areas of plenty came agriculture, the deliberate tending of crops and livestock to produce food, feed, fiber, and fuel. Geographer Carl Sauer believed the experiments necessary to establish agriculture and settle in one place would occur in lands of plenty. Only in such places could people afford to experiment with raising plants or take the time to capture animals and breed them for domestication. Sauer studied the geography of the First Agricultural Revolution, focusing on the location of agriculture hearths and what kinds of agricultural innovations took place in those hearths.

Where did **plant domestication** begin? Sauer, who spent a lifetime studying cultural origins and diffusion, suggested that Southeast and South Asia may have been the scene, more than 14,000 years ago, of the first domestication of tropical plants. There, he believed, the combination of human settlements, forest margins, and fresh water streams may have given rise to the earliest planned cultivation of **root crops**—crops that are reproduced by cultivating either the roots or cuttings from the plants (such as tubers, including manioc or cassava, yams, and sweet potatoes in the tropics). A similar but later development may have taken place in northwestern South America.

The planned cultivation of **seed crops**, plants that are reproduced by cultivating seeds, is a more complex process, involving seed selection, sowing, watering, and well-timed harvesting. Again, the practice seems to have developed in more than one area and at different times. Some scholars believe that the first domestication of seed plants occurred in the Nile River Valley in North Africa, but the majority view is that this crucial development took place in a region of Southwest Asia (also called the Fertile Crescent), through which flow the two major rivers of present-day Iraq: the Tigris and the Euphrates (Fig. 11.3). The cultivation of seed crops marked the beginning of what has been called the **First Agricultural Revolution**.

Archaeologists note that a number of changes occurred in Southwest Asia along with plant domestication. First, the plants themselves changed because people would choose seeds from the largest, hardiest plants to save for planting, yielding domesticated plants that grew larger over time than their counterparts in the wild. Archaeologists in Southwest Asia have found preserved seeds, which tell them which plants were being domesticated and when. The grain crops wheat and barley grew well in the warm Southwest Asian climate. Soon, people found that the river-inundated plains of Mesopotamia provided irrigable fields for farming. Agriculture provided a reliable food source, and grain surpluses enabled people to store grain for long-term distribution and use and to settle permanently in one place. In the process, the population of settlements began to increase.

Figure 11.4 depicts the global distribution of plant domestication hearths. In Southeast Asia (Region 1), taro, yams, and bananas were the leading food plants. In Southwest Asia (Region 4), plant domestication centered on wheat, barley, and other grains. In the Mesoamerican region (Region 6), the basic plants were maize (corn), squashes, and several kinds of beans.

Archaeologists continually find new sites to excavate, and as places are analyzed further, academics revise their

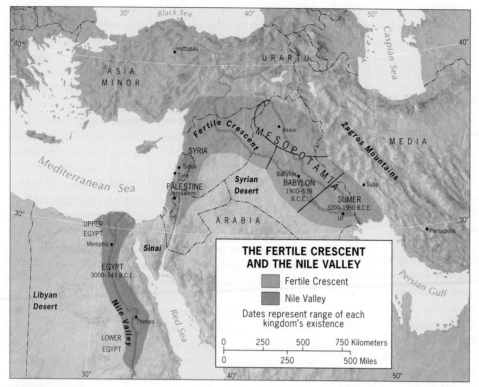

■ **Figure 11.3**

**The Fertile Crescent and Nile River Valley.**   The Fertile Crescent and Nile River Valley were two hearths of the First Agricultural Revolution. Modern political boundaries are shown for reference. © E. H. Fouberg, A. B. Murphy, H. J. de Blij, and John Wiley & Sons, Inc.

among the world's first. Another agricultural source region lies in West Africa (Region 9). Archaeological research on agriculture in this area is relatively recent, and analysts are not certain whether agriculture developed independently there.

Table 11.1 may be overwhelming at first glance, but it is worth careful attention. It reveals the enormous range of crops that were cultivated around the world, as well as how, at various times and in different locales, particular groups of crops became the mainstays of life. Soon the knowledge needed to farm such crops diffused outward from these agricultural hearths. For example, both millet and sorghum diffused from the West African region—millet to India and sorghum to China.

In many cases, what we now think of as centers of production of particular crops are not the places where those crops were originally domesticated. The corn (maize) we associate with the American Corn Belt diffused from Mesoamerica (Region 6) into North America. Later, the Portuguese brought it across the Atlantic and into Africa, where it became a staple in some regions. The white potato we associate with Ireland

assumptions about the timing of the emergence of agricultural hearths. The Central China hearth (Region 7) has recently attracted greater attention because new evidence supports a much earlier development of agriculture in this region—so early, in fact, that Chinese farmers may have been

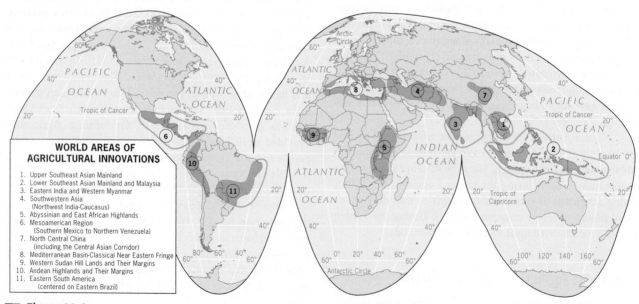

■ **Figure 11.4**

**Agricultural Hearths.**   Cultural geographer Carl Sauer identified 11 areas where agricultural innovations occurred. *Adapted with permission from*: C. O. Sauer, *Agricultural Origins and Dispersals*. New York: American Geographical Society, 1952, p. 24.

**TABLE 11.1**

**Chief Source Regions of Important Crop Plant Domestications.** *Adapted with permission from*: J. E. Spencer and W. L. Thomas, *Introducing Cultural Geography*, 1978, John Wiley & Sons, Inc.

### A. Primary Regions of Domestications

**1. The Upper Southeast Asian Mainlands**

| | | | | | | | |
|---|---|---|---|---|---|---|---|
| Citrus fruits* | Bamboos* | Yams* | Rices* | Eugenias* | Lichi | Teas | Ramie |
| Bananas* | Taros* | Cabbages* | Beans* | Job's tears | Longan | Tung oils | Water chestnut |

**2. Lower Southeast Asian Mainland and Malaysia (including New Guinea)**

| | | | | | | | |
|---|---|---|---|---|---|---|---|
| Citrus fruits* | Taros* | Pandanuses | Breadfruits | Lanzones | Vine peppers* | Nutmeg | Areca |
| Bananas* | Yams* | Cucumbers* | Jackfruits | Durian | Gingers* | Clove | Abaca |
| Bamboos* | Almonds* | Sugarcanes | Coconuts | Rambutan | Brinjals* | Cardamom | |

**3. Eastern India and Western Burma**

| | | | | | | | |
|---|---|---|---|---|---|---|---|
| Bananas* | Beans* | Millets* | Grams | Vine peppers* | Mangoes | Safflower | Lotus |
| Yams* | Rices* | Sorghums* | Eggplants | Gingers* | Kapok* | Jute | Turmeric |
| Taros* | Amaranths* | Peas* | Brinjals* | Palms* | Indigo | Sunn | Hemp |

**4. Southwestern Asia (Northwest India-Caucasus)**

| | | | | | | | |
|---|---|---|---|---|---|---|---|
| Soft wheats* | Peas* | Rye* | Beets* | Hemp | Soft Pears* | Pomegranates | Walnuts |
| Barleys* | Oil seeds* | Onions | Spinach | Apples | Cherries* | Grapes* | Melons |
| Lentils* | Poppies | Carrots* | Sesames | Almonds* | Plums* | Jujubes* | Tamarind |
| Beans* | Oats* | Turnips | Flax | Peaches* | Figs | Pistachio | Alfalfa |

**5. Ethiopian and East African Highlands**

| | | | | | | | |
|---|---|---|---|---|---|---|---|
| Hard wheats* | Sorghums* | Barleys | Beans* | Oil seeds* | Melons* | Coffees | Okras |
| Millets* | Rices* | Peas* | Vetches | Cucumbers* | Gourds* | Castor beans | Cottons* |

**6. Meso-American Region (Southern Mexico to Northern Venezuela)**

| | | | | | |
|---|---|---|---|---|---|
| Maizes | Taros* | Tomatoes* | Avocados | Muskmelons | Cottons* |
| Amaranths* | Sweet potatoes | Chili peppers | Sapotes | Palms* | Agaves |
| Beans* | Squashes | Custard apples | Plums* | Manioc | Kapok |

### B. Secondary Regions of Domestications

**7. North-Central China (including the Central Asian corridor)**

| | | | | | |
|---|---|---|---|---|---|
| Millets* | Soybeans | Naked oat* | Mulberries | Bush cherries* | Peaches* |
| Barleys* | Cabbages* | Mustards | Persimmons | Hard pears* | Jujubes* |
| Buckwheats | Radishes* | Rhubarb | Plums* | Apricots | |

**8. Mediterranean Basin—Classical Near Eastern Fringe**

| | | | | | | |
|---|---|---|---|---|---|---|
| Barleys* | Lentils* | Grapes* | Dates | Parsnips | Lettuces | Carrots* | Sugar beet |
| Oats* | Peas* | Olives | Carobs | Asparagus | Celeries | Garlic | Leek |

**9. Western Sudan Hill Lands and Their Margins**

| | | | | | |
|---|---|---|---|---|---|
| Sorghums* | Rices* | Yams* | Peas* | Melons* | Oil palms | Kola nut |
| Millets* | Fonio | Beans* | Oil seeds* | Gourds* | Tamarind* |

**10. Andean Highlands and Their Margins**

| | | | | | |
|---|---|---|---|---|---|
| White potatoes | Tomatoes* | Beans* | Quinoa | Cubio | Ulluco |
| Pumpkins | Strawberries | Papayas | Oca | Arrocacha | |

**11. Eastern South America (centered on eastern Brazil)**

| | | | | |
|---|---|---|---|---|
| Taros* | Peanuts | Cashew nut | Cacao | Cottons* |
| Beans* | Pineapples | Brazil nut | Passion fruits | Tobaccos |

*Source*: J. E. Spencer and W. L. Thomas, *Introducing Cultural Geography*: 1978. Reproduced by permission from John Wiley & Sons.

*The asterisk indicates domestication of related species or hybridized development of new species during domestication in some other region or regions. Some of these secondary domestications were later than in the original region, but evidence of chronologic priority seldom is clear-cut.

The plural rendering of the crop name indicates that several different varieties/species either were involved in initial domestication or followed thereafter.

The term *oil seeds* indicates several varieties or species of small-seeded crop plants grown for the production of edible oils, without further breakdown.

In regions 2 and 3 the brinjals refer to the spicy members of the eggplant group used in curries, whereas in region 3 the eggplants refer to the sweet vegetable members.

None of the regional lists attempts as complete listing of all crop plants/species domesticated within the region.

The table has been compiled from a wide variety of sources.

and Idaho came originally from the Andean highlands, but was brought to Europe in the 1600s where it became a staple from Ireland to the eastern expanses of the North European Plain. The banana we associate with Mesoamerica came from Southeast Asia, as did a variety of yams. Diffusion of crops and seeds was greatly accelerated by worldwide trade and communications networks established with the development of mercantilism and European colonialism.

## Domestication of Animals

Some scholars believe that animal domestication began earlier than plant cultivation, but others argue that animal domestication began as recently as 8000 years ago—well after crop agriculture. Whichever is the case, goats, pigs, and sheep became part of a rapidly growing array of domesticated animals, and in captivity they changed considerably from their wild state. As with the growing of root crops, the notion of **animal domestication** must have emerged over time, in stages.

The process of animal domestication began as people became more sedentary. People kept animals for ceremonial purposes as well as for pets or for other reasons. Quite possibly, animals attached themselves to human settlements as scavengers (foraging through garbage near human settlements) and even for protection against predators, thus reinforcing the idea that they might be tamed and kept. Orphaned young probably were adopted as pets; some wild animals were docile and easily penned up. Goats were domesticated in the Zagros Mountains (in the Fertile Crescent) as long as 10,000 years ago; sheep some 9500 years ago in Anatolia (Turkey); and pigs and cattle shortly thereafter. The advantages of animal domestication—their use as beasts of burden, as a source of meat, and as providers of milk—stimulated the rapid diffusion of this idea among interlinked places and gave the sedentary farmers of Southwest Asia and elsewhere a new measure of security.

Archaeological research indicates that when animals such as wild cattle are penned in a corral, they undergo physical changes over time. In a pen, animals are protected from predators, allowing the survival of animals that would have been killed in the wild. Our domestic versions of the goat, the pig, the cow, and the horse differ considerably from those first kept by our ancestors. In early animal domestication, people chose the more docile, often smaller animals to breed. Archaeologists discern the beginnings of animal domestication in a region by inspecting the bones of excavated animals. They look for places where bones get smaller over time, as this usually indicates early domestication.

As with plant domestication, archaeologists can use the combination of bone fragments and tools to identify general areas where the domestication of particular animals occurred. In Southwest Asia and adjacent parts of the Mediterranean Basin, people domesticated the goat, sheep, and camel. Southeast Asians domesticated several kinds of pigs, the water buffalo, chickens, and some water fowl (ducks, geese). In East India and West Burma (South Asia), people domesticated

cattle, which came to occupy an important place in the regional culture. In Central Asia, people domesticated the yak, horse, some species of goats, and sheep. In the Mesoamerica and the Andean Highlands, early Americans domesticated the llama and alpaca, along with a species of pig and the turkey.

Some species of animals may have been domesticated almost simultaneously in different places. The water buffalo, for example, was probably domesticated in both Southeast and South Asia during the same period. Camels were domesticated in both western and eastern ends of Southwest Asia. The pig was domesticated in numerous areas. Different species of cattle were domesticated in regions other than South Asia. Dogs and cats attached themselves to human settlements very early (they may have been the first animals to be domesticated) and in widely separated regions. Single, specific hearths can be pinpointed for only a few animals, including the llama and the alpaca, the yak, the turkey, and the reindeer.

Efforts to domesticate animals continue today. In East Africa, people are attempting to domesticate the eland, to serve as a source of meat in a region where a stable protein source is greatly needed. Several experimental stations in the savanna are trying to find ways to domesticate Africa's wildlife. They have had some success with a species of eland, but less so with various species of gazelles; they have been unable to domesticate the buffalo (Fig. 11.5). In fact, throughout the world only some 40 species of higher animals have ever been domesticated—and most of these were domesticated long ago. Jared Diamond, author of *Guns, Germs, and Steel*, explains that only five domesticated mammals are important throughout the world: the cow, sheep, goat, pig, and horse. According to Diamond, if we select only the big (over 100 pounds), herbivorous, terrestrial animals, we have 148 species that meet these criteria in the "wild." Only 14 of those 148 have been domesticated successfully, and each of these 14 was domesticated at least 4500 years ago. Modern attempts at animal domestication, even those driven by knowledgeable geneticists, have failed because of problems with the animal's diet, growth rate, breeding, disposition, or social structure.

Thus, the process of animal domestication, set in motion more than 8000 (and perhaps as long as 14,000) years ago, continues. The integrated use of domesticated plants and domesticated animals eased the work burden for early farmers. Animal waste fertilized crops, animals pulled plows, and crops fed animals. The first place where domesticated plants and animals were successfully integrated was Southwest Asia (the Fertile Crescent).

## Subsistence Agriculture

**Subsistence agriculture**—growing only enough food to survive—was the norm throughout most of human history. Subsistence farmers often hold land in common. Surpluses are shared by all the members of the community, accumulation of personal wealth is restricted, and individual advancement at the cost of the group as a whole is limited. Subsistence agriculture declined during the 1900s with the diffusion of

# FIELD NOTE

"Attempts to tame wildlife started in ancient times, and still continue. At Hunter's Lodge on the Nairobi-Mombasa road, we met an agricultural officer who reported that an animal domestication experiment station was located not far into the bush, about 10 miles south. On his invitation, we spent the next day observing this work. In some herds, domestic animals (goats) were combined with wild gazelles, all penned together in a large enclosure. This was not working well; all day the gazelles sought to escape. By comparison, these eland were docile, manageable, and in good health. Importantly, they also were reproducing in captivity. Here, our host describes the program."

© H. J. de Blij

■ **Figure 11.5**
**Nairobi, Kenya.**

industrialized agriculture and the goal of constantly increasing production both to feed growing populations and to sell more agricultural goods. The United States and other industrialized countries sought to move farmers "beyond" subsistence into industrialized production as part of development programs begun in the 1960s (see Chapter 10).

A return to subsistence agriculture has taken hold in parts of the world where farmers feel production for the global market has not benefited them either financially or culturally. For example, indigenous people in the southern Mexican states of Oaxaca, Chiapas, and Guerrero have largely returned to subsistence agriculture. *The Nation* reported in 2010 that Zapatista farmers have "in effect chosen to withdraw from the national economy, some weaning themselves off expensive chemical fertilizers and subsisting on corn they can grow, harvest, and barter."

Some subsistence farmers are sedentary, living in one place throughout the year, but many others move from place to place in search of better land. The latter engage in a form of agriculture known as **shifting cultivation**. This type of agriculture is found primarily in tropical and subtropical zones, where traditional farmers had to abandon plots of land after the soil became infertile. Once stripped of their natural vegetative cover and deprived of the constant input of nutrients from decaying vegetative matter on the forest floor, soils in these regions can quickly lose their nutrients as rainwater leaches out organic matter. Faced with these circumstances, farmers move to another parcel of land, clear the vegetation, turn the soil, and try again. Shifting cultivation gave ancient farmers opportunities to experiment with various plants, to learn the effects of weeding and crop care, to cope with environmental vagaries, and to discern the decreased fertility of soil after sustained farming.

With shifting cultivation, parcels of land are worked successively. The farmers first clear vegetation from a parcel of land. Next they plant crops that are native to the region: tubers in the humid, warm tropical areas; grains in the more humid subtropics; and vegetables and fruits in cooler zones. When the village grows too large and the distance to usable land becomes too great, part of the village's population may establish a new settlement some distance away. Population densities in areas of shifting agriculture cannot be very high; therefore, shifting cultivation continues only in areas where population densities are low.

One specific kind of shifting cultivation is **slash-and-burn agriculture** (also called swidden, milpa, or patch agriculture), reflecting the central role of the controlled use of fire in places where this technique is used. Trees are cut down and all existing vegetation is burned off. In slash-and-burn, farmers use tools (machetes and knives) to slash down trees and tall vegetation, and then burn the vegetation on the ground. A layer of ash from the fire settles on the ground and contributes to the soil's fertility.

As we discuss in the next section, agriculture has fundamentally changed since shifting cultivation was the global norm, but hundreds of millions of farmers continue to practice some form of subsistence agriculture.

thinking
*geographically*

Settling down in one place, a growing population, and the switch to agriculture are interrelated occurrences in human history. Hypothesize which of these three happened first, second, and third, and explain why.

# HOW DID AGRICULTURE CHANGE WITH INDUSTRIALIZATION?

For the Industrial Revolution (see Chapter 12) to take root, a **Second Agricultural Revolution** had to take place—one that would move agriculture beyond subsistence to generate the kinds of surpluses needed to feed thousands of people working in factories instead of in agricultural fields. Like the Industrial Revolution, the Second Agricultural Revolution was composed of a series of innovations, improvements, and techniques, in this case initially in Great Britain, the Netherlands, Denmark, and other neighboring countries.

By the seventeenth and eighteenth centuries, European farming underwent significant changes. New crops came into Europe from trade with the Americas, including corn and potatoes. Many of the new crops were well suited for the climate and soils of western Europe, bringing new lands (previously defined as marginal) into cultivation.

The governments of Europe helped create the conditions necessary for the Second Agricultural Revolution by passing laws such as Great Britain's Enclosure Act, which encouraged consolidation of fields into large, single-owner holdings. Farmers increased the size of their farms, pieced together more contiguous parcels of land, fenced in their land, and instituted field rotation. Methods of soil preparation, fertilization, crop care, and harvesting improved.

New technologies improved production as well. The seed drill enabled farmers to avoid wasting seeds and to plant in rows, making it simpler to distinguish weeds from crops.

By the 1830s, farmers were using new fertilizers on crops and feeding artificial feeds to livestock. Increased agricultural output made it possible to feed much larger urban populations, enabling the growth of a secondary (industrial) economy. In 1831, Cyrus McCormick, a farmer in Lexington, Virginia, perfected his father's design for a mechanical reaper (Fig. 11.6). At the time, farmers were limited in their production not by what they could sow (plant), but what they could reap (harvest) because harvesting required much more time and labor than planting. Harvesting involved laborers cutting grain with a scythe followed by more laborers who bundled the grain into bales. McCormick's mechanical reaper, which was pulled by horses, both cut and bundled grain. His invention diffused quickly during the 1840s, reportedly increasing yields of individual farmers by at least ten times. McCormick's company eventually became International Harvester and now Case IH, one of the largest agriculture implement companies in the world today.

Advances in breeding livestock enabled farmers to develop new breeds that were either strong milk producers or good for beef. The most common breeds of dairy cattle found in North America today trace their lineage back to the Second Agricultural Revolution in Europe. In the 1700s and 1800s, European farmers bred dairy cattle to adapt to different climates and topography. For example, the black and white Holstein dairy cow came from the Netherlands and is well suited to graze on grass and produce high quantities of milk. Scottish farmers bred the red and white Ayrshire breed of dairy cattle to produce milk well suited for butter and cheese and to forage for food in rough, rocky topography.

Innovations in machinery that occurred with the Industrial Revolution in the late 1800s and early 1900s helped sustain the Second Agricultural Revolution. The railroad helped move agriculture into new regions, such as the United States' Great Plains. Geographer John Hudson traced the major role railroads and agriculture played in changing the landscape of that region from open prairie to individual farmsteads. The railroad companies advertised in Europe to attract immigrants to the Great Plains region, and the railroads took the new migrants to their new towns, where they transformed lands from prairie grass to agricultural fields. Later, the internal combustible engine made possible the invention of tractors, combines, and a multitude of large farm equipment. New

**■ Figure 11.6**

**Midwest, United States.** Pioneers in 1870 used the mechanical reaper designed by Cyrus McCormick to cut and bundle grain on the prairie. Pulled by horses, the mechanical reaper sped up harvesting and diffused around the world.

© Hulton-Deutsch Collection/© Corbis

banking and lending practices helped farmers afford the new equipment.

## Understanding the Spatial Layout of Agriculture

When commercial agriculture is geared to producing food for people who live in a nearby town or city, a geographical pattern of land use based on the "perishability" of products and cost of transportation often emerges. In the 1800s, Johann Heinrich von Thünen (1783–1850) experienced the Second Agricultural Revolution firsthand: He farmed an estate not far from the town of Rostock, in northeast Germany. Studying the spatial patterns of land use around towns such as Rostock, von Thünen noted that as one moved away from the town, one commodity or crop gave way to another. He also noted that this process occurred without any visible change in soil, climate, or terrain. When he mapped this pattern, he found that each town or market center was surrounded by a set of more-or-less concentric rings within which particular commodities or crops dominated.

Nearest the town, farmers generally produced commodities that were perishable and commanded high prices, such as dairy products and strawberries. In this zone, much effort would go into production in part because of the value of the land closer to the city. In von Thünen's time, the town was still surrounded by a belt of forest that provided wood for fuel and building; but immediately beyond the forest the ring-like pattern of agriculture continued. In the next ring, crops were less perishable and bulkier, including wheat and other grains. Still farther out, livestock raising began to replace field crops.

Von Thünen used these observations to build a model of the spatial distribution of agricultural activities around settlements (Fig. 11.7). As with all models, he had to make certain assumptions. For example, he assumed that the terrain was flat, that soils and other environmental conditions were the same everywhere, and that there were no barriers to transportation to market. Under such circumstances, he reasoned, transport costs would govern the use of land. He reasoned that as distance to market increased, the higher transport costs had to be added to the cost of producing a crop or commodity.

The **Von Thünen model** (including the ring of forest) is often described as the first effort to analyze the spatial character of economic activity. The Thünian patterns discerned in many parts of the world are not solely the result of the forces modeled by von Thünen. Differences in climate type and soil quality weigh heavily in the kinds of goods produced in a place. Yet if you drive east out of Denver, heading for Nebraska, you cannot miss a certain zonation that puts dairying and market gardening nearest the city, cash grains such as corn (plus soybeans) in the next zone, more extensive grain farming and livestock raising beyond, and cattle ranching in the outermost zone.

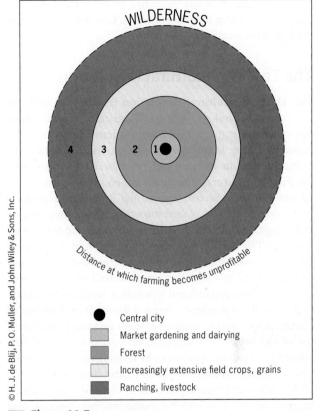

© H. J. de Blij, P. O. Muller, and John Wiley & Sons, Inc.

- ● Central city
- ▢ Market gardening and dairying
- ▢ Forest
- ▢ Increasingly extensive field crops, grains
- ▢ Ranching, livestock

■ **Figure 11.7**

**Von Thünen's Model.** The key influence on land use in the Von Thünen model is the cost of transporting goods to market.

Geographer Lee Liu studied the spatial pattern of agricultural production in one province of China, giving careful consideration to the intensity of the production methods and the amount of land degradation. Liu found that the farmers living in a village would farm lands close to the village as well as lands far away from the village with high levels of intensity. However, the methods used varied spatially, resulting in land improvements close to the village and land degradation farther from the village. In lands close to the village, farmers improved lands through "decades of intensive care," in particular putting organic material onto the fields, which made the grasslands close to the village "fertile and productive." In lands more remote from the village, farmers tended to use more "chemical fertilizer, pesticides, and herbicides" and fewer conservation tactics, resulting in land degradation whereby "the originally fertile remote land became degraded." Liu argued that this pattern in modern China occurs in large part because farmers live in the village, not in the remote fields, and therefore put most of their time and energy into the fields closest to their places of residence.

Even when agricultural production does not conform to the concentric rings of von Thünen's model, his underlying concern with the interplay of land use and transportation costs still explains many agricultural patterns. The fresh flowers grown in the Caribbean for sale in New York City could be viewed as the application of the von Thünen model on a larger scale, for it is less expensive to grow flowers in the Caribbean and ship them to New York City than it is to grow them in other locations.

## The Third Agricultural Revolution

The **Third Agricultural Revolution** is associated with the use of **biotechnology** to expand agricultural production. Agricultural scientist Donald Baker suggests one way to think about the three agricultural revolutions is to consider the "critical factor" in spurring each revolution. He explains that the First Agricultural Revolution depended on a change in human effort, the Second Agricultural Revolution hinged on increasing the amount of seed sown through improvements in technology, and the Third Agricultural Revolution is based on land use. The science that went into the Third Agricultural Revolution enables farmers to produce crops more intensively on the land and to bring more, marginal land into production.

The Third Agricultural Revolution relies on hybridization of seeds to produce a more stable crop in a variety of circumstances (wind resistant, drought resistant), intensified use of technology and irrigation, and expanded use of land either by not leaving it fallow or by farming on marginal land. The Third Agricultural Revolution dates back as far as the 1930s, when agricultural scientists in the American Midwest began experimenting with technologically manipulated seed varieties to increase crop yields. In the 1940s, American philanthropists funded research on maize (corn) production in Mexico, trying to find a hybrid seed that would grow better. They did, and by 1960 Mexico was no longer importing corn because production within the country was high enough to meet demand. In the 1960s, the focal point of the Third Agricultural Revolution shifted to India, when scientists at a research institution in the Philippines crossed a dwarf Chinese variety of rice with an Indonesian variety and produced IR8. This new rice plant had a number of desirable properties: It developed a bigger head of grain, and it had a stronger stem that did not collapse under the added weight of the bigger head. IR8 produced much better yields than either of its parents—giving rise to the **Green Revolution**.

The term *Green Revolution* refers the use of biotechnology to create disease-resistant, fast growing hybrid seeds—particularly of staple crops such as rice and wheat. The impact of the Green Revolution in India and other developing countries was so great that the term is often used as a synonym for the Third Agricultural Revolution. Building on the success of IR8, in 1982 scientists produced IR36, bred from 13 parents to achieve genetic resistance against 15 pests and a growing cycle of 110 days under warm conditions, thus making possible three crops per year in some places. By 1992, IR36 was the most widely grown crop on Earth, and in September 1994, scientists developed a strain of rice that was even more productive than IR36. The Green Revolution also brought new high-yield varieties of wheat and corn from the United States to other parts of the world, particularly South and Southeast Asia.

The increased yields of the Green Revolution came at a time of increased concern about global hunger and thus attracted enormous attention. In subsequent decades, most famines resulted from political instability rather than failure in production. India became self-sufficient in grain production by the 1980s, and Asia as a whole saw a two-thirds increase in rice production between 1970 and 1995. These drastic increases in production stemmed not only from new seed varieties but also from the use of fertilizers, pesticides, irrigation, and significant capital improvements.

The geographical impact of the Green Revolution is highly variable, however. Its traditional focus on rice, wheat, and corn means that it has had only limited impact throughout much of Africa, where agriculture is based on different crops and where lower soil fertility makes agriculture less attractive to foreign investment. But innovations are continually being developed. Research has already led to methods for producing high-yield cassava and sorghum—both of which are grown in Africa. Beyond Africa, research on fattening livestock faster and improving the appearance of fruits is having an impact in North and South America.

The promise of increasing food production in a world in which almost a billion people are malnourished has led many people to view the Green Revolution in distinctly positive terms. Others, however, worry about associated social changes, health risks, and environmental hazards. The large-scale monocropping that is often part of Green Revolution agriculture can make farms vulnerable to changes in climate or the infestation of particular pests. Higher inputs of chemical fertilizers, herbicides, and pesticides that go along with Green Revolution agriculture can lead to reduced organic matter in the soil and to groundwater pollution. Moreover, the Green Revolution has worked against the interest of many small-scale farmers who lack the resources to acquire genetically enhanced seeds and the necessary chemical inputs to grow them. One particularly vocal opponent of the Green Revolution in India, Vandana Shiva, argues that

> [T]he Green Revolution has been a failure. It has led to reduced genetic diversity, increased vulnerability to pests, soil erosion, water shortages, reduced soil fertility, micronutrient deficiencies, soil contamination, reduced availability of nutritious food crops for the local population, the displacement of vast numbers of small farmers from their land, rural impoverishment and increased tensions and conflicts. The beneficiaries have been the agrochemical industry, large petrochemical companies, manufacturers of agricultural machinery, dam builders and large landowners.

It is no easy matter to weigh the enormous increases in food production that have occurred in places that have adopted Green Revolution approaches against the types of social and environmental issues highlighted by Shiva.

A 2005 report in *Scientific American* contends that many small farmers have not benefited from the Green Revolution: "The supply-driven strategies of the Green Revolution, however, may not help subsistence farmers, who must play to their strengths to compete in the global marketplace. The average size of a family farm is less than four acres in India, 1.8 acres in Bangladesh and about half an acre in China." Smaller farmers are in a poor competitive position, and their position is further undermined by the fact that a few large corporations with the seed patents for biotechnologically altered grains and a virtual monopoly of the needed chemical inputs can have tremendous power over the agricultural production process. In addition, the need for capital from the West to implement Green Revolution technologies has led to a shift away from production for local consumers toward export agriculture. In the process, local places become subject to the vicissitudes of the global economy, where a downward fluctuation in the price of a given crop can create enormous problems for places dependent on the sale of that crop.

Researchers at the International Rice Research Institute, with help from an $18 billion grant from the Bill and Melinda Gates Foundation, bred a genetically modified "Green Super Rice" that will not have to be transplanted as seedlings but can be seeded directly in the paddy soil. It may yield nearly twice as much rice per acre than the average for strains in current use. The charting of the genome of rice (the 12 chromosomes that carry all of the plant's characteristics) may make it possible to transform rice genetically so that it will continuously acquire more new properties that could make it resistant to a wider spectrum of diseases and pests. The variety is going through its last testing phases and will be available to African and Asian farmers in 2015.

## New Genetically Modified Foods

Social scientists are now trying to differentiate the Green Revolution, which is largely based on hybridization of cereal crops, from the biotechnology revolution now underway. Agricultural scientists are now altering the chemical makeup of crops and modifying the genes of plants (genetically modified organisms, GMOs) to create new crops through biotechnology. A few researchers are calling the agricultural revolution in biotechnology a fourth revolution. Agricultural scientist Donald Baker suggests the critical factor in this revolution may be yield per dollar—as farms work directly with giant agribusinesses to produce as much food as possible for each dollar spent.

An entire field of biotechnology has sprung up in the wake of the Third Agricultural Revolution, and the development of genetically engineered crops (GE) or **genetically modified organisms (GMOs)** is its principal target. Since the origin of agriculture, people have experimented with hybrid crops and cross-breeding of animals. What is different today is that genetic modification involves splicing together genes from different species (e.g., tomatoes and salmon) to achieve a particular end. Genetically modified corn has been grown in substantial quantities in the United States for decades. The turn toward other types of GMOs has accelerated over the past 20 years. According to the Grocery

Manufacturers of America, GMOs are now found in 60 to 70 percent of all processed foods in the United States. The United States leads the world in the production of genetically engineered crops, with 88 percent of all acres in corn (up from 25 percent in 2000) and 93 percent of all acres in soybeans (up from 54 percent in 2000) sown with genetically engineered seeds.

A major debate has developed around GMOs. Proponents argue that GMOs can help feed an expanding world population and that hard evidence of negative consequences to their use is lacking. Opponents contend that GMO companies are releasing organisms into the environment without adequate understanding of their environmental, health, or socioeconomic consequences. A particular concern is the impact of pollen dispersal from GMOs on other organisms and the potential for disease-resistant plants to spur the evolution of super-pests.

Some regions have embraced genetically engineered crops, whereas others have banned them. The United States has largely been in the former camp, though there is a growing movement to require labeling of products containing GMOs. In contrast, ideological resistance to genetically engineered foods is strong in western Europe. Agricultural officials in most west European countries have declared GMOs to be safe, but labeling is required and there is strong public reaction against GMOs based on combined concerns about health and taste. Such concerns have spread to less affluent parts of the world as well. In many poorer regions, seeds are a cultural commodity, reflecting agricultural lessons learned over generations. In these regions, many resist the invasion of foreign, genetically engineered crops. But in their search for new markets, major GMO companies are promoting their products in the global periphery and semiperiphery. Many regions there do not have access to the necessary capital and technology to move forward, but the stage is set for growing conflict over GMOs.

## Regional and Local Change

Recent shifts from subsistence agriculture to commercial agriculture have had dramatic impacts on rural life. Land-use patterns, land ownership arrangements, and agricultural labor conditions have all changed as rural residents cope with shifting economic, political, and environmental conditions. In Latin America, dramatic increases in the production of export crops (or *cash crops* such as fruits and coffee) have occurred at the expense of crop production for local consumption. In the process, subsistence farming has been pushed to ever more marginal lands. In Asia, where the Green Revolution has had the greatest impact, the production of cereal crops (grains such as rice and wheat) has increased for both foreign and domestic markets. In Subsaharan Africa, total commercialized agriculture has increased, but African farms have remained relatively small and dependent on intensified manual labor.

## GUEST FIELD NOTE

### Gambia

I am interested in women and rural development in Subsaharan Africa. In 1983, I went to Gambia to study an irrigated rice project that was being implemented to improve the availability of rice, the dietary staple. What grabbed my attention? The donors' assurance that the project would benefit women, the country's traditional rice growers. Imagine my surprise a few months after project implementation when I encountered hundreds of angry women refusing to work because they received nothing for their labor from the first harvest.

In registering women's traditional rice plots as "family" land, project officials effectively sabotaged the equity objectives of the donors. Control now was concentrated under male heads of household who reaped the income produced by female labor. Contemporary economic strategies for Africa depend increasingly upon labor intensification. But whose labor? Human geography provides a way of seeing the significance of gender in the power relations

■ **Figure 11.8**
**Gambia.**

that mediate culture, environment, and economic development.

*Credit: Judith Carney, University of California, Los Angeles.*

What this regional-scale analysis does not tell us is how these changes have affected rural communities. These changes can be environmental, economic, and social. A recent study in the small country of Gambia (West Africa) by Judith Carney has shown how changing agricultural practices have altered not only the rural environment and economy, but also relations between men and women (Fig. 11.8). Over the last 30 years, international developmental assistance to Gambia has led to ambitious projects designed to convert wetlands to irrigated agricultural lands, making possible production of rice year-round. By the late 1980s, virtually all of the country's suitable wetlands had been converted to year-round rice production. This transformation created tensions within rural households by converting lands women traditionally used for family subsistence into commercialized farming plots. In addition, when rice production was turned into a year-round occupation, women found themselves with less time for other activities crucial for household maintenance.

This situation underscores the fact that in Africa, as in much of the rest of the less industrialized world, agricultural work is overwhelmingly carried out by women. In Subsaharan Africa and South Asia, 60 percent of all employed females work in the agriculture sector. A geographical perspective helps to shed light on how changes in agricultural practices throughout the world not only alter rural landscapes but also affect family and community relationships.

## The Impacts of Agricultural Modernization on Earlier Practices

In the modern world, hunter-gatherers live in the context of a globalized economy and experience pressures to change their livelihoods. In many cases, the state places pressures on hunter-gatherers to settle in one place and farm. Cyclical migration by hunter-gatherers does not mesh well with bounded, territorial states. Some nongovernmental organizations encourage settlement by digging wells or building medical buildings, permanent houses, or schools for hunter-gatherers. Even hunter-gatherers who continue to use their knowledge of seeds, roots, fruits, berries, insects, and animals to gather and trap the goods they need for survival do so in the context of a highly interconnected economic world.

Unlike hunting and gathering, subsistence farming continues to be a relatively common practice in Africa, Middle America, tropical South America, and parts of Southeast Asia (Fig. 11.9). The system of cultivation has changed little over thousands of years. The term *subsistence* can be used in the strictest sense of the word—to refer to farmers who grow food only to sustain themselves and their families, who find building materials and firewood in the natural environment, and who do not enter into the cash economy at all. This definition fits farmers in remote areas of South and Middle America, Africa, and South and Southeast Asia. Yet many farm

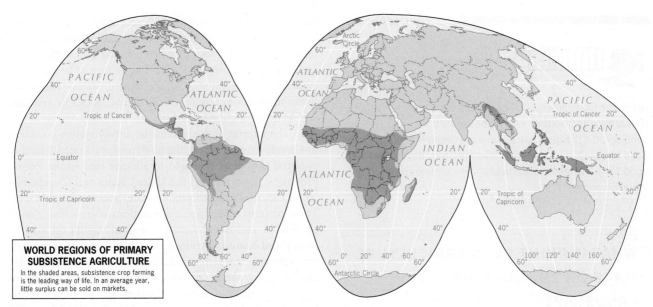

■ **Figure 11.9**

**World Regions of Primarily Subsistence Agriculture.**    Definitions of subsistence farming vary. On this map, India and China are not shaded because farmers sell some produce at markets; in Equatorial Africa and South America, subsistence farming allows little excess, and thus little produce is sold at markets.    © E. H. Fouberg, A. B. Murphy, H. J. de Blij, and John Wiley & Sons, Inc.

families living at the subsistence level periodically sell a small quantity of produce (perhaps to pay taxes). They are not subsistence farmers in the strict sense, but the term *subsistence* is surely applicable to societies where farmers with small plots sometimes sell a few pounds of grain on the market but where poverty, indebtedness, and tenancy are ways of life. For the indigenous peoples of the Amazon Basin, the sedentary farmers of Africa's savanna areas, villagers in much of India, and peasants in Indonesia, subsistence is not only a way of life but a state of mind. Experience has taught farmers and their families that subsistence farming is often precarious and that times of comparative plenty will be followed by times of scarcity.

Subsistence farming has been in retreat for centuries. From 1500 to 1950, European powers sought to "modernize" the economies of their colonies by ending subsistence farming and integrating farmers into colonial systems of production and exchange. Sometimes their methods were harsh: By demanding that farmers pay some taxes, they forced subsistence farmers to begin selling some of their produce to raise the necessary cash. They also compelled many subsistence farmers to devote some land to a crop to be sold on the world market such as cotton, thus bringing them into the commercial economy. The colonial powers encouraged commercial farming by conducting soil surveys, building irrigation systems, and establishing lending agencies that provided loans to farmers. The colonial powers sought to make profits, yet it was difficult to squeeze very much from subsistence-farming areas. Forced cropping schemes were designed to solve this problem. If farmers in a subsistence area cultivated a certain acreage of, say, corn, they were required to grow a

specified acreage of a cash crop as well. Whether this crop would be grown on old land that was formerly used for grain or on newly cleared land was the farmers' decision. If no new lands were available, the farmers would have to give up food crops for the compulsory cash crops. In many areas, severe famines resulted and local economies were disrupted.

Subsistence land use continues to give way to more intensive farming and cash cropping—even to mechanized farming in which equipment does much of the actual work. In the process, societies from South America to Southeast Asia are being profoundly affected. Land that was once held communally is being parceled out to individuals for cash cropping. In the process, small landowners are often squeezed out, leaving the land in the hands of wealthier farmers and the owners of commercialized farming operations.

For too long, the question has been how "to tempt [subsistence farmers] into wanting cash by the availability of suitable consumer goods," as A. N. Duckham and G. B. Masefield wrote in *Farming Systems of the World* in 1970. In the interests of "progress" and "modernization," subsistence farmers were pushed away from their traditional modes of livelihood even though many aspects of subsistence farming may be worth preserving. Regions with shifting cultivation do not have neat rows of plants, carefully turned soil, or precisely laid-out fields. Yet shifting cultivation conserves both forest and soil; its harvests are often substantial given environmental limitations; and it requires better organization than one might assume. It also requires substantially less energy than more modern techniques of farming. It is no surprise, then, that shifting cultivation and specifically slash-and-burn agriculture have been a sustained method of farming for thousands of years.

Many arguments have been raised about the impacts of the Green Revolution, both pro and con. How might the scale at which the Green Revolution is examined affect the arguments that are made about it? What types of factors are likely to be considered if the question is, "has the Green Revolution been good for Asia?" as opposed to "has the Green Revolution been good for a village or a particular agricultural community in India?"

## WHAT IMPRINT DOES AGRICULTURE MAKE ON THE CULTURAL LANDSCAPE?

Flying from the West Coast of the United States to the East Coast, if you have a window seat you will see the major imprint agriculture makes on the cultural landscape. The green circles standing out in the grain belts of the country are places where center-pivot irrigation systems circle around a pivot, providing irrigation to a circle of crops. The checkerboard pattern on the landscape reflects the pattern of land survey system and land ownership in much of the country.

The pattern of land ownership seen in the landscape reflects the cadastral system—the method of land survey through which land ownership and property lines are defined. Cadastral systems were adopted in places where settlement could be regulated by law, and land surveys were crucial to their implementation. The prevailing survey system throughout much of the United States, the one that appears as checkerboards across agricultural fields, is the **rectangular survey system**. The U.S. government adopted the rectangular survey system after the American Revolution as part of a cadastral system known as the **township-and-range system**. Designed to facilitate the settlement of non-Indians in the farmlands of the interior of the United States, the system imposed a rigid grid-like pattern on the land (Fig. 11.10). The basic unit was the 1 square mile *section*—and land was bought and sold in whole, half, or quarter sections. The section's lines were drawn without reference to the terrain, and

they thus imposed a remarkable uniformity across the land. Under the Homestead Act, a homesteader received one section of land (160 acres) after living on the land for five years and making improvements to it. The pattern of farms on the landscape in the interior of the United States reflects the township-and-range system, with farms spaced by sections, half sections, or quarter sections.

The imprint of the rectangular survey system is evident in Canada as well, where the government adopted a similar cadastral system as it sought to allocate land in the Prairie Provinces. In portions of the United States and Canada, different cadastral patterns predominate, however (Fig. 11.11). These patterns reflect particular notions of how land should be divided and used. Among the most significant are the **metes-and-bounds survey** approach adopted along the eastern seaboard, in which natural features were used to demarcate irregular parcels of land. One of the most distinctive regional approaches to land division can be found in the Canadian Maritimes and in parts of Quebec, Louisiana, and Texas, where a **long-lot survey system** was implemented. This system divided land into narrow parcels stretching back from rivers, roads, or canals. It reflects a particular approach to surveying that was common in French America.

Many parts of the world do not have cadastral systems, so field patterns are irregular. But whether regular or irregular, societies with property ownership have parcels of land divided into neat, clearly demarcated segments. The size and order of those parcels are heavily influenced not just by land partition schemes, but also by rules about property inheritance. In systems where one child inherits all of the land—such as those associated with the traditional Germanic

© Alexander B. Murphy

■ **Figure 11.10**

**Willamette Valley, Oregon.** The township-and-range system has left its imprint on the landscape near Eugene, Oregon, where the grid pattern of six-mile-by-six-mile townships and the sections of one square mile each are marked by property lines and roads.

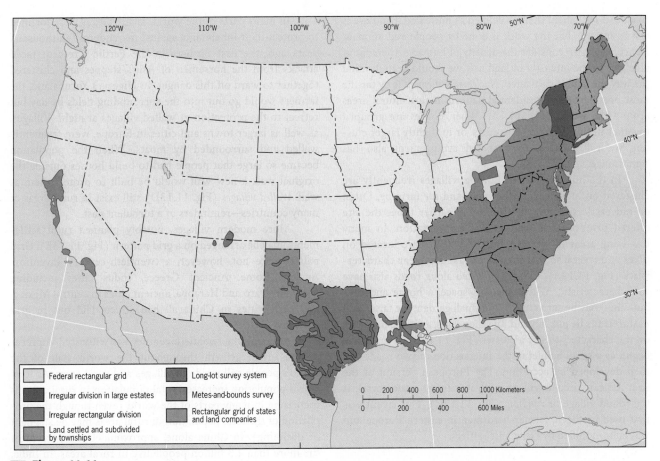

**■ Figure 11.11**
**Dominant Land Survey Patterns in the United States.**    *Data from*: Edward Price, Dividing the Land: *Early American Beginnings of Our Private Property Mosaic. Chicago*: University of Chicago Press, 1995, p. 8 and several other sources.

practice of **primogeniture**, in which all land passes to the eldest son—parcels tend to be larger and farmers work a single plot of land. This is the norm in Northern Europe and in the principal areas of Northern European colonization—the Americas, South Africa, Australia, and New Zealand.

In areas where land is divided among heirs, however, considerable fragmentation can occur over time. The latter is the norm throughout much of Asia, Africa, and Southern Europe, as well as most of the allotted Indian reservations in the United States. Therefore, farmers living in villages in these areas tend a variety of scattered small plots of land. In some places, land reform initiatives have consolidated landholdings to some degree, but fragmentation is still common in many parts of the world.

## Villages

Throughout this book we take note of various core–periphery contrasts which our world presents. Such contrasts are prominent in rural as well as urban areas. Traditional farm–village life is still common in India, Subsaharan Africa, China, and Southeast Asia. In India, farming, much of it subsistence farming, still occupies over 60 percent of the population. As

we have seen, however, in the world's core areas agriculture has taken on a very different form, and true farm villages, in which farming or providing services for farmers are the dominant activities, are disappearing. In the United States, where farming once was the leading economic activity, only some 2 percent of the labor force remains engaged in agriculture, and the population of most rural villages and towns is a mix of farmers and people who commute to work in urban areas.

Traditionally, the people who lived in villages either farmed the surrounding land or provided services to those who did the farming. Thus, they were closely connected to the land, and most of their livelihoods depended, directly or indirectly, on the cultivation of nearby farmland. As such, they tended to reflect historical and environmental conditions. Houses in Japanese farming villages, for example, are so tightly packed together that only the narrowest passageways remain between them. This village form reflects the pressure to allocate every possible square foot of land to farming; villages must not use land where crops could grow.

Unlike Japan, in the United States Midwest individual farm houses lie quite far apart in what we call a *dispersed settlement* pattern; the land is intensively cultivated but by machine rather than by hand. In the populous Indonesian island of Java, villages are located every half mile or so along a rural road, and settlement there is defined as nucleated. Land use is just as intense, but the work is done by people and animals. Hence, when we consider the density of human settlement as it relates to the intensity of land use, we should keep in mind the way the land is cultivated. *Nucleated settlement* is by far the most prevalent rural residential pattern in agricultural areas around the world (Fig. 11.12). When houses are grouped together in tiny clusters or hamlets, or in slightly larger clusters we call villages, their spatial arrangement also has significance.

In the hilly regions of Europe, villages frequently are clustered on hills, leaving the level land for farming. Often an old castle sits atop the hill, so in earlier times the site offered protection as well as land conservation. In many low-lying areas of western Europe, villages are located on dikes and levees, so that they often take on linear characteristics (Fig. 11.13A). Villages oriented along roads also have this characteristic. Where there is space, a house and out-buildings may be surrounded by a small garden; the farms and pasturelands lie just beyond. In other cases, a village may take on the characteristics of a cluster (Fig. 11.13B). It may have begun as a small hamlet at the intersection of two roads and then developed by accretion. The European version of the East African circular village, with its central cattle corral, is the round village or *rundling* (Fig. 11.13C). This layout was first used by Slavic farmer-herdsmen in eastern Europe and was later modified by Germanic settlers.

In many parts of the world, farm villages were fortified to protect their inhabitants against marauders. Ten thousand years ago, the first farmers in the Fertile Crescent faced attacks from the horsemen of Asia's steppes and clustered together to ward off this danger. In Nigeria's Yorubaland, the farmers would go out into the surrounding fields by day but retreat to the protection of walled villages at night. Villages, as well as larger towns and cities in Europe, were frequently walled and surrounded by moats. When the population became so large that people had to build houses outside the original wall, a new wall would be built to protect them as well. *Walled villages* (Fig. 11.13D) still exist in rural areas of many countries—reminders of a turbulent past.

More modern villages, notably planned rural settlements, may be arranged on a grid pattern (Fig. 11.13E). Grid patterns are not, however, a twentieth-century invention. Ancient Rome, Ancient Greece, Indus cities including Mohenjo-Daro and Harappa, ancient cities in central Mexico, and early cities in China all had streets laid out in grid patterns.

Although the twentieth century has witnessed unprecedented urban growth throughout the world, half of the world's people still reside in villages and rural areas. As total world population increases, total population in rural areas is increasing in many parts of the world (even though the proportion of the total population in rural areas may be stagnant or declining). In China alone, approximately 50 percent of the more than 1.3 billion people live in rural areas. In India, with a population of over 1 billion, between 60 and 70 percent of the people live in places the government defines as nonurban. Small rural settlements are home to most of the inhabitants of Indonesia, Bangladesh, Pakistan, and other countries of the global economic periphery, including those in Africa. The agrarian village remains one of the most common forms of settlement on Earth.

In some places, rural villages have changed as the global economy has changed. For example, Mexico has experienced rapid economic change since passage of the North American Free Trade Act (NAFTA) in 1992. Along with major shifts in industrial production (see Chapter 12), major changes in agricultural production and village life have occurred in Mexico. Before the passage of NAFTA, the Mexican government protected corn production

© Barbara A. Weightman

■■ **Figure 11.12**
**Aquitaine, France.** The agricultural landscape of Aquitaine demonstrates three features of rural France: people living in nucleated villages, a highly fragmented land ownership pattern, and land divided according to the French long-lot system.

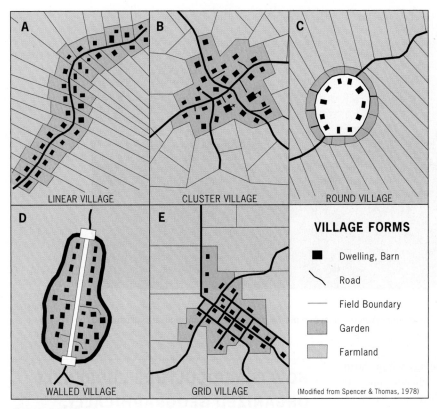

LINEAR VILLAGE

CLUSTER VILLAGE

ROUND VILLAGE

WALLED VILLAGE

GRID VILLAGE

**VILLAGE FORMS**

■ Dwelling, Barn

╱ Road

─ Field Boundary

▨ Garden

▧ Farmland

(Modified from Spencer & Thomas, 1978)

■■ **Figure 11.13**
**Village Forms.**   Five different representative nucleated village layouts are shown here. *Adapted with permission from*: J. E. Spencer and W. H. Thomas, *Introducing Cultural Geography.* New York: John Wiley & Sons, Inc., 1978, p. 154.

## Functional Differentiation Within Villages

Villages everywhere display certain common qualities, including evidence of social stratification and differentiation of buildings. The range in size and quality of houses, representing their owners' wealth and standing in the community, reflects social stratification. Material well-being is the chief determinant of stratification in Western commercial agricultural regions, where it translates into more elaborate homes. In Africa, as in most other places, a higher social position in the community is associated with a more impressive house. The house of the chief or headman may not only be more elaborate than others but may also be in a more prominent location. In India, caste still strongly influences daily life, including village housing; the manors of landlords, often comprising large walled compounds, stand in striking contrast to the modest houses of domestic servants, farm workers, carpenters, and craftspeople. The poorest people of the lowest castes live in small one-room, wattle-and-thatch dwellings. In Cambodia, the buildings in stilt villages built throughout the Mekong Basin look similar (Fig. 11.14).

because white corn is a staple crop used to make tortillas, a principal component of the Mexican diet. Through protection, Mexico's corn prices were higher than those in the United States. With the passage of NAFTA, Mexico entered a 15-year transition away from protecting its corn production. Economists believed the price of corn in Mexico would fall and in turn Mexicans would produce less corn.

What happened instead is that corn prices in Mexico fluctuated over time, tortilla prices rose, and then production of corn in Mexico increased. Tortilla prices rose in response to higher prices for corn in the United States as a result of corn being used for fuel. Mexican farmers increased corn production both because of a higher demand for corn in the United States and Mexico and also because indigenous farmers in the south switched to subsistence farming of corn to provide for their families and to remove themselves from the fluctuating global agriculture market and the uncertainties of NAFTA.

© Alexander B. Murphy

■■ **Figure 11.14**
**Siem Reap, Cambodia.**   A stilt village along the shores of Tonle Sap, the largest lake in Cambodia. The houses in this village in the Cambodian countryside are designed on stilts or floats to handle seasonal changes in water levels in the Tonle Sap Lake. In the dry fall and winter, the lake reduces in size and the stilts of the houses are exposed. In the wet spring and summer, the lake swells and inundates the village, covering the stilts with water.

■■ **Figure 11.15**

**Winthrop, Minnesota.**    The modern American farm typically has a two-story farm house surrounded by several outbuildings.

The functional differentiation of buildings within farm villages (like the functional zonation of cities whereby different areas of the village play different roles and function differently) is more elaborate in some societies than in others. Protection of livestock and storage of harvested crops are primary functions of farm villages, and in many villages where subsistence farming is the prevailing way of life, the storage place for grains and other food is constructed with as much care as the best-built house. Moisture and vermin must be kept away from stored food; containers of grain often stand on stilts under a carefully thatched roof or behind walls made of carefully maintained sun-dried mud. In India's villages, the paddy-bin made of mud (in which rice is stored) often stands inside the house. Similarly, livestock pens are often attached to houses, or, as in Africa, dwellings are built in a circle surrounding the corral.

The functional differentiation of buildings is greatest in Western cultures, where a single farmstead may contain as many buildings as an entire hamlet elsewhere in the world. A prosperous North American farm is likely to include a two-story farm house, a stable, a barn, and various outbuildings, including a garage for motorized equipment, a workshop, a shed for tools, and a silo for grain storage (Fig. 11.15). The space these structures occupy can exceed that used by entire villages in Japan, China, and other agrarian regions where space is at a greater premium.

Think of an agricultural region where you have visited or lived. Describe the imprint of agriculture on the landscape and consider what the cultural landscape tells you about how agriculture is produced in this region or how production has changed over time.

## HOW IS AGRICULTURE CURRENTLY ORGANIZED GEOGRAPHICALLY, AND HOW HAS AGRIBUSINESS INFLUENCED THE CONTEMPORARY GEOGRAPHY OF AGRICULTURE?

Understanding global agricultural patterns requires looking at more than market location, land use, and transportation costs—the factors analyzed by von Thünen. We must also consider the effects of different climate and soil conditions, variations in farming methods and technology, the role of governments and social norms, and the lasting impacts of history.

Commercial farming has come to dominate in the world's economic core, as well as some of the places in the semi-periphery and periphery. Commercial farming is the agriculture of large-scale grain producers and cattle ranches, mechanized equipment, and factory-type labor forces. It is a world apart from the traditional farms of Asia and Africa.

The spatial expansion of modern **commercial agriculture** began in the eighteenth and nineteenth centuries when Europe became a market for agricultural products from around the world: Moreover, European countries manufactured and sold in their colonies the finished products made from imported raw materials. Thus, cotton grown in Egypt, Sudan, India, and other countries colonized by Europe was bought cheaply, imported to European factories, and made into clothes—many of which were then exported and sold, often in the very colonies where the cotton had been grown in the first place.

Major changes in transportation and food storage, especially refrigeration, further intertwined agricultural

# FIELD NOTE

"The technology of refrigeration has kept pace with the containerization of seaborne freight traffic. When we sailed into the port of Dunedin, New Zealand, I was unsure of just what those red boxes were. Closer inspection revealed that they are refrigeration units, to which incoming containers are attached. Meats and other perishables can thus be kept frozen until they are transferred to a refrigerator ship."

© H. J. de Blij

**Figure 11.16**
**Dunedin, New Zealand.**

production and food processing regions around the world during the twentieth century (Fig. 11.16). The beef industry of Argentina, for example, secured a world market when the invention of refrigerated ships made it possible to transport a highly perishable commodity over long distances. European colonial powers required farmers in their colonies to cultivate specific crops. One major impact of colonial agriculture was the establishment of **monoculture** (dependence on a single agricultural commodity) throughout much of the colonial world. Colonies became known for certain crops, and colonizers came to rely on those crops. Ghanaians still raise cacao; Moçambiquans still grow cotton; and Sri Lankans still produce tea. The production of cash crops in poorer countries is perpetuated by loan and aid requirements from lending countries, the World Trade Organization, the International Monetary Fund, and the World Bank (see Chapter 10).

## The World Map of Climates

Before we can study the distribution of agriculture in the world today, we need to examine Figure 11.17, the distribution of climate zones. All of the elements of weather, absorption of the sun's energy, rotation of the Earth, circulation of the oceans, movement of weather systems, and the jet stream, produce a pattern of climates represented in the map—and those climate patterns have a profound impact on what can be grown where. We owe this remarkable map to Wladimir Köppen (1846–1940), who devised a scheme called the **Köppen climate classification system** for classifying the world's climates on the basis of temperature and precipitation.

Köppen's map provides one means of understanding the distribution of **climatic regions** (areas with similar climatic characteristics) across the planet. The legend looks complicated, but for present purposes it is enough to get a sense of the distribution of the major types of climate. The letter categories in the legend give a clear indication of the conditions they represent.

The (A) climates are hot or very warm and generally humid. The "no dry season" (Af) regions are *equatorial rainforest* regions. The "short dry season" (Am) climate is known as the *monsoon climate*. And if you can envisage an African savanna, you know what the (Aw, *savanna*) designation means.

Once you realize that the yellow and light brown colors on the map represent dry climates (BW, *desert* and BS, *steppe*), it becomes clear how much of the world has limited water availability. Nonetheless, some very large population clusters have developed in these water-deficient regions, especially at lower (and warmer) latitudes. The world faces a long-term water crisis, and the Köppen map helps show why.

The (C) climates also have familiar names. The (Cf) climate, represented by dark green, prevails over the southeastern United States. If you know the local climate in Atlanta or Nashville or Jacksonville, you understand why this climate is often called "humid temperate." It is moist, and it does not get as cold as it does in Canada or as warm (continuously, anyway) as in the Amazon Basin. If you have experienced this kind of climate, the map gives you a good idea of what it's like in much of eastern China, southeastern Australia, and a large part of southeastern South America.

# WORLD CLIMATES
## After Köppen–Geiger

**A HUMID EQUATORIAL CLIMATE**

| Af | No dry season |
| Am | Short dry season |
| Aw | Dry winter |

**B DRY CLIMATE**

| BS | Semiarid |
| BW | Arid |

h=hot
k=cold

**C HUMID TEMPERATE CLIMATE**

| Cf | No dry season |
| Cw | Dry winter |
| Cs | Dry summer |

a=hot summer
b=cool summer
c=short, cool summer
d=very cold winter

**D HUMID COLD CLIMATE**

| Df | No dry season |
| Dw | Dry winter |

**E COLD POLAR CLIMATE**

| E | Tundra and ice |

**H HIGHLAND CLIMATE**

| H | Unclassified highlands |

0    1000    2000    3000 Kilometers
0    1000    2000 Miles

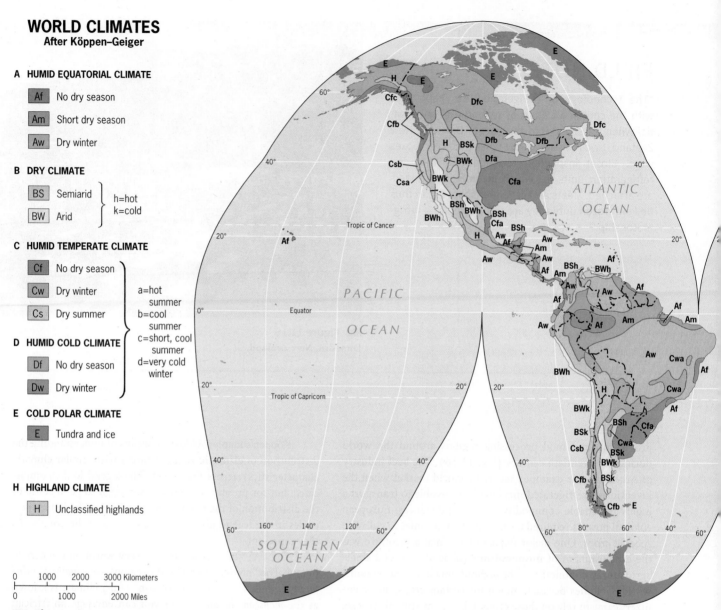

■ **Figure 11.17**

**World Climates.** The Köppen map of world climates, as modified by R. Geiger. Climates generally follow lines of latitude because the amount of incoming solar radiation varies by latitude. Climates are shaped further by the presence of mountains, as is seen in western North and South America and by the proximity to warm or cold ocean currents, as is evidenced on the west coast of southern Africa and the east coast of the United States.

The "dry summer" (C) climates are known as *Mediterranean* climates (the small s in Cs means that summers are dry). This mild climate occurs not only around the Mediterranean Sea, and thus in the famous wine countries of France, Italy, and Spain, but also in California, Chile, South Africa's Cape, and southern parts of Australia.

Farther toward the poles, the planet gets rather cold. Note that the (D) climates dominate in the United States' upper Midwest and Canada, but it gets even colder in Siberia. The "milder" (Da) climates (here the key is the small a, which denotes a warm summer) are found only in limited parts of Eurasia. Winters are very cold in all the (D) climates and downright frigid

(and long) in the (Dfb) and (Dfc) regions. (D) climates are generally continental, on the interior of continents, instead of on coasts. Continental locations make (D) climates generally drier than (C) climates. The continentality of (D) climates also contributes to the large range of temperatures found across the year because land heats and cools much faster than water.

*Polar* climates, where tundra and ice prevail, are found poleward of (D) climates. The polar location of (E) climates means temperatures are cold throughout the year. As a result, plant life does not break down and nourish the soil during the year, and also a layer of permafrost (frozen ground) exists year round.

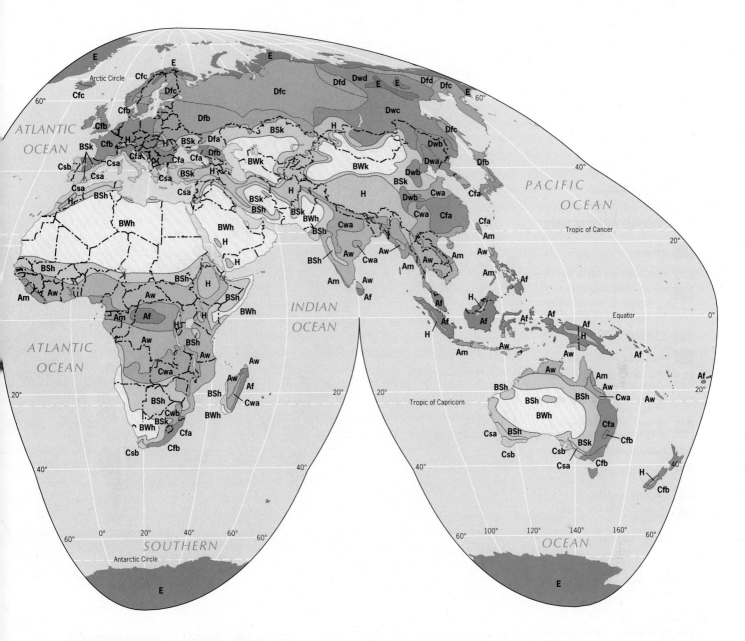

## The World Map of Agriculture

When comparing the world map of agriculture (Fig. 11.18) with the distribution of climate types across the world (Fig. 11.17), we can see the correlation between climate and agriculture. For example, drier lands rely on livestock ranching, whereas moister climates are characterized by grain production. Understanding the major agricultural zones shown in Figure 11.18 requires looking at both environmental and social variables.

### CASH CROPS AND PLANTATION AGRICULTURE

Colonialism profoundly shaped nonsubsistence farming in many poorer countries. Colonial powers implemented agriculture systems to benefit their needs, a practice that has tended to lock poorer countries into production of one or two "cash" crops. Cash farming continues to provide badly needed money, even if the conditions of sale to the urban-industrial world are unfavorable. In the Caribbean region, for example, whole national economies depend on sugar exports (sugar having been introduced by the European colonists in the 1600s). These island countries wish to sell the sugar at the highest possible price, but they are not in a position to dictate prices. Sugar is produced by many countries in various parts of the world, as well as by farmers in the global economic core (Fig. 11.18). Governments in the core place quotas on imports of agricultural products and subsidize domestic production of the same commodities.

Occasionally, producing countries consider forming a cartel in order to present a united front to the importing countries and to gain a better price, as oil-producing states did during the 1970s. Such collective action is difficult to coordinate, as the wealthy importing countries can buy products from countries that are not members of the cartel.

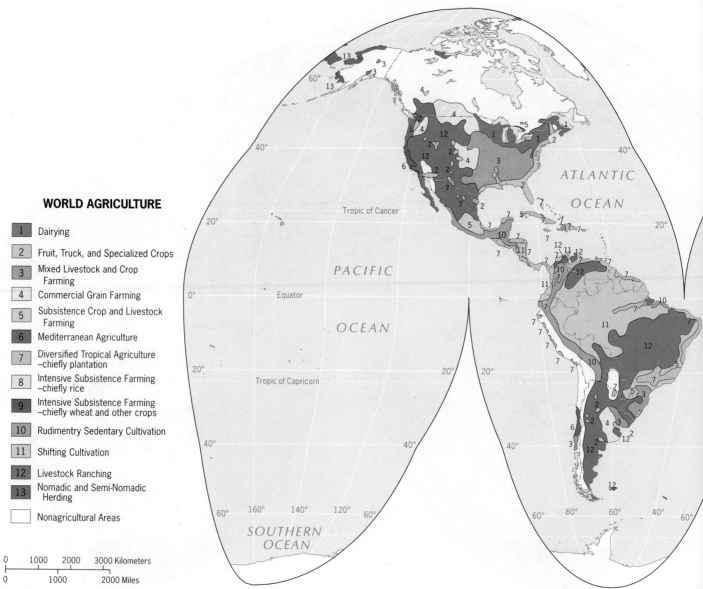

## WORLD AGRICULTURE

1  Dairying

2  Fruit, Truck, and Specialized Crops

3  Mixed Livestock and Crop Farming

4  Commercial Grain Farming

5  Subsistence Crop and Livestock Farming

6  Mediterranean Agriculture

7  Diversified Tropical Agriculture –chiefly plantation

8  Intensive Subsistence Farming –chiefly rice

9  Intensive Subsistence Farming –chiefly wheat and other crops

10  Rudimentry Sedentary Cultivation

11  Shifting Cultivation

12  Livestock Ranching

13  Nomadic and Semi-Nomadic Herding

Nonagricultural Areas

**Figure 11.18**

**World Agriculture.** The type of agriculture practiced varies with climate. Compare this map with Figure 11.17. Livestock raising is common in semi-arid and savanna climate zones. Crop farming and commercial grain farming are found in places that receive higher rainfall. Dairy production generally occurs where climates are cooler. In addition to climate, land ownership patterns factor into the type of agricultural production globally. Where parcels of land are small, farmers generally focus on subsistence production. *Adapted with permission from*: Hammond, Inc., 1977.

Also, the withholding of produce by exporting countries may stimulate domestic production among importers. For example, although cane sugar accounts for 75 percent of the commercial world sugar crop each year, farmers in the United States, Europe, and Russia also produce sugar from sugar beets. In Europe and Russia, these beets already yield 25 percent of the annual world sugar harvest.

When cash crops are grown on large estates, we use the term **plantation agriculture** to describe the production system. Plantations are colonial legacies that persist in poorer, primarily tropical, countries along with subsistence farming. Figure 11.18 shows that plantation agriculture (7 in the legend) continues in Middle and South America, Africa, and South Asia. Laid out to produce bananas, sugar, coffee, and cocoa in Middle and South America, rubber, cocoa, and tea in West and East Africa, tea in South Asia, and rubber in Southeast Asia, these plantations have outlasted the period of decolonization and continue to provide specialized crops to wealthier markets. Many of the most productive plantations are owned by European or American individuals or corporations.

Multinational corporations have tenaciously protected their economic interests in plantations. In the 1940s and 1950s, the Guatemalan government began an agrarian reform

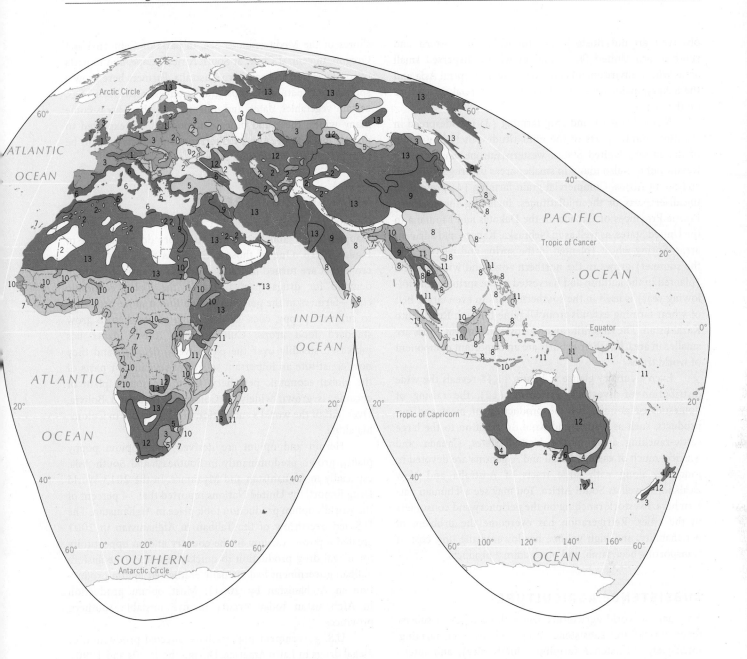

program. The plan entailed renting unused land from foreign corporations to landless citizens at a low appraised value. The United Fruit Company, an American firm with extensive holdings in the country, was greatly concerned by this turn of events. The company had close ties to powerful individuals in the American government, including Secretary of State John Foster Dulles, CIA director Allen Dulles (the two were brothers), and Assistant Secretary of State for Inter-American Affairs John Moors Cabot. In 1954, the United States supported the overthrow of the government of Guatemala because of stated concerns about the spread of communism. This ended all land reform initiatives but led many commentators to question the degree to which the United Fruit Company was behind the coup. Indeed, with the exception of President Dwight Eisenhower, every individual involved in the decision to help topple Guatemala's government had ties to the company. This example illustrates the inextricable links between economics and political motivations—and it raises questions about the degree to which multinational corporations based in wealthy countries influence decisions about politics, agriculture, and land reform in other parts of the world.

## COMMERCIAL LIVESTOCK, FRUIT, AND GRAIN AGRICULTURE

As Figure 11.18 shows, by far the largest areas of commercial agriculture (1 through 4 in the legend) lie outside the tropics. Dairying (1) is widespread at the northern margins of the midlatitudes—particularly in the northeastern United States and in northwestern Europe. Fruit, truck, and specialized crops (2), including the market gardens von Thünen observed around Rostock, are found in the eastern and southeastern United States and in widely dispersed small areas where environments are favorable. In Central Asia and the Sahara, major oases stand out as commercial agriculture on the map.

Mixed livestock and crop farming (3) is widespread in the more humid parts of the midlatitudes, including much of the eastern United States, western Europe, and western Russia, but it is also found in smaller areas in Uruguay, Brazil, and South Africa. Commercial grain farming (4) prevails in the drier parts of the midlatitudes, including the southern Prairie Provinces of Canada, in the Dakotas and Montana in the United States, as well as in Nebraska, Kansas, and adjacent areas. Spring wheat (planted in the spring and harvested in the summer) grows in the northern zone, and winter wheat (planted in the autumn and harvested in the spring of the following year) is used in the southern area. An even larger belt of wheat farming extends from Ukraine through Russia into Kazakhstan. The Argentinean and Australian wheat zones are smaller in area, but their exports are an important component of world trade.

Even a cursory glance at Figure 11.18 reveals the wide distribution of **livestock ranching** (12), the raising of domesticated animals for the production of meat and by-products, such as leather and wool. In addition to the large cattle-ranching areas in the United States, Canada, and Mexico, much of eastern Brazil and Argentina are devoted to ranching, along with large tracts of Australia and New Zealand, as well as South Africa. You may see a Thünian pattern here: livestock ranching on the periphery and consumers in the cities. Refrigeration has overcome the problem of perishability, and high volume has lowered the unit cost of transporting beef, lamb, and other animal products.

## SUBSISTENCE AGRICULTURE

The map of world agriculture labels three types of subsistence agriculture: subsistence crop and livestock farming, intensively subsistence farming (chiefly rice), and intensively subsistence farming (chiefly wheat and other crops). In some regions that are labeled as subsistence, that label does not tell the whole story. For example, in Southeast Asia, rice is grown on small plots and is labor-intensive, so that subsistence and export production occur side by side. Despite the region's significant rice exports, most Southeast Asian farmers are subsistence farmers. Thus, Southeast Asia appears on the map as primarily a subsistence grain-growing area.

## MEDITERRANEAN AGRICULTURE

Only one form of agriculture mentioned in the legend of Figure 11.18 refers to a particular climatic zone: **Mediterranean agriculture** (6). As the map shows, this kind of specialized farming occurs only in areas where the dry summer Mediterranean climate prevails (Fig. 11.17): along the shores of the Mediterranean Sea, in parts of California and Oregon, in central Chile, at South Africa's Cape, and in parts of southwestern and southern Australia. Farmers here grow a special combination of crops: grapes, olives, citrus fruits, figs, certain vegetables, dates, and others. From these areas come many wines; these and other commodities are exported to distant markets because Mediterranean products tend to be popular and command high prices.

## DRUG AGRICULTURE

Certain important agricultural activities cannot easily be mapped at the global scale and therefore do not appear in Figure 11.18. One of those activities is the cultivation of crops that are turned into illegal drugs. Because of the high demand for drugs—particularly in the global economic core—farmers in the periphery often find it more profitable to cultivate poppy, coca, or marijuana plants than to grow standard food crops. Cultivation of these plants has increased steadily over the past several decades, and they now constitute an important source of revenue for parts of the global economic periphery. Coca, the source plant of cocaine, is grown widely in Colombia, Peru, and Bolivia. Over half of the world's cultivation of coca occurs in Colombia alone.

Heroin and opium are derived from opium poppy plants, grown predominantly in Southeast and South Asia, especially in Afghanistan and Myanmar. In the 2013 World Drug Report, the United Nations reported that 74 percent of the world's opium production took place in Afghanistan. The U.S.-led overthrow of the Taliban in Afghanistan in 2001 created a power vacuum in the country and an opportunity for illegal drug production to quickly rebound (the austere Taliban government had virtually eradicated opium production in Afghanistan by 2001). Most opium production in Afghanistan today occurs in five unstable southern provinces.

U.S. government policies have affected production of illegal drugs in Latin America. During the 1980s and 1990s, the U.S. government worked with local authorities to crack down on coca production in Colombia. As a result of this crackdown, much of the drug production and trafficking moved north to northern Mexico. In June 2005, *The Economist* quoted one American official as reporting that "Mexican criminal gangs 'exert more influence over drug trafficking in the U.S. than any other group.' Mexicans now control 11 of the 13 largest drug markets in the United States." Marijuana and opium production in Mexico is on the rise, and the United States Drug Enforcement Agency (DEA) is concerned about the high potency of marijuana coming out of Mexico and Canada. Despite Afghanistan's dominance as a heroin producer, most heroin (which is derived from opium) consumed in the western United States comes from opium grown in Mexico, whereas the heroin consumed in the eastern United States comes from opium grown in Colombia.

Drug cartels that oversee the drug trade have brought crime and violence to the places where they hold sway (Fig. 11.19). There are areas in Rio de Janeiro where the official police have little control, and drug lords have imposed reigns of terror over swaths of the countryside in parts of Central and South America, Southwest Asia, Southeast Asia, and elsewhere. The drug trade depends on the voracious appetite for mind-altering substances in North America and Europe in particular.

The supply of marijuana in the United States traditionally came from Mexico and Canada, as the DEA has reported. But an increasing amount of marijuana consumed in the United States is grown in the United States. Since 1996, a total of 16 states in the United States—mostly in the West—have legalized marijuana for medicinal purposes, and in 2013 Colorado and Washington legalized it entirely (though they forbid consumption in public places and they have placed additional restrictions on cultivation for personal use and the amount of marijuana people can purchase). An April 2011 article in the *New York Times* valued marijuana production at

$40 billion, "with California, Tennessee, Kentucky, Hawaii and Washington the top five production states," despite the fact that medicinal marijuana is not legal in Tennessee or Kentucky.

Marijuana production has more than a monetary impact. Marijuana grown indoors consumes massive amounts of electricity. The cost of indoor production includes grow lamps that are the kinds used in operating rooms, dehumidifiers, air conditioners, electric generators, water pumps, heaters, carbon dioxide generators, ventilation systems, and electrical control systems. Energy analyst Evan Mills published a study in April 2011 estimating the energy costs of producing marijuana in the United States costs at about $5 billion a year (i.e., around 1 percent of all power consumed in the United States). Marijuana grown outdoors has much lower energy costs than marijuana grown indoors. Growers plant crops on public lands, especially in the West, because the remote location of public lands makes detection less likely. Also, the land is public and therefore not owned by any one person to whom a crop could be traced.

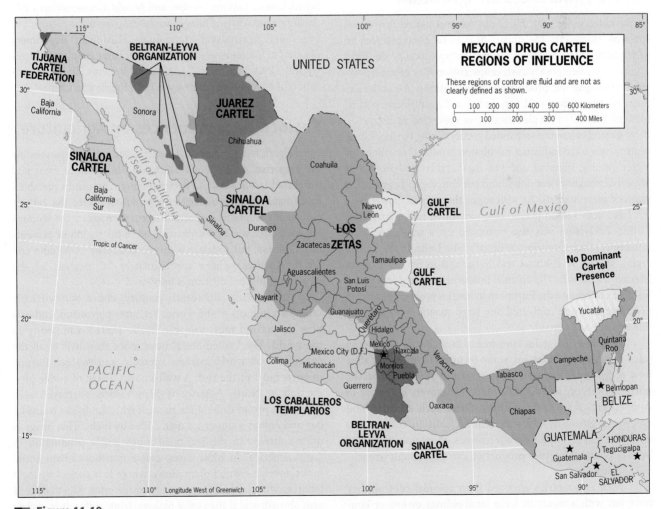

**■ Figure 11.19**

**Mexican Drug Cartel Regions of Influence in Mexico.**    Mexican drug cartels claim swaths of the country and fight with each other for control of territory. Control of territory is important in order to move cocaine, methamphetamine, and marijuana into the United States. The cartels involved and their territorial control has changed as the Mexican government has worked to disrupt the control of the cartels since their war on drugs began in 2006.    *Courtesy of*: Food and Agriculture Service. http://www.fas.org/sgp/crs/row/RL34215.pdf.

## INFORMAL AGRICULTURE

Small-scale informal agricultural activities are also missing from maps of global agricultural patterns, yet these play an important role in the contemporary world. Millions of people cultivate small plots of land in and around their homes for domestic consumption or to trade informally with others. These activities are not captured by formal agricultural statistics, but the food that is grown in this fashion plays a vital role in the lives of literally billions of people. Even city dwellers in many parts of the world are involved in small-scale agricultural activities—cultivating or raising livestock in small plots of land around their dwellings, on rooftop gardens, or in community gardens. Such practices are encouraged in some places—notably China—but more often they are ignored, or even discouraged. Yet the contribution urban agriculture can make to the food security of city dwellers is attracting growing attention, and it is likely to grow in importance in the coming years.

## Political Influences on Agriculture

As we noted above, the European colonial period provides a stunning example of the impact of political circumstances on agricultural practices. Consider, for example, one of the most significant contemporary **cash crops**: cotton. The colonial powers encouraged the production of plantation-scale cotton in many regions of the world (e.g., India) and established a trading network that led to the globalization of the cotton industry.

Cotton cultivation expanded greatly during the nineteenth century, when the Industrial Revolution produced machines for cotton ginning, spinning, and weaving that increased productive capacity, brought prices down, and put cotton goods within the reach of mass markets. As with sugar, the colonial powers laid out large-scale cotton plantations, sometimes under irrigation. Cotton cultivation was also promoted on a smaller scale in numerous other countries: in Egypt's Nile Delta, in the Punjab region shared by Pakistan and India, and in Sudan, Uganda, Mexico, and Brazil. The colonial producers received low prices for their cotton, and the European industries prospered as cheap raw materials were converted into large quantities of items for sale at home and abroad.

Wealthier countries continue to buy cotton, and cotton sales remain important for some former colonies. But they now compete with cotton being grown in the United States, northeast China, and Central Asia. Moreover, cotton is in competition today with synthetic fibers such as nylon and rayon. As global supply and demand shift in response to changing markets and new alternatives, economies that have been built around cotton production can go through wrenching adjustments.

Even as countries emerged from colonial control, they were left with a legacy of large landholdings owned or controlled by wealthy individuals or business entities. That legacy contributed to uprisings among the rural poor in places such as Mexico, Cuba, and Guatemala. The efforts of governmental authorities in some former colonies to confront this situation provide a different example of the impact of politics on agriculture. In some cases, governments enacted policies that perpetuated preexisting inequalities; in others, land reforms were introduced that served to redistribute land to individuals or communities. The latter effort was common in parts of Central and South America, leading to a substantial reorganization of the rural landscape—sometimes spreading wealth more broadly. Pressure for land reform continues in many countries, and land issues are at the heart of many social movements in the global economic periphery and semiperiphery.

A more mundane, but common, way in which governments influence agriculture is through tax regulations and subsidies favoring certain land uses. The U.S. government currently spends more than $10 billion subsidizing large-scale farmers. Pushed by a strong farm lobby, these subsidies guarantee floor prices for staple crops and protect farmers in bad years. They give large-scale agriculture an advantage over smaller scale alternatives. But in the past 60 years perhaps the most dramatic examples of politics affecting agriculture have come from the communist world. The governments of the former Soviet Union, eastern Europe, and Maoist China initiated far-reaching land reforms that led to the creation of large collective farms and agricultural communes. This giant experiment resulted in the massive displacement of rural peoples and irrevocably altered traditional rural social systems. Today privatization of farming is under way in both Russia and China.

## Sociocultural Influences on Agriculture

Agriculture is also affected by social and cultural factors. As incomes rise, many people start consuming more meat and processed foods, seek out better-quality fruits and vegetables, or demand fresh produce year round. Consider the case of coffee, one the most important **luxury crops** in the modern world. Coffee was first domesticated in the region of present-day Ethiopia, but today it is grown primarily in Middle and South America, where approximately 70 percent of the world's annual production is harvested.

In the early eighteenth century, coffee was virtually unknown in most of the world. Yet, after petroleum, coffee is now the second most valuable legally traded commodity in the world. The United States buys more than half of all the coffee sold on world markets annually, and western Europe imports most of the rest. A well-known image of coffee production in North America is Juan Valdez, portrayed as a simple yet proud Colombian peasant who handpicks beans by day and enjoys a cup of his own coffee by night. This image is quite contrary to the reality of much coffee production in Latin America. In most cases, coffee is produced on enormous, foreign-owned plantations, where it is picked by local laborers who are hired at very low wage rates. Most coffee is sent abroad; and if the coffee pickers drink coffee, it is probably of the imported and instant variety.

In the past few decades, however, coffee production has undergone changes as more consumers demand fair trade coffee and more coffee producers seek fair trade certification.

**■ Figure 11.20**
**Los Altos, Chiapas, Mexico.**   A Mayan farmer picks ripe coffee beans for sale to North American customers as fair trade coffee.

The aim of fair trade is to raise the income of certified producers by reducing the number of actors in the supply chain. Coffee producers form democratically run cooperatives that, if certified, can be registered on the International Fair Trade Coffee Register. Coffee importers then purchase the fair trade coffee directly from the registered cooperatives. Being registered guarantees coffee producers a "fair trade price" of $1.40 per pound of coffee (plus bonuses of $0.30 per pound for organic). Over 1.3 million farmers and workers in 70 countries, mainly in the periphery and semiperiphery, are connected to the 1150 fair trade certified producer organizations worldwide (Fig. 11.20). The fair trade campaign pressured Starbucks into selling fair trade coffee. Starbucks buys around 20 million pounds of fair trade coffee each year. That amounts to just 5 percent of its total purchases, but it is the largest purchaser of fair trade coffee in the world. Other retailers have followed suit; for example, all espresso sold at Dunkin' Donuts in North America and Europe is fair trade certified. Fair trade coffee is available at large retail outlets and under corporate brands at Target, Wal-Mart, and Sam's Club. The corporate embrace of fair trade coffee has boosted the movement considerably, though it has also raised concerns about corporate cooptation of fair trade standards.

The push for fair trade production shows how social movements can influence agriculture. And fair trade goes beyond coffee. Dozens of commodities and products, ranging from tea, bananas, fresh cut flowers, and chocolate to soccer balls, can be certified fair trade. According to Fair Trade International, consumers spent more than $6.5 billion on fair trade certified products in 2012.

People's changing tastes also shape the geography of agriculture. Tea is a rather recent addition to the Western diet. It was grown in China perhaps 2000 years ago, but it became popular in Europe only during the nineteenth century. The colonial powers (mainly the British) established enormous tea plantations in Asia and thus began the full-scale flow of tea into European markets. Tea was one of the first plantation-produced products to receive fair trade certification. Both the fair trade and the traditionally traded varieties are on the rise globally to meet the increasing demand.

Even as social preferences shape agricultural production, the consumption of particular products can have social consequences. Just a few decades ago, city dwellers in West Africa primarily consumed grains grown from nearby fields. Over the past three decades, relatively cheap imported rice from Malaysia and Thailand has become an important food source, and many locals came to prefer the taste of the imported rice. This set of circumstances left West Africa vulnerable when the price of imported grains skyrocketed in 2008. Local riots broke out and a food crisis ensued.

## Agribusiness and the Changing Geography of Agriculture

The commercialization of crop production and the associated development of new agricultural technologies have changed how agricultural goods are grown and have sparked the rapid growth of agribusiness. **Agribusiness** is an encompassing term for the businesses that provide a vast array of goods and services to support the agricultural industry. Agribusiness serves to connect local farms to a spatially extensive web of production and exchange. At the same time, it fosters the spatial concentration of agricultural activities. Both of these trends are revealed in the development of the poultry industry in the United States.

Early in the twentieth century, poultry production in the United States was highly disaggregated, with many farmers raising a few chickens as part of a multifaceted farming operation. Over the past 50 years, however, poultry production has fundamentally changed. Today, the farmers on the Delmarva Peninsula east of Washington, D.C., account for 8 percent of poultry production in the United States, and they do so by contracting and working directly with four major poultry companies. In an article on modern agriculture, David Lanegran summarized the impact of this transformation as follows:

> Today, chickens are produced by large agribusiness companies operating hatcheries, feed mills, and processing plants. They supply chicks and feed to the farmers. The farmers are responsible for building a house and maintaining proper temperature and water supply. Once a week the companies fill the feed bins for the farmers, and guarantee them a price for the birds. The companies even collect market-ready birds and take them away for processing and marketing. Most of the nation's poultry supply is handled by a half dozen very large corporations that control the process from chicks to chicken pieces in stores.

Lanegran goes on to show how selective breeding has produced faster growing, bigger chickens, which are housed in enormous broiler houses that are largely mechanized.

Broiler houses are concentrated in northwestern Arkansas, northern Georgia, the Delmarva Peninsula (Delaware, Maryland, and Virginia), the Piedmont areas of North Carolina, and the Shenandoah Valley of Virginia (Fig. 11.21). Lanegran

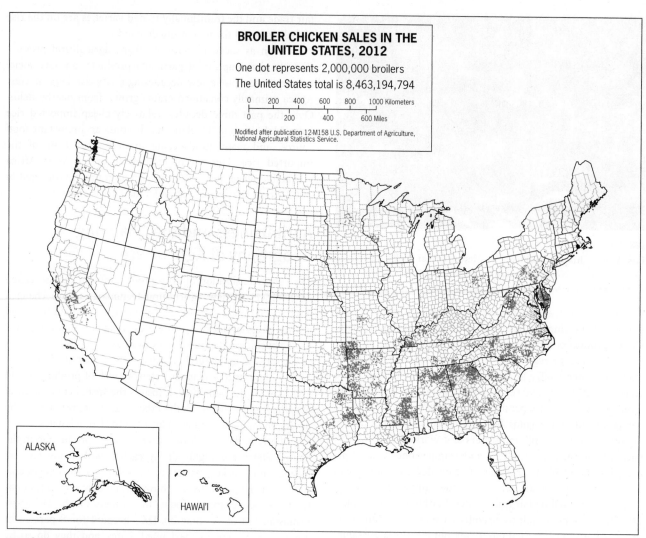

BROILER CHICKEN SALES IN THE
UNITED STATES, 2012

One dot represents 2,000,000 broilers
The United States total is 8,463,194,794

Modified after publication 12-M158 U.S. Department of Agriculture,
National Agricultural Statistics Service.

**■ Figure 11.21**

**Broiler Chicken Sales in the United States, 2012.**   Broiler chickens are grown for meat, which means they will be processed and consumed once sold. The chickens are produced at the locations on this map that shows sales. Farmers typically sell broiler chickens to one of 40 large processing companies including Tyson and Purdue. Ninty five percent of broiler chickens in the United States are produced by farmers who are under contract with a large processing firm and are required to follow their standards and use their feed from hatched egg to table.   *Courtesy of*: United States Census of Agriculture, National Agricultural Statistics Service.

shows that in many respects the "farmers" who manage these operations are involved in manufacturing as much or more as farming. They are as likely to spend their time talking to bank officers, overseeing the repair of equipment, and negotiating with vendors rather than tending their animals. As such, they symbolize the breakdown between the rural and the urban in wealthier parts of the world—as well as the interconnections between rural places and distant markets.

The poultry example is not unusual. During the 1990s, hog production on the Oklahoma and Texas panhandles increased rapidly with the arrival of corporate hog farms. John Fraser Hart and Chris Mayda described the quick change with statistics. In 1992, the U.S. Census of Agriculture counted just over 31,000 hogs marketed in Texas County, Oklahoma, and just four years later "the panhandle was plastered with proliferating pork places, and Texas County alone produced 2 million hogs. It was the epicenter of an area

that produced 4 million hogs, 4 percent of the national total and one-seventh as many finished hogs as the entire state of Iowa." The availability of both inexpensive water and natural gas on the Oklahoma panhandle was enticing for corporate hog farms, which require both. Hart and Mayda explain that the "reasonable" price of land and the accessibility to "growing metropolitan markets of the South and the West" also made the region attractive for hog production. As in poultry production, a corporation built a processing plant, and production (both by farms owned by the corporation and those owned privately) increased to meet the demand (Fig. 11.22).

Because of agribusiness, the range and variety of products on the shelves of urban supermarkets in the United States is a world apart from the constant quest for sufficient, nutritionally balanced food that exists in some places. A global network of farm production is oriented to the one-fifth of the world's population that is highly urbanized, wealthy, and powerful. Few

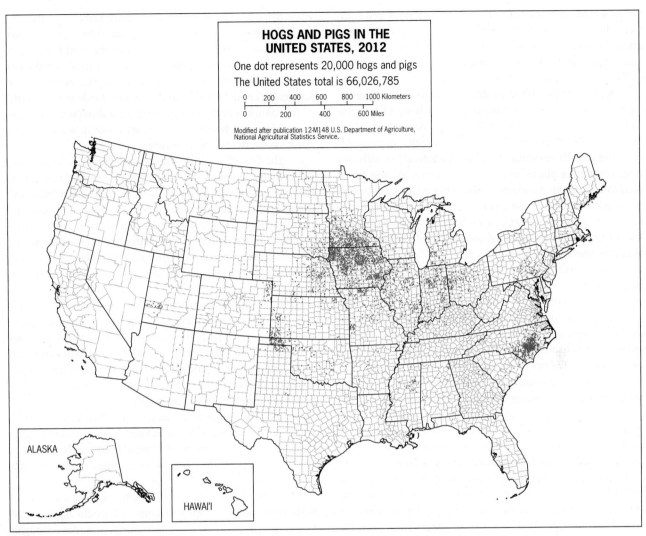

**HOGS AND PIGS IN THE UNITED STATES, 2012**

One dot represents 20,000 hogs and pigs

The United States total is 66,026,785

Modified after publication 12-M148 U.S. Department of Agriculture, National Agricultural Statistics Service.

ALASKA

HAWAI'I

■ **Figure 11.22**

**Hogs and Pigs in the United States, 2012.**   Hog and pig production is concentrated in the Corn Belt in and around Iowa and in North Carolina. The earliest stages of hog production are done inside buildings using systems designed to reduce the possibility of disease spreading among the livestock.   *Courtesy of*: United States Census of Agriculture, National Agricultural Statistics Service.

farmers in distant lands have real control over land-use decisions, for the better-off people in the global economic core play a disproportionate role in deciding what will be bought at what price. The colonial era may have come to an end, but as the map of agricultural regions reminds us, its imprint remains strong.

## Environmental Impacts of Commercial Agriculture

Commercial agriculture produces significant environmental changes. The growing demand for protein-rich foods and more efficient technologies are leading to overfishing in many regions of the world. In many places fish stocks are declining at an alarming rate. From mid-century to the late 1980s, the fish harvest from oceans and seas increased fivefold, and there seemed to be no limit to it. Countries quarreled over fishing rights, poorer countries leased fishing grounds to richer ones,

and fleets of trawlers plied the oceans. International attempts to regulate fishing industries failed. Then in the 1970s and 1980s, overfishing began destroying fish stocks. The cod fisheries on Canada's Grand Banks off Newfoundland collapsed. In 1975, biologists estimated the Atlantic bluefin tuna population at 250,000; today the western stock is listed as critically endangered, and the stock in the Mediterranean is listed as endangered. From ocean perch and king crabs off Alaska to rock lobsters and roughies off New Zealand, fish and shellfish populations are depleted. The total annual catch is also declining and may already be beyond the point of recovery. Much of the damage has already been done, and fishing industries in many parts of the world have reported dwindling harvests and missing species.

If you travel to Mediterranean Europe today you will see a landscape that reflects the clearing of forests in ancient times to facilitate agriculture and trade. Look carefully at many hillslopes and you will see evidence of terraces cut into the hills many centuries ago. The industrialization and commercialization of agriculture has accelerated the pace and extent of agriculture's impact on the environment in recent times. More land has been cleared, and the land that is under cultivation is ever more intensively used.

Significant agriculturally driven changes to the environment go far beyond the simple clearing of land. They range from soil erosion to changes in the organic content of soils to the presence of chemicals (herbicides, pesticides, even antibiotics and growth hormones from livestock feces) in soils and groundwater. In places where large commercial crop farms dominate, the greatest concerns often center on the introduction of chemical fertilizers and pesticides into the environment—as well as soil erosion. And, as we have seen, the movement toward genetically modified crops carries with it another set of environmental concerns.

The growth of organic farming (discussed at the beginning of the chapter) and the move toward the use of local foods in some communities can benefit the environment. Yet such initiatives have had only modest impacts on the majority of the world's peoples and places. A telling sign is that the organic movement has had little effect on the production of the staple foods on which billions of people depend. Moreover, large corporate entities are playing an increasingly prominent role in the organic movement—raising concerns about standards and rendering illusory the ideal of an independent organic farmer engaged in "sustainable" agriculture. Nonetheless, better regulated organic farming and local food initiatives are clearly on the rise. Their proponents argue that they are priced out of the market by subsidies favoring large farms and by the failure of most agribusiness to incorporate the environmental and health costs of large-scale, intensive farming, into their production costs.

The environmental impacts of large-scale intensive agriculture can be particularly severe when agriculture moves into marginal environments, as has happened with the expansion of livestock herding into arid or semiarid areas (see the map of world climates, Fig. 11.17). The natural vegetation in these areas cannot always sustain the herds, especially during prolonged droughts. As a result, ecological degradation and, in some areas, desertification are the result.

In recent decades, the popularity of fast-food chains that serve hamburgers has led to the deforestation of wooded areas in order to open up additional pastures for beef cattle, notably in Central and South America. Livestock ranching is an extremely land-, water-, and energy-intensive process. Significant land must be turned over to the cultivation of cattle feed, and the animals themselves need extensive grazing areas. By stripping away vegetation, the animals can promote the erosion of river banks, with implications for everything from water quality to wildlife habitat.

## The Challenge of Feeding Everyone

Food riots that break out in low-income countries and stories of famine in countries such as Somalia, Sudan, Malawi, and Zimbabwe remind us that food security remains a challenge for millions of people around the globe. Although food production has expanded in some parts of the world, food production per capita has actually declined in Africa over the past decade. Worldwide, nearly 1 billion people are malnourished. Currently, enough food is produced worldwide to feed Earth's population, but in the face of inadequate distribution systems and widespread poverty, food security looms as a significant issue for the twenty-first century.

The United Nations World Food Program defines hunger as living on less than the daily recommended 2100 calories the average person needs to live a healthy life. While news stories focus on starving populations in the wake of wars and natural disasters, acute emergencies account for less than 8 percent of the global hungry. Chronic undernourishment is a much greater problem, impeding childhood development, weakening immune systems, and undermining the social fabric of communities. Malnutrition is a key factor in the death of more than 2.3 million children who do not reach the age of 5.

In response to widespread malnourishment and famine, in 1985 the U.S. Agency for International Development created the Famine Early Warning System, which now collaborates with other organizations worldwide to monitor food stores and predict food insecurity. Many governments and nongovernmental organizations provide food aid to populations in need. The UN World Food Program is the largest source of food aid in the world. It delivers food that is tailored to meet the nutritional needs of particular groups. A typical food basket includes a staple food such as wheat flour or rice; a protein, often lentils or other legumes; vegetable oil; sugar; and salt.

Despite these initiatives, the battle against malnutrition is far from won, and climate change is introducing new challenges in places that are confronting extended droughts, exacerbated threats from new pests, and altered growing conditions for traditional crops (see Chapter 13). For the moment, however, the global food supply remains adequate to meet the needs of the human population, meaning that malnutrition and famine are at heart political and social problems. In their landmark work on vulnerability, geographers Michael Watts and Hans Bohl point to three interrelated causes of food insecurity: declining control over local food resources, lack of political power, and political-economic structures that foster inequality. With government corruption, institutional inefficiencies, and power struggles layered on top of these, the stage is set for the hunger problems described above.

Of course, many people in poorer countries do not suffer from malnutrition, and malnutrition is not limited to the periphery. There are children in virtually every county in the United States who do not have access to adequate food. That reality gave rise to the No Kid Hungry Campaign, which provides breakfasts to children who come to school hungry. Research shows that students who are hungry do not perform well in school, and that breakfast is critical to academic success. No Kid Hungry also helps ensure children receive lunches during the summer, when school is out and children cannot take advantage of school lunch programs.

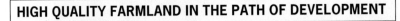

## HIGH QUALITY FARMLAND IN THE PATH OF DEVELOPMENT

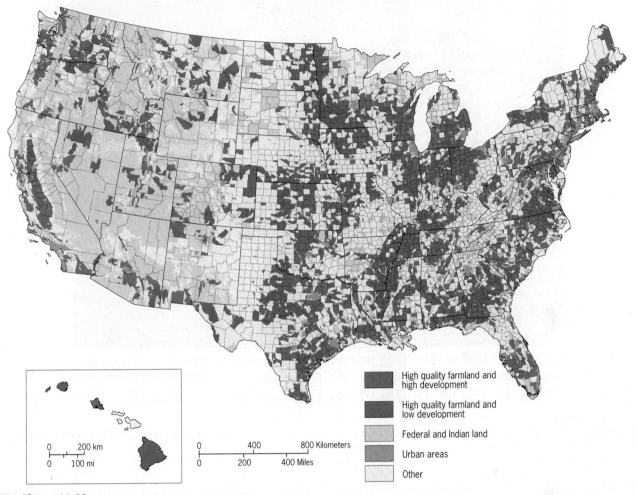

High quality farmland and high development

High quality farmland and low development

Federal and Indian land

Urban areas

Other

■■ **Figure 11.23**

**Farming on the Edge: High-Quality Farmland in the Path of Development, 2002.**  This map from American Farmland Trust, whose charge is to preserve farmland, highlights farmland that is endangered of being suburbanized as cities expand into neighboring farmlands.  *Courtesy of*: American Farm Trust, http://www.farmland.org/farmingontheedge/maps.htm, last accessed November 2005.

Looking ahead, there is growing concern in the United States and beyond over the loss of fertile, productive farmlands to housing and retail developments (Fig. 11.23). Many cities were established amid productive farmlands that could supply the needs of their inhabitants. Now the cities are absorbing the productive farmlands as they expand. Between 1987 and 1992, China lost more than one million hectares of farmland to urbanization. In the United States, the American Farmland Trust identified 12 U.S. areas where farmland was giving way to urban uses at a rapid rate in the 1990s, including California's Central Valley, South Florida, California's coastal zone, North Carolina's Piedmont, and the Chicago–Milwaukee–Madison triangle in Illinois–Wisconsin. These 12 areas represent only 5 percent of U.S. farmland, but they produce 17 percent of total agricultural sales, 67 percent of all fruit, 55 percent of all vegetables, and one-quarter of all dairy products. Figures for other countries in the richer parts of the world (such as Japan) as well as for poorer countries (such as

Egypt) prove that urban expansion into productive farmland is a global problem with serious implications for the future.

The conversion of farmlands into housing developments is not confined to areas close to major cities that could become suburbs. Expendable wealth and the desire to have a place to "get away from it all" have led highly productive commercial agricultural areas to be converted into regions for second homes. On the Delmarva Peninsula in the United States, for example, where poultry production is concentrated, the price of land rose as urbanites from Pennsylvania, Washington, D.C., Maryland, and New York bought land on the eastern shore to build second homes. Many of the new residents on the peninsula are demanding higher environmental standards. Rising land prices and stricter environmental standards are placing a squeeze on the cost of chicken production. As urban population continues to grow and expendable wealth increases for the wealthiest of the population, more agricultural lands will be converted to housing

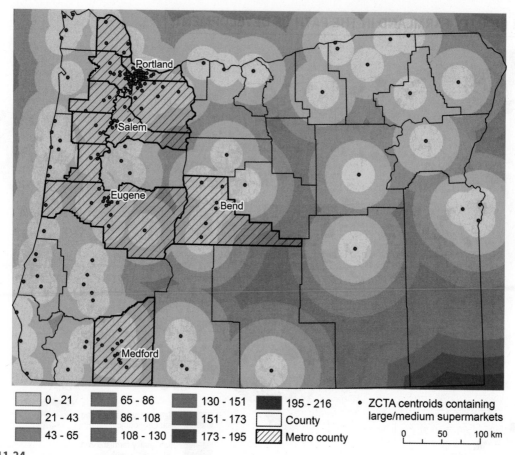

**■■ Figure 11.24**

**Food Deserts in Oregon, 2010.** Mean distance (km) from population-weighted ZIP Code Tabulation Area (ZCTA) centroids containing large or medium supermarkets in Oregon. *Map courtesy of*: Aki Michimi, 2011.

developments, especially lands in beautiful areas with recreational amenities.

Population growth, the loss of agricultural land, and the types of political-economic factors highlighted by Watts and Bohle help explain why global food prices have been on the rise for more than a decade. Further pressure on food prices is coming from consumption increases in countries experiencing rapid development (e.g., China) and from a trend toward using food crops for biofuel production. These factors were behind an almost 50 percent surge in global food prices between April 2007 and March 2008. Food riots broke out in some cities, and the specter of large-scale famine grew. Another more recent spike in food prices was one factor in the outbreak of revolutions in North Africa and Southwest Asia in spring 2011. A convergence of changing land use, increasing use of grains for fuel, corrupt governments, and environmental impacts works against the provision of adequate food at reasonable prices for the world's poor.

Despite the severity of the situation, in today's world it is possible for many people to put farming largely out of their minds. As a result of the industrialization of agriculture and improvements in transportation, consumers come in contact with farmers much less frequently than did previous generations. On a freezing cold winter day in Cincinnati,

Ohio, consumers can purchase fresh strawberries grown in Chile. Consumers can also purchase highly processed foods with long shelf lives and forget where the item was purchased, much less think of the farm work that went into the ingredients.

As a result of the growing distance between farmers and consumers, geographers have sought to draw attention to **food deserts**—areas where people have limited access to fresh, nutritious foods (Fig. 11.24). Urban food deserts are typically found in low-income neighborhoods where medium-size and large grocery stores are largely absent; instead, the only grocery stores within easy reach are small ones filled mainly with processed, energy-dense but nutrient-poor food. British geographer Hilary Shaw (2006) found that consumers in urban food deserts were more likely to purchase unhealthy foods because these foods were cheaper than fresh fruits and vegetables.

Geographers Akihiko Michimi and Michael Wimberly found that rural food deserts lack not only larger grocery stores but also public transportation to reach larger grocery stores. In their study of food deserts and access to fruits and vegetables, the geographers found that since the 1980s in rural areas of the United States a "restructuring of food retail industries has occurred such that local grocery stores that once served small rural communities have been closed" and replaced with larger national chains in regional trade centers. Michimi and Wimberly also found a difference between food deserts in metropolitan and nonmetropolitan areas of the United States. In metropolitan areas, obesity rates increased and the rate of fruit and vegetable consumption decreased with increasing distance from grocery stores. They did not find the same correlation in nonmetropolitan areas.

## Summary

Agricultural production has changed drastically since the First Agricultural Revolution. Today, agricultural products, even perishable ones, are shipped around the world. Agriculture has industrialized, and in many places, food production is dominated by large-scale agribusiness. A major commonality between ancient agriculture and modern agriculture remains: the need to change. Trial and error were the norms of early plant and animal domestication; those same processes are at play in the biotechnology-driven agriculture of the contemporary era. Whatever the time period or process involved, agriculture leaves a distinct imprint on the cultural landscape, from land surveys to land ownership to land use. Globalization has made an imprint on landscapes and agribusiness. What is produced where is not simply a product of the environment and locally available plants; the modern geography of agriculture depends on factors ranging from climate and government regulation to technology and shifting global consumption patterns.

## Geographic Concepts

organic agriculture
agriculture
primary economic activity
secondary economic activity
tertiary economic activity
quaternary economic activity
quinary economic activity
plant domestication
root crops
seed crops
First Agricultural Revolution
animal domestication
subsistence agriculture

shifting cultivation
slash-and-burn agriculture
Second Agricultural Revolution
von Thünen model
Third Agricultural Revolution
biotechnology
Green Revolution
genetically modified organisms
   (GMOs)
rectangular survey system
township- and range-system
metes-and-bounds system
long-lot survey system

primogeniture
commercial agriculture
monoculture
Köppen climatic classification system
climatic regions
plantation agriculture
livestock ranching
Mediterranean agriculture
cash crops
luxury crops
agribusiness
food desert

## Learn More Online

About food production and development
www.foodfirst.org

About the preservation of agricultural lands
www.farmland.org

## Watch It Online

Guns, Germs, and Steel
www.pbs.org/gunsgermssteel

Loss of agricultural land to suburbanization in Chicago
www.learner.org/resources/series180.html#program_descriptions
click on video on demand for program 24

Russia's Farming Revolution
www.learner.org/resources/series180.html#program_descriptions
click on video on demand for program 7

Sustainable agriculture in India
www.learner.org/resources/series180.html#program_descriptions
click on video on demand for program 17

# INDUSTRY AND SERVICES

## Containing the World-Economy

I found myself mesmerized by the loading of a container ship at the port just outside of Copenhagen, Denmark. The crane reached over to the ship, picked up each container, and slowly lowered the container onto the neatly organized dock. Slowly the stack of containers on the ship shrunk, each one emblazoned with a label of a shipping company based in one country or another: Germany, China, the United States, Japan, Sweden, Australia. The crane continued to unload goods produced in Asia. From the port in Copenhagen, the containers will be shipped by road, railroad, and barge to destinations throughout Scandinavia and to countries around the Baltic Sea.

The container ship is the backbone of globalization and has dramatically changed the economic geography of the planet since the first one sailed in 1956. Before containers, a ship would arrive at port with various, odd-sized crates and boxes. Hundreds of longshoremen would flock to the dock to unload the goods by hand. With **containerization**, ports now have relatively few employees who operate the high-tech cranes, moving standard-sized containers from ship to dock or dock to ship with precision. Cranes move containers with the goal of unloading a massive container ship within 24 hours of reaching port.

Nearly 90 percent of long-distance cargo is now shipped in standard containers. With a volume in excess of 2250 cubic feet (more than 65 m³), one container can accommodate goods worth millions of dollars. Steel containers are structurally sound and can be stacked and moved from truck to rail to ship without worrying about how fragile the contents of the containers are.

The container ship in Figure 12.1 is small compared to the *Marco Polo*, the world's largest container ship. Although the *Marco Polo* is the length of four football fields, it was designed to fit through the Suez Canal, making transportation of massive amounts of goods from Asia to Europe possible. The larger the ship, the less expensive it is to transport each container. So, shipbuilders keep going larger. Certain bottlenecks of shipping routes, including the Panama Canal,

© Alexander B. Murphy

■■ **Figure 12.1**
**Copenhagen, Denmark.** Cranes and container ships.

the Suez Canal, and the Straits of Magellan (at the tip of Malaysia) limit, how large the ships can be built. Most container ships are too large for the Panama Canal, but ships going from Asia to Europe are carefully designed to still use the Straits of Magellan and the Suez Canal.

Containerization has even changed the map of major port cities. Ports have become inter-modal hubs, and port authorities and managers are constantly expanding and improving their infrastructure and systems to attract more cargo through their port. Ports don't solely attract cargo, as the cruise ship in the background of Figure 12.1 demonstrates. In 2014, the Copenhagen Malmo Port completed construction on a cruise ship quay with three terminal buildings so that the port can serve more cruise ships and passengers.

Ports such as San Francisco declined because their piers were not well suited to the load-ing and unloading of containers. Others such as nearby Oakland boomed—capitalizing on a container-friendly port retrofit that made it one of the most important shipping centers along the West Coast of the United States. With proximity to customers less important than it once was, small ports such as Busan, South Korea, expanded dramatically, and previously nonexis-tent ports such as Tanjun Pelepas, Malaysia, were built. They have emerged as significant port cities because containerization made it economical to sell local goods in New York, London, and Buenos Aires.

The geography of industry and services is a product of shifting developments that have shaped production and consumption over time. In this chapter, we begin by looking at the ori-gins of the Industrial Revolution in Great Britain and its diffusion into mainland Europe. In addi-tion, we look at the rise of manufacturing belts in Europe, Asia, and North America. We then explore how industrialization has changed, focusing on the emergence of global labor networks and such concepts as flexible production and the global division of labor. We also consider how the expanding service economy is changing the nature of employment and the economic bases of many places.

# Key Questions FOR CHAPTER 12

1. Where did the Industrial Revolution begin, and how did it diffuse?
2. How have the character and geography of industrial production changed?
3. How have deindustrialization and the rise of service industries altered the economic geography of production?

## WHERE DID THE INDUSTRIAL REVOLUTION BEGIN, AND HOW DID IT DIFFUSE?

The manufacturing of goods began long before the Industrial Revolution. In **cottage industries**, families in a community worked together, each creating a component of a finished good or the good itself. For example, in a small town in England, a few families would receive a shipment of wool from a merchant and then prepare the wool and pass it on to families who would spin the wool into yarn. The families who made the wool into yarn passed the yarn to weavers who made blankets and other wool products. Typically, this work was done over the winter, after harvest and before planting the next year's crop. In the spring before planting, the mer-chants returned to pick up the finished products and pay for the production. Merchants shipped the goods around the world.

In the 1800s, as global trade intensified with the avail-ability of steam-powered ships, goods produced in cottage industries in India were in demand around the world. Indian cottage industries produced goods made of iron, gold, silver, and brass, Indian woodworkers produced hand-carved items that were in demand wherever they could be bought. India's textiles, made on individual spinning wheels and hand looms, were considered the best in the world. India's textiles were so finely produced that British textile makers rioted in 1721, demanding legislative protection against imports from India. China and Japan also possessed a substantial industrial base of cottage industries, long before the Industrial Revolution.

The transition from cottage industries to the Industrial Revolution happened in the context of changing **economies of scale**. Europeans sought to capitalize on economies of scale, to generate a greater profit by producing larger quantities of the goods in high demand, which in turn decreased the average cost of producing the good. European industries, from the textile makers of Flanders and Britain to the iron smelters of Thüringen, had become substantial operations. However, in price and quality, Europe's products could not match those of other parts of the world. European commercial companies, including the Dutch and British East India Companies, sought to gain control over local industries in Indonesia and India, respectively, in the 1700s and 1800s.

Both the Dutch and British companies were privately owned and operated under the flag of their country. Each company established battalions of soldiers as they sought to politically and economically control the sectors of production in Southeast and South Asia. The European presence on the ground created political chaos, and the Dutch and British companies profited from the political chaos, pitting local factions against one another. British merchants exported tons of raw fiber from India to expand textile industries in northern England, including Liverpool and Manchester.

The wealth brought into the Netherlands and England through trade (Fig. 12.2) funded technological innovations in manufacturing in Europe and fueled the expansion of production through the Industrial Revolution. The wealth was so great that the monarchs of both the Netherlands and England eventually stepped in and directly colonized Indonesia and South Asia in an effort to squelch the political chaos created by the companies and to secure the continued flow of wealth into European coffers. Through the mass production of goods, brought about by the Industrial Revolution, Europe eventually flooded global markets with inexpensive products, burying cottage industries at home and in Asia. Colonies were no longer merely sites of production and resource extraction.

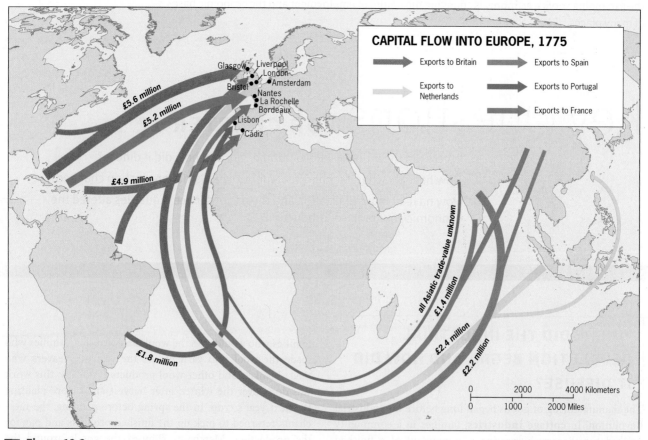

**■ Figure 12.2**

**Capital Flows into Europe During the Period of European Colonialism.**    This map shows the major flows of capital into Europe from Europe's colonies. The capital helped fuel Europe's Industrial Revolution at the end of the 1700s and into the 1800s.    *Adapted with permission from*: Geoffrey Barraclough, ed., *The Times Concise Atlas of World History,* 5th ed., Hammond Incorporated, 1998.

When Europe exported inexpensive, mass-produced products globally, colonies became customers, places where European goods were purchased.

## The Industrial Revolution

The first steps in industrialization occurred in northern England, where cotton from America and India was shipped to the port of Liverpool. Textile factories in the British Midlands, south of Manchester, took advantage of rivers and hills to power cotton spinning machines by water running downhill.

The hearth of the Industrial Revolution was England in the eighteenth century. Wealth brought to Europe through the colonization of and trade with South Asia, Southeast Asia, the Americas, and Africa funded inventions, including the spinning jenny and the steam engine (Fig. 12.2). James Watt is credited with improving the steam engine by creating a separate chamber to house the steam and by perfecting the pistons and getting them to perform correctly. The invention did not happen overnight: A series of attempts over a few decades finally worked when Watt partnered with toymaker and metal worker Matthew Boulton, who inherited great wealth from his wife (her father had amassed wealth as a global cloth trader). Boulton financed the final trials and errors that made the Boulton & Watt steam engine functional and reliable. Coal powered the steam engine, which fueled water pumps, trains, looms, and eventually ships.

The steam engine, trains, and railroads were all made of iron. Before Boulton and Watt could perfect the steam engine, inventors needed a reliable way to heat up iron so that it could be poured into cast molds to make the same product over and over again. In Coalbrookdale, England, in 1709, iron worker Abraham Darby found a way to *smelt* iron. By burning coal in a vacuum-like environment, the English already knew they could cook off impurities, leaving behind coke, the high-carbon portion of coal. Darby put iron ore and coke in a blast furnace and then pushed air into the furnace. This combination allowed the furnace to burn at a much higher temperature than wood charcoal or coal allowed. Mixing the iron ore with limestone (to attract impurities) and water and smelting it with coke enabled iron workers to pour melted iron ore into molds (instead of shaping it by hammering against anvils), yielding *cast iron*. The use of molds allowed more consistency in iron parts and increased production of iron components. As the toponym indicates, the residents of Ironbridge, a town neighboring Coalbrookdale, still take pride in their town's bridge, the first in the world to be constructed entirely from cast iron in 1779 (Fig. 12.3).

During the early part of the Industrial Revolution, before the railroad connected nodes of industry and reduced the transportation costs of coal, manufacturing needed to be located close to coal fields. Manufacturing plants also needed to be connected to ports, where raw materials could arrive and finished products could depart. In the first decades of the Industrial Revolution, plants were usually connected to ports by a broad canal or river system. In Britain, densely populated and heavily urbanized industrial regions developed near the coal fields (Fig. 12.4). The two largest centers of industry in Britain were an iron-working region in the Midlands, where Birmingham is located, and a textile production region in the Northwest, where Liverpool and Manchester are located.

The steam engine had a dramatic impact on industry and helped concentrate even more industrial production in the Midlands and Northwest. Industrialists used the steam engine to pump water out of coal mines, enabling coal workers to reach deeper coal seams, to power spinning wheels that spun 100 plus spools of thread at a time, to power dozens of looms in a factory all at once, and to create a new mode of transportation: the railroad. The first commercial railway connected Manchester, a center of textile manufacturing, along 35 miles of track to the port of

© John Robertson/Alamy Images

■ **Figure 12.3**

**Ironbridge, England.**   The world's first bridge made entirely of cast iron was constructed in the late eighteenth century near Coalbrookdale, England, reflecting the resources, technology, and available skills in this area at the time.

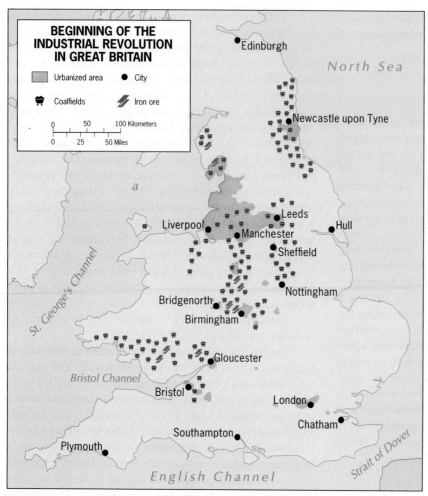

**BEGINNING OF THE INDUSTRIAL REVOLUTION IN GREAT BRITAIN**

Urbanized area    ● City

Coalfields    Iron ore

0    50    100 Kilometers

0    25    50 Miles

Edinburgh

North Sea

Newcastle upon Tyne

Leeds

Liverpool

Manchester

Hull

Sheffield

Nottingham

Bridgenorth

Birmingham

Gloucester

Bristol

London

Chatham

Southampton

Plymouth

St. George's Channel

Bristol Channel

English Channel

Strait of Dover

■ **Figure 12.4**

**The Origins of the Industrial Revolution.**    The areas of Great Britain that industrialized earliest were those closest to the resources needed for industrialization: coal, iron ore, and capital. Large areas of urbanization grew near industrial zones and in the port cities where materials came in and from which industrialized products went out.    *Adapted with permission from: Geoffrey Barraclough, ed., The Times Concise Atlas of World History, 5th ed., Hammond Incorporated, 1998.*

With the advent of the railroad and steamship, Great Britain enjoyed even greater advantages over the rest of the world than it did at the beginning of the Industrial Revolution. British investors and business leaders held a near monopoly over the manufacture of many products that were in demand around the world. The British perfected coal smelting, cast iron, the steam engine, and the steam locomotive. The railroad pioneer George Stephenson, who led the building of the railway between Manchester and Liverpool, set the standard gauge for the railroad track that is still used for about 60 percent of the world's railroads today. The Industrial Revolution increased Britain's influence globally. The British had the know-how, the experience, and the capital to diffuse the Industrial Revolution into the Americas and continental Europe.

## Diffusion to Mainland Europe

In the early 1800s, as the innovations of Britain's Industrial Revolution diffused into mainland Europe, the same set of **locational criteria** for industrial zones applied: sites needed to be close to resources and connected to ports by water. Coal and iron ore were heavy, and transportation of both resources was costly. The first manufacturing belts in continental Europe were located close to coal fields and connected by water to a port so that raw materials could be imported from the Americas and Asia and finished products could be exported. A belt of major coal fields extends from west to east through mainland Europe, roughly along the southern margins of the North European Lowland—across northern France and southern Belgium, the Netherlands, the German Rühr, western Bohemia in the Czech Republic, and Silesia in Poland. Colonial empires gave France, Britain, Belgium, the Netherlands, and, later, Germany access to the capital necessary to fuel industrialization and in some cases the raw materials necessary for production. Iron ore is dispersed along a similar belt, and the map showing the pattern of diffusion of the Industrial Revolution into Europe shows industrial production was concentrated along the coal and iron ore belt through the middle of mainland Europe (Fig. 12.6).

Liverpool in 1830. Sited where the River Mersey flows into the Irish Sea, Liverpool faces west, toward Britain's colonies in the Americas. Cotton and tobacco arrived in Liverpool, and were transported by rail or canal to Manchester, which was a center for textile manufacturing. Coal from Leeds, northeast of Manchester, was transported to Manchester. The coal, cotton, and textile plants were located close to each other, helping the area become the center for mechanized textile manufacturing in the Industrial Revolution.

The new transportation system of the railway diffused as thousands of miles of iron and then steel track were laid, fundamentally changing the quantity of and speed at which goods could be transported over land. The steam engine made its mark on sea transportation, as the first steam-powered vessel crossed the Atlantic Ocean in 1819, shrinking the time it took to travel across seas and also enabling shipbuilders to design larger vessels that could transport more goods (Fig. 12.5).

When industry developed in one area, economic growth had a **spillover effect** on the port cities to which

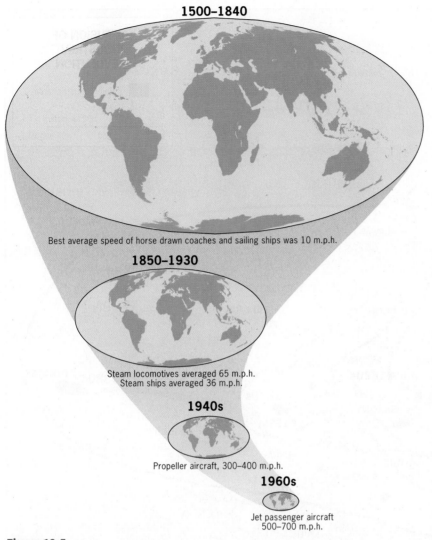

**1500–1840**

Best average speed of horse drawn coaches and sailing ships was 10 m.p.h.

**1850–1930**

Steam locomotives averaged 65 m.p.h.
Steam ships averaged 36 m.p.h.

**1940s**

Propeller aircraft, 300–400 m.p.h.

**1960s**

Jet passenger aircraft
500–700 m.p.h.

**Figure 12.5**
**The World Shrinks Through Transportation Innovations.** This diagram helpfully illuminates how much more quickly goods and people can move over land and sea after 1960 compared to 1650. The maps are slightly misleading, though, because these new transportation technologies do not connect every single place on Earth. Places close to airports and seaports are more connected to each other than places away from transportation nodes. Time–space compression tells us the world is shrinking, but unevenly as some places are closer and some are relatively farther away than ever before. *Figure courtesy of*: Peter Dicken, Global Shift.

they were linked by river or canal. For example, one of the largest industrial centers in continental Europe was the Rühr area of present-day Germany (Germany was not consolidated into a single country until the 1870s). The Rühr is connected to the port of Rotterdam, the Netherlands by the Rhine River. Each port has a **hinterland**, or an area from which goods can be produced, delivered to the port, and then exported. A port also serves its hinterland by importing raw materials that are delivered to manufacturing sites for production. In other words, Rotterdam is the port, and its hinterland includes the region along the Rhine, including the Rühr in Germany. Rotterdam is considered to be a port

sited in the mouth of a delta (Rodrigue 2014).

Over the last 200 years, the Dutch have radically altered the port, expanding it from the mouth of the delta west to the coast of the North Sea. With each change in the situation of the global economy, Rotterdam built new facilities to accommodate the new production and transportation needs. For example, in the 1950s, Rotterdam Municipal Port Management recognized the growth in oil dependency and built the Europoort, extending pipelines and a deep canal to allow the importation of oil, which was then distributed into the port's hinterland. In the 1980s, Rotterdam saw an opportunity to connect the port with the interior of continental Europe by railroad. It extended the port further west and built the Betuweroute rail line, which connects Rotterdam with Genoa, Italy. Rotterdam is both the starting and end point for goods along the corridor. It continues to expand to meet the changing situation of the global economy. In 2007, Rotterdam added land to the western end of the port, constructing a deep seaport to better serve larger container ships. The economic landscape of the port of Rotterdam has changed as the port managers have adjusted to the changing world-economy in order to facilitate transportation and solidify its position as the most important port in Europe and a hub of global commerce.

Once railroads were well established in Great Britain and continental Europe, the factors that determine where to locate, or site, manufacturing facilities changed. Transportation is a major cost in the production of a good, and railroads lowered the cost of transporting bulk and heavy goods. Companies could locate manufacturing plants away from coal and iron ore and in major cities, like London and Paris. Cities could import raw materials, produce goods drawing from the larger labor supply, and sell the goods to the larger population of consumers found in cities. Industrialization was slow to reach London because it lacked easy access to coal and iron ore until the railway expanded through Great Britain. London became a particularly attractive site for industry at this point because of its port location on the Thames River and, more importantly, because of its major role in the flow of regional and global capital.

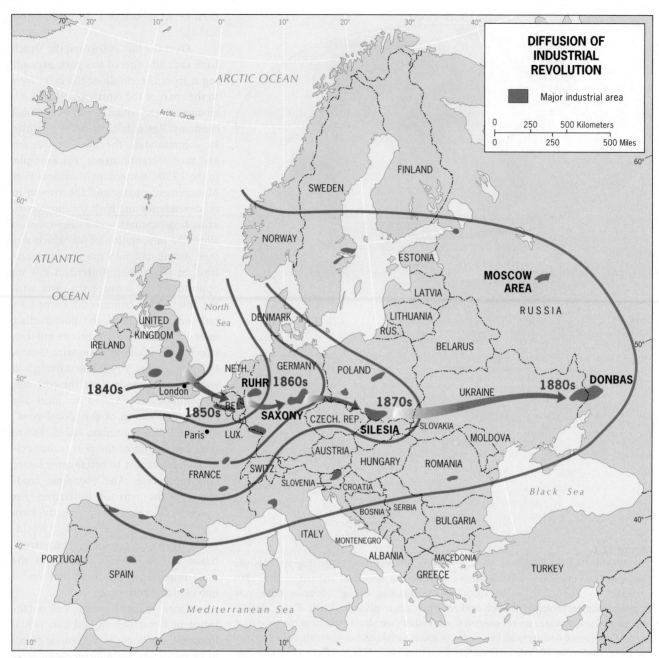

**Figure 12.6**

**Diffusion of the Industrial Revolution.**    The eastward diffusion of the Industrial Revolution occurred during the second half of the nineteenth century.    © H. J. de Blij, P. O. Muller, and John Wiley & Sons, Inc.

By choosing a site, or location, in London, a manufacturing company put itself at the center of Britain's global network of influence. Paris was already continental Europe's greatest city, but like London, it did not have coal or iron deposits in its immediate vicinity. When a railroad system was added to the existing network of road and waterway connections to Paris, however, the city became the largest local market for manufactured products for hundreds of miles. Paris attracted major industries, and the city, long a center for the manufacture of luxury items (jewelry, perfumes, and fashions), experienced substantial growth in such industries as metallurgy and chemical manufacturing. With a ready labor force, an ideal regional position for the distribution of finished products, the presence of governmental agencies, a nearby ocean port (Le Havre), and France's largest domestic market, Paris's development as a major industrial center was no accident.

London and Paris became, and remain, important industrial complexes not because of their coal fields but because of their commercial and political **connectivity** to the rest of the world (Fig. 12.7). Germany still ranks among the world's leading producers of both coal and steel and remains

## FIELD NOTE

"Paris and the Paris Basin form the industrial as well as agricultural heart of France. The city and region are served by the Seine River, along which lies a string of ports from Le Havre at the mouth to Rouen at the head of navigation for oceangoing ships. Rouen has become a vital center on France's industrial map. As we approached on the river, you could see the famous cathedral and the city's historic cultural landscape to the left (north), but on the right bank lay a major industrial complex including coal-fired power facilities (although France leads Europe in nuclear energy), petrochemical plants, and oil installations. It is all part of the industrial region centered on Paris."

© H. J. de Blij

■ **Figure 12.7**
**Rouen, France.**

Europe's leading industrial power (Table 12.1). By the early twentieth century, industry began to diffuse far from the original European hearth to northern Italy (now one of Europe's major industrial regions), Catalonia (anchored by Barcelona) and northern Spain, southern Sweden, and southern Finland.

## Diffusion Beyond Europe

Western Europe's early industrialization gave it a huge economic head start, or a **first mover advantage**, putting the region at the center of a quickly growing world-economy in

the nineteenth century. Industrialization began to diffuse from Europe to the Americas and Asia in the nineteenth century, and **secondary hearths** of industrialization were established in eastern North America, western Russia and Ukraine, and East Asia. Each of the primary industrial regions established by the 1950s were close to coal, which was the major energy source, connected by water or railroad to ports, and heavily invested in by wealthy persons already in the region and by merchants from Europe (Fig. 12.8).

### NORTH AMERICA

By the beginning of the twentieth century, the only serious rival to Europe was a territory settled predominantly by Europeans and with particularly close links to Britain, which provided links to the capital and innovations that fueled industrialization there: North America. Manufacturing in North America began in New England during the colonial period, but the northeastern States were not especially rich in mineral resources. North America, however, benefited from the ability of its companies to acquire needed raw materials from overseas sources.

Industries developed along the Great Lakes where canal, river, and lakes connected with railroads on land to move resources and goods in and out of industrial centers. The industrial region benefited from a ready supply of energy to fuel industrialization. Coal was the chief fuel for industries at the time, and there was never

### TABLE 12.1
**World's Largest Oil Producers.**

| TOP OIL PRODUCERS (BARRELS PER DAY) | | | |
|---|---|---|---|
| 1. Saudi Arabia | 11,730,000 | 12. Nigeria | 2,524,000 |
| 2. United States | 11,110,000 | 13. Venezuela | 2,489,000 |
| 3. Russia | 10,440,000 | 14. Norway | 1,902,000 |
| 4. China | 4,197,000 | 15. Algeria | 1,875,000 |
| 5. Canada | 3,856,000 | 16. Angola | 1,872,000 |
| 6. Iran | 3,594,000 | 17. Kazakhstan | 1,606,000 |
| 7. United Arab Emirates | 3,213,000 | 18. Qatar | 1,579,000 |
| 8. Iraq | 2,979,000 | 19. Libya | 1,483,000 |
| 9. Mexico | 2,936,000 | 20. India | 990,200 |
| 10. Kuwait | 2,797,000 | 21. Indonesia | 974,300 |
| 11. Brazil | 2,652,000 | 22. Colombia | 969,100 |

*Data from*: United States Central Intelligence Agency, *World Factbook*, 2014.

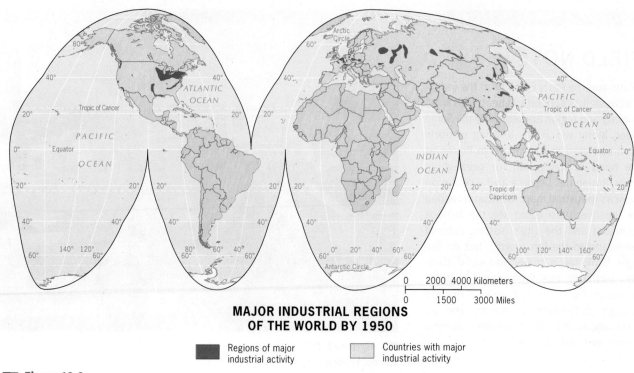

## MAJOR INDUSTRIAL REGIONS
## OF THE WORLD BY 1950

Regions of major industrial activity

Countries with major industrial activity

■■ **Figure 12.8**
**Major Industrial Regions of the World in 1950.**    This map shows the major industrial districts of Europe, North America, Russia, and East Asia in approximately 1950.    © E. H. Fouberg, A. B. Murphy, H. J. de Blij, and John Wiley & Sons, Inc.

any threat of a coal shortage in the United States: U.S. coal reserves are among the world's largest and are widely distributed, being found from Appalachian Pennsylvania to the northwestern Great Plains (Fig. 12.9).

### RUSSIA AND UKRAINE

The St. Petersburg region is one of Russia's oldest manufacturing centers. Tsar Peter the Great planned and constructed the city not only to serve as Russia's capital but also to become the country's industrial core. Peter the Great encouraged western European artisans with skills and specializations to migrate to the region, and he imported high-quality machine-building equipment to help fuel industrialization. The St. Petersburg region soon attracted industries including shipbuilding, chemical production, food processing, and textile making. After World War I, the newly formed Soviet Union annexed Ukraine and took advantage of its rich resources and industrial potential, especially in the coal-rich Donbas region, to become an industrial power. The Soviet Union (and Russia today) was resource rich. Soviet leaders directed an economic plan to industrialize the Moscow region. They developed industries in Nizhni Novgorod, a river port located at the confluence of the Volga and Oka rivers, 270 miles southeast of Moscow. Following the Volga River, goods can be imported or exported from Nizhni Nogorod to the Black Sea or the Caspian Sea.

### EAST ASIA

After Japan opened its economy through a change in government policy in 1868, the Industrial Revolution diffused to Japan. Japan began industrializing with its military sector and encouraged Japanese men to study sciences in universities abroad so they could bring their knowledge back to Japan and create industries. With limited natural resources, Japan depended on raw materials imported from other parts of the world for manufacturing. In the late 1800s and early 1900s, Japan colonized Korea, Taiwan, and portions of mainland China, which brought capital and resources for industry. Japan's dominant region of industrialization and urbanization is the *Kanto Plain* (Fig. 12.7), which contains about one-third of the nation's population and includes the Tokyo–Yokohama–Kawasaki metropolitan area. Japan's second largest industrial complex extends from the eastern end of the Seto Inland Sea to the Nagoya area and includes the Kobe–Kyoto–Osaka triangle, which is a vast industrial region with steel mills, a major chemical industry, automobile manufacturing, shipbuilding, textile factories, and many other types of production.

**thinking**
*geographically*

Examine the map of diffusion of the Industrial Revolution into Europe (Fig. 12.6) and hypothesize what other variables (aside from the presence of coal) were necessary for industrialization to take hold in these regions.

■ **Figure 12.9**

**Major Deposits of Fossil Fuels in North America.**    North America is one of the world's largest energy consumers, and the continent is also endowed with substantial energy sources.    © H. J. de Blij, P. O. Muller and John Wiley & Sons, Inc.

## HOW HAVE THE CHARACTER AND GEOGRAPHY OF INDUSTRIAL PRODUCTION CHANGED?

Economic geography provides context for understanding a multitude of human geographic developments. In this book, we have already made reference to economic geography to help explain globalization in Chapter 1, local and popular cultures in Chapter 4, identities and scale in Chapter 5, language loss and toponyms in Chapter 7, colonialism and political disputes in Chapter 8, and the geography of development in Chapter 10. In this section of the chapter, we incorporate economic geography principles we introduced in earlier chapters with other economic geography concepts to provide a context for understanding changes in the character and geography of manufacturing and service industries since World War II.

In Chapter 1, we defined **globalization** as a set of processes that are increasing interactions, deepening relationships, and heightening interdependence without regard to country borders. Globalization is also a set of outcomes that are felt from these global processes—outcomes that are unevenly distributed and differently manifested across the world. Improvements in transportation and communication technologies are at the root of globalization. The improvement of sailing ships and navigation methods helped establish global trade routes and the first wave of colonialism (Chapter 8). The advent of the steam ship, the diffusion of railroads, and the invention of the telegraph and then the telephone quickened global trade and connected empires in the second wave of colonialism. Through colonialism and trade, capitalism became the economic foundation of the world-economy (Chapter 8).

## Fordist Production

The manufacturing boom of the twentieth century can be traced in part to early innovations in the production process. Perhaps the most significant of these innovations was the mass-production assembly line pioneered by Henry Ford, which allowed the inexpensive production of consumer goods at a single site on a previously unknown scale. So significant was Ford's idea that the dominant mode of mass production that endured from 1945 to 1970 is known as **Fordist**. In addition to its role in facilitating mass production, economic geographers also see the Fordist system as encompassing a set of political-economic structures and financial orders that supported mass production by corporations. In Fordist production, corporations and political institutions were the political-economic structures that supported each other in growing the world-economy. The predominant financial order was the Bretton Woods arrangement, negotiated in 1944, under which countries adopted the gold standard, agreeing to peg the values of their currency to the price of gold. These structures created a degree of stability in international exchange that encouraged global mass production of goods.

The Fordist period is marked by a surge in both mass production and mass consumption. On the Ford assembly line, machines replaced people, and unskilled workers instead of craftsmen worked on the assembly lines. Ford paid his workers

a good wage, and droves of job seekers migrated to the Detroit area to work in the automobile industry (see Chapter 9). Ford's goal was to mass produce goods at a price point where his workers could afford to purchase them. Production of automobiles at Ford's River Rouge plant in Dearborn, Michigan (Fig. 12.10) exemplified the **vertical integration** of production common during the Fordist period. Ford imported raw materials, from coal to rubber to steel, from around the world and brought them to his plant on the River Rouge in Dearborn, just west of Detroit. The massive River Rouge Ford plant is better described as an industrial complex. The Henry Ford Foundation describes Ford's goal in building the complex of 93 buildings with more than 120 miles of conveyor belts that covered an area 1 by 1.5 miles as follows: "Henry Ford's ultimate goal was to achieve total self-sufficiency by owning, operating and coordinating all the resources needed to produce complete automobiles." The River Rouge complex included a power plant, boat docks, and a railroad. The complex had up to 100,000 employees, a fire station and a police department, prompting the Henry Ford Museum to describe it as "a city without residents."

**■ Figure 12.10**

**Dearborn, Michigan.**    The industrial complex of the Ford River Rouge Plant as it stood in the 1940s. In Fordist production, the corporation imported raw materials, bringing them by barge and rail to the Ford River Rouge Plant. The complex included a power plant, steel production, and the manufacturing of component parts of automobiles. Nearly everything Ford needed to produce an automobile was brought together at the factory complex where up to 100,000 employees (at its peak in the 1930s) labored to manufacture components and assembled automobiles.

Under Fordist production, distance was a major consideration in the location of industry. For example, in the United States, furniture manufacturing shifted from Boston in 1875 to Cincinnati by 1890 and then Grand Rapids, Michigan, by 1910. Furniture manufacturing took off in North Carolina when northern entrepreneurs built manufacturing plants there in the early 1900s to take advantage of North Carolina's "abundance of lumber, low-cost labor combined with Reconstruction era wood-working skills and attitudes" (Walcott 2011). The presence of infrastructure, nearness to customers, and humid climate (which kept wood from cracking) were also reasons furniture manufacturers located in close proximity to one another in North Carolina. High Point and other furniture centers agglomerated, or clustered together, to take advantage of not only the location and resources but also the services and infrastructure that grew to accommodate and aid furniture manufacturers in the region.

Finished furniture is a bulky commodity. Whenever furniture manufactures have considered locating outside of North Carolina and the Piedmont region or moving operations abroad, one of the key issues has been the **friction of distance**: the increase in time and cost that usually comes with increased distance over which commodities must travel. If a heavy raw material is shipped thousands of miles to a factory, the friction of distance increases. Friction of distance accounts for the raw materials that go into a product and prompts manufacturers to locate their plants close to raw materials if needed raw materials, such as coal and iron ore, are heavy.

A corollary to the concept of the friction of distance focuses on the location of customers instead of on the transport of raw materials. **Distance decay** (see Chapter 4) assumes the impact of a function or an activity will decline as one moves away from its point of origin. Distance decay suggests that manufacturing plants should be more concerned with serving the markets of nearby places than more distant places. This basic principle is important in understanding the locational dynamics of furniture manufacturing. Locating in North Carolina allows furniture manufacturers to reach nearby places, in the Northeast and Southeast, where the vast majority of their customers live, in less than a day.

## AGGLOMERATION

British economist Alfred Marshall (1842–1924), a leader in economic theory who is often credited with pioneering the field of industrial **location theory**, argued that a particular industry, whether automobile manufacturing or furniture production, clusters in an area. He called this process *localization*, and later theorists called it agglomeration. Marshall held that localized industries could attract workers with industry-specific skills, be able to share information, and attract support services specific to the industry.

Marshall explained *why* industries would cluster, and German economic geographer Alfred Weber (1868–1958) developed a basic model explaining *where* industries would cluster. Weber helped develop locational studies in economic geography by focusing on the location of manufacturing facilities. In *Theory of the Location of Industries* (1909), Weber focused on specific factors that pull industry to particular locations.

Weber's **least cost theory** focused on a factory owner's desire to minimize three categories of costs. The first and most important of these categories was *transportation*. Weber suggested that the site where transportation costs are lowest is the place where it is least expensive to bring raw materials to the point of production and to distribute finished products to consumers. The second cost was that of *labor*. Higher labor costs tend to reduce the margin of profit, so a factory farther away from raw materials and markets might do better if cheap labor compensates for the added transport costs.

The third factor in Weber's model was similar to Marshall's theory of localization. Weber described the advantages that came about when similar industries clustered together, which he termed **agglomeration**. When a substantial number of companies that produce the same or similar goods cluster in one area, as with furniture manufacturing in North Carolina, Weber held that the industries can assist each other through shared talents, services, and facilities. For example, all the furniture companies will need access to lumber, textiles, ports, and skilled employees. By clustering together in the High Point region of North Carolina, all the furniture manufacturers benefit because the government builds better infrastructure they can all share and business services, like accountants and lawyers who specialize in contracts and trade, will open offices to offer services the companies need. In 2012, local governments in the High Point region invested in a system of wireless Internet access so that the 75,000 furniture buyers who go to market to buy furniture in High Point twice a year can use the wireless systems on their iPads and tablets as they seal deals (Fig. 12.11). Agglomeration can make a location more attractive for a company, potentially overcoming higher transportation or labor costs.

Taking these three factors together, transportation, labor, and localization (agglomeration), Weber determined that the least cost location for a manufacturing plant could be determined by a *location triangle* (Fig. 12.12). Economic geographer Jean-Paul Rodrigue (2014) explains that "solving Weber's location model often implies three stages; finding the least transport cost location, and adjusting this location to consider labor costs and agglomeration economies." Weber reasoned that industry will be located close to raw materials in order to lower transportation costs, but that availability of labor (either particularly skilled or cheap) and agglomeration of industry will "pull" where to locate the industry in two other directions.

Weber's theory of location was written over a century ago and is built on the assumption that a manufacturer will choose where to locate in order to minimize the cost of transportation. The cost of transporting goods has changed a great deal since then with the diffusion of container ships after 1956. When Weber was writing, transportation costs accounted for upwards of 50 percent of the cost of a good; today, transportation costs account for less than 5 percent of

■■ **Figure 12.11**

**High Point, North Carolina.**   Twice a year 75,000 furniture buyers descend on the High Point Furniture Market in North Carolina. Purchasing goods to sell in furniture stores throughout the country and beyond, the buyers are attracted to 180 buildings and 11.5 million square feet of furniture show floor.

over the world, and then quickly shift where they manufacture their products in response to adjustments in production costs or consumer demand. These systems are designed to respond to consumers who want the newest/best/greatest offering or and also to enable manufacturers to lower cost of production by moving around the world.

Capitalism persists as an economic system not only because people consume but also because producers create and respond to consumer demand. Companies adapt to changing consumer preferences and commodify goods. Through the process of **commodification**, goods that were not previously bought, sold, and traded gain a monetary value and are bought, sold, and traded on the market. A new good, such as a mobile tablet, starts at a high price and becomes somewhat of a status symbol because of its high cost. The longer the mobile tablet is on the market and the greater the number of firms producing mobile tablets, the lower the price drops. Eventually, companies move the production of mobile tablets to lower the price of production and the price of

the cost of a good. This shift in transportation cost limits the value of Weber's theory today, except in the case of goods that rely on heavy raw materials (Rodrigue 2014).

## Flexible Production and Product Life Cycle

Fordist production was based on both mass production and mass consumption. Money flowed through the world-economy as consumers purchased goods manufactured in large-scale complexes. As the global economy became more integrated and transportation costs decreased, the advantages of concentrating production in large-scale complexes declined. As a result, in the latter third of the twentieth century many enterprises began moving toward a *post-Fordist*, flexible production model. The post-Fordist model refers to a set of production processes in which the components of goods are made in different places around the globe and then brought together as needed to assemble the final product in response to customer demand. The term **flexible production** is used to describe this state of affairs because firms can pick and choose among a multitude of suppliers and production strategies all

**WEBER'S LOCATION TRIANGLE**

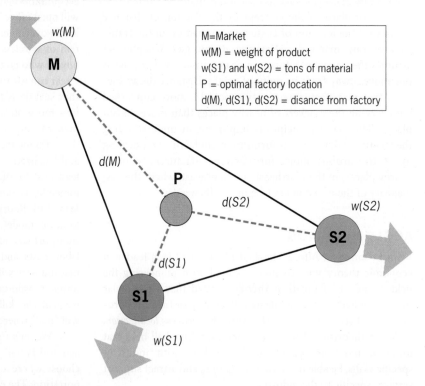

M=Market
w(M) = weight of product
w(S1) and w(S2) = tons of material
P = optimal factory location
d(M), d(S1), d(S2) = disance from factory

■■ **Figure 12.12**

**Weber's Location Triangle.**   Weber assumed that the cost of transporting goods was the same in all directions and increased at an equal rate in all directions. He also assumed that water was available everywhere but that labor was available only in certain population centers.

the good, in order to compete. Changes in the production of a good over time take place as part of a **product life cycle**.

The production of televisions over time and space is a good example of how a product life cycle moves through four states: introduction, growth, maturity, and decline. Commercial production of television sets began after World War II, with a variety of small and medium-sized firms in Europe, Asia, and North America involved in production in the *introduction stage*. Firms in the United States, including Zenith, were the dominant producers of televisions until the 1970s. The cost of producing and purchasing televisions is high in the introductory stage because the company has invested a great deal in developing the technology but has not sold enough units to lower the cost.

During the 1970s and 1980s, in the *growth stage*, a dramatic shift occurred, with a small number of large Asian producers—particularly in Japan—seizing a much larger percentage of the market and with a few European firms increasing their position as well. The growth of television sales and the generation of profits from sales during this stage encouraged companies to focus on economies of scale to produce and sell massive numbers of televisions. During the 1970s, major firms moved the manufacture of components and assembly of televisions out of their home countries. U.S. firms moved these functions to the *maquiladora* of Mexico (discussed in Chapter 10) and the special economic zones of China (described in Chapter 9); Japanese firms moved component manufacturing and assembly to Taiwan, Singapore, Malaysia, and South Korea. Because the assembly stage was the most labor intensive, television manufacturers tapped into the global labor market, locating assembly plants not just in Mexico, China, and Southeast Asia, but also in India and Brazil.

In the *maturity* stage, few manufacturers continue to make small changes to the product and invest in marketing to secure their market share. Manufacturing of televisions became more mechanized, and with more technology and lower wage costs, companies moved production closer to consumers. By 1990, ten large firms were responsible for 80 percent of the world's color television sets; eight of them were Japanese and two European. Only one firm in the United States, Zenith, remained, and its share of the global market was relatively small.

In the *decline* stage, fewer consumers are demanding the product, and manufacturers shift to research and development of new goods or production of other, higher-demand goods. In the twenty-first century, electronics companies, including Samsung and Panasonic, invested in research and development of high-definition and plasma televisions, leading to production of these high-end televisions in Japan—and more recently into China and South Korea. These investments began a new product development cycle for high-definition electronics.

## The Global Division of Labor

Tracing the production of televisions throughout the world over time helps us see how the **global division of labor** (also called the new international division of labor) currently works. Production of mass numbers of well-established goods is concentrated in the global economic periphery and semiperiphery to take advantage of lower labor costs, whereas research and development for new products is primarily located in the core. Fewer factors are fixed in flexible production, and as methods of assembly and products themselves change, production may be moved to take advantage of infrastructure, skilled labor, and accessible markets.

Geographically, the concept of **time–space compression** is the easiest way to capture the dramatic temporal and spatial changes taking place in the contemporary global economy. Time–space compression is based on the idea that developments in communication and transportation technologies have accelerated the speed with which things happen and have made the distance between places less significant (see Chapter 4). David Harvey, who coined the term *time–space compression*, argues that modern capitalism has so accelerated the pace of life and so changed the nature of the relationship between places that "the world seems to collapse inwards upon us." Fluctuations in the Tokyo stock market affect New York just hours later. Overnight, marketing campaigns can turn a product innovation into a fad in far-flung corners of the globe. Kiwis picked in New Zealand yesterday can be in the lunch boxes of boys and girls in Canada tomorrow. And decisions made in London can make or break a fast-developing deal over a transport link between Kenya and Tanzania.

Time–space compression shapes the global division of labor. When the world was less interconnected, most goods were produced not just close to raw materials, but close to the point of consumption. Thus, the major industrial belt in the United States was in the Northeast both because of readily available coal and other raw materials and because the major concentration of the North American population was there. With **just-in-time delivery** this has changed. Rather than keeping a large inventory of components or products, companies keep just what they need for short-term production and new parts are shipped quickly when needed. In turn, corporations can draw from labor around the globe for different components of production.

Advances in information technologies and shipping coupled with the global division of labor enable companies to move production from one site to another based on calculations of the "new place-based cost advantages" in a decision process geographer David Harvey has called a **spatial fix** (Walcott 2011, 7). In choosing a production site, location is only one consideration. "Distance is neither determinate nor insignificant as a factor in production location decisions" today (Walcott 2011, 9).

Major global economic players, including General Motors, Philips, Union Carbide, and Exxon, take advantage of low transportation costs, favorable governmental regulations, and expanding information technology to construct vast economic networks in which different facets of production are carried out in different places in order to benefit from the advantages of specific locations. Publicly traded companies, whose stock you can buy or sell on the stock exchange, are pressured by shareholders to grow their profits annually. One way to grow profits is to cut costs, and labor (wages, benefits, insurance) makes up a sizable proportion of production costs. Most multinational corporations have moved labor-intensive manufacturing, particularly assembly activities, to peripheral countries where labor is cheap, regulations are few, and tax rates are low. The manufacturing that remains in the core is usually highly mechanized. Technologically sophisticated manufacturing also tends to be sited in the core or semiperiphery because the expertise, infrastructure, and research and development are there.

## Flexible Production of Nike

We can use Weber's location theory to consider the site for a factory producing lightweight consumer goods, including textiles and shoes, during the first half of the twentieth century. In the triangle of factors, the most important for lightweight consumer goods is a ready supply of low-cost *labor*. Being close to the *raw materials* is less of a concern, as shipping low-weight components is relatively inexpensive. *Agglomeration* is drawn for production of lightweight consumer goods so that component producers locate nearby and serve more than one company.

Companies that specialized in manufacturing components would locate close to the manufacturer of the final product. For example, companies that made shoe laces would locate close to shoe manufacturers. In the 1920s in the United States, towns near Boston, Massachusetts—great "shoe towns" including Haverhill, Brockton, and Lynn—were home to shoe factories specializing in both men's and women's shoes. About 300 shoe factories had sales offices "within a few blocks of each other in Boston" (Smith 1925), and in a leather district close to the city, tanneries prepared hides imported from around the world.

Economic geographer J. Russel Smith (1925) described the economic landscape of the shoe factory town of Lynn:

> *Walking the streets of Lynn one realizes what concentration an industry can have; the signs upon the places of business read—heels, welts, insoles, uppers, eyelets, thread, etc., etc. It is an astonishing proof of the degree to which even a simple commodity like a shoe, so long made by one man, can be subdivided and become the work of scores of industries and thousands of people.*

Shoe salespeople periodically flocked to shoe company headquarters in Boston to learn about the company's newest offerings and filled their sample suitcases with shoes to show their clients as they made the rounds of their sales territories.

With flexible production systems and container ships, lightweight consumer goods still need to be located close to low-cost labor, but another important consideration is connectedness to an intermodal port where components can be imported by ship, rail, or truck. The production of shoes is no longer concentrated in a handful of shoe towns on the East Coast. One of the most famous brands of shoes, Nike, demonstrates how selecting manufacturing sites for components and products has changed with the advent of just-in-time production and globalization. The transformation from producing shoes in a few shoe towns to producing shoes through an elaborate global network of international manufacturing and sales did not happen overnight.

University of Oregon track coach Bill Bowerman and one of his former runners, Phil Knight, founded Nike in 1961. Knight designed a trademark waffle sole that would create more traction for runners. Nike sold $8000 in footwear in its first year. The company established headquarters in Beaverton, Oregon, a suburb of Portland. Nike began production in the 1960s by contracting with an Asian firm to manufacture its shoes. In 1974, Nike set up its first domestic shoe manufacturing facility in the small town of Exeter, New Hampshire, just 46 miles from Lynn, Massachusetts. By the end of that year, Nike's workforce was still modest in number. Nike employees in Oregon concentrated on running the company and expanding sales, while employees who worked directly for Nike in New Hampshire and Asia produced shoes.

Nike has grown to be a giant in the shoe and apparel business, with sales of over $27.8 billion in fiscal year 2014. Although several thousand people work for Nike in Beaverton, not a single individual in Oregon is directly involved in the process of putting a shoe together. Worldwide, some 40,000 people work directly for Nike today, and according to Nike, nearly one million workers are employed by Nike's 719 contract factories in 44 countries (Fig. 12.13).

Nike grew to become the world's leading manufacturer of athletic shoes, with an 18.6 percent share of the world's athletic shoe market and up to 60 percent of the U.S. market. Its employment numbers skyrocketed, and many new manufacturing plants were established in Asia and beyond. Today no manufacturing takes place at or near the headquarters in Beaverton. Employees at Nike headquarters are designers, planners, financial administrators, marketing and sales specialists, information technology directors, computer technicians, lawyers, and support personnel. The local social and economic geography of Beaverton bears little resemblance to what one might have expected in a town housing an important shoe company. Each **node**, or connection point in a network, of the Nike network is functionally specialized, dependent on other nodes, and influenced by the niche it occupies in the network.

## Distribution in the Commodity Chain

The largest producer of furniture in the world is not located in High Point, North Carolina, but in Sweden. Ikea, a global company with sales of $37.38 billion in 2013, is the world's largest producer, distributor, and seller of furniture. Ingvar Kamprad founded the company in 1943 at the age of 17. Kamprad, a born entrepreneur, first sold matches from door to door in his neighborhood in Sweden. He expanded his

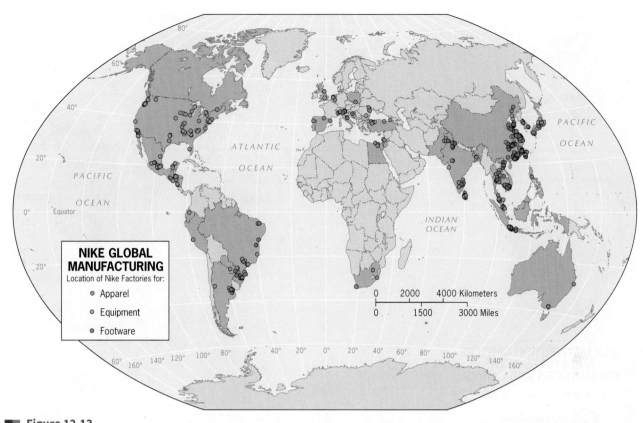

**Figure 12.13**

**Nike Production Facilities and Contract Factories.** Nike uses flexible production to manufacture shoes and apparel in 719 contract factories around the world. Nike plans short- and long-range contracts with factories, constantly assessing the best possible places to manufacture shoes, apparel, and equipment.

offerings to pens, Christmas decorations, and greeting cards during his teenage years. Pens were one of the main offerings in Ikea when he founded the company in 1943. According to the history told by Ikea, Kamprad first produced and sold furniture in 1948, using wood from Sweden's expansive forests. The company expanded in product offerings and locations since, focusing on producing modern and classic furniture at an affordable price point.

With approximately 300 stores in 26 countries, Ikea created and controls its own commodity chain. Ikea designs the furniture, sources the materials, and produces its famous products, including its best-selling product, the Billy bookcase. The company has over 1200 suppliers located in 55 countries (Krewson 2010). The company's volume of production and sales is so high that it has to consider carefully where to locate distribution centers to serve its stores. In the United States, Ikea has five distribution centers: Port Wentworth, Georgia (near Savannah), Perryville, Maryland (near Baltimore), Tejon, California (near Los Angeles), Westhampton, New Jersey (near Philadelphia, Pennsylvania), and Brossard, Quebec (near Montreal, Canada) (Fig. 12.14). Ikea has plans to build distribution centers in Joliet, Illinois (near Chicago), and Tacoma, Washington (near Seattle).

Ikea chooses the sites for its distribution centers with an eye on where stores are and where store expansion will occur.

The Savannah distribution center is one of its newest, and locating in Georgia allowed Ikea to reduce transportation time and cost from distribution (formerly from Perryville, Maryland) to its stores in Orlando, Tampa, and Atlanta. The new distribution center also enabled Ikea to open more locations in Florida and allows for further expansion in the Southeast. The Savannah distribution center is a model of efficiency. Thirteen computerized robotic cranes move Ikea products into the distribution center and then pull goods out for distribution to stores. The goal is for a crane not to return empty handed. So the same crane that is loading goods into the distribution center from a ship is also finding and loading goods onto truck and rail for transport to stores.

Controlling a large proportion of the commodity chain allows Ikea to operate at incredibly high volume with low prices, generating small profits for the company along each step in the commodity chain. Ikea invests in distribution logistics in order to keep transportation costs as low as possible. According to Ikea, the company is reorganizing its distribution center structure so that low-flow products (products that do not turn over in stores quickly) will be stored in a central distribution center and high-flow products will be stored closer to stores so they can quickly replenish supply.

Ikea is leading innovations in distribution of goods and is also a leader in Green technologies. The company is

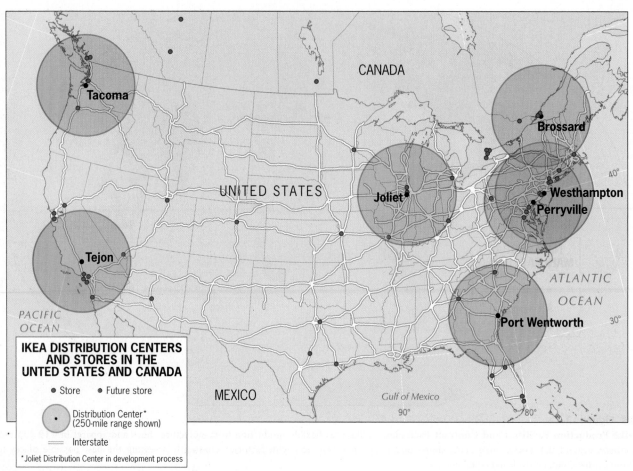

**Figure 12.14**
Ikea Distribution Center and Store Map.

generating its own electricity through solar and wind energy both as a Green initiative and also to manage costs of heating and cooling its buildings. As of 2014, Ikea was producing about half the energy it uses. Ikea is also working with the United Nations High Commissioner on Refugees (UNHCR) to create a new housing system for the world's refugees. The tents the UNHCR currently distributes are designed to last 6 months, and they do little besides providing shelter. Ikea's new house designed for refugees comes in flat boxes and can be assembled in a day. They are made of plastic that keeps the interior cool during the day and allows privacy so people outside the tent cannot see shadows from the tent at night. They include a solar panel that generates enough energy to power one light and a USB charging port. And, they last for about 3 years. The Ikea refugee houses are now being used in Syria and Ethiopia, with hopes of much broader distribution and a better quality of life for the world's refugees (see Chapter 3).

## Outsourcing: Business Product Outsourcing and Global Sourcing

Where to produce or assemble a good is only one small aspect of decisions made in a **commodity chain** (see Chapter 10)

for any good produced in an economy based on flexible production. A large part of business decision making today focuses on outsourcing and global sourcing, on where to extend contracts to complete projects and where to have component parts produced and assembled.

Economic geographers originally used the term *outsourcing* to describe a company moving production or services abroad. In the first model of outsourcing, a global corporation moved a certain division of its production, whether assembling the final product or supplying telephone support for software, to another country. In the 1990s and into the twenty-first century, outsourcing implied taking work that would normally be done in America and moving it abroad. The media focused on the outsourcing of manufacturing jobs to China and the outsourcing of call centers to India.

Using this basic concept of outsourcing is misleading in the world-economy. The global division of labor and growing connectivity, accompanied by fundamental shifts by Chinese and Indian companies, have deepened globalization and created a new world-economy. **Outsourcing** is now an umbrella term for globalized production in which a defined segment of the commodity chain is contracted abroad, either through business process outsourcing (BPO) or through global sourcing.

In the world-economy, the new model of outsourcing has developed out of the growth of Indian companies, including Tata, Infosys, and Wipro, who specialize in completing projects and fulfilling contracts by becoming experts in outsourcing themselves. Imagine that a global company, headquartered in the United States, produces and sells accounting software. A major regulation changes in the United States, and the company now needs someone to reprogram the software to account for the complexities of the new regulation. The company can hire an Indian company that specializes in BPO. The two companies contract the work to reprogram the software. The ball is then in the Indian company's court. It has to produce a finished product by the date on the contract in order to get paid, and it can do so however it sees fit. In many cases, the Indian company outsources the work itself, keeping tabs on and testing the product before delivering it to the company in the United States. BPO includes completing projects, as in this example, and it includes turning certain business functions, such as call centers, human resources, accounting, or software engineering, over to the Indian BPO in a longer-term contract.

Maximizing profits when producing goods is no longer as simple as moving around to take advantage of lower labor costs. China has capitalized on the desire of companies to produce goods globally by becoming the world leader in **global sourcing**. Say you are daydreaming and you think of a great new product, like sunglasses with windshield wipers on them. You no longer need to figure out where to make your product. You can mock up a prototype and take it to a global sourcing fair in Las Vegas, Mexico City, Johannesburg, or São Paulo and meet with dozens of Chinese global sourcing firms (Fig. 12.15). They will give you a bid on what it will cost to produce your awesome new product, and they will tell you when it can be done. You sign a contract, and you receive shipment of your product without ever having set foot in China. The Chinese global sourcing firm is connected to manufacturers throughout Asia, Africa, and the Americas, Your windshield wiper sunglasses may be stickered "Made in Mexico" when you receive them. If your product flies off the shelf and you order another shipment, your Chinese global sourcing company may ship the next order with stickers saying "Made in China." The global sourcing firm is connected and nimble so you do not have to be. The global sourcing firm controls a larger part of the commodity chain and can generate more wealth for itself by making the lowest cost production decisions.

Business process outsourcing and global sourcing both fall under the umbrella of outsourcing. Both take a segment of the commodity chain and move it to another country with full responsibility for that segment of the commodity chain in the contracted company's hands. BPO is typically for services, whether tertiary, quaternary, or quinary (Chapter 10). Global sourcing is typically for the secondary, or manufacturing, sector of the economy. However, global sourcing includes quite a bit of service work because the Chinese sourcing company develops the relations with the manufacturers, uses its knowledge of trade regulations, and manages a large sector of the product's commodity chain.

Supporting the global division of labor and global sourcing are elaborate trading networks and intricate financial relations. Trade itself is a tertiary economic activity of considerable importance to the global economy. Regardless of where goods are produced, consumption is still concentrated in the core and, increasingly, among the wealthy and middle classes of the semiperiphery.

**■ Figure 12.15**

**New York.** Business people visit booths to find producers at China Textile and Apparel Sourcing Expo.

## Made in America or Designed in America?

In 2011, ABC World News featured a segment called "Made in America," where journalists knocked on doors and challenged homeowners to look at every item in their home for the "made in" sticker. The news crew then helped families move all goods not "Made in America" onto the street so the family could visualize how much of what is in their home is made in the United States and how much is made elsewhere in the world. The ABC World News crew then, according to their website, "took on the challenge of trying to fill three rooms in a home entirely with 100 percent American-made products."

Would an iPod get to stay in the house redesigned by ABC World News? When you open a new iPod or other Apple product, a sticker greets you that says "Designed in California." The iPod would not pass the ABC "made in" test, but we should ask whether it is better for the American economy for a good to be made in or designed in America. Three authors asked this exact question in the journal *Communications of the*

## BREAKDOWN OF THE COST OF A $299 IPOD

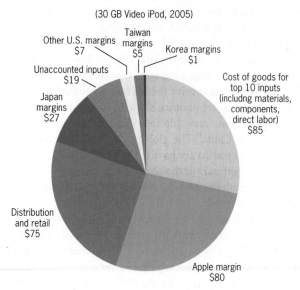

**Figure 12.16**

**Breakdown of the Cost of a $299 iPod.** *Courtesy of*: Greg Linden, Kenneth L. Kraemer, and Jason Dedrick. Who captures value in a global innovation network? The case of Apple's iPod. *Communications of the ACM*, 52, 3, March 2009.

*ACM* in 2009. Linden et al. asked who captures the value in a $299 iPod touch.

Using published sources on computer machinery and component parts, the authors figured out the iPod supply chain and calculated the value added at each step in the commodity chain (Fig. 12.16). The components of an iPod are produced by companies in Japan, Korea, Taiwan, and China. The most expensive component in the iPod is the hard drive, which is produced and designed by Toshiba, a Japanese company. One component that sets the iPod apart from other MP3 players is the microchip that controls access to songs and movies on the iPod. The microchip is housed in a wheel on the iPod classic and is produced by PortalPlayer, a California company with offices in India.

In his piece on PortalPlayer called "The World in an iPod," journalist Andrew Leonard explained that PortalPlayer has a 24-hour development cycle because engineers in California and in India can work around the clock (with time zones 12 hours apart) to design and redesign the microchip. The actual microchips are created in Taiwan. The commodity chain for PortalPlayer (Fig. 12.17) reveals how people and places around the world interconnect to design and create the company's microchip.

Linden et al. estimate that the PortalPlayer component is a small fraction of the cost of an iPod but that the research and

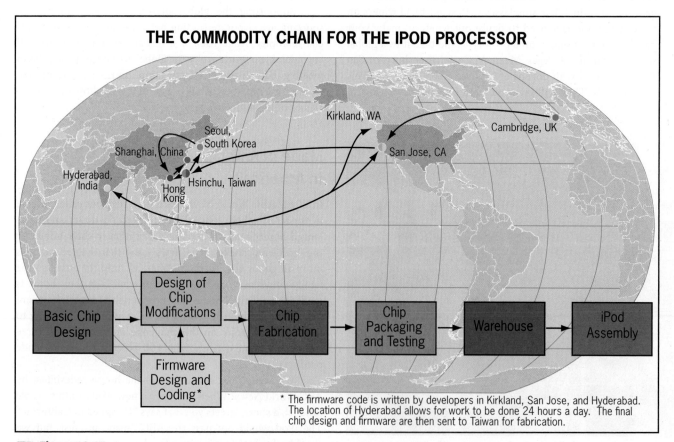

**Figure 12.17**

**Inside an iPod: The PortalPlayer World.** *Map designed by Stephen P. Hanna, based on information from*: Andrew Leonard, "The World in the iPod," *Spiegel Online*, August 8, 2005.

development that go into PortalPlayer and other innovative components that differentiate the iPod from its competitors derive more value from the sale of one iPod than does Invotec, the company that actually assembles the iPod. Linden et al. concluded that "while the iPod is manufactured offshore and has a global roster of suppliers, the greatest benefits from this innovation go to Apple, an American company, with predominantly American employees and stockholders who reap the benefits" (2009, 143) and that the second greatest benefit goes to the two Japanese companies that produce components that help differentiate the iPod, the hard drive, and the display screen.

The act of consumption is an end point of a commodity chain. It is also the beginning of the product's afterlife. What happens when you discard or donate the item? What are the costs or benefits created by the funds (whether funds for a charity or profits for a corporation) generated by your purchase? Corporations such as Apple, which sells the iPod, work to reduce consumer waste by recycling iPods and computers, and by offering discounts to consumers who recycle their old iPods. Nonetheless, in many global cities in poorer parts of the world, adults and children work in garbage dumps to recover valuable copper wire and other components of computers and related electronic devices made by Apple and its competitors.

Tracing the commodity chain of the iPod demonstrates that rarely does the consumption of a particular product have an unambiguous positive or negative consequence. In addition to the fact that components are made all over the world and assembly is only one small part of the commodity chain, we should consider the environmental consequences of steps in commodity chains. Jobs created by industry in one place can cause environmental damage in another. Consumption, or purchasing an item, is the end point in a commodity chain that affects places in a variety of different ways. The importance of studying the geography of commodity chains is that such an undertaking sheds light on the origins of products and helps explain why production occurs where and how it does and how production affects places and peoples at each step in the chain.

## Major Influences on the Contemporary Geography of Manufacturing

As the iPod example illustrates, multinational corporations frequently subcontract many of the steps in the production and retailing process to outside companies or subsidiaries, through BPO and global sourcing contracts, including the extraction of raw materials, engineering, manufacturing, marketing, distribution, and customer support. Weber's location theory no longer works for most products, except those that rely on heavy raw materials. With networks of global cities, container ships crossing the oceans in regular patterns, and flexible production, choosing an industrial location depends on labor costs, transportation (as Weber suggested), and also on regulatory constraints, expertise, and access to energy.

### TRANSPORTATION

Relatively inexpensive transportation is one of the foundations on which the flexible production system rests. In the early 1900s, the cost of transportation accounted for half or more of the final price of many goods traveling over significant distances. Transportation now accounts for 5 percent or less of the cost of most goods. In an era of vastly improved infrastructure, relatively cheap oil, and container ships, spatially disaggregated production systems are cost effective.

Efficient transportation systems enable manufacturers to purchase raw materials from distant sources and distribute finished products to widely dispersed consumers. Cost is not the only issue. Manufacturers also consider the availability of alternative systems in the event of emergencies (e.g., truck routes when rail service is interrupted). Since World War II, major developments in transportation have focused on improving **intermodal connections**, places where two or more modes of transportation meet (including air, road, rail, barge, and ship), in order to ease the flow of goods and reduce the costs of transportation.

The current volume of resources and goods shipped around the globe daily could not be supported without the invention of the container system, whereby goods are packed in containers that are picked up by special, mechanized cranes from a container ship at an intermodal connection and placed on the back of a semitrailer truck, on a barge, or on a railroad car. This innovation lowered costs and increased flexibility, permitting many manufacturers to pay less attention to transportation in their location decisions. Refrigerated containers also ease the shipment of perishable goods around the globe.

Jacques Charlier has studied the major changes to the Benelux (Belgium, the Netherlands, and Luxembourg) seaport system and the role containerization played in these changes. Charlier stressed the importance of containerization to the growth of sea trade in the Benelux ports and explained the locational advantage of Rotterdam, which is no more than six hours by rail or truck from 85 percent of the population of western Europe.

The container system and the growth in shipping at Rotterdam and other Benelux ports have combined to foster the development of other industries in the region, helping to make the Netherlands, in Charlier's words, a warehouse for Europe. The Netherlands is now home to more than 1800 U.S. firms, including call centers, distribution centers, and production centers, especially for food. Over 50 percent of all goods entering the European Union pass through Rotterdam or Amsterdam (also in the Netherlands).

### REGULATORY CIRCUMSTANCES

Regional trade organizations including the Association of Southeast Asian Nations (ASEAN), the North American Free Trade Agreement (NAFTA), and the European Union (EU) have trade agreements that influence where imported goods (and components of goods) are produced. Similarly, governments have individual agreements with each other about production and imports, and most governments (160 as of 2014) are part of the World Trade Organization (WTO), which works to negotiate rules of trade among the member states.

The WTO promotes freer trade by negotiating agreements among member states, typically dismissing import quota systems and discouraging protection by a country of its domestically produced goods. Agreements negotiated under the WTO are typically enacted in steps in order to avoid a major shock to a state's economy. In 2001 when Europe and the United States agreed to allow China to become a member of the WTO, they also agreed to remove the quota system that restricts the importation of Chinese goods into Europe and the United States. Soon after these quotas were eliminated, both the United States and the European Union issued "safeguard quotas" against certain Chinese imports. These quotas buffered the impact of Chinese goods on domestic producers. But most of the quotas have now expired, paving the way for mass importation of Chinese goods in the United States and Europe.

In addition to the growth of the purview of the WTO, the proliferation of regional trade associations in the last two decades is unprecedented. The list of acronyms for regional trade associations is almost overwhelming: EU, NAFTA, MERCOSUR, SAFTA, CARICOM, ANDEAN AFTA, COMESA, to name but a few (see Chapter 8). The World Trade Organization estimates that more than 360 regional trade agreements are in existence. Regional trade agreements are similar to bilateral agreements on trade between two countries, although they involve more than two countries. Most regional trade agreements encourage movement of production within the trade region and promote trade by diminishing (or deleting) trade quotas and tariffs among member countries. A regional trade agreement sets up a special free trade agreement among parties to the association, leaving nonmember countries to trade through the rules of the WTO or an existing bilateral agreement. Whether regional or global, trade agreements directly affect the location of production and even what is produced in a place.

Regulations at the state and local scales also matter. Not infrequently, the location of industrial operations is influenced by a range of state and local regulations that influence the cost of production. These range from tax regulations to environmental and safety standards. In many cases, governments actively seek to recruit industry through incentives that include tax breaks, subsidies, and exemptions from particular bureaucratic requirements. Export processing zones such as the *maquiladoras*, discussed in Chapter 10, provide a case in point. There are now many hundreds of such zones around the world, and they are shaping the global geography of industry.

## ENERGY

The role of energy supply as a factor in industrial location decisions has changed over time. Earlier in the chapter, we explained that at the start of the Industrial Revolution manufacturing plants were often established on or near coal fields. During the mid-twentieth century, the use of coal as an energy source in industry increasingly gave way to oil and gas. Today major industrial complexes are not confined to areas near oil fields. Instead, a huge system of pipelines and tankers delivers oil and natural gas to manufacturing regions throughout the world. For some time during and after the global oil supply crises of the 1970s, fears of future spikes in oil costs led some industries that require large amounts of electricity to move to sites where energy costs were low. When the crisis waned, national energy-conservation goals were modified. Energy supply has become a less significant factor in industrial location, but securing an energy supply is an increasingly important national priority.

U.S. consumption of petroleum and natural gas today is about 20 percent of the annual world total. By 2007, the United States required more than 20.6 million barrels of petroleum per day to keep its power plants, machinery, vehicles, aircraft, and ships functioning. However, U.S. production of oil in recent years has averaged about 10 percent of the world total, and even including the known Alaskan potential and the oil and natural gas in shale, U.S. oil reserves are estimated to amount to only about 4 percent of the world total. More so than many countries, the United States taps the oil that it has. In 2009 the country was the third largest oil producer in the world (Fig. 12.18). Even with this level of production, the United States remains heavily dependent on foreign oil supplies, with all the uncertainties that involves. There is, consequently, a push for the United States to begin large-scale fracking of oil and natural gas shale and to expand offshore drilling in the hope of expanding its production of oil. Opposition to the environmental and social consequences of fracking is growing, but the wealth being generated for corporations and state governments is hard to resist. Opposition to offshore drilling is also based on environmental grounds that were heightened by the major BP oil spill that occurred in the Gulf of Mexico in 2010—an example of what can happen when offshore oil resources are exploited without careful safeguards.

The United States leads world demand and consumption not just in oil, but in natural gas as well. As Figure 12.18 shows, natural gas often occurs in association with oil deposits. The use of natural gas has increased enormously since World War II. One result of the increased use of natural gas is the proliferation of pipelines shown on the map. In the United States in 2013, there were 2.4 million miles (over 4 million km) of pipelines, with 2.1 million miles of the pipelines providing local distribution of natural gas. Countries with large reserves of oil and natural gas—Saudi Arabia, Kuwait, Iraq, Russia, and others—occupy a special position in the global economic picture. None of these countries except Russia is a major industrial power, but they all played a key role in the industrial boom of the twentieth century. And while oil has brought wealth to some in Southwest Asia, it has also ensured that outside powers such as the United States and Great

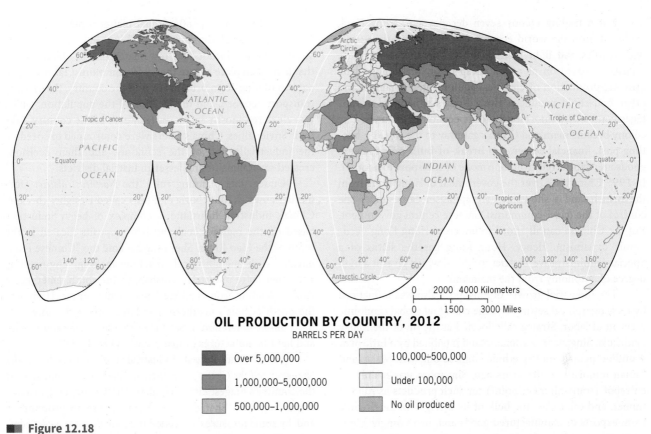

**OIL PRODUCTION BY COUNTRY, 2012**
BARRELS PER DAY

- Over 5,000,000
- 1,000,000–5,000,000
- 500,000–1,000,000
- 100,000–500,000
- Under 100,000
- No oil produced

■ **Figure 12.18**
**Oil Production by Country, 2012.**    Saudi Arabia, the United States, and Russia each produce more than 10 million barrels of oil per day.
*Data from*: United States Central Intelligence Agency, World Factbook, 2014.

Britain are involved and invested in what happens in the region. This set of circumstances has produced an uneasy relationship (at best) between countries in the oil-producing region and the major industrial powers of the "West."

## New Centers of Industrial Activity

As a result of advances in flexible production, over the last 30 years many older manufacturing regions have experienced **deindustrialization**, a process by which companies move industrial jobs to other regions, leaving the newly deindustrialized region to work through a period of high unemployment and, if possible, switch to a service economy (see the last major section of this chapter). At the same time, the places with lower labor costs and the right mix of laws attractive to businesses (often weak environmental laws and pro-free-trade laws) have become newly industrial regions. The new industrial regions are emerging as shifts in politics, laws, capital flow, and labor availability occur.

East Asia has become a particularly important new region of industrialization. From Taiwan to Guangdong and from South Korea to Singapore, the islands, countries, provinces, and cities fronting the Pacific Ocean have gotten caught up in a frenzy of industrialization that has made the geographic term *Pacific Rim* synonymous with manufacturing.

## THE RISE OF EAST ASIA

Throughout the better part of the twentieth century, Japan was the only global economic power in East Asia, and its regional dominance seemed beyond doubt. Other nodes of manufacturing existed, but these were no threat, and certainly no match, for Japan's industrial might. The picture began to change with the rise of the so-called Four Tigers of East and Southeast Asia: South Korea, Taiwan, Hong Kong, and Singapore in the 1960s and 1970s. Benefiting from the shift of labor-intensive industries to areas with lower labor costs, government efforts to protect developing industry, and government investment in education and training, the tigers emerged as **newly industrializing countries (NICs)**.

South Korea developed significant manufacturing districts exporting products ranging from automobiles and grand pianos to calculators and computers. One of these districts is centered on the capital, Seoul (with 10 million inhabitants in the city proper and some 25 million in the metropolitan area), and the two others lie at the southern end of the peninsula, anchored by Pusan and Kwangju, respectively. Taiwan's economic planners promoted high-technology industries, including personal computers, telecommunications equipment, precision electronic instruments, and other high-tech products. More recently, the South Koreans have moved in a similar direction.

Just a trading colony seven decades ago, Hong Kong exploded onto the world economic scene during the 1950s with textiles and light manufactures. The success of these industries, based on plentiful, cheap labor, was followed by growing production of electrical equipment, appliances, and other household products. Hong Kong's situational advantages contributed enormously to its economic fortunes. The colony became mainland China's gateway to the world, a bustling port, financial center, and **break-of-bulk point**, where goods are transferred from one mode of transport to another. In 1997 China took over the government of Hong Kong from the British, and a showplace of capitalism came under the control of the quasi-communist Chinese central government. But the Chinese can ill afford to undercut Hong Kong's economic dynamism. Hence, Hong Kong has the status of a Special Administrative District in China, which gives it a high degree of autonomy from the mainland.

The industrial growth of Singapore also was influenced by its geographical setting and the changing global economic division of labor. Strategically located at the tip of the Malay Peninsula, Singapore is a small island inhabited by a little over 4 million people, mostly ethnic Chinese but with Malay and Indian minorities. Fifty years ago, Singapore was mainly an entrepôt (transshipment point) for such products as rubber, timber, and oil; today, the bulk of its foreign revenues come from exports of manufactured goods and, increasingly, high-technology products. Singapore is also a center for quaternary industries, selling services and expertise to a global market.

Rapid economic growth entails risks, and in 1997 risky lending practices and government investment decisions caused Thailand's currency to collapse, followed by its stock market; banks closed and bankruptcies abounded. Soon Malaysia and Indonesia were affected, and by early 1998 one of the Four Tigers, South Korea, required a massive infusion of dollars (provided by the International Monetary Fund, a Washington-based bank) to prevent economic chaos. But the reforms that allowed the region to overcome these economic troubles served to strengthen East and Southeast Asia's economies, and the Four Tigers continue to exert a powerful regional—and international—economic role.

## THE CHINESE JUGGERNAUT

Although some industrial growth occurred in China during the period of European colonial influence, and later during the Japanese occupation, China's major industrial expansion occurred during the Communist period. When communist planners took over in 1949, one of their leading priorities was to develop China's resources and industries as rapidly as possible.

China is a vast country and has a substantial resource base. The quality of its coal is good, the quantity enormous, and many of the deposits are near the surface and easily extracted. China's iron ores are not as productive and are generally of rather low grade, but new finds are regularly being made.

Until the early 1960s, Soviet planners helped promote China's industrial development. China was spatially constrained by the location of raw materials, the development that had taken place before the 1949 communist takeover, the pattern of long-term urbanization in the country, the existing transport network, and the location of the population, which was clustered mostly in the eastern part of the country. Like their Soviet allies, China's rulers were determined to speed up the industrialization of the economy, and their decisions created several major and lesser industrial districts.

Under state planning rules, the *Northeast district* (formerly known as Manchuria and now called Dongbei) became China's industrial heartland, a complex of heavy industries based on the region's coal and iron deposits located in the basin of the Liao River. Shenyang became the "Chinese Pittsburgh," with metallurgical, machine-making, engineering, and other large industries. Anshan, to the south, emerged as China's leading iron- and steel-producing center. Harbin to the north (China's northernmost large city, with more than 5.4 million inhabitants) produced textiles, farm equipment, and light manufactures of many kinds (Fig. 12.19).

The second largest industrial region in China, the *Shanghai and the Chang Jiang district*, developed in and around the country's biggest city, Shanghai. The Chang Jiang district, containing both Shanghai and Wuhan, rose to prominence and, by some measures, exceeded the Northeast as a contributor to the national economy. Another industrial complex that developed farther upstream, along the Chang Jiang River, focused on the city of Chongqing. The Chang Jiang district has become a pacesetter for Chinese industrial growth—if not in terms of iron and steel production, then at least in terms of its diversified production and local specializations. Railroad cars, ships, books, foods, chemicals—an endless variety of products—come from the Chang Jiang district.

In Chinese cities including Dalian, Shanghai, Zhuhai, Xiamen, and Shenzhen, pollution-belching smokestacks rise above the urban landscape. Streets are jammed with traffic ranging from animal-drawn carts and overloaded bicycles to trucks and buses. Bulldozers are sweeping away the vestiges of the old China; cottages with porches and tile roofs on the outskirts of the expanding city must make way for often faceless tenements (Fig. 12.20). Decaying remnants of the old city stand amid the glass-encased towers that symbolize the new economic order. Modern skyscrapers now dominate the skyline of the cities at the top of the Chinese urban-economic and administrative hierarchy—including Beijing, Shanghai, and cities in SEZs. China's major cities now play host to gleaming new airports, daring architecture, spectacular public projects, and the terminuses of efficient high-speed railroads.

At the same time, the Northeast has become China's "Rust Belt." Many of its state-run factories have been sold or closed, or are operating below capacity. Unemployment is high, and economic growth has stalled. Eventually, the Northeast is likely to recover because of its resources and its favorable geographic site, but under the state's new economic policies, the dynamic eastern and southern provinces have

# FIELD NOTE

"Humen is one of the Pearl River Delta cities that has been transformed by the rise of China. The small textile factory I visited provided insights into the opportunities and challenges that are confronting China today. The 40 or so employees were mostly young, but there were a few older folks. They were making women's clothes for the French market. Most of them made the clothes from start to finish, although there were a few unskilled laborers who were ironing the fabric, cutting off loose ends of thread, and so on. Into each of the items of clothing was sewn a label with a fancy-sounding Italian name. The clothes are sold in Humen for the equivalent of $1.50–$2.50 each, but most of them were destined for France, where they would be sold for 20 times that amount. The employees work under a contract that stipulates a 9-hour day and a base wage of about $275/month plus basic room and board. They can work more hours, however, and are compensated based on how much they produce during the extra hours. Apparently, almost all employees choose to work extra hours—typically seven days a week, with breaks only on Sunday evenings and one day at the beginning of each month. If they work that hard, they can earn the equivalent of close to $500/month. The main workroom had decent lighting and ventilation (it was hot, of course). The manager told me there had been significant upward pressure on the wages of employees in the last few years, making it harder for him to earn much of a profit. He worried about factories relocating to lower-wage countries. In addition, he said that he was having an increasingly difficult time recruiting employees. He also noted with some mixture of amusement and annoyance that the people who had made out the best in his part of the city were the former farmers, who either had received substantial compensation (in the form of apartments) for being displaced or who were getting some share of rent for buildings constructed on the land they used to farm."

© Alexander B. Murphy

■ **Figure 12.19**
**Humen, China.**

grown into major manufacturing belts and have changed the map of this part of the Pacific Rim.

Today, the Chinese government is pushing industrialization into the country's interior, with new investment flowing into poorer parts of the central and western portions of the country. China is also looking to take advantage of its proximity to South and Southeast Asia through efforts to deepen transnational economic cooperation. From a global perspective, what is particularly striking is the magnitude and influence of the Chinese economic juggernaut. On August 15, 2010, China officially surpassed Japan as the world's second largest economy. China has become the world's largest exporter, and its energy and raw materials demands are now affecting the global supply of key resources. Today more passenger vehicles are purchased in China each year than in the United States, and China invests more domestically than any other country in the world.

None of the foregoing means that China will inevitably become the dominant power of the twenty-first century. China's economy still depends heavily on exports and foreign investment, and China's GDP per capita, while on the rise, is 10 times smaller than Japan's and 12.5 times smaller than that of the United States. Moreover, there are potentially destabilizing social and environmental costs to China's rapid rise, and with labor costs growing in China relative to Southeast Asia, China could be vulnerable to some of the very forces that gave it an advantage over other places not long ago.

## THE WIDER WORLD

Other newly industrializing countries have become increasingly significant global nodes of production. Over the past decade manufacturing has surged in South and Southeast

# FIELD NOTE

"Beijing, Shanghai, and other Chinese cities are being transformed as the old is swept away in favor of the new. Locals, powerless to stop the process, complain that their neighborhoods are being destroyed and that their relocation to remote apartment complexes is a hardship. Urban planners argue that the 'historic' neighborhoods are often dilapidated, decaying, and beyond renovation. The housing shown in Figure 12.20a was demolished to make room for what is going up in Figure 12.20b, a scene repeated countless times throughout urbanizing China."

■ **Figure 12.20a**
**Beijing, China.**

■ **Figure 12.20b**
**Beijing, China.**

Asia, in South Africa, and in parts of Central and South America. Brazil, Russia, India, China, and South Africa are increasingly grouped under the acronym BRICS (each letter standing for one of these countries) because these are the countries that demonstrate a shift in global economic power away from the traditional economic core. As we have seen, China is currently leading the way, but India has recently become the world's sixth largest economy. Although industrial production in India is modest in the context of the country's huge size and enormous population, major industrial complexes have developed around Calcutta (the Eastern district, with engineering, chemical, cotton, and jute industries, plus iron and steel based on the Chota Nagpur reserves), Mumbai (the Western district, where cheap electricity helps the cotton and chemical industries), and Chennai (the Southern district, with an emphasis on light engineering and textiles) (Fig. 12.21).

India has no major oil reserves, so it must spend heavily on oil energy. On the other hand, the country has a great deal of hydroelectric potential and access to ample coal. Its Bihar and Karnataka iron ore reserves may be among the largest in the world. With a large labor force, a growing middle class,

and a location midway between Europe and the Pacific Rim, India's economic influence is clearly on the rise.

## WHERE FROM HERE?

The diffusion of manufacturing activity to the semiperiphery and periphery and the associated sensation of a shrinking world have led a few commentators to suggest that we are entering an era characterized by the "end of geography." Alvin Toffler first suggested this idea in his *Future Shock* (1970). More recently, Richard O'Brien advanced a similar idea in *Global Financial Integration: The End of Geography* (1992) and Thomas Friedman suggested *The World Is Flat* (2005). Each author argues that a combination of technological changes and developments in the global economy have reduced the significance of location and made place differences increasingly insignificant. Geographers who study industrial production recognize that the nature and meaning of location and place have changed greatly in recent times, but they also note that these changes do not create a geographically undifferentiated world. Hence, what is needed is a greater understanding of how places have changed as a

■■ **Figure 12.21**
**Mumbai, India.** The cotton industry has been a major part of Mumbai's economy since the first cotton mill in India was built in 1854 in the city.

result of new production methods, new corporate structures, and new patterns of industry, as well as an examination of how the interplay between global processes and local places is creating opportunities and constraints for different parts of the planet.

Think about a cutting-edge, high-technology product that is still quite expensive to purchase and not yet broadly used (perhaps something you have read about but not even seen). Using the Internet, determine where this product is manufactured and assess why the product is manufactured there. Hypothesize where production of the good is in its production cycle, where production may shift to in the future, and how long it might take for production costs (and the price of the product) to decrease substantially.

# HOW HAVE DEINDUSTRIALIZATION AND THE RISE OF SERVICE INDUSTRIES ALTERED THE ECONOMIC GEOGRAPHY OF PRODUCTION?

Service industries—tertiary, quaternary, and quinary sectors—produce ideas, advice, innovations, and assistance to businesses and individuals. *Tertiary* services include a broad range of actions that aid people and businesses, including personal services such as cutting hair and giving massages, as well as entertainment, transportation, and retail. Quaternary industries are for the collection, processing, and manipulation of information and capital (finance, administration, insurance, legal services, computer services) and *quinary* industries are for activities that facilitate complex decision making and the advancement of human capacities (scientific research, higher education, and high-level management).

Distinguishing among types of services is useful, given the extraordinary growth in the size and complexity of the service sector. In the global economic core, service industries employ more workers than the primary and secondary industries combined, yet these service industries range from small-scale retailing to tourism services to research on the causes of cancer. Placing all of these activities in a single category seems unwarranted.

Specificity in terminology is also useful in highlighting different phases in the development of the service sector. In the early decades of the twentieth century, the domestic and quasidomestic tertiary industries were experiencing rapid growth in the industrialized world. With the approach of World War II, the quaternary sector began expanding rapidly, and this expansion continued after the war. During the last three decades, both the quaternary and quinary sectors have experienced very rapid growth, giving greater meaning to the term *postindustrial*.

The expanding service sector in the core economies is only one aspect of the changing global economy. Accompanying, and in some cases driving, this expansion are several other developments that have already been mentioned: the increasing mechanization of production, particularly in manufacturing enterprises operating in the core; the growth of large multinational corporations; and the dispersal of the production process.

Not all services contribute to an economy equally. Consider that you can pay $20 for a haircut and $20,000 for a surgery, and both are part of the service industry. An alternative way to think about the wealth generated through the service industries is to think about services in terms of *low cost, low benefit* versus *high cost, high benefit*. When you pay $20 for a haircut, the money goes to the person who cut your hair, and in turn the stylist puts some of the money toward rent to the salon owner and some of the money to buying groceries on the way home. That fraction that went to rent multiplies, as it helps pay the utilities in the salon and the beauty companies where the salon purchases products. With the $20,000 surgery, you are paying part of the income of the surgeon, the anesthesiologist, and the nurses. You are paying the hospital, which in turn purchases utilities and all kinds of medical products. For each service you purchased, think about the persons being paid as having a wake (like that caused by a boat) behind them. The stylist can pay for only a small part of the rent and a couple of groceries from your $20—low cost, low benefit to the economy. The surgeon can pay part of a child's private school tuition, part of a Disney vacation, and an entire month's worth of groceries—high cost, high benefit to the economy.

## Geographical Dimensions of the Service Economy

Deindustrialization and the growth of the service economy unfolded in the context of a world-economy that was already characterized by wide socioeconomic disparities. Only areas that had industry could deindustrialize, of course, and at the global scale the wealthier industrial regions were the most successful in establishing a postindustrial service economy. Deindustrialization did little to change the basic disparities between core and periphery that have long characterized the global economy. Even in the manufacturing realm, the availability of capital, mechanization, and innovative production strategies allowed the core industrial regions to retain their dominance. In the first decade of the twenty-first century, eastern Asia, western Russia and Ukraine, western Europe,

and North America still accounted for well over 75 percent of the world's total output of manufactured goods.

Despite its continued dominance in the manufacturing arena, the core has experienced some wrenching changes associated with the economic shifts of the past four decades. Anyone who has ever spent time in Detroit, Michigan, the British Midlands, or Silesia (southern Poland and northeastern Czech Republic) knows that there are pockets of significant hardship in relatively prosperous countries (Fig. 12.22). These are the result of large-scale deindustrialization. In the United Kingdom, the major industrial zones of Newcastle, Liverpool, and Manchester lost much of their industrial bases during the 1960s and 1970s. Similarly, the industrial zone of the northeastern United States (around the Great Lakes) lost much of its industrial base in the same time period, with steel manufacturing jobs moving to areas of the world with lower wages. This region of the United States, which used to be called the Manufacturing Belt, is now commonly called the **Rust Belt**, evoking the image of long-abandoned, rusted-out steel factories (Fig. 12.23). More recently, the global economic downturn that began in 2008 has resulted in devastating job losses in communities dependent on both secondary and tertiary industries. These examples serve to remind us that not all deindustrialized regions find their niche easily in the new service economy and that a tertiary economy, once established, does not necessarily buffer places from recessionary trends.

Nonetheless, some secondary industrial regions have made the transition to a viable service economy fairly successfully. The **Sun Belt** is the southern region of the United States, stretching through the Southeast to the Southwest. Both the population and economy of this region have grown over the last few decades, as service sector businesses have chosen to locate in areas such as Atlanta and Dallas where the climate is warm and the local laws welcome their presence. The eastern part of the Sun Belt served as an early industrial region, with Birmingham developing an iron and steel economy and Atlanta an industrial economy around cotton, tobacco, and furniture. In recent decades, high-tech and financial industries changed the economy and landscape of the Sun Belt, as can be seen in the names of stadiums in the region, such as EverBank Field in Jacksonville, Florida; Bank of America Stadium in Charlotte, North Carolina; and AT&T Center in San Antonio, Texas.

### NEW PATTERNS OF ECONOMIC ACTIVITY

With the striking growth of the service sector and information technologies, new factors have come into play that are affecting patterns of economic activity. Most service industries are not tied to raw materials and

**■■ Figure 12.22**
**Liverpool, England.** With the deindustrialization of the Liverpool region, the city has lost thousands of jobs and the city's population has decreased by one-third. Abandoned streets, such as this one, are a reflection of the city's industrial decline.

© Richard Klune/Corbis

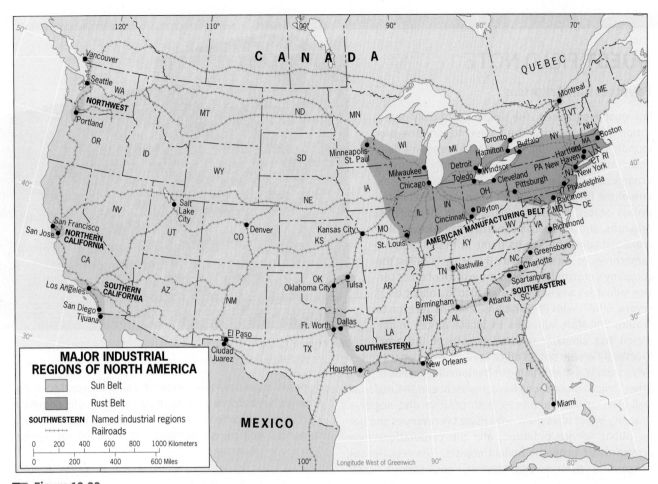

**■ Figure 12.23**

**Major Manufacturing Regions of North America.**   North American manufacturing has dispersed to the Sun Belt, and deindustrialization has taken hold in much of the American Manufacturing Belt, now known as the Rust Belt.   © E. H. Fouberg, A. B. Murphy, H. J. de Blij, and John Wiley & Sons, Inc.

do not need large amounts of energy. Market accessibility is more relevant for the service sector, but advances in telecommunications have rendered even that factor less important for some types of service industries.

To understand the influences that shape the location of services, it is useful to go back to our distinction among tertiary, quaternary, and quinary industries. Tertiary services related to transportation and communication are closely tied to population patterns and to the location of primary and secondary industries. As the basic facilitators of interaction, they are strongly linked to the basic geography of production and consumption. Other tertiary services—restaurants, hotels, and retail establishments—are influenced mainly by market considerations. If they are located far from their consumers, they are unlikely to succeed.

Employing technologies such as geographic information systems (GIS) (see Chapter 1), geographers can model the best locations for new businesses, office complexes, government centers, or transportation connections. Major retailers not only shape the landscapes of the places where they choose to put stores, but they also change the economic prospects and physical landscapes of the places where their headquarters

are located. Wal-Mart's headquarters in Bentonville, Arkansas, provides a particularly striking example. If producers of consumer products want to sell their goods in Wal-Mart stores, they must travel to Bentonville, Arkansas, to negotiate deals with Wal-Mart. In order to provide low prices to consumers, Wal-Mart negotiates very low prices with major producers. To create lower-priced products, companies have moved production abroad, and to create good relationships with the world's number one retailer (with sales of $405 billion in fiscal year 2010), a variety of companies have moved into Arkansas (Fig. 12.24). Those companies, along with an array of other businesses supporting their activities (hotels, restaurants, copy centers, delivery services), have fundamentally transformed the city.

The locational influences on quaternary services—high-level services aimed at the collection, processing, and manipulation of information and capital—are more diverse. Some of these services are strongly tied geographically to a particular locus of economic activity. Retail banking and various types of administrative services require a high level of interpersonal contact and therefore tend to be located near the businesses they are serving. Other types of quaternary services can

# GUEST FIELD NOTE

## Fayetteville, Arkansas

For most geographers, the simple act of daily observation of the world around them becomes a profoundly satisfying habit. For the last 17 years, my daily observations have been of the rapidly changing urban/economic landscape of northwest Arkansas, one of the fastest growing metropolitan areas in the United States. Wal-Mart originated in Bentonville, Arkansas, and as it became increasingly successful, it remained committed to its home in this affordable, rural corner of the mid-South. By the early 1990s, the company's growth had fueled the growth of other service industries and had contributed to the retention of several other major corporations. A recent decision to require Wal-Mart suppliers to locate offices in the region has similarly boosted growth in the area. Procter & Gamble put its office in Fayetteville only 25 miles from Wal-Mart's home in Bentonville. Dozens of other major corporations have a presence in the region as well. The results have been both positive and negative. Property prices have risen, with rising tax revenues and better public service provision, and the corporations have proven to be generous philanthropists. However, sprawl, congestion, overcrowded schools, and serious waste

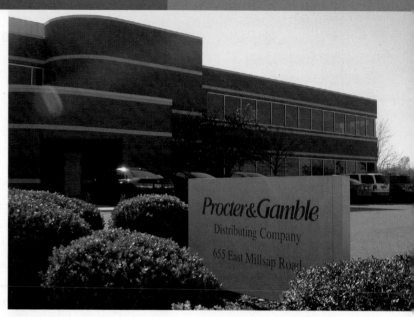

■ **Figure 12.24**

disposal issues have also followed. This once-rural corner of America has become a metropolitan growth pole, complete with national coffee shops, rush hour congestion, and sprawling golf-course subdivisions of 6000-square-foot "European" mansions.

*Credit: Fiona M. Davidson, University of Arkansas.*

---

operate almost anywhere as long as they have access to digital processing equipment and telecommunications. When you send in your credit card bill, it is unlikely to go to the city where the headquarters of the issuing bank is located. Instead, it is likely to go to North Dakota, South Dakota, Nebraska, or Colorado. Similarly, many "back-office" tasks related to insurance are performed in places such as Des Moines, Iowa, not Chicago or Hartford.

Many of the call centers for technical help for computers and related industries (software, hardware) are located in India and the Philippines. Given the relatively high levels of college education and the vast numbers of English speakers in these places, as well as the ease of routing phones through the Internet, "help desks" need not be located down the hall or even down the street. These locational curiosities occur because technological advances in the telecommunications sector have made it possible for all sorts of quaternary industries to be located far away from either producers or consumers. What matters most is infrastructure, a workforce that is sufficiently skilled but not too expensive, and favorable tax rates.

Those who work in the quinary sector tend to be concentrated around governmental seats, universities, and corporate headquarters. Corporate headquarters tend to be located in large metropolitan areas, whereas seats of government and

universities can be found in places that were chosen long ago as appropriate sites for administrative or educational activities based on cultural values or political compromises. The American ideal of the "university town" (which originated in Germany) led to the establishment of many universities at a distance from major commercial and population centers, in such towns as Champaign-Urbana, Illinois; Norman, Oklahoma; and Eugene, Oregon. Political compromises led to the establishment of major seats of government in small towns. Ottawa, Canada, and Canberra, Australia, are examples of this phenomenon. The point is that historical location decisions influence the geography of the quinary sector. And it is not just university professors and government officials who are affected. All sorts of high-level research and development activities are located on the fringes of universities, and a host of specialized consultants are concentrated around governmental centers. These then become major nodes of quinary activity.

## High-Technology Clusters

A **high-technology corridor** is an area designated by local or state government to benefit from lower taxes and high-technology infrastructure, with the goal of providing high-technology jobs to the local population. The goal of a high-technology corridor is to attract designers of computers, semiconductors, telecommunications, sophisticated medical equipment, and the like.

California's Silicon Valley is a well-known example of a high-technology corridor. Several decades ago a number of innovative technology companies located their research and development activities in the area around the University of California, Berkeley, and Stanford University, both near San Francisco, California. They were attracted by the prospect of developing links with existing research communities and the availability of a highly educated workforce. Once some high-technology businesses located in the Silicon Valley, others were drawn to the area as well. The area became what geographers call a **growth pole**, not just because other high-technology businesses came to Silicon Valley, but because the concentration of these businesses spurred economic development in the surrounding area.

Today, Silicon Valley is home to dozens of computer companies, many of which are familiar to the computer literate (such as Cisco Systems, Adobe, Hewlett-Packard, Intel, and IBM). The resulting collection of high-technology industries produced what Manuel Castells, Peter Hall, and John Hutriyk call a **technopole**, an area planned for high technology where agglomeration built on a synergy among technological companies occurs. A similar sort of technopole developed outside Boston, where the concentration of technology-based businesses close to Harvard University and the Massachusetts Institute of Technology gave rise to what is called the Route 128 high-technology corridor. The Route 128 corridor has been largely supported by the federal government rather than the local government, which supports many other technopoles.

Technopoles can be found in a number of countries in western Europe, East Asia, North America, and Australia. Few are on the scale of Silicon Valley, but they are noticeable elements of the economic landscape. Many of them have sprung up on the edges of good-sized cities, particularly near airports. In Brussels (Belgium), for example, the route into the city from the airport passes an array of buildings occupied by computer, communication, and electronics firms. In Washington, D.C., the route from Dulles International Airport (located in the Virginia suburbs) to the city passes buildings housing the headquarters of companies such as AOL, MCI, and Orbital Sciences (the Dulles Corridor). In the Telecom Corridor of Plano-Richardson (just outside of Dallas, Texas), telecom companies such as Nortel and Ericsson have taken root, but so too have numerous high-technology companies that are not telecom related (Fig. 12.25). In each of these technopoles, the presence of major multinational companies attracts other startup companies hoping to become major companies, provide services to major companies, or be bought by major companies.

Many of the technology firms are multinationals, and like their counterparts in other countries, they function in an

ASSOCIATED PRESS

■ **Figure 12.25**

**Plano-Richardson, Texas.** The Plano-Richardson Telecom Corridor is located just north of Dallas and is home to telecom corporate headquarters, such as Electronic Data Systems Corporation's headquarters in this photograph.

information environment and market their products all over the world. Being near raw materials or even a particular market is unimportant for these firms; what matters to them is proximity to major networks of transportation and communication. High-technology industries have become such an important symbol of the postindustrial world that local, regional, and national governments often pursue aggressive policies to attract firms in this sector. Bidding wars sometimes develop between localities seeking to attract such industries. Although high-technology industries often bring a variety of economic benefits, they have some drawbacks as well. Communities that have attracted production facilities find that the manufacture of computer chips, semiconductors, and the like requires toxic chemicals and large quantities of water. And even more research-oriented establishments sometimes have negative environmental impacts in that land must be cleared and buildings constructed to house them. Despite these drawbacks, the high-technology sector is clearly here to stay, and areas that can tap into it are likely to find themselves in an advantageous economic position in the coming years.

## Tourism Services

Every service industry has its own locational characteristics, but tourism is almost in a class by itself due to its geographical extent and economic significance. Once a relatively small activity confined to a set of specialized locations, tourism is now the world's largest service sector industry.

Tourism grew dramatically during the second half of the twentieth century. The tourism boom began in the global economic core as incomes and leisure time increased for a rapidly expanding segment of the population. Over the past three decades, the number of East and Southeast Asian tourists has risen much faster than the global average, reflecting the economic boom in many of the Pacific Rim countries. The combination of a weakening global economy and concerns over political stability caused noticeable dips in travel at the beginning and end of the first decade of the twenty-first century, but absent a major economic or geopolitical crisis, tourism is likely to continue to expand.

In Chapter 10 we looked at some of the social and cultural impacts of tourism, but it is important to recognize that tourism is a major industry as well. Communities all over the world have worked hard to promote tourism, and many are now notably reliant on tourist receipts. The tourist industry has transformed downtowns, ports, hinterlands, parks, and waterfronts. High-rise, ultramodern hotels dominate urban skylines from Boston to Brisbane. The Port of Miami and Fort Lauderdale's Port Everglades have been reconstructed to serve the cruise industry, and many ports from Tokyo to Tampa have added cruise terminals complete with shopping malls and restaurants. Theme parks such as Disney's establishments near Orlando, Paris, Tokyo, Hong Kong, Shanghai, and Los Angeles draw millions of visitors and directly and indirectly employ thousands of workers. Dubai has constructed an indoor ski run in the Mall of the Emirates in an effort to attract more visitors. Once-remote wildlife parks and nature reserves in East Africa and South Asia now receive thousands of visitors, requiring expanded facilities and sometimes causing ecological damage. Formerly isolated beaches are now lined by high-rise hotels and resorts; in the Caribbean and the Pacific, some entire islands have been taken over by tour operators.

The economic impacts of tourist-related development are far-reaching. The monetary value of goods and services associated with tourism is now conservatively estimated at more than $2 trillion—and if spillover effects are taken into consideration, the figure could be twice as large. With the growing middle class in China and India and with increases in average life expectancy, the figure is likely to continue to grow, affecting the prospects of places all over the world.

## Place Vulnerabilities in a Service Economy

Every type of economy carries with it potential vulnerabilities. In the early stages of industrialization, the economic destinies of places were tied to their manufacturing operations. As a result, such places were vulnerable to wrenching adjustments when demand shifted for the goods produced by local manufacturers or when the changing costs of transportation or labor led business owners to downscale or shift production elsewhere. Many older industrial areas in the United States and Europe experienced such adjustments, and their best hope for rebuilding often lay in the service economy. Thus, in Duisburg—a city at the heart of Germany's Ruhr Valley—abandoned steel mills were turned into tourist

attractions and warehouses were converted into retail establishments, restaurants, and offices (Fig. 12.26).

Service economies have their own vulnerabilities. Tourism can fall off in the face of economic downturns or natural hazards, and office work can be outsourced to distant places. Mechanization can also have a negative impact. We usually think of manufacturing jobs being affected by mechanization, but service jobs are vulnerable as well. In recent decades, countless jobs in the travel planning industry have been lost to the Internet, scanning machines in supermarkets have reduced the need for employees, and automated answering services have taken the place of live voices in many businesses. Changes of this sort can create the same sorts of hardships and pressures for economic readjustment that communities reliant on secondary industries face.

At a different spatial scale, the very geographical structure of large-scale service economies can affect the fortunes of places, regions, countries, and even the globe. Places dominated by the service sector cannot exist without extensive connections with other places because those living in such places still need food and material products, and they often need a large market to sustain their services. Hence, the dramatic shift away from the primary and secondary sectors that has taken place in some parts of the world is inextricably tied to economic globalization. But economic decision making in a globalized economy can easily become disconnected from the fate of individual places and regions.

The burgeoning financial service industry provides a case in point. That industry has grown explosively over the past few decades with the development of increasingly innovative products and arrangements. Some people made spectacular amounts of money in the process, but in recent

© Alexander B. Murphy

■■ **Figure 12.26**

**Duisburg, Germany.** The old industrial canal corridor is being converted to a pedestrian district that local authorities hope will attract locals and tourists.

decades key financial instruments and procedures were developed based on unrealistic assumptions about concrete circumstances. Banks made loans they should not have made, and mortgages were issued to people who were unlikely to be able to meet their payments. These practices helped to bring about the dramatic economic downturn that began in 2008, when a housing slump precipitated high levels of defaults on so-called subprime mortgages. A banking crisis ensued that rippled throughout the economy and, in our interconnected world, affected the fortunes and prospects of places near and far. The crisis serves as a reminder of the continuing vulnerabilities of places in a service economy, even in the absence of any direct challenge to the specific service industries on which particular local economies are based. It also raises a key question with a geographical foundation: What are the consequences of divorcing the development of wealth in a knowledge economy from the fate of individual places, regions, or countries?

How does a place change when deindustrialization occurs? Consider a place that has experienced deindustrialization, and research recent news articles on the Internet to find out how the economy of the place has changed since the loss of industry. What has happened to the place and its economy?

## Summary

The Industrial Revolution transformed the world economically, politically, and socially. Many of the places where industrialization first took hold have since become deindustrialized, both with the relocation of manufacturing plants and with the outsourcing of steps of the production process domestically and offshore. With changing economics, places change. Some now look like ghost towns, serving merely as a reminder that industrialization took place there. Others have booming economies and are thriving, having kept industry or having successfully developed a service economy. Still other places are redefining themselves. In the next chapter, we consider another lasting effect of industrialization and deindustrialization: environmental change.

## Geographic Concepts

containerization
cottage industries
economies of scale
locational criteria
spillover effect
hinterland
connectivity
first mover advantage
secondary hearths
globalization
Fordist
vertical integration

friction of distance
distance decay
location theory
least cost theory
agglomeration
flexible production
commodification
product life cycle
global division of labor
time–space compression
just-in-time delivery
spatial fix

node
commodity chain
outsourcing
intermodal connections
deindustrialization
newly industrializing countries
break-of-bulk point
Rust Belt
Sun Belt
high-technology corridor
growth pole
technopole

## Learn More Online

About the port of Rotterdam:
www.portofrotterdam.com
www.portofrotterdam.com/en/Port/port-in-general/Documents/20100726_EN/index.html

About Nike
www.nikebiz.com/company_overview

About Global Sourcing in China
http://www.forbes.com/sites/allbusiness/2014/01/06/sourcing-goods-and-suppliers-in-china-a-how-to-guide-for-small-businesses/

## Watch It Online

About Wal-Mart's influence on Bentonville, Arkansas
www.pbs.org/wgbh/pages/frontline/shows/walmart

# CHAPTER 13

# THE HUMANIZED ENVIRONMENT

## Disaster Along Indian Ocean Shores

**W**atching the horrors of the tsunami of December 26, 2004, unfold on screen (Fig. 13.1), I found it quite eerie to see such devastation in places where earlier I walked, drove and rode—like that Sri Lankan train on which I took a group of students in 1978—now smashed by the waves, the carriages toppled, killing more than a thousand passengers, some of them tourists. And the beaches near Phuket in Thailand, so serene and beautiful in memory, now proved a fatal attraction leading to disaster for thousands more, tourists and workers alike.

I went online to follow the events of that day and those that followed, horrified by the rising death toll and by the images of destruction and devastation. The in-box of my e-mail began to include messages from former students who remembered my in-field assessment of the tsunami risks in Southeast Asia. But I had not been especially prescient. Just like people farming the fertile soils on the slopes of an active volcano, people living at or near sea level near an earthquake zone live with risk.

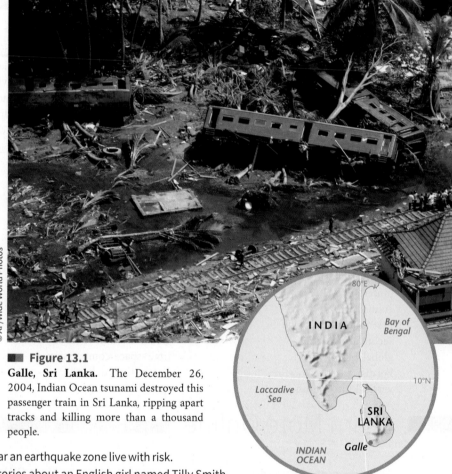

© AP/Wide World Photos

■ **Figure 13.1**
**Galle, Sri Lanka.** The December 26, 2004, Indian Ocean tsunami destroyed this passenger train in Sri Lanka, ripping apart tracks and killing more than a thousand people.

A few weeks later I began to hear and read stories about an English girl named Tilly Smith, who had been vacationing with her parents at a hotel on the beach at Phuket and was on Maikhao Beach when she saw the water suddenly recede into the distance. Tilly had just taken a geography class in her school not far from London, and her teacher, Mr. Andrew Kearney, had told the class what happens when a tsunami strikes: The huge approaching wave first sucks the water off the beaches, and then the sea foams, rises, and returns as a massive, breaking wall that crashes over and inundates the whole shoreline. Tilly saw what was happening and alerted her parents, her father told hotel security, and they ran back and forth, screaming at beachgoers to seek shelter on higher ground in the hotel behind them. About a hundred people followed the Smith family into the building, and they all survived. Of those who stayed behind, none did.

Being aware of some of the basics of physical geography has its advantages, and Mr. Kearney clearly had the attention of his students.

Newspaper editors could use some of this awareness. Many headlines referred to the tsunami as a tidal wave, but a tsunami has nothing to do with the tides that affect all oceans and seas. A tsunami results from an undersea earthquake involving a large displacement of the Earth's crust. Most submarine earthquakes do not generate tsunamis, but in some cases, fortunately relatively rare ones, a large piece of crust is pushed up or pulled under (or both), and this causes the water overhead to pile up and start rolling away in all directions. If you were on a cruise ship somewhere in the middle of the ocean, nothing catastrophic would mark the passing of this tsunami wave; your ship would be lifted up and then lowered, but it would not overturn. But when such a huge wave reaches a beach, it does what all waves do: It breaks. Most of us have seen this happen with waves several feet (or even tens of feet) high. But imagine a wave over 200 feet high approaching a beach. As it begins to break, it pulls the water away, exposing wide swaths of muddy bottom. Then it comes crashing into the shore, pushing deep inland.

Tsunamis of the magnitude of 2004 are not common, but as the deadly tsunami that struck the northeast coast of Japan in 2011 reminds us, the hazard is continuous. As the Earth's human population has grown, so have the numbers of people vulnerable to such a calamity. And as human land use along and near coasts intensifies, so too can the impacts of tsunamis. In the case of the 2004 tsunami, significant destruction of mangroves to make way for shrimp farms in Southeast Asia exacerbated the impacts of the disaster.

As we learn more about the submarine zones where earthquakes are most likely to occur, and couple that understanding with an appreciation of the human patterns discussed in other chapters, we can begin to determine where the hazards are greatest. Here we combine two major fields of study in geography, physical geography and human geography. Geographers who work in this arena study human-environmental relationships—the reciprocal relationships between human societies and natural environments. The environment is not a passive stage, and environmental change affects human societies. At the same time, humans have an impact on their natural environments. The study of hazards, not just from tsunamis but also from volcanic eruptions, terrestrial earthquakes, landslides, floods, avalanches, and other threats, is a key part of this research.

The tsunami that struck coasts along the Indian Ocean from Indonesia to Somalia and from Thailand to the Maldives resulted from a violent earthquake measuring more than 9.0 on the (10-point) Richter scale off the west coast of the island of Sumatra (Indonesia).

There, two of the planet's tectonic plates are colliding, forcing one beneath the other (Fig. 13.2). A series of tremors and quakes affects the crust in such subduction zones, but sometimes a major shock occurs. In this case, the towering wave generated by the December 26 earthquake had but a short distance to travel to reach northern Sumatra, where it struck in full force. By the time it had done its damage in remote Somalia (in Africa), it had claimed approximately 300,000 lives and ruined the livelihoods of millions more. The 2004 Indian Ocean tsunami illustrated one consequence of the tourist industry: Drawing millions of tourists and workers to coasts makes them more vulnerable to coastal hazards.

Geography is a discipline in which the relationship between humans and environment is a primary concern. One of the most influential nineteenth-century texts on this relationship, *Man and Nature* (1865), was written by the geographer George Perkins Marsh. In 1955, geographers were centrally involved in an international interdisciplinary symposium on "Man's Role in Changing the Face of the Earth." This symposium, like Marsh's earlier book, focused primarily on local and regional changes. More recently, a symposium led by geographers on "The Earth as Transformed by Human Action" picked up where the 1955 discussion left off, addressing global environmental changes. The geographer's concern with how things are organized on Earth and how places are connected provides an analytical platform from which to consider human-induced environmental change.

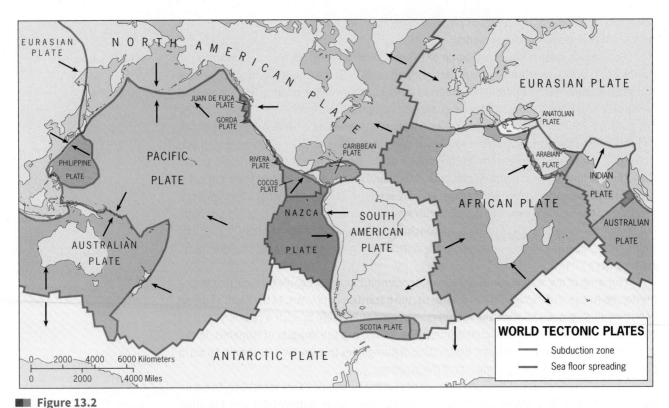

■■ **Figure 13.2**
**World Tectonic Plates.** The places at or near where tectonic plates meet are parts of Earth's surface most susceptible to earthquakes and volcanism. © H. J. de Blij, P. O. Muller, and John Wiley & Sons, Inc.

As the study of environmental change has moved forward, one of the most important lessons we have learned is that global environmental systems are interconnected. For example, the release of **chlorofluorocarbons** (CFCs) in the Northern Hemisphere in past decades contributed to a hole in Earth's ozone layer over Antarctica. Industrial production in the Netherlands and Germany contributes to acid rain in Scandinavia. The use of water from the Rio Grande for irrigation in northern New Mexico affects the amount and quality of the river's water that flows along the Texas–Mexico border. Human actions—the activities we undertake individually and collectively—are increasingly important factors in all sorts of global environmental changes. To confront these changes, we must consider the complex relationship between humans and environment.

# Key Questions FOR CHAPTER 13

1. How has Earth's environment changed over time?
2. How have humans altered Earth's environment?
3. What are the major factors contributing to environmental change today?
4. What is the international response to climate change?

# HOW HAS EARTH'S ENVIRONMENT CHANGED OVER TIME?

Environmental variation, spatial as well as temporal, is one of Earth's crucial characteristics. Temperatures rise and fall, precipitation waxes and wanes. Forests flourish and wither, deserts expand and contract. Humanity has evolved during a series of alternatively warm and cold phases of an Ice Age that is still in progress. But today humanity itself is part of the process.

Modern *Homo sapiens* emerged less than 200,000 years ago (and possibly not much more than 100,000 years ago). Humans altered their environment from the beginning by setting fires to kill herds of reindeer and bison, or by hunting entire species of large mammals to extinction. The Maori, who arrived in New Zealand not much more than 1000 years ago, greatly altered native species of animals and plants long before the advent of modern technology. Elsewhere in the Pacific realm, Polynesians reduced forest cover to brush and, with their penchant for wearing bird-feather robes, exterminated more than 80 percent of the regional bird species by the time the first Europeans arrived. Europeans ravaged species ranging from Galapagos turtles to Antarctic seals. European fashions had a disastrous impact on African species ranging from snakes to leopards. Traditional as well as modern societies have had devastating impacts on their ecosystems (ecological units consisting of self-regulating associations of living and nonliving natural elements) as well as on ecosystems into which they migrated.

Human alteration of the environment continues in many forms today. For the first time in history, however, the combined impact of humanity's destructive and exploitative actions is capable of producing environmental changes at the global scale. Consider for a moment the history of human life on Earth. Early human societies had relatively small populations, and their impacts on the physical environment were limited in both duration and intensity. With the development of agrarian and preindustrial societies, human alterations of the physical environment increased, yet the effects of these early activities were still limited in scale. Even the onset of urbanization and the development of urban centers, which concentrated large numbers of people in particular places, had relatively limited effects on a global scale.

Over the last 500 years, however, both the rate and the scale at which humans modify Earth have increased dramatically. Particularly during the last half-century, every place on Earth has been transformed, either directly or indirectly, by humans. The twentieth-century surge in the size of the human population, combined with a rapid escalation in consumption, magnifies humanity's impact on Earth in unprecedented ways. To acknowledge the incredible role humans play in shaping Earth's environment, atmospheric chemist Paul Crutzen argues that we have entered a new geologic epoch, the **anthropocene**.

## Tectonic Plates

How representative is the short-term present of the long-term past? Over the past century, geographers and other scientists have been engaged in a joint mission to reconstruct our planet's history on the basis of current evidence. One of them, the climatologist–geographer Alfred Wegener, used his spatial view of the world to make a key contribution. Viewing the increasingly accurate maps of the opposite coastlines of the North and South Atlantic oceans, he proposed a hypothesis that would account for the close "fit" of the shapes of the facing continents, which, he argued, would be unlikely to be a matter of chance. His continental drift hypothesis required the preexistence of a supercontinent, which he called **Pangaea**, which broke apart into the fragments we now know as Africa, the Americas, Eurasia, and Australia (Fig. 13.3). Wegener's hypothesis spurred thinking about plate tectonics and crustal spreading. Scientists now know that Pangaea and its fragmentation were only the latest episodes in a cycle of continental coalescence and splintering that spans billions of years. This latest Pangaean breakup, however, began only a little over 200 million years ago and continues to this day.

At plate boundaries, **tectonic plates** either *diverge* (spread apart), *converge* (come together), or *transform* (slide past one another). In the Atlantic Ocean, the North American plate is diverging from the Eurasian plate. Along this plate boundary, new oceanic crust is constantly being created where the plates diverge. A chain of volcanoes called the Mid-Atlantic Ridge has formed on the ocean floor.

Where the Indian plate meets the Eurasian plate, the two plates are converging. The Himalaya Mountains on this plate boundary were built through convergence. The Himalayas are still rising, and earthquakes are relatively common in the region as a result. When an oceanic plate converges with a continental plate, it is called a subduction zone. Along a subduction zone, the denser oceanic plate subducts under the continental plate, creating a trench along the boundary as well as volcanoes and strong earthquakes. Most of the strongest earthquakes that occur, including those in Haiti, Chile, and Japan in 2010 and 2011, happen along subduction zones.

## Ocean and Atmosphere

Earth is often called the Blue Planet because more than 70 percent of its surface is covered by water and views from space are dominated by blue hues and swirls of white clouds. The surrounding atmosphere was once loaded with the gas carbon dioxide ($CO_2$), and if you could have looked up at the sky it would have been bright red because $CO_2$ scatters red light. Eventually, however, the primitive ocean, still heated from below, began to absorb $CO_2$ in enormous quantities. A very long time passed before oxygen became a substantial gas in the atmosphere. Around 1500 million years ago, green algae started to spread across Earth's ocean surfaces, and as their colonies grew, their **photosynthesis** (the conversion of carbon dioxide and water into carbohydrates and oxygen

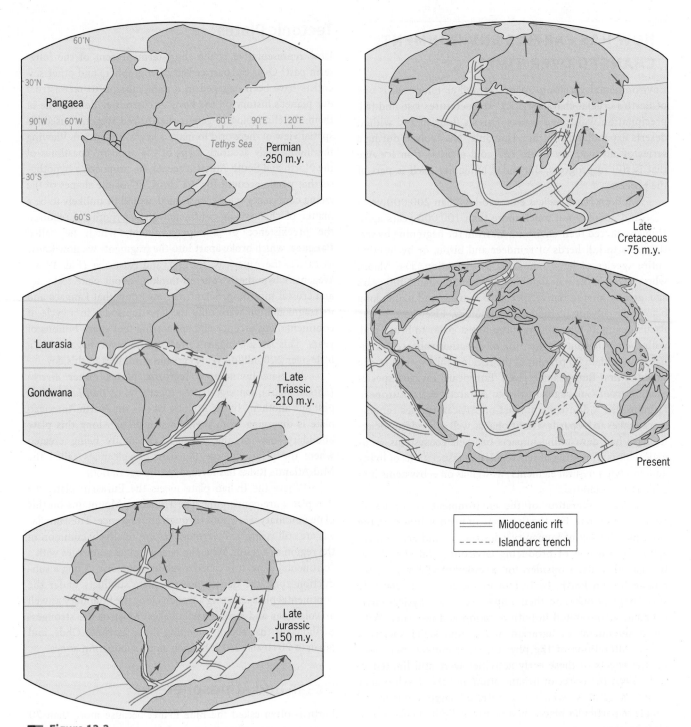

**Figure 13.3**

**Breakup of Pangaea.**   Pangaea broke up over millions of years, as reflected in this series of diagrams.   *Redrawn and simplified from*: Maps by R. S. Dietz and J. C. Holden, *Journal of Geophysical Research*, vol. 75, pp. 4943–4951, Figures 2 to 6.   © By the American Geophysical Union. Used by permission.

through the absorption of sunlight) raised the atmosphere's oxygen content. About 800 million years ago, the oxygen content in the atmosphere was about one-twentieth of its present strength, or just 1 percent of the total. But that was enough to support the emergence of the first single-celled animals, the protozoa.

# Fire and Ice

Today major volcanic eruptions happen infrequently enough that they make the news. Krakatoa (1883), Mount St. Helens (1980), Pinatubo (1991), and Merapi (2010) took many lives, damaged property, and, in the case of Pinatubo, even changed global climate slightly. In 2010, a relatively mild

## FIELD NOTE

"Kilauea has been erupting almost continuously since 1983, making it one of Earth's most active volcanoes. After flying over the volcano in a helicopter and looking down at the molten lava, I asked the pilot to take us to the coast where the lava was spilling into the sea. What we saw provided a stirring reminder that the environment is anything but static. Lava had poured across the road that ran along the coast, and the configuration of the coast was being remade before our eyes."

© Alexander B. Murphy

■ **Figure 13.4**
**The Southeast Coast of the Big Island of Hawai'i.**

eruption of the Icelandic volcano Eyjafjallajökull spewed enough ash in the air to disrupt air traffic across the northern Atlantic for more than a week. Over the past three decades, ongoing eruptions of the Kilauea volcano have altered the coastline of the Big Island of Hawai'i (Fig. 13.4) and displaced people along the slopes of Mount Etna in Sicily.

Yet such events are relatively minor compared to one billion years ago, when Earth's crust was still immature and subject to huge bursts of volcanic activity. Such episodes poured incalculable volumes of gases and ash into the atmosphere, perhaps contributing to the three **mass extinctions** (mass destruction of most species) known to have occurred over the past 500 million years.

The Earth's most recent experience with mass volcanism took place between 180 and 160 million years ago, when the supercontinent Pangaea was in the process of breaking apart. Lava poured from fissures and vents as South America separated from Africa and India moved northeast. Skies were blackened, the atmosphere choked with ash. Animals responded as they always have in time of crisis: by migrating, fragmenting into smaller groups, and speeding up their adaptive evolutionary response. Physical geographers hypothesize that the earliest phase of Pangaea's fragmentation was also the most violent, that the plate separations that started it all were driven by built-up, extreme heat below the supercontinent, but that the motion of the plates has since slowed down. The **Pacific Ring of Fire**—an ocean-girdling zone of crustal instability, volcanism, and earthquakes—is but a trace of the paroxysm that marked the onset of Pangaea's

breakup (Fig. 13.5). Yet, as we saw with the tsunami in Japan in 2011, modern tectonic events can cost millions of humans lives and alter the course of history.

When Pangaea still was a supercontinent, an Ice Age cooled Earth and may have contributed to, if not caused, the greatest known extinction crisis in the history of life on the planet. Ice Ages are not uniform cooling events: Surges of coldness and advances of glaciers are interrupted by temporary warming spells long enough to reverse much of the glacial impact.

The **Pleistocene** epoch, which began 2 million years ago (Fig. 13.6), was marked by long **glaciations** and short, warm **interglacials**. When the Pleistocene glaciations were most severe, permanent ice advanced deep into the landmasses of the Northern Hemisphere. Plants, animals, and hominids saw their living space diminished, their refuges shrunk, their niches unusable. Such glaciations could last as long as 100,000 years, but eventually a warming spell would arrive, the ice would recede, and space as well as opportunity expanded again. A warming phase of this kind occurred between about 120,000 and 100,000 years ago.

After this warm-up came the most recent glaciation of the Pleistocene, the **Wisconsinan Glaciation**, which left its mark on much of the Northern Hemisphere (Fig. 13.7). But resourceful humans managed to survive where their predecessors could not, and there is ample evidence of human occupation in southern Europe, ranging from cave art to tool kits. Even during a glacial advance brief periods of milder climate emerge. Thus, Figure 13.7 represents a glacial

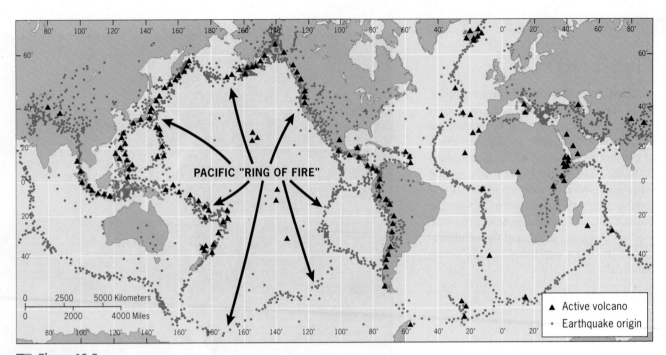

**Figure 13.5**
**Recent Earthquakes and Volcanic Eruptions.** © H. J. de Blij, P. O. Muller, and John Wiley & Sons, Inc.

## GEOLOGIC TIME SCALE

| Era | Period | Epoch | Age in Millions of Years Before Present |
|-----|--------|-------|-----------------------------------------|
| CENOZOIC | Quaternary | Present | |
| | | Holocene | 0.01 |
| | | Pleistocene | 1.6 |
| | Tertiary — Neogene | Pliocene | 5.3 |
| | | Miocene | 23.7 |
| | Tertiary — Paleogene | Oligocene | 36.6 |
| | | Eocene | 57.8 |
| | | Paleocene | 66.4 |
| MESOZOIC | Cretaceous | | 144 |
| | Jurassic | | 208 |
| | Triassic | | 245 |
| PALEOZOIC | Permian | | 286 |
| | Carboniferous — Pennsylvanian | | 320 |
| | Carboniferous — Mississippian | | 360 |
| | Devonian | | 408 |
| | Silurian | | 438 |
| | Ordovician | | 505 |
| | Cambrian | | 570 |
| PRECAMBRIAN | | | 4,550 |

extreme, not the whole picture. So human communities—fishing, hunting and gathering, and using increasingly sophisticated tools (and probably means of verbal communication)—exploited the milder times to expand their frontiers, then hunkered down when it got cold again.

About 73,500 years ago, something happened that appears to have come close to exterminating humanity altogether. A volcano, Mount Toba, erupted on the Indonesian island of Sumatra. This was not just an eruption: The entire mountain exploded, sending millions of tons of debris into orbit, obscuring the sun, creating long-term darkness, and altering global climate. Mount Toba's detonation could hardly have come at a worse time. Earth's habitable zone was already constricted because of glaciation. Anthropologists refer to this event as humanity's "evolutionary bottleneck," suggesting that much genetic diversity was lost. Today, the filled-in caldera marking Toba's cataclysm is 90 kilometers (55 miles) long and 50 kilometers (30 miles) wide, silent witness to the greatest threat to our existence ever to come from any source (Fig. 13.8).

The Wisconsinan Glaciation eventually gave way to a full-scale interglacial, the current warm interlude that has been given its own designation, the **Holocene** (Fig. 13.6). Global warming began about 18,000 years ago, and for the next 6000 years, temperatures rose rapidly. Although the ice sheets were thinning and giant, mud-laden floods sped down the Mississippi Valley, building the river's enormous delta, ice

**Figure 13.6**
**Stages in Earth History.**

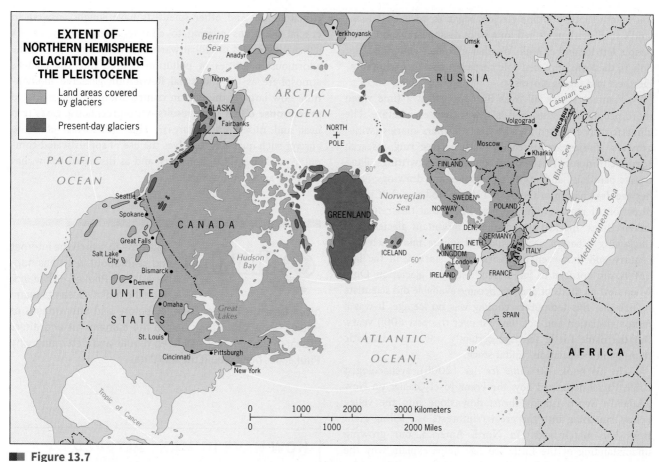

■ **Figure 13.7**

**Extent of Northern Hemisphere Glaciation.**   During the Late Pleistocene's Wisconsinan Glaciation, glaciers covered northern North America and Eurasia. The evidence on which this map is based includes glacial deposits and marks on bedrock cut by glaciers.   © H. J. de Blij, P. O. Muller, and John Wiley & Sons, Inc.

continued to cover most of northern North America as recently as 13,000 years ago.

To our human ancestors in the Northern Hemisphere, who inhabited much of western and eastern Eurasia and may just have been entering the Americas (some scholars argue that American Indians were here earlier), this warming must have been a welcome experience. So persistent was this most recent warming that people ventured farther and farther poleward.

## The Little Ice Age in the Modern Era

To the farmers, winegrowers, and seafarers of the fourteenth century, increasing cold, decreasing rainfall, frigid winds, and shortened growing seasons made for dwindling harvests, failing farms, and seas too stormy for fishing. By the turn of the

TeeJe/Flickr/Getty Images

**Figure 13.8**
**Mount Toba, Indonesia.**   The lake in this photo fills in the gigantic caldera left from the eruption of Mount Toba on the island of Sumatra in Indonesia.

fourteenth century, alpine glaciers began to advance. Greenland's small settlement had long since disappeared, and many people left Iceland as well. Weather extremes abounded, not only in the form of record cold snaps but also as searing summer heat and raging storms.

Famines struck all over Europe, just at a time when more people were clustered in towns than ever before. The climatic record, pieced together from farmers' diaries (winegrowers' diaries are especially useful), tree ring research (dendochronology), ice cores, contemporary writings, illustrative paintings, and surviving sketches and drawings, justifies the designation of the post–1300 period as a shift in the direction of reglaciation. We now know that this return to colder times, marked by advancing mountain glaciers and thickening subarctic ice, would end in the mid-nineteenth century and that even the worst of it, starting in the late 1600s, did not lead to full-scale Pleistocene glaciation. Only when new methods of analysis became available did scientists realize that this temporary cooling was no ice age: It was a minor glaciation and not the first over the past 6000 years. But the name **Little Ice Age** certainly was more dramatic than "Minor Glaciation," and it stuck.

In his book *The Little Ice Age* (2000), archaeologist Brian Fagan described how the Franz Josef Glacier on New Zealand's South Island "thrust downslope into the valley below, smashing into the great rainforests . . . felling giant trees like matchsticks." In North America, our growing understanding of the Little Ice Age helps explain why the Jamestown colony collapsed so fast, a failure attributed by historians solely to ineptitude and lack of preparation. Geographer David Stahle (1998) and his team, studying tree ring records that go back eight centuries, found that the Jamestown area experienced a seven-year drought between 1606 (the year before the colony's founding) through 1612, the worst in nearly eight centuries. European colonists and American Indians were in the same situation, and their relations worsened as they were forced to compete for dwindling food and falling water tables. The high rate of starvation was not unique to the colonists. They, and their American Indian neighbors, faced the rigors of the Little Ice Age as well.

As the Little Ice Age continued into the 1800s, a large-scale volcano had a major impact on human society. On April 5, 1815, the Tambora volcano on the island of Sumatra in what was then the Dutch East Indies, located not far east of Bali, rumbled to life. Less than a week later it was pulverized in a series of explosions that could be heard a thousand miles away, killing all but 26 of the island's population of 12,000. When it was over, the top 4000 feet of the volcano were gone, and much of what is now Indonesia was covered by debris. Darkness enveloped most of the colony for weeks, and tens of thousands died of famine in the months that followed. Colonial reports describe fields covered by poisonous ash and powder, waters clogged by trees and cinders, and air rendered unbreathable by a fog of acid chemicals.

Since the 1850s, when the Little Ice Age waned and a slow but nearly continuous warming phase began, climatologists and other scientists have sought answers to crucial questions relating to climate change: What causes alternating cycles of global warming and cooling? Given the enormous quantities of pollution poured into the planet's atmosphere as the Industrial Revolution gathered momentum, how large is the human contribution to the associated **greenhouse effect** (that results when greenhouse gases trap heat and raise temperatures)? This worldwide, effort to answer such questions involves the use of sophisticated computers and complicated models, and as discussed below, has achieved an alarming consensus.

Take time to search the Internet and read about what has happened to Phuket, Thailand, since the Indian Ocean tsunami hit in December 2004. Look for before and after images of Phuket—how did it look before the tsunami hit and after? Research how Phuket has been rebuilt and determine why Phuket has been rebuilt the way it has.

## HOW HAVE HUMANS ALTERED EARTH'S ENVIRONMENT?

Biologists estimate that as many as 25 million types of organisms inhabit Earth, perhaps even more. Most have not yet been identified, classified, or studied. No species, not even the powerful dinosaurs, ever affected their environment as much as humans do today. An impact by comets probably made the dinosaurs and many other species extinct. Some biogeographers suggest that the next great extinction is already occurring, and it is caused not by asteroids but by humans, whose numbers and demands are destroying millions of species.

The natural environment is being modified and stressed by human activity in many obvious and some less obvious ways. Some **environmental stress** is more obvious because it takes place around human habitats, such as cutting forests and emitting pollutants into the atmosphere. Less obvious environmental stress takes place away from dense concentrations of humans, including mountain-top mining, burying toxic wastes that contaminate groundwater supplies, and dumping vast amounts of garbage into waterways and the world's oceans. Humans have built seawalls, terraced hillslopes, dammed rivers, cut canals, and modified the environment in many constructive as well as destructive ways. All of these activities have an impact on environment and have given rise to a number of key concerns. Among these concerns are the future of water supplies, the state of the atmosphere, climate change, desertification, deforestation, soil degradation, and the disposal of industrial wastes.

## Water

Resources that are replenished even as they are being used are **renewable resources**, and resources that are present in finite quantities are **nonrenewable resources**. Water, essential to life, is a renewable resource. But the available supply of fresh water is not distributed evenly across the globe. Figure 1.11 shows the world distribution of precipitation, with the largest totals recorded in equatorial and tropical areas of Southeast Asia, South Asia, central and coastal West Africa, and Middle and South America. The volume of precipitation in the world as a whole is enormous; spread out evenly, it would cover the land area of the planet with about 33 inches (83 cm) of water each year. Much of that water is lost through runoff and evaporation, but enough of it seeps downward into porous, water-holding rocks called **aquifers** to provide millions of wells with steady flows. In the United States alone, it is estimated that there is 50 times as much water stored in aquifers as there is precipitation falling on the land surface every year.

Despite such favorable data, the supply of water is anything but plentiful (Fig. 13.9). Chronic water shortages afflict tens of millions of farmers in Africa and hundreds of thousands of city dwellers in Southern California; water rationing has been imposed in rainy South Florida and in Spain, which faces the Mediterranean Sea.

In many areas of the world, people have congregated in places where water supplies are insufficient, undependable, or both. In California, people are sometimes not allowed to wash their cars or refill their swimming pools; these are minor inconveniences compared to the fate faced by millions of Sudanese trying to escape violence in their country by fleeing to parched pans of the Sahara. In Florida, where the urban population depends on the Biscayne Aquifer for most of its water, the long-term prospect is troubled; whenever seasonal rainfalls do not reach their projected averages, Floridians overuse the Biscayne Aquifer, and saltwater enters the aquifer from the nearby Atlantic Ocean. The invasion of saltwater over time can permanently destroy a fresh water aquifer.

Hundreds of millions of people still cluster along several of Earth's great rivers. Indeed, nearly three-quarters of all the fresh water used annually is consumed in farming, not in cities. In California, where about 80 percent of available water is used for irrigation, an intense debate has emerged over whether cities should be provided with water at the expense of Central Valley farms, and whether fruits and vegetables should be bought from elsewhere, even overseas, rather than be grown locally?

As human populations have expanded, people have increasingly settled in arid regions. One of the great ecological disasters of the twentieth century occurred in Kazakhstan and Uzbekistan, whose common boundary runs through the Aral Sea. Streams that fed this large body of water were diverted to irrigate the surrounding desert, mainly for commercial cotton production. Heavy use of chemical pesticide ruined the groundwater below, causing a health crisis that some observers describe as an "ecological Chernobyl" (referring to the 1986 nuclear reactor meltdown in the Ukraine). In the meantime the Aral Sea began to dry up, and by the mid-1990s it had lost more than three-quarters of its total surface area (Fig. 13.10). In 2001, the Kazakhstan government, with a loan from the World Bank, began work to restore the lake. A dam was completed in 2005 and leaky irrigation canals have been fixed. As a result, the northern end of the lake is capturing more water from the Syr Darya River and the

## FIELD NOTE

"We drove north on Route 89 from Tucson, Arizona, across the desert. Drought rules the countryside here, and dams conserve what water there is. Snaking through the landscape are lifelines such as this, linking Coolidge Dam to distant farms and towns. In the vast, arid landscape, this narrow ribbon of water seems little more than an artificial brook—but to hundreds of thousands of people, this is what makes life possible in the Southwest."

© H. J. de Blij

■ **Figure 13.9**
**Tucson, Arizona.**

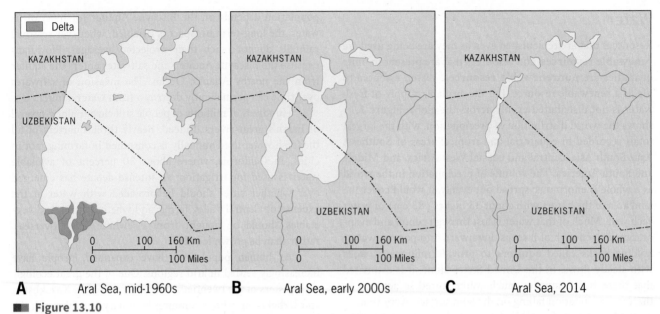

**Figure 13.10**

**The Aral Sea.** Affected by climatic cycles and afflicted by human interference, the Aral Sea on the border of Kazakhstan and Uzbekistan has shrunk. In a quarter of a century, it lost three-quarters of its surface area and more than 90 percent of its volume.    © E. H. Fouberg, A. B. Murphy, H. J. de Blij, and John Wiley & Sons, Inc.

fishing industry has rebounded slightly. But the general story is one or remarkable shrinkage.

The history of the Aral Sea highlights another aspect of the water story—the environmental concerns generated from damming rivers to generate hydroelectricity and capture water for rural and urban uses. In many of the wealthier parts of the world, dam building reached its peak in the middle of the twentieth century, and some dams are now slated for removal. But many dams are still being built in other parts of the world—along the Tigris and Euphrates, along the Mekong and its tributaries, along China's major rivers, and elsewhere. China's recently completed Three Gorges Dam, now the world's largest hydropower project, reduces the need to burn greenhouse-gas-producing coal, but its construction raised a host of concerns related to its impacts on forest cover, wildlife, sedimentation, and much more. And that dam is but one of many water-related projects in China. The geographical mismatch between population concentrations and available water is behind a decades-long project aimed at building a channel that can send water from the Yangtze River to the north. The project aims to meet the needs of a burgeoning urban population around Beijing and beyond, but the associated environmental alterations are tremendous.

School children are not typically taught to think about the geography of water—how varying precipitation and human uses of water affect its availability and quantity. Textbooks teach that water is a constant whose distribution is sustained through the **hydrologic cycle**, where water from oceans, lakes, soil, rivers, and vegetation evaporates, condenses, and then precipitates on landmasses. The precipitation infiltrates and recharges groundwater or runs off into lakes, rivers, and oceans. Physical geographer Jamie Linton questions the utility of any model of the water cycle that does not

take into account the role of humans and culture, suggesting that by "representing water as a constant, cyclical flow, the hydrologic cycle establishes a norm that is at odds with the hydrological reality of much of the world."

Linton argues that the hydrologic cycle does not take into account the norms of water in arid regions of the world, and it also assumes water cycles in a predictable, linear fashion. The amount of water cycling through is not a constant. For instance, land cover changes how much water is in the cycle. In the global south, Linton contends, forests "can actually promote evapotranspiration at rates much higher than for short crops," which has "the overall effect of *reducing* the quantity of water available for runoff or groundwater recharge."

Instead of the hydrologic cycle, Linton advocates thinking of water as a system rather than a cycle (Fig. 13.11). He defines the water system as the "integration of physical, biological, biogeochemical, and human components" of the global water system.

## WATER SECURITY

Throughout the world, people have come to depend on water sources with an uncertain future. Rocky Mountain and Sierra Nevada snows feed the Colorado River and the aquifers that irrigate the California Central Valley. Aqueducts snake their way across the desert to urban communities. None of this has slowed the population's move to the Sun Belt, and the water situation there is becoming problematic. In coastal eastern Spain, low water pressure in city pipes sometimes deprives the upper floors of high-rise buildings of water. In Southwest Asia and the Arabian Peninsula, growing populations strain ancient water supply systems, and desalinization plants that convert saltwater to fresh water are a necessity.

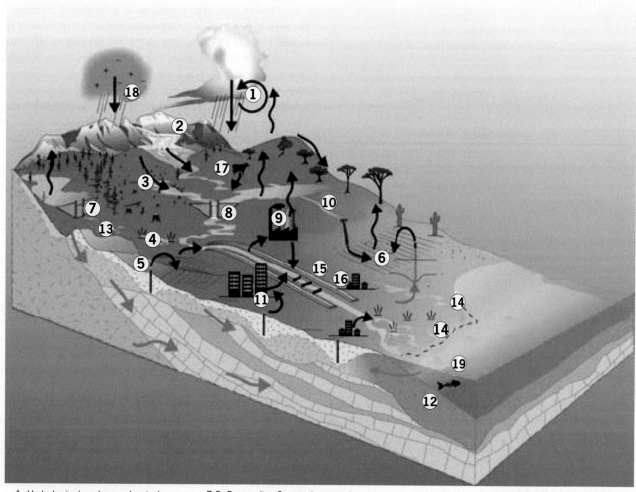

1. Hydrological cycle accelerated
2. Mountain snow and ice lost
3. Tree removal increases runoff, reduces transpiration, affects water table and landscape salinity
4. Wetlands dried up or drained
5,6. Ground- and surface water used for irrigated agriculture

7,8. Dams alter flow and reservoirs increase evaporation
9. Industrial water coolers release water vapor
10. Water transfers between basins
11. Urban, mining, and construction areas alter water flows and quality
12. Coastal saltwater intrudes inland

13. Impoundments reduce flows
14. Siltation, erosion, and nutrient flows change coastlines and affect water quality
15. Levees and locks modify flows and channels
16. Settlements alter floodplain landscapes
17. Grazing affects runoff and water quality
18. Industry causes acid rain
19. Coastal waters polluted and species lost

■■ **Figure 13.11**

**The Global Water System.** The human imprint is reflected in this diagram of the global water system. *Reproduced with permission from:* American Geophysical Union.

Water also plays a role in regional conflicts in places such as the Darfur region of Sudan. Consider, for example, the situation of Israel and its neighbors. With 8.1 million people, Israel annually consumes nearly three times as much water as Jordan, the West Bank Palestinian areas, and Gaza combined (total population: 11.7 million). As much as half of Israel's water comes from sources outside the Israeli state.

The key sources of water for the entire area are the Jordan River and an aquifer beneath the West Bank. When Israel captured the Golan Heights from Syria and the West Bank from Jordan during the 1967 war, it gained control over both of these sources, including the Jordan River's important tributary, the Yarmuk (Fig. 13.12). As the map shows, the Sea of Galilee forms a large fresh water reservoir in the Jordan River Valley. This is the source of the majority of Israel's water, though desalinization of sea water is increasingly important.

The water situation has the potential to further complicate relations between Israel and its neighbors. The aquifer

**Figure 13.12**
**Key Water Resources in the Middle East.** Here, as in many other places, meeting the needs of different populations for water requires cooperation among peoples and governments. © E. H. Fouberg, A. B. Murphy, H. J. de Blij, and John Wiley & Sons, Inc.

beneath the West Bank yields about 625 million cubic meters (22,071 cubic feet) of water through hundreds of wells linked together by a system of pipelines. Of this total, some 450 million cubic meters go directly to Israel; another 35 million are consumed by Israeli settlers on the West Bank, and only some 140 million are allotted to the West Bank's nearly 2 million Arabs. This is unfair, say the Palestinian Arabs: If the West Bank is to become an independent Palestinian territory, the water below the surface should belong to the Palestinians. But the Israeli cities of Tel Aviv and Jerusalem depend heavily on water from the West Bank, and Israel cannot survive without this source.

There are, however, signs of cooperation over water in the region. In late 2013 Israel, the Palestinian Authority, and Jordan signed an agreement to build the Red Sea–Dead Sea project (Fig. 13.12). A major desalinization plant will convert saltwater from the Red Sea into potable water that will be moved by pipeline to the north, and the briny runoff will be piped through Jordan to the Dead Sea to combat its rapid contraction. Israel and Jordan hope to gain between 8 and 13 billion gallons of water. Israel will also provide Amman with 8–13 billion gallons of fresh water from the Sea of Galilee, and the Palestinians can buy up to 8 billion gallons of

additional water from Israel at "preferential prices." The plan has been in the works for 20 years; it is hailed as a rare success in a region riven by conflict.

Nonetheless, water remains a geopolitical concern in the region. Israel might contemplate the return of most of the Golan Heights to Syria, but about 30 percent of all water reaching the Sea of Galilee comes from the Golan Heights. Israel might support the establishment of an independent state in the West Bank, but approximately 30 percent of Israel's water supply comes from the West Bank aquifer. Any effort to negotiate a lasting peace in the region will have to take these geographical circumstances into account.

## Atmosphere

Earth's **atmosphere** is a thin layer of air lying directly above the lands and oceans. We depend on the atmosphere for our survival: We breathe its oxygen; it shields us from the destructive rays of the sun; it moderates temperatures; and it carries moisture from the oceans over the land, sustaining crops and forests and replenishing soils and wells.

Scientists are concerned that human pollution of the atmosphere will result in long-lasting, possibly permanent damage. True, the air disperses even the densest smoke and most acrid chemical gases. However, anthropogenic sources of pollution from two centuries of industrial expansion are pouring into the atmosphere at an unprecedented rate. While the United States remains the world's largest per capita leader in terms of pollutants generated, China has overtaken the United States in total volume, India's share is rising rapidly, and other growing economies are compounding a problem that can only be solved by determined international action. Yet different national priorities, and the unequal distribution of contributors to the problem and beneficiaries of action, have worked against serious coordinated action.

### CLIMATE CHANGE

Growing populations and increased human activity, ranging from the burning of tropical forests to pollution of the atmosphere by industry and automobiles, are having an unprecedented impact on the atmosphere. The amounts of key "greenhouse" gases, carbon dioxide ($CO_2$), methane, and nitrous oxides in the atmosphere have been increasing at a rate of about 2 percent per decade; automobiles, steel mills, refineries, and chemical plants account for a large part of this increase. A simple experiment in a college chemistry lab shows that an increase in the level of $CO_2$ in the atmosphere traps more heat. Hence, it is not surprising that an overwhelming majority of climate scientists have concluded that *tropospheric* pollution from anthropogenic (human) sources is causing the Earth to retain increasing amounts of heat, with effects that will increase during the course of the twenty-first century and beyond.

While estimates of the degree of human-induced **climate change** differ, climate records from recent decades show that global temperatures are rising, which is why climate change is sometimes called global warming. Climate change is a more accurate term, however, because while the global temperature is rising, the outcome will vary greatly across regions of the world.

Sea-level rise is one aspect of climate change. While the rise in global temperatures will undoubtedly be interrupted by occasional spurts of cooling, computer models predict that warmer temperatures will melt polar and glacial ice and sea levels will rise as much as 50 centimeters or more during the twenty-first century. Certain calculations project an even greater sea-level rise. Low-lying islands in the Indian Ocean and the South Pacific have already disappeared beneath the waves. Alarmed government leaders in low-lying Pacific and Indian Ocean island nations talk of buying higher ground in other countries and of suing the governments of polluting states over lost real estate.

Changes in climate involve alterations in the amount of water vapor in the atmosphere, which affects patterns of precipitation. Changes in precipitation affect where certain types of vegetation can grow, altering everything from agricultural patterns to the location of animal habitats. Predicting exactly where, and in what magnitude, these changes will occur is difficult. What is clear is that those living on the margins of sustainability are facing even riskier futures.

Atmospheric scientists are investigating the relationship between current changes in the climate and extreme weather events. If you follow the news, you have read headlines from around the world about cold snaps that are the worst in the century, floods the highest in memory, and droughts the longest on record. Although the science is not completely settled, there is growing evidence of a link between warming global temperatures and the intensification of regional weather systems.

## ACID RAIN

A by-product of the enormous volume of pollutants spewed into the atmosphere is **acid rain**. Acid rain forms when sulfur dioxide and nitrogen oxides are released into the atmosphere by the burning of fossil fuels (coal, oil, and natural gas). These pollutants combine with water vapor in the air to form dilute solutions of sulfuric and nitric acids, which then are washed out of the atmosphere by rain or other types of precipitation, such as fog and snow.

Although acid rain usually consists of relatively mild acids, it can be caustic enough to harm certain natural ecosystems (the mutual interactions between groups of plant and animal organisms and their environment). Acid rain has acidified lakes and streams (with resultant fish kills), stunted growth of forests, and damaged crops in affected areas. In cities it has accelerated corrosion of buildings and monuments.

Areas affected by acid rain are generally downwind from industrial concentrations. In the United States and western Europe, compliance with legislated emission reductions is having positive results. In Canada as well as in Scandinavia, where acid rain from neighboring industrial regions damaged forests and acidified lakes, recovery came faster than most scientists

had predicted. This evidence is now encouraging other countries to impose stricter controls on factory emissions.

## The Land

Over the centuries, human population growth has put increasing pressure on land surfaces. More land is cleared and placed under cultivation, trees are cut down, and cities expand. The effects can be seen almost everywhere and are so extensive that it is often difficult even to reconstruct what an area might be like in the absence of humans. The human impact on Earth's land surface has several key aspects, the most significant of which are deforestation, soil erosion, waste disposal, and biodiversity loss.

### DEFORESTATION

Forests cover 31 percent of the total surface of the Earth from the tropical Amazon Basin to high-latitude North America and Eurasia. The world's forests, especially those of lower and middle latitudes, play a critical role in the **oxygen cycle**. Atmospheric oxygen is consumed by natural processes as well as by human activities. Forests counteract this loss through photosynthesis and related processes, which release oxygen into the atmosphere. The destruction of vast tracts of forest is called **deforestation**. Ecologists and others warn of unforeseeable and incalculable impacts not only for the affected areas but for the planet as a whole.

In the early 1980s, the Food and Agriculture Organization (FAO) of the United Nations undertook a study of the rate at which forests were being depleted. This analysis showed that 44 percent of the tropical rainforest had already been affected by cutting and that more than 1 percent was being logged every year (Fig. 13.13). A 2014 report revealed that Indonesia lost more than 6 million hectares of primary forest between 2000 and 2012.

In 2014, the FAO released its annual report on the world's forests with good news: The rate of deforestation worldwide declined in the last decade. According to the FAO, during the 1990s humans deforested 16 million hectares a year, mostly by converting tropical rainforests to agriculture land. Between 2000 and 2010, humans deforested 13 million hectares a year. Lower deforestation rates have been coupled with tree planting programs, especially in Brazil. As a result, the "net loss of forests was 5.2 million hectares per year between 2000 and 2010, down from 8.3 million hectares annually in the 1990s."

Deforestation is not a singular process: It has been going on for centuries, and the motivations for deforestation vary vastly. Forests are cut and reforested for wood and paper products; forests are preserved for the maintenance of biodiversity; and other forests are cleared for new agricultural production. The 2014 FAO report suggests that some 1.25 billion people depend on forest resources for their livelihood and argues that local economies need to do a better job at balancing resource extraction and conservation.

The reforestation (and harvesting) of deforested areas is not the whole answer to the problem, even if it could be done

# FIELD NOTE

"This was one of the most depressing days of this long South American field trip. We had been briefed and had seen the satellite pictures of the destruction of the rainforest, with ugly gashes of bare ground pointing like rows of arrows into the woods. But walking to the temporary end points of some of these new roads made a lot more impact. From the remaining forest around came the calls of monkeys and other wildlife, their habitat retreating under the human onslaught. Next week this road would push ahead another mile, the logs carted away and burned, the first steps in a process that would clear this land, ending billions of years of nature's dominance."

**Figure 13.13**
Para, Brazil.

on a large scale. Forests in the United States, for example, consist mainly of second-growth trees, which replaced the original forest after it was logged. However, the controlled second-growth forest does not (as the natural forest did) have many trees dying of old age after their trunks and limbs become soft from rot. As a result, many animal species that depend on holes in trunks and hollows in tree limbs cannot find places to nest (thus, the spotted owl dispute in the Pacific Northwest of the United States). For them the forest has ceased to be a favorable habitat. Moreover, reforested areas generally do not have the type of rich understory layer that can store substantial amounts of water and provide more organic input to the soil.

## SOIL EROSION

Soil erosion is caused by a variety of factors: Livestock are allowed to graze in areas where they destroy the natural vegetation; lands too dry to sustain farming are plowed, and wind erosion follows. Soil is a renewable resource because, with proper care, it can recover. However, it is being "mined" as if it were a nonrenewable resource.

The loss of potentially productive soil to erosion has been described as a "quiet crisis" of global proportions. Ecologists Lester Brown and Edward Wolf point out that the increasing rate of this loss over the past generation is not the result of a decline in the skills of farmers but rather of the pressures on farmers to produce more. In an integrated world food economy, the pressures on land resources are not confined to particular countries; they permeate the entire world.

Why has **soil erosion** increased so much? Part of the answer lies in population pressure: World population is over 7 billion. Associated with population growth is the cultivation of ever-steeper slopes, with hastily constructed terraces

or without any terraces at all (Fig. 13.14). As the pressure on land increases, farmers are less able to leave part of their soil fallow (unused) to allow it to recover its nutrients. Another part of the answer lies in rising levels of consumption accompanying industrialization and development (see below). As socioeconomic circumstances improve and people become more interconnected with the global economy, diets change and the demand for specialty items increases. Those changes in turn increase the pressure to farm marginal areas and to create large, monocropped factory farms that are less conservative of the soil than their small, multi-cropped counterparts.

Given that 99.7 percent of all human food is grown in soil (some is grown in water), the annual toll that soil erosion takes on the cropland available for agriculture is concerning. The dimensions of the problem are suggested by a 2006 study, which reported that globally about 37,000 square miles (10 million ha) of cropland are lost to soil erosion each year. An even more recent study suggests that soil is being lost at between 10 and 40 times natural replacement levels. International cooperation in food distribution, education of farmers and governments, and worldwide dissemination of soil conservation methods are urgently needed to address this "quiet crisis."

## WASTE DISPOSAL

If anything has grown faster than population itself, it is the waste generated by households, communities, and industries—much of it a matter of bulk, some of it a source of danger.

There is a strong correlation between level of socioeconomic well-being and solid waste production. The United States is one of the largest producers of **solid waste**, debris, and garbage discarded by those living in cities, industries, mines, and farms. According to current estimates, the United States produces about 4.5 pounds (2 kg) of solid waste per person per day, which adds up to more than 250 million tons (226 million metric tons) per year. But the United States is not alone. Other high-technology economies with a high ratio of disposable materials (containers, packaging) face the same problems.

Disposal of these wastes is a major worldwide problem. The growing volume of waste must be put somewhere, but space for it is no longer easy to find. In poorer countries, waste is often thrown onto open dumps where vermin multiply, decomposition sends methane gas into the air, rain and waste liquids carry contaminants into the groundwater below, and fires pollute the surrounding atmosphere. In countries that can afford it, such open dumps have been replaced by **sanitary landfills**. The waste is put in a hole that has been dug and prepared for the purpose, including a floor of materials to treat seeping liquids and soil to cover each load as it is compacted and deposited in the fill.

The number of suitable sites for sanitary landfills is decreasing, however, and it is increasingly difficult to design new sites. In the United States landfill capacity has been reached or will soon be reached in about a dozen States, most of them in the Northeast and Mid-Atlantic regions, and those States must now buy space from other States for this purpose. Trucking or sending garbage by rail to distant landfills is very expensive, but there are few alternatives.

Similar problems are evident on a global scale. The United States, the European Union, and Japan export solid (including hazardous) wastes to countries in Africa, Middle and South America, and East Asia. While these countries are paid for accepting the waste, they do not always have the capacity to treat it properly. So the waste often is dumped in open landfills, where it creates the very hazards that the exporters want to avoid. In the late 1980s, the wealthier countries' practice of "managing" waste by exporting it became a controversial issue, and in 1989 a treaty was drawn up to control it. The treaty did not (as many poorer countries wished) prohibit the exporting of hazardous waste, although it did place some restrictions on trade in hazardous materials.

It is useful to draw a distinction between **toxic wastes**, which are dangerous because of chemicals, infectious materials, and the like, and **radioactive wastes**, which are of two types: low-level radioactive wastes, which give off small amounts of radiation and are produced by industry, hospitals, research facilities, and nuclear power plants; and high-level radioactive wastes, which emit strong radiation and are produced by nuclear power plants and nuclear weapons factories.

© H. J. de Blij

■ **Figure 13.14**

**Guangxi-Zhuang, China.**    Overuse of land in this area of China has led to the collapse of formerly sound terracing systems.

In the United States, low-level radioactive wastes have for many years been disposed of in steel drums placed in six special government-run landfills, three of which are now closed.

High-level radioactive waste is extremely dangerous and difficult to get rid of. Fuel rods from nuclear reactors will remain radioactive for thousands of years and must be stored in remote places where they will not contaminate water, air, or any other part of the environment. In fact, no satisfactory means or place for the disposal of high-level radioactive waste has been found. Among many suggested disposal sites are deep shafts in the bedrock, chambers dug in salt deposits (salt effectively blocks radiation), ice chambers in Antarctica, sediments beneath the ocean floor, and volcanically active midocean trenches. Meanwhile, spent fuel rods (which last only about three years in the reactor) are put in specially designed drums and stored in one of about 100 sites, all of them potentially dangerous.

There is a related problem: transportation of waste. Even if secure and safe storage can be found for high-level radioactive waste, the waste has to be transported from its source to the disposal site. Such transportation presents an additional hazard: a truck or train accident could have disastrous consequences.

The dimensions of the waste-disposal problem are growing and globalizing. The threat to the planet's environment is not just over the short term but can exist for centuries, indeed millennia.

## Biodiversity

A significant change that is related to all of the developments discussed so far is the accelerating loss of **biodiversity**. An abbreviation of "biological diversity," biodiversity refers to the diversity of all aspects of life found on Earth. Although the term is commonly used when referring to the diversity of species, it encompasses the entire range of biological diversity, from the genetic variability within individuals of a species to the diversity of ecosystems on the planet.

Species are becoming extinct at a rapid rate. It is difficult to say exactly how quickly extinctions are occurring, since we do not know how many species there are. What is clear, however, is that although extinction is a natural process, humans have dramatically increased rates of extinction, particularly over the last few hundred years. Estimates from the United Nations Environment Program's Global Biodiversity Assessment indicate that 8 percent of plants, 5 percent of fish, 11 percent of birds, and 18 percent of the world's mammal species are currently threatened.

Whether a species is threatened with extinction depends on the range of the species, its scarcity, and its geographic concentration. If a species with a small range, a high degree of scarcity, and a small geographic concentration has its habitat threatened, extinction can follow. Because most species have small ranges, change in a limited area can affect a species. A 2005 report in *Scientific American* explained that "clearing a forest, draining a wetland, damming a river or dynamiting a coral reef to kill its fish can more readily eliminate species with small ranges than more widespread species."

Human impacts on biodiversity have increased over time. The domestication of animals, followed by the agricultural domestication of plant life, caused significant alterations in our relationship with other species. Large vertebrates have always been particularly hard hit by human activities. Many birds and mammals have been hunted not only for food but also for their skins, feathers, and so forth. During the eighteenth and nineteenth centuries, beaver populations in North America were drastically reduced as the beavers were trapped and skinned for their pelts. Many bird species were hunted for their feathers, which were sold to decorate fashionable hats. Worldwide, elephants and walruses continue to be hunted for their ivory tusks. From historical records we know that over 650 species of plants and over 480 animal species have become extinct in just the last 400 years. These represent only the documented extinctions. The actual number of extinctions that occurred during this period is almost certainly much higher.

Humans have also indirectly contributed to extinctions. Human travel, for instance, introduced new species to areas around the globe. Rats are among the more destructive of these; they have had devastating effects on oceanic islands. Introduced species may cause extinctions by preying upon native species or competing with them for resources. A famous example is the dodo bird (*Raphus cuculatus*), which was hunted to extinction by humans, dogs, and rats on the island of Mauritius. Introduced species may also carry new diseases, leading to the decimation and extinction of local populations. Species on islands are particularly susceptible to extinction because of the more insular ecosystems found on

islands. An estimated 2000 species of birds on tropical Pacific islands became extinct following human settlement.

Identifying the nature and extent of environmental changes is only a first step toward understanding the extent of human alteration of the planet. A second, and more complicated step is to consider the forces driving these changes.

What is the greatest environmental concern facing the region where you live, and in what other regions of the world is that concern also present? How do differences between your region and the other regions sharing the concern influence how it is understood and approached?

## WHAT ARE THE MAJOR FACTORS CONTRIBUTING TO ENVIRONMENTAL CHANGE TODAY?

Environmental change occurs at all levels of scale, from local to global. For example, deforestation has local effects by reducing the diversity of species even in a small area. It has regional consequences by increasing sediment runoff into streams and rivers. And, globally, it results in the increased release of carbon dioxide in the atmosphere, which affects the planetary climate.

Several interrelated factors influence the escalating impact of human activities on the natural environment. The past two centuries have witnessed dramatic growth in the human population, a fourfold increase (from about 1.5 billion to 6 billion) in the twentieth century alone. Per capita consumption of virtually everything, from water and farm products to metals and energy resources, has increased rapidly as well. Fast-developing technologies allow us to alter the natural environment ever more. Each of these interrelated factors that contribute to environmental change can be studied broadly, focusing on the general impacts of each factor on the global environment. Yet, when we shift scales to the local and regional, and we consider the context of human actions at these scales, we often find that the causes of environmental change vary depending on the local and regional context.

### Political Ecology

Leslie Gray and William Moseley describe the field of political ecology, which traces its roots to the 1960s and 1970s, as a way of considering the roles of "political economy, power and history in shaping human–environmental interactions." Political ecologists are interested in how environmental issues such as deforestation are affected by the ways in which political, economic, social, and ecological circumstances play out in individual places. As such, they focus attention on the spatial coalescence of processes operating at different scales on Earth's surface.

# GUEST FIELD NOTE

## Try, Mali

In this photo, a young man brings home the cotton harvest in the village of Try in southern Mali. Prior to my graduate studies in geography, I spent a number of years as an international development worker concerned with tropical agriculture—both on the ground in Africa and as a policy wonk in Washington, D.C. I drew at least two important lessons from these experiences. First, well-intentioned work at the grassroots level would always be limited if it were not supported by broader scale policies and economics. Second, the people making the policies were often out of touch with the real impacts their decisions were having in the field. As such, geography, and the subfield of political ecology, were appealing to me because of its explicit attention to processes operating at multiple scales, its tradition of fieldwork, and its longstanding attention to human–environment interactions. I employed a political ecology approach during fieldwork for my dissertation in 1999–2000. Here, I sought to test the notion that poor farmers are more likely to degrade soils than their wealthier counterparts (a concept widely proclaimed in the development policy literature of the 1990s). Not only did I interview rich and poor farmers about their management practices, but I tested their soils and questioned policymakers at the provincial, national, and international levels. My findings (and those of others) have led to a questioning of the poverty–environmental degradation paradigm.

*Credit: William Moseley, Macalester College.*

William Moseley, Macalester College

■■ **Figure 13.15**
**Try, Mali.**

Moseley, for example, has studied the conservation behaviors of farmers in southern Mali (Fig. 13.15). His research directly highlighted a fundamental fallacy in the widely held view that poorer people degrade the land more than wealthier people. Through extensive fieldwork, interviews, and soil surveys, Moseley found that poorer farmers in southern Mali were more likely to use organic materials to preserve topsoil, whereas wealthier farmers were more likely to use inorganic fertilizers and pesticides. The explanation for this outcome lies in the policies and power relationships at play in southern Mali. The government of Mali's agricultural extension service singled out the wealthiest households for cotton farming, which "helped these households become even wealthier in the short term." And the farmers, who (unlike their poorer counterparts) were able to afford inorganic fertilizers, turned to their use in the face of an increasingly competitive global market. Recognizing these points requires looking at the intersection of multi-scale political and economic influences on southern Mali.

## Population

Because humans across the world do not consume or pollute in exactly the same ways, we cannot make a simple chart showing that each additional human born on Earth results in a certain amount of consumption or generates a certain amount of pollution. Of course, all humans affect the environment, and a greater number of people on Earth necessarily translates into a greater capacity for environmental change, but the impacts of people in some places are much greater than those in other places.

Similarly, environmental change influences humans differently, depending in part on who they are and where they live. To underscore the spatial differences in environmental impact on humans, we can consider two maps of natural disaster hot spots published by the Earth Institute at Columbia University and the World Bank in a 2005 report. The maps highlight the places in the world most susceptible to natural disasters, whether caused by drought, tectonic activity (earthquakes and volcanoes), or hydrological hazards (floods, cyclones, and landslides) (Fig. 13.16). Comparing the map of

## MORTALITY RISKS

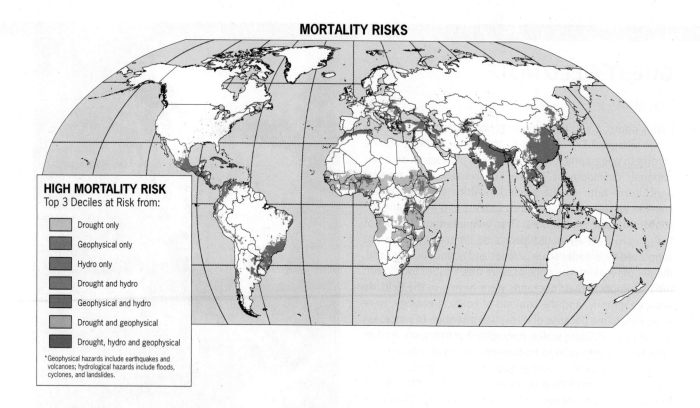

**HIGH MORTALITY RISK**
Top 3 Deciles at Risk from:

- Drought only
- Geophysical only
- Hydro only
- Drought and hydro
- Geophysical and hydro
- Drought and geophysical
- Drought, hydro and geophysical

*Geophysical hazards include earthquakes and volcanoes; hydrological hazards include floods, cyclones, and landslides.

## ECONOMIC LOSS RISKS

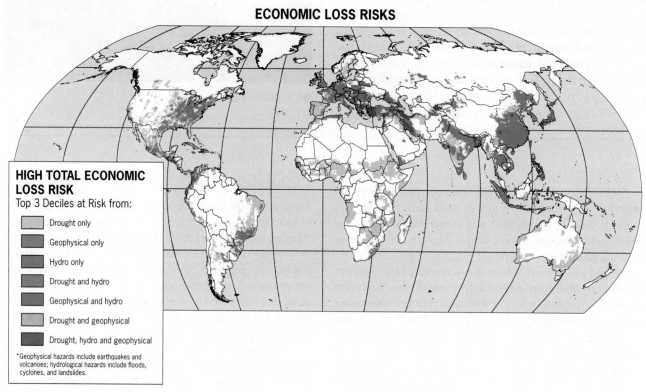

**HIGH TOTAL ECONOMIC LOSS RISK**
Top 3 Deciles at Risk from:

- Drought only
- Geophysical only
- Hydro only
- Drought and hydro
- Geophysical and hydro
- Drought and geophysical
- Drought, hydro and geophysical

*Geophysical hazards include earthquakes and volcanoes; hydrological hazards include floods, cyclones, and landslides.

■■ **Figure 13.16**

**Natural Disaster Hot Spots.**    The top map shows the potential mortality risks if major natural disasters occur in global natural disaster hot spots, and the bottom map shows the potential economic risks if major natural disasters occur in natural disaster hot spots.    *Courtesy of*: Center for Hazards and Risk Research at Columbia University and the World Bank, "Natural Disaster Hotspots—A Global Risk Analysis," March 29, 2005.

mortality risk with the map of total economic loss risk demonstrates that when a natural disaster hits a wealthier area, the place will more likely be hit financially, whereas in a poorer area of the world, the place will likely be hit by both financial loss and the loss of lives. Thus, when a devastating earthquake hit the Kobe region in Japan in 1995, there was enormous property damage, but fewer than 6500 people died. By contrast, when an earthquake of a similar magnitude struck Haiti in 2010, well over 100,000 people lost their lives.

## Patterns of Consumption

We humans rely on Earth's resources for our very survival. At the most basic level, we consume water, oxygen, and organic and mineral materials. Over time we have developed increasingly complex ways of using resources in pursuit of agricultural intensification and industrial production. Consequently, many societies now consume resources at a level and rate that far exceed basic subsistence needs. In a 1996 article on "Humanity's Resources" in *The Companion Encyclopedia of Geography: The Environment and Humankind*, I. G. Simmons notes that a hunter–gatherer subsisted, on average, on the resources found within an area of about 26 square kilometers (10 square miles). Today many people living in urban centers in the global economic core draw on resources scattered all over the planet.

The wealthier countries account for only a modest fraction of the human population (Chapter 2), but they make far greater demands on Earth's resources than do their counterparts in poorer countries. It has been estimated that a baby born in the United States during the first decade of the twenty-first century, at current rates, consumes about 250 times as much energy over a lifetime as a baby born in Bangladesh over the same lifetime. In terms of food, housing and its components, metals, paper (and thus trees), and many other materials, the consumption of individuals in affluent countries far exceeds that of people in poorer countries. Rapid population growth in poorer parts of the world tends to have local or regional environmental impacts, but expanding resource consumption in wealthier regions has greater global environmental consequences.

The foregoing discussion underscores the importance of thinking geographically about human impacts on the natural world. People living in the global economic periphery tend to affect their immediate environment, putting pressure on soil, natural vegetation, and water supplies, and polluting the local air with the smoke from their fires. The reach of affluent societies is much greater. The demand for low-cost meat for hamburgers in the United States has led to deforestation in Central and South America to make way for pastures and cattle herds. In the process, water demand has increased in such areas (Table 13.1). This example shows just one of the many ways in which the American (and European, Japanese, and Australian) consumer has an impact on distant environments.

The industrialized core has access to a vast array of transportation and communication technologies that allow

**TABLE 13.1**

**Estimated Liters of Water Required to Produce 1 Kilogram of Food.**

| ESTIMATED LITERS OF WATER REQUIRED TO PRODUCE 1 KILOGRAM OF FOOD | |
|---|---|
| **Food** | **Liters** |
| Chocolate | 17,196 |
| Beef | 15,415 |
| Chicken meat | 4,325 |
| Rice | 2,497 |
| Bread | 1,608 |
| Potatoes | 287 |

advertisers to stimulate demand for particular goods around the world and allow manufacturers to bring goods from distant places. The growing wealth over the last two decades in the semiperiphery, especially in India and China, has significantly increased the overall global consumption of consumer goods. The story of the Indian company Tata (which we described at the beginning of Chapter 4), however, illustrates the complexities of meeting growing demand. In 2008 Tata created the Nano, an automobile for the Indian market that was priced below $2500. Tata ramped up plans to produce 250,000 of the "people's car" a year. The Nano did not sell well, however; India's rising middle class wanted low-cost cars but not cars that appeared cheap. Tata initially spent $400 million to develop the vehicle, but it was then forced to spend considerably more to revamp it to meet the increasingly sophisticated tastes of Indian consumers.

As global consumption of consumer goods increases, the market for luxury goods has similarly expanded as more people around the world move into middle-class lifestyles. There is a rapidly growing market for luxury-brand leather handbags (Coach, Louis Vuitton, Gucci, and Chanel), particularly in Asia where American and European high-end brands are popular (and can be more affordable than a designer wardrobe). Japan and Hong Kong have the greatest market share of luxury-brand handbags in the region, and Chinese tourists account for a significant percentage of the designer bags purchased in the United States. In Hong Kong, a local money lender even allows women to hand over their designer bags as collateral to receive loans of up to 80 percent of the bag's value (though the lender only accepts four high-end brands!).

Beyond such stories is a more general growth in demand for natural resources in rapidly developing countries. China provides the most striking example. As recently as the 1980s, China's GDP was smaller than Spain's. Over the past few decades, however, the Chinese economy has surged forward. In 2010 it surpassed Japan to become the world's second largest economy, and in 2013 it became the world's second-biggest consumer country.

Overall consumer spending in the United States still significantly outpaces that in China, but China is gaining ground, and because of the size of its population, China surpasses the United States as a consumer in some areas. In 2010 China became the world's biggest consumer of energy, and it has led the world in the consumption of coal for many years. China has also emerged as one of the world's leading consumers of a wide variety of raw materials, from logs to iron ore to grains.

To meet the growing demand for natural resources, China has greatly expanded its overseas investments. From Africa to South America to other parts of Asia, Chinese firms are increasingly in evidence—extracting resources and shipping them back home. In the process, China's role in consumption-related environmental change now rivals that of the United States and the European Union. China's new international economic clout also carries with it predictable social consequences. In some places, Chinese investment is seen as a boost to the local economy and is welcomed. But there is growing concern that China is acting as a neo-colonial power, altering environmental and social systems while returning relatively little to the local economy.

## Industrial Technology

Technological advances have increased rapidly since the Industrial Revolution and today affect all aspects of our lives. We are continually developing technologies that we hope will improve our standard of living, protect us against disease, and allow us to work more efficiently. But these technologies come at a cost. Resource extraction practices such as mining and logging, which provide the materials to produce technologies, have created severe environmental problems. Technological innovations have produced hazardous and toxic by-products, creating pollution and health problems that we are only now beginning to recognize. In short, technology has enabled humans to alter large portions of the planet in a short period of time.

There are many dramatic examples of the role of industrial technology in environmental change. The impacts include degradation of the oceans (oil and gas exploitation and spills, pollution dumping, and massive overfishing), land surfaces (open pit and mountain top mining, dams, and irrigation projects), the biosphere (deforestation, vegetation loss), and the atmosphere (air pollution).

As the first parts of the planet to industrialize, western Europe and North America long led the world in industrial-related pollution. Now attention is turning to rapidly industrializing countries such as China, where the 2008 Beijing Olympics opened the world's eyes to the incredibly high emissions level in that country (Fig. 13.17).

According to the World Health Organization (WHO), anything over 10 micrograms per cubic meter of pollutant particles in the atmosphere represents a threat to human health. The most polluted city in the United States, Bakersfield, California, has days of 18.2 micrograms per cubic meter. By contrast, the ten most heavily polluted Chinese cities regularly see numbers above 100 and 150, and sometimes even above 250 micrograms per cubic meter—well beyond the limit of what the WHO considers "hazardous" air quality. The most polluted hour ever recorded was in Beijing between 11:00 P.M. and midnight on January 23, 2008. Extensive fireworks from Lunar New Year celebrations caused the already high pollution levels to rise to a frightening 994 micrograms per cubic meter.

These sustained levels of pollution, with smog so thick that it can be seen from space on the worst days, are raising alarm in China and beyond. In April 2014, China's national legislature made sweeping reforms to the country's environmental protection law, a sign the country is starting to take environmental issues more seriously.

## Transportation

Changing modes of transportation are a product of some of the most important technological advances in human history. Each innovation in transportation has required increased resource use, not only to make the vehicles that move people and goods, but also to build and maintain the related infrastructure—roads, railroad tracks, airports, parking structures, repair facilities, and the like. With each innovation the impacts

David G. McIntyre/epa/© Corbis

■■ **Figure 13.17**

**Beijing, China.**   Smog covers the traffic on a motorway in the central business district of Beijing just a few months before the opening of the 2008 Olympics in Beijing.

seem to widen. As David Headrick points out in a study discussed in the *Companion Encyclopedia of Geography*, Chicago's O'Hare Airport covers a larger area (approximately 28 square kilometers or 17 square miles) than Chicago's central business district (which covers approximately 8 square kilometers or 5 square miles). Moreover, transportation innovations offer access to remote areas of the planet. There are vehicles that allow people to travel through extreme climates, to the bottoms of the ocean, and across the polar ice caps. These places, in turn, have been altered by human activity.

Transportation is also implicated in global environmental change—albeit sometimes indirectly. Advances in transportation have produced significant pollution, as seen in the extent of oil spills along major shipping lanes (Fig. 13.18).

Transportation facilitates the types of global networks necessary to sustain the patterns of consumption outlined earlier. Many of the products available in stores—be they electronics or clothing or food—come from distant places. Resources are required to produce and ship them, and except those that meet basic subsistence needs, they all contribute to the greater strains placed on the environment that come from those living in wealthier parts of the world. This realization has led some individuals to reduce their levels of consumption or to consume more environmentally friendly, locally produced products. These changes have had some effect, but so far their impact on the geography of global consumption has been marginal.

## Energy

Consumption of material goods is closely linked to the consumption of energy. It takes energy to produce material goods, energy to deliver them to markets, and, for many products (such as appliances and automobiles), energy to keep them running. The resulting demands for energy are a factor in environmental change. Much of our energy supply comes from nonrenewable fossil fuels, such as coal, oil, and natural gas. Moreover, the evolution of tertiary, quaternary, and quinary economic activities has led to an increase in the consumption of nonrenewable resources. As populations grow, so does the demand for energy, and we can expect that over the coming decades energy production will expand to meet the increased demand. In developing countries in particular, demands for more energy are largely met by the burning of fossil fuels. This helps explain why, according to the United States Energy Information Administration (EIA), global oil production increased from 45.89 million barrels per day in 1970 to 90.1 million barrels per day in 2013.

Oil is a finite resource. It is not a question of *if* the world's oil supply will run out but *when*. Because discoveries of new reserves continue to be made, and because the extraction of fossil fuels is becoming ever more efficient, it is difficult to predict exactly how much longer oil will remain a viable energy source. Many suggest that the current level of oil consumption can be sustained for up to 100 years, although some argue for much shorter or much longer time frames. Despite the range of opinion, the majority of scientists believe that by the middle of this century alternative sources will have to play a much more significant role than they do now.

In recent decades, natural gas has emerged as an increasingly common alternative to oil. Natural gas can be extracted from the oil-refinement process, but major subsurface reservoirs of natural gas also exist, and they are being increasingly

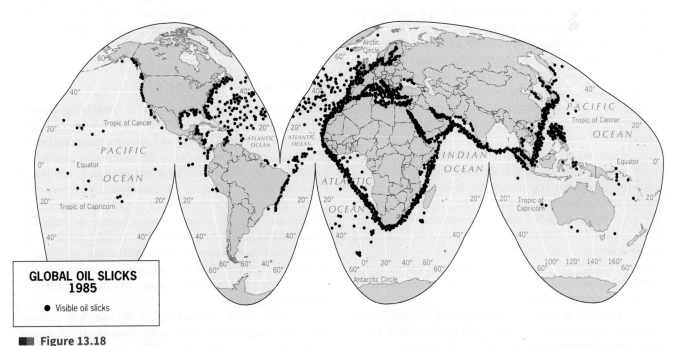

**GLOBAL OIL SLICKS
1985**

● Visible oil slicks

■ **Figure 13.18**

**Locations of Visible Oil Slicks.**   Oil slicks are a problem around the globe. This map was created in the 1980s, but the overall pattern has not greatly changed since then.   *Adapted with permission from*: Organization for Economic Co-operation and Development, *The State of the Environment*, 1985, p. 76.

tapped. Like oil, natural gas is a greenhouse gas, but it burns somewhat more cleanly. Natural gas is becoming increasingly common in energy production, and natural gas vehicles are even coming into wider use, particularly in Iran, Pakistan, Argentina, Brazil, India, and China.

Despite its advantages, natural gas is difficult to store and transport. To address this problem, scientists have figured out how to create liquefied natural gas (LNG), which is achieved by condensing natural gas at a very low temperature. The process is expensive, and LNG is highly flammable, but South Korea, Taiwan, and several European countries now import large volumes of LNG, and Japan turned to LNG after shutting down its nuclear power plants in the wake of the Fukushima nuclear power plant disaster. With countries ranging from Australia to Argentina to Qatar ramping up production, LNG's significance is growing.

In recent years, technological advances have also made it possible to access hard-to-reach pockets of natural gas trapped in shale. Rising energy prices have made it economical to use a costly technique called hydraulic fracturing, or fracking, to reach these pockets. Fracking operations inject a high-pressure fluid (typically water mixed with sand and chemicals) into deep-rock formations to create small fissures and release natural gas. The gas is then transported via pipeline to natural goas processing or LNG facilities.

Shale gas accounted for over 20 percent of natural gas production in the United States in 2010, and the EIA estimates that it will be 46 percent by 2035. Proponents hail the process because it is decreasing America's dependence on foreign oil. But fracking comes at a potentially high environmental cost. The extraction process uses a tremendous amount of water. In addition, the chemicals within fracking fluid may contaminate underground water supplies. Residents living near fracking operations periodically complain about foul-smelling odors. Moreover, the fracking process sometimes produces microseismic activity—earthquakes too small to be easily detectable, but with unknown long-term consequences. Finally, shale gas emits more greenhouse gases, particularly methane, than generic natural gas and oil, though coal tops them all.

When one considers that oil could become an increasingly scarce commodity within the lifetimes of many college students today, the importance of developing alternative energy sources becomes apparent. Adding further urgency to the quest are the pollution problems associated with burning fossil fuels and the geopolitical tensions that arise from global dependence on a resource concentrated in select parts of the world. Moving away from a dependence on oil carries with it some clear positives, but it could lead to wrenching socioeconomic adjustments as well.

The effects of a shift away from oil will certainly be felt to some degree in the industrial and postindustrial countries, where considerable retooling of the economic infrastructure will be necessary. It is the oil-producing countries, however, that will face the greatest adjustments. More than half of the world's oil supply is found in the Middle Eastern countries of Saudi Arabia, Iraq, Kuwait, the United Arab Emirates (UAE), and Iran. In each of these countries, the extraction and exportation of oil account for at least 75 percent of total revenue and 90 percent of export-generated income. What will happen to these countries when their oil reserves run dry?

Consider the case of Kuwait—a country in which the incomes of 80 percent of the wage earners are tied to oil. Kuwait's citizens are currently guaranteed housing, education, and health care, and each adult couple receives a one-time stipend when a child is born. All of these programs are provided tax free, and when workers retire, their pensions are close to the salaries they earned as active members of the workforce.

Concerns over the long-term implications of a decline in oil revenue in Kuwait have led to efforts to find an alternative source of wealth: potable water. In a part of the world that can go for months without rain, water is a most precious resource. Some people in Kuwait joke that for each million dollars spent in the quest for sources of fresh water, all that is found is a billion dollars' worth of oil! But where fresh water cannot be found, it can potentially be made, and Kuwait has positioned itself as one of the world's leaders in the field of desalinization. This is currently a very expensive process, but Kuwait has been able to devote some of its oil revenues to desalinization efforts. As a result, 90 percent of the small country's water supply is now generated from seawater. Absent a major technological breakthrough, in the short term income generated by desalinization will amount to only a tiny fraction of the income provided by oil production. The long term may be a different story, however. If not, Kuwait—and other countries in its position—will be facing a socioeconomic adjustment of enormous proportions.

## ALTERNATIVE ENERGY

Technology has played a key role in amplifying human-induced environmental change. At the same time, technologies are being developed to identify and solve environmental problems. Some of these technologies offer alternative approaches to local energy production. In recent decades, a number of countries have established implementation programs that encourage both the development of "clean" renewable energy technologies and increased energy efficiency in buildings, transportation, and manufacturing. Yet even alternative energy sources have environmental effects. At the core of the wind turbines that generate "clean" energy are rare earth minerals, the extraction and processing of which have negative environmental consequences.

A single wind turbine (Fig. 13.19), which is made of fiberglass, weighs hundreds of metric tons, stands 90 meters (196 feet) high, and "fundamentally relies on roughly 300 kilograms of soft, silvery metal known as neodymium—a so called rare earth" (Biello 2010, 16). Neodymium is used for

■ **Figure 13.19**

**Lake Benton, Minnesota.** The wind park near Lake Benton, Minnesota, was developed beginning in 1994 and now includes more than 600 wind turbines.

"thousands of times because the elements are so chemically similar" in order to separate the neodymium from other rare earth elements (Biello 2010, 17).

The chemical processing of rare earth elements uses electricity and water—leaving behind chemicals and residuals, including thorium (a radioactive metal) and salt. The environmental consequences of rare earth element mining have historically been costly enough that production stopped at Mountain Pass Mine in California in 2002, in part because of the cost of complying with environmental laws in the United States.

A combination of looser environmental laws and labor costs led to increased production of rare earth elements in China during the last decade (Fig. 13.20). In Inner Mongolia, China, the extraction of rare earth elements at the Bayan-Obo mine alone accounts for 40 percent of the world's supply. China closed off access to the mine to all outsiders, but the mine's enormous pits and waste ponds can still be viewed from space and even seen using Google Earth (Fig. 13.21).

Because rare earth elements can be used in weapons systems, the United States military blocked the sale of Mountain Pass Mine to a Chinese company as a matter of national security. Instead, Molycorp bought Mountain Pass Mine and has begun extracting rare earth elements again. China will likely remain the leading producer of rare earth elements in the near term. However, recycling rare earth elements from discarded devices and new mining efforts in the United States, Australia, and Vietnam will likely improve the availability of rare earth elements from sources outside of China in years to come.

the powerful magnets in a wind turbine that generate electricity. It is one of 17 elements on the periodic table that are considered rare earth elements.

**Rare earth elements** are in demand because they are used not only in wind turbines but also in alternative energy cars, computers, screens, compact fluorescent light bulbs, cell phones, MRI machines, and advanced weapons systems (Biello 2010). Rare earth elements are found in rock, and 97 percent of rare earth elements mined today come from China. Mining is only the first step in the exploitation of rare earth minerals because making them usable requires separating elements that are bound together in the rock. Hence, once the rocks are mined, Chinese companies intensively boil them in acid, repeating the process

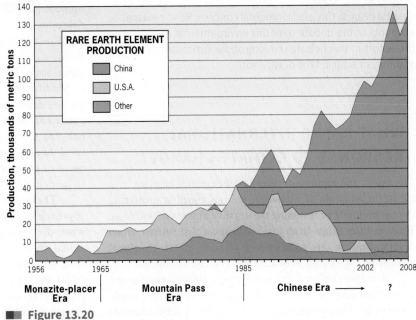

■ **Figure 13.20**

**Rare Earth Element Production Since 1964.** *Courtesy of:* USGS, http://files.eesi.org/usgs_china_030011.pdf.

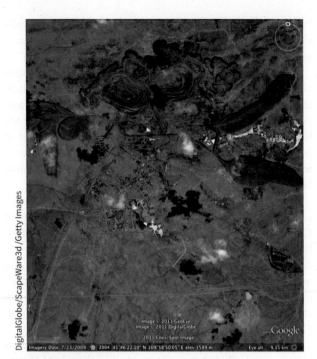

DigitalGlobe/ScapeWare3d/Getty Images

**■ Figure 13.21**
**Inner Mongolia, China.** GoogleEarth image of Bayan-Obo mine in Inner Mongolia, China. *Courtesy of:* Google Earth. © 2011 GeoEye © CNES 2011, Distribution Astrium Services/Spot Images S. A., France, all rights reserved.

Go back to the last Thinking Geographically question: What is the greatest environmental concern facing the region where you live? Now, add to your answer by concentrating on how people in the community (leaders, students, locals, businesses) discuss this environmental concern. Read newspaper accounts of the debate over this environmental concern. Are the actors in this debate thinking about processes operating at different scales? Why or why not?

## WHAT IS THE INTERNATIONAL RESPONSE TO CLIMATE CHANGE?

The extent and rapidity of recent environmental changes have led to the adoption of numerous policies aimed at protecting the environment or reversing the negative impacts of pollution. These policies range from local ordinances that restrict urban development in environmentally sensitive areas to global accords on topics such as biodiversity and climate change.

A major challenge in confronting environmental problems is that many of those problems do not lie within a single jurisdiction. Environmental pollution crosses political boundaries, and people sometimes move across those boundaries in response to environmental pressures. Designing policy responses is thus complicated by the fact that the political map does not reflect the geography of environmental issues. The problem is particularly acute when environmental problems cross international boundaries, for there are few international policymaking bodies with significant authority over multinational environmental spaces. Moreover, those that do exist—the European Union, for example—often have limited authority and must heed the concerns of member states. Those concerns, in turn, may not work in the interests of environmental sustainability. Within democracies, politicians with an eye to the next election may hesitate to tackle long-term problems that require short-term sacrifices. Most authoritarian regimes have an even worse record, as can be seen in the policies of the Soviet-dominated governments of eastern Europe during the communist era. Moreover, governmental leaders in poorer countries find it very difficult to take action when, as is often the case, action requires reductions in already marginal standards of living and even greater difficulties in meeting the kinds of debt payments discussed in Chapter 10.

Despite these obstacles, the growing extent and urgency of global environmental changes have led to a number of international agreements to address selected problems. Some of these agreements have been spearheaded by nongovernmental organizations (NGOs) that operate outside of the formal political arena. They tend to focus on specific issues and problems, often in particular places. With the 1972 *United Nations Conference on the Human Environment* in Stockholm, international governmental organizations began playing a major role in environmental policy.

The framework that currently guides international governmental activity in the environmental arena evolved from the United Nations Conference on Environment and Development (UNCED) held in Rio de Janeiro in June 1992. The delegates to UNCED gave the Global Environment Facility (GEF)—a joint project of the United Nations and the World Bank—significant authority over environmental action on a global scale. The GEF funds projects related to six issues: loss of biodiversity, climate change, protection of international waters, depletion of the ozone layer, land degradation, and persistent organic pollutants. The delegates to UNCED believed that significant progress could be made through these funded projects, along with bilateral (that is, government-to-government) aid. They also made it easier for NGOs to participate in international environmental policymaking.

These actions hold the promise of a more coherent approach to environmental problem solving than is possible when decisions are made on a state-by-state basis. Yet individual states continue to influence decision making in all sorts of ways. Take the case of the GEF. Between 1991 and 2010, the GEF provided $4.5 billion in grants, primarily to projects involving climate change or biodiversity. Even though the GEF is charged with protecting key elements of the global environment, it still functions in a state-based

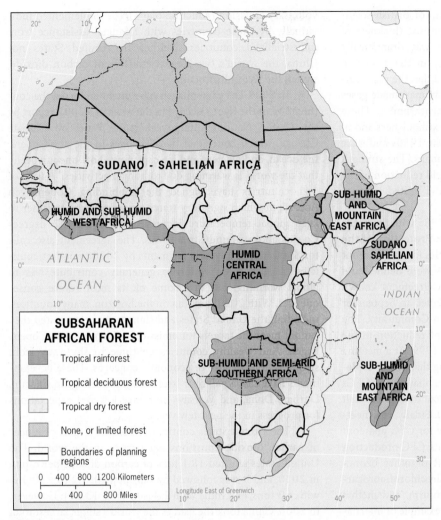

**SUBSAHARAN AFRICAN FOREST**

- Tropical rainforest
- Tropical deciduous forest
- Tropical dry forest
- None, or limited forest
- Boundaries of planning regions

0　400　800　1200 Kilometers

0　400　800 Miles

Longitude East of Greenwich

■■ **Figure 13.22**

**Major Regions and Forest Zones in Subsaharan Africa.** This map is based on a figure in a World Bank technical paper on the forest sector in Subsaharan Africa. The map shows major forest regions crossing state boundaries, but planning regions adhere to state boundaries. *Adapted with permission from*: N. P. Sharma, S. Rietbergen, C. R. Heimo, and J. Patel. A Strategy for the Forest Sector in Sub-Saharan Africa, World Bank Technical Paper No. 251, Africa Technical Department Series (Washington, DC: The World Bank, 1994).

world, as suggested by Figure 13.22—a map from a 1994 World Bank technical report on the forest sector in Subsaharan Africa that divides the realm into "major regions" that follow state rather than ecological borders. Nonetheless, the GEF serves the important role of providing financial resources to four major international conventions on the environment: the Convention on Biological Diversity, the United Nations Framework Convention on Climate Change, the United Nations Convention to Combat Desertification, and the Stockholm Convention on Persistent Organic Pollutants.

A few global environmental issues are so pressing that efforts are being made to draw up guidelines for action in the form of international conventions or treaties. The most prominent examples are in the areas of biological diversity,

protection of the ozone layer, and global climate change.

## Biological Diversity

International concern over the loss of species led to calls for a global convention (agreement) as early as 1981. By the beginning of the 1990s, a group working under the auspices of the United Nations Environment Program reached agreement on the wording of the convention, and it was submitted to UNCED for approval. It went into effect in late 1993; as of 2011, 168 countries had signed it. The convention calls for establishing a system of protected areas and a coordinated set of national and international regulations on activities that can have significant negative impacts on biodiversity. It also provides funding for developing countries that are trying to meet the terms of the convention.

The biodiversity convention is a step forward in that it both affirms the vital significance of preserving biological diversity and provides a framework for cooperation toward that end. However, the agreement has proved difficult to implement. In particular, there is an ongoing struggle to find a balance between the need of poorer countries to promote local economic development and the need to preserve biodiversity, which happens to be richest in parts of the global economic periphery. Also, there has been controversy over the sharing of costs for conservation programs, which has led to heated debates over ratification of the convention in some countries. Nevertheless, this convention, along with a host of voluntary efforts, has helped to focus attention on the biodiversity issue and to promote the expansion of protected areas. Whether those areas will succeed in providing long-term species protection is an open question that will occupy geographers and biologists for years to come.

## Protection of the Ozone Layer

When found in the troposphere (0 to 16 km or 1.0 to 10 mile altitude), ozone ($O_3$) gas is a harmful pollutant closely associated with the creation of smog. However, a naturally occurring **ozone layer** exists in the stratosphere (between 30 and 45 km altitude). The ozone layer is of vital importance because it protects Earth's surface from the sun's harmful ultraviolet rays. In 1985, a group of British scientists working in Antarctica discovered that the thickness of the ozone layer above the South Pole was dramatically reduced, from 300 Dobson units (DUs) in the 1960s to almost 200 DUs by 1985. Studies revealed that the main culprits in ozone depletion were a group of human-made gases collectively known as CFCs (chlorofluorocarbons). These gases, used mainly as refrigerants in fire extinguishers and in aerosol cans, had only been in use since the 1950s and were thought to be completely harmless to humans. The strength of the scientific evidence pointing to a rapid reduction of the ozone layer led to an unusually rapid and united international response.

International cooperation began in 1985 with the negotiation of the **Vienna Convention for the Protection of the Ozone Layer**. Specific targets and timetables for the phaseout of production and consumption of CFCs were defined and agreed upon as part of the international agreement known as the **Montreal Protocol**, which was signed in September 1987 by 105 countries and the European Community. The original agreement called for a 50 percent reduction in the production and consumption of CFCs by 1999. At a meeting in London in 1990, scientific data showing that ozone depletion would continue for many years after a phaseout of CFCs led the signatories of the Montreal Protocol to agree to halt CFC production entirely by the year 2000. Finally, at a meeting in Copenhagen in 1992, the timetable for CFC phaseout accelerated. Participants agreed to eliminate CFC production by 1996 and to accelerate the phaseout of other ozone-depleting chemicals such as halons, hydrochlorofluorocarbons, carbon tetrachloride, methyl chloroform, and methyl bromide. This response is an encouraging example of international cooperation in the face of a significant, albeit clearly defined, problem.

## Global Climate Change

Beginning in the late 1980s, growing concern about climate change led to a series of intergovernmental conferences on the nature and extent of human impacts on climate. In December 1990, the United Nations General Assembly approved the start of treaty negotiations. A draft convention called on developed countries to take measures aimed at reducing their emissions to 1990 levels by the year 2000 and to provide technical and financial support for emission-reduction efforts in the developing countries. The European Community (precursor to the European Union) and 154 other states signed the convention, commonly called the Earth Summit, in Rio de Janeiro.

In 1997, the Kyoto Agreement set a target period of 2008–2012 for the United States, the European Union, and Japan to cut their greenhouse gas emissions by 7, 8, and 6 percent, respectively, below 1990 levels. The agreement reached in Kyoto did not obligate less developed countries to adhere to specific reduction goals; instead it called for

voluntary emission reduction plans to be implemented individually by those countries with financial assistance from industrialized countries. Neither the United States nor China, the world's two largest emitters of carbon dioxide, signed the Kyoto Protocol.

In 2009, the Copenhagen Agreement endorsed the continuation of the Kyoto Accord in the wake of a 2007 report by the United Nations Intergovernmental Panel on Climate Change, which concluded that "changes in the atmosphere, the ocean, and glaciers and ice caps now show unequivocally that the world is warming due to human activities." A total of 141 countries have signed the nonbinding Copenhagen Accord, in which signatory states agreed to work together to keep global temperature increases to less than 2 degrees Celsius above preindustrial levels. The agreement also calls for $100 billion in yearly payments by 2020 to poorer countries because those countries generally contribute less to global warming, but face some of its most severe consequences. With 2020 looming on the horizon, many countries, including the United States and Canada, have suggested they cannot meet the targets for emission reduction set in Copenhagen. And wealthy countries continue to shy away from strong action because of economic concerns. These developments have cast a pall over later summit meetings in Cancun, Durban, Doha, and Warsaw, and have lowered expectations for progress in the next few years.

The United States continues to be the largest producer of carbon dioxide emissions per person in the world. The United States emitted 18.1 tons of carbon dioxide per capita in 2010, and it was followed by Europe with 7.2 tons, China with 6.3 tons, and India with 1.4 tons (Fig. 13.23). However, in 2006, China took the lead as the world's single largest total emitter of carbon dioxide, pushing the United States out of the top spot.

With most countries continuing to prioritize economic concerns over efforts to make serious inroads in the reduction of greenhouse gases, there is much doubt as to whether significant progress will be made in confronting the human role in climate change. Hence, policymakers and scientists are increasingly focusing their attention on adaptation strategies.

## Water Scarcity

One-fifth of the world's population lives in regions confronting water scarcity. Yet to date there have been few conflicts among states over water. On the contrary, geographer Aaron Wolf has shown that cooperation between states tends to increase in the face of growing water concerns. Cooperation usually takes the form of transboundary or multilateral treaties governing the use and protection of water resources. During the past half century, the world's states have entered into some 150 such agreements. From the Mekong to the Ganges to the Indus to the Niger, treaties have helped to promote the equitable management of river-basin waters.

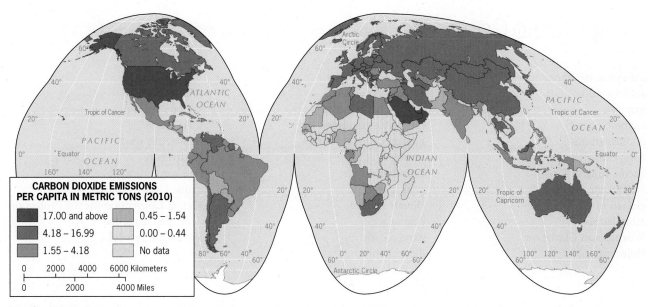

**■■ Figure 13.23**

**Carbon Dioxide Emissions per Capita, 2004.**   Recently, China's total carbon dioxide emissions exceeded those of the United States. However, in per capita emissions of carbon dioxide, mapped here, the United States, Canada, and the United Arab Emirates are the highest.   *Data from*: United Nations Development Programme, Human Development Report, 2007/2008.

Despite the many examples of cooperation, water-management challenges abound. In many cases monitoring is inadequate, enforcement mechanisms are lacking, and provisions do not exist to address more extreme variations in water availability. The last-named issue in particular is looming ever larger because the current structure of agreements may well not be adequate to cope with the more significant shifts in water availability that are likely to occur (indeed, are already occurring) in the face of climate change. Against this backdrop, a 2014 World Bank working paper (Dinar et al.) foresees the potential for growing political tensions over water in the coming years.

 Examine the map of global carbon dioxide emissions and explain the pattern you see. What other geographic patterns are correlated with those shown in the map?

# Summary

What will the future be like? Many would agree with geographer Robert Kates, who foresees a "warmer, more crowded, more connected but more diverse world." As we consider this prospect, we must acknowledge that global environmental changes are among the most pressing issues facing the world today, but also illustrate the limits of what we know about our planet. Global environmental change is not always anticipated and is often nonlinear. Some changes are "chaotic" in the sense that future conditions cannot be reliably predicted. Nonlinearity means that small actions in certain situations may result in large impacts and may be more important than larger actions in causing change. Thresholds also exist in many systems, which, once past, are irreversible. Irreversible changes occur, for example, when the habitat for a species is diminished to the point where the species quickly dies off.

Unfortunately, we may not be able to identify these thresholds until we pass them. This leaves open the possibility of "surprises"—unanticipated responses by physical systems.

The complexity and urgency of environmental change will tax the energies of the scientific and policy communities for some time to come. Geography must be an essential part of any serious effort to grapple with these challenges. The major changes that are taking place have different origins and spatial expressions, and each results from a unique combination of physical and social processes. We cannot simply focus on system dynamics and generalized causal relationships. We must also consider emerging patterns of environmental change and the impacts of differences from place to place on the operation of general processes. Geography is not the backdrop to the changes taking place; it is at the very heart of the changes themselves.

# Geographic Concepts

chlorofluorocarbons
anthropocene
Pangaea
tectonic plates
photosynthesis
mass extinctions
Pacific Ring of Fire
Pleistocene
glaciation
interglacials
Wisconsinan Glaciation
Holocene

Little Ice Age
greenhouse effect
environmental stress
renewable resources
nonrenewable resources
aquifers
hydrologic cycle
atmosphere
climate change
acid rain
oxygen cycle
deforestation

soil erosion
solid waste
sanitary landfills
toxic waste
radioactive waste
biodiversity
rare earth elements
ozone layer
Vienna Convention for the Protection
   of the Ozone Layer
Montreal Protocol

# Learn More Online

About geography and environmental hazards
www.bbc.co.uk/scotland/education/int/geog/envhaz/index.shtml

Forest change
http://earthenginepartners.appspot.com/science-2013-global-forest

Oxford's Environmental Change Institute
www.eci.ox.ac.uk/

Time-lapse imagery of environmental change
http://world.time.com/timelapse/

United Nations Framework Convention on Climate Change
http://unfccc.int/2860.php

About Rare Earth Minerals
http://ngm.nationalgeographic.com/2011/06/rare-earth-elements/folger-text

# Watch It Online

About Climate Change
http://youtu.be/2JmrmwIyhAE

About Tsunamis
http://video.nationalgeographic.com/video/101-videos/tsunami-101

About Desertification and Climate Change
http://www.ted.com/talks/allan_savory_how_to_green_the_world_s_deserts_and_reverse_climate_change

# GLOBALIZATION AND THE GEOGRAPHY OF NETWORKS

## Happiness Is in the Eye of the Beholder

Traveling through a rural village in Andhra Pradesh, India, we stopped to take in a weekend morning market. Women sold spices stored in heaps of colored flakes; a man had a chair set up and was cutting a little boy's hair; a group of men sold rebar from shops behind vegetable stands. I was used to seeing the colorful sarees and salwar kameez worn by Indian women. Then, an older woman from one of India's scheduled tribes caught my eye. I first noticed her clothing. The colors were as bright as any saree, but the silver, mirrors, and beads adorning her dress stood out. I looked up at her, our eyes connected, and then she smiled (Fig. 14.1). I asked if I could take her picture, and she nodded yes.

I think of her when I am teaching human geography. Often, students in their first college-level geography class are excited at the end of the semester to have learned so much about the world. Some have had their eyes opened to the world for the first time as an adult. Others have finally understood the roots of a conflict they have only heard about on television. And many feel overwhelmed. Too much information. Too many people. Too little they can do to help.

Everyone feels this frustration to some degree, since no one can understand all of the complexities that govern life on Earth. But the ideas and perspectives set forth in this book give you insight into what it means to think geographically. That type of thinking is critical if you are to raise the types of questions that go beyond the generalizations and stereotypes that can work against deeper understanding. So many books try to simplify the world in an alarmist way. The world is flat (Thomas Friedman)! There's a population

■ **Figure 14.1**
**Andhra Pradesh, India.** A woman who is a member of a scheduled tribe in India smiles in the middle of a Saturday morning market. The government has affirmative action programs where they reserve seats in universities and government for Indians in scheduled tribes (also called Adivasis), scheduled castes (known as Dalits and formerly as Untouchables), and the lowest castes (called "other backwards castes"). The scheduled tribes are India's indigenous population, and they comprise an estimated 8.2 percent of India's 1.27 billion people.

© Erin H. Fouberg

bomb (Paul Ehrlich)! We live in a post-American world (Fareed Zakaria)! Such books often start from an interesting observation but then overlook how geography affects what is happening.

Each of us can attest that the world is anything but flat. Millions of people in India may be competing on a more level playing field with those in North America than was true in the past, but many other millions live in a different world that we ignore at our peril. As geographer Yi Fu Tuan said, "People make places." Each place is an imprint of culture, a reflection of diffusion, and a dynamic entity. Each place has its own identity that makes it unique.

It is important not just to understand that the world is diverse, but to appreciate that the uniqueness of places cuts against the stereotypes that circulate about them. The image of the tribal woman in India is the counterbalance to the images of the developing world I saw when I was growing up. I remember seeing pictures of women in remote parts of South America wearing exotic clothing. I also saw television coverage of children in Subsaharan Africa with distended stomachs and hunger in their faces. But in these images of the developing world that I saw as a child, no one was smiling. The images I saw growing up formed the perceptions I had of the developing world and the people who live there. My experiences since then have changed the ways I see the world and my own place in it.

The king of Bhutan, a small country nestled in the foothills of the Himalayas, decided that statistics that calculate the wealth of a country (Chapter 10), from gross national income (GNI) to Internet access, did not accurately measure the state of people's lives. In the 1970s, the preceding king of Bhutan coined the term *gross national happiness*, stating that the government needed to focus on achieving happiness instead of focusing on gross domestic product (GDP). In 2008, the current leader of Bhutan, King Wangchuck, released a new measurement, an index called gross national happiness (GNH) (Fig. 14.2). King Wangchuck explained that measurements such as GDP or GNI emphasize production and consumption instead of conservation of resources and environment.

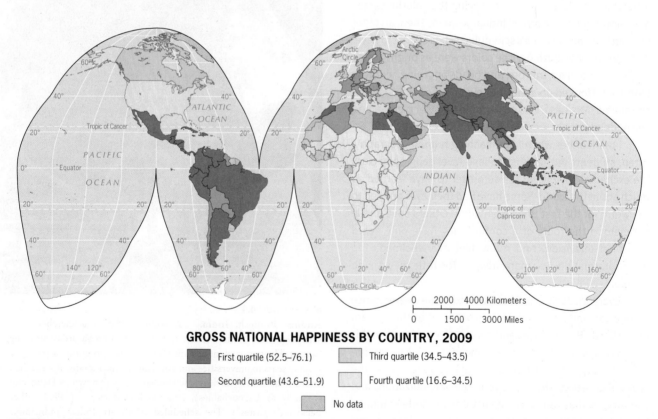

**GROSS NATIONAL HAPPINESS BY COUNTRY, 2009**

First quartile (52.5–76.1)     Third quartile (34.5–43.5)

Second quartile (43.6–51.9)    Fourth quartile (16.6–34.5)

No data

■■ **Figure 14.2**

**Gross National Happiness, 2010.**    Instead of measuring income, the government of Bhutan measures happiness, how well the people in the country are, using nine markers, including health, education, environment, and governance.    *Data from*: Centre for Bhutan Studies.

The Center for Bhutan Studies measures nine dimensions of happiness and calculates a single numerical index reported as GNH. The nine dimensions include measurements of psychological well-being, time use, community vitality, culture, health, education, environmental diversity, living standard, and governance. Regardless of the accuracy of the GNH index, we welcome a critical and reflective look at how we measure our world.

Our hope is that this book has helped you think through the ways you make sense of the world. In this chapter, we consider how identities have changed in a globalizing world. In an effort to deepen our understanding of globalization, we also examine how networks operate in our world, in order to encourage you to consider the possibilities for tomorrow.

# Key Questions FOR CHAPTER 14

1. How have identities changed in a globalized world?
2. What is globalization, and what role do networks play in globalization?
3. How do networks operate in a globalized world?

## HOW HAVE IDENTITIES CHANGED IN A GLOBALIZED WORLD?

Gillian Rose defines identity as "how we make sense of ourselves." She explains that we have identities at different scales: We have local, national, regional, and global identities. At each scale, place factors into our identities. We infuse places with meaning and emotions based on our experiences in those places. Relatively few people living in today's globalized world are world travelers. And many of those who have traveled the globe have missed out on the uniqueness of place by visiting only global cities, living the lives of businesspeople (visiting airports, office buildings, and hotels), or staying in luxurious resorts (separated from the "local") as tourists. How, then, can a person have a global identity if he or she has not experienced the globe?

Globalization networks link us with other people and places, and the flow of information technology is a daily way in which we are interlinked. A person may be overwhelmed by the flow of information and choose to ignore it, but even such a person has a global identity. People identify themselves by identifying with or against others at local, regional, and global scales. We make sense of the world by identifying with people and places.

In 1995, *National Geographic* discussed the future of the digital age and argued that as a result of technological advances and the Internet, people were interacting in person less. However, the author (Swerdlow 1995) also claimed that people would continue to have "a need for skin," a desire to interact with other humans in person. As evidence, the author cited how busy a mall is when the people in the mall could just as easily be ordering all of their purchases from home on the Internet.

This discussion of a pull between a faceless Internet and the "need for skin" took place nine years before Mark Zuckerberg created Facebook in 2004. People with Facebook or Twitter accounts (see Chapter 4) can feel connected without sharing skin by posting a quip or thought, which friends around the world can respond to immediately. Psychologists also recognize that the proliferation of reality television shows is connected to declining human interaction. Service organizations and clubs that used to be a major way for young members of a community to connect are generally experiencing membership declines in the United States.

In the 1990s, at the launch of the digital revolution, psychologists predicted that people would have poorer social skills because of the lack of personal or face-to-face interaction in the digital age. We can certainly see evidence of this in our daily lives, from people answering a phone call or text message when they are in the middle of a conversation with someone in person to students texting or multitasking on laptops during a geography lecture. Today, psychologists recognize that the networks created among people through digital technology also enable greater personal interaction and opportunities for empathy. Someone with medical problems can post a journal on a site such as Caring Bridge, and hundreds can follow the person's recovery and offer words of support. A young boy with a medical condition that makes it difficult to leave home can post lip-synched videos on YouTube, develop followers around the world, and end up with recording artists stopping by to lip sync with him. Social networks can be used for good or for ill, but either way, they tend to be a major way by which individuals, in a global, digital age, can develop a sense of belonging and a personal connectedness to people who are separated by computer screens.

## Personal Connectedness

Sixteen years before hundreds of millions around the world watched a live feed of the wedding of Price William and Catherine Middleton (Chapter 4) on the Internet and on television, the news that Prince William's mother, Princess Diana, had died traveled quickly from global television, radio, and print media sources among friends, family, and even strangers. Many felt the need to mourn for a princess they had never met in a place they had never been. Some wanted to leave a token offering for the princess: a rose, a note, a candle, a photograph. Impromptu shrines to Princess Diana cropped up at the British embassy in Washington, D.C., and at British embassies and consulates around the world. People in Britain left countless flowers at the royal palace in London, where Princess Diana resided.

In an incredibly divided world, in which the rift between rich and poor is growing at the global scale, what made people feel connected to a woman who was a royal, a member of a family that presides over a modest-sized country? Why do we relate to someone from an elite group of people of wealth and privilege? What, 16 years later, made people want to see how her son turned out and "get to know" who he was marrying by watching television programs and reading stories online and in print about Catherine Middleton leading up to the wedding?

The idea that people who do not personally know each other and likely never will are linked and have shared experiences, including death, tragedy, sorrow, and even joy, draws from Benedict Anderson's concept of the nation as an **imagined community** (see Chapter 8). When massive tragedies such as 9/11, Hurricane Katrina, or the Japan tsunami occur, people often talk about someone they knew who was in the place (or had been at some point), someone who died (even those they did not know but heard about in the news), or an act of bravery or triumph that occurred in the midst of tragedy. The desire to *personalize*, to *localize*, a tragedy or even a joyous event feeds off of the imagined global community in which we live. In the process of personalizing and localizing, events can be *globalized* in an effort to appeal to the humanity of all people with the hope that all will feel or experience the loss or joy tangentially.

In a world where some commentators argue that place and territory are unimportant because things like global superhighways of information transcend place, people continue to recognize territories and create places. In the case of a death or a tragedy, how do people choose a local space in which to express a personal and/or global sorrow? In the case of Princess Diana's death, people created hundreds of spaces of sorrow to mourn the loss of a seemingly magnanimous

person whose life was cut short. In the case of September 11, people transformed homes, schools, public spaces, and houses of worship into spaces of reflection by creating human chains, participating in moments of silence, or holding prayer vigils for the victims.

In his book *Shadowed Ground: America's Landscapes of Violence and Tragedy*, Kenneth Foote examines the "spontaneous shrines" created at a place of loss or at a place that represents loss and describes these spontaneous shrines as a "first stage in the commemoration of a disaster." Foote drew from extensive fieldwork that he conducted while visiting hundreds of landscapes of tragedy and violence in the United States to show how people mark or do not mark tragedy, both immediately with spontaneous shrines and in the longer term with permanent memorials (Fig. 14.3). He examines the struggles over whether and how to memorialize significant people or experienced tragedy. His research focuses on the United States, and after tracing and following the stories of hundreds of people and places, Foote concludes that "the debate over what, why, when, and where to build" a memorial for a person or event is "best considered a part of the grieving process."

Foote realized that the ways sites are memorialized or not vary over time and across a multitude of circumstances, depending on whether funding is available, what kind of structure is to be built, who is being remembered (only those who died or also those injured?), whether the site represents a socially contested event (which often happens when racism is involved), and whether people want to remember the site. In recent American history, major terrorist attacks have been memorialized, often with the word "closure" evoked. Oklahoma City permanently memorialized the site of a terrorist attack at the Murrah Federal Building on the five-year anniversary of the tragedy. Other tragedies, such as that experienced at the World Trade Center in New York City on September 11, 2001, take longer to memorialize. Millions of people feel a personal connection to the World Trade Center site, and so choosing a design and building a memorial took longer (Fig. 14.4).

The mass of information coming our way each day is often overwhelming. As people filter through or ignore the flow of information, they may personalize the information and either make a connection or differentiate themselves from particular people or places. In the end, many people's identities are shaped by developments unfolding at the global scale. Living in a world, at a scale we have not experienced previously, changes us and profoundly changes places. Globalization, for good or for ill, has modified how we interact with one another and has shaped how we make sense of ourselves in our world, our state, our region, and our locality.

**thinking** *geographically* Think of a national or global-scale tragedy, such as September 11 or World War II. In what ways do memorials of that tragedy reflect both globalization and localization at the same time?

# GUEST FIELD NOTE

## Columbine, Colorado

I took this photo at the dedication ceremony for the memorial to the victims of the Columbine High School shooting of April 20, 1999. Columbine is located near Littleton, Colorado, in Denver's southern suburbs. The memorial, dedicated on September 21, 2007, provides a quiet place for meditation and reflection in a public park adjacent to the school. Hundreds came to the ceremony to honor those killed and wounded in the attack, one of the deadliest school shootings in U.S. history.

After tragedies like the Columbine shootings, creating a memorial often helps to rebuild a sense of community. Public ceremonies like this can set an example for survivors who may otherwise have difficulty facing their loss in private. A group memorial helps to acknowledge the magnitude of the community's loss and, by so doing, helps assure families and survivors that the victims did not suffer alone—that their deaths and wounds are grieved by the entire community. Memorials are important too because they can serve as a focus for remembrance and commemoration long into the future, even after all other evidence of a tragedy has disappeared.

In my research for *Shadowed Ground*, I have visited hundreds of such places in the United States and Europe. I am

■ **Figure 14.3**

still surprised by the power of such places and the fact that shrines and memorials resulting from similar tragedies are tended lovingly for decades, generations, and centuries. They produce strong emotions and sometimes leave visitors—including me—in tears. But by allowing individuals to share loss, tragedy, and sorrow with others, they create a sense of common purpose.

*Credit: Kenneth E. Foote, University of Colorado at Boulder.*

■ **Figure 14.4**

**New York, New York.** The 9/11 Memorial commemorates those who died in the terrorist attacks on the World Trade Center on September 11, 2001. The wall includes the names of those who died in each tower, the first responders, those who died at the Pentagon, and those who died on each flight involved in that day's attacks. Additionally, the memorial includes the names of those who died during the first attack on the World Trade Center, a bomb detonated in the parking garage of the North Tower on February 26, 1993. A total of 2983 names are etched in the walls around the memorial pools of the North and South Towers, the footprints of the former buildings.

© Richard Baker/In Pictures/Corbis

## WHAT IS GLOBALIZATION, AND WHAT ROLE DO NETWORKS PLAY IN GLOBALIZATION?

Whether you are in favor of or opposed to globalization, we all must recognize that globalization is "neither an inevitable nor an irreversible set of processes," as John O'Loughlin, Lynn Staeheli, and Edward Greenberg put it. Andrew Kirby explains that globalization is "not proceeding according to any particular playbook. It is not a smoothly evolving state of capitalist development." Rather, it is fragmented, and its flows are "chaotic in terms of origins and destinations."

**Globalization** is a "chaotic" set of processes and outcomes created by people, whether they are corporate CEOs, university administrators, readers of blogs, electrical engineers, or protesters at a trade meeting. The processes of globalization and the connectedness created through globalization occur across scales and across networks, regardless of state borders.

The backbone of economic globalization is trade; so, debates over globalization typically focus on trade. To visualize how trade fosters globalization, examine a map of shipping routes (Fig. 14.5). The density of the networks on the map tells us how extensively connected the world really is. But what are the consequences of those connections? The arguments in favor of globalization, as explained by economist Keith Maskus (2004), are that "free trade raises the well-being of all countries by inducing them to specialize their resources in those goods they produce relatively most efficiently" in order to lower production costs, and that "competition through trade raises a country's long-term growth rate by expanding access to global technologies and promoting innovation."

The view that free trade raises the wealth of all countries involved underpins a set of neoliberal policies known as the **Washington Consensus**. The World Bank, the International Monetary Fund, the World Trade Organization, and investment banks are all part of the Washington Consensus. Together, these institutions created a set of policies, including structural adjustment loans, that encouraged neoliberalism (Chapter 10). Not everyone accepts this "consensus." Leaders in both the developing and developed countries questioned the underlying assumptions of the Washington Consensus, especially after the global economic downturn began in 2008.

Opponents view this set of policies as part of a Western-dominated effort to get the rest of the world to privatize state-owned entities, to open financial markets, to liberalize trade by removing restrictions on the flow of goods, and to encourage foreign direct investment (Fig. 14.6). They argue that the countries of the global economic core continue to protect their own economies while forcing the countries of the semi-periphery and periphery to open their economies in ways that can have significant negative local consequences. According to Maskus, the rules negotiated for the World Trade Organization "inevitably reflect the economic interest of powerful lobbyists" in places such as the United States and the European Union, and have heightened wealth differences between

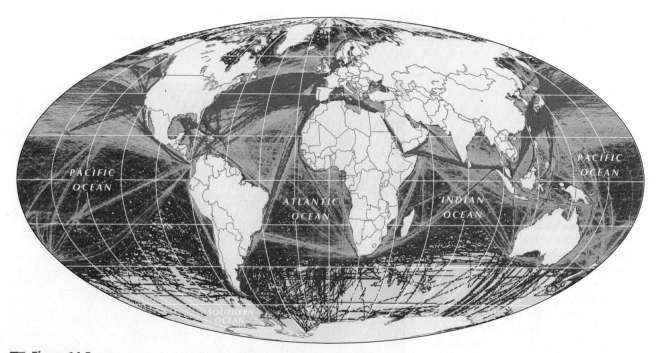

■■ **Figure 14.5**

**Global Shipping Lanes.**    The map traces over 3000 shipping routes used by commercial and government vessels during 2006. The red lines mark the most frequently used shipping lanes. *Courtesy of*: National Center for Ecological Analysis and Synthesis, http://ebm.nceas.ucsb.edu/GlobalMarine/impacts/transformed/jpg/shipping.jpg, last accessed August 2008.

# FIELD NOTE

"'You cannot come to southern Brazil without seeing our biggest city,' said the vintner who was showing me around the Cooperativa Aurora, the huge winery in Bento Gonçalves, in the State of Rio Grande do Sul. 'Besides, it's January, so they'll be having the big marches, it's almost like carnival time in Rio!' So I headed for Porto Alegre, only to find that a hotel room was not to be had. Tens of thousands of demonstrators had converged on the State's capital, largest port, and leading industrial city—and what united them was opposition to globalization. It was not quite a carnival, but the banners held aloft by the noisy, sometimes singing and dancing demonstrators left no doubt as to their common goals. The World Social Forum has become an annual event held in cities around the world, with ever-larger marches and meetings to protest the actions of the world's dominant states, especially the United States. The World Social Forum is a network of antiglobalizationists—people who seek an alternative economic reality for the globe, one not centered on accumulation of capital. Socialist economic views, leftist political leanings, and support for minority causes combine each year at the World Social Forum in a show of strength."

Lima Agliberto/Gamma-Presse/Zuma Press

■ **Figure 14.6**
**Porto Alegre, Brazil.**

more and less prosperous regions, and deepened the inequalities of the global system.

Whether or not you support neoliberalism, the globalizing trends of the last few decades mean that we are, in many respects, living on an unprecedented scale. In Andrew Kirby's words, we are living "not so much in a world without boundaries, or in a world without geography—*but more literally in a world*, as opposed to a neighborhood or a region" (emphasis added).

## Networks

Manuel Castells defines **networks** as "a set of interconnected nodes" without a center. A nonhierarchical network is horizontally structured, with power shared among all participants and ideas flowing in all directions. The multitude of networks that exist in the world—financial, transportation, communication, kinship, corporate, nongovernmental, trade, government, media, education, social, and dozens of others—enable globalization to occur and create a higher degree of interaction and interdependence among people than ever before in human history. Deeply entrenched hierarchies in the networks knit together the contemporary world, and these affect the character of different places and the interactions among them.

While networks have always existed, Castells says that they have fundamentally changed since 1995 as a result of the diffusion of information technology that links places in a global, yet uneven, way. Through information technology networks, Castells argues that globalization has proceeded by "linking up all that, according to dominant interests, has value anywhere in the planet, and discarding anything (people, firms, territories, resources) which has no value or becomes devalued." Information technology networks link some places more than others, helping to create the spatial unevenness of globalization as well as the uneven outcomes of globalization.

## Time–Space Compression

Access (or lack of access) to information technology networks creates time–space compression, which means that certain places, such as global cities (especially in the core), are more interconnected than ever through communication and transportation networks, even as other places, such as those in the periphery, are farther removed (Chapters 1 and 4). According to Castells (2000), the age of information technology networks is more revolutionary than the advent of the printing press or the Industrial Revolution. He claims that we are just at the beginning of this age "as the Internet becomes a universal tool of interactive communication, as we shift from computer-centered technologies to network-diffused technologies, (and) as we make progress in nanotechnology (and thus in the diffusion capacity of information devices)."

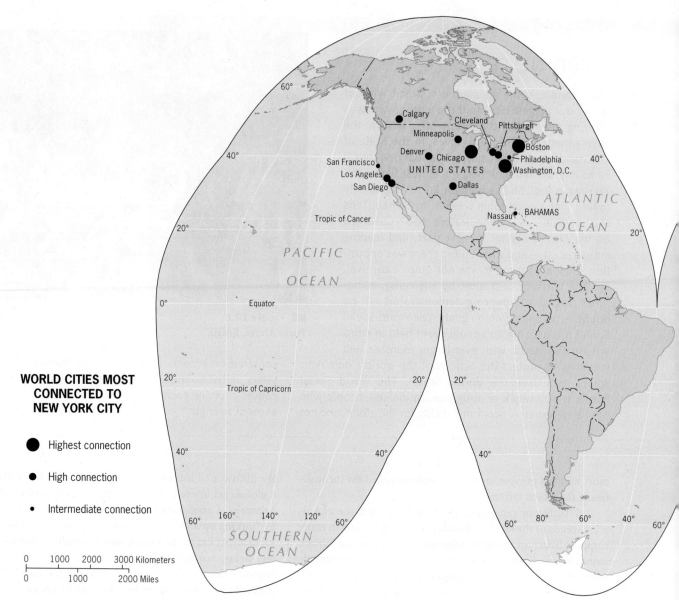

**WORLD CITIES MOST CONNECTED TO NEW YORK CITY**

● Highest connection

● High connection

· Intermediate connection

```
0    1000   2000   3000 Kilometers
0         1000        2000 Miles
```

■ **Figure 14.7**

**World Cities Most Connected to New York City.** This map shows the 30 world cities that are the most connected to New York City, as measured by flows in the service economy.    *Data from*: P. J. Taylor and R. E. Lang, "U.S. Cities in the 'World City Network,'" The Brookings Institution, Survey Series, February 2005. http://wwwe.brookings.edu/dybdocroot/metro/pubs/20050222_worldcities.pdf, last accessed September 2005.

A major divide in access to information technology—sometimes called the **Digital Divide**—is both a hallmark of the current world and an example of the uneven outcomes of globalization. The International Telecommunications Union reported the levels of digital access for developing and developed regions of the world. In 2014, the World Bank reported that on average developed (high-income) states had 42 landline telephone connections, 120 mobile cellular connections, and 78.2 Internet users for every 100 people. On average, developing (low- and middle-income) states had 10 landline telephone connections, 86 mobile cellular connections, and 29.1 Internet users for every 100 people.

The quickening pace of technological change is another hallmark of globalization and magnifies the global technological divide. We may be shocked to see how quickly technology has changed and diffused. In 1992, the highest-income states had on average only 10 cellular subscribers and 2.5 Internet users per 1000 people.

## GLOBAL CITIES

Time–space compression has helped to create and reinforce a network of highly linked global cities. In Chapter 9, we discussed the growth of *global cities* in the core, semiperiphery, and periphery and the deepening of their connectedness. We considered research published by geographers in the Globalization and World Cities group based in the United Kingdom, who use network analyses to examine levels of connectivity among

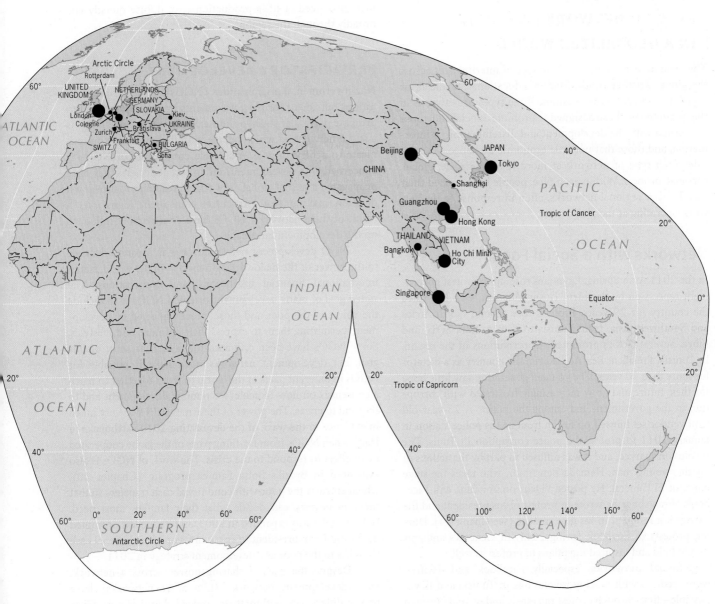

cities, based on such factors as air travel between cities, and the interpenetration of financial and advertising networks.

These researchers generated data for 315 global cities, measuring the information technology flows among the cities by tracking the flow of advanced services among them, focusing on accounting, advertising, banking/finance, insurance, law, and management consulting. Figure 14.7 shows the 30 cities they found to be most connected to New York City, as measured by the flow of producer services. By tracking flows, the authors found that Miami, not Los Angeles, is the U.S. city most closely linked to Latin America and that New York is the second most *globally* linked city in the world (behind London and ahead of Tokyo). Chicago is also a highly ranked member of the global city network, coming in seventh. The researchers found that New York and Chicago stand apart from other world cities in that these American cities have greater domestic linkages than global cities in the Pacific Rim or the European Union.

The linkages among global cities provide insights into the spatial character of the networks that underlie globalized processes. A multitude of globalized processes such as financial transactions and flows (represented here by banking/finance and accounting) occur across the network of global cities. Similarly, this network reflects the flow of advertising and marketing consultation services, which in turn reflects the flow of ideas through the media across the globe.

Castells claims that the age of information technology is more revolutionary than either the advent of the printing press or the Industrial Revolution. Do you agree with him? Write an argument in support of your position, drawing on your understanding of the expansion of the world-economy since 1500.

# HOW DO NETWORKS OPERATE IN A GLOBALIZED WORLD?

The term *network* defines any number of interlinkages across the globe, whether transportation, educational, financial, or social. In this section we examine three types of networks in the world today: those designed to promote a social end, those concerned with the development and dissemination of information, and those that underlie economic exchange. We consider each type of network at more than one scale: global, regional, or local. Within each type, people have created their own local or regional networks, often in response to the network operating at the global scale.

## Networks with a Social Focus

In the 2011 Arab Spring, Egyptians rose up to protest government repression by President Hosni Mubarak, who had ruled the country for 29 years. Protests rose around North Africa and Southwest Asia, from Tunisia to Yemen, Iran, Syria, and Libya. Several factors prompted the revolutions in the region. In Tunisia, President Ben Ali had run the country as a dictator for more than 20 years. The younger generation saw little hope for their future and grew increasingly frustrated with corruption in the government and among the police. A 23-year-old fruit vendor set himself on fire in front of the police station in January 2011 to protest the police corruption in Tunis. The revolution sparked, and it was diffused in part by the actions of another young man, Hamada Ben Amor, who takes the stage name of El Général. He posted videos on YouTube and Facebook of rap songs he wrote in protest of his president and the corruption rampant in his government (see Chapter 4). During protests in Egypt in spring 2011, El Général's anthems caught hold and inspired Egyptians to protest as well.

**Social networks**, especially Facebook and Twitter, were credited with making revolutions in Tunisia and Egypt possible—first, through protest rap music and second, through construction and completion of plans for protest. In Egypt, a Google employee anonymously created a Facebook page titled "We are all Khaled Said" in honor of a young Egyptian businessman who was beaten and killed by two police officers. The page garnered 473,000 supporters, and it "helped spread the word about the demonstrations in Egypt, which were ignited after a revolt in neighboring Tunisia toppled the government there" (Preston 2011, 1).

Rap or hiphop music diffused among protesters who shared the Arabic language. Islam, the predominant religion in the region, instructs followers to learn the Arabic language, and most people in the region can speak Arabic (Chapters 6 and 7). El Général's raps, spoken in Arabic, were readily understood by Arabic speakers around the region. He rapped, "My president, your country is dead/People eat garbage/Look at what is happening/Misery everywhere/Nowhere to sleep/I'm speaking for the people who suffer/Ground under feet." The accessibility of social media helped the video of a young man, produced at little production cost, diffuse quickly and broadly through the region.

## PARTICIPATORY DEVELOPMENT

Nongovernmental organizations (NGOs) are nonprofit institutions outside of formal governments that are established to promote particular social or humanitarian ends. Each NGO is a social network in which people with like interests communicate to achieve a goal. A sizeable community of NGOs is concerned with development, and in recent decades they have propagated a web of global networks in response to top-down decision making (e.g., structural adjustment loans). As a result of their networks, NGOs have considerable influence on the development landscape.

NGO development networks serve as a counterbalance to the power of the major decision makers in the world, states, international financial institutions, and corporations. The stated goal of many development-oriented NGOs is to include the voices of the poor and those directly affected by development, permitting them to express their opinions and lifestyles. Some NGOs have been criticized for falling far short of this goal, but development networks now make it possible for NGOs in different parts of the world to work together to reach a consensus on how to achieve economic development and to respond to crises. The power of these networks was very much in evidence in the wake of the devastating 2010 earthquake in Haiti, when NGOs from far-flung parts of the globe cooperated in an effort to respond to the crisis. The work of NGOs is also evidenced in Brazil's Bolsa Familia program (Chapter 10), which entrusts the poor with conditional cash transfers so that those in poverty can decide what their families most need. Bolsa Familia was expanded in 2003, and its success prompted the World Bank president to speak in favor of conditional cash transfers to the poor as a development strategy in 2011.

Despite the goal of sharing power across a network, most development networks (like other networks) have power differences within them. Indeed, Leroi Henry, Giles Mohan, and Helen Yanacopulos (2004) find that power relationships exist both within and between networks—often privileging the views of NGOs headquartered in the core, as opposed to those in the periphery.

A growing number of development entities are promoting local solutions to development. **Participatory development**—the idea that locals should be engaged in deciding what development means for them and how to achieve it—is another response to top-down decision making. Stuart Corbridge has studied how the global push for participatory development has encouraged the government of India to enact participatory development programs. Corbridge and his colleague Sanjay Kumar describe the goal of participatory development as giving the people who are directly affected by policies and programs a voice in making the policies and programs—that is, to use local networks to shape development for local goals. Kumar and Corbridge found that "[t]here can be no doubting the sincerity of" participatory development programs "to engage the rural poor" in India. However, they also found that local politics factor into the distribution of poverty alleviation schemes because richer farmers and elites in rural areas tend to be most involved with development program.

This situation is a failure not of development, they maintain, but rather of the definition of success. The goal of the program they studied in India was to get seeds to farmers and to create irrigation schemes. The program has succeeded in this respect for many farmers, though not for the poorest farmers. Their lack of participation is not a reason to abandon the participatory program, however. According to Kumar and Corbridge, the program (like other participatory development programs) has to "operate in an environment that is dominated by better off farmers and particular community groups." They argue that the definition of success must change because development organizations cannot expect the poorest to "participate in groups that have little meaning for them." In other words, Kumar and Corbridge contend that it is worthwhile to invest in participatory development, even if existing political and economic divisions among the poor influence who receives assistance. They conclude that efforts to move decision making to those most affected represent a move in the right direction and should not be cast aside.

The World Bank, the International Monetary Fund, and even state governments are increasingly embracing the ideal of participatory development, loosening demands for trade liberalization in the periphery and semiperiphery. As Kumar and Corbridge explain, politics will enter participatory development, just as it enters the development networks and the global development organizations. The goal of participatory development is worthwhile, even if the short-term results do not mesh with Western concepts of success.

## Networks and Information

The diffusion of products and ideas associated with popular culture depends largely on globalized media and retail store networks, as well as the advertising practices in which both engage. Today's media encompass much more than print, radio, and television. With technological advances, media include entertainment, music, video games, streaming media sites, smart phone apps, and social networks. Generation Like (Chapter 4) relies on social networks, and the teenagers and young adults who use them generate and diffuse popular culture.

Through a series of mergers and consolidations occurring mostly in the post–Cold War era, global media are controlled largely by six globe-spanning corporations: Time-Warner, Disney, Bertelsmann, Viacom, News Corporation, and Vivendi Universal. These six media corporations (along with other media corporations) are masters of **vertical integration**. A vertically integrated corporation is one that has ownership in all or most of the points along the production and consumption of a commodity chain.

Media companies compete for three things: *content, delivery,* and *consumers* (Pereira 2003). Through consolidation and mergers, vertically integrated global media companies such as the Walt Disney Corporation (Fig. 14.8) control

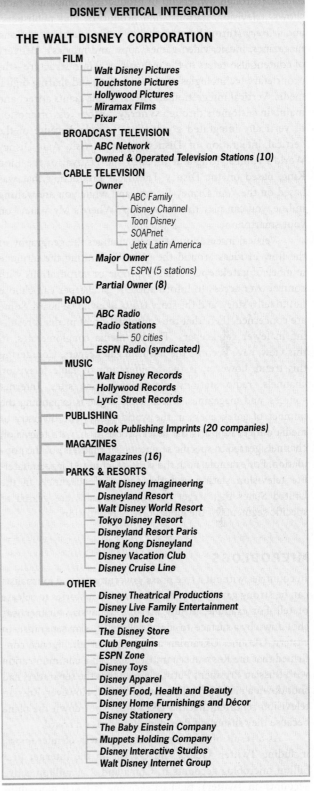

**■ Figure 14.8**

**The Walt Disney Corporation.** A list of companies that are part of the Walt Disney Company, based on data collected by the Columbia School of Journalism in 2013. By owning film, television, radio, and publishing, Disney can keep its message intact through vertical integration and synergy.  *Data from*: Columbia Journalism Review, Who Owns What. http://www.cjrarchives.org/tools/owners/disney.asp

*content* (through ownership of production companies, radio shows, television stations, film producers, and publishers) and *delivery* (through ownership of radio, television stations, magazines, music, video games, apps, and movies). Delivery of content also refers to the technological infrastructure—the proprietary technologies used for creating and sharing digital media. Vertical integration also helps media giants attract and maintain customers through **synergy**, or the cross promotion of vertically integrated goods. For example, because of the vertical integration of Disney, you can visit Walt Disney World's Animal Kingdom to catch the Festival of the Lion King, based on the Disney Theatrical Production that was based on the Walt Disney Picture, and while you are waiting in line, you can play the Disney app "Where's My Water" on your smartphone.

Vertical integration of media changes the geography of the flow of ideas around the globe by limiting the ultimate number of **gatekeepers**, that is, people or corporations with control over access to information. A gatekeeper can choose not to tell a story, and the story is less likely to be heard. Some are concerned, then, that the consolidation of media is resulting in fewer gatekeepers. The big media conglomerates, in this view, have become the ultimate gatekeepers. Countering this trend, however, is the proliferation of cable television channels, radio stations, streaming media sites, Internet sources, and magazines, which some argue is expanding the number of gatekeepers in the world today. The diversity of media outlets supports the latter proposition, with television channels geared to specific segments (or markets) of the population. For example, both the wide-reaching Al-Jazeera satellite television station and the new cable channels in the United States that target Muslim Americans are geared to specific segments of the global or U.S. population.

## MICROBLOGS

In countries without a free press, governments and journalists can be strong gatekeepers by choosing what stories to release or tell. For example, in July 2014, a Malaysian airliner was shot down by a surface-to-air missile by Russian separatists in eastern Ukraine. Ukrainian and American intelligence confirmed that the Russian separatist leader, in a communication with Russian President Putin, claimed that the separatists had shot down a plane (The Economist 2014). However, Russian television reported that the Ukrainians shot down the plane because they suspected President Putin was on board.

As a result of the extraordinary growth of microblogs, including Twitter, Weibo, and Qzone, on the Internet (1.3 billion microblog accounts in China and 271 million active accounts on Twitter), tight gatekeeping is much more difficult. A microblog allows individuals, without cost, to post thoughts, photographs, and experiences, albeit in a limited number of characters, and to spread word about a cause or concern through hashtags. The person or organization behind each account can represent actors and networks at local, regional, national, or global scales.

# Networks and Economic Exchange

Unlike traditional vertically integrated media, social media are more often horizontally integrated. A horizontally integrated corporation is one that acquires ownership of other corporations engaged in similar activities. The retail industry may appear to be dominated by a large number of different companies; however, many retail companies bearing different names are in fact owned by the same horizontally integrated parent corporation.

With **horizontal integration**, similar products are owned by one company, but they are branded separately so that consumers may think they are separate companies. Horizontal integration is common in clothing companies and housewares. Williams-Sonoma, West Elm, and Pottery Barn are separate stores in a mall, but they are all owned by the same parent company. Likewise, Athleta, Old Navy, Gap, and Banana Republic are separate stores in a mall but are all owned by Gap, Inc.

The incentive for horizontal integration is that a company successful in producing one good can replicate its success, share costs (like websites), and increase profits at different price points or slightly different genres of the same good. Facebook bought Instagram, another social media network, in 2012. In 2014, the messaging app What's App gained in popularity, and so Facebook purchased it as well. Facebook's goal is to be involved in some way each time Generation Like consumes or shares online.

## COMMUNITY-SUPPORTED AGRICULTURE

In the von Thünen model (Chapter 11), farms surrounded urban areas in a regular pattern, and farmers provided fresh food to the people in cities by bringing their products to markets. With the industrialization of agriculture (Chapter 11), the distance between farmers and consumers has increased, figuratively and literally. Consumers often do not consider the source of their food, and some processed foods look so little like natural foods that it is all too easy to forget farmers were involved in producing the food.

Container ships and refrigerated trucking and shipping (Chapter 12) now allow consumers in cold regions of the world in winter months to purchase fresh fruits and vegetables grown thousands of miles away, in warmer climates. In 2007, when the United States conducted its last Census of Agriculture, it found the number of principal operators of farms in the United States had grown by 4 percent, to 2.2 million people. According to geographer Steven Schnell (2007), one of the reasons the number of farmers in the United States has increased is the growth in the number of **community-supported agriculture** groups, known as CSAs (Fig. 14. 9). Schnell explains that CSAs began in Japan in the 1960s when a group of women "dissatisfied with imported, processed, and pesticide-laden food, made arrangements directly with farmers to provide natural, organic, local food for their tables."

From its hearth in Japan, CSAs diffused to Europe and then to the United States. The first CSA in the United States

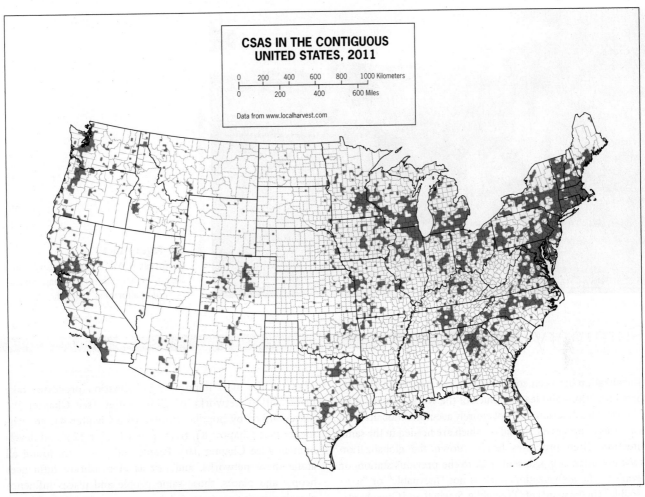

■ **Figure 14.9**
**CSAs in the Contiguous United States, 2011.** Schnell (2007) found that CSAs are more likely to be found in urban or suburban areas where people have higher levels of education and are actively involved in discussing politics. *Courtesy of:* Local Harvest.org.

was in the Berkshire Mountains of Massachusetts. By 2011, the number of CSAs in the United States had risen to over 4000, according to Local Harvest, an organization that maps CSAs to help consumers and farmers connect (Fig. 14.10).

Through a CSA, a farmer and consumers create a network whereby both assume risk. Consumers pay for a share of the farmer's harvest, typically fruits and vegetables, before the growing season begins. Farmers use the cash to purchase seeds, then plant, harvest, and deliver goods to consumers over a period of weeks during the growing season. Both Schnell and Local Harvest agree that CSA farmers typically use organic growing standards (Chapter 11) but do not take the time to certify their land and produce as organic.

Analyzing the global consolidation of media, the networking of NGOs concerned with development, and the global presence of retail corporations helps us see the diversity of global networks, with some increasingly centralized and others increasingly disaggregated. Aside from the spatial

characteristics of the network itself, what is interesting for geographers is the impact of these networks on local places, for globalized networks do not affect individual places in the same way. People interact with the global network, shaping it, resisting it, embracing it, and responding to globalization in unique ways.

Think about the information you are exposed to through the Internet, television, and other social media each day. Make a list of the companies that publish or produce these news sources you use. Go to *Columbia Journalism Review's* website, Who Owns What (http://www.cjr.org/resources/). Determine how many gatekeepers control the information you use to make decisions and understand your world.

Jeff and Meggan Haller/Keyhole Photo/© Corbis

■ **Figure 14.10**
**Belforest, Alabama.** Buford and Stewart Foster count and bag corn to be sold at a farmers' market.

## Summary

Globalization has been compared to a runaway train blowing through stations and leaving much of the world to stare at its caboose. This description is not entirely accurate. Globalization is a series of processes, not all of which are headed in the same direction. Even processes headed down the globalization track are often stopped, sent back to the previous station, or derailed. The globalization track is not "inevitable" or "irreversible" (in the words of O'Loughlin, Staeheli, and Greenberg).

Many of the most important globalization processes take place within networks of global cities (see Chapter 9), places linked by popular culture (see Chapter 4), governments (see Chapter 8), trade (see Chapter 12), and development (see Chapter 10). People and places are found all along these networks, and just as globalization influences people and places, those same people and places influence globalization's trajectory and future.

## Geographic Concepts

imagined community
globalization
Washington Consensus
networks

Digital Divide
social networks
participatory development
vertical integration

synergy
gatekeepers
horizontal integration
community-supported agriculture

## Learn More Online

About media ownership
*Columbia Journalism Review's* Who Owns What Website
www.cjr.org/tools/owners/

About the Network of World Cities
www.brook.edu/metro/pubs/20050222_worldcities.pdf

About the World Social Forum
www.forumsocialmundial.org.br/

## Watch It Online

About Gross National Happiness in Bhutan
http://youtu.be/CXJwNSkdTH0

About the Growth of the World City of Lagos, Nigeria
http://youtu.be/x5_9m4je3ck

# AREA AND DEMOGRAPHIC DATA FOR THE WORLD'S STATES

# Appendix B: Area and Demographic Data for the World's States

| Country | Land Area sq. km. | Land Area sq. mi. | Arable Land in sq. km. | Population 2013 (millions) | Population 2025 (millions) | Population Density Arithmetic | Population Density Physiologic | Total Fertility Rate (TFR) | Life Expectancy Male (years) | Life Expectancy Female (years) | Infant Mortality per 1,000 | Natural Increase (percent) | Net Migration per 1,000 | Urban (percent) | Poverty Index | GINI Index | Human Development Index (HDI) | Corruption Index | GNI per Capita | CO₂ Emissions per Capita |
|---|---|---|---|---|---|---|---|---|---|---|---|---|---|---|---|---|---|---|---|---|
| WORLD | 134,134,451 | 51,789,601 | 49,194,729 | 7,137 | 8,095 | 53.21 | 145.08 | 2.5 | 68 | 73 | 40 | 1.2 | 0 | 52 | | | 0.702 | | $11,690 | |
| SUBSAHARAN AFRICA | 22,434,378 | 8,661,914 | 9,591,310 | 1,100 | 1,464 | 49.03 | 114.69 | 4.8 | 57 | 60 | 68 | 2.6 | 0 | 40 | | | | | | |
| Angola | 1,246,700 | 481,351 | 591,900 | 21.6 | 31.6 | 17.33 | 36.49 | 6.3 | 50 | 53 | 98 | 3.2 | 1 | 59 | | 42.66 | 0.526 | 23 | 4580 | 1.6 |
| Benin | 112,622 | 43,483 | 37,000 | 9.6 | 13.4 | 85.24 | 259.46 | 5.2 | 58 | 60 | 70 | 2.9 | 0 | 45 | 0.401 | 43.53 | 0.476 | 36 | 750 | 0.5 |
| Botswana | 581,730 | 224,606 | 258,870 | 1.9 | 2.1 | 3.27 | 7.34 | 2.7 | 47 | 46 | 33 | 0.7 | 2 | 24 | | 60.46 | 0.683 | | 7650 | 2.7 |
| Burkina Faso | 274,200 | 105,869 | 120,700 | 18 | 25.6 | 65.65 | 149.13 | 6 | 55 | 56 | 73 | 3.1 | -2 | 27 | 0.508 | 39.78 | 0.388 | 21 | 670 | 0.1 |
| Burundi | 27,830 | 10,745 | 19,330 | 10.9 | 15.5 | 391.66 | 563.89 | 6.2 | 51 | 55 | 89 | 3.2 | 1 | 11 | 0.442 | | 0.389 | | 240 | 0 |
| Cameroon | 475,440 | 183,567 | 97,500 | 21.5 | 29.5 | 45.22 | 220.51 | 5.1 | 53 | 55 | 62 | 2.7 | -1 | 52 | 0.260 | 40.72 | 0.504 | 25 | 1170 | 0.4 |
| Cape Verde | 4,033 | 1,557 | 750 | 0.5 | 0.6 | 123.98 | 666.67 | 2.4 | 70 | 78 | 18 | 1.5 | -9 | 63 | | 43.82 | 0.636 | | 3830 | 0.7 |
| Central African Republic | 622,984 | 240,534 | 50,800 | 4.7 | 6.1 | 7.54 | 92.52 | 6.2 | 47 | 51 | 116 | 3.2 | 0 | 39 | 0.424 | 56.30 | 0.341 | 25 | 510 | 0.1 |
| Chad | 1,284,000 | 495,752 | 499,320 | 12.2 | 17.8 | 9.50 | 24.43 | 7 | 49 | 51 | 106 | 3.6 | -2 | 22 | | 43.30 | 0.372 | 19 | 770 | 0 |
| Comoros | 2,235 | 863 | 1,580 | 0.8 | 1 | 357.94 | 506.33 | 4.3 | 59 | 62 | 69 | 2.3 | -3 | 28 | | | 0.488 | 28 | 840 | 0.2 |
| Congo | 342,000 | 132,046 | 106,000 | 4.4 | 5.8 | 12.87 | 41.51 | 5 | 56 | 59 | 66 | 2.8 | -1 | 64 | 0.192 | 40.17 | 0.564 | 22 | 2550 | 0.5 |
| Congo, Dem. Rep. | 2,344,858 | 905,350 | 260,100 | 71.1 | 99.7 | 30.32 | 273.36 | 6.3 | 48 | 51 | 111 | 2.9 | 0 | 34 | 0.399 | | 0.338 | 22 | 230 | 0 |
| Cote d'Ivoire | 322,463 | 124,503 | 206,000 | 21.1 | 27.5 | 65.43 | 102.43 | 5 | 49 | 51 | 68 | 2.2 | -1 | 51 | 0.307 | 43.19 | 0.452 | 27 | 1220 | 0.3 |
| Djibouti | 23,200 | 8,958 | 17,020 | 0.9 | 1.1 | 38.79 | 52.88 | 3.7 | 59 | 62 | 58 | 2 | -4 | 77 | 0.127 | | 0.467 | 36 | | 0.6 |
| Equatorial Guinea | 28,051 | 10,830 | 2,840 | 0.8 | 1 | 28.52 | 281.69 | 5.1 | 51 | 54 | 65 | 2.3 | 6 | 39 | | | 0.556 | 19 | 13560 | 6.7 |
| Eritrea | 117,600 | 45,405 | 75,920 | 5.8 | 8 | 49.32 | 76.40 | 4.9 | 59 | 64 | 46 | 3.1 | 2 | 21 | 0.537 | | 0.381 | 20 | 450 | 0.1 |
| Ethiopia | 1,104,300 | 426,370 | 364,880 | 89.2 | 118.1 | 80.78 | 244.46 | 4.8 | 61 | 64 | 52 | 2.6 | 0 | 17 | | 33.60 | 0.435 | 33 | 380 | 0.1 |
| Gabon | 267,667 | 103,346 | 51,600 | 1.6 | 2.1 | 5.98 | 31.01 | 4.1 | 62 | 64 | 43 | 2.2 | 1 | 86 | 0.073 | | 0.674 | 34 | 10040 | 1.7 |
| Gambia | 11,295 | 4,361 | 6,050 | 1.9 | 2.7 | 168.22 | 134.05 | 5.8 | 57 | 60 | 81 | 3.3 | -2 | 57 | 0.329 | | 0.441 | 28 | 510 | 0.3 |
| Ghana | 238,533 | 92,098 | 157,000 | 26.1 | 32.7 | 109.42 | 166.24 | 4.2 | 60 | 62 | 53 | 2.4 | 0 | 52 | 0.144 | | 0.573 | 46 | 1550 | 0.4 |
| Guinea | 245,857 | 94,925 | 144,000 | 11.8 | 15.7 | 48.00 | 81.94 | 5.1 | 55 | 56 | 67 | 2.6 | 0 | 35 | 0.548 | 33.68 | 0.392 | 24 | 440 | 0.1 |
| Guinea-Bissau | 36,125 | 13,948 | 16,300 | 1.7 | 2.2 | 47.06 | 104.29 | 5 | 52 | 55 | 96 | 2.5 | -2 | 44 | 0.495 | | 0.396 | 19 | 510 | 0.2 |
| Kenya | 580,367 | 224,080 | 274,300 | 44.2 | 59.2 | 76.16 | 161.14 | 4.5 | 59 | 62 | 54 | 2.7 | 0 | 24 | 0.226 | | 0.535 | 27 | 860 | 0.3 |
| Lesotho | 30,355 | 11,720 | 22,853 | 2.2 | 2.5 | 72.48 | 96.27 | 3.1 | 48 | 48 | 65 | 1.2 | -2 | 28 | 0.227 | 54.17 | 0.486 | 49 | 1380 | 0 |
| Liberia | 111,369 | 43,000 | 27,100 | 4.4 | 6 | 39.51 | 162.36 | 5.7 | 59 | 61 | 63 | 3.3 | 2 | 48 | 0.459 | 38.16 | 0.412 | | 370 | 0.2 |
| Madagascar | 587,041 | 226,657 | 414,050 | 22.5 | 31.2 | 38.33 | 54.34 | 4.6 | 62 | 65 | 39 | 2.8 | 0 | 33 | 0.420 | 40.63 | 0.498 | 28 | 430 | 0.1 |
| Malawi | 118,484 | 45,747 | 57,350 | 16.3 | 22.7 | 137.57 | 284.22 | 5.6 | 54 | 54 | 89 | 2.9 | 0 | 16 | 0.332 | 46.18 | 0.414 | | 320 | 0.1 |
| Mali | 1,240,192 | 478,838 | 416,510 | 15.5 | 21.8 | 12.50 | 37.21 | 6.1 | 52 | 56 | 58 | 3.1 | -3 | 35 | 0.533 | 33.02 | 0.407 | 28 | 660 | 0 |
| Mauritania | 1,030,700 | 397,953 | 396,610 | 3.7 | 4.9 | 3.59 | 9.33 | 4.8 | 60 | 63 | 73 | 2.6 | -1 | 41 | 0.362 | 40.46 | 0.487 | 30 | 1110 | 0.6 |
| Mauritius | 2,040 | 788 | 870 | 1.3 | 1.3 | 637.25 | 1494.25 | 1.4 | 70 | 77 | 12.9 | 0.4 | 0 | 42 | | | 0.771 | 52 | 8570 | 3.2 |
| Mozambique | 799,380 | 308,641 | 499,500 | 24.3 | 33.5 | 30.40 | 48.65 | 5.9 | 49 | 50 | 64 | 3 | 0 | 31 | 0.390 | 45.66 | 0.393 | 30 | 510 | 0.1 |
| Namibia | 824,292 | 318,259 | 388,090 | 2.4 | 3 | 2.91 | 6.18 | 3.2 | 61 | 66 | 36 | 1.9 | -2 | 38 | 0.200 | 61.32 | 0.624 | 48 | 5610 | 1.5 |
| Niger | 1,267,000 | 489,189 | 447,820 | 16.9 | 27 | 13.34 | 37.74 | 7.6 | 57 | 58 | 71 | 3.8 | 0 | 18 | 0.584 | 31.16 | 0.337 | 34 | 390 | 0.1 |
| Nigeria | 923,768 | 356,667 | 720,000 | 173.6 | 239.9 | 187.93 | 241.11 | 6 | 51 | 52 | 97 | 2.8 | 0 | 50 | 0.239 | 42.95 | 0.504 | 25 | 1440 | 0.5 |
| Reunion | 2,510 | 969 | 350 | 0.8 | 1 | 318.73 | 2285.71 | 2.4 | 77 | 83 | 7 | 1.2 | 0 | 94 | | | | | | |
| Rwanda | 26,338 | 10,169 | 18,568 | 11.1 | 15 | 421.44 | 597.80 | 4.7 | 61 | 65 | 51 | 2.9 | -1 | 19 | 0.352 | 50.82 | 0.506 | 53 | 600 | 0.1 |
| São Tomé and Príncipe | 964 | 372 | 497 | 0.2 | 0.3 | 207.47 | 402.41 | 4.6 | 64 | 68 | 44 | 3.1 | -2 | 63 | 0.217 | 33.87 | 0.558 | | 1310 | 0.6 |
| Senegal | 196,722 | 75,954 | 90,150 | 13.5 | 18.5 | 68.62 | 149.75 | 5 | 62 | 65 | 51 | 3.1 | -2 | 47 | 0.390 | 40.31 | 0.485 | | 1030 | 0.5 |
| Seychelles | 455 | 176 | 30 | 0.1 | 0.1 | 219.78 | 3333.33 | 2.4 | 69 | 78 | 9.8 | 1.1 | -3 | 54 | | 65.77 | 0.756 | 54 | 12180 | 7.8 |
| Sierra Leone | 71,740 | 27,699 | 40,970 | 6.2 | 7.7 | 86.42 | 151.33 | 4.9 | 45 | 45 | 128 | 2 | 0 | 41 | 0.405 | 35.35 | 0.374 | 30 | 580 | 0.1 |
| Somalia | 637,657 | 246,199 | 441,290 | 10.4 | 14.6 | 16.31 | 23.57 | 6.8 | 53 | 56 | 83 | 3.2 | 4 | 38 | 0.500 | | | 8 | | 0.1 |
| South Africa | 1,219,090 | 470,691 | 963,410 | 53 | 56.9 | 43.48 | 55.01 | 2.4 | 56 | 60 | 45 | 1 | 4 | 62 | 0.041 | 65.02 | 0.658 | | 7460 | 9.2 |
| South Sudan | 644,329 | 248,775 | 285,332 | 9.8 | 13.5 | 15.21 | 34.35 | 5.1 | 53 | 55 | 81 | 2.4 | 16 | 18 | | 45.53 | | 14 | 790 | .. |

## Appendix B: Area and Demographic Data for the World's States (Continued)

| Country | Land Area sq. km. | Land Area sq. mi. | Arable Land in sq. km. | Population 2013 (millions) | Population 2025 (millions) | Population Density Arithmetic | Population Density Physiologic | Total Fertility Rate (TFR) | Life Expectancy Male (years) | Life Expectancy Female (years) | Infant Mortality per 1,000 | Natural Increase (percent) | Net Migration per 1,000 | Urban (percent) | Poverty Index | GINI Index | Human Development Index (HDI) | Corruption Index | GNI per Capita | CO₂ Emissions per Capita |
|---|---|---|---|---|---|---|---|---|---|---|---|---|---|---|---|---|---|---|---|---|
| Swaziland | 17,364 | 6,704 | 12,220 | 1.2 | 1.4 | 69.11 | 98.20 | 3.5 | 49 | 48 | 68 | 1.6 | -1 | 21 | 0.113 | 51.49 | 0.530 | | 2860 | 0.9 |
| Tanzania | 947,300 | 365,753 | 406,500 | 49.1 | 69.1 | 51.83 | 120.79 | 5.4 | 59 | 61 | 52 | 3.1 | -1 | 27 | 0.335 | 37.82 | 0.488 | 33 | 570 | 0.2 |
| Togo | 56,785 | 21,925 | 38,500 | 6.2 | 8.2 | 109.18 | 161.04 | 4.7 | 55 | 57 | 69 | 2.6 | 0 | 38 | 0.260 | 45.96 | 0.473 | 29 | 500 | 0.2 |
| Uganda | 241,038 | 93,065 | 142,620 | 36.9 | 55.4 | 153.09 | 258.73 | 6.2 | 57 | 59 | 54 | 3.5 | 1 | 16 | 0.359 | 44.55 | 0.484 | 26 | 480 | 0.1 |
| Zambia | 752,618 | 290,586 | 238,360 | 14.2 | 21.5 | 18.87 | 59.57 | 5.9 | 54 | 57 | 69 | 3.3 | 1 | 39 | 0.318 | 57.49 | 0.561 | | 1350 | 0.2 |
| Zimbabwe | 390,757 | 150,871 | 162,000 | 13 | 17.9 | 33.27 | 80.25 | 3.8 | 55 | 56 | 41 | 2.2 | 0 | 39 | 0.181 | | 0.492 | 21 | 650 | 0.7 |
| **NORTH AFRICA AND SOUTHWEST ASIA** | 12,710,422 | 4,907,492 | 4,893,118 | 251 | 307 | 19.75 | 51.30 | 2.9 | 70 | 75 | 27 | 1.8 | 2 | 70 | | | | | | 1.4 |
| Algeria | 2,381,741 | 919,590 | 414,320 | 38.3 | 46.5 | 16.08 | 92.44 | 3 | 76 | 77 | 23 | 1.9 | 0 | 73 | 0.002 | 30.30 | | 36 | 3720 | 1.4 |
| Armenia | 29,743 | 11,484 | 16,830 | 3 | 3 | 100.86 | 178.25 | 1.6 | 71 | 78 | 11 | 0.4 | 0 | 63 | 0.009 | 33.06 | | 28 | 6220 | 5.1 |
| Azerbaijan | 86,600 | 33,436 | 47,683 | 9.4 | 10.4 | 108.55 | 197.14 | 2.3 | 71 | 77 | 11 | 1.3 | 0 | 53 | | | | 48 | 19560 | 19.3 |
| Bahrain | 760 | 293 | 86 | 1.1 | 1.4 | 1447.37 | 12790.70 | 1.9 | 75 | 78 | 7 | 1.2 | -40 | 100 | | | | | 26110 | 7 |
| Cyprus | 9,251 | 3,572 | 1,249 | 1.1 | 1.4 | 118.91 | 880.70 | 1.5 | 76 | 81 | 6 | 0.6 | 14 | 62 | 0.008 | 41.35 | | 49 | 3290 | 1.4 |
| Egypt | 1,001,450 | 386,660 | 36,120 | 84.7 | 100.1 | 84.58 | 2344.96 | 3 | 69 | 72 | 24 | 1.8 | -1 | 43 | 0.052 | 29.54 | | 16 | 6130 | 3.7 |
| Georgia | 69,700 | 26,911 | 24,650 | 4.5 | 4.2 | 64.56 | 182.56 | 1.7 | 70 | 79 | 13 | 0.2 | 5 | 58 | 0.004 | | | 45 | 32030 | 9.3 |
| Iraq | 438,317 | 169,234 | 76,570 | 35.1 | 49.3 | 80.08 | 458.40 | 4.3 | 66 | 73 | 28 | 2.6 | -1 | 71 | | 33.69 | | | 4670 | 3.4 |
| Israel | 20,770 | 8,019 | 5,232 | 8.1 | 9.8 | 389.99 | 1548.17 | 3 | 80 | 84 | 3.5 | 1.6 | 2 | 91 | | | | 28 | 9190 | 31.3 |
| Jordan | 89,342 | 34,495 | 10,423 | 7.3 | 9.1 | 81.71 | 700.37 | 3.5 | 72 | 74 | 17 | 2.4 | 11 | 83 | 0.007 | | | 47 | | 4.7 |
| Kuwait | 17,818 | 6,880 | 1,520 | 3.5 | 4.3 | 196.43 | 2302.63 | 2.4 | 74 | 76 | 8 | 1.7 | 37 | 98 | | | | | | 20.4 |
| Lebanon | 10,400 | 4,015 | 7,330 | 4.8 | 5 | 461.54 | 654.84 | 1.5 | 77 | 82 | 9 | 0.9 | 18 | 87 | | 41.10 | | | 24310 | 0.6 |
| Libya | 1,759,540 | 679,358 | 153,550 | 6.5 | 7.5 | 3.69 | 42.33 | 2.5 | 73 | 77 | 15 | 2.4 | -6 | 78 | | | | 46 | | 40.3 |
| Morocco | 446,550 | 172,413 | 304,030 | 33 | 38.2 | 73.90 | 108.54 | 2.7 | 69 | 72 | 28 | 1.4 | -3 | 59 | 0.024 | | | | 10830 | 17 |
| Oman | 309,500 | 119,498 | 14,728 | 4 | 5.2 | 12.92 | 271.59 | 2.9 | 74 | 78 | 9 | 1.8 | 42 | 75 | | | | 17 | 38620 | 2.9 |
| Palestinian Territory | 6,260 | 2,417 | 3,730 | 4.4 | 5.9 | 702.88 | 1179.62 | 4.1 | 71 | 74 | 20 | 2.9 | -2 | 83 | | 40.04 | | 50 | 1270 | 4.1 |
| Qatar | 11,586 | 4,473 | 657 | 2.2 | 2.7 | 189.88 | 3348.55 | 2.2 | 77 | 79 | 7 | 1.1 | 49 | 100 | 0.191 | | 0.717 | 18 | 5020 | 19.9 |
| Saudi Arabia | 2,149,690 | 829,995 | 1,733,900 | 30.1 | 36.7 | 14.00 | 17.36 | 2.9 | 73 | 75 | 16 | 1.8 | 2 | 81 | | | 0.682 | 36 | 2980 | 1 |
| Sudan | 1,861,484 | 718,719 | 1,127,020 | 34.2 | 44.7 | 18.37 | 30.35 | 4.6 | 60 | 63 | 56 | 2.2 | -4 | 33 | 0.036 | | | 32 | 2960 | 3.3 |
| Syria | 185,180 | 71,498 | 139,210 | 21.9 | 27.9 | 118.26 | 157.32 | 3.1 | 72 | 78 | 17 | 2.2 | -14 | 54 | | 30.75 | 0.784 | 15 | 1500 | 2.6 |
| Tunisia | 163,610 | 63,170 | 100,790 | 10.9 | 12.1 | 66.62 | 108.15 | 2.2 | 73 | 77 | 16 | 1.2 | -1 | 66 | | | 0.617 | 37 | 4150 | 9.8 |
| Turkey | 783,562 | 302,533 | 384,070 | 76.1 | 85.5 | 97.12 | 198.14 | 2.1 | 71 | 76 | 21 | 1.2 | 0 | 77 | | 40.88 | | 11 | 2960 | 1.6 |
| United Arab Emirates | 83,600 | 32,278 | 3,970 | 9.3 | 11.5 | 111.24 | 2342.57 | 1.9 | 76 | 78 | 7 | 1.5 | 11 | 83 | | 35.29 | 0.473 | | 1500 | 0.3 |
| Western Sahara | 266,000 | 102,703 | 50,040 | 0.6 | 0.8 | 2.26 | 11.99 | 2.5 | 65 | 69 | 39 | 2.3 | 18 | 82 | 0.006 | 35.79 | 0.721 | | 4150 | 2.5 |
| Yemen | 527,968 | 203,848 | 235,410 | 25.2 | 34 | 47.73 | 107.05 | 4.9 | 61 | 63 | 72 | 2.7 | -1 | 29 | | | | | | |
| **SOUTH ASIA** | 6,779,264 | 2,617,474 | 3,098,440 | 1,779 | 2,047 | 3,664 | 10,631 | 2.6 | 65 | 68 | 47 | 1.6 | -1 | 32 | | | | | | |
| Afghanistan | 652,230 | 251,826 | 379,100 | 30.6 | 39.6 | 46.92 | 80.72 | 5.4 | 59 | 61 | 71 | 2.8 | -5 | 24 | 0.293 | | | 8 | 680 | 0.3 |
| Bangladesh | 143,998 | 55,598 | 91,250 | 156.6 | 177.9 | 1087.52 | 1716.16 | 2.3 | 69 | 71 | 35 | 1.5 | -3 | 26 | 0.237 | 32.12 | | 27 | 840 | 0.4 |
| Bhutan | 38,394 | 14,824 | 5,200 | 0.70 | 0.9 | 18.23 | 134.62 | 3.6 | 65 | 69 | 4 | 1.5 | 0 | 36 | 0.128 | 38.73 | | | 2420 | 0.7 |
| India | 3,287,263 | 1,269,212 | 1,793,000 | 1,276.50 | 1,443.30 | 388.32 | 711.94 | 2.4 | 65 | 68 | 44 | 1.5 | -1 | 31 | 0.282 | 33.60 | | 36 | 1550 | 1.7 |
| Iran | 1,648,195 | 636,368 | 491,310 | 76.5 | 87 | 46.41 | 155.71 | 1.9 | 72 | 75 | 19 | 1.4 | -1 | 71 | 0.008 | | | 25 | 5750 | 7.7 |
| Maldives | 298 | 115 | 70 | 0.4 | 0.4 | 1342.28 | 5714.29 | 2.3 | 73 | 75 | 9 | 1.9 | 0 | 35 | | | | | | 3.3 |
| Nepal | 147,181 | 56,827 | 41,210 | 26.8 | 30.4 | 182.09 | 650.33 | 2.6 | 66 | 69 | 46 | 1.7 | -5 | 17 | 0.197 | 32.82 | | 31 | 700 | 0.1 |
| Pakistan | 796,095 | 307,372 | 270,400 | 190.7 | 245.9 | 239.54 | 705.25 | 3.8 | 65 | 67 | 74 | 2.3 | -2 | 35 | 0.237 | 29.63 | | 28 | 1260 | 0.9 |
| Sri Lanka | 65,610 | 25,332 | 26,900 | 20.5 | 22 | 312.45 | 762.08 | 2.1 | 71 | 77 | 12 | 1.2 | -2 | 15 | | 36.40 | | 37 | 2920 | 0.6 |
| **SOUTHEAST ASIA** | 4,494,507 | 1,735,330 | 1,285,456 | 612 | 699 | 136.17 | 476.10 | 2.4 | 68 | 73 | 28 | 1.3 | -1 | 47 | | | | | | |
| Brunei | 5,765 | 2,226 | 134 | 0.4 | 0.5 | 69.38 | 2985.07 | 1.6 | 77 | 79 | 7 | 1.4 | 3 | 72 | | | | | | 22.9 |
| Cambodia | 181,035 | 69,898 | 57,550 | 14.4 | 17.2 | 79.54 | 250.22 | 2.8 | 61 | 64 | 45 | 1.8 | -4 | 20 | 0.211 | 31.82 | | 20 | 880 | 0.3 |

# Appendix B: Area and Demographic Data for the World's States (Continued)

| Country | Land Area sq. km. | Land Area sq. mi. | Arable Land in sq. km. | Population 2013 (millions) | Population 2025 (millions) | Pop. Density Arithmetic | Pop. Density Physiologic | Total Fertility Rate (TFR) | Life Exp. Male (years) | Life Exp. Female (years) | Infant Mortality per 1,000 | Natural Increase (percent) | Net Migration per 1,000 | Urban (percent) | Poverty Index | GINI Index | Human Development Index (HDI) | Corruption Index | GNI per Capita | $CO_2$ Emissions per Capita |
|---|---|---|---|---|---|---|---|---|---|---|---|---|---|---|---|---|---|---|---|---|
| Indonesia | 1,904,569 | 735,354 | 565,000 | 248.5 | 290.6 | 130.48 | 439.82 | 2.6 | 68 | 72 | 32 | 1.5 | -1 | 50 | 0.024 | 38.14 | | 32 | 3420 | 1.8 |
| Laos | 236,800 | 91,428 | 24,690 | 6.7 | 7.9 | 28.29 | 271.36 | 3.2 | 66 | 69 | 68 | 2 | -2 | 27 | 0.186 | 36.22 | | 26 | 1270 | 0.3 |
| Malaysia | 329,847 | 127,354 | 77,495 | 29.8 | 34.3 | 90.34 | 384.54 | 2.1 | 72 | 77 | 7 | 1.3 | 4 | 64 | | 46.21 | | 50 | 9820 | 7.7 |
| Myanmar | 676,590 | 261,232 | 105,770 | 53.3 | 57.7 | 78.78 | 503.92 | 2 | 63 | 67 | 52 | 1 | -2 | 31 | 0.038 | | | 21 | | 0.2 |
| Phillippines | 300,000 | 115,830 | 123,950 | 96.2 | 115.8 | 320.67 | 776.12 | 3 | 66 | 72 | 22 | 1.5 | -2 | 63 | | 43.03 | | 36 | 2500 | 0.9 |
| Singapore | 697 | 269 | 7 | 5.4 | 6.4 | 7747.49 | 771428.57 | 1.3 | 80 | 84 | 1.8 | 0.6 | 19 | 100 | | | | 86 | 47210 | 2.7 |
| Thailand | 513,120 | 198,116 | 218,600 | 66.2 | 67.1 | 129.01 | 302.84 | 1.6 | 71 | 78 | 11 | 0.4 | 0 | 46 | 0.004 | 39.37 | | 35 | 5210 | 4.4 |
| Timor-Leste | 14,874 | 5,743 | 3,840 | 1.1 | 1.3 | 73.95 | 286.46 | 5.7 | 65 | 68 | 45 | 2.7 | -14 | 30 | 0.322 | 30.41 | | 30 | 3620 | 0.2 |
| Vietnam | 331,210 | 127,880 | 108,420 | 89.7 | 100.1 | 270.83 | 827.34 | 2.1 | 70 | 76 | 16 | 1 | 0 | 32 | 0.026 | 35.62 | | 31 | 1550 | 1.7 |
| EAST ASIA | 11,796,361 | 4,554,575 | 6,378,919 | 1,594 | 1,641 | 135.13 | 249.89 | 1.5 | 73 | 78 | 15 | 0.4 | 0 | 57 | | | | | | |
| China | 9,596,960 | 3,705,386 | 5,145,530 | 1,357.40 | 1,406.10 | 141.44 | 263.80 | 1.5 | 73 | 77 | 16 | 0.5 | 0 | 53 | 0.026 | 37.01 | | | 5720 | 6.2 |
| China, Hong Kong SAR | 1,104 | 426 | 51 | 7.2 | 7.9 | 6521.74 | 141176.47 | 1.3 | 81 | 86 | 1.4 | 0.7 | 2 | 100 | | | | 75 | 36560 | 5.2 |
| China, Macao SAR | 28 | 11 | 0 | 0.6 | 0.7 | 21428.57 | 600000.00 | 1.4 | 79 | 86 | 3 | 1 | 34 | 100 | | | | | | |
| Japan | 377,915 | 145,913 | 45,490 | 127.3 | 120.7 | 336.85 | 2798.42 | 1.4 | 79 | 86 | 2.2 | -0.2 | 1 | 91 | | | | 74 | 47870 | 9.2 |
| Korea, North | 120,538 | 46,540 | 26,300 | 24.7 | 26.2 | 204.91 | 939.16 | 2 | 65 | 73 | 27 | 0.5 | 0 | 60 | | | | 8 | | 2.9 |
| Korea, South | 99,720 | 38,502 | 17,800 | 50.2 | 52 | 503.41 | 2820.22 | 1.3 | 78 | 84 | 3 | 0.4 | 1 | 82 | | | | | 22670 | 11.5 |
| Mongolia | 1,564,116 | 603,905 | 1,133,958 | 2.8 | 3.3 | 1.79 | 2.47 | 2.8 | 65 | 72 | 36 | 2.1 | -1 | 63 | 0.077 | 36.52 | | | 3160 | 4.2 |
| Taiwan | 35,980 | 13,892 | 9,790 | 23.4 | 23.7 | 650.36 | 2390.19 | 1.3 | 76 | 83 | 4.2 | 0.3 | 1 | 78 | | | | | | |
| EUROPE | 5,992,312 | 2,313,634 | 2,541,948 | 740 | 746 | 123.49 | 291.12 | 1.6 | 74 | 81 | 5 | 0 | 2 | 71 | | | | | | |
| Albania | 28,748 | 11,100 | 12,013 | 2.8 | 2.9 | 97.40 | 233.08 | 1.8 | 74 | 80 | 14.4 | 0.5 | -15 | 54 | 0.005 | 28.96 | | 31 | 4030 | 1.4 |
| Andorra | 468 | 181 | 202 | 0.1 | 0.1 | 213.68 | 495.05 | 1.2 | - | - | 1.9 | 0.5 | 4 | 90 | | | | | | 6.6 |
| Austria | 83,871 | 32,383 | 31,600 | 8.5 | 8.9 | 101.35 | 268.99 | 1.4 | 78 | 83 | 3.1 | 0 | 5 | 67 | | | | | 47850 | 8 |
| Belarus | 207,600 | 80,154 | 87,960 | 9.5 | 8.9 | 45.76 | 108.00 | 1.6 | 67 | 78 | 3.4 | -0.1 | 1 | 76 | 0.001 | 26.46 | | 29 | 6530 | 6.6 |
| Belgium | 30,528 | 11,787 | 13,330 | 11.2 | 12 | 366.88 | 840.21 | 1.8 | 78 | 83 | 3.3 | 0.2 | 6 | 99 | | | | 75 | 44720 | 10 |
| Bosnia-Herzegovina | 51,197 | 19,767 | 21,590 | 3.8 | 3.8 | 74.22 | 176.01 | 1.2 | 73 | 78 | 5 | -0.1 | 0 | 46 | 0.006 | 33.04 | | | 4750 | 8.1 |
| Bulgaria | 110,879 | 42,810 | 51,230 | 7.3 | 6.7 | 65.84 | 142.49 | 1.5 | 71 | 78 | 7.8 | 0.6 | -1 | 73 | | 34.28 | | | 6840 | 5.9 |
| Croatia | 56,594 | 21,851 | 13,277 | 4.3 | 4.1 | 75.98 | 323.87 | 1.5 | 74 | 80 | 4.7 | -0.2 | -1 | 56 | | 33.61 | | 48 | 13490 | 4.7 |
| Czech Republic | 78,867 | 30,451 | 42,250 | 10.5 | 10.7 | 133.14 | 248.52 | 1.5 | 75 | 81 | 2.6 | 0 | 0 | 74 | | 26.39 | | 48 | 18130 | 10.6 |
| Denmark | 43,094 | 16,639 | 26,240 | 5.6 | 5.8 | 129.95 | 213.41 | 1.7 | 78 | 82 | 3.4 | 0.1 | 4 | 87 | | | | | 59870 | 8.3 |
| Estonia | 45,228 | 17,463 | 9,560 | 1.3 | 1.3 | 28.74 | 135.98 | 1.6 | 71 | 81 | 3.6 | -0.1 | -5 | 69 | | 32.69 | | 78 | 16270 | 13.7 |
| Finland | 338,145 | 130,558 | 22,851 | 5.4 | 5.7 | 15.97 | 236.31 | 1.8 | 78 | 83 | 2.4 | 0.1 | 3 | 68 | | | | 89 | 46490 | 11.5 |
| France | 643,801 | 248,572 | 288,390 | 63.9 | 67.3 | 99.25 | 221.57 | 2 | 79 | 85 | 3.3 | 0.4 | 0 | 78 | | | | | 41750 | 6.7 |
| Germany | 357,022 | 137,846 | 166,640 | 80.6 | 80 | 225.76 | 483.68 | 1.4 | 78 | 83 | 3.3 | -0.2 | 5 | 73 | | | | 78 | 45070 | 5.6 |
| Greece | 131,957 | 50,949 | 81,600 | 11.1 | 11.3 | 84.12 | 136.03 | 1.4 | 79 | 83 | 3.4 | 0 | -1 | 73 | | | | | 23660 | 9.1 |
| Hungary | 93,028 | 35,918 | 53,380 | 9.9 | 9.8 | 106.42 | 185.46 | 1.3 | 71 | 78 | 4.9 | -0.4 | 1 | 69 | | 28.94 | | 54 | 12410 | 7.7 |
| Iceland | 103,000 | 39,768 | 18,722 | 0.3 | 0.4 | 2.91 | 16.02 | 2 | 81 | 84 | 1.8 | 0.8 | -1 | 95 | | | | 78 | 38270 | 5.1 |
| Ireland | 70,273 | 27,132 | 45,330 | 4.6 | 4.9 | 65.46 | 101.48 | 2 | 78 | 83 | 3.5 | 1 | -7 | 60 | | | | 72 | 39020 | 6.2 |
| Italy | 301,340 | 116,347 | 137,285 | 59.8 | 61.6 | 198.45 | 435.59 | 1.4 | 79 | 85 | 3.2 | -0.1 | 4 | 68 | 0.007 | | | 43 | 34640 | 8.9 |
| Kosovo | 10,887 | 4,203 | 5,700 | 1.8 | 2 | 165.33 | 315.79 | 1.9 | 67 | 71 | 10 | 1 | -2 | 38 | | | | 33 | 3600 | 6.7 |
| Latvia | 64,589 | 24,938 | 18,410 | 2 | 1.9 | 30.97 | 108.64 | 1.4 | 69 | 79 | 6.3 | -0.5 | -2 | 68 | 0.005 | 36.03 | | 53 | 14060 | 3.4 |
| Liechtenstein | 160 | 62 | 60 | 0.04 | 0.04 | 250.00 | 666.67 | 1.4 | 79 | 84 | 1.6 | 0.4 | 3 | 15 | | | | | | |
| Lithuania | 65,300 | 25,212 | 28,422 | 3 | 2.8 | 45.94 | 105.55 | 1.4 | 68 | 79 | 3.9 | -0.4 | -7 | 67 | | 32.63 | | | 13820 | 4.1 |
| Luxembourg | 2,586 | 998 | 1,314 | 0.5 | 0.6 | 193.35 | 380.52 | 1.5 | 78 | 83 | 3.4 | 0.4 | 19 | 83 | | | | 80 | 71640 | 21.4 |
| Macedonia | 25,713 | 9,928 | 12,670 | 2.1 | 2.1 | 81.67 | 165.75 | 1.5 | 73 | 77 | 10 | 0.2 | 0 | 65 | 0.007 | 43.56 | | 44 | 4620 | 5.2 |
| Malta | 316 | 122 | 103 | 0.4 | 0.5 | 1265.82 | 3883.50 | 1.5 | 79 | 83 | 6.3 | 0.3 | 3 | 100 | | | | | 19710 | 6.2 |
| Moldova | 33,851 | 13,070 | 24,600 | 4.1 | 3.8 | 121.12 | 166.67 | 1.3 | 67 | 75 | 10 | 0 | 0 | 42 | 0.005 | 30.63 | | 35 | 2070 | 1.4 |

## Appendix B: Area and Demographic Data for the World's States (Continued)

| Country | Land Area sq. km. | Land Area sq. mi. | Arable Land in sq. km. | Population 2013 (millions) | Population 2025 (millions) | Pop. Density Arithmetic | Pop. Density Physiologic | Total Fertility Rate (TFR) | Life Exp. Male (years) | Life Exp. Female (years) | Infant Mortality per 1,000 | Natural Increase (percent) | Net Migration per 1,000 | Urban (percent) | Poverty Index | GINI Index | Human Development Index (HDI) | Corruption Index | GNI per Capita | $CO_2$ Emissions per Capita |
|---|---|---|---|---|---|---|---|---|---|---|---|---|---|---|---|---|---|---|---|---|
| Monaco | 2 | 1 | 1 | 0.04 | 0.04 | 20000.00 | 40000.00 | 1.4 | - | - | - | 0 | 13 | 100 | | | | | | .. |
| Montenegro | 13,812 | 5,333 | 5,130 | 0.6 | 0.7 | 43.44 | 116.96 | 1.7 | 72 | 77 | 5.6 | 0.3 | 0 | 64 | 0.012 | 30.63 | | 44 | 7220 | 4.2 |
| Netherlands | 41,543 | 16,040 | 18,417 | 16.8 | 17.4 | 404.40 | 912.20 | 1.7 | 79 | 83 | 3.7 | 0.2 | 1 | 66 | | | | 83 | 48000 | 11 |
| Norway | 323,802 | 125,020 | 9,917 | 5.1 | 5.8 | 15.75 | 514.27 | 1.8 | 79 | 83 | 2.4 | 0.4 | 9 | 80 | | | | 86 | 98780 | 11.7 |
| Poland | 312,685 | 120,728 | 145,290 | 38.5 | 38.2 | 123.13 | 264.99 | 1.3 | 72 | 81 | 4.7 | 0 | 0 | 61 | | 32.78 | | | 12660 | 8.3 |
| Portugal | 92,090 | 35,556 | 36,360 | 10.5 | 10 | 114.02 | 288.78 | 1.3 | 77 | 83 | 3.4 | -0.2 | -4 | 38 | | | | | 20640 | 4.9 |
| Romania | 238,391 | 92,043 | 137,330 | 21.3 | 20.7 | 89.35 | 155.10 | 1.4 | 70 | 77 | 9.4 | -0.3 | 0 | 55 | | 27.33 | | | 8560 | 3.7 |
| San Marino | 61 | 24 | 10 | 0.03 | 0.04 | 491.80 | 3000.00 | 1.5 | 82 | 86 | 3.1 | 0.2 | 7 | 84 | | | | | | .. |
| Serbia | 77,474 | 29,913 | 50,530 | 7.1 | 6.8 | 91.64 | 140.51 | 1.4 | 72 | 77 | 5.4 | -0.5 | 1 | 59 | 0.001 | 29.65 | | | 5280 | 6.3 |
| Slovakia | 49,035 | 18,932 | 19,274 | 5.4 | 5.4 | 110.13 | 280.17 | 1.3 | 72 | 79 | 5.8 | 0.1 | 1 | 54 | | 26.58 | | 47 | 17190 | 6.6 |
| Slovenia | 20,273 | 7,827 | 4,797 | 2.1 | 2.1 | 103.59 | 437.77 | 1.5 | 76 | 83 | 1.6 | 0.1 | 0 | 50 | | 24.87 | | | 22810 | 7.5 |
| Spain | 505,370 | 195,123 | 269,600 | 46.6 | 45.2 | 92.21 | 172.85 | 1.3 | 79 | 85 | 3.1 | 0.1 | -3 | 77 | | | | | 29270 | 5.9 |
| Sweden | 450,295 | 173,859 | 30,486 | 9.6 | 10.5 | 21.32 | 314.90 | 1.9 | 80 | 84 | 2.6 | 0.2 | 5 | 84 | | | | 89 | 56120 | 5.6 |
| Switzerland | 41,277 | 15,937 | 15,287 | 8.1 | 8.6 | 196.24 | 529.86 | 1.5 | 80 | 85 | 3.8 | 0.2 | 8 | 74 | | | | 85 | 80970 | 5 |
| Ukraine | 603,550 | 233,031 | 412,970 | 45.5 | 41.8 | 75.39 | 110.18 | 1.5 | 66 | 76 | 8.5 | -0.3 | 1 | 69 | 0.002 | 24.82 | | 25 | 3500 | 6.6 |
| United Kingdom | 243,610 | 94,058 | 171,820 | 64.1 | 69.8 | 263.13 | 373.06 | 2 | 80 | 84 | 4.2 | 0.4 | 2 | 80 | | | | 76 | 38500 | 7.9 |
| **NORTH AND CENTRAL EURASIA** | 21,101,693 | 8,147,363 | 4,983,193 | 66 | 78 | 3.13 | 13.24 | 2.6 | 64 | 72 | 38 | 1.7 | -2 | 47 | | | | | | |
| Kazakhstan | 2,724,900 | 1,052,084 | 2,079,750 | 17 | 19.4 | 6.24 | 8.17 | 2.6 | 64 | 74 | 28 | 1.4 | 0 | 55 | 0.004 | 28.56 | | 26 | 9780 | 15.2 |
| Kyrgyzstan | 199,951 | 77,201 | 105,913 | 5.7 | 6.6 | 28.51 | 53.82 | 3.1 | 66 | 74 | 27 | 2.1 | -7 | 34 | 0.013 | 33.39 | | 24 | 990 | 1.2 |
| Russia | 17,098,242 | 6,601,631 | 2,143,500 | 143.5 | 143.1 | 8.39 | 66.95 | 1.7 | 64 | 76 | 7.4 | 0 | 2 | 74 | | 39.69 | | 28 | 12700 | 12.2 |
| Tajikistan | 143,100 | 55,251 | 48,750 | 8.1 | 10.1 | 56.60 | 166.15 | 3.7 | 64 | 71 | 34 | 2.5 | -1 | 26 | 0.031 | 29.88 | | 22 | 880 | 0.4 |
| Turkmenistan | 488,100 | 188,455 | 338,380 | 5.2 | 6 | 10.65 | 15.37 | 2.5 | 61 | 69 | 49 | 1.4 | -2 | 47 | | | | 17 | 5410 | 10.5 |
| Uzbekistan | 447,400 | 172,741 | 266,900 | 30.2 | 35.7 | 67.50 | 113.15 | 2.3 | 65 | 71 | 46 | 1.6 | -2 | 51 | 0.013 | | | 17 | 1720 | 3.7 |
| **NORTH AMERICA** | 19,811,345 | 7,649,160 | 4,740,525 | 352 | 386 | 17.77 | 74.25 | 1.9 | 77 | 81 | 6 | 0.4 | 3 | 81 | | | | | | |
| Canada | 9,984,670 | 3,855,081 | 653,460 | 35.3 | 39.7 | 3.54 | 54.02 | 1.6 | 79 | 83 | 4.9 | 0.4 | 7 | 80 | | | 0.902 | 81 | 51570 | 14.6 |
| United States | 9,826,675 | 3,794,079 | 4,087,065 | 316.2 | 346.4 | 32.18 | 77.37 | 1.9 | 76 | 81 | 5.9 | 0.5 | 2 | 81 | | | 0.914 | 73 | 52340 | 17.6 |
| **LATIN AMERICA AND THE CARIBBEAN** | 20,543,351 | 7,931,787 | 7,491,294 | 606 | 682 | 29.50 | 85.98 | 2.2 | 72 | 78 | 19 | 1.3 | -1 | 79 | | | | | | |
| Antigua and Barbuda | 443 | 171 | 90 | 0.1 | 0.1 | 225.73 | 1111.11 | 2.1 | 74 | 80 | 16 | 0.8 | 0 | 30 | 0.015 | 43.57 | | | 12480 | 5.9 |
| Argentina | 2,780,400 | 1,073,512 | 1,487,910 | 41.3 | 46.8 | 14.85 | 27.76 | 2.4 | 72 | 80 | 11.7 | 1.1 | -1 | 93 | | .. | | 34 | | 4.5 |
| Bahamas | 13,880 | 5,359 | 140 | 0.3 | 0.4 | 21.61 | 2142.86 | 1.7 | 72 | 78 | 16 | 0.7 | 6 | 84 | | | | 71 | 20600 | 6.8 |
| Barbados | 430 | 166 | 140 | 0.3 | 0.3 | 697.67 | 2142.86 | 1.8 | 73 | 77 | 12 | 0.4 | 1 | 44 | | .. | | 75 | 15080 | 5.4 |
| Belize | 22,966 | 8,867 | 1,600 | 0.3 | 0.4 | 13.06 | 187.50 | 2.6 | 71 | 77 | 14 | 1.8 | 5 | 45 | 0.030 | | 0.732 | | | 1.4 |
| Bolivia | 1,098,581 | 424,162 | 375,150 | 11 | 12.5 | 10.01 | 29.32 | 3.2 | 65 | 69 | 40 | 1.9 | 0 | 67 | 0.097 | 46.64 | | 34 | 2220 | 1.5 |
| Brazil | 8,514,877 | 3,287,594 | 2,756,050 | 195.5 | 214.1 | 22.96 | 70.93 | 1.8 | 71 | 78 | 21 | 0.9 | 0 | 85 | 0.012 | 52.67 | | | 11630 | 2.2 |
| Chile | 756,102 | 291,931 | 158,090 | 17.6 | 19.2 | 23.28 | 111.33 | 1.9 | 76 | 82 | 7.4 | 0.9 | 0 | 87 | | 50.84 | | 71 | 14310 | 4.2 |
| Colombia | 1,138,910 | 439,733 | 426,176 | 48 | 54.6 | 42.15 | 112.63 | 2.3 | 70 | 77 | 17 | 1.4 | -1 | 76 | 0.032 | 53.53 | | 36 | 7020 | 1.6 |
| Costa Rica | 51,100 | 19,730 | 18,850 | 4.7 | 5.4 | 91.98 | 249.34 | 1.9 | 77 | 81 | 9.1 | 1.2 | 3 | 73 | | 48.61 | 0.763 | 53 | 8820 | 1.7 |
| Cuba | 110,860 | 42,803 | 64,060 | 11.3 | 11 | 101.93 | 176.40 | 1.8 | 76 | 80 | 4.9 | 0.4 | -4 | 75 | | | | 46 | | 3.4 |
| Curacao | 444 | 171 | 44 | 0.2 | 0.2 | 450.45 | 4545.45 | 2.1 | 72 | 80 | 7.6 | 0.5 | 19 | - | | | | | | |
| Dominica | 751 | 290 | 260 | 0.1 | 0.1 | 133.16 | 384.62 | 2 | 71 | 77 | 15 | 0.5 | -6 | 67 | | | | | 6440 | 1.9 |
| Dominican Republic | 48,670 | 18,791 | 24,970 | 10.3 | 11.6 | 211.63 | 412.49 | 2.6 | 70 | 76 | 27 | 1.6 | -3 | 67 | 0.026 | 45.68 | | 29 | 5470 | 2.1 |
| Ecuador | 283,561 | 109,483 | 75,069 | 15.8 | 18.7 | 55.72 | 210.47 | 2.7 | 72 | 78 | 20 | 1.7 | 0 | 67 | | 46.57 | | 35 | 5170 | 2.2 |
| El Salvador | 21,041 | 8,124 | 15,670 | 6.3 | 6.7 | 299.42 | 402.04 | 2.2 | 67 | 77 | 8 | 1.2 | -8 | 65 | | 41.80 | | | 3590 | 1 |
| French Guiana | 88,150 | 34,034 | 121 | 0.2 | 0.3 | 2.27 | 1652.89 | 3.4 | 76 | 83 | 10 | 2.3 | -1 | 76 | | | | | | |
| Grenada | 344 | 133 | 110 | 0.1 | 0.1 | 290.70 | 909.09 | 2 | 70 | 75 | 5 | 0.8 | -8 | 39 | | | | | 7220 | 2.5 |
| Guadeloupe | 1,690 | 652 | 210 | 0.4 | 0.4 | 236.69 | 1904.76 | 2.2 | 77 | 84 | 7.9 | 0.6 | -6 | 98 | | | | | | |

# Appendix B: Area and Demographic Data for the World's States (Continued)

| Country | Land Area sq. km. | Land Area sq. mi. | Arable Land in sq. km. | Population 2013 (millions) | Population 2025 (millions) | Population Density Arithmetic | Population Density Physiologic | Total Fertility Rate (TFR) | Life Expectancy Male (years) | Life Expectancy Female (years) | Infant Mortality per 1,000 | Natural Increase (percent) | Net Migration per 1,000 | Urban (percent) | Poverty Index | GINI Index | Human Development Index (HDI) | Corruption Index | GNI per Capita | CO$_2$ Emissions per Capita |
|---|---|---|---|---|---|---|---|---|---|---|---|---|---|---|---|---|---|---|---|---|
| Guatemala | 108,889 | 42,042 | 44,290 | 15.4 | 20.3 | 141.43 | 347.71 | 3.9 | 68 | 75 | 25 | 2.6 | -2 | 50 | | 52.35 | | 29 | 3120 | 0.8 |
| Guyana | 214,969 | 83,000 | 16,780 | 0.8 | 0.8 | 3.72 | 47.68 | 2.6 | 63 | 69 | 29 | 1.4 | -8 | 28 | 0.031 | | | 27 | 3410 | 2.2 |
| Haiti | 27,750 | 10,714 | 17,700 | 10.4 | 12.5 | 374.77 | 587.57 | 3.5 | 61 | 64 | 59 | 1.7 | -4 | 53 | 0.242 | | | 19 | 760 | 0.2 |
| Honduras | 112,090 | 43,278 | 32,350 | 8.6 | 10.8 | 76.72 | 265.84 | 2.9 | 71 | 76 | 24 | 2.2 | -2 | 52 | 0.098 | 57.40 | | 26 | 2120 | 1.1 |
| Jamaica | 10,991 | 4,244 | 4,490 | 2.7 | 2.9 | 245.66 | 601.34 | 2.1 | 71 | 76 | 22 | 0.8 | -6 | 52 | | | | | 5130 | 2.6 |
| Martinique | 1,060 | 409 | 110 | 0.4 | 0.4 | 377.36 | 3636.36 | 1.9 | 79 | 85 | 9 | 0.4 | -5 | 89 | | | | | | |
| Mexico | 1,964,375 | 758,445 | 1,067,050 | 117.6 | 132.8 | 59.87 | 110.21 | 2.2 | 75 | 79 | 15 | 1.5 | -2 | 78 | 0.024 | 48.07 | | 34 | 9640 | 3.8 |
| Nicaragua | 130,370 | 50,336 | 50,710 | 6 | 7 | 46.02 | 118.32 | 2.6 | 71 | 77 | 18 | 1.9 | -5 | 58 | 0.088 | 45.73 | | 28 | 1650 | 0.8 |
| Panama | 75,420 | 29,120 | 22,650 | 3.9 | 4.6 | 51.71 | 172.19 | 2.6 | 74 | 80 | 15 | 1.5 | 1 | 75 | | 51.90 | | 35 | 8510 | 2.6 |
| Paraguay | 406,752 | 157,047 | 215,000 | 6.8 | 8.2 | 16.72 | 31.63 | 2.9 | 70 | 74 | 31 | 1.8 | -1 | 62 | | 48.01 | | 24 | 3400 | 0.8 |
| Peru | 1,285,216 | 496,222 | 243,260 | 30.5 | 34.4 | 23.73 | 125.38 | 2.6 | 72 | 77 | 17 | 1.5 | -3 | 75 | 0.043 | 45.33 | | | 6060 | 2 |
| Puerto Rico | 13,790 | 5,324 | 1,968 | 3.6 | 1.6 | 261.06 | 1829.27 | 1.6 | 76 | 83 | 7.7 | 0.3 | -8 | 99 | | | | | 18000 | |
| St. Lucia | 616 | 238 | 106 | 0.2 | 0.2 | 324.68 | 1886.79 | 2 | 72 | 77 | 11 | 0.9 | 1 | 18 | | | | | 6890 | 2.3 |
| St. Kitts-Nevis | 261 | 101 | 60 | 0.1 | 0.1 | 383.14 | 1666.67 | 1.8 | 72 | 77 | 18 | 0.6 | 1 | 32 | | | | | 13610 | 4.8 |
| St. Vincent and the Grenadines | 389 | 150 | 100 | 0.1 | 0.1 | 257.07 | 1000.00 | 2.2 | 70 | 74 | 17 | 1.1 | -9 | 49 | | | | | 6400 | 1.9 |
| Suriname | 163,820 | 63,251 | 830 | 0.6 | 0.6 | 3.66 | 722.89 | 2.3 | 67 | 74 | 19 | 1.1 | -2 | 70 | 0.033 | | | 36 | 8680 | 4.5 |
| Trinidad and Tobago | 5,128 | 1,980 | 540 | 1.3 | 1.3 | 253.51 | 2407.41 | 1.8 | 68 | 74 | 25 | 0.6 | -2 | 14 | 0.007 | | | | 14710 | 38.2 |
| Uruguay | 176,215 | 68,037 | 152,590 | 3.4 | 3.5 | 19.29 | 22.28 | 2 | 73 | 80 | 8.9 | 0.4 | -2 | 94 | | 41.32 | | 73 | 13580 | 2 |
| Venezuela | 912,050 | 352,143 | 216,000 | 29.7 | 34.4 | 32.56 | 137.50 | 2.4 | 72 | 78 | 11.6 | 1.7 | 0 | 89 | | | | 20 | 12460 | 6.9 |
| **PACIFIC AND AUSTRALIA** | 8,560,172 | 3,305,083 | 4,190,526 | 38 | 45 | 4.44 | 9.07 | 2.4 | 75 | 79 | 20 | 1.1 | 6 | 66 | | | | | | |
| Australia | 7,741,220 | 2,988,885 | 4,054,740 | 23.1 | 27.1 | 2.98 | 5.70 | 1.9 | 80 | 84 | 3.4 | 0.7 | 10 | 82 | | | | 81 | 59260 | 16.9 |
| Federated States of Micronesia | 702 | 271 | 220 | 0.1 | 0.1 | 142.45 | 454.55 | 3.5 | 67 | 68 | 36 | 1.9 | -15 | 22 | | | | | 3230 | 1 |
| Fiji | 18,274 | 7,056 | 4,250 | 0.9 | 0.9 | 49.25 | 211.76 | 2.6 | 67 | 72 | 26 | 1.2 | -8 | 51 | | 42.83 | | | 4110 | 1.5 |
| French Polynesia | 4,167 | 1,609 | 455 | 0.3 | 0.3 | 71.99 | 659.34 | 2.1 | 74 | 78 | 5.5 | 1.1 | 0 | 51 | | | | | | |
| Guam | 544 | 210 | 180 | 0.2 | 0.2 | 367.65 | 1111.11 | 2.9 | 75 | 81 | 10.5 | 1.5 | -10 | 93 | | | | | | |
| Kiribati | 811 | 313 | 340 | 0.1 | 0.1 | 123.30 | 294.12 | 3.6 | 62 | 67 | 38 | 2 | -1 | 54 | | | | | 2520 | 0.6 |
| Marshall Islands | 181 | 70 | 130 | 0.1 | 0.1 | 552.49 | 769.23 | 3.9 | 70 | 74 | 21 | 2.5 | -18 | 65 | | | | | 4040 | 2 |
| New Caledonia | 18,575 | 7,172 | 1,840 | 0.3 | 0.3 | 16.15 | 163.04 | 2.2 | 74 | 81 | 5 | 1.2 | 4 | 58 | | | | | | |
| New Zealand | 267,710 | 103,363 | 112,803 | 4.5 | 5 | 16.81 | 39.89 | 2 | 79 | 83 | 4.2 | 0.7 | 0 | 86 | | | | 91 | 36900 | 7.2 |
| Palau | 459 | 177 | 50 | 0.02 | 0.02 | 43.57 | 400.00 | 2.2 | 66 | 72 | 20 | 0.6 | 0 | 77 | | | | | 9860 | 10.6 |
| Papua New Guinea | 462,840 | 178,703 | 11,900 | 7.2 | 9.1 | 15.56 | 605.04 | 4 | 61 | 66 | 45 | 2.1 | 0 | 13 | | | | 25 | 1790 | 0.5 |
| Samoa | 2,831 | 1,093 | 350 | 0.2 | 0.2 | 70.65 | 571.43 | 4.5 | 72 | 74 | 21 | 2.2 | -17 | 21 | | | | | 3260 | 0.9 |
| Solomon Islands | 28,896 | 11,157 | 1,070 | 0.6 | 0.8 | 20.76 | 560.75 | 4.6 | 66 | 69 | 40 | 2.7 | -17 | 20 | | | | | 1130 | 0.4 |
| Tonga | 747 | 288 | 310 | 0.1 | 0.1 | 133.87 | 322.58 | 3.9 | 70 | 75 | 19 | 2 | -17 | 23 | | | | | 4220 | 1.5 |
| Tuvalu | 26 | 10 | 18 | 0.01 | 0.01 | 384.62 | 555.56 | 3.1 | 63 | 67 | 17 | 1.4 | -9 | 47 | | | | | 5650 | |
| Vanuatu | 12,189 | 4,706 | 1,870 | 0.3 | 0.3 | 24.61 | 160.43 | 4 | 70 | 73 | 21 | 2.6 | 0 | 24 | 0.135 | | | | 3000 | 0.5 |

Sources for Country Data Table

Data for population 2013, population 2025, total fertility rate, life expectancy–male, life expectancy–female, infant mortality rate, natural increase, net migration, and percent urban are from the Population Reference Bureau, 2013 World Population Data Sheet (http://www.prb.org/pdf13/2013-population-data-sheet_eng.pdf). Data for total land area are from the CIA *World Factbook*, 2014. Data for arable land, GINI Index, GNI per capita, and carbon dioxide emissions per capita are from World Bank, 2013 (http://data.worldbank.org/). Population density data are calculated by dividing total population by land area and arable land, for arithmetic and physiologic density, respectively. Data for poverty index are from Multidimensional Poverty Index, revised specifications are from the United Nations Development Program (http://hdr.undp.org/en/content/multidimensional-poverty-index-mpi). Data for corruption index are from Transparency International (http://www.transparency.org/cpi2013).

# GLOSSARY

**Absolute location** The position or place of a certain item on the surface of the Earth as expressed in degrees, minutes, and seconds of **latitude**, 0° to 90° north or south of the equator, and **longitude**, 0° to 180° east or west of the **Prime Meridian** passing through Greenwich, England (a suburb of London).

**Accessibility** The degree of ease with which it is possible to reach a certain location from other locations. Accessibility varies from place to place and can be measured.

**Acid rain** A growing environmental peril whereby acidified rainwater severely damages plant and animal life; caused by the oxides of sulfur and nitrogen that are released into the atmosphere when coal, oil, and natural gas are burned, especially in major manufacturing zones.

**Acropolis** Literally "high point of the city." The upper fortified part of an ancient Greek city, usually devoted to religious purposes.

**Activity (action) space** The space within which daily activity occurs.

**Agglomeration** A process involving the clustering or concentrating of people or activities. The term often refers to manufacturing plants and businesses that benefit from close proximity because they share skilled-labor pools and technological and financial amenities.

**Agora** In ancient Greece, public spaces where citizens debated, lectured, judged one another, planned military campaigns, socialized, and traded.

**Agribusiness** General term for the businesses that provide the vast array of goods and services that support the agriculture industry.

**Agricultural surplus** One of two components, together with **social stratification**, that enable the formation of **cities**; agricultural production in excess of what the producer needs for his or her own sustenance and that of his or her family and that is then sold for consumption by others.

**Agricultural village** A relatively small, egalitarian village, where most of the population was involved in agriculture. Starting over 10,000 years ago, people began to cluster in agricultural villages as they stayed in one place to tend their crops.

**Agriculture** The purposeful tending of crops and livestock in order to produce food and fiber.

**AIDS (Acquired Immune Deficiency Syndrome)** Immune system disease caused by the Human Immunodeficiency Virus (HIV), which over a period of years weakens the capacity of the immune system to fight off infection so that weight loss and weakness set in and other afflictions such as cancer or pneumonia may hasten an infected person's demise.

**Animal domestication** Genetic modification of an animal such that it is rendered more amenable to human control.

**Animistic religion** The belief that inanimate objects, such as hills, trees, rocks, rivers, and other elements of the natural landscape, possess souls and can help or hinder human efforts on Earth.

**Anthropocene** geological epoch defined by atmospheric chemist Paul Crutzen to acknowledge the central role humans play in shaping the Earth's environment.

**Aquifers** Subterranean, porous, water-holding rocks that provide millions of wells with steady flows of water.

**Arable** Literally, cultivable; land fit for cultivation by one farming method or another.

**Area** A term that refers to a part of the Earth's surface with less specificity than **region**. For example, "urban area" alludes very generally to a place where urban development has taken place, whereas "urban region" requires certain specific criteria on which a delimitation is based (e.g., the spatial extent of commuting or the built townscape).

**Arithmetic population density** The population of a country or region expressed as an average per unit area. The figure is derived by dividing the population of the areal unit by the number of square kilometers or miles that make up the unit.

**Assimilation** The process through which people lose originally differentiating traits, such as dress, speech particularities or mannerisms, when they come into contact with another society or culture. Often used to describe immigrant adaptation to new places of residence.

**Asylum** Shelter and protection in one state for refugees from another state.

**Atmosphere** Blanket of gases surrounding the Earth and located some 350 miles above the Earth's surface.

**Authenticity** In the context of local cultures or customs, the accuracy with which a single stereotypical or typecast image or experience conveys an otherwise dynamic and complex local culture or its customs.

**Backward reconstruction** The tracking of **sound shifts** and hardening of consonants "backward" toward the original **language**.

**Barrioization** Defined by geographer James Curtis as the dramatic increase in Hispanic population in a given neighborhood; referring to *barrio*, the Spanish word for neighborhood.

**Biodiversity** The total variety of plant and animal species in a particular place; biological diversity.

**Biotechnology** Technology designed to manipulate seed varieties to increase crop yields.

**Blockbusting** Rapid change in the racial composition of residential blocks in American cities that occurs when real estate agents and others stir up fears of neighborhood decline after encouraging people of color to move to previously white neighborhoods. In the resulting outmigration, real estate agents profit through the turnover of properties.

**Boundary** Vertical plane between states that cuts through the rocks below, and the airspace above the surface.

**Bracero Program** A 1940s-era U.S. government program designed to encourage Mexicans to come to the United States to work as contract laborers.

**Break-of-bulk point** A **location** along a transport route where goods must be transferred from one carrier to another. In a port, the cargoes of oceangoing ships are unloaded and put on trains, trucks, or perhaps smaller riverboats for inland distribution.

**Buddhism** Religion founded in the sixth century BCE and characterized by the belief that enlightenment would come through knowledge, especially self-knowledge; elimination of greed, craving, and desire; complete honesty; and never hurting another person or animal. Buddhism splintered from **Hinduism** as a reaction to the strict social hierarchy maintained by Hinduism.

**Cadastral map** A large-scale map, usually created at the scale of 1:2500, depicting the value, extent, and ownership of land for purposes of taxation.

**Capitalism**   Economic model wherein people, corporations, and **states** produce goods and exchange them on the world market, with the goal of achieving profit.

**Cartography**   The art and science of making maps, including data compilation, layout, and design. Also concerned with the interpretation of mapped patterns.

**Caste system**   The strict social segregation of people—specifically in India's Hindu society—on the basis of ancestry and occupation.

**Census**   A periodic and official count of a country's population.

**Central Business District (CBD)**   The downtown heart of a **central city**, the CBD is marked by high land values, a concentration of business and commerce, and the clustering of the tallest buildings.

**Central city**   The urban area that is not suburban; generally, the older or original **city** that is surrounded by newer **suburbs**.

**Central place**   Any point or place in the urban hierarchy, such as a town or city, having a certain economic reach or hinterland.

**Central Place Theory**   Theory proposed by Walter Christaller that explains how and where **central places** in the **urban hierarchy** should be functionally and spatially distributed with respect to one another.

**Centrality**   The strength of an urban center in its capacity to attract producers and consumers to its facilities; a city's "reach" into the surrounding region.

**Centrifugal**   Forces that tend to divide a country—such as internal religious, linguistic, ethnic, or ideological differences.

**Centripetal**   Forces that tend to unify a country—such as widespread commitment to a national culture, shared ideological objectives, and a common faith.

**Chain migration**   Pattern of **migration** that develops when migrants move along and through kinship links (i.e. one migrant settles in a place and then writes, calls, or communicates through others to describe this place to family and friends who in turn then migrate there).

**Child dependency ratio**   The number of people between the ages of 0 and 14 for every 100 people between the ages of 15-64.

**Child mortality rate**   A figure that describes the number of children that die between the first and fifth years of their lives in a given population.

**Chlorofluorocarbons (CFCs)**   Synthetic organic compounds first created in the 1950s and used primarily as refrigerants and as propellants. The role of CFCs in the destruction of the ozone layer led to the signing of an international agreement (the **Montreal Protocol**).

**Christianity**   Religion based on the teachings of Jesus. According to Christian teaching, Jesus is the son of God, placed on Earth to teach people how to live according to God's plan.

**Chronic (or degenerative) diseases**   Generally long-lasting afflictions now more common because of higher life expectancies.

**City**   Conglomeration of people and buildings clustered together to serve as a center of politics, culture, and economics.

**Climatic regions**   Areas of the world with similar climatic characteristics.

**Cognate**   A word that has the same linguistic derivation as another word (i.e., the word comes from the same root as another word).

**Colonialism**   Rule by an autonomous power over a subordinate and alien people and place. Although often established and maintained through political structures, colonialism also creates unequal cultural and economic relations. Because of the magnitude and impact of the European colonial project of the last few centuries, the term is generally understood to refer to that particular colonial endeavor.

**Colonization**   Physical process whereby the colonizer takes over another place, putting its own government in charge and either moving its own people into the place or bringing in indentured outsiders to gain control of the people and the land.

**Commercial agriculture**   Term used to describe large-scale farming and ranching operations that employ vast land bases, large mechanized equipment, factory-type labor forces, and the latest technology.

**Commercialization**   The transformation of an area of a **city** into an area attractive to residents and tourists alike in terms of economic activity.

**Commodification**   The process through which something is given monetary value. Commodification occurs when a good or idea that previously was not regarded as an object to be bought and sold is turned into something that has a particular price and that can be traded in a market economy.

**Commodity chain**   Series of links connecting the many places of production and distribution and resulting in a commodity that is then exchanged on the world market.

**Complementarity**   A condition that exists when two regions, through an exchange of raw materials and/or finished products, can specifically satisfy each other's demands.

**Community-supported agriculture (CSA)**   Network between agricultural producers and consumers whereby consumers pledge support to a farming operation in order to receive a share of the output from the farming operation.

**Concentric zone model**   A structural model of the American **central city** that suggests the existence of five concentric land-use rings arranged around a common center.

**Confucianism**   A philosophy of ethics, education, and public service based on the writings of Confucius and traditionally thought of as one of the core elements of Chinese culture.

**Connectivity**   Connectedness of a node in the world economy to other nodes along networks.

**Conquest theory**   One major theory of how **Proto-Indo-European** diffused into Europe which holds that the early speakers of Proto-Indo-European spread westward on horseback, overpowering earlier inhabitants and beginning the **diffusion** and differentiation of Indo-European tongues.

**Contagious diffusion**   The distance-controlled spreading of an idea, innovation, or some other item through a local population by contact from person to person—analogous to the communication of a contagious illness.

**Context**   The geographical situation in which something occurs; the combination of what is happening at a variety of **scales** concurrently.

**Core**   Processes that incorporate higher levels of education, higher salaries, and more technology; generate more wealth than **periphery** processes in the world-economy.

**Core area**   In geography, a term with several connotations. Core refers to the center, heart, or focus. The core area of a **nation-state** is constituted by the national heartland—the largest population cluster, the most productive region, the area with greatest **centrality** and **accessibility**, probably containing the capital city as well.

**Cottage industries**   Small-scale production of goods, typically by hand or with low technology In a home or small workshop.

**Creole language**   A language that began as a **pidgin language** but was later adopted as the mother tongue by a people in place of the mother tongue.

**Critical geopolitics**   Process by which geopoliticians deconstruct and focus on explaining the underlying spatial assumptions and territorial perspectives of politicians.

**Crude Birth Rate (CBR)**   The number of live births yearly per thousand people in a population.

**Crude Death Rate (CDR)**   The number of deaths yearly per thousand people in a population.

**Cultural appropriation**   The process by which cultures adopt customs and knowledge from other cultures and use them for their own benefit.

**Cultural barrier**   Prevailing cultural attitude rendering certain innovations, ideas or practices unacceptable or unadoptable in that particular **culture**.

**Cultural complex**   A related set of **cultural traits**, such as prevailing dress codes and cooking and eating utensils.

**Cultural diffusion**   The expansion and adoption of a cultural element, from its place of origin to a wider area.

**Cultural ecology**   The multiple interactions and relationships between a culture and the natural environment.

**Cultural hearth**   Heartland, source area, innovation center; place of origin of a major **culture**.

**Cultural landscape**   The visible imprint of of human activity and culture on the landscape. The layers of buildings, forms, and artifacts sequentially imprinted on the landscape by the activities of various human occupants.

**Cultural trait**   A single element of normal practice in a **culture**, such as the wearing of a turban.

**Culture**   The sum total of the knowledge, attitudes, and habitual behavior patterns shared and transmitted by the members of a society. This is anthropologist Ralph Linton's definition; hundreds of others exist.

**Custom**   Practice routinely followed by a group of people.

**Cyclic movement**   Movement—for example, nomadic migration—that has a closed route and is repeated annually or seasonally.

**Definition**   In political geography, the written legal description (in a treaty-like document) of a boundary between two countries or territories. See also **delimitation**.

**Deforestation**   The clearing and destruction of forests to harvest wood for consumption, clear land for agricultural uses, and make way for expanding settlement frontiers.

**Deglomeration**   The process of industrial deconcentration in response to technological advances and/or increasing costs due to congestion and competition.

**Deindustrialization**   Process by which companies move industrial jobs to other regions with cheaper labor, leaving the newly deindustrialized region to switch to a service economy and to work through a period of high unemployment.

**Delimitation**   In political geography, the translation of the written terms of a boundary treaty (the **definition**) into an official cartographic representation.

**Demarcation**   In political geography, the actual placing of a political boundary on the landscape by means of barriers, fences, walls, or other markers.

**Democracy**   Government based on the principle that the people are the ultimate sovereign and have the final say over what happens within the state.

**Demographic transition**   Multistage model, based on Western Europe's experience, of changes in population growth exhibited by countries undergoing industrialization. High birth rates and death rates are followed by plunging death rates, producing a huge net population gain; this is followed by the convergence of birth rates and death rates at a low overall level.

**Dependency theory**   A structuralist theory that offers a critique of the **modernization model** of development. Based on the idea that certain types of political and economic relations (especially **colonialism**) between countries and regions of the world have created arrangements that both control and limit the extent to which regions can develop.

**Deportation**   The act of a government sending a migrant out of its country and back to the migrant's home country.

**Desertification**   The encroachment of desert conditions on moister zones along the desert margins, where plant cover and soils are threatened by desiccation—through overuse, in part by humans and their domestic animals, and, possibly, in part because of inexorable shifts in the Earth's environmental zones.

**Deterritorialization**   the movement of economic, social and cultural processes out of the hands of states.

**Devolution**   The process whereby regions within a **state** demand and gain political strength and growing autonomy at the expense of the central government.

**Dialect**   Local or regional characteristics of a **language**. While *accent* refers to the pronunciation differences of a standard language, a dialect, in addition to pronunciation variation, has distinctive grammar and vocabulary.

**Dialect chains**   A set of contiguous dialects in which the dialects nearest to each other at any place in the chain are most closely related.

**Diaspora**   From the Greek "to disperse," a term describing forceful or voluntary dispersal of a people from their homeland to a new place. Originally denoting the dispersal of Jews, it is increasingly applied to other population dispersals, such as the involuntary relocation of Black peoples during the slave trade or Chinese peoples outside of Mainland China, Taiwan and Hong Kong.

**Diffusion**   The spatial spreading or dissemination of a culture element (such as a technological innovation) or some other phenomenon (e.g., a disease outbreak). See also **contagious, expansion, hierarchical, relocation**, and **stimulus diffusion**.

**Diffusion routes**   The spatial trajectory through which **cultural traits** or other phenomena spread.

**Digital divide**   The gap in access to telecommunications between developed and developing regions.

**Disamenity sector**   The very poorest parts of **cities** that in extreme cases are not even connected to regular city services and are controlled by gangs or drug lords.

**Distance**   Measurement of the physical space between two places.

**Distance decay**   The effects of distance on interaction, generally the greater the distance the less interaction.

**Dollarization**   When a poorer country ties the value of its currency to that of a wealthier country, or when it abandons its currency and adopts the wealthier country's currency as its own.

**Dot map**   Maps where one dot represents a certain number of a phenomenon, such as a population.

**Doubling time**   The time required for a population to double in size.

**Dowry death**   In the context of arranged marriages in India, disputes over the price to be paid by the family of the bride to the father of the groom (the dowry) have, in some extreme cases, led to the death of the bride.

**Eastern Orthodox Church**   One of three major branches of **Christianity**, the Eastern Orthodox Church, together with the **Roman Catholic Church**, a second of the three major branches of Christianity, arose out of the division of the Roman Empire by Emperor Diocletian into four governmental regions: two western regions centered in Rome, and two eastern regions centered in Constantinople (now Istanbul, Turkey). In 1054 CE, Christianity was divided along that same line when the Eastern Orthodox Church, centered in Constantinople; and the Roman Catholic Church, centered in Rome, split.

**Economies of scale**   Increasing production of a good so that the average cost of the good declines.

**Edge cities**   A term introduced by American journalist Joel Garreau in order to describe the shifting focus of **urbanization** in the United States away from the **Central Business District (CBD)** toward new loci of economic activity at the urban fringe. These cities are characterized by extensive amounts of office and retail space, few residential areas, and modern buildings (less than 30 years old).

**Emigrant**   A person migrating away from a country or area; an out-migrant.

**Emigration**   The act of a person leaving a country or area to settle elsewhere.

**Endemic**   A disease that is particular to a locality or region. See also **pandemic**.

**Environmental determinism**   The view that the natural environment has a controlling influence over various aspects of human life, including cultural development. Also referred to as environmentalism.

**Environmental stress**   The threat to environmental security by human activity such as atmospheric and groundwater pollution, deforestation, oil spills, and ocean dumping.

**Epidemic**   Regional outbreak of a disease.

**Ethnic religion**   A religion that is particular to one, culturally distinct, group of people. Unlike **universalizing religions**, adherents of ethnic religions do not actively seek converts through evangelism or missionary work.

**Ethnic neighborhood**   Neighborhood, typically situated in a larger metropolitan city and constructed by or comprised of a **local culture**, in which a local culture can practice its customs.

**Ethnicity**   Affiliation or identity within a group of people bound by common ancestry and culture.

**Eugenic population policies**   Government policies designed to favor one racial sector over others.

**Expansion diffusion**   The spread of an innovation or an idea through a population in an area in such a way that the number of those influenced grows continuously larger, resulting in an expanding area of dissemination.

**Expansive population policies**   Government policies that encourage large families and raise the rate of population growth.

**Export Processing Zones (EPZs)**   Zones established by many countries in the **periphery** and **semi-periphery** where they offer favorable tax, regulatory, and trade arrangements to attract foreign trade and investment.

**Extinct language**   Language without any native speakers.

**Extremism** see **religious extremism**

**Federal (state)**   A political-territorial system wherein a central government represents the various entities within a **nation-state** where they have common interests—defense, foreign affairs, and the like—yet allows these various entities to retain their own identities and to have their own laws, policies, and customs in certain spheres.

**Feng Shui**   Literally "wind-water." The Chinese art and science of placement and orientation of tombs, dwellings, buildings, and cities. Structures and objects are positioned in an effort to channel flows of *sheng-chi* ("life-breath") in favorable ways.

**Fertile Crescent**   Crescent-shaped zone of productive lands extending from near the southeastern Mediterranean coast through Lebanon and Syria to the alluvial lowlands of Mesopotamia (in Iraq). Once more fertile than today, this is one of the world's great source areas of agricultural and other innovations.

**Fieldwork**   The study of phenomena by visiting places and observing how people interact with and thereby change those places.

**First Agricultural Revolution**   Dating back 10,000 years, the First Agricultural Revolution achieved **plant domestication** and **animal domestication**.

**First mover advantage**   The benefit first innovators or first in a market have over later entries.

**First Urban Revolution**   The innovation of the **city**, which occurred independently in five separate **hearths**.

**Five themes (of geography)**   Developed by the **Geography Educational National Implementation Project (GENIP)**, the five themes of geography are **location, human-environment, region, place**, and **movement**.

**Flexible production system**   a system of industrial production characterized by a set of processes in which the components of goods are made in different places around the globe and then brought together as needed to meet consumer demand.

**Folk culture**   **Cultural traits** such as dress modes, dwellings, traditions, and institutions of usually small, **traditional** communities.

**Folk-housing region**   A region in which the housing stock predominantly reflects styles of building that are particular to the culture of the people who have long inhabited the area.

**Food desert**   An area characterized by a lack of affordable, fresh and nutritious food.

**Forced migration**   Human **migration** flows in which the movers have no choice but to relocate.

**Fordist**   A highly organized and specialized system for organizing industrial production and labor. Named after automobile producer Henry Ford, Fordist production features assembly-line production of standardized components for mass consumption.

**Formal economy**   The legal economy that is taxed and monitored by a government and is included in a government's **Gross National Product (GNP)**; as opposed to an **informal economy**.

**Formal region**   A type of **region** marked by a certain degree of homogeneity in one or more phenomena; also called uniform region or homogeneous region.

**Forum**   The focal point of ancient Roman life combining the functions of the ancient Greek *acropolis* and *agora*.

**Friction of distance**   The increase in time and cost that usually comes with increasing **distance**.

**Functional region**   A **region** defined by the particular set of activities or interactions that occur within it.

**Functional zonation**   The division of a **city** into different regions or **zones** (e.g. residential or industrial) for certain purposes or functions (e.g. housing or manufacturing).

**Fundamentalism**   see **religious fundamentalism**

**Galactic city**   A modern city in which the old downtown plays the role of a festival or recreational area, and widely dispersed industrial parks, shopping centers, high-tech industrial spaces, edge-city downtowns, and industrial suburbs are the new centers of economic activity.

**Gated communities**   Restricted neighborhoods or subdivisions, often literally fenced in, where entry is limited to residents and their guests. Although predominantly high-income based, in North America gated communities are increasingly a middle-class phenomenon.

**Gatekeepers**   People or corporations who control access to information.

**Gender**   Social differences between men and women, rather than the anatomical, biological differences between the sexes. Notions of gender differences—that is, what is considered "feminine" or "masculine"—vary greatly over time and space.

**Gendered**   In terms of a place, whether the place is designed for or claimed by men or women.

**Genetic or inherited diseases**   Diseases caused by variation or mutation of a gene or group of genes in a human.

**Genetically modified organisms (GMOs)**   Crops that carry new traits that have been inserted through advanced genetic engineering methods.

**Gentrification**   The rehabilitation of deteriorated, often abandoned, housing of low-income inner-city residents.

**Geocaching**   A hunt for a cache, the **Global Positioning System (GPS)** coordinates which are placed on the Internet by other geocachers.

**Geographic concept**   Ways of seeing the world spatially that are used by geographers in answering research questions.

**Geographic Information System (GIS)**   A collection of computer hardware and software that permits spatial data to be collected, recorded, stored, retrieved, manipulated, analyzed, and displayed to the user.

**Geography**   From the Greek meaning "to write about the Earth." As a modern academic discipline, geography is concerned with the analysis of the physical and human characteristics of the Earth's surface from a **spatial** perspective. "Why are things located where they are?" and "What does it mean for things to be located in particular places?" are central questions that geographical scholarship seeks to answer.

**Geography Educational National Implementation Project (GENIP)**   Joint effort undertaken in the 1980s by the American Geographical Society, the Association of American Geographers, the National Council for Geographic Education and the National Geographic Society designed to bring together the many subfields of human geography and to explain to nongeographers the discipline of geography; developed the **five themes** of geography: **location, human-environment, region, place**, and **movement**.

**Geometric boundary**   Political boundary **defined** and **delimited** (and occasionally **demarcated**) as a straight line or an arc.

**Germanic languages**   Languages (English, German, Danish, Norwegian, and Swedish) that reflect the expansion of peoples out of Northern Europe to the west and south.

**Gerrymandering**   Redistricting for advantage, or the practice of dividing areas into electoral districts to give one political party an electoral majority in a large number of districts while concentrating the voting strength of the opposition in as few districts as possible.

**Glaciation**   A period of global cooling during which continental ice sheets and mountain glaciers expand.

**Global division of labor**   Phenomenon whereby corporations and others can draw from labor markets around the world, made possible by the compression of time and space through innovation in communication and transportation systems.

**Global language**   The **language** used most commonly around the world; defined on the basis of either the number of speakers of the language, or prevalence of use in commerce and trade.

**Global-local continuum**   The notion that what happens at the global scale has a direct effect on what happens at the local scale, and vice versa. This idea posits that the world is comprised of an interconnected series of relationships that extend across space.

**Global positioning system (GPS)**   Satellite-based system for determining the **absolute location** of **places** or geographic features.

**Global scale**   Interactions occurring at the scale of the world, in a global setting.

**Global warming**   Theory that the Earth is gradually warming as a result of an enhanced **greenhouse effect** in the Earth's **atmosphere** caused by ever-increasing amounts of carbon dioxide produced by various human activities.

**Globalization**   The expansion of economic, political, and cultural processes to the point that they become global in scale and impact. The processes of globalization transcend state boundaries and have outcomes that vary across places and scales.

**Glocalization**   The process by which people in a local place mediate and alter regional, national, and global processes.

**Gondwana**   The southern portion of the primeval supercontinent, Pangaea.

**Gravity model**   A mathematical prediction of the interaction of places, the interaction being a function of population size of the respective places and the distance between them.

**Green Revolution**   The recently successful development of higher-yield, fast-growing varieties of rice and other cereals in certain developing countries, which led to increased production per unit area and a dramatic narrowing of the gap between population growth and food needs.

**Greenhouse effect**   The widely used analogy describing the blanket-like effect of the atmosphere in the heating of the Earth's surface; shortwave insolation passes through the "glass" of the atmospheric "greenhouse," heats the surface, is converted to long-wave radiation that cannot penetrate the "glass," and thereby results in trapping heat, which raises the temperature inside the "greenhouse."

**Griffin-Ford model**   Developed by geographers Ernst Griffin and Larry Ford, a model of the Latin American city showing a blend of traditional elements of Latin American culture with the forces of globalization that are reshaping the urban scene.

**Gross Domestic Product (GDP)**   The total value of all goods and services produced within a country during a given year.

**Gross National Income (GNI)**   The total value of what is produced in a country in addition to the income received from investments outside of the country and minus payments to other countries around the world.

**Gross National Product (GNP)**   The total value of all goods and services produced by a country's economy in a given year. It includes all goods and services produced by corporations and individuals of a country, whether or not they are located within the country.

**Guest worker**   Legal **immigrant** who has a work visa, usually short term.

**Hajj**   The Muslim **pilgrimage** to Mecca, the birthplace of Muhammad.

**Hearth**   The area where an idea or cultural trait originates.

**Heartland theory**   A geopolitical hypothesis, proposed by British geographer Halford Mackinder during the first two decades of the twentieth century, that any political power based in the heart of Eurasia could gain sufficient strength to eventually dominate the world. Mackinder further proposed that since Eastern Europe controlled access to the Eurasian interior, its ruler would command the vast "heartland" to the east.

**Hierarchical diffusion**   A form of **diffusion** in which an idea or innovation spreads by passing first among the most connected places or peoples. An **urban hierarchy** is usually involved, encouraging the leapfrogging of innovations over wide areas, with geographic distance a less important influence.

**High-technology corridors**   Areas along or near major transportation arteries that are devoted to the research, development, and sale of high-technology products. These areas develop because of the networking and synergistic advantages of concentrating high-technology enterprises in close proximity to one another. "Silicon Valley" is a prime example of a high-technology corridor in the United States.

**Hinduism**   One of the oldest **religions** in the modern world, dating back over 4000 years, and originating in the Indus River Valley of what is today part of Pakistan. Hinduism is unique among the world's religions in that it does not have a single founder, a single theology, or agreement on its origins.

**Hinterland**   An area of economic production that is located inland and is connected to the world by a port.

**Holocene**   The current **interglaciation** period, extending from 10,000 years ago to the present on the geologic time scale.

**Homo sapiens**   The only living species of the genus *Homo*; modern humans.

**Horizontal integration**   Ownership by the same firm of a number of companies that exist at the same point on a **commodity chain**.

**Huang He (Yellow) and Wei (Yangtzi) River Valleys**   Rivers in present-day China; it was at the confluence of the Huang He and Wei Rivers where chronologically the fourth urban **hearth** was established around 1500 BCE.

**Human-environment**   The second theme of geography as defined by the **Geography Educational National Implementation Project**; reciprocal relationship between humans and environment.

**Human geography**   One of the two major divisions of **geography**; the spatial analysis of human population, its cultures, activities, and landscapes.

**Human territoriality**   A term associated with the work of Robert Sack that describes the efforts of human societies to influence events and achieve social goals by exerting, and attempting to enforce, control over specific geographical areas.

**Human trafficking**   A form of **forced migration** in which organized criminal elements move people illegally from one place to another, typically either to work as involuntary laborers or to participate in the commercial sex trade.

**Hydrologic cycle**   The system of exchange involving water in its various forms as it continually circulates among the atmosphere, the oceans, and above and below the land surface.

**Identifying against**   Constructing an **identity** by first defining the "other" and then defining ourselves as "not the other."

**Identity**   Defined by geographer Gillian Rose as "how we make sense of ourselves;" how people see themselves at different scales.

**Imam**   The political head of the Muslim community or the person who leads prayer services. In **Shiite** Islam the Imam is immune from sin or error.

**Immigrant**   A person migrating into a particular country or area; an in-migrant.

**Immigration**   The act of a person migrating into a new country or area.

**Immigration laws**   Laws and regulations of a state designed specifically to control immigration into that **state**.

**Immigration wave**   Phenomenon whereby different patterns of **chain migration** build upon one another to create a swell in **migration** from one origin to the same destination.

**Independent invention**   The term for a trait with many **cultural hearths** that developed independent of each other.

**Indigenous religions**   Belief systems and philosophies practiced and traditionally passed from generation to generation among peoples within an indigenous tribe or group.

**Indus River Valley**   Chronologically, the third urban **hearth**, dating to 2200 BCE.

**Industrial Revolution**   The term applied to the social and economic changes in agriculture, commerce and manufacturing that resulted from technological innovations and specialization in late-eighteenth-century Europe.

**Infant Mortality Rate (IMR)**   A figure that describes the number of babies that die within the first year of their lives in a given population.

**Infectious diseases**   Diseases that are spread by bacteria, viruses, or parasites. Infectious diseases diffuse directly or indirectly from human to human.

**Informal economy**   Economic activity that is neither taxed nor monitored by a government and is not included in that government's **Gross National Product (GNP)**; as opposed to a formal economy.

**Interface areas**   Places where neighborhoods associated with different religions meet.

**Interfaith boundaries**   Boundaries between the world's major faiths.

**Interglacials**   Warm periods during an ice age.

**Interglaciation**   Sustained warming phase between glaciations during an ice age.

**Intermodal (connections)**   Places where two or more modes of transportation meet (including air, road, rail, barge, and ship).

**Internal migration**   Human movement within a **nation-state**, such as ongoing westward and southward movements in the United States.

**Internal displaced persons**   People who have been displaced within their own countries and do not cross international borders as they flee.

**International migration**   Human movement involving movement across international boundaries.

**Intervening opportunity**   The presence of a nearer opportunity that greatly diminishes the attractiveness of sites farther away.

**Intrafaith boundaries**   Boundaries within a single major faith.

**Islam**   The youngest of the major world **religions**, Islam is based on the teachings of Muhammad, born in Mecca in 571 CE. According to Islamic teaching, Muhammad received the truth directly from Allah in a series of revelations during which Muhammad spoke the verses of the *Qu'ran* (*Koran*), the Islamic holy book.

**Island of development**   Place built up by a government or corporation to attract foreign investment and which has relatively high concentrations of paying jobs and infrastructure.

**Isogloss**   A geographic **boundary** within which a particular linguistic feature occurs.

**Isotherm**   Line on a map connecting points of equal temperature values.

**Jihad**   A doctrine within **Islam**. Commonly translated as "Holy War," jihad represents either a personal or collective struggle on the part of Muslims to live up to the religious standards set by the *Qu'ran*.

**Judaism**   Religion with its roots in the teachings of Abraham (from Ur), who is credited with uniting his people to worship only one god. According to Jewish teaching, Abraham and God have a covenant in which the Jews agree to worship only one God, and God agrees to protect his chosen people, the Jews.

**Just-in-time delivery**   Method of inventory management made possible by efficient transportation and communication systems, whereby companies keep on hand just what they need for near-term production, planning that what they need for longer-term production will arrive when needed.

**Kinship links**   Types of **push factors** or **pull factors** that influence a migrant's decision to go where family or friends have already found success.

**Köppen climate classification system**   Developed by Wladimir Köppen, a system for classifying the world's climates on the basis of temperature and precipitation.

**Landscape**   The overall appearance of an area. Most landscapes are comprised of a combination of natural and human-induced influences.

**Language**   A set of sounds, combination of sounds, and symbols that are used for communication.

**Language convergence**   The collapsing of two **languages** into one resulting from the consistent **spatial interaction** of peoples with different languages; the opposite of **language divergence**.

**Language divergence**   The opposite of **language convergence**; a process suggested by German linguist August Schleicher whereby new **languages** are formed when a language breaks into dialects due to a lack of **spatial interaction** among speakers of the language and continued isolation eventually causes the division of the language into discrete new languages.

**Language family**   Group of **languages** with a shared but fairly distant origin.

**Latitude**   An imaginary line running parallel to the equator that is used to measure distance in degrees north or south from the equator.

**Laws of migration**   Developed by British demographer Ernst Ravenstein, five laws that predict the flow of migrants.

**Leadership class**   Group of decision-makers and organizers in early **cities** who controlled the resources, and often the lives, of others.

**Least Cost Theory**   Model developed by Alfred Weber according to which the location of manufacturing establishments is determined by the minimization of three critical expenses: labor, transportation, and **agglomeration**.

**Life expectancy**   A figure indicating how long, on average, a person may be expected to live. Normally expressed in the context of a particular state.

*Lingua franca*   A term deriving from "Frankish language" and applying to a tongue spoken in ancient Mediterranean ports that consisted of a mixture of Italian, French, Greek, Spanish, and even some Arabic. Today it refers to a "common language," a language used among speakers of different languages for the purposes of trade and commerce.

**Little Ice Age**   Temporary but significant cooling period between the fourteenth and the nineteenth centuries; accompanied by wide temperature fluctuations, droughts, and storms, causing famines and dislocation.

**Livestock ranching**   The raising of domesticated animals for the production of meat and other byproducts such as leather and wool.

**Local culture**   Group of people in a particular **place** who see themselves as a collective or a community, who share experiences, customs, and traits, and who work to preserve those traits and customs in order to claim uniqueness and to distinguish themselves from others.

**Local Exchange Trading System (LETS)**   A barter system whereby a local currency is created through which members trade services or goods in a local **network** separated from the **formal economy**.

**Location**   The first theme of geography as defined by the **Geography Educational National Implementation Project**; the geographical **situation** of people and things.

**Location theory**   A logical attempt to explain the locational pattern of an economic activity and the manner in which its producing areas are interrelated. The agricultural location theory contained in the **von Thünen** model is a leading example.

**Locational interdependence**   Theory developed by economist Harold Hotelling that suggests competitors, in trying to maximize sales, will seek to constrain each other's territory as much as possible, which will therefore lead them to locate adjacent to one another in the middle of their collective customer base.

**Longitude**   An imaginary line circling the Earth and running through the poles. Used to determine the location of things by measurement of the angular distance, in degrees east or west, from the **Prime Meridian**.

**Long-lot survey system**  Distinct regional approach to land surveying found in the Canadian Maritimes, parts of Quebec, Louisiana, and Texas whereby land is divided into narrow parcels stretching back from rivers, roads, or canals.

**Luxury crops**  Non-subsistence crops such as tea, cacao, coffee, and tobacco.

**Majority-minority districts**  In the context of determining representative districts, the process by which a majority of the population is from the minority.

**Malaria**  Vectored disease spread by mosquitoes that carry the malaria parasite in their saliva and which kills approximately 150,000 children in the global **periphery** each month.

**Manufacturing export zones**  A feature of economic development in peripheral countries whereby the host country establishes areas with favorable tax, regulatory, and trade arrangements in order to attract foreign manufacturing operations. The goods manufactured in these export zones are primarily destined for the global market.

**Maquiladora**  The term given to zones in northern Mexico with factories supplying manufactured goods to the U.S. market. The low-wage workers in the primarily foreign-owned factories assemble imported components and/or raw materials and then export finished goods.

**Mass extinctions**  Mass destruction of most species.

**Material culture**  The art, housing, clothing, sports, dances, foods, and other similar items constructed or created by a group of people.

**McGee model**  Developed by geographer T.G. McGee, a model showing similar land-use patterns among the medium-sized cities of Southeast Asia.

**McMansions**  Homes referred to as such because of their "super size" and similarity in appearance to other such homes; homes often built in place of **tear-downs** in American suburbs.

**Medical geography**  The study of health and disease within a geographic context and from a geographical perspective. Among other things, medical geography looks at sources, diffusion routes, and distributions of diseases.

**Mediterranean agriculture**  Specialized farming that occurs only in areas where the dry-summer Mediterranean climate prevails.

**Megacities**  cities with 10 million or more residents.

**Megalopolis**  Term used to designate large coalescing supercities that are forming in diverse parts of the world; formerly used specifically with an uppercase "M" to refer to the Boston—Washington multimetropolitan corridor on the northeastern seaboard of the United States, but now used generically with a lower-case "m" as a synonym for conurbation.

**Mental map**  Image or picture of the way space is organized as determined by an individual's perception, impression, and knowledge of that space.

**Mercantilism**  In a general sense, associated with the promotion of commercialism and trade. More specifically, a protectionist policy of European **states** during the sixteenth to the eighteenth centuries that promoted a state's economic position in the contest with other countries. The acquisition of gold and silver and the maintenance of a favorable trade balance (more exports than imports) were central to the policy.

**Mesoamerica**  Chronologically the fifth urban hearth, dating to 200 BCE.

**Mesopotamia**  Region of great cities (e.g. Ur and Babylon) located between the Tigris and Euphrates Rivers; chronologically the first urban **hearth**, dating to 3500 BCE, and founded in the **Fertile Crescent**.

**Metes and bounds system**  A system of land surveying east of the Appalachian Mountains. It is a system that relies on descriptions of land ownership and natural features such as streams or trees. Because of the imprecise nature of metes and bounds surveying, the U.S. Land Office Survey abandoned the technique in favor of the **rectangular survey system**.

**Microcredit program**  Program that provides small loans to poor people, especially women, to encourage development of small businesses.

**Migration**  A change in residence intended to be permanent. See also **chain, forced, internal, international, step**, and **voluntary migration**.

**Millennium Development Goals**  A set of markers outlined by the United Nations with the aim of improving quality of life and the economy in developing countries.

**Minaret**  Tower attached to a Muslim mosque, having one or more projecting balconies from which a crier calls Muslims to prayer.

**Modernization model**  A model of economic development most closely associated with the work of economist Walter Rostow. The modernization model (sometimes referred to as modernization theory) maintains that all countries go through five interrelated stages of development, which culminate in an economic state of self-sustained economic growth and high levels of mass consumption.

**Monoculture**  Dependence on a single agricultural commodity.

**Monolingual states**  Countries in which only one **language** is spoken.

**Monotheistic religion**  Belief system in which one supreme being is revered as creator and arbiter of all that exists in the universe.

**Montreal Protocol**  An international agreement signed in 1987 by 105 countries and the European Community (now European Union). The protocol called for a reduction in the production and consumption of chlorofluorocarbons (CFCs) of 50 percent by 2000. Subsequent meetings in London (1990) and Copenhagen (1992) accelerated the timing of CFC phaseout, and a worldwide complete ban has been in effect since 1996.

**Movement**  The fifth theme of geography as defined by the **Geography Educational National Implementation Project**: the mobility of people, goods and ideas across the surface of the planet

**Multilingual states**  Countries in which more than one **language** is spoken.

**Multinational state**  **State** with more than one nation within its borders.

**Multiple nuclei model**  A structural model of the American city that suggests a decline in significance of the **central business district** and the concomitant rise in significance of regions within metropolitan areas with their own nuclei.

**Multistate nation**  Nation that stretches across borders and across states.

**Mutual intelligibility**  The ability of two people to understand each other when speaking.

**Nation**  Legally, a term encompassing all the citizens of a state. Most definitions now tend to refer to a tightly knit group of people possessing bonds of language, ethnicity, religion, and other shared cultural attributes. Such homogeneity actually prevails within very few states.

**Nation-state**  Theoretically, a recognized member of the modern state system possessing formal **sovereignty** and occupied by a people who see themselves as a single, united **nation**. Most nations and states aspire to this form, though it is realized almost nowhere. Nonetheless, in common parlance, nation-state is used as a synonym for country or state.

**Natural increase**  Population growth measured as the excess of live births over deaths. Natural increase of a population does not reflect either **emigrant** or **immigrant** movements.

**Natural resource**  Any valued element of (or means to an end using) the environment; includes minerals, water, vegetation, and soil.

**Neocolonialism**  The entrenchment of the colonial order, such as trade and investment, under a new guise. See also **postcolonialism**.

**Neoliberalism**  Policies based on the economic theory that government should not intervene in markets.

**Neolocalism**  The seeking out of the regional culture and reinvigoration of it in response to the uncertainty of the modern world.

**Networks**  Defined by Manuel Castells as a set of interconnected nodes without a center.

**Newborn mortality rate**  The number of infants who die within the first month of life per 1,000 live births.

**New urbanism**  Outlined by a group of architects, urban planners, and developers from over 20 countries, an urban design that calls for development, urban revitalization, and suburban reforms that create walkable neighborhoods with a diversity of housing and jobs.

**Newly industrializing countries**   States that underwent industrialization after World War II and whose economies have grown at a rapid pace.

**Nile River Valley**   Chronologically the second urban **hearth**, dating to 3200 BCE.

**Node**   Connection point in a network, where goods and ideas flow in, out, and through the network.

**Nomadism**   Movement among a definite set of places—often **cyclic movement**.

**Nongovernmental organizations (NGOs)**   International organizations that operate outside of the formal political arena but that are nevertheless influential in spearheading international initiatives on social, economic, and environmental issues.

**Non-material culture**   The beliefs, practices, aesthics, and values of a group of people.

**Nonrenewable resources**   Resources that are present in finite quantities because they are not self-replenishing or take an extraordinarily long time to replenish.

**North American Free Trade Agreement (NAFTA)**   Agreement entered into by Canada, Mexico, and the United States in December, 1992 and taking effect on January 1, 1994, to eliminate the barriers to trade in, and facilitate the cross-border movement of goods and services between the countries.

**Official language**   In multilingual countries the **language** selected, often by the educated and politically powerful elite, to promote internal cohesion; usually the language of the courts and government.

**Offshore**   With reference to production, to **outsource** to a third party located outside of the country.

**Old age dependency ratio**   The number of people 65 years of age for every 100 people between the ages of 15-64.

**One-child policy**   A program established by the Chinese government in 1979 to slow population growth in China.

**Opinion leaders**   People in social networks who have millions of followers and help diffuse new ideas and products hierarchically.

**Organic agriculture**   Approach to farming and ranching that avoids the use of herbicides, pesticides, growth hormones, and other similar synthetic inputs.

**Outsource**   With reference to production, to turn over in part or in total to a third party.

**Oxygen cycle**   Cycle whereby natural processes and human activity consume atmospheric oxygen and produce carbon dioxide and the Earth's forests and other flora, through **photosynthesis**, consume carbon dioxide and produce oxygen.

**Ozone layer**   The layer in the upper atmosphere located between 30 and 45 kilometers above the Earth's surface where stratospheric ozone is most densely concentrated. The ozone layer acts as a filter for the Sun's harmful ultraviolet rays.

**Pacific Ring of Fire**   Ocean-girdling zone of crustal instability, volcanism, and earthquakes resulting from the tectonic activity along plate boundaries in the region.

**Pandemic**   An outbreak of a disease that spreads worldwide. See also **endemic**.

**Pangaea**   The primeval supercontinent, hypothesized by Alfred Wegener, that broke apart and formed the continents and oceans as we know them today; consisted of two parts—a northern Laurasia and a southern **Gondwana**.

**Participatory development**   The notion that locals should be engaged in deciding what development means for them and how it should be achieved.

**Pastoralist**   Person involved in a form of agricultural activity that involves the raising of livestock. Many peoples described as herders actually pursue mixed agriculture, in that they may also fish, hunt, or even grow a few crops. But pastoral peoples' lives revolve around their animals.

**Pattern**   The design of a **spatial distribution** (e.g. scattered or concentrated).

**Peace of Westphalia**   Peace negotiated in 1648 to end the Thirty Years' War, Europe's most destructive internal struggle over religion. The treaties contained new language recognizing statehood and nationhood, clearly defined borders, and guarantees of security.

**Per capita GNI**   The **Gross National Income (GNI)** of a given country divided by its population.

**Perception of place**   Belief or "understanding" about a place developed through books, movies, stories or pictures.

**Perceptual region**   A **region** that only exists as a conceptualization or an idea and not as a physically demarcated entity. For example, in the United States, "the South" and "the Mid-Atlantic region" are perceptual regions.

**Periphery**   Processes that incorporate lower levels of education, lower salaries, and less technology; and generate less wealth than core processes in the world-economy.

**Periodic Movement**   Movement—for example, college attendence or military service—that involves temporary, recurrent relocation.

**Photosynthesis**   The formation of carbohydrates in living plants from water and carbon dioxide, through the action of sunlight on chlorophyll in those plants, including algae.

**Physical geography**   One of the two major divisions of systematic geography; the spatial analysis of the structure, processes, and location of the Earth's natural phenomena such as climate, soil, plants, animals, and topography.

**Physical-political (natural-political) boundary**   Political boundary **defined** and **delimited** (and occasionally **demarcated**) by a prominent physical feature in the natural landscape—such as a river or the crest ridges of a mountain range.

**Physiologic population density**   The number of people per unit area of **arable** land.

**Pidgin language**   When parts of two or more languages are combined in a simplified structure and vocabulary.

**Pilgrimage**   Voluntary travel by an adherent to a **sacred site** to pay respects or participate in a ritual at the site.

**Place**   The fourth theme of geography as defined by the **Geography Educational National Implementation Project**: uniqueness of a **location**.

**Placelessness**   Defined by geographer Edward Relph as the loss of uniqueness of **place** in the **cultural landscape** so that one place looks like the next.

**Plant domestication**   Genetic modification of a plant such that its reproductive success depends on human intervention.

**Plantation agriculture**   Production system based on a large estate owned by an individual, family, or corporation and organized to produce a cash crop. Almost all plantations were established within the tropics; in recent decades, many have been divided into smaller holdings or reorganized as cooperatives.

**Pleistocene**   The most recent epoch of the Late Cenozoic Ice Age, beginning about 1.8 million years ago and marked by as many as **20 glaciations** and **interglaciations** of which the current warm phase, the Holocene epoch, has witnessed the rise of human civilization.

**Political ecology**   An approach to studying nature-society relations that is concerned with the ways in which environmental issues both reflect, and are the result of, the political and socioeconomic contexts in which they are situated.

**Political geography**   A subdivision of **human geography** focused on the nature and implications of the evolving spatial organization of political governance and formal political practice on the Earth's surface. It is concerned with why political spaces emerge in the places that they do and with how the character of those spaces affects social, political, economic, and environmental understandings and practices.

**Polytheistic religion**   Belief system in which multiple deities are revered as creators and arbiters of all that exists in the universe.

**Popular culture**   **Cultural traits** such as dress, diet, and music that identify and are part of today's changeable, urban-based, media-influenced western societies.

**Population composition**   Structure of a population in terms of age, sex and other properties such as marital status and education.

**Population density**   A measurement of the number of people per given unit of land.

**Population distribution**   Description of locations on the Earth's surface where populations live.

**Population explosion**   The rapid growth of the world's human population during the past century, attended by ever-shorter **doubling times** and accelerating rates of increase.

**Population pyramids**   Visual representations of the age and sex composition of a population whereby the percentage of each age group (generally five-year increments) is represented by a horizontal bar the length of which represents its relationship to the total population. The males in each age group are represented to the left of the center line of each horizontal bar; the females in each age group are represented to the right of the center line.

**Possibilism**   Geographic viewpoint—a response to determinism—that holds that human decision making, not the environment, is the crucial factor in cultural development. Nonetheless, possibilists view the environment as providing a set of broad constraints that limits the possibilities of human choice.

**Post-Fordist**   World economic system characterized by a more flexible set of production practices in which goods are not mass-produced; instead, production has been accelerated and dispersed around the globe by multinational companies that shift production, outsourcing it around the world and bringing places closer together in time and space than would have been imaginable at the beginning of the twentieth century.

**Postcolonialism**   A recent intellectual movement concerned with examining the enduring impacts of **colonialism**, not just in economic and political relations (the focus of **neocolonialism**), but especially in cultural terms. Postcolonial studies examine the ways in which basic concepts of culture and forms of cultural interaction continue to be shaped by the hegemonic ideas and practices of colonialism.

**Primary economic activity**   Economic activity concerned with the direct extraction of **natural resources** from the environment—such as mining, fishing, lumbering, and especially **agriculture**.

**Primary industrial regions**   Western and Central Europe; Eastern North America; Russia and Ukraine; and Eastern Asia, each of which consists of one or more core areas of industrial development with subsidiary clusters.

**Primate city**   A country's largest city—ranking atop the **urban hierarchy**—most expressive of the national culture and usually (but not always) the capital city as well.

**Prime Meridian**   An imaginary north-south line of **longitude** on the Earth grid, passing through the Royal Observatory at Greenwich in London, defined as having a longitude of 0°.

**Primogeniture**   System which the eldest son in a family—or, in exceptional cases, daughter—inherits all of a dying parent's land.

**Product life cycle**   The introduction, growth, maturation and decline of a product.

**Protestant**   One of three major branches of **Christianity** (together with the **Eastern Orthodox Church** and the **Roman Catholic Church**). Following the widespread societal changes in Europe starting in the 1300s CE, many adherents of the Roman Catholic Church began to question the role of religion in their lives and opened the door to the Protestant Reformation wherein John Huss, Martin Luther, John Calvin, and others challenged many of the fundamental teachings of the Roman Catholic Church.

**Proto-Eurasiatic**   Linguistic hypothesis proposing the existence of a language or group of languages that predated, and gave rise to, **Proto-Indo-European** and other language families with Eurasian origins.

**Proto-Indo-European (language)**   Linguistic hypothesis proposing the existence of an ancestral Indo-European **language** that is the **hearth** of the ancient Latin, Greek, and Sanskrit languages; this hearth would link modern languages from Scandinavia to North Africa and from North America through parts of Asia to Australia.

**Pull factor**   Positive conditions and perceptions that effectively attract people to new locales from other areas.

**Push factor**   Negative conditions and perceptions that induce people to leave their abode and migrate to a new locale.

**Quaternary economic activity**   Service sector industries concerned with the collection, processing, and manipulation of information and capital. Examples include finance, administration, insurance, and legal services.

**Queer theory**   Theory defined by geographers Glen Elder, Lawrence Knopp, and Heidi Nast that highlights the contextual nature of opposition to the heteronormative and focuses on the political engagement of "queers" with the heteronormative.

**Quinary economic activity**   Service sector industries that require a high level of specialized knowledge or technical skill. Examples include scientific research and high-level management.

**Race**   A categorization of humans based on skin color and other physical characteristics. Racial categories are social and political constructions because they are based on ideas that some biological differences (especially skin color) are more important than others (e.g., height, etc.), even though the latter might have more significance in terms of human activity. With its roots in sixteenth-century England, the term is closely associated with European **colonialism** because of the impact of that development on global understandings of racial differences.

**Racism**   Frequently referred to as a system or attitude toward visible differences in individuals, racism is an ideology of difference that ascribes (predominantly negative) significance and meaning to culturally, socially, and politically constructed ideas based on phenotypical features.

**Radioactive waste**   Hazardous-waste-emitting radiation from nuclear power plants, nuclear weapons factories, and nuclear equipment in hospitals and industry.

**Rank-size rule**   In a model urban hierarchy, the idea that the population of a **city** or town will be inversely proportional to its rank in the hierarchy.

**Rare earth elements**   Seventeen chemical elements that commonly occur together but are difficult to separate. They are commonly used to make high tech electronics and weapons systems.

**Reapportionment**   Process by which representative districts are switched according to population shifts, so that each district encompasses approximately the same number of people.

**Rectangular survey system**   Also called the Public Land Survey, the system was used by the U.S. Land Office Survey to parcel land west of the Appalachian Mountains. The system divides land into a series of rectangular parcels.

**Redlining**   A discriminatory real estate practice in North America in which members of minority groups are prevented from obtaining money to purchase homes or property in predominantly white neighborhoods. The practice derived its name from the red lines depicted on **cadastral maps** used by real estate agents and developers. Today, redlining is officially illegal.

**Reference maps**   Maps that show the absolute location of places and geographic features determined by a frame of reference, typically latitude and longitude.

**Refugees**   People who have fled their country because of political persecution and seek asylum in another country.

**Refugee camps**   Temporary settlements set up to accommodate people who flee their homelands in the face of civil unrest, oppression, or warfare.

**Region**   The third theme of geography as defined by the **Geography Educational National Implementation Project**: an **area** on the Earth's surface marked by a degree of formal, functional, or perceptual homogeneity of some phenomenon.

**Regional scale**   Interactions occurring within a **region**, in a regional setting.

**Relative location**   The regional position or **situation** of a place relative to the position of other places. Distance, **accessibility**, and connectivity affect relative location.

**Religion** Defined by geographers Robert Stoddard and Carolyn Prorak in the book *Geography in America* as "a system of beliefs and practices that attempts to order life in terms of culturally perceived ultimate priorities."

**Religious extremism** **Religious fundamentalism** carried to the point of violence.

**Religious fundamentalism** Religious movement whose objectives are to return to the foundations of the faith and to influence state policy.

**Relocation diffusion** Sequential **diffusion** process in which the items being diffused are transmitted by their carrier agents as they evacuate the old areas and relocate to new ones. The most common form of relocation diffusion involves the spreading of innovations by a migrating population.

**Remittances** Money migrants send back to family and friends in their home countries, often in cash, forming an important part of the economy in many poorer countries.

**Remote sensing** A method of collecting data or information through the use of instruments (e.g., satellites) that are physically distant from the area or object of study.

**Renewable resources** Resources that can regenerate as they are exploited.

**Renfrew hypothesis** Hypothesis developed by British scholar Colin Renfrew wherein he proposed that three areas in and near the first agricultural hearth, the **Fertile Crescent**, gave rise to three language families: Europe's Indo-European languages (from Anatolia [present-day Turkey]); North African and Arabian languages (from the western arc of the Fertile Crescent); and the languages in present-day Iran, Afghanistan, Pakistan, and India (from the eastern arc of the Fertile Crescent).

**Repatriation** A refugee or group of refugees returning to their home country, usually with the assistance of government or a non-governmental organization.

**Rescale** Involvement of players at other scales to generate support for a position or an initiative (e.g., use of the Internet to generate interest on a national or global scale for a local position or initiative).

**Residential segregation** Defined by geographers Douglas Massey and Nancy Denton as the degree to which two or more groups live separately from one another, in different parts of an urban environment.

**Restrictive population policies** Government policies designed to reduce the rate of natural population increase.

**Reterritorialization** With respect to popular culture, when people within a place start to produce an aspect of popular culture themselves, doing so in the context of their local culture and making it their own.

**Roman Catholic Church** One of three major branches of **Christianity**, the Roman Catholic Church, together with the **Eastern Orthodox Church**, a second of the three major branches of Christianity, arose out of the division of the Roman Empire by Emperor Diocletian into four governmental regions: two western regions centered in Rome, and two eastern regions centered in Constantinople (now Istanbul, Turkey). In 1054 CE, Christianity was divided along that same line when the Eastern Orthodox Church, centered in Constantinople; and the Roman Catholic Church, centered in Rome, split.

**Romance languages** Languages (French, Spanish, Italian, Romanian, and Portuguese) that lie in the areas that were once controlled by the Roman Empire but were not subsequently overwhelmed.

**Root crop** Crop that is reproduced by cultivating the roots of or the cuttings from the plants.

**Russification** the Soviet policy to promote the diffusion of Russian culture throughout the republics of the former Soviet Union.

**Rust belt** a region in the northeastern United States that was once characterized by industry. Now so-called because of the heavy deindustrialization of the area.

**Sacred site** **Place** or **space** people infuse with religious meaning.

**Sanitary landfills** Disposal sites for non-hazardous solid waste that is spread in layers and compacted to the smallest practical volume. The sites are typically designed with floors made of materials to treat seeping liquids and are covered by soil as the wastes are compacted and deposited into the landfill.

**Scale** Representation of a real-world phenomenon at a certain level of reduction or generalization. In **cartography**, the ratio of map distance to ground distance; indicated on a map as a bar graph, representative fraction, and/or verbal statement.

**Second Agricultural Revolution** Dovetailing with and benefiting from the **Industrial Revolution**, the Second Agricultural Revolution witnessed improved methods of cultivation, harvesting, and storage of farm produce.

**Secondary economic activity** Economic activity involving the processing of raw materials and their transformation into finished industrial products; the manufacturing sector.

**Secondary hearth** An area to which an innovation diffuses and from which the innovation diffuses more broadly.

**Sector model** A structural model of the American city that suggests that low-rent and other types of areas can extend from the **central business district** to the city's outer edge, creating zones that are shaped like a piece of pie.

**Secularism** The idea that ethical and moral standards should be formulated and adhered to for life on Earth, not to accommodate the prescriptions of a deity and promises of a comfortable afterlife. A secular state is the opposite of a **theocracy**.

**Seed crop** Crop that is reproduced by cultivating the seeds of the plants.

**Selective immigration** Process to control immigration in which individuals with certain backgrounds (i.e. criminal records, poor health, or subversive activities) are barred from immigrating.

**Semi-periphery** Places where **core** and **periphery** processes are both occurring; places that are exploited by the core but in turn exploit the periphery.

**Sense of place** State of mind derived through the infusion of a place with meaning and emotion by remembering important events that occurred in that place or by labeling a place with a certain character.

**Sequent occupance** The notion that successive societies leave their cultural imprints on a place, each contributing to the cumulative **cultural landscape**.

**Shamanism** Community faith in traditional societies in which people follow their shaman—a religious leader, teacher, healer, and visionary. At times, an especially strong shaman might attract a regional following. However, most shamans remain local figures.

**Shantytown** Unplanned slum development on the margins of cities, dominated by crude dwellings and shelters made mostly of scrap wood, iron, and even pieces of cardboard.

**Sharia law** The system of Islamic law, sometimes called *Qu'ranic law*. Unlike most Western systems of law that are based on legal precedents, Sharia is based on varying degrees of interpretation of the *Qu'ran*.

**Shifting cultivation** Cultivation of crops in tropical forest clearings in which the forest vegetation has been removed by cutting and burning. These clearings are usually abandoned after a few years in favor of newly cleared forestland. Also known as **slash-and-burn agriculture**.

**Shintoism** **Religion** located in Japan and related to **Buddhism**. Shintoism focuses particularly on nature and ancestor worship.

**Shi'ites** Adherents of one of the two main divisions of Islam. Also known as Shiahs, the Shiites represent the Persian (Iranian) variation of Islam and believe in the infallibility and divine right to authority of the **Imams**, descendants of Ali.

**Site** The internal physical attributes of a **place**, including its absolute location, its spatial character and physical setting.

**Situation** The external locational attributes of a place; its **relative location** or regional position with reference to other nonlocal places.

**Slash-and-burn agriculture** See **shifting cultivation**.

**Slavic languages** Languages (Russian, Polish, Czech, Slovak, Ukrainian, Slovenian, Serbo-Croatian, and Bulgarian) that developed as Slavic people migrated from a base in present-day Ukraine close to 2000 years ago.

**Social networks**  Interconnections among individuals that foster social interaction.

**Social stratification**  One of two components, together with **agricultural surplus**, which enables the formation of **cities**; the differentiation of society into classes based on wealth, power, production, and prestige.

**Soil erosion**  The wearing away of the land surface by wind and moving water.

**Solid waste**  Non-liquid, non-soluble materials ranging from municipal garbage to sewage sludge, agricultural refuse, and mining residues.

**Sound shift**  Slight change in a word across **languages** within a **subfamily** or through a language family from the present backward toward its origin.

**Sovereignty**  A principle of international relations that holds that final authority over social, economic, and political matters should rest with the legitimate rulers of independent states.

**Space**  Defined by Doreen Massey and Pat Jess as "social relations stretched out."

**Spaces of consumption**  Areas of a city, the main purpose of which is to encourage people to consume goods and services; driven primarily by the global media industry.

**Spatial**  Pertaining to space on the Earth's surface; sometimes used as a synonym for *geographic*.

**Spatial distribution**  Physical location of geographic phenomena across **space**.

**Spatial fix**  The movement of production from one site to another based on the place-based cost advantages of the new site.

**Spatial interaction**  The degree of flow of people, ideas, and goods among places. See **complementarity** and **intervening opportunity**.

**Spatial perspective**  Observing variations in geographic phenomena across **space**.

**Special Economic Zone (SEZ)**  Specific **area** within a country in which tax incentives and less stringent environmental regulations are implemented to attract foreign business and investment.

**Splitting**  In the context of determining representative districts, the process by which the majority and minority populations are spread evenly across each of the districts to be created therein, ensuring control by the majority of each of the districts; as opposed to the result of **majority-minority districts**.

**Standard language**  The variant of a **language** that a country's political and intellectual elite seek to promote as the norm for use in schools, government, the media, and other aspects of public life.

**State**  A politically organized territory that is administered by a sovereign government and is recognized by a significant portion of the international community. A state has a defined territory, a permanent population, a government, and is recognized by other states.

**Stateless nation**  Nation that does not have a state.

**Stationary population level**  The level at which a national population ceases to grow.

**Step migration**  **Migration** to a distant destination that occurs in stages, for example, from farm to nearby village and later to town and city.

**Stimulus diffusion**  A form of diffusion in which a cultural adaptation is created as a result of the introduction of a **cultural trait** from another **place**.

**Structural adjustment loans**  Loans granted by international financial institutions such as the World Bank and the International Monetary Fund to countries in the **periphery** and the **semi-periphery** in exchange for certain economic and governmental reforms in that country (e.g. privatization of certain government entities and opening the country to foreign trade and investment).

**Structuralist theory**  A general term for a model of economic development that treats economic disparities among countries or regions as the result of historically derived power relations within the global economic system.

**Subfamilies (language)**  Divisions within a **language** family where the commonalities are more definite and the origin is more recent.

**Subsistence agriculture**  Self-sufficient **agriculture** that is small scale and low technology and emphasizes food production for local consumption, not for trade.

**Suburb**  A subsidiary urban area surrounding and connected to the central city. Many are exclusively residential; others have their own commercial centers or shopping malls.

**Suburban downtown**  Significant concentration of diversified economic activities around a highly **accessible** suburban location, including retailing, light industry, and a variety of major corporate and commercial operations. Late-twentieth-century coequal to the American central city's **Central Business District (CBD)**.

**Suburbanization**  Movement of upper- and middle-class people from urban **core areas** to the surrounding outskirts to escape pollution as well as deteriorating social conditions (perceived and actual). In North America, the process began in the early nineteenth century and became a mass phenomenon by the second half of the twentieth century.

**Succession**  Process by which new **immigrants** to a **city** move to and dominate or take over areas or neighborhoods occupied by older immigrant groups. For example, in the early twentieth century, Puerto Ricans "invaded" the immigrant Jewish neighborhood of East Harlem and successfully took over the neighborhood or "succeeded" the immigrant Jewish population as the dominant immigrant group in the neighborhood.

**Sunbelt**  The South and Southwest regions of the United States

**Sunnis**  Adherents to the largest branch of Islam, called the orthodox or traditionalist. They believe in the effectiveness of family and community in the solution of life's problems, and they differ from the **Shiites** in accepting the traditions (*sunna*) of Muhammad as authoritative.

**Supranational organization**  A venture involving three or more **nation-states** involving formal political, economic, and/or cultural cooperation to promote shared objectives. The European Union is one such organization.

**Syncretic**  A blend of religious beliefs and traditions, often forming a new religion.

**Synekism**  The possibility of change that results from people living together in cities.

**Synergy**  The cross-promotion of vertically-integrated goods.

**Taoism**  **Religion** believed to have been founded by Lao-Tsu and based upon his book entitled "Tao-te-ching," or "Book of the Way." Lao-Tsu focused on the proper form of political rule and on the oneness of humanity and nature.

**Tear-downs**  Homes bought in many American suburbs with the intent of tearing them down and replacing them with much larger homes, often referred to as **McMansions**.

**Technopole**  Centers or nodes of high-technology research and activity around which a **high-technology corridor** is sometimes established.

**Tectonic plates**  Large pieces of rock that form portions of the Earth's mantle and crust and which are in motion.

**Terra incognita**  Areas on maps that are not well defined because they are off limits or unknown to the map maker.

**Territorial integrity**  The right of a **state** to defend soverign territory against incursion from other states.

**Territorial representation**  System wherein each representative is elected from a territorially defined district.

**Territoriality**  In **political geography**, a country's or more local community's sense of property and attachment toward its territory, as expressed by its determination to keep it inviolable and strongly defended. See more generally **human territoriality**.

**Tertiary economic activity**  Economic activity associated with the provision of services—such as transportation, banking, retailing, education, and routine office-based jobs.

**Thematic maps**  Maps that tell stories, typically showing the degree of some attribute or the movement of a geographic phenomenon.

**Theocracy**  A **state** whose government is under the control of a ruler who is deemed to be divinely guided, or of a group of religious leaders, as in post-Khomeini Iran. The opposite of a theocracy is a secular state.

**Third Agricultural Revolution**  Currently in progress, the Third Agricultural Revolution has as its principal orientation the development of **genetically modified organisms (GMOs)**.

**Three-tier structure**  With reference to Immanuel Wallerstein's **world-systems theory**, the division of the world into the **core**, the **periphery**, and the **semi-periphery** as a means to help explain the interconnections between places in the global economy.

**Thunian pattern**  See **Von Thünen Model**.

**Time-Distance decay**  The declining degree of acceptance of an idea or innovation with increasing time and distance from its point of origin or source.

**Time-space compression**  A term associated with the work of David Harvey that refers to the social and psychological effects of living in a world in which **time-space convergence** has rapidly reached a high level of intensity.

**Time-space convergence**  A term coined by Donald Janelle that refers to the greatly accelerated movement of goods, information, and ideas during the twentieth century made possible by technological innovations in transportation and communications.

**Toponym**  Place name.

**Total Fertility Rate (TFR)**  The average number of children born to a woman during her childbearing years.

**Township-and-range system**  A rectangular land division scheme designed by Thomas Jefferson to disperse settlers evenly across farmlands of the U.S. interior. See also **rectangular survey system**.

**Toxic waste**  Hazardous waste causing danger from chemicals and infectious organisms.

**Trade area**  **Region** adjacent to every town and **city** within which its influence is dominant.

**Traditional**  Term used in various contexts (e.g., traditional religion) to indicate originality within a culture or long-term part of an indigenous society. It is the opposite of modernized, superimposed, or changed; it denotes continuity and historic association.

**Trafficking**  When a family sends a child or an adult to a labor recruiter in hopes that the labor recruiter will send money, and the family member will earn money to send home.

**Transhumance**  A seasonal periodic movement of **pastoralists** and their livestock between highland and lowland pastures.

**Unilateralism**  World order in which one state is in a position of dominance with allies following rather than joining the political decision-making process.

**Unitary (state)**  A **nation-state** that has a centralized government and administration that exercises power equally over all parts of the state.

**Universalizing religion**  A belief system that espouses the idea that there is one true religion that is universal in scope. Adherents of universalizing religious systems often believe that their religion represents universal truths, and in some cases great effort is undertaken in evangelism and missionary work.

**Urban (area)**  The entire built-up, nonrural area and its population, including the most recently constructed suburban appendages. Provides a better picture of the dimensions and population of such an area than the delimited municipality (central city) that forms its heart.

**Urban hierarchy**  A ranking of settlements (hamlet, village, town, city, metropolis) according to their size and economic functions.

**Urban morphology**  The study of the physical form and structure of urban **places**.

**Urban realm**  A **spatial** generalization of the large, late-twentieth-century **city** in the United States. It is shown to be a widely dispersed, multicentered metropolis consisting of increasingly independent zones or realms, each focused on its own **suburban downtown**; the only exception is the shrunken central realm, which is focused on the **central business district (CBD)**.

**Urban sprawl**  Unrestricted growth in many American **urban** areas of housing, commercial development, and roads over large expanses of land, with little concern for urban planning.

**Urbanization**  A term with several connotations. The proportion of a country's population living in urban places is its level of urbanization. The process of urbanization involves the movement of people to, and the clustering of people in, towns and cities—a major force in every geographic realm today. Another kind of urbanization occurs when an expanding city absorbs the rural countryside and transforms it into suburbs; in the case of cities in the developing world, this also generates peripheral **shantytowns**.

**Urbicide**  The deliberate killing of a city, as happens, for example, when cities are targeted for destruction during wars.

**Variable costs**  Costs that change directly with the amount of production (e.g. energy supply and labor costs).

**Vectored disease**  A disease carried from one host to another by an intermediate host.

**Vertical integration**  Ownership by the same firm of a number of companies that exist along a variety of points on a **commodity chain**.

**Vienna Convention for the Protection of the Ozone Layer**  The first international convention aimed at addressing the issue of ozone depletion. Held in 1985, the Vienna Convention was the predecessor to the **Montreal Protocol**.

**Voluntary migration**  **Movement** in which people relocate in response to perceived opportunity, not because they are forced to move.

**Von Thünen Model**  A model that explains the location of agricultural activities in a commercial, profit-making economy. A process of spatial competition allocates various farming activities into rings around a central market city, with profit-earning capability the determining force in how far a crop locates from the market.

**Washington Consensus**  Label used to refer to the following fundamental principles of free trade: 1) that free trade raises the well-being of all countries by inducing them to devote their resources to production of those goods they produce relatively most efficiently; and 2) that competition through trade raises a country's long-term growth rate by expanding access to global technologies and promoting innovation.

**Wisconsinian Glaciation**  The most recent glacial period of the Pleistocene, enduring about 100,000 years and giving way, beginning about 18,000 years ago, to the current interglacial, the Holocene.

**World city**  Dominant **city** in terms of its role in the global political economy. Not the world's biggest city in terms of population or industrial output, but rather centers of strategic control of the world economy.

**World-systems theory**  Theory originated by Immanuel Wallerstein and illuminated by his **three-tier structure**, proposing that social change in the developing world is inextricably linked to the economic activities of the developed world.

**Zero population growth**  a state in which a population is maintained at a constant level because the number of deaths is exactly offset by the number of births.

**Zionism**  The movement to unite the Jewish people of the **diaspora** and to establish a national homeland for them in the promised land.

**Zone**  Area of a **city** with a relatively uniform land use (e.g. an industrial zone or a residential zone).

**Zoning laws**  Legal restrictions on land use that determine what types of building and economic activities are allowed to take place in certain areas. In the United States, areas are most commonly divided into separate zones of residential, retail, or industrial use.

# INDEX

Piazza della Transalpina, 232, 232f
Pidgin language, 161, 162
Pilgrimages, 190, 199, 200f
Pine Ridge Indian Reservation, 305
Place(s):
    authenticity of, 98–101
    gendered, 130
    and identity, 127–130
    influence of language on, 164–169
    sense of, 9, 127
    space vs., 130
    as theme of geography, 9
Placelessness, 111
Place vulnerabilities, in service industry, 376–377
Plank, Kevin, 24, 25
Plano-Richardson, Texas, 375, 375f
Plantation agriculture, 334, 335
Plant domestication, 315–318, 317t
Pleistocene epoch, 383
Plymouth, Montserrat, 72
Polar climates, 332
Politics:
    and agriculture, 338
    and development, 305–309
    geopoliticians' influence on, 235–236
    migration related to, 71
Political corruption, 301–302
Political ecology, 27, 394, 395
Political geography, 211–244
    boundaries and boundary disputes, 230–234
    European Union, 211–213
    spatial organization of governments, 222–230
    states and nations, 213–222
    study of geopolitics, 234–237
    supranational organizations, 237–243
Political power, 221–222
Political stability, 301–302
Pollution, 302, 390, 398, 402
Polytheistic religions, 175
Popular culture, 102–115
    in cultural landscape, 111–115
    diffusion of, 102–110
    and local culture, 91–93
    replacement of local culture by, 109–110
Population, 29–59
    causes of change in, 36–46
    and environmental change, 395–397
    and government, 56–58
    influence of health on, 47–56
    and infrastructure in China, 29–30
Population composition, 46
Population density, 31–36
    arithmetic, 31–32
    physiologic, 32
    and population distribution, 33–36
    of world, 33f–34f
Population distribution, 33–36, 33f
Population explosion, 41
Population growth, 36–46, 40f
    within countries, 41–42
    and demographic transition, 43–45
    government influence on, 56–58
    predictions about, 45–46
    regional and national, 38–41
    worldwide, 37–38, 37f
Population pyramids, 46–47, 46f, 47f, 57f
Pork production, 174f
PortalPlayer, 364, 364f, 365
Port cities, 346–347
Port Gentil, Gabon, 218, 307, 308, 308f
Portland, Oregon, 269
Porto Alegre, Brazil, 413, 413f
Possession toponyms, 165
Possibilism, 27
Postindustrial (term), 371

Potsdamer Platz (Berlin, Germany), 284
Poultry industry, 339–340, 340f
Powell, Colin, 84
Power:
    devolution of, 223–227
    political, 221–222
Power relationships, 130–141
    among ethnic groups, 137–141
    and dowry deaths in India, 136–137
    and migration, 70–71
    and value of work by women, 132–133
    vulnerable populations in, 134–135
    of women in Subsaharan Africa, 135–136
Precipitation, 14f–15f
Preconditions of takeoff stage (development), 295
Presho, South Dakota, 311f
Primary economic activities, 313
Primate cities, 260
Primogeniture, 327
Printing press, 161
Product life cycle, 359
Prorak, Carolyn, 173
Protestantism, 185, 207
Protestant Reformation, 184
Protestants, in Northern Ireland, 171–172, 206–207
Proto-Eurasiatic language, 154
Proto-Indo-European language, 154–156, 155f, 157f
Puerto Rico, 126
Pull factors (migration), 69–71
Push factors (migration), 69–71
Putin, Vladimir, 418
Putrajaya, Malaysia, 307f

Qin Xi Huang, 251, 251f
QQ application, 102, 103
Quaternary economic activities, 313
Quaternary industries, 371
Quaternary services, 373, 374
Quebec, Canada, 149, 237
Queer theory, 130
Quinary economic activities, 313
Quinary industries, 371
Quinary services, 374
Quota market, 306
Qzone, 102

Race:
    and identity, 119–125
    and power relationships, 132
    residential segregation based on, 123–125
    U.S. Census questions on, 120f
    of U.S. population, 121–122, 122f, 123f
Racism, 120
Radioactive waste, 393
Raleigh, North Carolina, 71
Ranching, 336, 342
Rank-size rule, 260
Rare earth elements, 401, 401f
Ratzel, Friedrich, 234–235
Ravenstein, Ernst, 69
Raw materials, for flexible production, 360
Reagan, Ronald, 236
Reapportionment, 229
Rectangular survey system, 326
Redlining, 273
Red Sea-Dead Sea project, 390
Reference maps, 11, 12
Reform Judaism, 183
Refugees:
    countries of origin of, 80f–81f
    housing for, 362
    migration by, 79–85
    regions of dislocation for, 81–85
Refugee camps, 61

Regions, 9, 18–22
Regional migration flows, 75–78
Regional population growth, 38–41
Regional supranational organizations, 240–241
Reincarnation, 179
Relative location, 12
Relict boundaries, 233
Religion, 171–210. See also specific religious groups
    in cultural landscape, 190–200
    in culture, 172–175
    diffusion of, 175–190
    and fundamentalism/extremism, 207–209
    global distribution of, 176f–177f
    and peace walls in Belfast, 171–172
    in political conflicts, 200–209
    and rural local culture, 94–96
Religious extremism, 207–209, 243
Religious fundamentalism, 207–209, 243
Religious prohibitions against pork, 174f
Relocation diffusion, 26
Relph, Edward, 111
Remittances, 61
Remote sensing technology, 13
Renewable energy sources, 400–401
Renewable resources, 387
Renren, 102, 103, 103f
Repatriation, 81
Rescale (term), 18
Residential areas, 262
Residential segregation, 123–125, 272–273
Restrictive population policies, 57
Reterritorialization, 106, 107f, 243
Reverse remittances, 61
Revolutions, 167
Rhythm Road, 106
Rihanna, 93f
Rio de Janeiro, Brazil, 267, 267f
Rituals, religious, 173
Rivoli, Pietra, 306
Robinson, K. W., 223
Robson, Elsbeth, 53–55
Rodrigue, Jean-Paul, 357
Roman Catholic Church, 58, 184, 207
Romance languages, 158
Roman Empire, 184f, 253–254, 254f
Romania, 216, 217, 217f
Rome, Italy, 253–255, 255f
Roost, Frank, 283, 284
Root crops, 315
Rosati, Clayton, 109
Rose, Gillian, 119, 127, 409
Roseville, Minnesota, 111f
Rostow, Walt, 295–296, 298
Rotterdam, Netherlands, 351
Rouen, France, 353, 353f
Route 128 corridor, Massachusetts, 375
Ruhr Valley, Germany, 258, 351
Rundling, 328
Rural life, 323–324
Rural local culture, 94–98
Rural-to-urban migration, 60–63
Rushkoff, Douglas, 106
Russia. See also Soviet Union
    in geopolitical world order, 237
    Industrial Revolution in, 354
    life expectancy in, 50
    national migration flows in, 79
    population polices in, 56
    St. Petersburg region, 354
    secularism in, 189
    Sochi, 108f
    toponyms in, 167
Russification, 79
Rust Belt, 372
Rwanda, 71, 81, 136, 299

# THE WONDERFUL WORLD OF AP®
# HUMAN GEOGRAPHY

Greg Sherwin

Paul T. Gray, Jr.

**W**elcome to the Wonderful World of AP® Human Geography. We realize that for many students this might be your first Advanced Placement® course and we think that many of you might be unaware or nervous about what to expect.

With that in mind, the purpose of this part of the book is to help you understand what AP® Human Geography is and how the program works. Completing an AP® course can be a very enriching educational experience and taking the AP® exam is a tremendous achievement that can earn you college credit. That bears repeating: *taking this class in high school can earn you credit at the university or college you will be attending.*

We certainly want you to have a successful experience and we want you to know what to expect. So we have divided this portion of the book into five sections that should clarify the program, explain what is covered on the exam, and address how the AP® exam is structured.

# Key Questions FOR AP® HUMAN GEOGRAPHY UNIT

1. What are the Most Frequently Asked Questions about the Program?
2. What are the Topics Covered in AP® Human Geography?
3. What are the types of Multiple Choice Questions on the AP® Exam?
4. What are the types of Free Response Questions on the AP® Exam?
5. What are final reminders I should be aware of for the day of the AP® Exam?

## ABOUT THE AUTHORS

Mr. Paul Gray and Mr. Greg Sherwin are high school teachers who teach AP® Human Geography. In fact, they have combined experience of over 25 years teaching the course. These dedicated professionals have a clear understanding of what students need to do to be successful in the class and on the exam. Both of them have served on the College Board's Test Development Committee, a group responsible for structuring the AP® Human Geography exam. They have also co-authored an AP® Human Geography Teacher's Guide published by the College Board.

In addition, they have created the Advanced Placement® Workbook that accompanies *Human Geography: People, Place, and Culture*. The workbook is designed to help high school students understand what they are reading more clearly. You can order yours at wiley.com/college/fouberg

## WHAT ARE THE MOST FREQUENTLY ASKED QUESTIONS ABOUT THE PROGRAM?

Let's start our journey into Advanced Placement® Human Geography by looking at the Top Ten most frequently asked questions about the program.

### 1. What is the Advanced Placement (AP®) program?

AP® stands for Advanced Placement® and it is a program of college-level courses and exams that gives high school students the opportunity to receive advanced placement and/or credit from the college they attend. AP® courses reflect the content and goals of a first-year college course that is offered by a large number of colleges and universities.

The Advanced Placement® Program is administered and managed by the College Board, the same organization that offers the SAT each year.

## 2. What is the format of the AP® Human Geography exam?

The AP® Human Geography exam lasts 2 hours and 15 minutes. It contains two sections:

1. 75 Multiple Choice Questions (MCQs): Students will have 1 hour to complete this portion. Each question will have 5 choices (A through E). We will explain to you the types of questions to anticipate in section 3 in this unit.

2. 3 Free Response Questions (FRQs): Students will have 75 minutes to answer these questions. FRQs take reflection time before you respond. FRQs also take a significant effort to write. We will explain these types of questions and how to answer them in section 4 of this unit.

Each portion of the test is worth 50% of a student's grade. In order to be successful on the exam, a student should have a clear understanding of how all of these questions work.

The MCQ portion of the exam is given first. Then, after a short break, students answer three FRQs (each FRQ averages 25 minutes).

## 3. How many students are involved in the AP® Human Geography program?

The number of students taking AP® Human Geography has grown tremendously because high schools are increasingly seeing the benefits of having a course that focuses on the world in an era of globalization.

### AP® Human Geography: By the Numbers—History of the Exam

| Year | # of Exams | % Change | # Schools |
| --- | --- | --- | --- |
| 2001 | 3,272 | – | 305 |
| 2002 | 5,286 | 62 | 402 |
| 2003 | 7,329 | 39 | 473 |
| 2004 | 10,471 | 43 | 561 |
| 2005 | 14,139 | 35 | 702 |
| 2006 | 21,003 | 38 | 890 |
| 2007 | 29,005 | 49 | 1,083 |
| 2008 | 39,878 | 37 | 1,380 |
| 2009 | 50,730 | 27 | 1,618 |
| 2010 | 68,397 | 35 | 1,951 |
| 2011 | 82,692 | 21 | 2,347 |
| 2012 | 98,697 | 19 | 2,652 |
| 2013 | 114,055 | 17 | 3,049 |
| 2014 | 137,044 | 20 | 3,531 |

*Source*: Constructed from information provided by Jon Moore—Educational Testing Service, Personal communication to Paul Gray (email), June 27, 2014.

## 4. How are the exams scored?

Multiple Choice Questions are scored by machine. Therefore, it is very important to fully erase any answers you want to change.

FRQs are more complicated. They are scored by a large number of college geography professors and Advanced

Placement® Human Geography teachers who meet during the first weeks in June. These professors and teachers work in groups and focus on one of the questions using a standard rubric.

Each exam receives a final score based on a five-point scale:

5 Extremely well qualified
4 Well qualified
3 Qualified
2 Possibly qualified
1 No recommendation

## 5. How can I earn college credit and placement?

According to the College Board website, more than 90% of four-year colleges in the United States and colleges in more than 60 other countries give students credit, advanced placement, or both on the basis of AP® exam scores.

Each college and university sets its own policies on what scores, if any, it will accept for credit and/or advanced placement. But you can go to the College Board website or http://collegesearch.collegeboard.com/apcreditpolicy/index.jsp for more specific information.

Below are some sample university policies:

**Florida State University (Tallahassee, Florida)**
"Students who have participated in the AP® Program in high school and received a score of 3 or better on the national examinations will receive college credit in the appropriate subject areas. Please refer to our website for information about specific scores and credits." (Source: http://admissions.fsu.edu/freshman/admissions/accelerated.cfm)

**University of Idaho (Moscow, Idaho)**
"Credit is granted for Advanced Placement® courses completed in high school in which a grade of 5, 4, or 3 is attained in College Board Advanced Placement® exams." (Source: http://www.uidaho.edu/registrar/transfer/ap)

**Drake University (Des Moines, Iowa)**
"Drake University awards advanced standing credit through several programs. In consultation with faculty advisers, all credits accepted are applied toward completion of Drake curriculum, major or elective requirements." (Source: http://drexel.edu/provost/aard/course-placement/credit-policies/)

(Florida State and University of Idaho accept AP® Human Geography credit with a score of 3 or higher; Drake University accepts a score of 4 or higher.)

## 6. How much does it cost to take the Advanced Placement® Human Geography exam?

As of 2015, the fee for each exam is $91.

Some states pay all fees for students to take AP® exams (check with your teacher or your school to find out more information).

To encourage AP® access and equity, most states offer discounted fees for students whose families may not be able to afford the cost of the AP® exam. Check with your high school counselor or AP® teacher for more information on whether you qualify for reduced exam fees.

We are very sensitive to the fact that $91 per AP® exam is a lot of money for many families. We encourage students whose families have financial need to go to the College Board website and click on the links for more information about state and federal fee reductions for those who qualify. For more details on exam costs and financial assistance, visit http://apcentral.collegeboard.com/apc/public/exam/calendar/190165.html

### 7. Should I take the Advanced Placement® exam?

To best answer the question, we need to start with a new one: "Why would you NOT take the AP® exam?" After all, being in the course all year and not taking the exam is like going to basketball practices all year and never playing a game.

Here are some thoughts:

1. By taking a college-level exam, you get a great sense of what it feels like to be in college and how prepared you are among your peers.

2. By taking a challenging exam, you are pushing yourself to become smarter.

3. A low score doesn't hurt your high school G.P.A. A high score can get you college credit for less than $100! Sweet!

4. A high score on AP® exams can also help you gain admission to colleges or universities.

Taking the AP® Human Geography exam could be one of the best investments you can make. College courses cost thousands of dollars. According to the College Board, many students who have done well on several AP® exams can actually finish college in 3 years or complete a double major in four years. Our advice is, as long as money isn't the issue, take the exam and grow from the experience.

### 8. When will I find out my score?

AP® scores are available online by the College Board each July. More information about scores is available on the College Board website: apscore.org

The College Board will send your score to one college you select for free. Sending your score reports to additional colleges can be done for a fee.

### 9. What if I have more questions about the AP® exam?

The best resources for you are your AP® teachers, the College Board website, and the AP® coordinator at your school. Every school should have an administrator in charge of Advanced Placement®. Those individuals will have detailed information specific to each school. It is not a bad idea for you to find out who that person is as early as possible—just in case. Your teacher should be able to tell you who the AP® coordinator is for your school or district.

### 10. How should I prepare for the exam?

Great question! We will help you in the next sections understand the topics you will learn in class and finally the types of questions that are asked on the AP® Human Geography Exam.

## WHAT ARE THE TOPICS COVERED IN AP® HUMAN GEOGRAPHY?

### 1. Course Description

The MOST IMPORTANT information about the AP® Human Geography exam and how to prepare for the course is in a small booklet called AP® Human Geography: Course Description published by the College Board. You can download it free at: https://apstudent.collegeboard.org/apcourse/ap-human-geography OR you can simply search the web for "AP® Human Geography Course Description" and the pdf should be available for you.

Now, why is this the MOST IMPORTANT information about the AP® exam?

Simply put, the people who created this booklet create the exam! So, in essence it is the closest you will get to understanding what the "AP® Gods" are thinking. There are even practice questions in the booklet.

We will give you a glimpse into that booklet and the thinking in the sections below.

### 2. The Five Major Goals of AP® Human Geography-http://media.collegeboard.com/digitalServices/pdf/ap/ap-human-geography-course-description.pdf

The people who designed the AP® Human Geography exam based the content on *five college-level goals* that build on the National Geography Standards. These five goals truly describe what this course is about and what skills you should have acquired after completing the class. As the booklet points out, if you successfully complete the course and do well on the exam, you should be able to do the following:

- "**Interpret maps and analyze geospatial data.**
  Geography is concerned with the ways in which patterns on Earth's surface reflect and influence physical and human processes. As such, maps and geographic information systems (GIS) are fundamental to the discipline, and learning to use and think about them is critical to geographical literacy. The goal is achieved when students learn to use maps and geospatial data to pose and solve problems, and when they learn to think critically about what is revealed and what is hidden in different maps and GIS applications.

- **Understand and explain the implications of associations and networks among phenomena in places.**
  Geography looks at the world from a spatial perspective, seeking to understand the changing spatial organization and material character of Earth's surface. One of the critical advantages of a spatial perspective is the attention it focuses on how phenomena are related to one another in particular places. Students should thus learn not just to recognize and interpret patterns but to assess the nature and significance of the relationships among phenomena that occur in the same place, and to understand how cultural values, political regulations, and economic constraints work together to create particular landscapes.

- **Recognize and interpret the relationships among patterns and processes at different scales of analysis.** Geographical analysis requires a sensitivity to scale, not just as a spatial category but as a framework for understanding how events and processes at different scales influence one another. Thus students should understand that the phenomena they are studying at one scale (e.g., local) may well be influenced by processes and developments at other scales (e.g., global, regional, national, state, or provincial). They should then look at processes operating at multiple scales when seeking explanations of geographic patterns and arrangements.

- **Define regions and evaluate the regionalization process.** Geography is concerned not simply with describing patterns but with analyzing how they came about and what they mean. Students should see regions as objects of analysis and exploration and move beyond simply locating and describing regions to considering how and why they come into being and what they reveal about the changing character of the world in which we live.

- **Characterize and analyze changing interconnections among places.** At the heart of a geographical perspective is a concern with the ways in which events and processes operating in one place can influence those operating at other places. Thus students should view places and patterns not in isolation but in terms of their spatial and functional relationship with other places and patterns. Moreover, they should strive to be aware that those relationships are constantly changing, and they should understand how and why change occurs."

(Source: AP® Human Geography Course and Exam Descriptions, Effective Fall 2013.

Copyright © 2013 The College Board.

Reproduced with permission. http://apcentral.college-eboard.com.)

### 3. Topics in AP® Human Geography

AP® Human Geography covers seven major topics throughout the year. The following lists the topics in the order assigned by the College Board (please note that teachers sometimes will cover these topics in a different order):

| Content Area (Topic) | Percentage Goals for Exam |
|---|---|
| I. Geography: Its Nature and Perspectives | 5–10% |
| II. Population | 13–17% |
| III. Cultural Patterns and Processes | 13–17% |
| IV. Political Organization of Space | 13–17% |
| V. Agriculture and Rural Land Use | 13–17% |
| VI. Industrialization and Economic Development | 13–17% |
| VII. Cities and Urban Land Use | 13–17% |

The percentages mark the range of multiple choice questions that will be on the AP® exam from each section.

## WHAT ARE THE TYPES OF MULTIPLE CHOICE QUESTIONS ON THE AP® HUMAN GEOGRAPHY EXAM?

Remember, an AP® Human Geography exam is 75 Multiple Choice Questions in 60 minutes followed by three FRQs in 75 minutes. It can be overwhelming the first time a student takes it, but here are some approaches to the exam.

### 75 MULTIPLE CHOICE QUESTIONS (MCQ)—THE SHOTGUN APPROACH

The purpose of the MCQ portion of the exam is to assess the *breadth* of a student's geographic knowledge. The MCQs, therefore, will assess concepts, terms, models, and theories from every section of the APHG Course Outline as well as from every chapter in the textbooks. In other words, just as a shotgun "sprays" shot everywhere, think about the MCQs as "spraying" all kinds of geography everywhere. Again, be prepared to answer MCQs from every part of the course.

### THREE FREE RESPONSE QUESTIONS (FRQ)—THE DRAGNET APPROACH

FRQs on the APHG exam should be answered using the *Dragnet Approach*, or *Just the Facts, Ma'am*. That is, just as the old TV detective Joe Friday told witnesses, you need to answer the question as it is posed and provide only what is being asked. Don't meander around as you answer—just the geographic facts are needed. Look for more details on answering FRQs below.

### MULTIPLE CHOICE QUESTIONS

On the AP® exam, every Multiple Choice Question has five choices. However, the type of Multiple Choice Questions may differ in difficulty based on how the question is asked. Some Multiple Choice Questions are designed for simple recall of facts; others ask you to analyze a statement; and some others might ask you to interpret a map, chart, or other data. We have included a series of types of Multiple Choice Questions you could have in class throughout the year, as well as on the APHG exam.

1. *Recall:* These are fact-based questions that require students to recollect specific information.

People who practice slash and burn agriculture make their living as:

A. subsistence farmers
B. nomadic herders
C. hunters and gatherers
D. guest workers
E. stateless migrants

2. *Determining Cause:* The word "because" is almost always part of the stem in this category of question. The student is expected to identify a reason for something.

Supranational organizations have become a contemporary reality largely because:

A. the collapse of the Soviet Union and the end of the Cold War have increased polarization among nation-states

B. globalization has made it more difficult for states to act alone

C. states must act unilaterally if they are to achieve their goals

D. states in the developed realm need a power base to check the ambitions of states in the developing realm

E. a world government is essential if there is to be international peace

3. *Except Questions:* AP® Multiple Choice Questions are never framed using negatives. Rather, the stem contains an "except" as a way of having students discriminate among possible responses.

All of the following have typically been true of plantation agriculture in Middle America except:

A. it produces crops for export

B. it is an inefficient operation

C. it produces only a single crop

D. the capital and skills necessary to support it are imported

E. labor on the plantations is seasonal

4. *Effects:* This is a modification of the recall-type question except that the student is challenged to identify *why* some phenomenon occurs.

In human geography, the process of expansion diffusion involves:

A. the spread of some innovation by a migrating people

B. the development of culture hearths in different places at different times

C. the use of innovation waves in controlling the movement of refugees

D. an innovation wave meeting with an absorbing barrier

E. the movement of a new idea or technology through an established or fixed population

5. *True/False:* From a series of statements or phrases, the student selects the one that is accurate. Very often these are just variations of the recall-type inquiries because they expect students to identify information they have memorized.

Which of the following statements accurately describes MacKinder's heartland theory?

A. it proposed land-based power rather than ocean dominance as the determining factor in ruling the world

B. it established that a multipolar world will ensure shared power among nations

C. it hypothesized that because centripetal forces seldom counterbalance centrifugal forces, conflict within the international community is a constant reality

D. it concluded that a pivot area in the center of a landmass will always be the key factor in making a nation globally dominant.

E. it argued that regardless of a state's location, power would always be determined by the abundance of its natural resources.

6. *Analyzing a Statement:* This type of question is a test of reading skills. The student is given a statement several sentences in length and asked to interpret it.

National flags within a region often share common designs but differ in colors and scales. They also reflect cultural values. The flags of Scandinavia are a good example. What is the symbol found on the flags of these countries that is a mark of their cultural identity?

A. a five-pointed star

B. a two-edged sword

C. a Latin cross

D. a gold crescent

E. a darkened oval

7. *Interpreting Maps and Other Graphics:* Students are provided with a visual prompt that they must analyze and then identify the correct answer.

According to the map on pages 44–45, World Population Density, which of the following statements is accurate?

A. the Western Hemisphere has a majority of the densest locations in the world

B. the further away you go from the equator, the more dense the population becomes

C. East Asia's density issue is due to lack of family planning options

D. coastal areas and those along rivers tend to contain larger population densities than the interior

E. Canada's population density is oriented to markets in China

## KEY FOR QUESTIONS:

1) A   2) B   3) E   4) E   5) A   6) C   7) D

## WHAT ARE THE TYPES OF FREE RESPONSE QUESTIONS ON THE AP® HUMAN GEOGRAPHY EXAM?

There are three FRQs on the AP® Human Geography exam. We imagine that your teachers will work with you throughout the year with FRQs as assessment items. It probably doesn't matter whether you read this at the beginning of the year or at the end of the year. If you read this at the end of the year, consider this a review of the key elements of writing an effective FRQ.

### 1. Obey the Speed Limit

Before we give you an example of an FRQ, you need to learn (or review) how to *actively* read an FRQ. Knowing how to read an FRQ actively will help you perform better on the APHG exam. Too many students speed-read through the question only to get it wrong because they didn't read it correctly. In our minds, the worst thing that could happen is to give a great but wrong answer to a question because you didn't read it correctly. So, slow down.........

### 2. FRQ Rules!!

FRQ stands for FREE RESPONSE QUESTION. So, it is a QUESTION to which you will RESPOND in a FREE manner. That is, you have a lot of flexibility in the way you write your responses. A well-written APHG FRQ should contain relevant geographic information. So, RESPOND FREELY to the QUESTION, making sure you provide the geographic information for which the question is asking.

#1) *The questions usually begin with an opening statement*: This basically gives you background for the question—it creates a framework.

#2) *FRQs are multipart questions*: There is nearly always an "A" and "B" and "C" (and sometimes a "D") part in an FRQ Question. Each part has functions that we will consider in the pages to come.

#3) *Look for the key verbs*: THIS IS THE MOST IMPORTANT THING YOU WILL DO!!! If you find the key verbs in the question, you'll know what to write to answer the question. This is so IMPORTANT that we will dedicate more to verbs in the pages to come.

#4) *Underline and highlight other key words*: Once you find the key verbs, then you want to underline the other key terms in the question. Terms are going to be very important, but other words that help indicate what you need to do are also important. Conjunctions like "and" or "or" are extremely important. Also, numbers play a major role in what you need to do. So, if it states "define TWO terms," make sure you write about two and not just one. Conversely, if the question asks for two items and you give three or more, only the first two answers you provide will be scored.

#5) *Responses to FRQs are not five-paragraph themes*: You DO NOT need to write an introduction, body, and conclusion as a response. Writing in complete sentences is essential. However, an FRQ is not an English essay. You should just answer the question.

### 3. LAW and ORDER: KVU (Key Verbs Unit)

Have you ever watched any of the versions of the television show *Law and Order*? Each show always starts with a crime scene. The detectives look over the crime scene to see what they can learn about what happened and formulate hypotheses. In this section, we will—sticking with our *Law and Order*

theme—do an autopsy on MRQs and FRQs so we can understand how they are structured.

Okay, not to sound morbid, but the cause of "death" on many FRQs is not being able to find the key verbs. We really do want you to learn how to watch for key words– especially certain verbs—what we like to call the "operative action verbs." Wow! They sound important and they are.  So here goes the autopsy of APHG FRQs.

| Between 2001 and 2014, the APHG Exam used the following verbs most frequently: | |
| --- | --- |
| Verb Used | Number of Uses 2001–2014 |
| **Explain** | 24 |
| **Identify** | 13 |
| **Discuss** | 5 |
| **Define** | 3 |
| **Describe** | 5 |
| **Compare and Give** | 1 each (**Compare** first used in 2014) |

So, which 3 or 4 of these are we most likely to see on the exam? Be sure to study what *EXPLAIN, IDENTIFY, DISCUSS, DESCRIBE and DEFINE really mean*. Understand **what and how much you should write** to use these verbs.

## KEY VERBS TO *UNLOCK* THE APHG FRQS*

Use this chart to see exactly what verbs have been used on the APHG exam in the past. The chart also shows you what actions to take as you use each verb in a FRQ response. For example, as you look down the page, the arrow indicates more complexity. The print size indicates how much is required to respond appropriately to each verb prompt. The larger the print, the more action and depth is required in your answer.

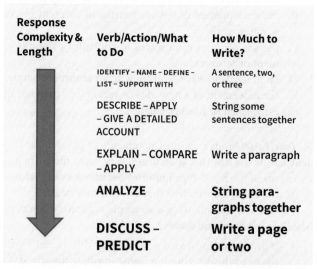

| Response Complexity & Length | Verb/Action/What to Do | How Much to Write? |
| --- | --- | --- |
| | IDENTIFY – NAME – DEFINE – LIST – SUPPORT WITH | A sentence, two, or three |
| | DESCRIBE – APPLY – GIVE A DETAILED ACCOUNT | String some sentences together |
| | EXPLAIN – COMPARE – APPLY | Write a paragraph |
| | ANALYZE | String paragraphs together |
| | DISCUSS – PREDICT | Write a page or two |

* Verbs used on APHG Exam FRQs 2001–2014 and data collated from: http://apcentral.collegeboard.com/apc/members/exam/exam_information/2004.html#name12

# Used only once on APHG exams 2001–14. Our advice is to treat this verb like Discuss.

Probably the best thing we can do for you right now is give you an example of a FRQ. As you read the question, the first thing you should do is find the VERBS—THESE ARE THE KEY WORDS TO SUCCESS ON THE FRQ.

Sample FRQ:

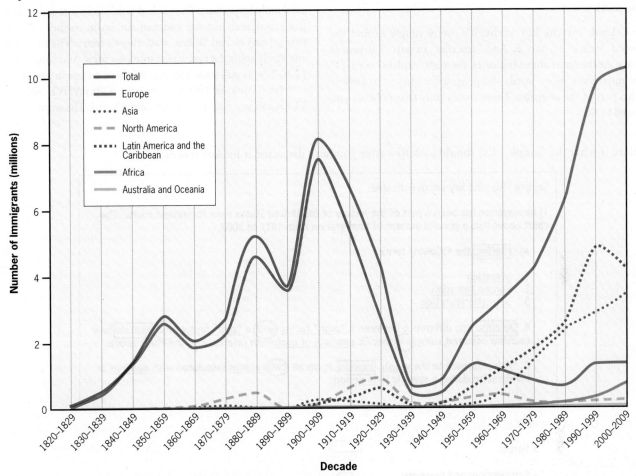

**Immigration to the United States by Region, 1820 to 2010.**    During the first wave of migration to the United States, from 1820 to 1930, the vast majority of migrants to the United States came from Europe. During the second wave of migration, from 1930 to the present, a shift occurred and migrants to the United States mainly come from Latin America and Asia.    *Data from:* United States Census Bureau, 2012.

Immigration has been a part of the history of the United States from its earliest roots. The chart above shows a general pattern of immigration from 1821 to 2010.

A.  Define the following terms:

1.  Migration

2.  Forced Migration

3.  Selective Migration

B.  Describe the difference between a "push" factor and a "pull" factor and explain how each has occurred, using one specific example of each with reference to the chart above.

C.  With reference to the graph, explain in detail two reasons for the declines in immigration that occurred during a specific time period.

## Dissecting the Sample Free Response Question (FRQ)

As we stated above, there are five things you need to learn about an FRQ. Let's dissect the question by looking at all five of those components.

**#1.  The questions usually start with an opening statement:** Here we have an opening statement, but is it really telling you anything you couldn't figure out on your own? Nope. Again, the purpose of the opening statement is to frame the question and help you "get in the zone." Cover up the opening statement. Could you still answer the question? Probably . . . so as long as you have studied the material.

**#2. FRQs are multipart questions:** There is always an "A" and a "B" section to an FRQ. Typically you'll see questions with two or three parts. In order to receive full credit, you must answer all three parts. On AP® exams, you don't know how much each section is weighted and they may or may not be equal.

**#3. Look for the key verbs:** It's pretty simple to find the word "define" in part A. And "describe" in part B is just as easy. As the chart above indicates, the verb "explain" in part C requires both more words and geographic content to answer this part of the question. These words truly tell you what you need to do.

**#4. Underline and highlight other key words:** Look at part B of the question. There is one other word that is essentially the next important word after the OPERATIVE ACTION VERBS. Hopefully, you see that the word is "and" AND it is used twice. Both times the use of the term is extremely important. The second "and" links a second operative action verb into the fold: explain. So, in essence, you have two actions in Part B. But, wait, there's more. The first "and" effectively splits the first action into two parts. And simple math $(2 \times 2 = 4)$ will show you that you have 4 steps in part B.

Now look at Part C. After the OPERATIVE ACTION VERB, can you find the next important word? The word is "two".

**Here is what the Sample FRQ should look like after you have dissected it for key words:**

Sample FRQ with key words indicated:

1) Immigration has been a part of the history of the United States from its earliest roots. The chart above lists a general pattern of immigration from 1821 to 2000.

    A) Define the following terms:

1. Migration
2. Forced Migration
3. Selective Migration

B. Describe the difference between a "push" factor and a "pull" factor and explain how each has occurred, using one specific example of each with reference to the chart above.

C. With reference to the graph, explain in detail two reasons associated with declines in immigration during a specific time period.

KEY:

• Verbs:

• Conjunctions and Numbers:

• Other Key Words: _____

Read the question with just the highlighted words. A bit confusing? Perhaps, but we think you could answer the question effectively if you knew just those words. Notice we didn't highlight any of the words in the opening statement. We suppose you could and the opening statement is helpful, but we feel it isn't essential to answering the question. Having said that, it is very important to read the question in its entirety. This is because some of the words which you may not have highlighted can be important as well. One example would be the inclusion of a date range in the question. Dates (such as "the late twentieth century") are intended to frame what might be included in your answer. The bottom line is to be careful to read every part of the question.

**#5. Responses to FRQs are not five-paragraph themes:** Let's look at Part A. There is no need for an introduction or conclusion. Just give the definitions using complete sentences. Really, could you imagine writing an introduction like this:

"There are many terms used to describe immigration and migration. I will successfully define three specific terms related to immigration: migration, forced migration, and selective migration."

This is boring—and a time waster. Just write in complete sentences, as the exam instructions dictate. A very acceptable practice (and a good idea) would be to underline the term you are defining.

Look at Part C again. An acceptable practice (and another good idea) would be to list your two points by starting with "1" and "2."

**Example:**
C. (1) One reason immigration declined in the 1930s was the Great Depression. With unemployment soaring, America no longer was a source of jobs.

(2) Immigration also declined in the 1930s because of quotas imposed by such legislative acts as the National Origins Law. These quotas limited the number of immigrants allowed into the United States. Many of these laws were passed by politicians who blamed immigration for high unemployment in the United States.

## Exam Day Final Preparation

The following is a list of best practices for the day before and day of the APHG exam. Rules, conditions, and situations in your particular school or testing center may vary. However, we believe if you follow these suggestions, you will create opportunities to do well on the APHG exam.

### Tips for the Day of the Exam

- Get plenty of sleep the night before the exam.
- Eat a protein-rich breakfast. Protein fires up your brain and can help you get ready to think.
- Be on time for the exam—be 10 minutes early. Some testing centers will lock the doors and not allow you to enter if you are late.
- Bring #2 pencils and black or dark blue pens—erasable if desired. Pencils are used on the MCQs and pens are used on the FRQs.
- NO CELL PHONES IN THE TESTING ROOM—Having a phone in the exam room/center can result in you having your test scores canceled.
- The MCQ section is first, has 75 questions, and is 60 minutes in length.
- Be careful with NOT and EXCEPT items. In other words, read carefully, as all the answers on these items are correct except for one.
- If you have any time remaining and you have finished the MCQs, go back and check your answers for accuracy.
- Remember, when the APHG exam is over, you may NEVER discuss the MCQs! You signed an agreement to this extent when the APHG exam began.
- THERE WILL BE A 15-minute BREAK AFTER THE MCQs.
- At the break get up, walk around, go outside. Get your blood flowing and clear your head. You still have the other half of the exam to take.
- Be on time coming back after the break.

- The FRQ section has 3 questions to answer in 75 minutes.
- For up to 5 minutes, read all three FRQs and make a short outline or write down key words to help with possible answers.
- **Important:** Any notes you make on the three question pages ARE NOT SCORED! Be sure to put any of your notes you want in your answer on the answer pages!
- Determine which questions you consider the easiest to most difficult to answer. Remember not to go over the 5-minute time frame.
- Start on the easiest question and take up to 10–15 minutes to answer it.
- When finished with your easy question, attack the next easiest question and allow 15–20 minutes to answer it.
- Finally, attack the last question, allowing 25–30 minutes to answer it.
- If you use all of the maximum times here, you will still have 5 minutes left over. It is likely you will have a lot more time left.
- Use any remaining time to review answers and/or add items to your answers.
- Always skip space between FRQs. This gives you space to go back and add material that was not written during your first attempt.
- Skipping space also allows ease of reading for the reader of your exam paper.
- Feel confident! Having a positive attitude can make a difference.

After the exam is over, you truly need to pat yourself on the back! You just completed a college-level course and a college-level exam. No matter what score you get on the exam, you have become a better learner and, since you took Human Geography, a better global citizen. Congratulations!

We wish you the best of success.

☐ Fraser Island Trek (Australia)
☐ 'Freighter to Paradise' (French Polynesia) see Aranui Cargo Boat
☐ From Tozeur to Douz across the Chott el-Djerid (Tunisia)

☐ Galician Carpathians (Poland)
☐ Gambia River (The Gambia) see Cruise the Gambia River
☐ Ganges (India) see Source of the Ganges
☐ Garden Route (South Africa)
☐ Georgian Military Road (Georgia)
☐ Georgian Valleys (Turkey)
☐ Gerlos Alpenstrasse (Austria)
☐ German Avenues: North to South (Germany)
☐ The Ghan (Australia)
☐ Gibb River Road (Australia)
☐ Glacier Express (Switzerland)
☐ Glasgow to Mallaig (Scotland-UK)
☐ Goa (India) see Beaches of Goa
☐ Gobi Desert Trek (Mongolia)
☐ Going-to-the-Sun Road (USA)
☐ 'Golden Valley' (Tajikistan) see Fergana Valley
☐ Golden Pass Panoramic Express (Switzerland)
☐ Golden Ring Towns (Russia)
☐ Gorges du Verdon (France)
☐ Gota Canal (Sweden)
☐ Grand Canal (China) see Suzhou to Hangzhou on the Grand Canal
☐ Grand Canal (Italy)
☐ Grand Canyon du Verdon (France) see Gorges du Verdon
☐ Grand Circle Road Trip (USA)
☐ Grand Teton National Park (USA)
☐ Great Divide Trail (Canada/USA)
☐ Great Dolomites Road (Italy)
☐ Great Ocean Road (Australia)
☐ Great Wall of China (China) see Walking the Great Wall
☐ Green Spain (Spain)
☐ Grossglockner Hochalpenstrasse (Austria)
☐ Gunung Agung Volcanic Scenic Route (Indonesia)
☐ Gunung Rinjani Trek (Indonesia)
☐ Gustav Mahler Cycle Trail (Czech Republic)

☐ Hærvejen Oxen Trail (Denmark)
☐ Haleakala Highway (Hawaii)
☐ Hanoi Unification Express (Vietnam)
☐ Haraz Mountain Trek (Yemen)
☐ Headwaters of the Amazon (Peru)
☐ Heaven's Gate Pass (Vietnam)
☐ Helicopter Ride over Franz Josef Glacier (New Zealand)

☐ Hell Valley Railway (Germany)
☐ Helsinki to Tampere (Finland)
☐ Hetta-Pallas Winter Ski Trail (Finland)
☐ Heysen Trail (Australia)
☐ High Atlas Mule Trek (Morocco)
☐ High Coast Trail (Sweden)
☐ Highway 901 (Puerto Rico)
☐ Hill Country Scenic Train Ride – Colombo Fort to Badulla (Sri Lanka)
☐ Himalayas see Fly over the Himalayas
☐ Historic Route 66 (USA)
☐ Ho Chi Minh Trail (Laos)
☐ Höga Kusten (Sweden) see High Coast Trail
☐ Höllental (Germany) see Hell Valley Railway
☐ Holy Spirit Island (Mexico) see Espiritu Sanctu and Isla Partida
☐ Home of the Sun God (Bolivia)
☐ Hortobagy Great Plains (Hungary)
☐ Houseboat Cruise through the Kerala Backwaters (India)
☐ Huangshan Trek (China)
☐ Huay Xai to Luang Prabang (Laos) see Mekong River Voyage
☐ Huayhuash Circuit (Peru)
☐ Huckleberry Mountain Horse Trail (USA)
☐ Hudson River Trip (USA)
☐ Hue to Hoi An on Highway 1 (Vietnam)

☐ Icefields Parkway (Canada)
☐ Ile de Gorée (Senegal)
☐ Inca Trail (Peru)
☐ Incense Road (Yemen)
☐ Indian Pacific Railway (Australia)
☐ Ingapirca Inca Trail (Ecuador)
☐ Inlandsbanan (Sweden)
☐ Inside Passage Ferry (Canada)
☐ International Selkirk Loop (Canada)
☐ Into the Khentii Mountains (Mongolia)
☐ Ioaninna to Méteora Road (Greece)
☐ Isfahan River Bridges Walk (Iran)
☐ Island hop along the Dalmatian Coast (Croatia)
☐ Isle of Man Steam Railway
☐ Istanbul to Aleppo on the Toros Express (Turkey)
☐ Itria Valley Trulli (Italy)

☐ Jakarta to Bandung (Indonesia)
☐ Jebel Musa (Mount Moses) (Egypt) see Follow the Footsteps of Moses up Mount Sinai
☐ Jebel Nafusa Mountain Drive (Libya)
☐ 'Jerusalem of the West' (Spain) see Via de la Plata, Santiago de Compostela Pilgrim Route
☐ Jerusalem: The Via Dolorosa (Israel)
☐ Jiuhuashan Trek (China)

☐ Jiuqu River (China) see Rafting Nine Bends River
☐ Jobo Mountain Adventure Drive (Lesotho)
☐ John Muir Trail (USA)
☐ Jonte River Gorge (France)
☐ Jungfraujoch Cog Railway (Switzerland)

☐ Kackar Mountains (Turkey)
☐ Kalka to Shimla on the 'Toy Train' (India)
☐ Kamchatka Ring of Fire Trek (Russian Federation)
☐ Kanchenjunga Trek (Nepal)
☐ Karakoram Highway (Pakistan)
☐ Keukenhof Gardens (The Netherlands)
☐ King's Road Trail (Finland)
☐ Kokoda Track (Trail-Papua New Guinea)
☐ Kolkata Heritage City Walk (India)
☐ Kom Emine Trail (Bulgaria)
☐ Krom River Trail (South Africa)
☐ Kullu Valley Trek (India)
☐ Kuranda Scenic Railway (Australia)

☐ La Méridienne Scenic Route (France)
☐ La Pedriza (Spain)
☐ La Rioja (Spain)
☐ La Ruta del Sol (Ecuador)
☐ La Ruta Maya (Guatemala)
☐ La Soufrière Summit Hike (Guadeloupe)
☐ Lake Issyk-Kul Trek (Kyrgyzstan)
☐ Lake Manyara National Park (Tanzania)
☐ Lake Sevan to Vayots Dzor (Armenia)
☐ Lake Waikaremoana (New Zealand)
☐ Lake Windermere (England-UK)
☐ Land's End to John o' Groats (England/Scotland-UK)
☐ Lauterbrunnen to Schilthorn (Switzerland)
☐ Lawrence of Arabia Camel Trek (Yemen)
☐ Le Petit Train Jaune (France)
☐ Le Train des Pignes (France)
☐ Le Tunnel (Sous la Manche) see Channel Tunnel by Eurostar
☐ Lewis & Clark's National Scenic Trail (USA)
☐ Lhasa-Gyantse-Xigatse Scenic Drive (Tibet)
☐ Lima to Huancayo (Peru)
☐ 'Limes' Route (Germany)
☐ Lisbon Tram Line 28 (Portugal)
☐ Little Yellow Train (France) see Le Petit Train Jaune
☐ Llangollen Canal (Wales/England-UK)
☐ Lofoten Islands (Norway)
☐ Loire Valley (France)
☐ London Market Walk (England-UK)
☐ London River Journey (England-UK)
☐ London to Australia (England-UK)
☐ London to Birmingham by Grand Union Canal (England-UK)
☐ London to Edinburgh on the Flying Scotsman

# 501
## MUST-TAKE JOURNEYS

# 501
## MUST-TAKE JOURNEYS

**Bounty Books**

**Publisher**: Polly Manguel

**Project Editor**: Emma Beare

**Publishing Assistant**: Sarah Marling

**Designer**: Ron Callow/Design 23

**Picture Researcher**: Vickie Walters

**Production Manager**: Neil Randles

**Production Assistant**: Gemma Seddon


First published in Great Britain in 2008 by
Bounty Books, a division of Octopus Publishing Group Limited
2-4 Heron Quays, London E14 4JP
www.octopusbooks.co.uk
Reprinted 2010
An Hachette UK Company
www.hachette.co.uk

A CIP catalogue record is available from the British Library

ISBN: 978-0-753720-01-1


Printed and bound in China

**Please note:** We now know that political situations arise very quickly and a city or country that
was quite safe a short time ago can suddenly become a 'no-go' area. Please check with the
relevant authorities before booking tickets and travelling if you think there could be a problem.

Where a journey crosses country borders, it appears in the chapter that relates to its starting point.

# Contents

# Introduction

Journeys – journeys to work, to school or university, to the theatre or cinema, to do the shopping or laundry or pick up the kids – most of us are taking journeys every day. We see the same old sights each time and mostly we let our brains work on automatic, failing to derive any pleasure from the actual trip, because we just don't expect to. Our most ardent wish, if ever expressed, would be for the journey to be over with just a click of the fingers. The destination is all.

Many sun-seeking holiday makers would also much rather reach their seaside holiday destination without the trials of the trip there – the queues at the airport, the flight, the walking, the traffic. Yet in recent years increasing numbers of people, though still not immune to the occasional lazy pleasures of beach life, have become fascinated by the variety of interests and challenges presented by all manner of different journeys. They have realized that to take a journey can enable them to have more unusual experiences, to encounter and interact with local peoples, to observe and explore new places, different cultures, historic landmarks and superb scenery.

There's an eclectic variety of fascinating journeys described in this book – some of them take only an hour or two to complete while others could last up to six months. Most modes of transport are covered: on foot, by bicycle, car, boat, train, plane, horse, mule and even dog sled. There are trips to be taken at different times of year, through mountains and valleys, jungles and pine forests, rivers and seas, from the snowy wastes of the Arctic Circle to the mind-numbing heat of the Sahara Desert. They encompass journeys taken for the extraordinary beauty of the landscape, to reach ancient monuments, to meet people living in remote regions and to see wildlife of all descriptions.

Whether it's canoeing down the Yukon, mountain trekking in Bulgaria, a boat trip up the Norwegian coast, a rail trip in the Himalayas, touring the Chilean vineyards or cycling in Northern Australia – there are journeys here to satisfy even the most jaded of travelling palates.

Some of the journeys – the walk along the Great Wall of China, or driving the famous US Route 66, or a camel trek from

Timbuktu on part of the old Salt Road – are well known classics; others are little known and rarely travelled. Some require feats of endurance and that you are at the very peak of fitness. On others you can relax in the lap of luxury with very little physical exertion: South Africa's famous Blue Train, for example, provides you with 5-star accommodation and haute cuisine as you travel from Cape Town to Pretoria and marvel through the window from the comfort of your carriage at the landscape, the elephants striding across the plains and the herds of giraffes and antelopes grazing peacefully before you. Quite a few of the journeys can be taken more or less on the spur of the moment; other very different types of journey in some distant land could involve months of planning.

There are all sorts of reasons for making a journey. You might want to see mysterious Mayan pyramids, or make a pilgrimage to an important religious site. You might want to feel at one with nature in part of the Canadian wilderness or simply walk an ancient trail beside a lake. Perhaps you are an active person, one whose idea of bliss is to trek through rainforest, or cycle in southern Italy – or you might want to keep the kids happy with a trip inland from a seaside resort. You may have a special interest: bird watching, whale watching, art, the Roman empire, food or wine – whatever your preferences, there is certain to be a journey to take that will fulfil your dream.

Having made your choice of journey, you should take the time to read and research it as thoroughly as possible. You need to be prepared, to take appropriate clothing and footwear, maps, medication, food and water, camping gear – anything you may need en route. While some journeys are easy, and you will never be far from help, others are seriously remote, and what you carry with you is desperately important.

Happily much of the time it's not a question of either the destination or the journey – you can have both! In many cases you have the opportunity to visit your chosen destination and have an exciting and interesting trip as well. The beautiful city of Luang Prabang in Laos is truly a joy to behold, but if you are able to reach there by gently travelling down the Mekong River from Huay Xai, then your whole experience of the visit will be much enhanced.

So have a good look through this book, find a journey that speaks to your soul – and get going.

# Around the World in 80 Days

Undoubtedly the most dramatic journey you can ever undertake – circumnavigating the world in 80 days, following in the footsteps of fiction's Phileas Fogg, created by 19th-century author Jules Verne, and TV globetrotter Michael Palin. This is definitely not a matter of booking long-distance flights that get you back to your starting point in a few days. Instead, you must follow Phileas Fogg's 45,000 km (28,000 mi) route as closely as possible, using only transport methods available in Jules Verne's time.

The journey starts outside the Reform Club in London's Pall Mall. To follow Palin's route, take a train to Folkestone, ferry to France and train to Venice via the Alps, Switzerland, Liechtenstein, and Austria. From there, a boat through the Corinth Canal takes in Greece, Crete and Egypt.

After boat-hopping down the Persian Gulf, visiting Saudi Arabia, Qatar and the United Arab Emirates, a week on a traditional sailing dhow brings you to Mumbai (Bombay), from whence a train across India leads to a sea passage to Singapore and on to Hong Kong. A railway marathon across China to Shanghai is followed by a ferry to Japan, and then a monotonous crossing of the Pacific on a container ship. The journey across the USA is by train. From New York another ship will return you to England and journey's end – Palin made it with a few hours to spare.

There's ample scope for planning an individual itinerary packed with plenty of interesting stops and fascinating sights. Though the basic methods of transport are boat and train, half the fun is finding alternative means of progress. For example, Phileas Fogg travelled by elephant and sledge, whilst Palin rode a camel and took a hot-air balloon trip. Not many have done it, because this really is the epic journey of a lifetime!

*TOP: Venice; MIDDLE: Sailing through the Corinth Canal; RIGHT: The Parthenon at the Acropolis in Athens; FAR RIGHT CLOCKWISE FROM TOP: The Great Pyramid of Giza; India Gate in Mumbai; The skyline of Singapore; A bullet train speeds past Mount Fuji; Hong Kong Harbour; A minaret amongst skyscrapers in Dubai*

**HOW:**
Various!
**WHEN TO GO:**
Any time you can arrange a very long vacation.
**TIME IT TAKES:**
80 days (if you don't fall behind schedule).
**HIGHLIGHTS:**
Venice – use a precious day to explore this special city, once a stop on another great journey – the 8,000-km (5,000-mi) Silk Road linking the Orient with the Mediterranean.
The Great Pyramid of Giza, near Cairo, and the enigmatic Sphinx – the former is the last survivor of Seven Wonders of the Ancient World.
Great Nicobar – this sparsely populated island is India's southernmost point, largely covered by a unique rainforest Biosphere Reserve.
Trying to emulate Michael Palin's big win at Hong Kong's spectacular Happy Valley racecourse.
**YOU SHOULD KNOW:**
Although many people associate travelling by hot-air balloon with *Around the World in Eighty Days*, this method of travel was never actually used by Phileas Fogg and his French valet Passepartout.

# AMERICAS AND THE CARIBBEAN

*A wall of yellow and green trees in front of a cloud-covered Mount Robson*

# Trans-Canada Train Journey

**HOW:**
By train
**DEPART:**
Halifax, NS
**WHEN TO GO:**
Year round, but schedules can be disrupted in winter (November to April)
**TIME IT TAKES:**
Plan your schedule and book tickets in advance. Currently it takes about six days with a long stopover in either Montreal or Toronto. If you want to see a lot of Canada allow two weeks and spend time in Montreal, Toronto, Jasper and Vancouver.
**HIGHLIGHTS:**
The Thousand Islands – the islands that gave you the dressing.
Old Montreal – fabulous, French and funky.
Mount Robson and Pyramid Falls – in the Rockies.
Vancouver – it really is as good as they say: the sea, mountains, excellent affordable eating and really friendly people.
**YOU SHOULD KNOW:**
The combination of harsh weather, 1950s rolling stock and the prevalence of mega-weight goods trains can make this a bumpy ride, but who needs sleep anyway when you're having such a good time?

There is no rule which states that crossing a whole continent will ever be easy and this journey certainly tests the mettle of the traveller. Nevertheless, the sights you see and the people you meet on this epic trip will stay in the memory for the rest of your life. Nearly all those who make the journey from Halifax to Vancouver do so for fun (flying is cheaper and quicker) – and this gives the whole experience a real party feel.

Completing the journey currently comprises three stages. The first from Halifax to Montreal takes you from the extremely picturesque Nova Scotia coast, through New Brunswick. Skirting the Appalachian Mountains, you are then transported to Montreal, the beating heart of French Canada. The second leg allows you to sample the most modern railway Canada has to offer. The Montreal to Toronto link feels strangely normal compared with the rest of the trip. Business people barely look up from their laptops as the train passes along the St Lawrence River, past the Thousand Islands and along the shore of Lake Ontario.

From Toronto, Canada's most modern of cities, you embark on the truly monumental part of the train ride. The seemingly endless forests of Northern Ontario eventually give way to wide open prairies as you cross the Continent's interior – the vastness of it all is quite breathtaking. After two nights on board, the train approaches the Rockies. Waterfalls and sheer rock faces heave in to view one after another and this is the time to grab a seat in the panoramic dome car. After this, Kamloops is the last major stop before arriving in Vancouver and your chance to experience the city often voted the 'World's Best Place to Live'.

# Fraser Discovery Route on the Rocky Mountaineer

**HOW:**
By train
**DEPART:**
Whistler, BC
**WHEN TO GO:**
The service only operates between mid-May and mid-October.
**TIME IT TAKES:**
Two days
**HIGHLIGHTS:**
Mount Robson – the Canadian Rockies may not be as tall as those south of the border, but you are looking at it from near sea level. Mount Robson is the biggest vertical rockface you will find anywhere on Earth.
The Fraser River – which in spring is one of the fastest flowing rivers in the world.
The chance to see bear, wolves and elk – and more – along the way.
Jasper – unspoilt by mass development and well preserved – it's an ideal town to end your journey and tarry for a while.
**YOU SHOULD KNOW:**
The service on board is first class, but it doesn't come cheap. However most people who have made this journey will tell you that there is no better way to spend the kids' inheritance…

If you could design your own railway journey, it would probably look something like this one. Opened in 2006, this latest addition to the Rocky Mountaineer experience offers the best service and the most spectacular scenery Canada has to offer. It even has the added benefit of stopping overnight so that you can get a good sleep and miss nothing that the Rockies have to offer.

Leaving the hustle and bustle of the ski resort of Whistler behind you and with a glass of champagne in hand, you travel eastbound through the rich farmland of the Pemberton Valley. It is time now to climb the stairs to the domed observation car as the train wends its way along the shores of Anderson and Seton Lakes, which are framed by the picturesque mountain scenery. Breathtaking views of the Fraser Canyon feed the eye as you near the improbably high Deep Creek Bridge. The train runs alongside the mighty Fraser River until it reaches the sleepy town of Quesnel where it stops for the night, allowing you to explore one of the Canadian interior's oldest towns and home to the world's largest gold pan.

The next morning your journey continues eastward to the main Canadian Rockies. Entering the Rocky Mountain Trench and the upper reaches of the Fraser River, you are surrounded by mountains on all sides. The route then leaves the Fraser River at Tête Jaune Cache, and climbs past majestic Mount Robson, the highest peak in the Canadian Rockies at 3,954 m (12,972 ft) and the highlight of the journey.

It is now time to put your watches forward one hour as the train crosses the top of the Yellowhead Pass and the border to the province of Alberta. The journey ends as the Rocky Mountaineer descends through Jasper National Park to the perfect little town of Jasper.

*Sunset over the Fraser River*

# The Skeena Train

*Fishing boats docked in Prince Rupert.*

Billed as Canada's best-kept secret, the 1160-km (721-mi) long Skeena Railway is probably the most scenic journey you can take in the whole of North America.

Taking passengers between Jasper National Park and Prince Rupert on the Pacific coast, it is more than just a tourist track. The railroad links many otherwise isolated communities and gives travellers a chance to view hidden Canada at first hand. This region is one of North America's last great wildernesses and it's sprinkled with tantalizing reminders of its rich First Nations history and the spirit of the pioneer.

Soon after leaving Jasper, the train passes Mount Robson and the Pyramid Falls, two of the most stunning sights the Rockies have to offer. The track then heads in a north-westerly direction, skirting the spectacular Columbia Mountains alongside the Fraser River and down to Prince George for an overnight hotel stop.

This sumptuous land of waterfalls, huge rivers, lakes and wilderness is home to bear, elk, wolves and moose and such is the gentle pace of the train that the driver often slows down for people to take photographs. The Story poles (or Totem poles) of the region offer great depictions of the area's fauna and often make good resting points for eagles scouring the landscape for prey.

The last leg of the journey, between the 'two Princes' takes you to ever more remote communities. There is ample opportunity for people-watching at the request stops on the way, recalling a golden era when the railway rolling into town was big news. Following the Skeena River, the train then reaches its final destination – Prince Rupert, gateway to Haida Gwai, northern Vancouver Island and Alaska.

**HOW:**
By train
**DEPART:**
Jasper, AB
**WHEN TO GO:**
The train operates year round, but snow can disrupt services any time between October and May.
**TIME IT TAKES:**
Two days with a compulsory overnight stop in Prince George.
**HIGHLIGHTS:**
The Rockies – the wow factor never goes away.
The chance to glimpse wildlife feeding and grazing on the riverbanks.
Stopping at small communities such as Dorreen (Pop 1) – and wondering if the passenger bought a return ticket…
The abundance of excellent First Nations art and culture.
**YOU SHOULD KNOW:**
It is important to book your hotel in Prince George in advance. It is also a good idea to ask around your fellow travellers to see if you can share a cab to your lodgings. Taxis and rooms are a scarce commodity when the train comes to town.

*Webster's Falls*

# The Bruce Trail

**HOW:**
On foot and by bike
**DEPART:**
Niagara, ON
**WHEN TO GO:**
During the fall colours (September-October) is best, but really any time from May to October is good.
**TIME IT TAKES:**
An experienced hiker could expect to complete the trail inside 20 days, but, since 200 km (125 mi) of the Bruce is paved road, it is probably best tackled in sections.
**HIGHLIGHTS:**
Blue Mountains Section (Lavender to Craigleith).
Beaver Valley Section (Craigleith to Blantyre) – offering fine views of rocky crevasses.
Sydenham Section (Blantyre to Wiarton) – teeming with nature.
The camaraderie of the campgrounds.
**YOU SHOULD KNOW:**
If you are backpacking you need to be in good shape. The rocky terrain can make this journey treacherous and it can be slippery in wet weather. Campfires are not allowed and drinking water must be treated.

At 800 km (500 mi) the Bruce trail in Ontario is the oldest and longest marked trail in Canada, taking the hiker along the Niagara Escarpment from Niagara to the tip of the Bruce Peninsula. There are also about 300 km (187 mi) of additional side trails that link well with the Bruce. The iconic waterfalls at Niagara are a great place to start and having left with the sound of crashing water in your ears and ozone in your lungs, it is a short hike to the main trail proper.

This well-maintained trail, with its clear markings and efficiently run campgrounds is the most ambitious of projects. The nine chapters of the Bruce Trail Association work hard at protecting this UNESCO World Biosphere Reserve, acquiring new land and opening up this most beautiful, fragile environment for all to see. Hence, it is important to take nothing and leave nothing, except memories and photographs. The fact that the campsites provide all necessary camping gear, to avoid outside contamination, means that you can travel light and cover more ground than you would otherwise.

This ancient escarpment shelters a rare bio-diversity and is home to an array of woodland dwellers, from chipmunks to bear and chickadees to Canada geese. The further north you venture the more isolated the trail becomes and the more likely you are to witness the resident fauna in its natural environment. A good pair of binoculars and a soft step is all you need – enjoy.

# The East Coast Trail

The 540 km (337 mi) East Coast Trail hugs the scenic shores of the Avalon Peninsula of Newfoundland and Labrador. This grand trail is very much a work in progress, with 220 km (138 mi) of the trail well marked. The remainder of it is accessible but un-signposted and provides a greater challenge to the more experienced hiker.

The marked section of the Trail stretches from Fort Amherst, in historic St. John's, to Cappahayden, on the beautiful southern shore. It is equipped with trail signage, maps and supporting trail information to enhance your hiking experience along the coast and through the wilderness. It consists of a series of 18 paths each with a northern and a southern trailhead. Each of these paths can be hiked individually, some are easy strolls, whilst others are longer and more demanding.

As is fitting for a trail of this magnitude there is much to see and explore. This system of what were backcountry routes and hunting trails takes the hiker through provincial parks, national historic sites and ecological reserves. Sustenance and rest can be taken at any one of the charming fishing villages which line the route.

There are currently plans by the volunteer East Coast Trail Association to expand the marked route to Trepassey in the south and Topsoil in the north. The Association should be your first port of call when attempting this epic trail as their encyclopaedic knowledge of the area can prove invaluable to even the most seasoned of hikers.

**HOW:**
On foot
**DEPART:**
Fort Amherst, NL
**WHEN TO GO:**
More navigable from May to October.
**TIME IT TAKES:**
Allow a month to complete the whole trail.
**HIGHLIGHTS:**
The Spout (a wave driven geyser)
The National Historic Sites of Cape Spear, Signal Hill, and Cape Race.
The suspension bridge at the historic abandoned community of La Manche.
Witless Bay Seabird Sanctuary
**YOU SHOULD KNOW:**
The trail is left intentionally unpaved and unspoiled. This means that underfoot conditions can be slippery and several of the walks are close to cliff edges. Therefore, hiking the trail has an inherently greater risk than taking a stroll in an urban park. Risks to a reasonably fit, prepared and cautious hiker are, however, minimal.

*The Cape Spear Lighthouse, Newfoundland, is located on the most easterly point of North America.*

# The Mantario Trail

Located 150 km (94 mi) east of Winnipeg in Manitoba, The Mantario Trail has become a magnet for seasoned hikers, mountain bikers and skiers alike. Running along part of the Canadian Shield, this most inviting of trails offers dramatic views at every turn. The landscape consists of imposing rocky outcrops, marshes, lakes, rivers, beaver dams and forest. The area is also replete with wildlife and muskrat, snapping turtles, black bear, coyote and wolf are common. Look skywards and it is likely that you will see bald eagles or turkey vultures circling.

A large portion of the 63 km (39 mi) trail is a dedicated Wilderness Zone, where hunting and motorized vehicles are forbidden. This gives the whole hiking experience a pedestrian feel in the best sense of the word, with only the sound of the wildlife, the wind through the trees and the sound of your step breaking the silence. Each stage of the hike takes you up and along granite ridges, which offer wonderful panoramic views of lakes and gullies.

Variety is the watchword for this well maintained trail. Spruce, balsam, jack pine and white birch all thrive here, giving the forest a wonderfully diverse feel. Overseen by the Manitoba Naturalists Society, this is a perfect family hike. Campgrounds are plentiful and in good order and the huge variety of outdoor activities should keep all happy. The fact that vehicular access is confined to the north and south trailheads adds to the sense of being alone with nature. Once you have unloaded the car, it is just you, the landscape and the abundant flora and fauna.

# Across Vancouver Island

There are two main ways to cross Vancouver Island, Canada's largest Pacific island. A seaplane ride from Vancouver takes you over the Lions Gate Bridge and across the Georgia Strait giving you a first full glimpse of this most verdant of lands. When reaching the island you fly over the sunshine coast resorts of Parksville and Qualicum, to the north the glaciers of Strathcona stand out, whilst to the south the mountains of Washington State appear magically close on a clear day. But above all the lush ancient forest, specked with the odd lake, feeds the eye. About halfway across, the Alberni Inlet guides the plane along to the Pacific Rim National Park with its long sandy beaches framed by rich temperate rainforest. Then finally you land in the heart of Tofino.

Since the locals will tell you that everything runs in the laid-back 'Tofino time', it is perhaps better to arrive by road. There is a good bus service linking the main ferry terminal at Nanaimo to both Ucluelet and Tofino, but it affords little opportunity for stop-offs; that said the views along the route are spectacular. Leaving Highway 1 from Nanaimo you turn onto Highway 4 and enter Cathedral Grove, an area of 800-year-old majestic Douglas firs, some measuring 9 m (29.5 ft) in circumference. After Port Alberni you come to Sproat Lake with an opportunity to stumble across the abundant wildlife in the area. In spring brown bears, waking from hibernation, come to eat the dandelion heads that grow near the road – don't leave your vehicle but have your camera ready. Finally the road winds its way past Kennedy Lake and then onto the Pacific Rim Highway that runs parallel to the golden sands of Long Beach.

**HOW:**
By seaplane or car and ferry

**WHEN TO GO:**
June to August can get busy, as can the storm-watching season (December to January). Between times (the 'shoulder seasons') are less crowded.

**TIME IT TAKES:**
Vancouver to Tofino by air 1 hour 15 minutes. By road, Nanaimo to Tofino, 3 ½ hrs without stopping.

**HIGHLIGHTS:**
Long Beach – a 16-km (10-mi) long stretch of pristine Pacific sandy beach.
Tofino Botanical Gardens – a wonderfully unconventional garden with boardwalks and paths through sculptures and forest.
The Pacific Rim Whale Festival in early March – where people gather to watch the 20,000 or so grey whales on their migration.
First Nations culture – there are few places in Canada where the native people live and thrive alongside the settler population better than on the west coast of Vancouver Island.

**YOU SHOULD KNOW:**
The road from Nanaimo to Parksville is deceptively good. After that Highway 4 can get tricky in bad weather so check your oil and tyres. The seaplane journey can be very bumpy in bad weather.

# The P'tit Train du Nord

The P'tit Train du Nord is the most innovative of trails and cries out to be used all year round. Running north from St-Jérôme to Mont Laurier it utilizes an old railway line, decommissioned in 1989, and is popular with hikers and cyclists in summer, while the winters are given over to Nordic skiing and other snow-based activities. If most of Canada is the Great Outdoors, then this is the very good outdoors, offering the feeling of seclusion whilst never straying too far from civilization. The dozen or so villages linked by the trail in the Laurentian hills north of Montreal, offer fine-dining and bountiful delicatessens as befits French Canada.

Good use has been made of the defunct stations and many are given over to service areas. As one would expect of a former railway, the gradients are not steep, making it a perfect trail for groups of all ages and abilities. However, it is sometimes surprising how high you can get – and the views of this rolling countryside are quite lovely from the several 'peaks' along the way. The trail is very much a work in progress, with some of the gravel tracks being upgraded to paved roadways making it even more accessible for summer visitors. In winter the area changes markedly and becomes the domain of cross-country skiers, the toughest sportsmen and women to be found anywhere in the world. Gentle inclines become muscle-testing mountains, as the sub-zero temperatures attempt to freeze every inward breath and the need to carry emergency supplies adds to the challenge.

The trail was designed with people in mind. Be it in summer or winter, the thrill of going from station to station and from village to village provides a perfect structure for those wishing to explore this most pleasant corner of Canada.

*A view across the Laurentian hills*

**HOW:**
On foot or by bike
**DEPART:**
St-Jérôme, QC
**WHEN TO GO:**
It is open all year round although most of the amenities operate shorter winter (November to April) opening hours.
**TIME IT TAKES:**
The full 200 km (125 mi) of the trail can easily be cycled in a week. Skiers should probably allow 10 days.
**HIGHLIGHTS:**
The wildflower meadows in spring (April/May).
The fragrant smell of the pine forests from late May to September.
The bucolic charm of the settlements along the way.
Lac-Saguay – a beautiful lake just a short hop from the trail.
**YOU SHOULD KNOW:**
Nordic skiing is not for beginners as it puts a strain on almost every part of the body. Start slowly and then with the aid of gym work, build up to the challenge.

# The Dempster Highway

Head north to the Yukon for the most exciting drive of your life. An engineering miracle, first opened in 1979 to link the mineral wealth of the north with southern Canada, this gravel road has now become a magnet for thrill seekers from around the globe. Those who like their roads even and services regularly spaced should keep away. This is the most challenging journey of them all, through the most magnificent of Arctic landscapes. From the Klondike gold fields to the Mackenzie Delta you cross mountain ranges, traverse valleys and have the chance to view nature red in tooth and claw.

The area is home to all the wildlife you would expect in northern Canada – and more. Both black and grizzly bear can be found as well as a host of caribou, sheep and mountain goats. With such a bountiful supply of food, predators are plentiful, so keep your eyes open for lynx, foxes and above all any patrolling wolves, the most magical of sights.

Each season brings new wonder, from the midnight sun in the summertime to the icy calm of winter, when ferries on the route are replaced by ice bridges, thus obliging you to place your trust in nature even as you marvel at it. Rarely can completing a road journey be greeted with such a sense of achievement, but the 741 km (463 mi) highway is a true test of man (or woman) and machine. Along the way there are abundant opportunities for adventure, so load up your kayak, pack your hiking boots and prepare to explore and enjoy this amazing wilderness.

**HOW:**
By car
**DEPART:**
Dawson City, YT
**WHEN TO GO:**
Year round, although less arduous from June to August.
**TIME IT TAKES:**
Very variable according to conditions, allow a good few days.
**HIGHLIGHTS:**
The sheer magnitude of it all, as you cross rivers and negotiate mountain passes.
The explosion of colour which heralds the short Arctic summer (July-August).
You can't help but notice the trees, which because of the frozen sub-soil, point in all directions to create a unique landscape.
**YOU SHOULD KNOW:**
Be prepared for almost anything. Sudden changing weather can force you to camp overnight at any time of the year. When camping hang your provisions away from the ground.

*The Dempster Highway links Dawson City and Inuvik.*

# The Coquihalla Highway

The Coquihalla Highway (pronounced 'coke-a-hal-a') is a major toll highway that connects the Greater Vancouver region with the interior of British Columbia. It was constructed in the 1980s to shave a couple of hours off travelling times, but it is much more than just a short cut. It is a four-seasons-in-one-day, peddle-to-the-metal, ear-popping, super highway through the magnificent Cascade Mountains. The dramatic changes of environment are always exhilarating, as you go from misty coastal cedars and tall firs to bright sunlight on the high rock faces in the space of half an hour.

The Coq, as it is affectionately known, travels northwards from Hope to Kamloops via Merritt on Highway 5, passing through Monck and Lac Le Jeune Provincial Parks. The road then climbs through the Great Bear Snow Shed to the summit of the Coquihalla Pass, at 1,240 m (4,068 ft), then crosses the top of the Thompson Plateau, with side roads leading off into rolling countryside speckled with fishing lakes. The route is particularly scenic in the early fall (October), when rolling fields and forest foliage take on a golden glow.

The forest around Merritt provides the greatest diversity of flora and fauna. Pine, spruce and Douglas fir can be found at the lower elevations and the extensive grasslands support moose, mule deer, bear and elk. Also keep your eyes peeled for wolves and mountain goat along the ridges to the side of the road. The sheer strain that the many inclines put on vehicles means that there is less commercial traffic than on many of the region's roads, so you are always guaranteed a smooth passage – weather permitting. Buckle up and prepare for the drive of your life.

*Orchards in the Okanagan Valley*

# The Cabot Trail

Located in the Cape Breton National Park in Nova Scotia, the Cabot Trail, which opened in 1939, winds spectacularly along the flanks of the mountains, offering astonishing vistas at every turn.

The 282 km (175 mi) Cabot Trail loop is popular with experienced cyclists, being both arduous and rewarding. The route meanders up ravines and plummets back down towards the coast. One breathtaking view after another unfolds, and the plunging descent from Mount MacKenzie to Pleasant Bay will be one you will never forget.

The park has 27 hiking tracks branching off the Cabot Trail. Many excursions are quite short and have the feel of a relaxed amble rather than a hearty tramp, but those who welcome a challenge will find something to suit. All trails are listed on the reverse side of the map you receive when you pay your entry fee to the park.

If you're looking to leave the crowds behind, the Glasgow Lake Lookoff is a relatively gentle 8 km (5 mi) round-trip hike that takes you through barren and scrub forest to a rocky bald headland overlooking a series of pristine highland lakes, with distant views of the ocean. The trail is alternately swampy and rocky, so strong footwear is advised.

Further along the Cabot Trail, the 0.8 km (0.5 mi) Bog Trail offers a glimpse of the tableland's unique bogs from a dry boardwalk. Lone Shieling is an easy 0.8 km (0.5 mi) loop through a verdant hardwood forest in a lush valley that includes 300-year-old sugar maples (most stunning in fall). A re-creation of a Scottish crofter's hut is featured along this trail.

**HOW:**
On foot or by bike
**DEPART:**
Port Hastings, NS
**WHEN TO GO:**
Popular year round, but the weather is best from late May to September.
**TIME IT TAKES:**
You could drive it in a day if so inclined, cyclists generally allow a week.
**HIGHLIGHTS:**
The almost vertigo-inducing descent to Pleasant Bay (when travelling clockwise).
Cheticamp – an Acadian village famous for fish and fiddle playing.
St Ann's – home to the world-renowned Gaelic College of Celtic Arts and Crafts.
**YOU SHOULD KNOW:**
This is the most undulating of roads on a grand scale, so whatever your mode of transport, check your brakes before starting and be aware of other road users, particularly in summer when inexperienced trailer-home drivers head off for their summer vacation.

*An uphill struggle near Pleasant Bay, Cape Breton Island*

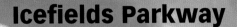

# Icefields Parkway

**HOW:**
By car
**DEPART:**
Lake Louise, AB
**WHEN TO GO:**
May to September offers the best weather.
**TIME IT TAKES:**
Around four hours without stopping, but allow a full day for picnic breaks.
**HIGHLIGHTS:**
The Columbia Icefield – a chance to witness a pristine wilderness.
Lake Louise – with its turquoise lake and overhanging glacier.
The Crossings – a chance to reflect and anticipate.
Arriving in Jasper, a rather special town set on a small plateau surrounded by a spectacular panoramic mountain backdrop.
**YOU SHOULD KNOW:**
Even in good weather the sheer elevation of this highway can mean that road conditions can change rapidly, so come prepared for all eventualities.

The magnificence of the Icefields Parkway (Hwy 93) can scarcely be overstated – a 230 km (144 mi) road from Lake Louise to Jasper through the heart of the Rockies, it ranks as one of the world's ultimate drives. Its seemingly unending succession of enormous peaks, vast glaciers, iridescent lakes, wild-flower meadows, wildlife and forests – capped by the sheer majesty of the Columbia Icefield – is utterly overwhelming.

Fur traders and First Nations peoples dubbed it the Wonder Trail, though the current road owes much to the depression era works programme and it was only opened in 1940 in its present incarnation.

Leaving the iconic image of Lake Louise behind you, the first 40 km (25 mi) of the road climbs steadily north through forest, until you reach the alpine meadow at Bow Summit, the journey's highest point. The next section, which drops down to the Saskatchewan River, offers the best chance to see black bears and moose. The Crossings marks the transition from the jaw-droppingly good to the truly awesome. This 50 km (31 mi) section is

famous the world over for its breathtaking scenery as Mount Athabasca and the Columbia Glacier heave into view.

Mountain goats, bighorn sheep and elk are common along the final 100 km (62 mi) of the Parkway. The road ascends Tangle Ridge, then drops down through forest and follows the Sunwapta and Athabasca Rivers into the charming little town of Jasper. The outstanding features of this final leg of the journey are the Sunwapta and Athabasca Falls and the opportunity to spot grizzly bears and mountain caribou.

Although over a million people make the trip each year to experience this 'window on the wilderness', the sheer vastness of the landscape still means it can rarely seem crowded.

*Sunlit peaks form a stunning backdrop for the still waters of Lake Louise, Banff National Park, Alberta.*

# Canoe down the Yukon River

**HOW:**
By canoe
**DEPART:**
Whitehorse, YT
**WHEN TO GO:**
When the ice has melted – late June
to early September.
**TIME IT TAKES:**
Sixteen to 20 days, allowing for
delays caused by bad weather.
**HIGHLIGHTS:**
Fort Selkirk – a renovated pioneer
and First Nations settlement.
The abandoned settlement at
Hottalinqua.
The vibrant colours of the glacial
melt waters.
**YOU SHOULD KNOW:**
Whilst bears pose little danger to
humans, you should be aware that
you are entering their domain. It is
important to keep all food tied up
above ground and if you see bears
leave the area immediately.

Starting at Whitehorse near the border with northern British Columbia, this 580 km (362 mi) canoe trip down the Yukon should only be undertaken by the most experienced of adventurers. Even the name of the river conjures up images of the frontier, and this journey takes you through early Canadian history as the river propels you on your way. So harsh is this environment that forward planning is a must. Sudden storms can cause long delays and the area is home to around 5,000 grizzly bears, so great care needs to be taken when setting up camp.

Such is the power of the Yukon, which is fed by melting ice, that it is possible to cover great distances in one day. The spectacular Lake Lebarge offers a good target for your first stop. 48 km (30 mi) long and on average 5 km (3.1 mi) wide, the lake offers the most challenging of paddles. Almost benign on a calm day, it can without much warning turn in to a bubbling cauldron and pose great danger to both man and canoe.

Once through the lake, the river gathers pace and takes you past abandoned wood yards and gold-mining settlements – a reminder of the folly of yesteryear, when the lure of potential wealth brought many to the region. Carmacks, some 350 km (219 mi) into the trip, offers the first opportunity to stock up and this cute little town of 500 even has a couple of hotels and restaurants.

The snow-covered mountains, shining in the midnight sun, frame the river as it runs fast towards the Arctic Circle and your final destination, Dawson City.

*Canoeing along the
Yukon River.*

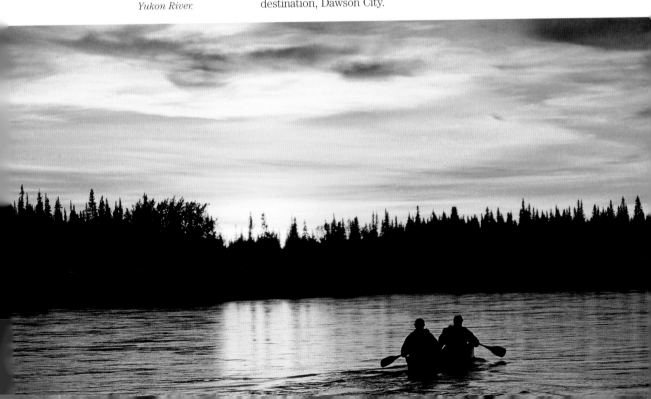

# The Inside Passage Ferry

The Inside Passage can be travelled as part of a longer cruise between California and Alaska. However it is difficult to beat the intimacy and affordability of the regular ferry service between Port Hardy on Vancouver Island and Prince Rupert in northern British Columbia. This 500-km (312-mi) voyage is one of North America's truly great journeys.

The first two hours of the trip involves crossing the open sea between Vancouver Island and Rivers Inlet and offers a chance to grab a coffee, soak up the atmosphere on board and get to know your fellow passengers. Soon it will be time to climb to the sometimes optimistically named sundeck, as the spectacular Central Coast Archipelago heaves into view. The route north then meanders through a narrow maze of channels, passes and reaches. The mountains soar up majestically from the ocean floor, their peaks covered in snow and ice.

So rugged is most of the coast here that if you were exploring by kayak, you would struggle to find a welcoming landing site. Passengers should keep their eyes peeled for whales or dolphins in Queen Charlotte Sound. With a little luck, you might even see a white-coated Kermode bear on Princess Royal Island's lengthy shoreline. Snow capped peaks delight the eye as the vessel travels through the improbably narrow channel between Pitt and Banks Islands. The open waters of Chatham Sound then await you before Prince Rupert comes in to view. This BC Ferries operation is more than just a tourist route, it forms part of a vital network connecting outlying communities – your co-travellers may therefore be your best interpreters.

**HOW:**
By ferry
**DEPART:**
Port Hardy, BC
**WHEN TO GO:**
Best in the summer months (May to September) when the voyage takes place entirely in daylight.
**TIME IT TAKES:**
15 hours
**HIGHLIGHTS:**
The sight of schools of migrating whales and dolphins.
Campania Island – a perfectly formed rocky island.
The never-ending wonders of the amazing scenery.
Prince Rupert – a cosmopolitan town full of surprises.
**YOU SHOULD KNOW:**
Unless you are travelling on to Haida Gwai or Alaska, the most affordable way back is by ferry, so be prepared for a round-trip. Also you should book your hotel in Prince Rupert well in advance, as rooms are scarce when the ferry pulls in to town.

*A Kermode black bear on Princess Royal Island, in its white colour phase; it is also known as the Spirit Bear.*

*Thousand Islands Park
in the fall*

# Sail up the St Lawrence

The main pleasure of riverboat cruising is in its constant proximity to the land, meaning that almost every moment brings something new to see and learn. The spotlight is always on the river and its environs, rather than the on-board 'entertainments' associated with ocean cruising.

Your boat up the St Lawrence heads eastwards from Kingston, with Lake Ontario behind you, and after it has rounded Wolfe Island you are greeted by one of North America's most fabulous sights, the iconic Thousand Islands. As most of the islands are the exclusive preserve of the rich or reserved for nature, this really is the best way to see them. From your ringside seat you can marvel at such sights as the abandoned Boldt Castle, while other islands are little more than rocky bird sanctuaries.

The St Lawrence Seaway, a triumph of co-operation between the US and Canada, opens up the heart of the Great Lakes to the Eastern Seaboard. Its strategic importance is evidenced by the prevalence of settlements visible on both banks. For the next 100 km (62.5 mi), rolling pastures frame the river on both sides until it widens at Lac St-François and Lac St-Louis. The names of the towns tell you that you are entering French Canada and that grande dame of Canadian cities, Montreal comes quickly in to view. Most notable among all Montreal's wonderful French colonial architecture is the magnificent dome of St Joseph's Oratory, rising magically above the city.

The final leg of the voyage is its most charming. Settlements become more spaced out and the hills of Parc National De La Maurice to your left contrast with the bucolic flatland to the right. The river then widens and the St Lawrence wends its way to Quebec City, the traditional heart of French Canada.

# Nahanni River on a raft

A Nahanni rafting expedition is truly a trip of a lifetime. Over the course of this 94 km (150 mi) journey from Virginia Falls to Blackstone Landing, this fast flowing river drops a heart pumping 396 m (1,300 ft). Each section of this epic voyage takes you through canyons, over rapids and past some of the most stunning scenery on Earth.

Even the names conjure up images of danger and excitement as you tumble through Hell's Gate, pass Headless Creek and camp out in Deadmen Valley. So remote is this region of north-western Canada that the only practical way to arrive is by air. This start to the voyage could not be more spectacular, as you land alongside the towering Virginia Falls.

Fed by the melt waters of the Mackenzie Mountains, the Nahanni River provides the rafter with the most thrilling of rides. From the figure-of-eight rapids of Hell's Gate to the giant waves of George's Riffle, this is a true test of oars, people and raft. The welcome respite of overnight camping could not be in more imposing surroundings, and the 1,200 m (3,900 ft) walls of Third Canyon are the most magnificent of sights to wake up to in the morning.

The rushing noise of the river is constant and reminds you of the challenges that lie ahead. Towards the end of this epic voyage you pass, as if by design, Kraus' Hotsprings where you can soothe your aching limbs, rejoice in nature and congratulate yourself on nearly completing this most exhilarating of journeys. It is then just a short paddle along the braided channels of The Splits where the river finally loses some of its rage.

**HOW:**
By raft
**DEPART:**
Virginia Falls, NWT
**WHEN TO GO**
June to August, when the ice has melted.
**TIME IT TAKES:**
About one week
**HIGHLIGHTS:**
Virginia Falls – difficult to tear oneself away.
The thrilling run through Painted Canyon.
The view of Tlogotsho Plateau from Deadmen Valley.
The lush steep-sided forest as you near Blackstone Landing.
**YOU SHOULD KNOW:**
The beauty of rafting is that even a relative beginner can tackle the hardest of runs if accompanied by experienced people. You do have to be fit however, as there is a lot of equipment to be carried on trips such as these.

*Virginia Falls in Nahanni National Park Reserve, Northwest Territories, are twice as high as Niagara Falls.*

# The International Selkirk Loop

The International Selkirk Loop is a 450-km (281-mi) scenic drive, which takes you through some of the most remote, undeveloped and spectacular regions of south-eastern British Columbia, northern Idaho and north-eastern Washington. It's an area of forested hillsides, dazzling waterfalls, snow-capped rocky peaks, and charismatic small towns and is popular with cyclists, recreational vehicle owners and bikers alike.

Much of the land within the Loop is protected National Forest. Hundreds of miles of trails are available for all levels of hiking, biking, horseback riding, skiing and snowmobile touring. You can hit the Loop at any point, but there is no better place to start than the sleepy town of Nelson. Tucked away in the interior of British Columbia, this idyllic place has over 350 heritage homes, though its laid-back townsfolk make it feel like somewhere out of the 1960s. Having stocked up, it is a short ride to Balfour to take the longest free ferry ride in the world, across the Kootenay Lake.

Verdant forests and the lake's deep blue water continue to enrich the senses as you head across the American border. Once into Idaho, every few miles seems to herald a new trail with new possibilities and the only difficulty is choosing when to stop. With the majestic Cabinet Mountains behind you, the Loop takes you into Washington State and the most beautiful corner of America.

The main achievement of the Loop is that it connects Americans and Canadians in a historic relationship of living, working and playing in a spectacular setting. The excellent provision of campgrounds and RV parks is married with the need to preserve the region's wildlife. It is home to endangered species such as the woodland caribou, grizzly bear and the white sturgeon deer, in addition to the more commonly found elk and moose.

**HOW:**
By car
**DEPART:**
Nelson, BC
**WHEN TO GO:**
April to October, but most spectacular in the fall (September-October) when the first dustings of snow cover the mountains.
**TIME IT TAKES:**
The compactness of the Loop makes for a good week's vacation.
**HIGHLIGHTS:**
The tree-covered hills around Kootenay Lake.
The area is home to numerous artists, who are only too happy to explain and sell their work. Look out for 'Open Studio' signposts.
The Pend Oreille County Museum – a museum recording pioneer life.
**YOU SHOULD KNOW:**
Good hiking gear is required when tackling the trails that branch off the Loop. However, it is still an enjoyable tour for those less able or those who simply want to enjoy nature from the comfort of their RV.

*Pine trees at Dog Lake, Kootenay National Park, British Columbia.*

# The Great Divide Trail

Created by the Adventure Cycling Association of North America with the goal of staying within 80 km (50 mi) of the Continental Divide, this is the mother and father of all bike rides. Originally confined to the USA, it was recently extended to include southern Canada, making the journey an epic 4,238 km (2,711 mi). It has become customary to ride The Divide from north to south but you are not obliged to do so.

The route begins in the glacial valleys of Banff National Park in the Southern Canadian Rockies. It then passes through the densely forested mountains of Montana and Idaho, wends its way down into the barren high desert lands of Wyoming's Great Basin, rises again up and over several 3,000 m (10,000 ft) passes in Colorado, before switching back through rugged mountainous sections of New Mexico and it finally drops down into the Chihuahuan Desert.

The route's highest point, Indiana Pass in Colorado, is around 3,600 m (11,910 ft) above sea level. The first half of the Albertan section and the segments in Montana and New Mexico are the most rugged and challenging, but such is the magnitude of this journey that difficulties can crop up at any point. Violent thunderstorms are common and can be the biggest obstacle to your progress as they often make the riding surface impassable. Be prepared to stop and take stock at a moment's notice. Carrying good lightweight camping gear is essential.

The sense of achievement is almost overpowering as you near the Mexican border. It is at this point that even a few miles can feel like a marathon. The incentive provided by doing the journey as a sponsored ride can add power to your legs as you near the finishing line. Only then can you take in what you have seen and done.

**HOW:**
By bike
**DEPART:**
Banff, AB
**WHEN TO GO:**
The degree of difficulty is less from April to September, although you always have to tread a fine line between extreme cold and extreme heat.
**TIME IT TAKES:**
Three months at a leisurely pace, two months for a more experienced rider or under 18 days if you want to break the record.
**HIGHLIGHTS:**
The Canadian Rockies – the ride south from Banff is spectacular.
The mountains of Southern Colorado.
The Flatlands of New Mexico – a chance to build up some strength in your legs.
Getting to the end!
**YOU SHOULD KNOW:**
You have to be fit – very fit – to complete this ride within any reasonable timescale. It is best tackled in a group of people of similar ability. Take advice from the people who designed the route, namely the Adventure Cycling Association.

*The Spanish Peaks in Southern Colorado*

# Historic Route 66

**HOW:**
By car
**DEPART:**
Chicago, IL
**WHEN TO GO:**
April to October for easy driving conditions.
**TIME IT TAKES:**
Allow several weeks for a realistic attempt to travel the entire length of Historic Route 66.
**HIGHLIGHTS:**
The Historic Odell Standard Oil Gasoline Station in Illinois, opened beside Route 66 in 1932 and now restored to its original condition.
The National Museum of Transportation in St Louis, Missouri, with a huge collection of historic vehicles and memorabilia, including a unit from the old Coral Court Motel that once fronted Route 66.
The National Route 66 Museum in Elk City, Oklahoma, that allows visitors to recreate a journey along the entire length of Route 66.
The first-ever Big Mac was munched on 66 in San Bernadino and the site is now the glitzy McDonalds Route 66 Museum, full of McDonalds memorabilia and home of the California Historic Route 66 Association. Two for one!
**YOU SHOULD KNOW:**
American fast food culture was born on Route 66, when Red's Giant Hamburgs in Springfield, Missouri became the world's first drive-through restaurant in the late 1940s.

With vast distances and a well-developed railroad system, the USA had roads that were little more than local tracks until well into the 20th century. In 1919 the War Department's first Transcontinental Motor Convoy – an expedition that included future World War II Supreme Commander Dwight Eisenhower – took months to cross from east to west. When a Federal highway system was developed, Route 66 – established in 1926, signed in 1927 and fully paved by 1938 – was one of the first.

This iconic road – from Chicago to Los Angeles through eight states and the heart of America, covering some 3,940 km (2,450 mi) – was nicknamed 'The Main Street of America', bringing prosperity to towns along the way and serving as the major route for westward migration during the Great Depression of the 1930s and industrial boom of World War II. Subsequently, Route 66 facilitated tourist development and acquired legendary status, featuring widely in literature (John Steinbeck christened it 'The Mother Road'), films and popular music. But its death warrant was signed in 1956 by the aforementioned Dwight Eisenhower – by then President – when he put his name to the Interstate Highway Act, which led to today's freeway network and made US-66 redundant, though it didn't vanish from maps until 1985.

Many sections were incorporated into freeways, and it is now impossible to follow the original route, which anyway varied over the years. But happily nostalgia soon set in and much of the old road has been designated – and marked – as Historic Route 66, with new sections constantly being added. These may be found especially in Illinois, New Mexico and Arizona, and with the help of patience and specialist maps, those who warm to the romance of this famous road can still retrace much of its length – or simply drive individual sections for a reminder of the way America once travelled, not so long ago.

*One of the Historic Route 66 signs*

# Florida Keys Scenic Drive

*Highway 1 passing over Pigeon Key in the Florida Keys.*

From the tip of Florida, the Overseas Highway (US-1) runs along a chain of subtropical isles where the Atlantic meets the Gulf of Mexico, connected by over 40 bridges. It runs for 203 km (126 mi) through a brilliant tropical landscape of blue sea, reefs and lush vegetation. Mile Marker 126 is just below Florida City on the mainland, starting the countdown to Key West.

The highway crosses the southern edge of the famous Everglades to bustling Key Largo, the largest and northernmost key. It continues through Plantation Key before sweeping across Snake Creek and on to Windley Key. The Middle Keys begin at Islamorada (Purple Isle), where a memorial at Mile 82 commemorates victims of a 1935 hurricane that was one of the most powerful ever recorded in the USA.

US-1 hurries across Long Key Viaduct to tiny Conch Key, then crosses Grassy Key to Marathon, the sprawling commercial heart of the Middle Keys, before taking the spectacular Seven Mile Bridge, one of the world's longest. Now, the keys seem to become more isolated, and wildlife becomes more obvious – like the endangered miniature deer on Big Pine Key (visit their sanctuary) and a profusion of birds such as eagles, red-tailed hawks and falcons.

For the final section, the road crosses a succession of small keys that almost seem to merge, before arriving at the end of the line – Key West, a quirky place that seems to owe more to Caribbean culture than American. It is truly eccentric and unlike anywhere else in the USA, and this is one drive where both journey and destination more than come up to expectations. It is possible to do the return trip in a day, but with plenty of attractions to explore along the way most visitors prefer a leisurely drive that includes an overnight stop.

**HOW:**
By car
**DEPART:**
Florida City, FL
**WHEN TO GO:**
October through March to avoid storms and scorching summers.
**TIME IT TAKES:**
Half a day
**HIGHLIGHTS:**
John Pennekamp Coral Reef State Park – the first underwater state park in the USA, featuring the coral reefs found only in Florida, for diving, snorkelling or reef trips in glass-bottomed boats.
The Theatre of the Sea on Windley Key, featuring performing sharks, dolphins and sealions.
At Crane Point Hummock on Marathon – the combined Museum of Natural History of the Florida Keys and Florida Keys Children's Museum.
The Ernest Hemingway Home and Museum in Whitehead Street, Key West.
**YOU SHOULD KNOW:**
The southernmost house in the continental USA – a wonderful turreted Victorian confection in pink, may be found at 1400 Duval Street in Key West.

# Coast Starlight Train

**HOW:**
By train
**DEPART:**
Seattle, WA
**WHEN TO GO:**
Any time of year.
**TIME IT TAKES:**
Official journey time is 35 hours, though some travellers stop off to see some of the many sights to be found en route.
**HIGHLIGHTS:**
Before embarking, visit Seattle's popular landmark Space Needle, built for the 1962 World's Fair.
Informative on-board talks by guides from the Klondike Gold Rush National Historical Park between Seattle and Portland, then Klamath Falls and Eugene.
A break in Paso Robles, with dozens of wineries to tour...before relaxing in the rejuvenating waters of natural hot springs.
**YOU SHOULD KNOW:**
The route has sometimes been disrupted by mudslides, so it's wise to check that there are no problems before planning a trip.

Who says the romance of rail travel is dead? It isn't if you save up your pennies and travel on Amtrak's Coast Starlight service, connecting Seattle's King Street Station with Union Station in Los Angeles via Portland, Eugene-Springfield, Klamath Falls, Sacramento, Oakland, the San Francisco Bay area, Salinas and Santa Barbara. Along the 2,216 km (1,377 mi) route, the train passes through some truly spectacular West Coast scenery encompassing virgin forests, snow-capped mountains, lush valleys...and long stretches of fabulous and unspoiled Pacific coastline. No wonder it's rated as one of the world's most beautiful rail journeys. Amtrak gives every passenger a Route Guide that details what to look out for along the way and includes photo symbols indicating the most photogenic spots.

To take full advantage of all that natural beauty, the train uses double-decker Superliner rolling stock, including a Sightseer Lounge car with floor-to-ceiling windows. If you did indeed accumulate those pennies, you can travel in pampered luxury in the first-class Pacific Parlour Lounge car, with sleeping berths, a library, wine tasting, movie theatre and complimentary drinks. For little people, there's a Kiddie car packed with a variety of distractions. There is a Dining Car for full meals and Café Car for those who want their sightseeing with snacks. To complete the unique ensemble, luggage travels in a Heritage Baggage Car and the train is hauled by Amtrak's mighty Genesis series locomotives.

A gentle word of warning – the Coast Starlight has sometimes arrived up to eleven hours late, though timekeeping has recently improved dramatically.

*A vineyard in Paso Robles, California*

# California State Route 1

Often called Highway 1, this classic West Coast road runs for 1,055 km (655 mi) along much of California's beautiful Pacific shoreline. It starts in Orange County to the south and ends in Mendocino County to the north. Different sections have different names, including Pacific Coast Highway, Cabrillo Highway and Shoreline Highway.

Along the way, this rewarding route can be multi-lane highway or two-lane blacktop, and driving its entire length produces extraordinary contrasts between urban sprawl and some of the finest coastal scenery in the USA, plus the opportunity to visit many important heritage sites. Highway 1 has mile markers that help locate any listed feature or attraction, numbered from south to north, each bearing the abbreviated name of the relevant county. Highway 1 is best driven from south to north as the reverse direction ends anti-climactically with Los Angeles smog.

Starting in San Juan Capistra, the road travels through Los Angeles and the Beach cities, Santa Monica, Malibu, Santa Barbara, Lompoc, Santa Maria, San Luis Obispo, Morro Bay, Carmel (former Mayor – Clint Eastwood), Pacific Grove, Monterey, Watsonville, Santa Cruz, Half Moon Day, Pacifica, San Francisco, Mill Valley and Fort Bragg. It terminates at Leggett, where it meets US Highway 101 (with which it actually shares several sections of the coastal route) for the last time. Many of the place names serve as a reminder of California's historical ties with Spain, and there are a number of old Spanish settlements along Highway 1.

Despite some stretches that are inescapably modern freeways, the leisurely traveller best remembers the characteristic feel of a narrow, winding coast road amidst stunning scenery – not for nothing is it said that to drive Highway 1 is to understand the heart and soul of California.

*Pacific coast, Big Sur, California*

**HOW:**
By car
**DEPART:**
San Juan Capistra, CA
**WHEN TO GO:**
Any season – catch this delightful drive when you can!
**TIME IT TAKES:**
It can theoretically be done in an over-long day, but take two or three and enjoy the sights.
**HIGHLIGHTS:**
Unspoiled Big Sur with its rugged cliffs, where the residents are environmentally conscious and not a billboard is to be seen beside the highway.
Half way between Los Angeles and San Francisco – Hearst Castle in San Simeon, the extravagant edifice built by newspaper tycoon William Randolph Hearst, the model for Xanadu in Orson Welles's film *Citizen Kane*.
Piedras Blancas Lighthouse at the northern entrance to San Simeon Bay, first illuminated in 1875 and still used as a navigational aid – but the real attraction is the vast colony of elephant seals.
**YOU SHOULD KNOW:**
Be prepared to duck a couple of hours into the journey – Route 1 passes beneath the busy runways of LA International Airport.

*Yosemite Valley in Yosemite National Park, Sierra Nevada Mountains, California*

**HOW:**
On foot or by bike

**WHEN TO GO:**
The Trail (starting at the Mexican border) is best between March and September.

**TIME IT TAKES:**
To hike the entire trail without pause you should allow between four and six months.

**HIGHLIGHTS:**
The Ansell Adams Wilderness in California's Sierra Nevada, named after the famous 20th century landscape photographer who was inspired by these mountains.
Yosemite National Park, a World Heritage Site that covers a large area on the western slopes of the Sierra Nevada mountain chain.
Crater Lake National Park in Oregon, the most notable feature of which is the eponymous Crater Lake, a volcanic caldera lake famous for its deep-blue colour.
A civilized stop-off at Timberline Lodge, built within Oregon's Mount Hood National Forest as a work-generation project in the Great Depression, now a National Historic Landmark and popular tourist destination.

**YOU SHOULD KNOW:**
It really can be done – some 300 so-called 'thru hikers' start out along the PCT each spring, and around 200 make it all the way.

# Pacific Crest Trail

Also known as the Pacific Crest National Scenic Trail or simply PCT, this long-distance hiking route is only for the super-fit (and mightily determined!), although some make the going easier by taking to the saddle. The Trail stretches from the Mexican border up into Canada, a distance of 4,240 km (2,650 mi), following the high country of the Sierra Nevada and Cascade Range, inland from and parallel to the USA's West Coast. The highest point is Forester Pass in the Sierra Nevada at 4,000 m (13,150 ft), the low point is sea level at the Columbia River on the Oregon Washington borders.

The PCT mostly crosses forests and protected wilderness, avoiding civilization and even roads wherever possible, ensuring that the intrepid hiker sees and enjoys America's wild grandeur at its pristine best. Those who just wish to experience a section of this rugged Trail – or don't have time for more – often opt for the northern section in Washington, which has much to offer. Start at the Bridge of the Gods across the Columbia River; from there on it's uphill most of the way, as the Trail goes through National Forests, skirts Mount Adams and crosses a vast wilderness area. From there, it enters Mount Rainier National Park, and then continues via Chinook, Snoqualmie and Stevens Passes into the Lake Chelan National Recreational Area and North Cascades National Park. If you get there you've missed Stehekin, the last town near the Trail, and must cross into Canada where the PCT ends in British Columbia's EC Manning Provincial Park.

Oh, when you finally rest those blistered feet after hiking the Pacific Crest Trail from start to finish, take a short break then go for the USA's Triple Crown of long-distance hiking – the Appalachian and Continental Divide Trails await!

# Minnesota State Highway 61

Once the northern extremity of US Highway 61, the great pre-freeway route from New Orleans in the Deep South through the American heartlands up into Canada, State Highway 61 was created in 1991 when a new Interstate was built. It is in the northeastern part of Minnesota, running for 243 km (151 mi) from Duluth to the Canadian border.

MS-61 is a designated scenic highway that follows the rocky North Shore of Lake Superior, offering great lake vistas and soaring views of the Sawtooth Range to the northwest. It passes through three counties – St Louis, Lake and Cook – beginning with a four-lane expressway from Duluth to Two Harbours. Those who prefer more traditional progress can take the original road, now designated County/Scenic 61 (generally known as North Shore Scenic Drive). The road then passes through the lakeshore communities of Silver Creek, Castle Danger, Beaver Bay, East Beaver Bay, Silver Bay, Illgen City, Little Marais, Schroeder, Tofte, Lutsen and Grand Marais, before reaching Grand Portage.

The quality of this impressive landscape may be judged by the large number of forests, state parks, landmarks and features to be found along Highway 61. The road passes through Superior National and Grand Portage State Forests. State parks include Gooseberry Falls, Tettegouche alongside Silver Bay, Temperance River, Cascade River and Judge C R Magney State Park. Grand Portage lies within an Indian Reservation, and the landmark Grand Portage National Monument celebrates the Ojibwa, the third-largest group of Native Americans in the USA after Cherokees and Navajos. The Monument also acknowledges the importance of the fur trade in times past, sitting as it does on the historic trade route to the Canadian interior used in pre-industrial times. It's a reminder of how tough the original inhabitants and pioneers must have been to survive in this rugged terrain.

**HOW:**
By car
**DEPART:**
Duluth, MN
**WHEN TO GO:**
Minnesota Highway 61 is best travelled between April and September.
**TIME IT TAKES:**
A day will suffice, but two days would allow some of the natural wonders to be properly explored.
**HIGHLIGHTS:**
Palisade Head, the highest lakeside cliff in Minnesota – right beside the main entrance to Tettegouche State Park at the end of the Baptism River.
Grand Portage National Park – containing Minnesota's highest waterfall at 37 m (120 ft), the obstacle on the Pigeon River that required 'portage' (using a path to carry canoes and stores past the falls).
An outing on Lake Superior from Grand Portage – take either the *Wenonah* or *Voyageur II* and visit the Isle Royale National Park on the lake's largest island.
**YOU SHOULD KNOW:**
Local boy Bob Dylan (born Robert Zimmerman in Duluth) celebrated his local scenic route in the album and song Highway 61 Revisited (1965).

*The lighthouse at Split Rock, Lake Superior, Michigan*

# Lewis & Clark's National Scenic Trail

**HOW:**
By car and boat
**WHEN TO GO:**
Northern winters can be harsh, so it's best to trace the Trail between April and September.
**TIME IT TAKES:**
By car, the entire Trail can be followed inside two weeks without hurrying (careful planning required!).
**HIGHLIGHTS:**
The Lewis and Clark Memorial in a small park on the Kansas City river bluff, overlooking the confluence of the Kansas and Missouri Rivers.
Historic side-wheel dredging vessel *Captain Meriwether Lewis* in the Brownville State Recreation Area, now converted into a floating museum.
South Dakota's Calumet Bluff, where the expedition held council with the Yankton Sioux, now interpreted at Gavins Point Oam Visitor Centre and at nearby Lewis & Clark State Recreation Area.
A boat trip along the Upper Missouri National Wild and Scenic River, a 240-km (150-mi) section from Kipp State Park upstream to Fort Benton – little changed from 1805-06 when the expedition passed through.
**YOU SHOULD KNOW:**
In 1806, starting a tradition that persists in the US hunting field to this day, expedition leader Meriwether Lewis was shot in the leg by a short-sighted companion while hunting elk.

If there's one thing the USA isn't short of, it's long distances. Lewis & Clark's route across North America underlines the point, covering 5,960 km (3,700 mi) from Illinois to the Pacific. Meriwether Lewis and William Clark undertook their two-year saga from 1804 to 1806 at the instigation of President Thomas Jefferson, who dreamed of exploiting unexplored lands to the west, recently acquired via the Louisiana Purchase. The two men – accompanied by 45 men, three boats and (appropriately) a Newfoundland dog – set off to find a viable route to the west coast, with orders to record every detail of the people, places and things they saw, which they did...meticulously.

Nowadays, the trail they blazed is the second longest of the USA's 23 National Scenic and Historic Trails. Starting at Hartford, Illinois, it goes through ten more states – Missouri, Kansas, Iowa, Nebraska, South Dakota, North Dakota, Montana, Idaho, Oregon and Washington. It is not literally possible to follow in their pioneering footsteps – unless you have a couple of years to spare, 45 men, three boats and an Alreadyfoundland dog!

But many retracement opportunities are available, organized by state, local and private interests under the auspices of the National Park Service. Water segments follow parts of the expedition's waterborne route by boat or canoe. Overland hiking and horse-riding sections are being established and there are marked motor routes where roads nearly or precisely follow the original trail. Perhaps the most complete option is to follow the Lewis & Clark Trail Highway established in the 1960s, allowing one of the most significant journeys in American history to be approximated by car along modern roads. Helpful maps and information can be obtained from state and local tourism agencies, historical societies, chambers of commerce and Federal or state agencies managing lands or waters that are part of the Trail.

*The Missouri River from White Rocks*

# Appalachian Trail

Officially known as the Appalachian National Scenic Trail – unofficially the AT – this marked trail in the eastern USA is a magnet for thousands of hikers each year. Some 3,200 km (2,000 mi) long, it runs from Springer Mountain in Georgia to Mount Katahdin in Maine, passing through North Carolina, Tennessee, Virginia, West Virginia, Maryland, Pennsylvania, New Jersey, New York, Connecticut, Massachusetts, Vermont and New Hampshire as it goes. After that, you know you've had a serious stroll – mostly enjoying the solitary splendour of unspoiled wilderness, though a few stretches do traverse towns.

Many attempt the full length in one hit and about a third of these 'thru hikers' make it. Many more are so-called 'sectional hikers' who either complete the AT bit by bit over a number of years, or just choose one or more choice sections to hike and never essay the whole. Thru hikers generally start in Georgia in early spring to take advantage of warm weather moving north. There are numerous simple shelters along the AT, but these get crowded in summer and most hikers carry basic camping gear. Indeed, living rough on the Trail is very much part of the attraction and this is definitely not an adventure for the faint-hearted (or ill-prepared).

The Appalachian Trail is largely owned by the National Park Service and has been fully mapped and marked to assist hikers. The main markers are white blazes on trees, with blue blazes indicating side trails to shelters, viewpoints, parking areas and even (whisper it if you dare!) short cuts.

A word of warning – the Maine section is particularly tough and demanding. And speaking of Maine, don't start along the wrong trail by mistake! The International Appalachian Trail goes north from Maine into New Brunswick and Quebec, with an extension to Newfoundland planned.

**HOW:**
On foot
**WHEN TO GO:**
Best between April and mid-October (after which hiking in Maine is seriously discouraged).
**TIME IT TAKES:**
A complete 'thru hike' takes four to seven months.
**HIGHLIGHTS:**
Flora – the Appalachian Trail passes through spectacular forests that vary enormously, depending on climate and elevation, and there are a number of sub-alpine and alpine sections with interesting plant life.
Fauna – there are numerous animals, birds and reptiles to be seen along the trail, including black bear, deer, elk, moose, smaller mammals, rattlesnakes...and (on the down side) a variety of biting insects.
So-called 'trail magic' – the AT is maintained by dozens of voluntary organizations and individuals, and is renowned for the generous help given to hikers, often anonymously.
The ultimate colour display of New England's trees along the AT in Vermont during the fall.
**YOU SHOULD KNOW:**
For an idea of what lies in store before starting the epic journey, read *A Walk in the Woods* by humorous writer Bill Bryson.

*Mount Katahdin on the Appalachian Trail*

*Rafter in Rogue River Rapids*

# Rogue River Trail

Wild and rugged are adjectives that spring readily to mind when describing the Rogue River's wilderness surroundings and seething white water, so typical of the northwestern USA. The river rises in Oregon's Cascade Range and rushes down to the Pacific Ocean with plenty of Grade IV rapids along the way (they're almost as difficult as rapids can get, whilst remaining runnable). That makes the river hugely popular with rafters, and there are also fascinating jet boat trips along some 160 km (100 mi) of the Rogue's course.

But for those who get seasick, or prefer to enjoy outstanding natural beauty at walking pace, there is an excellent trail for hikers. The 65-km (40-mi) Rogue River National Recreation Trail along the river's north bank offers a splendid way of seeing the impressive Rogue River Canyon. The western trailhead is at Foster Bar, some 50 km (31 mi) inland from the coastal town of Gold Beach. The eastern trailhead is at Grave Creek, the same distance down river from Grants Pass. Both trailheads (and the middle of the trail) can be reached by road. Most people hike in an easterly direction so the sun is on their backs in the afternoon.

The Trail is not too demanding terrain-wise, with a well-constructed trailbed and moderate grades, though it should not be attempted by the inexperienced or unfit. It is necessary to backpack, carrying adequate water and supplies along with camping gear, though it is possible to restock along the way. For those who prefer not to camp, lodge accommodation is available (pre-booking essential) at regular intervals. Potential hazards along the Trail include black bears, rattlesnakes, ticks and poison oak, but those risks are a small price to pay for the pleasure of experiencing an accessible piece of spectacular American wilderness.

# Oregon Coast Trail

The Oregon Coast Trail (OCT) follows the state's Pacific coastline, from Astoria on the Columbia River in the north to the California border near Brookings – a distance of 600 km (360 mi). It clings to the shoreline, with only an occasional short inland detour where the beach is impassable, usually at rocky headlands like Cape Kiwanda. Where the Trail goes through a coastal town, it usually follows the streets closest to the water.

The OCT experience can only be described as breathtaking. This is one of the most beautiful and dramatic coastlines to be found anywhere in the USA (maybe the world!) where the hiker truly feels at one with awesome Nature. Many travel the Trail and camp as they go. Camping is allowed on many beaches and where it is forbidden (within state parks) there are alternative campgrounds. Others prefer the many yurts along the way – conical shelters modelled on the Mongolian original that can be used for a small fee. There are also plenty of bed-and-breakfast establishments that offer walkers a warm welcome and hot showers. Be aware that some sections of the Trail can only be walked at low tide, necessitating a hold-up or sometimes-demanding detour if you arrive at the wrong time.

Oregon's Pacific beaches certainly justify a visit, even if you have no intention of travelling the whole Trail. An excellent way of experiencing this wild and unspoiled coastline is to choose a section of the trail that can be walked in a day – there will almost always be a local bus to return you to your starting point at the end of the leisurely hike. For those who don't 'do' walking, US-101 more or less follows the OCT (and is, indeed, part of the Trail for some of its length).

**HOW:**
On foot
**WHEN TO GO:**
May to September (but hang tough and go out of season, and you'll have the OCT to yourself!)
**TIME IT TAKES:**
From a single day for one short section to a couple of months for the entire Trail.
**HIGHLIGHTS:**
Oregon Dunes National Recreation Area – south from the Siuslaw River in Florence to the Coos River in North Bend, this is 65 km (40 mi) of the most extraordinary sand sculpture in the USA.
The secluded section of the OCT between Port Orford and Brandon – offering four days of pristine wilderness hiking for those willing to camp...and swim a river along the way.
A night in the yurt at Beachside State Park, just south of Waldport – you'll never see a better ocean view.
The most spectacular one-day hike on the OCT – the sea-stack-strewn stretch between Cannon Beach South and Arch Point.
**YOU SHOULD KNOW:**
Access to the entire length of Oregon's coastline is guaranteed by state law – no private beachfronts here!

*Brandon Beach, Oregon*

# Shenandoah Valley

**HOW:**
By car
**DEPART:**
Roanoke, VA
**WHEN TO GO:**
March to October
**TIME IT TAKES:**
It can be done in a day, but is worth a week.
**HIGHLIGHTS:**
The Frontier Culture Museum at Staunton, with reconstructed early farms, rare breed animals and a working smithy.
Edinburg – a picturesque village on the banks of Stoney Creek in the Central Valley, preserving the charm of 19th century life in a modern world.
Shenandoah Valley Folk Art & Heritage Center in Dayton, Rockingham County – extensive exhibits of local culture and history.
Natural Bridge in suitably named Rockbridge County, one of the so-called 'seven wonders of the modern world' and a major tourist attraction for nearly 200 years.
**YOU SHOULD KNOW:**
The word 'Shenandoah' derives from a Native American expression meaning 'Beautiful Daughter of the Stars'.

One of the most historic locations in the eastern USA is the Shenandoah Valley, scene of ferocious conflict in the American Civil War when it was known as 'The Breadbasket of the Confederacy'. It lies between the Blue Ridge Mountains to the east and the Allegheny Mountains to the west, stretching for 320 km (200 mi) and consisting of seven counties in Virginia and two in West Virginia. It is a famously productive agricultural area and numerous heritage sites hark back to the efforts of early settlers.

The Shenandoah River runs for much of the valley's length, as does US Highway 11 and the newer Interstate 81. Ignore the Interstate. A journey through the Shenandoah Valley must involve leisurely progress along US-11 – a former turnpike known as 'The Great Valley Road' – from Roanoke in the south to Harpers Ferry in the north, turning off along the way to explore tempting side roads. This trip will allow you to experience traditional 'Mom and Apple pie America' at its very best and provide real insight into the pioneer spirit that made the country great. The people are friendly and there's usually some sort of festival, celebration or re-enactment to be found – history and tradition are important here.

Bounded by inhospitable mountains, the valley was not easily reached. But the relentless westward thrust of the pioneers saw Shenandoah's first settlements in the 1730s. The wooded valley was soon partially cleared, creating today's picture-postcard landscape that combines natural beauty with traditional farmsteads and historic towns with squares of buildings dating back to the 18th and 19th centuries, all testifying to the energy and industry of those early arrivals. It's said that such places are the backbone of America, and driving through the picturesque Shenandoah Valley it's easy to believe that's true.

*Shenandoah Folk Art & Heritage Center*

# Blue Ridge Parkway

How can you ignore the USA's most-visited National Park, which also happens to be the world's longest and narrowest? Of course you can't – this 755-km (469-mi) National Parkway and All-American Road must not be missed, running as it does through the famously scenic Blue Ridge mountain chain, part of the Appalachians. The road was a 1930s job-creation project in the states of Virginia (Milepost 0) and North Carolina (Milepost 469), though not finally completed as a throughway until 1987.

The effort was worthwhile – the scenery is stunning (those mountains really are a study in misty blues!), whilst the road passes through unspoiled lands maintained by the National Park Service and the US Forest Service. There are 26 tunnels along the way, together with six viaducts and 168 bridges that carry the parkway across ravines, rivers and across roads to ensure an uninterrupted journey. The Parkway starts at Rockfish Gap, Virginia, from the terminus of Shenandoah National Park's Skyline Drive (itself a rewarding journey). It ends in the Great Smoky Mountains National Park near Cherokee, North Carolina. Towns where you can stop off include Waynesboro, Roanoke and Galax in Virginia, or Boone and Asheville in North Carolina.

A drive along the Blue Ridge Parkway is a memorable experience, but to make the most of this unique landscape it really is necessary to stop frequently and explore some of the numerous side roads and trails which often lead to stunning vistas that change according to the seasons, with a variety of trees, colourful foliage and flowers to be enjoyed, especially in spring and autumn. There are also plenty of interesting heritage sites to remind the traveller of the simple lives those hardy mountain families once led.

**HOW:**
By car
**DEPART:**
Rockfish Gap, VA
**WHEN TO GO:**
May to October (the road is not maintained in winter and high sections are often closed).
**TIME IT TAKES:**
Two days, if you hurry along, but taking more time will allow you to explore properly.
**HIGHLIGHTS:**
The Mabry Mill by its tranquil pool at Milepost 176.1, where a trail leads to this vintage gristmill, sawmill and blacksmith shop where old-time skills are demonstrated throughout the summer.
The Blue Ridge Music Center at Milepost 213 near Galax, Virginia – a museum and concert centre with a busy summer schedule, mainly of country music.
Mount Mitchell – the highest point in eastern North America, reached via a road off the Parkway at Milepost 355.4...what a view!
The Folk Art Centre at Milepost 382, for sales and exhibitions of traditional and contemporary Appalachian crafts, with three galleries, a library, book store and interpretive programmes.
**YOU SHOULD KNOW:**
Frontiersman Daniel Boone blazed a pioneering trail to the west that crosses the Parkway near Milepost 285 in North Carolina.

*Great Smoky Mountain National Park.*

# Chesapeake Bay Bridge-Tunnel

There's a toll to pay, but it's well worth it for the pleasure of driving along 'The East Coast's Scenic Shortcut' – US Highway 13 across the Chesapeake Bay Bridge-Tunnel (CBBT) from Virginia's Eastern Shore at Cape Charles to the mainland at Virginia Beach near Norfolk (or vice versa!). The CBBT was opened in 1964 and forms part of the East Coast's Ocean Highway from Florida to New York. It is a dramatic 37-km (23-mi) crossing of Chesapeake Bay utilizing bridges and tunnels, the latter requiring artificial islands as portals, that is both a travel convenience and major tourist attraction. The actual water crossing over this ocean strait is some 28 km (17 mi) long and has been described as 'one of the seven engineering wonders of the modern world'.

This four-lane highway crossing has replaced a passenger and vehicle ferry service that ran from the 1930s and was by the 1960s offering around a hundred daily crossings with large ferries.

The CBBT consists of low-level trestle bridges connected by two tunnels beneath shipping lanes, then two high-level bridges over two other navigation channels. The motorist and passengers mainly have a view of the Atlantic seascape during the crossing, but the bridges do curve to give views of other sections of the CBBT and there are usually plenty of ships to be seen, often including US Navy warships. One novel option is making the crossing by night (perhaps a return journey after a daylight trip?), which offers a fascinating light show. And as a bonus, if you do decide to return within 24 hours, the toll is more than halved!

**HOW:**
By car
**WHEN TO GO:**
Any time of year.
**TIME IT TAKES:**
Half an hour one-way (without stops).
**HIGHLIGHTS:**
Fisherman Island at the entrance to the Bay – a barrier island traversed by US-13 that is part of a National Wildlife Refuge, the habitat of varied waterfowl, shorebirds and waterbirds. The Scenic Overlook on the tip of Virginia's Eastern Shore, for the perfect spot to admire (and photograph) this engineering marvel. A quick tour of the Atlantic marshes and the unspoiled countryside of Northampton County on the Eastern Shore.
**YOU SHOULD KNOW:**
The reason it's CBBT rather than plain CBB is that the US Navy feared that accident or hostile action would collapse a bridge-only crossing, thus trapping its Atlantic fleet in Norfolk Navy Base.

*Sunset over the Chesapeake Bay Bridge-Tunnel*

# Lower Manhattan

New Amsterdam, the Dutch colony that grew into New York City, has long disappeared under Lower Manhattan – yet it remains a fascinating part of the great city to explore. But first look from the water – ride the subway to South Ferry and take a free round trip on the Staten Island Ferry (try for one of the older boats with open decks). Those harbour views are to die for, and you can't help but admire New York's iconic skyline.

Back in Manhattan, walk into Battery Park, with its Castle Clinton National Monument and superb waterfront views of the Statue of Liberty and Ellis Island. Head up State Street to the Bowling Green at the foot of Broadway. The city's oldest park offers a fine view of the impressive Alexander Hamilton Customs House. Go down Whitehall Street to the junction with Water Street. Turn left, walk a block east and go left again up Broad Street, then right into Pearl Street. Go up Pearl (pausing for refreshment at the atmospheric Georgian Fraunces Tavern) and turn left into Wall Street, lined with spectacular skyscrapers and noble buildings, including the Stock Exchange, Morgan Guaranty Trust Company and Citibank. Rest awhile in the tranquil graveyard of Trinity Church at the junction with Broadway. Turn north past historic St Paul's Chapel and go on to City Hall Park, overlooked by the fabulous Woolworth Building and home to New York's venerable City Hall.

End the tour by strolling south down partially pedestrianized Nassau and Fulton Streets to the South Street Seaport Historic District, complete with its working Fulton Fish Market, pavement cafés, Victorian shop fronts, trendy boutiques, street entertainers... and tall ships. The old waterfront is the place to spend the rest of the day, enjoying one of frantic Manhattan's most relaxed quarters.

*A statue of George Washington overlooking the New York Stock Exchange.*

**HOW:**
On foot
**WHEN TO GO:**
Avoid mid-winter (December and January) and high summer (July and August).
**TIME IT TAKES:**
A leisurely day.
**HIGHLIGHTS:**
The suitably tiny Peter Minuit Park at the junction of Water Street and Whitehall Street – commemorating the shrewd Dutchman who purchased Manhattan Island for peanuts.
The Parthenon-like Federal Hall National Memorial on Wall Street, at the very spot where George Washington took the Oath of Office to become first President of the USA.
The Fulton Market Building at Fulton and Front Streets – the wet fish is all gone by dawn, leaving the restored building to interesting shops and tempting restaurants.
**YOU SHOULD KNOW:**
Wall Street used to be...a wall (built by the Dutch in 1653 to defend what is now Lower Manhattan from hostile Indians).

# Roosevelt Island Tramway

**HOW:**
Aerial Tram
**WHEN TO GO:**
Any time.
**TIME IT TAKES:**
Four-and-a-half minutes at a dizzying 26 kph (16 mph).
**HIGHLIGHTS:**
A quick tour of Roosevelt Island for a bargain 25-cent fare on the 'Red Bus' that meets each tram.
The extraordinary lighthouse on the north tip of Roosevelt Island, built in 1872 – a great viewpoint overlooking the river, Manhattan's Upper East Side and Triborough Bridge.
A night trip – the view of Manhattan, the East River and Queens is magnificent.
The mysterious castle-like Renwick Ruin at the south end of the island, named after architect James Renwick who designed this former smallpox hospital...and St Patrick's Cathedral on Fifth Avenue.
**YOU SHOULD KNOW:**
Sex symbol Mae West once served time in the Welfare Island Penitentiary (closed in 1935), for putting on a bawdy Broadway show entitled...*Sex*.

*The Roosevelt Island Tram above the East River*

Along with the day's other 10,000-odd commuters and rubberneckers, why not fly through the air with the greatest of ease on New York City's amazing Roosevelt Island Tramway? Completed in 1976, this aerial tramway (cableway to Europeans) spans the East River, connecting Manhattan to Roosevelt Island. Each car has a capacity of 125 people and there are 115 trips per day across the 940-m (3,100-ft) distance, the tramway climbing to a maximum height of 76 m (250 ft) during the journey. The Manhattan entrance to the system is at Tram Plaza (60th Street and 2nd Avenue). The closest New York City subway station is the Lexington Avenue/59th Street complex.

The Tramway runs parallel to the Queensboro Bridge, which crosses Roosevelt Island. Until the 1950s, a trolley (the last in New York) ran to the centre of the Queensboro Bridge, where the cars stopped to let passengers descend to Roosevelt Island by lift. This service was discontinued after a bridge from Queens was built, but there was no direct link to Manhattan until the aerial tram arrived. It was intended to be a temporary measure until the island's subway station was built, but when that was finally completed in 1989 the 'Tram' had become so popular it became a permanent fixture. It was grounded after malfunctioning twice, in 2005 and 2006, stranding passengers in mid-air. After refurbishment, the service was reinstated though (just in case) each car now carries blankets, food, water...and a toilet with privacy curtain.

Roosevelt Island had various names over the centuries – Minnahononck, Varckens Island, Manning's Island, Blackwell's Island and Welfare Island – before its final renaming in anticipation of a Presidential monument to Franklin Delano Roosevelt that never got built. In the 19th century hospitals, asylums and prisons were located on the island, it is now subject to intensive residential redevelopment.

# Hudson River Trip

The mighty Hudson River has made an essential contribution to the New York City we know today. The river rises in the Adirondack Mountains and is 507 km (315 mi) from source to sea. It is entirely in New York State, though in the lower reaches serving as the state line between New York and New Jersey. The Hudson is tidal right up to the Federal Dam south of Troy, which separates the Upper and Lower Hudson Valleys.

Looking out at the hustle and bustle of New York Harbour, it's easy to forget that the Hudson River – and indeed much of upstate New York State – also has a traditional character that's at complete odds with the vibrant modern city. The river has great historical significance, reflected in the Hudson Valley's status as a National Heritage Area. It attracted many of the earliest European settlers and a canal connection to the Great Lakes in the 19th century helped to open up the vast interior of this great continent.

A splendid way to appreciate the contrast is to take a Hudson River Cruise, thus enjoying this striking American landscape much as the pioneers first saw it. There are numerous operators offering cruises, from a week-long luxury trip upriver from New York to a wide selection of interesting day trips from locations along the river. Key ports of call are Tarrytown, Nyack, West Haverstraw, Peekskill, Garrison, Cold Spring, West Point, Newburgh, Poughkeepsie, Kingston, Catskill, Hudson, Albany (the state capital) and Troy. Day cruises can be taken from many of these places, most offering informative commentary that adds context to a dramatic journey that will not only include wonderful natural beauty but also historic sights – from splendid old plantation houses through the massive mansions of robber barons to battlefields and George Washington's Revolutionary War headquarters.

**HOW:**
By boat
**WHEN TO GO:**
Cruise season is May to October.
**TIME IT TAKES:**
From two hours to a week, depending on itinerary.
**HIGHLIGHTS:**
Bear Mountain Bridge, a suspension bridge carrying highways and the Appalachian Trail across the river, flanked on the west bank by Bear Mountain State Park in Rockland County.
The United States Military Academy at West Point, alma mater of so many great Americans.
Vanderbilt Mansion National Historic Site and Franklin D Roosevelt Presidential Library & Museum, both in Hyde Park township, Dutchess County.
Philipsburg Manor at Sleepy Hollow, an atmospheric historic house, water mill and trading site where the Hudson and Pocantico Rivers meet.
**YOU SHOULD KNOW:**
The river is named after Henry Hudson, an Englishman who explored it for the Dutch East India Company in 1609.

*Bear Mountain Bridge crosses the Hudson River at West Point.*

# Cape Cod Scenic Route 6A

*Wood End Lighthouse,
Provincetown*

The arm-shaped peninsula that forms the easternmost part of
Massachusetts is technically an island, following the completion of
the Cape Cod Canal in 1914, but few refer to it as such. Bridges
connect 'the Cape' to the mainland, and in summer they're busy
with holiday traffic rushing to enjoy the wonderful beachfronts and
small-town character of this unique part of New England. Vehicles
often back up (both ways), and if planning to leave on a Sunday it's
wise to do so before noon or in the early evening, to avoid the
inevitable jams.

Massachusetts Route 6A is the official title of parts of former US
Highway 6 on Cape Cod, generally known as the Old King's Highway,
which runs along the north coast that fronts the enclosed Cape Cod
Bay. This is considered to be the Cape's most historic and scenic
road, and a journey along it (and back) provides a rewarding
opportunity to explore an historic maritime landscape and its quaint
New England towns. Though signed, Route 6A can be hard to follow
in places and it doesn't officially exist in Eastham or Wellfleet
(though the modern US-6 does bridge the gap). Route 6A starts at
the Sagamore Bridge in Bourne, and travels for 100 km (62 mi) to
Provincetown via Sandwich, Barnstable, Yarmouth, Dennis,
Brewster, Orleans and Truro.

These delightful towns are all well worth exploring – full of
character, antique shops, galleries, craft outlets and seafood
restaurants...but also thousands of vacationers in high season. In
order to experience the beauty of Cape Cod without fighting
through hordes of like-minded visitors, a journey in late spring or
early autumn can pay dividends, though the weather may be cool
and some attractions will be closed.

# San Juan Skyway

It's a tongue twister – the San Juan Skyway Scenic Byway. And it's quite a journey – consisting of a 380-km (236-mi) loop through the heart of the snow-capped San Juan Mountains in Colorado.

Starting in Durango, the Skyway follows US Highway 160 to Cortez, before taking Colorado State Highway 145 through Dolores into the San Juan National Forest, over Lizard Head Pass on to Uncompahgre National Forest. It descends near the small town of Ophir, where a spur road leads off to the former silver mining camp of Telluride, now a winter sports centre. After following the San Juan River down to Placerville, the Skyway takes CO-62 over the Dallas Divide to Ridgway. Here, it parts company with the Rio Grande Southern Railroad, which it has shadowed from Durango, and turns south on US-550, through the old mining town of Ouray and Uncompahgre Gorge. The Skyway then crosses Bear Creek Falls and enters the valley of Ironton Park, before climbing over Red Mountain Pass, returning to the San Juan National Forest and descending through the Chattanooga Valley (no, not the Chattanooga of 'Choo Choo' fame, which is in Tennessee) to the historic mining town of Silverton, from whence the Skyway returns to its start point at Durango.

Those are the simple facts of this route, that hint at its rugged character. But in reality they can hardly begin to tell the story of an extraordinary journey. The fabulous mountain views, sheer cliffs, rushing rivers, plunging waterfalls, rocky terrain, old mines, ghost towns, historic railroads and Victorian towns make driving the Skyway a unique experience, as it snakes around mountains, twists through valleys and wriggles through canyons. It's no wonder the San Juan Skyway was designated by the US Government as an All-American Road in 1996. This is the highest possible classification, an accolade that's well deserved.

*The Cliff Palace is an ancient Anasazi cultural settlement in Chapin Mesa.*

**HOW:**
By car

**WHEN TO GO:**
Make the journey between April and October – this is a winter sports area known for avalanches!

**TIME IT TAKES:**
Five hours of non-stop driving, or one to two days for the full experience.

**HIGHLIGHTS:**
Before or after the road journey, take a trip on the Durango & Silverton Narrow Gauge Railroad, riding rolling stock dating back to the 1880s and hauled by classic steam locomotives.
Mesa Verde National Park near Durango – a UNESCO World Heritage Site famous for the many ruined houses, villages and cliff dwellings once occupied by the ancient Pueblo people (often referred to as the Anasazi).
Wonderful mountain vistas from the top of Lizard Head Pass – look for the signed El Diente Peak, Wilson Peak, Mount Wilson and Lizard Head Peak.

**YOU SHOULD KNOW:**
The 'Million Dollar Highway' from Ouray to Silverton is not for the nervous – this two-laner clings to the mountainside and has no guardrails.

*The Skywalk that overlooks the Grand Canyon on the Hualapai Indian reservation in Arizona.*

# Grand Circle Road Trip

**HOW:**
By car
**DEPART:**
Las Vegas, NV
**WHEN TO GO:**
April to October
**TIME IT TAKES:**
At least 10 days, to allow for rewarding time spent exploring this magical landscape.
**HIGHLIGHTS:**
Kolob Arch in Zion National Park, thought to be the world's largest free standing arch at 95 m (310 ft) – see it whilst exploring the amazing Zion National Park Byway.
Hell's Backbone Byway, a dramatic stretch of road near Boulder that travels a ridge with a sheer drop on each side.
Looking straight down into the Grand Canyon from one of the new glass-floored observation platforms – scary!
On the last day – a final stop in the Lake Mead National Recreation Area, just before reaching Las Vegas.
**YOU SHOULD KNOW:**
The famous 1939 John Ford movie *Stagecoach*, starring a young Marion Morrison (John Wayne to you), was shot in Monument Valley.

Viva Las Vegas! But having said that, move on for one of the best sight-seeing road journeys in the USA. This drive of some 1,915 km (1,190 mi) will eventually return you to the world's gambling capital, but not before you've seen some extraordinary natural marvels.

From Las Vegas, drive to St George on Highway 15, then turn off right onto US-89 for Springdale. The attraction here is Zion National Park (overnight in St George or Springfield). Take to the road again – and what a road. You'll be travelling Utah Highway Scenic Byway 12, voted one of the top scenic drives in America for good reason. It winds through National Parks, State Parks and endless scenic vistas encompassing sandstone spikes, petrified forest, high desert and snow-capped mountains.

First stop is Bryce Canyon National Park, with colourful rock formations known as 'hoodoos' (overnight in Bryce). Then take the long and winding road to Capitol Reef National Park (overnight at Torrey). Another long stint through stunning desert landscape will bring you to Arches National Park with its wealth of extraordinary rock arches (overnight at Moab). A short distance further down the road is the Canyonlands National Park, full of amazing canyons, spires, buttes, arches and rivers (overnight at Monticello).

Go on to Monument Valley Tribal Park, with some of the most famous scenery in America – huge sandstone towers amidst unspoiled wilderness (overnight at Kayenta). Last but not least, it's time for the South Rim of the Grand Canyon, 1,830 m (6,000 ft) deep and up to 20 km (15 mi) wide (stay at Grand Canyon village). It is possible to see the North Rim, but it's a long dead-end detour (overnight at Williams).

After all that excitement, the last day is spent driving back to the bright lights of Las Vegas, and more worldly distractions.

# Grand Teton National Park

Part of the Rocky Mountains, the snow-dusted Teton Range soars without foothills from the level floor of Jackson Hole, a long, narrow valley in Wyoming. This special place is preserved as Grand Teton National Park, named after the highest peak that rises to an impressive 4,200 m (13,775 ft). With over 320 km (200 mi) of roads and trails, the Park offers wonderful hiking and biking opportunities.

Mountain bikers can ride the Park from end to end, starting at Jackson, 8 km (5 mi) outside the south entrance. Stay on the road until it forks, giving a choice – Teton Park Road goes over the Snake River and up beside Cottonwood Creek to Jenny Lake, then on past Jackson Lake to rejoin the eastern route. The latter is more straightforward, following the Snake River all the way to Jackson Lake Lodge at the junction with the western route. Thereafter, the road continues alongside the water through Colter Bay Village, which has an informative Visitor Centre, to Lizard Creek at the head of Jackson Lake and then up (and up!) to Flagg Ranch Village. Shortly thereafter, the scenic journey is complete. Or is it? In fact, that may not be the end of the saga after all – as you exit Grand Teton National Park, you find yourself at the south entrance to the awesome Yellowstone National Park, so the temptation to peddle on may prove irresistible.

Be aware that cycling within Grand Teton is restricted to paved and unpaved roads, so hiking trails and the backcountry are no-go areas. Some roads are narrow and vehicle traffic can be heavy in high season, so caution is the watchword. There is accommodation within the Park (pre-booking advisable) or campgrounds for those who wish to explore Grand Teton thoroughly on two wheels or four.

**HOW:**
By bike
**WHEN TO GO:**
May to October
**TIME IT TAKES:**
At least two days – there are numerous scenic side roads providing great views of the Tetons.
**HIGHLIGHTS:**
American bison grazing the lowlands, survivors of the great slaughter in the 19th century that nearly drove them to extinction – just the more obvious representatives of the Park's abundant animal and bird life.
Menor's Ferry and the Chapel of Transfiguration, a historic district off Teton Park Road north of Moose dating back to 1894 – an old cabin, country store, chapel and ferry across the Snake River.
A side trip to the top of Signal Mountain via Signal Mountain Road – it's what your mountain bike is for!
**YOU SHOULD KNOW:**
If you haven't brought your own, it's possible to rent a bicycle in Moose, just inside the park.

*American bison in the Grand Teton National Park*

# Arkansas Highway 7

**HOW:**
By car
**WHEN TO GO:**
September or October for
sensational fall foliage.
**TIME IT TAKES:**
At least a day.
**HIGHLIGHTS:**
The terrific Arkansas Museum of
Natural Resources at Smackover –
1920s scene of one of the wildest
mineral booms in North American
history as up through the ground
came that bubbling crude.
A side-trip from Camden that takes
you to Poison Spring State Park, site
of the Battle of Poison Spring in the
American Civil War.
The best view in Arkansas, after a
short hike to the top of Pedestal
Rocks in the Ozark National Forest.
**YOU SHOULD KNOW:**
Mountain sections of Highway 7 are
not for faint-hearted drivers – they
have numerous steep gradients and
hairpin turns.

Arkansas bills itself as 'The Natural State' – and when you drive Highway 7, the first state-designated Scenic Byway, it's easy to see why. This 465-km (290-mi) journey shows you many different faces of Arkansas, starting just north of the Louisiana state line on the West Gulf Coastal Plain, where an oil boom began near El Dorado in 1921. From there, the road continues to Camden and Arkadelphia through rolling country of river valleys and dense forest.

Highway 7 then enters the Ouachita Mountains, famed for producing amazing quartz crystals, and passes De Grey Lake en route to Hot Springs National Park. The road continues through Ouachita National Forest, past Lake Nimrod and enters the level terrain of the Arkansas River Valley at Russellville. But not for long – it soon climbs into the Ozark Mountains, swinging through the Ozark National Forest, the town of Jasper and on to Harrison, the end of the line.

The journey can be done in a day if scenery is your thing, but Highway 7 deserves a more relaxed approach, with many worthwhile attractions (and distractions) to be found along the way. It's almost impossible not to linger in Hot Springs – the top tourist destination in Arkansas with numerous tempting excuses to pause... not least the USA's oldest National Park, pre-dating the much-touted Yellowstone by 40 years (plunging into therapeutic hot springs mandatory!). Lake Ouachita in the State Park of the same name is delightful, as is the Lake Dardanelle State Park near Russellville. Pedestal Rocks and the Great Arch at Alum Cove will encourage you to linger in the Ozark National Forest. Further north, the Buffalo River is one of the few remaining unpolluted and free-flowing rivers in the USA, as it cuts its way through the Ozarks between massive bluffs.

*Whitaker Point, Ozark National Forest, Arkansas*

# North Cascades Scenic Highway

Its formal name is Washington State Route 20, but the popular North Cascades Highway sounds more romantic. SR-20 runs across Washington State from Puget Sound in the west to Idaho in the east, crossing the Cascade Mountains on the way. This provides a long trip for anyone who wants to drive the whole road, a distance of some 700 km (435 mi), so most prefer to focus on the Scenic Highway, a 225-km (130-mi) section that has some of the most dramatic scenery in the northwestern USA – a trip that would not have been possible before 1972, when this spectacular road was finally completed after decades of argument and much expenditure.

The North Cascades Scenic Highway begins at Sedro-Woolley on SR-20 and enters the rugged North Cascade Range through the Skagit Wild and Scenic River Corridor, following the Skagit through Hamilton, Concrete (true!), Rockport and Marblemount, which has the last gas station before journey's end. The road then enters North Cascades National Park and a good stopping point before the demanding challenge that lies ahead is Newhalem, where the Park's Visitor Center provides information on the vast wilderness bisected by the Scenic Highway. The road continues through the National Park, passing dams that create Diablo and Ross Lakes, providers of hydroelectric power for energy-hungry Seattle.

The Scenic Highway then enters its most demanding stretch, climbing into the mountains towards two incredible high points – Rainy Pass and Washington Pass, each with scenic outlooks that take the breath away. From there, it's downhill all the way as the Highway completes the mountain traverse by winding down through Mazama to Winthrop, a 19th-century staging post for gold miners who flooded into the Slate Creek area. The town has retained much of its original American Old West character and charm.

**HOW:**
By car
**DEPART:**
Sedro-Woolley, WA
**WHEN TO GO:**
May to mid-November
**TIME IT TAKES:**
Five hours with irresistible stops
**HIGHLIGHTS:**
Gorge Creek Falls pull-off outside Newhalem, for an easy loop trail offering great views of the Gorge Dam. Diablo Lake Overlook for restrooms, an interesting geology exhibit and a wide-ranging view across the Cascades. Rainy Pass Picnic Area – take lunch and stop here, before taking a post-prandial stroll along an easy loop trail. Stopping off at the summit of Washington Pass, the journey's literal highlight at 1,699 m (5,477 ft) – admire jutting Liberty Bell and Early Winter Spires (amongst others).
**YOU SHOULD KNOW:**
The Highway is closed between Diablo and Mazama in winter, with a huge depth of snow accumulating on the road. It takes four to six weeks to clear ahead of reopening each spring.

*Liberty Bell Mountain*

# Rim of the World Drive

*Big Bear Lake, California*

Up, up and away...into the Californian mountains to experience the 172-km (107-mi) Rim of the World Drive. This National Scenic Byway runs along the crest of the San Bernadino Mountains, passing through magnificent scenery as it connects some of the most popular recreational destinations in the Greater Los Angeles area – Crestline, Lake Arrowhead, Running Springs and Big Bear Lake.

Despite serving these and other well-developed areas, now heavily populated by commuters, the Scenic Byway still manages to twist and turn through some of the last unspoiled country left in Southern California, offering great panoramas at almost every turn. It begins at the Mormon Rock Fire Station just west of Interstate-15 north of San Bernadino, then heads east on California State Road 138 towards the San Bernadino National Forest. At Cajon Pass, several historic routes intersect (the Old Spanish Trail, Santa Fe Trail, Santa Fe Railroad and John Brown's Toll Road). From there, the road goes through Horsethief Canyon, which tells its own tale, and climbs to Crestline.

Now you're up, it's time for the away part – SR-138 becomes SR-18 to carry the Scenic Byway along the rim, with great vistas across San Bernadino and the Los Angeles Basin. There are numerous stopping points and tempting side routes to explore. These lead to mountain communities such as Blue Jay, Twin Peaks, Arrowhead Lake, Skyforest and Running Springs. The next major destination is Big Bear Lake, where SR-18 and SR-38 merge. The Scenic Byway takes the North Shore route – necessitating a diversion along the South Shore to visit Big Bear Lake village. SR-38 then loops back on itself through delightful mountain communities to the Mill Creek Ranger Station at the Byway's end, just short of Redlands, back on the edge of the San Bernadino conurbation.

# San Diego Scenic Drive

This beautiful city in Southern California is just across the border from Tijuana, holiday destination of many-a-million Americans. But as they hurry across the border they are missing something, because San Diego is a major destination in its own right. To make full appreciation of this laid-back place easy for visitors, the 95-km (59-mi) San Diego Scenic Drive guides them around the city. It is clearly marked with blue-and-yellow signs, illustrated with a bold white seagull.

A good starting point is on Harbor Drive at the foot of Broadway, on the Embarcadero (waterfront). Follow the signs carefully and no important sights or outstanding attractions will be missed. Amongst too many to list individually, high points along the way include Harbor Island (wonderful views of San Diego Bay), Spanish Landing, Point Loma (historic lighthouse), Cabrillo National Monument (commemorates the first European visitor, Portuguese explorer Juan Rodriguez Cabrillo, in 1542), Sunset Cliffs, Ocean Beach, Mission Bay Aquatic Park (endless beaches), Soledad Mountain Park (best view in town), the University of California and Salk Institute, La Jolla Cove and Cave, Pacific Beach, Mission Beach, Sports Arena, Old Town State Historic Park (former Hispanic town centre), Hillcrest, Balboa Park (museum and cultural focus), the financial district, Seaport Village (a trendy shopping complex) and back to the starting point.

That's not quite it – the route continues on to the historic heart of San Diego, the Gaslamp Quarter – once the home of opium dens, gambling halls and saloons, now a vibrant entertainment district. If you're not sidetracked there, continue to the end of the San Diego Scenic Drive in the ultra-modern Horton Plaza, where you can spend the rest of the day shopping and dining...a fitting end to a rewarding day spent exploring this beguiling Californian city.

**HOW:**
By car
**WHEN TO GO:**
Any time
**TIME IT TAKES:**
A relaxed stop-and-go day
**HIGHLIGHTS:**
One of the world's best collections of historic ships at the Maritime Museum of San Diego, and the nearby aircraft carrier USS *Midway*, now a floating museum.
The SeaWorld Adventure Park – everything from performing orcas and sealions to a variety of thrill rides.
Balboa Park, largest urban cultural park in North America, complete with Spanish revival buildings dating from the Expositions of 1915 and 1935 – find 15 museums, the Old Globe Theatre complex and lush gardens. Also in Balboa Park – the world-famous San Diego Zoo and Wild Animal Park.
**YOU SHOULD KNOW:**
Be prepared to say 'Hello sailor' – San Diego is the traditional home base of the US Navy's mighty Pacific Fleet.

*The Plaza de Panama fountain in Balboa Park*

# Beartooth Highway

*Index Peak reflected in Mud Lake.*

It initially seems incongruous that so many scenic journeys in the USA are routinely described as 'the most beautiful drive in America' – or perhaps equally strange that several dozen are rated as 'one of America's Top 10 scenic drives'. But then the realization sinks in that there is so much wondrous natural beauty in this vast and varied country that it really is hard to choose the best. That said, few would disagree that the Beartooth Highway in Montana and Wyoming comes very close to the top of any list.

It is a section of US Highway 212 between Red Lodge, Montana and Cooke City, Montana – a journey of just 111 km (69 mi), but what a journey. It ascends to the Beartooth Plateau, zigzagging and switchbacking as it crosses the Montana-Wyoming state line, just north of Yellowstone National Park, climbing above the tree line to offer expansive views. To the south – canyons eroded by the Clarks Fork River over millennia. To the north – the Absaroka-Beartooth Wilderness, complete with the sharply etched spike known as Bear's Tooth that gave these massive mountains their name. Then the Highway climbs to the summit of mighty 3,345-m (10,974-ft) Beartooth Pass.

From there, it's a downhill run into lake country. There are over a thousand in the wilderness with Long, Little Bear, Island and Beartooth Lakes alongside the Highway. After passing a turnoff for Wyoming Highway 296 (the Chief Joseph Scenic Highway – take it for a full-day loop drive back to Red Lodge) the Beartooth Highway runs down into the old gold-mining town of Cooke City. This is the northeastern gateway to Yellowstone, and there will be time a-plenty to take a peek...if you're not already suffering from an overdose of memorable scenery.

# Peter Norbeck Scenic Byway

'Take me back to the Black Hills, the Black Hills of Dakota', croons the seductive song. It's certainly a trip worth making and one way of getting the most from a visit is to follow the Peter Norbeck Scenic Byway, named after the early-1900s South Dakota Governor and conservation-minded Senator. This 110-km (68-mi) route loops through the Black Hills National Forest and Custer State Park in southwestern Dakota, an area rather different from the state's classic rolling prairies.

Start at the town of Custer, named after the late, not-so-great General who camped here in 1874 on his first, not-so-fatal expedition to the Black Hills. Head north on Highway 89, to a section called the Needles Highway where the road winds around hillsides and through tunnels, all the while passing the spectacular granite spires that give the road its name. Turning north on Highway 87 takes you past Peter Norbeck Wildlife preserve, onto the aptly named Iron Mountain Road, famous for one-lane tunnels aligned with Mount Rushmore.

From there, take US-16A along to that iconic American monument – Mount Rushmore, where the faces of four great Presidents were carved into the mountain's solid granite by sculptor Gutzon Borglum and his crew between 1927 and 1941. After admiring Washington, Jefferson, Roosevelt and Lincoln, head on (pun intended) past towering Harney Peak on Highway 244 to the edge of the Black Hills National Forest, where Highway 87 and then Highway 89 will return you to the starting point at Custer. Along the way you will have seen the American West at its best – soaring mountains, rugged rock formations, caves, forests, grasslands, canyons, gulches, rushing rivers and lakes, all made accessible to the motor car by amazing roads built with ingenuity and engineering skills of the highest order.

*A model of Sioux Indian Chief Crazy Horse stands in front of Thunderhead Mountain.*

**HOW:**
By car
**DEPART:**
Custer, SD
**WHEN TO GO:**
May to October
**TIME IT TAKES:**
A day, allowing for sightseeing stops.
**HIGHLIGHTS:**
Pigtail bridges on Iron Mountain Road – you'll know why they're called that when you get to the first one.
The Sculptor's Studio at the foot of Mount Rushmore, providing fascinating insight into the creation of this great 20th-century work.
If you're impressed by Mount Rushmore check out nearby Crazy Horse Monument, an ongoing project to create a massive likeness of the mounted chief in solid granite, which will be the world's largest sculpture – alongside the Indian Museum of North America and Native American Cultural Center.
Wind Cave National Park, near Custer
**YOU SHOULD KNOW:**
If the famous Mount Rushmore Presidential heads had bodies, they would stand tall – 150 m (475 ft) tall.

# Old Spanish Trail

This trade route from Santa Fe to Los Angeles was explored by European pioneers in the 1770s and saw extensive use in the second quarter of the 19th century. It is about 2,000 km (1,200 mi) long, though there were several choices for travellers using the loose network of Indian footpaths crossing the Colorado Plateau and Mojave Desert. In its heyday the Trail was renowned for all the less endearing characteristics of the Wild West – rip-roaring frontier towns, naked commercial opportunism, banditry, horse stealing and raids – as mainly Mexican pack trains went from Sante Fe to Los Angeles to trade slaves and woollen goods for horses and mules raised on Californian ranches.

The demanding journey encompassed six modern states – New Mexico, Colorado, Utah, Arizona, Nevada and California, running through high mountains, deserts and canyon country. Today, few traces of the original Trail remain, though it is remembered by many historical markers, road and street names. The only way to retrace its course is by car. The Old Spanish National Historic Trail offers dramatic landscapes and a rich legacy of pioneering spirit, western adventure and American history, and you can plot your own journey or get a special map that does it for you.

Beginning in the plaza at Santa Fe, the Trail's main route follows the Rio Grande Valley, then veers north, crosses the Continental Divide and reaches the San Juan River in Colorado. It continues across Colorado, passes near Mesa Verde and enters Utah east of Monticello. From there it continues past Canyonlands and Arches National Parks before crossing the Colorado and Green Rivers, then cuts across the Great Basin to Mountain Meadows. It crosses the corner of Arizona, reaches Las Vegas and continues across the Mojave Desert to Los Angeles via Cajon Pass.

*The San Juan River winds its way through the Comb Ridge area in Utah.*

# Sante Fe Trail

Santa Fe was pivotal in the development of the American Southwest. This charming adobe city featured on the El Camino Real Trail up from Mexico and was both the starting point of the Old Spanish Trail to California and end-point of the Santa Fe Trail from Missouri through the modern states of Kansas, Oklahoma and New Mexico. The latter was a vital trade route from its inauguration in 1821 to 1880, when the railway's arrival at Santa Fe made it obsolete. Depending on the route, the Trail was around 1,255 km (780 mi) long.

The original Trail took a northern path. This was the Mountain branch, intersecting the historic California and Oregon Trails at Independence, Missouri. Thereafter it reached the Arkansas River at Great Bend and went upstream to Dodge City, Garden City and La Junta, from whence it swung down through the Raton Pass to Watrous and on to Santa Fe via Las Vegas (no gambling then at this one-horse town!), San José and Pecos. The southern route – the Cimarron Cutoff – was shorter but more dangerous, with little water. It went through the Cimarron River Valley to Boise City, Oklahoma and Clayton, New Mexico, before rejoining the northern route at Watrous.

There were many variations, especially of the Mountain Route, but those who wish to follow the Santa Fe National Historic Trail from beginning to end can do so on modern highways that duplicate the general course of both routes, though some sections are inaccessible. The Historic Trail is administered and promoted by the US National Park Service, who offer specialist maps and a wealth of useful information. Those who follow the Trail today (in vehicular comfort!) can only marvel at the courage and determination of those who travelled only on foot, horseback or by wagon.

**HOW:**
By car
**WHEN TO GO:**
Any season
**TIME IT TAKES:**
Five days, allowing some time for exploration.
**HIGHLIGHTS:**
Arrow Rock – a prominent bluff on west bank of the Missouri River, a major landmark, river crossing and staging post on the Trail.
A National Historic Landmark – the longest clearly visible section of the Trail near once-deadly Dodge City, Kansas.
Spotting wagon ruts – the Trail was so well used over time that deep wagon ruts are still visible at many points along both routes, and may be found by looking for historical markers along the Scenic Byways.
The Fort Union National Monument north of Watrous, New Mexico – a preserved fort and remains of another where the two branches of the Santa Fe Trail reunited.
**YOU SHOULD KNOW:**
At its peak, the Santa Fe Trail carried over 5,000 wagons a year, mostly overloaded with manufactured goods to be traded or sold at Santa Fe and points west.

*Remains of the Santa Fe trail's Mountain branch in western Kansas*

*A paddle steamer is docked below a suspension bridge.*

# Mississippi Riverboat Cruise

**HOW:**
By boat
**WHEN TO GO:**
Cruises are available all year round.
**TIME IT TAKES:**
Most cruises are seven nights, but there are shorter and longer options to be found.
**HIGHLIGHTS:**
Hearing (or even playing!) a calliope – these steam-powered organs were, and still are, very much a part of the riverboat scene.
Small-town America at its best (plus 29 locks) on an Upper Mississippi cruise from St Paul down to St Louis (seven nights).
All the charm and elegance of the old Deep South on a Lower Mississippi cruise from New Orleans to Memphis (seven nights).
**YOU SHOULD KNOW:**
Louis Armstrong sure knew what he was talking about when he sang the classic song 'Ol' Man River – he travelled up the river from New Orleans by paddle steamer, stopping at various towns along the way to play.

An enduring image of 19th-century America is the riverboat – a sternwheeler belching wood smoke from tall twin stacks as she dashed up and down the Mississippi, Ohio or Missouri Rivers. There was probably a high-stakes poker game going on within the fancy white superstructure, ending in gunplay when five aces came down in the same hand, whilst Mark Twain watched from the bank, pen in hand. Well, maybe it wasn't quite like that, but these stylish craft certainly played a vital role in developing the central-southern and mid-western USA.

Americans are good at marrying tradition with commerce, so it's still possible to experience the delights of this traditional river transport by taking a paddlesteamer trip. The modestly named Majestic America Line runs a variety of cruises using a couple of late 20th-century steamboats – *American Queen* (the largest river steamboat ever built) and the *Mississippi Queen*. Each is the ultimate in old-fashioned comfort and style, though *American Queen* is something of an impostor – she looks the part and has a sternwheel driven by steam, but her main source of propulsion is diesel-powered propellers. The company's *Delta Queen*, built in 1927, is a National Historic Landmark, but sadly her cruising future is on hold as a result of modern safety regulations.

These steamboats offer both a selection of 'see the river' cruises and theme cruises including the popular Jazz and Civil War itineraries. A cruise won't be cheap, but really is an opportunity to experience the elegant atmosphere and travelling style of a bygone era. Oh, the romance of paddle steamers is infectious. If you don't fancy the Mississippi, sternwheelers are now working Alaska's Inside Passage and the great rivers of the northwestern USA (Columbia, Willamette and Snake) for the first time in a century.

# Death Valley

Here's one for the tough and super fit – a cycle trip through notorious Death Valley in California and Nevada. It's the lowest place in America at 86 m (282 ft) below sea level, and also one of the hottest on earth with temperatures regularly reaching 54°C (130°F) in the day (but sometimes freezing at night). That makes it the ultimate cycling challenge.

Death Valley National Park is a unique environment, offering a wonderfully atmospheric landscape of sand dunes, salt flats, multicoloured rocks, canyons, snow-capped mountains and seemingly endless wilderness. The Park has a number of roads, mostly narrow and twisting, and not even the most dedicated mountain biker can be expected to explore them all.

A good journey follows California Route 190, which crosses the middle of Death Valley (albeit not in a straight line!) from Panamint Springs in the southwestern corner of the Park. From there it's a 29-km (18-mi) run to Emigrant, then another 13 km (8 mi) to Stovepipe Wells Village, which has all the facilities required for a little R&R. You'll need it – the next leg is the 44-km (28-mi) slog along CA-190, which turns sharply south before reaching the Furnace Creek Visitor Center. If you want to see that low point, detour to Badwater Basin, due south of the Visitor Center. If you can't face that 52-km (34-mi) round trip, continue on CA-190 and make the straight run to the Park exit and on to Death Valley Junction, a 45-km (28-mi) ride.

If that's not enough to test your cycling prowess, you can take the State Line Road to Pahrump, Nevada – or even (if you're feeling lucky) cycle on from there to Las Vegas. Wimps can do Death Valley by air-conditioned car – which does give them the opportunity to explore the Park's many wonders more thoroughly.

**HOW:**
By bike

**WHEN TO GO:**
November to March to avoid the worst heat conditions (and traffic).

**TIME IT TAKES:**
A day, if you don't keep stopping off to admire the sights.

**HIGHLIGHTS:**
A literal highlight – Towne Pass, a 1,510-m (4,955-ft) summit that greets you just inside the Park.
Mosaic Canyon near Stovepipe Wells – take the dirt road for sweeping views and extraordinary walls of polished multicoloured rock.
Zabriskie Point – no, not the iconic Antonioni movie, but the real thing, to be found shortly after the Furnace Creek Visitor Center – it's an amazing rock formation.
A long, cold shower and good night's sleep at journey's end, wherever that may be.

**YOU SHOULD KNOW:**
Death Valley is the low point, but the high point in the lower 48 states – Mount Whitney – is just 123 km (76 mi) west of Death Valley. After cycling the Valley, why not go on to climb the mountain?

*Rock formations at Zabriskie Point*

# Sea Islands

**HOW:**
By car
**DEPART:**
Jacksonville, FL
**WHEN TO GO:**
Any time of year
**TIME IT TAKES:**
Two days to explore properly as you go.
**HIGHLIGHTS:**
One of the main attractions in northeastern Florida – the Jacksonville Landing complex on the north bank of the St Johns River, with wonderful shopping facilities and a rolling programme of entertainment.
Savannah's captivating downtown area – one of the largest National Historic Districts in the USA.
A side-trip to Georgia's famed Golden Isles – Jekyll Island, St Simons Island, Sea Island and Little St Simons Island (they're well-signed off US-17 in the Brunswick area).
Rainbow Row in Charleston – historic merchants' waterfront houses now painted in a variety of pastel colours.
**YOU SHOULD KNOW:**
During the Civil War white residents fled the Sea Islands, leaving slaves to organize their own lives and effectively become the first in the Deep South to be emancipated.

*Houses on Rainbow Row in Charleston*

This chain of barrier islands runs down the USA's Atlantic Coast off South Carolina, Georgia and Florida. The Sea Islands are captivating and with over 100 to choose from it's possible to plan a journey with ample opportunity to explore this delightful coast. One excellent route is from Jacksonville in Florida to Charleston in South Carolina, allowing you to find and visit Sea Islands in all three states.

From Jacksonville, take State Route 10 before cutting left through Atlantic Beach and taking the Mayport ferry. Turn right along the coast road over Fort George Inlet, continuing through the Little Talbot and Big Talbot Island State Parks, across Nassau Sound and onto Amelia Island. Stay with the water until the road becomes State Route 200 and doubles back on itself. Follow SR-200 until the intersection with US Highway 17 past Yulee. Known as the Coast Road, this mainly follows the line of Interstate-95, but is a route that allows you to take interesting side-trips all the way to Charleston.

US-17 cuts inland to Woodbine and Spring Bluff before turning coastwards and running north though Brunswick, parallel with the Sea Islands. A number of roads lead down to the water if you want the sea for yourself, as there are no major resorts in this area. The next port of call is Savannah, and the historic Georgia town merits a long stop, with a wonderful waterfront and access to more islands. Take US-16 north out of Savannah – it turns into US-17 and you're back on track. At Hardeeville, take the loop through Beaufort on Port Royal Island, perhaps going on to Hunting Island State Park before returning on US-21 via Beaufort, following the road past the air station until it rejoins US-17. From there it's a straight run into the elegant southern city of Charleston.

# The Arizona Trail

Ambitious mountain biker? Be one of the first to cycle the newly signed Arizona Trail, designed to provide a physical challenge even as it showcases the widest possible variety of terrain and ecosystems (including lung-busting mountains!), together with Arizona's cultural and historic diversity. The idea is to keep things simple (primitive, even, though there are campgrounds) so this is a rough, tough adventure that will take you through some of the most rugged and spectacular scenery in western America. Ready, steady, pedal...

The Trail begins at the Coronado National Memorial near the Mexican border and goes north through the Huachuca, Santa Rita and Rincon Mountains. Before you can draw breath, you'll be in the Santa Catalina Mountains north of Tucson, then the Mazatzals. But there's more climbing in store, into the San Francisco Peaks. At last, there's easier going – the Coconino Plateau all the way to the Grand Canyon, across the Colorado River and the final Kaibab Plateau stretch to the Arizona-Utah border. Job done!

Actually, it's not that simple, which is good news and bad news. The bad news is that the Arizona Trail is still under development, and only some 1,207 km (750 mi) of the proposed 1,287-km (800-mi) route have been completed, so it isn't yet possible to travel from beginning to end. There are short breaks in Saguaro National Park, Boyce Thompson Arboretum State Park, Kaibab National Forest and approaching the Grand Canyon. The good news is that the Arizona Trail incorporates many established trails, so it is possible to pick and choose rewarding sections without doing the whole thing.

One thing's for sure – you won't see much human habitation. Apart from the tiny town of Patagonia shortly after starting, the only other place on the Trail is Flagstaff, and even there you can take a detour.

*Kitt Peak in the Saguaro National Park.*

**HOW:**
By bike
**WHEN TO GO:**
September to June to avoid the hottest months.
**TIME IT TAKES:**
Allow a month for an attempt on the complete Trail.
**HIGHLIGHTS:**
Kentucky Camp in the Santa Ritas – the Forest Service has turned it into a living history exhibit of early 20th-century mining.
Pusch Ridge Wilderness in the Coronado National Forest – terrific mountain views, abundant wildlife, an impressive variety of flora.
Saguaro National Park in the Rincons – established to protect those wonderful tall cacti with arms that feature along with the tumbleweed in any self-respecting Western.
Crossing the Grand Canyon by the South Kaibab Trail, then up the other side on the North Kaibab Trail – the experience of a lifetime!
**YOU SHOULD KNOW:**
The Coronada National Memorial celebrates the first European expedition to southwestern America, by Francisco Vásquez de Coronado in 1540, so the Trail follows in the hoof prints of conquistadors.

# The John Muir Trail

This is a terrific hike for those with strong legs and stronger lungs, running for 340 km (211 mi) along California's Sierra Nevada mountain range from the Happy Isles trailhead in Yosemite Valley to Mount Whitney in the south. And that's the direction to go on the John Muir Trail (JMT), allowing the hiker to become acclimatized to the thin atmosphere before tackling the more remote, demanding southern half. The JMT attracts plenty of day hikers, but the true challenge is backpacking the entire Trail. A permit is required to hike, to be obtained from the National Park or Forest where the journey begins.

Be prepared for some heavy breathing. After the initial climb out of Yosemite Valley, the JMT is mostly over 2,440 m (8,000 ft) in elevation, above and beyond the height most people ever experience for extended periods. And that's not all – the journey crosses six passes (Donohue, Muir, Mather, Pinchot, Glen and Forester). The last – Forester – is the highest at a mighty 4,010 m (13,155 ft). After running through Tuolomne Meadows the JMT parallels the main range of the Sierra Nevada thorough Yosemite National Park, Inyo and Sierra National Forests, Devils Postpile National Monument, Kings Canyon National Park and Sequoia National Park. Along the way it passes through some wild country, including the formally designated John Muir and Ansell Adams Wilderness Areas.

Even after gallantly reaching the end of the JMT by climbing to the summit of Mount Whitney, there's a sting in the tail – a further hike to civilization at the nearest trailhead at Whitney Portal, 18 km (11 mi) farther on. The effort is worthwhile. One of the true wonders of the USA is that – for all the country's sprawling and apparently insatiable urban development – it takes such care of (and pride in) pristine wilderness of the sort preserved along the JMT.

**HOW:**
On foot
**WHEN TO GO:**
July to September
**TIME IT TAKES:**
Allow at least two weeks – three to be sure.
**HIGHLIGHTS:**
Yosemite's most famous sight – the impressive granite Half Dome at the eastern end of Yosemite Valley.
The Devils Postpile near Mammoth Mountain – an extraordinary basalt cliff made up of old lava columns, topped by pine trees and standing above a slope of fallen columns.
Soaking those hard-working feet in soothing hot springs to be found within the John Muir Wilderness section of the Trail.
The breathtaking natural beauty of the Kings Canyon National Park – including Rae Lakes, Marie Lake, Upper Basin, Le Conte Canyon, Evolution Valley and McClure Meadow.
**YOU SHOULD KNOW:**
After hiking the John Muir Trail, you can also boast of hiking the much longer Pacific Coast Trail (well, the section it shares with the JMT!).

*Painted Lady in Kings Canyon National Park*

# Huckleberry Mountain Horse Trail

This glorious scenic journey is in the Ozark National Forest of northwest Arkansas, and for a short distance within adjacent Mount Magazine State Park. Anyone who wishes to tackle the Huckleberry Mountain Horse Trail has a choice of steeds – the good old-fashioned horses for which it was designed, the two well-shod feet of Shanks' Pony or the thoroughly modern lightweight alloy wheels of a mountain bike. That's not all. Sadly for the purists, this Trail is one of four within the National Forest that has been designated for use by those noisy and rather irritating All-Terrain Vehicles (ATVs). Take your pick!

The Trail shows the Ozarks at their best, offering a rugged landscape of shady forests and stunning mountain vistas. It consists of two loops, together offering some 55 km (34 mi) of well-marked scenic horseback riding, if that's the delightfully relaxed way you choose to travel. The terrain is varied – deep, winding valleys and creeks are overlooked by mountain bluffs. There are clear mountain streams and numerous trailside ponds for watering the horses.

The Apple Loop is the easy one – 19 km (12 mi) of old logging roads and existing forest tracks marked with orange signposts or horseshoe blazes on trees. The Huckleberry Mountain Loop is likewise marked, but is definitely more demanding. Some of the sections on the 36-km (22-mi) Horse Trail are quite difficult, and there is a shorter 12-km (9-mi) option within the Mountain Loop, covering easier country for those who do not wish to attempt the full circuit. After rain, some of the creeks and streams can become dangerous and should be crossed with extreme care – especially Shoal Creek. It's not difficult to stray off-route, so a Trail map is a wise investment.

**HOW:**
On foot, a horse, a bike or an ATV
**DEPART:**
St Louis, AR
**WHEN TO GO:**
March to September
**TIME IT TAKES:**
One day
**HIGHLIGHTS:**
The view from the top of Mount Magazine, the highest point in Arkansas – breathtaking.
Brightly coloured butterflies – you'll find an absolute profusion of them from April onwards.
For petrolheads in a hurry – guided three- or five-hour ATV tours of the Huckleberry Mountain Trail.
**YOU SHOULD KNOW:**
Parts of the Mountain Loop are closed in April and May for the turkey breeding season.

*The Ozarks and the Arkansas River Valley from the top of Mount Magazine*

# Tahoe Rim Trail

*Lake Tahoe with the Sierra Mountains in the background*

Stand by for a tall trail – the Tahoe Rim Trail (TRT) that ranges in elevation from a mere 1,900 m (6,240 ft) at the outlet end of Lake Tahoe to an altogether more impressive 3,150 m (10,335 ft) at Relay Peak, though it has been carefully constructed to ensure that the average gradient throughout is no more than 10 per cent. This long-distance hiking and equestrian route circles Lake Tahoe in the Carson and Sierra Nevada mountain ranges of Nevada and California. Mountain biking is allowed along most (but not all) sections of the TRT.

Lake Tahoe is a deep-blue, natural mountain lake, some 35 km (22 mi) long by 19 km (12 mi) wide. It is surrounded by snowcapped mountains, volcanic peaks, granite cliffs, lush forests, jewel-like small lakes, alpine meadows and a rich diversity of flora and fauna. The Tahoe Rim Trail that girdles this natural marvel is 266 km (165 mi) long, going through two states, six counties, one State Park, three National Forests and three Wilderness Areas. It's all demanding terrain that presents a real challenge to the dedicated hiker, who will need to carry all the essentials for survival in a single backpack. The reward for all that physical effort is experiencing the solitude and outstanding natural beauty of one of America's great trails.

The TRT is open to skiers in winter, but is not marked then. A permit is required to enter Desolation Wilderness (the Echo Lake to Barker Pass section of the Trail). There are blue triangular TRT markers at regular intervals, but anyone attempting the entire journey should get a detailed map. Those who don't have the time (or strength) to undertake the entire journey but wish to see something of this magical landscape can access the Trail at many points for a day hike.

# Mason-Dixon Trail

Connecting the Appalachian and Brandywine Trails, the Mason-Dixon Trail (M-DT) is 310 km (193 mi) long and starts in Pennsylvania at Whiskey Springs on the Appalachian Trail. It then goes east to the Susquehanna River, passing through Pinchot State Park along the way. The M-DT continues along the west bank of the Susquehanna south to Havre de Grace in Maryland, crosses the river and continues east through the Elk Neck State Forest into Delaware's Iron Hill Park. From there, the M-DT heads north along the Christina River and White Clay Creek to the White Clay Creek Reserve. It then turns northeast for the last leg to the eastern trailhead at Chadds Ford on the Brandywine River, back in Pennsylvania.

The Trail is well marked by blue blazes, but is no wilderness excursion designed to avoid human habitation. True, it does go through much pleasing open countryside, but in so doing often follows narrow back roads where traffic can be dangerous. It also passes through plenty of small towns and developed areas. That said, it does offer some fine vistas, along with long and scenic stretches of hilly, rolling terrain that is well wooded, plus rocky climbs out of side gorges along the Susquehanna River.

Though essentially designed for hikers, many sections of the M-DT are increasingly being used by mountain bikers. There is an active Trail Association that provides up-to-date maps and is constantly doing maintenance and improvement work on the M-DT, also dealing with the occasional outbreaks of friction between private owners and hikers that can cause the Trail to be slightly re-routed.

**HOW:**
By foot or by bike
**WHEN TO GO:**
April to October (but September tends to be very wet).
**TIME IT TAKES:**
Two weeks
**HIGHLIGHTS:**
Gifford Pinchot State Park – reverting farmlands and wooded hillsides with Pinchot Lake serving as the centrepiece.
Codorus Furnace, located along Codorus Creek – once owned by James Smith, a signatory of the Declaration of Independence, this furnace built in 1765 supplied ammunition to colonists during the American Revolution.
The Holtwood Environmental Preserve on the banks of the lower Susquehanna River, including the Lock 12 Historic Area.
**YOU SHOULD KNOW:**
The M-DT follows in the footsteps of Charles Mason and Jeremiah Dixon, who surveyed the Maryland-Pennsylvania border in 1764, thus establishing the historic dividing line between the USA's North and South.

*Sunrise over Pinchot Lake*

# Wonderland Trail

**HOW:**
On foot
**WHEN TO GO:**
Late July to October (to avoid possible snow coverage).
**TIME IT TAKES:**
Two weeks
**HIGHLIGHTS:**
An original ranger's cabin at Indian Henry's Hunting Ground, dating from the construction of the Wonderland Trail in 1915.
Mowich Lake, a pretty trailhead in the northwestern corner of the National Park that offers basic facilities to the weary hiker.
Longmire Buildings in the Nisqually River Valley – a brief dose of civilization with an inn, museum and Wilderness Information Center.
**YOU SHOULD KNOW:**
Each year, only two to three hundred people manage to complete the entire Wonderland Trail in a single, unbroken hike.

Up and down, up and down – the Wonderland Trail in Washington State is not for the faint-hearted or unfit. This rough-country route shuns roads and human habitation as it journeys around mighty Mount Rainier in the National Park of the same name, arriving back at the starting point after 150 km (93 mi). As to that up-and-down element, the cumulative elevation gain during the circumnavigation is around 6,000 m (20,000 ft), which adds up to a serious physical effort as the Trail crosses ridge after soaring ridge.

But Wonderland it is – the Mount Rainier National Park offers a variety of eco-systems, from lowland forest to sub-alpine meadows, and Mount Rainier itself reveals a series of spectacular glaciers as the journey unfolds. The Trail crosses many rivers, often by simple log bridges, occasionally by more dramatic suspension bridges. Though there are a number of trailheads that will be busy in summer, many stretches of the Trail provide complete solitude amidst natural grandeur. But hikers should be aware that weather conditions can be treacherous, with dangerous storms always a possibility (especially in September). This is definitely not a journey for the inexperienced, but only the hardened wilderness hiker.

There are several campgrounds on the Trail (booking advisable in mid-summer), together with 18 trailside campsites at regular intervals along the way, each with a nearby water source and a bear pole for hanging food safely. A backcountry permit is required to hike the entire Trail, and the challenge is so alluring that early application is advisable (in March), as a ballot is held in April to allocate a limited number of permits, thus ensuring the Wonderland Trail will never be spoiled by over-exploitation.

*Indian Bear shelter, Mount Ranier National Park*

# California Zephyr

No argument – this is one of the world's great train journeys, sheer heaven for the scenically minded. It covers 3,925 km (2,440 mi) from Chicago to the Pacific coast, traversing Illinois, Iowa, Nebraska, Colorado, Utah, Nevada and California. In so doing, it crosses the American Midwest before heading over the Rocky Mountains and Sierra Nevadas to California. This luxury service was inaugurated in 1949 and has gone through various changes since those early days, though things have stabilized since Amtrak initiated the modern Superliner service (choice of roomy coach seats or private sleepers) in 1983.

Heading westwards from Chicago, the California Zephyr (CZ) crosses the Great Plains, that expanse of corn country where once the buffalo roamed. After reaching Denver, the scenery changes dramatically as the train climbs into the amazing Rocky Mountains. It crosses the Continental Divide via the 10-km (6-mi) Moffat Tunnel, and then follows the Colorado River for hours as it turns from white-water channel to wide river. After Grand Junction the CZ parts company with Colorado and enters Utah. There, it travels the Book Cliffs range before entering the Wasatch Mountains on the Rockies' western fringe, crossing at Soldier Summit.

After Salt Lake City the CZ passes along the south shore of the Great Salt Lake, across Bonneville Flats (scene of many a land-speed-record attempt) and into Nevada. It crosses the Pequop Mountains via the Flower Pass Tunnel, before following the Humboldt River across Nevada until it vanishes in the desert. The Truckee River leads to Reno and California's Sierra Nevada, which are finally crested at the forbidding Donner Pass. The CZ descends to the lowlands and runs into Emeryville, a suburb of Oakland, from whence there's a bus transfer for those continuing to San Francisco. Or start at Emeryville and go east, young man!

*Salt Lake City with the snow capped Wasatch Mountains in the background*

**HOW:**
By train
**DEPART:**
Chicago, IL
**WHEN TO GO:**
Any day
**TIME IT TAKES:**
Roughly 51 hours and 20 minutes (give or take!).
**HIGHLIGHTS:**
Plainview above Denver, for a sensational view of the cities of both Denver and Boulder (and the Rocky Flats nuclear arms manufacturing plant!).
Ruby Canyon on the Colorado River, with its towering red sandstone formations – unless you raft in, the only way to see the place is from the Zephyr.
The amazing series of switchback turns the track takes as it descends from Soldier Summit in Utah's Wasatch Mountains.
Cape Horn near Colfax, California – before the CZ crosses a long trestle is Cape Horn, the steepest slope on the entire route (carved out by Chinese labourers lowered in baskets).
**YOU SHOULD KNOW:**
For those who are hooked on the romance of railways, it's possible to revisit the Zephyr's 'golden age' – an evocative collection of classic CZ silver rolling stock plus locomotive at the Western Pacific Railroad Museum in Portola, northeastern California.

# San Francisco Streetcar

Everyone who visits the Bay City should take a journey on one of the famous streetcars, which have a long history. The first streetcars (technically cable cars) capable of handling San Francisco's steep hillsides were introduced in 1873 and were an instant success – to such a degree that several new lines were opened. The boom was short-lived – cheaper electric streetcars arrived and the great earthquake of 1906 damaged many lines. By the 1940s the old streetcars were in terminal decline, as buses were by then capable of handling the acute gradients. Happily, a citizens' revolt saw the retention of three streetcar lines, which remain to this day as a much-loved part of the city's character.

The survivors are the Powell-Mason, Powell-Hide and California Street Lines, now used more by tourists than commuters. A journey on one or more of these splendid old streetcars (preferably hanging onto the outside!) is a mandatory part of the San Francisco experience. Powell-Mason (Line 59) and Powell-Hide (Line 60) serve residential, shopping and tourist districts (Union Square, Chinatown, North Beach, Nob Hill, Aquatic Park and Fisherman's Wharf). They share some track and both use single-ended, partially open cars that have to be rotated on turntables at the end of each run. Line 61 runs entirely on California Street, from a terminus at California and Market Streets, close to the waterfront, steeply through Chinatown up to the summit of Nob Hill, then down to Van Ness Avenue. It uses double-ended cars with open sides and an enclosed middle section.

To maintain the romance, all three lines use cars that are either restored originals or faithful replicas, and the changing views from the moving streetcars are among the best in the city.

**HOW:**
By streetcar
**WHEN TO GO:**
Any time of year
**TIME IT TAKES:**
Get a passport and ride all three lines in a day, hopping on and off to explore this vibrant city as the fancy takes you.
**HIGHLIGHTS:**
The Cable Car Museum beneath the car barn at Washington and Jackson Streets, where you can also look at the main power house and descend to a large basement where the thick haulage cables are routed to the street.
The famously laid-back Fisherman's Wharf area, not far from the Taylor and Bay terminus of Line 59.
Grant Street in Chinatown – a feast for the senses with its colourful shops and crowded sidewalks.
The Maritime National Historical Park with its classic ships, adjacent to Ghirardelli Square.

*The old tram climbs up Telegraph Hill.*

# Mount Washington Cog Railway

In 1858, after climbing Mount Washington ('home of the world's worst weather'), Sylvester Marsh, nicknamed 'Crazy' Marsh, rashly proposed building a railway to the summit, at the dizzy height of 1,917 m (6,288 ft). After the laughing stopped, the New Hampshire State Assembly granted permission for the summit. So guess who had the last laugh? The first loco ran in 1867 and the line was completed in 1869, since which time Sylvester Marsh's quirky creation has carried over five million passengers.

Laid on trestle all the way, this extraordinary engineering feat has a maximum gradient of 37.41 per cent, and custom-built steam engines push carriages up a 4.9-km (3.1-mi) track, belching smoke as they use a ton of coal and a 3,785 litres (1,000 gallons) of water on every journey. Many of the locomotives, each of which has a name, date back to the 19th century (though much rebuilt over the years) and today's passengers enjoy much the same experience as those who were first captivated by the Mount Washington Cog Railway 150 years ago.

The locos look weird on the flat, with forward-tilting boilers that are designed to be level when climbing and descending the mountain. Both engine and coach are pulled up the mountain (and eased back down) by a 19-tooth cog that meshes into the track's central rail. At the same time, reassuring ratchets that prevent backward slippage are engaged on ascents. After a scenic ride that offers majestic mountain vistas, be prepared to avert your eyes as the summit approaches – a trail crosses the tracks, and there's something of a tradition whereby hikers await the train and 'moon'.

In winter there is a limited service (mainly weekends and school holidays) up through the snow to Kroflite Camp at 1,250 m (4,100 ft).

**HOW:**
By train
**DEPART:**
Mount Washington, NH
**WHEN TO GO:**
May to October (limited winter service November-April).
**TIME IT TAKES:**
Three hours for a round trip, including 20 minutes at the summit.
**HIGHLIGHTS:**
Peppersass, named for its likeness to a pepper sauce bottle – the first engine used in the construction of the line from 1867, now on display at the Marshfield Base Station.
Jacob's Ladder, the steepest section of the track – an extraordinary raised trestle that angles round the mountainside.
A wander round the summit, known as 'the city in the clouds', with numerous buildings including the Mount Washington Observatory and Tip Top House (built in 1853) – some days you can see four states, Canada and the Atlantic Ocean, and on other days nothing but swirling cloud!
**YOU SHOULD KNOW:**
The greatest wind speed ever recorded on earth – 372 kph (231 mph) – hammered the summit of Mount Washington in 1934.

*Looks like a train crash, works like a dream.*

# Rio Grande

Big Bend National Park in Texas is like the state itself – larger than life and many countries. This vast area is bounded by the Rio Grande to the south, which forms the border with Mexico, and the Park is a land of extremes – from desert to mountain, majestic rivers to inaccessible wilderness. The variety of plants and wildlife – especially birds – is extraordinary, and the Park's facilities are often stretched during high season (cooler winter months). But there's one way of getting round that problem – taking to the water, to kayak through the Chihuahuan Desert with open views and a dramatic river-scape that includes canyons up to 460 m (1,500 ft) deep.

The Rio Grande runs for 190 km (118 mi) within the Park, and a further 205 km (127 mi) downstream is designated a Wild and Scenic River. There is plenty of calm water, but this is not a journey for beginners as there are periodic encounters with rapids of varying severity, especially when the water is high. Unfortunately, extraction means it often isn't. The preferred option for experienced paddlers is a one- or two-person inflatable kayak, and even then this magnificent river is so remote that most people travel with a guide or organised party. It is possible to use your own equipment or hire locally (though not in the Park). Permits are required for self-organized trips, allowing you to stop off and explore interesting side canyons.

To run the Rio Grande through the Park, start at Lajitas on Texas Highway 170. Be aware that there are few facilities and a limited number of take-outs along the route and plan accordingly. Unless you intend to run the full length of the Wild and Scenic section, you end this unique journey at the Highway 2627 bridge in La Linda. This is a 200-km (125-mi) trip.

**HOW:**
By kayak
**DEPART:**
Lajitas, TX
**WHEN TO GO:**
November to April
**TIME IT TAKES:**
Lajitas to La Linda takes 10-14 days, depending on stops and side-trips.
**HIGHLIGHTS:**
The beautiful journey through popular Santa Elena Canyon – great scenery, serenity...and the excitement of the Rockslide Rapids.
Sunset over Mexico's remote Sierra del Carmen (Carmen Mountains), south of the river.
Marsical Canyon, the most remote in Big Bend National Park – just 16 km (10 mi) long but with varied scenery, towering limestone cliffs, some rapids and ample stop-off points along the canyon bottom.
Rio Grande Village – one of the few places along the river that has all the facilities.
**YOU SHOULD KNOW:**
Always camp on the US bank and carry identity documents – the Border Patrol can show up at any time and needs to know you're not an 'illegal'.

*Sunrise at Santa Elena Canyon, Big Bend National Park, Texas*

# Going-to-the-Sun Road

Named after the mountain of the same name, Going-to-the-Sun Road runs through Glacier National Park in Montana. It was completed in the 1930s after a dozen years of construction, and this ambitious engineering project was one of the first National Park Service projects to be specifically undertaken with automobile-borne tourists in mind.

The massive construction effort was justified – the parkway runs for 85 km (53 mi) through the craggiest of mountain scenery. Strong nerves are required, as the roadway is both narrow and winding, often clinging to the mountainside without guardrails (they have been attempted, but always get swept away by late-winter avalanches). For those who prefer to watch scenery rather than the road, there is a fleet of shuttle buses that allow visitors to explore the route at their leisure, hopping on and off at any one of numerous stops and catching the first bus along when they've finished sightseeing or exploring.

Going-to-the-Sun Road crosses the Continental Divide that separates the watersheds of the Atlantic and Pacific Oceans. The Road's high point is Logan Pass, with a breathless (disembark and try running on the spot if you doubt that) elevation of 2,025 m (6,645 ft). There is a visitor centre near the Pass that has tremendous views, and there are short hiking trails that give access to an abundance of alpine flowers in summer. This is one of the hardest roads in the US National Park system to clear ahead of reopening – snow can be more than 25 m (80 ft) deep at the top of Logan Pass (even deeper on the east side) and the job takes ten weeks. So there's actually quite a short timeframe when this wonderful drive can be undertaken.

**HOW:**
By car or bus
**WHEN TO GO:**
Early June to mid-September
**TIME IT TAKES:**
Two hours without stops
**HIGHLIGHTS:**
St Mary Lake – so scenic that it has featured in at least two major movies – *Forrest Gump* and *The Shining*.
Wildlife – look out for mountain goats, bears and lots more.
Glacier watching – there is a superb view of Jackson Glacier from the purpose-built overlook to the east side of Logan Pass.
Bird Woman Falls, a snowmelt waterfall that plunges 150 m (490 ft) down the mountainside, nicely framed from the parkway by the V-shaped Mount Oberlin.
**YOU SHOULD KNOW:**
The park (and its stopping areas) can get crowded in peak season.

*St Mary Lake, with the cottonwood trees still showing their golden fall colour.*

# Seward Highway

Go north to go south for glory! That's the message to those determined enough to make the journey down from Anchorage to Seward in south central Alaska, the chilly 49th state. The sometimes-moody Seward Highway was completed in 1951 and is 204 km (127 mi) long, though it follows a route used by Russian fur traders in the 1700s and native peoples for thousands of years before that.

*A bull moose swims low in the water to avoid the moose flies that surround his head.*

**HOW:**
By car
**WHEN TO GO:**
Any time of year
**TIME IT TAKES:**
Five hours non-stop, two days to explore properly along the way.
**HIGHLIGHTS:**
A short but interesting side trip from Canyon Creek Bridge to the historic mining town of Hope.
The Tern Lake Overlook near Moose Pass for sensational panoramic views of the unique Alaskan landscape.
Great wildlife viewing along the way – look out for whales, bears, moose, Dall sheep, a variety of birds and salmon galore in season.
At journey's end, the entertaining Alaska Sealife Center in Seward.
**YOU SHOULD KNOW:**
Beware quicksands! The mudflats and beaches along the coast from Anchorage to Portage can be dangerous and should be approached with extreme caution.

This incredible road runs along the Turnagain Arm and across the Kenai Peninsula, whose collective scenic glories have earned a coveted triple classification: All-American-Road, US Forest Service Scenic Byway and Alaska Scenic Byway.

From Anchorage, driving that tough hire car down Alaska Route 1 beside the reflective waters of Turnagain Arm, the first stops are Girdwood and Alyeska Resort, Portage Glacier and Whittier. Next comes the challenging Turnagain Pass followed by the Chugach National Forest, then a climb and descent past Upper and Lower Summit Lakes. At Tern Lake Junction, Alaska 1 heads off through the Kenai Peninsula and the Seward Highway becomes Alaska Route 9. After that it's a shortish run through Moose Pass and Bear Creek into Seward on the shores of Resurrection Bay.

The natural beauty of the Seward Highway is unlike any other to be found in the USA – stunning fjords and crystal-clear lakes, glaciers and waterfalls, ridges and valleys, alpine meadows and a profusion of wild flowers in season. The area has become a magnet for adventurous tourists who, drawn by a plethora of outdoor recreational options, arrive all year round. Salmon season is May to mid-October and (ironically) the Seward Highway stays open all winter where many Scenic Byways in states farther south do not. That said, occasional avalanches do briefly close the road in winter, but the sweepers soon open it up again.

# El Camino Real Historic Trail

For decades before the Mayflower arrived in North America, El Camino Real de Tierra Adentro (Royal Road of the Interior) brought Europeans up from Mexico to Santa Fe in 'New Spain' (now New Mexico). The significance of this migration route has been recognized by classification of the 650-km (404-mi) US section (from El Paso, Texas to San Juan Pueblo, New Mexico) as a National Historic Trail. This status is relatively new, as are efforts to promote the Trail – so travelling it requires some ingenuity.

The Trail runs along today's Interstate-25 corridor, with the modern highway following much of the old route. Before they arrived at what is now the Mexico-US border, settlers had endured a three-month voyage from Spain, a trek across the rugged Sierra Madre Mountains to Mexico City then a gruelling 1,770-km (1,100-mi) wagon journey to the Rio Grande. The last leg through dangerously inhospitable country was still to come, a reality that discourages modern attempts to hike the Trail.

However, it is possible to plan a self-guided car journey that follows the Trail and sees some remaining sites. First visit the new El Camino Real International Heritage Center, midway between Socorro and Truth or Consequences on I-25 (Exit 115). It overlooks the Trail where it crosses the fearsome Jornado del Muerto (Journey of the Dead Man) desert basin, a reminder of the hazards facing early travellers. The Center contains a wealth of Trail information, plus artefacts, and offers helpful suggestions for exploring the Trail. One recommended journey (described in great detail on a three-CD audio guide available from the Heritage Center) involves journeying between the historic plazas of the main towns along the Trail – Santa Fe, Albuquerque, Socorro, Las Cruces and El Paso, stopping off to look at Trail heritage along the way.

**HOW:**
By car
**WHEN TO GO:**
Any time of year
**TIME IT TAKES:**
Five days for the recommended journey, including exploration time.
**HIGHLIGHTS:**
The Museum of New Mexico's Palace of the Governors in Santa Fe – dating from the early 17th century, now the state's history museum.
San Miguel Mission, also in Santa Fe – oldest church in the USA, built at the last major stopover on the Trail in the early 17th century.
Fort Selden near Las Cruces, a mid-19th-century army post designed to protect travellers and towns along the Trail as it became a major trade route.
The historic district in the heart of Socorro, around a plaza that still holds the essence of the Trail.
**YOU SHOULD KNOW:**
The Trail finally fell into disuse when the railroad reached New Mexico in 1880.

*The San Juan Miguel Mission, Socorro, New Mexico*

# The Pan-American Highway

*San Francisco Church, Quito*

The world's longest drivable road is the Pan-American Highway, a system with a total length of some 48,000 km (30,000 mi). It passes through Canada, the USA, Mexico, Guatemala, El Salvador, Honduras, Nicaragua, Costa Rica, Panama, Colombia, Ecuador, Peru, Chile and Argentina. With various branches the whole system adds up to a vast and rambling network.

The intrepid traveller must drive from Prudhoe Bay in Alaska down to the Panama Canal. Although the Pan-American Highway has no official status in the USA and Canada, the accepted route follows the Alaska Highway. After reaching Canada, the road splits at Edmonton, one route going via the Great Lakes, Minneapolis and Dallas, the other taking in Calgary, Denver and Albuquerque. The two meet at San Antonio in Texas, before reaching the 'official' Pan-American Highway at the Mexican border south of Monterrey. Thereafter it runs through Central America via Mexico City and San Salvador to Panama City. There the road stops, briefly broken by the Darién Gap, a 90-km (55-mi) stretch of rain forest that may be crossed on foot, by bicycle, motorbike or ATV by reckless adventurers willing to brave bandits, swamps and jungle.

Thereafter, the Highway resumes its often spectacular and sometimes dangerous journey, as the road follows the Pacific coast down through Cali, Quito, Antofagasta and Valparaiso, before cutting across to the Atlantic at Buenos Aires. That marks the official end of the Highway, but there are two unofficial branches – one continuing down the west coast from Valparaiso to Quellon, the other from Buenos Aires to Ushuaia at the tip of South America. This latter route is, of course, mandatory for anyone who wishes to be one of the few individuals on the planet to have travelled America from top to toe.

*Right: The Beagle Channel in Tierra del Fuego.*

# The Copper Canyon

Anyone who has marvelled at the Grand Canyon has an even bigger treat in store south of the Mexican border. The awesome Copper Canyon complex in the Sierra Tarahumara consists of six linked canyons, collectively four times larger (and deeper) than their not-insignificant northern neighbour. The Parque Nacional Barranca del Cobre (Copper Canyon National Park) has been established to protect this remote but beautiful area in southwestern Chihuahua State, home to ultra-traditional Tarahumara Indians.

*The Copper Canyon complex consists of six linked canyons.*

**HOW:**
By train
**DEPART:**
Chihuahua
**WHEN TO GO:**
Best months: October to December, March and April.
**TIME IT TAKES:**
About 16 hours (one way).
**HIGHLIGHTS:**
Chihuahua itself – a splendid historic city full of colonial treasures and monumental structures.
The view from Divisadero, where the train obligingly stops for 20 minutes, so passengers can enjoy the sensational vista of three canyons (Tararecua, Urique and del Cobre).
**YOU SHOULD KNOW:**
If you should come across one of the frequent Tarahumara Indian celebrations, respect their privacy – they are shy, proud people and it is polite to ask permission before taking photographs.

Happily, you don't have to hike this rugged country to experience Copper Canyon's incredible scenery, because you just have to catch a train and much (though not all) will be revealed. El Chepe, as the Chihuahua al Pacifico train is known, runs from the city of Chihuahua to Los Mochis near the Sea of Cortez, a distance of some 650 km (400 mi), traversing the principal canyon of Urique (North America's deepest). The line, completed in 1961, is a magnificent engineering feat, with 37 bridges and 86 tunnels. The quality of the scenery along the route is pretty good too – recognized by El Chepe's classification as 'one of the top ten most spectacular train trips in the world' in 2005. This accolade is justified – the extraordinary diversity of this unique landscape ranges from snow-capped mountains to tropical forests in canyon bottoms.

There are four departures daily – two from each direction, one luxury and one standard – as the line is extensively used both by tourists and locals. But if you don't wish to take the full train journey, it is possible to stop off along the way to hike in and see attractions such Candameñta Canyon's Piedra Volanda Falls (Mexico's highest) and the huge stone monolith known as Peña del Gigante. Guided tours are available to more remote destinations that El Chepe doesn't reach.

# Rio Sonora

To follow the Rio Sonora is to journey through Mexican history, experiencing both the harsh natural beauty surrounding this life-giving river and the traditional towns that have grown along its banks since the Jesuits first arrived in the 17th century. Rough terrain and an uncertain water supply have combined to ensure that the river communities retain their rural roots, so this really is a step back in time.

The river – and journey – starts just across from Arizona at Cananea. Highway 118 loosely follows the river all the way down to Mazocahui, where a right turn onto Highway 14 completes the route to Hermosillo for a total distance of some 320 km (200 mi). It's worth exploring along the way, as this is a journey that can offer fascinating insight into Old Mexico, framed by the sweeping vistas of typically arid Sierra Madre scenery.

Sonora is a mining town that's just a century old – and the massive copper mine west of the city is the largest in Mexico. The road next passes through a couple of ranching centres founded around 1650 – Bacoachi and Arizpe – before reaching Banamichi, settled by Jesuits in 1639. The town's Hidalgo Plaza contains the Piedra Historica, an ancient petroglyph thought to be an irrigation map. At Huépac, look inside San Lorenzo, a 17th-century church with a fine interior. The next port of call is Aconchi, where the Agua Caliente Water Park has hot springs said to possess curative powers. Bavicora has a wonderful tree-lined plaza overlooked by the impressive Nuestra Señora de la Concepción Cathedral. Ures was once the state capital of Sonora, and the town's historic roots are very evident in the Plaza Zaragoza and San Miguel Cathedral. Mazocahui is the last sleepy pueblo before you reach the bustling provincial capital of Hermosillo, one of the largest towns in northern Mexico.

**HOW:**
By car
**DEPART:**
Cananea
**WHEN TO GO:**
March-November
**TIME IT TAKES:**
A day or three, depending whether or not you set a sensible Mexican pace.
**HIGHLIGHTS:**
The magnificent 17th-century Nuestra Señora de la Asunción Church in Arizpe, amid period buildings and a fine plaza.
Delightful riverside walks in Bavicora, shaded by sweeping oak, aspen and walnut trees.
Near Bacoachi – the Sierra de los Ajos ecological park, for a close-up encounter with Rio Sonora's flora and fauna.
La Plaza de Armas in Ures, with four wonderful bronze statues.
**YOU SHOULD KNOW:**
If you visit in October and November there will be numerous bullfights and local celebrations accompanying the cane milling, peanut and chilli harvests.

*Cacti in the Sonoran Desert*

# Yucatán

**HOW:**
By car
**DEPART:**
Villahermosa
**WHEN TO GO:**
December to May (avoiding hurricane season).
**TIME IT TAKES:**
The journey can be done in a day, but far better to take a couple and see the sights.
**HIGHLIGHTS:**
A stopover in Ciudad del Carmen, the 'Pearl of the Gulf' – try the seafood for which the town is renowned.
Mérida's central Plaza, with America's oldest Cathedral (1556-1599), Palacio Municipal (1735) and Casa de Montejo (1542), former home of the founding conquistador.
An outing to the evocative Mayan ruins at Chichen-Itza and the nearby Caves of Balankanche.
Progresso – Mérida's busy port, 30 km (18 mi) to the north, for amazing salt flats and extraordinary flocks of flamingoes.

The Yucatán Peninsula in southeastern Mexico separates two great bodies of water – the Caribbean Sea and the Gulf of Mexico. It has been rapidly developed for tourism in recent years, with the once-tiny fishing port of Cancun now a thriving boom town and the Mayan Riviera on the east coast a major resort destination for those seeking sun-sea-and-sand holidays.

For those more interested in the ancestral heartland of the ancient Mayan civilization, the 300-km (185-mi) journey from Villahermosa in the adjacent state of Tabasco to Mérida, Yucatán's 'White City', will be fascinating. Until recently, Yucatán was isolated, looking more to its Mayan roots and out to the Caribbean than inwards to Mexico, so it has a unique atmosphere and culture. You will appreciate this as you drive, perhaps diverting to explore this special land of jungle, thorny scrub, hills, Mayan ruins, haciendas, colonial cities, wildlife preserves and pristine beaches...not to mention engaging with the most welcoming of people.

From Villahermosa, head north on Highway 180 through Frontera, where you reach the Gulf. Keep going, enjoying stunning coastal scenery all the way (especially the amazing bridge crossing of the Laguna De Términos through Zacatal, Ciudad del Carmen and Puerto Real) before continuing to Chapoton and Campeche. From there, stay with 180 as the road cuts inland and heads for Mérida, via Chencoyi, Tenabo and Calkini. Mérida is worth waiting for. Founded by conquistadors on the site of a Mayan city, it is the oldest continually occupied city in the Americas, and displays much of the traditional splendour and charm of colonial Mexico.

A word of warning. Don't assume upon arrival that you can park anywhere. It may look that way, but police can, and sometimes do, impound illegally parked vehicles – a nightmare, especially if yours is a rental.

*The former home of the 16th century Conquistador, Francisco Montejo in Mérida*

# Oaxaca City to Puerto Angel

*One of the many pretty squares in Oaxaca*

What a journey! Driving Highway 175 through the coastal Sierra Madre del Sur Mountains of southwestern Mexico must be one of the most scenic drives in the whole country.

The experience begins in Oaxaca City – but not before you've explored this UNESCO World Heritage Site with its fine colonial architecture and rich cultural traditions. But it's soon time to leave cosmopolitan distractions behind, finding Highway 175 and heading south. It won't be a straightforward trip – in fact just the opposite. This two-lane road twists and turns violently as it winds through the mountains, to the point where motion sickness is a real possibility. What's more, the road surface is rarely the best – rainy season always sees damage to 175, which in true Mexican style barely gets repaired before next rainy season, so there's every chance of coming across a rockslide or collapsed section that slows traffic to a crawl.

That's just fine. There's no point in hurrying. The Sierra Madre del Sur are noted for their biodiversity, and this extraordinary road reveals stunning new vistas at every turn – take a spare memory card for the camera! You will have pictures of cloud forests with pines in the mist and lush tropical forest when the road descends. What's more, the small villages along Highway 175 often have wonderful indigenous crafts on sale, and the variety of colourful birdlife is mesmerising.

But all good things come to an end, and eventually the road runs down out of the mountains towards the Pacific Ocean. At the junction of 175 with the coastal highway (200), cross over and continue to Puerto Angel, an old-fashioned harbour town crouched around an enclosed bay that provides safe haven for its fleet of small fishing craft.

**HOW:**
By car
**WHEN TO GO:**
October to April
**TIME IT TAKES:**
A day - it's a 240km (150 mi) journey
**HIGHLIGHTS:**
Oaxaca's Zócalo, one of the most beautiful central squares in Mexico, and a vibrant hub of city life.
San Pablo Guelatao, the village on Highway 175 that was the birthplace of self-made Mexican President Benito Juárez – take a break beside the lake and admire a statue of the great 19th-century liberal as a       boy shepherd.
Roadside banana sellers – be amazed by how many varieties you'll be offered, and as a bonus you get to see what a freshly gathered cashew nut looks like.
San José del Pacifico, a hillside community about halfway through the trip – a good (maybe the only) place to spend the night if you decide to break the journey.
**YOU SHOULD KNOW:**
Never attempt to drive Highway 175 at night – it's cold, lonely and hard to spot potentially dangerous potholes or other more serious water damaged places in the dark.

*Kayaking near Ensenada Bay.*

# Espiritu Sanctu and Isla Partida

Describe the difference between the Gulf of California, Sea of Cortez and Mar de Cortéz? Of course they're all the same place – that long, narrow body of water separating the Baja California Peninsula from the Mexican mainland. Most maps prefer one of the English versions; most locals naturally use the latter.

Either way, that's where you'll find the enchanting island of Espiritu Sanctu (oh, all right, Holy Spirit Island). It is connected by a narrow isthmus to Isla Partida, and together they are a protected UNESCO biosphere. Both are small. Espiritu Sanctu has an area of 80 sq km (31 sq mi) and Isla Partida is 15 sq km (6 sq mi). But that doesn't prevent them from being a magical destination.

These rocky wilderness islands with their breathtaking coastline lie in the Sea of Cortez north of La Paz on the rugged Baja California Peninsula, a bustling regional capital. The way to explore them is journeying by kayak, camping as you go, enjoying a memorable outdoor adventure. Take along a snorkel and flippers, as the diving is memorable. You can hire kayaks and canoes for a circumnavigation locally, or choose from a number of guided tours. It is possible to paddle out to the islands, though some prefer to be delivered by motorboat to allow the maximum possible time around the islands. Either way, you'll experience a classic sea-kayaking trip.

The Sea of Cortez is home to a fabulous variety of marine life, and being on the water gives you every opportunity to see many species – look especially for humpback whales, California grey whales, whale sharks, leatherback turtles, sea lions, dolphins and giant manta rays – along with a rich variety of colourful fish and a huge number of seabirds.

**HOW:**
By kayak
**WHEN TO GO:**
Any time of year (warm winters, hot summers).
**TIME IT TAKES:**
Four days allows ample time for exploration.
**HIGHLIGHTS:**
Interesting sea caves within walking distance of Isla Partida's south coast.
A mangrove bay on Espiritu Sanctu, providing a welcome mass of greenery that may be explored by kayak.
The Ensenada Grande beach on Isla Partida, voted by a travel magazine as the most beautiful in Mexico and one of the Top 12 beaches in the world...so don't expect to have it to yourself!
The Malecon waterfront promenade around the bay in La Paz, a quintessentially Mexican town that pays only lip service to tourism.
**YOU SHOULD KNOW:**
The famous French underwater explorer and oceanographer Jacques Cousteau described the Sea of Cortez as 'The World's Aquarium'.

# Rio Usumacinta

Ready for a real wilderness adventure? Something ever-so-slightly dangerous? Then a raft trip down Mexico's glorious Rio Usumacinta, the Sacred Monkey River, could be just the thing. But this is border country, where smuggling between Guatemala and southeastern Mexico is rife. Bandits stalk the roads. Zapatista rebels have been active, so the Mexican army is in evidence. But the security situation has improved and – as the only way to make this incredible journey is as part of an organized group with experienced guides – the danger is not acute.

The river is formed in a great natural basin by the merging of two others – the Salinas and Pasión Rivers – and serves as the border between the Mexican state of Chiapas and Guatemala, after which it wanders through the state of Tabasco to the Gulf of Mexico, forming the only physical boundary between the Yucatan Peninsula and the rest of Mexico. Various hydroelectric schemes have been proposed for the upper reaches of the river, but happily these have been shelved as the long-term benefits of eco-tourism become apparent, though other threats to this vast natural jewel remain.

A number of different trips are on offer. All will start with a drive of several hours' duration to the put-in point, which is often the tiny frontier post of Frontera Corozal. From there, a couple of inflatable rafts, carrying all the necessary stores and inflatable kayaks for side trips, will convey up to a dozen adventurers downriver.

The trip will be a voyage of discovery, with overnight camping on river beaches and numerous stops to swim or explore interesting features and historic sites along the banks. The scenery varies from jungle-covered bluffs, cascading waterfalls, through tumbling rapids and canyons to the broader, slower sections towards the take-out point at Tenosique.

**HOW:**
By car and boat
**DEPART:**
Frontera Corozal
**WHEN TO GO:**
Avoid the rainy season (May to November).
**TIME IT TAKES:**
Around 10 days for a 120-km (75-mi) raft journey.
**HIGHLIGHTS:**
Wildlife, from dazzling butterflies to howler monkeys that inhabit treetops all along the river – you can't miss them, because they really are noisy.
The ruined remains of two powerful cities of the ancient Maya civilization, Yaxchilán (just down river from the start point) and Piedras Negras (further down on the Guatemala bank).
Roaring falls where the Busiljá River enters the Usumacinta.
The Canyon of San José – a deep run with sheer rock walls that tower to over 300 m (1,000 ft).
**YOU SHOULD KNOW:**
Though relatively short in length, Usumacinta is the world's seventh-largest river by volume of water.

*Kayaking on Rio Usumacinta*

83

# La Ruta Maya

**HOW:**
By car
**WHEN TO GO:**
Year round
**TIME IT TAKES:**
Allow two weeks to complete the
Guatemalan stage of the route.
**HIGHLIGHTS:**
The magnificent Temple of
the Jaguar.
The surrounding Tikal National Park.
Chichicastenango – the most
colourful local market in
the Americas.
The glorious jungle flora and fauna
of the region.
**YOU SHOULD KNOW:**
Planning ahead is essential as
transport links in Guatemala can be
unreliable. It is probably advisable to
travel as part of a tour with a local
guide, so that you can appreciate all
that you see.

It may come as a surprise to the casual observer that La Ruta Maya, far from being a route trodden by the ancients, is a construct of 20th century American travel writing. This often-travelled route links sites which were mysteriously abandoned by the Mayan civilization over a thousand years ago. La Ruta starts in Southern Mexico and takes you down the spine of Central America to Belize. The least visited and perhaps the most mystical part of the route lies within the modern day boundaries of Guatemala.

As much of the route is a network of dirt tracks, good suspension is a prerequisite for any mode of road transport you choose, though as the crowning glory of the area is so remote many tourists decide to approach it by air. Hidden by thick jungle until the 19th century, Tikal is one of the most stunning archaeological sites to be found anywhere in the world. Once one of the largest and most influential cities of the Mayan era, the city disappeared over the centuries, swallowed up by the lush jungle. The scale of the development can be seen by climbing up Temple IV to view distant structures still half hidden in the forest canopy. It is estimated that the 16 sq km (6.2 sq mi) already uncovered is a mere fraction of the entire city.

This is but one of many important Mayan cities, hidden over many centuries and now re-discovered. Some were home to grand palaces; others were of more modest proportions. All however have something to reveal about the fascinating ancient Mayan empire.

*Temples I, II and III at Tikal*

# Volcano Pacaya

There are times in your life when you have to place total faith in science and the gods – bungee jumping and white-water rafting, to name but two. Walking up the side of an active volcano, as it belches angrily, certainly comes into this category.

Located in the south west coastal region of Guatemala, Pacaya began its most recent active phase in 1965, and since then has offered up a full array of volcanic activity. More often than not, the Pacaya Volcano spews little more than gaseous emissions and relatively small steam eruptions. However, from time to time it can experience more serious explosions that prompt the evacuation of the numerous villages found on its sides. Rising to 2,690 m (8,370 ft) above sea level, the Pacaya volcano is not the tallest in Guatemala, but it is certainly the most climbed. Its constant activity has made it a magnet for vulcanologists from around the globe and predictions of major eruptions such as the one in 2006 have increased in accuracy.

Hikers are charged a small fee that goes towards the maintenance of the trails. Facilities along the way are good, with rest stops and even some primitive washrooms. The main route to the summit takes you from the car park at San Francisco de Sales, up gentle slopes until you reach the rim of the old Cerro Chino crater. This is a chance to catch your breath and admire the stunning views. After this the final steep ascent begins and it is not easy. Loose ash and volcanic rock make walking difficult, while clouds of sulphur can hinder breathing. Hazards aside, when you reach the top the views are astounding, like standing in a lunar landscape.

**HOW:**
On foot
**DEPART:**
San Francisco de Sales
**WHEN TO GO:**
Year round although hottest from June to August.
**TIME IT TAKES:**
Allow a full day.
**HIGHLIGHTS:**
The sight of the volcano from below. The view of Acatenango, Fuego and Agua volcanoes as you near the Cerro Chino crater.
Being close to something so fundamental to the planet's ecosystem – the sheer power of it is almost overwhelming.
**YOU SHOULD KNOW:**
As a hangover from its recent civil war, Guatemala has a high gun-owning population and armed robberies, whilst falling in number, are still quite common. You are relatively safe within the boundaries of the park, where rangers are employed for security, but it is a good idea to travel in a group and avoid wearing flashy jewellery.

*Hiking on Volcano Pacaya near Antigua.*

*The Rio On storms through Mountain Pine Ridge Forest Reserve.*

# Mountain Pine Ridge Forest Reserve

**HOW:**
On foot
**WHEN TO GO:**
Year round – but expect rain at any time.
**TIME IT TAKES:**
You could do it in a day if really fit, but allow a week or two to soak up the park.
**HIGHLIGHTS:**
Barton Creek Cave – a cave system full of Mayan artefacts.
Green Hills Butterfly Ranch – a host of butterflies flutter by in a jungle setting.
The Hidden Valley Falls – a viewing platform gives a great vantage point to the 460-m (1,500-ft) high waterfalls.
Chiquibul Forest Reserve – home to many endangered species.
**YOU SHOUD KNOW:**
The reserve is recovering from a pine beetle infestation that wiped out as many as 60 per cent of the trees in 2000. This resilient forest is still recovering, but no less beautiful for it.

Pine forests are not the first things that spring to mind when you think of Central America, but the unique Mountain Pine Ridge in Belize has surprises around every corner. This 1020-m (3,400-ft) tall ridge is a natural wonderland of spectacular waterfalls, wild orchids, vibrantly coloured parrots, keel-billed toucans among a myriad of exotic flora and fauna.

Located in the Mountain Pine Ridge Forest Reserve, the trail leads you through thick jungle, past ancient rock formations and most notably to Caracol, the largest Mayan ruins in Belize. Excavation of these relics is still in its infancy – it's fascinating to see the forest slowly giving up its secrets.

All around you the forest invades the senses with ambient noise, colour and smell. Mossy ferns and abundant vegetation form a soft canvas, while exotic birds perch among the treetops and other wildlife plays between the branches. The area is dotted with cool mountain pools to swim in and caves to walk through – if only all life were like this! The tempo of this magnificent walk is perfect. The altitude of the climb takes the edge off the tropical heat and the often-misty summit of the ridge provides a magical backdrop.

It is probable that the forest is the remnant of a volcanic island that collided with the mainland several millennia ago. This would explain the feeling of isolation you get from climbing the trail. This is truly a paradise gained.

# Monteverde Cloud Forest

Bathed in a curtain of life-giving mist, the Monteverde Cloud Forest in the mountains of Costa Rica is a profusion of saturated greenery that stands as an icon of modern day conservation. Originally founded by Quakers fleeing the draft in 1960s America, this privately owned reserve has now been expanded to cover over 10,500 hectares (26,000 acres).

With altitudes ranging between 600 m and 1,800 m (1,970 and 5,900 ft), the Forest Preserve is one of the most flourishing biological sanctuaries in the world. Over 100 species of mammals, 400 species of birds, 120 species of amphibians and reptiles, and 2,500 species of plants, as well as tens of thousands of insect species reside within its borders. In addition, larger animal species including the jaguar, ocelot, resplendent quetzal and baird's tapir inhabit the Preserve's boundaries.

The reserve is best enjoyed at a leisurely pace and a boat trip on the adjacent Lake Arenal is a good way to get your bearings. From there it is possible to join a guided horseback trek around the lake's shores and on to Monteverde. From this vantage point you can marvel at the myriad of colours that surrounds you, whilst the sounds and scents of this most luscious of environments fills every sense. This area is a true haven for wildlife to flourish, protected from humans. It provides scientists with a great natural field station as well as delivering a wonderful, natural utopia for the more casual tourist to enjoy.

**HOW:**
By boat and on horseback
**WHEN TO GO:**
Year-round – though quieter from October to March.
**TIME IT TAKES:**
A combined boat and horseback trip takes around 5 hours.
**HIGHLIGHTS:**
The Butterfly Garden
The Orchid Garden
The World of Insects
The Monteverde Serpentarium
**YOU SHOULD KNOW:**
If travelling with a guide ask for testimonials or get a recommendation from the local tourist authority, as some operators can be less than scrupulous. Make sure that the horses you ride look healthy and that the guide keeps to well-trodden paths.

*Green-crowned Brilliant hummingbird feeding on a ginger flower.*

# Cerro Chirripo

**HOW:**
On foot
**WHEN TO GO:**
Year round, though it's less hot from
November to March.
**TIME IT TAKES:**
Allow two or three days to climb the
mountain or at least a week to enjoy
the surrounding National Park.
**HIGHLIGHTS:**
The sheer thrill of it all – the sounds
of the jungle, the forest scenery and
the panoramic views from the top.
The surrounding National Park – as
close to a pristine jungle as you
could wish to experience.
The descent – climbing the mountain
requires so much energy that it is
sometimes difficult to take in the
amazing jungle location. The descent,
though not easy, affords you that
luxury.
**YOU SHOULD KNOW:**
Do not be tempted to start the climb
without a permit. Sometimes the
rangers say there is a long waiting
list, when in fact there is none.

There can be few more intense fusions of pleasure and pain than the hike up Cerro Chirripo, with its 18-km (11-mi) climb to a 3,000-m (10,000-ft) high summit. If the gradient doesn't slow you down, then the diminishing oxygen at altitude will add extra pressure to the lungs. The rewards, however, for making it to the top are bountiful. On a clear day it's possible to see both the Pacific and the Caribbean by just turning your head!

A permit is needed to make this climb and the monies raised go towards trail maintenance and the employment of park rangers. So with ticket in hand and a rucksack stocked for all eventualities, it is time to breathe in the tropical air and start the climb. Everything from sun block to a sleeping bag is essential, as the hot tropical sun can easily burn you and it has been known to snow near the summit. Thankfully you don't need the added burden of a tent, as there are a couple of dormitory-style huts along the way.

As befits a jungle environment, the slippery trail can make progress hard work. Short of out-and-out mountaineering this is probably the most difficult 18 km (11.25 mi) you will ever travel in your life. Its inaccessibility is what keeps this area special and free from the development and exploitation that blights much of Central America. Besides the challenge of climbing Costa Rica's highest peak, there are numerous trails that wind through more ecological zones than you will find in most entire countries.

*The view from Cerro Chirripo*

# Panama Canal and Lake Gutan

*The Pedro Miguel locks and Centennial Bridge*

For sheer drama it is difficult to top the 77 km (48 mi) passage through the Panama Canal. Built to cut sailing times between the east and west coasts of America, one twentieth of the world's shipping now passes through its locks. It is the perfect marriage of engineering efficiency and Italianate architecture that makes it a true wonder of the modern world.

The locks themselves utilize the waters of the surrounding rainforest to send vessels on their way through improbably narrow passages. The region's rivers and lakes are dammed, and, along with the locks, these dams control the release of 236 million litres (52 million gallons) of freshwater per passing vessel. Where else in the world can you lean over the side of large cruise ship and touch land? When the ship is ready to change locks, it is mesmerising to look down from the stern. With only 10 m (33 ft) between propellers and lock gates the commotion caused by the water is quite incredible.

The canal marks the lowest point at which you can cross the American Continental Divide as you sail through the 13 km (8 mi) of the dramatic Gaillard Cut, where the mountain was literally sliced open to allow passage. Such is the dramatic nature of the scenery that it appears to the eye that you are heading straight towards a cliff as you head through the final lock that takes you into Lake Gutan. Here there is a chance to disembark or simply marvel at the sheer volume of shipping waiting to pass through the canal.

**HOW:**
By ship
**WHEN TO GO:**
The climate is pretty constant all year round.
**TIME IT TAKES:**
Allow a full day for a round trip through the canal and onto the lake.
**HIGHLIGHTS:**
Marvelling at the mechanics of it all.
The evergreen tropical jungle, which adorns both sides of the canal.
The contrast between the bubbling excitement of the canal and the tranquillity of Lake Gatun
Watching passing ships travel close by in the opposite direction on the section between Culebra Cut and Lake Gutan
**YOU SHOULD KNOW:**
The delicate eco-system that surrounds the canal is threatened by deforestation, as a result of illegal logging.

*Clouds drift among the forest trees.*

# Trail to Volcan Baru

**HOW:**
On foot
**WHEN TO GO:**
Year round – it's almost deserted between November and March.
**TIME IT TAKES:**
Allow a full day – 6 hours up, 4 hours down.
**HIGHLIGHTS:**
The sounds of the jungle.
The misty forest.
El Respingo – a bird-watcher's paradise, nearby.
The surrounding National Park.
**YOU SHOULD KNOW:**
In 2007 the volcano was the scene of one of the most astonishing stories of endurance when the only survivor of a plane crash, a 12-year-old girl, was found, injured but alive after spending two nights alone in the jungle.

Volcan Baru forms the focal point of a sumptuous National Park that shares its name. The highest point in Panama, it has become a Mecca for outdoor adventurers, bird-watchers and nature lovers of all kinds.

It is quite probable that your first view of this 3,474-m (11,398-ft) high iconic symbol of the Central American rainforest will be fleeting, as the summit is usually shrouded in cloud. This is an important consideration when planning a climb and an early morning start is vital in order to maximize your chances of enjoying good views from the top.

When the clouds clear, those who do make this arduous climb are greeted by the most wondrous of sights. A magnificent carpet of green lies before you, framed by the azure waters of both the Pacific Ocean and the Caribbean Sea.

Because of the volcano's height and isolation, this area is considered a bioclimatic island. Its forest is home to distinctive species of orchids and rare flora such as magnolia and giant oak trees, some of which are over 800 years old. You'll also see wild bamboo gardens and gigantic, knotted trees dripping with vines and sprouting prehistoric-looking bromeliads from their stems.

The rainforest also provides a home to over 200 species of bird, the most notable of which is the resplendent quetzal, whose extraordinary beauty puts it in the number-one spot on many bird-watchers' lists. Other rare birds here include the silky flycatcher, the three-wattled bellbird, and the hairy woodpecker.

In higher reaches, an intermittent cloud forest creates an eerie ambience. All said, it is a wonderful place to hike and immerse yourself in untamed beauty, but come prepared, with waterproof outerwear and shoes and a dry change of clothes just in case.

# Railway Trail

Since motor vehicles were given the freedom of Bermuda in 1946, they have become the only real threat to the island's balmy perfection. With 50,000 vehicles for 69,000 residents, clogged roads and noise risk overwhelming Bermuda's extraordinary natural beauty and wealth of history. The Railway Trail traces a traffic-free path through the archipelago – a thoroughfare and playground for walkers, pedal-cyclists and riders. It runs for some 34 km (21 mi) along the roadbed of the narrow-gauge railway torn up in 1948, its continuity broken into seven sections where original trestle bridges no longer exist. Sections are 3 to 6 km (1.75 to 3.75 mi) long, but more than 30 access points make it easy to return to main roads and get a bus if distances prove too much.

The Railway Trail is, in effect, Bermuda's backyard. From Sandys Parish in the west to St George's in the east, it bypasses every town and village, but provides tranquil access to all of them. It is a treasure trove of fascinating sights, unavailable any other way. It winds through sun-dappled countryside, revealing a succession of glorious seascapes. You see beautiful houses with characteristic Bermudan stepped roofs of whitewashed limestone, and skirt magnificent Georgian mansions. You pass pink sandy beaches, marshlands and mangroves. You share the scent of roses with the migrating birds in the upland forest sanctuary of Heydon Trust; and you enjoy the commanding view of the Sound from 19th century Fort Scaur, the smallest drawbridge in the world, and a dozen other wonderful ways to remove yourself from urban Bermuda.

At Store Hill, the Trail becomes more neighbourhood front porch; and the cliffs above Shelly Bay bring you to the Coney Island Road cricket pitch – where you must backtrack a little to take the ferry to St George's, the oldest English-speaking town in the New World, and the beginning of the seventh section.

**HOW:**
On foot or by bike
**WHEN TO GO:**
Year round. From April to September, walking and cycling is more comfortable in the early morning or late afternoon.
**TIME IT TAKES:**
Two to four hours per section
**HIGHLIGHTS:**
The quaint, garage-size old railway stations.
Gibbet Island, seen from the North Shore Road, where witches were burned and felons hanged.
The endemic flora of the farms and plantations of Paget Parish.
The Shelly Bay Nature Reserve.
**YOU SHOULD KNOW:**
In Bermuda, 'cyclists' or 'bikers' means 'motorcyclists': in conversation, and especially if hiring, you must refer to 'pedal-cyclists'.
Mopeds and motorbikes still occasionally abuse the Railway Trail, but local residents, and the police, are getting much tougher.

*Fort Scaur*

# Blue Mountain Downhill

*Ride the Blue Mountain Downhill at a leisurely pace!*

It is effortlessly simple. If you want to see the Blue Mountains, have yourself driven to the highest point accessible by vehicle, Hardware Gap (1,707 m/5,600 ft), deep in Holywell National Park and in the immediate shadow of the Blue Mountain peak itself, at 2,257 m (7,402 ft) the highest point in the Caribbean. The forest, Kingston and the sea are spread below you. All you have to do is put on the required helmet and knee pads, mount your bike, and roll gently downhill for 29 km (18 mi).

The actual riding time is about 2.5 hours, but the journey can take all day depending on your starting point. Enthusiasts come from as far as Ocho Rios, adding five hours driving to the ride. In any case, the downhill is punctuated by extremely well chosen photo opportunities and refreshment pauses, culminating in mid-afternoon with a short walk to a forest pool, with creepers and vines dangling from a rock face over which cascades a 30 m (100 ft) waterfall. You'll be ready for the swim. It's a chance to reflect on everything you've seen and everything you've been told about descending through several different ecosystems and the flora and fauna of each.

Because the mountain roads are small, and bikes don't make a lot of noise, you really do get close to some of the blazing colours of Jamaican bird species, and of the clouds of flowers that turn densely packed rainforest trees into floral totems. You can stop and listen any time, or take a better look at plants that catch your eye. But probably you'll be content to drift on down while all your other senses enjoy the feast. Those that want can go as fast as they like but more sensible cyclists ride the Blue Mountain Downhill at a leisurely pace.

# Trek to the Boiling Lake

The Boiling Lake trek is Dominica's ultimate trial of strength. The volcanic island is the most rugged and mountainous in the Caribbean, and its deeply incised valleys attract more rain than anywhere else. The combination of tropical location and active volcanism make it a rainforest paradise of streams and cascades – much of it protected in the wilderness National Park that surrounds its highest peaks, the Morne Trois Pitons. The Boiling Lake lies at its heart, a fittingly dramatic finale to what feels like a mythic adventure into a new world.

The trail starts by the waterfall and pools of the Titou Gorge, and follows the stream through emerald rainforest uphill to the Breakfast River, traditionally the first stop. Then you climb steeply to emerge on the razor edge of 1,020 m (3,168 ft) Morne Nicholls, from which you can touch the clouds and sky. The Valley of Desolation lies below, wreathed in the bubbling sulphur steam of 50 fumaroles and hot springs that colour rocks like stained-glass; and where water may flow black, milky, bright yellow or iron-red. But not even the bizarre formations or the mosses and rare orchids that survive here are preparation for the exhilaration of emerging suddenly, after another hard climb through clouds and steam, at the cliff edge of the Boiling Lake itself.

At 72 m (270 ft) across, the Lake is the second biggest flooded fumarole in the world; and though it can cool to a glassy pale green, it is usually a seething cauldron belching frankly dangerous fumes up its steep, slippery rock sides. Its sheer natural drama – a scorching, unpredictable hotpot 900 m (2,640 ft) up in the clouds – is enhanced by the total lack of visitor facilities. There's nothing to spoil it, and that vision energizes the trek home.

**HOW:**
On foot
**WHEN TO GO:**
Year-round. Outside the rainy season (June to October), the Lake's altitude means you can expect frequent rain squalls at any time, so the trail is usually both wet and muddy in places.
**TIME IT TAKES:**
Six to eight hours return journey
**HIGHLIGHTS:**
The change from the tropical rainforest glades characteristic of Dominica's natural glory, to the wind-battered vegetation of its high peaks, all in just 12 km (7 mi) from the sea.
The 360-degree panorama from Morne Nicholls.
The intensity of effort required for the trek, and proportionate sense of reward afterwards, when you drop into the hot pools of Titou Gorge to soak off the mud and massage weary muscles.
**YOU SHOULD KNOW:**
1. You must go with a guide, because the trail becomes indistinct, especially in the Valley of Desolation. 2. Wear proper footwear (not sneakers) and scruffy clothes – you will get dirty and (probably) wet. 3. Try to go in a group of six to ten, so that there is likely to be someone of similar ability to walk with. 4. The trail includes some relentless climbs, so there is no shame in deciding to stop early.

*Steam rises from the Boiling Lake.*

# La Soufrière Summit Hike

From Basse-Terre, the capital of Guadeloupe's western 'butterfly-wing', La Soufrière rises to an imposing 1,467 m (4,900 ft) only 13 km (7.5 mi) away. Even much closer, from the trailhead at the car park of Savane à Mulets, 1,142 m (3,800 ft) high at the foot of its summit cone, the dormant volcano reveals none of its secrets. To begin with, you follow the trail that climbs gently round the mountain, scrambling over fissures, and enjoying the mosses, lichens, mountain pineapples and panoramic views over the Caribbean. At the sheer 60 m (100 ft) rock crevice known as the 'Great Fault', you turn right and clamber up some very slippery rocks for ten minutes to reach 'La Dècouverte', the highest point – and enter another world, completely invisible from below.

Instead of a single immense crater, since the massive eruption of 1976 La Soufrière is capped by a cluster of eruptive vents arranged along the fracture zones. The pits and pools form a lunar landscape of damage where the hail of stones and sludge projectiles utterly destroyed previously lush vegetation. Green posts mark the trail through the mist of sulphurous fumes leaking from this wasteland, once so rich in plants it was called 'le jardin Herminier' (in honour of an early 19th century Guadeloupean doctor and botanist), and now known as 'la Porte d'Enfer'. Here you cross the 'Great Fault' by a natural rock bridge and loop right to the multiple fumaroles of 'Piton Napoleon', until you reach the bubbling cauldron of the south crater. Often invisible in fog or hidden by its own thick vapour, you can smell it and feel its radiating heat at some distance. In fact the hellish landscape is a fascinating demonstration of recovery. La Soufrière's summit plateau of bizarre rock formations is covered with the flora of recolonization – a wonderful surprise and a rewarding hike.

*La Soufrière volcano is a very rewarding hike!*

# The Road

Close to St Maarten, the peak of an extinct volcano called Mount Scenery rears out of the Caribbean, the centrepiece of Saba's 13 sq km (5 sq mi) of vertiginous cliffs and lush, forested mountains. So steep are its hills that for centuries the only way to get around was by hiking up long stone stairways, using donkeys to carry produce and household goods: the world's engineers agreed that it was impossible to build a road on Saba's rugged terrain. With the determination of a Joseph Conrad hero, a local man decided otherwise. Guided only by a correspondence course in engineering, between 1938 and 1961 he browbeat the rock into submission using just dedicated local labour and a wheelbarrow. The Road is his testament. It is literally the only road on the island.

The Road defies gravity, common sense, and all the rules of engineering. It's a stomach-churning 14 km (8.75 mi) switchback made of concrete, with no blacktop, edging or markings. It connects the airport on the northeast side and the harbour at Fort Bay on the southwest, twisting and turning through all four of Saba's villages en route. Mango, guava, avocado, lemon and banana trees line it where its narrow ribbon isn't already crowded by the uniform white, red-roofed houses walling its sides. It makes no concessions to fear or vertigo as it careers past sheer drops into the ocean, and plunges up, down and round within the villages. Sabans take it at speed – and wily locals choose laborious hiking trails rather than walk the Road.

Even by taxi, the Road is an adrenaline rush. Given Saba's incomparable flora, the natural beauty of its rainforest, and its reputation as a world-class dive site, it's appropriate that just travelling between its charms should be a unique journey in itself.

**HOW:**
By car

**WHEN TO GO:**
Year-round. Since Saba has no beaches, it doesn't observe seasons like other Caribbean islands. Some adrenaline junkies actually come to drive the Road during the tropical downpours of June to October.

**TIME IT TAKES:**
About 35 minutes end-to-end.

**HIGHLIGHTS:**
The incomparable views that change with every twist and turn, and pass through five of the six distinct ecosystems on the island.
The hairpin ascent up a near vertical slope from the airport to Hell's Gate. Vanishing into cloud on Mt Scenery – at 877 m (2,850 ft) the highest point in the whole of the Netherlands, of which Saba is a part.
The descent from Windwardside, the village where most visitors stay, via The Bottom to Fort Bay, where the dive boats depart. The 15-minute taxi drive combines the thrills of the Road with a temperature rise of 30 degrees at sea level.

**YOU SHOULD KNOW:**
As an hors d'oeuvre for the Road, be sure to arrive by plane – Saba's runway is just 400 m (1,200 ft) long with a sheer drop into the ocean at either end.

*An aerial view of Hell's Gate Village and the Road*

*Riding mules in the pristine wilderness of Pico Duarte.*

# Pico Duarte

**HOW:**
On foot
**WHEN TO GO:**
Year-round – but never without a waterproof coat, winter clothing, a sleeping bag and hiking boots. Traversing distinct climate zones almost guarantees unstable weather at any time of year.
**TIME IT TAKES:**
3 days, 46 km (28 mi) round trip (La Cienaga); 5 days, 90 km (56 mi) (Mata Grande); 6 days, 86 km (53 mi) (Los Corralitos); 6 days, 96 km (59 mi) (Sabaneta); 6 days, 108 km (67 mi) (Las Lagunas).
**HIGHLIGHTS:**
Climbing the highest mountain in North America, east of the Mississippi. The variety and numbers of birds – including trogons, hispaniolan parrots, palm chats, woodpeckers, red-tailed hawks, and zumbador hummingbirds. Riding mules (you can hire as many as you want: the rule of thumb is one guide and one mule for every five hikers).
**YOU SHOULD KNOW:**
With one or two extra mules, even small children can enjoy trekking on and around Pico Duarte. Some have been known to sleep happily while strapped to a mule on a 9-degree gradient.

Pico Duarte (3,087 m/10,128 ft)) is the highest mountain in the Caribbean. More significantly, it is the centrepiece of the huge Cordillera Central Reserve of Bermúdez National Park, and almost untouched by the kind of tourism that threatens to make a Disney World of other parts of the Dominican Republic. The Park is uninhabited, a pristine wilderness of clear mountain rivers, jungle forests alive with the darting colours of hummingbirds and parrots, and the most magnificent landscapes in the Caribbean. Pico Duarte itself is only one of several similar peaks, and incorporates distinct sub-tropical eco-zones ranging from coconut palms and swaying bamboo groves to humid mountain forest, mountain rainforest and cool alpine scrub and pine.

Of the five routes to Pico Duarte, all are strenuous hikes of between 3 to 6 days and 46 to 108 km (28 to 67 mi). The most popular starts 25 km (13 mi) south west of Jarabacoa, from the village of La Cienaga where you have to register for the 46 km (28 mi) round trip, and hire a guide and mule (the mule is all but mandatory – if only as insurance for porterage and safety). Early in the morning, you follow the bubbling rivers up into the wild woodlands, serenaded by Mourning Doves. The dense forest thins, and gaps in the canopy reveal more and more of Hispaniola's fabled, translucent beauty. By nightfall you reach a ramshackle cabin called La Compartición, where the trails meet and hiking parties prepare for the pre-dawn scramble up the last 5 km (3 mi), through scented pines and open meadows, to greet the sunrise from the bare, rocky summit.

On a clear day with the clouds flushed pink below you, with the emerald forest and blue sea sharp contrasts in the distance, Pico Duarte's rugged antiquity fully justifies its mythic status in the Caribbean imagination. A magical trek.

# Tren Frances

Cuba is so big, with so much to see, that sooner or later visitors need to get from one end of the country to the other. The most rewarding method of travel is the train – and the Tren Frances is FC's (Ferrocarriles de Cuba) flagship service. On odd days (1st, 3rd, 5th of the month, etc) it leaves Havana for Santa Clara, Camaguey and Santiago; and on even days (2nd, 4th, 6th, etc) it makes the return journey. It's a stately schedule befitting the air-conditioned, stainless steel rolling stock acquired from France in 2001 after its retirement as a workhorse of the Trans-Europe Express between Paris, Brussels and Amsterdam. With reclining seats, carpets and cafeteria service, the Tren Frances still offers two classes: basic leatherette *especial* (2 + 2 seats across) and *primera especial*, with fabric seats spaciously arranged 2 + 1 across the aisle. It's comfortable, fast and (despite frequent moans from downright unlucky passengers) relatively reliable. It has to be: if it's more than an hour late, you get the fare refunded in full.

But watching the backyard of Cuba's glorious countryside unfurl, punctuated by visions of its colonialist past and the grinding demands of its agro-industrial economic present, you realize quite how extraordinary this train really is in its Cuban context. It's a statement about the country's determined ambition to make do, mend and better itself on its own terms. The Tren Frances really is the best way to see the 'real' Cuba – and the daily evidence is the other passengers. Most are Cuban, keen to talk and share, and (in marked contrast to the grumpy clientele on the 'tourist-only' bus network) thoroughly cheerful about life and its vicissitudes. *Primera especial* may be grubby and worn, but only the Tren Frances provides a first-class insight to match the country you see from its windows.

**HOW:**
By train
**WHEN TO GO:**
Year-round
**TIME IT TAKES:**
Over 12 hours for the one-way journey of 861 km (533 mi)
**HIGHLIGHTS:**
The powerful air-conditioning.
Breaking the ice with fellow-passengers.
In Santiago, the station is opposite the Caney rum factory.
Sub-tropical dusk and dawn.
The sense of intimacy with Cuba you retain, even long after stepping off the train in either Havana or Santiago.
**YOU SHOULD KNOW:**
1. Foreign visitors pay more than Cubans for rail travel; and they pay neither in pesos nor dollars, but in Cuban Convertible dollars (CUC$). 2. It's best to reserve your seat at least 24 hours in advance, and at both Havana and Santiago stations you do so at a special booth (NOT the normal Booking Office). You may be asked to show your passport, and/or to confirm your ticket one hour before scheduled departure, at the same place.

*Cathedral Santiago de Cuba*

# Revolutionary Trail in the Sierra Maestra

**HOW:**
On foot
**WHEN TO GO:**
Year-round. Irrespective of seasons, the Sierra Maestra's super-lush north side has a wet microclimate, but its south side lies in a cacti-studded, semi-desert rain shadow: on Pico Turquino, fickle weather frequently changes from bright sunshine to thunderous rain in minutes.
**TIME IT TAKES:**
One day (La Comandancia); two days (La Comandancia with a visit to the bio-research centre of La Platica for the flora and fauna); two days (summit of Pico Turquino).
**HIGHLIGHTS:**
Listening to revolutionary songs performed by Quinteto Rebelde in Santo Domingo – these are the original performers from 1958, when they wrote these songs and played them in battle (on Radio Rebelde) to confuse Batista's troops. The band re-formed recently, and play regularly in a local hotel.
Getting politically hyped-up by the enthusiasm of fellow hikers along the trails or in the campsites. With history at every turn, the naturalist's paradise of the Sierra Maestra makes this some of the world's most stimulating trekking.
The friendly and informative researchers at the bio-stations.
**YOU SHOULD KNOW:**
You can stay any number of nights at the Park campsites for the price of a guide and a single entry permit, but you need to carry all the food and water you require with you. Remember to tip the guide.

When Fidel Castro led Cuba's successful revolution against the dictator Batista in 1959, he lit a fire that still burns. Whatever anyone thinks about Cuba's progress since, Castro, his brother Raul, Che Guevara and the other 79 young men who landed from the Granma motor yacht west of Santiago on Cuba's southeastern coast in December 1956 are enshrined in a romantic political vision that still enthralls every visitor to the country. The Sierra Maestra is the mountainous jungle stronghold from which Castro fed the tiny flame into a consuming firestorm.

Virtually unchanged since those momentous days, the entire Sierra Maestra region is full of important revolutionary sights – but the Sierra's status as a National Park derives equally from the necessity to preserve some of Cuba's most beautiful landscapes and very best wildlife. Trekking the revolutionary trail is therefore a double whammy for political and ecological heritage. To make the most of your visit, head for the small town of Santo Domingo (itself the site of a key battle) at the north entrance to the Park. From here, you can join tours (the only way to get the necessary permits) to however many sites you have time for. Two are essential. La Comandancia de la Plata was Castro's field headquarters, in a forest clearing on a western spur of Pico Turquino. The wooden huts where Castro lived, and Che (a qualified doctor) ran a tiny hospital, retain their full dramatic potency in their remote, desperate setting up a single tortuous track of mud and rocks. The other is the tough, two-day hike to Pico Turquino's summit, a ritual political pilgrimage for many young Cubans. A famous black-and-white picture shows Castro on the peak, gun in hand, looking imperiously over the country he was to rule for 49 years.

*View of the Sierra Maestra on the jungle trail from Alto del Naranjo to the Comandancia de la Plata. The rangers' hut on the right is where visitors must leave their photographic equipment before continuing the 2km (1.2 mi) to the Comandancia from where Fidel Castro's revolution was originally run.*

# Mariel to Valle de Vinales

Though relatively close to Havana, Cuba's far west has always been isolated from development or tourism by dense forests and rugged mountains. Its remote beauty has been made accessible by the extension of the Circuito Norte – the *autopista* that links Havana east and west along its north coast – to Pinar del Rio, and the paving of access roads close to some of the region's most breathtaking charms. Driving is certainly the most colourful way to see Cuba, and this is one of Cuba's very best scenic routes.

Once you clear the shabby suburbs of Havana, pure pleasure kicks in at Mariel, the fishing port once famous as the departure point for Cubans trying to reach Florida. With the sea sparkling on one side, you drive up into the green hills of the Sierra del Rosario, a protected UNESCO Biosphere Reserve of tropical mountain forests. Cut by numerous rivers and waterfalls, the Reserve is both stunningly beautiful and home to 100 bird species and more than half of Cuba's endemic species of flora and fauna. From the Circuito Norte it's easy to visit Las Terrazas, a woodland eco-community from which you can swim in the forest waterfalls and pools of the San Claudio Cascade, or the orchid gardens at Soroa.

It gets even better. The Valle de Vinales is a UNESCO World Heritage Site, designated as a cultural landscape both for its astonishing beauty, and for its vernacular architecture and traditions. Dramatic panoramas feature huge rocky outcrops called *mogotes*, like islands towering out of a sea of green fields; and huge caves (once the refuge of remnant Taino Indians and runaway slaves) dot surrounding cliff faces. The Valley is Cuba's soul: it is wholly appropriate that such a lovely place is the only source of Cuba's finest tobacco leaves.

**HOW:**
By car
**WHEN TO GO:**
Year-round
**TIME IT TAKES:**
Five hours, excluding detours and stops. The distance is only 170 km (106 mi) but allows for sometimes daunting obstacles (like sleeping cattle in the 'fast' lane) that you may encounter.
**HIGHLIGHTS:**
The short trek through the tropical forest to the falls at San Claudio.
Watching cigars being made in the Vuelta Abajo area of Vinales – like the mandatory five grades of leaves, the process is as rigidly traditional, and controlled, as that of making Burgundy's most illustrious Premier Crus.
The single-storey, wooden houses with characteristic porch-balconies that make the town of Vinales feel like a timewarp.
Driving 'Cuban style'.
**YOU SHOULD KNOW:**
This drive reveals Cuba at its loveliest and most fascinating. Even if you don't have time to linger en route, it's well worth doing.

*Countryside and mountains in the glorious Valle de Vinales*

# Highway 901

At the eastern end of Puerto Rico's Ruta Panoramica, in downtown Yabucoa, the major road ends, and a narrow country lane winds straight ahead into the rising hills. Highway 901 is a sideshow, a scenic corniche road that has so far escaped the horrifying urbanization and development of Puerto Rico's fabulous coastline. From Yabucoa it leads straight to the sea at Playa Lucia, a bedraggled but lovely palm-lined beach kept free of crowds by frankly dangerous currents. Highway 901 climbs quickly past the beach, rising to the very cliff edge some 100 m (328 ft) high above the Caribbean, curling round the tail of the Cuchilla de Panduras Mountains as they drop into the sea. From here, you get a glorious view along the top of the cliffs: with a classic white lighthouse drawing your eye to the distance. Driving is hair-raising enough without going fast, because at several points the edge of the road is the edge of the drop. The view is the compensation for frazzled nerves.

The lighthouse is not open to the public, but you can stop outside it to admire the vistas either side of Punta Tuna, on which it stands. Below the rocky promontory, on both sides sandy coves are hemmed in with thick vegetation bursting with colourful flowers, their scent on the air. In crowded Puerto Rico, the breezy solitude is pure balm for the soul: it's usually impossible to resist a scramble down to the beach itself before driving on. Above you, 901 swings back inland to join the roar of traffic at Maunabo, forming the northwestern boundary to the Punta Tuna wetland area of freshwater swamp and three kinds of mangrove. Like Highway 901, the reserve is tiny, beautiful, and a wonderful reminder that Puerto Rico's coast isn't all freeways and billboards.

# Ruta de las Nieves

From the coastal jungle around Maracaibo, Venezuela's cordillera rises rapidly to the thriving town of Valera. Now called the Trans-Andean Highway, the road twines upwards into the glories of the Sierra Nevada National Park, passing the Venezuelan Andes' highest peaks and most dramatic landscapes before dropping down to the lovely old colonial city of Mérida. Woven into the snow-capped mountains, the Ruta de las Nieves is an astonishing introduction to the extreme contrasts of Andean eco-systems, culture and way of life. Valley bottoms are a mesh of stone walls and streams enclosing trout fisheries or pasture for horses and cattle – a system as ancient as the carefully-tended terraces (*andenes*) that climb slopes 1,000 m (3,200 ft) high. The Ruta ascends through cloudforest to the high mountain *paramo* of windswept grassland, through 17th century stone villages like Mucuchies or its neighbour San Rafael, Venezuela's highest (3,140 m/10,330 ft) community. It follows the high ridge between Timotes and Apartaderos – said to be the most scenic drive or bike-ride in the country – with vast panoramas of the Sierra Nevada on either side. The greys and whites of the jagged upper peaks shift with pink and pale-gold reflections from banks of scree and snow; and 200 glacial lake surfaces race with the movement of the sky.

Marvellous as it is just to drive, the Ruta de las Nieves also provides access to some of Venezuela's best hiking, mountain-biking, riding, climbing and eco-tourism. In fact, Mérida is the epicentre for these and other sports like hang- or para-gliding, and the place to organize tours, equipment and guides. Locally, the Ruta de las Nieves is shorthand for two to eight day wilderness trips which start from one of its villages on foot, horseback, or bike. It is certainly one of the most dramatic and interesting Main Streets in the world.

**HOW:**
By car
**WHEN TO GO:**
Year-round, according to your preferred activity and level of difficulty. The hiking season is November to April.
**TIME IT TAKES:**
Three hours (by car, 128 km/79 mi Valera-Merida). In practice 4-8 hours to allow for food and fuel stops, and stops to gaze at the scenery and the craft shops along the way and in the villages.
**HIGHLIGHTS:**
The Sierra Nevada backcountry of the *paramo* eco-zone – high grassland full of wildflowers and the endemic, soft-green velvet frailejón, framing the glacial lakes.
Venezuela's highest pass, at 4,108 m/13,146 ft, on the Ruta at Pico del Aguila.
**YOU SHOULD KNOW:**
The Ruta is both an inspirational journey in its own right, and the gateway for some of the best adventures and recreation Venezuela has to offer.

*The Ruta de las Nieves winds upwards into the Sierra Nevada National Park.*

# Teleférico de Mérida

**HOW:**
By cable car
**WHEN TO GO:**
December to February offers the clearest weather, but many visitors prefer July to September when there is more snow on the mountains. Since thick fog often covers the area, choose any clear day, and go early for the best chance of the view.
**TIME IT TAKES:**
Ninety minutes non-stop. Unless you are both very fit and acclimatized to altitude, take a break of 15 to 20 minutes at each stop before joining the next cabin.
**HIGHLIGHTS:**
Standing higher than anywhere in Europe or North America (outside Alaska).
Skiing in the tropics – lots of visitors ski down to the lower stations when conditions allow it.
The astonishing views of Cordillera de la Culata and Quebrada de la Fria, the neighbouring ranges of the Sierra Nevada, from the Aguada-Loma section.
Los Nevados, a fascinating relic of a pre-Hispanic town, six hours on foot, or four hours by mule, from Loma Redonda. From the same station, in one hour you can reach Laguna del Espejo and Laguna de los Anteojos – a terrific way to get used to the altitude and temperature change
**YOU SHOULD KNOW:**
Be cautious, especially on arrival at Pico Espejo: your body will suffer from any quick or sudden movement. Remember that many long treks and climbs end at the Teleférico – so the people you see bounding about are probably experienced mountaineers.

*The Teleférico 'flies' over the Sierra Nevada National Park.*

This is the closest you will ever come to flying on a magic carpet. You start in balmy tropical air at 1,625 m (5,330 ft), and in just 90 minutes soar 12.6 km (7.9 mi) to the 4,765-m (15,629-ft) snowcapped Pico Espejo, adjacent to Venezuela's highest Andean peaks. This is the Teleférico de Mérida, the longest and highest cable car in the world.

The ascent is pure drama. Mérida is a lovely 16th century colonial city set like a bowl of flowers wedged into the green slopes of Venezuela's Sierra Nevada National Park. The Teleférico terminal just east of Plaza Bolivar makes a surreal contribution to the antiquity of Mérida's historic heart, and as the city dwindles into pint-sized perfection, most visitors are fixated by the contrast. The focal point changes at the first station, La Montana (2,542 m/8,338 ft). It's a good idea to walk about and breathe deeply, to get accustomed to the sudden increase in altitude – for now the true majesty of the mountains becomes apparent. During the next two sections (La Aguada 3,452 m/11,323 ft, and Loma Redonda 4,050 m/12,263 ft), huge vistas open up of the saw-toothed high peaks stacked behind one another. Reaching into the distance, you can see how Venezuela's cordillera shares the triple spine that characterizes the Andes through Peru, Bolivia and Chile; and nearer, how apparently insignificant trickles and water cascades have carved mighty canyons and broad river valleys. Finally, the Teleférico climbs into a world of ice, rock, glaciers and still lakes. A marble statue of the Virgin of the Snows marks the place for the finest panoramic views, including nearby Pico Bolivar (5,007 m/16,423 ft), highest of them all. The altitude can induce a state of super-exaltation in some visitors; the statue is a gentle reminder for humility in the face of such natural magnificence.

# Roraima Tepui Trek

The Gran Sabana of southeast Venezuela's Canaima National Park is a remote wilderness of jungle, tropical savannah, rain and cloud forests, rivers and waterfalls. Over 1,500 million years, erosion studded the region with huge table-mountains, once connected but now isolated into individual colossi whose sheer cliffs rise 1,000 m (3,280 ft) and much more. Roraima is the highest of these *tepuis*, and its 2,810-m (9,217-ft) summit is a geologist's and botanist's paradise. With a microclimate, topography and endemic flora and fauna evolved in virtual isolation, it is a fantastic world of surreal rock formations, fissures, gorges, pools, waterfalls and sandy 'beaches', valleys of sparkling multi-coloured crystals, insectivorous flowers in gaudy red and yellow, and flashing hummingbirds. Minerals in the rock turn streams into liquid rainbows of blue, red and green; and mist, fog, hot sunshine and driving rain make a lottery of the weather.

Getting there starts with a flight (by scheduled Cessna!) to Santa Elena, where you must buy all the food you will need, and then a 4x4 to the Pemon Indian village of Paraitepui, where you (or a tour agency) sort out the Park entrance fee, guides and porters. A full day's trek across rolling grassland, fording the Tek and Kukenan Rivers, brings you to the 1,800 m (5,900 ft) base of Roraima. It takes a further 4 to 5 hour (minimum) diagonal climb up 'the ramp', through cloud forest, waterfalls, and ancient rock formations to the top, where you camp in one of the sandy areas overhung by rock called *hoteles*. Trails lead in all directions to the summit's best sites, like the Valley of Crystals, but you'll need at least two days to explore any but the shorter ones. No matter: from the rim, you understand how Roraima's strange reality beggars imagination, and how it inspired Conan Doyle to believe in a 'Lost World'.

**HOW:**
By plane, 4x4 and on foot
**WHEN TO GO:**
Year-round, but most people prefer the dry season between December and April. At any time, rain can cause rivers to swell, and delay even roped-up crossings.
**TIME IT TAKES:**
Five days (minimum for experienced trekkers); 6-7 days, allowing 1-2 days on the tepui; 8-14 days, allowing a more circuitous approach and lots of time investigating the novelties of the *tepui*.
**HIGHLIGHTS:**
The Valley of Crystals – the river valley of the Arobopo (from its source on the *tepui*, it falls off the sheer rim and eventually reaches the Orinoco), an amphitheatre 'guarded' by weirdly-shaped black stone columns; the river runs over a bed of colourful crystals and crystal fragments.
The 'Kukenan Window' – a 2-hour dawn hike to catch the view of Roraima's eastern wall, with Matawitepui in the distance and the jungle of Guyana below, before the clouds form.
The guacharos (oil birds) in the massive vertical fissures on one section of Roraima's sheer rim: these are thought to be evidence of the break-up of the supercontinent Pangaea.
The swathes of colourful, trumpet- and other-shaped carnivorous plants, humming with greed.
Fording 50-m (164-ft) wide rivers shortly after upcountry rain.
**YOU SHOULD KNOW:**
1. Whatever you take up the *tepui*, you must take back down, including all forms of paper and other refuse.
2. Taking souvenirs – even a single stone or crystal – from the *tepui* is a serious offence; and your baggage is likely to be searched back in Paraitepui. 3. Hooray! There are no mosquitoes on the plateau; but you will need bug repellant for the vicious gnats (*jejenes*) of the sabana.

*Aerial view of the Roraima Tepui*

# Angel Falls

Sixteen times higher than Niagara, Angel Falls (Salto Angel) has an uninterrupted drop of 979 m (3,212 ft), and are the highest in the world. Their exotic reputation is enhanced both by their remote location in southeastern Venezuela, and by the myths they have attracted. The Falls plunge over the rim of the largest of the region's sandstone mesas (sheer-sided mountains of dense jungle), called Auyantepui (home of the god of evil) by the Pemon Indians who refused to venture onto it; and it was the direct inspiration for Conan Doyle's 'Lost World' of mystery, darkness and dinosaurs.

You might take two, or six or even ten days to reach Angel Falls by boat. Starting southeast of Auyantepui, you can explore the orchid and bird-filled jungle paradise skirting the mesa, spending an adventurous week aboard a motorized *curiara* (dugout canoe) and sleeping in a hammock. You pause to swim through canyons (*kavac*) and frolic underneath waterfalls tumbling out of tangled flowers and foliage high in the riverbanks (*toma de agua*). Eventually, you thread your passage through mild rapids on the Akanan River to the Carrao River, where you will meet other canoe parties heading for Angel Falls. Some will have flown direct to Canaima, intending to visit the Falls in two days: they will miss the pink and orange-coloured river beaches, the cascades glowing gold in the sunset, the insights into their river and rainforest world you glean from talking to your Pemon guides and the villagers at campsites – the richness of 'other world' experience that makes the breathtaking first sight of Angel Falls a culmination instead of a tick on a list. Every visitor follows the Churun River to Devil's Canyon, and Ratoncito Island. A short hike is rewarded by one of the world's genuinely awesome natural wonders – and just then, it's a pleasure to share it.

*Angel Falls – the world's longest drop*

# Rafting the Upano River

On its swift-flowing path from the Andes to the Ecuadorian Amazon, the Upano River becomes a broad jungle waterway spun with thrilling rapids. Occasional clearings in the dense forest on its banks are home to the indigenous Shuar people, whose frail balsa rafts are the only river traffic. The descending river powers through canyons trailed with vines and foliage, then twists into a narrow gorge choked by massive boulders. A dozen waterfalls crash hundreds of feet from the high canyon walls, adding their sparkle to the drenching spume of contorted water. It's spectacular, ecstatic, breathtaking – one of the best whitewater rafting adventures in the whole world.

Everything about the legendary five-day Upano raft trip is perfect. You join the river at the frontier town of Macas, where it runs broad, a flight path for egrets, parrots, raptors, and the darting brightness of songbirds galore. Shuar guides share their knowledge of the forest and of culture in the headwaters of the Amazon. After the Patuca Bridge, the Upano enters a series of rocky gorges, culminating in the Canyon of the Sacred Waterfalls. These are grade IV and V rapids, and all the more exciting because you have been well prepared for them (and the good rafting agencies send a super-stable 'cataraft' down behind you so you never have too far to swim!). Better still, though there are lots of them, they come in groups, so you won't get completely battered or exhausted. By the time you leave the river at Santiago, 104 km (65 mi) downstream,

you feel exhilarated not just by the speed thrills of distance rafting, but by the feeling of having learned a bit about the Shuar and the Amazon rainforest from the amazing side-trips and the evenings in camp. Better than Five Star: this is Wild Thing.

**HOW:**
By raft
**WHEN TO GO:**
November to January is the favourite time; but May to August is also popular. Water levels can fluctuate dramatically according to rainfall at any time, making grade II or III rapids into IV and V. More experienced rafters may prefer heightened thrills.
**TIME IT TAKES:**
Five days, including Put-in and Take-out.
**HIGHLIGHTS:**
The Logrono Caves – a side trip into the jungle, deep into caves of huge stalactites and falling water to the foot of a 23 m (75 ft) cascade. With Wagnerian noise and drama, the torrent crashes from the outside, through a rocky slit of sunlight, into the semi-darkness.
The roiling grade IV & V rafting along Namangosa Gorge.
The wind-whipped beauty of the multiple tributary falls in the Sacred Canyon – some as high as 244 m (800 ft).
Shuar guides and villagers including you in their evening circle of cooking, stories, gossip and speculation. They still use blowpipes for some of their hunting.
**YOU SHOULD KNOW:**
Previous rafting and camping experience is recommended but not compulsory. Rafting agencies permit one backpack (no suitcases) per person. All good agencies are responsible for supplying all rafting and safety equipment.

*One of the many waterfalls of the Upano River*

# La Ruta del Sol

**HOW:**
By car
**WHEN TO GO:**
December to August; from
September to November it is much
colder, and the §coast is often
shrouded in fog.
**TIME IT TAKES:**
Ten to twelve hours driving from
Salinas to Esmeraldas – but then you
wouldn't have time to see how
stupendous it is, or to divert to left or
right.
**HIGHLIGHTS:**
The Pacific Ocean sailing community,
who congregate in the Bahia de
Caraquez, providing a touch of
glamour to the eco-beach idyll.
The Awa and Cayapas Indian culture
still extant in Cotocachi-Cayapas, and
around the estuary of the Cayapas-
Mataje Mangrove Reserve near
Esmeraldas.
Swimming on the equator with a foot
in each hemisphere.
Spending all day in a hammock
beneath swaying palms near Santa
Elena, then partying all night with the
surfers in Montanita.

La Ruta del Sol is Ecuador's Pacific Coast Highway. Officially, the name applies to the southern stretch from Salinas north to Puerto Cayo, but in practice it extends all the way to Esmeraldas. It makes good sense, because La Ruta del Sol is a catch-all for Ecuador's best beaches, reef dive sites, loveliest and wildest coastal landscapes, party-town resorts, and National Parks along the way. But resort development scarcely exists except near the Ruta del Sol's southern end. Great surfing attracts an international crowd to la Punta and the closest town, Montanita; and it's the nearest good beach for Guayaquileños at weekends. The party only stops when you head north. Suddenly, beach follows deserted beach. Apart from small and ancient fishing communities, there are scarcely any buildings. La Ruta leads to a wilderness coastline that gets increasingly pristine the further north you get. The few small towns lining the highway are each of them gateways to delights like the reef at Isla de la Plata or the ecological marvel of the Machalilla National Park, which has both humid and dry tropical forests side by side. Also near Puerto Lopez is the tropical magnificence of Los Frailes beach.

Unfortunately, visiting cruise ships and a local USAF base have recently damaged the charm of Manta, once the source of Panama hat straw; but the best begins at Bahia de Caraquez. Close by are four distinct eco-systems, home to over 350 different bird species. You can go from mangroves to one of the last tropical dry forests in the world, where golden orioles nest in giant ceibo trees, and you can look down on estuarine marsh filled with roseate spoonbills. From June to December you can even watch humpback whales and their young. You can walk, cycle, ride or drive it: the Ruta del Sol seems to include almost everything people want to do for sport, pleasure, or curiosity.

*An empty beach between Chirije and Bahia de Caraquez*

# Devil's Nose Railway

*Tourists 'ride the roof' on the Devil's Nose Railway.*

The Devil's Nose Railway used to connect Quito with Guayaquil. Recently weather-damaged by El Niño, it now operates only between Riobamba and Alausi. It's a spectacular four-hour ride along twisting gorges and high bridges over ravines, and through fertile valley bottoms lined with colourful villages and small towns. But at Alausi, nobody leaves the train, because ahead lies the Devil's Nose itself. One of the world's greatest railway engineering feats, the track switchbacks down an almost perpendicular 1,000-m (3,250-ft) wall of rock to Sibambe. Unable to go any further, the train performs its technological marvel in reverse, and everyone disembarks back at Alausi.

Oh, but it's worth it. The descent from Alausi takes an hour of constant advancing and backing up, zigzagging across the sheer mountain side; and another to re-ascend. Meanwhile you have a matchless view, forever renewed as the train shifts position and height, of the patchwork panorama of fields: yellow, green and grey rectangles moulded to every contour on the hillsides. On most trains you can even sit on the roof for the entire journey, which turns the trip into something of a party. That may be the reason some trains (currently they are single-carriage *autoferros*) no longer allow the practice. In any case, the adrenaline of riding a narrow ledge hacked into andesite volcanic rock, over an Andean precipice inches away, unites even inside travelers in excitement, if not comfort.

The Devil's Nose Railway is enormous fun, and an ideal prelude for travelers intending to trek the Inca Trail to Ingapirca. From Alausi it's only a short drive to the mountain hamlet of Achupallas (3,300 m/10,824 ft) where the Trail begins. Alausi is also en route to the 16th and 17th century colonial splendour blended into the Inca city of Cuenca, the World Heritage Site to the southeast.

**HOW:**
By train
**WHEN TO GO:**
Year-round
**TIME IT TAKES:**
Six hours (Riobamba-Alausi-Sibambe-Alausi, including brief halts)
**HIGHLIGHTS:**
'Riding the Roof' through the indigenous farmland and remote Allot Indian villages of Chimborazo Province, on trains of mixed passenger and freight wagons that run as far as Alausi – locals and travellers make a happy gang crowded on top with their bags. The sensation, on the Devil's Nose, of being a fly on a wall.
**YOU SHOULD KNOW:**
1. Bring some warm clothes.
2. A trip on the Devil's Nose provides invaluable acclimatization for further Andean adventures.

# Ingapirca Inca Trail

**HOW:**
By car and on foot
**WHEN TO GO:**
Year-round
**TIME IT TAKES:**
Four days (including getting to Achupallas, via either the Valley of Volcanoes or the Devil's Nose Railway).
**HIGHLIGHTS:**
Condors wheeling above the pass at Tres Cruces.
The wilderness beauty of the yellow, green and grey grasslands of the *paramos*, populated only by your fellow-trekkers and pack mules.
The mighty stones that make up the 500 year-old Inca roadway – part of a continuous system that extended further than the Roman Empire's.
Crossing the streams and swampy valley floor before Paredones.
**YOU SHOULD KNOW:**
You must be fully acclimatized to altitude to undertake this moderate to challenging trek, with some previous camping experience.

The Ingapirca Trail is a 35 km (22 mi) remnant of the 5,000 km (3,125 mi) of well-maintained roads that united the Inca Empire from Chile to Ecuador. You reach it by driving southeast of Quito through the Valley of Volcanoes, a spectacular route that passes the snow-capped giants of Cotopaxi (5,897 m/19,342 ft), Illinizas (5,263 m/17,263 ft), and Chimborazo, Ecuador's highest (6,310 m/20,697 ft). Pausing only for provisions at one of the colourful Indian markets at Latacunga or Saquisili, you camp at Achupallas, set 3,300 m (10,824 ft) up in the mountains above Alausi.

At first the Inca road follows the Rio Cadrul across the hills and wild *paramos* (high grasslands) to the lake at Tres Cruces. It's clear that in 500 years, nothing very much can have changed in the spectacular landscape. But above Tres Cruces, at 4,300 m (14,104 ft) on the saddle of the pass and the trek's highest point, the panorama is breathtaking. You can gaze across the high peaks in every direction, and look down on blue gems of lakes in the valley pockets. You camp by one of them, Culebrillas, close both to the Inca ruins of a *tambo* (courier rest-stop) at Paredones, built by the Inca Tupac Yupanqui; and to the quarry where the Incas mined the igneous stone Diorite which they used to build Ingapirca.

Near Ingapirca, the close-set stones show the original Inca roadway to be 7 m (23 ft) wide, a colossal highway through the roof of the world. It's a powerful reminder that the temple to the sun and other buildings at Ingapirca whose walls have been tumbled by wind and grasses, was a mere motel to the culture that built Machu-Picchu. Ingapirca isn't as obviously dramatic as Peru's Inca ruins, but the absence of crowds makes the Inca Trail getting there much more impressive.

*Chimborazo volcano –
Ecuador's highest*

# Amazon Journey

The Amazon is navigable for 4,380 km (2,725 mi) from the Atlantic to the foot of the Peruvian Andes. For 3,600 km (2,240 mi) to Iquitos, it's the dramatic highway for people and freight to cross the continent to Colombia, Ecuador and Peru; and boats of all sizes and degrees of comfort make the trip. But although most travellers can enjoy the experience for itself, they have little opportunity to see anything of the rainforest, its indigenous people, or the unique flora and fauna it hides. The main river, for all its apparent emptiness, has too many settlers on its banks. Instead, from Manaus you can explore the pristine wilderness surrounding the confluence of the Amazon and its biggest tributary the Rio Negro. The Negro's waters are crystal clear, and stained dark with dissolved organic matter; unlike the muddy yellow of the main river, they carry no silt. Where the Negro meets the Amazon at Encontra das Aguas, the unified stream flows black and white for more than 32 km (20 mi).

West and north of the confluence the rainforest is almost untouched, and barely inhabited. Over a few days, you can reach deep into all three types – the *igapo*, seasonally flooded with dark water and an orchid-filled, bromeliad-trailing cathedral of fishing-birds; or *terre firme*, where giant trees with buttresses like rocket fins create the high canopy for howlers and other monkeys; and the *varzea*, flooded with rich silts and with a totally distinct flora that attracts large concentrations of birds, mammals and black caiman. You may be able to visit a deep-forest settlement, and learn something of the medicines as well as nourishment provided by the jungle, or stalk birds on aerial walkways 37 m (120 ft) up in the canopy. These are the things that distinguish adventure from a mainstream Amazon journey.

**HOW:**
By boat
**WHEN TO GO:**
In June, the Amazon and Negro reach their flood, which declines until October-November: the *igapo* rainforest, for example, will have depth variations of 12 m (40 ft). You can travel the Amazon year-round, but each year brings a fresh variation on how best to explore its ecology.
**TIME IT TAKES:**
5-7 days Iquitos-Manaus (typical 'line boat'); 8-14 days (tour boat, including excursions into the forest). 5-12 days Manaus-Rio Negro-Amazon round trip (various tour boats). NB. Allow 1-2 days longer upstream from Manaus.
**HIGHLIGHTS:**
Lazing in a hammock in the humid languor of midstream Amazon, overflown by blue and gold macaws. Threading the Anavilhanas Archipelago on the Rio Negro, within constant touching distance of dense unfettered wilderness. The jungle tower at Ariau, providing access to 5 km (3 mi) of aerial walkways within the forest canopy.
**YOU SHOULD KNOW:**
Whatever kind of boat you choose, and wherever your destination along the Amazon, watch out for your baggage in every port.

*The silt-laden waters of the Amazon meet the darker waters of the Rio Negro at Manaus.*

# Serra Verde Express

**HOW:**
By train
**WHEN TO GO:**
Year-round. Curitiba is notorious for its
fickle weather: summer or winter, the
temperature can change from 30 °C to
15 °C (86 °F to 59 °F) in 30 minutes,
and rainfall on the Serra do Mar is
colossal but short-lived in duration.
**TIME IT TAKES:**
3½-4 hours ('Litorina'); 4-6 hours
('Convencional'), to Paranaguá, when
either of them go the full distance.
They often don't, and schedules are
perpetually elastic. Curitiba-Morretes
(the interesting bit) is usually 2-2½
hours; and your ticket will remain valid
if you break the full journey to visit
Marumbi or Morretes.
**HIGHLIGHTS:**
Marumbi – nowhere else can you
access very rare Atlantic rainforest
so easily.
The Sao Joao Bridge, 55 m (180 ft)
above the riverbed, and spanning
113 m (370 ft) in a soaring arch.
The flat-topped Parana pine, or
candelabra tree. It's the symbol of
Parana State – and one of very few
gendered tree species, with male and
female counterparts.
**YOU SHOULD KNOW:**
On the crowded weekend and holiday
trains, vendors will try and sell you
souvenirs through the train window –
when all you really want is food or
drink. Travel with the workers.

*Passengers lean out of the train
windows to take in the view
and keep cool.*

The Serra Verde Express takes you from Curitiba in southeastern Brazil to Paranaguá on the coast. It's the most spectacular train ride in Brazil. Forty minutes after you leave the high-rise modernity of Curitiba and the conventional drab of its suburbs, you emerge from the first tunnel into the completely unexpected, revelatory world of the Serra do Mar. Buckled like a concertina into a series of soaring peaks and precipitous valleys, the Serra do Mar drops 900 m (2,950 ft) from Curitiba to the delicate old colonial town of Morretes at sea-level. These mountains form the largest and best-preserved slice of Brazil's pristine Atlantic rainforest, protected as the UNESCO World Heritage Site and Biosphere Reserve of Marumbi. The dense forest of banana trees, palmetto, hard woods, orchids and creeper vines is shot with rivers and waterfalls, and alive to the colour and movement of toucans and monkeys. Winding through these steep worlds within worlds, the train crosses 37 impossibly high girder bridges, and 13 major tunnels blasted through rock. If you sit on the left side of the carriage, you'll see the best of the staggering panoramas that change at every turn, and smell the sweet air that grows balmier as you descend.

There are two kinds of Serra Verde Express. The smart, expensive version is the weekend-only air-conditioned 'Litorina', which halts in the mountains for photo opportunities, but does continue to Paranaguá. It's always crowded. On weekdays, the third-class 'Convencional' chugs as far as Morretes, but stops at Marumbi (Km 59) for visitors to the Reserve. It's a working train – a passenger equivalent of the great freight trains that still haul produce out of the mountains to the sea. There is no on-board service, but at the frequent unscheduled halts, people offer you coffee, fruit, pastries and bottles of local banana liqueur through the window.

# Pantanal Fazendas

*Waterways in the Pantanal*

The Pantanal of southwestern Brazil covers 140,000 sq km (87,500 sq mi). Fourteen times bigger than Florida's Everglades, it's the world's largest freshwater marsh. Between October and March every year it floods, and plant life explodes across its vast network of rivers and black waterways, knee-deep floodplains, lush savannahs, ponds, thick forests and lily-covered lagoons. From April the waters recede, returning newly-refreshed pasture and habitat both to the staggering numbers and variety of birds and mammals who make it their home, and to the *fazendas* – the enormous cattle ranches of the region, whose prosperity depends on their ability to adapt to the dramatic annual transformation.

*Fazendas* exist throughout the Pantanal wherever the land remains higher than the surrounding floodwaters. They make it possible for travellers to find good (often deluxe) food and lodgings while exploring the region. They provide horses, canoes or boats, and above all, local knowledge and expertise in finding the best sites and species habitats, which vary from year to year. Some *fazendas* even offer visitors the opportunity to live like Panatanal cowboys, roping, herding and branding specially bred cattle. Horses make the best transport, providing the extra height you need to see down into the shallows, and a commanding view above the vegetation line and through the forest. Their stamina ensures you see much more than you could on foot; and by portaging canoes, or pre-arranging them, you can cross huge areas. You don't even have to retrace your steps – many *fazendas* co-operate so you can travel from one to another enjoying some of the 650 bird species, giant otter families taking breakfast, alligators, anacondas, howler monkeys, piranhas and even jaguars that contribute to giving the Pantanal one of the highest concentrations of wildlife on earth. *Fazendas* are part of the region's ecology and culture: use them to get the most from the Panatanal.

**HOW:**
On horseback or by boat
**WHEN TO GO:**
Year-round. Aquatic species are obviously at their best between November and April; but drought and tropical sunshine dries whole lakes and rivers by October, when land species concentrate close to remaining water sources. Whenever you come, you'll see different aspects of the Pantanal's uniquely abundant ecosystem.
**TIME IT TAKES:**
3-4 days for the barest idea of the Pantanal's character and natural personae; 8-10 days based on 3 or 4 *fazendas* for a glimpse of the range of its ecological variety; 14 days + to get to grips with the region's balancing act between earth and water.
**HIGHLIGHTS:**
The best birdwatching on the planet. Rarities in abundance, of aquatic, shore, field, forest and savannah, and of every size and colour.
Mammals and reptiles in and out of the water, mangroves, forest canopy or on open ground: if you've ever seen them, it was never this closely.
The blissful luxury available overnight at some *fazendas*.
Viewing the rainforest and flooded plains from horseback.
**YOU SHOULD KNOW:**
1.Some *fazendas* insist on previous riding experience – but all of them use horses bred to local conditions.
2. Make sure you choose *fazendas* with good access to whatever features of the Pantanal you want to see most.

*A typical house near Canela*

# Rota Romantica

**HOW:**
By car
**WHEN TO GO:**
Year-round. March/April is especially lovely. Come for the December Film Festival in Gramado, the biggest of various events along the Rota throughout the year.
**TIME IT TAKES:**
3-4 hours to drive from end to end. Most people come for 3-8 days.
**HIGHLIGHTS:**
The late 19th century medieval-style half-timbered buildings of Picada Café, along with Novo Petropolis, among the most obviously Germanic towns on the Rota.
The Plateau of Araucarias, part of the National Forest of Ibama, 6km (4 mi) from Canela. The 131m (430 ft) waterfall plunging off the cliff into the dense growth of Canela's Parque de Caracol – a landscape typical of the Serra Gaucha's beauty.
Vale dos Vinhedos, north and west of the Rota, centre of Brazil's best vineyards.
The grandeur of the Itaimbezinho canyon country in Aparados da Serra National Park, north of Gramado, a reminder of what Brazil is really like just beyond the charming Rota.
**YOU SHOULD KNOW:**
The temperature in Gramado, Canela and Novo Petropolis (580 m/1900ft up in the Serra Gaucha) is usually about 5 °C (41°F) lower than in Porto Alegre.

Rota Romantica is Portuguese for 'Romantic Route'. In the mountains of Rio Grande do Sul, Brazil's southernmost state; it's the name for the 184 km (114 mi) scenic road that winds from São Leopoldo to São Francisco de Paula through the Serra Gaucha. It is a fairytale landscape of wooded hills, vineyards, broad rivers, canyons, waterfalls, bluffs and green pastures. It looks almost European, a look enhanced by the predominant German and Italian cultures of its original colonists. Many of the local Brazilians have blond hair and look northern European; and even speak the local Riograndenser Hunsruckish German dialect. The towns are full of black-and-white half-timbered, or Swiss chalet-style, buildings. The shops are full of German and Italian specialities; and Oktoberfest is sacred. Add to this an arcadia worthy of Poussin, in all the moods and colours of four full seasons, and the Rota Romantica is unlike any other Brazilian experience.

For visitors, Gramado and Canela are the hub of the Rota Romantica's attractions, and of the *serra alemana*, the towns with the Rota's typical German flavour. From Gramado it is easy to join the Rota's sister routes, the Italian-influenced Caminhos da Colonia, which runs through the Italian wine-making towns in the parallel *serra italiana*, and the specifically wine-inspired Rota de Uva e o Vinho. Gramado, Canela and the shoemaking and dairy town of Novo Petropolis also form part of the stunning Região de Hortênsias – a shorter road tour through miles of dazzling blue hydrangeas. One of the region's greatest delights is the constant incongruity of its Euro-Brazilian character and the Rota Romantica's popularity thrives on it. It is also the Rota's only drawback: for many northern Brazilians, the emphasis on old-world cultures practised in the Serra Gaucha's communities is a political issue about 'being Brazilian'.

# Corcovado Rack Railway

The 38 m (125 ft) statue of Christ the Redeemer, standing arms outstretched on a mountain, is the symbol of Rio de Janeiro. The mountain is the 709 m (2,326 ft) Corcovado ('Hunchback'), and the Corcovado Rack Railway takes you up – and to the most sublime views of the world's most glittering city. The Rack Railway is itself a treat. Opened in 1884 by the Emperor Dom Pedro II, it runs on the Riggenbach ladder rack system for 3.8 km (2.4 mi) from Cosme Velho Station, climbing the steep, forested hillside to emerge just behind and below the statue. From here, you can choose to climb 222 steps to the statue itself, or take a panoramic elevator all the way.

The rail trip only takes 20 minutes, but there are just four electrically-driven trains with two cars each, so capacity is limited to 360 people an hour. You can wait hours for your turn, but the journey really is worth it. The rack cranks you up Corcovado's granite crags by way of the Tijuca Forest National Park. Originally cleared by early coffee growers, the mountain was replanted with native species between 1855-70 to safeguard the springs that supplied Rio with water. Now the Park is the biggest urban forest in the world, and for visitors to the viewing platform above it, a green frame to the 360 degree panorama of downtown Rio, the Sugarloaf (from its best 'sleeping giant' angle), the Lagoa, Copacabana, Ipanema, Niteroi and several favelas.

For those in the know, a special VIP version of the train is advertised as suitable for business presentations, sofa conversations, and the luxury of onboard cocktails or appropriate snacks. With background music and a tour guide for 20 minutes, it's the best train for the descent.

**HOW:**
By train
**WHEN TO GO:**
Year-round.
**TIME IT TAKES:**
Twenty minutes up and 20 minutes down. Trains leave Cosme Velho Station every half-hour, every day from 8.30 am to 6.30 pm.
**HIGHLIGHTS:**
The vast skies arcing across Rio's bays, beaches, and beautiful grography. The VIP train's 'office' suite – for one of the world's great views
Paineira Station – you can leave the train halfway up, take a walk in Tijuca Forest, and re-board with the same ticket (but caution: most of Corcovado is only safe for experienced climbers, not hikers).
**YOU SHOULD KNOW:**
If possible, avoid Christmas and Easter, when group pilgrimages to Christ the Redeemer make the wait for the train even longer.

*The road and railway wind up Corcovado Mountain to the statue of Christ.*

# Lima to Huancayo

**HOW:**
By train
**WHEN TO GO:**
Year-round (according to the often theoretical schedule), but between October and March, at least the Huancayo end of the trip will be balmier.
**TIME IT TAKES:**
11-12 hours (in daylight: depart Lima 7.00 am, via Ticlio, La Oroya, Concepcion, arrive Huancayo 6.00-7.00 pm).
**HIGHLIGHTS:**
The Desamparados railway station in Lima, built with flourish in 1912.
Coming out of a tunnel, along a cliff-edge gallery through an arch onto the Infiernillo Bridge over a deep chasm – a standout among spectacular thrills en route.
The Oxygen Matron, whose presence on the train is required by law; for which you will be grateful.
**YOU SHOULD KNOW:**
At the railway's highest point, there is 40 per cent less oxygen in the air than at Lima. People describe feeling drunk, shell-shocked or nauseous, and may stagger about or slump gasping. But help is at hand, and it will pass as you descend.

Second only to the Pan-Himalayan Railway in Tibet which opened in 2005, the Lima-Huancayo line soars 4,829m (15,839 ft) up into the Andes, a masterpiece of engineering and a thrilling ride. It took 38 years to build the 335 km (209 mi) railway, including some 59 bridges, 66 tunnels, and 22 zigzags where the train switchbacks up sheer cliff faces. Its completion in 1908 opened the huge mineral and agricultural wealth of the Andes to market at Lima and the port of Callao. It was, and still is a working train; and that's why it works so well as a visitors' introduction to Peru.

It's a comfortable train, and it needs to be. For six hours you climb steadily from sea level at Lima to the frozen wilderness of the high Andes, feeding your growing altitude headache with coca tea from the trolley. When you stretch your legs at what is still thought to be the world's highest station, Ticlio (4,758m/15,606 ft), you may gasp for air and need the help of the Oxygen Matron who patrols the train. Most people do. The cold is bitter but the scenery is breathtaking. It gets even better as you revive, watching flowing robes and llamas raising dust in the settlements of the altiplano. At La Oroya, you change tracks and direction. Nothing grows around La Oroya. It is the smelting centre for a collection of mining towns nearby, all overhung with the smell of sulphur. After the fantastic mountain panoramas before this section, it's a relief to leave the peaks and treeless tundra behind at Jauja, and descend through the fertile greenery of the Mantaro Valley, one of the greatest of all Andean craft centres. By the time you reach Huancayo, you feel you've travelled through the heart of Peru's economic future as well as its highland geography.

*The train soars up into the Andes*

# Cuzco to Machu Picchu

*Tavelling through the Urubamba Valley.*

Three kinds of train run between Cuzco, the Inca capital, and Machu Picchu, the 'Lost City' hidden in the high peaks of the Andes. The 'Backpacker' is the most economical, and usually more crowded. The 'Vistadome' offers the premium service of greater comfort, free onboard refreshments, and mostly-glass observation carriages. Both services leave Cuzco at 6 am for the roughly 4 hour, 112 km (70 mi) long journey, but spend the first half hour climbing steeply up a series of switchbacks called the Zigzag to Poroy, the first stop. The third kind of train starts its journey from Poroy: saving half an hour is the kind of luxury it represents. So is starting at 9 am – so that by the time its passengers arrive at the most glorious Inca ruins in the world, the other visitors will already be leaving. The luxury train is called the Hiram Bingham, and behaves like a 1920s Pullman service, including cocktails and lunch.

The railway runs through typical Andean valley farms, via the Pomatales River Gorge to Ollantaytambo, at the start of the sacred valley of the Urubamba. It passes whole hillsides of broken terracing, dotted with ruined Inca forts, and then follows the river into the Urubamba gorge. It climbs past the ruins of Qente into a valley where the microclimate is fed by a waterfall, and giant hummingbirds are common among the bright flowers of the morning. At Chachabamba, rocky outcrops are overhung with bromeliads and orchids, and tall ceibos crowd the train. Then the view opens as it pulls up at Machu Picchu Town, 2 km (1.25 mi) below the Citadel, and the place where passengers catch the 20-minute bus ride to the top. Anticipation alone makes this a great railway journey.

**HOW:**
By train
**WHEN TO GO:**
Year-round. All three services are more expensive between June and August, the dry season.
**TIME IT TAKES:**
Four hours (San Pedro Station, Cuzco to M Picchu); 3½ hours (Poroy to M Picchu).
**HIGHLIGHTS:**
The comfort, even on the Backpacker, and especially if you've been hiking or trekking.
The Qente waterfall, and the pristine subtropical flora around it.
The view up the Urubamba Valley on the return journey.
**YOU SHOULD KNOW:**
Though much improved, the train from Cuzco to Machu Picchu is notorious for opportunistic thieving. The views and the occasion are so exciting that it's easy to take your eye off the ball.

*A hiker on the trail to the Pisac ruins*

# The Inca Trail

The trek to Machu Picchu, the Lost City of the Incas, is one of the world's most famous. Even though the route to it is crowded, it's only because of the imaginative appeal of its destination. Crowds don't matter when you first arrive at the Trail's end – the stone portal of Intipunku, the Gateway of the Sun, through which you first see the ruins of Machu Picchu.

The traditional route begins at Cuzco, once the imperial capital of the Incas' Andean Empire. Most visitors choose to acclimatize to the altitude while browsing Cuzco's Inca and Spanish colonial history, architecture and artefacts.The trek leads up the Urubamba River valley from Chilca to the Inca ruins at Llactapata; past the gentle farmland slopes and woods of Wayllabamba to a steep climb through cloud forest to the second campsite at Llulluchapampa. The plants, flowers and birds are completely different in the open terrain before Abra de Huarmihuanasca, the 'Dead Woman's Pass', at 4,200m   (13,776 ft) the highest point of the trek; but the hard work of climbing at altitude is worth it for the panorama of the Vilcanota and Vilcabamba mountain ranges. The Trail drops to cross the Pacaymayo River but at the next pass, Runku Raccay, you come to a series of ancient stone steps descending to the Inca town of Sayac Marca, from which a still superbly-paved Inca highway disappears through amazing cloud forest to Phuyupatamarca ('Cloud-Level Town'). This campsite is close to the extensive Inca site of Huinay Huayna, from which the Trail drops through forest until it levels out and climbs to Intipunku itself. No photograph prepares you for the reality of Machu Picchu. The legendary magnificence of the panorama is magnified by the physical investment you make in Inca history and culture on the ascent.

# Cordillera Blanca

The Cordillera Blanca of central Peru is the world's highest tropical mountain range. With 29 summits over 6,000 m (19,680), its landscape of snowcapped peaks, glaciers, lakes, rivers and treeless tundra is among the most dramatic in the Andes. It is a magnet for serious climbers and experienced trekkers, but its paramount beauty can be equally appreciated from the hundreds of old horse trails weaving through its valleys and passes – the highways accessible to mountain bikers. There are few restrictions on biking in the Cordillera, so with a good guide, your choice of routes depends only on energy and the time available.

There's a classic 7-day circuit of the Cordillera that runs past Laguna Querococha, up over the watershed to the extraordinary archaeological ruins of Chavin de Huantar, and along the Conchucos Valley altiplano. The long return ascent brings you to the 4,750-m (15,580-ft) Portachuelo de Llanganuco Pass, and what is considered to be the most beautiful view in South America. With the Andes ranked behind them into the misty distance, you stand in what feels like touching distance of Nevado Huascaran, Chopicalqui, Chacraraju and Huandoy peaks. Then you launch into an incredible flying descent past the Llanganuco lakes to the route's end, at 2,500 m (8,200 ft), Yungay town.

You can acclimatize in and around 3,090 m (10,135 ft) Huaraz, the mountain-biking and trekking hub in the Callejón de Huaylas valley. You can explore the villages descending the Huaripampa Valley; follow the Ulta up to the Punto Olimpica Pass and a long thrilling ride down to San Luis; tour the glacial lakes full of coots and herons; break for a thermal bath set in the Quercos River Gorge; and always against the magnificent backdrop of Peru's loveliest mountains. The Cordillera Blanca makes you feel you reinvented mountain biking.

**HOW:**
By bike
**WHEN TO GO:**
May to September
**TIME IT TAKES:**
Four days (minimum for a short 'circuit'). 7-10 days is usual, to include 2 days acclimatization rides with a guide. It's possible for independent riders to go it alone – but parties of at least 2-4, plus a guide, are usual (and easy to arrange) for security and safety.
**HIGHLIGHTS:**
The Andean panorama, seen from the Llanganuco Pass.
The 'folded mountains' above the lovely Laguna Purhuay – a geological wonder of a mountain of rock apparently melted, like chocolate, and petrified in mid-flow.
The grove of Puya Raimondii cactus spikes, 3 m (10 ft) tall, each rising out of a ball of spiky fronds, near the rim of Laguna Quesquecocha.
Freewheeling through the Quechua farming communities of the temperate Conchucos Valley (adding cultural to the geographical shock!)
**YOU SHOULD KNOW:**
Most of the Cordillera Blanca falls within the Huascaran National Park, but the region is barely regulated or policed. On short or long trips, even on popular routes, you need to keep your wits about you, both on your bike and in camp.

*Puya Raimondii cactus plants tower over this tourist.*

# The Huayhuash Circuit

**HOW:**
On foot
**WHEN TO GO:**
May to September
**TIME IT TAKES:**
Twelve days (minimum for the full Circuit, including two 'rest' days for detour treks). Most travellers need to add at least two days for acclimatization, if not attached to a tour programme that already includes it. It is not at all unusual for trek agencies to propose Circuit treks of 18 to 22 days to allow plenty of time for detours during the trip.
**HIGHLIGHTS:**
The detour trek from the campsite at Laguna Carhuacocha to Laguna Siula, at the foot of Siula Grande itself.
The view from Punta Cayoc – north to the entire Huayhuash group of peaks, south to the Cordillera Raura, and immediately to one side of where you're standing, the glaciers of Puscanturpa.
The campsite at Laguna Jahuacocha – a beautiful lake reflecting Rondoy, Jirishanca, El Toro, Yerupaja, Siula Grande and Sarupo, among other snowy peaks.
Trekking with mules and Quechua muleteers.
**YOU SHOULD KNOW:**
Even highly experienced trekkers can be at risk of altitude sickness. Lack of regulation and policing in the Huayhuash range means that it is better to attempt the Circuit as part of a guided group, for security and safety.

The Cordillera Huayhuash (pronounced 'why-wash') is isolated, rugged, difficult and dangerous to trek in. The Circuit trek is the most challenging of all its routes. The reward for completing it – available only to experienced and determined travellers – is a mythic sense of communion with seriously high mountains. It is no coincidence that the Huayhuash Circuit goes close to Siula Grande, climbed in 1985 by Joe Simpson and Simon Yates, and the setting for Simpson's epic memoir of courage *Touching The Void*.

The Huayhuash repays adventurers with majestic vistas of some of Peru's highest peaks, high alpine valleys and turquoise lakes. The actual circuit begins in sight of Yerupaja (6,634 m/21,760 ft), Peru's second-highest mountain, at the Quechua town of Chiquian. Accompanied now by mules, you follow the Quero River to the meadows of Mitacocha and up to the wild terrain enclosing Laguna Sacracocha. By the fourth day, you leave the alpaca herds of Cartelhuain below to cross the Continental Divide, zigzagging to the Punta Cacanan pass (4,700 m/15,416 ft). From here, you look down on the idyllic meadow campsite of Laguna Mitacocha, famous for its trout and its birdlife, and the fabulous range of the Huayhuash high peaks, including 6,126 m (20,093 ft) Jirishanka. The panorama ahead improves each day as you follow the green valleys and high passes deeper into the mountains, but on the sixth day the terrain above the Atocshaico lakes becomes a lunar wilderness of boulder-strewn ridges before a steep descent through herds of grazing alpaca and vicuna to Huayhuash Village. Punta Cuyoc (5,050 m/16,564 ft) is the trek's highest point, and from here the Quebrada Huanactapay is the first of a series of valleys, passes, waterfalls, lakes and glaciers that ends after some twelve days at Laguna Jahuacocha, nestled in a huge amphitheatre of the Cordillera's most impressive peaks. This trek creates feelings that should be bottled.

*The infamous Siula Grande*

# Headwaters of the Amazon

Chiclayo is the major regional centre for northern Peru, the crossroads between the coast, the highlands, and the jungle. Iquitos lies on the other side of the Andes, a major city that can only be reached by air or by boat along the Amazon and its headwaters. Local businessmen in a hurry claim to make the trip in three full days. Nobody else would dream of taking fewer than seven days, and most opt for two to three weeks for the journey. There are far too many world-class distractions en route.

Scattered around Chiclayo are Peru's most important pre-Hispanic and pre-Inca cultural sites, including the massive citadel complex of Chan Chan, capital of the Chimu people, and Huaca Larga, the greatest adobe building in South America and one of 26 in Tucume's Valley of Pyramids. It's a 10-hour drive up and across the watershed to Chachapoyas, through the wonders of the cloud forest and mountain jungle; but curiosity will divert you to Cajamarca, where the conquistadors imprisoned Inca Atahualpa, or the fortress sites of Sipán and Kuelap. The region's rich history is hand in hand with its astonishing natural beauty. Tarapoto is as famous for the multiple waterfalls in its surrounding forests, and the variety of rare birds and butterflies, as for the Quechua music, art and dancing of local villages, and the 2,500 orchid species in its leafy environs.

The road ends at Yurimaguas, where cargo boats leave for the two-day journey to Iquitos. You watch the river grow – from the Huallaga to the Maranon, the Ucayali and the broad Amazon stream. You get some idea of how the forest people live, and the extraordinary biodiversity of the upper Amazon. Most of all, you feel an urgent desire to stop and explore.

**HOW:**
By bus or car and then by boat
**WHEN TO GO:**
Year-round; but the unpaved highland roads off the main route can be treacherously muddy in the December to March rainy season, and in the Peruvian Amazon lowlands it rains from December to May. Even the shallow Huallaga remains navigable in the 'dry' season of June to August.
**TIME IT TAKES:**
24 hours by bus or car from Chiclayo to Yurimaguas. Then two days minimum by boat to Iquitos. Coming the other way, any number of agencies will allow you to spend weeks or even months on the river system at various jungle reserves, eco-lodges, or Indian villages, before leaving you at Yurimaguas.
**HIGHLIGHTS:**
Swimming below 35 m (115 ft) Aguashiyacu waterfall.
The colossal Pacaya Samiria Reserve, the pristine jungle jewel of northern Peru – accessible only by boat, either from the riverboat stop at Lagunas, or as a side-trip from Iquitos. (NB it can take at least 3 days to get in and out of the Reserve, and with no tourist infrastructure, you need to hire or attach yourself to a guide).
**YOU SHOULD KNOW:**
At its shortest, this journey reveals greater natural, historical and cultural variety than any other in Peru.

*The citadel complex of Chan Chan*

# El Choro

*Hikers on the Chucuro Pass*

Bolivia may be the poorest country in South America but whatever it lacks in the way of material comforts is more than compensated for by an extravagance of cultural heritage and sublime natural scenery. Nowhere is this more evident than on El Choro, the 70-km (40-mi) long, ancient Inca road that connects the high mountains of the Altiplano with the sub-tropical jungle of Las Yungas.

From La Cumbre, near La Paz, you scramble your way up the barren mountainside to the Chucuro Pass, high above the tree line at nearly 5,000 m (16,000 ft). Toss a stone onto the cairn beside the statue of Jesus for good luck, then set off along the paved path, cut into the mountains a thousand years ago, now worn smooth and polished by centuries of human and animal feet. You wind your way down, past gushing waterfalls and torrential rivers, across old wooden bridges, alongside ancient dry stone walls, pre-Columbian ruins and isolated thatched huts. On your journey you will encounter itinerant Aymará Indians in their traditional brightly coloured costumes – traders and alpaca herdsmen, leading pack-llamas loaded with goods to sell in the Altiplano.

Desolate mountain rock gives way to the mysterious twisted and stunted trees of the Challapampa cloud forest – a magical place to stop for the night. The next day, as you continue your rapid descent, the rarified high-altitude air becomes ever more dense and humid, ripe with the smells of the rainforest, and the vegetation starts to grow luxuriantly thick and green. By the third day, you find yourself in a paradise of verdant jungle, with all your senses quickened by the exotic sights and scents and sounds of Las Yungas. You will reach the laid-back hill town of Coroico glowing with a real sense of achievement at having accomplished one of the best treks in South America.

# The Lost World of Huanchaca and the Caparú Plateau

The 600-m (1,968-ft) high Caparú Plateau emerges abruptly out of the midst of the primeval Huanchaca rainforest, a 1.5 million hectare (3.7 million acre) conservation area in northeast Bolivia. The awe-inspiring sight of this 150-km (95-mi) long pre-Cambrian sandstone mesa (table mountain) was first documented by the explorer Colonel Percy Fawcett in 1910 and the description of his journey through the wilderness inspired Arthur Conan Doyle to write his famous novel *The Lost World*.

Flor d'Oro, in the far north of Huanchaca National Park, is only accessible by light aircraft or a long boat journey up the River Iténez, the border with Brazil. On the flight from Santa Cruz, there are spectacular aerial views. The sky is reflected in the land below, an endless patchwork of rainforest, wetlands, and lakes threaded through with huge rivers. Out of this kaleidoscopic swirl of greens, greys and blues, a rust-red wall of cliff suddenly rises to the savannah plain of the Caparú – a complete contrast to the lowland tangle of jungle. From above, you witness the surreal spectacle of rivers tipping over the sheer edge of the plateau in huge cascades.

The region is one of the last virgin areas on the planet, with a diversity of habitats and species unmatched anywhere in the Americas. As you trek from Flor d'Oro to Lago Caiman and then scramble up Caparú, you will pass through four different eco-regions, seeing all sorts of exotic plants, birds and animals. Eventually you clamber up to Mirador de los Monos (Monkey Point) and, as you gaze down from the plateau at the rainforest and wetlands below, it strikes you that you are among the privileged few who have ever adventured this far into the wild.

*View of the rainforest from the Caparú Plateau*

**HOW:**
By plane or boat and on foot
**WHEN TO GO:**
May to October
**TIME IT TAKES:**
Flight two hours. Hike 10 hours. Allow between four and seven days to make the most of your visit to the region.
**HIGHLIGHTS:**
Aerial view of the plateau, rivers and waterfalls.
Swimming in the pool of El Encanto waterfall.
Sights of rare birds and animals including spider monkeys, jaguars and macaws.
Los Torres rocks.
View from Monkey Point.
**YOU SHOULD KNOW:**
The Huanchaca was renamed the Noel Kempff Mercado National Park after a famous Bolivian biologist. It is a controlled region and you must plan your itinerary with the authorities beforehand. The hike described here is moderately difficult and requires a good level of fitness. You can plan a less arduous route and/or explore by 4x4 or canoe.

*Isla del Sol and Lake Titicaca*

# To The Home of the Sun God

From the picturesque town of Copacabana, on the southwestern shore of Lake Titicaca, it is only a boat ride to the heartland of the Incas. In Incan mythology, the rugged island mountain of Isla del Sol is venerated as the birthplace of civilization. Here the Sun God created the first Incan, Manco Capac, out of the sacred waters of Lake Titicaca. Today, the Aymará Indians still cultivate the same ancient terraces that their ancestors carved into the mountainsides more than a thousand years ago.

The ferry is a small cabin boat into which you are packed like a sardine, or you must perch perilously on the almost equally crowded roof. The underpowered outboard motor splutters, straining to carry its load out into the lake. There is no doubt at all that the boat will capsize; you are entirely at the mercy of the gods. Since you are shortly going to drown, you may as well take a last glimpse at the world. And it is spellbinding. The lake stretches before you – 8,000 sq km (3,120 sq mi) of the bluest water you have ever seen, encircled by the tallest mountains in the western hemisphere.

Your joy at still being alive, as you tread the path along the island ridge, is soon replaced by a sense of wonder. You are in a place untouched by time: *campesinos* patiently till the unyielding soil with wooden hoes, bowler-hatted Aymará women trudge uphill bearing loads larger than themselves, and raggedy urchins scamper along the terraces after their skinny sheep. As you sit in the ruins of an Incan palace watching the sun go down over the lake, the glistening peaks of the Cordillera Real take on an almost mystical hue. It is only too easy to believe that you have reached the origin of the world.

# Torres del Paine 'W' Trail

The 'W' Trail through the Torres del Paine Biosphere Reserve is one of the world's classic treks. The spectacular scenery, shaped by the combined forces of glaciation and fierce Patagonian winds, is an extraordinary dreamlike landscape of spiky mountains, water and ice – a phantasmagoria of colour and form. You camp beside turquoise, aquamarine and green lakes strewn with icebergs, cross tumultuous rivers and waterfalls, walk through wild grasslands and primeval forests, gaze hypnotically at blue-tinted glaciers, and marvel at wondrous rock spires soaring to 3,000 m (9,800 ft).

An initial boat journey northwards across Lake Grey takes you to the trail head. From the boat, you will see great chunks of ice dropping off the face of Glacier Grey and icebergs drifting along the lake. The trail leads along the eastern shore where you can view Glacier Grey from above. This huge fractured river of ice, over 3-km (2-mi) wide, reflects the constantly changing skies, with a mesmerising effect of dancing shapes of light and shade.

The strenuous climb through French Valley – a cirque of spectacular sheer cliffs – leads you to a heart-stopping view over the lakes and another glacier. Walking the 13 km (8 mi) Sendero Paso los Cuernos (Horns Pass Way) along the northern shore of Lake Nordenskjold, you will see guanacos and humueles roaming the grasslands, and condors wheeling gracefully around the horned peaks of the bizarre bi-coloured slate and granite Cuernos mountains, possessing the sky.

The last leg of the trek is a scramble over a steep moraine of boulders to the most dramatic view of all – the Torres. These three stark granite monoliths, from which the Reserve gets its name, loom over the land like sentinels, dwarfing you beneath the power of nature.

**HOW:**
By boat and on foot
**WHEN TO GO:**
High season is from December to March when there is up to 18 hours of daylight.
**TIME IT TAKES:**
Four to six days
**HIGHLIGHTS:**
The lake crossing with views of Grey Glacier.
Mirador Francés
Cuernos del Paine
Torres del Pain
Wildlife sightings.
**YOU SHOULD KNOW:**
This is a moderately strenuous trek, difficult in parts, requiring a good level of physical fitness. There are overnight shelters and camping sites at regular intervals along all the trails. There are also facilities for cycling, horse riding and rafting. Despite its remoteness, the Torres del Paine attracts trekkers from all over the world and, at the peak of the season, can feel crowded.

*Sendero Paso los Cuernos in Torres del Paine National Park*

# Through the Patagonian Channels

**HOW:**
By boat
**WHEN TO GO:**
November to March
**TIME IT TAKES:**
Four days
**HIGHLIGHTS:**
Taitao Peninsula.
Messier Channel – the changing colours of the water from the rivers pouring down from the icefield.
Ultima Esperanza Sound – cascades tumbling over verdant cliffs.
Views of Pius XI and San Rafael Glaciers.
Whale sighting.
**YOU SHOULD KNOW:**
You can make this voyage equally well in either direction by cruise ship as well as the local cargo/passenger ferry described here. You can also go on sea-kayak expeditions through channels off the shipping route for a close-up experience. Anyone sailing their own boat must report to the port authorities twice a day with notice of their whereabouts.

The ferry that travels the wind-lashed west coast of Southern Patagonia takes you through the intricate glacial labyrinth of channels, islands and fjords at the tail end of the Andes Cordillera. It is a wonderful voyage past forest, river and mountain scenery and across a stormy stretch of open sea, accompanied by dolphins, albatross and even the occasional whale.

From the port of Puerto Montt, the ferry weaves through the Gulfs of Ancud and Corcovado, passing by picturesque wooden villages on stilts huddled on the shore of the UNESCO World Heritage Isla de Chiloé and the beautiful thickly forested islets of the Chonos Archipelago, before heading round the Taitao Peninsula, the westernmost promontory of the Chilean coast, and across the wild, windswept waters of the Golfo de Penas (Gulf of Sorrows). It almost defies belief that the Kawesqar Indians, the pre-Hispanic nomadic inhabitants of the Patagonian Channels, habitually crossed this tempestuous sea in their dugout canoes.

At the end of the Messier Channel, one of the deepest fjords in the world, the lush scenery becomes bleaker, and the further south you go, the lower the snowline creeps down the wild, barren mountainsides. The ferry calls in at Puerto Edén, the only settlement along this untamed stretch of coast, home to the last of the Kawésqars. The passage continues through miles of narrows, often scarcely wide enough for the boat to negotiate. It finally enters Ultima Esperanza (Last Hope) Sound, with stunning views of the mountains of the Patagonian Icefield, and journey's end at Puerto Natales, gateway to the iconic granite spires of Torres del Paine National Park. You will look back on your voyage with fond memories – as much for the atmosphere of human camaraderie among the disparate bunch of passengers and motley ship's crew as for the magnificent glacial scenery.

*The Patagonian Andes tower over Ultima Esperanza Bay.*

# Wine Route

*A vineyard in the Colchagua Valley*

The wine region is a fertile basin of eight upland valleys between the Andes and the Pacific extending 950 km (600 mi) southwards from Santiago, Chile's capital city. The conditions are perfect for vine-growing – crumbly loam and volcanic soils, clear unpolluted air, and a balmy frost-free climate of hot sunny days and cold nights with a long dry season, allowing for slow, steady maturation of the fruit to produce wines of superb taste and texture. Vines were first brought to Chile by 16th century Jesuits who, with a weather eye for potential converts, followed closely in the footsteps of the Spanish conquistadors. They zealously set about their missionary task, introducing the indigenous farmers to their sacramental joys and teaching them the art of viticulture.

The 120-km (75-mi) long Colchagua Valley produces the best world-class red wines of all and is Chile's first official Ruta del Vino. The route starts at San Fernando, heart of the country's Hispanic folk-culture, homeland of the rodeo and the *huaso* – the chic Chilean equivalent of a cowboy, kitted out in long leather silver-spurred boots, swirling poncho and broad-brimmed hat.

The Wine Train chugs through the scenic agricultural landscape of fruit orchards, wheat fields and wineries at a gentle 30-40 kph (20-25 mph), its 1920s German-built carriages pulled by a heritage Chilean steam engine. Passengers are treated to wine tastings as the train passes each beautifully tended vineyard. From the window, there are panoramic views of snow-capped Andean volcanoes, oak-forested hills, and *huasos* on horseback riding down country roads lined with slender poplar trees. Arriving at Santa Cruz, you find yourself in a charming traditional country town surrounded by wineries, where you can watch the production process and taste the new vintage direct from the vat.

**HOW:**
By train
**WHEN TO GO:**
November to April
**TIME IT TAKES:**
Train journey of 90 minutes plus a full day sightseeing.
**HIGHLIGHTS:**
Museum of Colchagua – a beautifully curated collection.
Casa Silva – the oldest and most traditional winery in the Colchagua Valley.
Santa Cruz – picturesque rural town surrounded by lakes and vineyards.
*Huasos* – Chilean 'cowboys' in traditional dress.
**YOU SHOULD KNOW:**
Chile is the only wine-producing country in the world free of the dreaded phylloxera pest that wiped out so many European vineyards in the 19th century. This means the vineyards do not have to constantly renew their root stock; some of the vines here are more than 100 years old, producing wines of exceptional character.

*A cyclist on the Carretera Austral road*

# Carretera Austral

**HOW:**
By bike or car and ferry
**WHEN TO GO:**
January or February
**TIME IT TAKES:**
Three to four weeks by bike. Seven to ten days by car.
**HIGHLIGHTS:**
Rio Negro Hornopirén – one of the loveliest villages in Chile, nestling in a bay enclosed by volcanoes.
Pumalín National Park
Queulat National Park – Pedro Aguirre Cerda Lagoon, glaciers, cascades.
Lago General Carrera – Catedrales de Mármol, village of Puerto Bertrand, and Rio Baker.
Caleta Tortel – picturesque coastal village, built on stilts.
**YOU SHOULD KNOW:**
Although only mountain bike aficionados with stamina and determination should attempt the entire route, any properly equipped enthusiastic cyclist can do a stretch without too much difficulty. If you want to go by car, it is advisable to use a 4x4. More sections of the road are being paved every year so no doubt it will not be long before droves of tourist buses are hurtling down it.

Otherwise known as 'Pinochet's Folly', the construction of the 1,200 km (750 mi) Carretera Austral trunk road was part of the Chilean dictator's scheme to open up the impoverished, sparsely populated region of Aisén. Thirty years and millions of dollars later, it is still a work in progress. It wends its tortuous way through the mountainous, fjord-fragmented terrain of North Patagonia, a potholed dirt and gravel track barely wide enough for two vehicles, only paved around the larger towns, with ferry crossings wherever the complex coastal topography bars its path – a nightmare for drivers but a dream come true for mountain bikers. From the port of Puerto Montt to the sleepy southern village of Villa O'Higgins on the edge of the Patagonian Icefield, the road carves a path through phenomenal scenery that makes the senses reel. You travel for miles without seeing a soul, camping by riversides on a journey through one of the world's most remote and rugged regions.

Within minutes of hitting the road you hop on and off a ferry into stunning volcanic scenery of sub-tropical rainforest. At the precipitous cliffs of Hornopirén you face more water – five hours crossing the bay to Caleta Gonzalo. This initial cyclist's frustration is worth enduring for what follows – hundreds of kilometres of fantastic cycling. After a bumpy ride through the glorious forest and fjord country of Pumalin National Park to the fishing town of Chaitén, you cycle 425 km (265 mi) along a switchback of mountain ridges and lush valleys, across tumbling rivers with glaciers and waterfalls to the beautiful turquoise lakes around Coihaique, the regional capital. A final 440 km (275 mi) stretch through the awe-inspiring, isolated mountain terrain around Cochrane and Tamango National Park takes you to road's end – the accomplishment of the 'ultimate' bike ride.

# Across the Patagonian Cordillera

A horse and a guide are prerequisites for a trek into the Cordillera. A packhorse is the only realistic means of travel in this uncharted Andean wilderness, a land that is just as it was 500 years ago when the first pioneers and missionaries made their way across it. There are no roads at all, only ancient Indian paths and drovers' tracks, known only to the *arrieros* (mule drivers) and *vaquearos* (cattle and sheep drovers) handed down from one generation to the next.

From Lago Puelo in Argentina, the Puelo River flows through Lago Inferior on the Chilean side of the border to the Reloncavi estuary on the Pacific Coast. This is the starting point for your ride into the wilds, some 100 km (60 mi) from the city of Puerto Montt.

The tranquil ride from the village of Puelo along the Reloncavi fjord is a scenic treat with the Yate Volcano towering ahead of you. After loading your horse onto the ferry to cross Lago Tagua-Tagua you then take to the narrow trails that lead through verdant rainforest scored with tumbling rivers, dramatic waterfalls and rapids, to high mountain plateaux of wild flower meadows, sparkling streams and azure lakes. Apart from the occasional isolated farmhouse, you really are in the back of beyond, entirely reliant on your guide to pick your way along the valleys and ridges, across the lakes and rivers to Lago Inferior on the border with Argentina.

You re-encounter the 21st century world in the form of the Chilean border police. Here you must say farewell to your horse and take a boat across Lago Inferior to Argentina where you disembark in the steppes of Lago Puelo National Park under the snowy peaks of Tres Picos, at the end of an amazing journey.

**HOW:**
On horseback
**WHEN TO GO:**
November to March
**TIME IT TAKES:**
Eight to ten days
**HIGHLIGHTS:**
Crossing Rio Puelo in a wooden boat with your horse swimming alongside.
La Pasarela del Rio Puelo – spectacular rapids and waterfalls.
Lago las Rocas – a beautiful lake in a glorious setting.
Staying in a traditional Chilean homestead.
**YOU SHOULD KNOW:**
It is easy to hire horses and guides. No previous experience of riding is needed but you should be reasonably physically fit. Treks vary in length; a single day's ride in this beautiful region is well worth doing even if you do not have the time or inclination for the full haul.

*Lago Puelo lies in the National Park of the same name.*

# Tren a las Nubes

Built in the 1940s, the Tren a las Nubes (Train to the Clouds) is the third highest railway in the world. It is worth travelling along for the sheer technical wizardry of the railway line itself, quite apart from the mind-blowing terrain it goes through on its skyward journey. American engineer Richard Fontaine Maury designed the track so that an engine could pull a train up the mountains by its own power alone without needing the conventional mechanism of a cog-and-pinion rackrail. The resulting train journey is a thrilling 220-km (136-mi) zigzag switchback ride crossing some of most complex topography on the planet by means of 13 viaducts, 29 bridges and 21 tunnels. There are two huge loops along the route where the track virtually doubles back on itself in order to gain height and you feel that you have been given a front row circle seat over the world as you gaze down from vertiginous mountain heights.

From the sub-tropical colonial city of Salta, the train travels up the Lerma Valley passing quaint mud-built villages and red-flowering ceibo trees as it heads into the Quebrada del Toro (Bull's Gorge) and across the rocky salt desert canyons of the Andes – the little-known lands of the Diaguita Indians. Awesome rock formations, blasted into grotesque shapes by aeons of erosion, appear in a kaleidoscopic whirl of colour where the earth has been tinted by rich veins of mineral ore – vivid shades of red, yellow, pink, green and orange.

The train stops along the way so that you can wander around in this strange land on your way to the altiplano copper-mining town of San Antonio de los Cobres. Here, standing at 4,230 m (13,900 ft) on the Polvorilla Viaduct among the snow-capped peaks, you will find the clouds really are drifting beneath your feet.

*La Polvorilla Viaduct near San Antonio de los Cobres*

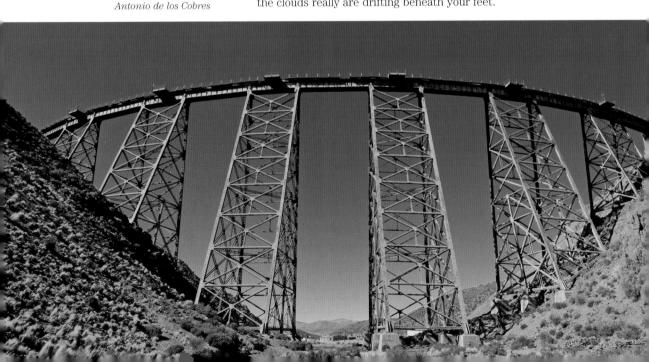

# The End of the World Train

*The End of the World Train*

This is a journey to delight any railway enthusiast. Not only are you travelling on the world's southernmost railway line but you are pulled by one of several heritage steam engines along a narrow gauge track with a fascinating past.

The railway starts 8 km (5 mi) from Ushuaia and runs for some 14 km (9 mi) into Tierra del Fuego National Park, a protected area of 630 sq km (240 sq mi) once inhabited by Yamaha Indians. As the train meanders along the River Pipo valley at a sedate 15 kph (9 mph) you have breathtaking views of the wild glacial landscape of the South Andes Cordillera – steep snow-capped mountains, rivers, waterfalls, woods and lakes interspersed with tundra plateau carpeted in lichens and mosses. The journey ends at Estación del Parque from where you can explore this remote region on foot.

Although today the End of the World Train is a tourist attraction, it was originally built to fulfil an altogether murkier purpose – the transportation of forced labour to the hinterland forest and of felled trees back to the coast. By the end of the 19th century the Argentinian authorities had established a penal colony as far away from civilization as possible, at the tip of South America. From these inauspicious beginnings emerged today's city of Ushuaia, its earliest buildings constructed by convicts using timber from the surrounding sub-polar forests. The prison was transformed into a naval base in 1947 and the railway was decommissioned in 1952 after an earthquake badly damaged the track. The growth of the travel industry led to its re-opening in 1994 as an environmentally-friendly means of conveying tourists to an otherwise inaccessible part of the National Park. Despite the best efforts of tourist brochures, the railway is still commonly known as 'The Prisoners' Train'.

**HOW:**
By train
**WHEN TO GO:**
All year
**TIME IT TAKES:**
One hour
**HIGHLIGHTS:**
Ushuaia Museo del Presidio – Prison Museum.
Cañadón del Toro gorge
Cascada La Macarena waterfall
Tree cemetery
**YOU SHOULD KNOW:**
To fully appreciate the trip it is a good idea to visit the Prison Museum first, where you will get atmospheric impressions of life in the penal colony and find out more about the railway and National Park.

# South Patagonia Ice Cap Trek

Los Glaciares National Park in the Patagonian Icefield is a 4,450 sq km (1,720 sq mi) wonderland – a maze of rivers and glaciers, milky glacial lakes, and mountain spires soaring like cathedrals into the sky. This is a landscape from another planet – unimaginably strange and overwhelmingly beautiful. At the heart of the Park are two huge glacial lakes, Lago Argentino to the south, the largest lake in Argentina, and Lake Viedma to the north, in the shadow of the 'ultimate' granite massifs of Mount Fitz Roy and Cerro Torre.

The starting point for any trek is El Chaltén, an isolated mountain village at the confluence of two rivers north of Lake Viedma. From here, after you have hiked through the romantic lenga beechwoods along the banks of the Rio Eléctrico, you hike up to Paso Marconi for incredible views of Mount Fitz Roy and don your snow shoes for the tough but scenic journey across the icefield, traversing the Viedma and Upsala glaciers through magical ice landscapes, bivouacking in rough shelters along the way.

At last, as you scramble across Upsala's rocky moraine ridge, Lake Argentino comes into view. The boat ride across the lake to the southern edge of the Park, passing the glacier faces, is a fitting grand finale to your trek – both spell-binding and scaring. These relentless rivers of ice make awesome creaking and juddering sounds as the iceface continually fractures and falls. Huge chunks come crashing down into the weird milky-green coloured water and then sail calmly off, littering the lake with icebergs.

You end your ice-journey at El Calafate, a friendly rustic town on the southern shore where nature once again wears a benign expression and you can mull over your unforgettable experience over a traditional meal of Patagonian lamb and home-made bread.

*Mt Fitz Roy in the Parque Nacional los Glaciares*

**HOW:**
On foot
**WHEN TO GO:**
December to March
**TIME IT TAKES:**
Seven to nine days
**HIGHLIGHTS:**
Rio Eléctrico – beechwoods, wildlife, rare birds and exotic flowers.
View of Mt Fitz Roy at dawn when the granite spires glow pink.
Snoe-shoeing on the Viedma Glacier.
Lago Argentino boat trip to see Perito Moreno.
Walichu Caves – palaeolithic cave paintings near El Calafate.
**YOU SHOULD KNOW:**
The South Patagonian icefield is the third biggest continuous stretch of ice in the world – only the ice caps of Antarctica and Greenland are larger. This trek is difficult; previous experience of hiking in winter conditions and good physical fitness is required. There are many other walks and hikes to suit all abilities from one day to two weeks.

# Cycle Across the Andes to the Atacama

The road between San Salvador de Jujuy in north-west Argentina and the Atacama, the world's driest desert, is the highest route in the Americas. It takes you through jaw-dropping World Heritage scenery and over the Paso Jama into Chile at an altitude of nearly 6,000 m (20,000 ft).

This is not a trip for the faint-hearted. It is 400 km (250 mi) of tough mountain road. You start gently enough, pedalling slowly along the ancient Camino Inca, constantly distracted by the incredible multi-coloured rock of the Quebrada de Humahuaca. After about 60 km (40 mi) you turn off to the picturesque mud-built village of Purmamarca, admire the Cerro de Siete Colores (Seven Coloured Mountain) and prepare for some serious cycling.

The Cuesta de Lipan is a hair-raising stretch of fiendish bends through desolate wilderness, spiralling up to 4,000 m (13,000 ft). From the top, you gaze down at a hallucinatory view of blank whiteness – the entrancing salt landscape of the Salinas Grandes. You cycle across in a light-headed haze to make the ascent to the remote border town of Susques, the place to take a break and wander round the ancient ruins.

After the triumph of crossing Paso Jama – Argentina's gateway across the Andes – the road, to your horror, goes uphill again. You stagger on, for what feels like forever. Just when you've decided you must be on the wrong road, you are suddenly there – at the top of the world. The Atacama Desert spreads below you, and beyond, the dream of the Pacific Ocean. The descent to San Pedro is fantastic. You hurtle downhill in a spirit of wild exhilaration to a tourist town chock-full of backpackers – the sort of place you might normally deride. For once, you will be only too grateful for the creature comforts it provides.

**HOW:**
By bike
**WHEN TO GO:**
April to October
**TIME IT TAKES:**
Three to five days (or 12 hours in a 4x4)
**HIGHLIGHTS:**
Quebrada (Gorge) of Humahuaca – UNESCO World Heritage Site
Purmamarca's beautiful 16th-17th century Chapel.
Salinas Grandes
Moon Valley rock formations San Pedro de Atacama.
Flamingoes at Salar de Tara, Atacama.
**YOU SHOULD KNOW:**
You need to be very fit for this difficult journey. You will be travelling through an isolated semi-desert region at an average altitude of 3,000 m (10,000 ft). Be properly equipped and take warm clothing – the temperature drops dramatically at night. To avoid altitude sickness you should spend a day at Purmamarca to acclimatize; don't eat before you travel, and drink *maté* (herbal tea) to help oxygenate the blood.

*The incredible salt landscape of the Salinas Grandes*

# Explore the Península Valdés

*A southern right whale erupts out of the water.*

If you are in search of an escape from the mundane, you would be hard put to find anywhere more inspiring than the windswept shores and blue waters of the Patagonian coast. This magical region of multi-coloured pebble beaches, steep cliffs, jagged rocks, and miles of sand flats is one of the most precious wildlife habitats in the world where, amongst a plethora of sea and land creatures, you can see dolphins playing, orcas out on a seal hunt, and the largest southern right whale breeding-grounds in the world.

The drive from Puerto Madryn, on Golfo Nuevo, along the Ameghino Isthmus to the tip of the World Heritage wilderness of Península Valdés, plunges you straight into the savage beauty of the natural world. You can hear the southern right whales calling to each other as you watch them play in the water along the remote shores of El Doradillo beach. You drive along dirt tracks through desolate country of steppe and saltpans where guanacos, rheas, maras and grey foxes roam at will among the sheep. On the mudflats of Puento Norte, while you watch the elephant seals and sea lions, you will see opportunistic orcas lurking offshore ready to pounce on any unprotected pup and drag it into the water. At Valdés Caleta, a long gravel spit, you can observe a colony of Magellan penguins among the thousands of seabirds that congregate here.

At the end of the road, at Punta Delgada lighthouse on the south-eastern tip of the peninsula, as you gaze down from the high cliffs at the huge colony of elephant seals on the beach below and out over the endless spread of the Atlantic Ocean, you feel you have reached the very edge of the earth, far beyond the clutches of the man-made world.

# Ruta de Las Siete Lagos

Imagine a giant-sized, untamed version of Switzerland and you will get some idea of the phenomenal scenic beauty of Argentina's Lake District. The 200-km (125-mi) drive from Bariloche on the southern shore of Lago Nahuel Huapi up to the mountain resort of San Martin takes you through two national parks along a winding road with panoramic views round every bend.

From the beautiful city of Bariloche, a scenic 70-km (40-mi) lakeside drive takes you to the charming resort town of Villa La Angostura, the starting point of the famous Ruta de las Siete Lagos (Road of the Seven Lakes). The road zigzags its tortuous way along the narrow river valleys and ridges of Nahuel Huapi, the oldest of Argentina's national parks. The lower slopes of the rugged Patagonian mountains are swathed in evergreen coigüe forest, lightened by paintbox colours of wild flowers and shrubs – eye-catching daubs of yellow, red, orange and pink. The savage dark rocks and snowy peaks tower above you and, at every turn, just when you think you have seen the view of a lifetime, you are greeted with yet another incredible sight to take your breath away.

The road takes you through Villa Traful, a picturesque Andean village of wood and stone houses overlooking a turquoise lake, past Lago Escondido (Hidden Lake) twinkling behind its forest canopy, the twin lakes, Villarino and Falkner, joined by an isthmus, and the most beautiful of all, Lago Hermoso. At the entrance to Lanín National Park the landscape becomes drier, the thick evergreen forest gives way to southern beech woods, and you soon catch sight of the immaculately still waters of Lago Machonico. The road ends at the tranquil tourist town of San Martin, nestling among the mountains on the shore of Lake Lácar.

*Lake Traful in Patagonia*

**HOW:**
By car or bike
**WHEN TO GO:**
September to April; December for wild flowers in full bloom.
**TIME IT TAKES:**
One day by car. Three days by mountain bike.
**HIGHLIGHTS:**
Valle Encantada – strange rock formations.
Los Arrayanes National Park on peninsula of Lake Nahuel Huapi – forest of rare 300-year old and 20-m (66-ft) high arrayán trees, said to be Disney's source of inspiration for the film *Bambi*.
Lake Traful vantage point
Vullinaco Waterfall
LagoHermoso
**YOU SHOULD KNOW:**
The Lake District is a very popular area for sports activities. Cerro Catedral, near Bariloche, is one of Argentina's main ski resorts. In the summer you can go sailing, rafting and fly-fishing as well as mountain hiking, horse riding, off-road driving and cycling.

*Iguazú Falls*

# The Northern Loop

**HOW:**
By car or bus
**WHEN TO GO:**
March to May
**TIME IT TAKES:**
Three to five weeks.
**HIGHLIGHTS:**
Aconacagua – the highest peak in the western hemisphere.
Sierra de las Quijadas National Park – other worldly fossil landscape.
Cachí and Las Cardones National Park – a beautiful town and scenic views.
Santa Ana, Our Lady of Loreto and San Ignacio Miní World Heritage Sites – eerie 17th century Jesuit ruins overgrown with jungle.
La Garganta del Diablo, Iguazú Falls – where the 2-km (1.25-mi) wide River Iguazú suddenly drops 70 m (230 ft).
**YOU SHOULD KNOW:**
Many people prefer to fly across the two cross-country sections of this route to avoid the less scenically interesting parts. This makes the journey much quicker but means you get no real sense of the vast space and contrasting landscapes and miss out on all the highs and lows that make a road trip such a satisfying experience. Argentina has one of the most extensive, reliable and comfortable bus networks in the world and the roads are virtually traffic free.

The eighth largest country in the world, Argentina has an amazing diversity of scenery, climates and cultural influences. This 5,000-km (3,000-mi) road trip enables you to see sights and landscapes that you would not even glimpse from a plane, takes you to four great cities, across the pampas, into the wine lands, up into the Andes, through desert, ending in the sinister rainforest borderland of Brazil and Paraguay, at the heart of South America.

From Buenos Aires, sultry tango capital, you start on the most gruelling stretch of road – 1,000 km (600 mi) cross-country through the stark monotony of the pampas. You are rewarded with an overwhelming buzz of accomplishment when you hit the hills of the wine country and the beautiful green city of Mendoza, gateway to the Andes.

You head north-eastwards through wild green mountains and picturesque hill villages to see the sublime colonial architecture of Córdoba, and continue north to Tucumán, 'the garden of the republic'. You will experience one of the most beautiful drives of your life in the polychrome desert canyons of Cafayate on the way to Salta, a charming sub-tropical colonial city on the edge of the Andes.

Travelling back eastwards through the cactus-dotted plains of the Chaco and the verdant wetlands of Corrientes you reach the historic north-eastern province of Misiones, a rainforest region of deep red ferrous earth and lush green jungle, named after the brutal Jesuit missionaries who converted the Guarani Indians to Christianity by force. The road to the Brazilian border ends at the spectacular Iguazú Falls, one of the greatest natural wonders of the world. The deafening roar of thousands of tons of water cascading down stirs feelings of fear, awe, wonder and respect at the indomitable power of nature. It's a sensational end to an incredible journey.

# The Beagle Channel & Magellan Strait

Short of travelling to Antarctica, the southern hemisphere's most incredible scenery is to be found in the crazy maze of channels, islands and bays that make up the south-western coastline of Tierra del Fuego. The sea passages that connect the Atlantic and Pacific Oceans are notoriously difficult to navigate. Changeable, often tempestuous weather and the narrowness of the straits promise to make the voyage from Ushuaia an unpredictable one. You will see dolphins, Magellan penguins, seals and cormorants, hear the creaking sounds of the glaciers and the thunderous crashes as great chunks of ice break off into the sea, and experience a sub-polar wilderness of forest and mountain.

The Beagle Channel is named after the eponymous surveying ship that the great naturalist Charles Darwin sailed on. His description of the landscape is just as valid today as it was in 1839: 'The lofty mountains on the north side...are covered by a wide mantle of perpetual snow... numerous cascades pour their waters through the woods into the narrow channel below...magnificent glaciers extend from the mountainside to the water's edge. It is scarcely possible to imagine anything more beautiful than the beryl-like blue of these glaciers and especially as contrasted with the dead white of the upper expanse of snow. The fragments which had fallen from the glacier into the water were floating away and the channel with the icebergs presented...a miniature likeness of the Polar Sea'.

You disembark at Punta Arenas, a charming colonial town of red-roofed houses and a lovely tree-lined central square. Here the statue of Ferdinand Magellan, the first explorer to sail from the Atlantic into the Pacific, reminds you of the full historical significance of your journey, adding an extra dimension to the wondrous spectacle of nature you have witnessed.

**HOW:**
By boat
**WHEN TO GO:**
November to March
**TIME IT TAKES:**
Four to five days
**HIGHLIGHTS:**
Cape Horn National Park – stark promontory with sheer 400-m (1,300-ft) cliffs.
Wulaia Bay – spectacularly beautiful Magellanic forest scenery.
Avenida de los Glaciares – stretch of the Beagle Channel lined with hanging glaciers.
Magdalena Island – Magellan penguin colony and lighthouse.
**YOU SHOULD KNOW:**
You can do this journey equally easily the other way round – starting in Punto Arenas, Chile and ending in Ushuaia, Argentina. Either way, the route is weather-dependent. In calm seas, the boat will make a diversion to Cape Horn National Park. There are several cruise companies or, for a truly authentic experience, you can go on a cargo boat if you are prepared to rough it a bit.

*Cormorants in the Beagle Channel*

# Che Guevara's Revolutionary Road

**HOW:**
By motorbike or bus and by boat
**WHEN TO GO:**
Year-round (remembering that in the southern hemisphere, June to August can be very cold; and rainy seasons vary, and are subject to micro-climates along some of the route).
**TIME IT TAKES:**
Che famously took nine months. Recently, two actors took a year, making a film on the way. You can travel the road by bus and boat in roughly a month, but nearer three months is considered the minimum.
**HIGHLIGHTS:**
The Chuquicamata copper mine, biggest open-pit mine in the world, in the Atacama Desert south of Iquique – primary source of Chile's wealth, and Che's indignation that it was US-owned.
The Amazon jungle around the leper colony of San Pablo – with indigenous Indian guides recounting tales and lore of the dense forest.
Cuzco, once capital of the Inca Empire, overprinted with the Hispanic colonial boot – a dangerous but charming city, and base for Machu Picchu.
**YOU SHOULD KNOW:**
1. Outside cities and major tourist attractions, a knowledge of Spanish is invaluable and occasionally vital. 2. Throughout South America, local rules and regulations may not always be those decreed by official federal agency. You must check at the time you want to go. 3. Check, if you plan to enter Colombia via Leticia, how you can proceed either into Colombia or elsewhere in the Amazon basin. It can be notoriously difficult to leave without great expense. Che flew to Bogota.
NB. On this journey, Che never visited Bolivia. But aficionados traveling from Chile to Peru may want to pause and take one of several Bolivian tours based on his later exploits.

Heading south from Buenos Aires in 1952, 23 year-old Che Guevara circled South America on a motorbike, with a friend. His diaries of their epic journey are a tale of high drama, low comedy, disaster and discovery. Retracing his route even approximately may not influence your political philosophy, but it will provide you with a particular insight into the nature of South America as a continent, and to the historical and geographic reasons for collective aspects of its social cultures. Of course, your trip will be much more comfortable: but if the main roads are paved, and you travel in an air-conditioned bus or car or train, you can still find the sleepy, sun and wind-parched villages in the dust of Patagonia or the Atacama desert, the stone hut shelters of the Andean altiplano, and the broiling humid shacks in the Amazon jungle in which Che sought to quantify 'workers' conditions'.

Down Argentina, across the Andes, up Chile to Peru, then from Cuzco through the Amazon headwaters to Iquitos and (via Leticia) Colombia and Venezuela – Che's diaries provide much more than just the inspiration to keep your eyes properly open. His carefree exuberance is infectious, a reminder to take opportunities to share the back of a dusty truck with whoever, or to swim when the ferry needs pushing. His route goes deep into remote backcountry, to borders and regions which can still be dangerous. Seek help where you can from local people – but use the tourist infrastructure where it is useful. Balance some of your curiosity with caution (eg when hitch-hiking, as Che did), but enjoy unexpected adventures when they happen.

Che's journey did not end in Venezuela. Choose to follow him, and nor will yours: you'll share his lifelong respect for the magnificence of South America, and of its peoples' durability.

*Inquisitive young villagers in Iquitos, Peru.*

AFRICA

# Krom River Trail

**HOW:**
On foot
**WHEN TO GO:**
October to May
**TIME IT TAKES:**
A few hours
**HIGHLIGHTS:**
A plunge into one of the splendidly cooling swimming pools that greet you enticingly at either end of the Krom River Trail.
Views of Du Toits Peak – highest point of the Limietberg Nature Reserve at 1,996 m (6,557 ft).
The animals and birds – including klipspringer, baboon, caracal, an occasional leopard, Cape sugarbird, protea canary and black eagle.
**YOU SHOULD KNOW:**
Be prepared to meet anglers along the Trail – the Krom is a popular trout-fishing river.

Sadly this great river, along with its associated wetlands, is coming under increasing pressure from the development demands of modern South Africa, with consequent degradation. But it is still possible to experience the pristine beauty of the Krom River and environs as it has always been by hiking various marked trails in Limietberg Nature Reserve, which is located in the De Toitskloof Pass between Paar and Worcester in the Western Cape. To hike the Krom River Trail, approach through the Huguenot Tunnel from the Worcester side and park. A permit from Cape Nature is required.

The Trail is 7 km (4.4 mi) long, and can be comfortably walked in half a day. No guide is needed, though sensible pre-hike precautions (appropriate clothing plus a basic supply of food and water) should be taken. The Trail crosses the Molenaars River and ascends along the right-hand slope above the Krom River. It passes through an area of indigenous forest and reaches a waterfall with pool beneath. There is then a hair-raising climb up a chain ladder to a second fall and pool – this waterfall in its lush setting is one of the very best in the whole Western Cape. The Trail then returns by the same route.

There are other rewarding trails in the park – each different, each taking no more than a day. The Rock Hopper Trail from Eerste Tol to Tweede Tol is more adventurous, and involves finding your own way down (or up) an 8-km (5-mi) stretch of the Witte River's boulder-strewn riverbed, using a combination of walking, swimming and rock-scrambling. This Trail requires a drop-off at the beginning and pick-up at the end. The Elands Trail initially involves a steep climb, providing great valley and river views, before descending to Fisherman's Cave with its inviting pool.

# Cape Wine Route

If you are interested in glorious scenery and delicious wines, a trip along Route 62, in South Africa's Western Cape region, is a must. Some 50 years ago, a highway was opened here, and Route 62 became a forgotten road, with little traffic and fewer visitors. Surprisingly, this was a godsend for the area: its fruitful farming communities were left in peace. The result is probably the longest wine route in the world, meandering through some of the most sublime scenery and prolific vineyards you can imagine.

*The Franschhoek Valley is one of the leading wine growing regions.*

Leaving Cape Town, the road climbs through majestic mountains, over a series of dramatic passes, alongside crystal clear streams, through fertile valleys rich with magnificent vineyards and orchards. The approach to Montagu, the first town en route, is astonishing. Set in a narrow valley, by a mountain stream, with towering ochre cliffs to either side, and peach and apricot trees laden with blossom, this Victorian era town might be in the Garden of Eden. Continuing through the Breede River Valley, the Worcester winelands provide 27 per cent of the country's wine as well as being the main brandy producing area.

Stop at some of the many wineries to taste both white and red wines – the gabled, Cape Dutch architecture, set in gold and green vineyards against a backdrop of mountains, makes a memorable sight. Farther on the road travels through the Klein Karoo region, a huge, khaki coloured, treeless space with flat-topped hills and small towns lying under the vast, cloudless African sky. Here are several small, picturesque towns such as Ladysmith, set at the foot of the Towerkop Mountain. Route 62 ends at Port Elizabeth, South Africa's water sports mecca. The splendid beaches, scuba diving, game fishing and whale watching tours could hardly be more different from the mellow journey you have just completed.

**HOW:**
By car
**WHEN TO GO:**
September to November, late January to April.
**TIME IT TAKES:**
About two days, but take a week to fully enjoy the experience.
**HIGHLIGHTS:**
The Robertson Wine Festival, which takes place over a week every October.
The historic town of Tulbagh, with its Cape Dutch architecture and lovely gardens.
Addo Elephant Park.
**YOU SHOULD KNOW:**
This is the first wine route in the world to produce a Braille wine bottle. A percentage of its sales go directly to the Institute for the Blind.

# Garden Route

**HOW:**
By car
**WHEN TO GO:**
November to May
**TIME IT TAKES:**
It is possible to drive in a day, but to enjoy and appreciate this trip you should spend several days, up to a week.
**HIGHLIGHTS:**
Watch the endangered southern right whales in their calving grounds, November and December.
Go cage diving with great white sharks at Gansbaii.
Cable slide across the rainforest canopy in Tsitsikamma.
Visit an ostrich farm at Oudtshoorn.
**YOU SHOULD KNOW:**
The Garden Route and the Wine Route are sufficiently close together to move easily between the two. If this is your plan, give yourself a few extra days.

South Africa's Garden Route is a spectacular road trip along the coast from Mossel Bay east to Storms River. Sandwiched between the Outeniqua and Tsitsikamma mountains and the Indian Ocean, the road is named not for its floral gardens but because of its lush and varied vegetation, so different from the country's harsh, dry interior.

From Mossel Bay, an old-fashioned seaside town, the N2 links a series of charming towns, with areas of great natural beauty in between. This is part of the Cape Floral Region, named a UNESCO World Heritage Site in 2004. It is famed for its *fynbos*, natural heathland vegetation that includes 9,000 species, 6,200 of which are endemic. Of these, many are flowering and others are fragrant. Rooibos and honeybush are both commercially harvested, and one of the many proteas, *Protea cynaroides*, is South Africa's national flower.

Pass through the Wilderness National Park – its lagoons and wetlands are home to 250 species of bird, including Knysna Lourie, a bright green bird with red wings, and many kingfishers. If you like oysters, you can feast on them here to your heart's content, and of course the local wines are excellent. From Plettenberg Bay, another seaside resort, the road descends sharply, winding through old growth forest until it reaches the finest stretch of untamed coastline in Tsitsikamma National Park, before reaching the journey's end at Storms River.

Along the way there is much to do, hiking, diving, kayaking or even playing golf. Keep an eye open for the very rare Knysna elephants – a handful are said to roam the magnificent yellowwoods between Knysna and Plettenberg. Perhaps you'd like to travel on the last continuously operating steam train on the continent, the steam train Choo Tjoe, currently running only between Mossel Bay and George, after mud slides in 2006 damaged the track.

*The Tsitsikamma Range in Eastern Cape Province.*

# The Blue Train

The Blue Train is one of the world's most prestigious train journeys, luxury on wheels, right up there with the Orient Express. Its origins go back to 1923, when trains were introduced to carry passengers from Johannesburg to Cape Town, where they embarked on the long voyage to England. In 1933, a dining saloon was introduced, and gradually further luxuries were added. After a break for World War II, the service returned, and this time it was named the Blue Train after its blue carriages. Three years after the end of apartheid, in 1997, the service was re-launched in all its present day glory, taking passengers from Cape Town to Pretoria.

Arriving at the station at 7.50 am, passengers are ushered into a splendid check-in lounge, where sparkling wine and delicious nibbles are offered before a butler takes you to your suite, where your luggage is already in situ. This is 5-star accommodation: top quality bed linen, goose down duvets, marble bathroom, a desk set by the window, even a multiple choice entertainment centre. Elsewhere, there are two comfortable lounges and a dining car, where elegant outfits are obligatory for dinner.

This is a fabulous journey – the train glides smoothly through superb scenery. From its windows you'll see tea and citrus estates, vineyards, thick, indigenous forests, cliffs and gorges, and deserts where giraffes, zebras and elephants roam in peace. Enjoy an off-train visit to the privately owned Aquila Game Reserve at Kleinstraat, where you can experience a close encounter with cheetahs. Back on board, wonder at the extravagant sunset as you sip your pre-dinner drink before enjoying a gourmet meal and a great night's sleep. After a leisurely breakfast in the morning, in your suite if you wish, the Blue Train reaches Pretoria, the end of its 1,600-km (1,000-mi) journey.

*The Blue Train has been operating for over a century.*

**HOW:**
By train
**WHEN TO GO:**
Any time of year but November to April is probably best.
**TIME IT TAKES:**
27 hours
**HIGHLIGHTS:**
The views from the top of Cape Town's Table Mountain.
A trip to the infamous, apartheid era prison on Robben Island.
Sitting in the Blue Train's observation car.
A driver's eye view of the unfolding journey ahead, shown both in the club car and on a TV channel in your suite, via a camera mounted on the front of the train.
**YOU SHOULD KNOW:**
There are two Blue Trains. Both travel at 90 kph (58 mph), are 336 m (1,102 ft) long, and consist of 18 carriages, 11 of which are for the use of the passengers. The beds are custom made, and are hidden in the wall during the day, when the suite is a sitting room. Some of the suites even have bathtubs rather than showers, and all bathroom fittings are gold.

*The very Orange River, running through the very orange mountains.*

# Running the Orange River

**HOW:**
By raft, kayak or canoe
**WHEN TO GO:**
March to January
**TIME IT TAKES:**
Four to six days for a typical journey.
**HIGHLIGHTS:**
Rapids like Dead Man's Rapid and Sjambok Rapid – not too dangerous, but definitely enough to get the blood pounding.
Birds – the water and banks are alive with species including cormorants, goliath herons, fish eagles and kingfishers.
Tall tales around the campfire under an amazing African sky at the end of a rewarding day's paddling.
**YOU SHOULD KNOW:**
If a custom journey doesn't appeal, various canoe societies in the Northern Cape organize annual marathons on the Orange River.

For those in search of adventure, running the Orange River in the Richtersveldt National Park on the border of South Africa and Namibia is just the ticket. In this isolated part of the Northern Cape, the Orange River's long journey from the Drakensberg range to the Atlantic Ocean finally ends. Here, this majestic river is a long, green-fringed oasis that offers scenic stretches of serene water as it twists and turns through a striking desert landscape, with occasional fun rapids to spice up the journey.

This is a river run to be undertaken with a guide, either solo or with a group. The Orange River is usually tackled using two-person inflatable rafts, kayaks or canoes, sometimes with the support of a larger raft carrying supplies. A typical trip will be around 80-km (50-mi) long and different guides and organizers use various starting and take-out points. There is usually a base camp at the start where personal belongings may be left, with transport back at the end of the trip. Most expeditions assemble at Viooolsdrift on the Namibian border, just upriver from the Park – and some 350 km (217 mi) from the mouth of the Orange River – from where paddlers are driven to base camp.

The Richtersveldt National Park has recently been made a UNESCO World Heritage Site and it's easy to understand why. The Richtersveldt is one of the most remote and unspoiled areas of South Africa, and one of the best ways to see this barren but extraordinary place is from the river that runs through it – some say the best way. It's a true wilderness experience, in a rocky landscape that one writer has eloquently called 'too beautiful to describe'. Somehow, that says it all – though that means you must see for yourself!

# Chapman's Peak Drive

The journey may not be long – just 9 km (5.6 mi) – but Chapman's Peak Drive on the Atlantic Coast at South Africa's southwestern tip is one of the world's most spectacular marine cliff roads. Starting from the picturesque horseshoe-shaped fishing harbour of Hout Bay, the Drive skirts Chapman's Peak, the southerly extension of Constantia Berg. It winds up towards Chapman's Point, offering views down to sandy coves below, from whence it descends to sea level at Noordhoek. That sounds simple enough, but doesn't begin to hint at the drama that will be enjoyed as this unique toll road unfolds.

It was constructed between 1915 and 1922, and has 114 bends and sections blasted out of sheer rock faces. The effort was worthwhile. The geology is fascinating – the road was cut where base granite meets sedimentary limestone above, creating brilliantly coloured layers of orange, red-yellow silt shot with lines of dark purple manganese. But that's not the main attraction, because Chapman's Peak Drive delivers almost unbelievable views of the Atlantic Ocean meeting and greeting the rocky coastline, as it snakes towards journey's end – a journey that seems far too short.

This is, of course, a two-way road, but those who wish to see the sights without worrying that it's dangerous to drive whilst eye-balling the views can take a bus. These may travel only from the Hout's Bay end in the interests of safety, though short tours that include Chapman's Peak Drive are freely available from various start points. This is the best direction to drive, too, as it makes pulling off into scenic overlooks easier. The Drive may be hiked from either end but not right through – walkers are barred from the central section. It is occasionally closed to all traffic as a result of adverse weather conditions.

**HOW:**
By car or bus
**WHEN TO GO:**
Any time of year
**TIME IT TAKES:**
Just 15 minutes end-to-end (without stopping).
**HIGHLIGHTS:**
Stopping at one or more of the many scenic overlooks above the sea to have a picnic – or simply drink in the staggering seascapes.
Sunset over Hout's Bay, seen from the Chapman's Point lookout.
Parking and hiking the trail to the top of Chapman's Peak for truly amazing views (four to five hours needed, take water).
**YOU SHOULD KNOW:**
The Drive was closed in 1999 after a motorist was killed by falling rocks, but it has since been improved by major works and is now much safer.

*Chapman's Peak Road winds around the cliffs.*

# Drakensberg Traverse

**HOW:**
On foot
**WHEN TO GO:**
March to May
**TIME IT TAKES:**
From one to three weeks depending
on Traverse chosen.
**HIGHLIGHTS:**
Photographic opportunities –
extraordinary landscapes and up-close
animals and birds.
Magnificent sunrises, sunsets and (way
above light pollution) starry nights of
unbelievable intensity.
The celebratory dinner at a mountain
lodge after the Traverse has been
completed – job
well done!
**YOU SHOULD KNOW:**
Drakensberg weather can be severe –
storms blow up from nowhere and,
whilst there are no snowfields,
snowfall has been recorded on every
day of the year.

Call it Quathlamba or call it Drakensberg, the end result is the same – the rugged mountain range that extends for 1,125 km (700 mi) from Mpumalanga (formerly Eastern Transvaal) to Eastern Cape Province. Traversing the Drakensberg (Dragon Mountains) involves a wilderness adventure, camping out (unless there's a handy cave as night approaches) and backpacking everything needed during the trip. This is a guided expedition, as only extremely experienced wilderness hikers could contemplate going solo. The main challenge is the altitude, with thin mountain air making physical effort more difficult, testing resolve and endurance to the limit. Daily distances of 8 km (5 mi) to 16 km (10 mi) are the norm.

There are lots of routes to choose from, in both northern and southern Drakensberg, usually titled according to length – Mini-Traverse (five days), Classic-Traverse (seven days), Super-Traverse (14 days) or Grand-Traverse (21 days). One option is trekking in the Drakensberg Park, two hours from Durban, with all the magic of these mountains plus ancient cave dwellings with rock paintings – now a UNESCO World Heritage Site.

Traverses begin with an ascent to the escarpment, either by climbing a steep pass or using the local specialty short-cut – metal ladders bolted to the sloping rock – after which each party treks for the set distance and time before descending back to civilization. Although the parameters of each Traverse are loosely established, the sort of flexibility dictated by unknown factors like weather conditions and the party marching at the pace of the slowest will determine final itinerary.

One thing never changes – these mountains always offer an opportunity to experience an enchanting wilderness of peaks and high escarpment, astonishing natural architecture, incredible views...and the sense of achievement that comes from undertaking and making one of the world's greatest hikes.

*A hiker enjoying the beautiful mountain view.*

# Table Mountain Aerial Cableway

Opened in 1929, and extensively refurbished in 1997 when new cars and double cabling were introduced, the Table Mountain Aerial Cableway has transported more than 16 million people to the top of Table Mountain, a dramatic ride which offers wonderful views of Cape Town and surrounds, both on the way up and from the summit.

This isn't a journey for the faint-hearted (or vertigo sufferers). Some 1,200 m (3,940 ft) of cable link the Lower Cable Station on Tafelberg Road near Kloof Nek with the Upper Cable Station on the westernmost end of the Table Mountain Plateau. In the course of their upward journey, the cars rise steeply from a height of 302 m (990 ft) to 1,067 m (3,500 ft). The latest Rotair cars can each carry 65 passengers, more than doubling the capacity of the old cars.

Once up, there are various pathways leading to stunning views over Cape Town, Table Bay, Robben Island, Cape Flats and the Cape Peninsula. There are three signed walks. Klipspinger Walk follows the plateau edge above Platteklip Gorge. Agama Walk has been designed to give wonderful all-round views of Cape Town. Dassie Walk offers spectacular views to the north, south and west. There are two free, guided plateau tours each day, at 10.00 am and noon.

Directions to the Cableway are found on all major roads into and in Cape Town – follow the brown information boards. There is ample parking near the lower cable station. You can't book in advance, but queuing is rarely necessary. Hours of operation vary according to season, and the service can be suspended at short notice if wind speeds become too severe. Always take a jacket, as it is usually much cooler above than below.

**HOW:**
By cable car
**WHEN TO GO:**
Any time of year
**TIME IT TAKES:**
Ten minutes
**HIGHLIGHTS:**
Seeing a 360° view of Cape Town during the journey, thanks to the cable car's rotating floor.
An extraordinary diversity of plant life on the summit – look especially for the sunshine conebushes in full flower (summer only).
Doing it the hard way – a serious hike from Plattklip Gorge to the Upper Cable Station, returning by cable car (or vice versa if you want gravity on your side).
**YOU SHOULD KNOW:**
The dassie, or rock hyrax – a small, rabbit-like creature likely to be encountered on the flat summit – is surprisingly the elephant's closest living anatomical relative.

*Robben Island with Cape Town and Table Mountain in the background.*

# Robben Island Ferry

**HOW:**
By ferry
**WHEN TO GO:**
Any time of year
**TIME IT TAKES:**
Allowing time for a prison tour and island stroll, the round trip takes three to four hours.
**HIGHLIGHTS:**
Cell number 46664, where Nelson Mandela was incarcerated for 18 years.
The Moturu Kramat, a sacred Muslim pilgrimage site dedicated to the Prince of Madura, a Cape Town imam who was exiled to Robben Island in the mid-1700s and died there.
The Robben Island lighthouse, built at the Island's (rather low) highpoint in 1863 to try and reduce the large number of ships regularly wrecked on the rocky shores.
Observation of the over-active and ever-entertaining penguin colony.
**YOU SHOULD KNOW:**
Have a beady-eyed look along the shoreline – a Dutch treasure ship was wrecked on Robben Island in the 17th century and the occasional gold coin still washes up today.

Cape Town's Victoria & Alfred Waterfront is the departure point for one of the city's essential activities – the 12-km (7.5-mi) ferry trip to Robben Island, for centuries a safe dumping ground for those deemed undesirable by the authorities, from Muslim leaders and Dutch colonial dissenters through lepers to anti-apartheid freedom fighters – among the latter Nelson Mandela, who went on to become a Nobel Peace Prize winner and South Africa's first black President. During the apartheid years the prison on Robben Island (established in 1959) became known for brutality designed to isolate opponents of the regime and crush morale. The harsh regime failed to achieve its objective and Robben Island became known in Africa and throughout the world as a symbol of resistance to tyranny and the triumph of the human spirit over adversity.

Today, Robben Island is a UNESCO World Heritage Site and the prison has become a living museum, where many of the guides are former political prisoners who really do know what they're talking about. After a period of neglect, resources are being devoted to sprucing up the prison in particular and the island in general.

In times past, the ferry journey from the mainland to Robben Island was notoriously unpredictable. Sailings by five ancient ferries were frequently cancelled as a result of mechanical problems, but the launch of a new 300-seater ferry, the Sikhululekile ('We are free'), has restored reliability to the service. Even so, the ferry journey can be an exciting roller-coaster ride – or not take place at all – if one of the sudden storms for which the area is famed blows up. It's a risk worth taking, as there are stunning bay views during the approach to Robben Island, with Table Mountain as the brooding backdrop.

# Trans-Oranje

One of South Africa's great train services is the Trans-Oranje's twice-weekly run between Cape Town and Durban (or vice versa), the longest inter-city train journey in South Africa. The operator is Shosholoza Meyl ('Pleasant journey') and this comfortable train is incredibly good value. The Wednesday tourist-class departure from Cape Town is the one to aim for, as the ticket includes a sleeper bunk, hot shower (bring your own soap and towel) and restaurant car. The Monday train is the much more basic economy class with few facilities, and is mainly used by locals for shorter hops (not recommended for the full journey).

Contrary to popular opinion, the recently refurbished Trans-Oranje is completely safe, with no danger to families or women traveling alone – it is carefully policed by courteous staff who take great pride in their train and the provision of high-level service. Travellers have the choice of an economy Sleeper-6 (formerly Second Class) with six same-sex bunks, Sleeper-4 (formerly First Class) with four same-sex bunks and the two-berth Coupés for couples.

From Cape Town, the multicoloured Trans-Oranje heads out across the arid Karoo Desert. It then passes the famous De Beers diamond mine in Kimberley, crosses the plains of the Orange Free State and continues on into Natal, passing through the mountainous landscapes of Cliffdale, Ntshongweni, Situndu Hills and Marianhill before arriving on the shores of the sparkling Indian Ocean at Durban, that humid city of bananas, sugar cane and fun. Along the way the train stops at names writ large in the annals of South African history, including Kimberley, Bloemfontein and Ladysmith. The ideal journey is a return trip, allowing full appreciation of the varied sights of this extraordinary land of contrasts afforded by a journey on the Trans-Oranje – from ever-changing scenery to shantytowns.

**HOW:**
By train
**WHEN TO GO:**
April to November (no air-conditioning on the train!).
**TIME IT TAKES:**
37 hours and 15 minutes each way (all being well).
**HIGHLIGHTS:**
The Karoo Desert landscape as night falls – the train is timed to allow travellers to enjoy spectacular sunsets.
The biggest man-made hole in the world, on the left just after Kimberley station.
The full 'English Farmhouse Breakfast' that awaits in the restaurant car each morning.
Pietermaritzburg Station, where the future great but humble Indian leader Mahatma Gandhi was thrown off a train in 1893.
**YOU SHOULD KNOW:**
The Trans-Oranje passes the spot where Winston Churchill was taken prisoner in the Boer War, when the armoured train he was on was derailed by insurgents.

*Sunflower fields in Freestate Province*

# Namib Desert

The name 'Namib' means 'Vast Dry Plain', and the Namib Desert extends along the Atlantic coast, with vast seas of towering dunes rolling inland towards gravel plains and isolated mountain ranges. This is one of the oldest and driest deserts in the world.

Windhoek, Namibia's capital, is a graceful city set on low hills; the road southwest (C26) crosses lovely countryside and desert hills. South of Solitaire on the C14 a signed road leads south to Sesriem and the Namib Dunes. These are 'dynamic' dunes – they shift and change shape, sculpted by the wind. They are made of quartz sand, and their colours also change, from cream to copper, red to violet. Some of these enormous sandhills are easily accessible, by foot or 4x4.

Sossusvlei, 60 km (37 m) deeper into the desert is the most photographed place in Namibia. It consists of a huge clay pan surrounded by massive red dunes, some as high as 300 m (975 ft). When the Tsauchab River fills and spills into it, this briefly becomes a turquoise lake, flocked by aquatic birds. The park opens at sunrise and closes at sunset; to experience the glorious technicolour effects it is necessary to stay around Sesriem.

The road northwest towards Swakopmund, the C14, runs along the eastern edge of the dunes then through the Gaub Pass and the Kuiseb Pass, turning west to cross the Namib-Naukluft Park, an area of gravel plains and occasional hills. It reaches the coast at Walvis Bay, a busy harbour town. Swakopmund, 30 km (19 mi) north, is an attractive German-colonial seaside resort, and Namibia's most popular holiday destination, with a wide range of adventure sports on offer on land and sea.

*The red dunes of Sossusvlei*

# Skeleton Coast

The Skeleton Coast stretches from Swakopmund to the Angolan border 500 km (300 m) north. This is an inhospitable place, where immense stretches of beach are beaten by breakers, engulfed by fog and cut off by trackless, shifting dunes. Early Portuguese sailors knew it as 'The Sands of Hell', for the crew of a foundering ship was doomed. The skeletons on this coastline are not just human: the bleached bones of innumerable whales, dating from the whaling industry's heyday, as well as the remains of countless ships swept ashore during the mercantile era, dot the sands. Pounded by the sea and blasted by sand the latter have been reduced to scraps of rusty metal, scattered planks and shattered masts, while the wrecks of later vessels, though more intact, are inaccessible.

The narrow strip of dunes was proclaimed a Nature Reserve in 1971. This ancient, untouched wilderness has a fascinating ecosystem – although almost rainless, the desert is moistened by the dense fogs that are brought by the icy Benuela Current and blown inshore. Plants and lichens adapt to the extreme conditions by taking on strange forms. Visits are limited to minimize human impact on this ecologically sensitive area. The coast road runs along the margin of the dunes, but there is no access. The northern section is a private concession, and offers fly-in safaris. However, a sightseeing flight from Swakopmund is a good option – these low-level flights allow a view of the vast graveyard of the shore and the mesmerising changing shapes and colours of the dunes.

*Walvis Bay on the Skeleton Coast*

**HOW:**
By plane
**WHEN TO GO:**
May to October
**TIME IT TAKES:**
About three hours
**HIGHLIGHTS:**
The remote wrecks, including the *Dunedin Star*, which ran aground in 1942.
The Ugab Formations, a moon-landscape whose black ridges contrast with the white desert.
The Clay Castles, fragile mud deposits laid down along the Hoarusib River when the area was a lake.
Sarusa Springs Oasis – a perennial water source.
**YOU SHOULD KNOW:**
The dense coastal fogs occur most mornings and evenings.

*The desert hills and gravel plains of Damaraland Plateau*

# Damaraland

**DEPART:**
Swakopmund
**HOW:**
By bike
**WHEN TO GO:**
May to October
**TIME IT TAKES:**
Five or six days
**HIGHLIGHTS:**
The Damaraland Plateau is well known for its desert-adapted elephants – you may meet some. The Petrified Forest, composed of fossilized logs, which were once driftwood, is 260 million years old. Twyfelfontein – more than 2,500 engravings are cut into the huge red rocks.
The strange *Welwitschia mirabilis*, or the living fossil plant, a tree dwarfed by the extremes of the desert, lives for over 1,000 years.
**YOU SHOULD KNOW:**
Any fit cyclist should be able to tackle this safari; a back-up vehicle will carry luggage and over-tired cyclists.

Damaraland occupies the area between the Skeleton Coast and Namibia's central plateau. It was named for the people who still occupy it as subsistence farmers – the Damara are one of the most ancient ethnic groups in the country. Here, desert hills are interspersed with mountains and gravel plains. The rugged landscape is networked by streams which streak the land with green, providing water for the Damara people and their livestock and for many desert-adapted, free-ranging animals including elephants, zebras and the rare black rhino.

This region is rich in geological features – mountains, craters, strange rock formations and the renowned petroglyphs. These paintings and engravings on rock are found near The Brandberg and at Twyfelfontein, a beautiful spot with a perennial spring which has always attracted not only wildlife but also hunter-gatherers. These recorded their rituals – hunting, and religious ceremonies – on stone, leaving a record of life as far back as the Stone Age. Twyfelfontein was made a UNESCO World Heritage Site in 2007.

Here are many quiet roads and tracks, off the main tourist routes, and some companies offer mountain bike safaris. These typically start from Swakopmund, with visits to the Spitzkoppe (the ''Matterhorn of Africa') and Namibia's highest mountain, the Brandberg. A night is spent in the remote and beautiful landscape of the Ugab River in a camp run by the Save the Rhino Trust, after which the route climbs the Damara steppe and eventually reaches Twyfelfontein. These safaris use carefully chosen routes to highlight the extraordinary geology of the region.

# Fish River Canyon Trail

The second largest canyon in the world, Fish River Canyon winds and twists (legend suggests it was formed by the frantic writhings of a giant serpent) for over 160 km (100 mi). It is actually formed of two canyons, the outer one up to 27 km (17 mi) wide, and the inner reaching a depth of 550 m (1,787 ft). The figures do not prepare the visitor for its enormous drama and beauty.

Because of flash flooding in the rainy season and the extreme heat of summer, the canyon is open for a limited season to trekkers for the challenging walk down the 85 km (52 mi) trail from Hobas to Ai-Ais near the southern end. From Hobas a gravel road leads to Hikers' Viewpoint, the start of the route, and from here those not braving the walk can enjoy an awe-inspiring panorama. The first part of the walk is the most rugged and exhausting, with the steep descent of the canyon wall and several miles of rough sand and boulders. On the canyon floor there is good, flat, sandy camping by the cool river pools (the river water is drinkable if boiled or sterilized); tents are unnecessary in the warm clear weather. The route follows the serpentine course of the river past sulphur springs, viewpoints and strange rock formations. There are recognized short cuts bypassing the longer bends.

The last section of the walk is relatively easy going, though by the end of the season the river will be dry and water must be carried. At Ai-Ais (the name means 'scalding hot') the weary but triumphant walker will find the Hot Springs Resort with all its welcome facilities.

**HOW:**
On foot
**WHEN TO GO:**
1 May to 30 September
**TIME IT TAKES:**
Five days plus
**HIGHLIGHTS:**
'Palm Springs' at the end of the demanding first section. This spot offers good camping and the bliss of a soak in the hot, bubbling sulphur springs.
The Grave of Lieutenant Thilo von Troths, a German killed in a skirmish with the Nama in 1905.
The amazing experience and sheer beauty of the canyon.
Reaching Ai-Ais, where the mineral rich thermal springs are piped into baths, jacuzzis and an outdoor pool.
**YOU SHOULD KNOW:**
This is a very tough walk and should not be attempted by inexperienced hikers.
A medical certificate is required.
The trek must be booked in advance; numbers are limited.
The rains shift sand and vegetation and the route can change from year to year.

*The descent into Fish River Canyon is not an easy hike.*

# Okavanga Delta

**HOW:**
By *Mokoro* or dugout canoe
**DEPART:**
Maun
**WHEN TO GO:**
July to September
**TIME IT TAKES:**
1, 2 or 3 days
**HIGHLIGHTS:**
Wildlife: you will spot hippos and
crocodiles in the waterways, and you
may see elephants and antelopes
while trekking.
Local knowledge: as well as
identifying wildlife, polers can explain
Delta life.
**YOU SHOULD KNOW:**
Wildlife can be dangerous: camp
sensibly and never swim without
checking with your poler.

The Okavango River rises in Angola, flows south through Namibia and into Botswana; then the river's waters spread, sprawling over the sandy wastes of the Kalahari Desert to form an immense, extraordinary inland delta. This maze of channels, islands, waterlily-covered pools and lagoons covers more than 15,000 sq km (6,000 sq mi). The waters of this, the largest landlocked delta in the world, never reach the sea; trapped in the parched Kalahari (which covers most of Botswana) this watery wilderness is a magnet for wildlife. In the lush forests and along the floodplains, hundreds of species of bird flourish and lions, elephants, hippos and crocodiles, as well as smaller animals, congregate.

Trekking trips and motorboat cruises are based at various lodges on the islands, but the perfect way to experience the beauty and serenity of the Delta is drifting along passageways of papyrus, gliding across the pale golden waters in a shallow-draft dugout canoe, a *mokoro*. Traditionally made from logs of ebony or sausage tree wood, these amazingly stable craft are now often constructed of fibreglass – international conservation groups encourage this to save the slow-growing trees. Generally a *mokoro* carries two passengers, supplies and a poler, who stands at the back with the *ngashi*, a long pole made from the mogonono tree. Day trips start at the town of Maun, which lies to the south of the Delta; two- or three-day trips can also be arranged, overnighting in campsites in the Delta. Trips combine poling and trekking – poling is hard work. Most polers speak some English, and are very knowledgeable about the flora and fauna, though they tend to be rather shy.

*A mokoro moves quietly through the marsh reed of the Delta.*

154

# Nxai Pan Old Cattle Trek

The Nxai, Sowa and Ntwetwe Pans, once part of a 'superlake' which evaporated leaving only salt, form northeastern Botswana's Makgadikgadi Pans National Park, which covers 12,000 sq km (4,800 sq mi) and protects large tracts of palm forests, grasslands, savannahh and salt pans. The parks complement each other in enabling wildlife migration.

In the heat of August this is a land of dizzying mirages, but with the rains, temporary lakes form in the depressions and the earth greens. Now herd animals, including elephant and zebra, arrive in their thousands and waterbirds, most spectacularly flamingoes, flock to feed on algae and crustaceans.

Nxai Pan lies north of the highway which cuts through the Park area. To visit, a 4 x 4 is essential, since the track to the entrance is loose sand, and the area is 2,578 sq km, (1,031 sq mi), with just three designated campsites, one of which has apparently been trashed by elephants. There are two viewing platforms. The permanent residents of the grassy expanse include lion, giraffe, kudu, impala and ostrich, and during the migration period the huge herds are followed by predators.

Running inside the western boundary is the Old Cattle Trek route, the Pandamatenga Trail. This once linked boreholes along the route – used till 1963, when stock fences were introduced – of cattle drives. It runs to the Zambian border. In a 4x4 it is still possible to follow this trail out of the Park, north-eastwards to Pandamatenga, some 200 km (125 mi) away. However, careful planning is essential: this seldom-used track is indistinct and the tall grasses conceal obstacles.

**HOW:**
By 4x4
**WHEN TO GO:**
All year, but November to April for the animal migration.
**TIME IT TAKES:**
Two days plus
**HIIGHLIGHTS:**
The wildlife
The vegetation – umbrella acacias, Mokolae palms (the nuts are eaten by elephants, the sap makes palm wine and the fronds, baskets).
Baines' Baobabs, immortalized by the artist/traveller in 1862 and little changed.
**YOU SHOULD KNOW:**
Visitors must have a campsite reservation.
The nearest fuel supply is 102 km (64 mi) east.

*Baobab trees in Naxi Pan National Park*

*Traditional houses in Malealea*

# Jobo Mountain Adventure Drive

**HOW:**
On foot, by 4x4 or on horseback
**WHEN TO GO:**
October, November, March to May
**TIME IT TAKES:**
Pony treks last from a few hours to three days; 4x4 treks last as long as you like.
**HIGHLIGHTS:**
Getting to know the friendly, cheerful Basuto people.
Basuto huts: many of the one-roomed huts (*rondavels*) are decorated with intricate, symbolic murals.
The Sani rock paintings, deep in a sheltering cave, are well preserved.
The view from Jobo Mountain is sensational.
**YOU SHOULD KNOW:**
Some 4x4 routes should only be attempted by experienced off-road drivers.
Each summer several people die from lightning strikes, so avoid high, open ground during storms.

Lesotho – the 'Kingdom of the Sky' – is a small, mountainous country surrounded by South Africa. Though British rule was resented in the 19th century, this British Protectorate (Basutoland) was not included in the Union of South Africa, and the peaceful kingdom avoided the long years of apartheid.

Rural Lesotho is perfect trekking country. Dominated by mountain ranges, this is a land without fences where herd-boys drive their flocks and blanket-wrapped farmers ride. In the south, a relatively small area around the village of Malealea seems to offer all the best features of the highlands. Here are precipitous mountains and gorges, ancient rock paintings, waterfalls and a scattering of remote villages fluttering with bright flags. These flags are colour-coded advertisements for the available comestibles – red and green for meat and vegetables, white and yellow for sorghum or barley beer. Fittingly, this area is reached through the Gates of Paradise Pass.

The lodge here will advise on routes for walkers and drivers of 4x4s and arrange pony treks. Ponies and guides are provided by the villages, and longer treks spend nights in village huts. The Basuto are a nation of horsemen and their small, strong, surefooted ponies are the ideal form of transport. No wild gallops here, though: the ponies pick their way carefully up and down the steep tracks. Very gentle, they are ideal for non-riders.

A trek to Jobo Mountain and village is one of the most rewarding and exciting journeys. The route covers the Sani rock paintings and the Botso'ela Waterfall and the final climb is along a precarious pass between two beautiful, deep gorges. Most 4x4 drivers prefer to walk the last, vertiginous section.

# The Tea Road

One of the smallest African countries, Swaziland, under its king Mswati III, has a strong sense of pride; the King represents and maintains the traditional way of life. This is an absolute monarchy and the power and clan links of the still highly revered King are perhaps the basis of Swaziland's continued stability. Many Swazis wear traditional robes and the high points of the year are the Incwala, the sacred ceremony of kingship and the Umhlanga, performed by the country's maidens.

The superb scenery of this relaxed and friendly country ranges from rainforest and savannah scrub to jagged mountains and high veld. Originally set aside for the royal hunt, several of the excellent game and nature reserves owe their existence to the monarch and this is one of the best areas to see rhinos, despite poaching. Happily, the King is on the side of the conservationists.

The Tea Road makes a good scenic circular tour for travellers with limited time. It is named after a failed project to establish tea plantations. The route runs north from the main road from Mbabane, climbing into the Mzdzimba Range, the burial place of the kings. The ridge provides a panoramic view of the beautiful Royal Valley, Ezulwini. At its centre, the town of Lobamba contains the palace, parliament and the royal kraal, where the King participates in the two magnificent annual ceremonies. A boulder marked gravel road crosses the mountains through Swazi villages and descends to the Malkerne Valley, a lovely area famous for skilled craftwork. North of the country road back towards Mbabne, the mountainous Miliwane Wildlife Sanctuary has a variety of wildlife and good walks.

**HOW:**
By 4x4
**WHEN TO GO:**
May, June and October
**TIME IT TAKES:**
One day
**HIGHLIGHTS:**
The view from Mdzimba includes Sheba's Breasts, twin peaks traditionally the site of King Solomon's Mines.
Even businessmen wear *emahiya*, the traditional dress of Swaziland. The cultural festivals are an extraordinary spectacle.
**YOU SHOULD KNOW:**
The gravel roads are often very steep and impassable during the rainy season.

*Traditionally dressed Swazi women taking part in a festival.*

# Bazaruto Archipelago

**HOW:**
By dhow
**WHEN TO GO:**
May to November
**TIME IT TAKES:**
One day or three to five days
**HIGHLIGHTS:**
A viable population of the endangered dugong inhabits the waters.
Excellent black marlin fishing can be found around Santa Carolina.
The top of the Bazaruto dunes gives a fine view over the archipelago.
The cooking of the dhows' resident chefs is famously good.
**YOU SHOULD KNOW:**
Rock reefs can be razor-sharp.
Winds, tides and sandbanks can be hazards for motorized dhows; if you arrange your own trip, check the reliability of your dhow with the tourist office.

Mozambique's attractive holiday resort, Vilankulo is a charming town with a lively market and lovely beaches, and the gateway to the Bazaruto Archipelago. The main islands of the chain, lying between 10 and 25 km (6 and 15 mi) offshore, are Bazaruto, Santa Carolina, Benguerra and Margaruque (which is close enough for a day-trip). The whole area is protected as a conservation area. The sand dunes, tidal flats and saline lakes support a wide variety of seabirds; the coral reefs teem with fish and marine mammals. Once this was a backpackers' dream, with nothing but campsites; now the islands offer luxury accommodation. The most enjoyable way to explore this tropical paradise is by dhow.

With billowing sails and graceful silhouettes, dhows epitomise a romantic dream of travel. In reality traditional, sail-only dhows, fighting wind, wave and current, becalmed or grounded, with nothing but a rudimentary toilet, have their drawbacks. Dhows with auxiliary outboards and more comfortable facilities offer catering and on-board sleeping arrangements and camping options.

Typically a trip will call at Margaruque for snorkelling and the beach and continue to Benguerra. The journey on to Bazaruto, with its high dunes, anchors at Two Mile Reef for diving. The deep waters around Santa Carolina offer good game fishing. All these low-lying islands have white, palm-fringed beaches – wild and wave-beaten on the windward side, calm turquoise waters and glorious sunsets on the leeward.

The diving in these protected reefs is first class. Uncrowded dive-sites have excellent visibility; as well as a rainbow of small fish, dolphins, rays, humpback whales and turtles are widespread.

*Isla Benguerra in the Bazaruto Archipelago*

# Zambezi River Cruise to Victoria Falls

David Livingstone first saw Victoria Falls in 1855. In awe he wrote that 'angels in their flight must have gazed' on such sights. Though he named the falls for his queen, the Kolola name, 'the smoke that thunders', is more evocative. Here, the Zambezi races over a cliff nearly 2 km (1.2 mi) wide and plunges into the Batoka Gorge more than 100 m (325 ft) below. When the river is in flood, the spray can be seen from miles away.

The falls must be seen, felt and heard from close quarters. At the Victoria Falls World Heritage National Monument Site a walk over a narrow footbridge leads to a buttress, the Knife Edge, with a dizzying view of the falls and the sheer drop. A steep track leads down to the river and a whirlpool called the Boiling Pot. There are advantages to visiting in both the wet season – the falls are at awe-inspiring full flow – and the dry when, though the flow is reduced, the size and structure can be seen clearly.

The range of adventure activities on offer around the foot of the falls includes abseiling, bungee jumping and river boarding as well as white water rafting. However, a river cruise is a leisurely and luxurious way to see the falls from the top and, on the stately progress upstream, watch for wildlife in the parks on both sides of the river. Various cruises are on offer, but the double-or triple-decker craft have a certain style. They leave from the Royal Mile, named for George VI, who visited the Falls in 1947. There is a choice of sunrise and sunset, breakfast, lunch and dinner cruises.

**HOW:**
By river cruiser
**DEPART:**
Livingstone
**WHEN TO GO:**
All year
**TIME IT TAKES:**
Most cruises last one to two hours
**HIGHLIGHTS:**
A sunset cruise with cocktails has a touch of colonial elegance.
Livingstone Island is in the middle of the river, right by the falls.
Wildlife – from the river you might be lucky enough to see a rhino as well as elephants and hippos.
The Monument Site Park opens during full moons for the mysterious lunar rainbow.
**YOU SHOULD KNOW:**
Prepare to get soaked while viewing the falls.

*Victoria Falls at the border of Zambia and Zimbabwe*

# The Albertine Escarpment

**HOW:**
By 4x4
**WHEN TO GO:**
December to February and June to
September
**TIME IT TAKES:**
The road can be driven in one
day but a break in the journey
is recommended.
**HIGHLIGHTS:**
The National Parks – large
populations of chimpanzee inhabit
Budongo and Kibale Forest Parks.
Semliki Forest Park is particularly
famous for its birdlife. Rwenzori Park,
home to many species of wildlife,
stretches over the foothills into the
mountains.
Birds of Semliki Forest – of the
hundreds of species, 35 are found
only here, including the Congo
serpent eagle and three types
of hornbill.
Views of the 'Mountains of the
Moon' from Fort Portal are often
misty but always impressive.
**YOU SHOULD KNOW:**
The situation on the northern border
with Sudan and the south-western
border with Congo is volatile.

Described by Winston Churchill as 'the pearl of Africa', Uganda has superb landscapes – mountain ranges, rolling countryside, lakes, rivers and waterfalls. Most of this landlocked country is fertile and the heat is tempered by altitude. Uganda's troubled recent history should not deter tourists.

In the west lie the Rwenzori Mountains (Africa's highest range). Permanently snow-capped, they are called the 'Mountains of the Moon'. Lake Albert stretches about 160 km (100 mi) along the Congo border to the Albert Nile and spectacular Murchison Falls, where the Victoria Nile rushes and tumbles on its way to Lake Albert.

Masindi, five hours west of Kampala, is the gateway to the Falls area. Between Masindi and the Lake lies the Budongo Forest National Park. The road south along the escarpment is not good: little used and often very steep, it can be a difficult drive, but it crosses some of the loveliest country in Uganda and, with a 4x4 and plenty of time, this is a pleasurable journey.

Ringed by eucalyptus trees planted in colonial times, Hoima lies on a plain. In 1862 it became the capital of the King of Banjora, and the throne room of the current Kitari is open by arrangement. South of Hoima the road rises again, passing through mountainous, lushly forested countryside where occasional cultivated areas allow views for miles around. Finally, the road reaches the hilly greenness surrounding Fort Portal.

One of the most attractive towns in Uganda, Fort Portal lies high in the well-watered foothills of the Rwenzie among tea-estates. With an excellent climate, this refreshing and pleasant spot is a good base for exploring the National Parks (Semuliki, Kibale and Rwenzori) that encircle it.

*A young chimpanzee stops playing to pose for the camera.*

# Mount Elgon & Sasa River Trail

A single, massive extinct volcano towering over the plains, Mount Elgon straddles Uganda's border with Kenya. Wagagi, the highest peak of the caldera ring, is, at 4,321 m (14,043 ft), East Africa's fourth highest mountain. It is an important water catchment and a conservation area of astounding richness. The ascent traverses fertile cultivated foothills (coffee and fruit), montane forest, bamboo and low canopy forest, heath and, above 3,800 m (12,350 ft), Afro-alpine moorland, supporting rare plants. The larger animal residents are rarely spotted, though the forest abounds in monkeys and, of the hundreds of bird species, many are restricted to this location.

Mount Elgon is uncrowded and unspoilt, a magnificent and fascinating wilderness of truly spectacular scenery. It rises in a series of quite gentle slopes punctuated by steep cliffs and scrambles, and is a straightforward climb which can be made by non-mountaineers. The Sasa Trail is the most direct route to the summit, though the first day is strenuous, scaling the cliff by the 'ladders', a series of steep steps and muddy passages. The descent can be made by the Piswa/Sipi Trail, ending at the pretty, relaxing resort at Sipi Falls.

Several companies run climbs. If you organize your own, guides, porters, permits and routes should be arranged at Budadiri, easily reached from Mbale. After the 'ladders' the trail leads through forests and open moorlands, affording breathtaking views. Wagagi is reached by way of Jackson's Hole; then the path follows the caldera rim and joins the Piswa Trail. This passes through lovely terrain – streams, waterfalls and gorges. The last leg follows the Sipi Trail down to Kapkwai, upstream from Sipi Falls.

**HOW:**
On foot
**WHEN TO GO:**
June to August and December to March
**TIME IT TAKES:**
Five days plus
**HIGHLIGHTS:**
Flowers – rare species include giant groundsel, giant lobelia, giant heather.
Bird – restricted range birds include Jackson's francolin, tacazze sunbird and the moustached green tinker bird. The endangered lammergeier may also be spotted.
Tutum Cave on Sipi Trail – a spectacular cave and waterfall hidden in the forest.
Sipi Falls is an impressive, three-tiered waterfall; the lowest section drops over a sheer cliff.
**YOU SHOULD KNOW:**
No specialized equipment or skills are needed, but altitude sickness can be a problem.
The area is subject to sudden weather changes.
All tourists must be accompanied by a licensed guide.

*Sipi Falls in the foothills of Mount Elgon*

**161**

*Waterbuck at Lake Mzizimia in
the Selous Game Reserve*

# Tazara Railway

**HOW:**
By train
**WHEN TO GO:**
June to February
**TIME IT TAKES:**
About 24 hours on the slow train, 19
on the fast (straight through).
**HIGHLIGHTS:**
The Pugu Hills begin just outside Dar;
the traveller is plunged straight into
green, rural Tanzania.
Selous Game Reserve – in the
daylight, elephants, zebras, giraffes,
monkeys and birds of all sorts are
easily spotted from the train.
**YOU SHOULD KNOW:**
Tickets must be booked in advance;
sleeping cars are single sex.

The Tanzania and Zambia Railway Authority runs trains from Dar es Salaam to Mbeya in Tanzania's Southern Highlands and on to Kapiri Mposhi in Zambia. This line was built by the Chinese while Tanzania was more or less communist and some of the poorly maintained rolling stock is still Chinese. This is a notoriously unreliable train service, particularly west to east, and catering can cease completely, though the food is good when the restaurant car is open and food sellers throng the platforms at every stop. Without the railway, however, much of the Southern Highlands is hard to reach and the journey is enjoyable – staff and passengers are friendly and the line runs through some marvellous countryside.

Two fast trains a week leave Dar in late afternoon, and one slow train in the morning. If time is of no concern and landscape is, take the slow train and break the journey at Ifakara, a leafy old trading-station town eight hours southwest of Dar. This means a daylight journey through the lovely, verdant countryside west of Dar and the huge expanse of the Selous Game Reserve where the train crosses woodlands, grasslands and waterways teeming with wildlife.

The fast train reaches Ifakara after midnight and, after some hours of darkness, offers views of the Highlands – the lushly forested slopes of the Udzungu Mountains towering to the north, the ranges, one after another, southwards towards Lake Nyasa. This train arrives in Mbeya at lunchtime. Mbeya, a major trade and transit centre, is set in low hills clothed in tea plantations, coffee, bananas and cocoa. It is surrounded by mountains and the climate is pleasantly cool.

# Lake Manyara National Park

Lake Manyara, a large, shallow, soda lake, is dramatically situated at the foot of the western escarpment of the Rift Valley. The National Park, a UNESCO World Biosphere Reserve, occupies its northwest corner; though one of the smaller parks – the road through it is only about 40 km (25 mi) long – it enjoys diverse vegetation, which provides a variety of habitats.

The wildlife species are not as numerous as in better known parks  (though this is home to the elusive tree-climbing lion), but the birdlife is a huge attraction, particularly flamingoes, which visit the lake in millions during the wet season.

Early morning is the best time to arrive, to catch the game drive. It is very peaceful, with more chance of spotting animals. The safari trips visit in the afternoons, when the Park can be crowded. The road runs the length of the park through marsh, savannah and acacia woodlands and close to the steep escarpment wall, where a variety of trees grow. It passes two sulphur springs, and ends. Tracks and loops off the main road, lead to different habitats – the lake, plains where buffalo, zebra and impala graze, and a pool which is home to hippo and flamingoes.

There are camps inside the Park, and the village of Mto wa Mbu just to the north has accommodation. Travellers who arrive by bus may rent 4x4s from the tourist hotels here.

**HOW:**
By 4x4
**WHEN TO GO:**
June to February (December to April for birding)
**TIME IT TAKES:**
One day plus
**HIGHLIGHTS:**
Elephants – their numbers have decreased, but they are relaxed around vehicles.
Hippos – it is possible to observe them at quite close range.
Flamingoes – during the rains, the lake can look rosy pink from a distance.
Tree-climbing lions are rarely seen; stop in the acacia woodlands and sit very still…
**YOU SHOULD KNOW:**
Walking is not allowed in the Park.

*Elephants on the edge of the Lake*

# Mount Kilimanjaro

Kilimanjaro's iconic snow-capped summit hovers above the lush rainforest and cultivated farmlands of equatorial Tanzania. This is Africa's highest mountain and one of the world's highest volcanoes. Uhuru Peak, one of a jagged group to the east of Kibo, reaches 5896m (19162 ft). Kibo itself appears as a snow-covered dome, but this is a dormant volcano and its caldera conceals a huge crater.

Every year hundreds set out – in theory no specialised expertise or equipment is needed – but a large percentage do not reach the summit. Though the climb can officially be undertaken all year, the rains make the paths slippery and the unpredictability of the weather should never be underestimated. Altitude sickness is a problem which can be alleviated by acclimatisation. What with Park and hut fees, obligatory guides and porters, camping and catering, this is an expensive venture. All treks should be organised through a tour company, but one essential is to allow enough time. Whatever route is chosen, variables such as local conditions and illness must be allowed for in flexible timetabling.

The Machame Route, though not the easiest, is one of the most scenic. It follows steep paths through magnificent forests and over moorland plains, followed by a long track running runs east below the precipitous glaciated cliffs, traversing scree and ridges. This leg importantly gives time to acclimatise at around 4,000 m (13,000 ft). After a night at Bafa Hut, the last day of the ascent involves and early start and a gruelling climb up a bleak and barren section (often snow-covered) to the caldera rim and onwards to Uhuru. The trek down is by the steeper but more direct Mweka Route.

*Reading the signposts on
Mount Kilimanjaro*

# Ngorongoro Crater Highlands Trek

*The still-active Ol Doinyo Lengai volcano*

Ngorongoro Crater is one of Africa's best known reserves, with its huge, steep-sided crater and an unequalled concentration of wildlife, though here tourists sometimes seem to outnumber animals. But the Crater is just part of the enormous Ngorongoro Conservation Area (a UNESCO World Heritage Site). The beautiful and rugged Crater Highlands, formed from volcanoes and collapsed volcanoes, extend in a chain along the east of the area. Several of the peaks top 3,000 m (9,750 ft), and the collapsed volcanoes have produced the eponymous craters. This remote and little-visited area offers remarkable scenery, plenty of wildlife and very good trekking.

All treks in the Highlands must be accompanied by a guide, and some use donkeys for portage and Maasai warriors as guides, who make up for their lack of English with botanical knowledge and ability to spot wildlife. The area is also home to the Datoga pastoralists and Hadzabae foragers, and guides may be able to negotiate visits to villages. Camping is often in 'cultural Bomas' where visitors can learn about Maasai life. Treks can last up to a week.

There are no designated routes in the Highlands, so the places visited will vary. Deserted Empakaai Crater, with its deep, flamingo-crowded lake, offers dramatic views over the whole area from the caldera rim; wooded Olmoti Crater is the source of the Munge River. The soda lakes of Eyasi and Makat are home to many waterbirds (and their predators) and the deep river gorges provide breeding grounds for raptors and water for the Maasai cattle. The higher peaks include Oldeani with its forested crater, and the still-active Ol Doinyo Lengai (Mountain of God). The acacia forests are rich in wildlife.

**HOW:**
On foot
**WHEN TO GO:**
June to February
**TIME IT TAKES:**
One to seven days
**HIGHLIGHTS:**
Acacia wildlife includes giraffes, impala and elephants.
Empakaai views – the Great Rift Valley, Lake Matron and even snow-capped Kilamanjaro.
Olmoti – the river pours through a notch in the rim in a spectacular waterfall.
Ol Doinyo Lengai – the brave and energetic can scramble up to watch the steaming, bubbling crater.
**YOU SHOULD KNOW:**
Treks into the craters must be with an armed ranger.
Weather in the Highlands can change to fog or rain very quickly; temperatures at night can fall to freezing.
Respect local customs and beliefs and learn a few phrases in Kiswahili from your guide or the villagers themselves.

# Mombasa to Zanzibar Cruise

Some companies now offer holidays that combine the glorious beach life of the Kenyan coast with a short cruise from Mombasa to Zanzibar. These are designed to give a taste of the pleasure of life at sea and a fascinating glimpse of East Africa and the Indian Ocean.

Mombasa has a very long history; Roman, Arabic and East Asian seafarers sheltered in its fine natural harbour. For centuries the Old Town saw bloody battles between the Portuguese and the Omani Arabs following the Portuguese seizure of the city in an attempt to break the Arab monopoly of the lucrative spice trade. Modern Mombasa, despite its turbulent history, is a fine city, and, with its laid-back Swahili culture, a relaxing one.

Simply the name conjures up exotic fairytale images, and Zanzibar in reality is a bewitching place. This fertile tropical island is clothed in spice plantations and ringed by picture-postcard beaches and perfect blue waters. The capital, Stone Town, is steeped in history; it is a maze of narrow winding lanes and hidden courtyards, minarets and mysterious, massive closed doors. Zanzibar, under the rule of the Omani Arabs, who moved their capital from Muscat, was the world's most important clove supplier. Now, though the sultans and slaves have gone, the spices remain.

Most cruises sail from Mombasa in the afternoon and, after a night on board, provide a tour of the island, visiting Stone Town and a clove plantation. The journey back to Mombasa may allow a day on the tiny coral islet of Misali, off the coast of Pemba, Zanzibar's northern neighbour. This is a marine haven, with idyllic beaches and fascinating nature trails.

# The Asmara to Nefasit Steam Train

The narrow gauge, Italian era steam train from Asmara to Nefasit is a joy, not just for steam train buffs but for anyone finding themselves in Eritrea's delightful capital city. Set high on the Kelbessa plateau, 2,350 m (7,755 ft) above sea level in the Eritrean Highlands, Asmara itself is delightful, but take a day out for this trip and you'll be richly rewarded.

The journey is just 25 km (16 mi) long, but from the moment you clamber aboard, you know it will be fun. Built between 1887 and 1938, this track was the brainchild of Mussolini, also responsible for the fabulous Art Deco and Modernist architecture of the city itself. With his demise, it sank into disrepair, but using the expertise of the old railway workers, brought out of retirement, and most of whom are now in their 70s and 80s, it was rehabilitated in the late1990s.

Pulling out of Asmara, the train chuffs and puffs along the track. Great plumes of dirty grey smoke rise into the air and urgent tooting alerts the world as it makes its way down the escarpment. The views are spectacular: dramatic mountains, deep valleys and forest. You'll pass traditional villages with orchards of lemon trees, banana plants and the ubiquitous prickly pears, and now and again you'll stop at a small station.

This was an amazing engineering feat – the downhill gradient is an almost constant 1 in 28, and the train negotiates its way through some 20 tunnels and over 65 bridges during the course of the journey. Some of the track runs along narrow ledges cut into the mountainsides, with a vertiginous drop to the valley below. These scenes are much as they must have been for hundreds of years, and now, thankfully, it is possible to enjoy them again.

**HOW:**
By train
**WHEN TO GO:**
September to March
**TIME IT TAKES:**
About an hour
**HIGHLIGHTS:**
The fabulous Art Deco architecture in Asmara, such as the Fiat building and the Impero Cinema.
TThe neo-Romanesque cathedral, with its plaque commemorating its benefactors – including Benito Mussolini himself.
The evening *passegiata*, where the town turns out to walk and talk.
Debre Bizen, a 14th century monastery set high above Nefasit, with its remarkable collection of medieval manuscripts. But beware – only men may enter!
**YOU SHOULD KNOW:**
The narrow gauge rails are 950 mm, the locomotives are pre-war 440 and 442 Mallets, the shunting tanks are Breda, built between 1927-1937 and the railcars are Art Deco style Fiat Littorinas, built in 1935.

*The old narrow gauge Italian steam train crosses one of the many bridges on the line.*

# The Blue Nile Gorge

**HOW:**
On foot
**WHEN TO GO:**
October to March
**TIME IT TAKES:**
At least one day
**HIGHLIGHTS:**
Bahir Dar, a beautiful, interesting town.
Lake Tana and its island monasteries.
Tis Issat Falls, one of Ethiopia's most famous scenic attractions.
**YOU SHOULD KNOW:**
You will need to be fit if you plan to trek in the gorge. There are many organised road trips, or you can bring bikes. If you are going to camp in the gorge, be careful not to be too close to the river – remember those crocodiles!

The Blue Nile Gorge is one of the world's most spectacular sights, rivalling, if not beating, America's Grand Canyon. The river itself flows south from its source near Lake Tana, and then north-west until it joins the White Nile at Khartoum in Sudan. Then, as the Nile, it flows through Egypt, eventually discharging into the Mediterranean. It is the longest river in the world, and the source of life for millions of people.

There are different methods of arriving at and travelling through some or all of the gorge. From Lake Tana, the road drops sharply for well over 300 m (1,000 ft), to the riverbed, with outstanding views in every direction. The closer you get to the bottom, the hotter and more humid it becomes, but the breathtaking views more than make up for this minor problem. Crossing an Italian era bridge over the river, you may be surprised to be strictly forbidden to take photographs – particularly since you will be approached by people selling postcards of it!

The gorge is glorious, covered in beautiful vegetation including dragon trees and junipers that jostle for space between small, terraced fields of a grain known as *teff*, used in Ethiopian flatbread, which sways and bows in the light breeze. Frankincense trees are grown as part of a project – they can be tapped for resin up to ten times annually. There are small Amharan villages to be seen, the round houses roofed with grass blending naturally into their surroundings. Baboons bound in and out of view, and birds include lammergeyers, bee-eaters and various raptors. The road is carried on Italian viaducts for part of the way – watch out for crocodiles and hippos down in the river beneath. People here are friendly folk, fascinated by foreigners, the women and girls often nonchalantly balancing huge, beautiful pots full of water on their heads. The climb out of the gorge is exhaustingly steep, but walking here is well worth the effort.

*The Tis Issat Falls drain Lake Tana into the Blue Nile near Bahir Dar.*

# Raft the Omo River

The Omo River rises in the Shewan Highlands, and tumbles south for 760 km (475 mi) before emptying into Lake Turkana on the border with northern Kenya. Its total fall is some 2,000 m (6,600 ft), and the only easily navigable stretch is in the far south. The entire river valley is archaeologically important, and after the earliest known fossil fragments of *Homo sapiens* were discovered in the southern reaches, a UNESCO World Heritage Site was declared. This is a truly remote region, not only rich in wildlife and birds, but also in the many unique tribal peoples, hunters and pastoralists, who inhabit the surrounding areas. The river passes through the Omo and Mago National Parks, two of the richest and least visited of East Africa's wildlife sanctuaries.

Starting the trip at the small town of Omorate, your raft carries you along the broad, brown river, which by now has levelled out and become quite placid. There are crocodiles sunning themselves upon the banks, and hippos to be seen as you glide through open forest of tamarind and figs. Colobus monkeys chatter and leap, baboons bark in the distance and the birds are magnificent – you will see goliath herons, kingfishers, turacos, fish eagles and more. The Omo Delta, a maze of islands and marshes, is inhabited by the Dassenach people. Pastoralists who practise flood retreat cultivation, they hunt crocodiles at night, by spearing them from small canoes – a small crocodile makes a large meal.

As Lake Turkana, the world's largest desert lake, is shrinking, so the delta is expanding, having reached 250 km (156 mi) at its widest point and becoming a wetland of international importance. Drifting closer to Lake Turkana, you will notice the silt-laden water gradually changing to the colour that gives the lake its other name – the Jade Sea.

**HOW:**
On a raft
**WHEN TO GO:**
November to January
**TIME IT TAKES:**
Between one and several days, depending on the tour company you are using.
**HIGHLIGHTS:**
Enjoying the sights and sounds of the wildlife and birds.
Visiting Mursi, Karo and Hamer Koke villages and meeting the tribal people.
Continue your journey into Kenya, exploring Lake Turkana and its National Parks, also a UNESCO World Heritage Site.
**YOU SHOULD KNOW:**
During five days in August 2006, the lower reaches of the Omo flooded, resulting in 456 deaths, and leaving 20,000 people stranded. Ethiopia's rivers are losing capacity as they are filling with silt.

*A Karo warrior*

*Looking towards the northern escarpment, near Sankabar*

# The Simien Mountains

**HOW:**
On foot
**WHEN TO GO:**
October to April
**TIME IT TAKES:**
Two to three days
**HIGHLIGHTS:**
Spotting endemic and rare species of mammals, birds and plants.
Axsum, Ethiopia's most ancient city, said to be the hiding place of the Ark of the Covenent and the home of the Queen of Sheba.
Lalibela, and its monolithic, rock hewn churches.
Ascend Rash Dashen, Ethiopia's highest peak at 4,600 m (15,159 ft) and the fourth highest on the African continent.
**YOU SHOULD KNOW:**
The Simien fox is actually a rare, red wolf. On the Internation Union for Conservation of Nature (IUCN) Red List, there are less than 500 individuals of this endangered animal left.

One of Africa's major massifs, and a UNESCO World Heritage Site, the magnificent Simien Mountains have to be seen to be believed. Formed some 40 million years ago by violent seismic activity, erosion produced the dramatic mountain-scapes we can enjoy today – dramatic escarpments, mile-deep gorges, sculpted mountains, plateaux, river valleys and *ambas*, sheer pinnacles of lava, the last remnants of ancient volcanoes. Many of the peaks rise above 4,000 m (13,000 ft), and snow and ice are often to be seen at the highest levels.

Despite the altitude and harsh terrain, villages and terraced fields are dotted about these mountains, linked by rough tracks. Starting the trek to Chennek from Sankabar, the most scenically exciting route takes you down into the Jinbar Wenz Gorge, across the river to Gich village, and up to Gich Camp. Situated at 3,100 m (1,900 ft), this manned park station looks across richly forested valleys and mountains bursting with wildlife, including large groups of the endemic Gelada baboon, also known as the Bleeding Heart baboon for the patch of deep red on the chests of the males. Here too are very rare Walia ibex and Simien fox. Take the opportunity to hike to the superb viewpoint of Imet Gogo, with its tremendous vistas across a vast canyon to the rock spires beyond – looking down you might see a Lammergeyer (Bearded vulture) repeatedly dropping its prey onto the rocks far below – a process designed to access the marrow by pulverizing the bones.

Following a tough, tussocked trail through magnificent Afro-alpine vegetation – giant heather, giant red hot pokers and endemic lobelia, you come at last to Chennek. Situated on a cliff edge, this is one of the world's most spectacular campsites: the dizzying views spreading below make you feel you are at the edge of the world.

# Timbuktu by Boat

Though Timbuktu remains a fabled place in the minds of many, today it is quite possible to reach. In order to do so, you can't beat travelling there by boat, along the mighty Niger, Africa's third longest river. Setting out from Mopti, to the west of Timbuktu, take a *pinasse*, a type of motorized canoe with a domed grass canopy, and enjoy the travelling as much as the arriving.

The flood plains around Mopti provide a wonderful habitat for birds of all sorts, including many migratory species, and the river itself is home to many fish, some of which will no doubt be caught and cooked for you. You may well see hippos, too – their large, irascible presence alerting you to the relative fragility of your craft. The river is full of activity: local boats carry goods and livestock, fast boats speed tourists to Timbuktu. Children shriek '*toubab*' (white man), and wave frantically as you pass, men fish, women wash clothes at the river's edge or pound millet in time-honoured fashion. Occasionally houses here have solar panels, often powering televisions – an unlikely sight indeed.

This journey is fun: from time to time the *pinasse* stops at a village, which you can explore while provisions are bought. Lunch is cooked on board, and at night tents are pitched on the riverbank, and dinner cooked over a fire. Gradually the scenery changes: marshlands give way to grasslands and finally, the desert. The trip ends at Korioume, just 10 km (6 mi) along a paved road from Timbuktu. Just a few decades ago the Niger ran through the town, but the desert has been encroaching. In 2007 a Libyan-built canal and reservoir was opened, joining Timbuktu to the river once again, and bringing a better water supply to this legendary but beleaguered city.

**HOW:**
By boat
**WHEN TO GO:**
November to March
**TIME IT TAKES:**
Two to four days, depending on your boat.
**HIGHLIGHTS:**
Visiting riverside villages, appreciating the Moorish mud brick architecture and meeting tribal people such as Fulani and Bozo.
Spotting birds and other wildlife – you might see a manatee.
Taking a camel trip to a Touareg village from Timbuktu.
The Festival in the Desert, held at Essakane each February, a 'must' for world music fans.
**YOU SHOULD KNOW:**
The late, great, musician, Ali Farka Touré owned a farm near Niafounke, on the banks of the Niger, not far from Timbuktu. Appointed mayor of the area in 2004, he introduced a tree planting scheme and modern irrigation systems and was living there when he died in 2006.

*An adobe village along the Niger River*

171

# The Salt Road from Timbuktu to Taoudenni

Azalai, as the camel caravans travelling from Timbuktu to Taoudenni are known, regularly trek some 800 km (500 mi) across one of the harshest regions of the Sahara desert. They have passed this way for over 1,000 years, ever since salt, which could be traded weight for weight with gold, was discovered in the area.

Join a Touareg caravan leaving from Timbuktu, or take a guide and a 4x4 – whichever way you go it will be the journey of a lifetime. There is austere beauty in the desert, and little sound other than the soft shoe shuffle of camels moving over hard sand and sharp stones. Sleeping under the stars in the immense silence of the desert is a profound experience.

Days begin before sun up, and the caravan travels doggedly until darkness falls. Strong, sweet mint tea is frequently brewed and begins to taste like nectar from the gods. At night, rice and dried meat is cooked and eaten, with a sprinkling of sand thrown in. Reaching the halfway point of Arouane, a tiny settlement en route, feels like a great achievement. From there on in, the desert is empty – no grass, no trees, just sand stretching to the horizon. There is little wildlife – desert rats, lizards, beetles and, perhaps, gazelles, but you may pass camel bones: bleached by the sun they underline the fact that your life is in the hands of your guide.

When the stony desert becomes sand dunes, you know you are within reach of Taoudenni. Here, in a vast basin that was once a sea, a couple of hundred men dig for salt, living in primitive, almost Biblical conditions. However, within 24 hours the camels are all fully loaded with their heavy cargo, and are ready to begin the trek back to Timbuktu and civilization.

*A Touareg caravan travelling along the Salt Road – the salt is transported in large rectangular-shaped slabs.*

# Mount Cameroon Trek

*The trail up to the volcano*

An active volcano (the last eruption was in 2000) rising steeply from the Gulf of Guinea, Mount Cameroon is, at 4,095 m (13,309 ft), the highest mountain in West Africa. It is a 'biodiversity hotspot', a scientifically important area with varied habitats and endemic plant and birdlife. The terrain ranges from farmland and dense rainforest to scrub savannah and a harsh tract of volcanic rock and ash up to the bare summit.

There are several routes up the mountain. The most direct, the Guinness Route, is straight up and down, very steep, and can be completed in a day and a half (the runners in the annual Race of Hope manage it in as little as five hours). But spending longer on the mountain is very rewarding and set hikes of several days, starting at Mann Spring or Buea and descending the northwest face by Elephant Opening allow time to appreciate the diverse vegetation, do some bird-spotting and admire the views.

An eco-tourism organization based at Buea, which works closely with the villages round the mountain, arranges various treks. It employs locals with specialized knowledge as guides and uses some of its profits for community projects. The climb to the summit is demanding: altitude sickness is common – because the mountain starts at sea level, a short climb brings a big change in altitude. The weather is notoriously changeable – even in the dry season trekkers can be engulfed in sudden tropical downpours and, at the summit, the temperature can fall below freezing. There are, however, a number of options for treks of different durations around the lower slopes. These include lava-flow walking, visits to the numerous craters, and bird-watching.

**HOW:**
On foot
**WHEN TO GO:**
November to April
**TIME IT TAKES:**
The ascent: three to five days. Other treks: one to three days.
**HIGHLIGHTS:**
A night on the mountain – the brightness of the stars and sunrise on the slopes.
Birds include the Cameroon pigeon, Purple-throated cuckoo-shrike and the Cameroon francolin.
**YOU SHOULD KNOW:**
The ascent requires a good level of fitness and preferably some climbing experience. The treks can be tailored to the individual's needs and abilities.

*Boats crossing the Gambia River at Basse Santa Su.*

# Cruise the Gambia River

**HOW:**
By boat
**WHEN TO GO:**
November to April
**TIME IT TAKES:**
Four hours or a day or two,
depending on whether you go direct
or overnight on board or at a lodge.
**HIGHLIGHTS:**
The Baobolong Wetland Reserve
Spotting birds and other wildlife
en route
Abuko Nature Reserve
The island of Janjangbureh and its
port, Georgetown
Wassu Stone Circles
The beautiful, empty beaches of
Kombo South.
**YOU SHOULD KNOW:**
The River Gambia was an important
slave trading route. Each year a
Roots music festival is held, named
after the book by Alex Hayley, whose
supposed ancestor lived in a small
village near Albreda, until he was
captured, enslaved and sent to
America.

Continental Africa's smallest country, The Gambia, is shaped like a wedge cut into the middle of Senegal. Dominated by the Gambia River, which runs from the Atlantic coast inland for some 320 km (200 mi), the country consists of the river and the land to either side of it. The river is the country's lifeblood, providing water and food in an otherwise arid region, and for those who like wildlife, and birdlife in particular, a cruise along all or part of this essential waterway is a treat.

Begin your trip at Bintang, a small town some 80 km (50 mi) from the capital, Banjul, and take a pre-arranged boat along the river to Farafenni, passing the renowned Baobolong Wetlands on the north bank. This is The Gambia's first designated RAMSAR site, and the country's largest nature reserve, covering 220 sq km (85 sq mi). It is a maze of small islands with waterways, or *bolongs*, weaving their way between them. Here you will see ancient mangroves, many over 19 m (60 ft) tall, as well as tidal mudflats and savannahh forest. It is home to up to 300 species of bird, including fishing owls, goliath herons, spoonbills, and much more besides. It's not uncommon to spot 60 or 70 species during a three-hour spell.

This is a gentle, pleasant jaunt, puttering along the river in the sunshine, binoculars at the ready, with the sounds of water, birds and chattering monkeys in the background. The river itself is full of life – you may see dolphins and otters, crocodiles and even hippos, and if you want to spend more time away from the tourist resorts of the coast, there are several lodges in which to stay and chill out in an unspoilt natural paradise.

# Ile de Gorée

Dakar, a huge, feverish city, brims with life. Here are all the sights, smells and sounds of Africa – noisy markets, great live music, fabulous street-food and exuberant nightlife. The sprawling city swarms with jet-setters, expats, French military types and the grindingly poor. A mere 20-minute ferry ride away lies the meditative calm of the Ile de Gorée.

Europeans first colonized the easily defensible island in 1444; power shifted between the Portuguese and the Dutch until the French took over in 1677. They stayed, with brief periods of British rule, till Senegalese independence in 1960. The colonial legacy is evident in the island's lovely old mansions, flower wreathed balconies and quiet unpaved lanes (there are no cars on the island).

Gorée became a centre of the West African slave trade – the first Portuguese slave house was established in 1536. The trade continued, officially and unofficially, under the French till 1848. Now the island's main draw is La Maison des Esclaves and its 'doors of no return', with its grim basement 'storage rooms' for slaves, the airy quarters for traders above. It has become a place of pilgrimage for African Americans, though it is debateable whether this was in fact a major shipping point for slaves – Gorée is a tiny island, and the Maison has no good moorings. But this UNESCO World Heritage Site is a universal heritage, which brings slavery's iniquities movingly to life. This is a brief journey, but memories of it will be long.

**HOW:**
Local ferry
**WHEN TO GO:**
January to May, November and December
**TIME IT TAKES:**
One day, or longer
**HIGHLIGHTS:**
Stay on Gorée – in one of the several pleasant hotels – and, outside weekends, enjoy the peace of this beautiful, faded place.
Museum – as well as the Maison des Esclaves there are some interesting museums and fortifications.
Sit on the mainland wharf at twilight and watch the low, rocky outline of Gorée fade into the night.
**YOU SHOULD KNOW:**
All museums on Gorée close on Mondays.

*Ile de Gorée*

# Mole National Park Safari

**HOW:**
On foot
**WHEN TO GO:**
November to February
**TIME IT TAKES:**
Walks last three hours. Four days
would allow for getting there and
away and time to enjoy the Park.
**HIGHLIGHTS:**
The animals – particularly elephants
bathing in the waterhole – they can
be approached to within a few yards.
The birds – Mole has the longest bird
checklist in Ghana. Even hardened
birdwatchers are thrilled by the
colourful, exotic and rare specimens.
The sounds of the savannah at night.
The staff canteen at the safari office
serves traditional Ghanaian food.
**YOU SHOULD KNOW:**
Closed shoes are mandatory for
guided walks.
Tsetse flies can be a nuisance on the
plain; carry netting to cover head and
shoulders.

Mole, an immense, remote tract of wooded savannah in northeast Ghana, is home to a huge range of animals (over 90 species including elephants, baboons, warthogs and antelope) and birds (300 species recorded, from tiny bee-eaters to vultures and eagles). However, its tourist potential is unrealized – 95 per cent of its area is unvisited even by rangers, which has allowed regular poaching. The game-viewing circuit is limited to a few miles of poor roads around the southeast corner.

The area is best seen on foot and, unusually, most visitors arrive by public transport. The daily bus from Tamale (four to six hours west by dirt road) comes right into the Park. This is a crowded, dusty uncomfortable ride, with frequent breakdowns, but it is regarded as a memorable part of the Mole experience. Mole Motel, where the bus journey ends, is the only place to stay. The buildings are old and basic, the accommodation far from luxurious, the water supply erratic, but its situation, high on a steep escarpment above the savannah, is superb, affording views of the untouched wilderness landscape, the glorious sunsets and of two waterholes and the animals which gather there to drink.

Outside the hotel grounds, walkers must be accompanied by armed rangers (rifles protect against poachers, not big cats – lions have not been observed for some time). The hotel runs 'walking safaris' in the early morning (cooler) and late afternoon, when more animals may be seen. These guided walks allow close-range observation of wildlife and can be tailored to the needs of the group.

*A troop of baboons take a stroll along the trail.*

# Marrakech Express

For the baby-boom generation, the Marrakech Express conjures up the old hippy days of the late 1960s and early 1970s, when everyone seemed to be discovering the wonders of Morocco, a country and culture so fascinatingly different from Europe, yet sitting on its doorstep. Immortalised by the eponymous song, the Marrakech Express remains an iconic journey.

Rabat is Morocco's capital. Less famous than other Moroccan cities, it is a delightful place, with a marvellous fortified Kasbah, and an ancient, walled medina, as well as a French-built new town. It is well worth spending a day or two here before taking the train.

The track follows the coastline south-west to Casablanca, passing the up-market beach resort of Skhirat, as well as Mohammedia, an industrial town but with a huge beach which draws tourists from both Casablanca and Rabat. All Morocco's cities pride themselves on their individuality, and Casablanca is no exception. Built mainly in the 20th century by the French, and boasting some fine Art Deco architecture, this is the country's business and financial hub.

Leaving Casablanca, the track veers inland, through the city's fertile, agricultural hinterland, past orange groves loaded with fruit and fields of crops and vegetables. Gradually the green fields are left behind as the train makes its way across a flat, increasingly barren plain. Scoured by the wind and sun for millennia, the deep red earth and rocky outcrops look bleak and under populated.

As the train approaches its goal, the scenery changes again and the magnificent range of the Atlas Mountains, with their snow-capped peaks, come into view. Finally, the spectacular, ancient, red mudbrick walled, Imperial city of Marrakech is reached. Founded in the 11th century, this tourist mecca and architectural gem demands that you explore its labyrinthine souks and remarkable, secret gardens.

*Marrakech city walls with the Atlas Mountains in the backgroud*

**HOW:**
By train
**WHEN TO GO:**
March to June and September to November. Try to avoid Ramadan.
**TIME IT TAKES:**
About four hours.
**HIGHLIGHTS:**
Marrakech's famous square, Djema el-Fna, crowded with exotic street entertainers and excellent street food.
The 12th century Koutoubia minaret
The Saadien Tombs
The Majorelle Gardens, founded by the artist Jacques Majorelle in 1917, the gardens were restored by Yves Saint Laurent and Pierre Berge who bought the property after Majorelle's death in 1962.
**YOU SHOULD KNOW:**
Trains in Morocco are frequent, efficient and reasonably priced, first class and second class compartments contain six or eight seats respectively, with air conditioning in first class on certain inter-city routes. Plans to build a high-speed link between Tangiers and Marrakech have been agreed, as has the building of a tunnel under the Mediterranean from Paloma, Spain to Tangiers.

# Rif Road Trip

**HOW:**
By car
**WHEN TO GO:**
March to June and September to
November
**TIME IT TAKES:**
A minimum of two days, but up to a
week or more if you want to explore
some of the fascinating towns
en route.
**HIGHLIGHTS:**
The Medersa Bou Inania, Fes.
The view of Fez from the
Merenid Tombs.
The Museum of Moroccan Arts and
Crafts in the Dar Batha Palace, Fes.
Friouato Cave, perhaps the deepest
and most impressive cave in North
Africa, 22 km (14 mi) from Taza.
Sidi Yahia, a lovely oasis and holy
place 6 km (4 mi) from Oujda.
**YOU SHOULD KNOW:**
There are alternative routes across
the Rif Mountains; the most
straightforward takes you through
awe-inspiring mountain scenery, via
the pleasant, coastal city of Al
Hoceima. Whatever you do, make
sure you avoid Ketama, the
dangerous town at the heart of the
drugs trade.

The highly scenic Rif Mountains stretch across northern Morocco, from Tangiers to Oujda on the Algerian border. Entirely separate geologically from the Atlas Mountains, they were originally part of Europe. With the highest of the craggy, limestone peaks rising to some 2,500 m (8,250 ft), this is Morocco's Wild West – untamed country, full of hidden valleys, gullies and streams. The only large towns lie on the foothills; otherwise the mountain settlements are merely extended villages. This is a lawless area, where much of the forest has been cut and the land put to *kif* (cannabis) and hashish production.

Driving from the port city of Tangiers, the road climbs to Tetouan, and then on to Chefchaouen, a beautiful town of blue and white houses, nestling on the edge of the wildflower-strewn mountainside. Continuing to Fez, the road twists and turns for 217 km (135 mi), through steep bends and dramatic scenery. Take a small detour to Ouezzane, a town honoured by Muslims and Jew alike, busy with craftsmen and surrounded by olive groves.

Fes is unique: its old town, one of the great medieval cities of the world, contains some of the most spectacular buildings in the country. The narrow, twisting alleys of the souks are extraordinary and thrilling to explore, your senses swamped by sights, sounds and smells that are both alien and bewitching.

Leaving Fes, the road takes a circuit around Jbel Tazekka, a high altitude national park of cork oaks and cedar forests, before reaching Taza. One of Morocco's oldest towns, Taza lies between the Rif and the Middle Atlas on the edge of a plateau. From here you pass over sparsely populated plains and plateaux, the countryside becoming increasingly green and fertile, until you reach Oujda, the capital of eastern Morocco and the gateway to Algeria.

*The city of Chefchaouen with the Rif Mountains beyond*

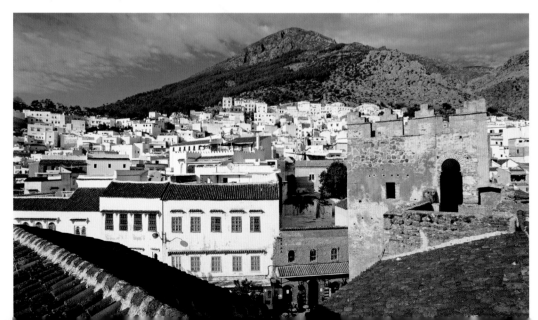

# High Atlas Mule Trek

*The Kasbah at Ait Ben Haddou*

Morocco's High Atlas mountain range stretches east from the Atlantic Ocean to the Algerian border. Centuries of erosion have produced rocky peaks that descend to deeply carved, green valleys. Djebel Toubkal, at 4,167 m (13,670 ft), the highest peak in North Africa, dominates the Toubkal National Park. Established in 1942, and situated 60 km (37 mi) south of Marrakech, this remote area is a traditional Berber homeland, and small settlements and villages are scattered throughout, clinging precariously to the mountainsides. Built of *pisé* (rammed earth), they blend perfectly into the environment.

From Tamatert, the highest village at about 2,000 m (6,600 ft), you set out, with mules and a guide, to ascend to the Tamatert Pass, trekking through terraced fields of wheat and barley, orchards of apples, cherries and walnuts, and finally forests of pine and junipers. Walking or riding is the only way to travel and transport goods in this region, and the undulating tracks, though sometimes rocky, are well maintained.

The views from the pass are vast, encompassing two separate valleys: this majestic sight can barely have altered in 1,000 years. The high peaks, including Toubkal itself, are the source of water for the Tamatert valley – a multitude of springs, fed by melting snow and ice, trickle, tumble and cascade downwards, irrigation canals ensuring every inch of fertile land is well watered. The golds and greens of the valley floor turn to purples, reds and browns as you gaze at the barren peaks above. In spring the mountainsides are covered in gorgeously colourful wildflowers, attracting scores of butterflies, some of which are endemic. Birds thrive here: Alpine accentor, chough, booted eagle – altogether about 50 different species can be seen, not to mention Barbary sheep, endangered through over-hunting, and shaggy mountain goats that skip up and down seemingly impossible inclines.

**HOW:**
On foot with mules
**WHEN TO GO:**
All year round, but if you don't want snow, go between April and October.
**TIME IT TAKES:**
There are treks to suit everyone, varying between about four hours and ten days. The latter means camping, but your guides will do all the hard work, including the cooking, and the mules will carry all the essentials leaving you free to enjoy the experience.
**HIGHLIGHTS:**
Climb Djebel Toubkal – you do not have to be a very experienced mountaineer to achieve this.
Trek to the lovely Lake Ifni, and its nearby waterfalls.
Visit traditional Berber villages including Sidi Chamharouch, a place of pilgrimage.
Visit Ait Ben Haddou, a remarkable fortified village and UNESCO World Heritage Site.
Spend a few days in Marrakech, a city unlike any other.
**YOU SHOULD KNOW:**
Even trekking with mules, you'll want to walk some of the time, and as the tracks are rocky and uneven, a walking pole will be a great help.

# From Tozeur to Douz across the Chott el-Djerid

The Chott el-Djerid is the largest saltpan in the Sahara, covering an area of over 5,000 sq km (1,900 sq mi) and separating the steppes of northern Tunisia from the Grand Erg Oriental desert in the south. In the summer, when the Chott is completely dried up, it is a vast gleaming expanse of apparently solid bluish-white crust. In spring and autumn, heavy rains transform it into a salt marsh, which soon evaporates into weird-shaped crystalline masses and pools. Whatever the season, it is incredibly dangerous to walk on. There are terrible local tales of it swallowing whole caravans of camels.

The only way to cross this forsaken land is by using the 250 km (155 mi) causeway that runs from the picturesque town of Tozeur on the northwestern fringes of the Chott, to Douz, on the border of the desert. As you leave Tozeur, the road runs through undulating hills where goats and camels graze. You cannot help but feel a sudden lurch of excitement when the Chott comes into view. The completely straight gypsum causeway plunges you into an eerie otherworld. This is like nothing on earth that you have even begun to imagine. As far as the eye can see, there is literally nothing but salt crusts gleaming in the sun against the straight line of the horizon. By the roadside there are lurid pink-tinted crystalline deposits, wherever you look there are shimmering reflections, and Fata Morgana mirages pop up out of nowhere.

Thoroughly disorientated and with some relief, you finally arrive at Douz, the 'gateway to the Sahara' – a date palm oasis inhabited by the Mrazig, a tribe of nomadic desert shepherds. Here you can do something 'normal' – like take a camel ride out into the dunes – to ground yourself back in reality.

*Tribesmen near Douz*

# Jebel Nafusa Mountain Drive

Once an international pariah but mellowed with age, Colonel Ghadaffi is almost respectable nowadays, entertaining world leaders in his desert tent. They're not the only ones who are welcome, as tourism is developed to supplement Libya's oil wealth. It's a great policy, because this Mediterranean country is full of sights that surprise and delight. A good way of seeing traditional Libya is to journey from Tripoli to the Jebel Nafusa Mountains and on to Nalut at their western extremity, up by the Tunisian border. Don't hurry to hit the road, though – take a day to explore the exotic capital city and see some of its famous sights.

Then head for the mountains. Apart from the narrow coastal trip, Libya is all Sahara Desert, and this 300-km (185-mi) journey is an ideal way to experience something of the unique atmosphere of that silent sea of sand. Head south from Tripoli through scrubby semi-desert for 80 km (50 mi) to Bi'r al Ghanam, where you meet the Jebel Nafusa Mountains, a harsh landscape of rocky escarpments and barren hills broken by fertile patches where olives, figs, apricots and grain are grown. This is the heartland of the Berber people and remains of their civilization dot the landscape, with ancient stone villages overlooking the plain from perches high above.

Follow the road along the northern foothills past Bi'r Ayyad, Qasr al-Hajj, Shakshuk, Tiji and Al Hawamid until – at the westernmost end of the Jebel Nafusa range, up by the Tunisian border – you reach Nalut. Then you'll appreciate the reason for choosing this destination. It's one of the finest Ghurfa (storage chambers) villages in Libya, in a commanding position with sweeping desert views, atmospheric twisting streets and an old town made up of over 400 extraordinary ghurfas.

**HOW:**
By car or 4x4
**WHEN TO GO:**
April to October
**TIME IT TAKES:**
A day
**HIGHLIGHTS:**
In Tripoli – the medina (old market quarter), castle, Jamahiriya Museum (impressive collection of classical statues, mosaics and artefacts), Gurgi Mosque, Roman Arch of Marcus Aurelius and Gazelle Fountain.
Gharyan, on the edge of the Nafusa Mountains – with extraordinary troglodyte dwellings dug straight down into the ground (a detour via Yefren on the return journey).
At Qasr al-Hajj – an extraordinary grain and oil store that is one of the best examples of Berber architecture.
In Nalut – the 300-year-old mud-brick ksar and the even-more-ancient Alal'a Mosque (rebuilt 1312).
**YOU SHOULD KNOW:**
Most Berbers belong to the Khariji sect of Islam, and females should sensibly cover their heads (besides, the sun can be fierce!).

*The Sahara Desert with mountains in the background*

# Follow the Footsteps of Moses up Mount Sinai

Mount Sinai, or Jebel Musa (Mount Moses) is of enormous spiritual significance in the shared Judaeo-Christian and Muslim Old Testament heritage, for it is here that Moses is supposed to have received the Ten Commandments. The local Bedouins have deep reverence for the sanctity of their land and for over 1,500 years pilgrims have journeyed here to make obeisance. Perched on the summit are both a Greek Orthodox chapel and a Muslim shrine. The 6th century St Catherine's Monastery, supposedly built around the Burning Bush, stands at the foot.

There are two routes up the 2,285-m (7,500-ft) high mountain. The Siket Sayidna Musa (Path of Our Lord Moses) – 3,750 Steps of Penitence hewn out of stone by the monks of St Catherine's – lead directly up a steep ravine to the summit. Or you can take a gentler, more winding path, the Siket El Bashait (Camel Path) either on foot or by camel. Most tourists are herded up the latter track, as likely as not having first been cajoled onto the back of a camel by persuasive Bedouins. The ease of this route is the only thing to recommend it. It is much less scenic and far more crowded. The two paths meet at Elijah's Basin, a sandy hollow where visitors can camp overnight before climbing the final 750 steps to the mountain summit.

As you tread the Steps of Penitence, you cannot help but be moved by its mystical connotations. From the summit, the view over Sinai is breathtaking. Wrinkled folds and ridges of red- and green-hued granite extend to the horizon in 'an ocean of petrified waves'. Even for the most sceptical, it is almost enough to stir some sort of faith in the supernatural.

**HOW:**
On foot or on a camel
**WHEN TO GO:**
October to March
**TIME IT TAKES:**
One to three hours, depending on your pace.
**HIGHLIGHTS:**
St. Catherine's Monastery – UNESCO World Heritage site containing the largest collection of early manuscripts outside the Vatican, irreplaceable works of religious art, mosaics and icons.
Shrive (Confession) Gate – stone hewn arch where pilgrims could have their sins forgiven.
Elijah's Basin – a 500-year-old cypress tree marking the spot where Elijah is said to have heard the voice of God.
The view from the summit.
**YOU SHOULD KNOW:**
Wear good hiking shoes and take plenty of water with you. The climb is a long one but is quite easy for anybody reasonably fit. Tourists are usually persuaded to climb Mount Sinai by night in order to greet the sunrise from the summit. Far better to forego the dawn view, which is accompanied by freezing cold and hordes of other trippers, for the sake of seeing all the amazing scenery on the way and having more space to yourself to contemplate the view.

*St Catherine's Monastery dates from the 6th century.*

# Up the Nile

The cruise from Luxor to Aswan takes you through the heartlands of the oldest nation state in the world, the cradle in which the whole of Western Civilization is rooted. The awesome River Nile, the longest waterway in the world, is the sustainer of all life in the desert, depositing the fertile black silt of its floodplain and supplying water for the crops that grow in it. As you sail past the timeless agricultural scenery of the valley, flanked by sheer desert cliffs up to 550 m (1,800 ft) high, five millennia of history unfolds before your eyes.

Luxor, the ancient city of Thebes, is 'the world's greatest open air museum'. Here is the stupendous Karnak Temple, the tombs of the Valley of the Kings and the Colossi of Memnon. At the great lock at Esna, the Nile is transformed into a chaotic water bazaar as garrulous traders in rickety boats besiege the river traffic, proffering scarves, trinkets and souvenirs. The Temple of Horus at Edfu is the best-preserved temple in Egypt, and on the riverbank at Kom Ombu a temple with beautiful relief carving stands as a wondrous reminder of the antiquity of this land.

The charming southern city of Aswan is a riot of new impressions – the vivid colours and smells of the souks, the tall graceful Nubian townspeople, the Nile at its most picturesque – all swaying palm trees, golden dunes and white-sailed feluccas (traditional wooden sailing boats). Here the river is studded with numerous beautiful islands. Elephantine, the largest, is one of the most ancient sites in Egypt. Just upstream is the first of the Nile's six huge cataracts (rapids), the High Dam and Lake Nasser – the boundary of Egypt and the gateway to Africa.

**HOW:**
By boat
**WHEN TO GO:**
November to April
**TIME IT TAKES:**
Five days
**HIGHLIGHTS:**
Karnak Temple – largest temple complex in the world.
Luxor Museum – stunning ancient Egyptian art collection.
Colossi of Memnon – statues more than 17m (50 ft) high.
Temple of Philae and the High Dam at Lake Nasser.
Sunset felucca trip around islands of Aswan.
**YOU SHOULD KNOW:**
You can take one of the numerous cabin cruiser floating hotels that ply the Nile or sail in a felucca – a rather less comfortable but altogether more liberating experience, sightseeing at whim rather than being restricted to a cruise itinerary. Whichever way you travel, you should study your ancient history to get the most out of the countless sights you will pass.

*A felucca on the Nile at Luxor*

# Oases of the Great Sand Sea

The Great Sand Sea is an uninhabitable belt of shifting golden dune ridges up to 100 m (330 ft) high, a natural impassable barrier between Egypt and Libya up to 300 km (200 mi) wide and extending for some 600 km (375 mi) north to south. Human habitation is only possible in the five remote oases at its edge, where mineral springs and waterholes enable life. On this 1,000 km (600 mi) road adventure, you will experience the magical stillness of elemental landscapes and wonder at the resilience of communities who have managed to preserve their culture, continuously since antiquity, in the face of such overwhelmingly hostile odds.

Siwa, Egypt's westernmost oasis is the site of the ancient Oracle of Amun, consulted by Alexander the Great. It is an 80 km (50 mi) swathe of date palms, olive trees and salt lakes inhabited by Berbers. The 400 km (250 mi) road along the ancient caravan route to Bahariya, is part rutted sand track, part concrete and part no road at all – just rough driving across the dunes in vaguely the right direction. From Bahariya, you cross the surreal White Desert with dramatic rock formations like giant mushrooms, to reach Farafra, one of the most isolated places in Egypt.

Compared to this tiny oasis, Dakhla seems huge – fourteen villages surrounded by fields of mulberry, citrus, datepalm and fig, overlooked by magnificent pinkish cliffs. It is perhaps the most beautiful stop on your journey and the village of Al-Qasr with its medieval architecture is one of the most significant archaeological sites of Egypt's Western Desert. Your final stop is Kharga on the notorious Forty Days Road, the slave route from the Sudan to Cairo. Once back in the tourist maelstrom of modern Egypt, you will immediately yearn to return to the mystical desert silence.

*White inselbergs dot the lunar-like landscape of the White Desert.*

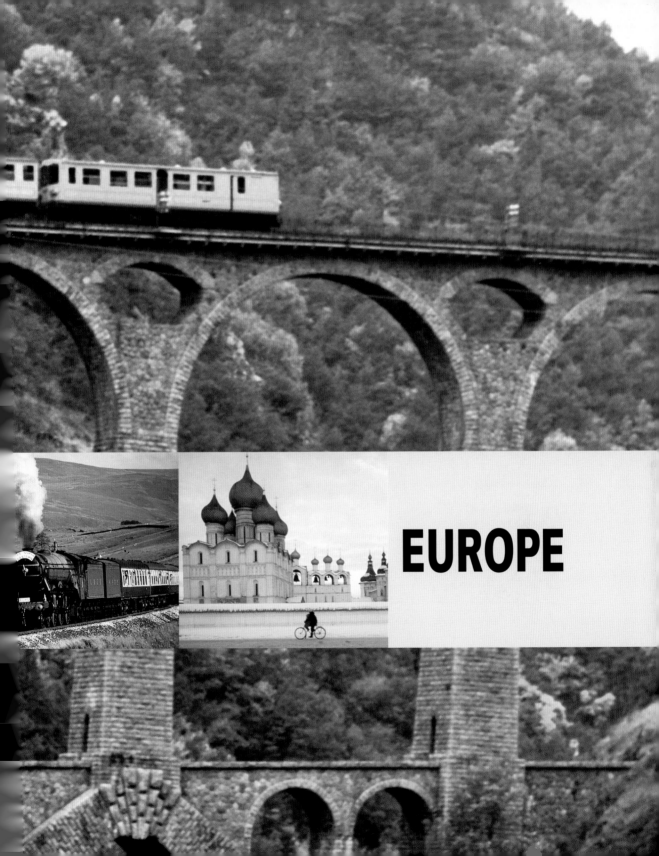

# EUROPE

# Snaefellsnes National Park

**HOW:**
On foot
**WHEN TO GO:**
May to June
**TIME IT TAKES:**
Six to eight hours
**HIGHLIGHTS:**
Bird colonies along the cliffs.
Badstofa Cave, Hellnar.
Mary's Spring – water emerging from
lava, thought to have healing powers.
The Midnight Sun
Spotting orca whales off the coast.
**YOU SHOULD KNOW:**
This walk is quite an easy one. There
are numerous trails and historical
sites in the Snaefellsnes National
Park. From Arnarstapi or Hellnar you
can hike up across the ice cap to the
volcano crater.

A continuously evolving landscape of volcanoes, geysers and lava fields, the whole of Iceland is a geological treasure; and the Snaefellsjokull is the absolute jewel in the crown. A mysterious 1,446 m (4,743 ft) high strato-volcano, with a 200-m (650-ft) deep ice-filled crater, shrouded in a 7 sq km (3 sq mi) ice cap, it has lain dormant for the past 1,800 years; ancient plaits of lava trail down its flanks across the plains of the Snaefellsnes Peninsula to the sea. It is one of the seven most potent 'energy sources' of the planet, the well-spring of Icelandic mythology, looming over a strange land where dwarves still lurk in the crannies, elves hide in the mossy banks and ogres stomp across the ice. Used by Jules Verne as the setting for his novel *Journey to the Centre of the Earth*, the Snaefellsjokull is an enduring source of inspiration for mystics, artists and poets.

From the romantic moonscape wilds of the Budir estuary you walk for 18 km (11 mi) in a surreal fairyland, across a moss-carpeted and rock-strewn lava plain to the picturesque fishing village of Arnarstapi. From here you can walk a further 8 km (5 mi) along a bizarrely beautiful coast of fantastic lava formations and spectacular caves. Fierce Atlantic breakers crash through holes in the rocks, hurling great fountains of spray up into the sky, and the basalt column cliffs are packed with birds – colonies of kittiwakes, fulmars, razorbills and arctic terns. Reaching the sheltered natural harbour by the hamlet of Hellnar you can stand beneath the Snaefellsjokull, only 10 km (6 mi) from the snowline, on the meeting point of the ley lines that supposedly carry currents of transcendental volcanic energy round the planet.

*Snaefellsjokull glacier*

# Lofoten Islands

*Vestvagoy island*

A cycling vacation along the Vestfjord route is a most memorable experience – new, breathtaking sights appear around every bend. Combining ferry trips with cycling, this route serves up almost everything Norway has to offer. White sandy beaches butt up against soaring mountain scenery. Archaeological relics and historical buildings satisfy those who seek more cultural pursuits, whilst for the more active there is ample opportunity to swim, hike or fish.

Idyllic little villages of brightly painted wooden houses line the route as you travel from island to island. It is easy to see why locals describe this area as the real Norway and the archipelago features prominently in Nordic art, film and literature. To cover the full 450 km (281 mi) would be to undertake a journey of epic proportions; however good transport links make it possible to get to almost any part of the trail quickly.

Old market centres such as Løvøy and Grøtøy have been faithfully restored, whilst Steigen is a real hidden gem, teeming with innumerable historical relics. Those who seek more adventure should explore the cave system at Nordskot, whilst those looking for a more sedate outdoor experience can soak up the sun on the wonderful white sandy beaches near Misten. The Vestfjord really does have something for everyone. All you need is a bicycle, good waterproofs, a ferry timetable and a spirit of exploration, and a new adventure awaits you around every corner.

**HOW:**
By bike
**WHEN TO GO:**
May to September provides the best weather.
**TIME IT TAKES:**
Around two weeks for the whole route
**HIGHLIGHTS:**
Tranøy Lighthouse – a fine example and open to visitors.
Steigen Fortidspark – where the past is re-enacted.
Raftsund – a narrow strait between Hinnøya and Austvågøya.
The Stone Age settlements and ruined boathouses on Gimsøya.
**YOU SHOULD KNOW:**
Forward planning is required to make the most of this trip. Although the ferries are reliable, the faster services take you to the most crowded sections. If you wish to leave the beaten track it may require taking two or more of the less frequent services.

189

*Folda Sound, Bodø*

# Trondheim to Bodø

This is an incredibly beautiful journey and, when taken in summer, the light evenings ensure that you miss nothing. The train transports you through pine forests, across foothills and alongside fjords and rivers. This sea of green and blue is broken only by the occasional red wooden farmstead.

It is a curious feeling to head towards something that you will never see, but the Arctic Circle announces itself in many ways. As you head north, the light changes imperceptibly. The snow, which was confined to the mountain tops moves ever nearer, whilst on the track the wooden tunnels, constructed to protect the line from avalanches, grow more numerous.

As the signs of human habitation thin out and the mountains get more rugged, the landscape becomes ever more hypnotic. Thoughts turn to wildlife watching and there is every chance that you will spot a majestic reindeer in its natural surroundings. The Arctic Circle is heralded not only by a hoot of the train's whistle and two cairns on the side of the track, but by curious rituals on the train. A party spirit suddenly erupts; some partake in illicit drinking, while others share food and sometimes kissing breaks out as though it were New Year's Eve. It does feel significant to have crossed 'the line' and it is always interesting to watch the impromptu ceremonies that mark it.

The final steep descent takes you from Arctic tundra towards the blue Atlantic Ocean. This is as far north as the railway goes and as the charming town of Bodø comes into view, you are left with the feeling that you have taken more than just a train journey.

# Spirit of Norway

It is hard to think of a better trip anywhere in the world that can be completed inside a single day. It could be that the Norwegians, ever mindful of their high cost of living, feel that most tourists want to get their money's worth. Several companies operate excursions that whisk you up mountain railways, along precipitous roads and then out to sea, to experience Norway's most famous feature, the iconic Fjords.

The typical journey starts with a ride on Northern Europe's highest-altitude railway line, the Bergen Railway. Exposed to harsh Atlantic weather systems, it is a huge engineering feat just to keep the line open, but you will be glad they do. The mountain views are stunning as the engine hauls you up incredibly steep inclines. From there the rollercoaster ride continues as you transfer to the Flåm Railway, a 20-km (12.5-mi) journey from the hill station of Myrdal, which runs alongside magnificent mountain scenery and tumbling waterfalls.

Beautiful though this all is, you quickly realize that it was merely the hors d'oeuvre. From Flåm the next leg of the excursion is completed by boat. Although the fjords are so obviously a symbol of Norway, one cannot tire of seeing them. These deep-sea gullies, carved by ice, take the breath away and the towering rock faces on both sides make it sometimes hard to believe that you are on water. Legendary, labyrinthine and starkly beautiful, a journey through the fjords leaves you with images that will stay with you for the rest of your life.

The last leg of this most fabulous of days out takes you, by coach, along the amazingly winding mountain road to your final destination of Stalheim. From there it is possible to transfer by train back to Bergen.

**HOW:**
By train and boat
**WHEN TO GO:**
Year round but best under the midnight sun – May to July.
**TIME IT TAKES:**
16 hours – but three days if you choose to stop.
**HIGHLIGHTS:**
The picturesque village of Flåm. The mountains around Sognefjord. The improbably narrow Naeroyfjord. The Folk museum at Stalheim – a celebration of traditional Nordic life.
**YOU SHOULD KNOW:**
Norway can be very expensive – there's no shame in taking your own lunch with you, in fact that is precisely what most locals do.

*The magnificent mountains around Sognefjord*

*The coastal village of Ballstad*

# Bergen to Kirkenes

**HOW:**
By postal boat
**WHEN TO GO:**
Year round
**TIME IT TAKES:**
Six or seven days one-way
**HIGHLIGHTS:**
The Lofoten Islands
The Sor-Varanger Museum
in Kirkenes.
Bergen – full of Hanseatic history.
The lovely town of Bodø.
**YOU SHOULD KNOW:**
Whilst the main purpose of these
vessels is to provide supplies to far-
flung communities, the operators do
cater well for the tourist trade. The
vessels alternate between day-time
and night-time deliveries, so that
anyone taking a round trip will
miss nothing.

Large cruise ships ply the 2,000-km (1,250-mi) voyage between Bergen and Kirkenes, but for sheer intimacy it's difficult to beat the more informal service offered by the 'postal' ships that serve outlying Norwegian coastal communities. This odyssey takes you around Norway's breathtakingly beautiful fjord coastline, stopping over thirty times and showing you a side of Norway inaccessible by any other means of transport.

The journey begins in Bergen, a harbour town founded by the Vikings almost a millennium ago, when it quickly became a vital hub, handling trade between Northern Europe and the British Isles. As you leave the port, the splendid 14th-century gabled buildings of the seafront slowly dwindle to nothing and your eyes are drawn to the wonderfully rugged coastline.

Along the way you will see glorious fjords, precipitous mountains and quaint fishing villages before crossing the Arctic Circle. Here, as you approach the North Cape, you will experience the midnight sun in the summer. Winter offers the chance to see the Northern Lights – the ultimate light show.

For much of the journey all eyes are fixed on the starboard side, where snow-capped mountains and fjords abound. This is until the vessel meanders between the Lofoten Islands whose stark, craggy beauty hits you from both sides. The trip gives you a true appreciation of this beautiful country and how most of its population clings to the coast. When you cross the Arctic Circle the population becomes more thinly spread and the scenery ever more dramatic. The awe-inspiring Laksefjorden and Tanafjorden lie ahead, before the vessel reaches its final destination, the sheltered port of Kirkenes.

# Raumabanen Railway

Now over 80 years old, the Raumabanen Railway has always unashamedly been a tourist track. Aside from a brief period when it was used to ferry around the country's gold reserves, it has operated to cater for the cruise ship trade arriving into Romsdalfjord and Åndalsnes. Whereas other railway journeys take you past wonderful sights as if by coincidence, the Raumabanen has a single purpose – to show off Norway at its finest.

This 114-km (182-mi) long marvel of 1920s engineering starts at Åndalsnes, the northern gateway to the fjords. Right from the start the views are spectacular and as the train climbs steadily, hugging the mountainside, you are treated to breathtaking views of the valley below. The imposing peaks of Romsdalhorn and Trollveggen soon dominate the skyline. You are torn between looking up or looking down as the train crosses Kyllingbrua, a startlingly high stone arched bridge which hangs high above the Rauma River.

It seems scarcely possible to climb any higher, but this is exactly what happens just after you pass Verma, as the train takes you through a corkscrew tunnel under the mountains. This really is a giant fairground ride for grown-ups. As you approach Dombås, the scenery opens up offering panoramic views of this most remarkable of lands. Here you can either continue to Oslo or Trondheim or, better still, go back and do it all again.

**HOW:**
By train
**WHEN TO GO:**
Year round – special steam trains serve the line in summer (June to August).
**TIME IT TAKES:**
Around three hours one-way, although a shorter journey between Åndalsnes and Bjorli is available for those wanting to make a quick round trip.
**HIGHLIGHTS:**
The Brudesløret (the bridal veil) – a spectacular waterfall.
The Kylling turning tunnel – quite a ride.
Lesjaskogsvatnet Lake
The procession of mountain peaks from Trollveggen, Romsdalshorn, Karlskråtind, Mongeura to Vengetindene.
**YOU SHOULD KNOW:**
The railway can get crowded and is more expensive in the high season (June to August). If you can be flexible, September or early October are good times to go and the evenings are still light.

*The stunning scenery of the western fjords*

# Lyse Road

The Lyse Road was constructed as a service route for a hydro-electricity station, but that bland description reveals nothing of the experience the road has to offer. It twists and sweeps, clinging precariously to the side of a mountain that rises out of one of Norway's most beautiful fjords, making it the ultimate challenge to your driving skills and a rush like no other.

Built in the 1980s, the 44-km (27-mi) long Lyse Road stands as the critical test for those who have a zest for driving on mountain roads. All along the route you are book-ended by magnificent mountains on one side and the shimmering darkness of Lysefjord on the other – this really is like a scene from a car advertisement.

Viewed from above it would seem as if someone had thrown a giant sidewinder onto the edge of a mountain. With 27 hairpin bends, the Lyse is the ultimate brake-tester. The views are always amazing, if at times a little disorienting – and the relative shallowness of parts of the fjord produces the most wonderful light.

There are a few places where you can stop and it is advisable to do so, if only for the sake of the driver, who should be concentrating so hard on the road that he/she will have little chance to enjoy the stunning scenery. Consideration for other users of the road must be a priority on this often single lane highway, but this is a top rate scuttle if you get a clear run.

**HOW:**
By car
**WHEN TO GO:**
The road is closed in winter – roughly between November and April.
**TIME IT TAKES:**
One to two hours
**HIGHLIGHTS:**
The hike to Pulpit Rock – with its views high above the fjord.
The view of the road from Øygardsstølen.
Tjodan hydro-electric power station – the reason for the road's existence.
The charming little town of Lysebotn.
**YOU SHOULD KNOW:**
Speed limits are rigorously enforced in Norway, so if you are tempted to speed, don't – this road demands the utmost respect and fines can be as steep as the road itself.

*Sightseers on Prekestolen (Pulpit Rock)*

# High Coast Trail

The Höga Kusten (High Coast) was formed when the region sank under a gigantic mass of ice during the last ice age. When the ice retreated, the land sprang back and it is still rising today. This has left a dynamic landscape of vertical cliffs and craggy outcrops, lined with tranquil sandy coves.

Accessibility and flexibility are the watchwords for the exciting 127-km (80-mi) trail that takes you through this terrain. Divided into thirteen stages, it offers the hiker a wide variety of challenges, whilst each stage is handily reachable by car. There are even organized self-guided tours where you can walk between lodgings, while your luggage is transported for you, allowing you to travel light.

This striking area has been given UNESCO World Heritage Site status and the hike takes you through Sweden's highest coastal area. A rich diversity of rivers, lakes, inlets and hills makes it a good test for hikers of all levels. Each day offers varying terrain as well as beautiful views out over the dark blue seas of the Gulf of Bothnia.

Starting near central Örnsköldsvik the trail presents the hiker with compact challenges. Mountains seem more climbable when you know that old-fashioned Swedish hospitality awaits you at the end of each day. Accommodation ranges from simple huts to guesthouses, but for a genuine Swedish welcome, nothing beats staying in a traditional farmhouse, several of which open their doors to tourists in summer.

**HOW:**
On foot
**WHEN TO GO:**
Fully accessible from May to October
**TIME IT TAKES:**
One to two weeks according to fitness levels
**HIGHLIGHTS:**
The Skuleskogen National Park
The imposing Slåtterdalsskrevan Gorge.
The suspension bridge near Härnösand.
Surströmming (fermented herring) – a local delicacy certain to greet you at the table at some point.
**YOU SHOULD KNOW:**
It is important not to be too ambitious. Don't be fooled by the relatively short distances between designated stops – the ruggedness of the terrain can often slow your progress.

*Slåtterdalsskrevan Gorge in Skuleskogen National Park*

# Gota Canal

**HOW:**
By boat and/or bike
**WHEN TO GO:**
Year round, but it springs fully into
life from June to August
**TIME IT TAKES:**
Two to six days by steamer
**HIGHLIGHTS:**
The gorgeous lakes of Vättern
and Vänern.
The Trollhätte Canal Museum
De la Gardie Palace – a wonderful
Baroque-style building.
Birka Viking settlement on
Björkö Island.
**YOU SHOULD KNOW:**
Organised tours, though usually all-
inclusive, can be expensive. With a
little forward planning, it is possible
to enjoy this magnificent waterway
for a fraction of the cost.

If you want to see Sweden at play, head straight for the Gota Canal. This marvel of 19th-century engineering stretches 190 km (118 mi) from Sjötorp on Lake Vänern to the Baltic Sea at Mem and is a real crowd-puller. Whether you are travelling on it or cycling alongside it you cannot help but be impressed by its sheer scale. Fifty-eight locks, some of them rising to an incredible 90 m (295 ft) above sea level, carry vessels through a chain of stunning natural lakes, making this one of the most impressive waterways anywhere on the planet.

The canal takes you through the heart of Sweden, passing historic sites, medieval churches, attractive towns and rich green forests along the way. Many steamers ply their trade along it and this gentle form of transport has much to recommend it. You can hop on and hop off these boats and, with the aid of a bicycle, it is possible to explore the wider environs.

For a more intimate experience there is nothing better than hiring a boat on any one of the stunningly beautiful lakes that grace the waterway, stopping only to have a picnic lunch by the shore. Most journeys are about getting somewhere, whereas riding the Gota Canal invites you to stop and marvel at every point. It offers great fishing, kayaking, Nordic walking and a whole host of other activities. Like one big joyful playground, it has become more than the sum of its parts – a wonderful potpourri of outdoor adventure.

*The charming city of Mariestad
on Lake Vänern*

# Padjelanta Trail

*Padjelanta National Park –
one of Europe's last
great wildernesses*

So remote as to be reachable only by helicopter, the 140-km (88-mi) Padjelanta Trail is nature at its most raw. Padjelanta translates as 'the higher land' and is the summer home to the Sami people who bring vast reindeer herds here to graze. Aside from the mountains of the Sarek National Park, the landscape is relatively flat and open, consisting mainly of rolling hills with a scattering of higher peaks. Located entirely above the Arctic Circle, trees are scarce, though there is a surprising abundance of flora, and there is no finer sight than the flowering of an Arctic meadow.

There are no roads in the area, adding to the feeling of complete isolation, and accommodation is rudimentary. This trek has the motto 'as nature intended' stamped all over it. There is no electricity and water is sourced from fast running streams. Heat comes from wood fires and bathing takes place outdoors. All this helps to keep the Padjelanta a pristine wilderness for the ambitious and rugged hiker to enjoy.

At the centre of Padjelanta lies a succession of four wondrous lakes, the Kutjaure, Sallojaure, Vastenjaure and Virihaure. It is here that the Sami set up their summer camps and invite visitors to sample their unique way of life. You soon get to learn that communal living and interdependence are essential in this starkly beautiful setting. This is a lesson that will stand you in good stead, as you continue on your way through this ever shifting landscape – one of Europe's last great wildernesses.

**HOW:**
On foot
**WHEN TO GO:**
June to August
**TIME IT TAKES:**
Four days to one week
**HIGHLIGHTS:**
Sitting out under the midnight sun.
Sleeping in a traditional Sami tent.
The comradely spirit engendered by the need to share.
The view across the spectacular Tarra Valley.
**YOU SHOULD KNOW:**
You really are cut off from most modern amenities on this trek. You should be fit and have a good knowledge of first aid and some basic survival skills. This is by no stretch of the imagination a 'walk in the park', there is little signage and pathways are often not very clear.

# Inlandsbanan

The 1,067-km (667-mi) Inlandsbanan (inland railway) carries you along the spine of central northern Sweden. Built to serve the logging industry, it has now diversified to cater for the burgeoning tourist trade. The pace of the train is very laid back. As befits a Swedish operation, you are transported at an average speed of 50 kph (30 mph) through magnificent pine and birch forests.

As the train departs Mora on its northbound journey, all eyes are drawn to the deep forest where yellow wild flowers line the track. This is an ideal habitat for bear, reindeer and moose and the train will conveniently slow down if any are spotted, so be sure to have your camera primed and ready. The train passes many water features on the way but the waterfalls at Strorstupet and Helvetesfallet are the most spectacular.

Whilst it is possible to make this gentle journey inside two days, it is best experienced in separate stages with stopovers between. Aside from the wonderful forest surroundings, there is much to enjoy on the way. The first main stop is at Östersund. More associated with winter sports, it takes on a different life in summer. A picturesque little town, it offers historic walks, a heritage museum and the splendid Lake Storsjön is nearby.

The next stop, Vilhelmina, is most worthy of exploration. Surrounded by invigorating fast flowing streams, it is home to many Sami artisans and has many naturally heated pools and an extensive cycleway.

As the train continues steadfastly towards the Arctic Circle, the forest becomes more untamed and the vista ever more beautiful. The train finally pulls in to Gällivare, a town where people successfully combine modern living with a more traditional way of life.

*A train crosses the steel bridge at Storstupet.*

# Norsjö Cable-Way

Originally built in 1943 to ferry ore buried deep in the mountains, the Norsjö Cable-Way seemed to have had its day by the end of the 20th century. It was then that the locals, some of whom could recall the great sacrifices that were made during its construction, rallied round to save it. At over 13 km (8 mi), it stands as the longest cable car journey in the world and now ferries tourists between Örträsk and Mensträsk, gliding at a majestic 10 kph (6.25 mph) high above the Västerbotten countryside.

Fourteen cabins ply their trade in each direction, offering the chance to enter a fragile woodland environment accessible by no other means. Reindeer and moose are common sights and, unlike other forms of transport, the relative quietness of the cable cars does not seem to disturb them too much. As you pass each concrete mast – there are 73 in all – you can't help but marvel at the amazing feat of engineering that produced this modern wonder.

It is a strange experience to be held aloft for so long and the cable-way provides a wonderful bird's eye view of this splendid environment. After the initial jolt into action, the cable-way provides a real Hansel and Gretel experience, soaring above lakes and forests through a dizzying expanse. All passengers have a window seat and the compact cabins have an intimate feel, each housing just four people. In summer, birdsong provides the perfect soundtrack to your voyage, whilst in winter snow and ice cling to the trees as if they were sculpted that way.

**HOW:**
By cable car
**WHEN TO GO:**
The service operates year round and each season has its own unique feel.
**TIME IT TAKES:**
One hour twenty minutes
**HIGHLIGHTS:**
The Cable-way Museum at Örträsk.
The pretty ski resort of Mensträsk
The film of how the cableway was built – shown in the cinema in Örträsk.
The charming little town of Örträsk.
**YOU SHOULD KNOW:**
Booking in advance is essential for this popular attraction. It should also be noted that currently only ten of the carriages are heated, so if you are travelling in winter check that you are in one of these, or wrap up warmly!

# The East Coast Route

**HOW:**
By bike
**WHEN TO GO:**
Year round
**TIME IT TAKES:**
It makes for a good week's holiday.
**HIGHLIGHTS:**
Grenen Museum of Art in Skagen.
Koldinghus – a beautifully
restored castle.
Moesgård Forhistoriske Museum – a
museum of the people, near Århus.
Sønderborg Castle overlooking the
dramatic Flensborg Fjord.

*The coastline of Skagen, with
the village of Skagen in
the background*

Denmark ranks as one of the most bicycle friendly countries in the
world. The Danes simply love cycling and any one of their eleven
National Cycle Routes provides the lover of two wheels with an
exciting and memorable holiday. At 650 km (406 mi), the East
Coast Route is the longest and most spectacular of the lot.
Stretching from Skagen to Sønderborg, the route meanders through
pretty Danish countryside, taking the rider along fjords, round bays
and peninsulas.

The towns that line the route are rich in tradition and culture.
Charming fishing villages are to be found along the northern
section, while to the south grand castles and sumptuous manor
houses grace the rolling landscape. You will always be cycling within
easy reach of the sea and the many secluded coves along the way

give you good reason to stop and take a dip.

Of all the towns along the route, Århus must be singled out for special mention. Nowhere in Denmark will you find a greater concentration of artists, museums, musicians and historically significant sites. Denmark's graceful and welcoming second city is a perfect place to make a break in your journey and, having explored it, you will probably want to stay for a day or two.

When you make this journey, you will realize how perfectly designed it is for cyclists. The towns that line the route are remarkably evenly spaced, so as the legs begin to tire, there is always something to stimulate the mind or satisfy the stomach.

**YOU SHOULD KNOW:**
Over 90 per cent of the route is asphalted, making cycling easy and fun. The route should present no problems for a reasonably fit cyclist with a good set of brakes. .

# Hærvejen Oxen Trail

If roads could speak this one would recount tales like few others.  Throughout history this route, which starts just the other side of the German border and runs down the spine of Jutland, has borne the weight of Danish hopes – as well as their livestock. A source of great pride for modern day Denmark, many of its secrets still lie by the roadside, yet to be discovered.  It is probable that the route has been trodden for millennia and an air of historical significance hangs over every part of it.

For much of the way it seems little more than a dirt track, while other sections are more like modern roads. Famous for its magnificent stone bridges, the Hærvejen is ideal for hiking or biking vacations. Whichever mode of transport you choose, you will want to stop and marvel at sights both ancient and modern. Runic stones, burial mounds and monoliths line the route and offer cryptic clues to the regions antediluvian past. More recent history is displayed in the German World War I bunkers and the Froslev Concentration Camp, where Danish Communists were imprisoned during World War II.

The road's elevation of some 92 m (300 ft) in places, gives you excellent wide views of the countryside and the ridge forms the source of Denmark's two longest rivers, the Skjernå and the Gudenå. All in all, this is a journey which can be relished as a trek through the tranquil Jutish countryside, or studied deeply like an ancient text. The choice is yours.

**HOW:**
On foot or by bike
**WHEN TO GO:**
Open all year, but the weather is best from May to September.
**TIME IT TAKES:**
Five days hiking or two days by bike.
**HIGHLIGHTS:**
The historic town of Vejen – the only major settlement on the route.
Roede Kro (the Red Inn) – a resource centre for the region.
Hairulf Stone – a splendid inscribed standing stone.
The stone bridge at Immervad – basic, symmetrical and symbolic.
**YOU SHOULD KNOW:**
Only a small part of the road is paved and much of the rest of it makes for a pretty bumpy bicycle ride. So make sure you have good suspension, or better still make the journey in the manner of the ancients and walk.

# Copenhagen Waterbus

**HOW:**
By boat
**WHEN TO GO:**
The service operates from May
to September
**TIME IT TAKES:**
You can buy one or two day passes
**HIGHLIGHTS:**
Frihedsmuseet – a museum
dedicated to those who resisted the
Nazis in World War II.
Little Mermaid statue – a perfectly
formed landmark.
Trekoner Fortress – an imposing
historical monument.
Christianborg Palace – a former
royal palace, now home to the
Danish government.
**YOU SHOULD KNOW:**
It is not possible to book a seat on
this journey and the boats can get
full, especially during the middle of
the day in July and August. If you do
find you are not able to board a
particular vessel, Copenhagen's
compactness means it is possible to
walk to your next destination.

Copenhagen is one of Europe's truly great cities. With its perfect blend of old and new, it is a city that demands to be explored. While most cities are only slowly waking up to the fact that their waterways are a vital resource for life, as well as for trade, Copenhagen has always known it. Most of its great sights are visible and accessible from the water and there is no better way to travel around it than by waterbus.

This hop-on, hop-off service calls at all of Copenhagen's major tourist attractions, as well as providing an important transport link for those who like to travel at a more relaxed pace. Several operators ply the route and offer up to 16 drop-off points. So with ticket and timetable in hand, it is time to climb aboard and investigate this wonderfully compact city. With forward planning, it's possible to stroll along the world famous Tivoli Gardens before having lunch in Nyhavn, the old sailors' quarter which brims with fabulous cafés. The afternoon can then be spent lapping up the cultural delights of the Frihedsmuseet and the Amalienborg Palace, before visiting the artists' district of Christiania. This can all be rounded off with a visit to the city's renowned Opera House.

The choice is really yours on this most flexible of tours. It is an excellent way to get to know your way around Copenhagen and for those who already know the city well, it affords a new perspective on this most magnificent of urban landscapes.

*Tour boats on the canal at Nyhavn*

# Over the Öresund Bridge

The people of the southern Swedish territory of Skåne have more in common with the Danes than they do with their fellow countrymen in the north. Even the relatively flat rolling landscape is remarkably similar. It is therefore no surprise to learn that these two areas were linked by land some 7,000 years ago. Only two courses of action were available to those who wanted to reunite these lands, one was to wait for another ice age, the other was to build a crossing.

Built in a true spirit of cooperation, what resulted was a wonder of modern construction, to rival that of the Channel Tunnel. Before the bridge was officially opened in 1999, the crossing between Copenhagen and Malmö was a joyless one. Coaches and hovercraft would ferry people who found cheap flights to Sweden via Denmark, and they would mingle with Swedes who were looking for bargains on the other side of the water.

The arrival of the combined rail and road crossing changed all this and it is now possible to make the excursion in comfort and with speed. As you depart Copenhagen, the Öresund has a surprise for you as it starts its life as a tunnel, to avoid interfering with the busy airport. Soon it emerges from the water, as a majestic bridge, providing fantastic views on both sides.

The crossing has really opened up this area of southern Sweden and re-attached it to the mainland. Once across, the opportunities to explore are numerous. Outside of the cities the most popular destination is the area around the Falsterbo Peninsula. With its long sandy beaches it draws hikers and sun-seekers from far and wide and transport links connect well with the bridge.

**HOW:**
By train or car
**WHEN TO GO:**
Year round
**TIME IT TAKES:**
Thirty-five minutes by train from downtown Copenhagen to downtown Malmö.
**HIGHLIGHTS:**
The view of the bridge from either shore.
Copenhagen – a compact city, worth a day or two's exploration.
Malmö – a city of green open spaces and a pretty town centre.
The university town of Lund – the jewel of southern Sweden, with its magnificent cathedral and numerous beautiful gardens.
**YOU SHOULD KNOW:**
A hefty toll is charged to road users who cross the Öresund Bridge. If you are intending to cross several times, period passes are available at a more reasonable rate.

*The Öresund Bridge joins Denmark and Sweden.*

# The King's Road Trail

**HOW:**
By bike
**WHEN TO GO:**
The weather is best from May to September
**TIME IT TAKES:**
It makes for a good week's cycling or hiking holiday.
**HIGHLIGHTS:**
Rauma – a superb mixed woodland and a UNESCO World Heritage Site.
Åland Islands – great to look at and full of maritime history.
Hvitträsk Villa – a fine example of modern architecture.
The Gallen-Kallela Museum – a beautiful building housing a good museum.
**YOU SHOULD KNOW:**
This journey should present little difficulty to even the novice hiker or cyclist. In fact the wide range of things to see and do makes the King's Road Trail perfect for a family vacation.

In it heyday the King's Road was as important to Northern Europe as the Silk Road was to Asia. Linking Bergen in the west to St Petersburg in the east, it provided a strategic link, greatly aiding the flow of people, goods and ideas. The Western King's Road that runs from Helsinki to Pohj, takes you on a 100-km (62.5-mi) journey through an area of great natural beauty as well as offering up a superb blend of old and new architecture.

There are many ways to make this journey and you can use a combination of car, train and even boat. However, cycling fits best with the tempo of the region and there is a well-maintained cycle route with good signage. The traveller is taken through forests of silver birch and fir trees, alongside the shimmering Baltic Sea, through picturesque towns and on towards the Russian border.

The King's Road offers a wonderful insight into traditional Finnish life and the route is filled with history and culture. Finland has always been a buffer between east and west and the influences on people, food and places are displayed fully on this trek. This area has long been a summer playground for Scandinavians and nowhere is this better shown than in Loviisa – with its delightful beaches, framed by subtly coloured wooden buildings, it is a seaside resort with few peers.

This is a journey that serves up great contrasts and gives the traveller a new perspective on Finnish life. It may not be too much of an exaggeration to say that without the King's Road Finland would not be the country it is today.

*The Åland Islands*

# The Hetta-Pallas Winter Ski Trail

The 55-km (34-mi) Hetta-Pallas Winter Trail is the Finnish section of the 800-km (500-mi) pan-Scandinavian Nordkalottleden Trail. The Trail passes through the Pallas-Yllästunturi National Park in Lapland, an area of fast-flowing rivers, turquoise lakes, lush forests and glacier-topped mountains. It is not an overly demanding trail for the experienced cross-country skier, as it follows mostly the lower slopes, apart from one ravine section where it travels above the tree-line. Its very simplicity adds to the hypnotic high, familiar to long distance skiers, and for a sense of true wilderness in all its luminous and silent beauty, it is hard to beat.

As Finland has common access to all its land enshrined in law, the intrepid skier is free to ski in any wilderness or forest area. However, the trail itself is well maintained and well marked and the best advice is to follow the signs. 'Wilderness huts' at manageable intervals are available to travellers. These wood cabins are basic and must be shared, though in winter they are rarely over-used and they're free.

In summer, the Hetta-Pallas Hiking Trail covers roughly the same route, though at higher altitudes, as the winter trails are too wet to be hiked in summer. The Trail goes through a ravishingly beautiful landscape of birch-clothed fell highlands and steep-sided ravines but, while the area is utterly wild, the trek can easily be undertaken by any reasonably fit and eager walker. The same wilderness huts are available in summer, though they can get crowded at the most popular times, so it is always wise to take a tent. In this land of the midnight sun, you can, of course, hike all night and find a place to rest in the morning.

*A snowshoer heads towards a wilderness hut along the Hetta-Pallas Winter Trail.*

**HOW:**
On skis or snowshoes in winter or on foot in the summer months

**WHEN TO GO:**
Winter trail – mid-February to end April; Summer hiking – late June to end September.

**TIME IT TAKES:**
Hiking the trail can be completed in four days; skiing, comfortably, in three days.

**HIGHLIGHTS:**
Fell Lapland Nature Centre. Chance to see the Northern Lights. The husky farm at Muonio, a short side trip from the trail.

**YOU SHOULD KNOW:**
It is probably best to avoid the area in July, as mosquitoes and black fly abound at this time.

*One of the many lakes that surround Tampere*

# Helsinki to Tampere

**HOW:**
By train
**WHEN TO GO:**
Year round
**TIME IT TAKES:**
Ninety minutes
**HIGHLIGHTS:**
The train is the real star, as you view pristine countryside through immaculately clean windows.
Helsinki Station – a green trimmed Art-Deco style masterpiece.
The 200 or so lakes that surround Tampere.
Central Museum of Labour (Tampere) a quirky museum full of interesting things.
**YOU SHOULD KNOW:**
One cannot say this too often: train travel in Finland is fun, affordable and stress-free.

The Finns are right to be proud of their trains. Fast, punctual and meticulously clean, they set a standard that is hard to match. In an age where people are increasingly looking for environmentally friendly holidays, VR Ltd Finnish Railways sets the benchmark, giving you every reason to leave the car at home.

If you can tear yourself away from the cultural and architectural delights of Helsinki, the train journey to Tampere is one of the real gems of European travel. This sparsely populated land is a place of great natural beauty, where the modern sits well with the traditional. Summer brings never-ending daylight, while the winter landscape has an ethereal elegance often lit up by the hauntingly beautiful Northern Lights.

As the majestic red and white train glides through the open countryside, passing lakes fringed by forest, you cannot help but be struck by the serenity of it all. It is hard to think of any other intercity journey in the developed world that passes through landscape of such untamed beauty.

The only complaint one could have is that the journey is over so soon. The memory of sumptuous lakes, verdant forests and grand farmsteads is one that will linger long in the mind. The next time you are on the train to work, you will be tempted to close your eyes and try to imagine that you are back on the Helsinki-Tampere Express.

# The Post Boat Route across the Kvarken

The passage across the Kvarken has always been inextricably linked with taxation. It is a long way around the Gulf of Bothnia and, in the 17th century, King Gustav II bestowed on the residents of Björkö the privilege of conveying goods over the water. In return they were excused military service and given tax breaks. Even up until the late 20th century, these waters were busy with vessels plying the lucrative duty-free trade. All this has now gone and the Kvarken has returned to a quiet normality.

Björkö, at the head of a handsome archipelago, still makes its living from the sea. The relatively shallow waters of the Kvarken are rich with fish and this is reflected in the local diet. Great hiking is to be found on this island group and all paths inevitably lead to the sea; as you gaze over the Kvarken an urge to cross it awakens in you.

It is still possible, by private charter, to make this historic crossing and as you set out, the full beauty of the island chain becomes apparent. Soon you are in open sea and the glimmering waters of the gulf surround you, until the imposing landscape of Sweden's High Coast heaves into view. The traditional landing for this journey is Holmön, an ideal place to end a perfect voyage.

Each year, just after the midsummer festival (late June), these superb waters spring to life. A flotilla of white-sailed boats sets out in a faithful re-enactment of the original post boat run – it's a magnificent spectacle to behold and a wonderful event to participate in.

**HOW:**
By boat
**WHEN TO GO:**
The relatively mild waters of the Kvarken mean that it is navigable nearly all year round. The worst weather is from November to March.
**TIME IT TAKES:**
Two to five hours, depending on the type of vessel and sea conditions.
**HIGHLIGHTS:**
Kvarken Archipelago – the first UNESCO World Heritage Site in Finland.
The picturesque town of Björköby (on Björkö).
Holmön Island – a nature reserve and the sunniest area of Sweden.
**YOU SHOULD KNOW:**
A good level of seamanship is required to undertake this trip. So if you do not have the necessary skills, it is advisable to engage the services of someone who does.

*Post boats sailing across the Kvarken.*

# The Curonian Spit Trail

**HOW:**
By bike or on foot
**WHEN TO GO:**
June to September
**TIME IT TAKES:**
Two days
**HIGHLIGHTS:**
Witches Hill – woodland path with beautifully carved wooden sculptures of mythological figures.
Great Dune of Parnidis 52 m (170 ft) high.
Dead dunes near Parvalka – where a whole village was swallowed up.
Thomas Mann's summerhouse and museum.
Traditional weathervanes – unique to the Curonian Spit.
**YOU SHOULD KNOW:**
Cycling is by far the most convenient way of getting around on the Curonian Spit. The bike paths are kept in good repair, making for easy pedalling.

The Curonian Spit is a 98-km (60-mi) long sand bar, a remarkable natural phenomenon created by the combined power of the sea and the wind in a continual cycle of sedimentation and erosion. It is an extraordinarily insubstantial landscape, continually battered by the howling gales of the Baltic Sea, a natural sea-wall of giant shifting dunes up to 60 m (200 ft) tall, held together by pine and birch forests. On its leeward side, it encloses the Curonian Lagoon, acting as a windbreak to ensure a millpond-like calm, in startling contrast to the open sea. The Spit is less than 4 km (just over 2 mi) across at its widest point and 350 m (0.25 mi) at its narrowest. Only the northern 52 km (33 mi) is in Lithuania; the southern section is Russian territory.

From the old port town of Klaipeda you take a ferry across the narrow channel at the mouth of the Curonian Lagoon to the northern tip of the Spit. From here a bike path runs southwards to Nida, the main town, built along the shore of the lagoon. There are several other picturesque hamlets along the way with old churches and traditional brown- and blue-painted tiled-roofed fishermen's cottages, mostly now inhabited by artists and writers.

You find yourself roaming through an eerily beautiful, remote land, crossing endless white-sand beaches and pine-forested dunes, passing old cemeteries where graves are marked by wooden crosses and outdated road signs for half-remembered villages that have been swallowed by the sand. The only sounds are the wind, the sea and the call of birds. A bike ride or walk along the length of the Spit is a wonderfully life-enhancing experience, giving you a heightened awareness of the power of the elements and the fragility of the environment.

*An aerial view of the Curonian Spit*

# The Baltic to Crimea

*An aerial view of typical Russian architecture in Lviv's Ploshcha Rynok*

For anyone in love with the romance of train travel, a journey by rail across Russia, Belarus, Moldova and Ukraine, through cities that have affected the course of European history for more than a millennium, is an eye-opening experience. This vibrant region of Europe, which for the greater part of the 20th century has been inaccessible, is buzzing with a sense of hard-won freedom and a youthful appetite for the future.

From the fabulous imperial city of St Petersburg, take a train down to Moscow then travel westwards through the eerie haunting beauty of the Belarus steppe to Minsk, an old-style Soviet city that now has a certain nostalgic charm, and then to Brest on the Polish border to visit the stupendous Soviet World War II fortress. Travelling southwards into Ukraine, the largest country in Europe, you cross a timeless land of black-earthed wheat fields, copses of silver birch, flower-strewn pastures, and ancient villages to stop at the wondrous World Heritage City of Lviv. Carry on heading south through the startlingly picturesque but little-visited wine country of Moldova – a landscape of rolling hills, tranquil lakes and whitewashed villages – to Odessa, a magnificent Black Sea city founded by Catherine the Great. Next stop is Yalta, a delightful resort on the beautiful Crimean coast and site of the Livadia Palace where Churchill, Roosevelt and Stalin held their fateful 1945 conference to discuss the post-war shape of Europe. Go to the naval base of Sevastopol, steeped in the history of the Crimean War, and visit Bakhchysaray, the 16th century capital of the Crimean khanate. Finally catch a train northwards to bring your journey to an end in the beautiful ancient city of Kiev in the heart of Ukraine.

**HOW:**
By train
**WHEN TO GO:**
May, when the spring flowers are at their height.
**TIME IT TAKES:**
Two weeks
**HIGHLIGHTS:**
St Petersburg – the Hermitage.
Moscow – the Kremlin and Red Square.
Lviv – Ploshcha Rynok, 16th century market square, a World Heritage Site.
Odessa – Potemkin Steps.
Yalta – Chekhov's house.
**YOU SHOULD KNOW:**
A private tour train, The Crimea Express, takes the above route. The advantage of travelling on it rather than ordinary scheduled services is simply the convenience of having the stops organized for you and luxurious accommodation. If you prefer to travel more spontaneously, planning your own itinerary, train services in Eastern Europe are cheap and reliable, especially in Ukraine.

**209**

# Golden Ring Towns

The Golden Ring is one of the best-known tourist routes in Russia, a 700-km (440-mi) circular tour of the ancient provincial towns and cities north-east of Moscow. The trip is a spectacular testament to Russia's past. You will see kremlins (fortresses), castles, monasteries, churches and cathedrals dating from the 12th to the 17th century. The fairytale splendour of the onion-domed architecture is fascinatingly unfamiliar to the western eye, and the depth and grandeur of the country's religious heritage is awe-inspiring. It is remarkable that, despite the turmoil of wars, revolution and years of Soviet governance, so much of Russia's spiritual history is still intact.

The journey makes a refreshing change from the noise and pollution of Moscow. Provincial life is surprisingly un-westernized and you will see a completely different side to Russian culture as you travel from town to town through tranquil countryside of cattle pastures, birch forests, fields and lakes.

There are seven main towns on the route. Nearest to Moscow is Vladimir, 12th century Russian capital. Travel on northwards to the rustic tourist town of Suzdal on the Kamenka River, stuffed with monuments; then to Kostromo on the River Volga, famous for

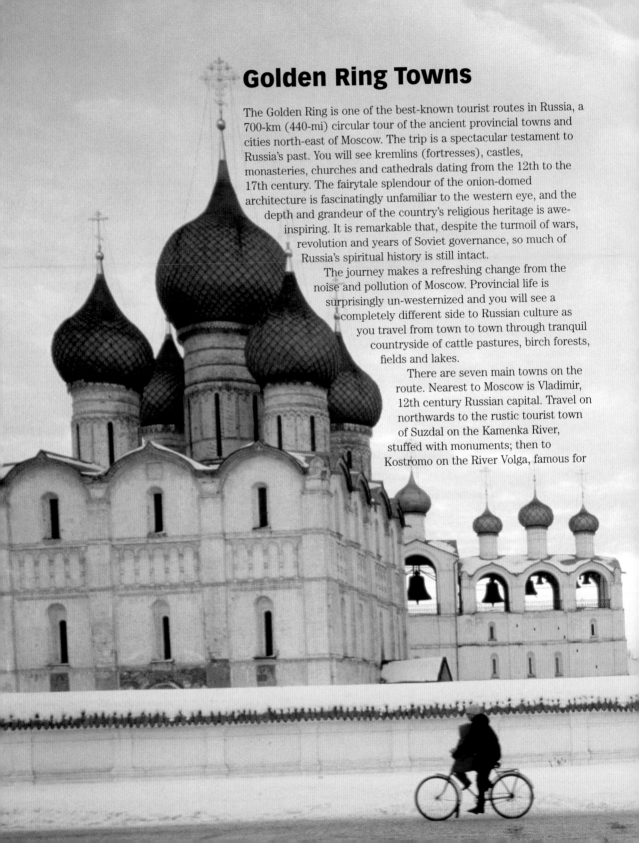

the 16th century Ipatievsky Monastery. Next is the historic city of Yaroslavl and, heading back towards Moscow, the sleepy little towns of Rostov Velikiy, once known as the 'eternal city', and picturesque Pereslavl-Zalesskiy on Lake Pleshcheveyo. The final Ring-town is Sergiev Posad, the 'Vatican' of the Russian Orthodox Church – a famous pilgrimage centre. The Holy Trinity Cathedral's breathtaking blue and golden domes provide a fitting finale to a journey that casts an entirely new light on the historical fabric underlying this influential corner of Europe.

*The Kremlin in Rostov Velikiy*

**HOW:**
By train or car
**WHEN TO GO:**
April to October
**TIME IT TAKES:**
Two weeks
**HIGHLIGHTS:**
Suzdal – St Euthymius Monastery and Church of the Annunciation.
Sergiev-Posad – World Heritage Site of Trinity-St Sergius Laura Monastery and Necropolis.
Rostov – 17th century kremlin, an architectural masterpiece.
Pereslavl-Zalesskiy – 17th century monastic architecture.
Yaroslavl – frescoes and ceramics.
**YOU SHOULD KNOW:**
Suzdal and Pereslavl-Zalesskiy can only be reached by road. The other towns are all accessible by train.

# The Trans-Siberian Railway

The legendary Trans-Siberian Railway is the greatest train journey in the world, an epic endurance test of nearly 10,000 km (more than 6,000 mi) across the vast Siberian steppe. The journey has such resonance that we have even invented the notion of 'The Trans-Siberian Express' – a mythical train that exists only in imagination. The Trans-Siberian Railway is in fact the collective name given to three routes between Moscow and the East, branching their separate ways at Ulan-Ude near Lake Baikal: the classic line to Vladivostok and alternative routes to Beijing – the Trans-Manchurian line via Harbin and the Trans-Mongolian line via Ulaanbaatar.

The Trans-Mongolian line across the Gobi Desert to Beijing is the usual tourist route. It is the shortest and most scenic. The classic journey from Moscow to Vladivostok is an entirely different experience. Few people travel the entire length of the line and even fewer are foreigners, so you will find yourself completely reliant on your own resources without the camaraderie of other tourists. However, it gives you an entirely authentic experience of this vast country, and with careful pre-planning you can stop off at places of interest on the way. For those who have the stamina to travel without a break, it is still a relief that the train stops every few hours so you can stretch your legs and stock up on food from the platform vendors.

For the first three days, whichever destination you aim for, you cross kilometre upon kilometre of apparently boundless Siberian steppe broken only by intermittent industrialized cityscapes. Whether you end up in Vladivostok or Beijing, the experience will provide you with lasting memories of an incredible journey. This is an epic trip to be undertaken purely for its own sake – for the joy of travelling rather than the anticipation of arrival.

**HOW:**
By train

**WHEN TO GO:**
All year. May to September is the peak time but the trains are well heated in winter and Siberia under snow is an incredible sight.

**TIME IT TAKES:**
One week

**HIGHLIGHTS:**
Yekaterinburg – Obelisk marking the boundary between Europe and Asia, 1,777 km (1,111 mi) from Moscow.
Views of Lake Baikal.
Ulan-Ude – historic Siberian town.
Khabarovsk Bridge – the longest bridge on the railway, 2,950 m (8,500 ft) across the River Amur.
Vladivostok Station – picturesque mock-17th century architecture and the last milestone of the railway.

**YOU SHOULD KNOW:**
A through train goes all the way from Donetsk in Ukraine to Vladivostok – technically the longest train journey in the world. From Vladivostok you can take a boat to Japan. The crossing takes 36 hours.

*The mock 17th-century train station in Vladivostok*

# The Volga-Baltic Waterway

By far the most memorable way of travelling between Moscow and St Petersburg is to take a river cruise along the Volga-Baltic Waterway, an extraordinarily complex network of canals, rivers and inland seas covering a total distance of 1,125 km (700 mi) and linking the mighty River Volga, the longest river in Europe, to the Baltic Sea.

The Volga-Baltic Waterway was part of Peter the Great's grand design. Having moved his capital to the Baltic, he dreamed of sailing from his new imperial city back to Moscow in the heart of the Empire. Construction began in 1709 and continued throughout the 18th and 19th centuries, making it possible to sail all the way from St Petersburg on the Gulf of Finland to Astrakhan on the Caspian Sea. With the completion of the 128 km (80 mi) Moscow-Volga Canal in 1937, Russia's capital was finally linked to this intricate system of canals and rivers.

You sail the Moscow Canal to the River Volga, through the Rybinsk Reservoir and the Mariinsk canal system, around Lake Onega and onto the River Svir to the southern coast of Lake Lagoda, the largest lake in Europe, finally connecting with the River Neva, having passed through 21 locks on your way. The tourist cruisers take a roundabout scenic route with wonderful natural and historic sights – Yaroslavl, a 'Golden Ring' city on the banks of the Volga; the red, blue and golden-domed churches of Uglich; the 14th century Kirillo-Belozersky monastery; the ancient wooden buildings of Kizhi Pogost; the scenic River Svir and beautiful coastline of Lake Lagoda.

By the time you arrive at St Petersburg, a city of haunting magnificence, you are amazed by the imagination and engineering skill involved in creating such a labyrinthine transport route, as well as the sheer size of this perplexing country.

**HOW:**
By boat
**WHEN TO GO:**
May and June are the best months, when everything is in full bloom but it is not yet too humid.
**TIME IT TAKES:**
Ten to thirteen days
**HIGHLIGHTS:**
Moscow Canal.
Yaroslavl – one of Russia's oldest cities.
Uglich – churches!
Kizhi Pogost – island of World Heritage medieval wooden buildings.
St Petersburg – the imperial city.
**YOU SHOULD KNOW:**
The ambitious traveller can travel by water the entire way along the ancient trade route from St Petersburg to Astrakhan, the ancient capital of the Tatars on the Caspian Sea.

*The Church of the Transfiguration in Kizhi Pogost*

*View of the River Dnieper, Kiev*

# River Dnieper to the Black Sea

**HOW:**
By boat
**WHEN TO GO:**
April to August
**TIME IT TAKES:**
Twelve days
**HIGHLIGHTS:**
Kiev – Monastery of the Caves; 11th century caves and tunnels.
Zaporizhzhya – display of Cossack horsemanship and music.
Seeing the backwaters and fishing villages at the river delta.
Yalta – Livadia Palace, Swallows Nest Castle and Chekhov's house.
Odessa – 18th and 19th century architecture.
**YOU SHOULD KNOW:**
You can take another onward boat from Yalta, Sevastopol or Odessa to Istanbul.

The third longest river in Europe, only outdone by the Volga and the Danube, the Dnieper is the lifeblood of Ukraine: vital water source for a country dependent on agriculture, massive hydro-electric power generator, and – not least – commercial corridor, transporting an endless stream of river traffic for the ten months of the year that it is ice-free. Passenger boats regularly ply this majestic river on an unhurried journey between Kiev, the 'Mother of Cities', and Odessa, the 'Pearl of the Black Sea', cruising through the heart of the largest country in Europe – a country steeped in a turbulent history of war and suffering that has somehow, against all odds, retained its distinctive culture and spirit.

After seeing the sights in the 9th century city of Kiev, voyage southwards past scenic forested ravines to Dnipropetrovsk, an old fortress town set in green hills, now a major commercial centre; cruise past the Dneproges Dam – a tour de force of design, one of the seven modern wonders of the world; and stop off at Zaporizhzhya, home of the Cossacks, the legendary warrior horsemen who dominated the southern steppes for four hundred years.

From the wetlands and backwaters of the river delta around Kherson, the boat strikes out along the glorious Mediterranean-like Black Sea coast of the Crimea to Sevastopol, the historic site of the Charge of the Light Brigade; and Yalta, 19th century haunt of the intelligentsia, where the Tsar had his holiday palace and Tolstoy and Chekhov spent their summers. Backtrack across the Black Sea to end your voyage at Odessa, fabled 19th century city of terraces.

# Settle-Carlisle Railway

This was the last great main rail line to be constructed in England, completed in 1876 by the Midland Railway Company after six years of blood, sweat and tears as the builders overcame major natural obstacles to create 116 km (72 mi) of track frequently described as 'the most scenic rail journey in England'. The romantic Victorians and Edwardians certainly thought so, as they loved taking this picturesque route when heading north for their annual summer holidays – using a through service from London to Scotland that lasted until 1977.

Those skilled 19th-century railway engineers built 14 tunnels and 17 major viaducts to create a route through the magnificent Yorkshire Dales, on through the lush, gently rolling hills of the Eden Valley with its charming villages and traditional market towns to Carlisle, gateway to Scotland. Their work has proved enduring, as the Settle to Carlisle line still has regular scheduled services much used by locals, as well as discerning tourists drawn by the opportunity to view some of the country's finest scenery from the comfort of a train seat.

The full journey actually begins in Leeds, with its connection to the intercity rail network. Also, the so-called 'Lancashire Dales Rail' service runs on many Sundays between the beginning of May and mid-October, offering a through trip from Blackpool via Preston and Blackburn on to Settle and Carlisle. This has associated guided walks and coach trips from certain trains to beautiful parts of the North Pennines and Yorkshire Dales. For those drawn by the romance of bygone travel, charter trains with vintage carriages – pulled by classic steam locomotives – regularly do the Settle to Carlisle run (usually as part of a longer journey). But whichever way you choose to go, it will be an experience to treasure.

**HOW:**
By train
**WHEN TO GO:**
April to October to see the countryside at its best.
**TIME IT TAKES:**
Just under two hours (Settle-Carlisle) or two-and-a-half hours (Leeds-Carlisle).
**HIGHLIGHTS:**
The amazing 24-arch Ribblehead Viaduct between Dent and Ribblehead.
The long tunnel beneath Blea Moor – as the train enters the southern entrance it passes under Force Gill Aqueduct that carries a stream over the line.
Delightful Appleby Station – built by the Midland Railway as one of the major stations on the line – spot the water tower and crane that service steam specials.
The Eden Lacy Viaduct between Langwathby and Lazonby, for as fine an English landscape view as you'll ever see.
**YOU SHOULD KNOW:**
When the Government proposed closing the line in 1988, a petition with the signatures of 32,000 protesters resulted in a change of mind.

*A train crosses the Ribblehead Viaduct.*

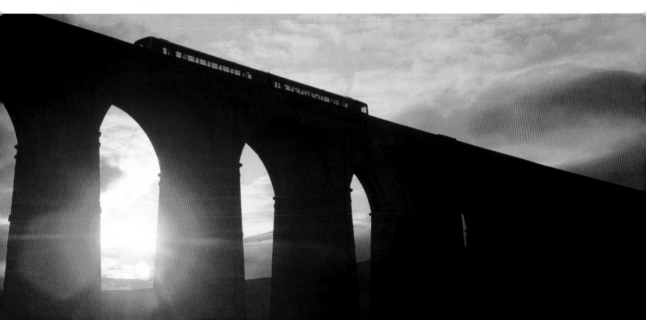

# The Ferry to Orkney

**HOW:**
By boat
**WHEN TO GO:**
May to September
**TIME IT TAKES:**
From 40 minutes (John o' Groats-Burwick) to six hours (Aberdeen-Kirkwall).
**HIGHLIGHTS:**
The famous waterside stack known as The Old Man of Hoy (take the Scrabster crossing for a sea view).
Scapa Flow Visitor Centre on Hoy, for fascinating insight into this great haven for the British Navy, where the German World War I High Seas Fleet was scuttled in 1919.
Magnificent St Magnus Cathedral in Kirkwall, begun in 1137 by Earl Rognvald – the most obvious reminder (among many) of Orkney's Norse heritage.
The Heart of Neolithic Orkney – a UNESCO World Heritage Site in West Mainland that includes some of the oldest and best-preserved Neolithic sites in Europe.
**YOU SHOULD KNOW:**
The world's shortest scheduled air service at two minutes is between the islands of Westray and Papa Westray – just a minute if the wind is right!

*The Standing Stones of Stennes, Orkney's oldest stone circle*

Sometimes the journey's the thing, other times it's the destination that counts – but when you sail to Orkney you get the best of both. This group of 67 islands is off Scotland's northeastern tip and 20 are inhabited, with most people living on Mainland, the largest island and home of Kirkwall, the administrative centre. Orkney is well served by air, but the way to go is by ferry for a scenic journey on the ocean wave (which, be warned, can be quite high). There is a choice of services.

From Aberdeen (to Shetland, calling at Kirkwall four days a week) a car ferry follows the coast past Peterhead, the gas terminal at St Fergus, Rattray Head lighthouse, Fraserburgh and Kinnaird Head, before heading out to sea. Land is sighted at Wick on the Caithness coast, before Duncansby Head lighthouse and Orkney – passing South Ronaldsay and East Mainland before docking in the Bay of Kirkwall.

The most scenic is the 90-minute crossing from Scrabster, near Thurso. The large MV *Hamnavoe* starts from the low cliffs near Holborn Head lighthouse, before crossing the Pentland Firth, where the Atlantic meets the North Sea head-on. Landfall is at Rora Head on the island of Hoy, after which the route passes through Hoy Sound with Graemsay to the right and round into Hamnavoe Inlet to dock at the picturesque port of Stromness on West Mainland.

For a cheap 'n' cheerful journey by the shortest, least expensive and most sheltered route, the hour-long car-ferry dash from Gills Bay to St Margaret Hope on South Ronaldsay is the one to choose.

In summer there is a short passenger ferry crossing from John o' Groats to Burwick on South Ronaldsay, usually taken in conjunction with various guided tours of Orkney that are offered as part of the service.

# North Yorkshire Moors Railway

Lovers of steam will be beguiled by this 29-km (18-mi) line, especially if they also appreciate the Yorkshire Moors. For those who just love wonderful landscapes, it is possible to travel the line in a train pulled by a heritage diesel loco – but how much better to take one of the steam trains that not only delivers scenery, but also nostalgic transport back to a bygone era?

The North Yorkshire Moors Railway (NYMR) runs from Pickering to Grosmont, from whence onward travel to Whitby is now available by steam train – a popular extension. The NYMR is a charitable trust, with trains mainly staffed by dedicated volunteers. From Pickering, trains run via Levisham, Newton Dale and Goathland to Grosmont.

Pickering station has been restored to 1937 condition, with wonderful period detail. Levisham is in pretty Newton Dale, two miles from the village it serves, and now represents a small North Eastern Railway station from around 1910. Newton Dale Halt is a remote request stop in splendid countryside, mainly used by walkers. Goathland was built in 1865 and is almost unchanged, now restored as a country station from the 1920s. Grosmont represents the British Rail era of the 1950s, where through travellers change for the charming old fishing port of Whitby.

The NYMR timetable is complex, in that not all trains from Pickering to Grosmont have an onward connection to Whitby. However, special Grosmont Day Rover or Whitby Day Rover tickets allow unlimited travel all day, permitting the journey to be broken by anyone who wishes to explore interesting diversions along the way.

Grosmont is also on the Esk Valley Line from Middlesbrough to Whitby, one of the most scenic rural lines in England, and this journey also offers fabulous scenery – trains are modern, though steam specials are run.

*The nostalgic North Yorkshire Moors steam train*

**HOW:**
By train
**WHEN TO GO:**
April to October (limited weekend service in winter).
**TIME IT TAKES:**
From Pickering to Grosmont takes 65 minutes, plus 20 minutes to Whitby.
**HIGHLIGHTS:**
In the busy market town of Pickering – an ancient castle and the Beck Isle Museum of rural life, also featuring superb old photographs of the town, its people and surroundings.
Goathland Station – recognize it from regular appearances in the TV drama series 'Heartbeat' (Aidensfield) and Harry Potter films (Hogsmeade).
Visiting artist-in-residence Christopher Ware – his studio at Levisham station is open whenever trains are running (and some other times too).
A visit to the engine sheds at Grosmont to see the old locomotives that are being painstakingly restored.
**YOU SHOULD KNOW:**
The Grosmont Tunnel is believed to be the oldest railway tunnel in the world, built in the 1830s when carriages and wagons on the line were horse-drawn.

*Boats moored at Ambleside, on the shore of Windermere*

# Lake Windermere

**HOW:**
By boat
**WHEN TO GO:**
April to October for summer services (winter services are limited).
**TIME IT TAKES:**
Just over an hour for the full length of the lake.
**HIGHLIGHTS:**
Windermere Steamboats Museum at Bowness, with a collection of craft that tell the story of lake cruising from its inception in the 19th century – don't miss Beatrix Potter's rowboat. The Aquarium of the Lakes, a unique freshwater aquarium on the southern shore of Windermere that recreates lake life around the world.
Brockhole Visitor Centre between Windermere and Ambleside, in a mansion with lovely gardens and lake frontage, designed to showcase the attractions of England's largest National Park.
A Windermere cruise plus a return steam journey on the preserved Lakeside & Haverthwaite Railway along the Leven Valley from the south end of the lake – combined tickets available.
**YOU SHOULD KNOW:**
The Lake was originally Winandermere, but the Victorian railway company thought that was too long, called their new station at Birthwaite 'Windermere'...and the name stuck for both town and lake.

England's largest natural lake, set within Cumbria's Lake District National Park, has been a popular holiday destination since 1847, when a branch of the Kendal and Windermere Railway was opened. This magical lake set amidst spectacular fells beneath a big sky has never lost its appeal, surely attracting more visitors now than ever it did during its Victorian and Edwardian heyday.

Windermere is a ribbon lake, some 17 km (10.5 mi) long and never more than 1.6 km (1 mi) wide, stretching from Newby Bridge in the south to Ambleside in the north. Ambleside is one of two towns on the lake, the other being Bowness-on-Windermere, half way along the east bank. Strangely, the town of Windermere does not itself have lake frontage, though it has effectively merged with Bowness, which does.

Although there is a road along the eastern shore of the lake, the best way to enjoy Windermere and its impressive surrounds is from the water.

There are any number of cruises on offer from three main departure points – Lakeside in the south, Bowness in the middle and Waterhead (Ambleside) in the north. A wide variety of options are offered, including travelling from end to end, a return journey from Lakeside to Bowness, a circular islands cruise from Bowness, a return journey from Waterhead to Bowness or circular lake tour from any departure point. All types of cruise boats operate, from large lake steamers, through mid-sized modern launches to smaller traditional wooden launches...and even the occasional vintage steam launch.

It is certainly a busy stretch of water in summer, but all that marine hustle and bustle – set against the majestic grandeur of the unchanging fells and mountains – seems part of Lake Windermere's timeless charm.

# Glasgow to Mallaig

Scotland's West Highland Line is a mighty fine line, especially for lovers of dramatic scenery. The WHL begins at Glasgow's Queen Street Station and takes a while to get going scenically – trundling through suburbs, Dumbarton and Helensburgh before turning north for Garelochhead. It gets up to landscape speed as it passes along the northwestern shore of Loch Lomond and reaches Crianlarich, where a western branch goes to Oban while the northern branch crosses wild Rannoch Moor before arriving at Fort William.

There beginneth one of the world's great scenic railway journeys, starting near Britain's highest mountain (Ben Nevis), crossing Britain's longest inland waterway (Caledonian Canal), visiting Britain's most westerly mainland station (Arisaig), passing Britain's deepest freshwater loch (Loch Morar), Scotland's whitest beach (Morar) and arriving at Europe's deepest sea loch (Loch Nevis). Nothing done by halves around these parts, then!

The train follows the rugged coastline, passing through many tunnels and small stations before reaching Mallaig, 265 km (165 mi) from Glasgow.

You don't have to stop there – ferries link Mallaig to the Kyle of Lochalsh, Armadale, the Small Isles and the Isle of Skye. It's easy to turn a memorable Highlands journey into an unforgettable Highlands and Islands expedition.

It is also possible to marry the romance of steam with that overdose of magnificent Highland scenery, by taking a trip from Fort William to Mallaig and back on The Jacobite, a special service that runs on weekdays between mid-May and mid-October, with added weekend services in July and August. This not only offers the Highland sights, but also the evocative sound of steam...plus a leisurely stop at Glenfinnan where Bonnie Prince Charlie raised his standard in 1745 and time to explore the thriving fishing community of Mallaig.

**HOW:**
By train
**WHEN TO GO:**
May to October (dour winter weather often obscures the scenery!).
**TIME IT TAKES:**
About five hours (Glasgow-Mallaig), of which the super-scenic Fort William to Mallaig leg takes 80 minutes.
**HIGHLIGHTS:**
Britain's only railway show shed, at Cruach Cutting shortly before the WHL's high point at Corrous Summit on vast Rannoch Moor.
At Banervie, where the WHL meets the Caledonian Canal – the amazing series of canal locks known as Neptune's Staircase.
Crossing the world-famous 21-arch Glenfinnan Viaduct in its truly spectacular setting.
The view from Arisaig Station on a clear day – spot the Small Isles of Rum, Eigg, Muck and Canna, plus the southern tip of Skye.
**YOU SHOULD KNOW:**
Having perversely looped down into Fort William from the northeast, the Glasgow train has to reverse back out of the station the way it came in order to continue the journey to Mallaig.

*Fort William with Ben Nevis in the background*

*The Flying Scotsman passing magnificent scenery.*

# London to Edinburgh on The Flying Scotsman

The Flying Scotsman is a rail route, train service and world-famous locomotive, in that chronological order. The route is the 627-km (390-mi) East Coast mainline from London King's Cross to Edinburgh Waverley, created by the combined efforts of three different Victorian railway companies.

The train service is the modern incarnation of one that began in 1862 as the Special Scotch Express, a daily train each way simultaneously leaving at 10.00. Renamed The Flying Scotsman in 1924, it began a non-stop run between the two capitals in 1928, a journey that reached luxury heights in the 1930s with on-board hairdressing, cocktail bar and a fine restaurant. World War II ended that, but the service survived rail nationalization in 1948, with journey times falling steadily as first diesels and then electric locomotives were introduced. After privatization in 1994, the Flying Scotsman was seen as a flagship asset and it continues running to this day.

The locomotive was built in 1923 and named The Flying Scotsman in 1924, to gain publicity for the newly acquired and recently re-titled service of the same name launched by the London Midland & Scottish Railway. At the end of the steam era it was sold, cashing in on its fame with tours of America and Australia before returning to Britain and ending up in the National Railway Museum in York.

Those wishing to ride a train pulled by this grand old loco will have to wait until completion of a lengthy refurbishment. However, it's still possible to enjoy both the route and the train service by travelling from London to Edinburgh, making a truly historic railway journey via Peterborough, Grantham, Doncaster, York, Darlington, Durham, Newcastle, Berwick-upon-Tweed and Dunbar. Many first-timers take the journey simply to see the magnificent coastal scenery before and after leaving England at Berwick.

**HOW:**
By train
**WHEN TO GO:**
Any time of year
**TIME IT TAKES:**
Four-and-a-half hours
**HIGHLIGHTS:**
Digswell Viaduct over the River Mimram (also called the Welwyn Viaduct) – a landmark on the East Coast Line between Welwyn Garden City and Digswell.
The long viaduct and splendid view of the magnificent Cathedral from the train window at Durham.
The King Edward VII Bridge crossing over the River Tyne at Newcastle, between the iconic Metro Bridge and Redheugh Bridge.
Arriving at Waverley, the grand (and vast!) Victorian station in the heart of Edinburgh, and going straight out onto the city's premier shopping street, Princes Street.
**YOU SHOULD KNOW:**
The Flying Scotsman locomotive was sold by canny British Rail for £3,000 in 1963 – and bought back by the nation in 2004 for over £2,000,000.

# Offa's Dyke Path

Who was Offa, and why his Dyke? The first is easy – Offa was the Anglo-Saxon King of Mercia, the great English kingdom that thrived in the Dark Ages, who ruled from 757 to 796. The next answer is more difficult. We know what Offa's Dyke is – a massive earthwork that roughly follows some of the modern English-Welsh border – but why it was created remains a mystery.

It certainly required effort, being some 103 km (64 mi) long, from Rushock Hill in the south to Llanfyndd in the north – not as once thought stretching from 'sea to sea', completely separating two countries. It consists of a ditch on the Welsh side and rampart on the English side, but patently couldn't be defended like that other great boundary construct, Hadrian's Wall. The best explanation is that the famously belligerent Offa built it because he could, simultaneously – like any top dog – marking his territory. The message to potential enemies was 'look how powerful I am because I can build such a mighty earthwork, so trespass across it at your peril'.

Be that as it may, today Offa's Dyke Path is one of the most attractive National Trails, passing through some of Britain's most beautiful countryside. Although following the full length of Offa's Dyke, it is actually longer than the original, running for 285 km (177 mi) from the Severn Estuary near Chepstow through the tranquil Welsh Marches and on to Prestatyn on Liverpool Bay.

Anyone who hikes the Dyke will see high moorland, wide river valleys, lush fields and ancient woodland. Along the way there are historic towns and lonely villages, castles and hill forts, churches and abbeys, together with rich and varied flora and fauna. In short, walking the Path is a wonderful journey of discovery.

**HOW:**
On foot
**WHEN TO GO:**
April to October
**TIME IT TAKES:**
Allow two weeks to hike from end to end, five days for the Offa's Dyke section.
**HIGHLIGHTS:**
The ruined but impressive White Castle on a low hill close to the village of Llantilio..
The ancient settlement of Clun, complete with castle ruins, ancient bridge and medieval houses.
The Offa's Dyke Centre in Knighton, a town that straddles the Dyke and is mainly in Wales but partly in England, for all the information you could want on the Dyke.
Crossing the amazing Pontcysyllte Aqueduct en route to the Welsh coast after Path and Dyke finally part company.
**YOU SHOULD KNOW:**
Much of Offa's ambitious Dyke may have survived for over 1,200 years, but it was historically obsolete early in the 9th century, soon after it was completed.

*Walkers take in the stunning scenery along Offa's Dyke.*

# Wainwright's Coast to Coast Walk

**HOW:**
On foot

**WHEN TO GO:**
May to September to take advantage
of the best (if still sometimes
unpredictable) upland weather.

**TIME IT TAKES:**
Around two weeks

**HIGHLIGHTS:**
Superb views over Buttermere after
the steep climb up Loft Beck.
The Pennine watershed at Nine
Standards Rigg – the Nine Standards
being nine massive cairns at the
summit.
The lovely ridge walk down towards
Egton Bridge, ending with a walk
along the River Esk and through
woods to the pretty village.
Stopping off at Grosmont Station
towards the end of the walk – have a
refreshing cup of tea and inspect
steam engines being restored by the
North Yorkshire Moors Railway.

**YOU SHOULD KNOW:**
Wainwright's description is A Coast-
to-Coast Walk rather than The Coast-
to-Coast Walk, and he encouraged
hikers to experiment with diversions
of their own devising.

Alfred Wainwright was a great hill walker – and writer on the subject – who devised his most ambitious route in 1973. This 305-km (190-mi) walking trail crosses northern Britain from side to side, from Irish Sea to North Sea. On the way it passes through three National Parks (Lake District, Yorkshire Dales and North Yorkshire Moors) that together offer some of England's finest upland scenery. Thousands hike all or some of this wonderful trail each year, stopping for the night at the friendly bed-and-breakfast establishments to be found in almost every one of the 40-odd hamlets, country villages and small towns along the Walk. Some stay at youth hostels and others with strong backs carry all they need for self-sufficiency and camp as they go.

The Walk is generally undertaken from west to east, starting at the sea cliffs of St Bees on the Cumbrian coast. The first port of call is the Lake District with its incomparable mountain scenery – and plenty of steep paths. After Shap the route crosses undulating farmland until it reaches the Yorkshire Dales at Kirkby Stephen, after which the hilly terrain returns, though the Pennines are not quite so demanding as Lakeland mountains. After Richmond there is another level march across the Vale of Mowbray to Ingleby Cross and from there on to the North Yorkshire Moors. This undulating last stretch over heather-covered hills leads to the North Sea and on to the bustling fishing village of Robin Hood's Bay – journey's end!

Though well recognized, the route is not generally way-marked, so map-reading skills are essential (even with the help of a GPS unit that co-ordinates with Ordnance Survey maps!). It can also be quite demanding in the hillier sections, so the rewarding but energetic Coast to Coast Walk should not be attempted by the unfit.

*Beautiful Lake Buttermere in the Lake District*

# Peddars Way & Norfolk Coast Path

*Windswept salt marshes along the Norfolk Coast Path*

Starting from the delightful little country park of Knettishall Heath near the village of Hopton in North Suffolk, Peddars Way travels through Norfolk for some 74 km (46 mi) to Holme-next-the-Sea, where it meets the Norfolk Coast Path. Together, these two routes form a National Trail that showcases some of East Anglia's most interesting landscapes and striking natural features.

Peddars Way follows the line of an old Roman Road built in AD 61 to help subdue those troublesome Iceni, whose warrior queen Boudicca had been doing a bit too much pillaging. The peaceful way-marked route is a pleasing mix of footpaths, tracks and country lanes that runs through Breckland, a uniquely East Anglian area of forest, heathland and shallow river valleys, before crossing rolling wooded farmland to the sea.

Upon reaching the Norfolk Coast Path there is a choice – left for the western end of the Path at the traditional seaside town of Hunstanton on The Wash, or right for the much longer 80-km (50-mi) stretch to the eastern end at Cromer. Many people choose to check out Hunstanton before retracing their steps, so they walk the whole length of this atmospheric route along North Norfolk's heritage coast, within an Area of Outstanding Natural Beauty.

Here, the sights are low clay cliffs that are under constant assault by the restless sea, abundant wildlife, windswept salt marshes punctuated by gutters and creeks, shifting sand dunes, wide beaches and pretty coastal villages notable for their brick-and-flint buildings, quaint quays and harbours. Finally, at Cromer (famed for crabs and classic pier) the journey ends. Or does it?

In truth, those who can't get enough of East Anglia's distinctive character will find connections to the Weavers Way and Angles Way that continue on through the Norfolk Broads to Great Yarmouth.

**HOW:**
On foot
**WHEN TO GO:**
April to October
**TIME IT TAKES:**
Around eight days
**HIGHLIGHTS:**
Historic Castle Acre with the extensive ruins of a priory and the castle that gives the village its name.
A famous seal colony at Blakeney Point – and the delightful coastal village of the same name.
The magnificent Palladian mansion of Holkham Hall in its parkland setting, plus a fascinating Bygones Museum (mainly summer opening, check times in advance).
The Wells to Morston stretch of the Norfolk Coast Path – one of the most remote and beautiful parts of this distinctive coast, with a wonderful river crossing.
**YOU SHOULD KNOW:**
It is possible to reach the start of Peddars Way by bus from Thetford (to Knettishall Heath) or Bury St Edmunds (to nearby Coney Weston).

# Pembrokeshire Coast Path

If someone said 'I'm off for a stroll from St Dogmaels to Amroth' few people would know what they were talking about – but those who love wild, unspoiled coastline should find out fast. For those places are at opposite ends of one of Britain's best long-distance walks, the 299-km (186-mi) Pembrokeshire Coast Path in West Wales. This splendid National Trail is not only a satisfying walk amidst the rugged beauty of an extraordinary coast, but also a hike through history.

For much of the wilder northern section the Path keeps to clifftops, giving marvellous views of beaches, cliffs and offshore islands, plus abundant seabird life. In spring, there is the added bonus of colourful wildflowers. The section from St Dogmaels to St Davids includes the rocky bay of Witches' Cauldron, Whitesands Bay (from where St Patrick set sail for Ireland), the Norman castle at historic Newport, the old harbour at Lower Fishguard and Porthclais (where St David was baptized).

The middle section to Milford Haven follows the sweeping St Brides Bay that has beautiful beaches, picturesque villages, Marloes Sands with extraordinary multi-coloured cliffs, a little chapel at St Ann's Head and the imposing Victorian fort at Dale Haven.

The southern section is gentler, passing along the shores of Milford Haven's great natural harbour (teeming with birdlife) before reaching some of the finest beaches in Wales – Freshwater West, Broad Haven South, Barafundle Bay and Freshwater East. There's also plenty of commanding cliff scenery, especially numerous stacks and arches on the Castlemartin Peninsula. There is plenty of heritage to enjoy, too, including Pembroke Castle and the village of Angle with its wonderful old church, Fisherman's Chapel, dovecote and medieval tower-house. The charming seaside town of Tenby is a worthy last stop before the Coastal Path ends at Amroth.

*Broad Haven South on the Pembrokeshire Coast*

# Land's End to John o' Groats

This one is reserved for dedicated charity walkers and bike riders (sponsored or not). It's the longest place-to-place journey in Britain, but there are obviously plenty of dedicated cyclists who seek to join the informal LEJoG Club, as several thousand are thought to undertake this marathon trip – the shortest route is 1,407 km (874 mi) – each year.

The start point at Land's End is the signpost giving the choice of New York or John o' Groats (most people choosing the latter) and the first decision is whether to leave the West Country by using the main A30 road, or choose one of the longer, hillier and scenic routes on minor roads. Such is the nature (and beauty) of this long trip – there is no 'official' route and time available can be balanced against the many sights to be found along the way to provide a customized trip.

After Cornwall and Devon it's into Somerset, through the Cotswolds towards Birmingham and then Staffordshire, where a strategic decision must be made – head due north on the western route, through the Lake District, or tack across to the Peak District and the eastern route through the Yorkshire Dales.

Whichever route is chosen, the intrepid cyclist will cross the line of Hadrian's Wall into the Scottish Lowlands, continue through the scenic Borders and on towards Glasgow (western route) or Edinburgh (eastern route). From there the western route takes in Fort William and the eastern route Aviemore and Inverness (capital of the Highlands) before they converge around Dingwall for the final run up the coast to John o' Groats. There aren't too many alternative roads in the Highlands, but those few are all scenic. John o' Groats is a small village and harbour, and nearby Dunnet Head is actually the most northerly point in mainland Britain.

*Hikers by Ashness bridge in the Lake District*

**HOW:**
By bike or on foot
**WHEN TO GO:**
April to September
**TIME IT TAKES:**
Under three weeks at comfortable cycling speed.
**HIGHLIGHTS:**
The Lake District (western route) or Yorkshire Dales (eastern route).
The Grey Cairns of Camster – ancient burial chambers that are remarkably well preserved, but especially stimulating as they're almost at journey's end.
Cycling the last 3 km (2 mi) from John o' Groats to Duncansby Head, the true completion of the end-to-end trip at the most northerly point that can be reached by road.
**YOU SHOULD KNOW:**
The record for bicycling from Land's End to John o' Groats is under 45 hours.

*Porthcurno in Cornwall*

# London River Journey

*Big Ben and the Palace
of Westminster*

Nearly two million commuters (a number that is rising fast) now travel to work on London's river each year, using stylish catamarans with on-board coffee bars, airline-type seats and bicycle racks for those who pedal on from boat to office. These frequent scheduled services run up the River Thames from Woolwich (which has a free car ferry across the river to North Woolwich) to Waterloo and Embankment in Central London, and downriver from Putney via Chelsea Harbour and Embankment to Blackfriars. Taking both trips will allow the voyager to see the many famous sights along the river.

However, there are some 25 major piers and terminals along the London river, and commuter services are supplemented by a wide variety of tourist boats, most of which offer a running commentary on the sights and history of this vibrant capital city as the Thames weaves its way through the heart of historic London and the chosen journey unfolds. Some of these sightseeing services extend the distances that can be travelled on the river down to the Thames Flood Barrier and up to Kew (for the world-famous Kew Botanical Gardens) and Hampton Court (Henry VIII's wonderful palace).

Most tourist cruises concentrate on the central area, from Westminster Pier (close to the Houses of Parliament and Westminster Abbey), Waterloo Millennium Pier (for the London Eye and South Bank arts complex), Tower Pier (Tower of London) and Greenwich Pier (National Maritime Museum, Queen's House, Old Royal Observatory and former Royal Naval College). It is possible to buy 'hop on, hop off' River Rover tickets that permit travellers to disembark at any pier to explore, before resuming their tour. These are also valid for the Docklands Light Railway, to enhance a day's exploration of the River Thames and its environs.

# London Market Walk

The exhilarating 8-km (5-mi) walk from the shabby chic of Portobello Market to the anarchic hippiedom of Camden Lock by the back way along London's canal paths reveals multifarious aspects of this schizoid metropolis – a city that is all things to all people, where wealth and squalor intermingle in a ferment of styles, cultures and creeds.

After a bit of dawdling among the picturesque antique shops, clobber stalls and costermongers' barrows of Portobello, stroll northwards through Golborne Road flea market, where old London scrap dealers, Portuguese pastry shops and Moroccan food stalls vie for trade, and head towards the Grand Union Canal.

Trellick Tower looms menacingly ahead – a 31-storey award-winning, ferro-concrete monolith, an undisguised homage to 1970s urban nihilism. In a triumph of London spirit over adversity, at its foot are lovingly tended community gardens. Escape onto the canal towpath, a haven of rural calm after the bedlam of the market – the occasional narrow boat chugging past, swans drifting serenely in pairs, a lone resident heron in graceful flight. Walk eastwards and, suddenly, the abandoned concrete cityscape morphs into another world – the graceful Victorian villas, brightly painted narrow boats and weeping-willow trees of Little Venice.

Where the Grand Union ends, at the shiny steel wharves and gleaming commercial buildings of Paddington Basin – icons of post-modern anomie, the Regent's Canal begins. Pick your way across the grimy Edgware Road into dank canal tunnels, under railway bridges, past the ramshackle moorings of motley canal-dwellers to emerge into fairyland: gleaming white stucco Regency palaces, rolling lawns and curtains of greenery trailing into the water. Follow the path to skirt Primrose Hill; cut through London Zoo, and along the backs of elegant early-Victorian terraces. Finally, dive into the sub-culture of Camden Lock – the hippest street market in London – for a shot of revitalizing urban energy.

*Camden Lock Market*

**HOW:**
On foot
**WHEN TO GO:**
Any time
**TIME IT TAKES:**
2 to 3 hours
**HIGHLIGHTS:**
Electric Cinema, Portobello Road – London's oldest working cinema; a listed art deco building opened in 1910.
Canal mural – an intricate collage depicting birds, boats, water and sky made entirely from rubbish dredged from the canal. A triumph of community enterprise.
Browning's Island, Little Venice – Robert Browning habitually rowed his skiff here to compose his poetry under the weeping willow trees.
London Zoo Aviary – designed by Lord Snowdon.
Primrose Hill – panoramic view over London.
**YOU SHOULD KNOW:**
A good alternative to walking the whole way is to catch the waterbus that leaves every half hour from Paddington Basin to Camden Lock – a delightful boat ride through Maida Hill tunnel and past London Zoo.
The Portobello Market operates on Fridays and Saturdays throughout the year.

# Ferry Across the Mersey

The short but impressive River Mersey runs for just 113 km (70 mi) from Stockport in Greater Manchester to the sea in Liverpool Bay, for some of its length now merged with the Manchester Ship Canal. It is the historic boundary between the counties of Lancashire and Cheshire and – perhaps more significantly – the river has played a huge part in shaping the character and fortunes of the great northern port city of Liverpool.

Its wide estuary is constricted as the Mersey passes between Liverpool and Birkenhead. There, it may be crossed by two road tunnels and a railway tunnel dating back to 1880 – but by far the most famous way of crossing the river is on the Mersey ferry, which runs from George's Landing Stage at the Pier Head in Liverpool to the terminals of Woodside in Birkenhead (opposite the Pier Head) and Seacombe in Wallasey on the Wirral Peninsula bank. There are triangular River Explorer Cruises with informative commentary that take in all three terminals and some of the river towards New Brighton.

But the real experience is the simple Ferry Cross the Mersey, as immortalized in song by Gerry and the Pacemakers as part of the 1960s explosion of musical creativity in Liverpool known as Merseybeat. There was a hit single, album, film, musical plus several cover versions of this well-known song – and the self-same ferries that inspired it are still running today. The three ferries are *Royal Iris of the Mersey*, *Snowdrop* and *Royal Daffodil* (originally *Mountwood*, *Woodchurch* and *Overchurch* after post-war housing developments in Birkenhead when launched in the late 1950s, all renamed after major refits in the 1990s). Ride one of these on the short river crossing and enjoy a wonderful view of the thing that made Liverpool great – its waterfront.

*The ferry heads towards Liverpool.*

# London to Birmingham by Grand Union Canal

Once an important commercial artery endlessly travelled by barge families who lived in cramped quarters aboard narrowboats that transported a huge variety of goods between the two great cities, initially pulled by horses and later propelled by chugging engines, the Grand Union Canal fell into disuse as the roads conquered all. In fact, despite the 18th- and early 19th-century origins of its component canals, the Grand Union is a relatively recent creation, formed by canal company mergers in 1929 in an ultimately doomed attempt to remain competitive.

Happily, this great engineering feat, with 166 locks on the main 220-km (137 mi) waterway (there are also various arms) has been revived by modern leisure interest, and it is now possible to make the signed towpath walk from Little Venice near Paddington in London into the heart of Birmingham. This not only offers a tranquil (and level!) hike through some beautiful countryside, but also passes some splendid canal architecture. From London, the Grand Union climbs into the Chiltern Hills, then on past the Northampton arm to Royal Leamington Spa, Warwick and Birmingham.

The same scenic pleasures are, of course, available to those who let a narrowboat do the walking, and make the trip in a manner that most nearly recreates the experiences of those old-time bargees (though accommodation is more spacious nowadays). The self-drive narrowboat is the craft of choice and most end-to-end cruises begin at Brentford, on an arm of the Grand Union that connects to the River Thames. In truth, most canal cruises either do a specific section of the Grand Union, or undertake journeys that include other scenic canals as well, as one thing to remember about canal journeys is that the boat usually has to end up back where it started!

*The Grand Union Canal in Warwickshire*

**HOW:**
On foot or by boat
**WHEN TO GO:**
April to October
**TIME IT TAKES:**
Around a week for the walk, at least five days for an end-to-end cruise.
**HIGHLIGHTS:**
Bull's Bridge Junction near Norwood where the two London arms of the Grand Union join – once the main dockyard of the Grand Union Carrying Company.
A fascinating Canal Museum and the Boat Inn at Stoke Bruerne, an old canal town.
The long tunnels at Blisworth, 2,813 m (1.75 mi), and Braunston, 1,867 m (1.16 mi) – boat only (no towpath).
The fabulous castle and medieval buildings of Warwick – well worth an exploration stop.
**YOU SHOULD KNOW:**
Fenny Stratford Lock near Milton Keynes raises and lowers the canal's water lever by a mere 30 cm (12 in).

229

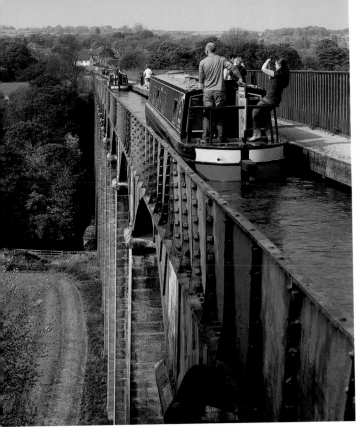

# Llangollen Canal

When canal cruising became popular, the original centre section of the Ellesmere Canal (later part of the Shropshire Union), was renamed the Llangollen Canal – deemed a more appropriate name to underline the wonderful scenery and stunning engineering features of 'Britain's most beautiful canal'. The 66-km (41-mi) route links Llangollen in North Wales to Hurleston in Cheshire, via Ellesmere in Shropshire.

The journey is worth it for two aqueducts alone, though the Canal also passes through wonderful countryside. The amazing 19-arch Pontcysyllte Aqueduct spans the River Dee and 10-arch Chirk Aqueduct crosses the River Ceirog. These were the audacious creations of Thomas Telford and William Jessop in the early years of the 19th century.

Pontcysyllte soars above the Dee Valley to a height of 38 m (125 ft) for a distance of 305 m (1,000 ft). This awe-inspiring engineering marvel certainly deserves its status as a Grade I listed Scheduled Ancient Monument. The water is carried by an iron trough that extends to just 30 cm (1 ft) above the water level, and though there is a towpath on one side, the other is unprotected. When travelling by narrowboat, this leads to the extraordinary sensation of floating through mid-air. The crossing is popular, especially in high summer, with a non-stop procession of boats and walkers experiencing this unique attraction. Chirk Aqueduct is less eye-catching than Pontcysyllte, but an equally clever piece of engineering, with the adjacent tunnel serving as a reminder of the challenges faced by its builders.

From the English end, the Canal passes through lush green countryside with the Welsh hills as a backdrop, then wends its way through foothills and ancient woodland before reaching the final stretch to Llangollen beneath limestone cliffs. Narrowboats are available for hire at Llangollen, Whittington, Trevor and Wrenbury, allowing for a choice of different journeys.

**HOW:**
By boat
**WHEN TO GO:**
April to October
**TIME IT TAKES:**
A week-long round trip along the canal from Llangollen and back involves some 36 hours of actual cruising.
**HIGHLIGHTS:**
Horseshoe Falls – a weir and pumping house on the River Dee near Llangollen built by Telford to supply the canal system with water.
Chirk Castle – a magnificent medieval fortress, the oldest castle built by Edward I that is still inhabited.
Lift bridges – the Llangollen Canal is noted for the number of ingenious lift bridges (operated by the lock key) that often have to be raised before a narrowboat can pass.
**YOU SHOULD KNOW:**
The joints on Pontcysyllte Aqueduct's iron trough are still sealed using the original mixture devised by the builders – a mixture of flannel and lead dipped in liquid sugar.

*The engineering marvel that is Pontcysyllte Aqueduct*

# Three Rivers Ride

This is part of Britain's National Bridle Network, a series of cross-country routes that is being developed for long-distance horse riders. The way-marked 153-km (95-mi) Three Rivers Ride through the glorious Welsh Marches starts at Tidbach near Bromyard in Worcestershire, enters Herefordshire at Wolferlow and crosses the Rivers Lugg and Wye before entering Wales at Hay Bluff and continuing through the Brecon Beacons National Park to the third and final river – the Usk – finally finishing at the Mountain Centre (Brecon Beacons Visitor Centre) near the town of Brecon.

This really is a scenic ride par excellence, with stunning views all the way. It is a journey of two halves. The first section in Worcestershire and Herefordshire offers a peaceful ride past cider orchards and through classic English countryside, across the rapidly flowing River Lugg and along the breathtaking Wye Valley. After crossing the Welsh border the second section runs through a sweeping bank of hills, along the Western flank of the Black Mountains, skirting the picturesque Llangors Lake and crossing the River Usk.

Some riders do the full journey, whilst others prefer to concentrate on the more dramatic mountain scenery of the 56-km (35-mi) Welsh section. The weather in the Brecon Beacons can be unpredictable, and the Path itself is often far from human habitation, so riders are advised to take appropriate all-weather gear and be sure to tell someone their plans before starting out for the day. Don't assume you can rely on a mobile phone to summon assistance if something goes wrong in the remote Welsh hills – there is rarely a signal.

Those who don't have their own horse will find several riding and trekking stables who can provide mounts for the Three Rivers Ride – including sturdy and locally bred Welsh cobs. A selection of bed and breakfast stops for both rider and horse can be found along the route, together with self-catering cottages that have stables.

*The Brecon Beacons National Park*

**HOW:**
On horseback
**WHEN TO GO:**
May to September for the best weather.
**TIME IT TAKES:**
At least a week for the full Ride – more if undertaking side exploration.
**HIGHLIGHTS:**
A bottle of locally brewed farm cider from one of the village shops in Herefordshire – rather stronger than most commercial brews!
Cefn Hill near Hay-on-Wye – for wonderful views of England to one side and of Wales to the other.
Lord Hereford's Knob – a striking hill on the northern edge of the Black Mountains – those who think the name a trifle rude may prefer to use the Welsh *Twmpa*.
**YOU SHOULD KNOW:**
There is a further riding trail at either end of the Three Rivers Ride – the Sabrina Way in England and the Epynt Way in Wales.

# The Ridgeway National Trail

**HOW:**
On foot
**WHEN TO GO:**
April to October
**TIME IT TAKES:**
About a week
**HIGHLIGHTS:**
The White Horse of Uffingham, cut
into the chalk hillside – the oldest
such figure in Britain, dating from
over 3,000 years ago.
Close to the Trail – the private drive
of Chequers in Buckinghamshire,
country home of British Prime
Ministers since 1921.
Getting there – you'll know the walk
is nearly over when you reach the
Boer War Memorial on Coombe Hill.
**YOU SHOULD KNOW:**
Motorcycles and 4 x 4 vehicles can
use stretches of the Ridgeway at the
western end in summer, and tend to
churn up the surface. Horse riders
and cyclists may also use much of
this National Trail.

*Burial mounds on the ancient
Ridgeway Trail at Avebury*

This chalk ridge path – a National Trail since 1973 – is known as 'Britain's oldest road', having been in use as part of an ancient trade route from the Dorset coast to The Wash since Neolithic times. Roman, Saxon and Viking armies used the Ridgeway and it became a medieval drovers' road. Following 18th-century Enclosure Acts the Ridgeway – formerly a loose collection of paths heading in the same direction – was consolidated into a single road defined by digging earth banks and planting thorn hedges and trees.

The National Trail runs for 139 km (87 mi) through the counties of Wiltshire, Berkshire, Oxfordshire and Buckinghamshire. It starts at Overton Hill near the prehistoric stone circle at Avebury, within a UNESCO World Heritage Site, then follows the high ground across the open, rolling expanse of the North Wessex Downs to the west of the River Thames. It runs alongside the Thames after crossing at Streatley and continues into the secluded beech woods (carpets of bluebells in spring, spectacular foliage in autumn) and gentle valleys of the Chiltern Hills, ending at the top of Ivinghoe Beacon (from whence the Icknield and Peddars Ways continue on to the North Norfolk coast at Hunstanton).

People have been using the Ridgeway for at least 5,000 years, leaving plenty of evidence of their passing. There are numerous ancient monuments to explore, especially in the western section, including the long barrow of Wayland's Smithy and splendid Iron Age forts such as Segbury Camp, Barbury, Uffington and Liddington Castles. The Ridgeway also follows the Iron Age Grim's Ditch, an 8-km (5-mi) earthwork adjacent to the River Thames. Whilst there will be short sections where the hiker meets other people, travelling the Ridgeway is likely to be a largely solitary experience, with the walker able to enjoy its wonderful landscapes without distraction.

# Isle of Man Steam Railway

Once upon a time there was a considerable network of steam railway lines in the ancient kingdom that is the Isle of Man, but time has taken its toll and only one remains – and that was saved from closure in the 1960s by the Marquis of Aisla, who funded the Southern Steam Railway personally until the Manx Government belatedly took it over as a tourist attraction in the 1970s. A further stretch is currently being restored by enthusiasts, and the Groudle Glen Railway provides a limited summer service along a scenic stretch of line near Douglas.

To travel this delightful line is to step back in history – the journey starts at a classic Victorian Station at the end of North Quay in Douglas, and the trains date back to the 1870s (with rolling stock and seven locomotives maintained in the same local workshops that were always used). Britain's longest narrow-gauge steam railway at 24 km (15 mi) runs from Douglas to Port Erin, via Port Soderick, Santon, Ballasalla, Ronaldsway, Castletown, Ballabeg, Colby, Level and Port St Mary. Several of these stations are request stops and passengers can hop on and off as the fancy takes them.

Each train has an open carriage, plus closed first- and second-class carriages. It's a case of 'first come, first served' when it comes to obtaining seating, with no premium fares. The route passes through pleasant countryside with distant sea views, climbing out of Douglas to a summit at Santon Station, before descending steeply towards Ballasalla with good views of sea-cliffs. The line then runs on across beautiful rolling farmland to the delightful seaside town of Port Erin, which has a Steam Railway Museum adjacent to the station.

*Beyer Peacock steam railway*

**HOW:**
By train
**WHEN TO GO:**
Mid-March to October
**TIME IT TAKES:**
About 45 minutes from end to end
**HIGHLIGHTS:**
The ancient Cistercian Monastery of Rushden Abbey at Ballasalla – recently restored and now with an interpretive visitor centre.
Milner's Tower on Breda Head, overlooking the bay at Port Erin – built in 1871 to represent a lock in honour of local benefactor William Milner, a Liverpool safemaker.
In Castletown – Castle Rushen, probably the finest medieval castle in the British Isles.
Ronaldsway Halt – close to the Isle of Man Airport, making this one of the few places in the world where one can travel from airport to town by steam railway.
**YOU SHOULD KNOW:**
There are other worthwhile railway journeys on the island – the Manx Electric Railway on the east side (Douglas to Ramsey tramway), the Snaefell Mountain Railway and Great Laxey Mine Railway.

# South West Coast Path

First trodden by vigilant excisemen who needed to see into every cove and bay in their unrelenting battle with smugglers, the South West Coast Path is a National Trail that hugs some of the most precious coastline in Britain, recognized by the formal status afforded to much if it – the Path goes through World Heritage Sites, National Parks, Areas of Outstanding Natural Beauty, Sites of Special Scientific Interest, a UNESCO Biosphere reserve, past offshore bird reserves... and of course follows a number of designated Heritage Coasts.

This is Britain's longest footpath, stretching for 1,014 km (630 mi) from Minehead in Somerset along the coasts of North Devon, Cornwall, South Devon and Dorset to Poole Harbour. The number attempting the whole path is small, but many hike individual sections or complete the full length in different visits over the years. Those willing to undertake the ultimate challenge must be fit – with all those undulations, walkers who take on the entire path will climb a total of some 27,000 m (88,500 ft) – that's three times the height of Mount Everest – cross 17 large rivers, 300 bridges, 900 styles, skip up 27,000 steps and pass 2,500 way-marks. An epic undertaking indeed!

The West Country is Britain's most popular holiday destination and – whilst there is beautiful countryside and many inland attractions – the real draw is the ocean, the dramatic coastline it sculpted and the heritage created by those who sought to make a living from the sea over countless centuries. Those who walk the length of the South West Coast Path will be rewarded by seeing it all – an extraordinary variety of terrain, dramatic landscapes, seascapes, breathtaking coastal vistas, bustling towns, quaint harbours, delightful villages, beautiful beaches, assorted wildlife and more. It really is the journey of a lifetime.

*An aerial view of Chesil Beach*

# Channel Tunnel by Eurostar

A tunnel linking England and France was first dreamed up around 1800, but Napoleon's rampages and invasion fears put an end to that. In fact, it took nearly two centuries for the dream to become reality, with the opening of the Channel Tunnel in 1994. Known in France as Le Tunnel sous la Manche or simply Le Tunnel, this 50-km (31-mi) double rail tunnel runs from Folkestone to Calais and handles both vehicle shuttle trains plus high-speed passenger services.

The latter are run by Eurostar, offering a fast journey at up to 320 kph (200 mph) between the city centres of London and Paris. With the (somewhat belated) completion of the high-speed line at the English end, it is now possible to take a day trip from one great capital to the other, to do business, shop or just look around.

From London, this stylish journey begins at the excellent new terminal within the magnificent, refurbished Victorian station of St Pancras. There, travellers find everything they need (such as a ticket office, currency exchange, newsagent, cafés and lounges) and some things that are more about setting the mood (like the Champagne Bar). Passengers may carry baggage straight onto the sleek, ultra-modern trains prior to their journey. After speeding through the English countryside via Ebbsfleet International and Ashford Stations, Eurostar shoots through the Tunnel before racing across France via Lille to Paris Gare du Nord. It's a great railway journey that everyone should do at least once.

There are different classes available – Business Premier, Leisure Select and Standard – and Eurostar regularly wins awards for the all-round quality of service it offers. As a result, the service is heavily used and it is advisable to book in advance to be sure of a seat on the train of your choice.

*The Champagne Bar at St Pancras – a fantastic 90 m (295 ft) long*

**HOW:**
By train
**WHEN TO GO:**
Any time of year (but who can resist Paris in the Spring?)
**TIME IT TAKES:**
The fastest London-Paris journey time is two-and-a-quarter hours.
**HIGHLIGHTS:**
A great view of the Dartford Crossing high-level bridge over the River Thames.
The old tunnel-boring machine on display near the English end of the Channel Tunnel.
Crossing beneath the English Channel in just 20 minutes (the ferry on the ocean wave above takes much longer!).
**YOU SHOULD KNOW:**
The American Society of Civil Engineers has included the Channel Tunnel on its prestigious list of Seven Wonders of the Modern World.

# Venice Simplon-Orient-Express

Sadly, one of the great rail journeys of all time – the Orient Express between Paris and Istanbul – ended in 1977 after reaching a peak of perfection in the 1930s when the crème de la crème of society, spies, film stars and the odd femme fatale used this famous service to cross

*One of the beautifully restored carriages*

Europe. The modern Orient Express is less glamorous – a practical, workmanlike sleeper from Strasbourg to Vienna.

Happily, the atmosphere of the original may be recaptured by taking the Venice Simplon-Orient-Express, which offers an old-fashioned leisure experience as it conveys pampered passengers from London to Venice in the lap of luxury. The first leg from London Victoria uses vintage British Pullman carriages, and after a swift trip through the Channel Tunnel the journey to Venice continues using original cars from the old Orient Express, clad in distinctive blue-and-gold livery.

As the train makes its way across France, via Paris, passengers relax in private compartments attended by a personal steward, before cocktails and dinner prepared under the direction of a top French chef. Afterwards, passengers congregate in the bar car, listening to the baby grand piano's tinkling ivories and making new friends. Then it's time to return to a compartment that has been transformed into a bedroom.

Morning sees the train amidst the Swiss Alps as breakfast is served in the compartment. The morning is spent in the bar car drinking coffee and admiring the passing Austrian scenery as Innsbruck comes and goes, before a three-course lunch is served. Then it's back to the bar car as the Italian Dolomites appear, before afternoon tea in the compartment. After crossing the Brenner Pass and passing Verona, just as people are thinking they could get used to travelling like this, the Orient Express crosses the Lagoon and pulls into Venice's Santa Lucia Station.

**HOW:**
By train
**WHEN TO GO:**
March to November
**TIME IT TAKES:**
Two days
**HIGHLIGHTS:**
Eating fine food served in meticulously restored period dining cars where fine linen, silver cutlery and crystal glassware are the norm.
A leisurely visit to the on-board boutique to spend a little pocket money.
Spectacular mountain scenery as the Orient Express passes through the Alps and Dolomites.
**YOU SHOULD KNOW:**
In 1934 fictional detective Hercule Poirot was forced to exercise his little grey cells to solve a murder on the Orient Express (a train which writer Agatha Christie had taken in 1928).

# London to Australia

Since hippies were invented (and gap years became popular), the scenic route from London to Australia has been well trodden by itchy feet. Of course it can be flown in a mere 22 hours, but the scenic overland route is a lot more fun – either going alone or with an organized group.

A classic journey involves travelling from London (by public transport or hitchhiking) through France, Belgium, Germany, the Czech Republic, Austria, Hungary, Romania, Bulgaria, Turkey, Iran, Pakistan, India, Nepal, Myanmar, Thailand, Malaysia, Indonesia, East Timor and (finally!) on to Darwin, Alice Springs, Adelaide and Sydney. The beauty of travelling alone or with a few companions is the fact that there are almost infinite possibilities for varying the route and taking interesting side trips – indeed, an essential part of this rewarding experience is remaining flexible and seeing where the fickle finger of fate points.

However, there are also advantages in joining a pre-arranged bus trip. This choice is good for anyone who has a firm schedule to keep, as arrival is guaranteed after a set period (usually three months), or worries about being on the road alone. It is also ideal for those who enjoy being part of a like-minded group, sharing chores, laughs, companionship and anything else that occurs en route. Also, the itinerary will be planned to provide the maximum number of highlights, including exotic places like the Mount Everest base camp that might not be easy for lone travellers to reach.

The ease of group travel must be set against the loss of freedom to play it by ear and stay or go on as the mood dictates, which many regard as the very essence of this adventurous journey from the top to the bottom of the world. But whichever way you choose it will be the experience of a lifetime.

**HOW:**
By bus/train/boat
**WHEN TO GO:**
Any time
**TIME IT TAKES:**
Three to six months depending on stops along the way.
**HIGHLIGHTS:**
Dracula's Castle in the Transylvanian Mountains of Romania – once the home of fearsome Vlad the Impaler.
Tabriz in the north of Iran – a city of stunning blue mosques and the sort of lively bazaars that are such an essential part of the journey.
World-famous Bagan in Myanmar (formerly Burma) – once capital of the powerful Burmese Empire, featuring literally thousands of amazing temples.
Approaching journey's end – Uluru (formerly Ayers Rock) near Alice Springs in the centre of Australia.
**YOU SHOULD KNOW:**
A certain element of pre-planning is required – many countries require visas that cannot be obtained upon arrival.

*The stunning sight of Uluru as you approach journey's end.*

# Cross the Atlantic on a Cargo Boat

**HOW:**
By ship
**WHEN TO GO:**
April to October
**TIME IT TAKES:**
About two weeks
**HIGHLIGHTS:**
Sunsets at sea.
Being up on the Bridge.
Spotting a whale.
Entering New York Harbor.

In a post-modern age of counting carbon footprints, freighter-travel is about as eco-friendly as it gets, short of a rowing boat. Cargo ships are the life-line of the global economy, transporting containers of goods all over the world. Although they do carry passengers, freighters don't advertise themselves. To book a passage you must be prepared to do plenty of research and be dedicated to the idea of a cryptic adventure into the unknown.

Of all the trade routes, the Trans-atlantic crossing is perhaps the most romantic, harking back to the belle époque, era of the ocean liner. The prospect of crossing the bleak immensity of the Atlantic without any organized on-board entertainment may seem a challenging one, but if you are self-reliant yet

*A container ship enters New York Harbor.*

congenial then a freighter is the ideal way to travel. There is enormous pleasure to be had in wandering between decks, mucking in with the crew, or just sitting outside your cabin reading *Moby Dick*.

On the voyage to New York from Tilbury, London's container port, there comes a point, after the ship has weighed anchor at Rotterdam and Le Havre and there is only ocean ahead, when you may fleetingly feel stir-crazy; until the mesmerizing effect of the sea suddenly makes you aware of your own insignificance in comparison to the immensity of nature and you start to experience a joyful sense of liberation from mundane responsibilities.

After days of nothing but sea and sky, the sight of the Statue of Liberty is both elevating and humbling. As you step down the gangplank into the Land of the Free, you cannot help sparing a thought for the countless numbers who made this crossing before you, at the same time as wondering how anyone could possibly be so foolhardy as to attempt it in a rowing boat.

**YOU SHOULD KNOW:**
Freighters carry a maximum of 12 paying passengers and sail to virtually every destination in the world at less than half the cost of a passenger liner. A certain amount of serendipity is involved in planning your trip since there aren't regular scheduled crossings as there are with passenger ships. Sailing dates as well as ports of embarkation and debarkation may suddenly change without notice. It is important to keep in mind that you are on a working ship and it is not part of the crew's job to entertain or serve you.

# Antrim Coast Road

**HOW:**
By car
**WHEN TO GO:**
Any time of year – winter weather
tends to be relatively mild, though
often wet.
**TIME IT TAKES:**
A mere hour non-stop – but if you
don't linger to enjoy some of the
many attractions along the way
you're not human.
**HIGHLIGHTS:**
Glendun's magnificent viaduct bridge
by engineer Charles Lanyon, built in
1832 – a fine example of the
engineering genius required to
construct the Antrim Coast Road.
Near Ballypatrick – Loghareema, the
vanishing lake…after rain it fills to a
considerable depth but a few days
later is empty again.
A worthwhile detour in Ballypatrick
Forest Park – a loop around
Carneighaneigh Mountain (don't miss
the Megalithic burial chamber).
Culfeightrin Church at Ballyvoy –
complete with exotic palm in the
graveyard and large standing stone
next to the door.
**YOU SHOULD KNOW:**
The Londonderry Arms is a delightful
old coaching inn (now a welcoming
traditional hotel) at Carnlough once
owned by Winston Churchill.

*Red Bay in the Glens
of Antrim*

With an end to the Troubles in Northern Ireland – when Protestant and Catholic activists squaring up to each other frightened away outsiders for several decades – the economy has boomed, especially tourism. It's hardly surprising – Ireland is a delightful country, and the North has its share of fabulous scenery. This is especially true of Northern Ireland's rocky coastline, and the best way to appreciate that is to take a leisurely drive along the Antrim Coast Road, unquestionably one of Ireland's most scenic drives.

This is part of the A2 road, which actually begins in Newry in County Down and runs through Belfast and on to Derry City. The two-lane Antrim Coast Road section was constructed in the 19th century to open up the hauntingly beautiful but then-isolated Glens of Antrim, and is quite an engineering feat. It starts at Larne, then follows the coast through Ballygalley, Glenarm, Carnlough, Waterfoot and Cushendun, where it leaves the sea for an inland stretch before rejoining the water at Ballycastle to complete the journey. However, it is possible to stay with the coast by turning off the A2 at Cushendun and finding Torr Road, a very narrow and winding road that will return you to the A2 at Ballyvoy. This detour delivers truly awesome coastal views, though you will miss the enchanting Ballypatrick Forest Park on the main road. Tough choice!

No denying it, the Antrim Coast Road is stunningly beautiful. Not only does it offer ever-changing vistas of this extraordinary coast, but it also passes glacial valleys, sandy beaches, wooded glens, waterfalls, picturesque villages and ancient sites. Taken together, it all adds up to a very special journey that becomes not only a magnificent scenic drive but also a fascinating voyage of discovery.

# Bushmills to Benone

This well-marked coastal cycle journey officially begins at the famous Giant's Causeway, just outside Bushmills in County Londonderry. The North Atlantic Coast section of the National Cycle Network Route 93 then runs beside the sea for some 32 km (20 mi) to Castlerock.

Bushmills is the first town along the way, after following the tracks of Northern Ireland's only heritage steam railway. Beware – before continuing along the cycleway it's very tempting to visit the famous distillery and take a glass or two of the finest Irish whiskey. Providing the hospitality doesn't get out of hand, the resumed ride passes Dunluce Castle, where the limestone cliffs of the White Rocks end in a dark basalt outcrop crowned by this ancient castle joined to the mainland by an arched walkway, beneath which lies Mermaid's Cave.

It's hard not to pause at either Portrush (built out on the peninsula of Ramore Head) or nearby Portstewart (with the wonderful long beach of Portstewart Strand). These two coastal resorts enjoy wonderful natural settings and have a full range of facilities. From Portstewart Route 93 drops down to the large, bustling town of Coleraine at the mouth of the River Bann. There's no avoiding the crowded streets, because this is the first point at which it's possible to cross the impressively wide river, but that's no bad thing – the town has a fine central square.

After Coleraine, the cycleway follows the river to the seaside village of Castlerock. The North Atlantic Coast section actually ends here, as Route 93 turns away from the sea towards Limavady, so many cyclists simply return to their start point along the main A2 coast road. However, before doing that it's worth going on through Downhill to Benone Strand, one of the longest beaches in Northern Ireland.

**HOW:**
By bike
**WHEN TO GO:**
May to September
**TIME IT TAKES:**
A leisurely three hours end to end.
**HIGHLIGHTS:**
The Giant's Causeway itself – the amazing grouping of interlocking basalt columns that are one of Ireland's most famous (and impressive) natural features. Mountsandel Forest near Coleraine, containing the ancient site of Mount Sandel Fort – said to be the oldest site of human habitation in Ireland. The ruined mansion at Downhill built by Frederick Hervey, Earl of Bristol and Bishop of Derry in the 1770s – see also the circular Mussenden Temple, his library.
**YOU SHOULD KNOW:**
Bushmills is the world's oldest legal distillery, founded under licence from King James I in 1608.

*White Rocks near Portrush*

# Carrick-a-Rede Rope Bridge

**HOW:**
On foot
**WHEN TO GO:**
March to October
**TIME IT TAKES:**
At least two minutes
**HIGHLIGHTS:**
Fabulous views from Carrick Island across to Rathin Island and Scotland. Abundant seabird life around the rocky coastline, plus unique geology, flora and fauna to be found within this Site of Special Scientific Interest. A relaxing cup of tea in the tearoom after completing that daring return journey across the bridge.
**YOU SHOULD KNOW:**
There is a small charge for crossing the bridge, levied by the National Trust – though some suggest they should be paid for trying it!

Only those with the strongest head for heights should make the swaying journey across the rope bridge at Carrick-a-Rede near Ballintoy in County Antrim. Mind you, it's not quite as perilous as it was until recent years, when this rope suspension bridge from the mainland across to tiny Carrick Island consisted of widely spaced wooden slats and a single-strand handrail. At least the modern bridge is a little more substantial, having been rebuilt as a Millennium project by local rock climbers.

It is at the end of a short footpath that offers wonderful coastal vistas, and crosses a chasm that is 23 m (75 ft) deep (don't look down!) between the mainland and the small T-shaped island. The bridge itself is around 20 m (65 ft) long with a pronounced dip in the middle. It was traditionally erected by salmon fishermen who laid their nets off Carrick Island but it's now a magnet for visitors – some 140,000 of them every year, drawn by the magnificent scenery and the challenge of crossing the bridge. It can get crowded in high summer, and as only eight people are allowed on the bridge at any one time it is best to go early (it opens at 10 o'clock every morning).

The bridge is now taken down around the end of November and not replaced until the beginning of March, depending on the weather, as attempts to cross during windy winter conditions would be both foolhardy and dangerous. Although there are no reports of anyone actually having fallen from the bridge, it's not always a return journey. Every year a number of people who have made it across to Carrick Island simply can't face a second trip, and have to be taken off by boat.

*Tourists on Carrick-a-Rede Rope Bridge*

*Weathered trees at Ballydowane Cove*

# Copper Coast Drive

This should be in England's West Country, the old centre of tin and copper-mining in the British Isles. But it isn't, because Country Waterford also has its mining heritage – its cliffs were mined for lead, silver and copper in the 18th and 19th centuries. Mining finished in 1880, but the name Copper Coast remains.

The short journey along this magical road from the seaside town of Tramore offers haunting views of the Comeragh Mountains to one side and the wild splendour of cliffs, beaches, coves and caves to the other. The scenery is indeed magnificent, but that's not all there is to enjoy – the road passes through six delightful villages and each has something to offer.

Fenor has peaceful Kilfarrasy Beach, plus forest and lakeside walks and the Bog of Fenor. Annestown is a tiny hillside village, overlooking a scenic valley and wide bay with a sandy beach and rock pools. Dunhill has ancient Stone Age dolmens and a traditional Irish shop and pub that is an ideal refreshment stop, plus a church on the hill – a superb vantage point.

Boatstrand is a picturesque little harbour, with a path to imposing Dunabrattin Head. To the east, beaches and stacks lead towards Sheep Island, whilst to the west successive headlands recede to Helvic Head. Mining Bunmahon's cliffs gave this coast its name, and evidence of this activity may be seen in the cliffs that flank the beach. There is also evidence of an older occupation – the ruined monastery – and a geological garden. The last of these delightful villages is Stadbally, an ancient place with three beaches and a medieval church and tower. The Copper Coast ends at the harbour town of Dungarvan – a journey long to be remembered.

**HOW:**
By car
**WHEN TO GO:**
April to October
**TIME IT TAKES:**
Allow a full day to see the sights.
**HIGHLIGHTS:**
The ruins of Dunhill Castle, destroyed by the hated Oliver Cromwell in 1649.
One of the best coves on the Copper Coast – Ballydowane Cove near Bunmahon.
The cliff-top mining trail at Bunmahon, with the well-preserved remains of a Cornish-style engine house.
Dungarvan Castle, with a shell keep dating from the time of King John, who appointed the first constable in 1215.
**YOU SHOULD KNOW:**
There are 17 designated UNESCO European Geoparks and the only one in the Irish Republic is...the Copper Coast.

# North Mayo Drive

**HOW:**
By car
**WHEN TO GO:**
Year round, but the weather is best
from March to October.
**TIME IT TAKES:**
Three hours without stopping, but
best enjoyed as a 2- or 3-day jaunt.
**HIGHLIGHTS:**
The archaeological site of the
Ceide Fields.
The glistening Lough Conn.
Rathfran Abbey – one among many.
The stretch around Lackan Bay and
Downpatrick Head.

Drama underpins everything about North Mayo, whether it's the rugged landscape or its often-troubled history. Although only a few hours' drive from Dublin or Belfast, it feels light-years removed from them. The area's population is now lower than it was before the potato famine and those who remain are among the hardiest and most welcoming people to be found anywhere.

The 173-km (108-mi) North Mayo Drive takes you in a loop that starts and finishes in the county's largest town, Ballina. A choice of over fifty hostelries awaits you and good simple food is prepared in most of them. The drive, in essence, links ten communities, each with its own distinct feel. In between there is ample opportunity to visit magnificent abbeys or simply wander along any one of many riverside trails.

Driving counter-clockwise, the road hugs the Atlantic coast before turning inland at Belderrig. From there it travels alongside the picturesque Carrowmore Lough, a perfect place to pull over and have a picnic. As the road swings round and you start the journey back towards Ballina, the peaks of the Nephin Beg Range dominate the landscape and the charming town of Bangor Erris demands that you stop and dwell a while. For those wishing to engage in more rugged outdoor pursuits, a well-appointed hiking trail leads off to the mountains.

This drive is a must for anyone who wants to experience the real Ireland. Around every corner there are symbols of martyrdom and sainthood, of suffering and triumph. It is a land of desolate beauty, where the pace is gentle and the *Craic* is at its most genuine.

*A sea stack at Downpatrick Head*

# The Wicklow Way

**HOW:**
On foot
**WHEN TO GO:**
Year round; more crowded and better weather from May to September.
**TIME IT TAKES:**
Five to ten days depending on fitness or ambition.
**HIGHLIGHTS:**
The views from Croaghanmoira Mountain.
The boardwalk climb up White Hill.
Byrne's pub in Greenane – traditional Irish hospitality.
Powerscourt Gardens – one of Ireland's treasures
**YOU SHOULD KNOW:**
Ireland's reputation for rainfall is well deserved. A good set of waterproofs is a must. Public transport in the area is pretty infrequent, so forward planning is required. Thankfully most of the hoteliers in the area will offer to take you short distances.

The countryside of Ireland is a collage of many different landscapes, including several mountainous and upland areas. One of the most spectacular of these is in County Wicklow, just south of Dublin. Despite its closeness to the capital, the county contains many large stretches of delightfully unspoilt mountain trails of which the Wicklow Way is the best known. In fact, the Wicklow Way was the first such trail in Ireland, having been formally established in 1980.

The Wicklow Way begins in Dublin's southern community of Rathfarnham and travels in a south-westerly direction across the Dublin and Wicklow uplands, then it goes through the rolling hill country of southwest County Wicklow to finish in the small, County Carlow village of Clonegal some 132 km (82 mi) later.

A mixture of suburban parkland, forest trails, wild and scenic mountain landscape and, finally, gently sloping countryside, the trail offers a wonderfully varied experience for the enthusiastic hill-walker. En route the Wicklow Way passes tarns, ruined buildings, occasional memorials to historic events of past centuries and extensive remains of the early Christian monastic settlement in the stunning Glendalough Valley. The central section is covered by the Wicklow Mountains National Park and its headquarters in Glendalough are well worth a visit.

This is a pleasurable, well-marked trail, with tougher sections of the track graded to prevent erosion. The route occasionally follows the Military Road, constructed by the British in the early 19th century in an attempt to root out rebels hiding in the hills. The only downside of the trail is its reliance on forest paths to avoid walking on private land, which at times limits views. However this does little to detract from the superb scenery, craggy narrow valleys and fabulous hills.

# The Ring of Kerry

The Ring of Kerry is the jewel in the crown of Irish tourism; it is easy to see why visitors return time and again to this 178-km (112-mi) circuit of the Iveragh Peninsula. This is a wild and out-of-the-way region, sparsely populated inland but lined with quaint little towns along the coast. Superb scenery bombards the senses at every turn; rugged mountains, perfectly sculpted by the last ice age 10,000 years ago, frame 120 km (75 mi) of unspoilt beaches.

Several operators offer coach tours, but for those wanting greater flexibility, travelling by bicycle or car is the best option. Starting from Killarney, with the wonderfully named Mcgillycuddy's Reeks (Ireland's highest point) to your left, the first port of call is Killorglin, a town where time has stood still. Replete with traditional Irish fare, it is an excellent place to stock up or simply relax and have a meal. From here on the views get even more spectacular and the road between Glenbeigh and Kells offers the most magnificent coastal scenery.

The area is brimming with history and if you can take your eyes off the natural spectacle, the Ring of Kerry provides fascinating glimpses of the ancient heritage of Ireland – Iron Age forts, Ogham Stones and monasteries abound. The route then hugs the coastal road, offering several chances to cross to the Skellig Islands, a paradise for birdwatchers. The loop takes you through the charming towns of Waterville, Caherdaniel and Castlecove, all of which are worthy of exploration and, if you time it right, the sunsets over the Atlantic can be sensational.

The final stretch runs along the Kenmare River until finally, with the water behind you, the road passes through the wooded Killarney National Park, full of rivers, waterfalls, lakes and wildlife.

**HOW:**
By bike or car
**WHEN TO GO:**
Year round
**TIME IT TAKES:**
It can be done inside a day, but the longer you take the more you see. It is worthy of a least a week of anybody's time.
**HIGHLIGHTS:**
Killorglin – home of the pagan Puck Fair.
The beach at Waterville.
Caherdaniel – Derrynane Estate home of Daniel O'Connell.
The 2,500-year-old Staigue Fort.
Picture-postcard-pretty Kenmare.
**YOU SHOULD KNOW:**
The Ring can get monstrously busy in high season (June to August). Just before and just after these times it is quieter and more rewarding.

*Spectacular scenery in the Ring of Kerry*

# Connemara Coast Trail

**HOW:**
On horseback or on foot
**WHEN TO GO:**
Year round, although horse riding is
generally offered from May
to October.
**TIME IT TAKES:**
Around ten days for the experienced
hiker; horse-riding tours are generally
five to seven days.
**HIGHLIGHTS:**
The ferry ride to Inishbofin Island.
Omey strand – a beach par
excellence.
The views over the Atlantic from
Mace Head.
The smoked salmon – the area
produces some of the finest to be
found anywhere.
**YOU SHOULD KNOW:**
Before setting out you should be
equipped for any weather. Storms
can roll in quickly from the ocean
and disappear just as quickly. Good
waterproofs are therefore a must.

Founded in the late 1980's, the Connemara Coast Trail takes you through a landscape of untamed beauty and serves up the most stunning scenery Ireland has to offer. Refreshed by salty zephyrs from the Atlantic Ocean, the traveller is treated to a wonderful mélange of unspoilt valleys, bogs, shimmering lakes and fabulous mountains. The coast itself is blessed with spectacular rocky inlets and the most magnificent long white sandy beaches.

Connemara translates from Gaelic as 'inlets of the sea' and there are dazzling views that greet you at every twist and turn. The trail presents a good challenge for the experienced rider or hiker and has the added bonus of taking you through the Gaelic heartland of Ireland. Even the smallest of settlements is teeming with Celtic culture and history and whilst you would be hard pushed to find someone who didn't speak any English at all, it is a good idea to have a couple of words of Irish, even if it is only to say hello or order a drink.

At all times the views out to sea and the sight of the brooding Twelve Bens inland both compete for your attention. But even in a place so consistently beautiful, the stretch of the coast between Roundstone and Moyrus stands out. Taking you around the dark recesses of Bertaghboy Bay you are treated to ever changing light as the curving pathway seamlessly changes the view.

The coastal trail and its inland sister trail make up one of the most invigorating outdoor experiences in Ireland. It is home to a community intent on preserving what it has and which takes great pride in showing it off to the rest of the world. Come and enjoy.

*Dawn reflections of the
Twelve Bens in Derryclare
Lough, Connemara*

# Sligo Yeats Trail

Nothing evokes the spirit of old Ireland better than the sight of horse and rider silhouetted against the setting sun, and there is no better place to ride than the captivating coastline of Sligo, an area steeped in history and blessed with natural beauty.

Many operators cater for those who wish to indulge in what is now called the Yeats Trail. The preferred option for the experienced rider has to be a self guided tour riding between lodgings. A typical tour starts near the exquisite Streedagh Beach, which is your first chance to slacken the reins and experience the gallop of a lifetime along the wonderful long golden sands. If the tides are right it is possible to ride across to the magical Dernish Island, scene of many a shipwreck. A long soak in the bath, a hearty meal and a pint of the black stuff (Guiness) are your rewards at the end of a long day in the saddle.

The new day arrives with the sun rising over the towering rocks of Benbulben. It is time to shake off any saddle-soreness and remount. This stage takes you along small tracks and down country lanes and then on to the magnificent white sands of Trawbawn. It is then but a small climb to the Cullumore cliffs for an amazing view over Sligo Bay.

Having fed and stabled your horse and done the same for yourself, the final leg of the trip takes you towards Ardtarmon Castle, both sumptuous and rich in history. A ride along Lissadell Beach then takes you on the most challenging part of the trip as you climb steadily up the foothills of Benbulben.

**HOW:**
On horseback
**WHEN TO GO:**
Year round, but best in May and June when the wild flowers are in bloom.
**TIME IT TAKES:**
Allow anywhere between a couple of days to a week.
**HIGHLIGHTS:**
The long sandy beaches – the perfect place to ride.
Inishmurray Island – a monastic settlement founded about 500 AD.
Ardtarmon Castle – family home of Countess Markievicz.
Drumcliffe Churchyard – burial place of William Butler Yeats.
**YOU SHOULD KNOW:**
Intermediate to advanced riding skills are required for this trip. Most operators also do not allow children less than 13 years old.

*Galloping along the golden sands.*

*Arran Quay along the Liffey*

# Cruise the Liffey

**HOW:**
By boat
**WHEN TO GO:**
River cruises operate from Easter to September.
**TIME IT TAKES:**
45 minutes on the water but allow a full day to explore the river and its environs.
**HIGHLIGHTS:**
A stroll through Trinity College.
O'Connell Bridge – a world-class structure.
The nearby fish, fruit and vegetable markets – great for people watching.
Dublin Castle – a short walk south from Grattan Bridge.
**YOU SHOULD KNOW:**
The Liffey is subject to high tidal variation. This can affect the route of the river trip and in some instances lead to cancellation, so check before you set out.

No trip to Ireland's resplendent capital is complete without a trip along its iconic river. So much has changed in recent years for this tiger economy of the Eurozone, and nowhere is the transformation better exemplified than along the shores of the Liffey. It was not so long ago that Dubliners referred to their river as 'the slime' and those who walked near it could not help but notice its special aroma. Much effort and money has been put in it to changing this and, as people started to return to living by the water's edge, the river has improved markedly.

Now proud of its river, the city offers cruises through this most magnificent of urban landscapes. Old and new sit side-by-side, offering up a wonderful mix of historical buildings and stunning new architecture. The downstream journey takes you beneath the world famous Ha'penny Bridge while the commentator waxes lyrical on Dublin's past, taking you on a journey through time, from before the Viking invasion to the point where Cromwell first landed through to the present day.

There are great sights to be seen along the way, most notably Trinity College and the Spire in O'Connell Street. However Dublin does not have a waterfront to rival that of London or Paris. To get the full benefit of what the river has to offer, a cruise should form part of a wider walking tour. Using Fleet Street and Abbey Street as your southern and northern boundaries you can cross the Liffey several times and get a most rewarding view of this wonderful city and its fabled river.

# Amsterdam Tram

Unlike their counterparts in many other European cities, citizens of the Dutch capital never lost their trams – but by the end of the 20th century Amsterdam's extensive network was getting tired, with antiquated cars that were constantly out of service for repair. By 2003, a fleet of new Combino trams came into service, with wheelchair-friendly low floors. These sleek blue-and-white trams have become a welcome sight, operating alongside a number of older cars that have been retained.

Riding the trams is an excellent way of seeing Amsterdam for those who don't have time for the water tour, and the Combinos with their large windows provide a great view of 'The Venice of the North'. New trams went hand in hand with a major refurbishment and extension of the network, a work in progress, but the first fruit was the introduction of a new route – Line 26 from Central Station to the new housing developments of IJburg on artificial islands reclaimed from the vast (and equally artificial) IJsselmeer inland sea – the former being yet another example of the Dutch genius for turning water into dry land, and the latter of their ability to turn salt water into fresh.

Line 26 is inevitably known as the IJtram. This 8.5-km (5-mi) route runs mainly through residential areas, rather than amidst heavy city traffic, and includes the 1.5-km (1-mi) Piet Hein Tunnel. Happily for commuters, it is the only tramline in Amsterdam that accepts non-folding bicycles. It also provides an interesting return journey from the city centre, passing the spectacular new Muziekgebouw concert hall, the passenger terminal where cruise ships dock, the Lloyd Hotel and Eastern Docklands, before crossing IJburg's successive islands. This is not a particularly scenic journey, but the opportunity to see the on-going work of redeveloping Amsterdam's waterfront and IJburg should not be missed.

**HOW:**
By tram
**WHEN TO GO:**
March to October to avoid short days and sometimes bitterly cold winter weather.
**TIME IT TAKES:**
The IJtram takes just 18 minutes from Central Station to the Harbour Island terminus in IJburg.
**HIGHLIGHTS:**
The heart of the old city around Central Station, for the scenic Amsterdam of canals and tall houses at its best.
A visitor centre near the Vennepluimstraat stop on Line 26, which explains the ambitious creation of IJburg.
Crossing the impressive Enneus Bridge that carries both the IJtram and the only road to and from IJburg.
**YOU SHOULD KNOW:**
Amsterdam's trams cross more than 1,500 bridges, often after making the sharpest of turns.

*Riding trams is a great way of seeing Amsterdam.*

# Waterway Cruise

**HOW:**
By boat
**WHEN TO GO:**
April to September
**TIME IT TAKES:**
Around a week from Sneek to Loosdrecht, including time for exploration.
**HIGHLIGHTS:**
Fields full of contented black-and-white Friesian cattle that – unlike others the world over – have never moved from their region of origin.
Mooring up right in the centre of Amsterdam – nip ashore to visit the world-famous Rijksmuseum and the Van Gogh Exhibition.
Loosdrecht Broad, full of uninhabited islands and alive with water birds.
Utrecht – cruise from Amsterdam on the River Vecht, via Loosdrecht, and moor at the quay opposite the Cathedral of Saint Martin.
**YOU SHOULD KNOW:**
There is often a small toll to pay at the well-maintained locks and lifting bridges on Dutch waterways.

The Netherlands is awash with waterways, and one of the very best ways of seeing this distinctive country is by taking a self-drive boat cruise. This is a country where boating is not just a way of spending leisure time but is still very much a part of commercial life, with free mooring everywhere and plenty of shops, bars, cafés and restaurants along the waterside to cater for passing boat traffic. As serene progress is made along rivers, canals and through lakes, the traditional Dutch picture of big skies, windmills (actually they're mostly wind pumps), dykes and other craft of all sorts is constantly repainted – and there will be plenty of interesting towns and villages to see, too.

There is, of course, an almost endless selection of worthwhile routes that may be cruised – and a wide range of hire craft to choose from. But one excellent journey is from Sneek in Friesland to the north, down to Loosdrect south of Amsterdam. Confined only by the length of time for which the cruiser has been booked, the beauty of this trip – and Holland's huge variety of waterways – is that part of the pleasure is planning an interesting individual itinerary with stops and diversions, or simple cruising wherever the mood suggests.

However, the basic route south from Sneek is via Joure (where the world-famous Douwe Egberts trading company was founded in 1753), Ossenzijl (turn off here for the Friesian Lakes), Giethoorn (known as 'Little Venice of the North', with no roads in the old village, which must therefore be explored by water or bicycle), Zwartsluis (home to a fleet of heritage fishing and inland cargo vessels), Strand Horst (a major boating centre), Spakenburg (spot local women wearing traditional costume), Muiden (for Amsterdam side trip, or moor up at nearby Weesp and take the train) and finally Loosdrecht.

*The windmills along the canal at Kinderdijk*

# Keukenhof Gardens

There's only a limited opportunity to enjoy the vast 'Kitchen Garden', which opens for a few short weeks each year. Contrary to its name, Keukenhof has some seven million flower bulbs, which provide an amazing display of spring colour (mid-April sees the daffodils, crocus, narcissi, tulips and hyacinths all in bloom), so is perhaps best described by its alternative name, 'The Garden of Europe'. The world's largest flower garden is located near Lisse, in an area southwest of Amsterdam called the Dune & Bulb Region.

Whilst a visit to the Keukenhof Gardens is an experience to savour, it may be combined with a cycle journey through the surrounding fields, which together deliver an equally spectacular collection of flowering bulbs. Taken together, the garden tour and cycle ride go a long way to explaining Holland's preeminence in the world of horticulture in general and bulbs in particular.

The gardens are easily reached by bus from Amsterdam, The Hague, Leiden, Haarlem and Schipol Airport. Cycles are not allowed within the gardens, but may be hired at the main entrance. A number of proven scenic cycle routes are recommended, ranging in distance from 5 km (3 mi) to 25 km (16 mi). Any of these may be combined with a visit to Keukenhof, or the gardens can be a major port of call on a tour of the bulb fields.

One 'must see' on every cycle tour is the Tulipland Panorama in nearby Voorhout. This mural depicts the bulb fields as they were half a century ago. It is a work in progress, but has already attained a size of some 65 m (215 ft) long by 4 m (13 ft) high. There's only one word for this extraordinary artistic effort and the bulb fields themselves...and that's 'amazing'.

*The tulips at Keukenhof Gardens*

**HOW:**
By bus and bike
**WHEN TO GO:**
Last week in March to mid-May for the Keukenhof Gardens (may vary slightly depending on the weather).
**TIME IT TAKES:**
Allow a full day for visiting Keukenhof Gardens plus a cycle journey – half a day for each.
**HIGHLIGHTS:**
Within Keukenhof Gardens – the largest fountain in Europe, plus an unusual 700-tree labyrinth.
Aalsmeer Flower Auction from the viewing gallery – the largest flower auction in the world held in the world's largest commercial building.
Spring Flower Parade – a wonderful day-long carnival procession through the bulb-growing region every April, from Noordwijk to Haarlem via Lisse.
**YOU SHOULD KNOW:**
You won't exactly have Keuchenhof Gardens to yourself – around 750,000 visitors drop by to be dazzled each spring.

# North Holland's Historic Triangle

**HOW:**
By train and boat
**WHEN TO GO:**
April to September
**TIME IT TAKES:**
Hoorn to Medemblik by steam train
takes an hour (or 15 minutes more
with the intermediate stop at Twisk).
Medemblik to Enkhuizen by boat is
around 75 minutes.
**HIGHLIGHTS:**
The steam museum in Hoorn – for a
splendid collection of vintage
locomotives, rolling stock and
bygone railway artefacts.
Impressive former Dutch East India
Company building in Hoorn
and Enkhuizen.
Zuiderzeemuseum in Enkhuizen –
reached only by water, this is an
atmospheric recreation of a working
fishing village from the past.
**YOU SHOULD KNOW:**
Hoorn is just 30 minutes from
Amsterdam by thoroughly modern
double-decker train.

The 'Historic Triangle' in Noord Holland consists of three small but charming former ports – Hoorn, Medemblik and Enkhuizen. Once fronting the Zuiderzee, since 1932 they have been contained within the freshwater IJsselmeer, the largest lake in western Europe. This area due north of Amsterdam not only offers classic Dutch landscapes of dykes and patchwork fields, but also well-preserved historic towns and villages that grew wealthy in the 17th century as the Dutch East India Company thrived. As always, wealth translated into fine architecture, and there are many splendid buildings from that opulent colonial era to admire.

The classic way of seeing these three is by taking the steam train from Hoorn to Medemblik. With lots of stops and starts for crossings, the preserved 'steam tram' (as the Dutch describe narrow-gauge railways), resplendent in original 1920s livery, chugs and whistles through the countryside, past incurious sheep and cattle and restored stations to Medemblik, complete with period extras that make it perfectly possible to imagine the reality of travelling this delightful line in its heyday.

From there, a steamer takes you on to Enkhuizen from whence the 'Historic Triangle' can be completed by returning to Hoorn by the scheduled train service. It is possible to book combined tickets for the train and steamer legs of the trip, with a 'hop on, hop off' option that allows ample opportunity to explore. But do consult a timetable before attempting to undertake this rewarding journey to be sure you won't be disappointed. The steam train doesn't run between December and February, and there is a limited service only in March, October and November. The train does not always operate on Mondays, so a little pre-planning is required.

*The historic steam train travels through patchwork fields.*

# Luxembourg City Walk

This was one of many tiny fiefdoms that made up the jigsaw of medieval Europe, and the Grand Duchy of Luxembourg has retained its independence to this day. At its heart is the old part of Luxembourg City, once a mighty fortress. Most of the defensive walls were demolished in the 19th century, but the impressive ramparts that remain are now a UNESCO World Heritage Site.

The defensive qualities that made Luxembourg so important in the Middle Ages are based on its location – high above two rocky gorges at the confluence of the Rivers Alzette and Pétrusse. These narrow valleys are up to 70 m (230 ft) deep and spanned by many bridges and viaducts that connect the 24 quarters of this complicated place, which perches atop crags and spills down into the depths. This is also a city of green spaces, at dramatic odds with its bustling streets and squares.

An ideal way to appreciate the unique combination of the city's heritage and natural beauty is to take the well-signed Wenzel Walk – a circular stroll around the oldest areas that is boldly billed as 'a thousand years in a hundred minutes'. This journey through European history focuses on the defensive stronghold at the heart of the old city, beginning at the historic Bock Promontory where Count Siegfried built his castle in the 10th century.

It then visits the Chemin de la Corniche, old city gates, the Wenzel defensive wall, medieval bridges, the Alzette Valley with its medieval waterside buildings and explores extraordinary Spanish and French military works. There are frequent information boards that put the sights along the way into context, or it is possible to take a guided tour. As a bonus, the Wengel Walk not only delivers fascinating insight into Luxembourg's heritage, but also stunning scenic panoramas from commanding vantage points.

**HOW:**
On foot
**WHEN TO GO:**
April to October
**TIME IT TAKES:**
Less than two hours
**HIGHLIGHTS:**
An informative visitor centre in the archaeological crypt beneath Bock Promontory and the Jacob Tower. The red sandstone Castle Bridge, built in 1735 – providing access to the Bock Promontory both on the surface and beneath the ground. The splendidly fortified Rham Plateau with its defensive towers and gates. A warren of underground casements and tunnels hewn into the solid rock by Spanish and French engineers in the 17th and 18th centuries.
**YOU SHOULD KNOW:**
The Wenzel Walk is named after a 14th-century ruler, Duke Wenceslas II, many of whose ambitious fortifications may still be seen.

*Houses on Chemin de la Corniche in the old town*

# Flanders Fields

*Tombstones mark the graves of British soldiers killed in the Third Battle of Ypres, Passchendaele.*

Some of World War I's most intensive fighting took place in the 'Fields of Flanders'. Medieval Flanders no longer exists, but loosely corresponds to the Flemish area in southern Belgium. Around 550,000 soldiers were killed there, with countless more wounded. There are still plenty of reminders of those dark days and a tour of Flanders Fields gives some idea of what that awful conflict was like – though it's hard to equate today's peaceful countryside with vast expanses of liquid mud, shattered trees and ruined towns that characterized the hellish battlefields that once were here.

The place to start is Ypres (in Flemish, Ieper), the medieval city that became the centre of fighting in Flanders. It doesn't have one building more than 85 years old, as the place was reduced to rubble during 1915. The In Flanders Field Museum is on the second floor of the rebuilt Cloth Hall and it provides real insight into the nature of the conflict and the lives (and deaths) of the ordinary soldiers who fought hereabouts.

There are guided minibus tours of key locations for those who appreciate informative commentary, but battlefield maps are available and it is possible to make a more reflective journey alone. Sadly, the hardest moments will be in one or more of 200 beautifully maintained cemeteries containing war dead of all nationalities, known and unknown. Passchendaele was the sight of one of World War I's bloodiest battles in 1917, reflected in Tyne Cot Cemetery, where 12,000 lie. The Sanctuary Wood Museum has thousands of artefacts and photographs, plus a preserved section of battlefield. The eerie Hill 60 is another historic battlefield. There are other evocative locations, too – but whatever route you choose, this is sure to be one of the most moving journeys you ever make.

# Gorges du Verdon

Provence in summer is magical, with superb weather that sets off magnificent landscapes and ancient villages to perfection. One of the most dramatic geological features in the region is the Verdon Gorge, a 25-km (15-mi) long ravine that ranges from 6 m (20 ft) to 100 m (330 ft) wide at the base, 200 m (660 ft) to 1,500 m (4,920 ft) across the top and 300 m (990 ft) deep. Carved from limestone by the turquoise Verdon River, this is the world's second-largest gorge – one French name is Grand Canyon du Verdon. It is also, by general agreement, the most beautiful in Europe.

There are hiking routes within the Gorge, but most people prefer to enjoy its unique charms by driving or cycling one of two winding rim roads. The northern route from Castellane follows the D952 road to Moustiers-Sainte-Marie. The south side may be seen to great advantage by leaving Aiguines on the D71, twisting and turning towards the spectacular Corniche Sublime, one of the very best scenic sections overlooking the Gorge.

For a round trip, take the northern route, but before reaching Moustiers-Sainte-Marie turn south on the D957 along the lakeshore and take the D19 to Aiguines. From there, follow the southern route until it leaves the Gorge at Le Petit Saint-Maymes and continue on the D71 to Comps-sur-Artuby. Turn north onto the D995 to rejoin the D952, and return along the Gorge to the start point at Castellane.

These popular cycling routes are not for the faint of heart or weak of leg – they are strenuous rides that should not be attempted by those lacking fitness. That said, the dividend for those who are up to the challenge is considerable, with sensational views all the way to complement that sense of physical achievement.

**HOW:**
By car or boat
**WHEN TO GO:**
April to September
**TIME IT TAKES:**
Two hours by car (round trip), a full day by bicycle (round trip).
**HIGHLIGHTS:**
The section between Castellane and Rougon where the road runs alongside the river, before plunging into the Gorge at the Point Sublime.
The Museum of Prehistory at Quinson – celebrating primitive man's presence in the area, in a thoroughly modern building designed by English architect Norman Foster.
The large reservoir known as Lac de Sainte Croix where the Verdon River emerges from the Gorge.
On the southern route – the Fayet Tunnel with viewports cut into the walls, followed by the striking Chaulière Bridge over the River Artuby.
**YOU SHOULD KNOW:**
Cyclists should carry an ample supply of liquid – dehydration can be a problem on this physically demanding journey and water sources are few and far between.

*The stunning Gorges du Verdon – France's 'Grand Canyon'*

# Aiguille du Midi Cable Car

*The cable car above the Dent
du Geant*

Once, only a very few people could enjoy the sensational views from the top of the Aiguille du Midi, a sharp-topped peak in the Mont Blanc Massif in the French Alps – and they were intrepid Alpine climbers capable of reaching the summit under their own steam. Nowadays, the panorama may be enjoyed by anyone who rides up from the centre of Chamonix by cable car, in two stages, enjoying terrific mountain scenery all the way.

The pre-war Téléphérique fell into disuse but it was rebuilt, extended and reopened in the 1950s, for many years offering the world's most elevated cablecar journey. It has lost that distinction, but still delivers the world's highest vertical ascent, from 1,035 m (3,400 ft) up to 3,842 m (12,608 ft), with the first stage to the Plan de l'Aiguille at 2,300 m (7,500 ft). The second stage traverses the Pelerins Glacier before rising up the mountain's North Face. Once all the way up, it's possible to enjoy those amazing 360° views of the Swiss, French and Italian Alps, have a cup of coffee and check out the gift shop before catching a return car. But in fact there are other options, winter and summer.

The famed Vallée Blanche ski run begins here, and the nearby Cosmiques Refuge is the starting point of a climb to the summit of Mont Blanc. In summer only, there is another cable car – the 5-km (3-mi) Panoramic Mont Blanc route, open from mid-March to September – across the Geant Glacier to Helbronner Point on the Italian side of the massif. From there, another cable car runs to and from the Italian village of La Palud in the Aosta Valley, facilitating one of the world's most unusual border crossings.

# Paris

An excellent way of conserving shoe leather, whilst seeing Paris, is to ride L'autobus 38 from south to north through the centre of this romantic capital city. As the delightful journey unfolds, the traveller will not only see famous sights but also the hustle and bustle of everyday Paris.

The ancient southeastern gate of Paris, Porte d'Orléans, is the starting point of Route 38's green single-deckers. From there, they pass the Church of St Peter of Montrouge and the superb Metro entrance at Mouton Duvernet. Observatoire de Paris, with its lovely gardens, was created at the behest of Sun King Louis XIV, and appropriately the first map of the moon was made there. Note the chic La Closerie des Lilas in passing – a restaurant once frequented by the likes of Verlaine, Lenin and Ernest Hemingway.

Route 38 passes the 17th-century Luxembourg Palace and Gardens, built for a homesick Italian Queen. A short distance away is the Panthéon, where many of France's greatest citizens are interred and the Sorbonne, where most were educated. Break the journey at Saint-Michel – the square and boulevard are famous meeting-points – then wander over the River Seine to the Ile de la Cité, enjoying a wonderful close-up of Notre Dame Cathedral before catching a Route 38 bus in front of the historic Palais de Justice, passing the grand Hôtel de Ville and reaching the terminal at rue de Victoria. Half the buses stop here.

Those that continue go through what Emile Zola described as 'The stomach of Paris' – Les Halles market area (now the Forum shopping centre). Then it's the George Pompidou Centre and the triumphal arch of Porte Saint-Martin before Route 38 nears journey's end, reaching the magnificent Gare de l'Est and terminating at another piece of splendid Victorian railway architecture – the Gare du Nord.

**HOW:**
By bus
**WHEN TO GO:**
Any time
**TIME IT TAKES:**
This is not a bus journey to take in one go – allow at least half a day to get off and explore along the way… or better still make it a day.
**HIGHLIGHTS:**
The unostentatious monastery shop at avenue Denfert Rocherau, opposite rue Cassini, for a wide range of hand-made goods produced throughout France by monks.
The Musée de Cluny in its 15th-century building at Boulevards Saint-Michel and Saint-Germain – a fabulous collection of medieval artefacts and pictures.
The 136 statues of the great and the good from French history on the façade of the Victorian Hôtel de Ville.
Interesting passages (small covered streets) between Boulevard de Strasbourg, rue du faubourg St-Denis and rue du Faubourg St-Martin.
**YOU SHOULD KNOW:**
Route 38 follows in famous footsteps – Porte d'Orléans is where General LeClerc, greeted by ecstatic flag-waving crowds, entered Paris to liberate the city from German occupation in 1944.

*The Hôtel de Ville*

# Route Napoléon

You may be forgiven for thinking the 'N' in Route N95 stands for Napoléon, especially when you keep passing gilded imperial eagles on stone plinths bearing the legend ROUTE NAPOLEON. Actually, it stands for National as in Route National, but there is a strong connection with the Great Emperor (or Little Corporal, depending on your point of view).

For this 325-km (200-mi) journey from the French Riviera to Grenoble is the route travelled by Napoléon Bonaparte upon returning from Elban exile in 1815, determined to overthrow Louis XVIII. What followed is history – one hundred days that culminated in the Battle of Waterloo, which finally ended the Napoleonic era. He may have had other things on his mind as he journeyed north, but the comeback kid must surely have appreciated the rugged beauty of the mountainous landscape as he went, using a remote route unlikely to bring him into conflict with hostile Royalists.

Starting from Golfe-Juan, Route Napoléon passes through Cannes, where Napoléon's party spent the first night, and up to Grasse with its sweeping coastal views. From there, the road winds to Séranon, where they slept. They proceeded via Castellane to Barrême through heavy snow on day three. On the fourth day it snowed again but they pressed on, taking lunch at Digne-les-Bains before following the River Bléone to Malijai. On the fifth day they progressed through Sisteron (another mandatory French lunch stop!) and Tallard to Gap. The next day saw them complete the demanding stretch over the Col Bayard to Corps, from whence they proceeded via La Mure to a triumphal entry into Grenoble on the final evening. Today N95 is a scenic through road – but in Napoléon's time it was no more than a series of mule tracks and rough trails through the mountains.

*Sisteron in Provence – the perfect spot for lunch!*

# La Méridienne Scenic Route

France's vast and rugged range known as the Massif Central traditionally made communication difficult and isolated southern France from the more economically advanced north. A railway was built through the mountains in the 19th century, but it was not until the end of the 20th century that a really good road was constructed.

The autoroute A75 runs from Clermont-Ferrand to Pézenas, a distance of 340 km (240 mi) and is a work in progress, with the final short section to Béziers still under construction. For all those who head for the Languedoc each summer (and the rather fewer number that use this spectacular road at other times of the year) this extraordinary constructional feat has proved to be a real blessing, offering an alternative route to the old and slow A6 road which became choked with traffic every summer.

Known officially as La Méridienne Bonne Route, the new A75 not only offers a fast, efficient route to the south, but also delivers a wonderful scenic drive as it snakes through the mountains, for much of its length at a height of 800 m (2,600 ft) or more. Along the way there are five mountain passes, three tunnels and eight major bridges or viaducts. Undoubtedly the most impressive engineering (and design) feat is the Millau Viaduct, designed by Norman Foster and appearing to be impossibly delicate as it crosses the Tarn Valley, reaching a greater height above ground than the Eiffel Tower.

Best of all, those enjoying this rewarding journey through the Massif do not have to pay a toll to use the road, which – unlike many French autoroutes – is free. But there is a small charge for crossing the Millau Viaduct, which seems like a bargain – especially to anyone who ever tried to drive through gridlocked Millau during the holiday season.

*A view across to the Millau Viaduct*

**HOW:**
By car
**WHEN TO GO:**
Any time of year
**TIME IT TAKES:**
Around five hours non-stop from end to end at sightseeing speed.
**HIGHLIGHTS:**
The Aire de Marvejols – a rest area with amazing mountain views that is ideal for a picnic.
South of St Flour – an excellent view of a 19th-century engineering marvel, the soaring Garabit Viaduct, a railway arch bridge built above the Truyère River in the 1880s by the master, Gustave Eiffel. Well worth the effort – a diversion from the autoroute at Exit 45 to visit the exhibition centre and (after a climb) the overview that gives a tremendous view of the Millau Viaduct (follow the signs for Observatory).
**YOU SHOULD KNOW:**
If a bottle of champagne had been accidentally dropped from Millau Viaduct's high point during the opening ceremony in 2004, it would have taken eight seconds to hit the ground.

# Chamonix-Zermatt Haute Route

**HOW:**
On foot or on skis
**WHEN TO GO:**
Any time of year
**TIME IT TAKES:**
No less that 12 days on foot and a week on skis.
**HIGHLIGHTS:**
Spectacular views all the way to the Matterhorn from the top of Col Superior du Tour at a dizzy altitude of 3,288 m (10,787 ft).
A welcome break at the picturesque Alpine village of Champex-Lac, surrounded by woods and with a beautiful lake.
A worthwhile short-cut by cable car from Le Chable up the mountain to Verbier – incredible views as you relax, recharge the batteries and let the winding gear take the strain.
Above the impressively sited Vignettes Hut – the best Alpine views you'll ever see from the Haute Route's high point at the 3,796-m (12,454-ft) Pigne d'Arolla summit.
**YOU SHOULD KNOW:**
Even in high summer the walking route is likely to involve crossing patches of snow, using crampons.

Why go on foot or skis when there's a car or public transport available? Actually, if the journey rather than the destination is the thing it makes perfect sense to give a simple answer – 'because I can'. In the case of the Chamonix-Zermatt Haute Route, that reply really means something – this is one of Europe's ultimate physical challenges, and anyone who successfully undertakes this 180-km (110-mi) traverse through the Alps from Chamonix to Zermatt (bridging the spectacular gap between those two iconic Alpine mountains, Mont Blanc and the Matterhorn) can feel proud indeed – around half fail, especially in winter.

The summer walking route, pioneered by 19th-century English mountaineers, crosses Alpine meadows, passes shining lakes, skirts glaciers, goes through forests and visits picturesque mountain villages. There are variations allowing for a personal itinerary. In the case of a summer hike, the basic choice is between the original 'high' route and a lower-level option that avoids collapsing glaciers that have made the high route even more difficult. Along the original route hikers mostly stay at mountain huts, whilst the lower route involves staying in village accommodation.

The winter route, first skied in 1911, is one of the world's most prestigious ski tours, making a tortuous way through the highest and most dramatic Alpine scenery with skiers staying at high huts that allow them to cover considerable distances each day. To carry off this hazardous enterprise, both snow conditions and weather need to be favourable and again there are route decisions to be made, with a number of established variations to choose from, including a reverse journey from Zermatt to Chamonix. Whatever the route, the rewards are exhilarating skiing amidst breathtaking scenery.

Be warned – the Haute Route should only be attempted by parties of super-fit, highly experienced and well-prepared adventurers.

*The best Alpine views you'll ever see from the Pinge d'Arolla summit.*

# Le Train des Pignes

This 150-km (130-mi) rail line, up through the mountains from Nice to Digne-les-Bains, is a nostalgic reminder of a bygone era of railway travel. It is the sole survivor of the Train des Pignes network built during the late 19th century, once consisting of four narrow-gauge lines. Even with the benefit of modern rolling stock the train bounces and rattles as the track follows rushing rivers through steep-sided mountain valleys, reaching places vehicles cannot and making the journey something of an adventure.

The section from Nice to Plan-du-Var is busy, but once the route follows the Var River into the rugged Vésubie Gorge the landscape improves dramatically. The train continues along the river, stopping at delightful old-fashioned stations until it finally parts company with the Var, climbing more steeply up the beautiful Vaire Valley, going through tunnels and looping back on itself to gain the necessary height to continue into the mountains, passing through a 3.5-km (2-mi) tunnel between Méailles and Thorame. The next stage is along the wide Verdon Valley, before another long tunnel carries the train beneath the Col des Robines and along another lovely valley. The final stretch follows rivers through the mountain park of Trois Asses and curves through gentler terrain to Digne-les-Bains, completing this scenic journey par excellence.

It is possible to buy a 'hop on, hop off' ticket for this route (either one-way or return) that allows passengers to disembark along the way, before re-boarding a later train. Picnic sites and walks are signed from many stations and there are plenty of historic villages to explore. For those with steam tendencies, there is a section of the line (between Puget-Théniers and Annot) where like-minded enthusiasts run a service pulled by old steam locomotives at weekends between May and October.

*The ancient walled village of Entrevaux*

**HOW:**
By train
**WHEN TO GO:**
April to October
**TIME IT TAKES:**
About three-and-a-half hours
**HIGHLIGHTS:**
The pretty station at Villars-sur-Var – now also operating as a restaurant and tempting chocolaterie.
A perfect stop-off – the ancient walled village of Entrevaux, complete with drawbridge, citadel, Gothic church and narrow streets.
The village of Saint-André-les-Alpes, at the head of Lake Castillon – the station has a picnic area shaded by giant sequoia trees.
The thermal baths that put 'les-Bains' into Digne-les-Bains – but don't think you're the first to find them (the Romans were here first).
**YOU SHOULD KNOW:**
The term Train des Pignes comes from the fact that pine cones were used as tinder in the fireboxes of the original steam engines.

# Rhône Cruise

**HOW:**
By boat
**WHEN TO GO:**
April to September
**TIME IT TAKES:**
A typical cruise from Chalons-sur-Saône to the sea, with daily sightseeing trips, will last six days.
**HIGHLIGHTS:**
Exploring the traffic-free narrow streets and alleys of the famous old St Jean Quarter in Lyon.
The famous medieval Pont d'Avignon, as immortalized in song, and the impressive Palais des Papes.
The ruined Crussol Castle near Valence – one of the most impressive sights in the entire Rhône Valley.
A visit to those famous free-roaming bulls and white horses in the Camargue's extensive marshlands.
**YOU SHOULD KNOW:**
Once steam propulsion came in during the 1830s, Rhône steamers cut the journey time from Lyon to Arles to just one day – horse-drawn barges took up to three weeks.

The mighty River Rhône rises in the Swiss mountains, flows through Lake Geneva and on into France. Joined by the River Saône, this fickle river used to be hazardous, with fierce currents, unexpected shallows and sudden spates. It was tamed in the 20th century with the construction of locks and other major works – a process that both improved navigation and created several hydro-electric plants.

A cruise down the Rhône is an excellent way to appreciate the river and some of the special sights to be found close to its banks – most organized cruises stop to offer passengers an opportunity to visit places of interest (of which there are many).

Most end-to-end cruises start at Chalons-sur-Saône, to offer an entrée to wine country in the form off those splendid Beaujolais and Mâconnais vineyards, all within easy reach of Bordeaux. The rivers merge at Lyon. From there the first port of call is Vienne, capital of the Roman province of Viennoise. As the ship heads for Tain l'Hermitage this too, is wine country – the famous vineyard-clad Cotes du Rhône slide by as the cruise passes Valence and Montelimar before reaching the delightful medieval village of Viviers. Below Viviers, the boat traverses the extraordinary Bollène Lock and cruises down to Avignon, home of 14th- and 15th-century Popes and Antipopes. It then continues to Arles, the important Roman city that retains many well-preserved reminders of that era. From there, you have a choice of route as the Rhône splits, its two arms (Grand Rhône and Petit Rhône) forming the fabulous Camargue Delta as they proceed to the Mediterranean.

For those who do not wish to take an extended luxury cruise there is, of course, a huge variety of day cruises and it is also possible to hire self-drive boats.

*Vienne on the banks of the River Rhône*

# Riviera Corniches

The French Riviera may be a playground for the rich and famous, but there's much more to the Côte d'Azur than casinos, exclusive villas and harbours stuffed with billion-dollar yachts. This delightful coast stretches from St Tropez to Menton on the Italian border, with Fréjus, Cannes, Antibes, Nice and Monaco along the way. There couldn't be a better way of appreciating the natural beauty and diverse character of this special place than by driving the three spectacular coast roads known as corniches, with each of these parallel highways delivering a different perspective on the Riviera.

The Grand Corniche (La Grande Corniche) is a 31-km (19-mi) cliff-top road, rising to a height of some 450 m (1,475 ft) as it passes above the Principality of Monaco. It was built at the beginning of the 19th century (following the line of the Roman Via Julia Augusta) to facilitate the movement of Napoléon's troops to Italy, and as such does not pass through many interesting places. No matter – the road itself is the star of the show, offering sensational far-reaching views. It is by far the most satisfying way of entering and leaving Nice, and the drive from there to sober Menton is unforgettable.

The 33-km (20-mi) Base Corniche (La Corniche Inférieure) along the shoreline is an altogether different experience – slow-moving and traffic-choked, it was built by a Prince of Monaco and visits each and every place on the Côte d'Azur in turn. This is the way to go if you're interested in the hothouse social and commercial street life of the Riviera.

The Middle Corniche (La Moyenne Corniche) runs between the other two roads, clinging to the escarpment's rocky backbone as it winds through the Mediterranean landscape, offering wonderful views of the coast and the Riviera's towns and villages below.

*Eze can be seen from the Middle Corniche.*

**HOW:**
By car
**WHEN TO GO:**
Any time
**TIME IT TAKES:**
Allow a day to drive all three in turn, with leisurely stops.
**HIGHLIGHTS:**
La Turbie on the Grand Corniche – the symbolic border between Gaul and Ancient Rome, with an impressive Roman colonnade.
On the Middle Corniche – the view of Cap Ferrat from the elevated Villefranche Neck, and (upon exiting a tunnel) the sudden appearance of the dramatic village of Eze, perched high on its soaring rock.
On the Base Corniche – Cap Ferrat... and of course Monte Carlo, where you definitely won't break the bank.
**YOU SHOULD KNOW:**
Princess Grace of Monaco died when her car mysteriously plunged from the Middle Corniche.

# Vosges Wine Route

**HOW:**
By bike or car
**WHEN TO GO:**
May to October
**TIME IT TAKES:**
Allow four days to cycle the Route du Vin at leisurely speed – or a day to drive it.
**HIGHLIGHTS:**
The red-roofed l'église Sainte Colombe in Hattstatt, begun in the 11th century with a 15th-century Gothic choir and 18th-century furniture.
Colmar – it's packed with tourists in mid-summer, but the well-preserved capital of the wine region is far too good to miss.
The Postal Museum at Riquewihr – actually that's a bonus, because the real attraction is that Riquewihr is one of the finest medieval villages in Alsace (which means it beats lots of competition).
The imposing restored castle of Haut Koenigsbourg above the village of Orschwiller.
**YOU SHOULD KNOW:**
The local dialect is more Germanic than French, and many street signs are bi-lingual.

*Riquewihr is one of the finest medieval villages in Alsace.*

Much of Alsace looks as though it has been created as the backdrop for a Hansel-and-Gretel fairy tale...or maybe a Disney film. The picturesque medieval villages with their brightly painted half-timbered houses vie with each other to put on the best floral display, as they sit in an undulating landscape beneath rocky crags topped with romantic ruined castles, surrounded by terraced vineyards that produce the region's famous white wines.

The 200-km (130-mi) Route du Vin runs through the foothills of the Vosges, following the western edge of the wide Rhine Valley from Marlenheim west of Strasbourg to Thann, near Mulhouse. It winds from north to south and biking is an excellent way of fully appreciating this delightful area, though fitness is required – there are plenty of thigh-sapping hills. For car drivers with a discerning palate, the journey can be a battle against temptation – there are free roadside *dégustations* (wine tastings) at almost every turn, along with endless *caveaux* (commercial wine cellars) imploring you to 'try before you buy'.

Apart from wine and related matters, the glory of this journey is the number of unspoiled Alsatian villages and small towns to be visited, each with its own unique selection of regional food and wine to be sampled. There are nearly 70 such villages and the Route du Vin is loosely divided into four stages: Thann to Wettolsheim; Colmar to Ribeauville; Bergheim to Bernarsdwiller; Obernai to Marlenheim. In summer and autumn there's a wine or food festival almost every weekend at one village or another, with generous wine tasting, a surfeit of local delicacies and hand-made arts and crafts on offer... just follow the unmistakable sound of traditional Alsatian music.

# Echoes of Rimbaud & Verlaine

*The old mill at Charleville-Mézieres*

The names of Jean-Nicholas-Arthur Rimbaud and Paul Verlaine may not mean all that much to today's world citizens, but these 19th-century literary giants are French national heroes. The poet Rimbaud made an enormous impact in his home country, and the older Verlaine was an eminent Symbolist poet who invited Rimbaud to Paris, where the pair soon started living a Bohemian life of hashish- and absinthe-fuelled excess.

Rimbaud was from the Ardennes, the region of rolling hill country and extensive forests that is mainly in Belgium and Luxembourg, but extends into France. He returned there after his relationship with Verlaine ended badly (the drunken Verlaine shot him in the hand), walking endlessly through the countryside and writing poetry. He then travelled extensively, working in many exotic parts of the world, before he died at the age of thirty-seven in Marseilles and was interred in the family vault at Charleville. Ironically, Verlaine also spent time in the Ardennes after Rimbaud had departed, working as a teacher.

Today, it is possible to follow in their footsteps through this beautiful region by taking the Route Rimbaud-Verlaine. This 150-km (95-mi) pilgrimage from the Old Mill in Charleville-Mézières to the Auberge du Lion d'Or in Juniville has been devised as a themed route that includes places where the poets lived, worked and caroused, and has therefore been well mapped and described for the would-be traveller. It is a journey that may be made on foot, bicycle or by car.

Although this is called the Rimbaud-Verlaine Route, and the links with the two poets form an interesting extra dimension, in truth this journey is really about exploring the beautiful and – in tourist terms – largely undiscovered Ardennes countryside and its interesting towns and villages.

**HOW:**
On foot, by car or bike
**WHEN TO GO:**
September or October for the splendid autumn foliage.
**TIME IT TAKES:**
Allow one day by car, two on a bike or around a week to complete the walk.
**HIGHLIGHTS:**
Rimbaud's grave and dedicated museum at the town where he was born – Charleville-Mézières.
Roche, where Rimbaud wrote his famous prose poem *Une Saison en Enfer* (*A Season in Hell*), supposedly in a laundry.
Rethel, where Verlaine taught at the higher education college and Coulommes, where he stayed.
**YOU SHOULD KNOW:**
Don't expect to find a coach tour that lets you do the Rimbaud-Verlaine Route the easy way – some of these tiny country roads are simply not suitable for buses.

*Hennessy Cognac tour boat on the River Charente*

# River Charente Cruise

**HOW:**
By boat
**WHEN TO GO:**
April to September
**TIME IT TAKES:**
At least two weeks for an end-to-end sightseeing cruise (a month's better if you can afford it!).
**HIGHLIGHTS:**
At Saintes – a large number of important Roman remains from the time when this was one of the most important towns in Gaul.
A trip on the *gabare* (traditional Charente cargo boat) *La Dame Jeanne* from the Quais du Port in Cognac.
Angoulême – a lovely old town with fine 17th- and 18th-century streets, plus Cathédrale de St Peter with its stunning Romanesque façade, a grand château and cartoon museum.
Tasting fine brandy – visit the famous names in Cognac itself (Hennessy, Martell, Rémy Martin among others) and nearby Jarnac (Courvoisier).
**YOU SHOULD KNOW:**
In the late 16th century King Henri IV of France described the River Charente as 'the most beautiful stream in my kingdom' – his favourite river must have been quite something!

It doesn't take long for a tamed river to revert to the wild, and that's pretty much what happened to the River Charente in western France after commercial traffic ceased in the 1950s. It rises in the Haute-Vienne and flows into the Bay of Biscay near Rochefort, just south of La Rochelle, once forming a major transport artery that brought prosperity to the Cognac region.

Happily, the Charente's fortunes have been restored by the arrival of waterborne tourism, with major works restoring navigability. It is now possible to sail down from Angoulême via delightful towns like Jarnac, Cognac and Saintes to the bustling ship building port of Rochefort. And this process is still new enough to ensure that the Charente isn't solid with boats from bank to bank all summer long.

That said, small (for up to eight people) boats are available for hire at many marinas along the Charente (by the day or for longer) and navigation is easy. The popular choice is a cruise that allows leisurely exploration of the chosen area. For those with deep pockets, an end-to-end trip from Fleac near Angoulême to Rochefort would deliver a dream holiday – along all 170 km (105 mi) of navigable water, passing through 21 locks on the canalized section as this idyllic river meanders through its beautiful valley.

Anyone who undertakes this journey will appreciate why so many put France at the top of their holiday wish list, because such a cruise ticks all the boxes that make the French countryside such a special destination – incomparable pastoral landscapes, a timeless river, ancient villages and towns with traditional markets, vineyards, fine churches and splendid châteaux, history everywhere. Of course the modern world has impinged on that idyllic image of rural France, but somehow that's easy to forget when cruising the Charente.

# The Loire Valley

The Loire Valley is known as 'The Garden of France and Cradle of the French Language'. The lush landscape combines with architectural and cultural heritage to make this an area of outstanding natural and cultural excellence. High on everyone's list of special attractions are the numerous châteaux along the river – around a thousand remain in the Loire Valley out of a total that was once much greater, with some 300 along the river itself. The reason for this over-abundance of great houses is simple – just about every one of the country's serious movers and shakers – from kings on down – built here over the centuries.

The Valley between Chalonnes-sur-Loire and Sully-sur-Loire is classified as a UNESCO World Heritage Site, and this is an ideal section for an extended cycle tour. Starting at Chalonnes and heading east, the route follows the river to Angers, Saumur, Tours, Amboise, Chaumont-sur-Loire, Blois, Beaugency, Orléans, Châteauneuf-sur-Loire and finally Sully. The distance is around 300 km (185 mi). The riding is not too hard, and this is a splendid way to see and appreciate the best that the Loire Valley has to offer – which is very good indeed.

What an experience – the banks of this delightful river are ablaze with sunflowers and home to the finest examples of the castle-builder's art, from imposing medieval fortresses like Angers and Amboise to Renaissance masterpieces like Chambord and Chenonceaux and spectacular gardens like Villandry. This is also the home of great white wines, with the vineyards of great domaines everywhere, so there will be plenty of opportunity to sample fine vintages and enjoy the distinctive local cuisine (river fish a speciality!).

Shops in most of the Loire towns rent bicycles by the day for those who prefer to explore locally rather than make the full journey.

**HOW:**
By bike
**WHEN TO GO:**
April to October
**TIME IT TAKES:**
A week to cycle from Chalonnes to Sully, with ample sightseeing time included.
**HIGHLIGHTS:**
The Royal Abbey at Fontevraud – resting place of the English King Henry II, his wife Eleanor of Aquitaine and their son Richard the Lionheart.
Leonardo da Vinci's manor house at Clos-Lucé near Amboise – now a museum dedicated to the great man and his revolutionary ideas.
The château at Cheverney – see stunning interiors full of original furniture, tapestries and paintings (plus a Tintin museum...this is Captain Haddock's Castle).
A side-trip to see the extraordinary troglodyte dwellings of Les Goupillières near Azay-le-Rideau on the banks of the Indre River – the caves were made by quarrying the limestone used to construct the magnificent château.
**YOU SHOULD KNOW:**
The fairy-tale château of Ussé, begun in the 15th century and re-modelled in the 1600s, provided inspiration for the timeless tale of Sleeping Beauty.

*A bridge crosses the Loire near Château d'Amboise.*

*Mountain bikers enjoy the view of the cliffs of the Gorge de la Jonte.*

**HOW:**
By bike
**WHEN TO GO:**
September or October to miss the crowds and enjoy spectacular foliage.
**TIME IT TAKES:**
It's well worth a full day for the round trip.
**HIGHLIGHTS:**
Be sure to stop and enjoy one of the very best viewpoints on the entire route – the Belvédère des Terrasses. A side-trip to the fabulous limestone cave of Aven Armand between Meyrueis and Saint Enimie.
The 16th-century Château de Roquedols near Meyrueis – a sturdy 15th- and 16th-century castle in the forest that doubles as an information centre for the National Park (castle open July and August only, grounds all year).
The bizarre Le Rozier Museum in a former priory – an extraordinary collection of miniature buildings loving created using tiny blocks of the region's natural stone (open June-September).
**YOU SHOULD KNOW:**
Birdwatchers flock to the Jonte Gorge for the rare opportunity to see three species of vulture circling (Black, griffon and Egyptian vultures).

# Jonte River Gorge

The Cévennes Mountains are in the southern part of the Massif Central, a place described as 'being between land and sky' – an assessment that's easy to appreciate when standing on high ground beneath a big sky, looking out over wooded hills that roll away into the far distance. This area has been accorded National Park status and is an unspoiled wilderness, but this land of dramatic moors and gorges, rivers and forests, medieval towns and little villages that cling to hillsides is a well-kept secret as far as mass tourism goes.

To get a feel for this special area, cycle the round trip along the short Gorge de la Jonte from Le Rozier to Meyrueis – but be warned that you will have to make a serious physical effort to earn those scenic rewards. The Jonte River rises in the Massif du Mont Aigoual within the Cévennes National Park and runs into the Tarn River at Le Rozier. The Jonte Gorge may not be quite as spectacular as the nearby Tarn Gorge, but it has a romantic charm all of its own.

For a ride to remember, this takes some beating. The outward journey from Le Rozier is the hard part. It's just 19 km (12 mi) long, though this is a demanding climb. But with the help of gravity the run back down from Meyrueis to Le Rozier makes all that effort worthwhile, as the narrow road snakes above the blue river, within the V-shaped Jonte Gorge with its rocky sides rising to the high plateau of the Grandes Causses. This really is a journey through breathtaking scenery – a genuine case of 'seeing is believing'. And if you duly like what you see, over 200 km (125 mi) of dedicated cycle paths await within the National Park...

# Brittany's Emerald Coast

Brittany is a jewel in France's coastal crown, as the soubriquet 'Emerald Coast' suggests. The Breton coast is a wonderland of cliffs and seascapes, magical islands and estuaries, beaches and coves, fishing villages and ports...and a gastronomic delight for lovers of seafood and rich regional cuisine. It's possible to spend a lifetime exploring this endless coastline but an excellent introduction to the sort of delights to be found is provided by a round-trip cycle ride from Saint Malo via Dinan to Dinard and back. This offers excellent seascapes, sandy coves, fishing villages and (as a bonus) some lush Breton countryside.

The easy journey (no steep hills!) starts beside the River Rance at Saint Malo (cycle hire available), setting off in an easterly direction along the D201 coast road that hangs above the sea, through Rothéneuf to Cancale – the picturesque fishing village famed for its delicious oysters. From there, head south to Les Portes Rouges and pick up the D155 – the spectacular Rue du Bord de Mer that hugs the coast to Le-Vivier-sur-Mer. Stay with the D155 as it turns south to Dol-de-Bretagne, then turn onto the D676 and ride to the walled town of Dinan, high above the River Rance. This last stretch provides an opportunity to enjoy rolling Breton countryside, as does the next.

From Dinan, take the D2 through La Hamonais to Ploubalay, where the D786 returns you to the coast at Lancleuc, from whence the road follows the sea to the Belle Epoque resort of Dinard, the 'Cannes of the north', via the charming fishing villages of La Chapelle and Saint-Lunaire. A ferry across the mouth of the Rance completes the scenic circuit to Saint Malo. Appetite whetted, you'll surely be back to see more of the Emerald Coast next year!

**HOW:**
By bike
**WHEN TO GO:**
April to October
**TIME IT TAKES:**
It can be done in a day, if you're not tempted to linger along the way (you will be).
**HIGHLIGHTS:**
Saint Malo – this dramatic walled port city is worth a day of anyone's time, with many splendid sights to see, including Chateau Saint Malo, Cathédral de St Vincent and the Solidor Tower.
Dinan – for historic attractions including the Chateau Dinan, Duchess Anne's Tower, the 13th-century Jacobins Theatre, St Saviour's Basilica and the flamboyant Gothic l'eglise de St Malo.
A side-trip from Dinan to the grand Château de la Bourbansais with its wonderful garden and appealing zoo that nurtures endangered species.
A treacherous skip across from Brittany into Normandy to visit one of France's most famous attractions – the Benedictine abbey and medieval dwellings of Mont St Michel.
**YOU SHOULD KNOW:**
The infamous house above the Bates Motel in Alfred Hitchcock's famous thriller *Psycho* was modelled on a villa near the Ecluse Beach in Dinard, where the great director spent many summers.

*Saint Malo*

# Normandy Beaches

It's easy to jump into a car and whiz along the Normandy Coast from the mouth of the River Orne to the Varneville Dunes on the Cotentin Peninsula. It's a pleasant journey, as the coast road passes sand dunes with wide expanses of sand beyond and a series of small seaside towns. For most visitors today, this is the place for relaxed sun, sand and seafood holidays.

Nothing hints at the drama played out here when Allied troops stormed ashore on D-Day – 6 June 1944 – to begin a fight to liberate France that saw 100,000 dead and dozens of Normandy's towns and villages destroyed. From east to west, the invasion beaches were codenamed Sword, Juno, Gold, Omaha and Utah. Sword stretches from Ouistreham to Saint-Aubin-sur-Mer, and here British forces came ashore. From Saint-Aubin to Courseulles-sur-Mer was Juno, where Canadians landed. Gold occupied the next 8 km (5 mi), again attacked by British troops. Omaha Beach was another stretch of

broad sand from Saint-Honorine-des-Pertes to Vierville-sur-Mer, where American troops sustained heavy casualties. By contrast, the Americans found Utah Beach between Pouppeville and La Madelaine to be lightly defended.

Little evidence of the furious battles that raged here survives, though the sheer size of these beaches makes it easy to imagine the enormous scale of operations. Some traces are left – like remains of the astonishing Mulberry Harbour that was towed across the Channel to Arromanches and many German bunkers, notably at Pointe du Hoc on Omaha beach, where cliffs are pitted with shell holes. Also, nearly every town has a D-Day museum and war memorial that helps to bring the reality of the savage fighting that took place along this coast to life, as do numerous Allied and German war cemeteries. It's a drive that's well worth making – a journey of solemn remembrance.

who died but were never identified for burial.

The modern Juno Centre above the beach of the same name, commemorating the Canadian involvement in D-Day. Here also is a memorial to the French Resistance and a preserved German bunker.

A side trip to Bayeux – damaged in the Battle of Normandy, sympathetically rebuilt and home of both the famous Bayeux Tapestry and a magnificent cathedral.

**YOU SHOULD KNOW:**
The first Allied soldier to die in combat on D-Day was Lieutenant Denholm Brotheridge, killed during the British glider-borne night attack on the now-famous Pegasus Bridge over the Caen Canal near Ouistreham.

*Gold Beach at Arromanches*

# Cathar Castle Walk

The Sentier Cathare is a 250-km (155-mi) trek from Port-La-Nouvelle on the Mediterranean near Narbonne, through the breathtaking Languedoc countryside. It is so called because – in crossing the Corbières and Pyrenean foothills of the Aude en route to Foix, in Ariège – the walk passes nine ruined Cathar castles. These 'castles in the sky' are picturesque ruins built high on rocky pinnacles by the Cathars, a Christian religious sect with mystic links to the Holy Grail that emerged in the 11th century, before being crushed as heretical by the Catholic Church in the bloody Albigensian Crusade of the early 1200s that is said to have cost over a million lives.

As a result, France acquired lands that were more Catalan than French, and it is through this wonderful terrain that the Sentier Cathare passes. The trail is way-marked with red-and-yellow signs (combining the colours of Languedoc and Catalonia), and is divided into manageable daily stages of around 20 km (12 mi). The trail is well maintained and – whilst there are some quite steep and rocky sections – it can be safely tackled by anyone who is fit. It might best be described as a challenging hike rather than demanding mountain trek, and there are rest houses and gites d'etape where travellers can bed down at the end of each day.

This exceptional walk combines a tangible sense of history with an exceptional landscape and the clean mountain air that together make it a joy to be afoot (or in the saddle, as the trail is also popular with horse-riders). Staging points on the journey are Durban, Padern, Duilhac, Galamus, Bugerach, Quillan, Puivert, Espezel, Comus, Montségur and Roquefixade. The western end of the Sentier Cathare towards Foix has the best Cathar remains, and also some of the best landscape.

*The remains of Château Peyrepertuse*

# Canal du Midi

In the 17th century boats provided the most efficient way to carry goods – but waterborne commerce between northern and southern France was fraught with danger, as ships had to sail around hostile Spain, running the gauntlet of Barbary pirates on a month-long voyage. Solution? Build a canal that links the Atlantic Ocean to the Mediterranean Sea.

The result was the 235-km (145-mi) Canal du Midi, connecting Toulouse on the Garonne River to the Mediterranean port of Sète. Opened in 1681, it was a monumental engineering achievement with over 300 significant structures, including more than 100 locks, many bridges, several dams and a tunnel. For three centuries this extraordinary waterway served its purpose well, bringing prosperity along its length, and since commercial traffic ceased in 1980 it has become Europe's most popular leisure waterway.

It's easy to understand why. The Canal du Midi goes through stunning countryside and time has been kind, mellowing the canal to the point where it seems like a graceful extension of the landscape as it meanders through Cathar country, passing towns and villages that have preserved their traditional character and charm. Cruising the canal is hugely popular and there are many options for those who wish to experience the delights of this unique waterway, now a UNESCO World Heritage Site.

It is possible to travel from end to end (either way) on cruise boats, which usually offer additional sightseeing opportunities along the way. This journey can also be done by hire craft, though the schedule often demands a hectic pace with little time to stop and explore. Most people prefer to focus on a section of the canal (often one with no locks!) and proceed slowly, opting for one of the many different types of craft on offer from numerous boat-hire establishments and enjoying a truly relaxing holiday in wonderful surroundings.

**HOW:**
By boat
**WHEN TO GO:**
April to October
**TIME IT TAKES:**
At least a week for an end-to-end cruise without sightseeing stops. Boat hire available from one day upwards for custom cruises.
**HIGHLIGHTS:**
The Malpas Tunnel, the world's first-ever canal tunnel, under Ensérune Hill in Herrault – there are now two more tunnels beneath it, a railway tunnel and a drainage adit.
A typical canal-side village – there are dozens to enjoy, but a fine example is Capestang with its fine stone bridge, splendid fortified church and picturesque central square.
Wine – the canal runs through France's most prolific wine-producing region, so there are endless opportunities to stop and taste.
Surrealistic wood sculptures lining the canal at Aiguille, near Puichéric – created by an artist who is also the lock-keeper (or the lock-keeper who is also an artist).
**YOU SHOULD KNOW:**
The Canal du Midi was created by visionary Languedoc tax collector Pierre-Paul Riquet, but the enterprise bankrupted him and debts incurred in building the canal were not paid off for 100 years.

*The Canal at Capestang*

# Le Petit Train Jaune

The Languedoc-Roussillon Region's Little Yellow Train – operated by the French national rail company SNCF – runs from Villefrance-de-Confluent over a 63-km (39-mi) route that climbs steeply to Bolquère in the Catalan Pyrenees – the highest station in France at a giddy 1,593 m (5,225 ft). From there, le Petit Train Jaune crosses the plateau beneath the brooding presence of the Cerdagne Massif to Latour-de-Carol, where it connects with two mainline services – to Barcelona and Toulouse.

In summer, these quirky red-and-yellow narrow-gauge trains are much appreciated by tourists, as they run through dramatic mountain scenery, passing through many tunnels and over viaducts and bridges. In winter (with a snow plough fitted to the front) the reduced twice-daily service carries skiers and acts as a lifeline for the isolated communities along the line.

This service has been running for over a hundred years, and (much to the dismay of purists) the characterful original rolling stock – which is becoming increasingly difficult to service and repair – has now been supplemented by modern units, though heritage trains still run all summer long. Both types are 'multiple units', where electric motors are spread along the length of the train to permit the train to climb (and more importantly descend!) steep inclines safely – until this was developed around 1900, a rack-and-pinion system would have been the only option for le Petit Train Jaune.

Things to watch out for along the way are the mountainside village of Olette (spot the tall houses jutting precariously over the river), the fortified village of Mont Louis and the futuristic 'solar oven' at Fort Romeu...and of course the mountain scenery, which speaks for itself.

**HOW:**
By train
**WHEN TO GO:**
Any time of year
**TIME IT TAKES:**
Around three hours (up) and about 20 minutes less (down).
**HIGHLIGHTS:**
Before starting – a tour of Villefrance-de-Confluent, an unspoiled medieval town within its original walls...don't miss sensational views from Fort Liberia above the town.
Riding at one with nature in one of the train's open-top carriages with bench seats, known by the locals as 'bathtubs'.
The splendid viaduct across a rocky valley at Séjourné – one of around 650 major engineering feats along the line.
**YOU SHOULD KNOW:**
With typical French ingenuity, the line is powered by its own hydro-electric generators on the River Têt.

*The Yellow Train passes over the viaduct at Séjourné.*

276

# Pyrenean Haute Route

This 800-km (500-mi) trek runs from Hendaye on the Atlantic to Banyuls-sur-Mer on the Mediterranean. It takes the high line along the spine of the mountains, avoiding centres of human activity. Though it rarely strays too far from useful facilities, the Haute Route Pyrénéenne (HRP) from one end of the Pyrenees to the other is not always well marked (good maps are essential) and there is little prospect of rescue in case of difficulty. It is therefore an undertaking reserved for adventurers experienced in demanding back-packing, as the sheer length of the journey precludes professionally guided trips. That said, many people choose to hike shorter sections of this superb mountain route alone or with an organized party.

The HRP is one of Europe's classic hikes and is definitely the highest, most beautiful, dramatic and challenging walk the Pyrenees can offer, as it weaves to and fro across the French-Spanish border. Although not way-marked, the path is generally well defined, and there are a number of refuges along the way that allow the intrepid walker to 'stay high' and rarely descend into the valleys. The true joy of walking the Pyrenees – apart from the rugged mountain scenery – is the fact that this is one of Europe's last great wilderness areas.

There are many variants along the HRP where trekkers can choose alternative paths – for example to avoid the few sections that require the use of crampons and an ice axe. If you are only able to spare a limited amount of time, be sure not to miss the section containing the spectacular Ordesa Gorge and the Cirque de Gavarnie, a breathtaking natural amphitheatre. Other rewarding short-trek options are the major summit ascents (choose from ten, Pico Aneto being the highest).

**HOW:**
On foot
**WHEN TO GO:**
Mid-June to mid-September
**TIME IT TAKES:**
Allow around six weeks for the sea-to-sea journey
**HIGHLIGHTS:**
The Pic du Midi d'Ossau (known as 'the Matterhorn of the Pyrenees'), a striking twin-headed peak.
Aigues Tortes National Park, an area of outstanding natural beauty sprinkled with deep-blue glacial lakes.
The Pic d'Ansabère, with extraordinary fingers of limestone rock that look like organ pipes.
**YOU SHOULD KNOW:**
Emergency rations are essential – one of the main difficulties in walking the HRP is that food supplies cannot be replenished every day.

*Wonderful scenery makes this very arduous trek worthwhile.*

# Corsican Mule Trails

**HOW:**
On foot
**WHEN TO GO:**
May to September
**TIME IT TAKES:**
At least two weeks for the entire GR20 route.
**HIGHLIGHTS:**
Reaching the summit of Mount Alcudina, the high point of the GR20's southern section at 2,134 m (7,001 ft) – see both coasts...and the demanding terrain that lies ahead! A short detour to the summit of a 'lookout mountain' – Paglia Orba with its stunning panoramic views. Meeting the shepherds who still take their flocks of sheep and goats to the high pastures in summer.
The lovely glacier lake, Lac de Nino – surrounded by greensward that is likely to be populated by grazing mules, ponies and cattle.
**YOU SHOULD KNOW:**
Napoléon was born in Corsica, and after hiking the GR20 you'll have a pretty good idea why he was such a determined character.

As its rises abruptly from the Mediterranean, with pink granite peaks that soar to a height of over 2,500 m (8,200 ft), Corsica is often described as the 'mountain in the sea'. What's more, many aficionados of the long-distance hike say that Corsica's Haute Route GR20 (GR stands for Grandes Randonnées) from coast to coast is Europe's finest mountain walk. There may be other contenders, but there can be no denying the fact that this is a supreme physical challenge.

Paths are well defined – most are former mule trails – and clearly marked. But they are often rough underfoot with many steep ascents and descents. It is rarely possible to progress for more than 16 km (10 mi) in eight hours of demanding hill walking. From south to north, the GR20 follows the high mountains that divide the island's two regions, starting amongst the soaring pinnacles around Conca.

The path goes through woods and alpine meadows, crossing high ridges, bare granite slopes and deep gorges. It demands fitness and endurance, but the reward is a fantastic experience – sensational scenery, nights spent in refuges or old shepherds' cabins and the opportunity to gain insight into one of the few mountain communities in Europe that still maintains a traditional way of life, barely changed for centuries.

This is not an adventure that can be fully vehicle supported and most people attempting the G20 from end to end do so as part of an organized party with logistical support, so they have to carry no more than the supplies needed for the day's hike. Alternatively, it is possible to arrange for a local guide, who will supply mules that carry everything needed to ensure that this spectacular journey may be made with little recourse to the modern world.

*Montemaggiore and the Corsican mountains*

# Via de la Plata, Santiago de Compostela Pilgrim Route

Santiago de Compostela, the 'Jerusalem of the West' was Europe's first tourist destination. Ever since the 9th century, when skeletal relics supposedly belonging to St James (Santiago's namesake) were discovered, people have been flocking here on the premise that the Way of St James pilgrimage cuts in half the time to be spent in purgatory. Walking along one of the many traditional routes that lead here from all over Europe is as popular a journey today as it has ever been.

The Via de la Plata is one of the least-travelled of the Ways of St James – an uplifting 1,000 km (625 mi) physical and spiritual trek for anyone who would prefer to walk in contemplative solitude rather than socialize with the throngs of wayfarers along the much better known Camino Francés. It follows the path of the old Roman Road from the orange groves of Seville to the northern market town of Astorga, where it merges with the Camino Francés east-west route. Much of the path is a reminder of how it must have been two thousand years ago, with Roman bridges and ruins, original paving and ancient milestones. You walk across open country of fields and olive groves, woods and moors, passing through some of Spain's most beautiful cities and stopping off at pilgrim *refugiós*.

The road runs through the hills and plains of the Extremadura taking you to Mérida, one of the richest Roman sites in Spain, and Cáceres, an intact medieval walled city, through the pastures and highlands of Salamanca, along the Duero River to the Romanesque city of Zamora, and into the verdant woodlands of Galicia. The final triumphant step of your pilgrimage is onto the carved scallop shell inscribed into the pavement of Santiago Cathedral, a ritual that supposedly purges you of your sins.

*The Cathedral at Santiago de Compostela*

**HOW:**
On foot
**WHEN TO GO:**
April to June or September to October. Avoid July and August when the heat is unbearable.
**TIME IT TAKES:**
Six to seven weeks
**HIGHLIGHTS:**
Mérida – Roman ruins.
Cáceres – city walls.
Zamora – Romanesque churches.
Salamanca – Plaza Mayor.
Santiago de Compostela Cathedral.
**YOU SHOULD KNOW:**
For the most part, the path is undulating but not too taxing. However, after you enter Galicia, there are some very steep climbs and descents that require a reasonable level of fitness. Pilgrims often wear a 'uniform' of cloak and wide-brimmed hat and carry a walking stick, a gourd (for drinking from wells) and a scallop shell (the St James' pilgrim symbol).

*The cathedral and castle in Zamora from the Duero River*

# A Coruña to Madrid

**HOW:**
By train
**WHEN TO GO:**
April to October
**TIME IT TAKES:**
Ten hours minimum
**HIGHLIGHTS:**
Tower of Hercules, A Coruña – the oldest lighthouse in the world, dating from the 2nd century with magnificent views from the top.
Scenic mountain landscape between Ourense and Zamora.
Duero Valley.
Castle of Medina del Campo.
**YOU SHOULD KNOW:**
If you have the time, this journey is interesting to do in stages, stopping off at Ourense and Zamora on your way.

Considering how long Spain has been a major tourist destination, its magnificent hinterland has remained remarkably undiscovered. There is no better way to see the interior of this beautiful country than catching the train from the lovely city of A Coruña, on the Galician coast, to Madrid – a 740-km (460-mi) scenic journey that takes you through a sparsely populated rural backwater of historic hill villages and ancient agricultural landscapes with breathtaking Mediterranean and Alpine views.

Leaving the dramatic coastal cliffs and bays of A Coruña behind, the train travels through the lush valleys and verdant woodlands of Galicia, up to the desolate romantic moorland around the city of Ourense on the banks of the River Miño, and through the virtually uninhabited borderlands of Spain and Portugal towards Zamora, across a mountain wilderness of rugged heath and forest where wolves still roam. Passing through countless tunnels, you cannot help thinking about the forced labour that built this section of the railway – half-starved Republican political prisoners of the 1940s and 50s, hacking their way through the mountain rock in pitch-darkness.

From Zamora, known as a 'museum of Romanesque art' for its 12th and 13th century churches, the railway meanders through the vineyards of the fertile Duero Valley and cuts across the ancient farmlands of the Tierra del Campo. The last leg takes you up past olive and citrus groves, oak and pine forests into the highlands north of Madrid. Finally you descend to the plain of Castilla-La Mancha and arrive at Spain's impressive capital city, by which time your head will be full of splendid scenic impressions and your appetite whetted to explore more deeply into this world away from the usual hackneyed tourist itineraries.

# Green Spain

The railway system that runs across northern Spain is a mere 1m (3 ft) wide, originally designed for transporting coal from the mines of the Cantábrican Mountains. The network runs for 800 km (500 mi) through the exuberant terrain of 'Green Spain', the fertile coastal strip between the stormy seas of the Bay of Biscay and the misty slopes of the Cordillera Cantábrica, from the French border town of Hendaye to the Atlantic port of Ferrol, near the pilgrim city of Santiago de Compostela.

Travelling on the little electric railway lines that weave their way along the coasts of four provinces – the Basque country, Cantabria, Asturias and Galicia – is an enchanting way of seeing the little-known Celtic face of Spain. You pass through magical landscapes of brooding mountain peaks and white-water rivers, verdant estuaries and craggy shorelines, vibrantly green valleys and luxuriant woods. There are more than 250 stops along the way – historic provincial capitals, market towns, fishing villages and remote hamlets in the heart of the countryside – with several changes en route. You are unlikely to encounter many other tourists as the train trundles through the back of beyond. Your travelling companions will be a miscellaneous assortment of commuters – local fishermen, housewives going to market, teenagers off for a day trip in the city, and the odd village priest.

Although the whole journey can be undertaken in one long day, it is far more fulfilling to take your time, seeing the city sights in Bilbao, Santander, Oviedo, Gijón and Avilés, branching off to visit the Gothic city of León and the gorges of the Picos de Europa, and spontaneously stopping at any number of picturesque seaside towns or country villages, spending the night at tourist guesthouses.

**HOW:**
By train
**WHEN TO GO:**
April to October
**TIME IT TAKES:**
Nineteen hours minimum
**HIGHLIGHTS:**
Bilbao – FEVE Railway station, a period masterpiece. Guggenheim Museum
Santander – Magdalena Palace and period architecture.
Churches and monuments of Oviedo.
**YOU SHOULD KNOW:**
An alternative means of exploring Green Spain is by taking an 8-day rail-cruise on El Transcantabrico, a FEVE Railway luxury tourist train which stops for sightseeing.

*The Santander a Bilbao station – a period masterpiece*

# Madrid to Barcelona

**HOW:**
By train
**WHEN TO GO:**
Anytime
**TIME IT TAKES:**
2 hours 38 minutes
**HIGHLIGHTS:**
Madrid – Prado Art Gallery
Zaragoza – Cathedral of San Salvador
Barcelona – Parc Güell and Sagrada
Familia Church both designed by
Antoni Gaudi.
Barcelona – Las Ramblas and Barri
Gòtic – old city centre
**YOU SHOULD KNOW:**
Spain is aiming to have more high
speed train lines than anywhere else
in the world by 2010. Travelling by
train creates four times less pollution
than air travel.

The Alt Velocidad Española, better known as the AVE ('bird' in Spanish), is a high-speed train capable of travelling at 350 kph (220 mph) – the Spanish super-equivalent of the French TGV. AVE trains have been running between Madrid and the south of Spain since 1992 but, until recently, it still took more than six hours to get to Barcelona, Spain's second most important city. Although construction of the high-speed line to Barcelona was a priority and started years ago, engineering problems caused by repeated land sinkage kept delaying its completion.

The Madrid-Zaragoza-Barcelona line was finally inaugurated in February 2008 with seventeen trains in each direction per day. It is one of the world's fastest trains covering a distance of 660 km (410 mi) in just 2 hours 38 minutes. This brand-new self-driving, high-speed train may well live up to its acronym and make air travel obsolete. The AVE takes hardly any longer than the plane once you include check-in times and the journey to and from the airport, and is far less hassle and much more comfortable.

Madrid's Atocha Station looks more like an airport terminal than a station, its huge central atrium decked in palm trees. The AVE glides away from the platform and is soon whizzing across the beautiful countryside of Aragon and Catalonia. But it goes so fast, the view from your window is a blur; you are more likely to pass the time reclining in the luxury of your swivel seat, relishing the Michelin-starred food that is served on board, and playing with the audio, video and internet technology at your fingertips. Before you know it, you are at the World Heritage city of Zaragoza and only a little while later pull into Sants Station in the vibrant heart of Barcelona.

*The Tower of St Magdalena and Pilar Basilica in Zaragoza*

# El Greco Walk, Toledo

Known as the 'city of three cultures', the World Heritage city of Toledo was renowned in medieval times for intellectual and religious tolerance. The expression of this can still be seen in the variety of the city's monuments – churches, synagogues, mosques, palaces and battlements built over the centuries in an exuberant blend of Gothic-Mujedar-Sephardic styles. Wandering through the twisting medieval streets and narrow covered passages, you feel as though you have been time-warped into a mysterious fairytale past.

The famous 16th century artist El Greco, born in Crete, settled in Toledo long after its heyday when the city was in the grip of a fervid mystical Christianity, which he translated into extraordinarily vivid visual imagery. Toledo itself, perched on a rocky hill enclosed on three sides by the deep ox-bow gorge of the River Tajo, appears in many guises as a favourite background in his paintings and is the subject of one of his most iconic – and haunting – works ('View of Toledo').

If you cross the 13th century five-arched Puente San Martin to the south bank of the Tajo and walk along the Carretera de Circunvalción, following the bend in the river all the way along the gorge to the restored Roman Puente de Alcántara, you can see the amazing views that were the inspiration for El Greco's Gothic masterpiece. The time-scoured city walls of earth-brown brick emerge from the hill in perfect harmony with the golden landscape, dark green olive groves contrast with the parched hills and the spire of the Cathedral, like a raised sword, stands guard over the land.

Your walk culminates in the magnificent spectacle of the four towers of the Alcazár fortress looming dramatically above you as you re-enter Toledo through the Baroque Gate of the Alcantara Bridge, and your head is filled with visions of this magical city from an entirely different perspective.

*The World Heritage city of Toledo is enclosed on three sides by the River Tajo.*

**HOW:**
On foot
**WHEN TO GO:**
April to October
**TIME IT TAKES:**
One to two hours
**HIGHLIGHTS:**
Toledo Cathedral – one of the largest in the world.
The Alcázar (Castle).
Museum of El Greco – re-creation of the artist's house with exhibits of his work.
Puerta Bisagra – main entrance gate to the Old City.
Iglesia de Santo Tomé – contains the famous El Greco painting *Burial of Count Orgaz.*
**YOU SHOULD KNOW:**
This walk is particularly lovely in the evening light. To even skim the surface of this beautiful historic town, you should aim to spend at least one night here.

# Montserrat Rack Railway

A railway to the legendary monastery of Montserrat was first opened in 1892, built for the ever-increasing number of pilgrims who trudged up the mountain to make obeisance at this centre of Catalan faith and culture, the home of La Moroneta (the Black Madonna). The disruption caused by war, followed by a number of nasty accidents and catastrophic floods resulted in its closure in 1957. Since then many attempts have been made to re-open it, culminating in the present state-of-the-art railway inaugurated in 2003.

From the town of Monistrol de Montserrat, the train makes a brief but thrilling, sometimes near-vertical journey along the original 5 km (3 mi) route through tunnels and across bridges with amazing views of the bizarrely-shaped granite teeth, for which Montserrat is so famous, outlined against the sky. You plunge into the darkness of the recently constructed La Foradada tunnel then across the 480-m (1,574-ft) long Pont del Centenari – an awesome engineering design of steel lattice supported by eight pillars – to arrive at Monistrol Vila Station. Here the rack rail section of the line begins and the cog-wheel kicks in to haul you farther up the mountain. Suspended between mountain and valley you continue your ascent in and out of tunnels to make one final spectacular upward heave to Montserrat Monastery, a gargantuan 19th century complex of buildings, complete with basilica and museum, resting on a broad ledge enclosed by steep cliffs that soar skywards.

After this sensational ride you may need a pause to get your breath back and see the sights before you feel ready to rise to the challenge of further thrills in the form of two funicular cableways, one transporting you to the mountain summit and the other down the sheer cliff-face to the shrine of Santa Cova.

*The Monastery was founded in 1025.*

**HOW:**
By train
**WHEN TO GO:**
April to October
**TIME IT TAKES:**
Fifteen minutes
**HIGHLIGHTS:**
Old Monistrol Vila Station exhibition. El Rosari Monumental – a series of sculptures by Gaudi and others along the path to the Santa Cova shrine.
Montserrat Nature Centre – panoramic views from the top of the mountain reached by the Sant Joan Funicular from Montserrat Monastery.
Basilica and Black Madonna.
Montserrat Museum.
**YOU SHOULD KNOW:**
Montserrat ("Jagged Mountain") is named after its bizarre spiky rock outcrops, dramatic formations of pink-hued rock that can be seen from miles away. This is a popular day-trip from Barcelona.

# La Pedriza

One of the many wonders of Madrid is its proximity to some astounding natural scenery. Less than an hour's bus ride northwards and you can breathe pure mountain air and escape the crowds in the wilderness of La Pedriza. This 32 sq km (12 sq mi) granite massif, a spur of the Sierra de Guadarrama, is a mind-blowing landscape of golden-pink granite spires and domes, veined with streams. Crazily complex rock formations sprout out of the woods, with names like El Pájaro (the Bird), La Foca (the Seal), and La Tortuga (the Tortoise). Wild goats roam among the granite slabs and falcons and vultures whirl through the sky.

La Pedriza is incredibly popular among Madrileños for the hiking and climbing here but it's not much frequented by tourists. There are numerous romantic legends and anecdotes attached to the area. It is all too easy to lose one's way among the granite cliffs and slabs, making it a haven for 19th century bandits and later a Republican hideout in the Spanish Civil War.

At the foot of La Pedriza lies Manzanares el Real, a faintly bohemian village inhabited by artisans, artists and musicians. From here you can walk along the tranquil tree-lined banks of the River Manzanares, swimming in one of the waterholes on your way up to the shrine of Peña Sacra for a spectacular view; or, for a more testing journey, take the 4-km (2.5-mi) zigzag route to El Yelmo (the Helmet), a high rock dome to the north of the village, perhaps the most famous feature of La Pedriza. Whichever route you take, you cannot fail to be awestruck by the beauty of this unique landscape.

**HOW:**
On foot
**WHEN TO GO:**
April to October
**TIME IT TAKES:**
A daytrip from Madrid with a 2-5 hour walk.
**HIGHLIGHTS:**
Castillo de Manzanares.
16th century Church of Nuestra Señora de las Nieves.
Panoramic view from La Ermita de Nuestra Señora de la Peña Sacra.
**YOU SHOULD KNOW:**
If you want La Pedriza to yourself, go on a weekday. You need to be fit to scramble across the granite slabs in your path. This is a great place for climbers of all levels.

*The Castillo de Manzanares*

# La Rioja

**HOW:**
By bike
**WHEN TO GO:**
April to October
**TIME IT TAKES:**
One week
**HIGHLIGHTS:**
Wine tasting
Romanesque architecture on Camino
de Santiago.
Rio Oja Valley
San Millán de la Cogolla – World
Heritage Site13th Century Yuso and
Suso Monasteries.
San Vicente de Sonsierra – Church of
the True Cross.
**YOU SHOULD KNOW:**
La Rioja is a good place to go for the
inexperienced cyclist, with little
traffic and easy-going terrain.

La Rioja is practically synonymous with wine. The economy of the Alavesa hills around the River Ebro has relied on wine production since Roman times and produces some of the most famous vintages in the world. The region is only 150 km (90 mi) long and 50 km (30 mi) wide, almost completely encircled by mountains, ensuring a perfect micro-climate for grape growing. It is brilliant cycling country – kilometre upon kilometre of quiet country road, sleepy villages, historic monuments and dozens of *bodegas* (wineries) where you can sample the wares on your way.

Laguardia, the heart of Alavesa, is a walled medieval hill-town with 320 cellars dating back to the late 18th century. From here you cycle along the banks of the Ebro, passing the historic towns of El Ciego and San Vicente de la Sonsierra, to Haro, where the 15th century monastery has been converted into a winery. Then, skirting the Ebro, wind your way through vineyards to reach the atmospheric town of Briones, cut almost vertically into the hillside.

Many of Spain's monasteries and convents are hidden in the mountains of the Sierra de Demanda, the south-western boundary of La Rioja. Cycle southwards through the densely wooded hills and verdant grasslands of the Cárdenas Valley to San Millán de la Cogola and see the World Heritage Yuso and Suso Monasteries. Go to Santo Domingo de la Calzada, beautifully situated at the foot of the highest peaks of the Sierra de Demanda, a famous stop on the Camino de Santiago pilgrimage route. Finally, cycle past ancient hamlets up through the meadows of the Oja Valley to the breathtaking evergreen mountains of Ezcaray.

By the end of your journey you will be sated with the combination of historic landscapes and heady wine-tastings, leaving you with many lasting memories.

*Vineyards around the
hilltop town of Laguardia*

# Ruta de Califato

Andalucia is a region steeped in history and legend, reflecting centuries of Arab influence. The Moorish occupation of Spain lasted for the best part of 800 years, reaching its zenith under the Caliphate of Cordóba. From the early 10th century Cordóba became the most important city in Europe, a bridge between east and west where new ideas flourished in an atmosphere of intellectual and artistic enlightenment. The Caliphate eventually collapsed through ruinous civil wars, leaving Granada as the last bastion of Moorish rule after the fall of Cordóba in 1031.

Today the remains of this Andalucian golden age are to be seen in the incredible Moorish monuments of the cities and startlingly picturesque architecture of the hill villages. Setting out from Cordóba for Alcala La Real, 125 km (78 mi) away, you drive through the olive groves, vineyards and fields of the Guadalquivir Valley, stopping at whitewashed hill villages bedecked with petunias, and admiring the rugged limestone scenery of the Sierra Subbéticas, clothed with wild olive and oak groves.

From Alcala, an ancient strategic stronghold dominated by its magnificent Moorish castle, you can either take the direct 50 km (30 mi) route to Granada, through the village of Pinos Puente, where Queen Isabella is said to have granted permission for Christopher Colombus to sail the Atlantic, or add a few kilometres to your journey by touring the Vega, frontier territory between the Moors and the Christians, where medieval fortified villages are dramatically perched on craggy outcrops of the Sierra de Huétor, guarding the plains below.

As you approach Granada, the snow-capped peaks of the Sierra Nevada, the highest mountains in Spain, gradually loom into view, a splendid backdrop to this glorious city of the Alhambra Palace, where Moorish culture achieved its spectacular climax.

*Zuheros is one of the 'white villages' of Andalucia.*

**HOW:**
By car or bike
**WHEN TO GO:**
March to June when the flowers are at their best, or September to October.
**TIME IT TAKES:**
Two to three days by car; seven days by bicycle.
**HIGHLIGHTS:**
Cordóba – the Mesquita.
Priego de Cordóba – historic town.
Alcala La Real – picturesque plaza and Moorish castle.
Villages of Subbéticas – Zuheros, Luque, Iznajar.
Granada – the Alhambra Palace.
**YOU SHOULD KNOW:**
Sierra Subbéticas is an area of outstanding natural beauty. There are alternative routes through it and lovely country walks.

# The Rapids of the Noguera Pallaresa River

**HOW:**
By kayak or raft
**WHEN TO GO:**
The best time is May and June when the river is in full flood but you can raft anytime between April and September.
**TIME IT TAKES:**
Four to eight hours
**HIGHLIGHTS:**
The thrill of running the rapids.
Romanesque churches of the Pallars Sobirà.
Castle of Gilareny
Collegats Gorge
Medieval bridge and Abbey of Gerri de La Sal.
**YOU SHOULD KNOW:**
The Pallars Sobirà is a paradise for camping, trekking, climbing and mountain biking holidays and, in winter, skiing and snowshoeing.

The 146-km (90-mi) long Noguera Pallaresa River is the most powerful river in the Pyrenees – a major source of hydro-electric energy. Its turbulent waters pour down from the 2,000-m (6,550-ft) high Val d'Aran in the Pyrenees through the beautiful lake and mountain scenery of the Pallars Sobirà. Over the past forty years, this romantic pastoral region of picturesque mountain villages, ancient stone houses, isolated churches and Roman ruins has become increasingly popular as a Spanish holiday destination for sports, nature and adventure enthusiasts but, so far, has been relatively free from international tourism. The reliable flow and relative safety of the unpolluted white water rapids make the Noguera Pallaresa perfect for rafting and kayaking.

There are charming cobble-stoned villages up- and down-stream, from any of which you can take a dramatic river journey through breathtaking countryside. You can run a 45-km (28-mi) stretch of water from the village of Escaló through Sort, the main sports centre for the area, to the Collegats Gorge. Or, for novices, the 14-km (9-mi) stretch between Llavorsi and Rialp, with eight rapids along the way, is a brilliant introduction to the joys of river navigation and a lot less dangerous than it feels: despite unpredictable rapids and a lot of boat-bumping as you swirl downstream, the worst that can happen is a good soaking. From Sort, you make a jaw-dropping descent down the fastest rapid of the entire river and float through the spectacular rock formations of the Collegats Gorge, an epic climax to a journey of thrills and spills. Whether you decide to test your solo oarsman-ship in a kayak or cling with several others to an inflatable raft, you will experience an exhilarating buzz of adrenaline that makes you want to take another trip as soon as you can.

*The Noguera Pallaresa River*

# Tarragona to Lleida

*Poblet Monastery*

When you have had your fill of the hedonism of the Catalan coast, it is time to head inland, to explore the agricultural heartlands of Catalonia where the villages have their own folklore, culture and customs, local festivals rooted in medieval tradition, and magnificent regional food and wines. The people of this fiercely independent, semi-autonomous province have a strong sense of nationalism. They are Catalan first and Spanish second, their identity clearly visible in their preference for speaking in their native tongue, a language very different from the Castillian Spanish spoken elsewhere.

Inhabited since prehistoric times, Tarragona, on the Costa Dorada, was the base from which the Romans set out to colonize Iberia. It is beautifully situated on a rocky outcrop overlooking the sea with a walled old quarter and impressively intact Roman remains both in and around the town. A 115-km (70-mi) cycling tour of the back roads to the pleasant inland town of Lleida on the River Segre gives you an insight into Catalan rural culture as you meander through the pretty farmlands from village to village, winding along country lanes, passing dry-stonewalled terraces of fruit and olive groves, visiting ancient chapels and monasteries, old farm buildings and windmills along the way.

Although this part of Spain is heavily dependent on tourism, the old quarters of the villages are still devoted entirely to food production, with a co-operative in each village. You pass the vineyards of Montsant and see the olive oil factory at El Soleras at work, the famous olive villages of Les Garrigues and the historic curiosity of the old oil mill at Albatàrrec. You will be able to gorge yourself on wonderful regional dishes as you exercise them off, ending your bike ride glowing with well-being at the gateway to the Pyrenees.

**HOW:**
By bike
**WHEN TO GO:**
October for the olive harvest.
**TIME IT TAKES:**
Two days
**HIGHLIGHTS:**
World Heritage monuments of Tarragona.
Monastery of Poblet.
Stone huts of Ulldemolins.
Seu Vella, Lleida – 12th-15th century Cathedral.
**YOU SHOULD KNOW:**
This is easy cycling over gently undulating or flat terrain.

# The White Villages of La Alpujarra in the Sierra Nevada

After the official expulsion of the Moors from Spain in 1492, refugees retreated into La Alpujarra, an inaccessible region of steep valleys in the southern Sierra Nevada, where they survived in isolated pockets for a further 150 years by cultivating the fertile silt washed down from the mountains. Today some 70 'white villages' are testimony to the Moorish cultural roots of the inhabitants. On a hike through this beautiful rugged country the Moroccan Berber influence can be seen all around – in the inimitable terracing of the fields, intricate irrigation techniques and cubic architecture.

The land is so steep that the quaint whitewashed houses with flat roofs and crooked clay chimneys seem to be piled on top of each other, each village an idiosyncratic jumble of narrow streets. The beautifully tended terraces of olive, fig, mulberry and nut trees are constantly watered by melting snow, directed down the mountains along *acequias* (irrigation channels). A network of ancient walled trails and mule paths takes you along ridges dotted with cacti, down into rocky wooded gorges, through almond groves and wildflower meadows, always with breathtaking views of the snowy peaks of the Sierra Nevada.

From Mairena, a typically picturesque white village, you head westwards to the charming village of Yegen, leaning precariously on a narrow ledge. The twisting trail leads through several hamlets up to the pretty village of Mecina Bombaron and then across ridge and river to Bérchules in the high mountain grasslands. A steep descent through pine forest followed by another climb through flower-filled meadows takes you to your destination – the village of Trevélez. Toppling over a frighteningly steep gorge, it is arguably the highest village in Spain. Here you can reward yourself for your long trek with what is indisputably the best-tasting Serrano ham in the country.

**HOW:**
On foot
**WHEN TO GO:**
March to May for the wild flowers or September to October for the autumn colour.
**TIME IT TAKES:**
Six to seven days
**HIGHLIGHTS:**
Moorish cubic architecture. Outstanding natural scenery. Trevélez – highest town in Spain with a church at 1,476 m (4,840 ft). Yegen – village made famous in the 1920s and 30s by the Hispanophile English writer Gerald Brenan, a friend of Virginia Woolf who came here to stay with him.
**YOU SHOULD KNOW:**
This is a moderately easy trek for anyone reasonably fit. La Alpujarra is excellent walking country, criss-crossed by trails of varying difficulty, but can equally well be toured by car, bike or horse.

*Pampaneira in the Sierra Nevada Mountains*

# Cross the Strait of Gibraltar

The ferry ride across the Strait of Gibraltar is a startling journey of contrasts and culture shock. You suddenly realise how incredibly close Europe and Africa really are, which makes the differences between them even more unaccountably stark. The Strait is very narrow indeed – only 13 km (8 mi) at its narrowest point, and 50 km (31 mi) separate Algeciras from Tangier.

Algeciras is not the sort of place that anyone goes to by choice. A sprawling industrialized city on the Bay of Gibraltar, at the bottleneck between the Mediterranean and Atlantic, it is one of the busiest ports in the world. But, for that very reason it is a peculiarly exciting city, with the highly-charged, chaotic atmosphere that invariably pervades a port. Once you start to explore, you will be pleasantly surprised by how attractive the older parts are.

Even before you step on the ferry you feel the presence of North Africa in the groups of djellaba-clad migrants and back-street tea shops. As soon as you are aboard this sensation is heightened. Everyone around you is suddenly speaking Arabic; you are the outsider. As the boat departs, you experience a surge of anticipation then, looking back to catch a last glimpse of the Rock of Gibraltar, a quite extraordinary sense of loss, only to be overwhelmed minutes later by the thrill of sighting the minarets of Tangier in the distance.

Landing in Tangier, your nostrils are assailed by the exotic smells in the air, and there's a sultry atmosphere that befits the city's reputation as a seedy adventurers' haunt. Tangier has a curious, fading grandeur about it and while it's by no means a typical Moroccan city or indeed an African one, it is an exciting and idiosyncratic introduction to an extraordinary continent.

**HOW:**
By boat
**WHEN TO GO:**
Any time
**TIME IT TAKES:**
70 minutes to 2½ hours depending on ferry speed.
**HIGHLIGHTS:**
Algeciras – Mercado de Abastos – main market,
Barrio San Isidro – old quarter of Tangier – Views of the Rock of Gibraltar and
Dar el Makhsen, Tangier – 17th Century sultan's palace housing vast art collection.
Drinking mint tea or coffee at one of the cafés in the Petit Socco in Tangier or having a drink at the (posh) Minzah Hotel or the (unposh) Muniria Hotel, where William Burroughs wrote *The Naked Lunch*.
**YOU SHOULD KNOW:**
You can also get to Tangier by the fast ferry from Tarifa in only thirty minutes – much quicker but far less thrilling.
Cecil Beaton, Tennessee Williams, Truman Capote, William Burroughs, Allen Ginsberg and Jack Kerouac are just some of Tangier's famous past residents and habitués. Though the Tangier of today is a pale shadow of its former self, it still has a certain seductive allure.

*The lighthouse in Algeciras*

# Mountains of Majorca

**HOW:**
By train
**WHEN TO GO:**
April to May or September
**TIME IT TAKES:**
1 hour 20 minutes
**HIGHLIGHTS:**
Palma Cathedral
Mountain views
Picturesque antique railway
carriages
Sóller – Plaça Consitució
**YOU SHOULD KNOW:**
The Serra de Tramuntana is brilliant
walking country with well-marked
trails to suit all levels of ability.

The reality of Majorca belies its reputation as a high-rise hell of commercialized tourism. Apart from the narrow coastal strip along the Bay of Palma and the grim east coast resorts, the island is startlingly beautiful, particularly in the Serra de Tramuntana, the rugged mountains of the north-west. Here are soaring peaks interspersed with valleys of olive and citrus groves, sheer cliffs plunging into the sea, and charming mountain villages tucked away in the hills.

By far the most enjoyable way of travelling to the mountains is to catch the quaint little antique train from Palma to Sóller, originally built for the orange merchants of Sóller who needed a more efficient means of getting to the island capital than the long circuitous haul across the mountains by horse and cart. The train has been running since 1912 and its mahogany panelled, brass-fitted wooden carriages take you a step back in time as you make the 28 km (17.5 mi) journey along a narrow gauge track through staggeringly beautiful countryside. The train winds its way northwards across the plain of Palma and climbs into the mountains across enchanting valleys thick with citrus groves. It stops at villages along the way and there are some astounding views as well as scarily long sections of tunnel that only end after you've begun to think they're never going to.

Sóller is a lovely mountain town, built on a slope around a main square with several cafés and bars. The town has miraculously retained a genuine, un-touristy atmosphere about it and you stroll through sleepy narrow streets of 18th and 19th century stone houses with huge wooden doors and wrought iron *rejas* (screens). It is a brilliant base for hiking expeditions or you can take an old-fashioned tram down to the coast.

*The town of Sóller hides at the foot of the mountains.*

# Peneda-Gerês National Park

Little known, Peneda-Gerês National Park is located in northern Portugal, part of a system of mountain ranges along the border with Spain. It is a glorious, unspoilt region of mountains, valleys, forests, lakes and rivers speckled with small, traditional farming communities linked by ancient footpaths, old paved tracks and even the remains of a Roman road.

Starting at Caldas do Gerês, an old spa village in a lovely, wooded valley, hike over the Serra do Gerês, past Campo do Gerês and on through woodland over Serra Amarela to the picturesque mountain villages of Brufe and Cutelo. Arable land is scarce and maize and grain are staples, grown on ancient terraces; the lush mountain pastures are grazed by the rare, long-horned Barrosao ox. From Ermida, a tiny, remote community not far from the splendid Arado waterfalls, trek through a wonderful valley to Soajo, well accustomed to visitors thanks to its collection of 18th and 19th century *espigueiros* – stone granaries – set on mushroom-shaped granite legs. Finally, make your way to Arcos de Valdavez, a lovely, welcoming, old market town.

The sense of wilderness is strong – tourism is light, and you will often find yourself alone for hours at a time, despite almost always being within easy reach of a village. The dense woodland includes birch, juniper, holly and several species of oak and silver birch at the rivers' edge. Peneda-Gerês is a rare refuge for both golden eagles and wolves, both of which were hunted remorselessly until recently, but there is more chance of seeing roe deer, otters or wild boar. There are birds, too – red kites, falcons and more. Gazing at the magnificent views, with buzzards wheeling in the sky and the ever-present sound of rushing water, the tourist towns and golf courses of the Algarve seem a world away.

**HOW:**
On foot
**WHEN TO GO:**
The Park is open all year and entry is free; hiking is best from May to October.
**TIME IT TAKES:**
About a week
**HIGHLIGHTS:**
Rio Caldo, a village surrounded by mountains with a large reservoir and water sports centre.
The Ethnographic Museum of Vilarinho da Furna, dedicated to the eponymous village that was 'drowned' to make way for a dam in 1972. If the water levels drop dramatically in summer, the village begins to reappear.
The ruined castle at Lindoso.
Soajo Festival, held each August, it features a 'corrida' or race, run on foot, not horseback, where the competitors carry water on their heads.
Arcos de Valdavez Festival, held during the second week of August.
**YOU SHOULD KNOW:**
There are various hiking trails in the Park as well as themed trails. You will need to carry a map and compass and be prepared for a challenging walk. It can be very hot in the uplands, so be careful not to start an accidental fire.

*The Peneda-Gerês National Park seen from the village of Brufe.*

293

*The train crosses the Tua River.*

# Tua Railway

**HOW:**
By train
**WHEN TO GO:**
May to October
**TIME IT TAKES:**
About two hours
**HIGHLIGHTS:**
The jet-ski championships held at Mirandela each year.
The narrow gauge Corgo line, from Peso de Regua to Vila Real.
The Parque Natural do Alvao, the smallest in the country.
Vila Real, with its Roman site at Panoias, and 18th century palace of Solar de Mateus.
**YOU SHOULD KNOW:**
There is an extra 4 km (2.5 mi) of track open between Mirandela and Carvalhais, which is also open, thanks to local enterprise.

The historic, narrow gauge railway line that runs from Tua to Mirandela is thought to be not only the most spectacular train journey in Portugal, but also of the entire Iberian Peninsula. The 54-km (34-mi) track clings to the rocky edge of a gorge as it carries you up into the Trás-os-Montes ('beyond the mountains') region, following the course of the Tua River valley. This major feat of engineering was completed in 1887, after three years of difficult, dangerous work, requiring vast quantities of dynamite to blast a track through these rugged mountains. Today the line is under threat of closure, so this is a journey you should take soon.

From the Douro River at Tua, the lime green and white diesel locomotive quickly leaves the town behind and begins to climb north towards Abreiro, the halfway point. For a while the main Douro line from Porto to Pocinho, of which this is an off-shoot, is visible beneath you, but you rapidly reach the most dramatic part of the journey, which takes you through narrow tunnels and over bridges, with exceptional views across the river on your left, which itself drops further and further away. Sometimes, looking out of the window, there appears to be absolutely nothing between you and a vertiginous drop of hundreds of feet to the water below, tumbling along at speed, over granite boulders, between the rocky walls of the gorge. After Abreiro the incline lessens as the train reaches the Trás-os-Montes plateau and its olive groves, before finally pulling in to Mirandela.

# Lisbon Tram Line 28

Lisbon's Tram Line 28 takes you across four of the seven summits upon which Lisbon stands, in the course of a classic journey through some of the most interesting areas of this historic city. In 1873, a mass public transport company called Carris began operations, gradually introducing electric trams and new routes across the city. Although most lines today use modern, articulated vehicles, Line 28 uses remodelled vintage beauties, which are entered at the front and exited at the rear.

The trams depart every seven minutes or so from Largo Martim Moniz, making their way up the Mouraria hill to Largo da Graça, before trundling down through Alfama, the oldest, most beautiful and best-known part of the city. The next port of call is Baixa, the lower city, which was rebuilt in French neo-classical style after the earthquake of 1755, by the Marques de Pombal. Climbing uphill again, the trams pass through the old city centre, replete with theatres, and on through the traditional nightlife areas, the Bairro Alto and the Bica, haunt of writers and artists. Rattling and clanking their way up and down the hills, through narrow streets, the trams pass many important sites, including handsome churches, the Parliament building and the Cathedral, before finally reaching the Cemitério dos Prazeres – Cemetery of the Pleasures – where members of Lisbon's noblest families are buried.

This trip is great fun. The trams are often crowded – people sometimes even hitchhike by hanging onto the outside as it rattles along. It's noisy with laughter, chitchat and occasional shouts of abuse at cars blocking the way. The bell rings to alert people and traffic to the tram's presence, and there are frequent stops. Your best bet is to buy a pass allowing you multiple journeys, in order to jump on and off whenever you want.

**HOW:**
By tram
**WHEN TO GO:**
All year round, but April to June and September to November are probably the best months.
**TIME IT TAKES:**
45 minutes, theoretically, but usually more like one hour plus.
**HIGHLIGHTS:**
Café A Brasileira – opened in 1905, this is Lisbon's most famous coffee house; a bronze statue of the poet and writer Fernando Pessoa sits outside.
The Basilica da Estrela and the Estrela Gardens.
The English Cemetery, where the author Henry Fielding is buried.
The Castello de Sao Jorge, originally the Moorish Governor's stronghold.
The Gulbenkian Museum, a superb collection of treasures.
**YOU SHOULD KNOW:**
Fado is Portugal's traditional music, and Lisbon is the best place to find it. During June, Fado singers accompany visitors along the route of Tram Line 28.

*The tram crosses the pedestrianized Rua Augusta.*

*Sunset at Cape St Vincent*

# Vicentine Coast

In 1995 a large stretch of Portugal's Atlantic coast was designated The South-West Alentejo and Vicentine Coast Natural Park. Consisting of a remarkably well-preserved landscape of outstanding natural beauty, this region is a remote and unusual area to explore by car or bike, though easily reached from either Lisbon or the Algarve.

Sagres in the south is well known throughout Portugal as it was here, during the 15th century, that Prince Henry the Navigator not only made his home, but also started his school of navigation. All the great Portuguese explorers of the age studied here, including Vasco da Gama and Magellan. From the beach halfway between Sagres and Sao Vicente, newly designed ships set sail into the unknown, thus launching Portugal's colonial empire. The town itself was damaged first by Sir Francis Drake and again during the earthquake in 1755, but it is still dominated by Prince Henry's impressive fortress.

The scenery along this coast is wild and exciting: towering cliffs, secluded, sandy coves, sand dunes, estuaries, rocks and islets provide many different types of coastal habitat. You will find rare, even unique, wildflowers that have adapted to life in sand or rocky crevasses, while inland are orchards of fig, orange and almond. This is a major migration route for birds of prey as well as a multitude of seabirds. You may see Bonelli's eagles, kites and fishing eagles, as well as rock doves and white storks, making their untidy nests on rocky pinnacles by the sea.

En route you'll pass through small villages of gleaming, white houses, where you can stay the night and enjoy delicious seafood, taking walks along tracks through flower-filled fields to the sea. Zambujeira do Mar, a pleasant, seaside village with a splendid beach, makes a convenient conclusion to your tour.

# Walking the Levada do Caldeirao Verde in Madeira

In the early 15th century, Portuguese settlers found an uninhabited, densely forested, mountainous island, which they named Ilha de Madeira, meaning 'Island of wood'. After clearing the mountain slopes for cultivation, they realized that although the north of the island had more water than it needed, the south – the best agricultural land – was dry for much of the year.

This led to the building of *levadas*, a huge system of irrigation channels that divert the excess water from the mountains to the rest of the island. Many were dug into the ground, but many others were hand-hewn into rock or tunnelled through mountains, often by slave labour from Portugal's colonial empire. Today the 2,000-km (1,250-mi) long system is still being expanded, and the footpaths alongside the *levadas*, essential for maintenance, are now a favourite destination for walkers, and a perfect way of exploring the stunning interior of the island.

The *levada* of Caldeirao Verde, (Green Cauldron) built in the 18th century, is a beautiful, steep walk, beginning at Queimadas Forestry Park, at an altitude of 890 m (2,900 ft). The path first takes you up through the forest of laurels, beeches, Japanese cedars and junipers, soon providing spectacular views of the terracotta roof tiles of the villages below. The route winds through four different tunnels, the second of which is 200 m (660 ft) long, each carved by hand, after which you will soon see the Caldeirao on your left – a natural, mossy rock bowl containing a waterfall-fed lake. All along the narrow path, moss, ferns and lichen growing to either side, you will see dramatic mountain scenery, and by the time you reach the Caldeirao you'll be glad to have a rest and, perhaps, a picnic, with just the sounds of splashing water and birdsong for company.

**HOW:**
On foot
**WHEN TO GO:**
April to November
**TIME IT TAKES:**
Two to three hours
**HIGHLIGHTS:**
Levada of 25 Fontes – where you will find 25 springs cascading into a lake.
Ribeiro Frio to Portela, through glorious heather forests.
The UNESCO World Heritage Nature Site (1999) of Madeira's Laurissilva Forest.
The volcanic caves of Sao Vicente.
**YOU SHOULD KNOW:**
Some *levada* walks are much harder than others. For this one, take walking boots and a torch for the tunnels.

*A hiker walks along a* levada.

# Amalfi Coast Road

Winding its way between Sorrento and Salerno, on the ankle of Italy's boot, is the famous Amalfi Coast Road. This heavily used stretch of tarmac, carved into the mountainsides, is renowned for its stupendous views and extraordinary hairpin bends. The route, along with the charming villages and towns along the way, has been one of Italy's major tourist attractions for decades.

Sorrento, situated on cliff-tops, overlooks the whole of the Bay of Naples. From here you can see Naples itself as well as Vesuvius and the island of Ischia. Steps and lifts drop down 45 m (150 ft) to the sea, where swimming is from wooden jetties rather than a straightforward beach. From here, the road twists around the rocky peninsula to Positano, where pastel hued houses of pink, peach and apricot, enhanced by brightly coloured flowers, seem to cling precariously to the mountainside, up which they scramble from the small beach below.

The road soars and descends, through occasional tunnels, curling round frightening bends where one false move could send you hurtling off into the sparkling blue sea, hundreds of metres below – these spectacular, dizzying views are unparalleled. Visit Amalfi, set at the foot of Monte Cerreto, and admire the magnificent 9th century cathedral, built when the town was a major maritime republic. Make the trip up to the stunning medieval hill town of Ravello, a tranquil gem of a place, boasting palaces, villas, gardens, narrow, cobbled lanes and a view which writer Gore Vidal rated as the most beautiful in the world.

From Amalfi, the road passes through Vietri, known for its ceramic production since the 15th century, and a mere 5 km (3 mi) farther, head into the bustling port area of Salerno, an historic town with a wealth of splendid palaces and churches.

*The Amalfi Coast Road winds its way around the beautiful town of Amalfi.*

# Via Ferrata High Route

The first via ferrate, iron roads, were built in the Dolomites during World War I. These high mountain routes consist of fixed steel cables, ladders and bridges, forming long trails through the mountains that are available to walkers and climbers of varying experience and ability. Originally built to help high altitude troop movements taking place in very harsh, winter conditions, these routes have not only been renewed and restored, but many others have been added, enabling access to much of the high Dolomites.

A great many towns and villages give access to via ferrate, but one of the most popular routes is Alta Via Uno. Beginning at Pragser Wildsee, near Toblach, this 120-km (75-mi) hike, ending at Belluno, takes days to complete and carries you through some of the most unforgettable scenery in the 'Pale Mountains'. The routes are all very well signed, and there are frequent refuges in which to stay, providing simple, inexpensive meals and beds for hikers. It is also possible to take a much shorter, weekend trip that ends at Passo Falzareggo.

These are mountains of exceptional beauty. Tranquil, gentle valleys are interspersed with soaring steeples and pinnacles reaching up to 3,000 m (9,900 ft). The sheer walls, and jagged ridges formed from dolomite rock change colour with the passage of the sun, glowing red, pink, yellow, grey and white. On your way you will see rivers, lakes and forests laid out around you, an endless variety of trees, orchids, edelweiss and thousands of wildflowers in spring. In the highest regions, Alpine chamois and steinbock can be seen – even brown bear have been spotted. Elsewhere there are weasel, marten and the ubiquitous marmot, standing to attention, checking out eagles on the hunt in the sky above.

*Climbing the Via Ferrata.*

**HOW:**
On foot
**WHEN TO GO:**
May to mid-September
**TIME IT TAKES:**
The entire length of Alta Via Uno will take up to two weeks to complete, but there are shorter sections that take only two to three days. Other via ferrate can be completed in a few hours.
**HIGHLIGHTS:**
Skiing and other winter sports in the region.
The spectacular, panoramic views.
Paragliding and hang gliding during the summer.
**YOU SHOULD KNOW:**
The name Dolomites derives from Deodat Gratet Dolomieu, the French mineralogist who first described the type of carbonate rock that forms these mountains.

# Great Dolomites Road

**HOW:**
By car
**WHEN TO GO:**
April to September
**TIME IT TAKES:**
About three hours, but you'll see more and have more fun if you spend a night or two en route.
**HIGHLIGHTS:**
The breathtaking views in every direction.
The South Tyrol Archaeological Museum, home to the 5,000-year-old mummy known as 'Otzi the Iceman'.
Bolzano's Gothic cathedral, started in1184 and completed in 1382.
The Tyrolean village of San Genesio, known for its celebrations, where the locals wear traditional Tyrolean costume.
**YOU SHOULD KNOW:**
Cortina d'Ampezzo, which was the host town of the Winter Olympics in 1956, has also hosted many a film crew. The surrounding mountains have been the location of several films, including *The Pink Panther*, *For Your Eyes Only* and *Cliffhanger*.

*The Great Dolomites are the setting for one of Europe's great road trips.*

There is no doubt that the journey along the Great Dolomites Road between Cortina d'Ampezzo and Bolzano is one of Europe's great road trips. It twists and turns, switchbacking around some of the highest peaks in the range, and passing through ski resorts and mountain villages along the way. This astonishing feat of engineering was built between 1895 and 1909, and provides a true feast for the eyes of those who travel along it.

From Cortina d'Ampezzo, a chic, expensive ski resort during the winter months, surrounded by magnificent peaks dotted with cable cars and funicular railways, the road ascends sharply to the high pass of Passo Pordoi. During the winter, when the mountains are covered with thick snow, the road may sometimes be impassable without chains, but in spring and summer the scene is verdant and the slopes are covered with a million wildflowers – buttercups, rhododendrons, Alpine poppies and more. The narrow road twists past the Stella mountain group, which looms above you and there is a superb view of Sassolungo thrown in.

As you descend towards Canazei, an attractive town in its own right and the halfway mark, you find yourself at the base of the area's tallest peak, the mighty Marmolada. At 3,342 m (10,000 ft) the mountain, with its pristine white glacier, is known affectionately as the Queen of the Dolomites. As the road drops down to Bolzano it passes through an amazing canyon, near vertical walls rising on either side. The town itself is enchanting: its historic centre rich with notable buildings, Hapsburg era churches and narrow, cobbled streets ensuring its enduring popularity as a tourist resort.

# Cinque Terre

The Cinque Terre are five little, coastal villages set in steep valleys surrounded by rugged, mountainous terrain. This region remained isolated until roughly 100 years ago, when a railway line was built, but the area's unique landscape and culture has been well preserved, and it's now a UNESCO World Heritage Site.

*Corniglia – one of the pretty villages in the Cinque Terre*

The Cinque Terre region is characterized by a multitude of terraces carved into the hillsides over hundreds of years. Vineyards and olives groves are cultivated here, and the villages are linked via a maze of footpaths. The main, coastal path, or Sentiero Azzuro, is the most direct, but there is another, more difficult ridge path too, and many shorter, ancient tracks up to the village sanctuaries.

Starting in the west, at Monterosso al Mare, the cactus lined trail climbs through terraces to Vernazza. This is the toughest section of the coastal path, but Vernazza is stunning – rose and ochre painted houses nestle at the base of the mountain, jutting out on a promontory beside a natural harbour, with the ruins of an ancient castle high above. Corniglia offers the Gothic-Ligurian style church of San Pietro (1334) while Manarola, situated beside a stream, is known for its wine. The famous 'Lovers Walk' starts here: a paved path through vineyards to Riomaggiore, the most easterly of the five villages. Here a picturesque cascade of pastel houses tumble down to the small dock below.

Whether you decide to walk the coastal path directly, or stay in one or two of the villages on the way, this is a magical place. The air is fragrant with wild herbs, the views inspiring, the wine and food delicious. Take your time, walk and swim, drink local wine in the sunshine, visit some beautiful churches – this is a splendid place for a break.

**HOW:**
On foot
**WHEN TO GO:**
April to November, but avoid July and August if you don't like crowds.
**TIME IT TAKES:**
Five to six hours direct, but so much more pleasurable to stay a night or two along the way.
**HIGHLIGHTS:**
Vernazzo – Santa Margherita di Antiochia
Manarola – San Lorenzo
Riomaggiore – San Giovanni Battista
Riomaggiore – The Sanctuary of Madonna di Montenero
The renowned local pesto – a sauce of basil, garlic, pine nuts, olive oil and pecorino cheese.
**YOU SHOULD KNOW:**
You don't have to walk the whole way. Instead, use the train, or go by boat, for part of the way. A small fee is payable to use some of the most popular trails.

# Sentiero del Viandante

**HOW:**
On foot
**WHEN TO GO:**
Late March to October
**TIME IT TAKES:**
Five to six hours
**HIGHLIGHTS:**
Fiume Latte – the shortest stream in Italy appears in spring from a grotto, white-ish in colour because of its steep descent.
Villa Cipressi – named for its Cyprus trees; now a hotel, its splendid gardens reach right down to the lakeside.
Villa Monastero – another historic building, now an international cultural and scientific centre, with a magnificent garden.
Take the ferry from Varenna to Bellagio and Menaggio.
**YOU SHOULD KNOW:**
In 2007 Lake Como was reported as being too polluted for swimming. Check on the situation before you dive in.

Lake Como, situated in northern Italy close to the Swiss border, has attracted visitors for centuries. Today, the actor George Clooney has a villa here, but wealthy Lombardians and Milanese holidayed here long before the region was 'discovered' during the 19th century, when Europe's writers, artists and composers began to arrive. The lake, shaped like an inverted 'Y', boasts a delightful, sub-tropical climate, and the resulting vegetation, olive and citrus groves, bougainvillea and palm trees, looks remarkable against the backdrop of snow-clad mountains.

The Sentiero del Viandante, or Wayfarer's Trail, is an ancient mule path connecting the villages along the lake, originally used for bringing goods both from Milan, to the south, and the northern plains. Nowadays it is a little piece of hiker heaven, with orange signs marking the route. Starting at Lierna, a lovely, medieval town with two of the lake's best beaches, follow the path up towards Ortanello, through the forest to the 13th century church of St Peter. This is a perfect spot for a picnic. A sunny, grassy space – complete with fountain, tables and even barbecue equipment – spreads out around the church, and by now you'll need a break.

Follow the trail through Ortanello and soon you'll be heading down to Varenna. You are now high over the lake and this is the trickiest part of the hike, but the views over the sparkling blue lake and the mountains are glorious. Visit the ruins of Vezio Castle – from the top of the tower you can see over the entire lake. Varenna, perhaps the most picturesque town on Lake Como, has steep, narrow lanes that wind down to the harbour, past lovely houses, their balconies a mass of colourful flowers. Here you can finally sit down and sip a glass of cold Prosecco whilst looking over the water.

*Varenna is perhaps the most picturesque town on Lake Como.*

# Rome to Catania

You may well puzzle over the idea of a train running all the way from Rome, in mainland Italy, to Catania in Sicily, but this is a rare journey where the train boards a ship to cross the sea. It may be faster to fly, but you would miss watching the landscape changing from a European aspect to a harsher, almost North African one as it slips by.

Leaving Rome's main station in the morning, the suburbs finally give way to plots of well cultivated land interspersed with small houses, many only half-built, multi-coloured washing flapping on lines in the sunshine. Yellow and white flowers brighten the fields and the trees begin to appear smaller and more gnarled.

After drawing into Naples, its shabby, colourful tenements strung with washing, the line turns to run parallel to the coast. You'll catch a glimpse of the island of Capri and the Sorrentine peninsula, and soon the landscape becomes one of bare, rocky hills, abandoned villages, with an occasional sprinkling of modern houses. The beach too, looks somewhat abandoned: with few people and just the odd fishing boat out to sea. Finally the train pulls into Villa San Giovanni, where the carriages, uncoupled, are rolled onto the ferry, and taken across the Straits of Messina, where they are rolled back onto tracks and re-assembled. During the crossing, passengers either stay in their compartments or climb the stairs to the deck, where they can relish the sight of Sicily and Messina gradually drawing closer.

The journey down Sicily's eastern coast takes you past citrus groves, crumbling castles, prickly pears and cactus. You even get a good enough look at Taormina to want to visit it properly, as well as passing the imposing mass of Mount Etna, before eventually arriving at Catania, the island's second city and seaport.

*Taormina with Mount Etna in the background*

**HOW:**
By train
**WHEN TO GO:**
All year round, but April to November is probably best.
**TIME IT TAKES:**
Ten to thirteen hours, depending on Italian Railways
**HIGHLIGHTS:**
The journey itself – having the time to realize you are travelling and watching southern Italy pass by.
The Vatican City and St Peter's.
Rome's famous ruins, such as the Colosseum, the Forum and the Catacombs.
Exploring Mount Etna.
Catania – the two markets in the historic centre
**YOU SHOULD KNOW:**
The Straits of Messina were described in Homer's *Odyssey* as one of the most treacherous passages on earth, guarded by sirens who tempted sailors to their deaths with songs. Ships had to pass between two monsters, Scylla, who plucked sailors from their ships and ate them alive, and Charybdis, who sucked entire ships into the whirlpool it created.

# Via Francigena Pilgrim Trail

**HOW:**
On foot
**WHEN TO GO:**
Late March to June, September to November. High summer is possible, but the towns can become over-crowded.
**TIME IT TAKES:**
About four days, but it depends on your pace, and how long you spend in the towns and villages you pass through.
**HIGHLIGHTS:**
Montaione – San Vivaldo, with its 17 chapels.
The Romanesque church of Santa Maria a Chianni.
Chianti Montespertoli and Chianti Colli Fiorentini, two excellent locally grown wines.
Castelfiorentino – The Baroque church of Santa Verdiana and Benozzo Gozzoli's frescoes.
Siena's annual medieval horserace, the Palio, which takes place in the Piazza del Campo.
**YOU SHOULD KNOW:**
The recent revival of interest in long distance walks and pilgrim trails has prompted the Italian government to plan to upgrade the route, which is less well known and less travelled than the trail to Santiago de Compostela.

*Monteriggioni in the Elsa Valley*

Originally going south to Bari, the launching point for Jerusalem, the Via Francigena is an ancient pilgrim trail stretching all the way from Canterbury to Rome. Much of the trail is relatively undeveloped and the paths are sometimes overgrown – thus allowing walkers to meditate on an enchanted landscape in peace.

One of the loveliest sections of the trail takes you through the Tuscan heartlands. Starting at Castelfiorentino, a fortified town in the Valdesa Valley with a superb Baroque church, the path follows the course of the River Elsa to Certaldo. Like many Tuscan towns, it rests upon a hill, 129 m (426 ft) above sea level, and from its walled, medieval centre you can see the modern section spreading out beneath, surrounded by fecund vineyards. Visible in the distance are the towers of San Gimignano.

The path continues through Poggibonzi: set on a small hill, its crucial position between the old states of Siena, Volterra and Florence provoked centuries of invasions and uprisings. A further 11 km (7 mi) and you reach San Gimignano, an almost perfectly preserved, absolutely gorgeous hilltop town. During the 10th century San Gimignano prospered from pilgrims and traders travelling the Via Francigeno, and art flourished in the many churches and monasteries. The magnificent frescoes in the Duomo are just a taste of the treasures to be found here.

Monteriggioni, the next fortified village en route, boasts almost intact 13th century walls, encompassing fourteen towers that are the largest of their kind in Tuscany. By now you are only some 15 km (9 mi) from Siena, the region's capital. On reaching the Piazza del Campo, one of Italy's most sublime squares, and the Piazza del Duomo, dominated by an astonishing cathedral, you can vividly imagine a medieval pilgrim's awed response to his surroundings. Your own will doubtless be much the same.

# Crete Senesi

*The glorious countryside around Asciano*

Cycling through the lovely landscapes of Crete Senesi is possibly the best way to see the part of Tuscany to the south of Siena. Meaning 'Siennese clays', the name refers to the greyish beige colour of the clay soil, which is used in the production of terracotta tiles and splendid, large olive jars.

Leaving the Val d'Orcia, its green, undulating hills occasionally interrupted by eroded gullies, make your way to Montepulciano. Topping a ridge, its superb views stretch out for miles. At the foot of the hill is the Renaissance church of San Biagio. Designed by Antonio da Sangallo, this is an exceptional building. The road from the church up to the town, however, is steep, and you'll need a glass or two of the excellent, local red wine by the time you get there.

Wheel along through vineyards and olive groves on unpaved roads that wind up hill and down vale. Catch glimpses of fortified hilltop villages and ancient farmhouses, and notice the vines giving way to fields of wheat and sunflowers swaying in the welcome breeze, Cyprus trees standing sentinel against the deep blue sky. Arriving in 15th century Pienza, you find a treasure trove of Renaissance architecture, built by order of Pope Pius II, whose birthplace it was. The piazza, with the Pope's family palazzo and a splendid cathedral, is a glorious sight.

Leaving Pienza, you head for Montalcino. Set on a hilltop overlooking the valleys beneath, the town has been settled since Etruscan times, though today it is far better known for its exceptional Brunello wines than for its historic architecture. Make sure you visit the nearby Sant'Antimo Abbey: started in the 9th century, it is a sublime example of monastic architecture. The mellow stone glows in the warm light of the surrounding countryside, forming a perfect, harmonious scene.

**HOW:**
By bike
**WHEN TO GO:**
April to October
**TIME IT TAKES:**
Three days or more, depending on how many places you decide to visit.
**HIGHLIGHTS:**
The Bravio delle Botti, an annual event occurring on the last Sunday in August, when competing teams push large wine casks up the hill.
Asciano, a small walled town in the heart of Crete Senesi, with mixed Romanesque and Gothic architecture.
San Quirico and Bagno Vignoni, popular for their spring water even in Roman times.
The Abbey of Monte Oliveto Maggiore and its famous frescoes.
The glorious landscapes through which you travel and the views from the hill towns.
**YOU SHOULD KNOW:**
The cycling varies from easy to really quite strenuous – bear in mind that this is a hilly region, and mountain bikes are needed.

# Umbria Hill Towns

A tour around the medieval hill towns of Umbria makes for the most pleasant of journeys. Pottering along the small back roads, amidst spreading chestnut trees and luxuriant elms on the hillsides, through valleys and beside clear sparkling streams, you are in a landscape captured by many a master painter. The popularity of nearby Tuscany has allowed Umbria to remain relatively unscathed, although Assisi and Orvieto have always drawn crowds.

*Orvieto's famous cathedral can be seen from miles away.*

**HOW:**
By car
**WHEN TO GO:**
March to May, September to November. High summer is usually pretty busy.
**TIME IT TAKES:**
You should spend at least a week, but three or four would be ideal!
**HIGHLIGHTS:**
Todi, with its ancient city walls.
Civita – an artist's paradise, built on a pinnacle and attached to the wider world by a narrow bridge.
Collevalenza – with its unique Sanctuary, built in 1965.
The church of Santa Maria degli Angeli, outside Assisi, which encloses another tiny church that was the first Franciscan friary.
Orvieto – Tempio Belvedere, the last above-ground Estruscan temple in Italy.
**YOU SHOULD KNOW:**
Not only were both St Benedict and St Francis born in Umbria, but also the painters Raphael and Pietro Perugino had their schools here.

Perugia is both beautiful and lively – home to the University for Foreigners and topped by the 16th century Rocca Paolina, Italy's largest fortress; the July Jazz Festival is colourful and exciting, thousands of people speaking hundreds of languages throng the streets and piazzas, enjoying free concerts late into the night.

Assisi, reconstructed after the shocking earthquake of 1997, is crowded with pilgrims coming to visit the Basilica of St Francis. He was born here in 1181. From the magical castle of Rocco Maggiore look out across the glorious Tiber Valley, which so inspired him. There are treasures to be found everywhere – countryside and town alike: Spello's ancient walls date back 2,000 years, and its 13th century church is illuminated with Pinturicchio's fabulous frescoes. The town itself is peaceful and traffic-free. Tiny Bevagna, for once not a hill town, has Roman remains, lovely churches and a marvellous 19th century theatre.

The road from Todi to Orvieto is particularly scenic, including views of Lake Corbara; Orvieto itself is visible from miles away, its world famous Duomo silhouetted against the deep blue Umbrian sky. The pedestrianized ancient city centre is reached either by funicular railway, or via escalators hewn into the soft, tufa stone cliff. The Piazza del Duomo and the cathedral itself are magnificent, and Orvieto also has an extraordinary labyrinth of underground passages beneath it, begun by the Etruscans and continued during the Middle Ages.

# Itria Valley Trulli

Until recently, Puglia, the easternmost part of the heel of Italy's boot, remained largely unknown, but today things are changing, and the region is recognized as a fascinating place, rich in architecture and lovely to behold. Farming is still the mainstay here – ancient, gnarled olive trees and verdant vines, luscious figs and almond trees emerge from the intense red soil, and deep green pines clothe the low hills.

Begin your journey at Monopli on the coast, with its defensive walls and towers that protect a once important harbour, dominated by an ancient castle. The pedestrianized centre is a charming maze of narrow streets, and there are imposing palaces and a splendid Cathedral to be seen. It's an easy ride from there to Conversano, inhabited since Palaeolithic times. Built by the Normans, part of the megalithic walls form the foundation of the trapezoidal castle, which today houses the town's picture gallery and Paolo Finolglio's 16th century frescoes.

Now ride through the gently undulating landscape of the Itria Valley, with its old fortified farmhouses, *masserie*, standing amidst the cherry trees and olive groves, to the UNESCO World Heritage Site of Alberobello, and its 1,500 14th-century trulli houses. Unique to this area, trulli are small, circular buildings made of limestone blocks, with conical roofs, originally constructed without mortar. The town is, of course, heavily visited, but more trulli are dotted around the countryside.

Finally, make your way back towards the coast to Ostuni, an architectural gem of a place. Known as La Citta Bianca – the White Town – for its brilliant, whitewashed houses, it is built on several levels, approached up steps, through arches and along little alleys. There are balconies and carved entryways everywhere, flowers trail from terracotta pots and from each corner you can see the sea.

**HOW:**
By bike
**WHEN TO GO:**
May to October
**TIME IT TAKES:**
About a week
**HIGHLIGHTS:**
Conversano – San Benedetto, 11th century monastery, with its two bell towers and medieval cloister.
Alberobello – The trullo church of St Anthony and the trulli museum.
Ostuni – 15th century, late Gothic-style cathedral, with its magnificent rose window.
The spectacular caves of Castellana Grotte, near Alberobello.
The 'Processione della Grata, a candlelit procession of up to 6,000 people that takes place on the second Sunday of August, going from the Sanctuary della Grata, outside Ostuni, into the centre of town.
**YOU SHOULD KNOW:**
Lack of water has long been a problem in Puglia – drinking water is brought by aqueduct across the Apennines from Campania.

*Alberobello has been named a World Heritage Site.*

# Selvaggio Blu Trek in Sardinia

**HOW:**
On foot
**WHEN TO GO:**
April to June, September to November – it's too hot during July and August.
**TIME IT TAKES:**
About eight days
**HIGHLIGHTS:**
Swimming at Cala Goloritze, perhaps Sardinia's most beautiful beach. The awesome views of the Orosei Gulf from the top of Punta Salinas. Lying under the night sky, listening to the Mediterranean Sea lapping on the shore.
**YOU SHOULD KNOW:**
Don't try to do this trek on your own – you really won't know where you are and could get into serious difficulties.

Said to be the toughest trek in Italy, as well as one of the most beautiful, Selvaggio Blu is a 45 km (28 mi) hike around the Gulf of Orosei on the east coast of Sardinia, the Mediterranean's second largest island.

In the late 1980s, Peppino Cicalo and Mario Verin, two Tuscans, conceived the idea of finding and linking a network of shepherds' and charcoal burners' paths, long unused, around the Gulf, keeping as close to the sea as possible. These paths are only used by wild pigs and sheep, and are so overgrown with Mediterranean vegetation that they are difficult to recognize – even the blue painted arrows that point the way quickly fade or become hidden, and taking a knowledgeable guide with you is a necessity.

Beginning at Pietra Longa, near Arbatax, the trek to Cala Gonone takes you through a wild, lonely landscape of rock and stone, through ancient forests of oak, canyons, rock gullies and limestone arches. There is no sign of human habitation; in fact you feel you are in an extraordinary space, totally alone, lost between the sky and the sea – your sole point of orientation. In parts you'll need to use ropes to climb or abseil, you'll walk along narrow ledges beside high cliffs, with the sea hundreds of metres beneath you – this is not a trek for the faint-hearted, or indeed for beginners.

Each night you make your way down to a small beach (*cala*) where you sleep under the stars, or perhaps take shelter in a 'sheepfold'. There is no support on this journey, no mountain huts or places to renew your supplies – even drinking water is scarce – but the payback is magnificent panoramas, a complete absence of 'civilization' and the true, unspoilt nature of the Mediterranean wilderness.

*The S'Architeddu Lupiru, one of the rock formations located along the way.*

# Grand Canal

Known as La Serenissima, Queen of the Adriatic and City of Light, Venice is certainly one of the wonders of our world. An archipelago of 118 islands formed by 150 canals within a marshy lagoon on the Adriatic, Venice relies upon her waterways for transport, with the Grand Canal as the principal highway.

Take vaporetto No.1 from Piazzale Roma, the gateway to Venice, and you can travel the whole length of the Grand Canal to St Mark's Basin, with perfect views of some of the finest architecture the city has to offer. Almost 200 remarkable buildings, most of which rise straight from the water, form the 'banks' of the canal in an extraordinary sequence of façades, their reflections rippling below. This was the most expensive and sought-after area in the city, and these fine palazzi were built by aristocrats and wealthy merchants between the 13th and 18th centuries.

The canal winds through the heart of Venice in an inverted 'S' shape, and the vaporetto zigzags across it to stops on either side, passing under three bridges, the 16th century, marble Rialto, the Academia, made of wood (1854) and the stone Scalzi (1858). Today a fourth bridge is being constructed, linking the railway station and the Piazzale Roma.

This is a breathtaking voyage, varied, colourful and surprising. You'll see the postman delivering by boat, gondolas carrying honeymoon couples to their waterfront hotel, and vaporetti that cross from side to side rather than up and down. You'll pass fifteen splendid churches, museums and galleries such as the Guggenheim Collection, housed in the Palazzo Venier dei Leoni. As you head towards San Marco the canal opens out to its widest point, merging with St Mark's Basin and the lagoon in a magnificent expanse of water dominated by the gleaming white façade of Santa Maria della Salute, which guards its mouth.

**HOW:**
By vaporetto
**WHEN TO GO:**
All year round, though there can be floods from November to March, and June to September can be very crowded.
**TIME IT TAKES:**
Under one hour – but buy a travel card and you can jump on and off at any number of stops to explore.
**HIGHLIGHTS:**
The fish and vegetable markets at the Rialto – go early in the morning.
The Venice Biennale – a major art exhibition every two years.
The Venice Film Festival – the oldest in the world and highly influential; it takes place in late August/early September.
The Carnival – one of the most famous in the world, with fabulously costumed and masked participants, it ends at midnight on Shrove Tuesday every year.
**YOU SHOULD KNOW:**
Venice, with its lagoon, is a UNESCO World Heritage Site. Visit if you possibly can, the entire place is a work of art.

*The Grand Canal with the domes of Santa Maria della Salute*

*Sailing along the dramatic Corinth Canal.*

# Venice to Patras

Travelling overland from Italy to Greece is a lengthy and expensive trip. If time is of the essence, take the ferry from Venice to Patras, thereby spoiling yourself with a mini-cruise into the bargain. Even a short stay in Venice can be exhausting, with so much to see, but a couple of days crossing the Adriatic will boost your energy levels.

Many ships leave from Venice port – large cruise liners as well as ferries head off in all directions. There is a frequent service to Patras, indeed some 40 ships ply this route during the summer season. The ferries are large, holding up to 1,600 people and their vehicles. Everyone uses them: locals, holiday-makers and long distance lorry drivers, all chatting in different languages as they explore their 'home' for the next two days.

The ferries are equipped with all mod cons: shops, restaurants, bars, discos, casinos and swimming pools, so there's plenty to keep you occupied if relaxing on a sun deck, gazing out to sea, begins to pall. There is also a choice of cabins, inside, outside, for two passengers or four, with or without shower facilities – and all fully air-conditioned. In fact the cheapest method is to camp on deck, and very pleasant too if the weather is balmy. If not, the campers move inside to corridors and lounges. This is a straightforward journey, stopping twice, once at Corfu and again at Igoumenitsa, the start of a motorway running all the way to Turkey.

Patras itself has a long and distinguished history. Built on the slopes of Mount Panachaikon, its old town is charming, full of neo-classical buildings, churches, monuments, narrow lanes and steps. Greece's third city and second largest port after Piraeus, Patras is large, lively and a good base for exploring.

# Riviera Day Train

The ancient city of Genoa is situated on the Ligurian Sea, on Italy's northern coast, not far from the border with France. Taking the train along the Italian and French Rivieras has been a classic journey ever since the railway arrived in the late 1800s. Prior to that, the coastline was largely unknown to the wider world, but the railway brought an influx of foreign visitors, including European royalty and artists who came for the climate, the lovely scenery and the clear, sharp quality of the light.

To best enjoy the trip, make sure you find a seat on the left side of the train, so your view of the dazzling green-blue sea is uninterrupted. The windows on the right look out mainly at high walls and lines of drying laundry. The train is heavily used, by people going to work, school or college, as well as by day-trippers and more serious travellers, and it stops at every little station along the way. From the windows you will see the gorgeous Mediterranean countryside, decked with flowering shrubs and palm trees swaying in the warm breeze. At Ventimiglia, close to the border, there's an addictive Friday morning market, which many French people come to each week – an easy jaunt as there are no border controls here.

Once in France, the famous towns of the Riviera come thick and fast, in an almost continuous line – gawp at Monte Carlo, home to the famous casino and principal town of the tiny, sovereign state of Monaco, its harbour bursting with millionaires' yachts. The train passes in and out of dark tunnels, making you blink each time you emerge into the golden sunlight. Look out for Eze, perched 400 m (1,300 ft) high above the sea, Beaulieu-sur-Mer, Villefranche and finally, Nice, the undisputed Queen of the Côte d'Azur.

**HOW:**
By train
**WHEN TO GO:**
From September to June to avoid the high season crowds.
**TIME IT TAKES:**
Roughly three hours, but these trains are notoriously late.
**HIGHLIGHTS:**
Genoa – historic centre, the largest in Europe.
The aquarium, the second largest in Europe.
Nice – the Cours Saleya Flower market and the Matisse Museum.
**YOU SHOULD KNOW:**
Genoa boasts many famous sons, including three popes, Christopher Columbus, the composer Niccolo Paganini and the 2002 Nobel Prize winner for Physics, Riccardo Giaccomo.

*Villefranche-sur-mer on the Cote d'Azur*

311

*The cable car to Schilthorn*

# Lauterbrunnen to Schilthorn

**HOW:**
By cable car
**WHEN TO GO:**
Year-round, the dramatic landscape
has no equal; but from May to
September/October, the wildflowers
and seasonal colours sharpen the
contrasts between mountain
and valley.
**TIME IT TAKES:**
20-25 minutes Lauterbrunnen-
Mürren cog railway (31 minutes via
Stechelberg cable-car station); 31
minutes Stechelberg-Schilthorn
cable car.
**HIGHLIGHTS:**
The incredible 'corkscrew' of the
waterjet of Trummelbach Falls in the
Lauterbrunnen Valley: inside the
mountain, and accessible by lift
installed in the rockface, the
Jungfraujoch meltwater pumps
20,000 litres (4,399 gallons) per
second through twisting, smooth-
bore chutes and curling ravines.
The view opening up as the train
passes Grutschalp.
In winter, skiing the black run from
Schilthorn.
**YOU SHOULD KNOW:**
Mürren is the highest, year-round
inhabited village in the Bernese
Oberland, and its peaceful wooden
charms are 700 years old. The slopes
around Mürren were the site of
Switzerland's first competitive skiing
activities – the slalom in 1922, and
the downhill in 1928.

The classic image of Switzerland – dramatic snow-capped peaks, icy
torrents crashing down the sombre grey of sheer cliffs, emerald
meadows studded with the white, gold and pink of wild flowers, and
endless vistas of Uhland-green forests and turquoise lakes beneath a
swollen arc of sky – belongs to Mürren in the Bernese Oberland.
Mürren is a car-free cluster of ancient wooden chalets, an eyrie set on
a ledge 800 m (2,100 ft) straight up (literally) from the
Lauterbrunnen Valley floor. You reach it on a cog railway from
Lauterbrunnen, itself impossibly pretty, and as the train passes
Grutschalp it leaps the valley wall, opening up the best views bar
none of the entire Jungfraujoch. It really is the ultimate: only from
Mürren do you get the slanting range of the Eiger, Monch and
Jungfrau heaving their rocky mass out of the forests and meadows of
their flanking valleys. It's like looking through a cross-section of
natural beauty, of wilderness and domestic pastoral – and it is
especially intoxicating because the view is revealed only as the train
ascends, improving with every metre climbed.

You can ascend much higher than Mürren, on the cable car from
Stechelberg to the dizzy heights of Schilthorn (2,970 m/9,742 ft). If
anything, the panorama – from Bern to Mont Blanc – is even more
magnificent, but from the summit you see an exclusively Alpine world
of peaks and skyscapes. The softer valleys and lakes that from
Mürren balance earth with heaven are lost in this airy empire. On the
other hand, when you regain your powers of speech, you can enjoy a
drink in the revolving restaurant on Schilthorn's summit – made
famous by the James Bond film *On Her Majesty's Secret Service*.
Equally stunning in summer or winter, Lauterbrunnen to Schilthorn is
the best railway journey in Switzerland.

# Bernese Oberland Hike

The Bernese Oberland is famous even among Switzerland's exceptional landscapes. It is home to the great peaks, glaciers, forest valleys, vivid green pastures, rugged gorges and mare's tail waterfalls that form the composite quilt of Switzerland's most potently attractive image. There is a discreet network of trails and paths that enables you to go just about anywhere within its sphere of mythic mountain splendour. You will never be disappointed – but as an introduction to the region, the day's hike from Meiringen to Grindelwald is perfect.

At Meiringen, breakfast on a meringue (invented here) before following the angry Reichenbach torrent up the densely wooded flank of the Haslital to the Falls. Any irritation you may feel about the constant reminders of Sherlock Holmes in the area is quickly subsumed by the sublime beauty of the path ahead. At Kaltenbrunnen you burst out of the trees to get the first, exquisitely framed view of the snowy mountains. Every little valley here is another Shangri-La of flower-strewn meadow, bubbling stream, forest, and soaring cliff-faces; but ahead and behind, the view gradually gets bigger and bigger. Suddenly, you stand on the Grosse Scheidegg Pass itself. From 1,962 m (6,434 ft), with the Wetterhorn to one side close by, you look down across the upper Grindelwald glacier to the wisps of cloud hovering above village and valley. To your left, far along the ridge of snow and rock, the Eiger stands out as a perfect pyramid, blue on the misty horizon. Behind it looms the bulk of the Jungfraujoch; below, Kleine Scheidegg, with the Mannlichen Ridge and the Faulhorn to the right. This is beauty on an epic scale, a breathtaking and worthy partner to the vast arc of the sky; and it is classic Bernese Oberland. Walk down to Grindelwald, where locals understand your shining eyes and eager, wordless happiness.

**HOW:**
On foot
**WHEN TO GO:**
June to September
**TIME IT TAKES:**
Six to seven hours (Meiringen to Grindelwald via Grosse Scheidegg). There are a number of variations on the route, and of alternative means of transport for different parts of it. In a full day, you can hike the route and still enjoy some of the distractions en route as well.
**HIGHLIGHTS:**
The historic cog railway to the Reichenbach Falls – opened in 1899, it runs across cast-iron arched bridges, and the 100-year-old carriages have been rebuilt and two wooden 1899 semi-open cars have been copied from photographs, and re-introduced.
The magical tranquility of the remote and enclosed glen at Rosenlaui, beneath the Wetterhorn.
Riding a sledge or *velogemel* (snow bicycle) at night, in winter, from Grosse Scheidegg to Grindelwald , as fast as you dare down the 7-km (4-mi) ice-covered, snow-banked road.
Drinking in the view behind to Meiringen, and ahead to Grindelwald, from the hotel terrace at Grosse Scheidegg.
**YOU SHOULD KNOW:**
The infinite variety of walks and hikes in the Bernese Oberland means you need never do the same one twice.

*The glorious scenery around Grindelwald*

# Lucerne to Flüelen

**HOW:**
By boat
**WHEN TO GO:**
April to October; but the full
steamship service runs only between
June and late September.
**TIME IT TAKES:**
About three hours by steamer from
Lucerne to Flüelen. The ticket usually
allows you to make excursions from
any of the stops, and continue the
journey on a later sailing, and in either
direction.
**HIGHLIGHTS:**
The panorama across and down the
lake from Lucerne, where the water
is widest.
The needle dam in the Reuss River
outside Lucerne. The dam maintains
the Lake's level at the point where the
river leaves it.
The oldest alpine resort of
Burgenstock, a place of utter calm and
peace set on the low hills of a wooded
peninsula, seemingly set on the water.
William Tell's chapel, near Flüelen.
**YOU SHOULD KNOW:**
Swiss Railways' Flexi-Pass systems
frequently allow you to incorporate all
or part of the steamer journey from
Lucerne to Flüelen in a more
comprehensive travel plan.

*One of the 100 year-old paddle
steamers on Lake Lucerne*

Lake Lucerne is also known as 'Vierwaldstadtsee', the Lake of the Four Forest Cantons through which it winds. Its complicated shape contorts through forested mountains that rise steeply from its shore, opening fresh panoramas of alpine magnificence under the vast, shifting skies that inspired the British artist Turner and a dozen other world-class painters. On its southeastern shore lies the Rutli Meadow, traditional site of the founding of the Swiss Confederation, and it is lined by many of Switzerland's oldest communities like Vitznau, Brunnen and Treib. From Lucerne to Flüelen, at the foot of the Lake's wildest and most remote arm, these ancient villages and towns are oases of highly picturesque domesticity set against dramatic peaks that change character with benign or savage weather.

The unlikely combination is even more impressive when you enjoy it from one of the fin-de-siècle paddle steamers that turn the journey to Flüelen into a stylish rite. It's not nostalgia but glamour that makes the journey such fun: the historic boats seem appropriate to the grandeur of the waters they patrol. They fit into a scenario that includes castles on promontories, timber-framed villages huddled round 12th century stone-quoined ports, waterfalls cascading down sheer granite cliffs, mountain meadows folded into rock-filled ravines, and the brooding menace of mountains like Rigi, forever changing mood, reflected in the sparkling water. Other boats might reach Flüelen more quickly; the steamers add grace to breathtaking landscapes that seldom look quite the same twice.

# Alpine Pass Hike

The Alpine Pass route is one of the great European hikes. It crosses Switzerland from Sargans in the east on the Lichtenstein border, to Montreux in the west on Lac Lèman. It crosses sixteen passes along its 354-km (220-mi) length, and completing it involves climbing and descending a total of 19,500 m (63,960 ft), the equivalent of going up and down Mount Everest more than twice! The reward is some of the world's most spectacular mountain scenery, with the additional satisfaction of passing through historically important passes and alpine towns.

The Hike is usually divided into fifteen stages of 9 to 28 km (5.6 to 17.5 mi), but with bad weather and rest days, it's generally regarded as a minimum 19 to 20 day journey. Of course you can undertake any of the stages as shorter excursions: the stages are calculated to connect with a variety of cable cars, chairlifts, funiculars, buses and trains for the weary, footsore and pressed for time. The important thing is to give full vent to the sheer enjoyment of the landscape. You'll pass the Wetterhorn, Eiger, Monch, Jungfrau, Gspaltenhorn, Blumlisalp and Les Diablerets – mountains of consummate grace and charisma. You'll cross huge glaciers in the high wilderness, traverse grassy saddles of alpine meadow, and drop deep into steep valleys of velvet emerald pasture. From the wilder shores of Lake Lucerne at Flüelen, the Bernese Oberland rises in majesty, and the Alpine Pass route weaves over, round and through the best of it. Ancient villages like Meiringen, Grindelwald, Mürren and Kandersteg typify regional variations in decorative architecture, cooking and local tradition – and good planning can make any part of the Hike coincide with the fairs and festivals on local calendars. Best of all: the Alpine Pass Hike needs relatively little preparation to transform it into a genuinely life-enhancing experience.

*The Alpine Pass runs through some of the world's most spectacular mountain scenery.*

**HOW:**
On foot
**WHEN TO GO:**
June to September, when the alpine wild flowers are at their best; every mountain hut and farmstead is welcoming, and good weather prevails.
**TIME IT TAKES:**
About twenty days, including at least fifteen days of actual walking. But with so much to see, and so many brilliant excursions, it's normal to complete the Hike at weekends, over months or even years.
**HIGHLIGHTS:**
The enormous differences between the passes – from the remote needle of Richetli to the spectacular rocky crest of Bunderchrinde or the tourist-thronged Kleine Scheidegg.
Climbing out of the Lauterbrunnen Valley via the Trummelbach Falls.
The changing panorama, familiar but subtly different every day.
**YOU SHOULD KNOW:**
1. Pre-conditioning on similar terrain is valuable if you intend to spend more than 2 days at a time walking; and even in high summer you'll need clothing suitable for the unreliable temperatures.
2. Taking a guide is not mandatory, but highly advisable in the remoter sections like Griesalp-Kandersteg-Adelboden. In any case, guides' intimate knowledge of mountains and folk-lore adds a whole dimension to the hike.

*The beautiful Simmental Valley*

# Golden Pass Panoramic Express

**HOW:**
By train
**WHEN TO GO:**
April to October. The service operates year-round, but many of the excursions that make breaking the journey so exciting do not.
**TIME IT TAKES:**
7 hours 20 minutes (Zurich to Geneva, including 5 hours 18 minutes Lucerne to Montreux). But the onward Golden Pass ticket remains valid however long you take to travel its different sections.
**HIGHLIGHTS:**
The pedestrian suspension bridge over one of Europe's most spectacular gorges near Aareschlucht Ost, Innertkirchen (part of an excursion including the Reichenbach Falls).
The super-privileged view from the very front of the train (beneath the driver's elevated cab), going up the giant horseshoe curve out of the gorgeous Simmental above Gstaad.
The intricate carvings, decorations and paintings on the huge, 113-windowed chalet at Rossiniere, in the distinctive style of the thickly wooded Pays d'Enhaut pre-Alpine region.
The quite stupendous view during the switchback hairpin descent into Montreux – the nearest a railway can get to a mountain road.
**YOU SHOULD KNOW:**
Reservations are necessary for seats in restaurant and 'panoramic' cars; and especially for the 'driver's seats' at the front of the train.

Officially, the Golden Pass links Zurich and Geneva, but its real purpose is to offer travellers a means of exploring the heart of Central Switzerland between Lucerne and Montreux without doubling their tracks. Each of the stops (Lucerne-Interlaken-Zweisimmen-Montreux) is a gateway to a choice of extraordinary excursions and activities in the area. The Golden Pass is designed to make them accessible and heavily discounted when the invitations to linger become irresistible. Otherwise, the scenic beauty and variety of the basic five hour eighteen minute journey is just an exercise in frustration. From Lucerne you can take a paddle steamer across the Lake to the cog railway up Rigi, the artist J.M.W. Turner's 'mountain of infinite mood'; or plunge into the gloomy splendour of the gorges leading to the dramatic Reichenbach Falls. At Interlaken, you can take one of several funiculars or mountain railways into the soul of the Bernese Oberland – even to the top of the Jungfrau itself. The onward journey is always magnificent, past the lakes of Brienz and Thun, through Spiez to the Simmen Valley, guarded at Wimmis by a fairytale 15th-century castle.

At Zweisimmen, you change trains to the special gauge Golden Pass Panoramic train designed by Ferrari's Pininfarina for the best possible views. The train climbs slowly enough to see the intricate and elaborate carvings typical of the region's chalets. These designs change radically from the steep-sided alpine pastoral valleys above Gstaad, to the gentler landscapes of French-speaking Switzerland near Chateau d'Oex (where a perfect sheltered microclimate makes it a world centre for hot-air ballooning). Then, as a visual crescendo of Wagnerian proportions, the train climbs a series of mountains, bridges and viaducts, through the summit tunnel to Les Avants, to emerge with the French Alps spread before you, beyond Montreux and the beckoning sparkle of Lac Lèman below.

# Glacier Express

As befits a service connecting two of the most glamorous resorts in the Alps, Zermatt and St Moritz, the Glacier Express is the last word in panoramic luxury. It needs to be, because in just eight hours it traverses the heart of Switzerland's highest mountain ranges. The journey starts at the foot of the twisted pyramid of the Matterhorn and skirts the Bernese Oberland, following the valley floors (in summer, riotous profusions of wild flowers) where the Rhône and the Rhine begin, and just below the line where glaciers spill out from the high passes. The landscape is a roll call of iconic names. The snow-capped summits of Schilthorn, Jungfrau, Monch and Eiger pass in distant backdrop, and the high peaks close in around the climbing train. Soaring viaducts arch above cloud-filled chasms, carrying it up and over the 2,033 m (6,668 ft) Oberalp Pass. Edging round sheer precipices, across 291 bridges and through 91 tunnels, the Glacier Express brings you so close to the mountains you can actually see the occasional chamois looking outraged at having to share the elemental magnificence of its rocky perch.

In fact, the train is every bit as first-class as the scenery. Though it has both 1st and 2nd class seating, everyone sits (in great comfort) beneath a glass roof, with good services at their disposal. The difference is that 2nd class is more crowded, an indicator of the train's popularity throughout the year. In summer it provides access to some of the finest high alpine walks; in winter it serves three of Switzerland's most justly celebrated skiing areas. But most people take the Glacier Express for the sheer joy of sightseeing in luxury – and then high-stepping off the train in the unadulterated chic of St Moritz or Zermatt.

**HOW:**
By train
**WHEN TO GO:**
Year-round. Seat reservations are mandatory, and lunch on the train should be pre-booked.
**TIME IT TAKES:**
About eight hours (Zermatt to St Moritz, via Visp, Brig, Andermatt and Chur). The unhurried pace of the ascents and descents justifies the route's nickname of 'the Slowest Express Train in the World'.
**HIGHLIGHTS:**
The tunnel at Furka – with its viaduct approaches and staggering ravine views, both a technological and scenic triumph.
The view from the top of the Oberalp Pass, looking along the length of the Alps. On a really clear day you see some 50 peaks in serried ranks leading to Mont Blanc.
The descent from Chur (Switzerland's historic and oldest township) to St Moritz.
**YOU SHOULD KNOW:**
The Glacier Express also has a 'Premium' service available for private parties of a single carriage or even whole trains.

*The Glacier Express travels from Zermatt to St Moritz.*

# Lötschberg

Two very different trains combine to make the shortest route between Bern and Lake Maggiore, and one of the greatest scenic journeys anywhere in Europe. The Lötschberg Line connects the UNESCO World Heritage city of Bern with the Jungfrau-Aletsch-Bietschorn, the Alpine world's first UNESCO World Heritage Landscape. It's a grand Euro-train, powering through the Simplon Tunnel to Italy, where Domodossola is effectively a terminus of the Swiss Railway system. Here the Lötschberg transfers its passengers to the delightful blue and white carriages of the narrow-gauge Centovalli Railway, which takes them back into Switzerland at Locarno, at a fraction of the pace but with scenery every bit as magnificent as the Aletsch Glacier north of the mountains. In just five hours, you see some of the very best pre-alpine landscapes – utterly different north and south – either side of the splendours of the Bernese Oberland.

The miniature-scale Centovalli Railway always connects with the Lötschberg, but it runs many more trains on its dedicated section. The route potters for 20 km (12.5 mi) to its highest point at Santa Maria Maggiore (830 m/2,722 ft), before dropping dramatically to Valle Vigezzo and leaving Italy at Ponte Ribellasca. Dense chestnut forests, studded with tranquil, ancient stone-built hamlets fill the web of steep valleys. Slowly inching across deep ravines on seemingly precarious viaducts and bridges, and through 22 short tunnels, the route offers staggering views of Mediterranean Alpine scenery as it cuts across some of the 'hundred valleys' between Camedo and Locarno. The 'panoramic' carriages of the Express are worth the supplement – but the region's incredible beauty is best appreciated if you stop (for lunch, a drink, a short hike or some other local activity) and breathe it in before catching the next train onwards. The Centovalli Railway guarantees you can have your cake and eat it too.

*The iron viaduct over the Isorno River Gorge*

# Andermatt to Grindelwald

The yellow livery of the Alpine Postbus Network is a national institution in Switzerland. Punctual and ubiquitous, the buses reach the country's remotest corners, heedlessly coping with the steepest switchback roads and the highest passes. They even have a special, triple-toned horn based on a sequence from Rossini's opera *William Tell*. A series of Express routes covers the most spectacular roads across and between the high passes, and among the best is the 'Romantic Route'. It starts from the rustic village of Andermatt at the foot of the St Gotthard Pass, and climbs a terrifying sequence of hairpins rising 1,000 m (3,280 ft) in 18 km (12 mi). Coming over the Furka Pass, the road down to Gletsch follows the hillside above the awesome Rhône Glacier, before ascending the Grimsel Pass. From here you get one of the best panoramas in the Bernese Oberland, the classic grandeur of the triple-peaked ridge of the Eiger, Monch and Jungfrau (the Ogre, the Monk, and the Virgin).

Most people fall silent as the Postbus weaves past gentle reservoir lakes, dropping over 1,500 m (4,900 ft) to Meiringen on the Reichenbach Valley floor. This is where every dream about the Bernese Oberland is fulfilled. Rugged mountain drama yields to lucid green meadows in their summer glory of wild flowers; and the climb back up to Grosse Scheidegg, on to Grindelwald itself, is a landscape of the kind of beauty that robs you of speech. Every hamlet, farm, cow and cowbell seems in its proper firmament – and that's why the journey is called 'Romantic'. In fact, there's a lot of romance about: the route is so popular that double-decker Postbuses are used. If even that's not good enough, historic Postbuses are available for private charter.

*The road to the Furka Pass winds to the right of the Rhône Glacier.*

**HOW:**
By postbus
**WHEN TO GO:**
June to September, to include the wild flower finery of the valleys.
**TIME IT TAKES:**
Five hours (driving time); up to seven hours (travel time, depending on frequency and duration of stops of certain services).
**HIGHLIGHTS:**
The Rhône Glacier, already an image of nature at its grandest, here at the mighty river's source.
The melodious tinkle of big cowbells, answered by the frequent triple horn of the bus – the sound of alpine Switzerland.
Stopping for a meringue at Meiringen, where it was invented.
The north face of the Eiger seen from near Grindelwald.
**YOU SHOULD KNOW:**
Despite modern interpretations, the 'Romantic' Bernese Oberland got its nickname from the Romantic aesthetic popularized by Goethe, Mendelssohn and Lord Byron, all of whom were entranced by the landscape of the Jungfrau region.

# Jungfraujoch Cog Railway

**HOW:**
By train
**WHEN TO GO:**
Year-round; but many of the services
and adventure attractions based in
Jungfraujoch 'village' are only open
from June to September.
**TIME IT TAKES:**
4 hours 45 minutes round trip from
Interlaken (2 hours 25 minutes
Interlaken-Lauterbrunnen-
Jungfraujoch; 2 hours 25 minutes
Jungfraujoch-Grindelwald-Interlaken).
**HIGHLIGHTS:**
Using the big permanent telescopes
at Kleine Scheidegg to watch
climbers on the North Face of the
Eiger, towering above you.
Posting a letter at Europe's highest
post office, next to Jungfraujoch
Station.
The close-up of the Aletsch Glacier
from the Sphinx Observation
Platform, accessible by lift, and the
highest point of Jungfraujoch.
**YOU SHOULD KNOW:**
The Jungfraujoch Railway ascends so
high, so relatively quickly, that many
people are troubled by the thin air. If
you are affected, tell the nearest
official; he/she will arrange
immediate help.

*The Jungfraubahn on the way
up from Kleine Scheidegg.*

The Jungfrau Railway leads to the highest railway station in Europe, at 3,454 m (11,333 ft). It is literally the zenith of a circular route from Interlaken round the heart of the Bernese Oberland, connecting its most famous resorts and providing access to the very best of the region's incomparable scenery and topographical splendour. The train engages its sturdy cog-wheels at Lauterbrunnen, ready to climb parallel to the fabled Lauberhorn Downhill World Cup course past pretty Wengen to Kleine Scheidegg, 2,061 m (6,762 ft) up at the foot of the fateful North Wall of the Eiger. Then it doglegs up to Eigergletscher, famous for its polar dog kennels (it is also the start of a difficult ski run called 'Oh, Hell!'), before hauling through the 7.3-km (4.6-mi) Eiger Tunnel to Eigerwand and Eismeer Stations. At each, it pauses for five minutes for travellers to gasp at the view unfolding through the giant windows hacked through the rock – but then it reaches the top at Jungfraujoch Station, a haven in the middle of glaciers and still-higher peaks of perpetual snow. In every direction, mountains pierce the clouds in the valleys far below, and in the intense blue clarity of the sky you can see as far as the Vosges Mountains in France, and the Black Forest in Germany. Here on the Jungfraujoch – the saddle connecting the Eiger, Monch and Jungfrau peaks among others – the Aletsch Glacier begins, the longest (22 km/14 mi) river of ice in the Alps.

In summer, there are husky-drawn sleigh rides at Jungfraujoch, as well as glacier skiing and a snowboard park; and it's the jump-off for some of Europe's best hiking and climbing. But winter or summer, it's the sensation of standing on the top of Europe that keeps firing the imagination.

# Val Tremola

If no longer the most famous, the St Gotthard is certainly the most historic of all Alpine passes. It opened to regular foot traffic in about 1200, and the first vehicle crossed in 1775. Its importance to both Switzerland and Italy is demonstrated both by the autoroute and rail tunnels underneath it, and the recent building of a new road over it. Take it if you're in a hurry to reach Bellinzona and Milan. But better by far is the much quieter old cobbled road that branches off just after Andermatt. You get a taste of how spectacular (and how worryingly lonely) Alpine travel must have been – until you reach the wild and windy top of the Pass, where you meet the new road, and where a new hotel and the old St Gotthard Hospice building (now a museum) sit by a small lake surrounded by picnicking families. From here the buses and nearly all the traffic follow the new road down to Airolo. Instead, find the old road which restarts behind the hotel. Now virtually deserted after centuries, it switchbacks in broad hairpins down the Val Tremola (the 'Trembling Valley'). The slick cobbles, hammered and rutted with use, cling to the steep green hillside, with some of its 38 bends propped up by precarious retaining walls. Drivers will be delighted. Passengers will be absorbed in the astounding vistas first, down into the heart of the valley; then along the length of the Ticino Valley (here called the Val Leventina) as it opens up below, descending in a blue haze to distant Bellinzona.

You pass wild gorges and waterfalls as the Alps give way to chestnuts and walnut trees – but the core of the journey is the Val Tremola. For centuries, all Europe passed this way.

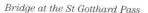

*Bridge at the St Gotthard Pass*

**HOW:**
By car
**WHEN TO GO:**
May to October. The roads over the St Gotthard are not always open during winter.
**TIME IT TAKES:**
One to three hours, depending on how awestruck you are.
**HIGHLIGHTS:**
Finding yourself alone on the old road, able to pause when you want.
The engaging Museo Nazionale del San Gottardo (formerly the St Gotthard Hospice) at the summit of the Pass.
The natural rock arches of the Stretto di Stalvedro, at the mouth of the wild Val Canaria, between Airolo and Biasca.
The three castles of the World Heritage Site of Bellinzona, including 14th century Castelgrande, built on a Roman castle/palace, and now a museum of archaeology and arts.
**YOU SHOULD KNOW:**
Beware the Val Tremola in wet weather – not because of the rain itself, but because some motorcyclists view driving the wet cobbled bends as a desirable challenge to be attempted at speed.

# The Spree and Havel Rivers

**HOW:**
By boat
**WHEN TO GO:**
Year-round. Each season renews the whole gamut of watery landscapes, from the Biosphere wildernesses of the Spreewald and Havel lakes, to Potsdam's inner city grandeur and elegance, or Berlin's industrial, residential and commercial exuberance.
**TIME IT TAKES:**
1 hour (city tour on River Spree); 3 hours (circular tour to/from Charlottenburg Palace Bridge via Landwehrkanal, Kreuzberg, Old Berlin and Mitte district); 3-8 hours (Spree-Wannsee-Havel by various routes, most including Potsdam with or without a stopover at Sans Souci Palace); 2-21 days (Spree-Wannsee-Havel, always including Berlin and Potsdam, but going increasingly further afield in Mecklenburg and Brandenburg).
**HIGHLIGHTS:**
Stepping off a boat at Grunewaldsee (the first of Berlin's western lakes) – right behind Ku'dam, Berlin's most fashionable shopping avenue.
The hauntingly romantic vision of Potsdam's palaces, lawns, parks and colonnaded avenues dripping icicles and stilled by a shroud of snow.
The hidden corners of Old Berlin, seen from the waterways beneath some of its 1700 bridges, especially around Museum Island in the Mitte district.
**YOU SHOULD KNOW:**
There are more than 6,500 km (4,062 mi) of waterways in the Berlin-Mecklenburg-Brandenburg system dominated by the Rivers Spree and Havel, to be enjoyed in a canoe, punt, cruiser, dinghy, sailing yacht, luxury gin palace or scow. It is a natural paradise and a cultural and historic revelation.

The Spree River joins the larger Havel at Spandau. It flows from the huge, car-free network of broadleaf woods and *fliesse* (waterways) comprising the benign wilderness of the Spreewald Biosphere Reserve southeast of Berlin. It brings Berlin most of its water – and the opportunity to float through the heart of Germany's capital on practically any kind of boat, and in any kind of style that you choose. The Havel continues to the palaces and pleasure grounds of Potsdam, Germany's former royal capital, and onwards west and north. It bulges with lakes, leading eventually to the forested seclusion of the Shorfeide-Chorin UNESCO Biosphere, but it shares its enchanting natural wonders with evidence of Germany's most illustrious history. The Elector's Castle at Oranienburg, and Brandenburg an der Havel, the medieval town set on three islands in mid-river, are just two of hundreds of jaw-dropping surprises.

Most importantly, the Spree and the Havel form Berlin's alternative transport system. Using the Landwehrkanal linking the Upper and Lower Spree (at Schlesisches Tor and Charlottenburg) you can visit the Reichstag and the very centre of the reunited city. But you can also see the 19th-century elegance of lovely Nikolaiviertel, and the thirty historic ships still working at Berlin's oldest quarter, the old harbour of Fischerinsel in Kreuzberg. Berlin is veined with waterways based on its two rivers, and the options are endless. Wannsee is Berlin's main water playground, and the site of festivals like 'Wannsee in Flames', a September parade of boats with music, dance and spectacular fireworks. Potsdam's gardens, lakes and parks match its peerless architectural magnificence: like Berlin in its variety of historic and modern moods, these treasures acquire a completely novel perspective, seen from the water. Short or long, a cruise on the Spree and Havel will forever change the way you think about Germany.

*With the Cathedral in the background, the tourist boats glide along the Spree River.*

# Berlin Wall Bike Trail

*The heavily illustrated segment
of the Berlin Wall*

It appeared in 1961 without warning, and disappeared just as suddenly in 1989. Now, the very few fragments of the original Berlin Wall still in situ are themselves protected by fencing from souvenir hunters. Once an embarrassment, the Wall is now regarded as the defining icon of the reunited, reconstructed and re-born capital of Germany. Recently, Berliners completed a bike trail that follows its path for a meandering 106 km (66 mi) across the city and its suburbs. Where railway lines or reconnected streets forced long detours, tunnels and bridges now link the obstructed sections; and as nature has reclaimed the open spaces originally cleared to make a 'killing ground' along its length, the Wall is now represented by a ribbon of green in a grey urban landscape. This chilling 'death strip' was 5 to 100 m (16 to 330 ft) wide – big enough to get lost in the sprouting birch trees and thick underbrush if you miss one of the grey 'Mauerweg' ('Wall Trail') signs at intersections.

The Trail provides a privileged green access corridor to the heart of Berlin and the best of its sights and amenities. But every inch of it is also a confrontation with some of the city's – and Germany's – worst historical nightmares. Bravely, modern Berliners embrace the past as inevitable. They've rescued one piece of their history, the Brandenburg Gate, from isolated sterility in former no-man's-land, but kept the flaking concrete pillbox watchtower column behind it, from which guards sniped at and killed dozens who made their pitiful dash for freedom. The Trail helps explain how optimism triumphed over the institutionalized violence implicit in the Wall's graffiti-ed concrete and its associated artefacts. It is gut-wrenchingly successful, and a brilliant introduction to modern Berlin.

**HOW:**
By bike
**WHEN TO GO:**
Year-round. Berlin Wall Bike Trail guided tours are only scheduled from May-September, but can be arranged with most tour agents throughout the year. So can the information packs, bike rentals and anything else you need for a self-guided tour.
**TIME IT TAKES:**
Four to five hours (scheduled tour), but with or without a guide, you could easily spend days or weeks refining your explorations.
**HIGHLIGHTS:**
Just think – you're riding the path used by heavily-armed DDR Customs, Police and Army patrols 24/7 throughout the Wall's existence. About 3,200 people were arrested trying to cross it; and 270 died trying to get over, under or through it.
The wackiness of having this parkland 'highway' through a major capital city – in it, and very much of it, but still utterly distinct from it.
**YOU SHOULD KNOW:**
Endlessly fascinating, this is one of the great bike trails in the world, combining the exercise with the highest standard of visual, cultural and historical interest. What it reveals about the Cold War remains a work in progress, of relevance to all of us.

323

*The Rathaus (town hall) in Bremen*

# Bridges Cycle Route

The web of rivers, lakes and canals spread across the flatlands of Germany's northwest corner is cycling heaven. Easy riding leaves you plenty of energy to enjoy the succession of nature reserves, moors and wetlands that stud the rich loam of Lower Saxony's northern farmland. Isolated now, the region's small villages and towns once stood on some of Europe's busiest trade routes. The Bridges Cycle Route follows one of them, from Osnabrück to Bremen. Both cities rose to prominence under Charlemagne at the turn of the 8th/9th centuries, but the region had been prized long before by the Romans (whose ubiquitous relics of defeat are a matter of great local pride). Osnabrück's market place and old town comprise one of the most beautiful survivals of urban medieval architecture anywhere (and the treaty of Westphalia was signed here in 1648, ending the Thirty Years War); while still evident behind Bremen's bustling modernity is the equally ancient city of Roland, who held the pass at Roncesvalles for his King, Charlemagne.

Between them the cycling is mostly asphalt, with some forest, farm and gravel tracks in the nature reserves along the way. Dummer Lake is home to every kind of watery recreation, besides providing sanctuary to a huge variety of waterfowl and bird species. Goldenstedt has an ingenious tunnel to introduce you to moorland ecology; and the historic wonders of Diepholz, Löhne and Vechta are matched by the megalithic tombs and historical monuments of the Wildeshauser Geest. You pick your way across water and wetness on every kind of imaginable bridge: plank, wooden arch, Roman (Bohmte/Hunteburg), medieval stone, moated drawbridge, sculpted Baroque or railway viaduct. The final bridge takes you across the River Weser straight to Bremen's Schlachte, the promenade of restaurants in the heart of the city. Cyclists can even park there.

**HOW:**
By bike

**WHEN TO GO:**
April to October, but experienced bikers may also enjoy the vast skies and misty, diffused light of winter, when icy roads are not recommended for novices.

**TIME IT TAKES:**
Four to five days

**HIGHLIGHTS:**
The ancient battle site of Kalkriese (aka. 'Varus battle'), near Bramsche, where Roman legions suffered a devastating rout in 9 AD at the hands of Germanic tribes, and never got this far again. The museum has original artefacts of the battle, and colourful re-enactments.
The moated castle at Diepholz.
The citadel and armoury museum at Vechta.

**YOU SHOULD KNOW:**
The defeat by Arminius of the Roman legions under Varus has been the subject of centuries of myth, disbelief, and speculation. Only in 1987/88 did anyone find sufficient evidence (thousands of coins, weapons, and many other relevant objects) to show that the battle really did take place on the scale lauded in German poetry.

# The Romantic Road

Beloved by Germans as one of their favourite holiday routes, the Romantic Road starts by the River Main at the Prince-Bishopric fortress town of Wurzburg. Picking its way through rural backwaters of stunning beauty, it seeks out some of Germany's least-famous but most magnificent castles, palaces, old towns and topographical curiosities; crosses the Danube at Donauwörth, and follows the bubbling torrent of the alpine Lech River all the way to King Ludwig II's 19th century fairytale extravaganzas of Neuschwanstein and Hohenschwangau. Finally, it crosses the Alps in a flourish of jagged peaks to the Austrian Tyrolean city of Innsbruck. It's a route that is archetypically German, a visual poem of misty, chivalrous romance.

Across Francony, Swabia and western Bavaria you pass through the topography of feudalism in all its degrees. Commanding each valley, river junction, or broad plain, a huge castle-palace proclaims the regional duke of yore; a cathedral lends him spiritual authority; in nearby towns, lesser towers and imposing manors announce his fiefs; and his borders are marked and guarded by gigantic fortresses. In each city, town and village, this hierarchy is repeated on a half-timbered domestic scale of wonderful subtlety, their buildings and services ranked according to the medieval or Renaissance priorities when they were built.

The discovery makes the journey entrancing. The system may repeat itself, but even within short distances, the landscapes and styles change completely. Vagaries of history mean you encounter Baroque, medieval, Renaissance and Gothic styles at random, just as you cross ranges of hills, river gorges, and meadow plains before the journey's dramatic finale among Alpine peaks. Tranquil, vivacious, and tempestuous by turn, the Romantic Road generates both cause and effect.

**HOW:**
By bike or car
**WHEN TO GO:**
April-October
**TIME IT TAKES:**
12-14 days (by bike, 576 km/360 mi)
**HIGHLIGHTS:**
Making the rounds with the night watchman in the walled Gothic town of Rothenburg.
The oddity of Nördlingen, an ancient town with the only completely preserved medieval walls in Germany, sitting in the middle of a huge, 15-million year old meteorite crater.
The medieval city centre of Landsberg, set romantically in the wild river bed of the Lech.
Neuschwanstein Castle – especially the Music Room, a great hall on the top floor, its ceiling painted the dark blue of night, set with a thousand stars.
The magnificent mountain landscapes on the Austrian side, near Imst.
**YOU SHOULD KNOW:**
If you take your time, this journey can be just as romantic by car.

*The gloriously romantic Neuschwanstein Castle*

# Middle Rhine Valley

The Middle Rhine Valley from Strasbourg to Koblenz is a slow crescendo culminating in Germany's most iconic geographical feature. By car, train, bicycle or boat, your path runs between the Black Forest and the more rugged Pfälzerwald to the west. The river broadens and unwinds lazily into the wetland sanctuaries downstream around Worms and Mainz. Gaining momentum with the added mass of the river Main, it fusses its way to Bingen before unleashing itself into the 65 km (43 mi) gorge twisting north to Koblenz. Celebrated in painting, poetry, music and the grandest of opera, the Rhine Gorge here is a byword for wild, dramatic beauty – but in fact it is a cultural landscape fashioned not by Nature but by Man.

UNESCO designated its World Heritage status by citing 'the continuous evolutionary nature of the cultural environment'. Meaning that with a railway and two roads (upper and lower) on each vineyard-terraced bank, the Rhine's importance as a highway for commerce and tourism is undiminished in 2,000 years – and we visitors are participants in the continuing process. The Middle Rhine Valley is the gateway to central Europe. The castles, towns and villages perched on its jagged rocks, unable to expand and unwilling to modernize the genuinely historical 'look' that helps to stimulate the mythic notions called 'Rhine Romanticism', have become their own industry. By boat, there are no tollgates but your fare contributes to the river. In a car or on a bike, you tap more directly into the symbiosis of trade and beauty that remains so attractive; but you can only see things on the other bank, where they are unreachable. However you travel, the Middle Rhine Valley is a cultural mirror of venerable age and insight, and should be respected as much as admired.

*Marksburg Castle sits above the town of Braubach.*

# Hell Valley Railway

Höllental (Hell Valley) is a 'V'-shaped gash 9 km (5.4 mi) long in the rocks of the Black Forest in southwest Germany. Its imposing slopes are 600 m (1,970 ft) high, pulled into a gorge so narrow that at one point, a bronze statue high on a crag commemorates a stag that famously escaped its hunters with one gigantic bound right across it. The Valley was typical of the dense impenetrable forest of legend until just 150 years ago, when the only mule track became a narrow road, inspiring the Railway of 1889-1901 that connects Freiburg with Donaueschingen. The Railway's engineering is as awesomely dramatic as the views to which it gives access. It is 25.4 km (15.8 mi) long, rising from 278 m (912 ft) in Freiburg to 885 m (2,903 ft) at Hinterzarten (Donaueschingen); built as a cog railway, its 5.5 per cent average gradient provoked the development of ordinary trains powerful enough to keep traction on the ascent. The new technology improved railways everywhere.

Now, the locomotives are still stubby, but sleeker. They pull double-decker carriages to cope with the large number of travellers seeking the thrill of one of western Germany's most dramatic mountain routes. Even if you're saturated with lovely Freiburg, the trip is a beautiful surprise. The 'Hirschsprungfelsen' is one of several rock formations that make whole mountains look sculpted, but the natural landscapes are enhanced by nine tunnels and a series of impossible viaducts – like the Ravennaschlucht, 222 m (728 ft) long and 42 m (138 ft) high – that carry you up to Doeggingen. Without overt fuss, in the middle of a 535 m (1,755 ft) tunnel, the line crosses Europe's principal watershed, and drops you, blinking in the bright light, in the beautiful high woods where the River Danube springs forth.

**HOW:**
By train
**WHEN TO GO:**
Year-round
**TIME IT TAKES:**
Forty to fifty minutes
**HIGHLIGHTS:**
Lake Titisee/Neustadt – set into the hills and fringed with woods, and a magnet for sailing and canoeing.
Hiking in the Wutach Gorge: the viaduct at Kappel Gutachbrucke crosses the foaming Wutach at the very head of its beautiful gorge. A 13-km (8-mi) trail traces its wildest corners across rocks and wet, slippery, plank footbridges. A Nature Reserve of maple, oak, lime and mulberry trees, it's home to 1,200 rare species, 30 orchids, 100 species of birds (including kestrels, kites and kingfishers) and butterflies, and a vanishing river.
The ceremonial coach and other treasures of the Furstenberg family, at their 1723 *Schloss* in Donaueschingen. In 1806, everything passed to Baden-Wurttemberg, so the coach looks particularly forlorn.
The 'Donauquelle' – the actual spring, in the *Schlosspark*, of the Danube, on its way to the Black Sea.
**YOU SHOULD KNOW:**
In 1770, the Höllental region of the Black Forest belonged to Austria, so when Marie-Antoinette, daughter of the Austrian Emperor, came to meet her future bridegroom, Louis XVI, she rested here. Being (technically) still in Austria, she was fed Vienna roast a la Black Forest.

*The imposing Hell Valley*

# The Alpine Road

The German Alpine Road belongs to the heyday of motorcar 'Touring', when Bugatti battled with Daimler-Benz on road rallies like Italy's Mille Miglia. The Alpine Road was built in the 1930s to stimulate the new mobility, but Hitler, ambitious to impress, annexed the project. Germany's Alpine Road was to be altogether more grand, more sweeping and more beautiful than anyone else's – and 26,000 labourers were to build 105 bridges, 15 tunnels, and ten viaducts to make it so, joining Lindau on Lake Constance with Berchtesgaden in the heartland of the Bavarian Alps. In fact, it was only completed in 2002. Now it carves boldly through some 450 km (281 mi) of Germany's loveliest mountain scenery. Through the Allgau and up into the Alps it winds past 21 turquoise and lapis lakes, 25 castles including the inspired fantasy of Neuschwanstein, and brooding dark green forests cut with secret valleys, where ancient moss soaks emerald in angry waterfalls. Imperiously the Alpine Road swings back and forth, cresting precipices and swaying round the long corniches. It's designed to be driven for fun, and fun it is.

Stunning though it is for people who love their machines, the road owes its sublime pleasures to its fundamental natural magnificence. From the grand, Italianate, gabled houses of medieval Lindau, prettily reflected in the lake, the landscapes are composed of drama and varied history, and each little town has a facet to add to its regional culture. Lakeside Bregenz, woodcarving Oberammergau, Mittenwald where violins are made in one of Bavaria's most evocative villages, Füssen and the high alpine market towns make the perfect domestic foil for the rugged wilderness of their settings. With obvious draws like Schwangau, the Bavarian Rococo ten-sided church of Kloster Ettal near Garmisch, and charming Berchtesgaden itself, the Alpine Road is like a handsome, dashing charmer who will never be out of style.

*The road winds through one of Germany's most dramatic and romantic natural landscapes.*

# Rennsteig Trail

Although the term 'rennsteig' ('racing steep') has been applied to many of Germany's ancient trade routes, 'The Rennsteig' refers exclusively to the famous high altitude trail through the Thuringian Forest. For 168 km (106 mi) it follows a ridge connecting the highest peaks between Blankenstein on the Upper Saal River, and Horschel near Eisenach. The path has served as a geographical and political border as well as a highway for over 1,000 years, but it has been relatively inaccessible until recently. That has helped revive its natural ecology, and the region has become a wildlife haven despite its popularity with summer crowds.

Known as the 'green heart' of Germany, an upland corridor of emerald forest some 20 km (12 mi) broad stretches 60 km (37 mi) northwest, (roughly) from Greiz to Eisenach. This highland plateau includes the Thuringian Forest's most dramatic, unspoilt and beautiful natural scenery. Its hills are bounded by fault lines, rising in steep scarps from the spruce and broadleaf woods whose canopy is broken only by a few open pastures close to the smallholdings of ancient hamlets. Within the forest, the highest peaks are only about 985 m (3,230 ft), but they are geological marvels of gneiss, porphyry and granite. The Rennsteig weaves between them, taking in the best vistas of its pastoral idyll, and occasionally opening up superb panoramas on either side to one of the peaceful, romantic villages folded into the hollows.

Access to the Rennsteig is well supplied by public transport: before reunification some of its sections were the favourite destinations of East German campers and schoolchildren. It also has any number of places to rest and shelter – some recalling the ridge-way's illustrious history as an Imperial messenger route, when it passed through a dozen different states and principalities. The Rennsteig's history is almost a match.

*Hikers on the Rennsteig Trail in the Thuringian Forest*

**HOW:**
On foot
**WHEN TO GO:**
April to October. It can be just as wonderful in winter, but fewer facilities make it advisable to walk only short sections at a time.
**TIME IT TAKES:**
8-14 days, depending on walkers' age and experience. None of the stages are difficult, but there are some lengthy ascents when endurance will be at a premium.
**HIGHLIGHTS:**
The satisfaction of the first day, walking far above Blankenstein, looking back across the Saal and its lakes spread below.
The highest section of the ridge, Beerberg (982m/3,221 ft), part of the astonishingly lovely view from Schmucke.
The summer toboggan run at Brotterode – just off the Rennsteig, but worth the detour for its 12 steep curves to the racing kilometer, taken full pelt.
**YOU SHOULD KNOW:**
The Rennsteig is so nearly perfect that some walkers get irritated by the presence of others using it. It can happen to anyone – but truly the landscapes are wonderful enough to share in peace.

*Burghausen and the Salzach River*

# The Benedict Trail

The Benedict Trail is a six-day biographical bike tour round the heart of rural Upper Bavaria. It's a circular route 'in the footsteps' of Pope Benedict XVI. Joseph Ratzinger was born, raised, educated, and found his vocation in the region. He still has family here, and it remains very close to his heart. After his clerical studies, he (and his brother) celebrated their 'Primiz' – the first Mass of a newly-consecrated priest – in Traunstein; and at his Papal inauguration in the Vatican he was handed a special memento of the 'Black Madonna' of Altötting, to whom he had proclaimed devotion as a boy. She has been venerated for 500 years as special to Bavaria, and is one of Germany's greatest centres of pilgrimage. It is as much a compliment to this most devout region of ultra-Catholic Bavaria, where Benedictine educational tenets have been entrenched for centuries, as to the Saint, that the Pope chose Benedict's name for himself. The Trail opens a window into that culture.

The scenic marvels – rivers, forests, ancient hamlets still toting their manorial loyalties on banners and chivalric regalia, massive fortresses, needle-spired churches and capitals of forgotten dukedoms by lakes – unfold forgivingly on the eye. These are landscapes familiar from 15th-17th century oil paintings, and not a lot has changed on the Trail's constantly stimulating historic byways. Pope apart, it's as good as a week's cycling can get. But the Papal associations (domestic and spiritual) are potent enough to re-route the imagination. His life inspires a rare intimacy between visitor and place, bringing the region's history, living, into the present. Piety in this part of Bavaria built and maintains these religious establishments in the context of a community and culture. It nurtured a Pope.

# Rasende Roland

Rugen, the Baltic island close to Germany's northeast border with Poland, has been a popular holiday resort for generations of visitors. Rasende Roland has been one of its greatest attractions for over 100 years. It's a vintage, steam-puffing, narrow gauge train service that connects Putbus with Rugen's southeast resorts of Binz, Sellin and Göhren. Its track is only 750mm (2 ft 6 in) wide and 24 km (15 mi) long, and its immaculately maintained engines and carriages – to the same scale – reinforce its appearance as an overgrown children's toy. In fact, Rasende ('Racing' or 'Runaway') Roland is a year-round scheduled service, and its significance is that only its miniature size permits it to run wholly within the boundaries of the UNESCO Biosphere Reserve that fills Rugen's southeast corner.

It's a region of peninsulas, small islands, hooked spits and sand bars; and it includes the Granitz Forest, the Mönchgut peninsula, and Vilm – a small island whose oak and beech forest has remained untouched for whole centuries, and whose unique flora can only be visited by appointment. Dogged and unobtrusive, Rasende Roland runs just inside the Reserve's edge. Thirteen stations provide access to the many natural wonders and variety of sights and entertainments. Roland is happy to be a bus. At Sellin, you can take a little funicular to the beach and pier below. Get off at Baabe for biking round leafy lanes and blueberry woods, or Göhren, to cycle through the coastal forest to Thiessow, where you can sit near a small café to watch the waders and waterfowl in the marshy lagoons. From Göhren you can also cycle back to Binz by way of long strands of white beach, ice creams and swimming.

Rasende Roland is so right for Rugen. Steam rail enthusiasts swear by its technical brilliance in miniature. The rest of us just enjoy it.

**HOW:**
By train
**WHEN TO GO:**
Year-round (Putbus-Göhren). From May to September, the number of trains between Binz and Göhren is doubled; and the line is extended from Putbus to Lauterbach, the harbour where Roland connects with the boat to and from Vilm.
**TIME IT TAKES:**
About 1.25 hours (Putbus-Göhren); about 4.5 hours (Putbus-Lauterbach-boat to Vilm-Putbus).
**HIGHLIGHTS:**
Rasende Roland's vintage engines – their steaming, hissing tubes and polished brasses are irresistible and glamorous, and each has a special character.
Jagdschloss Granitz Castle, near Binz – rosy pink crenellated towers and an astounding collection of shooting trophies in its 19th century luxurious interior.
Walking through the woods between Binz and Sellin (the train stops at both). Very Grimm!
**YOU SHOULD KNOW:**
Dreams can come true. You can take a 10-day course on how to drive a steam locomotive, supervised by a regular driver with whom you will work during his normal shift. It's the real thing, and you get a certificate as an 'Honorary Engine Driver' of Rasende Roland.

*Rugen's little steam train*

# The Eagle's Nest

The 'Eagle's Nest' is the nickname given by the American occupying forces of 1945 to Hitler's lodge on the 1,834 m (6,017 ft) peak of Mount Kehlstein, pressed against the Bavarian Alps' border with Austria. It commands a 360 degree panoramic view across the mountains, fulfilling the intentions of Martin Bormann and Hitler's innermost circle, who conceived the lodge as a 50th birthday present that would symbolize the singular height and endurance of Hitler's authority. Inevitably, the hubris of that intention makes the Eagle's Nest one of Bavaria and Germany's biggest tourist magnets. Be warned: it is a stunningly beautiful place, but despite local people's most fervent wish it is tainted by history, and no euphemism can change that.

Even so, getting there is a unique journey. There is only one way. You must take the bus from Obersalzberg, because the road (closed to normal traffic) is like no other in the world. From Obersalzberg to the top, it is designed so that in a 700-m (2,296-ft) vertical ascent over 6.5 km (4 mi), there is only one bend, and you cross the steep northwest face of the Kehlstein twice. Your ears pop and you might not look if your eyes weren't glued wide-open. At the upper car park, you are directed into an imposing, marble-lined tunnel that cuts 124 m (406 ft) straight into the mountain, where an ornate, brass-frilled and ornamented lift whisks you up to the inside of the Eagle's Nest buildings in just 41 seconds. The walls are a metre thick, and the place is a fortress. The conference and domestic rooms and the terraces would be mundane except that imagination is in full flow, reconciling extraordinary location and engineering with all the rest. You set out joking, excited. You come back speechless.

# Southern Wine Road

A towering stone archway called the Weintor ('Wine Gate') marks the beginning of Germany's Southern Wine Road, at the French/German border town of Schweigen in the Pfalz (Palatinate). From here, the Road curls through the small river valleys carved out of the foothills of the Pfälzerwald, a huge UNESCO Biosphere Reserve of upland forest, moors and sandstone crags; then emerges into the broad reaches of the Rhine, where an almost Mediterranean climate makes the low hills ideal for viticulture (the Romans introduced the vines, along with the almond trees, figs, lemons and kiwis which grow here). It is scenic, gentle countryside, set with small castles on promontories and little villages of intricately carved, half-timbered antiquity. Only Neustadt a.d.Weinstrasse, the regional centre, reveals the industrial aspects of the massive wine industry, but its giant silver tanks offer more promise than offence.

The Southern Wine Road continues north as far as Durkheim, September site of the world's biggest wine festival (held around the world's biggest wine-barrel). Durkheim is the centre of a marvellous loop hike through especially picturesque and historic villages, but the Road to Neustadt and Landau is in any case a sybarite hiker's dream – wonderful landscapes, welcoming towns and villages and festivals of some sort in every one. The trip is more intense in the hills between Landau, Bergzabern and Schweigen. Each valley is more isolated and each tiny town more distinct. Filled with flowers and vines trailing across narrow streets and ancient buildings, hamlets like Dörrenbach, Gleiszellen-Gleisorbach or Oberotterbach nevertheless have characters as different from each other as their wines. Dramatically placed between steep terraces of vines, or huddled under cliff-faces (so the higher ground is free for vineyards) they demand that you sit and drink in what makes them special.

*The church and vineyards at Siebeldingen near Landau*

**HOW:**
On foot

**WHEN TO GO:**
April-October. Even from March, there are countless festivals, including Mandelblutenfest (Almond Blossom Festival) in Gimmeldingen (March), Erlebnistag Weinstrasse (Wine Road Day) everywhere (last Sunday in August); and Neustadt's October Deutsches Weinlesefest (Wine Harvest Festival), when the German Wine Queen is crowned.

**TIME IT TAKES:**
6-8 days (Bad Durkheim-Neustadt-Bergzabern-Schweigen, 110-130 km (69-81 mi) allowing for a very short day at least once, following a night's inevitable celebrating en route).

**HIGHLIGHTS:**
Federweisser (featherwhite) wine – 'a cloudy, sweet, bubbly almost-wine' still in the process of fermenting, and much more potent that it tastes. Walking from Deidesheim across the 'Pfalz balcony', with the hills rising on one side and stunning vistas across the Rhine plain, full of ancient and beautiful wine estates.

**YOU SHOULD KNOW:**
A new route opened in 2008 called the Pfälzer Mandelpfad (Almond Trail). It's a 50-km (31-mi) hiking trail through vineyards and long rows of almond trees, from Maikammer to Bergzabern.

# Castle Road

Travelling on Castle Road across Germany to the Czech Republic feels like leafing through a storybook. One day might be a chivalric adventure of knights-at-arms. The next, a Renaissance romance of courtly manners, or a poetic extravaganza of Baroque magnificence, or the military reminiscences of a Roman soldier. There are more than sixty notable castles and palaces between Mannheim and Prague, each one with a 500 to 1,000 year-old history written into its fabric. Individually fascinating benchmarks of power, strength, wealth and pleasure during many eras, they tell an even more absorbing collective tale of German cultural evolution and of its contribution to a shared European heritage.

Castle Road is roughly 1,000 km (625 mi) long, with Nuremberg approximately halfway. Its byways wind through local, provincial and regional capitals from the Neckar Valley to the magic sylvan tranquility along the course of the Jagst and Tauber rivers. It crosses the green, picture-perfect range of Franconian Switzerland and the Main River into the crags of Francony's huge forest and the Fichtelgebirger, with Bohemia beyond. Like the natural landscapes, the castles and great houses range in style and setting from the graceful, gentle and elegant, to the sophisticated, imposing and grand. Some swagger with brooding magnificence. Others inspire frightful awe. After Bamberg (a UNESCO World Heritage Site of breathtaking historical magnitude), the terrain is wilder, and huge fortresses at Coburg and Kronach, along with a dozen medieval masterpieces farther on, show how might was usually found to be sufficiently right. Castle Road passes through whole medieval towns, like Rothenburg, Schwabisch Hall, or Kirchberg on the Jagst, where town and castle clearly show the Rennaissance and Baroque additions on their medieval origins. Castle Road's real achievement is to combine the roll call of towns and the disparate virtues of their unique structures into a single fanfare for Germany's richest history.

*Horneck Castle in Gundelsheim*

# The Route of Emperors and Kings

For more than 1,000 years, the Danube has been the principal highway for the exercise of power in central Europe. It connects major capital cities east and west. Between Regensburg and Budapest especially, its banks are studded with the towns, abbeys, fortresses, palaces and cathedrals built to demonstrate the temporal power of bishops, princelings, dukes and oligarchs whose shifting allegiances raised Kings and lowered Emperors. The gorges of the Danube still echo hallowed names – Charlemagne, Attila, Wittelsbach, Hohenzollern, Hapsburg, Esterhazy – whose assaults and confrontations have left their stamp. Journeying along it now from Germany to Austria, Slovakia and Hungary you could feel that little has changed in centuries – except that modern travellers do so in much greater comfort.

Most go by boat, which certainly offers a unique visual perspective on the Danube's natural wonders as well as its sights. Rounding a curve to your first sight of the Benedictine Abbey at Melk, in the UNESCO World Heritage Cultural and Natural Heritage Site of leafy Wachau Valley, is just one of the princely landscapes you can't see any other way. Even so, lots of people choose to travel the Danube by bike. You can speed or tarry at will, and because the special bike route follows the old towpath, the going is flat the whole way. If you're prepared to use an agent to smooth your path, you can combine bike and boat, either for excursions in Passau, Linz, Durnstein, Vienna and Budapest, or as alternative transport  through the woods, terraced vineyards, orchards and meadows between stops like the venerable towns of Aggspach, Spitz and Weissenkirchen.

Like the emperors and kings who have preceded you, allow plenty of time, however you travel. The wealth of history, culture and giddy-making surprises is too rich, and the Danube too beautiful, to rush.

*The Danube in Budapest*

**HOW:**
By boat and/or bike
**WHEN TO GO:**
April to November. Winter boat services are infrequent, and at the mercy of heavy rains/river levels.
**TIME IT TAKES:**
6-7 days by boat (Regensburg-Passau-Durnstein-Vienna-Bratislava-Esztergom-Budapest); 14-16 days by bike (including 2 rest/excursion days); 19-21 days (bike and boat, with many short excursions and including rest days).
**HIGHLIGHTS:**
Discovering Regensburg to be one of Germany's most complete medieval cities.
Tulln – with its baroque old town.
Brooding medieval magnificence and baroque exuberance – the hallmarks of the Danube's royal cities and towns.
**YOU SHOULD KNOW:**
1. By bike, travel the Danube from west to east – there's an overall incline in your favour, and both the prevailing wind and afternoon sun will be on your back. 2. If you start your journey mid-week, you'll avoid the large numbers who set out at weekends. 3. Follow the route by car only if you have no other option – you'll miss so much

# 'Limes' Route

The longest heritage route in Germany immerses you in the oldest period of German history. From Bad Honningen near Koblenz to Kelheim outside Regensburg, the 550-km (344-mi) route – all of it a UNESCO World Heritage Site – marks the line of forts, watchtowers, earthen palisades and stone walls which 2,000 years ago formed the border between the Roman Empire and the Germanic tribes Romans called 'barbarians'. 'Limes' is the Latin for 'border defences': this route is part of Roman 'limes' stretching over 6,000 km (3,750 mi) round the Middle East, North Africa, Spain and France, at the moment of the Empire's greatest expansion in circa 150. The Upper German and Rhaetian 'Limes' meet at Aalen on the upper reaches of the Kocher River. In fact, for a short way the trail is shared with the 330-km (206-mi) Kocher-Jagst Cycle Route, a delightful circular riverside ramble through the meadowlands of the Kocher and Jagst – but evidently not topographically attractive to Roman commanders.

Working its way from the Rhine-Westerwald nature reserve to the solid walls of Regensburg's Porta Praetoria ('Guardian Gate') in Bavaria, the route is a constant scenic surprise. The Lahn Valley, Nassauer region, Upper Taunus nature reserve, the Wetterau, Main Valley, Odenwald and Franconian forests, Swabian Alb and fabulous Altmuhl Valley nature reserve proffer a selection of the best German landscapes. Woven into them, in addition to original Roman remains, there are any number of reconstructions, restorations and excavations that help illustrate military and domestic life at that time – and many of them offer a range of recreational possibilities to entertain families as well as antiquarians. The German 'Limes' is a route to tackle in short stages.

**HOW:**
By bike
**WHEN TO GO:**
April to October. There are many Roman-themed guided tours, activities, festivals and re-enactments along the route. The Aalen Roman Festival takes place every even-numbered year and is especially worthwhile.
**TIME IT TAKES:**
10-14 days (by bike, and by car too, if you actually want to stop to look at some of the route's attractions and wonders).
**HIGHLIGHTS:**
The reconstructed Roman fort at Saalburg, near Bad Homburg.
The archaeology park, fort and Roman baths, and the 'Limes' museum at Aalen.
The Roman museum and 'Limes' information centre at Weissenburg.
Miltenberg's special, 19-km (12-mi) 'Roman Route' for cyclists and hardy walkers.
The reconstructed Pompeii-style villa, and ruins of the Roman Baths at Aschaffenburg.
**YOU SHOULD KNOW:**
Julius Caesar's history 'The Conquest of Gaul' tells many stories of repelling ferocious 'Alemanni' and other Germanic tribes of 'barbarians' – but the German 'Limes' were never so much a fortress defence as a line of demarcation to demonstrate Rome's authority.

*The reconstructed Roman fort at Saalburg*

# German Avenues: North to South

Germany's longest scenic route picks its way from the dazzling wall of pure white cliffs at Cape Arkona on the Baltic island of Rugen, to the flowered gardens of Reichenau, the island gem in the temperate beauty of Lake Constance. For 2,500 km (1,562 mi) between Poland in the extreme north and the southern borders with France and Switzerland, it wends through central Germany's most vivid scenery. It's a leisurely road, but it is not random. Its path is determined by the avenues of trees that line what used to be trade routes and super-highways, and are now forgotten byways. The trees were planted centuries ago as windbreaks, and to provide summer shade. Now, they provide an almost unbroken, leafy canopy of continuous charm that crosses eight of Germany's federal states – a magical path that brings travellers close to some of the country's finest cities and landmarks, without ever losing its own transcendental quality of peacefulness.

After the rivers, lakes and shimmering water-worlds of Mecklenburg and Brandenburg, the Avenues Route splits at Rheinsberg. One branch continues into Saxony-Anhalt on its way to Goslar (one of dozens of UNESCO World Heritage Sites and Biosphere Reserves in transit) before turning south above Göttingen; the other leads to Dresden and the extraordinary pristine landscapes of the Erzegebirge mountains along the Czech border, then twists along the river gorges and remote forested hills of Thuringia. Linden trees, oaks, maples, chestnuts and poplars alter the road's character with the seasons. Framing castles and palaces, fields of yellow rapeseed and open tracts dotted with red poppies and blue cornflowers, the promise of the Avenues is renewed and fulfilled down the Lahn Valley and above the Rhine gorge, to the Black Forest and up into the Alps. It's one of Germany's very best surprises.

**HOW:**
By motorbike or car
**WHEN TO GO:**
May to October
**TIME IT TAKES:**
7-10 days by motorbike or car, but motorbike clubs recommend allowing at least 14 days.
**HIGHLIGHTS:**
Meissen's porcelain, the Bauhaus at Dessau, Dresden's Zwinger Palace, Saalfeld's fairy grottoes, Bad Kreuznach's medieval bridge-houses, castles at Rheinsberg, Koblenz and 100 other stunning sites.
The 'secret corridor' – if you don't actually visit any of the cities on the Route, you could believe from the Avenues that Germany was to a large extent a vast nature park.
The UNESCO World Heritage site of Reichenau – Germany's oldest monastery complex, and repository of its historic Benedictine soul.
**YOU SHOULD KNOW:**
It's a miracle the Avenues Route still exists. Under an EU ruling, France has been forced to cut down swathes of its own trees along its famous poplar-lined highways because of the 'risk' of 'strobe-effect' when you drive down them very fast in sunshine.

*The Romanesque church of Saint Peter and Paul on Reichenau Island.*

# Zillertalbahn

The little steam train that chugs up the Zillertal (Ziller Valley) in the heart of the Tirol runs on a track only 760 mm (2 ft 6 in) wide. It is the most famous narrow gauge railway in Austria; as well as being a means of transport it's a visible reminder of the valley's history.

The railway was built in 1901-2, in the days when the local inhabitants depended on agriculture, mining and forestry for their living. They desperately needed a freight line to transport timber and minerals down the valley, to replace a thoroughly inadequate road – a tortuous track that was only negotiable by mule. Although the railway's prime purpose was to ensure that the existing economy prospered, it had the secondary unforeseen benefit of opening up the valley to tourism. Throughout the 20th century the Zillertal grew in popularity, attracting skiers, climbers and walkers with the allure of its unspoilt natural surroundings. The picturesque agricultural villages along the railway are now charming little resorts.

The Zillertal inclines gently southwards towards the Zillertaler Alps, enclosed by the Kitzbüheler Alps to the east and the Tuxer Mountains to the west. It is not only the largest valley branching from the Inntal but also the loveliest – a scenic delight of alpine pastures and forests surrounded by mountain peaks. The railway runs for 32 km (20 mi) between Jenbach, on the River Inn, and Mayrhofen, under the Hintertux Glacier, with 14 stops on the way. The train is pulled by a heritage steam engine at a maximum speed of 35 kph (22 mph). It takes you on a romantic journey back in time, in a classic passenger car, listening to the soothing repetitive clickety-clack of the wheels and the intermittent hissings and puffings of the engine, while you admire the unspoilt pastoral beauty of the valley all around you.

*The Zillertalbahn near Mayrhofen*

# The Arnoweg

*Hotels in the 19th century spa town of Bad Gastein*

In 1998, the 1,200-km (750-mi) Arnoweg long-distance hiking trail was established to celebrate 1,200 years of history, dating from the Vatican's decision in 798 to raise the status of the city of Salzburg by creating an archbishopric. The trail is named after Archbishop Arno, a friend of the Emperor Charlemagne, who was the first appointee to the post. The route combines several well-established alpine trails in a circuitous tour around Salzburgerland with 60 signposted stages and alpine huts along the way. It cuts through three national parks, climbs to heights of over 3,000 m (9,800 ft) and passes innumerable sites of cultural significance.

The Arnoweg is a challenging hike through some of the most beautiful scenery in the world. You feel as though you have stepped straight into the film set of *The Sound of Music* – a land of soaring mountains, precipitous gorges, flower-filled pastures, sparkling streams, medieval castles and picturesque towns.

You hike along mountain ridges, past the medieval town of Hallein to the Hohenwerfen fortress for a spectacular view over the Salzach Valley, then into the lush valleys and glaciated peaks of the Hohe Tauern National Park where eagles and bearded vultures circle the skies. Visit the 16th century gold-mining town of Rauris and the famous 19th century spa town of Bad Gastein, and see the medieval Mauterndorf fortress – hunting castle of the Archbishop. Stroll through the gently contoured landscape of the Grasberge and Nockberge seeing marmots, mountain hares and herds of chamois, and scramble up scree crags in the Niedere Tauern. Hike across gentle hills in the lower Alps to reach the last leg of the trail through the lakes region to the historic city of Salzburg – and return to the real world exhausted but fulfilled.

**HOW:**
On foot
**WHEN TO GO:**
June to September
**TIME IT TAKES:**
Six to nine weeks to do the whole route. Many people just do one or two sections.
**HIGHLIGHTS:**
Hohensalzburg Fortress – the largest medieval fortress in Europe.
Krimml Falls – the largest waterfall in Europe.
Grossglockner – the highest mountain in Austria at 3,798 m (12,460 ft).
Neukirchen – a beautifully situated village.
Dürrnberg Salt Mine – the oldest in the world.
**YOU SHOULD KNOW:**
This hike is not to be undertaken lightly. Some sections merely require stamina and sure-footedness but others demand previous alpine experience and the use of crampons, ice-pick and harness. You should make sure you are properly equipped and always carry a whistle to blow a distress call in an emergency.

# Grossglockner Hochalpenstrasse

**HOW:**
By car or bike
**WHEN TO GO:**
May to October
**TIME IT TAKES:**
Though it takes less than an hour by car/motorbike or 3 hours by bike, it's worth allowing a full day, making stops along the way to walk around and admire the views.
**HIGHLIGHTS:**
Hochmais – a 1,850-m (6,068-ft) viewing point over the impressive glaciers of the beautiful Feirleiten Valley.
Edelweisssptize – take a side road up to panoramic views from a height of 2,571m (8,433 ft).
Fuscher Törll viewing point, at an altitude of 2,428 m (7,964 ft).
Fuscher Lacke, a picturesque mountain lake.
Pasterze Glacier.
**YOU SHOULD KNOW:**
The Grossglockner is a toll road open only in daylight hours and in the summer months. There are plenty of parking spaces at the scenic spots along the way.

The Grossglockner High Alpine Road is one of the most spectacular scenic routes in Europe. It was first opened in 1935, specifically constructed as a tourist attraction – 48 km (27 mi) of death-defying hairpin bends winding far above the snowline with breathtaking views over the idyllic pastoral landscapes of the Hohe Tauern National Park.

The road runs across the highest pass in the Austrian Alps, between the village of Bruck on the edge of the Hohe Tauern and Heilgenblut at the foot of the Grossglockner, climbing through pastures and forests to craggy snow-covered mountain peaks. The landscape is especially striking in early summer when fingers of un-melted snow from the previous winter still reach down into the green valleys.

From Bruck the road heads southwards towards a 10 per cent incline. Make a detour up the steep little side road leading to Edelweissspitze for a mind-blowing panoramic view over the pass before heading up to Fuscher Törll, from where you get your first sighting of Grossglockner, the highest mountain of the Austrian Alps at 3,798 m (12,457 ft). From Hochtor, the highest point of the road at 2,504 m (8,213 ft), descend to Kaiser-Franz-Josef-Hohe, the most dramatic lookout point of all – Grossglockner towers directly in front of you with an incredible view of the Pasterze, the longest glacier in the Eastern Alps. The road winds downwards from the snowline through alpine meadows into the valley below, where the unbelievably quaint village of Heiligenblut sits peacefully at the foot of the Grossglockner.

Although the Hochalpenstrasse is as touristy as it gets, with signage at every bend and information points along the way, nothing can detract from the unbelievable beauty of the dramatic scenery and the thrill of the zigzagging road. This is an absolutely unmissable trip.

*The Grossglockner High Alpine Road*

# Semmering Railway

The train travels over Kalt
Rinne viaduct.

The 160-year-old World Heritage Semmering Railway is the most
scenic route in Austria, running for 41 km (26 mi) across the
Semmering Pass in the mountains between Vienna and Graz. Built
between 1848 and 1845 in the pioneering days of railway
construction, it became the prototype for all high-mountain
railways. It is an inspired feat of engineering with sixteen viaducts,
fifteen tunnels, and a gradient five times greater than anything that
had been built before.

In 1842 Austrian State Railways commissioned Carlo di Ghega, a
Venetian engineer, to design a line that would not detract from the
beauty of the natural surroundings. It was the last link in the
Südbahn line, to create a continuous track between Vienna and
Trieste on the Adriatic Sea. The resulting section of railway is a
work of art that led to Semmering becoming a fashionable fin de
siècle tourist resort, attracting visitors as much for the train journey
as for the destination.

The line runs from the country town of Gloggnitz in the
Schwarza Valley up to Semmering, a charming 19th century ski
resort that today has a distinctly quaint feel about it. The highest
point of the railway is 898 m (2,945 ft). It then descends the
southern slopes of the mountains to Mürzzuschlag, a small provincial
town where Johannes Brahms composed his Fourth Symphony.

The dramatic landscape of sheer gorges, craggy mountains and
forest makes for a hair-raising ride – winding round sheer rock faces,
shooting into tunnels and crossing precipitous ravines. Despite the
progress in engineering techniques since the line was built, you
cannot fail to admire the harmonious design. If you only do one train
journey in Austria, make it this one.

**HOW:**
By train
**WHEN TO GO:**
Any time of year
**TIME IT TAKES:**
40 minutes
**HIGHLIGHTS:**
Gloggnitz Castle, originally an 11th
Century Benedictine monastery.
Incredible mountain views.
Kalt Rinne Viaduct
Südbahn Kulturbahnhoff – Railway
museum at Mürzzuschlag.
**YOU SHOULD KNOW:**
There is a hiking track over
Semmerling Pass following the route
of the railway line.

341

*Cattle graze the alpine meadows.*

# Gerlos Alpenstrasse

**HOW:**
By car or bike
**WHEN TO GO:**
Any time
**TIME IT TAKES:**
1-2 hours by car; 4-5 hours by mountain bike.
**HIGHLIGHTS:**
Zell am Ziller – picturesque tourist town.
Piesendorf, Neukirchen – quaint villages.
Krimml Falls – highest waterfall in Europe, and one of the top eight in the world.
Zell am See – Scenic views of the Ziller and Pinzgau Mountains.
13th century Church of St Hippolyte
**YOU SHOULD KNOW:**
This is a toll road, open all year round.

The main road from the old gold-mining town of Zell am Ziller in the Tirol to the lakeside town of Zell am See in the province of Salzburg is a favourite amongst cyclists and motor-bikers. It is a winding route along a panoramic stretch of road, crossing the Gerlos Pass at an altitude of 1,530 m (5,020 ft) and descending through enchanting mountain countryside, with an amazing view of the famous Krimml Falls, the longest waterfall in Europe.

The history of the road goes back to the 17th century, when gold was discovered in the Ziller Valley. Rather than risk transporting the precious metal through what were then the foreign states of Bavaria and Tirol, the prospectors widened the mule track over the Gerlos Pass so that cartloads of gold could be carried into the safe territory of Salzburg for smelting. After the gold rush, the road fell into disrepair and the Salzach and Ziller Valleys were once again cut off from each other. Amidst much bureaucratic bickering, plans were finally drawn up for a proper highway in 1949 but the road was not completed until 1962.

The present road zigzags its way up from Zel am Ziller in the Ziller Valley to the high moorland at the top of the pass, then descends through the Salzach Valley alongside the innaccessible narrow wooded valleys and fissured gorges of the Pinzgau Mountains, along the edge of the Hohe Tauern National Park. The Krimml Ache River flows through just such a valley, making a sudden plunging drop of 380 m (1,250 ft). Tons of water thunder down in three great cascades, sending clouds of mist into the air – a truly awesome force of nature that will impress itself on your memory.

# The Brine Trail

The Salzkammergut, the old salt-mining region of Austria, is one of those rare parts of the world where mankind has managed to leave its mark without blighting the natural environment. Now designated as a World Heritage Cultural Landscape, the region is not only scenically breathtaking but also architecturally beautiful. Historic palatial buildings and picturesque villages nestle around clear-watered lakes under the silver crags and green forested slopes of the Dachstein Mountains as though they belonged naturally as an integral part of the landscape.

Of all the many charming villages, the old salt-mining town of Hallstatt is the most enchanting – a cobble-stoned lakeside town straight out of the pages of a picture book. Its fairytale 16th and 17th Century houses are squeezed into every square inch of space on a precipitous mountainside, expanding upwards on terraces and outwards into Lake Hallstätter, on piles driven into the lakebed.

The 10-km (6-mi) walk from Hallstatt to the quaint market town of Bad Goisern follows the course of a historic pipeline used for transporting brine from the salt-mine to the trading town of Ebensee on Lake Traunsee, 40 km (25 mi) away. The path, known as the Soleweg (Brine Trail), is cut into the rock face 200 m (650 ft) above the western bank of the lake. As you amble through romantic countryside of woods and pastures, spotting wildlife and breathing pure mountain air, you are accompanied by a heart-stopping view of the opposite shore – the towering crags of the Sarstein Ridge mirrored in the water. The beauty of the pastoral surroundings induces a sensation of mild euphoria and by the time you reach Bad Goisern you will be completely smitten with this glorious part of Austria.

**HOW:**
On foot
**WHEN TO GO:**
June to September
**TIME IT TAKES:**
Three hours
**HIGHLIGHTS:**
A tour of Hallstätt salt mine.
Gosauzwang Bridge – impressive 38-m (125-ft) bridge built on enormous stone piles over the rushing torrent of the Gosau River.
Breathtaking views of the Dachstein Mountains.
**YOU SHOULD KNOW:**
This is a straightforward family walk for young and old. The Salzkammergut is wonderful hiking and cycling country. There are hundreds of trails of all lengths and levels of difficulty leading around and between the lakes and up into the Dachstein Mountains.

*Evening falls over Lake Hallstätter.*

*St Gilgen on Wolfgangsee*

# Mozart Cycle Path

**HOW:**
By bike
**WHEN TO GO:**
June to September
**TIME IT TAKES:**
Seven to eight days
**HIGHLIGHTS:**
Salzburg – Mozart's birthplace and
UNESCO World Heritage City.
Herrenchiemsee – island in the
Chiemsee with fairytale castle.
Waging am See – picturesque
lakeside town.
Wasserburg – historic Bavarian salt-
trading town on the River Inn.
Mattsee Abbey,
**YOU SHOULD KNOW:**
This route is easy or moderate
cycling, much of it on cycle paths.
The route is well signposted with
hotels and guesthouses where
cyclists are welcome and there are
bike repair shops in almost
every town.

This 450-km (280-mi) cycling route in the borderlands of Austria and Bavaria is a wonderfully relaxing way to unwind, dawdling along through enchanting pastoral scenery of rolling fields, mirror-like lakes and alpine meadows with the snowy peaks of the mountains always in the background. The region was once the centre of the European salt trade, which brought in huge amounts of money. Its legacy can be seen in the architecture of the old market towns and picturesque villages that you pass – quaint period buildings, beautiful churches and magnificent castles.

From Salzburg you cycle north to Oberndorf, the site of the 'Silent Night Chapel', where the world's best-loved Christmas carol was first sung in 1818, and into the Chiemgau region of Bavaria. Pass the Waginger See, a pretty oxbow lake set in rolling farmland, and cycle along the shore of Bavaria's largest lake, the Chiemsee or 'Bavarian Sea'. The route continues past the Seeon Benedictine Monastery to the lovely old market town of Wasserburg, sited picturesquely on a bend of the River Inn, and follows the course of the river before heading back eastwards through the historic salt-mining towns of Bad Reichenhall and Berchtesgaden to the

Königssee, a beautiful fjord-like lake set in the mountains of Berchtesgaden National Park. The first circle of your journey completed, you head back into Austria through St Gilgen on Wolfgangsee, the village where Mozart's mother was born, along the shore of Wallersee to the final lake of your tour, the charming Mattsee, surrounded by hills and woods, only a few kilometres north of Salzburg. By the end of your journey you will have a marvellous sense of physical tiredness and mental well-being – your legs may ache but your head will be full of the wonderful landscapes you have seen.

# Wild Waters Hike to the Reisach Waterfall

Squeezed between the glaciated peaks of the Hohe Tauern and the limestone spires of the Dachstein, the landscape of the Niedere Tauern is a gorgeous district of lakes and tarns set in rounded mountains and plateaux veined with rivers and streams, reminiscent of Scotland. The Hochgolling, a great stone giant of a mountain, juts out at the end of the range at a height of 2,863 m (9,390 ft), towering over the mountains around the old Styrian mining town of Schladming in the Upper Enns Valley.

Better known as a cross-country ski resort, Schladming is also a great place to come in the summer. Surrounded by nature reserves, it is superb walking country – pastoral mountain scenery of rivers, pastures and woods with tumbling streams and a network of over 500 km (300 mi) of hiking trails.

The 12-km (7.5-mi) Wild Waters Trail leads from the town up through the steep Untertal valley, passing a quaint old mill and through a nature reserve, alongside a river that flows in intermittent bursts of rippling cascades. It is fed by two creeks: the Steinriesenbach, from the direction of Hockgolling, and the Reisachbach. Following the course of the Reisachbach, the valley gets ever steeper and narrower until you reach the Reisach, the longest waterfall in Styria – a violent avalanche of water that pounds down through a cleft in the rocks and drops a distance of 140 m (460 ft) over two steps. After watching this dramatic spectacle, it is worth summoning the energy to continue climbing. Carry on up the steps of Höll, a steep mountain path, and across a perilous suspension bridge to the Reisachsee, a tranquil alpine lake where you can sit and relax, admiring the silver peaks of the Dachstein Mountains in the distance.

**HOW:**
On foot
**WHEN TO GO:**
May to June – to see the waterfall at its most dramatic.
**TIME IT TAKES:**
Four to five hours
**HIGHLIGHTS:**
Hochgolling Mountain.
Views of the Dachstein Mountains.
Reisach Waterfall.
Höll Suspension Bridge.
Reisachsee – alpine lake.
**YOU SHOULD KNOW:**
This is quite a strenuous but not too difficult walk for anybody reasonably fit, including children.

# Carnic Peace Trail – Via Alpina

The Via Alpina is a network of trails traversing the Alps all the way from Trieste on the Adriatic to Monaco on the Mediterranean. It was established in 2005 to create a single cohesive route out of the countless existing trans-Alpine paths. The main artery, known as the Red Trail, is some 2,400 km (1,500 mi) long, broken down into 161 manageable stages as it weaves its way back and forth across the borders of all the Alpine countries.

The summit trail along the ridge of the Carnic Alps in eastern Austria has been integrated into the Red Trail. It was the front-line between the Austrians and Italians in World War I and, in the 1970s, the supply paths used by the troops were linked up and given the symbolic name of the 'Carnic Peace Trail' in remembrance of the devastating loss of life here – as many soldiers died from the freezing weather conditions as were killed by the enemy.

Easily as beautiful as anywhere else in the Alps, the Carnic Peace Trail is one of the less touristy sections of the Via Alpina. You enter a timeless country of traditional villages and flower-strewn pastures, make hair-raising 750 m (2,500 ft) ascents and scramble across valleys, wash in sparkling mountain water and wake each morning in a different mountain hut but to the same inevitable tinkling of cowbells and chorus of moos.

A hike through the Austrian Alps really is the perfect way of getting away from it all – walking through some of the world's most beautiful scenery, spending the night in the shelter of spartan but adequate mountain huts, and living on the staple alpine diet of cured ham and un-pasteurised cheese, you cannot fail to be satisfied.

**HOW:**
On foot
**WHEN TO GO:**
June to September
**TIME IT TAKES:**
A week (four months for the whole Via Alpina).
**HIGHLIGHTS:**
Lienz – beautiful historic town.
Traces of trenches, battery positions and bivouacs from World War I.
Medieval villages.
Outstanding natural scenery.
**YOU SHOULD KNOW:**
The Carnic Peace Path is not technically difficult and requires no climbing equipment, merely sure-footedness and a good level of fitness. In July and August you will be hard put to find yourself walking completely alone. Hordes of trekkers flock to the Alps at this time of year.

# Vrsic Pass Road

**HOW:**
By car, bike or on foot
**WHEN TO GO:**
May to October. Cyclists come for the first Sunday in September, when over 1,000 of them race the 12 steep and winding km to Vrsic Pass.
**TIME IT TAKES:**
1.5-2 hrs (by car, Bovec to Kranjska Gora); 1-2 days (by bicycle); 3-4 days (hiking). Cyclists may prefer to make the round trip of Kranjska Gora-Bled-Bohinj-Tolmin-Bovec-Vrsic-Kransjka Gora, a 5-6 day tour for the experienced
**HIGHLIGHTS:**
The Valley of the Triglav Lakes.
The view from Vrsic to the awesome Martuljek mountain triangle.
The glorious concentration of rarities in the Juliana Alpine Garden, set at 800 m (2624 ft) at the southern foot of Vrsic Pass, in the valley where the mild Mediterranean climate still has influence.
The Russian Chapel at the northern foot of Vrsic Pass. Just one of many moving memorials along this road, this one commemorates the death of more than 300 Russian PoWs in an avalanche in 1916.
**YOU SHOULD KNOW:**
The Vrsic Pass is part of the arena where the young Ernest Hemingway witnessed the daily horror and bitter experience that inspired *A Farewell To Arms*.

Triglav National Park fills the northwest pocket of Slovenia, where it meets both Austria and Italy. It protects Slovenia's Julian Alps, returned to their pristine remoteness since their mutilation during some of the bloodiest and longest battles of World War I. Untouched since, what little development had taken place has now been reversed. Only one road remains across it from which to gauge the stunning landscape of winding glacial valleys, torrent-filled gorges, forested ridges and stark mountains. It follows two of the most beautiful valleys of all. From Bovec, on the Park's southern edge, it traces the milky turquoise Soca River up the last of the narrowing Upper Trenta Valley to the alpine watershed of the Vrsic Pass. The road seems to end before a towering ridge of forest that rises high beyond the tree line to the snowy peaks of Jalovec (2,645 m/8,676 ft) on one side, and Slovenia's highest mountain, Triglav (2,864 m/9,394 ft) on the other; but it twists its way steeply to Vrsic itself, Slovenia's highest pass at 1,611 m (5,284 ft). A short walk to one side leads you to the Soca's source – a cave from which, in spate, a torrent jets out into a series of falls and descending ravines.

From the top of Vrsic, the hairpin descent is dizzying. So is the panorama, of one the most picturesque of all alpine valleys. Zgornjesavska is a Hollywood dream Alpine set of meadow, mountain, snow, stream and forest; and its fame is global thanks to the World Cup skiing venue of Kranjska Gora on its far side (just outside the Park). It's hard to believe that the bitter events of World War I could take place in the face of such beauty – but there is a stream of small monuments and memorials among the rare alpine flora on either side of the road.

*Lake Bohinj in northwest Slovenia*

# Rafting down the Drava River

Born as a mountain torrent in the Julian Alps in Austria, the River Drava is significantly broad and deep by the time it flows through Dravograd into Slovenia, through which it runs for 102 of its total 720 km (450 mi). Since Roman times it has been the region's sole highway – not just for ordinary trade, but also for the lumber industry in the surrounding heavily forested mountains. Rafting lumber became the most important economic activity, and towns and villages grew up along the Drava's banks on the profits. The trade centred on the ancient city of Maribor, where the development of an enormous raft harbour (the 'Lentstatt') attracted the parallel growth of riverside facilities and entertainments. Today, the Lent district is still Maribor's most beautiful, authentically old and cobbled, and lively. Only the Drava has been tamed. Hydro-electric dams slowed its legendary boiling currents to a broad, placid stream; and it's become a watery theatre for Slovenians to re-enact their cultural traditions for visitors.

Which means there are two ways to go rafting on the Drava. If you're determined and lucky, you can raft from Dravograd all the way to Maribor or even Ptuj, passing through the most beautiful section of the entire river's course, camping or sleeping in hotels as your own pace dictates. Otherwise, you join a raft at Koblarjevzaliv (an artificially-wide but very pretty section of river near Maribor) with anything from five to forty others. Unfortunately, each raft promises to send '2 rafters plus a rafter's girl' with you, and their function is not just to steer, but to sing you their selection of hearty Slovenian folk songs, and stuff you full of (quite good) wine.

**HOW:**
By raft

**WHEN TO GO:**
May to October/November (depending on the weather). Come for the Lent Festival, when throughout June Maribor's left bank district celebrates its oldest traditions.

**TIME IT TAKES:**
1 hour is the standard Maribor rafting experience, but you can arrange as long a trip as you want. Rafting from Dravograd to Maribor usually takes 2-3 days, but there are many good wildlife, landscape and history reasons along the Drava that could tempt you to spend much longer.

**HIGHLIGHTS:**
The early mists and high summer noon, and water so still you can hear the scurried 'rustle…plop!' of a water-vole.
The lack of river traffic (until very recently, all navigation was banned), which may not last, as jetfoils have now been allowed access.

**YOU SHOULD KNOW:**
If the Slovenian equivalent of Caribbean 'pirate cruises' is what it takes to raft the Drava, it's still worth it. It's fun, too.

*Ptuj on the banks of the Drava River*

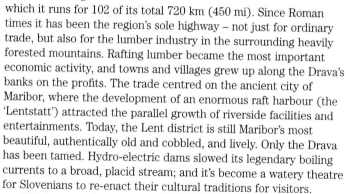

# The Bohinj Railway

**HOW:**
By train
**WHEN TO GO:**
April to early November. If you ride
the train only part of the way, you
can link the journey to one of the
spring or summer festivals that
abound in the region, or to one of
many natural attractions in the
Triglav National Park.
**TIME IT TAKES:**
3-3.5 hours (Jesenice to Gorizia, with
a stopover before the return of about
4 hours, in either direction).
**HIGHLIGHTS:**
The steam engines – you don't have
to be a train enthusiast to appreciate
the various engines, borrowed from
the Railway Museum at Ljubljana.
The very curious, double Savica
Waterfall, near Ukanc village – one of
many splendours on Bohinj Lake, it
appears to thread itself through two
sinkholes, re-emerging lower down.
A ride on a 'Lucija' riverboat – a
paddlewheel – on the emerald water
of the Soca River at Most na Soci.
The waft of Mediterranean mountain
scents as you descend closer to the
Friuli.
**YOU SHOULD KNOW:**
All the way along the Bohinj Railway,
not one inch of landscape is less
than sensational.

The Bohinj Railway is an authentic classic steam train trip on a historic line through some of Europe's loveliest mountain scenery. It runs between Jesenice, just inside Slovenia's border with Austria, to Gorizia in Italy, along what used to be the Austro-Hungarian 'Transalpina' railway from Vienna to Trieste, inaugurated in 1906. Although the service is scheduled (at roughly fortnightly intervals), it's definitely an excursion train. You can get on or off at any of the stops, and rejoin it after your own sightseeing, but the full trip incorporates a bus tour to the Friuli vineyards, staff in period uniforms, tour guides for railway enthusiasts, and entertainment staff to make sure travellers match Slovenian standards of enthusiastic merrymaking.

Partying aside, the Bohinj Railway takes you through countryside so beautiful it will twang your heartstrings. From Jesenice, you steam along the Sava River past the alpine dreamscape lake at Bled (where, if you started your journey in Italy, the medieval castle will be your vineyard-equivalent lunchtime goal). After Bohinj itself, the jewel of Slovenia's alpine crown, a 6.33-km (3.93-mi) tunnel cuts through the Bohinj Mountains to the southern side of the Julian Alps, and skirts the Triglav National Park until it turns southwest along the Soca Valley at Most na Soci. The bridges, viaducts and gradients must have represented extraordinary engineering at the time they were built, and they are still spectacular. The most famous bridge of all is at the Gorizia end of the line. The Solkanski Most features the longest (220 m/721 ft) stone railway arch in the world, with 4,533 chunks of limestone in the principal arch. Bohinj Railway staff have been known to tease travellers by testing their memory for these important facts – after the vineyard visit. The fun is deemed essential to the journey.

*Lake Bled*

# The Amber Trail

*Orava Castle in the Orava River Valley*

For 1,000 years, amber has been traded between the Baltic and Hungary. All along this route you will find amber for sale and as decoration. Exploring the route by bicycle brings you into first-hand contact with people whose lives and culture have been shaped by the rich, golden-brown fossil resin. If you travel with a guide, he or she will be one of them; and an invaluable mentor of the fine details in the rich historical quilt ahead of you. The daily stages of the bicycle tour read like a catalogue of 2,000 years of violent cultural collisions. Between Budapest and Kracow you pass six UNESCO World Heritage Sites, and numerous castles of varying beauty, puissance and repair, attesting conflicts of Roman, Barbarian, Lithuanian, Polish, Ostrogoth, Turkish, Austro-Hungarian, Hapsburg, Nazi German, Soviet Russian, and (most recently) economic origin. Soaring pinnacles on cathedrals, palaces, and public buildings reveal the complex bargains of Church and State at Esztergom, Banska Bystrica, Orava and Kracow. Evidence of more humble aspirations and compromises – at Banska Stiavnica, Vikolinec, Liptovsky Mikulas, Lanckorona, Kalwaria Zebrzydowska and the Wieliczka salt mine – adds an equally stunning perspective of daily lives under feudalism and communism.

The revived Amber Trail is now an outstanding example of central European co-operation: three countries (Hungary, Poland and Slovakia) reserving a corridor across some of their loveliest hills, rivers, and plains for international enjoyment. The Danube Valley and the Great Bend, the Fatra and Tatra sections of the Carpathian Mountains, and the Northern Plain in Poland, include magical landscapes of every variety; and the Trail route follows the smallest back roads. There are wetland meadows as well as mountain beech forests and river gorges. Tranquility has returned to this newly pristine countryside, enfolding former turbulence into exquisite villages happy to extend their welcome to passing travellers.

**HOW:**
By bike
**WHEN TO GO:**
May to October
**TIME IT TAKES:**
Ten days (Budapest to Kracow, 330 km/206 mi by Amber Trail, cycling 40-50 km /25-32 mi in 4-5 hours on 8 days, with one rest day). Guided groups have a back-up vehicle for transfers in case of unspeakable weather or weariness.
**HIGHLIGHTS:**
Riding the length of Szentendre Island in the middle of the Danube as it reaches the Great Bend at Esztergom (and the view of the Bend from Visigrad Castle when you get there).
The UNESCO-cited historic old centre of Banska Stiavnica.
The wooden church at Lestiny, built without a single nail; and the wooden rugmaking looms in Malatina. Both villages are typical of the Chocsky and Oravsky Hills.
The huge Gothic fortress of Orava Castle commanding its world from high above the river at Oravsky Podzamok – you're afraid to imagine what its history signifies.
**YOU SHOULD KNOW:**
With a guide and backup transport options, which can include boats or an enchanting miniature train (near Kremnica and its beautiful 7 peaks), the Amber Trail is suitable for anyone reasonably fit. The route has surprises and entertainments en route to keep the most demanding travellers of any age group riveted and eager for more.

*The horses await you.*

# Hortobagy Great Plains

**HOW:**
On horseback
**WHEN TO GO:**
April to November
**TIME IT TAKES:**
7-14 days for a number of scheduled tours; but most are of negotiable length and direction if the right numbers (4-12 usually) want to make the trip.
**HIGHLIGHTS:**
The Kisber horses, mainly chestnuts with some greys, trained to standards of responsiveness and endurance that make you aspire to be a better rider (but be prepared to let them have their eager heads on the canters).
Miles and miles of gently rolling, poppy-filled, long-grass pastures at Hortobagy.
The 'Puszta Otos'('Great Plains Five') – when a *csiko* (horse-herder) stands with one foot on each of two horses, while driving three (or even more) others, unyoked, before him, at a full gallop. Circuses perform a yoked version at a trot. At full pelt, screaming in the Puszta wilderness, it's an elemental glory. Ask, and you may receive.
**YOU SHOULD KNOW:**
Your back recovers.

Unless they are actually cowboys, even experienced riders like their comfort on a long journey, so the most popular way to ride Hungary's 'Puszta' (Great Plains) is to ride from place to place, but to stay in hotels rather than camp. It's possible, but difficult, to do it any other way. And you do need to be experienced for a journey across northern Hungary's vast grasslands to its greatest vineyards at Eger and Tokaj. Depending on your choices, you could take seven to fourteen days, riding steadily with long canters, for five or six hours. There's scarcely a fence or manmade obstacle to bar the way through hundreds of kilometres of woods, shrub-studded hills and a horizon of stirrup-high grasslands. You get to feel the Puszta intimately; and the only people you're likely to see will be herders, practicing inbred equine traditions going back 600 years. If you're lucky, they might show you some of their astounding accomplishments with horses.

After the exhilaration of each day's riding, it's equally stimulating to arrive at places emblematic of Hungary's history and culture. If you start from a stud farm for the Kisber horses you will be riding, you might visit the UNESCO World Heritage village of Holloko, gallop through the beech forests of the wild Bükk Hills to a stud farm for Lipizzaners, spend a day in the beautiful Baroque city of Eger with its 1,000 year-old history, and another week in and beyond Hortobagy, before reaching Tokaj, home to Hungary's most princely history and vines. You arrange your own route and timescale in conjunction with others wanting to go a similar direction – but like most keen riders, after a couple of days you'll be so enthralled by the willing intelligence of your Kisber transport, you'll just want to stay in the saddle forever.

# Poznan to Warsaw Scenic Road

The drive between the two major Polish cities of Poznan and Warsaw can, of course, be made on a multi-lane highway. It's much better though, if you have the time, to take the scenic route, a lovely trip through the Weilkopolska lakelands, passing small towns, old churches, castles and palaces.

Poznan itself is a historically significant city on the Warta River. At one time the capital of Greater Poland, it contains the oldest cathedral in the country, built in the 10th century. Today it is the region's administrative capital, and a commercial and industrial centre. Just a few miles to the south, and a slight detour off your route to the village of Kornik, lies the Weilkopolska National Park, a peaceful area of forests and lakes, cut with a few, well-signed trails. Set on a lake, Kornik boasts a splendid, moated castle, with a landscaped arboretum that includes trees and shrubs from around the world. At Rogalin, not far away, stands a beautiful 18th century palace, with 3 protected oak trees in the grounds that are over 1,000 years old.

The journey takes you to several more castles and palaces before reaching the city of Kalisz, generally considered Poland's oldest city as it was mentioned as being a trading post by Ptolemy in 200 BC. Avoiding heavily industrial Lodz, travel south to Piotrkow, site of the first Jewish ghetto in the country, built in 1939. Outside the town is the infamous Rakow Forest, where memorials stand testament to the 600 Jews massacred here in 1942, and to the 7,000 Polish and Russian prisoners also killed here. Now you are about an hour's drive from Warsaw, Poland's lively capital city. Remarkably, brilliantly rebuilt after World War II, its historic old town is inscribed on the UNESCO World Heritage List.

**HOW:**
By car
**WHEN TO GO:**
May to September
**TIME IT TAKES:**
Can be done in a day, but you may well want to stay en route, perhaps in a restored palace or an eco-farm.
**HIGHLIGHTS:**
The annual Classical Music Festival in Poznan.
Smielow Palace, late 18th century, it is set in a large nature park.
Goluchow Castle, where you can see Polish bison in the grounds.
**YOU SHOULD KNOW:**
The Gothic Cathedral of St Peter and Paul, built on an island in the river at Poznan, contains the tomb of Mieszko 1, the founder of Poland, and of his son Boleslaus the Brave, the first King, crowned in 1025.

*The old town hall in Poznan*

353

# Galician Carpathians

Tucked away in the far south-eastern corner of Poland is the Bieszczady National Park. Located in the Carpathian Mountains, which rise in Slovakia and stretch through Poland, Ukraine and into Romania, the Park protects the Bieszczady Mountains, in the eastern section. It has been enlarged four times since its creation in 1973, when this unique region became the world's first tripartite International Biosphere Reserve, encompassing areas lying in Slovakia and Ukraine.

The mountains comprise three zones: foothills forested with willow, ash, sycamore and grey alder, ancient beech forests interspersed with firs and maples at about 900 m (3,000 ft) and high pastures, known as *poloniny*, from 1,050 m (3,500 ft). This gorgeous, Alpine-type grassland includes scree and rocks covered with rare lichen and mosses. Elsewhere, endemic wildflowers as well as Alpine and sub-Alpine species carpet the mountain meadows. Bieszczady National Park has 132 km (83 mi) of marked trails, providing hikes of relative ease. One of the best is the hike to the top of Mount Tarnica, at 1,364 m (4,500 ft) the Park's highest peak.

Starting at Ustrzyki Gorne walkers can follow the red path through the forest, which probably looks at its best when decked in glowing autumnal colour. If you start early enough you may see deer, but these forests are rich with flora and fauna, including wolves, bears, elk, lynx, wildcats, wild boar and beavers, which have been successfully introduced into the creeks and streams. As the trail leaves the forest for the *poloniny*, the landscape opens out around you, the wind ruffles through the grasses, and an extraordinary range of raptors can be seen – honey buzzards, goshawks, sparrow hawks, perhaps even a golden eagle. On reaching the top of Mount Tarnica, the 360-degree views over the whole Park are quite something to behold.

*Bieszczady National Park*

# Dunajec Gorge

*Rafting down the river.*

Way down in the south of Poland, on the border with Slovakia, is the little-known Pieniny National Park, through which the Dunajec River flows. An important tributary of the Vistula, the river cuts through the narrow Pieniny Mountain range, and over the centuries its waters have gouged a splendid gorge through the limestone crags. For 18 km (11 mi) the river forms the border with Slovakia, and since both countries joined the European Community in 2004, rafting downstream has become a popular jaunt for tourists from many destinations.

The Flisaki raftsmen have been active on the Dunajec for centuries, transporting goods, fishing for the salmon that were once plentiful here, and steering log-booms. In 1832 tourism began on the river, and just over 100 years later, the Flisaki registered as an organization. Today some 500 men work about 250 wooden rafts, each carrying ten passengers, and accompanied by two raftsmen, wearing traditional round-brimmed, black felt hats, usually decorated with white cowry shells or embroidery.

Starting from the marina in Sromowce-Katy, the rafts set out on their voyage, bobbing down through rapids which give onto more placid stretches of water, and finding their way around seven loops in the river, changing direction by more than 90 degrees many times over the whole course. On the way they pass through wonderful limestone scenery – 500 m (1,600 ft) cliffs, partially tree-clad, forests and fields, even two formidable castles, one on either side, built as strategic fortresses during the 13th and 14th centuries.

The Flisaki are knowledgeable guides as well as being very experienced raftsmen, and they delight in educating their passengers about the mountains and their folklore. The trip ends in Szczawnica, a charming mountain resort in the Grajcarek Valley, with vistas towards the highest peaks of the Pieniny range.

**HOW:**
By raft
**WHEN TO GO:**
April to October, but late May to mid-September is probably the best time.
**TIME IT TAKES:**
About 2 hours 15 minutes
**HIGHLIGHTS:**
Czorsztyn Castle, a partially restored ruin.
Niedzica Castle, beautifully maintained this is a hotel as well as housing an interesting museum.
Walk the new, 90-m (295-ft) bridge from Poland's Sromowce Nizne, at the foot of the Three Crowns mountains, to the picturesque village of Cerveny Clastor (Red Monastery) in Slovakia.
**YOU SHOULD KNOW:**
You can raft the river every day during the season except for two religious holidays – Corpus Christi and the first day of Easter.

*A view of the beautiful city of Prague*

# Vltava River Cruise

Since the advent of cheap flights the ancient and magnificently beautiful city of Prague has become a popular destination for short and long breaks and at times it can seem uncomfortably crowded. The river, always an important part of the life of the city, offers a breathing space. Sightseeing cruises of various durations are available and in summer a regular ferry runs north to the suburb of Troja and south, through lovely countryside, to Slapy Dam.

Prague Castle, the best-known image of the city, occupies the heights of the Left Bank. The long, almost blank palace façade is crowned by the irregular Gothic spires and pinnacles of the St Vitus Cathedral. Below are the narrow, hilly streets, steep roofs, towers and cupolas and terraced gardens of Mala Strana, 'Little Quarter'. To the south rises the big, wooded hill of Petrin with its funicular railway.

On the Right Bank, several of the imposing buildings of Stare Mesto, 'Old Town', can be seen, including the Smetana Museum and the National Theatre with its gold-topped roof. From here down to Vysehrad, 'High Castle', with the dominating spires of the neo-gothic St Peter and St Paul, the river side of Nove Mesto – 'New Town' – is lined with fine mansions and commercial buildings, including the Art Nouveau House of the Hlahol Choir.

Boat trips offer good views of some of the city's many bridges and of the islands. On Slovansky Ostrov stands the Baroque Sitka Tower; Kampo, near the weir built in the 19th century to help navigation, has peaceful gardens and an old mill, now an art gallery.

# Gustav Mahler Cycle Trail

This cycle trail, one of a number of well-planned and mapped tours in the Czech Republic, runs from Jihlava in the heart of the Bohemian-Moravian highlands northwards to Kutna Hora in Central Bohemia, west of Prague. The trail covers about 83 km (52 mi) of track, with short country road sections, through wooded, rolling hills, river valleys, villages, and two charming towns with Mahler connections.

In medieval times this was a wealthy and important silver-mining region. Jihlava was founded by King Wenceslas in the 13th century and prospered. However, it never recovered from the ravages of the Thirty Years' War, though it still has many fine medieval and renaissance buildings. In 1865 the Mahler family moved here; Gustav attended the grammar school and learnt music; his love of Czech folk tunes was life-long. His parents are buried in the Jewish cemetery.

Humpolec is another old town with a history of silver mining, though it became better known as a centre for the cloth trade. The art nouveau Town Hall houses a museum with a Gustav Mahler gallery. The hilltop village of Kaliste, with its lovely views over the countryside, was Mahler's birthplace. The tiny cottage has been reconstructed and is visited by music lovers from all over the world.

For a change from Mahler, a restored castle above the Sazava River bridge at Ledec nad Sazavou offers a collection of handicrafts, weapons and coins.

Beautiful Kutná Hora became the favourite residence of several Bohemian kings and rivalled Prague economically, culturally and politically, though after years of warfare and the flooding of the silver mines it fell into decline. Now, with its wealth of Gothic and Baroque buildings, this delightful town is a UNESCO World Heritage Site.

**HOW:**
By bike
**WHEN TO GO:**
May, June, September and October
**TIME IT TAKES:**
2 or 3 days
**HIGHLIGHTS:**
Kutná Hora holds a splendid Gothic pageant every June.
The Gothic Cathedral of St Barbara is spectacular with a 5-aisled nave and a roof of 3 tent-like towers.
In the ossuary at Sedlec is a chandelier constructed from bones.
**YOU SHOULD KNOW:**
This scenic, rural touring cycle route should pose no problems.

*The Cathedral of St Barbara in beautiful Kutná Hora*

357

# Island hop along the Dalmatian Coast

**HOW:**
By boat
**WHEN TO GO:**
May, June, early July, September and October
**TIME IT TAKES:**
At least a week
**HIGHLIGHTS:**
Split – Diocletian's Palace. Built for the Emperor's retirement, the walls of this UNESCO World Heritage Site enclose Roman buildings converted over the centuries.
Brac – the Supetar town cemetery is a dreamlike conglomeration of monuments by Ivan Rendic, one of Croatia's leading sculptors.
Lopud, Kolocep and Sipan – the only inhabited islands in the Elaphite chain. Beautiful and unspoiled they are a day trip from Dubrovnik.
Dubrovnik's city walls: the circuit of the battlements gives splendid views of the roofs, towers and domes and the grid plan of the town.
**YOU SHOULD KNOW:**
The island routes will present no difficulties for regular cyclists. Ferry tickets must be purchased before the journey.

Dalmatia's dramatically beautiful coastline is fringed by hundreds of small, enticing islands. Those south of Split are easily reached and, despite their popularity, peaceful. They offer fine cycling – quiet roads through fertile, hilly, well-wooded countryside, tiny coves, pretty villages, and no long distances. Combined yacht and cycle trips are becoming popular, but bike rental is available in many places and the bike fares on the car ferries are modest. Split is a big, hectic, vibrant city centred on an old town built around and into the massive remains of Diocletian's Palace. The regular ferry connecting Split and Dubrovnik calls at Brac, Hvar, Korcula and Mljet. Wooded Solta and rugged, remote Vis are easily reached from Split but not by the connecting route.

Brac produces good wine and its lustrous white building stone is prized worldwide. The south coast has several seaside villages, including Bol, famous for its lovely beach and for its windsurfing.

Ancient little harbour towns nestle in the deep bays of Hvar's green, indented coastline, but, with its harbour and fortress, Renaissance square and Gothic palaces, Hvar Town is the main attraction.

Popular Korcula, a perfect miniature medieval city, perches on a steep headland. Marco Polo was born here during the long Venetian rule that shaped the glorious architecture of the town.

The island is thick with orchards and vineyards and ringed by fishing villages.

Mljet, with its fertile farmland, untouched forest and salt-water lakes, quiet villages and fine monastic buildings, is seductively tranquil. Much of the island is a National Park.

Dubrovnik, a medieval city reshaped by the Baroque and now carefully reconstructed after its infamous shelling in 1991-2 is, with its pearly marble streets, rich history and culture, and setting of lushly wooded mountains and breezy blue waters, enchanting.

*Korcula old town*

# Budva Riviera

The beautiful Budva Riviera, with its azure water, background of mountains and string of bays, coves and fine sand beaches, runs only about 35 km (23 mi) from Budva to Petrovac. Some of the settlements that punctuate the coast date back to Roman, Greek and even Phoenician times, though little archaeological evidence remains. A walk along the Riviera, either on the beaches, by the coast road or on the peaceful hillside path parallel with the old road, allows breaks or overnight stays at irresistible beaches and exploration of the inland villages and old, frescoed monasteries.

Budva is a delightful place. The old town was built on a headland and is surrounded by 15th century walls. This busy tourist town offers old buildings, churches and museums, festivals and a lively nightlife. Southwards, a promenade walk follows the bay round to Becici beach. Milocer, once a royal holiday spot is, with its two beaches – King's and Queen's – and lush parkland setting, a fashionable resort. Sveti Stefan is reached by a causeway; built on a tiny island as a fishermen's village in the 15th century, it is now an exclusive and beautiful hotel complex.

Between here and Petrovac are several small, secluded beaches and an interesting inland area, the peach and pomegranate clad Pastrovici Hills. This was once a semi-autonomous Dukedom with its own language and traditions.

Petrovac, with its spectacular setting and red sand, is an attractive and very popular town. It retains charm and intimacy, but is threatened by the density of recent construction. A walk south to Lucice beach, or on to the relatively undeveloped Buljarica beach escapes the crowds.

*The island of Sveti Stefan on the Adriatic*

**HOW:**
On foot
**WHEN TO GO:**
May, June and September
**TIME IT TAKES:**
Three days plus, depending on stops
**HIGHLIGHTS:**
Views from the battlements over the whole of Budva, Saint Nikola Island and Sveti Stefan.
The little port village of Przno (before it is over-developed) for a sunset drink on the waterfront.
**YOU SHOULD KNOW:**
Accommodation can be over-subscribed and expensive.

# Dajti Express Cable Car

**HOW:**
By cable car
**WHEN TO GO:**
April to June, September and October
**TIME IT TAKES:**
One day or less
**HIGHLIGHTS:**
There are some good restaurants,
including one with fish straight from
its own pools.
In the late spring, alpine strawberries
grow among the trees.
You may come across one of Enver
Hoxha's domed anti-invasion bunkers
in the woods.
**YOU SHOULD KNOW:**
The summit of Mount Dajti is
still fenced off, occupied by
military installations.

Tirana, the capital of Albania, has its own eccentric charm – hospitable natives, orange trees in the streets, some old Ottoman buildings and a glorious street market. From the chaotic jumble of poverty, hastily erected buildings and traffic which is the city centre, the dark bulk of Mount Dajti, 25 km (15 mi) to the east can, smog permitting, be seen.

This spacious and easily accessible National Park is a favourite excursion and escape for city-dwellers. It has been inhabited from early times and the name could be linked with the ancient cult of Diktynna, a mother goddess venerated around the Mediterranean. Its relatively low altitude – 1,610 m (5,232 ft) – allows forest cover and pleasant shady walking in the summer.

Until 2005 the only approach was by road, passing through the city outskirts and fashionable new housing, winding along the

contours of the mountain. Inside the Park, low-key tourist developments are built around restaurants and the road finishes at a large, green area which is used for picnics and barbecues. This is also the terminus for the Dajti Express Cable Car, an Austrian-built enterprise which runs from the edge of town. The 4-km (2.5-mi) ride up to 1,230 m (3,998 ft) takes just fifteen minutes. The views over the mountain range, the sprawl of Tirana and the eastern lowlands are excellent. From the Dajta Field, paths lead through attractive beech woods and areas of pine and fir. These quiet wooded slopes are home to many flower and plant species and to small mammals including red squirrels and beech martens.

The woods are cool and peaceful, a perfect respite from the city.

*Views over the mountains from
the Dajti Cable Car*

# The Albanian Coast from Corfu

The southern Albanian coast is very close to Corfu and, since the 7th century BC when Greece established colonies in what was then Illyria, strong trade and cultural links have existed. Now regular short ferry and hydrofoil crossings from Corfu make it easy to reach Saranda and the remarkable UNESCO World Heritage Site at Butrint. It is just possible to make a day-trip of it.

Sunny Saranda is an attractively situated port and seaside town, a pleasant place to stay. An ancient city, it has Roman and Byzantine remains, though little archaeological work has been undertaken. On the Butrint road south lie the interesting ruins of the Byzantine Monastery of Shen Gjergi, a lovely spot with views of the Adriatic and good bird watching in the marshes. Further south, the pleasant beach-resort of Kasmili makes an alternative base.

Butrint is one of the most exciting sites in the Balkan Peninsula. Set against a background of hills and largely bounded by water (ancient Butrint was effectively an island), this extensive and complex site has remains dating from periods covering 2,500 years. The excellent guide to Butrint by Neritan Ceka is essential for serious exploration. The massive perimeter walls, some dating from the 5th century BC, shelter Roman baths, a Venetian tower, a Greek lustral well, fragments of early Christian buildings and a large complex known as the Tri-conch Palace. Finely carved gates pierce the walls, two opening onto the lakeshore, where the ancient harbour lay. The inner fortress contains temples and baths, a gymnasium, a Roman house, Greek theatre and acropolis and an early Christian baptistery. Many of these have fine mosaic floors.

*The Basilica at Butrint near Saranda*

**HOW:**
By boat and car
**WHEN TO GO:**
Late April to October
**TIME IT TAKES:**
It's possible to complete the trip in 1 day, but much better to make it a jaunt of at least 3 days.
**HIGHLIGHTS:**
The enormous baptistery is a building of great beauty and tranquillity.
Kasmili has an idyllic beach, clean, clear blue water and good fish restaurants.
Sunset on Saranda's waterfront, when Corfu seems to drift in a haze.
**YOU SHOULD KNOW:**
Get hold of the guidebook to Butrint before your visit as it's rarely available on site.
The mosaics at Butrint are usually sand-covered for protection.

*A view from the ferry bus as it crosses Lake Komani*

# Crossing Lake Komani

**HOW:**
By boat
**WHEN TO GO:**
June to September
**TIME IT TAKES:**
At least two days
**HIGHLIGHTS:**
Shkorda – Rozafa Castle, a medieval/Venetian fortress high above the confluence of three rivers.
The Phototheque a selection of photographs from a huge 19th century archive, a unique record of historical and everyday life in Northern Albania.
An easy trip from Bajram Curri is to lovely Valbona Valley with its plunging waterfalls.
**YOU SHOULD KNOW:**
Catering on the ferry is rudimentary. The tunnel to the ferry is unlit, mud-roofed and often flooded.

Lake Komani was formed when the River Drin was dammed in 1970 as part of a huge hydroelectric scheme. It winds, fjord-like, from the huge Vau i Dejax dam near Shkodra to the Fierza Dam. The memorable ferry ride is the best way to reach the remote and spectacular Tropoja region – the road is dreadful. From Tirana a minibus leaves to link with the RORO ferry and continues to Bajram Curri from Bregluna at the Fierza end; the return trip leaves early next day.

Another ferry plying the waters is the local waterbus, a ramshackle-looking craft created by welding an old bus onto a hull. This takes about four hours – twice as long as the car ferry – but it provides links for the remote dwellings of the lake and offers a unique insight into the life of the area. A night in Shkodra (old Scutari) makes catching this early ferry bus possible. This interesting old city was, under Ottoman rule, the largest town in Albania; it is still predominantly Muslim, and very traditional. The road to the ferry station – about 35 km (22 mi) follows the river valley and passes through a narrow tunnel. The ferry journey is superb, following the twists and turns of the lake whose deep, still, jade-green waters reflect the precipitous tree-clad gorges. In places the deciduous woods have been cleared, the ground terraced to allow those whose homes are clustered high above the lake to scratch a living.

Bajram Curri is a windy, ugly little town set in magnificent scenery. Named after a key figure in the liberation of Albania from Ottoman rule, it is a good base for exploring the huge lakes and towering mountains of this otherwise inaccessible area.

# Dracula's Transylvanian Tour

Transylvania, part of Hungary and then of the Ottoman Empire, became Romanian in 1918. The name now is synonymous with spiky mountains and castles, dark forests, werewolves and Dracula the Vampire Count. For Romanians and historians, Vlad Tepes, the Impaler, son of Vlad Dracul, was a fierce fighter and ruthless ruler. Though rumoured to be in league with the devil, he was not known as a vampire. Vampirism is an accepted part of folklore. Bram Stoker, after much research but no visits, set his tale in Transylvania and invented Count Dracula. History and fantasy meet in a 'Dracula tour'.

The inhabited, fortified citadel Sighisoara was the birthplace of Vlad Tepes; with its jagged skyline of battlements and spires, it looks the part. If time allows, a visit to the northern town of Bistrita and the Bargau Valley with its saw-tooth peaks and lonely hamlets reveals Stoker's well-described locations. The tour-bus magnet though is Bran, south of Brasov. 'Dracula's Castle', perched on a crag and bristling with turrets, may have inspired Stoker, but was never inhabited by Vlad. The sprawling hilltop castle in nearby Rasnov is more atmospheric and the countryside around both is wild and untouched. Vlad was a Wallachian prince; he spent his boyhood in the Princely Court in Targoviste. A monastery on a tiny island in Lake Snagov is probably his burial place.

This north-south journey ends in Bucharest, but a westward loop back to Sighisoura passes the brooding, little-visited Poenari Castle where the Impaler spent years in refuge before escaping the Turks aided by the villagers of Arefu. The fine Saxon city of Sibiu was briefly his home, and the cathedral contains the tomb of his son, Mihnea the Bad.

*The multi-turreted Bran Castle*

**HOW:**
By car or organized coach tour
**WHEN TO GO:**
June to September
**TIME IT TAKES:**
At least a week
**HIGHLIGHTS:**
Lively Baroque Brasov makes a good base to explore the old towns, fortresses and villages.
The road north to Sibiu: cross the mountains by Red Tower Pass or (summer months only) by the breathtaking Transfagarasun Highway.
Vlad Dracul House in Sighisoara houses a medieval-themed restaurant.
**YOU SHOULD KNOW:**
Poienari Castle is reached by climbing 1,400 steps.

# The Danube Gorge

**HOW:**
By bike and boat
**WHEN TO GO:**
April to June, September and October
**TIME IT TAKES:**
Two or three days
**HIGHLIGHTS:**
Nine massive towers, the remains of
a medieval fort, stand on the Serbian
bank of Golubac Gorge.
The Tabula Traiana (a carved stone
with Roman inscriptions) was laid in
AD 103 to mark the start of
construction of the road and of
Trajan's famous bridge, the first
across the Danube and the largest in
the Roman world.
On the Romanian side, a 40 m (130
ft) face of Decebal, the Dacian chief,
is carved into the rock.
A boat trip with lunch is a good way
to relax and see the gorges from a
different angle.
**YOU SHOULD KNOW:**
The route is not hilly and the wind
usually blows from the west.
Most of the road is quiet though it
becomes busy after Orsova.

The Iron Gate, Portile de Fier, now refers to the 117 km (73 mi) stretch of the Danube from Moldova Veche to the huge dam upstream of Drobeta-Turnu Severin. This joint Romanian and (then) Yugoslavian hydroelectric project was completed in 1972. As well as taming a notoriously dangerous river, this raised the water level by over 30 m (97 ft) and changed the whole character of the landscape.

This popular section of the Danube Bike Trail passes through four gorges. Bazias, where the river enters Romania, was once a busy freight station; it is a convenient point to join the route. At the little port of Moldova Veche the waters divide around an island and flow into the Golubac Gorge. Though the town here was submerged, some castle ruins remain. The second gorge, Gospodin Vir, is, like Golubac, about 15 km (10 mi) long and as little as 220 m (715 ft) wide. Kazan Gorge remains spectacular; here the cliffs tower to 700 m (2,300 ft) and the twisting chasm narrows to just 150 m (492 ft). The Romans built an extraordinary planked road here, inserting supporting beams into the rocks. Upstream from Orsova on the Serbian side a plaque commemorates this road and Trajan's Bridge.

Downstream to the dam with its twin power stations is the true Iron Gates gorge, once the most perilous stretch for shipping and now effectively a reservoir. Beneath the calm deep waters lies Ada Kaleh, an island famous for its independent Turkish community and the site of a Hapsburg fortress (now rebuilt downstream). Local companies run boat trips through the dam's navigational canal and up to the Kazan Gorges.

*The Tabula Traiana along
the Danube*

# Kom Emine Trail

*The Central Balkan National Park*

Between Mount Kom on the Serbian border and Cape Emine on the Black Sea coast stretches the Stara Planina (Old Mountain) range along which runs the Kon Emine Trail, part of the trans-European E3 trek. The whole walk – about 700 km (438 mi) will take about a month. The railway and road which follow the southern contours permit breaks in interesting, historical towns and villages where, as well as rest and provisions, information and advice on routes and day walks can be obtained.

The western and central sections of the range contain the highest peaks – many over 2,000 m (6,500 ft) – and the most demanding terrain. From the ridge the views are superb – south over green undulating foothills, north over sheer rock walls and deep gorges. Large areas are National Parks, rich in birds and wildlife. The weather is fickle; spring is particularly wet.

The trail begins at Berkovitsa, in the northwest – a lovely area of deep wooded valleys and remote monasteries; it can also be reached from Sofia in the south. The Troyan Pass (a link between provinces in Roman times) gives road access, as does the Shipka Pass. Here, the road south leads to Kazanlak, the 'capital' of the rose-growing region and the 'Valley of the Thracian Kings', with many burial mounds. The pleasant town of Slivan is the start of shorter walking trails.

Sleepy, attractive Kotel is a good starting point for the Eastern section where the range is still a dominating north/south barrier. Near the ancient village of Emona on the forested southern slopes, high cliffs run to where Cape Emine juts into the Black Sea. South lie sandy beaches and rolling farmland.

**HOW:**
On foot
**WHEN TO GO:**
July to September
**TIME IT TAKES:**
A month plus for the whole walk; at least a week for road travel combined with walks.
**HIGHLIGHTS:**
Access from Sofia passes the spectacular Iskar Gorge and an impressive waterfall.
Brown bears and wolves are still found in the Stara Planina, which is home to many rare birds including golden eagles.
The road to Emona gives glorious and welcome views of the sea.
The Shipka Pass allows sweeping panoramas north and south; here too is the impressive Shipka Monument to Freedom.
**YOU SHOULD KNOW:**
This is a strenuous trail; hikers who attempt it should be fit and experienced. Day walks offer an easier way into the mountains.

**365**

# Attic Coast Road

*A small church on Lake Vouliagmeni*

Cape Sounion is the windy southern tip of Attica, 69 km (43 mi) from Athens. Here on a rocky cliff-top spur high above the Aegean stands a Doric temple to Poseidon, god of the sea. It was built in 444 BC, the same time as the Parthenon, and its brilliant white columns have been a welcome landmark to seafarers ever since. The marble, quarried at nearby Agrileza, contains no iron and retains its whiteness over centuries. Of the original 34 slender columns, 15 survive; Lord Byron set an unfortunate precedent in 1819 when he carved his name on one of them. The sacred site was sealed by massive walls; these can be followed down to the bay and the remains of ancient boathouses, which later became a pirates' lair.

The coast road along the Attic Riviera passes many busy and commercialized beaches and resorts. South of Vouliagmeni and Varkiza with their marinas and luxury clubs, the road is lined with quieter coves and tavernas and exclusive villas. There are regular buses from Athens to Sounion, and it is a popular outing – an early morning visit avoids some of the crowds. It is possible to drive back round the Cape and a little north to the rather desolate town of Lavrio. The Mineralogical Museum is a reminder of its wealthy past as a silver-mining centre. A loop inland rejoins the coast road at Anavysos.

# Samarian Gorge Hike

The Samarian Gorge now seems to be an essential part of a Cretan holiday. It is a long – 16 km (10 mi) plus 3 km (2 mi) to the coast – and gruelling walk. Wardens, donkeys and helicopters are on hand – every year injured walkers are rescued – and flash floods are not uncommon early and late in the season – weather warnings must be heeded. But this is an exciting trek, with magnificent scenery and remarkable flora and fauna. The Gorge is home to hundreds of bird species and to the shy and elusive kri-kri, the Cretan ibex. Herbs scent the air, and Cretan dittany, used medicinally since ancient times, grows on the rocks.

Organized trips usually arrive early (the Gorge opens at 6.00 am), with boats from the bottom of the gorge to the waiting coaches at Hora Sfakion. This can be done independently, by public bus. A south to north walk is quieter, but uphill, and against the tide of trekkers coming down.

The precipitous early stages of the Gorge, a spectacular gash in the Omalos Plateau, are fitted with wooden rails. At the bottom, ancient cypresses surround a chapel; from here the path follows the stream to Samaria, a village abandoned when the Gorge was made a Park in 1962. The Gorge deepens and narrows, the stream filling its bed and the track crosses it by stepping-stones and wooden walkways. At the short stretch known as the Iron Gates, the walls close in to little more than 3.5 m (11 ft) and soar sheer to almost 300 m (1,000 ft). At the end of the Gorge itself lies the old deserted village of Ayia Roumeli, and a half hour's hot walk over a stony wilderness to the sea. Here the new village provides weary hikers with cold drinks, swimming, ferries and accommodation.

*The stunning Samarian Gorge*

**HOW:**
On foot
**WHEN TO GO:**
1 May to 31 October
**TIME IT TAKES:**
4-7 hours
**HIGHLIGHTS:**
The first view of the Gorge with its startlingly sudden plunge can be enjoyed by non-walkers.
In spring, the Gorge is brilliant with wild flowers including anemones, irises and orchids.
Bird watching: owls, falcons and eagles are frequently seen; the endangered lammergeier (bearded vulture) may be spotted.
Frescoes in the 14th century church in Samaria.
**YOU SHOULD KNOW:**
Walkers should be fit and accustomed to long walks over rough terrain.
Beware of falling rocks.
Obey the Park Rules (these include no smoking and no singing!)

*The town of Ermoupoli*

# The Piraeus to Santorini Ferry

Sailing the Aegean between the Isles of Greece may be a dream, but the ferry journey from Piraeus to Santorini is a pleasant reality. Several shipping lines operate but the daily, early ferry via Syros, Paros, Naxos and Ios allows a day of sea travel with glimpses of interesting islands.

The ship leaves the chaotic sprawl of Piraeus, heading south east, and sails round either the rocky north or the greener south of Syros, into the handsome port of Ermoupoli. This, the largest town in the Cyclades, was, in the 19th century, Athens' main port. Its opera house is based on La Scala! On two hills behind the harbour are a medieval quarter and a fine domed church.

The ferry runs south to Paros whose single central peak is ringed by fishing villages, beaches and little bays. The busy harbour at Parikia is the hub of inter-island transport, but behind it, ranks of tightly packed square white houses rise gently to an old kastro. Just an hour west, Naxos is big, beautiful and, unusually, very fertile. Fishing boats and restaurants crowd the harbour and narrow, ancient alleyways climb through stone archways to the fine mansions of the fortified Venetian town. Midway between Naxos and Santorini, the little 'party island', Ios, has one of the prettiest harbours in the Aegean: linked by a stepped path to the port at Yialos, hilltop Hora has snowy houses, blue domed churches and a windmill, all flanked by palm trees.

Santorini (Thira) was part of the Minoan civilization till (probably around 1640 BC) a cataclysmic eruption when its high centre sank to form a deep lagoon around which the island – actually the partial rim of the crater – curves. Above black sand beaches and tiny fishing villages tower darkly striated pumice cliffs; hundreds of feet up, the brilliantly white settlements of Ia and the capital, Fira, cling to the caldera ring.

**HOW:**
By ferry
**WHEN TO GO:**
May, June, September and October
**TIME IT TAKES:**
Ten to twelve hours
**HIGHLIGHTS:**
The traveller entering Naxos harbour has been greeted for 2,500 years by the colossal marble portal of an unfinished temple to Apollo.
While the ferry is moving slowly, dolphins may swim alongside and play for a while.
Indigo sea, sunshine, the misty outlines of the clustered Cyclades, the joy of 'island hopping' for a day.
The extraordinary thrill of entering the great bay of Santorini.
**YOU SHOULD KNOW:**
Buy ferry tickets on the day – weather can cause disruption to schedules.
The last major earthquake on Santorini was in 1956.

# Patras to Messolonghi

A short ride east by back roads from Patras, the attractive port village Rio is the southern entry point for the Charilaos Trikoupis Bridge. Named after the 19th century statesman who first suggested a bridge here, it was opened in 2004 at the time of the Olympic Games. The overall length is 2,880 m (9,449 ft) and its cable-stayed suspended deck is the longest in the world. Designed to improve road communications between mainland Greece and the Peloponnese it has, in addition to toll-paying traffic lanes, a designated bicycle/pedestrian lane which offers, for those with a head for heights, a spectacular crossing of the Gulf of Corinth.

A ferry still runs between Rio and Antirio – both villages still have the forts which guarded this, the 'Little Dardanelles', the narrowest point in the Gulf. On both sides, fertile coastal plains, backed by mountains, are dotted with small seaside resorts. Just east of Antirio is Nafpaktos, ancient Lepanto, where in 1571 the sea battle that ended Turkish domination of the Mediterranean took place. To the west the road passes through coastal villages and over flat swampland to the serene area of salt marsh, reeds and calm waters (a protected biodiversity zone) of Kolsova Lagoon. On its banks lies Messalonghi, once a collection of stilted fishermen's huts, now a lively modern town, usually visited for historical reasons. Lord Byron came here to join battle in the struggle for independence, but died of fever in 1824. His death brought the war to international attention, and he became a national hero. In 1826 after a bitter siege the townspeople abandoned their fallen city by the Gate of Exodus, which still stands. Most were recaptured and killed. The town was awarded the honorary title of Hiera Polis (Sacred City) for its heroic part in the War of Independence.

**HOW:**
By bike
**WHEN TO GO:**
May, June, September and October
**TIME IT TAKES:**
One or two days
**HIGHLIGHTS:**
The fine Castle of Morea, the moated fortress at Rio.
The view from the bridge – lush hillsides, towering mountains and the water, busy with shipping, far below.
The statue of Lord Byron in the Garden of the Heroes in Messalonghi; beneath it is buried his heart.
Bird watching in the wetlands (Greece's largest); many winter migrants visit, and rare species breed.
**YOU SHOULD KNOW:**
Much of the ride is fairly level. The roads between Antirio and Messalonghi can be busy.

*The Rio-Antirio Bridge offers a spectacular crossing of the Gulf of Corinth.*

# Vouraikos Gorge Railway

**HOW:**
By train
**WHEN TO GO:**
May to early July, September and
October (avoiding weekends)
**TIME IT TAKES:**
At least two days
**HIGHLIGHTS:**
The lovely landscapes of the Gorge.
The two original steam engines are
displayed, one at each end of
the line.
Kalavryta Museum is a dignified,
undramatized and moving memorial
to the 1,436 men who died.
**YOU SHOULD KNOW:**
It is worth buying a first class ticket,
as this allows seating in the front
and back of the train.
It is a very small train; buy
tickets early.

Diakofto is a peaceful village on the Gulf of Corinth. It has a small beach and a background of steep mountains, olive groves and citrus orchards and it is the end of the remarkable Vouraikos Gorge Railway. This was built between 1889 and 1896 to transport ore from the Kalavryta region to the coast. The short – 22.5 km (14 mi) – journey is memorable and enjoyable; the track climbs 700 m (2,275 ft) using a rack-and-pinion system for traction over the steep gradients. The best view of the mechanism is from the front of the train; the very back gives wonderful views of the scenery.

After a gentle ascent through the lush landscape of the valley, the line criss-crosses the river; the gorge narrows and the train enters the first of fourteen tunnels, then runs along a ledge above the river. The only stop is at the picturesque, unspoilt settlement of Zahlorov – there is accommodation and good walking here. The journey continues beside the river in the shade of plane trees, and over open country to Kalavryta.

This is a delightful spot. At 756 m (2,457 ft), with fresh air, bubbling springs and tree-shaded *plateia* (town square), it is a favourite with At henians for weekends. Some miles south of the village the deep Cave of the Lakes has fine stalactites and a chain of deep stone basins which run with water in the spring. Little Kalavryta is famous nationwide – the War of Independence started officially here in 1821, and in 1943 it saw one of the worst atrocities of World War II when the Nazis executed all the men of the area.

*Great views of the Gorge can be enjoyed from the train.*

# Nestos Valley

The Nestos River, which forms the boundary between Macedonia and Thrace, rises in the lofty Rodopi range in Bulgaria. It flows south through craggy mountains, gorges and deep forests to spreading fertile plains and a wetland delta fed by dozens of tributaries. The valley makes a glorious mountain bike ride; some of it is tough going, some uses well-marked donkey tracks, old roads, or paths alongside the railway line.

*The Nestos River*

The mountain road from Drama to Xanthi crosses the valley at the village of Paranesti, from where it is possible to cycle a 'there and back' loop into the remote mountains, a region of hidden waterfalls, thick flower-scattered woodland, a refuge for many animals and birds. From Paranesti downstream the river runs through forested foothills and fields of sunflowers, past isolated villages. Stavroupolis is the only place with facilities for tourists. Here, as well as accommodation, information on cycling, organised hikes and kayaking is available.

South, the thick beech woods are full of birdlife. Now the river flows into The Narrows, a remarkable protected landscape of seven successive hairpin bends. The railway and the track cut along above the river and allow views of the tight meanders and the lush, undisturbed – there's no road access – wildlife habitat.

From Toxotes, the route crosses a huge area of corn and tobacco at the apex of the delta and then the river threads through a protected region of wetland – salt marshes, freshwater lakes and extensive riparian forest. Here, in the green shady tree tunnels, the only sounds are the calls of thousands of birds.

**HOW:**
By bike
**WHEN TO GO:**
May to early July and September
**TIME IT TAKES:**
At least four days
**HIGHLIGHTS:**
Bird watching: forest and river woodland species include peregrines, golden orioles and flycatchers; the delta is home to large numbers of storks, herons and egrets.
Wildlife: bears are occasionally spotted in the mountains. The residents of the Narrows include otters and wildcats.
Stavroupolis is a lovely village with traditional stone houses and a tree-shaded square.
**YOU SHOULD KNOW:**
Sections of this route are very demanding.
Stavroupolis is an ideal place to break the journey, but there is little accommodation and it may be necessary to go by road to Xanthi.

# Ioaninna to Méteora Road

Ioaninna, a lively and attractive town on the shores of Lake Pamvotis, is the capital of Epirus. During Ottoman rule the city prospered; it was at this time that the famous Crafts Guilds of Epirus were started by those driven by poor land to practise skills from silversmithing to baking. The old, walled Turkish town is built on a headland and the despot, Ali Pasha, made it his capital. Now the town has several interesting museums.

The scenic road northeast climbs steadily to the Katara Pass through the Pindus Mountains. This massive range, snow-capped from October till May, stretches to the Albanian border. Below the pass lies Metsova, still the 'capital' of the Vlachs, mountain-dwelling shepherds who speak a dialect of Latin. Metsovo also flourished under Turkish rule and later those who grew rich elsewhere re-invested in their home-town. Here, stone lanes wind between fine old houses and many of the traditional crafts survive.

Méteora – 'suspended in air' is, with its monastery-crowned pinnacles of rock, an astonishing sight. From the 11th century, solitary hermits occupied the caves; Turkish raids in the 14th century drove monks to live here, between heaven and earth, and by the 16th there were twenty-four monasteries. These were built with materials hauled up ladders and winched up in nets, and this means of access allowed the monks to seal themselves off from the world. Steps were cut in the 20th century, and now just six monasteries are occupied and open to visitors. The village of Kastraki at the foot of the rocks off the main road is a good base for exploring Méteora.

*Roussanou Monastery is perched precariously on its rock pinnacle.*

# Prespa Lakes from Kastoria

Set on a promontory in Lake Orestiada and surrounded by mountains, Kastoria in western Macedonia is one of Greece's loveliest towns. Its name means 'place of beavers' and it has long been a centre of the fur trade. After the beavers became extinct in the 19th century, the trade continued with imported fur. The town is architecturally outstanding. Many of the 17th and 18th century merchants' mansions survive and there are 54 Byzantine and medieval churches. Some, tiny and hidden away, were built as private chapels; these are often closed but their exteriors are interesting, with frescoes and geometric masonry. Panaghia Koumbelidhiki has an unusual tall, drum-shaped dome; 10th century Aghia Anarhyri overlooks the lake.

A side road 36 km (22 mi) north leads through fertile meadows to the Prespa Basin where Greece's borders with Albania and the Republic of Macedonia run through the two Prespa Lakes. This was a politically sensitive, little visited place, but now the Prespa Lakes National Park is a Transnational Park and though still remote this beautiful and serene area is more accessible. The huge Megali Prespa has steep, rocky shores interspersed with lush wetlands; Mikri Prespa and its encircling reed-beds is a protected area – among the many birds breeding there is the endangered Dalmatian pelican.

The region has several villages. Agios Germanos is an attractive agricultural settlement with the excellent Prespa Information Centre, which can arrange guided bird-watching tours of the Park. It has two frescoed Byzantine churches, and the hills outside the village give panoramic views over the lakes. The only Greek village on Megali Prespa is Psarades, a lovely traditional fishing village. Fishermen sometimes offer trips to see the lake and the scattered churches on its shores. A floating footbridge leads to the islet of Ayios Ahillios with two ruined Byzantine churches.

**HOW:**
By car
**WHEN TO GO:**
May to early July, September
**TIME IT TAKES:**
At least three days
**HIGHLIGHTS:**
The Folk Museum in Kastoria is housed in an old, sumptuously furnished fur-trader's mansion.
Birdwatching: storks, egrets, herons and white pelicans are among the water birds frequently seen around the lakes.
Boat trips visit painted cave-shrines, old monasteries and the 15th century Panayia Eleoussas, a rock church deep in a chasm.
Tavernas on Psarades waterfront serve fish straight from the lakes.
**YOU SHOULD KNOW:**
Be careful not to wander into the protected reed beds of Mikri Prespa.

*The 15th century rock church
Panayia Eleoussas*

*The Temple of Tholos in the sanctuary of Athena in Delphi*

# Sacred Way

**HOW:**
On foot
**WHEN TO GO:**
April to June, September and October
**TIME IT TAKES:**
One day
**HIGHLIGHTS:**
The Museum – with a superb collection of the sculpture, friezes and artefacts from the site.
The stadium where the Pythian Games took place every 4 years still has a starting line of marble slabs with grooves for the runners' toes.
The Tholus, or Rotunda, a very beautiful construction in the Sanctuary of Athena, the postcard image of Delphi.
The views – beyond the grey crags, green valleys studded with olives roll down to the sea, sparkling in the Gulf of Itea.
**YOU SHOULD KNOW:**
The extensive site is steep, rocky and uneven.
Carry provisions; there are plenty of excellent picnic spots and it's a long walk down to catering facilities.

The Sanctuary of Apollo at Delphi took shape from the 8th to the 7th century BC, centred on a temple guarding the centre of the world, the Omphalos (Navel), the chasm of the Oracle. Here Pythia, the priestess, perched above the void and spoke the words of the god; a priest interpreted the often-ambiguous pronouncements to the waiting supplicants. From the 6th to the 4th century BC, Delphi was the spiritual centre of the ancient world and an international political centre, for warriors and kings joined the worshippers. Great wealth and power were amassed – in addition to ritual cleansing and sacrifice, those seeking advice paid tribute. Individuals and cities erected dedications to Apollo – statues and small buildings (treasuries) and the Sanctuary grew. Under Roman rule, the power of the Oracle declined, and in the Christian 4th century it was declared defunct.

Delphi spreads over a natural amphitheatre of rocks and cliffs in the foothills of Mount Parnassus. The Sanctuary – the Sacred Precinct – is part of a larger complex that includes a gymnasium, stadium and sanctuary to Athena. The entrance is through the Roman agora; the Sacred Way, a paved path, zigzags up the terraces and slopes. The lower section is flanked by plinths and niches, which once held more than 3,000 votive statues, and the remains of the treasuries. Above these, the Spring of Gaia and the Rock of the Sibyl pre-date the building of the temple. The Athenian Stoa acts as a gateway to the Temple, which now consists of foundations and a re-erected line of Doric columns. The Sacred Way ends at the 5,000-seat rock-cut theatre, which still has remarkable acoustics.

# Mani Peninsula

The middle of three rocky fingers extending from the Peloponnese, the Mani is a mountainous, harsh region. Outer Mani, south of Kalamata, is watered by streams from the thickly forested Taiyetos Range. Inner, or Deep Mani, is barren, rock-strewn, starkly dramatic – blank tawny hills bristling with tower-villages, scattered with tiny churches, tangled with prickly pear. Until Greek independence in 1832, Maniots lived in chieftain-led clans, in villages of almost windowless towers, defence against invasion and blood feuds. Until recently no roads penetrated the mountains; now the little ports, then so vital, are ghost towns. Christianity was not accepted till the 9th century, and then zealously; many of the tiny Byzantine chapels and churches are strikingly frescoed and carved.

Areopolis, named for the god of war, is the chief town of the Inner Mani.  From here to Cape Matapan, southernmost point of mainland Greece, about 36 km (22 mi) of very scenic road follows the western 'shadowed' coast, linked by a network of unmetalled roads and stone tracks to villages and churches in the foothills of the mountainous spine and the coves and bays of the jagged rocky coast. From Pyrgos Dirou, where a track leds to the famous Diros Caves, the road runs south to Gerolimenas, a sheltered harbour and fishing village with accommodation. The road onwards crosses the coastal plain to Alika, climbs steeply past Vathia, hugs the cliff edge and turns east to Porto Kayio. This village in a sheltered bay was once a fortified harbour; now it offers rooms and a walk on good tracks south to Cape Matapan, or Tenaron. Tenaron, the legendary entrance to the underworld, is a cave in Asomati Bay just north of the Cape.

**HOW:**
On foot
**WHEN TO GO:**
Late April to June, September to early October
**TIME IT TAKES:**
At least three days
**HIGHLIGHTS:**
Areopolis  – several of the churches in have been restored; the frescoes are superb.
Vathia – the most spectacular of the tower villages; the narrow towers cluster in a maze of cobbled streets. It is almost deserted.
Asomati Bay – as well as the rather dull 'entrance to the underworld', there are scattered remains of an ancient settlement and temple to Poseidon.
Relaxed Porto Kayio has good harbour-side fish restaurants.

*Vathia is the best preserved Mani village.*

**EASTERN
MEDITERRANEAN
& MIDDLE EAST**

# Blue Voyage

Cevat Sakir Kabaagac, a Bodrum writer, recounted his travels by boat around the Carian and Lycian coasts and now the title of his book *Blue Voyage*, describes cruises in these Turkish waters. With rocky coastlines backed by dramatic forested mountains and waters of heavenly peacock hues, this is an idyllic region for a leisurely sea-voyage.

Gulets are the graceful traditional Turkish motor-yachts, still constructed locally of the red pine that covers the hillsides. Most are now built for the tourist business and they're comfortable and well equipped. They may be chartered by groups, or a cruise can be an alternative 'package' holiday.

A typical Blue Voyage will sail from Bodrum to Marmaris by way of pretty Gökova, mooring here or at one of the neighbouring fishing villages or coves, and along the north of the narrow Datça Peninsula, doubling back to Datça, with its busy harbour and waterfront. Fjord-like Keci Buku Bay provides anchorage on the journey east to Marmaris, at the traditional fishing village of Selimye, or Bozburun, renowned for its boat building. Just short of huge, hectic Marmaris lie the more tranquil bays of Turunc and Kumlubük.

The gulet will be at sea for several hours each day – possibly under sail – anchoring for swimming, visiting fishing villages or, for those withan interest in history, archaeological sites. The captain will establish his passengers' preferences. Scattered around the Gulf of Gökova are the remains of several ancient towns; at the tip of the Datça Peninsula the ancient city of Cnidos, and on a promontory south of Bozburun, are the ruins of Loryma, with its sheltered harbour.

**HOW:**
By gulet
**WHEN TO GO:**
Late April to June, September and October
**TIME IT TAKES:**
One week
**HIGHLIGHTS:**
The Crusader castle of Saint Peter dominates Bodrum Harbour; it contains the fascinating Museum of Underwater Archaeology.
Cnidos is an important site in a wild and beautiful location. A steep street flanked by the remains of houses, a temple and theatre, overlooks ancient twin harbours.
Swimming from the gulet in deep, transparent, cool, blue sea.
At anchor in a quiet bay – watching shooting stars and listening to the lullaby of gently lapping waves.
**YOU SHOULD KNOW:**
Children under 12 are not usually allowed on gulet cruises.

# The Lycian Way

**HOW:**
On foot
**WHEN TO GO:**
Late March to early June, late September to November
**TIME IT TAKES:**
The whole walk takes about a month, sections from one day or more.
**HIGHLIGHTS:**
Patara has a village, the extensive site of a Hellenistic city, and miles of undeveloped (protected) sandy beach.
The Lycians of Olympos worshipped a god of fire manifested in the Chimaera where inextinguishable flames still leap from crevices in the rocks. Best seen at night.
The wildlife – wild boar are found in the mountains; tortoises are frequently seen. Stretches of the coast are turtle nesting sites. The many bird species include winter and summer migrants.
**YOU SHOULD KNOW:**
Anything more than one of the day-walks requires good fitness. Walking in summer months is unwise; the heat is extreme, and the water sources dry up.

The Lycians settled the wide peninsula between Telmessos (present-day Fethiye) and Antalya around 1400 BC. Their legacy includes a partly deciphered script and many archaeological remains, including the unique rock-tombs which dot the whole area.

The 500-km (300-mi) Lycian Way, a way-marked footpath (with signed detours to places of interest) was inaugurated in 2000. The walk roughly follows the Turquoise Coast, sometimes cutting inland. The terrain is varied – rocky cliff-tops, steep scrambles down to isolated beaches, open stony hillsides, dense forest and shady valleys. You pass many archaeological sites and cross wonderfully unspoiled countryside – wreathed with flowers in spring, in autumn purple with crocuses and heather. The views over the sea to the misty outlines of the Greek islands, or down towards the brilliant water, are stunning. In some places, villages or resorts are accessible, in others, free camping is permitted. An excellent detailed guide to the walk is available.

This is a long and, in many places, demanding path. Many walkers opt for sections of the Lycian Way; others find a base and walk for separate days. Between Fethiye and Patara, along the western stretch, are the Lycian sites of Tlos, Pinara, Letoon and Xanthos and the Ottoman Greek ghost town, Kayakoy. South-coast Kas has a beautifully sited theatre, and Lycian tombs; the path east twists inland before descending to Ucagiz and a cluster of historical sites along the shore and on Kekova Island. At Demre, a church is dedicated to St Nicholas, who was bishop here, and impressive ancient Myra lies nearby. Below Mount Olympos (on the south-east coast) lie traces of the eponymous city and on its slopes, the mysterious Chimaera. Near Tekirova, the picturesque ruins of Phaselis are grouped around three small bays.

*A Lycian necropolis*

# Georgian Valleys

The mountainous region north of Erzurum towards Artvin was part of the medieval kingdom of Georgia, which embraced Christianity early, remained autonomous under the Seljuks and was partitioned between the Ottomans and the Persians after the Mongol invasion. Most Georgians had converted to Islam by the 17th century, but the people here are racially distinct and the Georgian language survives in some remote parts of the far northeast. The area is known unofficially as Turkish Georgia.

This is an area of green valleys, waterfalls and orchards; the high forests are home to wild boar and ibex, the slopes are planted with fruit and vegetables, cotton and tea. Relics of Christian Georgia are the churches in the scattered villages. Some have been converted to mosques, and are well preserved; others are in ruins.Most are built in the Armenian style, with drum and cone domes.

Erzurum, always a transport and military centre, is the largest city on the high plateau of Eastern Anatolia. The road northeast crosses a bleak, sparse landscape and drops into the valley of the Tortum, passing Tortum Lake. The river joins the Çoruh at the alpine town of Yusufeli; in places, the Çoruh Valley narrows to a gorge whose reddish cliffs tower above the rushing river. Local lads have always enjoyed spinning down the race on home made rafts; now this is a popular location for white water rafting, which can be organised in Yusufeli, which also makes a good base for exploring the countryside. Further north, the pleasant little town of Artvin clings to the mountainside and is surrounded by dramatically situated villages, churches and monasteries, with ruined castles and citadels perched on the crags.

**HOW:**
By 4x4 and on a raft
**WHEN TO GO:**
May and June, after the snow has melted, for the best rafting; May to September for exploring.
**TIME IT TAKES:**
Four days plus
**HIGHLIGHTS:**
A popular traditional festival, Kafkasor Yaylasi, held near Artvin in late June, includes dance, music, acrobats, etc; the main attraction is (bloodless) bull wrestling.
The churches are fascinating; for example, Haho Church (10th century) has carved reliefs of biblical scenes such as Jonah and the Whale; massive, elaborate Osk Vank has fine frescoes.
In June, the cherry and apricot orchards are in bloom.
**YOU SHOULD KNOW:**
Some of the white-water runs are very challenging.
Many of the villages can only be reached by 4x4.
Accommodation in this little-visited area is basic.

*One of the fascinating churches in the Georgian Valleys*

# Kackar Mountains

**HOW:**
On foot
**WHEN TO GO:**
July to September
**TIME IT TAKES:**
One to seven days or longer
**HIGHLIGHTS:**
The Hemsinlis – the people of the lovely, verdant valleys spend summers in the mountains with their flocks and herds. They live in pastoral dwellings, *yaylas*, moving upwards as the snows recede.
Wildlife – the slopes are full of flowers – rare orchids as well as lilies, primula and delphiniums; the mountains are a good place to spot birds of prey, including the lammergeier.
**YOU SHOULD KNOW:**
There are no good large-scale maps of the region.
Place names can be confusing; they may be Turkish, or Georgian/Armenian.

The Kackar Mountains are part of the Pontic Alps, the formidable range running along the Black Sea coast, which for centuries provided defence against invasion and a refuge for minorities. The coast enjoys a damp climate and the lower slopes of the mountains are clothed in tea plantations, beech and chestnuts, with dense pine and 'rainforest' higher up; the southern slopes are alpine, with steep high summer pasture.

The Kackars cover a relatively small area, but their close-packed snow-clad peaks, many of which are well over 3,000 m (9,750 ft), block paths from the valleys.

The mountains are increasingly popular with trekkers, and this is a lovely and rewarding area, rich in wildlife, dotted with small lakes and home, in the summer, to flocks and herdsmen. On the Black Sea sections, Ayder and Cat are good bases; both are reached via the beautiful Hemsin Valleys. On the southern side, above the Coruh and reachable from the Western Georgian valleys, Barhal, Hevek, Meretet and Tekkule are good starting points. The hikes are more gruelling from the south, but the weather is much better; the gentler northern slopes are covered in dense, damp cloud most afternoons. The villages have accommodation, and it is possible to hire guides or join an organised trek of anything from a day to a week. The highest mountain is Kackar Dagi – 3,932 m (12,779 ft) – and there are several others almost as high; climbing the peaks requires full kit and some experience, but there are some glorious one- and two-day walks below the highest sections.

*Trekking in the Kackar Mountains.*

*The Galata Tower watches over the Bosphorus.*

# Bosphorus Ferry Trip

Istanbul, capital of mighty Christian and Islamic empires, was always a bridge between east and west; now Europe and Asia are linked by road, but ferries remain essential to life in this great city. Tour companies run Bosphorus Cruises with fast boats, but a leisurely zigzagging trip on a regular ferry from the centre of Istanbul to a village close to the Black Sea is a good antidote to sightseeing fatigue.

The Bosphorus, the 30-km (19-mi) strait linking the Black Sea with the Mediterranean, remains an important trade route; in the past, it was also a defence and a summer escape from the heat and disease of the city. Along both banks are royal residences (including the splendid Beylerbeyi Palace), villas, fashionable suburbs, boatyards, fortresses and working villages. Not many of the beautiful wooden *yalis*, the summerhouses of the wealthy, survive – many burned down, or were demolished before preservation laws came into force.

The waterfronts are punctuated by mosques, including the distinctive Ortaköy Mosque, just below the Atatürk Bridge. South of soaring Fatih Bridge, the twin castles – small Anadolu Hisar and the massive Rumeli Hisar, the Fortress of Europe – could effectively 'lock' the Bosphorus. Inland from the fashionable settlements on the European shore is Belgrade Forest, once a hunting preserve for the Sultans. The last ferry stop is at Anadolu Kavagi, on the Asian shore. Here there is time to explore and have a meal, or plan a return journey by bus, dolmus, and short ferry hops, visiting some of the places glimpsed on the journey.

**HOW:**
By ferry
**WHEN TO GO:**
The ferry runs all year
**TIME IT TAKES:**
About 1 hour 30 minutes each way
**HIGHLIGHTS:**
Kucuksu Kasri, near Anadolu Hisari. The shady site was long a royal favourite for picnics; in the 19th century, the wooden kiosk was replaced with an exquisite tiny Rococo palace.
Sariyer – a fish market and good restaurants, and the private Sadberk Hanim Museum, which displays a fascinating collection in a *yali*, with rooms arranged in the Ottoman style.
Anadolu Kavagi – a lovely village, with old wooden houses and waterfront fish restaurants. From the top of the huge ruined castle there is a panoramic view to the Black Sea. The Istanbul skyline from the water, especially at dusk, is spellbinding.
**YOU SHOULD KNOW:**
There is a reduced ferry service out of season – check timetables.

# Istanbul to Aleppo on the Toros Express

The original Istanbul to Baghdad railway was largely planned and financed by Germany, but the Toros Express (named for the mountain range it crosses) was inaugurated in 1930 by the Compagnie Internationale des Wagons-Lits, to extend its Orient Express service. Though trains no longer continue to Iraq, and the opulence has vanished (along with Belgian detectives), the Toros Express now runs from Istanbul to Aleppo once a week. Haydarpasa Station, on the waterfront south of Usküdur, is reached by ferry from Galata. This grandiose building, with its wood panelling and fine stained-glass, was presented to the Sultan by Kaiser Wilhelm in 1908.

The Syrian sleeping car, with its two-bed compartments and friendly, tea-making steward, is attached to a Turkish train. It heads out of Istanbul by the Sea of Marmara, and then eastwards along a broad valley. Then the line climbs southwards, and continues (past Afyon, where an ancient citadel crowns a dark crag) to the empty, arid plateau, where views expand – tawny plains, distant peaks, isolated villages and minarets. It is late by the time the train arrives in Konya (home to fine carpets and whirling Dervishes); overnight it runs, by way of innumerable tunnels and bridges, through the huge Toros range. In the early morning the train descends the southern slopes towards Adana. Then the line runs east through fertile plains to Febsipasa, where the sleeping car is uncoupled and joined to another train. At the border, after the normal delays, the train is coupled to a Syrian locomotive, and the journey continues through rocky hills and olive groves to the beautiful Syrian city of Aleppo.

**HOW:**
By train
**WHEN TO GO:**
March to November
**TIME IT TAKES:**
About 30 hours
**HIGHLIGHTS:**
The sheer romance of a journey like this – heading into the huge, changing landscape of Turkey and on into Asia Minor.
Descending the Toros at dawn: distant views from the craggy mountains of the green plain below, glimpses of the distant Mediterranean as first light touches it.
Finally arriving in Aleppo: a beautiful, exciting but easy-going city.
**YOU SHOULD KNOW:**
Tea-making is the only catering for the sleeping car. Take ample provisions and liquids.  Also take toilet paper.

*Al Khosrowiyya Mosque in Aleppo*

# Cappadocia Cross-Country Ride

This part of Central Anatolia is famous for bizarre scenery, underground settlements and frescoed churches. The weird 'fairy chimneys' – toadstools, cones and pleated domes – were formed by erosion of the soft, volcanic tufa; unusually – most volcanic rock is black or grey – here the colours are soft golds and reds. These easily worked rocks have always provided refuge from raids and persecution; the underground towns were probably dug in Hittite times – 1900-1200 BC – and used, extended and elaborated over the centuries. St Paul brought Christianity to Cappadocia, though most of the cave churches are Byzantine. Caves are still used for stabling, storage and to keep pigeons; cultivation has also been continuous – the Hittites made wine, and grapes are still grown; the fertile soil also produces fruit.

Many of the tourists who throng a few popular areas are day-trippers, but Cappadocia repays a longer stay. An excellent escape from the crowds into the extraordinary landscape is on horseback; several ranches offer anything from short sunset rides to cross-country trips of a week or more. These combine riding – through fertile valleys, narrow gorges, along winding tracks among the fairy chimneys and over the high volcanic *mesas* with visits to villages and sites of interest. Time is usually allowed in Göreme, where villagers are still troglodytic, to explore the Göreme National Park, an open- air museum of many exceptional churches.

**HOW:**
On horseback
**WHEN TO GO:**
April to November
**TIME IT TAKES:**
Seven days plus
**HIGHLIGHTS:**
Enjoyable riding – the small, nimble horses are happy picking their way over rocky mule tracks or cantering along sandy valleys.
The plain exteriors of most of the rock-cut churches give no clue to the glorious interiors with Byzantine carving and superb frescoes.
The underground settlements (some home to as many as 20,000): complex warrens descending many levels, with deep ventilation shafts, wells, escape routes and sealable doors.
**YOU SHOULD KNOW:**
Riding standard is intermediate; riders should be fit – most days entail 5 or 6 hours in the saddle.

*The Zelve Valley in Cappadocia*

385

# St Paul Trail

**HOW:**
On foot
**WHEN TO GO:**
May, June, September and October
**TIME IT TAKES:**
Organized treks last about a week,
the whole trail, four to five weeks.
**HIGHLIGHTS:**
Adada – some well-preserved
buildings and tumbled stones in a
lovely hillside setting – the Greco-
Roman road, made of huge stone
slabs, can be followed from
the south.
Wildlife – the beautiful forests are
rich in birds and flowers. The
Volcanic Oak is unique to Kasnak
Forest, south of Egirdir.
Egirdir – superbly sited on the huge
lake, backed by mountains, is a good
place to relax, swim and eat fresh
lake fish.
Following ancient travellers who
walked the King's Way from Ephesus
to Bablyon, and St Paul along roads
he actually trod.
**YOU SHOULD KNOW:**
The demanding trail requires a good
level of fitness.

*Egirdir Lake*

St Paul, a native of Tarsus in south-east Turkey, was, as an educated man and a citizen of the Roman Empire, able to travel and communicate freely. He spent about twenty years spreading Christianity and part of his first journey in AD 46 was from Perge near the Mediterranean coast to Antioch in Pisidia, a Roman colonial town north of Lake Egirdir.

Researched and established, like the Lycian Way, by Kate Clow, the St Paul Trail opened in 2004. The walk starts from Perge, skirting the Yazili Canyon, or from Aspendos, via the Koprolou Canyon. The routes into the wild hills of the Toros range meet at Adada, a little-visited site north of Sutculer, then pass Egirdir, crossing the lush agricultural western lakeshore to the attractive village of Barla. After a boat crossing comes a long climb to the Anatolian plateau and Antioch in Pisidia. Though little is left of the Church of St Paul, the extensive site is impressive.

The way-marked tracks – in all around 500 km (300 mi) – sometimes follow Roman roads or stretches of the Ancient 'King's Way', often lead through beautiful mixed forests of oak, juniper and cedar or chestnut, or by narrow stony tracks over ridges, skirting and scaling gorges, waterfalls and lakes. The trail passes isolated villages and, in summer, the tented settlements of the Yoruk people on the hillsides with their flocks. For the historian, there are sites to visit, for the naturalist flora and fauna and for the climber, some high peaks. There is an excellent guidebook. Some of the villages now offer accommodation, while Egirdir, Sütçüler or Barla make good bases for day-treks, or sections of the route. Several companies offer guided walks.

# The Georgian Military Road

Its name seems to encapsulate everything modern, so the first great surprise is that the Georgian Military Road is the historic name for the 2,000 year-old route linking Georgia with Russia, across the Caucasus Mountains. Apart from the 4 km (2.5 mi) Caspian coastal strip, completely blocked at Derbent in Russia, it's the only major route through the Caucasus. Just a rugged track until Russia annexed Georgia, the road was only surfaced between 1799-1863. For 208 km (130 mi) it follows the Kura River out of Tbilisi, climbing the Aragvi River Valley to the 2,379-m (7,815-ft) Krestovy Pass. The landscape is as wild and lawless as its history. Always magnificent, the looming crags and peaks now crowd into the awesome Baidarka Canyon, below Mount Kazbegi, Georgia's highest (5,033 m/16,508 ft) peak. Here, at the Russian border, the road runs for several kilometres on a shelf cut into the granite walls of the Darial Gorge – rising sheer for 1,500 m (4,900 ft) on both sides – before descending through the helter-skelter of the Terek River Valley tunnels to Vladikavkaz in Russia.

Its treacherous hairpins and precipitous drops can still be genuinely frightening – but the road's natural drama is magnified by the accrued wealth of history along its length. At the UNESCO World Heritage city of Mtskheta, cathedrals, monasteries and palaces still guard Georgia's religious soul as they have since the 3rd century, 500 years before Christianity ever reached Russia or Germany. Church and state again combine at the medieval fortress of Ananuri, with two beautiful churches within its crenellated walls; and at the Church of the Trinity, the landmark on the skyline of Mount Kazbegi. The ruins of castles and forts dating to the 3rd century BC are testament to an even older sequence of invasions, tribal migrations, and trade incursions.

*Djvari Monastery overlooks the Aragvi River.*

**HOW:**
By car or bus

**WHEN TO GO:**
June-September. The road can usually be driven year-round, even though there can be deep snow at the pass in May. Georgia's ski resort at Gudauri is always accessible.

**TIME IT TAKES:**
5-9 hrs (by car/bus, direct); 2-4 days (by car/bus, stopping briefly at some of the major sites of man and nature).

**HIGHLIGHTS:**
Svetitskhoveli Cathedral at Mtskheta, architectural symbol of Georgia's religious philosophy and the country's most sacred site. One of the world's greatest cathedrals.
Tamara's Castle, at the southern entrance to the, vertiginous, gloomy magnificence of the Darial Gorge.
The tetraconch plan – prototype for the whole of the south Caucasus – of the Great Church of the 6th century Djvari Monastery.
The contrast between the Georgian and Russian sides of the mountains, like summer and winter.

**YOU SHOULD KNOW:**
1. Delays at the border are frequent, especially on the Russian side. 2. The Georgian Military Road is part of Georgia's national psyche, embodying the drama of its landscape and history. Its romantic imaginative appeal has inspired writers including Pushkin, Tolstoy, Dumas, Gorky, Lermontov and the hero/saint of Georgian nationalism, Ilya Chavchavadze.

# Monasteries Hike

**HOW:**
On foot
**WHEN TO GO:**
Late May to early July, September
**TIME IT TAKES:**
Two days plus
**HIGHLIGHTS:**
Debed Canyon is richly green, well
watered and densely wooded; it is a
lovely place to walk, either along the
shady riverbed or the canyon rim.
Sanahin Monastery – the mossy
complex of church, shadowy
chapels, ancient graves open
archways and scattered *khatchkars*
is bewitching.
Haghpat Monastery – the extensive
walled complex, built in the 12th
century, includes bell tower, library,
refectory and chapel as well as the
fine main church. The views over
the canyon are superb.
**YOU SHOULD KNOW:**
Some of the walking can be muddy.

Armenia became Christian in 301 AD (around 90 per cent of Armenians are members of the Armenian Apostolic Church) and the lovely countryside is scattered with old churches and monasteries and elaborately carved stone crosses, *khatchkars*. Beautiful, green Lori province has a concentration of medieval monasteries along the spectacular Debed Canyon. Both the railway and the road north to Georgia follow the line of the Canyon, but if time is not pressing this makes an excellent walk. Distances are small, several of the villages have accommodation and climbs are not demanding.

From Tumanyan, the ruined 13th-century convent and the hamlet of Kobayr are visible. Stone steps from the railway line lead up the hill. The roofless church still has some frescoes. The large village of Odzun sits on a shelf over a steep drop to the Debed River; in the centre of the village, the sturdy church is 17th century, with an arcaded cloister once used as a school. On the edge of the cliff is another church and the remains of Horomayri Monastery cling to the slopes a little to the south.

Alaverdi is a quiet town lying in a bend of the canyon. There is a 12th century hump-backed stone bridge over the river, but this is mainly a modern copper-mining town. The cable car (which runs to the shift timetable at the mine) provides an easy way up to the canyon edge, and the villages of Sadahart and Sanahin. Sanahin Monastery is a UNESCO Word Heritage Site. The oldest building dates to 928; this was the seat of an archbishop and there is a funeral chapel for the royal Zakarian family.

Another UNESCO World Heritage Site, Haghpat Monastery, founded in 976, perches on the edge of the canyon and combines superb architecture with a tremendous location.

*Haghpat Monastery and bell tower*

# Lake Sevan to Vayots Dzor

*Lake Sevan*

This huge mountain lake, lying at just less than 2,000 m (6,500 ft) and covering nearly 1,000 sq km (400 sq mi), is famous for its glorious blueness, changing from duck-egg to turquoise to ultramarine with the weather. The fresh air and the white sand beaches make this a popular summer destination for city-dwellers; the 'Armenian Riviera' gets very busy.

Sevanank peninsula – an island till the water level dropped following irrigation/hydroelectric projects – is crowned by two early monastery churches; the climb to the hilltop gives views over the lake to a jagged skyline of surrounding volcanic peaks. South of Sevan town, well preserved Hayravank Monastery stands on a promontory, and the lovely old village of Noratus has a fine church, ruined basilica, enormous cemetery, and access to a quiet beach. At the medieval/modern cemetery the traveller may come across a Karasoonk marking the 40th day after a death – family, friends and musicians gather at the graveside before retiring for food, drink and storytelling.

From Martuni on the southern shore the newly repaired road runs through the Selim Pass to Yeghegnadzor, the main town of the remote region of Vayots Dzor. Small country roads lead off to hidden valleys and architectural delights.

Yeghegnadzor is set in an agricultural river valley. The road west leads to the wild and mountainous Arpa Valley, near the Azerbaijan border. This is a quality-wine producing area. Areni, and several of the nearby villages, have wineries and accommodation.

**HOW:**
By car or 4x4
**WHEN TO GO:**
Late May, June and September
**TIME IT TAKES:**
Two days plus
**HIGHLIGHTS:**
Noratus – the largest *khatchkar* cemetery in Armenia, bristles with the intricately carved upright stone slab crosses dating from the 9th-15th century. Modern memorials often carry etched portraits of the deceased.
The Selim Caravanserai is the best preserved in Armenia. Built in 1332 of basalt blocks, it housed travellers and animals on the Silk Route. Take a torch.
Vayots Dzor has many exceptional early churches; the Veghegis Valley and the areas around Yeghegnadzor and Vayk are particularly rewarding.
**YOU SHOULD KNOW:**
The condition of country roads is often very poor; it is worth hiring a car – preferably a 4x4 – with driver.

**389**

# Rub'al Khali – The Empty Quarter

**HOW:**
By car
**WHEN TO GO:**
November to March
**TIME IT TAKES:**
Two days plus
**HIGHLIGHTS:**
The Wadi Dawkah Frankincense Park
is a UNESCO World Heritage Park.
Trees of 5 m (16 ft) or more are over
200 years old.
Camel racing takes place at Thumrait
in November and January.
Camping in the desert: sunset, the
true silence of night, the cool beauty
of first light.
**YOU SHOULD KNOW:**
Reduce tyre pressure for driving on
sand. Hire a guide and/or driver.
Light boots are the best footwear –
the sand gets very hot.

Covering most of Saudi Arabia and slices of Yemen, Oman and the UAE, Rub'al Khali, the world's largest sand desert, occupies nearly a quarter of the Arabian Peninsula. Wilfred Thesiger crossed this harsh land with companions from the Bait Kathir tribe of southern Oman and his famous book *Arabian Sands* describes its hardships and its spell.

Oman is a peaceable country, politically stable, with a calm, tolerant populace who are in no rush to sacrifice their national identity to tourism. Here, half a day's drive allows a visit to the great desert, and a night or two in the sands, independently or on an organized trip.

The road from Salalah, a colourful south-coast port city with good beaches, crosses the fertile rolling plains and the Jebel Gara Mountains. This area enjoys monsoon rains, and is popular with Arabian visitors during the 'winds of plenty'. The landscape changes to dark gravel hills and narrow wadis – the home of the strange, gnarled frankincense tree. Thumrait, a stopping point for the ancient caravan routes, has a camel racetrack. Sisr, to the north, enjoys year round water; nearby Ubur is the site either of the 'Atlantis of the Sands', a lost Koranic city, or one of the caravanserai. Several towers, a waterhole and thousands of artefacts have been excavated.

The margins of the Empty Quarter are sparsely inhabited by lizards, hawks, small mammals and Bedouin tribes, but off the Desert Highway the traveller enters a world of towering sand dunes, shimmering mirages and colours that shift, red, orange, violet, with the light. On the edge of this fabled wilderness, the emptiness is awe-inspiring.

*Camels on their way across the Star Dunes.*

# The Incense Road

*The city of Sana'a*

The wealth of the ancient kingdoms of Yemen depended on trade in frankincense and myrrh, highly valued throughout the civilised world. Part of the overland Incense Road, which stretched through Arabia to the Mediterranean, passes through several historically important places in Yemen, which owed their power to taxes from the enormous camel caravans. Before making this journey now, check with the authorities – access to some areas of Yemen is restricted or prohibited.

Yemen's capital, Sana'a (a UNESCO World Heritage Site) has one of the oldest intact medinas in the Arab world, a jumble of mosques, markets and unique tower houses. From Sana'a the road climbs through the mountains and descends to the eastern desert where, in the 8th century BC, a huge dam was built in what became known as Wadi as-Sudd (Wadi of the Dam) and the city of Ma'rib became capital of the Kingdom of Saba. The kingdom fell, the incense trade declined, the dam collapsed. Temples sunk in the desert and the empty mud brick towers of Old Ma'rib are all that survive, though a new dam and oil finds offer new prosperity.

The old city of Shabwa lies across the Ramlat as Sab'atayn desert. From the hill, where its remains are engulfed by sand and salt, a dramatic panorama covers the eastern end of the mighty Wadi Hadramawt, the largest wadi in the Middle East, named for the ancient people who first inhabited it. The fertile main valley extends 160 km (100 mi) westward; its main town Sayun is an ancient caravan-route market town, with beautiful mosques, fine mud-brick buildings – and an airport. At the Wadi's heart lies Shibam, another UNESCO World Heritage Site, a compact walled city tightly packed with hundreds of five to seven storey medieval mud brick tower houses.

**HOW:**
By car
**WHEN TO GO:**
March to June, October and November
**TIME IT TAKES:**
3 days plus
**HIGHLIGHTS:**
Sana'a's towers have lower storeys of dark basalt, upper of reddish brick; the top floors are mud-plastered, often whitewashed, the facades decorated with white patterns.
The 'Palace' hotels in Sana'a – these converted tower houses have traditional interiors and views over the city, including the hidden network of walled gardens.
A day or two spent exploring the Wadi Hadramawt and the pretty villages, mosques, tombs and historical sites scattered over its tributaries.
The first sight of Shibam, the 'Manhattan of the desert', rising from the valley.
**YOU SHOULD KNOW:**
Check government guidelines on travel in Yemen.

*The cliff–top village of Shahara in the Haraz Mountains*

# Haraz Mountain Trek

**HOW:**
On foot
**WHEN TO GO:**
April, May, September and October
**TIME IT TAKES:**
Three days plus
**HIGHLIGHTS:**
The breathtaking, peaceful countryside, and the uncommercialized villages.
Some of the narrow terraces are the width of just one row of crops – from a distance they look like giant ladders.
The ubiquitous Yemeni tower houses in the villages are stone; the decoration often consists of ornate windows of coloured glass.
**YOU SHOULD KNOW:**
Most of the villages in the Haraz lie at around 2,000 m (6,500 ft) – climbing even the higher peaks (just under 3,000 m/9,750 ft) is fairly straightforward.
Sudden bursts of heavy rain can reduce temperatures and send large boulders rolling down the slopes.

The Haraz Mountains, west of Sana'a, is an area of step hillsides, high peaks and lovely stone villages. From the 12th century, the mountains served as refuge for descendents of the Ismaili Sulayhids, and many of the villages date from this period. During Ottoman occupation this was a strategic area where cannons guarded mountain passes. Farming is intensive – even the steepest slopes have been terraced, and monsoon rain is gathered for irrigation. A large proportion of Yemen's scarce arable land lies in these mountains and a wide variety of crops are grown.

Trekking in Yemen is not organized, with no maps or marked trails, but the Manakha area is perfect for day-treks. Two of the villages, Manakha and Al Hajjara, have facilities for visitors and make good bases. Hostel accommodation offers packed lunches and evening entertainment of local music and dance, and can arrange guides and camping equipment for longer treks. Manakha is the market town for the surrounding region; Al Hajira, to the west, is a lovely fortified hilltop village.

There are many enjoyable circular day-walks using the network of paths between villages – south to Al-Khutayb, an Ismaili pilgrimage site, west to Jabal Masar and a scattering of historic hamlets, or Jabal Shibam, the highest peak in the region. Longer treks to the edge of the mountains, where peaceful villages look down over steep escarpments, or north and south out of the Manakha region can be arranged. Guides will arrange camping outside villages.

# Petra Monastery Hike

Visitors to Petra may choose to escape the crowds and see Little Petra, a few miles north. This was an important suburb of Petra, a re-supply post for travellers and traders. Its Arab name is Siq Barid, 'The Cold' – it is entered by a slit in the rocks so narrow the sun scarcely filters through. The 400-m (1,300-ft) siq opens up into wider areas where the rock walls are crowded with houses, temples and triclinia, linked by rock-cut stairways in the cliff face. Floods have eroded lower facades but some of the higher ones are well preserved. As well as the dining rooms, there are a number of water channels and cisterns. A set of stairs at the bottom of the siq leads to a hidden canyon with views of the surrounding countryside.

A little south are the ruins of Al Beidah, a Neolithic village and one of the oldest sites in the Middle East. The remains are unremarkable, but some of the items found, dating to around 7000 BC, bear witness to early experiments in settled agriculture.

The path drops to a wadi and from here a fairly easy hour's walk reaches the Monastery of Al Dier. Following small wadis through the rocks cuts out some of the hundreds of steps up to this inspiring monument. Near the top views open up over the mountains and valleys. The Monastery was actually a single chamber temple dedicated to a Nabatean king, probably used later as a church. The flat plaza to the front was levelled for ceremonials; the massive façade – nearly 50 m (162 ft) square – is carved into the mountainside; the doorway is bigger than a house.

*Siq Barid in Petra*

# Lawrence of Arabia Camel Trek

**HOW:**
On a camel
**WHEN TO GO:**
March to May, October and
November
**TIME IT TAKES:**
Five days
**HIGHLIGHTS:**
The spectacular landscape and the
sheer scale of Wadi Rum.
'Lawrence's Spring', Ain ash-
Shallaleh, is a peaceful, ferny spot,
the head of a Nabatean rock-cut
aqueduct.
The camel-mounted Desert Patrol
Corps can be a stirring sight, robed
and armed to the teeth.
Bedouin hospitality and nights in the
desert: shared food, glorious sunsets,
myriad stars, the jangling of a camel-
harness accentuating the silence.
**YOU SHOULD KNOW:**
Wear suitable clothes for camel
riding; the traditional head wrapping
keeps out sun and sand.
Desert nights can be very chilly.

In 1917, with Emir Faisal and the Arab warriors (and the support of General Allenby), T. E. Lawrence took Aqaba; he also attacked the Hejaz Railway on several occasions. The railway was originally built to transport pilgrims to Medina, but was used by the Turks as a vital supply line. Now a few trains run from Damascus, but only as far as Amman.

Lawrence had a deep love for the Arab world and the Bedouin, and he spent some time in the Wadi Rum, one of a huge network of valleys in the sandy southern desert. His lyrical descriptions of the great stone jebels rising sheer from the desert floor, weathered into domes and ridges, which appear almost liquid, ring true today. Parts of *Lawrence of Arabia* were filmed here. The area around the main Bedouin settlement, Rum, is very busy, but even on foot it's possible to escape the crowds of day-trippers, exploring red sand corridors through ravines and valleys.

The ideal way to explore the desert is on a camel, with nights in Bedouin encampments. Basic camel riding can be quickly learned and most riders become fond of their silent mounts, despite their grumpy expressions. Long treks include the journey to Mudawarra on the Saudi border, where a railway carriage blown up by Lawrence in 1917 (he made the trip in three days on a racing camel) still lies by the disused track.

After the daunting red cliffs of the Wadi Rum, the trek threads it way south east through small wadis and hidden valleys to flatter terrain and darker rocks. Wadi Mhask is suddenly green (it lies above a huge underground water source); the jagged rocky cliffs near Mudawarra conceal canyons, home to wildlife including ibex and wolves.

*Wadi Rum at sunset*

# Jerusalem: The Via Dolorosa

Ancient Jerusalem has many sites of immense spiritual importance; for Judaism, the massive Western Wall is all that remains of the Great Temple; the majestic Dome of the Rock is, for Islam, more shrine than mosque. For Christianity, the Church of the Holy Sepulchre enshrines the last resting place of Christ, while the Via Dolorosa marks His final journey from trial to crucifixion.

The Roman Empire adopted Christianity in the 4th century and since then believers have retraced this walk. The route has changed over the centuries, though the destination is the same. Pilgrims from all over medieval Europe came to share Jesus' suffering at the Stations of the Cross and the ritual was adopted universally.

The location of Calvary is undisputed, but Pilate probably lived in what is now the Citadel, not the Antonia Fortress (now a Muslim Madrasah) where the 'Way of Sorrows' begins. The 'Stations' of the Via Dolorosa, which runs east-west through the narrow streets of the Muslim Quarter, are marked with oratories and chapels (modest by comparison with the Gothic and Baroque splendours of Europe), plaques, crosses, and Roman columns. In the Christian Quarter, commerce and spirituality join in the 'pilgrim trade' shops lining the road to Calvary. A jumble of churches and hospices surrounds the huge Church of the Holy Sepulchre (originally built by Constantine at the request of his mother, St Helena), where the tenth to fourteenth Stations are located.

For Christian visitors, joining the Franciscan friars' Friday walk, pausing for devotion at each 'Station', is a very powerful experience. For others, just to walk and reflect can be moving.

**HOW:**
On foot
**WHEN TO GO:**
March to May, September and October
**TIME IT TAKES:**
One hour plus
**HIGHLIGHTS:**
Christ's Tomb – A 19th century rotunda houses the Holy Sepulchre; here a marble slab covers the place where Christ's body is believed to have been laid.
Golgotha – part of the Church where the Greek Orthodox altar is built on the rock of the Crucifixion, and the Catholic chapel has a bronze and silver altar given by Ferdinand de Medici.
In the Convent of the Sisters of Sion, near the start of the walk, is part of the 'Ecce Homo Arch', an ancient rock-cut cistern, and the lithostrotos, a stone-slab pavement where incised gaming boards for dice games recall the soldiers casting lots.
**YOU SHOULD KNOW:**
Unless visiting Jerusalem specifically for a festival, the city is best avoided during Christian and Jewish holidays, when it becomes impossibly crowded.

*The Church of the Holy Sepulchre*

*The ruins of the Arab castle of Qalaat Jaber*

# Along the Euphrates

**HOW:**
By car, bus or train
**WHEN TO GO:**
March to May, September and October
**TIME IT TAKES:**
Four days plus
**HIGHLIGHTS:**
Resafe is a fascinating site in the middle of nowhere. The great walls contain (among much else) extensive remains of a very early basilica and the massive cisterns of the ancient city.
The Archaeological Museum in Deir ez-Zur is outstanding, with excellent well-labelled sections on Dura Europos and Mari.
The first sight of the walls of Dura Europos, standing high above the river, across the parched desert.
Mari was founded in 2900 BC and destroyed in 1759 BC; the foundations of the Royal Palace, with more than 300 rooms, give an idea of its scale. At present, it is the only easily accessible Mesopotamian site.
**YOU SHOULD KNOW:**
Because of the Iraqi border's proximity, police checks are frequent on the road to Mari. Carry documents.
The desert sites can be extremely hot and dusty.

The mighty green Euphrates rises in the mountains of eastern Anatolia and cuts a fertile swathe for 2,700 km (1,700 mi) through the deserts of Syria and Iraq; this was home to great civilisations and city-states. Control of the flow of water has always been contentious; following massive hydroelectric and irrigation projects by Syria and more recently by Turkey, tension has grown.

Along the Euphrates lie some fine archaeological sites. Travel is straightforward – roads with good bus links, and there's a railway line as far as Deir ez-Zur. East of Aleppo, Lake Assad is the huge reservoir formed by damming the Euphrates. From Ath Thawra (purpose built for construction workers and displaced villagers) a road runs over the dam to Qalaat Jaber castle, once high above a river crossing, now on the lakeshore.

Though little is left of busy Raqqa's former glory, a short detour south leads to Resafe, a remarkable ancient walled city in the desert. Downstream, twin Roman forts stand on either side of the river: Halebiye – built by Palmyra's rebel queen Zenobia – still has extensive walls; Zalebiye is fragmentary. Both have great views over the valley and desert.

Deir ez-Zur, a pleasant desert town, is a good base for visiting the southern sites (Abu Kamal is too close to the sensitive Iraqi border). Here, an elegant pedestrian suspension bridge crosses the wide, shallow river.

Dura Europos, an extensive, mainly Roman, garrison town is famous for finds which have been removed – notably the remarkable frescoed synagogue, now in a purpose built wing of the Damascus Museum. Little remains of the mud-brick Mesopotamian city, Mari, but this is an archaeological site of great significance.

# Isfahan River Bridges Walk

Isfahan is one of the most beautiful cities in the Islamic world. In the 16th and 17th centuries under the Safayids (particularly the inspirational Shah Abbas I), it was a city of exquisitely tiled mosques and palaces, paradise gardens, teahouses, fine carpets, and was a centre for the arts. Today, the old city remains a treasure house – squares, domes, minarets, courtyards, and an ancient covered bazaar. The Zayandeh River crosses the city just south of the centre – five of its eleven bridges are old and its banks make a fine walk. The teahouses built under or on the bridges make excellent refreshment stops.

From the bustle of Engelab-e Eslami Square, a path leads southeast to the river and a view of the Si-o-Seh Pol – The Bridge of 33 Arches – a very recognizable landmark, built in 1602. Walking east, the Chubi Bridge, designed to irrigate the gardens, was once joined to a canal system.

Khaju Bridge, built by Shah Abbas II, is two-layered; the bottom section, with locks incorporated into the arches, regulated the flow of the river. Stairs lead to the upper storey. A quiet walk east – 3.5 km (2.2 mi) – leads to the oldest bridge, Sharestan; a mostly stone and brick structure dating from the 12th century. The pleasantly shady south bank is popular with Isfahani picnickers.

South west of the Si-o-Seh Bridge is Jolfa, the Armenian quarter established by Shah Abbas I, whose residents still worship in the many medieval churches. The last Safayid bridge is the short Marnan Bridge, west of the centre.

**HOW:**
On foot
**WHEN TO GO:**
March to May, September and October
**TIME IT TAKES:**
One day
**HIGHLIGHTS:**
The pretty teahouse in the centre of Chubi Bridge is considered one of the best in the city.
The upper story of Khaju Bridge, with niched seats, remains of frescoes and an octagonal pavilion built for the Shah, was a place for meeting and talking.
Vank Cathedral in Jolfa is richly decorated inside with Islamic tiles and magnificent frescoes. There is a small museum.
Sunset and early evening at Si-o-Seh Pol when the light softens on the river and the distant mountains, and the bridges are illuminated.
**YOU SHOULD KNOW:**
The black, tent-like *chador* is issued for mosque visits, but even on the riverbank women must cover heads, arms, legs and general outline; colours are acceptable but never wear red.

*The Khaju Bridge over the River Zayandeh*

*The mountain village
of Masuleh*

# Chalus Scenic Road

Tehran lies in the relatively temperate foothills of the Alborz
Mountains that run the length of the Caspian Sea coast. The road
from Tehran runs west, then north through the mountains. This
marvellously unspoilt forested region of high peaks – several are over
4,000 m (13,000 ft) – is sadly threatened by plans for the Tehran-
Somal Highway, which seem to be going ahead despite environmental
objections. The road down allows panoramic views of the blue
Caspian (rich in caviar and salmon) and the bright green coastal
plains, where rice, cotton and citrus orchards thrive in the
humid climate.

The development of the coast has been piecemeal – the
previously charming twin villages of Chalus and Nosahar are now
sprawling towns, though east of leafy Nosahar are some pleasant,
undeveloped beaches. West of Chalus at Namak Abrud the popular
cable car ascends the wooded slopes of Mt Medvin. Ramsar, where
the coastal plain narrows and the mountains are a dramatic
backdrop, is one of Iran's most pleasant seaside resorts. This is a
relaxed, attractive place with good accommodation. In the little town
of Lahijun, which still has some traditional Caspian architecture, is a
museum of tea history – tea has been grown successfully in the
Alborz foothills since about 1900.

The large city of Rasht (the wettest place in Iran) is popular
with Tehranis; it has an airport, and makes a good base for exploring
the area. The road to the beautiful mountain village of Masuleh
passes Fuman, whose wide streets are lined with date palms and
plastercast statues.

# Baku to Sheki Scenic Road

Until independence in 1991, Azerbaijan was ruled by great powers including Persia, Mongolia and Russia. Now this beautiful, hospitable little country is a Muslim state with a relaxed attitude to women's dress, alcohol and other faiths, and it's become an exciting tourist destination.

Nineteenth century Baku was a major oil exporter, and international investment has once again made the big, cosmopolitan capital an oil-boom town. The old city seems unaffected by the turbulent 20th century: within its walls, amid cobbled lanes, colourful markets and medieval mosques, stands the massive Maiden's Tower (assumed to be defensive, but possibly an ancient Zoroastrian temple) and the medieval seat of Azerbaijan's ruling dynasty. Among several interesting museums is an excellent Carpet Museum. Along the bustling waterfront, the Caspian is turquoise, but thick with oil.

Outside Baku are bleak reminders of the Soviet petrochemical industry, with views over the desolate coastal town of Sumquayit. Westward, the road hugs the foothills of the Caucasus. Shemaka lies in rolling countryside luxuriant with fruit, vegetables and vineyards; little remains of the ancient city but the hilltop ruins of Gulistan Castle. From Ismayilli, a scenic cliff top road leads to Lahic, a beautiful mountain village whose skilled carpet makers claim descent from the Persians. Near the pleasant market town of Qabala is the site of one of the oldest towns in Azerbaijan, dating from around the 3rd century BC.

Sheki, in its glorious mountain setting, was a major staging post on the Silk Road – in its heyday there were five caravanserai – and its silk weaving industry continues, though now restricted to small workshops. This lovely town has museums, a royal palace and an attractive old town by the stream beneath a fortress.

**HOW:**
By car or bus
**WHEN TO GO:**
June, early July and September
**TIME IT TAKES:**
Three days plus
**HIGHLIGHTS:**
The recently restored Palace of the Shirvan Shahs in Baku is a complex, fascinating site – a fine example of Shirvan architecture.
In the mountain village of Pirquli near Shamaka, the Observatory, an important Soviet space research centre, is open to visitors.
The Khan's Palace, Sheki, is beautifully decorated with tiles and carvings; the interior has murals of flowers and birds, battles and hunting scenes.
One of Sheki's caravanserai has been converted into a fascinating hotel.
**YOU SHOULD KNOW:**
Driving can be hazardous – hire a driver, take a tour or use public transport.
Azerbaijan suffers from pollution and environmental degradation.

*The courtyard of the Caravanserai Hotel in Sheki*

ASIA

*The River Lena is one of the ten longest rivers in the world.*

# River Lena Cruise

**HOW:**
By boat
**WHEN TO GO:**
June to September
**TIME IT TAKES:**
Six days
**HIGHLIGHTS:**
Yakutsk – coldest city on earth.
Confluence of Vilui River – pastoral scenery for forest walks and swimming.
Zhigansk – first settlement beyond the Arctic Circle, founded in the 17th century.
Kyusyur – regional cultural centre inhabited by native hunters and reindeer farmers.
Delta wetlands.
Tiksi – strategic Arctic Ocean settlement, only accessible by boat.
**YOU SHOULD KNOW:**
Cruises start from Yakutsk, from where you can go northwards to the Arctic or southwards towards Baikal. Each voyage is equally interesting in its own way.

A voyage along the River Lena is an eye-opening cultural and ecological adventure, taking you to the shores of the Arctic Ocean through a vast tract of virgin territory, only recently opened to tourists. From its source in the Baikal Mountains of Central Asia, the Lena flows for 4,400 km (2,800 mi) through Siberia. It is among the ten longest rivers in the world, a huge waterway, up to 25 km (15 mi) wide, that is an indispensable transport route through the inaccessible Sakha Republic (Yakutia).

This sparsely populated region of northeastern Siberia contains the largest area of permafrost in the world – where deep-frozen woolly mammoths have been uncovered, perfectly preserved. For most of the year it is a silent frozen land wrapped in snow and darkness, but come spring, a magical transformation takes place – the ice thaws, the river flows and the tundra suddenly bursts into life with an exuberance of leaf, blossom and birdsong.

In the 17th century, the first Cossack adventurers to sail along the Lena discovered a wilderness inhabited by semi-nomadic horsemen, cattle breeders and reindeer herdsmen. Today, little has changed. You voyage through a timeless land of desolate beauty and awesome space, completely forgotten by the march of mankind; disembarking at picturesque riverside villages, you will observe the fascinating world of a self-contained shamanic folk culture.

As you approach the Arctic Ocean, the huge river starts to break up into an increasingly complex labyrinth of channels, islands and streams as it gradually spreads into a 400-km (250-mi) wide delta – a 60,000 sq km (37,500 sq mi) lush summer wetland, the largest nature reserve in the Russian Federation. This unique habitat is a vital breeding ground and safe haven for millions of birds, fish and sea mammals – an ecological paradise.

# The Amur Highway

The Trans-Siberian Highway has to be one of the world's ultimate road trips, along an 11,000 km (7,000 mi) network of roads all the way from St Petersburg to Vladivostok. The Amur Highway, still under construction, is by far the most challenging section – an epic adventure in itself.

This infamous 2,200 km (1,375 mi) stretch of road runs between Chita, historic city of revolutionary exiles, and the picturesque city of Khabarovsk on the River Amur, carving its way through the inhospitable, sparsely populated swamplands of eastern Siberia and the impenetrable taiga forests of Russia's Far East, closely following the route of the Trans-Siberian Railway. It is a prestigious engineering project, bulldozing its way across savage terrain regardless of the natural obstacles in its path. Construction continues relentlessly 24 hours a day, seven days a week, but even so, much of the road is still potholed and rock-riddled gravel or dirt track that all too easily turns into a mud bath whenever it rains. Despite its incomplete state, the road was officially opened by Vladimir Putin in 2004, in a triumph of illusory hope over harsh reality; it is due to be fully asphalted by the end of 2008 but nobody believes this date to be anything other than an official fantasy.

When the Amur Highway is finally completed, it will be a far tamer trip than the one you make today. Gradually, the road is evolving into a four-lane superhighway that will present little challenge other than distance. As yet it is still one of the world's great adventure drives through a vast, untamed wilderness where you stop at isolated villages, camp by the wayside, negotiate with road gangs and test your vehicle's, and your own, stamina to its limits.

**HOW:**
By car, motorbike or bike
**WHEN TO GO:**
Mid-June to mid-August unless you are prepared to brave sub-zero temperatures and ice roads.
**TIME IT TAKES:**
3-4 days by motorbike or car, 9-12 days by bike.
**HIGHLIGHTS:**
Khabarovsk – picturesque city.
River Amur – 9th longest river in the world.
Taiga scenery.
Mikhailo-Arkhangelskaya Museum, Chita – 18th century wooden church now a museum dedicated to the Decembrist anti-tsarist revolutionaries.
**YOU SHOULD KNOW:**
This is a trip through wilderness for which you should be well prepared before you set out. Fuel is sold by the roadside, but there are few places to stay or buy supplies between Khabarovsk and Chita.

*The River Amur flows through the forest near Khabarovsk.*

# Trekking in the Golden Mountains of Altai

**HOW:**
On foot or on horseback
**WHEN TO GO:**
July to August
**TIME IT TAKES:**
12 to 18 days
**HIGHLIGHTS:**
Mount Belukha
Crossing the Karatyrek Pass.
Kucherla Valley
Sighting a snow leopard.
**YOU SHOULD KNOW:**
You must travel with a guide or on an escorted trip. Organized treks vary in length and difficulty but you need a good level of fitness in order to cope with altitudes above 3,000 m (10,000 ft) and long days of walking or riding. If you go on a riding trek some previous horse-riding experience is desirable.

Straddling the borders of China, Mongolia, Kazakhstan and Siberia, the Altai ('golden') is a rugged World Heritage wilderness, a remote land of snow-capped mountains, torrential rivers, glaciers, lakes and waterfalls where wild animals roam in the pastures and forests, and humans are few and far between. This was once the heartland of the Turkik tribes, the savage hordes of Ghengis Khan who swept down from the mountains into the plains of Central Asia. Their descendants are peaceful nomads who live traditional pastoral lives scattered through the mountains with their herds. There are no towns, no villages and no roads – just a vast expanse of soul-stirring nature.

The Altai is not easy to reach. A four-hour flight from Moscow gets you to the pleasant provincial city of Barnaul, then you spend another two days on a bumpy bus ride through the steppe. At last you reach Tyungur, a small village at the edge of the mountains where you equip yourself with supplies, and a packhorse to carry them, for a trek into the back of beyond.

Taking ancient herdsmen's trails, you tramp through sweet-scented pine forest and climb across jagged ridges above the tree line, scrambling over moraine and rambling through remote valleys full of wild flowers. Pick luscious clusters of wild currants, camp by clear mountain streams, and wonder at primeval stone mounds that mark the hill-tops as you get closer to Mount Belukha. This sacred twin-peaked mountain towers 4,506 m (14,780 ft) into the sky, clothed in snow and half-hidden behind its veil of clouds. According to shamanistic tradition, you are in Shambhala – the mythical kingdom of Tibetan scripture that holds the secrets of the Earth. The mountain radiates a mysterious silence, overwhelming in its intensity, giving you a strange feeling that the shamans could very well be right.

*The highest mountain in Siberia – Mount Belukha*

# Circum-Baikal Railway

*The train hugs the shores of Lake Baikal.*

A journey along the Circum-Baikal Railway line is an incomparable cultural, historical, technical and scenic experience. It is one of the most complex railway lines in the world, running for 89 km (56 mi) along a narrow mountain shelf, going through 56 tunnels and galleries and over 248 bridges and viaducts, and passing more than 170 architectural and natural monuments.

Lake Baikal, the world's deepest lake, lies directly in the path of the Trans-Siberian Railway and, before the Circum-Baikal was built, trains had to be uncoupled and transported across the lake by ferry. The Russo-Japanese War of 1904 made it imperative that this final link in the Trans-Siberian line was completed to carry troops and supplies. Huge sums of money and the forced labour of thousands of convicts were thrown at the problem of constructing a railway along the vertical granite mountainsides of the lake's southern coast. In terrible conditions, constantly threatened by landslides and mudflows, the prison work-gangs hacked out ledges and tunnels using only chisel and sledge hammer. The line became operational in 1905 and, in reference to its massive cost, rapidly acquired the sobriquet 'the golden buckle in the steel belt'.

The Circum-Baikal became redundant in the 1950s when a hydroelectric project necessitated flooding a section of line and building a by-pass. Today it is a quiet back-route, serviced by excursion trains that trundle along at 25-30 kph (15-20 mph), stopping every so often for passengers to look at the incredible engineering – all the more incredible for having been built without the aid of machines. The railway runs through a region of outstanding natural beauty with breathtaking views of Lake Baikal's astounding scenery. It is a spectacular testament to Russian skill in engineering and design, quite unlike any other railway journey in the world.

**HOW:**
By train
**WHEN TO GO:**
May to October
**TIME IT TAKES:**
4 hours and 40 minutes
**HIGHLIGHTS:**
Ulanovo – see the remains of the original railway sleepers and tunnels.
Local culture in villages along the route.
Beautiful scenery.
Belaya Valemka (White Cutting) – marble outcrop, rare combination of minerals of outstanding geological significance.
Polovinnaya and Shabartuysky Bridges – ferro-concrete arched viaducts.
**YOU SHOULD KNOW:**
You can also explore the railway line on foot, going through disused tunnels and over viaducts as you hike along the lakeshore.

# Kamchatka Ring of Fire Trek

**HOW:**
On foot
**WHEN TO GO:**
June to September
**TIME IT TAKES:**
Two weeks
**HIGHLIGHTS:**
Climbing Mutnovsky 2,323 m
(7,620 ft) high – glaciated caldera.
Ash cones, geysers, fumaroles and
mud pools.
Zhirovskye and Viluchinskye hot
springs.
Kurilskoye Lake – see brown bears
and sea eagles.
Klyuchevskaya Volcano – largest
active volcano in Eurasia.
**YOU SHOULD KNOW:**
Much of the Kamchatka is still
uncharted wilderness and there is no
tourist infrastructure. You need to be
extremely physically fit, adventurous
and prepared to rough it. As well as
adventure eco-trekking, you can also
go on birdwatching, fishing and
rafting expeditions and coastal
cruises.

A remote peninsula at the far edge of Russia's Far East, Kamchatka is more or less the same size as Britain, and on the same latitude. But it could not be more different. Barely touched by man, with only a single rough road, it is one of the world's greatest ecological treasures – a rugged wilderness in a constant state of geothermal flux containing some of the world's most spectacular volcanoes. With more than 400 glaciers and 160 volcanoes, it is one of the most active regions in the Ring of Fire volcanic belt that girdles the Pacific.

A journey into Kamatchka is like entering a dreamland – a surreal world of elfin cedar trees and giant savannah grasses; boiling mud pots and blue-algae lakes; blackened lava desert and dense primeval forests; steaming sulphur springs and swirling icy rivers. Brown bears roam in the woods, the rivers are stuffed with salmon and the surrounding seas are rich fishing grounds where whales, sea-lions and sea otters flourish. In the autumn, the swathes of luxuriant green forest turn to fiery shades of brilliant reds, yellows, pinks, purple and gold, transforming the landscape into a dazzling rainbow of colour before the leaves fall and the long dark arctic winter sets in.

You trek through highlands and lowlands, scrambling down steep ravines and wading through rivers, wandering through the woods and along the seashore, camping by clear-watered streams, bathing in hot springs and climbing to the summits of snow-capped volcanoes. At the rim of the Mutnovsky Volcano, you peer down into the caldera through a sulphurous veil of fumaroles to glimpse a sparkling wall of ice crystals – an incredible climax to an awesome eco-adventure at the very edge of the world.

*Mud face packs for these two soaking in the hot spring.*

# Lake Issyk-Kul Trek

*Lake Issy-Kul – one of the world's highest lakes*

Lake Issyk-Kul, the 'Pearl of the Tien Shan Mountains' in northern Kyrgyzstan, is one of the world's highest (1,610 m/5,280 ft) lakes. Yet despite being fed by the icy water of 118 rivers and streams, and the melt-water of the soaring peaks that surround it, it never freezes, because of the slightly saline springs bubbling up in its centre. This quirk, combined with Issyk-Kul's huge size (its shore is 700 km/437 mi long), has resulted in a microclimate that has transformed the adjacent mountains. They should be barren, rugged, windswept and bitterly cold. Instead, below a snowline consistently higher than 4,000 m (13,000 ft), the Tien Shan Mountains here are a hiker's paradise of thick forests, small lakes of vivid colours in rolling alpine pastures, waterfalls and torrents gurgling along valley floors. The lake itself is edged with sandy beaches and the most unlikely of all, flower-filled meadows – and the water's temperature is 24 °C (75 °F) from June to September.

Issyk-Kul's extraordinary climate has made it a favourite resort for visitors from Bishkek and Alma-Ata – but only the north shore has been heavily developed. The best trekking routes are based on Karakol (formerly known, and still often referred to as, Przheval'sk, after the Russian explorer), at the lake's eastern end. Typically, seven to fourteen day treks cherry-pick the region's best two to three day hikes, driving up to 150 km (95 mi) between the most scenic landscapes. From the Dzhetyoguz Valley you cross the Tilety Pass and clamber up the Karakol and Keldyke gorges to beautiful Ala-Kul Lake, from which you can look along the magnificent 5,000 m (16,400 ft) plus peaks of the Terskei Ala-Too range. More remote, and lovelier in all its variety is the Sarydzhaz river valley to Mertsbakher Lake trek. Provided you stay largely on the southern shore, Issyk-Kul offers a pristine wilderness of gentler terrain than you expect in the heart of central Asia.

**HOW:**
On foot
**WHEN TO GO:**
June to October
**TIME IT TAKES:**
7-21 days (including one day's travel each way from Bishkek/Alma-Ata to Przheval'sk).
**HIGHLIGHTS:**
Staying in a yurt, the traditional collapsible and portable nomadic dwelling, made of felt stretched over a birch lattice framework, with a hole (*tunduk*) in the top for ventilation.
The view from Djuuku Pass of Ara-Bel Valley, Djuuku Gorge and Djashyk-Kyol (Green Lake).
Drinking *Kymyz* (mare's milk) in a yurt camp, listening to the guide/shepherd's stories about the beautiful red rocks known as 'Seven Bulls' and 'Broken Heart' in the Sarydzhaz Valley.
Sunbathing on a sandy beach 1,524 m (5,000 ft) up in Central Asia.
**YOU SHOULD KNOW:**
1. Make sure your papers are in perfect order, especially if you are coming from Kazakhstan.
2. Difficult access to health and transport facilities on the south side of Issyk-Kul make trekking inadvisable for children under twelve.

407

# The Fergana Valley

Known as the 'Golden Valley', the Fergana is a 22,000-sq km (8,500-sq mi) wedge of rich arable land enclosed by the Tien Shan and Pamir Mountains. The 300-km (190-mi) long valley is a picturesque ethnic melting-pot with a distinguished history. In 329 BC Alexander the Great founded the city of Khujand and, some 200 years later, the inhabitants of the valley began trading with China – the origins of the Silk Road. The 7th to 8th century Arab Empire introduced Islam from the west; and Babur, 16th century descendant of Ghengis Khan, spread the splendours of Fergana's Moghul culture into South Asia. In the 1920s Stalin carved up this prosperous province between Tajikistan, Uzbekistan and Kyrgyzstan, creating today's crazily illogical borders.

As you travel up the valley from Khujand, an important Tajik city on the Syr Darya River, you will find yourself drawn into an intriguing cultural adventure. The diversity of customs, costumes and language is fascinating and you may often be surprised by the contradictions between ancient and modern, Islamic and communist ideals. Head northeast through cotton and wheat fields, orchards and vineyards into Uzbekistan, to the historic capital of Kokand; and Margilan, a market town famous for its silks. Admire the faded 19th century grandeur of the elegant tree-lined streets in Fergana town, and visit Andijan, the city where Babur was born. Cross into Kyrgyzstan, a remote mountainous country of breathtaking natural beauty, ending your travels in fairytale surroundings of sparkling alpine lakes, wild walnut orchards and snow-capped mountain peaks.

On your journey, you will see countless historic monuments, haggle in colourful bazaars, relax under the ornately painted roofs of wayside *chaikhanas* (traditional tea houses); and find yourself welcomed into people's homes with a heartfelt hospitality that transcends cultural barriers, leaving you with many fond memories of this remarkable part of the world.

*Fergana Valley with the Tien Shan Mountains in the background*

# The Pamir Highway

The Pamir Highway is one of the highest, most thrilling, least-travelled routes in the world. Here, at the meeting point of the Tien Shan, Hindu Kush and Karakoram mountain ranges, is some of the most extraordinary and beautiful terrain on the planet, an eerie empty land of parched ochre rock, hot springs and turquoise glacial lakes set amongst the magnificent snow-capped peaks of the world's highest mountains.

Built by the Russians as a Soviet supply road, the Highway runs for some 1,250 km (780 mi) from Dushanbe to Osh along an ancient Silk Road route across the Pamir Plateau. Subject to erosion, earthquakes and landslides, the road is in a constant state of disrepair, making for a journey full of sudden unforeseen hazards. There is almost no traffic and, apart from shepherds herding their flocks, scarcely a soul to be seen. You will, however, stumble upon plenty of monuments – petroglyphs, ancient temples, Buddhist stupas and ruined fortresses, charting several millennia of history.

The Highway runs eastwards from Dushanbe across the plains, winding steeply upwards through rugged mountains to Khalaikum. You pass rusting hulks of abandoned Russian tanks and lurid signs warning of minefields as you manoeuvre your way through old landslips and uncontained streams sloshing across the road. The air grows colder and howling winds blow through an increasingly desolate landscape as you climb over the Koi-Tezek Pass at 4,200 m (13,775 ft) and set out across the Pamir Plateau towards China. At the frontier, the road turns northwards along the Chinese border up to Ak-Baital Pass at 4,655 m (15,270 ft) before descending to the hauntingly beautiful Lake Kara-Kul, through the lush pastures and dramatic gorges of the Alai Valley in Kyrgyzstan, to end this epic road trip at the colourful city of Osh.

*The highway slices through the Karakoram Mountains.*

**HOW:**
By 4x4 or bike
**WHEN TO GO:**
July to September
**TIME IT TAKES:**
Five to seven days by 4x4, three weeks by mountain bike
**HIGHLIGHTS:**
Yamchun – 12th century fort with spectacular view.
Bathing in the Garm-Chashma and Bibi Fatima hot springs.
Lake Karak-Kul – salt lake formed by meteorite impact millions of years ago.
Views from the Ak-Baital Pass, 4,655 m (15,270 ft).
**YOU SHOULD KNOW:**
This is a demanding journey whether you travel by jeep or bike. You will be travelling at very high altitudes so must be physically fit. You can shorten the journey by taking a plane part of the way, from Dushanbe to Khorugh – a spectacular scenic flight through the mountains that is an experience in itself.

**409**

*The new bridge over the River Oxus*

# Follow the Footsteps of Alexander across the Oxus

**HOW:**
By car, motorbike or bike
**WHEN TO GO:**
April to June or September to October
**TIME IT TAKES:**
Two to three days by car/motorbike; four to six by mountain bike.
**HIGHLIGHTS:**
Tajikistan – 18th century Hissor Fort.
Ajina-Teppa – 7th century Buddhist monastery complex.
Spectacular view from top of Nurek Dam, one of the tallest dams in the world.
Afghanistan – Blue Mosque of Mazar-i-Sharif.
Balkh – medieval ruins and early Islamic monuments.
**YOU SHOULD KNOW:**
Most governments advise against any unnecessary travel in Afghanistan but, depending on local conditions at the time of travel, the north is not unduly hazardous. Never travel without a knowledgeable local guide and make thorough enquiries beforehand. Afghan visas can be obtained in Dushanbe.

Crossing the Oxus into Afghanistan, one of the most wonderful countries in the world, is a lot easier now than it was two millennia ago when Alexander the Great's armies floated across the fast-flowing river by clinging onto their leather tents converted into makeshift rafts. In 2007, an imposing 670-m (2,200-ft) long bridge was opened, a vital link in a 21st century 'Silk Road' that aims to connect landlocked Central Asia to the Indian Ocean port of Karachi.

The legendary River Oxus (nowadays known as the Amu Dariya) separates Tajikistan and Afghanistan. The people on either side share the same ethnic bonds but for decades they have been divided by political turmoil and the barrier of the river itself, which was crossable only by an intermittent ferry service. The bridge will eventually help regenerate a remote area that is still suffering the aftermath of thirty years of war. Right now it enables the intrepid traveller to undertake a fascinating trip at the cutting edge of adventure tourism.

The spanking new bridge seems utterly incongruous in comparison to its surroundings. As soon as you cross it, you are hurled back through time into a biblical landscape – a startling contrast to southern Tajikistan where the intensively farmed fields and ancient remains of the historic Hissor and Vakhsh Valleys all testify to millennia of civilization.

It may take a while to see beyond the poverty but persevere along the dusty road to Mazar-i-Sharif, the cultural capital of northern Afghanistan, and you will soon be filled with respect for the dignified bearing and beautiful manners of this resilient people; and you will be completely overawed by the staggering beauty of the Blue Mosque – a cogent reminder of the sophisticated civilization in Afghanistan at a time when the West was stuck in the Dark Ages.

# Orkhon Valley

Mongolia is the most sparsely populated country in the world, a vast untamed expanse of mountain, forest, desert and plateau. In this nomadic land where more than thirty per cent of the population are still herdsmen and there are scarcely any roads, riding is the normal means of getting around. Mongolians have an almost symbiotic relationship with their horses – calm, surefooted ponies that easily handle the rough terrain unshod.

An expedition by horse to the Orkhon Valley will open your eyes to a way of life that is utterly unfamiliar. The Orkhon is the cradle of Central Asian nomadic societies, a World Heritage Cultural Landscape where the inhabitants live in harmony with nature, continuing pastoral traditions and shamanic religious practices that have remained unchanged for some two millenia.

As you ride through the wildflower pastures by the River Orkhon, the only signs of human life are the scattered *gers* (yurt tents) of nomad families. A camping trek of some 200 km (125 mi) along the river valley and up into the Khangai Mountains, through verdant, volcanic plains and forested gorges to the dramatic cascade of the Orkhon waterfall is a liberating escape from the complexities of the post-modern age. Here there is just you, your horse and nature in the raw.

Incredible as it may seem, you are travelling through the heart of the largest empire in the history of the world. At its height in the 13th century, the Mongol Empire stretched across Central Asia from Beijing to the borders of Hungary. Ghengis Khan held sway over more than a 100 million people from his capital city of Kharkhorum in the Orkhon Valley. The remnants can be seen today – ruins standing as testaments that this remote valley was once the centre of the world.

**HOW:**
On horseback
**WHEN TO GO:**
May to October
**TIME IT TAKES:**
Ten days
**HIGHLIGHTS:**
Galloping across the steppe.
Staying in a traditional *ger* camp.
Ruins of Kharakhorum – Ghengis Khan's capital.
Erdene Zuu Monastery – most ancient Buddhist monastery in Mongolia.
Drinking fermented mare's milk.
**YOU SHOULD KNOW:**
You should be a reasonably competent horse rider to go on this trek. Alternative means of transport are yak cart, mountain bike or 4x4.

*The Orkhon Valley*

# Gobi Desert Trek

**HOW:**
On a camel or by 4x4
**WHEN TO GO:**
May to October
**TIME IT TAKES:**
Eight to nine days
**HIGHLIGHTS:**
Bayan Zag flaming cliffs
Hongor Sands
Yol Valley glacier
Staying with local herdsmen in a
ger village.
Seeing rare wildlife.
**YOU SHOULD KNOW:**
According to National Geographic
*Adventure Magazine,* the Gobi is one
of the top six trekking destinations.
The Gobi is a wild and remote region
with no roads and dangerously
powerful winds. You should not
attempt to explore it without a guide.

The Gobi is one of the strangest places on the planet. The largest desert in Asia and the fourth largest in the world, it is a cold desert of high plateau and mountain where it is not uncommon to see frost. It stretches some 1,600 km (1,000 mi) east to west, covering the whole of southern Mongolia and extending into northern China, gradually expanding southwards all the time. Although at first sight it looks totally barren, the Gobi supports many unusual mammals and more than 200 species of bird as well as endemic plants.

From Dalandzadgad, a town 540 km (336 mi) south of Ulaanbaatar, you can ride either by camel or jeep through the stunning landscapes of Gurvansaikhan National Park where three mountain ridges rise up to 2,600 metres (8,500 ft). The dramatic scenery is extraordinarily varied – rocky and sandy desert, precipitous cliffs and ravines, oases and saltpans. You can climb to the top of Hongor Sands, a giant 180-km (110-mi) long 300-m (1,000-ft) high sand dune, explore the glaciated Yol Valley, and wander in the other-worldly terrain of the Bayan Zag 'flaming cliffs' – a vast red sandstone amphitheatre of weirdly eroded pillars, rock canyons and ridges, where in 1923 Roy Chapman Andrews famously discovered dinosaur remains and fossilized eggs.

The surreal empty landscapes and the insubstantial beauty of the dunes give you a strangely comforting sense of your own insignificance. You are surrounded by silence, only the singing of the wind; and at night, the only light is a twinkling sky thick with stars. A trek into the Gobi is a life-changing experience that leads one to re-assess man's place on the planet.

*A camel caravan crosses Hongor Sands, the biggest dune in the Gobi Desert.*

# Into the Khentii Mountains

*Terelj National Park*

Mongolia is generally associated with endless empty desert, but a trip through Terelj National Park into the lower Khentii Mountains soon puts paid to any such pre-conceptions. From a lush marshland veined with rivers and streams, where bizarrely shaped granite outcrops rise dramatically from meadows strewn with wild flowers, you clamber through a glorious mountainous landscape of wooded hills and valleys. Apart from the odd nomad camp, the wilderness stretches out before you all the way to Siberia, a paradise for the numerous animals and birds that thrive here.

As you climb from the meadows into the mountains you can watch birds of prey patrolling the huge skies, see wild horses, red elk, moose, wolves and even spot a brown bear. Walk along the banks of clear-watered rivers, catch fish in Khagiin Khar, a 20-m (66-ft) deep glacial lake, and dip a toe in the Yestii hot water springs. Climb to the top of Altan Ulgii, at 2,646 m (8,680 ft) the highest mountain of the Khentii, for wonderful panoramic views and wander round the spooky Gunjin Sum Monastery, deep in the larch forest. Only the outer walls are intact but many old tales are attached to it that will send a shiver down your spine.

Only 80 km (50 mi) from the capital, Ulaanbaatar, and easily accessible by one of the few roads in this vast country, the Terelj National Park and Khentii Mountains cover an area of some 2,864 sq km (1,100 sq mi) with some of the most beautiful scenery in Mongolia. Miles from any signs of civilization, dependent on your own resources, this is a trip for the nature lover in search of a genuine backwoods experience and a complete release from the pressures of urban life.

**HOW:**
On foot
**WHEN TO GO:**
May to October
**TIME IT TAKES:**
Ten days
**HIGHLIGHTS:**
Ulaanbaatar – Gandan Monastery, a functioning Buddhist monastery.
Seeing wildlife.
Weird rock formations
Ruins of the Gunjin Monastery
Altan Ulgii – highest mountain of the Khentii
**YOU SHOULD KNOW:**
Most of the trek is relatively easy-going, although it's steep in parts so you need to be reasonably fit. The Terelj National Park is beginning to cater for tourists at its edges and you can take much shorter trips from Ulaanbaatar to go rock-climbing, rafting, mountain biking and horse riding.

413

*The road runs parallel to the Yarlung Tsangpo River.*

# Lhasa-Gyantse-Xigatse Scenic Drive

**HOW:**
By car or 4x4
**WHEN TO GO:**
May to June or September to October
**TIME IT TAKES:**
Two to three days
**HIGHLIGHTS:**
Lhasa – Jokhang Temple, the holiest shrine in Tibet.
Yamdrok Lake
Karola Glacier
Khumbum Pagoda
Tashilhunpo Monastery
**YOU SHOULD KNOW:**
Foreigners require entry and travel permits. The whole of Tibet is at very high altitude so it is best not to fly in from a low altitude country but acclimatize yourself gradually by travelling through increasingly high altitude zones on your way here.

Tibet, for so long closed to outsiders, is the world's largest and highest plateau, a land of snow-clad mountains, turquoise lakes, rolling pastures and cobalt skies – the Shangri-La of western imaginings, an ancient spiritual culture that is being slowly crushed by the inexorable march of progress.

Lhasa is not at all the 'Place of the Gods' that you expect. The ancient city has long since been engulfed by concrete and commerce. You have to look hard to find the prayer wheels, exotic temples and cymbal-clashing saffron-robed monks that you pictured. You must leave the city to discover Tibet – an enchanting pastoral world of nomad tents and yaks, wild plateau horsemen, brightly costumed women leading pack-mules, and everywhere pervaded by the mysteries of an ancient shamanic Buddhism.

The road southward from Lhasa crosses the Yarlung Tsangpo (Brahmaputra) River and climbs through the scenic Kyi Chu Valley to the 4,794-m (15,725-ft) Ganba Pass, where prayer flags flutter in the wind. Below you is the sacred Yamdrok Lake – a truly breathtaking sight. You carry on through a ravine up across the Karo Pass, more than 5,000 m (16,500 ft) high, seeing lakes and glaciers, and descend to Gyantse, a charming traditional market town in a fertile valley 265 km (165 mi) southwest of Lhasa. Here you will find the Palkhor Monastery and the staggering 32-m (105-ft) tall Khumbum Stupa, one of the most magnificent buildings in Tibet.

Carry on to Xigatse, ancient seat of the Panchen Lamas and visit the temples and monasteries round about. The Tashilhunpo Monastery is a breathtaking complex of golden-roofed buildings where you can see the incredible 35-m (115-ft) high Thangka Wall, built by the first Dalai Lama in 1468. This is the glorious Tibet that you imagined.

# Mount Kailash Kora

A massive peak, more than 6,600 m (21,700 ft) high in the remote Gangdisé Shan mountain range, Kailash is not only revered in the shamanistic Bön religion of Tibet but equally among Buddhists, Hindus and Jains. It is believed to be the sacred centre of the world and, among Hindus, the home of Lord Shiva.

Pilgrims travel for days through the wilds of western Tibet to make a *kora* (ritual circumambulation) of Mount Kailash in the hope of a better life. The more circuits that are completed, the more auspicious it is. Thirteen is considered especially lucky, while 108 rewards you with instant nirvana. Exceptionally devout believers prostrate their way around the circuit – flinging their entire body flat out on the ground with every step.

The 52-km (32-mi) circular walk starts and finishes at Darchen, a nondescript mud brick village in a tranquil plain of grazing yaks. It is a mortal sin to set foot on the mountain itself. The pilgrim trail leads round the edge through green valleys and narrow gorges to the Drolma Pass at 5,600 m (18,370 ft). This is the high point of the *kora* where celebrating pilgrims chant, prostrate themselves at stone *chortens* (stupas) and tie their prayer flags, adding to the myriad of multi-coloured tattered cloths torn into shreds by the howling wind. As you descend round the other side, the view of the striated north face of the mountain is dazzlingly perfect – alternate lines of black rock and shimmering ice, rising to an unsullied glistening cone of snow outlined by the deep blue of the Tibetan sky.

There is something extraordinarily uplifting about walking with pilgrims. The intensity of their faith creates an inspirational atmosphere and joyful spirit of shared endeavour as you make your personal *kora*.

**HOW:**
On foot and 4x4
**WHEN TO GO:**
May to June or September to October
**TIME IT TAKES:**
Seven days – four days 4x4 journey from Lhasa and three days walking.
**HIGHLIGHTS:**
La Chu glacial valley
Gori Kund frozen lake
Milarepa's Cave
Lake Manosarovar
**YOU SHOULD KNOW:**
Be sure that you are acclimatized to the altitude before setting out. It is the height rather than the terrain that makes the Kailash circuit a demanding walk. Apart from one or two steep rocky parts that require good shoes, it is fairly easy trekking.

*Buddhist prayer stones at the sky burial site above Tarboche in La Chu glacial valley*

# Roof of the World Express

The world's highest railway line, the 'Roof of the World Express' was opened in 2006. It runs for 1,142 km (710 mi) between Lhasa, capital of Tibet and Xining in China, crossing the Tibetan Plateau more than 5 km (3 mi) above sea level. It reaches its highest point at the Tanggula Pass (5,231m/17,158 ft) and goes through the Fenghuoshan, the highest tunnel in the world at 4,905 m (16,093 ft). There are 675 bridges and 45 stations along the line, and more than half the track is laid on permafrost in a miracle of engineering.

The railway is the fulfilment of China's long-term ambition to join its western province with the rest of the country, to promote economic progress and cultural unity. The Tibetans view it rather differently – as yet another threat to their ancient indigenous culture; and environmentalists are concerned about the disruption to the region's delicate ecology. Whatever the rights and wrongs, it cannot be denied that it is both an incredible journey and an inevitability in a globalized economy.

Most of the journey is at an altitude of over 4,000 m (13,000 ft). The carriage windows are tinted to block out harmful ultra-violet rays and every berth has a personal oxygen canister in addition to the oxygenated air that is pumped round the train. As you cross the desolate treeless Tibetan plateau – the 'Rooftop of the World' – you enjoy a spectacular moving picture of the surreal scenery. You pass the highest lake in the world, see yak, wild antelope and donkeys grazing and watch golden eagles cruising through the sky. Puffy white clouds hang in the cobalt blue Tibetan sky above a vast moonscape of yellows, ochres and browns, and a skyline of sharply etched snow-capped peaks glows golden in the sun. This is the train-ride of a lifetime.

**HOW:**
By train
**WHEN TO GO:**
May to June or September to October
**TIME IT TAKES:**
14 hours
**HIGHLIGHTS:**
Lhasa – Johkang Temple
Tanggula Pass.
Qinghai Lake – largest lake in China.
Xining – Kumbum Monastery, one of the most important Buddhist sites in China.
**YOU SHOULD KNOW:**
You can now travel all the way across China on a single train journey between Lhasa and Beijing in three days.

*The Qingzang/Qinghai-Xizang train approaching Lhasa.*

416

# Sacred Valleys Trek

By anybody's reckoning Bhutan is a most extraordinary country. Tucked away in the folds of the eastern Himalayas, and surrounded by China and India, this remote, mountain kingdom is the last place in the Himalayas where Mahayana Buddhist culture survives intact, informing every aspect of life here. First opened to the world in 1974, the present King's policy has been tailored to keep Bhutan's traditional culture and pristine environment untouched by outside influences and so far, so good.

Bumthang is a complex of four, beautiful valleys, lying at about 2,600 m (8,500 ft). Buckwheat, barley, potatoes and apples grow in profusion, and this tranquil landscape is Bhutan's sacred heart, containing many of its most revered temples. Trek alongside the Chamkhar River, famed for its trout, visit Thamshing Lhakang Temple, built in the 7th century, and Membar Tsho (Burning Lake) where Guru Rimpoche, who brought Buddhism here from Tibet, hid some sacred scriptures.

Walk through traditional villages of unique architecture, meet delightful local people, marvel at gorgeous handicrafts, climb up to Phephela Pass through serene forests of miniature bamboo, rhododendrons and pine. Follow the course of the river up to the base camp of Gangkhar Puensum. Bhutan's highest mountain at 7,570 m (24,000 ft) is the world's highest, unclimbed mountain. Various attempts to climb it have failed, and mountaineering has been forbidden since 2003 because of local religious beliefs.

Flora and fauna flourish in this environment of respect for all living things, and over 600 bird species can be found, including ten that are endangered. There are 165 different mammals including red panda, Himalayan black bear and tiger. Takin, the national animal, can be seen grazing in alpine meadows, also home to some of the country's remarkable flora. What with temples and fortresses, natural beauty and charming people, trekking Bhutan's Sacred Valleys is a magical experience.

**HOW:**
On foot
**WHEN TO GO:**
March to June, September to November
**TIME IT TAKES:**
Up to two weeks
**HIGHLIGHTS:**
The colourful festivals that take place in the valleys during spring and autumn.
Thanbi Temple, founded in 1470.
Thimpu, Bhutan's capital city.
**YOU SHOULD KNOW:**
Bhutan, (known by its people as 'the Land of the Thunder Dragon') accords great respect to the mountain Gangkhar Puensum. According to folklore it is the source of three major Bhutanese rivers, the Kuru, Chamkhar and Mangde. When they first appeared, the rivers proposed a race, but Chamkhar said she would rather take her time and enjoy the views. This is why the Trongsa and Lhuntse valleys are narrow and steep, while Bumthang valley is wide and lush.

*The beautiful and remote mountain kingdom of Bhutan*

417

# Barsey (Vershay) Rhododendron Sanctuary Trek

**HOW:**
On foot
**WHEN TO GO:**
March and April for the rhododendrons
**TIME IT TAKES:**
About one week
**HIGHLIGHTS:**
Watching the sunrise over Kanchenjunga.
The amazing sight of miles and miles of flowering rhododendrons.
Kechopalri Lake, revered by Buddhist and Hindu alike for its miraculous, healing properties.
**YOU SHOULD KNOW:**
Sikkim is the least populated state in India, and its official language is…English.

*Rhododendrons in bloom at the Barsey Rhododendron Sanctuary*

The landlocked state of Sikkim is small, but due to its position tucked into the Himalayas, its climate, flora and fauna is very varied, with elevations that range from 280 m (900 ft) to the summit of Kanchenjunga, the world's third highest mountain standing at an impressive 8,598 m (28,208 ft).

One of the loveliest treks here takes you through the Vershay Rhododendron Sanctuary. Starting from Rinchenpong, a small market village, climb through well-cultivated land, past fruit orchards and plots of rice, maize, millet and vegetables, to Hi Barmoik. This attractive village of wood and stone houses is spread across the wooded mountainside at an altitude of 2,200 m (7,000 ft).

Climbing higher, the trek takes you through mixed forest to Barsey, where the altitude goes up to 4,100 m (13,500 ft), producing habitats that support everything from bamboo to Alpine wildflowers. This is a wonderful area for birds – over 200 species have been recorded here, and mammals include leopard, marten, civet, barking deer and red panda. Barsey lies on a huge ridge, covered with silver fir, hemlock, magnolia, orchid and, of course, rhododendrons. In spring, the sheer quantity of millions of brilliantly coloured rhododendron flowers, (from thirty different species), is overwhelming, and the clear air is redolent with their fragrance.

There are wonderful views too, of the high peaks. At Phoktay Dara there is a superb, panoramic viewing point, where you can see the magnificent snow-capped mountains, including both Kanchenjunga and Mount Everest in all their glory. Passing through flower-filled meadows, and across clear streams you descend to the Khalej Valley before visiting Pamayangtse Monastery, one of the oldest and most revered Buddhist monasteries in Sikkim. Situated on a hill at about 2,000 m (6,500 ft), it commands another spectacular view of the Himalayas and Kanchenjunga. Inside, you can marvel over ancient carvings, frescoes, and a marvellous, seven-tiered wooden sculpture of Heaven.

# Annapurna Circuit Trek

The Annapurna circuit, stretching for 300 km (187 mi), is one of the classic Nepal Himalayan trails – a gruelling, exhilarating, life-enhancing trek through some of the most spectacular mountain scenery the world has to offer. The trail is mostly well maintained, but some snow and ice will almost certainly be encountered, particularly when crossing the high pass of Thorong La, at 5,416 m (17,800 ft.).

*A trekker looking out over the old fortified village of Jharkot along the Annapurna circuit.*

From Besisahar, at about 500 m (1,600 ft), you ascend gently through brilliant, green rice paddies and numerous small streams. As you climb higher, you'll see marijuana fields, goats at pasture, apple and apricot orchards and barley, as well as small villages scattered amongst the terraced farmland. After a few days the trail becomes steeper and you find yourself passing through temperate and coniferous forests, alpine meadows, finally climbing beyond the tree line.

Sometimes you'll spend two nights in one place in order to acclimatize your body – the air is thin up here and altitude sickness can be a problem – but by now you are living in a different world, where the sound of rushing water from streams and waterfalls replaces that of cars and machinery. The villages become more Tibetan the higher you go, and Buddhism takes over from Hinduism. People here seem genuinely friendly and welcoming, and there are many lodges in which to stay.

By the time you reach Thorong La pass and make the descent to Muktinath, an important religious site, you will have seen the most extraordinary, panoramic views of the snow-laden Annapurnas, crossed high suspension bridges, waded through rivers, and eaten masses of dal and vegetable curry. At Tatopani, relax in the welcome hot springs. Watch the sunrise from Poon Hill in Ghorepani, or gaze at the amazing, high altitude lake at Tilicho before descending to the 'real' world once again.

**HOW:**
On foot
**WHEN TO GO:**
Late September to December
**TIME IT TAKES:**
About three weeks
**HIGHLIGHTS:**
The beautiful, terraced valley of Marsyangdi.
The walk between Chame and Manang via Upper Pisang with its stupendous, inspirational views.
The Hindu and Buddhist temples at Muktinath.
**YOU SHOULD KNOW:**
This trek is strenuous – you'll be walking for up to 7 hours per day, carrying a light rucksack. It is also very cold, especially above 3,000 m (10,000 ft). Rent rather than buy everything you need for the trek, and pay the entrance fee to the Annapurna region in Kathmandu or Pokhara.

*Mount Kanchenjunga*

# Kanchenjunga Trek

In remote, north-eastern Nepal, on the borders of Sikkim and Tibet, the magnificent mountain Kanchenjunga rises to the sky. At 8,598 m (28,300 ft), this is the world's third highest peak, now part of a conservation area. First climbed in 1955, the region was opened to group trekkers 20 years ago. A climate of high rainfall, humidity, frost and snow together with isolation, has created a region of unique mountain ecosystems, supporting snow leopards, Himalayan black bears, goral, blue sheep, yak, serow and red panda.

The long, arduous trek takes you from from the village of Taplejung, gradually ascending through fertile, cultivated hillsides – rice and cardomom – before entering forests of oak, Himalayan larch, rhododendron and pine. There are 69 varieties of orchid to be found amongst the 1,200 species of flowering plants, and the numerous waterfalls are testament to the heavy monsoon rains.

For the first few days you will camp in villages, mostly populated by Limbu people, recognizable by their *topi* hats, which are larger and more colourful than those worn by most Nepalis. The Limbus, along with the Rais, make up the famous Gurkhas of the British and Indian armies. As you climb higher, you'll camp in ever more remote locations, in the midst of magnificent mountain scenery.

Climbing ever more steeply, the forest gives way to high Alpine meadows where yaks graze beside the moraine. You'll pass lakes, some frozen, ford streams, traverse many high passes and cross the Yalung Ri glacier, shortly after which you'll suddenly see the immense, southern wall of Kanchenjunga and its three major summits, in particular Jannu and its glaciers. Crossing the Mirgin Pass another spectacle awaits you – the extraordinary sight of Everest, Lhotse, Chamalang, Maluku and Gyankung Kang on the horizon, and mighty Jannu so close you feel you could touch it.

# Fly over the Himalayas

The Himalayan Mountains are the highest in the world. Of the thirty one summits over 7,600 m (25,000 ft), 22 rise in Nepal, including Everest and seven other great giants that are over 8,000 m (26,000 ft). If you have limited time here but still wish to see some of the highest peaks and do a little trekking, one option is to take the mountain flight from Pokhara to Jomson, where you can take a short trek into the Annapurnas.

Pokhara is the second largest tourist centre after Kathmandu, beautifully situated beside Lake Phewa, and several flights leave here every morning for Jomson. Within 30 km (19 mi) of the town, the elevation changes drastically from 900 m (3,000 ft) to 8,000 m (26,000 ft), and as the small plane takes off it rises sharply, giving you a view of the white, hilltop World Peace Stupa at the edge of town.

The flight is short but spectacular, passing through a narrow corridor between Dhaulagiri, 8,167 m (27,000 ft), and Annapurna, 8,019 m (26,500 ft). You also have wonderful views of Manasulu, Nilgiri and of Machapuchere, with its instantly recognizable fishtail peak. These mountains are seen at eye level, and on a clear day you can see folds and ravines in the rock face as well as a perfect view of the snowline. Sometimes it can be cloudy, but even then you'll suddenly see a towering snow-capped, glacier-draped pinnacle looming majestically beside you.

On sunny days the plane's shadow races along the bare, brown rock face beneath you. Scattered mountain villages, paths and rivers snaking through deep valleys are clearly visible. Suddenly the plane dives steeply into a valley, making alarmingly tight turns as it aligns itself to the runway. Don't worry - moments later you'll be breathing the pure, crisp air of the high Himalayas.

**HOW:**
By plane
**WHEN TO GO:**
March to May and late September to end November
**TIME IT TAKES:**
About 30 minutes
**HIGHLIGHTS:**
The superb views of some of the Himalayas' most majestic mountains. Trekking in the Annapurnas. The fortress town of Kagbeni. Muktinath, a place of pilgrimage and a major religious site.
**YOU SHOULD KNOW:**
The Nepalese word 'himal' means 'snow covered mountain'. The Himalayan glaciers, the source of Asia's largest rivers, are at risk. A UN climate report states that global warming could melt them all by 2035, causing flooding followed by drought in Nepal, India, China, Pakistan and Burma.

*Flying above the clouds, alongside the Himalayas.*

# Swat Valley

Although the country of Pakistan was only created in 1947, it was born from a culture that goes back thousands of years, as is evident from the ancient remains, historic monuments, beautiful architecture and the dignified demeanour of its people.

Swat, the 'Switzerland of Asia', was an independent princely state ruled by the Wali of Swat until 1969, when he ceded his authority to the central government. People have lived here for more than 2,000 years and there are plentiful remains from the Gandhara Buddhist civilization (and plenty of people claiming to be descendants of Alexander the Great). Situated in the foothills of the Hindu Kush, it is a spectacularly beautiful region where snow-capped mountains enclose small enchanting valleys, each a magical self-contained world of lakes, forests and waterfalls.

Battered Suzuki jeeps ply the main valley, piled high with passengers hanging onto the tailgate, and they career along in a cavalier fashion that, at first, is frankly terrifying. But, have faith – your driver knows every twist, turn, bump and pothole of the narrow road. Only an attitude of oriental fatalism will enable you to appreciate the captivating scenery as your vehicle whizzes alongside the River Swat taking you from the charming main town of Mingora to the villages of the upper valleys. As the road winds upward, the mountains start to close in and the river becomes increasingly turbulent. Steep verdant slopes, terraced with fruit orchards and poppy fields, reach up to deep green forest and a skyline of glistening icy peaks. The mountain village of Kalam is secreted 100 km (60 mi) up the valley, in the depths of the forest beside a tumultuous river swollen with glacial water. The comparison with Switzerland is belittling. This is an altogether greater, wilder and more mysterious land – a sort of savage Paradise.

*River crossing near Mingora in the Swat Valley*

# Travelling the Grand Trunk Road

According to Rudyard Kipling, the Grand Trunk Road was 'such a river of life as exists nowhere else in the world', the lifeblood of the Indian sub-continent along which the ideas that have shaped its culture have flowed for more than 2,000 years. The Buddhist, Hindu, Jain and Sikh religions sprang up around it, Alexander the Great marched his army across the Indus on it and the Mughals spread the might of their empire along it. Known to 17th century British travellers as the 'Long Walk', the Grand Trunk Road runs for 2,400 km (1,500 mi) between Kabul and Kolkata, passing through the historic cities of Peshawar, Islamabad, Rawalpindi, Lahore, Amritsar, Delhi, Agra and Varanasi.

From the romantic Mughal city of Lahore, the heart of Pakistan, whether you travel northwards toward the Afghan border or south into India, you get swept up in the life of the road. The stream of traffic moves at a cracking pace as motley bullock carts, bicycles, auto-rickshaws and battered 1950s cars play chicken with the psychedelic trucks and buses. These dazzling works of art on wheels are practically a national symbol of Pakistan, each exquisitely painted carriage-work a unique story, telling of the owner's region, ethnic origin, interests and personality in emblematic form of brilliant colour and calligraphy.

In the shade of the wayside trees are street vendors and caravanserais (truckstops), men lolling on charpoys (string beds), children playing in the dust, loose livestock wandering into the traffic, graffiti and garish advertisements on every inch of wall. It feels as though the entire world is on the move. As you cross the Jehlum River, where Alexander defeated the armies of Porus in an epic battle of 326 BC, you are exultantly aware of your own small part in this endless sea of humanity.

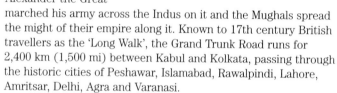

*Not just red buses in Lahore!*

**HOW:**
By car or bus
**WHEN TO GO:**
September to April
**TIME IT TAKES:**
As long as you like
**HIGHLIGHTS:**
Qissa Khawani bazaar (Bazaar of the Storytellers) in Peshawar
Badshahi Mosque in Lahore
Bazaars of Rawalpindi
Wah Garden at Hasan Abdal
Greco-Buddhist ruins in Taxila
**YOU SHOULD KNOW:**
At the time of writing, the political situation in Pakistan is very dynamic and most governments advise against all non-essential travel.

423

*The Biafo Glacier*

# Snow Lake Trek

Said to be the 'Most Beautiful Place in the World', Snow Lake is certainly one of the most remote. This is the land of the yeti, an icy mountain wonderland, a week's trek from the nearest human habitation – itself a far-flung outpost in the mountain wilds of Baltistan.

Snow Lake belies its name – it is not a lake at all but a huge ice-basin, 16 km (10 mi) wide and thought to be around 1.6 km (1 mi) thick, enclosed by the stupendous 6,000-m (20,000-ft) peaks of the Karakoram Mountains. It lies at the head of the Biafo and Hispar glaciers, which spread down from the 5,151-m (16,895-ft) high Hispar Pass to form the longest glacier system outside the polar regions, a massive ice highway connecting the ancient mountain kingdoms of Baltistan and Hunza.

From Skardu, capital of Baltistan, a jeep takes you on a white-knuckle ride through the Braldu Gorge where hairpin bends are too tight to take in one go and the wheels constantly threaten to slip over the edge of sheer precipice. Thrilled to be alive, you reach Askole, gateway to the highest mountains in the world – a medieval village in the middle of nowhere. Over the next fortnight, you will trek 120 km (75 mi) through an enchanted land of blue ice pinnacles, deep glacial caves, gorges, crevasses and hanging glaciers – up the Biafo Glacier to Snow Lake and across the pass to descend the Hispar Glacier into Hunza. Climbing 300 m (1,000 ft) a day, camping in remote valleys, scrambling over rocky moraine and using ropes to cross crevasses, you test your stamina to the limit – to collapse, exhausted but elated, amid the terraced orchards and lush wildflower meadows of the Hunza Valley.

# The Karakoram Highway

The Karakoram Highway is perhaps the 'ultimate' road. A marvel of civil engineering, long considered impossible, it was a joint construction project between Pakistan and China across the highest international pass in the world in a region of hazardous weather and high tectonic activity, with constant risk of landslides. By the time of its completion in 1986, it had taken twenty years and the lives of almost 900 workers. The decrepit concrete huts by the wayside are poignant reminders of the road gangs' harsh working conditions.

The Highway covers a distance of some 1,300 km (800 mi) connecting Islamabad to Kashgar in China – a daunting but thrilling scenic drive by way of the Karakoram and Pamir Mountains. You roller-coaster up the Indus Valley through barren foothills until quite suddenly, without any apparent gradation, you are enclosed by craggy, ice-covered peaks. A mellow stretch through the beautiful scenery of the Hunza Valley, with wonderful views of terraced slopes covered in fruit trees and isolated villages clinging to rugged cliffs, takes you up to one of the highest altitude national parks in the world – an icebound wilderness that is the hideout of the elusive snow leopard.

Wind your way up treacherous hairpin bends, passing spectacular glaciers that practically drop into the road, to the Khunjerab Pass at 4,730 m (15,500 ft) and across 120 km (75 mi) of desolate no-man's land into China.

The road surface improves dramatically this side of the border and the landscape is transformed from the savage glacial peaks of the Karakorams to rounded ochre Pamir hills. You descend to the Taxkorgan Valley, pass Karakul, a surreal lake on the Pamir plateau at the edge of the Taklimakan desert sands to finally arrive at the ancient Silk Road oasis of Kashgar with a triumphant sense of mission accomplished.

**HOW:**
By car or bus
**WHEN TO GO:**
June to September
**TIME IT TAKES:**
Four days to three weeks, depending on stops and means of transport.
**HIGHLIGHTS:**
Balti Fort and picturesque Hunza Valley market town of Karimabad.
Khunjerab Pass.
Lake Karakul and Muztag Ata Mountain.
Kashgar – Id Kah Mosque
**YOU SHOULD KNOW:**
The Khunjerab Pass is closed between October and May because the road is blocked by snow. You drive on the left in Pakistan so remember to change sides of the road when you enter China. (At the time of writing Pakistan is politically volatile and most governments have issued travel warnings, but you can still get to the top of the Khunjerab Pass from Kashgar in China).

*The beautiful Hunza Valley*

# The Palace on Wheels

**HOW:**
By train
**WHEN TO GO:**
Year round
**TIME IT TAKES:**
Seven days for this tour – there are other tours lasting up to ten days
**HIGHLIGHTS:**
Ram Ganj Bazaar in Jaipur.
The Taj Mahal – even more majestic during a full moon.
The 'Lake City' of Udaipur
The Train – it really is the star of this journey; from the food to the service to the décor – everything about it is first class.
**YOU SHOULD KNOW:**
Despite the high cost, demand for this journey greatly outstrips supply. You therefore need to book a couple of years in advance or find a travel agent who has block bookings. If you can be flexible, it's possible to be put on a reserve list and hope for cancellations.

The Palace on Wheels train, which runs from Delhi through Rajasthan, is perhaps the most audacious feat of recycling in transport history. In 1981, the former royal train was faithfully restored with the aim of bringing a regal experience to a much wider audience. Although replaced with a newer model some ten years later, it still provides a feast of luxury living for those who travel on it. With its bars, restaurants, personal attendants and even a library, the Palace on Wheels pampers the traveller like no other train journey.

The journey starts and ends at Delhi's Safdarjung Railway Station and takes you to some of the finest sights that there are in this northwest corner of India. The first stop on the week-long excursion is the magnificent 'Pink City' of Jaipur, offering a chance to stretch your legs whilst marvelling at the astonishing architecture of Rajasthan's capital city. The many bazaars within the city give the traveller a real feel of the tastes, colours and smells of India.

The train then continues on its way, allowing you to sample the delights of Jodhpur, the 'Sun City', and Udaipur, the 'Venice of the East'. More colours feast the eye as the train heads back towards Delhi and the vibrant red city of Fatehpur Sikri awaits you. This is a journey that leaves the best to last, as if compensating you for soon having to give up such luxury. The contrast between the heavily industrialized city of Agra and its world famous monument – the Taj Mahal – could not be greater. Though the 'Taj' is one of the most photographed buildings in the world, nothing can match the breathtaking splendour of seeing it up close.

The short journey back into Delhi gives you one last chance to relax and enjoy the opulence of the train.

*The opulent Palace on Wheels*

*The wonderfully preserved steam train*

# Darjeeling Himalayan Railway

The Darjeeling Himalayan Railway is the most fascinating of all the 'toy train' routes in India. With a 610 mm (2 ft) gauge, it's the narrowest to be found on the subcontinent and it has the unique attraction for a mountain railway of having no tunnels – thus allowing passengers an uninterrupted view of the beautiful Himalayan landscape.

Starting from New Jalpaiguri, this wonderfully preserved steam train meanders its way along an 86 km (54 mi) route, making a dozen or so stops along the way before journeying through picturesque tea plantations, and finally reaching the charming hill station of Darjeeling. Aside from the marvellous views, the climb itself is something to behold. Starting at an altitude of 100 m (330 ft), the train reaches an elevation of 2,000 m (6,600 ft) by the time it arrives at its destination. Several hair-raising bends greet you along the way, as the train seems to cling to the hill face like a mountain goat. At the aptly named 'Agony Point', the tightest bend on the line, the train seems to change direction completely in the blink of an eye.

Whilst this journey can be taken in one go, there are several places along the route that are worth exploring. Most notable are the village of Tindharia, which houses a railway workshop, and Ghum, the highest station in India and home to a railway museum.

Having taken this amazing trip, it's easy to see why railway enthusiasts often list it in the world's top ten journeys. This diminutive railway was declared a UNESCO World Heritage Site in 1999, and while many stations are little more than wooden shacks, the sheer effort that has gone into keeping the line open is evident in its well maintained track, burnished engines and comfortably upholstered seats.

**HOW:**
By train
**TIME IT TAKES:**
Around eight hours one-way
**WHEN TO GO:**
Avoid the monsoon season (June to September). Otherwise the climate is good year round.
**HIGHLIGHTS:**
The views of Khanchenjunga – the third highest peak in the world.
The Happy Valley Tea Estate – well worth a visit to see how they produce what some regard as the best tea in the world.
Giddapahar Mandir – a temple dedicated to Lord Shiva, just outside Kurseong.
The Buddhist Monastery at Ghum – home to ancient texts and beautiful murals.
**YOU SHOULD KNOW:**
The area around Darjeeling is subject to periods of unrest, which can cause the line to be closed. You should always check the situation before travelling and take advice from your embassy.

*Rice fields in the valley*

# Kullu Valley Trek

**HOW:**
On foot
**WHEN TO GO:**
Best from April to June or September
and October
**TIME IT TAKES:**
Allow three weeks to explore the
whole valley
**HIGHLIGHTS:**
The Dhoongri Temple – a magnificent
wooden structure near Manali.
The charming little village of
Jagatsukh – a perfect place to stop
for a while.
Old Manali, with its stone and timber
buildings.
The hot sulphur springs at the scenic
village of Vashisht.
The views from the Rohtang Pass at
3,915 m (12,845 ft).
**YOU SHOULD KNOW:**
A reasonable degree of fitness is
required to attempt the higher
passes of the Kullu Valley. Weather
conditions can deteriorate rapidly, so
allow extra time when tackling the
more difficult stretches of the trek.

The Kullu Valley in the northern state of Himachal Pradesh is far removed from the stereotype of India as a country of heat and dust. For many Westerners the valley is merely part of the hippy trail, but to Indians it is a highly productive agricultural area. Freshened by the glacial waters of the Beas River, the valley is home to a major apple-growing industry and is flanked by paddy fields during the monsoon season and wheat fields for the remainder of the year. With conifers and rhododendrons lining the upper slopes, the Kullu Valley is one of the most sumptuous parts of India.

Several operators offer guided tours tailored to meet all requirements and abilities, but a better experience may be gained by hiring a cook and a guide in Manali and venturing out in a smaller group. Engaging locals ensures that you will see the best the area has to offer. Since travelling in nearby Kashmir has become too dangerous, more people are choosing the Kullu Valley as a safer option. However it is still possible to escape the crowds at higher elevations, where you can enjoy the fresh pine forests and the stunning mountain scenery.

Walking over mountain passes and between remote villages, you cannot help but be struck by the beauty of the area. At the higher altitudes craggy outcrops replace the lush vegetation and the snow-capped peaks of the Himalayas frame every scene. There are hot springs to warm you and mountain streams to cool you down. The area is also a hive of outdoor activity, including rock climbing, skiing, rafting and paragliding.

# Manali to Leh

It is difficult to comprehend the sheer magnitude of the Himalayas – while most of the world's great mountain ranges can be traversed inside a day or two, the Himalayas seem to go on forever. They fill the horizon like a giant cumulous cloud – indomitable, magnificent and often impenetrable.

The 3,900-m (12,800-ft) high Rohtang Pass, closed to traffic for most of the year, springs to life when the thaw arrives. It provides a vital lifeline for remote communities, as well as the most memorable of bus journeys. On leaving Manali, the road starts its long ascent towards the pass; beneath you are forests and mountain pasture, whilst ahead lies the permanent snow of Solang Nala. A temple sits at the crown of an escarpment, and the bus usually stops here to allow passengers to gain sustenance and acclimatize to the thin air. From this vantage point the panoramic views over the Beas Valley are simply stunning.

The next couple of hours provide the most spectacular scenery of the entire journey. As the bus negotiates its way along the inclines of the valley, you see soaring peaks and suspended glaciers. You are now well above the tree line and surrounded by the most amazing green and red scree, as the bus continues ever upwards. After an overnight stop at Sarchu Serai and an early start, the bus ascends to a head-spinning 5,328 m (17,475 ft) and the brilliant white of the snow-capped peaks surrounds you. Patches of green return, in land fed by the Indus River, as you gradually make the descent into the beautifully tranquil town of Leh, once the capital of the Himalayan kingdom of Ladakh.

**HOW:**
By bus
**TIME IT TAKES:**
24 hours with an overnight stop
**WHEN TO GO:**
The Rohtang Pass is only open from May to early November, weather permitting.
**HIGHLIGHTS:**
The Buddhist monasteries between Upshi and Leh.
The views over the Bhaga Valley.
Moray Plains – an astonishing plateau, surrounded by white peaks.
The palace at Leh – a Tibetan-style ruin and the focal point of the town.
**YOU SHOULD KNOW:**
Such is the altitude of Rohtang La that disruption can happen even in summer, so be prepared for unscheduled stops. It is recommended that you stay in Leh for a few days to acclimatize to the thin air at this altitude.

*Leh is dominated by the ruins of the Royal Palace.*

429

# The Matheran Hill Railway

Opened in 1907, this narrow-gauge railway is a charming and rather eccentric example of early 20th century engineering enterprise. Traversing difficult mountainous terrain, the train chugs along a track that has over 200 sharp bends and crosses 120 bridges. With a sometimes-cramped capacity of 100, it links the foothill town of Narel to the beautiful little hill station town of Matheran, covering a distance of 30 km (18.6 mi) at an average speed of 15 kph (9.3 mph).

The atmosphere on board is at times one of barely organized chaos, as food vendors and rhesus monkeys climb on board and vie for your attention. The former try to sell you pastries and the latter immediately try to steal them – you can't help but admire the symmetry of the situation.

As it's the only motorized form of transport that is allowed to enter Matheran, the train enjoys a privileged position, but at times the pace is so sedentary that walking would be a quicker option. Matheran translates as 'jungle at the top' and this becomes ever more real to you as the train struggles to climb the very steep tropical terrain.

The views from the train are incredible, with wide-open valleys to one side and steep, mountain faces to the other. The ozone produced by the numerous waterfalls is refreshing even on the sultriest of days. When the train finally pulls into Matheran you realize that the relaxed pace of the journey was entirely appropriate. The town is all about taking it easy, and there's a peaceful, unhurried air about the place. There is no finer feeling than relaxing with your evening tipple on the verandah of your hotel while marvelling at the sunset over the densely forested hills.

*A train winds its way down into the valley.*

# Kalka to Shimla on the 'Toy Train'

*The Kalka to Shimla 'Toy Train'*

An air of excitement builds audibly as the train pulls in to Kalka Station. Railway enthusiasts crowd round to examine the powerful little engine, as street food sellers jostle for your attention. A piercing whistle announces that it's time to board the train and head towards the 'Queen of the Hill Stations' – Shimla. This important rail link was built in 1924 and its 'toy trains' still do a roaring trade running on an improbably small 760 mm (2 ft 6 in) narrow gauge set of rails. The construction was an incredible feat of engineering – the track passes through more than 100 tunnels and over 960 bridges, up into the stunning mountain scenery of the Himalayan foothills.

Immaculately maintained stations line the route and the arrival of the train elicits intense interest from locals at every stop along the way. You are carried along the crests of rich green valleys, climbing inexorably at a sedate 25 kph (16 mph). The charming station at Solan marks the halfway point on this stately excursion, and it is from here that you catch the first sight of Shimla high in the distance. The snow-capped peaks of the Himalayas appear in all their majestic beauty as the forest thins to reveal ever more spectacular vistas.

When the train draws serenely in to Shimla at an altitude of 2,420 m (7,940 ft), it becomes immediately apparent why the British chose the town as their summer capital. While Delhi swelters in the summer sun, Shimla delights in a near perfect 20 °C (68 °F). The town itself is worthy of a day or two's exploration – with its striking Victorian architecture surrounded by magnificent mountain scenery.

**HOW:**
By train
**WHEN TO GO:**
May to July and September to November (July and August are the rainy season)
**TIME IT TAKES:**
Around six hours
**HIGHLIGHTS:**
The Gurkha Castle at Solan – a reminder of the area's former rulers. Shimla State Museum – a great place to learn about the often-turbulent history of the region.
Shri Sankat Mochan Temple – a beautiful Hindu temple located 5 km (3 mi) outside Shimla.
Dyer-Meakin Brewery – a beer producer founded by Germans in Solan.
**YOU SHOULD KNOW:**
The railway is very popular in high season, particularly during June and July, and advance booking is recommended. There are also many interesting places to see along the way, so breaking your journey is well worth considering.

*Sandstone cenotaphs, built to honour past rulers, lie just outside Orchha.*

# Temple City Journey

**HOW:**
By local bus

**TIME IT TAKES:**
It can be done in three days, but allow a week or two to explore the area fully.

**WHEN TO GO:**
Avoid the monsoon season between June and September when it can be very wet and stiflingly hot. October to March sees the most temperate weather.

**HIGHLIGHTS:**
Gwalior Fort – sitting high above the town with its 3-km (2-mi) long and 10-m (33-ft) high walls.
Man Mandir Palace – A 15th century palace in Gwalior, with an extraordinary network of chambers and dungeons.
The 14 sandstone cenotaphs, built to honour past rulers – just outside Orchha.
The 1,100-year-old granite Brahma Temple in Khajuraho.
The Museum of Man – a wonderful museum of anthropology with an open-air exhibition of the region's history.

It is possible to book this tour on the Internet, travel in air-conditioned coaches and even have your bags carried from hotel to vehicle for you. However for an up-close-and-personal view of this most holy of trails, a far better option is to place yourself in the hands of one of the local tourist bus operators. Sometimes infuriating but always interesting, the buses seem to run to no known schedule. But if you have the time and the inclination these trips offer up a real India from which luxury travel detaches you.

Starting in Gwalior, with its imposing hilltop fort, you enter a region rich in history and legend. This lively city has changed hands countless times over the centuries and its history is etched in the buildings and the faces of the people. The Tuscan and Corinthian style architecture, mixed with more traditional Hindu Mogul temples, makes Gwalior worthy of thorough exploration. From here it is a 120-km (75-mi) journey to Orchha, founded in the 16th century by Hindu rulers. Located on the banks of the meandering Betwa River, this once great city's population has dwindled over the years. It is now eerily quiet with no defined centre, but it's a great place simply to wander around and stumble upon treasures.

After a further 160 km (100 mi) you reach Khajuraho, the 10th century religious capital of the Chandela dynasty and a town now so rural and isolated that it's hard to imagine that it was once a thriving metropolis. Of the 80 or so temples built there, 22 remain and bear testimony to the city's cosmopolitan, multi-faith past. Temples mirror the peaks of the nearby Himalayas, and Jain and Hindu gods sit side by side. Famed for its erotic statues and the extraordinary regularity of its temples, Khajuraho is a place to marvel at.

**YOU SHOULD KNOW:**
How and where to buy tickets for buses in India can be confusing, so ask advice at your hotel. Also, if you board a near-empty bus be prepared for a long wait, as they rarely leave until they're full.

# Saputara Scenic Road

Saputara's location, 1,000 m (3,280 ft) up on the edge of a plateau, coupled with its congenial climate, pure air and breathtaking views of beautiful scenery, has resulted in some modern luxuries being brought to this picturesque hill station. For more than a century Saputara has offered an increasing number of visitors a respite from the often-oppressive heat of Mumbai and it now boasts first class accommodation and several tourist attractions.

Buses to Saputara run from the main metropolitan centres of western India, but a journey undertaken by car or motorbike allows you to create your own unique experience of this lovely area. The 50-km (30-mi) journey from Waghai is short but rewarding, and there is much to distract the curious tourist with time on their hands. You can stop to breathe in the ozone by one of the many waterfalls or linger at a particularly enchanting lookout spot. The whole area is home to many traditional Gujarati villages, whose masked dances and handicrafts are renowned throughout India.

Ancient mixed forests start to crowd in as you near Saputara. Barely touched by human intervention, the forests provide a wonderful habitat for a wide range of wildlife. The dense growth makes a good home for tigers, leopards, pangolins, pythons and four-horned antelope as well as for a great variety of birdlife. The deep forest is also reputed to offer refuge to higher beings – legend has it that the Hindu deity Lord Rama spent 11 years of his exile here.

Whether you start your journey in Mumbai, 265 km (166 mi) away, or from Waghai, the area has such a magnetic quality that you are always left with the feeling that there was so much more to see.

**HOW:**
By car, motorbike or bus
**TIME IT TAKES:**
Two hours driving without stopping (from Waghai), but allow at least a week to explore the area.
**WHEN TO GO:**
The area has a good climate all year round. It is best experienced during the monsoons from March to November when the waterfalls are at their best.
**HIGHLIGHTS:**
Pushpak Ropeway – India's longest cableway, offering a 10-minute ride across the valley.
Sunrise Point – there are great views from here at any time of day, but, as its name implies, they're even better in the morning.
Vansda National Park – a small but thriving wildlife park (entry permit required).
The spectacular Gira Falls – 1 km (0.6 mi) off the Waghai-Saputara road.
Unnai Mata Temple (near Waghai) – a fabulous temple with hot springs.
**YOU SHOULD KNOW:**
While the Saputara-Waghai road itself is in relatively good shape, if you want to make detours to see any of the neighbouring attractions it is advisable to hire a car suitable for off-road driving.

433

*The morning wash on Ganga Ghat*

# The Source of The Ganges

**HOW:**
On foot and by car
**TIME IT TAKES:**
seven to ten days
**WHEN TO GO:**
April to July
**HIGHLIGHTS:**
The sight of the breathtakingly beautiful azure Gangotri Glacier.
The temple at Mukteshwar Mahadeva – a shrine to the goddess Ganga.
Dashashwamedh Ghat adjacent to the Vishwanath Temple in Varanasi.
The Golden Temple – a focal point in Varanasi.
The shopping area of Vishwanath Lane in Varanasi.
**YOU SHOULD KNOW:**
To Hindus this journey is a pilgrimage of huge religious significance. Be mindful of the fact that there are restrictions on footwear, photography and even the presence of women in certain buildings. If you are not of the Hindu faith then it is always advisable to ask whether you can enter temples and shrines.

There are times while making the climb towards the source of the Ganges when you wonder whether the two-day trek to Gaumukh from Gangothri is really worth it. As you climb up the steep hills, your mind is more focused on the ascent than on the astounding mountain scenery. But the Ganges is no ordinary river and to view its source is to witness the birth of the earthly manifestation of a god. It is said that the goddess Ganga was sent down to earth after a heavenly feud, that her descent was broken by Lord Shiva's matted locks and that she finally reached earth as seven streams.

The forbiddingly beautiful Shivling Mountain hangs 6,543 m (21,470 ft) above the blue-green Gangotri Glacier, which marks the emergence of this great river. When looking at the Ganges here in its purest state it's hard to imagine how mighty and muddy this holiest of rivers will become downstream. To journey down it is not only to follow the path of a geographical feature, but also to look deep into the heart and soul of India. Millions come to her to wash their bodies and to wash away their sins. Rivers are central to Hindu culture and they play pivotal roles in life and death; this trip takes you through some of India's most significant holy places.

After journeying back to Gangotri you can travel by road to the hallowed cities of Rishikesh, Haridwar, Garh-Mukteswar and Prayag, before finally arriving at the most sacred city in India – Varanasi. Once there, the true significance of this great river becomes apparent, as worshippers line its steps and magnificent temples, forming a procession along the riverbanks. Few rivers, if any, are granted such high status and the sheer power of the Ganges to draw you and thousands of others towards it is awe-inspiring.

# Kolkata Heritage City Walk

To the outsider, Kolkata (formerly Calcutta) may conjure up images of Mother Theresa nursing the poor, and to the casual visitor it often seems to be an amorphous urban sprawl with poor signage. Thankfully an organization was set up in the early 1990s to change these perceptions. A small group of mainly young volunteers run Cruta (Conservation and Research of Urban Traditional Architecture) and offer walking tours through the meandering streets of this great city. All the proceeds from these tours go to maintaining Kolkata's architectural splendour.

There are two main tours; the first is a short affair focusing on the city centre. Starting at Dalhousie Square, the visitor is taken around fifteen or so historical buildings, including the impressive Writers Building, the Town Hall, St John's Churchyard and the celebrated Metcalfe Hall. But for a taste of the 'real' Kolkata, the North Calcutta Walking Tour is a must. With the aid of a local guide it is possible to venture into areas otherwise inaccessible to most visitors. There are slums and shantytowns and the streets do seem to be totally covered in litter in some places, but there are hidden gems to be found. Several wonderful secluded courtyards as well as the House of Rabindranath Tagore and the Marble Palace stand out in this old mercantile quarter.

Combined, these tours show the visitor both sides of this truly amazing city. Change is happening fast and at times it seems to have left some behind, but at least the members of Cruta are preserving Kolkata's amazing heritage whilst providing employment to local people.

**HOW:**
On foot
**TIME IT TAKES:**
A full day for both tours
**WHEN TO GO:**
The best time to visit Kolkata is from the end of October through to the middle of March, when the weather is pleasant. During the monsoon season (June to September) the rains can cause severe flooding.
**HIGHLIGHTS:**
New Market – a market of over 2,000 stalls specializing in silk and silver. Eden Gardens – a nice park and home to the test cricket stadium. Saint Paul's Cathedral Paresnath Jain Temple
**YOU SHOULD KNOW:**
It is inadvisable to venture into North Kolkata alone. It is easy to get lost as most of the street signs are in Bengali, where they exist at all. It is also not advisable to display your wealth in the form of jewellery or cameras whilst walking through the shanty towns.

*Paresnath Jain Temple*

# Cycle in the Cardamom Hills

**HOW:**
By bike
**WHEN TO GO:**
December to February sees low rainfall and lower temperatures. February to May is dry and hot. May to September is the monsoon season.
**TIME IT TAKES:**
Allow 2 weeks for a thorough exploration of the hills.
**HIGHLIGHTS:**
The tea plantations at Munnar. Mangaladevi Temple near Kumily. Sri Ayappan forest shrine at Sabarimala – off the beaten track but worth the effort.
**YOU SHOULD KNOW:**
A reasonable level of fitness and good suspension are needed to enjoy this cycling tour. Several companies offer all-in deals with food and lodgings provided. However for the more adventurous it is possible to hire bikes locally and go it alone.

India is a country of such vastness and complexity that it can be tempting to do too much in too little time. A day in Agra, another in Kolkata and one in Chennai (Madras) – soon the images of red forts can merge into one and you are left with a muddle of memories. A cycling tour in the Cardamom Hills reveals India at its simple best. The slow pace of travel through these fabulously pretty hills on two wheels provides a vacation filled with exploration and discovery of an India that, through increased industrialization, is fast disappearing.

The Cardamom Hills form a long narrow chain at the southern end of the Indian sub-continent. Their ridge acts as the boundary between the states of Tamil Nadu and Kerala, extending from the Palghat Gap in the north and running 280 km (175 mi) to Cape Comorin in the south. Aside from the crop from which they take their name, the hills are renowned for tea production, and the plethora of the other spices produced in the area provides a wonderful gift for your sense of smell.

The region is also home to a wide variety of wildlife, most notably elephants and some big cats and it is very likely that you will encounter the former. Cats however are shy of human contact, so the best chance of seeing them is in one of the local nature parks. The freedom gained by cycling, whilst allowing you to cover ground quickly, fits well with the surroundings. Life here is conducted at a slower pace than in much of the rest of India, and while the Himalayas may have more to offer in the way of spectacular scenery, the Cardamom Hills are more accessible and have their own unique charm.

*Tea pickers in Kerala*

# Houseboat Cruise through the Kerala Backwaters

There can be few more relaxing journeys than floating along the waters of Kerala in a traditional houseboat. The backwaters of Kerala are a labyrinthine network of lakes, canals, and the estuaries and deltas of the 44 rivers that drain into the Arabian Sea. It's a wonderful ecosystem teeming with life – over a quarter of India's plant species are found here. There is such an abundance of flora and fauna, nourished by the tropical sun and generous rainfall, that it's easy to understand why Kerala is sometimes called 'God's Own Country'.

The houseboats, known as kettuvallam, are magnificent creations that blend in perfectly with their environment. They are made with only the locally grown renewable resources of bamboo and coconut fibre – no nails are used in their construction. They were originally designed to carry crops to outlying communities, but since that trade has now sadly all but ceased, many of them have been converted into luxury houseboats for the tourist trade.

With nearly 1,000 km (625 mi) of navigable waterways at your disposal, you are spoiled for choice when it comes to thinking about what route to take, but wherever you go you will see a traditional India, not visible from any other means of transport. It's a tranquil world of ancient fishing methods, huge water lilies, verdant paddy fields, and villages with thatched roof houses and rustic shrines. Gliding sedately along, with the songs of birds as your soundtrack and towering coconut palms sheltering you from the beating sun, there is surely no better place on Earth.

**HOW:**
Houseboat
**WHEN TO GO:**
October to February; avoid the monsoon season – June to August.
**TIME IT TAKES:**
Two weeks is fine but a month would be even better.
**HIGHLIGHTS:**
Periyar Wildlife Sanctuary
Rajamala National Park
The Dutch Palace at Cochin
Kerala is home to Ayurvedic massage – a real therapeutic treat.
**YOU SHOULD KNOW:**
Don't be afraid to haggle over price, especially if you are planning an extended journey. If you haven't booked in advance and are reliant on a local tourist office, take a step back. Those who approach may have paid for the privilege of being there, while just a few hundred metres away there could be a houseboat owner who would offer you the same trip for a fraction of the price.

*A houseboat awaits your arrival.*

# Nilgiri Mountain Railway

If trains have personalities, and there are some people who think they do, the engines that ply the Nilgiri Mountain Railway are redoubtable little fighters. Now over 100 years old, this 'toy train' route is an engineering achievement that almost defies gravity. So steep is the gradient that a system of racks and pinions was developed to stop the train sliding back down the track, making it unique in all of India.

The line never really paid its way as a carrier of goods, but thankfully it has been kept open and it's now one of India's most spectacular tourist railway trips. For reasons of safety, the train travels at an average speed of less than 10 kph (6.25 mph), making it the slowest train in India. Linking Mettupalayam near Coimbatose with the celebrated hill station of Udagamandalam (Ooty) in Tamil Nadu, the mountain railway was recently declared a UNESCO World Heritage Site.

The train's sedate tempo allows travellers to take in the captivating beauty of these seemingly endless hills. At every point on its steadfast journey, you are surrounded by lush mountain vegetation, as the train meanders its way around spine-tingling curves, through tunnels and alongside deep ravines. An added charm is that it is often possible to get off the train and walk beside it, without any fear of being left behind – such is the serene pace of this journey.

**HOW:**
By train
**TIME IT TAKES:**
Three to four hours each way
**WHEN TO GO:**
Year round
**HIGHLIGHTS:**
Udagamandalam (Ooty) – the 'Queen of Hill Stations'.
The Nilgiri Hills – literally the 'Blue Mountains'.
Idugampalayam Aanjineyar Temple at Mettupalayam.
The Rose Garden at Udagamandalam (Ooty).
**YOU SHOULD KNOW:**
The railway is very popular all year round and it is advisable to book well in advance. Also be prepared for a noisy journey, created by the effort required to climb such steep hills.

*The narrow gauge rack train*

# The Beaches of Goa

Goa has long been India's good-time Riviera, renowned for its sun-kissed beaches, vibrant markets and an energetic nightlife unrivalled anywhere on the subcontinent. This tiny state is blessed with almost year-round sunshine and a coastline graced with long sandy beaches. Each of these many beaches has its own character – some are crowded, others are almost deserted; some have white sands, others are dark brown. Each beach is worthy of exploration if you want to enjoy the total Goan experience.

Several operators offer packages that take you to different beaches each day, but for a more rewarding hike it is hard to beat a self-guided tour. The 120-km (75-mi) coastline is interrupted only by the seven rivers that flow into the Arabian Sea. With judicious use of taxis and local fishermen, who run unofficial ferry services, it is possible to sample all that this amazing coast has to offer.

Starting at the ruggedly beautiful Harmal Beach in the north and journeying to the wonderfully secluded Palolem Beach in the south, you are taken on an odyssey of high contrast. Near the capital, Panaji, the noise of the water gives way to the hubbub of people, as the town seems to spill over into the sea. Venturing south again takes you to Colva, the most popular beach in southern Goa, and it is easy to see why. Golden sands are lapped by the azure sea, while traders, fishermen and visitors give the whole area a wonderful market feel.

The crowds thin out once again as you head towards the silver sands of Palolem Beach. Also known as Paradise Beach, it is framed by the hills of the Western Ghats and lined with cute bamboo huts. It is a perfect spot to unwind.

**HOW:**
On foot
**WHEN TO GO:**
Anytime except the rainy season, which usually lasts from June to August.
**TIME IT TAKES:**
Five to seven days
**HIGHLIGHTS:**
Canacona Island – a ferry ride from Palolem Beach.
The view over the Arabian Sea from Harmal Beach.
Chapora Fort – a 500-year-old Portuguese fort, near Varca Beach.
Albuquerque Mansion – near Anjuna Beach.
**YOU SHOULD KNOW:**
The coast of Goa can get maddeningly busy at times. If it all gets too much for you, remember that the further you go from Panaji, the quieter it will be.

*Anjuna Beach*

# Hill Country Scenic Train Ride – Colombo Fort to Badulla

**HOW:**
By train
**WHEN TO GO:**
December to March
**TIME IT TAKES:**
Eleven to twelve hours
**HIGHLIGHTS:**
Kandy, home of Sri Lanka's most important Buddhist relic, Buddha's Tooth.
Nuwara Eliya – the old British hill station where the colonials spent their summers.
Horton Plains and World's End National Park.
Ella, with its magnificent view and excellent hill walking.
Take a tour of a tea factory, and take some home with you.
**YOU SHOULD KNOW:**
To enjoy this trip to the full, make sure to book the first class observatory carriage. Tickets must be booked at least ten days in advance.

Most travellers to Sri Lanka fly into Colombo, the capital city, and base themselves either there or at the beaches just to the north. If you have only limited time, but would like to see something different, take the train to Badulla for some of the loveliest landscapes the island has to offer.

Starting at crack of dawn from Colombo Fort, the train sets out towards the hills, running alongside the Muthurajawela Marshland, a protected area teeming with birds. Before long you enter the first of the journey's 46 tunnels and begin the ascent, through lush hardwood forests, to Kandy, the spiritual and cultural centre of the Sinhalese.

As the native forest gives way to pines and eucalyptus, you'll notice that the temperature is cooler and more pleasant. Glossy green tea plantations cover the hillsides, and brightly dressed Tamil women pick the leaves into baskets carried on their backs. From time to time you'll see splendid waterfalls and, as the train climbs slowly up towards Nanu Oya, the dramatic, triangular point of Adam's Peak, 2,243 m (7,400 ft), can be seen to the south. Higher still, tea gives way first to vegetable gardens and then more forest before reaching Pattipola, the highest station in the country. Now you are on a fascinating piece of line, known as the 'Lizard's Spine' where, between tunnels, you can see both north and, more spectacularly, south – way down to the coast.

The train descends through wonderful countryside, crossing an amazing nine-arch bridge connecting two mountains instead of spanning a river. One last treat, particularly for train buffs, comes at Demodara, where the line loops around a steep hill with two stations, one 27 m (90 ft) above the other. After a few more miles of magnificent views, you reach your destination, Badulla.

*Tea plantations cover the hillsides.*

# Sri Pada (Adam's Peak) Pilgrim's Route

*The shadow of Adam's Peak on the clouds*

While Adam's Peak, at 2,243 m (7,400 ft), is not Sri Lanka's highest mountain, its sharply triangular silhouette and religious importance makes it the country's most famous landmark. A place of pilgrimage for over 1,000 years, the mountain resonates in four major religions and, as a result, the thousands of pilgrims who make their way to the top each year are an eclectic mix of nationalities and ages.

The purpose of the pilgrimage is not just to see the Sacred Footprint at the summit, but also to see the dawn break over the mountain. Moments later, the sun produces a unique phenomenon called *irasevaya*, throwing a perfect shadow of the cone onto the clouds. As the sun rises, this shadow retreats down and across the valley below, before disappearing at the base of the peak.

Leaving Dalhousie before dawn for the 7-km (4-mi) climb – the shorter of the two main routes – you join many pilgrims walking beneath the stone arch that marks the start. Soon you reach steps – over 5,000 of them must be climbed – making this a hard slog. Helpfully, there are rest stops and teahouses en route, and the trail is strung with lights that snake ahead of you up the mountain. The eclectic mix of people – fathers carrying babies, bare footed women, children, elderly folk and tourists make this pilgrimage a remarkably friendly one.

Reaching the small, summit temple produces such feelings of euphoria that the fact the 'real' footprint is apparently beneath the cast you can see, detracts not at all. As dawn breaks pink and gold, you'll see the Hill Country rising to the east, while to the west you look all the way down to Colombo and the coast. Catching the awesome shadow on the clouds is the icing on the cake.

**HOW:**
On foot
**WHEN TO GO:**
December to April
**TIME IT TAKES:**
Allow four hours
**HIGHLIGHTS:**
The spectacle of dawn breaking from the top of Adam's Peak.
Visiting nearby tea estates.
Kandy and the Temple of the Sacred Tooth.
The camaraderie en route.
Reaching the 5,000th step!
**YOU SHOULD KNOW:**
The Sri Pada or 'sacred footprint' is a revered site for Buddhists, Hindus, Christians and Islamists alike, but long before the development of these religions, the mountain was worshipped by the aboriginal inhabitants of Sri Lanka, the Veddas. Their name for the peak was 'Samanala Kanda'; Saman being one of the four guardian deities of the island.

# Ngong Ping 360

Ngong Ping is a concept experience for tourists. Like a Disneyland, it is a shopping and recreational opportunity disguised as a theme park, reflecting the 'cultural and spiritual integrity' of its locale on Ngong Ping plateau, high above Hong Kong's Lantau Island. The inspiration for it however, and still Ngong Ping's greatest attraction, is Ngong Ping 360, the amazing cable car ride that gets you there.

From Tung Chung, on Lantau's waterfront, Ngong Ping 360's bi-cable gondola lift system crosses the bay to Hong Kong's new Airport Island, turns a 60-degree angle without stopping and heads up hill and over dale for 5.7 km (3.6 mi) to the plateau village. The 25-minute ride is certainly spectacular – and beautiful when fingers of sea mist thread the rolling grasslands of North Lantau Country Park below. The 360-degree panoramas from the gondolas make the most of the islands scattering the South China Sea to Macau; of the techno-sprawl of Chek Lap Kok's airport complex; of Lantau's own mountain crags (rising to 934 m/3,064 ft); and finally of Po Lin Monastery and the 250-ton, 34-m (112-ft) giant Buddha outside it.

The Tian Tan Buddha motivates many visitors to come here – but neither it nor the monastery is historic or even venerable, and what sincerity exists is brought and taken away by individual visitors. The palpably commercial atmosphere is at odds with Ngong Ping's claim to be the centre of Buddhist interest in Hong Kong, and only your wallet will feel enlightened.

Despite the overly commercial flavour of much of the whole Ngong Ping project, a trip on the Ngong Ping 360, the biggest cableway in Asia, is certainly a once in a lifetime experience.

# Maclehose Trail

The Maclehose Trail is an eye-opening 100-km (62-mi) hike across Hong Kong's New Territories behind Kowloon. Most visitors to Hong Kong – and even a number of habitués – have no idea that huge tracts of beautiful hills and rugged wilderness exist so close to the compressed bustle of one of China's most dynamic cities.

The Maclehose, named after Hong Kong's longest-serving Governor during the colonial era, begins in Pak Tam Chung, among the coves and rocky inlets of the Sai

*Kowloon from Lion Rock Peak*

Kung peninsula where, despite the millions living nearby, the green hills drop to totally empty, curving white sand beaches like Tai Long Wan ('Big Wave Bay'). Most of Sai Kung's natural beauty is protected by Country Parks, but their rural isolation is real. No towns ever existed here, and as the terrain grows more rugged it becomes barely inhabited. By the fifth of its ten stages, the Trail runs through woodland to the vast rock bulwark of Lion Rock, an abrupt cliff with Kowloon spread in miniature below. From there to Tuen Mun, the Trail is a series of glorious upland hikes round the slopes of Tai Mo Shan, Hong Kong's highest peak. There are streams and waterfalls in deep ravines full of subtropical birds and dense foliage, grassy moorlands, forests, and ancient hamlets and farms. Near Tai Po Road monkeys may mob you, demanding tolls of bananas or nuts, but wildlife isn't predominant. The Maclehose is an adventure in Chinese landscapes, and every stage provides new surprises.

Once a year, four-person teams compete to race the Maclehose Trail against the clock for charity. Normal hikers reckon on 35-37 hours of actual walking. Star winning teams take a little over 14 hours. But the record is held by four soldiers of the Gurkha Regiment – an incredible 11 hours 56 minutes.

**HOW:**
On foot
**WHEN TO GO:**
Year-round
**TIME IT TAKES:**
35-37 hours of actual hiking; with only two difficult stages, most hikers allow seven days.
**HIGHLIGHTS:**
Post-hike rest & recreation – Hong Kong Central (Wan Chai) is never more than an hour away.
The secret coves of Sai Kung – either deserted or with just a local bar.
Pak Sha O – a wonderfully preserved village on the Sai Kung peninsula.
Ng Tung Chai, on the northern slopes of Tai Mo Shan – a completely secluded series of high waterfalls in a really lush ravine of mosses, ferns and trees growing out of the water-washed boulders.
**YOU SHOULD KNOW:**
Tai Mo Shan means 'Big Hat Mountain'.

# Walking the Great Wall

The Great Wall of China is over 7,200 km (4,500 mi) long, and so familiar that it can seem to be universal property. In fact it was built over 2,000 years and consists of a network of structures reflecting China's expansion west and north. Its magnificence owes much to a breathtaking assumption about where civilization begins (or ends). Archaeologists and historians might choose the most remote earthworks, huge sections of which are still being revealed as far away as Gansu province, even if most people's choice of which section to walk is limited to the best preserved, if not best restored, and to the distance of those sections from major tourist hubs. Nothing could connect you to the past more than the Han Dynasty (206 BC – 220 AD) Wall of concrete-hard reeds and mud, austere and magnificent in the wind-whipped wilderness of the Gobi Desert. Shorn of any outer brick casing, the two gateways of Yumenguan and Yangguan, near Dunhuang still bear majestic witness to imperial power as the two western gateways into 1st century China.

Far fewer people walk the Wall east of Beijing. From Simatai you can follow one of the steepest and most dramatic sections through Huangyaguan, across razor-sharp mountain ridges with a watchtower on every one, to Jinshanling. But to appreciate the culture underwriting the Wall, you need to walk the long western stretches around Datong, beyond the Beijing crowds, but crammed with rich evidence of the Ming, Han, Qin and Wei Dynasties. In fact, for anything less than fourteen days, use a car or bus to cherry-pick the Wall's greatest features from Hongcibao, Motianling, Qidun, Kouzishang and Huashijian, staying in local farmers' houses alongside the Wall itself. Here, the Wall is no theme park. It feels more disused than ruined, and its threatening majesty retains all its power to shock. Sublime hiking.

*The Wall at Badaling*

**HOW:**
On foot

**WHEN TO GO:**
Year-round – especially close to Beijing, sections of the Wall are always open to visitors. Further afield, schedules vary; but the most remote sections have no controls at all.

**TIME IT TAKES:**
1-35 days (of which up to seven might be by car/bus, bypassing less interesting sections to walk) to get any real impression of the Wall's architectural and cultural complexity.

**HIGHLIGHTS:**
The fortified stairways, cannon platforms and other Ming Dynasty (circa1350) military detailing close to Jinshanling (northeast of Beijing). The only surviving wooden city gate in China, at Deshengbao (west of Beijing). The watchtowers of Xusi and Jinpai. The huge fort and establishment at Yanmenguan Pass near Shuozhou – one of the most strategic sites and the scene of many famous battles.

**YOU SHOULD KNOW:**
Fortresses along the Wall had a social hierarchy reflecting the rest of society. The preserved ruins of the biggest garrisons include still-existing villages or small towns that were originally established as markets for nomad traders from the other side.

# Huangshan Trek

Huangshan means 'Yellow Mountain'. It's in Anhui province, south of the Yangtse flood plains and vast rice paddies, and it is China's most famous mountain. In fact, along with the Great Wall, its image is an iconic representation of China itself; and its grandeur and beauty are acknowledged by its listing as a UNESCO World Natural and Cultural Heritage Site.

*The terrifying path up Huangshan*

The region includes dozens of peaks over 1,000 m (3,280 ft) and three ('Lotus', 'Brightness Apex' and 'Celestial Capital') over 1,800m (6,000 ft). The steep stone steps and chainlink rail to the summit of 'Celestial Capital' are typical of the often hair-raising paths and approaches to Huangshan's finest panoramas – but there are hundreds of beauty spots (with a directory of exotic names like 'Two Immortals Playing Chess', 'Grasping Beautiful Scenes Bridge', 'Beginning to Believe Peak', or 'Monkey Gazing at the Sea') which identify every rock, pine tree, cloud or hot spring. Huangshan is said to combine these four essences of aesthetic pleasure in perfect balance and harmony. Nobody would argue otherwise, but it has a lot more besides. Its terrain and microclimate engenders distinct frigid, temperate and subtropical zones of flora and fauna; and 2,000 years of unabashed tourism means its vegetation is that of ancient China.

There are centuries-old pines, gingkoes, sweet gums, camphor and magua trees; 300 kinds of medicinal herbs; goddess-flowers, crepe myrtles, lilies and orchids. Pine Valley has a 1,100-m (3,609-ft) descent of 6,500 steps to the Emerald Pool's double (reflected) image of mountains and sky; and Huangshan has any number of dramatic waterfalls, curiously-shaped formations, hot springs and cool streams.

The mountain is especially significant to honeymooners and couples, who fasten padlocks even on the remotest trees and rocks to symbolize their union. In Huangshan, you walk in beauty, among people's most cherished dreams.

**HOW:**
On foot
**WHEN TO GO:**
Year-round
**TIME IT TAKES:**
One to ten days, much longer if you open up to the authentic poetic pulling power of this mountain.
**HIGHLIGHTS:**
The beautiful calligraphy inscribed on rocks at beauty spots. You may need someone to tell you just how good the poetry really is, but it looks terrific and many examples are by some of China's greatest poets and emperors.
The inexhaustible magic of pine trees silhouetted against mist curling round precipitous crags and steep forests – like Huangshan's 'Pine Greeting a Guest', or 'Unity', named for its 56 branches matching the exact number of China's ethnic minorities.
Tunxi Ancient Street – astonishingly well-preserved trade centre of the ancient Southern Song Dynasty.
**YOU SHOULD KNOW:**
There may be some truth in the assertion by Chinese poets and artists that once you've been to Huangshan, it is pointless ever to visit another mountain.

# Jiuhuashan Trek

Of China's four Buddhist sacred mountains, Jiuhuashan represents the South. Its temples are dedicated to Bodhisatva Ksitigarbha, lord of the earth and underworld. It rises on the northern edge of the Yangtze flood plains in Anhui Province, west of Shanghai. Above the glassy terraces of rice paddy, the road climbs into ragged pine forests, twisting deep into a landscape of forest-capped cliffs, cascades and massive, bizarre rock formations. In the mist creeping up from the valleys, shapes form in the washed-out colours of ancient Chinese paintings, and you feel a déja-vu familiarity. Though there are tea and vegetable plantations among the blossoming azaleas, these are cultivated by the monks and nuns of some 80 temples and sacred institutions, and they don't impinge on the otherwise authentic wilderness. But more than 1,500 years of sanctity means that Jiuhuashan's nine principal peaks, and every cave, stream, path, promontory, pool, waterfall, cliff, temple, pagoda and even the 'Ten Perfect Views', have names of meditational significance (like 'Celestial Presence at the Heavenly Pillar') – which transforms hiking on the mountain into an involuntary pilgrimage whenever genuine pilgrims pause on the often narrow path.

It's no hardship. The goodwill you encounter trekking on Jiuhuashan enhances what is already an exceptionally lovely region. There is no development other than the stunning temple complexes, all of them integrated into the dramatic landscape according to the principles of the Tang, Ming and Qing dynasties in which they were built. You choose temple guesthouses over campsites, and seek out some of their 1,500 Buddha statues and thousands of important cultural relics – because rapidly you realize how their existence gives meaning to every rock and tree that you might hike past. With wafting incense, temple bells and a shrine on every corner, this is not normal hiking – but Jiuhuashan's natural magnificence and spiritual integrity make it abnormally rewarding.

*The temples of Jiuhuashan are integrated into the dramatic landscape.*

# Shanghai's Maglev Train

A ride on Shanghai's Maglev (magnetic levitation) Train is a journey into the future of transport. The Maglev rail system might be only 30.5 km (19 mi) long, but that's enough to demonstrate its potential to transform national and international economies by bringing the most remote areas within reach of trade and tourism.

Although Maglev was created and developed in Germany, Shanghai is the first place in the world to use it successfully in a scheduled service, or indeed in any commercial venture at all, and the statistics are amazing. The train can reach 350 kph (220 mph) in two minutes, and is designed for normal operation with a maximum speed of 431 kph (268 mph). But during tests, the train reached a top speed of 501 kph (311 mph), an indication of what it holds in reserve. With no conventional engine, and on a (necessarily) dedicated track of electromagnetic power and guidance coils, the impetus of acceleration is spread throughout the train. The ride is as smooth as an airborne aircraft, without even the spine-pinning surge of 'take-off'. Looking ahead from the Maglev, you see how the swooping concrete curves of the track are banked; inside, you barely feel it. Once on board, a flickering display charts even the slightest variation in speed, and you can't help sharing the thrill of streaking past the fastest cars on the adjacent expressway.

So far, the Shanghai Maglev only connects Pudong International Airport and Longyang Road, a suburb of the business district, and a long way from downtown. Despite some legitimate misgivings yet to be resolved, plans to extend the line to 160 km (99 mi) between downtown Shanghai and Hangzhou are going ahead. Then you will be able to transfer the 55 km (34 mi) between Shanghai's two airports in 15 minutes – like flying at zero altitude.

**HOW:**
By train
**WHEN TO GO:**
Year-round. Initially, you could only travel on the Maglev as part of an organized tour. Now that it is integrated into the regular transport system, you can ride it at any time.
**TIME IT TAKES:**
Usually 7 minutes 20 seconds (the taxi ride over the same route takes at least 1 hour).
**HIGHLIGHTS:**
No fossil fuel! (The Maglev may not be environmentally perfect, but it's in the right direction.)
Seeing the driver of a Ferrari on the expressway shaking his fist at the Maglev speeding past.
Floating on a magnetic cushion – a thought worthy of both Confucius and China's most imaginative poets.
The exhilaration of pure speed intensified the first time by just a twinge of apprehension, and on subsequent occasions by excited anticipation.
**YOU SHOULD KNOW:**
This technology is going to happen all over the world, and you don't need to know anything about science to share the thrill of it.

*The Maglev train pulls into the station at Longyang Lu.*

*The Grand Canal, Suzhou*

# Suzhou to Hangzhou on the Grand Canal

**HOW:**
By boat
**WHEN TO GO:**
Year-round. Hangzhou has four
distinct seasons, but its subtropical,
monsoon climate makes it neither
too hot not too cold.
**TIME IT TAKES:**
Three hours (Suzhou-Wuxi); 14-16
hours (Suzhou-Hangzhou, overnight);
2-4 days (Grand Canal Cruise on
special 'hotel boats', stopping for
sight-seeing and excursions).
**HIGHLIGHTS:**
The 18 bridges, reflecting the styles
of different dynasties, and ten richly-
decorated and colourful land and
water city gates opening onto the
Grand Canal at Suzhou.
The Lingering Garden and the Garden
of the Master of the Nets –
ingenious, beautiful, and
consummately Confucian.
The Six Harmonies Pagoda at West
Lake, octagonal and with 13 curling
roofs, representing the six
fundamental precepts of Buddhism.
Qing He Fang Street in Hangzhou,
much of which survives from the
Southern Song Dynasty (1127-1279),
and where the shops still sell silks,
brocades, parasols, Hangzhou's
speciality fans, and the exquisite teas
for which the region is revered.

China's Grand Canal is 2,000 years old, 1,764 km (1,103 mi) long, and dwarfs any other man-made waterway on earth. Running south from Beijing, it connects all China's major, east-west running rivers, and thus most of its major cities, in a single, gigantic system. No longer significant to modern transport, communications or defence, the Grand Canal remains as a unique guardian of Chinese history and culture – and nowhere on its length is that more evident than its southernmost stretch from Suzhou to its terminal at Hangzhou. The beauty of both cities is legendary, and the Grand Canal between them passes ancient water towns and villages, lakes and hanging gardens draped in antiquity, and the wood and stone infrastructure of generations of Chinese lives. It is a privileged view of history, and China's greatest poets and artists have recognized and celebrated it since the Sui Dynasty 1,500 years ago: even at its inception, this section of the Grand Canal was imbued with an aesthetic to please.

From Suzhou's gardens, waterways and pagodas, you cruise past a traditional China from the 13th or 14th centuries to Wuxi, the 'Radiant Pear' of Taihu, a lake dotted with islands and gorgeous temples. There you can take a painted dragon-boat across the lake to Tongli, a medieval town split into seven parts by the fifteen river courses flowing through it. Living history just keeps coming for 147 km (92 mi), through Zhenjiang (girlhood home of American writer Pearl S. Buck), to the incomparable natural beauties of Hangzhou itself. The canal passes by ancient stone farmhouses where silk production became famous in the 6th century, but West Lake is Hangzhou's masterpiece, praised by Su Dongpo and Marco Polo, and a major reason for the Grand Canal's citation as a UNESCO World Cultural Heritage Site.

# Pearl River Twilight Cruise

*The port city of Guangzhou*

The Pearl River Delta has been China's southern gateway for nearly 2,000 years, and the city of Guangzhou has been its significant port since the Tang dynasty (618 to 917). Formerly known as Canton, it accommodated first the Portuguese, then the British as predominant trade partners. Today, it is still one of China's fastest-growing cities, and just as devoted to international trade; but its success has been achieved at the cost of pretty well anything that speaks of its history or ancient culture. Instead, Guangzhou is a testament to China's perception of modernity. Concrete confections stretch for blank miles along the Pearl River's broad stream, and river mists turn brown along the banks where they mix with traffic fumes. This is 'Metropolis', and even its residents criticize its lack of redeeming features. Guangzhou's (self-assessed) greatest attraction is to flee the fumes by boat – if only to cruise a short distance up and down the endless concrete shore. Then night falls, and the gorgeous butterfly of the Pearl River takes wing.

Where the Pearl River runs through the city, at night Guanghzou celebrates its industrial heritage and future in a blaze of lurid yellow, red and orange illuminations. Tombstone slabs of daytime grey become canvases for flashing, spinning, flickering sequences of neon. Hotels, shopping malls and high-rise office blocks on both banks create what look like rainbows arcing across the shimmering water. Some co-ordinate lighting sequences, creating themed patterns with names like 'Night Moon Over Goose Pool' and 'Red Heart of the Pearl River'. Multicoloured stroboscopic displays bounce reflections off every ripple, suggesting the hidden pulse of this endlessly energetic city. At any other time of day, a cruise on the Pearl River is merely dull. In the gloaming, the conspiracy of colour in frantic motion reminds you of Guangzhou's ancient, subtle, colourful Chinese soul.

**HOW:**
By boat
**WHEN TO GO:**
Year-round
**TIME IT TAKES:**
1.5-2.5 hours (a leisurely loop between the Guangzhou Bridge in the east, Bai Hedong ('White Crane') Bridge in the south, and the west side of the Shamian district. Duration depends on the size of the cruise ship and the degree of luxury.
**HIGHLIGHTS:**
The Great Bridge of the People – in the heart of the city, it looks its futuristic best by artificial light (or moonlight on its own).
The old colonial villas and cobbled, tree-lined avenues of the Foreign Enclave in Shamian district.
The '13 Hongs' – the line of warehouses along the Shamian waterfront where 19th century foreign traders were allowed to do business. For a long time, these *hongs* were the front line of the opium and silk trades, profits from which flowed to the safety of Hong Kong.
The co-ordinated light shows – even the advertisements look terrific.
**YOU SHOULD KNOW:**
Different cruise companies operate from different wharves. Tianzi Wharf, centrally located near Haizhou Square, is most frequently touted; but many cruises leave from White Goose Wharf in Shamian, usually much more convenient for visitors.

# Tiger Leaping Gorge

Where the Yangtze, Mekong and Salween Rivers rush side-by-side out of Tibet and south along China's border with Burma, the towering ridge of Yulong Xueshan (Jade Dragon Snow Mountain) forces the Yangtze into an abrupt change of direction known as The Great Bend. It turns north, the mountains close in, and the river enters Hutiao (Tiger Leaping) Gorge, one of the world's deepest.

It is narrowest at its start, where a large rock in the middle defies the ferocity of the torrent in a chasm only 30 m (100 ft) wide. This is where a tiger once leaped across it – but its legendary name derives not from tigers' agility, but from their unpredictable savagery. Entering its middle section, the water drops another 100 m (328 ft) without warning. Now at racing speed, whole blocks of water thunder and crash onto sharp outcrops of rock, and you can hear the greedy sucking of deep whirlpools pulling at the air. The third section of Hutiao's 15 km (9 mi) is even more dangerous and spectacular. The steeply-angled (70 to 90 degree) cliffs rise a sheer 18 to 2,400 m (6 to 8,000 ft) from the water, twisting and turning in a surge of high waves and filling the canyon in a haze of frothing spew. Just looking at it is one of the glories of nature, and you can hike along it in two days (rafting it is suicidal!). Beyond the gorge itself, the Great Bend continues for about 190 km (120 mi), turning south and east. For experienced rafters, the prolonged wave-trains and grade IV rapids are one of the world's greatest six to eight day expeditions. For everyone, the proximity of the Gorge to Lijiang, cradle of China's traditional Naxi and Dongba cultures, justifies including this journey in any top-three wish list.

*The calm section of Tiger Leaping Gorge*

# Rafting Nine Bends River

Wuyi Shan, in northern Fujian province, is southeast China's most remote mountain region. Its incomparable scenic beauty was recognized 4,000 years ago by the Yue people, and it became a site of pilgrimage for Taoism, Buddhism and Confucianism. Already a protected area for 1,500 years before gaining the UNESCO grand slam of World Biosphere and World Natural, Cultural and Historical Heritage Site, Wuyi is the ultimate Chinese expression of the potential for harmony between nature and man. Its heart-stirring landscapes are littered with the temples, palaces and pavilions created in tribute to the aesthetics of Confucian philosophy, whose greatest spear-carrier, the 10th century neo-Confucian Zhu Xi, lived and taught here for fifty years.

Jiuqu (Nine Bends) Gorge, a 10-km (6-mi) section of the 63-km (39-mi) Jiuqu River, is the geographical heart of this summation of Chinese history and culture – and the water element in the formula for harmony. So when you raft the Jiuqu Gorge, you embrace a welter of Chinese philosophy which dictates significance in every rock, every mist of spray, the towering cliffs and solitary, jungle-topped stacks wreathed in cloud; and in the deep placid green pools, the wind-dashed waterfalls and squabbling, rock-strewn rapids of the watercourse. The rafting itself needs no crash-helmet commando training: you sit on bamboo chairs set on six, lashed-together bamboo poles, and swirl gently down stream.

It really is worth reading about Wuyi before you raft the Nine Bends. Each bend reveals a new set of surprises, a geography saturated with sophisticated meaning: with just an inkling of the nature of the reverence in which the Nine Bends are held, you get a four-dimensional view of what are otherwise merely world-class panoramas. On the water, with visual stimuli at maximum pleasure, this is one of the few places you can go 'holistic' rafting.

**HOW:**
On a raft
**WHEN TO GO:**
Year-round.
**TIME IT TAKES:**
1.5-2 hours (Xingcun – Wuyi Town, through the Nine Bends); one to two days (starting further upriver enables you to reflect in peace on the extent of the region's natural beauty, and renders you immune to the noisy crowds of rafters along the Nine Bends stretch when you get there).
**HIGHLIGHTS:**
The Palace complex and other Minyue remains at Xingcun – the most extensive and best preserved of all South China's Han Dynasty sites, over 2,000 years old.
The Wuyi Nature Reserve (of which the Nine Bends is part) – 95 per cent intact sub-tropical forest.
The green triangles of small terraces backed up in the gullies along the river bank – source of China's rarest and most precious Rock teas, like Dahongpao ('Grand Red Robe').
The 'fairy boats' – the boat-coffins dating back 4,000 years, stuffed into caves and fissures all along the soaring rock walls of the gorge, representing the philosophical and mystical unities of dozens of contrasting dynasties and regimes.
**YOU SHOULD KNOW:**
You can save a lot of time and anxiety at the raft pier by pre-booking through a tour agent.

*Tourists on rafts in the Jiuqu Gorge*

*The entrance to Qutang Gorge*

# Three Gorges: cruising the Yangtze

**HOW:**
By boat
**WHEN TO GO:**
Year-round. With the Three Gorges
Dam now operating, navigation is
much less dangerous, and unlikely to
be cancelled even when rains swell
the Yangtze, which with its huge
catchment area can happen at any
time of year.
**TIME IT TAKES:**
24-28 hours (Yichang or Zhongbao,
the granite island on which the dam
is based, to Baidicheng, including an
overnight stop at Fengjie, whose
massive towering gates face the
Yangtze at the division between Wu
and Qutang Gorges); 8-14 days
(Shanghai-Chongqing).
**HIGHLIGHTS:**
Xiling 100-li Art Gallery – the high
cliffs of Yellow Ox, Light Shadow and
Yellow Cat gorges, filled with mist
and mystery, and said to be like
travelling through a painting.
The 12 Peaks of the Wushan
Mountains, spread along both shores
of the Wu Gorge.

From east to west, Xiling, Wu and Qutang Gorges stretch for 192 km (120 mi), compressing China's mighty Yangtze River into an angry torrent between Hubei and Sichuan Provinces. For millennia, the gorges have been celebrated for their uniquely dramatic scenic splendour, and as one of the most important focal points of Chinese history and culture. You could spend a lifetime of fascinating study among the temples, castles, cities, shrines and man-made treasures lining their banks; and the same again, lost in wonder at the natural formations of caves, grotesque rock formations, juddering whirlpools and soaring cliffs that represent so much of China's folk memory – its mythology and legend writ in stone (and in many cases, on it as well: China's most famous poets and artists have left long testaments inscribed on the rock walls).

The Three Gorges may be the highlight of any journey along the Yangtze, but since the building of the new dam, there are only two ways to experience them. Either you can take a short, local cruise from the dam site to Baidicheng ('White Emperor Town'), at the western end of Qutang's north shore and a breathtaking sight of 2,000 year-old vermilion walls and flying eaves; or you must cruise from Shanghai all the way to Chongqing on one of the new 'tourist boats' which are now the only ones to be allowed to use the dam's five locks above Yichang, the eastern gateway to the gorges. You can no longer cruise just from Wuhan to Chongqing. Hopefully, visitors in the future may be allowed to travel on the Chinese commercial boats that lack any comfort, but stop everywhere, enabling you to handpick sites along the gorges, and still enjoy their context – as treasures along the much greater highway of the whole Yangtze River.

**YOU SHOULD KNOW:**
The rising waters of the dammed Yangtze may slightly diminish the immensity of the Gorges' cliffs, but the region is so crammed with extraordinary treasures that it can't really matter in the greater scheme of things.

# Dalian Coastal Drive

At the southern tip of northeast China's Liaodong Peninsula, Dalian is northern China's biggest port and a former colony of both Russia and Japan. Set between the hills of its own sub-peninsula, the city is unusual in China, because it is full of parks, woods, and green spaces that make the most of the beaches along its twisting shoreline. Dalian's deep-water industrial port is miles away – and the same meteorological quirk that keeps it ice-free makes Dalian a major domestic tourist resort. Since 1955, when the city became exclusively Chinese, its authorities have sought to retain some of the European ideas brought by the Russians – of wide boulevards, and, especially, the wonderful corniche called the Binhai Road.

The Binhai Road runs for 42.5 km (26.6 mi) to Heishijiao, following every cove and promontory around the west and south of the city. It perches between the golden beaches (including 2 of China's designated top ten judged by colour, curve, breadth and fineness of sand) and the coastal hills of the nature park that fills most of the sub-peninsula. Visually, you could be near Sorrento or Cannes above the Mediterranean; but the thicker weight of the air and the sea mists are unmistakably oceanic. Dalian's city fathers proudly refer to their 'dancing silk ribbon', which begins at Asia's biggest plaza, Xinghai Square, and curls out and away among the woods and flower-filled cliff-sides. It's extremely pretty, but the Binhai Road is the centrepiece of a resort region, and nature has been tamed to comply. At regular intervals, close to the beaches, formal entertainment facilities and attractions remind you of how crowded it gets in the summer. There are scenic spots like Wooden-Club Island, the Black Rock Reefs and the novelty sculptures of Donghai Park; and at Tiger Beach, rides like the Jurassic Riptide Adventure and Viking Village...

**HOW:**
By car or on foot
**WHEN TO GO:**
June to October. Come in April only for the blossoming of 3,000 cherry trees (planted by the Japanese in the 1920s) at nearby Long Wangtang.
**TIME IT TAKES:**
1-2 hours (by car); 8-9 hours (steady hiking)
**HIGHLIGHTS:**
Russian Street in central Dalian – the best concentration of buildings among several pockets of architectural history.
Fujiazhuang Beach – the most popular and by far the most fun (but with a steep drop-off 100 m (328 ft) offshore).
The 'Strange Slope' of part of the road called '18-Hairpin Bend' at Donghai Park – a genuinely disturbing optical illusion where your car appears to roll away uphill.
Yanwoling ('Swallow Nest Mountain') – one of Binhai Road's loveliest stretches.
**YOU SHOULD KNOW:**
At Tiger Beach's Ocean Park, the 'Pirate Village' attraction simulates boats in a violent storm at sea, and offers visitors 'an experience of being robbed'.

# The Silk Road

**HOW:**
Various!
**WHEN TO GO:**
Year-round, according to which section you want to travel. A French team recently demonstrated that with meticulous planning, and travelling on horseback, you can travel the entire distance at the optimum season for each region.
**TIME IT TAKES:**
Many agencies offer tours of one or more sections of the Silk Road, ranging from 10-23 days, and including short treks on foot and by camel. Typically, 12-14 days for sections within Turkmenistan, Uzbekistan, Kyrgyzstan and Tajikistan; 14-23 days for sections within China (Kashgar, Xi'an, the Great Wall West Gate at Jiahuagan and Beijing); 15 months (Venice-Beijing, by horse). Most agencies will help you personalize their advertised tours.

The wayposts of the Silk Road are a litany of adventure and romance crossing half the world. Already ancient when Marco Polo set out from 13th century Venice, the 13,900-km (8,700-mi) route to Kublai Khan's capital of Beijing is still fraught with the same historic dangers. War, pestilence, religious confrontation and plain banditry continue to influence travellers' choices – and are the reason why the Silk Road is not one, but a series of fragmented routes which tell a collective history.

Created by trade, the Silk Road has always been even more important as a conduit for ideas. The exchange of science and technology, of philosophy, religion and artistic culture has scored a trail of monumental magnificence across two continents. Venice, Istanbul, Bukhara, Samarkand, Tashkent, Kashgar, Urumqi, Dunhuang, Lanzhou and Xi'an stand out, but the mountain ranges, deserts, steppes, rivers and other natural obstacles between them hide a thousand treasures ranging from whole medieval cities to the most exquisite Islamic and oriental objets d'art. There are only two rules for travellers who want to make the most of the Silk Road: always expect the unexpected, and embrace cultural differences to the best of your diplomatic ability.

In many ways, the present Silk Road is the legacy of Kublai Khan. From Turkey to the China Sea he established the 'Ulak' system of caravanserais, where travellers could rest, and his

*The walled fort city of Jiahuagan lies at the western terminus of the Great Wall in China.*

couriers could change horses (he could send a message from Beijing to Damascus and get a reply in six weeks). You find them, a Byzantine arch or a quintuple-tiered pagoda, on the horizon of mountains and deserts – and just as welcome whether you arrive on foot, by camel train or truck. Kublai Khan's 'Big Idea' always was communication between peoples – and there's no better way on earth than to chase it down the Silk Road.

*The blue domes of the Registan in Samarkand, Uzbekistan*

**HIGHLIGHTS:**
Riding in a camel train on the southern edge of the Taklamakan Desert.
The very rare 'Singing Sand Dune' of Moon Lake.
The maze of markets and alleyways in Kashgar, where colourful traditional dress and a myriad range of Kyrgyz, Uighur, Tajik, Kazakh and Chinese faces demonstrate its historic importance as a melting pot for trade and culture. The Sunday market draws 100,000 people.
Wherever you are on it, just the idea of being 'on the Silk Road' is totally exhilarating – even when things aren't especially comfortable or easy to handle.

**YOU SHOULD KNOW:**
The title of 'Silk Road' was invented by the 19th century German historian and geographer, Ferdinand von Richtofen, father of the 'Red Baron', the World War I Luftwaffe flying ace.

*Donkeys carry bales of hay at the Sunday market in Kashgar.*

# Xinjiang to Tibet Highway

Getting into Tibet isn't always easy unless you fly direct to Lhasa. Of the five overland routes, the highest and most remote is the Xinjiang to Tibet Highway, so desolate a road that despite a regular military presence it offers travellers blessedly little bureaucratic interference. The Highway begins at Yecheng (Kargilik) in Chinese Turkestan, and climbs straight up the eastern edge of the Karakoram to Dahongliutan, at 4,900 m (16,000 ft) only just higher than the average altitude of the entire Highway. You need to be prepared, either with time to acclimatize, or ancillary oxygen. The 2,743-km (1,714-mi) journey takes from 9 to 16 days on largely unpaved road; and the very few villages and truck stops may be unable to offer you bed, food or even water. That said, usually you find that truckers will happily share their steaming pot of noodles, and every day you'll find some sort of establishment with hot food and a roof.

The rewards of entering Tibet this way are enormous. Over the Kunlun Mountains you skirt the western Tibetan plateau. Instead of people there are birds thronging the small lakes, and wildlife in extraordinary numbers. Mountain peaks form blue on vast horizons of grassland and rocky scrub. There will be a moment when you feel chastened by the biblical immensity of sky and earth and loneliness; and grateful for a human voice. Along the north slopes of the Himalayas into the desert terrain between Gerze and Nyima, only herds of antelope and wild yak disturb the ghosts at the ancient rock paintings at Rutog, among the ruins of the Guge Kingdom. It's a relief to joke with living monks at Tuolin, Sagya, and Tashilunpo monasteries. The contrast makes you realize how this brilliant wilderness journey is also a subtle, cultural introduction to Tibet.

*The Highway near Xinjiang*

# The Romantic Road

One of the loveliest but least known of Japan's scenic routes is the Romantic Road through the mountain heartland of central Honshu. It begins in the historic city of Ueda, once the feudal castle citadel of the Sanada family, and picks its way along the quietest backroads through the mountains of Gunma Prefecture to Utsunomiya. The only logic to its weaving route is to connect landscapes of transcendent beauty, from the cherry blossom of spring pastures to the full-throated blaze of autumn in the mountain forests. It leads to the double waterfalls of Fukiware, the rugged splendour of Lake Chuzenji and the natural glory of Nikko National Park; and to countless shrines, pagodas, castles, hot springs of all shapes, size and location, and ancient towns and villages that reveal some of old Japan's most enduring characteristics.

For some 50km (31 mi) of its 350 km (219 mi) length, the Romantic Road follows the base of Mount Asama, an active volcano. Old and new Japan accommodates itself to nature's dangerous beauty first, with a 1,000 year-old, three-storied pagoda of inspired grace, built at Miyota as protection against eruption; and second, with a miniature version of Tokyo's Ginza shopping district at the upmarket mountain resort of Karuizawa, farther along the road. Both are charming. In the same way, the route passes by traditional and modern hot springs. The old style is for traditional architecture, and a beautifully composed natural setting; some of the newer springs like Kusatsu are factories of hydrotherapy.

You need a car to follow Japan's Romantic Road. It would be worth it even if you stopped only at the ultimate jewel – the World Heritage Sites of Nikko, home to Japan's most lavishly decorated shrine complex, and set in outstanding natural magnificence.

**HOW:**
By car
**WHEN TO GO:**
May to October
**TIME IT TAKES:**
Two to five days
**HIGHLIGHTS:**
The impressive view of Mount Asama from the sylvan beauty of Onioshidashi Park, formed round a stream of solidified lava from a previous eruption.
The completely traditional, small hot spring resort of Shima Onsen, in the northern mountains of Gunma.
The glorious twin cascades of Ryuzu Falls, tumbling through the gold and red of autumn forests.
The Yomeimon at the Toshogu shrine complex of the spectacular Tokugawa Mausoleum, just one of Nikko's stunning historical and religious sites.
**YOU SHOULD KNOW:**
For sheer romance, time your visit for the annual historical festival in August in the rural paradise of Numata, nestled at the foot of the Tamahara Highlands.

*Toshogu shrine pagoda in Nikko*

457

# Walking the Nakasendo

Developed from the 7th century onwards, the Nakasendo was formalized at the beginning of the Tokugawa Shogunate (1600-1868) as one of the five official roads for the use of the shogun and government dignitaries in ruling their territory. The Nakasendo was one of two highways connecting Edo (Tokyo) and Kyoto, and it runs through the forested heart of Japan across the mountains of Honshu and along its misty, green river valleys. There were 69 post towns and smaller stations established along its 534 km (332 mi) length – and long stretches, especially in the mountainous areas, remain now almost exactly as they were in the 17th century. Despite inevitable modernizing, it's still possible to hike the entire Nakasendo – but most visitors choose to spend one to twelve days on its pristine central section from Ena to Narai.

Between these beautifully preserved Edo towns lies the fabulous Kiso Valley, a living vision of ancient, rural Japan. Huge stretches of the road are paved with their original *ishidatami* cobbles, curling through pedestrianized villages of traditional wooden houses, and stepped to follow the steep gradients of the forest hillsides. With volcanic Mount Ontake as a backdrop, the road reaches its zenith as custodian of Japanese rural cultural tradition between the villages of Tsumago and Magome. Achingly picturesque combinations of rocky hillsides, rivers, waterfalls and forests confound touristic cynicism with their enduring natural beauty. So much so that you appreciate the fact that even the postmen here wear full Edo-period costume. From Magome, some of the Nakasendo's loveliest landscapes unfurl on the steep climb to the Torii Pass, and culminate in the 17th to 19th century treasures of Narai.

One terrific feature of the Nakasendo is the chance to stay in traditional *minshuku* – family-run inns where everyone eats and talks together. It's a rare opportunity for visitors to meet local people – it illuminates the journey.

*The highway weaves its way through villages like Magome.*

**HOW:**
On foot
**WHEN TO GO:**
April to October. Each season creates a new version of the Nakasendo's magic.
**TIME IT TAKES:**
1-12 days. The most popular stretch, Tsumago-Magome, is a 3-4 hour slow ramble, usually as part of a 1-day excursion. Ena-Narai is an easy to moderate 12-day hike of up to 20 km (12 mi) a day, with 2 rest days.
**HIGHLIGHTS:**
The hilarity of composing haiku, partly in sign language, for the Japanese families who run the *minshuku,* where all activities like eating and bathing are communal.
The historical integrity of the road – the restoration along the Ena-Narai section far transcends the usual 'theme-park' approach. This is all genuine and surprisingly moving.
The early morning mists, reinforcing the most powerful aesthetic in the predominant image of old Japan.
**YOU SHOULD KNOW:**
Among the *minshuku* along the Nakasendo's central section are some of Japan's oldest and most famous inns – astonishingly, unwilling to capitalize on their fame and therefore still accessible to all travellers. That really is a cultural shock!

# Shinkansen – the Bullet Train from Osaka to Hiroshima

The high-speed Shinkansen is the pride of Japan Rail, and the core of its entire railway system. Even so, it has its own hierarchy. Though it serves all Japan's major cities, its newest, sleekest, fastest version is reserved for the Tokaido/Sanyo Shinkansen. Powered by the 300-km/188-mph Nozomi Super-Express, it's the Tokyo-Kyoto-Osaka-Hiroshima-Hakata service, connecting the capital with the beautiful coastal region of Sanyo, the southern half of Honshu Island's panhandle, facing the Inland Sea. The Sanyo Shinkansen runs extra services on its section of the route, between Osaka and Hiroshima. The region is a mixture of fruit trees and pasture, backed by wooded hills full of craggy ravines and tumbling streams, but with a fretwork of bays, promontories, coves and offshore islands to further embellish its popularity.

The Shinkansen runs on a route parallel to the much older Sanyo Railway, celebrated for over 100 years as one of Japan's most scenic routes. Much like a dragon on old porcelain, the silver starship of the Shinkansen snakes through the traditional Japanese landscape of ancient, historic towns and villages, and of woods, water and arched bridges. It's a mighty metaphor for Japan's ability to synthesize the future with the past.

As metaphors go, both Osaka and Hiroshima are equally powerful – Osaka, because its history is that of Japan's greatest internal dynastic struggle between the Toyotomi and the Tokugawa; and Hiroshima because of its importance as a symbol of resurrected humanity. In Osaka, the huge castle is a colossus of war, though beautiful and compelling; in Hiroshima, even Peace Park and the Torii Gate on Miyajima reinforce visitors' confrontation with desolation – if only of the mind and common memory. On the Shinkansen between the two cities, you have time for these thoughts.

**HOW:**
By train
**WHEN TO GO:**
Year-round.
**TIME IT TAKES:**
Around two hours (Shin-Osaka to Hiroshima Station)
**HIGHLIGHTS:**
The 16th century Ujo ('Raven') Castle, of Okayama.
The 17th century Koraku-en Garden – one of the three Major Gardens of Japan, it took 14 years to build.
Peace Park in Hiroshima.
Miyajima ('shrine island'), about 40 minutes by local train and ferry from Hiroshima – a profoundly moving memorial of consummate Japanese style.
**YOU SHOULD KNOW:**
Talking on mobile phones is forbidden on all Japanese trains, except in the entrance sections of Shinkansen carriages.

*The Shinkansen speeds through Tokyo.*

459

# The 88 Temples of the Shikoku Pilgrim Route

In Shikoku, ancient Japan is no ghost. The smallest of Japan's four main islands, it remains isolated by the Inland Sea despite the increasing development of its north coast cities in the wake of recently improved access to Honshu and Kyushu. Away from this densely populated ribbon of conurbation, Shikoku remains the loveliest and most bucolic region in the country. The south, especially, fits a traditional image of Japan – of fabulous mountain scenery, samurai castles, craft workshops, farming villages where oxen pull creaky wagons, and of small terraces of vegetable or orange trees cut into the hillsides of dense woodland.

This warming, humane landscape is the backdrop to Japan's oldest pilgrim circuit – the 1,450-km (906-mi) journey to 88 shrines established by the 9th century Buddhist priest Kobo Daishi. Every year, more than 100,000 of his followers – called *henro* – complete the rite. Most, devout and determined but subject to modern pressures, do so by bus or car. A small proportion travel on foot, fulfilling the 'walk of life' that Kobo Daishi proposed as an opportunity for self-examination by confrontation with the unexpected and unknown.

And you do confront it: even those who set out merely to enjoy the hiking discover that as a *henro*, they are drawn into a quite novel experience. Pilgrims wear white to show their status. Throughout Shikoku, they find they are the recipient of 1,000 small charities or gifts of food or money. These they must accept in humility as *o-settai*, gifts to help them on their way from people who cannot make the journey themselves. The constant exchange of moral responsibilities and actual goods adds a revelatory dimension to the usual introspections of a long, long hike. However, 1,000 years of pilgrims' comments indicate that the 88 temples hike benefits much more than just leg muscles or lungs.

*A statue stands guard over one of the temples.*

*The pearl farms of Ago Bay*

# The Pearl Road

The Pearl Road is a skyline drive across the coastal edge of the Ise-Shima National Park on the Kii Peninsula in Mie Prefecture east of Nagoya and Nara. It overlooks the saw-tooth ria formations of deep indented bays and complicated fjords facing the Pacific, notably Ago-wan (Ago Bay), south of Toba city, where in 1893 Mikimoto Kokichi produced the first cultured pearl; and which is still the main centre of Japanese pearl production. In fact the Pearl Road begins at Mikimoto Pearl Island, where in addition to memorial statues and pearl museums, you can see the pearl *ama* – the highly trained, women pearl free-divers – at work. But Toba city is principally a resort centre, full of theme parks and huge groups looking for cheap excursion fun, and the Pearl Road provides an escape route to the tranquility of the lovely hills behind the otherwise gorgeous coastline.

It's fair to point out that the unbridled coastal development at Toba and elsewhere in the vicinity (all made misty by distance when you look down from the Pearl Road Observatory) owes its tacky existence to its proximity to one of Japan's most sacred Shinto shrines at Ise City. With so many visitors to the double shrines of Geku and Naiku, it's no wonder developers moved in to cater for them. From the Pearl Road, one side looks down on the shrine precincts. The stylized, traditional wooden buildings are set in ancient forests of sugi (giant cryptomaeria trees), with lakes, ponds and large stone formations of unfathomable symbolism all around. Established in the 3rd and 5th centuries, it's the image of the shrines and not the touristy horrors that you take away with you. They will outlast any modern development – and so will the Pearl Road's naturally beautiful marine landscapes.

**HOW:**
By car or bus
**WHEN TO GO:**
Year-round, it's a lovely region in which to unwind – and easily accessible.
**TIME IT TAKES:**
One hour
**HIGHLIGHTS:**
The Isa Grand Shrines – Naiku houses the sacred mirror of the Emperor – one of the three essential pieces of regalia of the Imperial family.
The isolated, but perfect white sand of Goza Shirahama beach.
A boat trip among the coves and islets of Ago Bay, a marine landscape that changes dramatically with the weather, but always enhanced by the sight of the *ama* (female divers) diving for pearls.
**YOU SHOULD KNOW:**
In the historic city of Matsukaka, below the walls of the magnificent castle there is a row of 19 houses dating back to 1603. Six of them are still occupied by descendants of their original samurai owners.

461

# The Tokaido Highway

**HOW:**
By car or on foot
**WHEN TO GO:**
Year-round (May to October if you plan to hike and/or camp)
**TIME IT TAKES:**
Traditionally, over the 489 km/303 mi route – 15 days (women), 12 days (men), 90 hours (professional and official messengers, operating in relays). Now, 4-12 day tours offer selective highlights and the time to marvel at them.
**HIGHLIGHTS:**
Comparing Hiroshige's 19th century picture of Satta Pass and Yui Town near Mt Fuji – once a very dangerous, narrow section of the Tokaido, now shared with the JR Tokaido Line, the Japan National Highway 1 and the Tomei Expressway.
The 1.5 km (1 mi) of Edo-era merchant and domestic buildings at Seki in Mie Prefecture – completely undisturbed since.
The mountain villages and forested hills around Hakone.
Arriving at Kyoto's To-ji, one of its most important temples.
**YOU SHOULD KNOW:**
Official *shukuba* ('post-houses') on the Tokaido had to include a *toiya-ba* (courier depot) with horses and personnel at the ready; a *sekisho* ('entrance gate') where papers, permits and goods were officially examined; and one or more *hatago* ('basket of grass', originally for horses, and thus 'accommodation facility'). There were often more than one of these travellers' inns: Miya-juku, now Atsuta in central Nagoya City, had 248 *hatago*.

The Tokaido was designated Japan's most important thoroughfare at its creation in 1603. It was to be the Number One highway from the shogun's capital in Edo (Tokyo) to the imperial capital in Kyoto: the coastal route was easier than the alternative mountain route (the Nakasendo). In 1619, it was extended to Osaka, and the 57 official post houses between the Nihonbashi Bridge in Tokyo and Umeda in Osaka defined the heart of Japan's political, economic and social structure. Goods, people, and most of all information passed up and down the Tokaido's length, strictly regulated and efficiently serviced.

They still do, only now they travel on Japan National Route 1 or the Shinkansen, both of which parallel the old road. But the modern highway and express train both cut through hills and shave awkward angles in the name of passenger comfort; and their ribbons of steel and asphalt are anyway hemmed in by buildings and advertising. Almost forgotten, alongside but very much intact, the Tokaido remains, some of it accessible by car, and in some areas like Mie Prefecture, it is 95 per cent intact. Even where the new road is literally on top of the old, the Tokaido is signalled by the shrines, temples and official buildings of its former official status; and one section, in the lovely mountain region between Hakone and Machi has been officially 'preserved' – each November a Daimyo Gyoretsu ('feudal procession') of about 200 people acting as servants, porters, palanquin-carriers and spear-carrying guards re-enacts typical history. Of the rest – the majority – it is astonishing how much survives of the original road fabric. You could use the 1830 pictorial guide of the Tokaido's stages, and still recognize most of it. It is one of Japan's most exciting surprises that you can get so close to its social history.

*The busy Satta Pass, shared by the JR Tokaido Line, the Japan National Highway 1 and the Tomei Expressway.*

# Tokyo Water Cruise

Partly because nobody thinks of Tokyo as a waterfront city, a ride in a *suijo basu* (river bus) provides a completely novel perspective on one of the world's most densely-packed, urban maelstroms. From Hinode Pier green-glassed, sleek double-decker boats like rocket-ships make a futuristic statement for the Sumida River ferry, a service that started in 1885. Now, the ferry carries far more Japanese tourists and visitors than commuters on the 40-minute ride from the mouth of the Sumida River on Tokyo Bay upstream to Asakusa.

The frenzy of the city recedes on the water, and you get an unexpected, 'back-door' view of its working heart. You pass Tsukiji's colossal Wholesale Market for fish and produce; the tidal duck ponds of the moated Hama-Rikyu Tei-En ('Detached Palace Garden'); old lumberyards and warehouses; the landmark green roof of the Kokugikan, housing the arena, museum and HQ of Japanese Sumo Wrestling; and, at Asakusa itself, the giant red lantern of Sensoji Temple, much loved by elderly Japanese.

Four other *suijo* lines start from Hinode, in various guises. The Harbor Cruise Line is a stern paddle-wheeler with a stovepipe stack – take it at dusk as the lights start to twinkle along the shore and across the Rainbow Bridge. Two more serve Odaiba, the massive artificial island in Tokyo Bay. The Odaiba Line goes to Seaside Park, where city folk come to frolic on the shipped-in beach and to practise romance on the boardwalk; the Tokyo Big Sight Line serves the monolithic convention centre and its asphalt grid of office blocks, and the Palette Town shopping malls. Other lines thread the network of manmade islands to the aquarium or the Kasai Sealife Park in Chiba. Travelling by river bus, you get a chance to reflect on what makes Tokyo's energy so exciting.

**HOW:**
By river bus
**WHEN TO GO:**
Year-round (but the illuminations on the Rainbow Bridge and Odaiba shore are revamped for a spectacular evening show throughout August, each year).
**TIME IT TAKES:**
40 minutes (Sumida Line, Hinode-Asakusa); 50 mins (Harbor Cruise Line); 30 minutes (Odaiba Line, Hinode-Seaside Park); 35 minutes (Tokyo Big Sight Line, Hinode-Palette Town); 1 hour (Kasai Sealife Park Line, Hinode-Kasai Rinken Koen/Chiba); 50 minutes (Canal Cruise Line, Hinode-Shinagawa Aquarium).
**HIGHLIGHTS:**
Venus Fort, one of the giant shopping malls in Odaiba.
Plum Grove, at the eastern tip of the 62-acre Hama-Rikyu Gardens – an oasis of sylvan beauty and tranquility, right next to the *suijo* landing stage.
The Museum of Maritime Science on Odaiba: six stories high, shaped like a full-sized ocean liner.
Watching fugu-fish being dissected at the Central Market – only licensed experts are trusted to remove the lethal poisonous bits of one of Japan's most famous delicacies.

*A Tokyo river bus—more like a rocket-ship!*

# Enoshima Electric Railway

**HOW:**
By train
**WHEN TO GO:**
Year-round
**TIME IT TAKES:**
34 minutes (Fujisawa-Kamakura)
**HIGHLIGHTS:**
The woods and flower displays at
Inamuragasaki Park, from which you
get a wonderful view down the
coastline from Shichirigahama to
Enoshima, with the Izu islands and
Mt Fuji in the misty distance.
The flower temples of Kamakura –
like Kaizuoji, Eishoji and
Jyoukoumyouji.
Taking an escalator through the
woods to the highest point of
Enoshima Island – where among the
trees is the lovely Enoshima
Benzaiten Shrine, a triple Shinto
Shrine to the three sister goddesses
of the sea.
**YOU SHOULD KNOW:**
The Tokeiji Temple in Kitakamakura
(a short walk from the Railway
terminus) is particularly famous as a
place to break off personal
relationships.

*The train arrives in the popular
seaside resort of Enoshima,
with Enoshima Island in
the background.*

It looks like a train, but the Enoshima Electric Railway has the soul of the much-appreciated local tram it used to be. It runs from Fujisawa, 51 km (32 mi) southwest of Tokyo, to the popular seaside resort of Enoshima and on to Kamakura, once capital of Japan and still the religious and historic hub of the Shonan region. The Railway has 15 stations on its 10 km (6 mi) length, with eclectic attractions in the vicinity of each, and there are special tourist tickets available to ensure you miss none of them.

Not even new rolling stock can disguise the Railway's alter ego of Tram. It follows the original tramlines laid out before 1910, at slow speeds determined by the sharp curves between the older buildings. Only near Enoshima Station does it run along the street. Otherwise its narrow-gauge track squeezes between the backs of residential blocks and houses, bursting free of the inelegant tangle of wires and backyard detritus that makes all train journeys fascinating to reveal a procession of sights of extraordinary variety and interest. Most are partly visible from the train itself – like the unusual lighthouse at Enoshima Island, and some of the many shrines and temples for which Hase and Kamakura are famous. Flowers of every colour adorn everything (Meigetsun Temple is actually dedicated to hydrangeas), confirming the region's reputation.

The Enoshima Electric Railway is a humble vehicle, but it takes you to some magical places. Get off at Hase for the 700 year-old brass Great Buddha at Kotoku-in Temple; or Kamakura, with 65 Buddhist temples, 19 Shinto shrines, and historic buildings going back to the city's foundation in 1192. Enoshima Island, a short walk away, offers amazing views of Mount Fuji in the distance, and a restful panorama of the beaches below. It's a marvellous little train.

# The Winding Paths of Soraksan

*Pine trees above the Chonbuldong Valley*

Soraksan (*san* means 'mountain') Nature Reserve sits on the east coast of the central Korean peninsula, behind the South Korean resort city of Sokch'o. The region is a tumbling mass of cracked granite and gneiss peaks, many over 1,200 m (3,936 ft), spread around the highest point, the 1,708 m (5,602 ft) Tae-ch'ongbong.

Threaded with plunging ravines of thick forest, streams and waterfalls, Sorak is full of hidden valleys and unexpected panoramas that take your breath away. A lattice of pathways and hiking trails leads into its remotest depths, but near the Reserve's entrance (just a 15-minute drive from Sokch'o's lovely beaches and resort razzmatazz) you understand what it means to be one of South Korea's most popular recreation sites. Even so, Soraksan has the grandeur to awe the biggest crowds, especially in autumn when its deciduous forests blaze with colour.

Its popularity as a natural wonder is combined with its cultural significance: several of South Korea's most famous temples can be found here. One, Allak-am, is placed above the Yukfam and Piryong waterfalls, celebrating their visual pleasure as an act of worship. Others, ancient structures like Shinhungsa and Anyang-am, are part Buddhist shrine, part working monastery (you may not actually enter the buildings), and part contemplative platform for some of the fantastic rock formations like Biseondae, a platform in the middle of a rushing torrent, or Heundeulbawi, a 5 m (16ft) spherical stone monster on a flat ledge. For centuries, pilgrims and visitors have tried to move it. It rocks but never rolls.

Deep within the Reserve, the hiking paths are rocky, narrow and steep – but effort is rewarded with constant surprise at Soraksan's variety of natural magnificence. In fact, the longer you stay, the more it's clear that Soraksan's paths demonstrate as much of Korea's soul as of its landscapes.

**HOW:**
On foot
**WHEN TO GO:**
Year-round. You can ski in winter, and Sorak's waterways and valleys respond to every shift of season and daily weather – but the reds and golds of autumn are glorious.
**TIME IT TAKES:**
1-14 days. Soraksan's legendary beauty is seductive, and it has many repeat visitors who stay longer each time.
**HIGHLIGHTS:**
The Sorak Cable Car to the Kwongumsong mountain. One way looks out to Sokch'o and the East Sea (NB in Korea you never refer to the Sea of Japan); the other to the immense mysteries – and invitations - of Soraksan's interior.
Trying to move Heundeulbawi.
The tributary streams and valleys of the Chonbuldong Valley – the main route into the heart of Soraksan.
**YOU SHOULD KNOW:**
Throughout Sarokson, especially near the temples, you'll find *ajimas* (temporary stands) selling snacks. One of the local favourites is boiled silkworms, which you recognize by the disgusting smell.

465

# A Trip to Anak Krakatao

**HOW:**
By boat
**WHEN TO GO:**
Dry season (May to September)
is best.
**TIME IT TAKES:**
Carita to Anak Krakatao and back
(including a climb to the edge of the
caldera) can be done in a day.
**HIGHLIGHTS:**
The islands of Rakata (another name
for Krakatao), Panjang and Sertung –
for a chilling perspective on the size
of the explosion that reduced the
original large island to these three
outlying fragments.
A side trip to Welcome Bay in the
mainland portion of the Ujung Kulon
National Park – don't miss the white
rhino skeleton at the ranger station.
A canoe trip along Ujung Kulon's
Cigenter River through dense tropical
forest teeming with wildlife.
**YOU SHOULD KNOW:**
Hollywood geography isn't all it
should be – the 1969 adventure
movie featuring Krakatao's 1883
eruption was titled *Krakatoa, East of
Java* when in fact the volcano is due
west of Java.

Anak is the offspring of the vanished volcanic island of Krakatao (sometimes incorrectly called Krakatoa). Located in the Sunda Strait between Java and Sumatra, the parent island famously blew apart in the great eruption of 1883, with ensuing tsunamis killing tens of thousands after a 'big bang' that was heard 5,000 km (3,000 mi) away. Starting in 1929, the new island of Anak Krakatao emerged from the sea as the centre point of three encircling islands – the remains of the original Krakatao.

It is an active volcano that is growing steadily. It lies within the remote Ujung Kulon National Park in West Java, created by the Dutch in the late 19th century, and it is possible to find a good selection of cruises that include Anak Krakatao on an itinerary designed to explore this fascinating refuge, which comprises the western tip of Java. This is both

rewarding and the easy way to go – Ujung Kulon is an extraordinary wilderness with no tourist infrastructure, so a do-it-yourself journey to this magical place is a real backpacking adventure.

Even so, those who are interested only in vulcanology can make a dedicated journey to Anak Krakatao. Depending on current volcanic activity, it is possible to land and camp on the vegetated eastern shore of this young volcano before scrambling to the cone's summit – a demanding hike up a steep slope covered in lightweight ejecta (pumice-like rocks) that will take around two hours. But this is not a simple enterprise – the jump-off point is the port of Carita, a 120-km (75-mi) drive from Jakarta that alone takes the best part of half a day. From there, it is possible to hire a dilapidated fishing boat out to the Krakatao Islands, for the unique pleasure of exploring the world's most violent volcano.

# Gunung Agung Volcano Scenic Route

The island of Bali is Indonesia's top tourist destination and – with stunning sandy beaches in white (to the south) or black (to the north) – it's easy to understand why so many people flock to this tropical paradise. And the island has a warm heart – the active volcano of Gunung Agung in East Bali's traditional Karangasem region, where local culture survives largely intact. This impressive peak rises above the mountains that form Bali's spine, towering to a height of 3,142 m (10,308 ft), and it is the site of Pura Besakih, Bali's sacred mother temple. The peak appears conical, but this fact actually conceals a massive summit crater. Strangely, Gunung Agung is covered in lush vegetation on the western side, whilst the eastern flank is barren.

The best way to appreciate the brooding presence of this mighty volcano is to drive (or cycle) the scenic route along Gunung Agung's southern side from Rendang to the village of Bebandem near Amlapura (there is no public transport to speak of). This delightful road runs through exceptional countryside with water flowing everywhere, descending gradually as it proceeds in an easterly direction.

Reached via an attractive minor road from Bangli, Rendang is a pretty little town. From there, the winding road passes through the village of Muncan, set amidst some of the most attractive rice country on the island. The next ports of call are Selat and Pura Pasa Agung – starting point for the easier southern hiking route up Gunung Agung (the northern route is tougher, and the two are entirely separate). The road continues through Duda, and Sibetan to Bebandem. From there, it's a short step to the bustling centre of Amlapura – this old royal town is still the capital of East Bali, though somewhat reduced in importance after being isolated for three years following Gunung Agung's last major eruption, in 1963.

*Rice fields below Mount Gunung Agung*

# Jakarta to Bandung

One striking landmark in the centre of Jakarta in West Java is Gambir Station, with its lime green ceramic façade. Built by the Dutch colonial authorities in the 1930s and recently renovated, this is the main starting point for long-distance trains to other major cities in the south and east – including one of Indonesia's most scenic railway journeys, the 180-km (110-mi) trip from Jakarta to Bandung.

The trains to choose between are the fully air-conditioned Argo Gede executive express and the Parahyangan executive and business class express (no air-con in the latter category, a feature which anyone who wilts in tropical heat will definitely miss!). These trains travel in daylight hours to ensure that visitors can appreciate the passing countryside. This is a rewarding exercise, as the route goes through some fabulous scenery. The Argo Gede is more expensive and faster, the Parahyangan slightly cheaper and slower.

To be sure of securing an A seat that delivers the best views on the outward journey (from the left side of the train) it is wise to book in advance. As the train begins its journey south from Jakarta, the outlook seems pleasant enough if rather ordinary – but don't demand your money back, as the most impressive landscapes will appear during the latter part of the trip, after the line starts climbing into the tranquil highlands. Along the way it passes through tunnels, also crossing spectacular viaducts, huge bridges and steel trestles constructed more than a century ago by Dutch engineers. The lush scenery has – to a degree – been shaped by man, with endless terraced rice paddies against a mountain backdrop.

Bustling Bandung is located in the highlands – a factor that made it a classic hill station in colonial times, where the Dutch could retreat to obtain cool relief from the sweltering lowlands.

*Crossing a high trestle-bridge near Bandung.*

**HOW:**
By train
**WHEN TO GO:**
Any time of year
**TIME IT TAKES:**
Just under three hours (by Argo Gede), three-and-a-half hours (by Parahyangan)
**HIGHLIGHTS:**
The Cibodas Botanical Garden at Cianjur – this fabulous garden at the foot of Mount Gede near Jakarta displays the tropical and highland flora of western Indonesia.
Factory shop outlets – find them everywhere in Indonesia (but especially Jakarta and Bandung).
The extraordinary Pasupati Bridge in Bandung, opened in 2005, boldly crosses above residential areas.
Bandung's wealth of fine colonial-era buildings erected by the Dutch, many in the splendid tropical Art Deco style.
**YOU SHOULD KNOW:**
Beware aggressive Madurese ticket touts at Gambir Station – use only the special offices that sell tickets for the luxury trains.

# Gunung Rinjani Trek

**HOW:**
On foot
**WHEN TO GO:**
April to November (to avoid the rainy season)
**TIME IT TAKES:**
Four days
**HIGHLIGHTS:**
Forest life – a huge variety of birds, butterflies and (if you're lucky) a glimpse of a rare black ebony leaf monkey.
Bathing away the aches and pains of a hard day's trekking in the hot springs of the crater lake.
Sunrise at the summit – the final climb is always done before dawn, so trekkers can enjoy the truly awe-inspiring sunrise.
**YOU SHOULD KNOW:**
The name 'Gunung Rinjani' comes from an old Chinese word meaning 'the place where a child was born' – and indeed a new caldera is rising within the summit lake.

One of the most spectacular volcanoes in Indonesia is Gunung Rinjani on the island of Lombok. The forested sides of the country's third-tallest mountain rise to a height of 3,726 m (12,224 ft) and the spectacular summit crater contains the vast, sacred lake of Segara Anak. Despite frequent eruptions, the lower slopes are intensely cultivated.

There are many well-used routes up Gunung Rinjani from surrounding villages, as locals believe the volcano is the abode of deities and make regular pilgrimages to the lake, where they leave offerings and try to bathe away illness in the hot springs. The most usual start point for a climb to the summit is Sembalun Lawang to the east.

For those who want more than a simple ascent, one of the best short expeditions in Southeast Asia is the Rinjani Trek from Senaru in the north, over the summit and down to Sembalun Lawang. Gunung Rinjani is a National Park, and this rewarding trek is a model for eco-tourism. The Rinjani Trek Centre in Senaru embodies a partnership between the National Park, local people and the tourist industry, which should ensure that – whilst this special place can be enjoyed by those prepared to make the effort – it will never be spoiled.

And effort is required, though any reasonably fit participant can undertake the tough challenge. This is a guided trek that involves overnight camping on the mountain. It begins with a steep ascent through tropical forest and alpine meadows to the Senaru crater rim. The route traverses the spectacular rim ridge and descends to the emerald crater lake, before climbing back up the steep crater to the Sembalun rim. From there it's a hard climb to the summit, before the final descent to Sembalun Lawang to complete a memorable adventure.

*The still active volcano rumbles on.*

# Puerto Princesa Subterranean River Trip

*Entering the cave at Sabang Beach.*

If you want to visit a UNESCO World Heritage Site like no other, the Puerto Princesa (sometimes Saint Paul's) Subterranean River National Park offers a unique experience. Located in the Saint Paul Mountains 50 km (30 mi) north of the city of Puerto Princesa on the island of Palawan, the Park consists of a dramatic limestone karst landscape with a full mountain-to-sea ecosystem that includes important forests.

But the star feature is undoubtedly the navigable underground river that winds through a cave before discharging directly into an aquamarine lagoon on the South China Sea, a fact that makes the lower reaches of the river tidal. Access is from Sabang Beach – but be warned: the last part of the journey there will rattle your teeth, as the unmade road is awful. Once at Sabang, a permit to travel the river is obtainable from the National Park office. A 30-minute boat ride with great landscape views takes you to the river entrance. Alternatively, this can be a pleasant 90-minute hike along the Monkey Trail that takes in a great swimming beach along the way (no swimming is permitted near the river mouth).

From there, the journey continues in an outrigger canoe, a single lamp illuminating the extraordinary geological formations of the lofty cavern within. The knowledgeable guide will be a mine of information on life within this wondrous place – including fish, bats and the swiftlets whose nests are coveted for soup – as he quietly paddles around showing you the best stalactites and stalagmites. Although 8 km (5 mi) of this hauntingly beautiful underground river has been mapped, only 4 km (2.5 mi) is deemed navigable. A special permit is required to explore the full navigable stretch, as the regular tour covers just 1.5 km (1 mi).

**HOW:**
By boat
**WHEN TO GO:**
Any time of year
**TIME IT TAKES:**
Around an hour for the basic river tour.
**HIGHLIGHTS:**
The leisurely 20-hour ship crossing from Manila's South Harbour to Palawan – a worthwhile journey in its own right.
Exploring the amazing forests and limestone formations to be found above ground in the National Park.
Getting up close to the extraordinary (and fearless) monitor lizards that frequent the forest and shoreline.
**YOU SHOULD KNOW:**
If you have a picnic in the National Park don't look away for a second – the long-tailed macaque monkeys are grand masters of food-theft strategy.

*Rice fields at Banaue*

# Banaue to Sagada By Road

Asia's cities are mostly dirty, crowded places full of frenetic activity, but the very opposite is true of vast swathes of the continent's unspoiled countryside, where life often seems to go on pretty much as it has for centuries. Nowhere is this contrast more obvious than on the island of Luzon. To the south is the sprawling metropolis of Manila complete with 14 million people, while to the north is the sparsely populated Cordillera mountain range that forms the island's spine.

Enjoying the unspoiled delights of the latter is no mean feat – by definition there is little tourist infrastructure and – far from the heavy hand of central government – the local Igorot people seem to be inclined to make sure that it stays that way. The two villages that must be seen are Banaue and Sagada. Reaching Banaue is a fairly major undertaking, with the usual method being jeep rental (with or without driver) in Manila, followed by an all-day drive. Be sure to make an early start, as Banaue shuts down for the night in the early evening.

The drive from Banaue to Sagada is awesome. The mountain scenery alone is breathtaking, with countless rushing streams and hilltops rolling away to the distant Mount Pulog, Luzon's highest point. But the bonus is the display of extraordinary rice terraces, created on the hillsides by Igorots over millennia. The road winds down into Bontoc Valley, and then makes the steep climb back up to Sagada, dramatically presented against a backdrop of limestone cliffs and pine forests.

It's more than tempting to make a full day of it, stopping to explore rice paddies, caves, forests and waterfalls, with a leisurely pause for a lunch of smoked meat, red rice and corn washed down with a glass (or two) of the local wine.

# Rice Terrace Hike

Once you've braved the difficulties of reaching the Cordilleras of northern Luzon, it's imperative to make the most of a very special place. The most striking feature of these mountains is provided by serried ranks of narrow rice terraces that climb the hillsides – now collectively listed as a UNESCO World Heritage Site. After allowing the high-maintenance terraced paddies to decline somewhat, the local Igorot people have found a new pride in their heritage following the UNESCO listing and a profitable trickle of tourists.

The way to appreciate fully the endeavour that went into creating and maintaining these extraordinary two-thousand-year-old man-made ledges is to get up close and personal by taking a hike. The paddies, with their high earthen walls, green pools and constantly trickling water, are often divided by bright red chongla plants. They are criss-crossed with paths and steps and there are numerous farms and dwellings that often look identical. It's easy to get disorientated, but local children are happy to act as guides for a few pesos and this is a worthwhile investment.

Having reached bustling Banaue, an onward trek to the less busy village of Batad shows the rice terraces at their very best. It is necessary to drive from Banaue to the Batad junction, and from there up to the Saddle, which is the jumping-off point for the hike. There is ample casual accommodation in the village, and it is best to stay overnight rather than make it a day trip – the return journey to the Saddle up the steep mountain path is strenuous and can take two hours or more. The village sits at the bottom of a natural amphitheatre formed by the curving, terraced hillsides, and the opportunity to stay for a while and do some exploring should not be missed.

**HOW:**
On foot
**WHEN TO GO:**
April or May when the swaying expanses of rice are at their pre-harvest best.
**TIME IT TAKES:**
About 90 minutes (by car) to the Saddle, then another 90 minutes from there down to Batad.
**HIGHLIGHTS:**
Extending the hike to the fabulous Tappiya Falls beyond Batad, where the superb outlook and a cooling swim will be a great reward for the climb.
A 15-minute side trip down steep steps from the Banaue-Sagada road to the unspoiled and traditional farming village of Bangaan amidst its own rice terraces.
Whilst in the Banaue area – a visit to Poitan, a village noted for artisan weaving and wood carving.
**YOU SHOULD KNOW:**
The rainy season (June to August) often makes roads and tracks in the area impassable.

*The rice terraces of Bangaan*

# Death Railway and the Bridge over the River Kwai

The journey along the infamous Death Railway and across the Kwai River Bridge is one of Thailand's best-known journeys, taken by thousands of people each year. Some simply want to experience the place, but others come to visit the spot where family members lost their lives.

In 1942, the Japanese needed an alternative supply route for their forces in Burma other than the dangerous sea voyage where they were under attack. They decided on a railway that had to be cut through difficult terrain of remote, jungle-clad hills. Tragically, there was an unlimited workforce to hand – 61,000 Allied prisoners of war, of whom 16,000 died here, and an enslaved population of some 200,000 Burmese, Thais, Malaysians and Indonesians, of whom 80,000 lost their lives.

Trains leave from Bangkok's Thonburi station, along the Death Railway line itself, reaching Kanchanaburi, before crossing the bridge. You can descend at the station just south of the Bridge and walk across the wooden planks, or just stay on board and rattle over at 10 km (6 mi) per hour. If you continue to the terminus at Nam Tok you will pass over the Wampo Viaduct, also POW-built. Looking at the lush vegetation and the tranquil river views it seems unimaginable that some of the worst horrors of war took place here less than 70 years ago.

About 80 km (50 mi) north of Kanchanaburi, on a section of line that has long been disused, is Hellfire Pass. Here the Australian Government, in collaboration with the Thais, has founded a museum and cleared a 7-km (4-mi) piece of track along which are memorial plaques to the fallen. Walkers leave mementos such as flowers, letters, even jars of vegemite: a sight that almost moves you to tears even if you have no direct involvement.

*Bridge over the River Kwai*

# Cheow Lan Lake and Nam Talu Cave

Located in Thailand's southern province of Surat Thani, roughly halfway between the country's two coastlines, is the wonderful Khao Sak National Park. Covering an area of 739 sq km (285 sq mi), the park comprises the largest area of ancient rainforest in southern Thailand, complete with stunning karst topography – the highest formation is 960 m (3,200 ft). There are several different trails within the park, but one of the most exciting is to explore Cheow Lan Lake and Nam Talu Cave.

Cheow Lan was formed when the Ratchaprapha Dam was built in 1982. Some 169 sq km (65 sq mi), it is surrounded by rainforest and limestone crags, and contains over 100 islands. Basing yourself at one of the simple, bamboo floating bungalow operations, you can enjoy a few days of swimming and exploring the lake by kayak or canoe,

This is the best way of viewing the wealth of wildlife in the surrounding forests, and admiring the multitudes of birds, in particular, hornbills – Helmeted, Great and Wreathed hornbills live here, along with kingfishers, parrots, flycatchers, herons and many more. Sitting quietly in a small cove, you'll see gibbons and macaques in the trees nearby, apparently totally unconcerned by the presence of humans.

Your local guide will take you through the rainforest to Nam Talu cave. After beaching the kayak, you walk for a couple of kilometres looking out for tree snakes, orchids and otters, which inhabit the stream that winds its way through the jungle, to the 30-m (99-ft) entrance, inside which you will see stalactites, stalagmites and eroded stone formations. Thousands of bats inhabit this cave, which takes 90 minutes to walk through, but be warned: a stream runs through it, waist deep in parts, which has to be waded through.

*Canoe and raft house on
Cheow Lan Lake*

**HOW:**
On foot and by kayak
**WHEN TO GO:**
December to April
**TIME IT TAKES:**
1 to 3 days or more
**HIGHLIGHTS:**
The extraordinarily diverse rainforest –
tall trees, bamboo, ferns, lianas, etc.
The rich and varied wildlife, including
wild Asian elephants.
Rafflesia kerri – the second largest
flower in the world.
The reflections of the islands and
surrounding limestone peaks in the
calm, green water of the lake.
**YOU SHOULD KNOW:**
The region receives a great deal of
rain, so bring good walking shoes,
insect repellent, sunscreen, and a
change of clothing in case you get
soaked. In 2007 six tourists and two
guides were drowned in a flash flood
in Nam Talu Cave – take advice and
use your own common sense before
going there.

**HOW:**
By train
**WHEN TO GO:**
All year round, but best between
October and April
**TIME IT TAKES:**
About one hour from end to end
**HIGHLIGHTS:**
The views over Bangkok from the
elevated trains.
The welcome respite from the
heat.
Nipping up to Mo Chit station on
the Sukhumvit line to visit
Chatuchak Weekend Market.
Saphan Taksin Station where you
can join an express boat and take
a trip on the river.
Siam station, where you can
change lines or jump out and walk
to one of the many shopping malls
for some retail therapy.
**YOU SHOULD KNOW:**
Bangkok now has a super modern
metro that covers different areas
to the Skytrain. There are currently
three interchanges with Skytrain,
and the metro does go to Hua
Lamphong, the main train station.

# Bangkok Skytrain

The Skytrain has changed the face of travel in Bangkok. It used to be a nightmare of a city where one could easily spend two hours travelling a distance of about 5 km (3 mi) because the weight of traffic was bringing the whole place to a grinding halt. All this changed on 5 December 1999, King Bhumibol's birthday, when the Skytrain opened.

Approached by stairs and escalators, the ultra-modern elevated stations are airy, spacious, clean and safe. The platforms are marked to show where the carriage doors will open and, at rush hour, passengers queue up behind one another at these entry points, rather than filling the whole space. Inside there is plenty of sitting and standing room, and air-conditioning ensures a pleasant temperature even when it is sweltering outside.

After a slow start, the Skytrain has really taken off, carrying passengers throughout the day, from 6.00 am to midnight. Apart from the miracle of being able to get around speedily, the train is fun to be on. Passengers get a fascinating, bird's eye view of the city. Not only is one amazed by the vast quantity of skyscrapers, a symphony of chrome, steel, glass and concrete but, in amongst the hyper-modernity are glimpses of ancient temples, their sweeping roofs glittering red and gold in the sunlight, housing stock that varies from villas with flower-decked gardens to slums whose grimy windows are cheek by jowl with the track, advertising hoardings, monuments, traffic circulating and Thais going about their business.

Several of the stations are linked to 'skywalks', elevated walkways leading to nearby shopping malls and other amenities such as the National Stadium, the Chao Praya River and the wonderful Chatuchak Weekend Market. The Skytrain, due to be extended, will eventually cross the river to Thonburi, and run out to Bangkok's new airport.

# Maeklong Railway – Bangkok to Samut Songkhram

*The Damnoen Saduak Floating Market*

Built privately around the turn of the last century, the Maeklong Railway brought seafood from the fishing ports of Samut Sakhon and Samut Songkram to Bangkok – a distance of about 75 km (47 mi). The line was never connected to the main rail system, no longer carries freight, and is one of the capital's better-kept secrets.

Leaving from Bangkok's west bank Wong Wian Yai station, take the train to Mahachai. Trundling along a single narrow track, you soon leave the city behind and find yourself in a fertile landscape of coconut palms, banana plants, lychee, guava and white pomelo orchards, interspersed with canals. There are numerous tiny stations along the way – blink and you'll miss them – and the train slows as it approaches barrier-free road crossings, so the driver can check that there is no approaching traffic.

Mahachai, confusingly, is the station for Samut Sakhon. Renowned for its fish, it has a fabulous fresh seafood market and a multitude of restaurants. It is also where you leave the train to take a small ferry across the Tha Chin River to the station on the other side. Here you take another train to Samut Songkhram's Maeklong terminus. This second section of line passes through an area of salt production and prawn farms. Sitting on the left side, you see fields full of shallow, saltwater ponds. When drained, the salt is raked into piles, bagged up and sent off by road.

All too soon the journey comes to an end – but this is almost the best bit, as the line goes through the middle of a large, colourful market. Stallholders clear awnings and goods from the track as the train approaches, putting them all back together again the moment it has passed, like the sea closing behind the wake of a ship.

# Scenic Route to Chiang Dao Caves

The lovely northern city of Chiang Mai makes an excellent base for many different explorations. For this journey you'll need your own transport, to enable you to enjoy a roundabout journey to the Chiang Dao Caves, taking in some unusual, and un-touristy places en route.

Travelling north from Chiang Mai, take Route 107 – you'll soon see a sign to your left pointing to the Hill Tribe Museum. Set in Rama IX Lanna Park, which also contains a golf course, shooting range, fishing lake and the city's racecourse, this interesting little museum contains a wealth of information about Thailand's six main hill tribes as well as other, minor tribal groups. Continuing north you will find the Model Centre of Learning, a project where young Thais learn various handicrafts, and where visitors can see how raw cotton and silk are turned into beautiful lengths of fabric.

The next stop on your journey is the Dara Pirom Palace, former home of Princess Dara Rasamee and an absolute gem of a place, full of fascinating personal effects and objects that give an insight into the royal lifestyle as it was lived about 100 years ago. Further north still and you turn off onto the small Route 3010, winding through the forest to the much-revered Four Buddhas' Temple. Redeveloped over the years, it stands in a tranquil forest setting, little visited by foreigners.

Finally, return to the main road, and head to Chiang Dao. You'll pass an elephant training camp on the way – well worth a visit if you have time. The cave complex is well signed and much visited: there are 100 named caves here, stretching over 10 km (6 mi) into the mountain. Currently only five can be explored, and you'll need to take a guide with a lantern for three of them.

*Elephant camp near Chiang Dao*

**HOW:**
By car
**WHEN TO GO:**
Any time but October to April is probably best.
**TIME IT TAKES:**
This is a day trip
**HIGHLIGHTS:**
Doi Suthep, Chiang Mai's 1676-m (5,500-ft) peak, with its sacred temple, winter palace and delightful National Park.
Trekking in the mountains north of Chiang Mai.
Rafting on the Kok River from Fang.
Pai – this is some peoples idea of heaven.
**YOU SHOULD KNOW:**
North east of Chiang Mai is the area known as the Golden Triangle, where Thailand, Burma and Laos meet, and where many of the world's opium poppies are grown. These days you'll notice the tourists rather than the opium dens, but it is still exciting to stand in one country and see two more across the river.

479

*The red roofs of Lang Co village*

# Hue to Hoi An on Highway 1

**HOW:**
By car
**WHEN TO GO:**
January to April
**TIME IT TAKES:**
4 – 5 hours
**HIGHLIGHTS:**
The Cham Museum, founded in 1915, with its wonderful selection of ethnic sculpture and carving dating from the 7th to 15th centuries.
The Bach Ma National Park, 40 km (25 mi) south of Hue – a mountain nature reserve with waterfalls, lush vegetation and superb coastal views.
A stop at the fabulous Lang Co beach south of Hue, with the great backdrop of the Rang Cua Mountains.
The thousand stone-carving craftsmen of Non Nuoc village at the foot of the Marble Mountains near Da Nang.
**YOU SHOULD KNOW:**
Take a half-empty suitcase and buy some custom-made 'designer' clothes in Hoi An – the many skilled local tailors can copy anything (from a magazine picture) at bargain prices.

The Hue, Da Nang and Hoi An coastal strip is one of the most-visited areas in Vietnam, with a great deal to offer. It is close to the former DMZ (Demilitarized Zone) between the old North and South, which were divided by the Ben Hai River. Much of the fighting in the 1960s Vietnam War took place thereabouts, and many interesting relics of that traumatic time remain to this day.

The Vietnamese Imperial City of Hue suffered serious damage in the conflict, but this UNESCO World Heritage Site remains a fascinating place that merits exploration. Hue is also the starting point for the drive south along Highway 1 via Da Nang to Hoi An. This magnificent coastal route is in much better shape than many roads in Vietnam, twisting and turning above the sea and rising to a dramatic high point at the Hai Van Pass (though a tunnel is under construction) where the panoramic view is sensational.

After crossing the pass, it's worth stopping at Da Nang to relax for a while on the splendid China Beach – though in fact there are other, rather more cultural side trips to consider here. These include the World Heritage Site of My Son, centre of the ancient kingdom of Cham and the extraordinary Marble Mountains, which are sculpted limestone hills containing pagodas, temples and grottos dedicated to Buddhist, Taoist and Confucian divinities.

Upon completing the scenic journey to Hoi An, the first thing to do is to explore the quaint old town, yet another World Heritage Site – be sure not to miss the Hoi An Museum, Phuc Kien Communal House, the Japanese Covered Bridge and the ancient Vietnamese houses. Another worthwhile outing is up the Thu Bon River to see traditional boatbuilding, woodworking and pottery-making villages like Kim Bong and Thanh Ha.

# Heaven's Gate Pass

Fancy going to Heaven...on a bicycle? It can be arranged in Vietnam's Northern Highlands, also known as the Tonkinese Alps, where one of the most scenic bike rides in South-east Asia can be experienced. The Heaven's Gate Pass (Tram Tom in local parlance) is the literal high point, but for those who want more it's possible to plan a longer guided trip that will tour through hill country along the Chinese border – a place populated by tribes with a distinctive culture that wear beautiful local dress and have definitely not been turned into hustlers by the few tourist dollars that have come their way.

To undertake this marvelous cycle ride, first take the overnight train from Hanoi across the Red River and on to Lao Cai. From there, a minibus will convey you and your trusty steed up through an impressive landscape of rice terraces to the picturesque village of Sa Pa, below Heaven's Gate. The onward climb from Sa Pa is steep, but the effort is worthwhile – after a refreshing pause at the Silver Waterfall, 3 km (2 mi) from the summit, more physical effort gets you to the top of the world...and the considerable rewards for Herculean pedal-pushing.

You've reached the summit of the highest pass in Indochina, and the views of mountains and the Hoang Lien Valley below are breathtaking (assuming you've got any breath left to take). Having made it to the top, it's possible to turn around and let gravity hurry you back down to Lao Cai. Alternatively, you can coast down the far side into a land of precipitous rice paddies, remote traditional villages, rickety suspension bridges, stilt houses and ox carts. For those who love wild and unspoiled places, that is indeed a heavenly journey.

**HOW:**
By bike
**WHEN TO GO:**
March to May or September to November
**TIME IT TAKES:**
4-5 hours of hard pedaling from Sa Pa to the summit of Heaven's Gate Pass.
**HIGHLIGHTS:**
Sa Pa's Bac Ha bustling market for a slice of local life at its most authentic...and colourful.
Village-made tamarind candy – washed down with a slug of cassava, the local firewater.
A trip to Hoang Lien National Park near Sa Pa, where one of the most diverse landscapes and ecosystems in Indochina is being preserved.
The wonderful view of the lofty Fansipan peak from the summit of Heaven's Gate (assuming it isn't shrouded in mist!).
**YOU SHOULD KNOW:**
Don't be surprised if you get smiles from the locals that cause you to do a double take – the women of the local Lu tribe dye their teeth black.

*The terraced farmland around Sa Pa*

# Hanoi Unification Express

**HOW:**
By train
**WHEN TO GO:**
Any time of year.
**TIME IT TAKES:**
Between 30 hours and 41 hours depending on the choice of train.
**HIGHLIGHTS:**
A side trip to Cu Chi, the impressive underground tunnel network used by the Viet Cong during the Vietnam War.
Taking a welcome break at Nha Trang to enjoy the fabulous white-sand beach before resuming the journey.
The scenic section through the mountains alongside the Hai Van Pass and along the coast to Hue.
Exploring Hanoi, the refined city of delightful colonial architecture and traditional charm.
**YOU SHOULD KNOW:**
Carry your papers at all times in Vietnam – especially when trying to buy a train ticket, which will cost foreigners double the local price.

*All aboard!*

This is a train journey that time forgot. The term 'express' is used loosely, as in averaging around 50 kph (30 mph) as opposed to the 15 kph (10 mph) achieved by local trains on the single track connecting Ho Chi Minh City (formerly Saigon) to Hanoi in the north. This amazing 1,725-km (1,100-mi) railroad was built by the French along Vietnam's coastal spine a century ago and passes through wonderful countryside, though in truth the real reason for riding the Unification Express is to experience a railway journey like no other. There are four trains a day in each direction, ranging from the slow to the very slow. For all that, the service is reliable and does get there eventually.

Rolling stock is old-fashioned (with crude toilets amongst other drawbacks) and the train will be hot and crowded. There is a choice of seat (hard or not-very-soft) and sleeper (yes, hard or not-very-soft). Possessions left unwatched for a second will vanish like smoke in the wind. There will be frequent stops on sidings to allow trains to pass in the opposite direction and hordes of hustlers selling everything from food and drink to fake designer goods will appear at every stop. But this is a fascinating and worthwhile journey that will not only convey you through beautiful scenery, but also provide the opportunity to meet the people and experience the reality of Vietnamese life.

For those who don't want to experience the rough-and-tumble of an end-to-end journey on the Unification Express, there are organized guided tours that make use of the train with plenty of stop-offs and side trips to see selected sights along the way. In any event it is possible to break the journey without penalty for a little self-chosen exploration.

# Perfume River Dragon Boat Trip

*A Dragon Boat on the Perfume River*

Though not yet described as 'The Venice of the East', the imperial city of Hue – former capital of Vietnam's Nguyen Dynasty – is divided by the Perfume River and has numerous canals. So taking to the water is a great way to see the city's sights, and the famed Hue Dragon Boats – the local motorized equivalent of Venetian gondolas – are the way to travel. These long-tailed, brightly painted boats ply the Perfume River, and most do indeed have some resemblance to those fearsome if mythical fire-breathers, though tending to be of rather haphazard construction.

It's possible to enjoy the Dragon Boat experience by taking one as though it were a water taxi. Any trip around town will have the added dimension of revealing the sights and sounds of Hue's busy river life, with houseboats everywhere, laden sampans heading for market or undertaking another important mission like sand dredging...and of course there are more of those in-your-face Dragon Boats at every turn. This in itself is a worthwhile outing.

But the Hue area has many fascinating monuments and historical sights, and a Dragon Boat journey up river through lush countryside is a splendid way of visiting some of the best. There are many options to choose from, but a typical tour will include the Linh Mu (Thien Mu) Pagoda, Hon Chen Temple, Tu Duc Tomb, Emperor Minh Mang's Tomb amidst tranquil gardens and lakes and Khai Dinh Tomb. Some require a moto-taxi from the bank and the stops (usually 30 to 45 minutes) are not long enough to allow proper exploration, as these tombs are often large complexes. However, the Dragon Boat trip is an experience in its own right, and it's always possible to return on another day and spend more time at particular sights.

**HOW:**
By boat
**WHEN TO GO:**
Any time (January to April is best; from June to August it sometimes rains very hard).
**TIME IT TAKES:**
Around eight hours for a typical day tour by Dragon Boat.
**HIGHLIGHTS:**
A Dragon Boat ride to Thuan An Beach for a bit of typical tropical sun-sea-and-sand relaxation.
Sunset over the Perfume River – take a stroll beside the river as night falls for a wonderfully romantic light show.
A side trip to the Imperial Citadel of the Nguyen Dynasty, damaged by American bombing during the Tet Offensive of 1968 but partially restored and still mightily impressive.
**YOU SHOULD KNOW:**
The Perfume River is so named from the traditional ritual of scattering flower petals on the water.

# Saigon to Angkor Wat

**HOW:**
By bike
**WHEN TO GO:**
November to February
**TIME IT TAKES:**
Allow at least 10 days, with a day each in Phnom Penh and Angkor Wat.
**HIGHLIGHTS:**
A visit to the extraordinary Caodai Great Temple at Tay Ninh, headquarters of Caodaism, one of Vietnam's most interesting religions.
A tour of Phnom Penh, 'The Pearl of Asia' – Cambodia's capital with its wonderful Khmer temples and classic colonial architecture.
Taking a side trip into the beautiful Kiriom National Park with its pine forests, orchids, waterfalls and the Cham Bok Pagoda.
The temples of Angkor Wat, abandoned for centuries, rediscovered in the 1800s and justifiably regarded as one of the wonders of the world.
**YOU SHOULD KNOW:**
If cycling isn't your thing, the Saigon-Angkor Wat journey can be done on water, cruising up the mighty Mekong and along the Tonlé Sap River.

Don't be afraid to refer to Ho Chi Minh City as Saigon – most of the local people still do. And it's from Saigon that one of Indochina's great cycling expeditions begins, taking the adventurous pedal-pusher from the former capital of South Vietnam through the Mekong Delta and on to the drier country and contrasting sights of Cambodia, ending at the ancient city of Angkor Wat. This fabulous testament to the Khmer civilization was built between the 9th and 12th centuries and is now a stunning UNESCO World Heritage Site.

With proper planning this can be a solo journey, though it does involve travelling light, buying provisions and finding accommodation as you go. It is also possible to find organized groups who are undertaking this marathon ride, where kit can be sent on ahead to pre-booked overnight stops – these are often sponsored trips arranged by charities. There are endless choices of route to follow, but one well tried and proven journey is from Saigon via My Tho, Tra Vinh, Can Tho, Long Xuyen, Chau Doc, Nha Bang (on the Cambodian border), Takeo, Phnom Penh, Tang Krasang and Phumi Loveay to Siem Riep (from whence to Angkor Wat).

This scenic route is not physically demanding, as the countryside is fairly flat. It weaves through rubber plantations, crosses rivers and passes through the paddy fields and lush countryside of the Mekong Delta before crossing into Cambodia – a land of traditional villages, busy markets, ancient temples and colourful pagodas. The locals do not see many foreigners, and those who venture into remote country areas on uncrowded back roads are invariably the subjects of great curiosity, especially to children. But the interesting passers-by from another world are invariably received with warmth and hospitality in these rural backwaters.

*Cyclists at sunrise, with Angkor Wat in the background*

# Ho Chi Minh Trail

The Ho Chi Minh Trail began in North Vietnam, cut through the mountains and wound its way hundreds of miles south through both Laos and Cambodia and the various mountain passes along the way enabled access to South Vietnam. It was not simply a single road, but a maze of up to 19,000 km (12,000 mi) of trails passing through triple canopy jungle, karst mountains and open grassland.

This remarkable route enabled troops, arms and supplies to be moved south towards Saigon. As much of it was invisible from the air, the USA began a massive, secret campaign of bombing and defoliation, particularly in Laos, a country with which they were not at war. Between 1964 and 1973, over two million tonnes of bombs were dropped on Laos, making it the most heavily bombed country in history. Absolutely no reparations were offered subsequently, leaving eastern parts of Laos littered with UXO (unexploded ordnance) that kills and maims people to this day.

It is possible to travel on parts of the trail in Laos, by mountain bike, motorbike or 4x4, but you must take a guide, and follow the route faithfully – exploring here could be fatal. Starting from Xepon, you can go as far north as the Mu Gia Pass, travelling through beautiful, mountainous rainforest, across rickety log bridges over rivers, past tribal villages where, for a small contribution, you may be able to stay the night. Along the way you will see the debris of war – burnt out tanks, heavy artillery, scattered UXO and bomb craters. You will also see flowers planted in bomb casings, fences made from war detritus, tank treads used as bridges, and you will meet some amazing people, most of whom, remarkably, seem to hold no grudge.

**HOW:**
By bike, motorbike or 4x4
**WHEN TO GO:**
November to March
**TIME IT TAKES:**
Anywhere between one day and two weeks depending on how far you want to go.
**HIGHLIGHTS:**
Visit the UXO office in Xepon, view the collection of disabled ordnance here and talk to the experts who are clearing this deadly inheritance.
See the enormous Australian/Lao goldmine outside Xepon.
Visit the village of Ban Dong, on the Laos/Vietnam border, site of a major battle.
Enjoy the fabulous journey through the forest, the birds, butterflies and tropical flowers you will see, and thank your lucky stars bombs are not raining down on your head.
**YOU SHOULD KNOW:**
The Ho Chi Minh trail was so named by Americans, after the North Vietnamese president, who came to be known as Uncle Ho. He oversaw the end of the French Indo-Chinese Empire, but died in Hanoi in 1969 without seeing America defeated and Vietnam re-united.

*Rice fields amid the bomb craters in Khammouane along the Ho Chi Minh Trail*

*Tourist boats line up outside Pak Ou Cave.*

# Mekong River Voyage – Huay Xai to Luang Prabang

**HOW:**
By boat
**WHEN TO GO:**
November to March
**TIME IT TAKES:**
Two days and one night
**HIGHLIGHTS:**
The Bokeo gem mines near Houay Xai.
The views over the river from the slow boat.
The Pak Ou Buddha Caves, 25 km (16 mi) up-river from Luang Prabang.
The exquisite temple complex of Wat Xiang Thong, possibly the most beautiful in the whole of Laos.
**YOU SHOULD KNOW:**
Apart from slow boats and speedboats (very uncomfortable and rather dangerous), there is at least one other more expensive and more comfortable cruise boat you can book. Right down in southern Laos, there are other Mekong River journeys to be taken, from Pakse down to Si Phan Don.

Since Laos re-opened its borders to westerners in the late 1980s, the Mekong River voyage from Houay Xai to Luang Prabang has become an absolute classic. Crossing the river from Thailand takes a matter of minutes, and you will soon find the 'slow boats' that will carry you downstream.

These are either cargo boats with enclosed sides, or riverboats that have a roof but are open-sided – the better choice. The luggage is stored at one end, and passengers sit on narrow, wooden benches that get less comfortable the longer you sit on them – take a cushion or something to sit on if at all possible. Bring your own food and drink – you can buy drinks on board but of course they are more expensive than they should be.

Discomfort notwithstanding, it is perfectly lovely to be on the Mekong. Most of the passengers are young backpackers, and the atmosphere is sociable. You pass few villages en route, but you'll see fishermen on the river and people on the sandy beaches – tiny glimpses of local life – as well as lovely, riverside scenery. Arriving at the village of Pak Ben, your overnight stop, there seem to be more foreigners in Pak Ben than there are locals – all the slow boats stop here – and it's crammed with guesthouses, small shops and eateries.

In the morning, off you go again on this peaceful voyage: the sound of the water slipping past is hypnotic, though occasionally broken by noisy speedboats that complete the trip in a few hours. As you reach your destination, more villages and fantastic vegetable plots at the river's edge can be seen. The Mekong is wide and beautiful at Luang Prabang, with temples visible on each bank, and you'll be glad to reach dry land once more.

# Siem Reap to Battambang

In the northwestern rice-growing region, Battambang is Cambodia's second largest town, an interesting place with an old-fashioned provincial atmosphere as yet unaffected by the invasion of mass tourism. The architecture is a mixture of traditional Cambodian and French colonial, with streets shared by motorcycles, cars and horse-drawn vehicles. And for those who wish to see unspoiled rural Cambodia there couldn't be a better starting point – within a short distance of the town is a timeless land of small villages, rice paddies and farmland. There also may be found Angkorian ruins, pagodas, waterfalls and caves.

Interesting though Battambang may be, the real attraction is getting to the place by boat from Siem Reap – a trip generally considered to be Cambodia's most scenic river journey. A ferry leaves at 7 o'clock every morning, following a picturesque route across the northern tip of Tonlé Sap and up the Sangker River.

The Tonlé Sap becomes Asia's largest lake when it quadruples in size during the rainy season. It is a huge expanse of water that makes a vital contribution to the Cambodian economy, and the banks are lined with fishing communities. From there, the ferry enters the winding Sangker River and follows it for 40 km (25 mi) upstream to Battambang, through fields and forest, passing numerous villages before the boat moors at the first of three bridges in the town.

Apart from passing through splendid scenery, this fascinating journey is part of everyday Cambodian life. The Sangker (unlike the Mekong River) has no tourist boats and the ferry is a genuine local service. Water is the lifeblood of the local communities, and at every turn there will be something new to see along the bank – and there will be frequent stops for sampans that have urgent business with the crowded ferry.

**HOW:**
By boat
**WHEN TO GO:**
March to October to avoid the rainy season (though it makes the boat trip longer and less predictable).
**TIME IT TAKES:**
4-8 hours by boat from Siem Reap to Battambang, depending on water conditions.
**HIGHLIGHTS:**
Riding a Bamboo Train – with typical creative flair, these bamboo carts powered by a motorcycle engine chug along the regular rail tracks transporting people, animals and cargo, before being whipped off the line when a proper train comes along.
The intriguing floating village of Prek Tol, outside Battambang – actually, most of the houses are on tall stilts.
A side trip to the fabled temples of Angkor Wat from Siem Reap.
**YOU SHOULD KNOW:**
The boats from Siem Reap are rickety (expect frequent breakdowns) but the risk is worth taking – this is indeed a memorable journey.

*The floating village of Chong Kneas on Tonlé Sap Lake*

# Selangor River Cruise

**HOW:**
By boat
**WHEN TO GO:**
April to October
**TIME IT TAKES:**
The 'Firefly Cruise'
usually lasts for
around 45 minutes.
**HIGHLIGHTS:**
Touring the twin forts of Kuala Selangor,
originally built to guard the mouth of
the Selangor River in the early 16th
century and subsequently expanded.
The village of Tanjung Keramat with its
picturesque lake and the fast vanishing
ruins of another major fort.
A visit to the Kuala Selangor Nature
Park, home to a huge variety of wildlife
including numerous species of resident
and migratory birds.
Wonderful local seafood – eat lunch or
dinner (or buy at the market) at the
fishing village of Pasir Penambang at
the mouth of the Selangor River.
**YOU SHOULD KNOW:**
Fireflies are lit up by the rare chemical
luciferin, which scientists have
synthesized for use in important
medical research.

Despite intensive exploitation of Malaysia's abundant natural resources, many of this fascinating country's estuaries, rivers and jungles remain unspoiled – for now, so perhaps it's a case of 'catch them while you can'. One of Malaysia's natural wonders that you can't catch – but can definitely see – is the display put on as night falls by the fireflies (kelip kelip) that feed on the nectar of mangrove trees (berembang) near the mouth of the Selangor River. Colonies gather in individual trees and flash rapidly in unison as the insects seek mates.

A new dam upriver has disturbed the habitat and numbers are dwindling. Even so, this is still an amazing light show. Proceed to Kuala Selangor, northwest of Kuala Lumpur. This once-sleepy town has started to show signs of tourist exploitation, but there is tasteful accommodation to be found on the riverbank for those who wish to stay over and explore the area's other attractions. But the main event is undoubtedly staged by the fireflies, which are actually small Lampyridae beetles.

Starting points for river cruises are the villages of Kampung Kuantan and Bukit Belimbing, where it is possible to embark on a small rowboat (tongkang) after 7.30 pm (though in the way of these things some cruises are now propelled by silent electric outboard motors). Most of the 'flashers' have found a mate and switched off by late evening but in the meantime the synchronised, rhythmic (three flashes a second) display of blinking green lights puts the average Christmas tree to shame. No flash photography, noise or torchlight is permitted during the cruise, to ensure that the habitat of the fireflies is not unduly disturbed. For the most impressive display, it is wise to avoid rainy evenings and those when the moon is near full.

*The Selangor River*

# Taman Negara Expedition

One of the finest jewels in Malaysia's somewhat tarnished ecological crown is the vast and ancient (it's 130 million years old) rainforest within the Taman Negara National Park, in the formidable Titiwangsa Mountains of Pahang State. The Park has been protected for seventy years and remains a treasure trove of Mother Nature's riches – with undisturbed habitats and wonderful flora and fauna that have evolved undisturbed over countless millennia. This magical place may be reached by bus from Kuala Lumpur, with the final leg by boat from Kuala Tembeling Jetty. Once in the Park, it is possible to stay in an eco-friendly lodge, of which there are several.

The high point (literally) of any visit to Taman Negara is a journey along the extraordinary Canopy Walkway. This apparently flimsy ropewalk looks as though it's been there for generations, but is of fairly recent construction and is entirely safe. At 510 m (1,675 ft) it's the world's longest, weaving through the very tops of the trees at a height of 45 m (150 ft) to give a unique view of a sunlit jungle world that can only be guessed at from ground level.

But that's not all Taman Negara has to offer. There is a great variety of animal life within the Park – including headline species like elephants, tigers, leopards, sun bears and Sumatran rhino – but these are shy and rarely seen. However, long-tailed macaque monkeys are a common sight and there is plenty of visible bird life (over 300 species recorded), plus reptiles aplenty. The adventurous visitor can undertake guided jungle treks by day or night, stroll along marked nature trails or even shoot the rapids on the Tembeling River. Rewarding though these activities may be, it's that swaying journey through the treetops that will be truly memorable!

**HOW:**
On foot
**WHEN TO GO:**
March to October
**TIME IT TAKES:**
Around half an hour to complete an aerial journey along the Canopy Walkway.
**HIGHLIGHTS:**
A night of animal watching from a hide – to give visitors the best chance of observing larger animals, there are a number of observation hides overlooking clearings and salt licks. Visiting a settlement occupied by the semi-nomadic Batek people, who still practise their traditional way of life as hunter-gatherers within the Park. The ear-shaped Gua Telingga Cave near the little town of Kuala Tahan.
**YOU SHOULD KNOW:**
Taman Negara was King George V National Park until the name was changed following independence – *taman negara* translating as (surprise!) 'national park'.

*Steady nerves are needed on this tree-top jungle walkway.*

489

# Cameron Highlands Road

After driving north from Kuala Lumpur for 90 minutes on the modern Expressway, take the turn-off for the town of Tapah and discover another world. For this is the gateway to the Cameron Highlands, named after a certain William Cameron who appreciated in the 1880s that these fertile mountains would be ideal for growing tea. The slopes were soon covered in plantations, and the British, who supervised humid lowland rubber plantations and tin mines, soon discovered that the cooler Highlands provided an ideal summer retreat.

Today, relaxing colonists have been replaced by holidaymaking city dwellers who also appreciate the cool, fresh climate. The journey up into the Highlands from Tapah is a drive to remember, as the old road (Route 59) is very narrow, twisting and turning sharply through beautiful scenery. The tea industry remains, but today all sorts of vegetables, fruit (especially strawberries) and flowers are grown on farms mixed in with tea plantations in the hilly green landscape. The route goes through Ringlet, Habu and Tanah Rata to Brinchang.

Until recently, this was the only way into the hills, though there is now access from the north and east, so it's possible to enter or leave the Highlands via Gunung Brinchang (to the west) or Tringkap (to the east). This improved access will be sure to increase tourist and commercial pressure. There is already some modern tourist development, but for now the Cameron Highlands preserve much of their original character, with many bungalows from the colonial era still standing in stunning hillside locations. But the Highlands are becoming so popular that (even with the new roads) traffic is often slow-moving or at a standstill. To dodge the busiest times, plan a journey that avoids local school holidays – especially the long Christmas break from mid-November through December.

*A tea estate in the Cameron Highlands*

# Penang Ferry

*The ferry sets out for Penang Island.*

In the 1780s, the port of Penang was established on the tropical island of the same name by Captain Francis Light of the British East India Company. From small beginnings, this strategically located Malaysian port in the Malacca Straits has become a major Far Eastern commercial centre with Freeport status. The capital of Penang State – George Town – is on the island, along with extensive port facilities and numerous high-tech industries. Railway access is to Butterworth at the mouth of the Perai River, facing Penang across a 3-km (2-mi) channel.

From there, there's only one way for self-respecting travellers to proceed to Penang Island – by ferry (though in truth it is now possible to get there via a modern road bridge). The famous Penang vehicle and passenger ferry service is the oldest in Malaysia, having been established in 1920, and has long enjoyed iconic status. It connects the Sultan Abdul Halim ferry terminal near the station in Butterworth to the Raja Tun Uda terminal in George Town. The fleet of eight double-decker ferries constantly plies the waters of Penang's port from early morning until well after midnight. Once known as 'The Big Yellow Ferry', the boats have recently been repainted in an assortment of bright colours – oranges, yellows, reds, blues and greens – making them an even more distinctive feature of the busy waterway.

From the ferry's top deck there is an excellent view of the impressive 13.5-km (8-mi) Penang Bridge. The 21st-century skyline of George Town is not up to New York standards, though this is undoubtedly a work in progress. But still ferry voyagers enjoy one of the world's great 'must see from the water' sights – the historic town (yet another one known as 'The Pearl of the Orient') set against the timeless forested hills of the island's interior.

**HOW:**
By boat
**WHEN TO GO:**
November to March, June and July
**TIME IT TAKES:**
Around 15 minutes
**HIGHLIGHTS:**
Penang Bird Park (Taman Burung Perang) in Butterworth – for a fabulous display of over 300 bird species from South-east Asia.
In George Town – Beach Street and the streets leading off it, at the heart of the old colonial commercial quarter.
Fort Cornwallis – an old star-shaped fort on the north-eastern coast of Penang Island, rebuilt in 1804.
**YOU SHOULD KNOW:**
It's only necessary to pay on the outward ferry journey – the return trip from Penang Island is free.

# Mount Kinabalu Trek

The two-day trek up Mount Kinabalu in the Malaysian state of Sabah on Borneo follows a well-trodden path, but this doesn't mean it's easy. The mountain is located in Kinabalu National Park, a World Heritage Site noted for extraordinary biodiversity. Kinabalu is South-east Asia's fourth-highest mountain at 4,095 m (13,345 ft). The freezing summit at Low's Peak may be reached by anyone who is physically fit, without mountaineering equipment. However, the climb may be attempted only with an experienced local guide. The journey begins with a stay at Park Headquarters, followed by a walk or minibus transfer to Timophon Gate at 1,800 m (5,900 ft). From there, the route continues up to the Laban Rata Guesthouse at 3,300 m (10,800 ft). Supplies to the hut are carried by porters, so that trekkers can enjoy a few basic home comforts like hot food, drinks and showers before attempting the final climb the next day. Some start to suffer altitude sickness at this height and should on no account continue the ascent.

The trek is quite often timed so climbers arrive at Laban Rata around dusk, to enjoy the fabulous sunsets and skyscapes, with an early start the following morning delivering a magnificent sunrise over the mountains, sometimes above the clouds. The final stretch to the summit is mainly over bare granite rock and – once there – panoramic views on a clear day are magnificent. The descent is steep and trekkers are more likely to suffer injury (happily usually minor) coming down than going up.

There is now an alternative route – the rugged Mesilau Trail – from the Mesilau resort some 15 km (9 mi) from Park HQ. This newer summit trail up the other side of Mount Kinabalu is much more challenging than the established route and thus appeals to those with a sense of adventure.

*A hiker in Kinabalu National Park*

**HOW:**
On foot
**WHEN TO GO:**
March to October
**TIME IT TAKES:**
Four to six hours for the ascent to Timophon Gate, two to four hours from Laban Rata Guesthouse to the summit (spread over two days).
**HIGHLIGHTS:**
Plants galore – Kinabalu National Park is full of rare (often unique) plants.
A trip to Poring, 40 km (25 mi) to the southeast of Park HQ – for a great view of the mountain, hot springs, a butterfly farm, orchid centre and canopy walkway.
A side trip to nearby Tuaran Village to visit the crocodile farm – be there at feeding time for an impressive show of reptilian greed.
**YOU SHOULD KNOW:**
The trek is popular, so it is necessary to book accommodation at Park HQ and Laban Rata Guesthouse well in advance – no accommodation, no trek.

# Skrang River Safari

Sarawak is located in northwestern Borneo, and is one of two Malaysian states on the island (the other being Sabah). With large tracts of tropical rain forest, Sarawak is separated from the Indonesian part of Borneo by the central mountain range, where several rivers rise. These include the shallow, fast-flowing Skrang River, fiefdom of the fearsome Dayak Iban headhunters. They believed that freshly gathered heads led to an abundant rice harvest, and celebrated their headhunting in the form of elaborate tattoos. Women, too, often bore tattoos that celebrated their skills as weavers.

The Skrang Ibans still have a traditional way of life, but happily there are no fresh heads hanging in the rafters of their huge longhouses along the riverbanks – just a few ancient skulls. Instead, the Ibans now supplement their subsistence economy by welcoming a select number of guests. But first there's a five-hour drive from the state capital of Kuching to the river, from whence a motorised longboat takes over.

It is possible to make scenic river trip through longhouse country, enjoying the verdant rainforest. This a is a genuine jungle safari, sometimes beneath overhanging foliage, and it may be necessary to hop out if the boat grounds in the shallow water to help re-float it before continuing. There are also plenty of white-water rapids to add to the excitement.

However, most people prefer to arrange a stop at one of the riverside longhouses. Once there, visitors are shown around before being entertained by the residents, who put on a wonderful show of tribal music and dancing – not to mention a feast washed down with liberal helpings of tuak rice wine. You can sometimes stay in the longhouse itself, or in some places there may be a simple but comfortable guesthouse.

**HOW:**
By boat
**WHEN TO GO:**
March to August; October and November
**TIME IT TAKES:**
Up to four hours for the scenic journey along the Skrang River to see longhouses.
**HIGHLIGHTS:**
On the way from Kuching to the Skrang River – a stop at Serian to visit the bustling produce market.
An amazing display of deadly blowpipe skills by proficient Iban hunters.
Seeing the rich flora and fauna of the jungle that surrounds the longhouses, with the help of a local guide.
**YOU SHOULD KNOW:**
If you are visiting a longhouse it is customary to bring small presents for your Iban hosts.

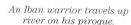

*An Iban warrior travels up river on his pirogue.*

# AUSTRALASIA
# AND
# THE PACIFIC

# Great Ocean Road

The Great Ocean Road belongs in an élite group of classic coastal drives, which includes California's Pacific Highway and Italy's Amalfi Coast Road. It runs 285 km (180 mi) along Victoria's south coast, west of Melbourne between the towns of Torquay and Warrnambool. Constructed originally to open up a previously inaccessible coastline for commerce, the Great Ocean Road has now become a major tourist attraction in its own right. Started in 1919 with the labour of ex-servicemen and completed 13 years later, this engineering marvel clings precariously to sheer cliff faces, snakes around inlets, crosses narrow gorges and passes through tunnels blasted out of solid rock.

Leaving the lively seaside resort of Torquay with its world-famous surf break at Bells Beach, the road hugs the shoreline as it passes through the pretty little towns of Anglesea and Lorne. As you negotiate sharp corners and descend into protected bays you are presented time and again with stunning views of the Southern Ocean, endless expanses of virgin sands and rugged cliffs stretching off into the distance. After Apollo Bay the route bears inland and crosses Otway National Park, part of the Otway Ranges, an area of dense temperate rain forest which offers one of your best chances of seeing a koala in the wild. These shy creatures are notoriously hard to spot, thanks to their camouflage and inertia during the day.

Appropriately enough, the highlight of this trip comes towards the end. Just 70 km (45 mi) before Warrnambool the Twelve Apostles rise proudly from the sea, like giant sentinels guarding the coast. These majestic limestone stacks, up to 45 m (150 ft) high, are the result of coastal erosion and they provide a justly famous spectacle at sunrise and sunset.

*The Twelve Apostles near the Great Ocean Road*

# Gibb River Road

Running straight across the heart of the Kimberley region in Australia's remote north-west, the Gibb River Road remains one of the country's great off-road driving adventures, although improvements in the road's condition has meant that there are many more travellers who take on the challenge than there used to be. Even so, there is still a real sense of achievement as you motor into the small towns of Derby at the western end or Kununurra at the eastern end, saddle-sore after 700 mostly bone-shaking kilometres (440 mi) and once you've cleared the last of the bulldust from your lungs.

'The Gibb', as the road is known locally, is serious 4x4 terrain. Apart from a short sealed stretch east of Derby, it is a red dirt and gravel track, fairly wide and smooth for the most part but badly corrugated in places from the effect of other vehicles and 'wash outs' from the wet season. All this might still be negotiated in a conventional car but what you really need the high clearance of a proper 4x4 vehicle for are the even rougher side tracks you must take in order to visit the main attractions along the route. Involving detours of up to 50 km (30 mi), places such as Bell, Adcock and the Manning Gorges showcase the natural features for which this ancient and rugged landscape is famed: narrow sandstone gorges, waterfalls, hidden creeks and tranquil pools.

Most travellers tackling the Gibb choose to camp along the way but there are accommodation options for those wanting more comfort. You can drive the road in either direction but as the majority of the big sights are in the western half you might prefer to start from the eastern end and save these delights for later.

**HOW:**
By 4x4
**WHEN TO GO:**
May to October
**TIME IT TAKES:**
At least five to six days if you want to make the most of being in this remarkable region.
**HIGHLIGHTS:**
Waterfalls in full flow in the gorges – but you need to go early in the season to see them (soon after the end of the 'wet').
Walking along beautiful Bell Creek and into the Gorge.
Swimming in a gorge pool (crocodile-free!).
The sunset over the Pentecost River and Cockburn Ranges from Home Valley Station.
**YOU SHOULD KNOW:**
Letting air out of your tyres before you set off will improve your journey considerably and reduce the likelihood of punctures. You must have a permit in advance to travel on any side tracks which cross Aboriginal land.

*The Pentecost River Crossing on the Gibb River Road*

# The Indian Pacific Railway

**HOW:**
By train
**WHEN TO GO:**
You can take this journey at any time of the year as the train is fully air-conditioned. If you get off the train at any of the outback stops, however, you should bear in mind that temperatures can climb well above 40 °C (104 °F) in the summer months (December to February).
**TIME IT TAKES:**
Three days, with three nights on board and extended stops for optional tours at Broken Hill, Adelaide and Kalgoorlie.
**HIGHLIGHTS:**
Early morning sightings of kangaroos and emus beside the line.
Experiencing something of the hard life of the miner on an underground mine tour in Broken Hill.
The majestic spectacle of a soaring wedge-tailed eagle, Australia's largest flighted bird and symbol of the Indian Pacific.
**YOU SHOULD KNOW:**
This route has only been possible as an uninterrupted journey from coast to coast since 1970, when standard gauge rail lines were adopted in the three states through which it passes.

This classic long-distance rail journey crosses the Australian continent from the Pacific Ocean in the east to the Indian Ocean in the west. Running twice weekly in each direction, trains are hauled by huge diesel locomotives and can be up to a kilometre (over half a mile) in length. From Sydney the journey provides an inspiring overview of many of the country's most distinctive landscapes: the lush, heavily forested slopes of the Blue Mountains give way to the sprawling rural heartland of New South Wales which in turn is succeeded by the bleak outback scenery of the Broken Hill mining region. Crossing into South Australia gives you fine views of the Flinders Ranges with their dramatic ridges.

After an extended stop in Adelaide the Indian Pacific heads north west along the Spencer Gulf to Port Augusta before embarking on the most forbidding part of the journey, across the vast and featureless Nullarbor Plain (which means literally 'empty of trees') – 1,200 km (750 mi) of red earth, low scrub and nothing else, which includes the longest straight stretch of railway track in the world (478 km / 300 mi). The bustling gold-mining centre of Kalgoorlie returns you to human activity with a jolt before your last night on board conveys you the final 600 km (375 mi) for a morning arrival in the West Australian capital of Perth.

The Indian Pacific is run by the same company that operates the Ghan Railway, and it offers the same range of travelling options. If your budget allows, the most comfortable option is to travel Gold Kangaroo class – a definite recommendation for the en-suite accommodation, full on-board catering and the attentive but relaxed service throughout your journey.

*The legendary Indian Pacific*

# The Ghan

One of the world's great rail journeys, the Ghan takes two days to bisect the Australian continent from Adelaide on the Southern Ocean to Darwin, Australia's most northerly city and its gateway to Asia. Over its 3,000-km (1,900-mi) course it crosses three distinct climate zones, from the fertile coastal plains of South Australia through the vast dry desert of the Red Centre to the luxuriant vegetation of the tropical Top End. The Ghan takes its name from the Afghan camel drivers who with their animals opened up 19th-century trading routes into the interior. Constructed originally between Adelaide and Alice Springs in 1929, the line was only completed to the northern coast in 2004. The camel has not been forgotten, though – there are now more in Australia than on the Arabian Peninsula.

The company running the Ghan manages quite a trick spoiling you with all the benefits of modern rail travel in comfortable, air-conditioned carriages and the highest standards of on-board service, while at the same time imparting a real sense that you are blazing an adventurer's trail as you travel across one of the world's harshest, least hospitable terrains. As you gaze out from the window of your compartment over the endless expanses of red earth and spinifex grass, the flat horizon only rarely broken by sandstone outcrops, you have ample time to reflect on those early pioneers, as well as the indigenous peoples who have sustained themselves for centuries in this very environment. Then, as the vivid desert sun sets and the train continues its measured progress, you can give thanks you don't have to do the same, before you make your way to the restaurant car to dine on kangaroo steak or barramundi fish.

*Twin locomotives pull the Ghan away from Alice Springs.*

**HOW:**
By train
**WHEN TO GO:**
April to October
**TIME IT TAKES:**
Two days and two nights, including two extended stops for local excursions (optional), at Alice Springs and Katherine; two to three days longer if you break the journey at Alice Springs to visit Uluru (Ayers Rock)
**HIGHLIGHTS:**
The welcome and send-off by the train staff on the departure platform at Adelaide.
Waking up on your first morning to the reds and ochres of the vast central desert.
Absorbing the unique atmosphere of Alice Springs, a town that's an awfully long way from anywhere.
Dining on the train under the stars of the desert sky.
**YOU SHOULD KNOW:**
Trains run twice weekly between Adelaide and Darwin in each direction. Alice Springs is the mid-way point, where you will find the Ghan logo of a camel with rider in sculptural form on the station platform (a popular spot for photos).

*The steamer near Nildottie*

# Paddle Steamer on the Murray River

The presence of Australia's principal river, the Murray, has been a key factor in turning the south east of the country into its most productive and heavily populated area. The American writer Mark Twain hailed the Murray as Australia's Mississippi, although in a country where water has always been a limited resource it lacks the flow of its mighty American counterpart. Like the Mississippi the Murray offered a means of navigation for the early European settlers to reach the rich pastoral country inland; and for over fifty years from the 1860s it reigned unchallenged as the main transport artery for the region, carrying livestock and produce downriver to the coast and bringing supplies back to the sheep and cattle stations.

As in America the paddle steamer was the dominant means of river transport in these years. Where once they had a strictly commercial, utilitarian role these elegant vessels now ply their trade on the Murray as leisure boats. There is no better way to enjoy the varied sights of this riverscape – the mighty cliff-faces, the stands of towering red gums, the wetlands with their abundant wildlife – than from the deck of a paddle steamer as you glide by in sedate comfort. At the historic river port of Mannum, on the Murray's lower reaches and an hour's drive east of Adelaide, you board the *Murray Princess* for an extended cruise upriver to the first lock near Blanchetown and back again, sleeping on board in well-appointed cabins. The rewards for opting for this slower and gentler form of transport are many, not least the grandstand views it gives you of the river's spectacular birdlife – pelicans, black swans and egrets are all commonly seen here.

# The Ned Kelly Trail

The short and violent life of Ned Kelly, Australia's most famous outlaw, or 'bushranger', has long since gained iconic status. You can compare the legend with the more humdrum realities of a life spent in rural poverty in this driving tour around its key locations. By Australian standards it is a relatively compact affair – some 650 km (400 mi) in a round trip from Melbourne – since Kelly never strayed far from his roots in the 'high country' of Victoria's northeast.

The Hume Highway, the main Melbourne to Sydney road, conveniently connects many of the Kelly sites. Beveridge and Avenel, an hour's drive north of Melbourne, were two of Ned's childhood homes; his ex-convict father John 'Red' Kelly died when Ned was twelve and is buried in Avenel. Ned robbed the bank in nearby Euroa, while the town museum in Benalla has a number of interesting Kelly-related exhibits.

The next stop, Glenrowan, marks the heart of the Kelly story. Here Ned and his gang made their famous last stand in the local inn. While the other gang members all died in the police siege, Ned himself was wounded when trying to break out wearing a suit of homemade armour. A pleasant country drive brings you to Beechworth, the furthest point on the tour, where you can still see the gaol in which the fifteen-year old served his first sentence.

There are fine views of the King valley and mountains on the journey back to Mansfield, which takes you via Power's Lookout and Stringybark Creek; an atmospheric walk through blue gums and blackwoods leads you to the site where Ned achieved national notoriety when the gang shot three policemen dead; their graves and a memorial can be seen in Mansfield.

**HOW:**
By car
**WHEN TO GO:**
September to May
**TIME IT TAKES:**
Allow one week if you want to see all the sites properly.
**HIGHLIGHTS:**
The green silk sash in Benalla Museum given to the ten-year-old Ned as a reward after he had saved a boy from drowning; the sash bears the marks of his blood as he was wearing it when he was wounded and captured at Glenrowan.
Kate's Cottage and Ned Kelly Memorial in Glenrowan, an evocative replica of the Kelly home.
Ned Kelly's death mask and the beam from which he was hanged on 11 November 1880, both in Old Melbourne Gaol.
**YOU SHOULD KNOW:**
1. The trail takes you close to some of Victoria's premier wine-producing areas.
2. Ned Kelly's armour has survived and can be seen on display in the State Library of Victoria in Melbourne.

*The Ned Kelly statue at Glenrowan*

# Matilda Highway

**HOW:**
By car
**WHEN TO GO:**
April to October to avoid the extreme summer temperatures
**TIME IT TAKES:**
Seven to ten days, allowing for one or two longer stops along the way.
**HIGHLIGHTS:**
The Stockman's Hall of Fame in Longreach, a lively and comprehensive guide to the outback way of life.
The Waltzing Matilda Centre in Winton.
Cloncurry, birthplace of the Royal Flying Doctor Service.
Watching the sunset with a 'tinny' (beer) and a fish supper at Karumba Point – journey's end.
**YOU SHOULD KNOW:**
The distances between the various settlements along the route can be very large, so you should ensure that you always have spare fuel and plenty of water with you.

The Matilda Highway is the main north-south route through the interior of the state of Queensland. Starting in Cunnamulla, the first town after the New South Wales border, it runs for 1,700 km (1,060 mi) in a north and north-westerly direction until reaching the Gulf of Carpentaria at Karumba. This is a classic drive through the great Australian outback, and if you like your roads straight and empty and your vistas boundless then you will enjoy this experience. But you should be warned that the landscape can be dauntingly unvarying: wide open expanses of grassland and low scrub, extending for kilometre after kilometre in every direction. Only as the highway approaches the Gulf in the north does it change somewhat to feature a coastal habitat of cracked saltpans – and to become, if anything, even flatter.

Many of the key towns of the Queensland outback line the route of the Matilda. Places such as Winton, Longreach and Charleville developed in the 19th century as supply and transportation centres for the vast and isolated sheep and cattle stations that cover much of the area. The towns themselves are not large and are relaxed and easy-going places in which to spend a day or two savouring the special atmosphere of the interior.

The Highway takes its name from the region's associations with 'Waltzing Matilda', Banjo Paterson's ballad which has become Australia's unofficial national anthem. You can visit the Combo Waterhole, the supposed setting for the story, outside Kynuna on the highway south of Cloncurry. The North Gregory Hotel in Winton is where 'Waltzing Matilda' is said to have had its first performance in April 1895 (although the hotel has since been rebuilt following a fire).

*The town of Winton along the Matilda Highway*

# Sydney to Melbourne Coast Road

The direct route linking Australia's two largest cities is the inland Hume Highway, but the coast road is unquestionably the more rewarding option, and the distance involved is not much greater. Known as the Princes Highway, this route follows the New South Wales coastline south from Sydney to the state border with Victoria, at roughly the halfway point on the 1,050-km (655-mi) journey. It then heads east across the Gippsland region towards Melbourne.

Leaving Sydney the Highway skirts Botany Bay, site of Captain Cook's famous first landing in 1770, before reaching the industrial city of Wollongong. The road then passes through a succession of small fishing villages and relaxed seaside resorts that stretch all the way down to the state border. Here you are rarely more than a few kilometres from the shoreline and there are regular opportunities to turn off for wonderfully secluded beaches. These, together with outstanding surfing and all manner of water sports, including diving and game-fishing, constitute the area's main attractions, but inland there are also easily accessible national parks, such as the Royal National (the second oldest national park in the world, after the USA's Yellowstone), Morton and Ben Boyd Reserves, which contain spectacular upland scenery and some of Australia's best-preserved temperate rainforests.

After the old whaling station of Eden, the Princes Highway strikes inland across southern Victoria and the fertile dairy-farming region of Gippsland. This is a land of gently rolling hills and forests of tall eucalypt. You brush the coastline once more briefly at Lakes Entrance, which as the name suggests is a good base for exploring the Gippsland Lakes, the country's most extensive network of inland waterways. And if you are after a bigger adrenalin rush, Ninety Mile Beach (which you can drive along!) is never far away.

*Ninety Mile Beach*

**HOW:**
By car or 4x4
**WHEN TO GO:**
Year-round
**TIME IT TAKES:**
Three to five days, if you allow time to explore the area's many natural beauties.
**HIGHLIGHTS:**
Mogo, site of a former gold mine where there is a reconstructed mid-19th century gold-rush town.
Take a trip out to sea to spot whales on their annual migration (June to November) at places like Jervis Bay, Narooma and Eden.
Croajingolong National Park in the far east of Victoria, over 100 km (62 mi) of isolated, unspoiled coastline with excellent bushwalking opportunities.
**YOU SHOULD KNOW:**
To get the most out of the many national parks along the route you will need a 4x4 vehicle and a good pair of walking boots.

*The Glass House Mountains*

# The Bruce Highway

**HOW:**
By car
**WHEN TO GO:**
Year-round
**TIME IT TAKES:**
One week, allowing for detours.
**HIGHLIGHTS:**
Australia Zoo, former home of the 'Crocodile Hunter', Steve Irwin.
Sampling the culinary delights of stylish Noosa, renowned throughout the country for its fine dining.
A day in a sailing boat, exploring the Whitsunday Islands.
Eating Queensland mangoes when in season (November to January) – they don't come bigger or juicier.
**YOU SHOULD KNOW:**
Deadly box jellyfish, known as 'stingers', populate the tropical waters north of Agnes Water during the summer months (October to April), so, however inviting it looks, you are strongly advised not to swim in the sea during this period.

Running between the state capital, Brisbane, and the bustling city of Cairns 1,720 km (1,075 mi) to the north, the Bruce Highway is Queensland's principal transport artery, connecting most of the main towns and cities of Australia's second-largest state. On this road you are rarely more than a few kilometres from the Pacific Ocean, so it is easy to relieve the tedium of highway driving with a short detour to chill out on a clean, deserted beach. Inland you are accompanied much of the way by views of the foothills, escarpments and plateaux of the Great Dividing Range.

On leaving Brisbane the Highway runs up the Sunshine Coast, more relaxed and less developed than its famous Gold Coast cousin. You cannot miss the striking profiles of the Glass House Mountains to your left, while to the north you will be hard put to resist the seductive seaside charms of Noosa. These coastal plains are rich agricultural country and intensive cultivation is evident throughout the journey: pineapples around Gympie, mangoes around Bowen, huge sugarcane fields in the Mackay region. At Rockhampton, self-styled 'beef capital' of Australia and a great place for a steak, you enter the Tropics and notice the vegetation becoming thicker and lusher as hills and rainforest edge ever closer to the coast.

A number of coastal towns north of Mackay provide excellent bases for exploring the Whitsunday Islands lying offshore and for longer trips to the Great Barrier Reef itself. Townsville is the region's main city; you certainly know you are in the Tropics wandering along its attractive promenade. And as you cover the final 300 km (190 mi) to Cairns you would be well advised to have some energy in reserve for the vast array of adventure activities offered by your destination city.

# Alice Springs to Coober Pedy

The vastness of the Australian continent is everywhere evident on this overland trip that takes you 700 km (440 mi) south from the centre. It follows the Stuart Highway, named after Scottish-born John McDouall Stuart, one of Australia's pioneering explorers who in 1862 finally succeeded, on his third attempt, in blazing a trail from south to north coast. This feat paved the way for the construction just ten years later of the Overland Telegraph Line linking Adelaide with Darwin; a further link to Java revolutionized communications between Britain and its far-flung colonies.

On leaving the lively town of Alice Springs you will not see another population centre until journey's end. Boundless stretches of flat highway extend to the horizon and are punctuated by occasional tiny roadside settlements like Kulgera and Marla, whose sole function is to service the needs of long-distance travellers. All the while you are surrounded by unbroken vistas of the great central Australian desert, one of the world's harshest, most arid environments. Amazingly, the earliest known evidence of animal life on the planet was found not far south from here, at Lake Torrens, while if you are lucky enough to be on the road following a desert rainstorm you will see the landscape transformed by a sudden profusion of wild flowers.

Coober Pedy, the self-styled 'opal capital of the world', is the place to come to gaze on this most beautiful and elusive of minerals. A huge range of stones are sold, but you can also try your luck at some 'fossicking' to find your own. The small town is not a lot to look at on the surface because much of it (including five churches) is built underground, where people have made their homes to escape the extreme summer heat.

**HOW:**
By car or 4x4
**WHEN TO GO:**
April to October
**TIME IT TAKES:**
You can do this trip in one day, although it is a long drive and you would be better advised to stay overnight at a roadhouse along the way.
**HIGHLIGHTS:**
Seeing the desert sun rise over the MacDonnell Ranges from a hot-air balloon above Alice Springs.
Shopping for Aboriginal art and crafts in Alice Springs' many galleries.
Staying in an underground hotel in Coober Pedy.
The Old Timers Mine in Coober Pedy for a historical perspective on opal mining.
**YOU SHOULD KNOW:**
Take care if you go hunting for opals yourself at Coober Pedy as there are many old disused shafts that are barely visible on the surface.

*The road to the opal town of Coober Pedy*

# Six Foot Track to the Blue Mountains

**HOW:**
On foot
**WHEN TO GO:**
March to May and September to November are the most pleasant times to do this walk.
**TIME IT TAKES:**
Three days, plus one to two days more for visiting the Jenolan Caves and the sights around Katoomba.
**HIGHLIGHTS:**
The views into the Jamison Valley from Echo Point at Katoomba.
Crossing Cox's River on the suspension footbridge, built by army engineers.
The spectacular limestone formations in the Jenolan Caves.
**YOU SHOULD KNOW:**
Take plenty of water on this hike, as well as warm clothing since spring and autumn nights can be quite chilly.

Easily accessible from Sydney, the Blue Mountains have been inspiring visitors since the early days of European settlement. This is a landscape of wooded slopes, dramatic escarpments and hidden valleys. The mountains really do look blue too, thanks to the mist given off by the ubiquitous eucalypt trees; it was this mist, indeed, which kick-started the tourism industry, when the first intrepid visitors came to savour the therapeutic benefits of the mountain air at the end of the 19th century.

The Six Foot Track, so named from the original specification for a track six feet wide, was created as a bridlepath back in the 1880s. Hiking its 42-km (26-mi) length from Katoomba to the Jenolan Caves remains one of the best ways to immerse yourself in the varied natural splendours of the area. There are several energetic climbs on a route that takes you up along high ridges and down into steep-sided valleys, dense with spreading ferns. The rewards for your efforts are panoramic views of distant canyon walls and sudden variations in habitat which increase your wildlife-spotting opportunities. Campsites at strategic locations along the way mean that you need not exert yourself to the extent of the doughty runners who compete every March in the Six Foot Track Marathon, billed as Australia's toughest off-road race.

Your best chances of seeing the local wildlife are at dawn and dusk when wallabies and kangaroos come out to graze, whilst many of the forest mammals – possums and gliders, for example – scavenge only at night. The birdlife is a different matter – you are unlikely to miss the brilliant hues of rosellas and lorikeets darting from tree to tree, and you may even be fortunate enough to come across the reclusive lyrebird foraging on the forest floor.

*The Blue Mountains in New South Wales*

# Kuranda Scenic Railway

Prolonged and torrential rains during the wet seasons in the early 1880s were making life very difficult for the tin miners of North Queensland. It became imperative to improve supply lines to their camps up on the Atherton Tablelands inland from Cairns, and so the line now known as the Kuranda Scenic Railway was born. There was fierce initial competition for the route up into the mountains, until the present one, which follows the course of the Barron River, prevailed. Opened in 1891, the line took five years to construct and is a remarkable feat of engineering. One thousand five hundred navvies, many of Irish and Italian extraction, used little more than hand tools, mules and dynamite to blast out fifteen tunnels and numerous cuttings, as well as to build bridges over the many steep-sided creeks.

You can begin your journey from the main station in central Cairns, or better still, join the train at Freshwater Station in the northern suburbs, where there are informative displays about the railway and its history as well as the chance to eat in a restored historic carriage. The line then winds for 30 km (19 mi) through the Barron Gorge, climbing all the while until it reaches Kuranda, an ascent of 330 m (1,100 ft). Each carriage is equipped with an audio-visual commentary on the route to enhance the unrivalled views of mountains, precipitous cliff-faces, waterfalls and a World Heritage rainforest. And if you are lucky your train might be drawn by the 1720 Class Diesel electric locomotive that has been painted to depict 'Buda-dji', the legendary carpet snake whose story from the Aboriginal Dreamtime you will hear during your journey.

**HOW:**
By train
**WHEN TO GO:**
Year-round, although the wet season (December to March) is best if you want to see the waterfalls in full flow.
**TIME IT TAKES:**
1.75 hours one-way
**HIGHLIGHTS:**
The Horseshoe Bend, a 180-degree curve which marks the start of the climb out of the coastal plain to Kuranda.
Stoney Creek Bridge on its three tall trestle piers.
The views of Barron Falls, especially during the 'wet'.
Getting away from the day-trippers and staying overnight in Kuranda, the 'village in the rainforest'.
**YOU SHOULD KNOW:**
The last train back from Kuranda leaves at 3.30 pm. For a different perspective on the landscape consider instead taking the Skyrail Rainforest Cableway down to Cairns.

*Kuranda Scenic Railway*

# Cape York Peninsula

The northernmost point of the Australian continent, lonely and remote, Cape York Peninsula has been described as one of the last great wild places on earth. The so-called 'Trip to the Tip' is a challenging one whichever mode of overland transport you choose. If you have the stamina and confidence, one of the best ways to encounter a landscape largely untouched by human hand is by mountain bike. Cairns is the place to organize your own transport or else sign up for an escorted tour. If you travel independently you should bear in mind that accommodation options are limited, so you need to take basic camping equipment as well as appropriate spares and supplies.

Most of the 1,000 km (625 mi) from Cairns to the Cape is on dirt tracks and unsealed roads. Whilst you have to be on constant alert for potholes and the heavy corrugations that form on many surfaces, you will find your progress is often not much slower than fellow travellers in motor vehicles. And your greater lightness and flexibility will give you the advantage when negotiating the many creek crossings with their swift-flowing streams and steep-sided banks.

The route from Cairns takes you up the coast through the Daintree Rainforest and on to Cape Tribulation and Cooktown, before heading inland across Lakefield National Park to join the main road running up the spine of the peninsula. The 160 km (100 mi) from the Wenlock River north to the Jardine River, which follows the route of the old Overland Telegraph Line, is a particularly exciting section. After a ferry crossing of the mighty Jardine River it is a relatively straightforward ride, via the small Torres Strait Islander town of Bamaga to Cape York itself, where a sign confirms you are at the tip of mainland Australia.

*Cycling through corrugations
on Cape York.*

# Skyrail Rainforest Cableway

The World Heritage-listed tropical rainforests of north Queensland are the oldest continually surviving rainforests on earth. The opening of the Skyrail Rainforest Cableway outside Cairns in 1995 has given visitors an entirely new perspective on this dazzlingly lush environment. From the safety and comfort of your enclosed gondola cabin you gaze down on a previously inaccessible world as the cableway carries you silently over the dense, verdant rainforest canopy. And with much of the natural activity taking place in the heights of the trees, you have a good chance on your trip of seeing sights that are simply unavailable from the forest floor up to 60 m (200 ft) below.

Skyrail connects Smithfield, a northern suburb of the coastal city of Cairns, with the small inland town of Kuranda, 330 m (1,100 ft) up on the edge of the Atherton Tablelands. At 7.5 km (4.5 mi) it is one of the world's longest cableways and can carry up to 700 passengers per hour. Not only is it an enjoyable way to travel, it is also good for the planet; Skyrail's operators pride themselves on its low environmental impact which has been recognized in numerous ecotourism awards.

There are two stops on the route, at Red Peak and Barron Falls. Both give you the chance to get off and explore the rainforest at ground-floor level along boardwalks and with the help of knowledgeable local rangers. Here you may well see a brush turkey foraging on the forest floor, while from your gondola you should catch flashes of brightly-coloured parrots, lorikeets and cockatoos; and although you are unlikely to see them, you can listen out for the whip-crack call of the whipbird and the cooing of the Wompoo pigeon, among the most distinctive sounds of the rainforest.

*The Skyrail 'hangs' above Barron Gorge.*

**HOW:**
By cableway
**WHEN TO GO:**
Year-round
**TIME IT TAKES:**
1.5 hours one-way, including stops,
**HIGHLIGHTS:**
The panoramic views of the Cairns coastline and the Coral Sea during the initial ascent.
The Ulysses butterfly, a true Australian star with its electric blue wings.
Kuranda, with its laid-back atmosphere and huge array of arts and crafts stalls.
The Barron Falls in full flow (wet season only – December to March).
**YOU SHOULD KNOW:**
For a change of transport and scenery you can opt to make the return journey on the 100-year-old Kuranda Scenic Railway.

# Fraser Island Trek

Anyone for the world's largest sandcastle? Sand-based Fraser Island off the southern coast of Queensland extends to 123 km (76 mi) from north to south and is 26 km (16 mi) across at the widest point. Managed by the Queensland Parks and Wildlife Service as part of the Great Sandy National Park, this extraordinary place is a UNESCO World Heritage Site.

It has a variety of habitats – from pristine rivers to freshwater lakes, lush subtropical rainforest to eucalypt forests, mangroves to melaleuca swamps, heaths and – of course – endless beaches. All are inhabited by a wealth of wildlife, including over 200 species of bird and a variety of reptile life, with migrating whales frequently spotted off shore.

The easy way to explore this popular destination is by 4x4 vehicle – or is it? Even these powerful monsters get marooned in Fraser's soft sand and a surer (if slower) way of seeing this enchanting island is to make the Fraser Island Trek – a hike that follows the continuous beach up the eastern coast with possible detours into the interior, starting at Hook Point on the island's southern tip. The first stop is Dilli Village, where accommodation can be booked in advance. From there, the hike continues to the outpost of Eurong and on to the island's main settlement, Happy Valley, where the trekker can find accommodation and replenish stores.

The onward march runs north alongside imposing cliffs called The Cathedrals that are characterized by multi-coloured layers. After Cathedral Beach Resort the route passes through Dundubara before reaching the basalt promontory of Indian Head, with superb views from the top of the headland. Many walkers end their journey soon afterwards at Orchid Beach, though determined hikers continue through awkward soft sand and around impassable rocky outcrops to the Trek's official end at Sandy Cape Lighthouse.

**HOW:**
On foot
**WHEN TO GO:**
Any time of year
**TIME IT TAKES:**
Allow five days to include selected inland detours.
**HIGHLIGHTS:**
Seeing a large number of dingoes – the purest strain left in Australia is on Fraser Island, as there has been little inter-breeding with domestic dogs.
A long side trip from Dilli – the Southern Lakes Drive covering many of the interior's best features including Lakes Boomanjin, Benaroon, Birrabeen and McKenzie with its white sand and blue water.
The rusting remains of the ocean liner *Maheno*, driven ashore in 1935 whilst on the way to a Japanese scrapyard.
**YOU SHOULD KNOW:**
Even when the tide is out and the beach is up to 100 m (330 ft) wide, great care should be taken when crossing sometimes-treacherous creeks and rock bars.

*The Flinders Ranges*

# The Heysen Trail

**HOW:**
On foot
**WHEN TO GO:**
April to October (the Heysen Trail is closed during fire-danger season).
**TIME IT TAKES:**
Around 60 days to hike the entire Trail in one go.
**HIGHLIGHTS:**
The stunning Wilpena Pound in the South Flinders Ranges, caused by millions of years of erosion, renowned for its unique geology and Aboriginal cultural significance.
Walking through the world-famous vineyards of the Barossa Valley in the northern part of the Mount Lofty Ranges (and managing the occasional tasting).
The home of the artist after whom the Trail is named – see Sir Hans Heysen's The Cedars near Hahndorf in the Adelaide Hills.
The sandy expanses of Tunkalilla Beach on the Fleurieu Peninsula facing the Southern Ocean.
**YOU SHOULD KNOW:**
Hikers should use special stations along the Trail to cleanse footwear, thus helping to inhibit the spread of the introduced root-rot fungus Phytophthora, which can devastate native plants.

Any super-fit backpacker with two months to spare can achieve the ultimate prize – an end-to-end certificate and badge to prove that they've tackled and beaten one of Australia's toughest official long-distance hikes, also recognized as one of the world's great long-distance walks.

The Heysen Trail runs from Parachilna Gorge in the Northern Flinders Ranges down to Cape Jervis on the southern tip of the Fleurieu Peninsula, passing Adelaide along the way. It traverses some of South Australia's most breathtaking landscape, providing an incredible variety of stimulating sights to reward determined hikers who follow the distinctive red-and-white markers with their stylized representation of the Trail crossing hills and valleys.

The Heysen Trail takes in rugged gorges, native bushland, pine forests and scenic coastal areas, also passing through rich farmland, vineyards and historic towns. The northern part through the South Flinders Ranges offers rocky landscapes, ridges, gullies, pines and gum-lined creeks. The central section crosses rolling hills, farmland and grazing country with patches of bushland and forest. The southern part of the Trail offers fabulous coastal views, towering cliffs, gullies, sand dunes and dense bush.

Those who lack the time and/or energy to tackle the complete Heysen Trail can still enjoy many of its splendours. It is well-mapped and has been specifically designed to facilitate day walks along individual sections, though it is a linear trail – so those who wish to make the most of their walk should make arrangements to be picked up at the end of the day, to avoid wasting time by retracing their steps. The southern section from Spalding down to Cape Jervis follows the Mount Lofty Ranges and is most suitable for day walks, especially for families, as the northern section is more rugged and isolated.

# Port Phillip Bay

It's possible to be one among thousands, or do your own thing. Australia's passion for pedalling comes to a grand climax during October every year with 'Around the Bay in a Day' – the country's greatest mass cycling event, when up to 15,000 cyclists gather in Melbourne to ride around Port Phillip Bay, each choosing the route that best suits their capabilities – distances on offer are 50 km (31 mi), 100 km (62 mi), 210 km (130 mi) and 250 km (155 mi).

Port Phillip Bay, with Melbourne at the top, is almost land-locked – access to the Bass Strait is via the narrow Rip between Port Lonsdale and Point Nepean. The Bay has an irregular coastline of some 265 km (165 mi) and the full circumnavigation by road is somewhat shorter. It has many inlets and beaches, with the western shore being somewhat swampy and the eastern shore characterized by sandy beaches. For those planning their own ride there are numerous options, though there is increasing suburban development and consequent road traffic around the Bay, especially on the eastern shore. A full circumnavigation at a sensible pace to include recreational stop-offs and side trips could take a few days.

Clockwise from Melbourne, the route passes through the suburbs to Frankston and follows the water to Sorrento, where a ferry crosses the Rip to Queencliff. Then the road goes through Geelong before travelling back up the more sparsely populated western shore to Altona Beach and back to Melbourne.

In truth, it's best to get the buzz from being part of the amazing 'Around the Bay in a Day' mass ride. The event is beautifully staged by the Bicycle Victoria organization, with all sorts of support services offered. Advance registration is required (available on line) and is the key to an unforgettable cycling experience.

**HOW:**
By bike
**WHEN TO GO:**
October for 'Around the Bay in a Day', any time for a solo spin.
**TIME IT TAKES:**
By definition, less than a day – a very long day of non-stop power cycling for the full circuit!
**HIGHLIGHTS:**
The high-rise skyline of downtown Melbourne viewed from Hobson's Bay. The revelling in Melbourne's Alexandra Gardens where the 'Around the Bay in a Day' event ends, including live music and entertainment.
**YOU SHOULD KNOW:**
Those stimulated by participating in 'Around the Bay in a Day' can go on to tackle another major event organized by Bicycle Victoria – the week-long 'Great Victorian Bike Ride'.

*St Kilda Beach, Port Phillip Bay*

# Perth to Adelaide Road Trip

**HOW:**
By car
**WHEN TO GO:**
September to May to avoid the hottest desert conditions .
**TIME IT TAKES:**
Eight or nine days
**HIGHLIGHTS:**
Wave Rock near the small town of Hyden, and also nearby Aboriginal paintings on the walls of Mulka's Cave.
The Old Telegraph Station near Eucla, where encroaching sand serves as a reminder of the harshness of the Nullarbor Plain's unforgiving conditions.
A short side trip from the Eyre Highway to the Head of Bight for great views – and southern right whales disporting between June and October.
A refreshing side trip to the world-renowned Barossa Valley at journey's end, to toast that 'Ultimate Road Trip' in fine Aussie wine.
**YOU SHOULD KNOW:**
As recently as the late 1950s much of this route consisted of little more than hard-packed dirt roads (of which there are still plenty to be found off the main highway).

Billed as 'Australia's Ultimate Road Trip', the journey from Perth in Western Australia to Adelaide in South Australia lives up to its name. This epic route stretches for 3,200 km (1,900 mi) along Australia's southern coastline, delivering an ever-changing drama of striking landscapes, soaring cliffs, azure sea – and the mesmerizing desert that is the Nullarbor Plain. It's a largely empty land, with few significant towns along the way, but there's plenty to see. That emptiness also requires pre-planning, with a need to carry spare fuel and adequate emergency water supplies, just in case.

From Perth, the journey begins with a sortie down the coast along Highway 1, passing through Bunbury to the South Coast at Walpole, then along to Albany and the charming seaside settlement at Esperance, where the road turns north and runs up country to Norseman. Alternatively, it's possible to head inland from Perth along the Great Southern Highway, with a quick stop in the small town of York with its 19th-century buildings, before continuing through the small settlements of Aldersyde, Gorge Rock, Hyden and Forestania to Norseman.

From Norseman the long-distance Eyre Highway begins a long straight run parallel with the coast through the fearsome Nullarbor Plain to Eucla, the largest place on the Plain. Between the tiny settlement of Nullarbor and Eucla there are half a dozen lookout points that offer superb views of the impressive cliffs of the Great Australian Bight. After Eucla one of the longest stretches of tarmac road in Australia follows the coast through Nullarbor National Park to Ceduna, from whence the Flinders Highway continues through Streaky Bay, Elliston, Port Kenny, Port Lincoln and Port Augusta. The picturesque coastal towns of the Eyre Peninsula give way to the Clare Valley and the final run down into Adelaide. An awesome journey safely completed!

*The impressive cliffs of the Great Australian Bight*

# Pinnacles Desert Walk

Within the Nambung National Park in Western Australia may be found an extraordinary natural phenomenon – the Pinnacles. These surreal limestone monuments have become one of Australia's major attractions, and it's easy to see why. After driving up the coast from Perth, into the Park and along the unmade 27-km (17-mi) access track to the Pinnacles area, visitors have an opportunity to park and explore this extraordinary place on foot.

*The Pinnacles in Nambung National Park*

The Pinnacles were formed over millions of years to create a unique landscape that contains over four thousand sculpted monuments, scattered across a vast and arid desert landscape of rippled quartz sand dunes. They have been likened in appearance to fingers, termite mounds or even tombstones, but one thing is certain – Pinnacles come in all sizes and shapes and every single one is different, ranging from tiny spikes to sturdy monoliths that rise to over 4 m (13 ft) in height.

There's a loop track from the end of the access road that can be driven but is much better walked, as this allows for exploration of interesting groups of stones, with every twist and turn opening up new vistas. For those who prefer their excursions to be well organized in advance, it is possible to join guided walks through the Pinnacles, an approach with the advantage of guaranteeing that some of the most interesting formations will be visited. Even so, most people like to make their own discoveries.

To make the very most of the Pinnacles, it is sensible to arrive early in the morning or late in the day. Then, the desert becomes an eerie wonderland of contrasting colours and extended shadows when viewed in dawn light or at dusk against the purple and orange hues of a big sky. Photographers become ecstatic whilst the rest merely marvel.

**HOW:**
On foot
**WHEN TO GO:**
August to October
**TIME IT TAKES:**
Half a day gives ample opportunity for a fascinating walk, ideally starting/ending at dawn/dusk.
**HIGHLIGHTS:**
A sensational spring display of seasonal wild flowers around the desert area in the Park.
An encounter with the western grey kangaroos and emus that frequent Nambung National Park.
A spot of relaxation on the pristine white beach at nearby Cervantes.
**YOU SHOULD KNOW:**
If you have a hire car be sure that the insurance covers travel on unsealed roads – this is often specifically excluded in Australia.

*Spring Creek Track in Purnululu National Park*

# Purnululu National Park

**HOW:**
On foot and by 4x4
**WHEN TO GO:**
Only in the dry season – April to December
**TIME IT TAKES:**
Three hours for the Spring Creek Track.
**HIGHLIGHTS:**
Alongside Spring Creek Track – the strange bottle-shaped baobab trees that are a more common sight in Southern Africa and Madagascar. The short walk through the narrow Echidna Chasm, with its towering walls and tall palm trees – one of the most mysterious places in Australia. Piccaninny Creek on the southern edge of the Bungle Bungles, an impressive winding gorge contained by the high walls of the domes. Cathedral Gorge – well named, it is impossible to remain spiritually unmoved within this spacious cavern that soars to the sky.
**YOU SHOULD KNOW:**
The area is rich in Aboriginal art and Purnululu National Park contains many sacred burial sites.

Lots of Australia is pretty remote – and Purnululu National Park is more remote than most. This stunning place lies in Kimberley, the empty northeastern corner of Western Australia that is often described as 'Australia's last frontier'. The Park lies between Halls Creek – 110 km (68 mi) to the south – and Kununurra – 250 km (155 mi) to the north.

Although Aborigines lived in the area for countless generations, it only became generally known in 1982 when a TV crew 'discovered' the extraordinary landscape of orange-and-grey-striped beehive sandstone formations (called the Bungle Bungles), cliffs, tropical pools, plunging chasms and gorges with elegant fan palms adorning the rocks. Such was the impact of their revelation that Purnululu was officially declared a National Park just five years later and has now been designated as a UNESCO World Heritage Site.

Tourists being tourists, the usual way to tick off the incredible sights to be found in the Park is to view them from the air – regular flights by light aircraft are available from specialists in Halls Creek or Kununurra. There is also a helicopter service from the nearby Turkey Creek Roadhouse at Warmun on the Great Northern Highway.

But of course the best option is to get in amongst the real thing on foot, for a day hike or camping trip, though this requires more effort than merely turning up and tramping the terrain. It is possible to arrange a vehicle tour with the air carrier, who will land on the edge of the Park for a rendezvous with the ground crew. For hikers and campers, however, the only way in is along the unmade Spring Creek Track. This dusty 80-km (50-mi) route is only passable by 4x4 vehicle, with four-wheel drive engaged all the way to avoid damaging the dry road surface.

# Tasmania Coast Trek

After exploring the mainland, a trip across the Bass Strait to Tasmania seems like a visit to another country. This island is the most distinctive of Australia's states, with the relatively unspoiled environment that permits its self-proclaimed status as 'The Natural State'.

Those who wish to underline Tasmania's eco-credentials – and prove their own advanced self-sufficiency qualifications – should undertake the marathon hike along the connecting South Coast and Port Davey Tracks in the vast Southwest National Park. This is an epic wilderness adventure often described as 'the hardest trek in Australia', so it isn't for the faint of heart or weak of leg.

The easy part is getting there, with regular shuttles from Hobart servicing each end of the route. The heaviest part is the pack, which must contain everything needed for two unsupported weeks. That includes food and camping gear (there are basic campgrounds at regular intervals), plus a selection of all-weather clothing. It is essential to get a Backpacker Pass in advance and sign the registration book before starting (and after finishing).

Any hike in Tasmania involves battling against mud. The 84-km (52-mi) South Coast Track has plenty of it, plus two mountain ranges to cross where the coast is impassable and shoreline sections where the waves can be dangerous. The route is Cockle Creek, South Cape Rivulet, Granite Beach, New River Lagoon, Deadmans Bay, Louisa River, Cox Bight and Melaleuca. The demanding 80-km (50-mi) Port Davey Track begins at Melaleuca and goes inland via Spring River, Watershed Camp and Junction Creek to Scott's Peak, offering serious tests like bottomless mud and leech-infested swamps. Those who crack can be airlifted out from the mining camp at Melaleuca, but otherwise the only way out of the spectacular but dangerous wilderness is on two feet – or feet first!

**HOW:**
On foot
**WHEN TO GO:**
December to March are the best months but can still produce cold winds and heavy rain – even snow flurries on the high tops!
**TIME IT TAKES:**
Eleven days if tramping the recommended daily sections.
**HIGHLIGHTS:**
Two rowboat crossings during the great trek – at New River Lagoon and Bathurst Narrows.
The beautiful Osmiridium Beach – check the map and look for a small path from the South Coast Track.
Staying in one of the hikers huts at Melaleuca – they may be primitive, but seem like the height of luxury after days of hard trekking.
A chance to see the rare and endangered orange-bellied parrot from the Deny King Memorial Hide near the airstrip at Melaleuca.
**YOU SHOULD KNOW:**
Some of the deadliest snakes on the planet lurk along the way – they tend to be shy but carry anti-venom in the First Aid kit, just in case!

*Louisa Bay on Tasmania's South Coast*

# Helicopter Ride over Franz Josef Glacier

**HOW:**
By helicopter and on foot
**WHEN TO GO:**
Any time of year
**TIME IT TAKES:**
A typical helicopter-dropped guided glacier walk on Franz Josef takes two hours.
**HIGHLIGHTS:**
The Lake Wombat Walk from Franz Josef township – up through lush ferns and rimu forest with abundant bird life to the lake named after the 19th-century gold prospector known as Wombat Jack.
The coastal walkway near Harihari – one of the West Coast's most scenic short hikes with great views of coastline, mountains, rivers and forests.
The classic reflection of New Zealand's highest peak, Mount Cook, in the steely waters of Lake Matheson.
**YOU SHOULD KNOW:**
The weather around the glaciers can be changeable, so walkers should be prepared for all conditions and let someone know where they intend to go.

The Franz Josef Glacier and its near neighbour, the Fox Glacier, are extraordinary natural phenomena on the West Coast of the South Island. Descending from the Southern Alps, they terminate less than 300 m (985 ft) above sea level in verdant rainforest. Classification of both glaciers and the surrounding Westland National Park as a UNESCO World Heritage Site is well deserved. Due to heavy snowfall, Franz Josef is one of the few glaciers in New Zealand that is still growing. It is around 12 km (7.5 mi) long and terminates just 19 km (12 mi) from the Tasman Sea.

The glacier is one of the country's top attractions, with the former mining township of Franz Josef catering for visitors. It is some 5 km (3 mi) from the glacier's face and from there it is possible to hike up to the glacier, either solo or as part of a guided group (basic mountaineering equipment required). However, this is a fairly demanding walk that terminates at the first icefall – a frozen near-vertical slope.

By far the most popular way of experiencing this extraordinary place is to take a helicopter tour from the heliport in Franz Josef. It is possible to take a scenic ride that shows the glacier in all its glory from the comfort of a helicopter seat, or alternatively a longer trip that is extended to include the Fox Glacier.

But most able-bodied visitors prefer to set foot on the ice – the helicopter drops its passengers between the first and second icefalls on Franz Josef Glacier, where they have a guided tour of awe-inspiring glacial landscape – a wonderland of pinnacles and brilliant blue ice with sensational views of surrounding mountains. This is undoubtedly one of the world's most spectacular glacier experiences – or perhaps the most spectacular.

*A helicopter landing on the Franz Josef Glacier*

# Walking the Kauri Coast

*In the Kauri forest*

For those who prefer to see their landscape from two feet rather than four wheels, and enjoy a bit of an adventure at the same time, walking the old Waoko Coach Road on the North Island is an ideal challenge.

This historic route is an example of pioneering road building, dating back to the early years of colonial New Zealand. The Coach Road was once the only link between Hokianga and Kaipara Harbour on the sparsely populated West Coast, and remains isolated.

It extends to 22 km (13 mi) between Taheke and Tutamoe, with the northern entry at Waima and the southern entry at Tutamoe. It is certainly the shortest route between the two points – the distance between the two ends of the Coach Road by the modern State Highway is 90 km (56 mi).

Along the way the old road passes through the Waima and Mataraua forests, which are impressively preserved examples of the kauri forests that used to cover the coastal area hereabouts. Hikers will have the forest pretty much to themselves – the route is not well marked and little used, so it is essential to take good maps, food, water and wet-weather clothing...and wear stout boots. The journey goes up hill and down dale to a maximum height of 700 m (2,300 ft) but the gradients were chosen to allow horses to pull up fully laden wagons, so are never too steep.

The weather can be unpredictable and anyone who gets caught in one of the occasionally violent rainstorms on the high plateau can head for the public shelter halfway along the Coach Road. For anyone who likes their adventures organized, there are guided trips that offer accommodation and transport along with the scenic tramp.

**HOW:**
On foot
**WHEN TO GO:**
Any time of year (but be warned – this is a high-rainfall area).
**TIME IT TAKES:**
Though the distance is not long, the route is demanding and a full day (each way) is required.
**HIGHLIGHTS:**
Taking the interesting side leg to Wekaweka Valley near Weimamaku. Spotting remnants of the original construction, like a number of hand-cut stone culverts that still function today.
Starting very early to see kiwis in their natural habitat and hear the amazing dawn chorus.
**YOU SHOULD KNOW:**
Only one vehicle ever managed to drive the Coach Road without stopping or changing horses – it carried the then Prime Minister Sir Joseph Ward in 1912.

*Paihia - the 'Jewel of the Bay of Islands'*

# Twin Coast Discovery Highway

A stunning circular route provides a superb scenic drive through New Zealand's Northland, starting at Auckland, travelling up the North Island's East Coast before returning down the enchanting West Coast. This unforgettable journey goes through Warkworth, Wellsford, Mangawhai, Waipu, Marsden, Whangarei, Kawakawa, Waitangi/Russell, Paihia, Kerikeri, Kaitaia, Hokianga, Waipoua Forest, Dargaville and back from there to Auckland. The length of the Twin Coast Discovery Highway is around 925 km (575 mi).

The first stretch up the East Coast ends at the vibrant Northland centre of Whangarei, with its wealth of activities and strong cultural aspect. Then it's on to the famous Bay of Islands area, where hundreds of coves, beaches and islands are just waiting to be found. This is also the place to explore New Zealand's heritage, especially at Waitangi (where a treaty with the Maoris was signed in 1840) and Russell, a former whaling port once known as the 'Hell Hole of the South Pacific' and one of the first European settlements in New Zealand. Don't expect flames – happily it's now a charming waterside village full of historic sites. Another mandatory stop is at the seaside settlement of Paihia, known as the 'Jewel of the Bay of Islands'.

After crossing over the northern tip with its dense subtropical forests, the next stop is Kaitaia, gateway to the far north. From here, it's possible to take a side-trip along Ninety Mile Beach or go up to the tip of New Zealand at Cape Reinga. But the Highway heads south to the beautiful harbour at Hokianga and thence down the Kauri Coast – once heavily forested before being logged out it is now rolling pastureland. After the little farming town of Dargaville, on the north shore of Kaipara Harbour, the Highway crosses back to Wellsford on the east coast route south of Whangarei.

**HOW:**
By car
**WHEN TO GO:**
Any time of year
**TIME IT TAKES:**
Don't stint on this one – allow several days (or even a week) to explore the wonderful landscape as you go.
**HIGHLIGHTS:**
First stop – the impressive hot springs of the Waiwere Thermal Reserve, near the delightful seaside town of Orewa with its golden beaches.
Chartering a boat at Opua (with or without a skipper) to explore the beaches and coves of the offshore islands.
Gumfields Historic Reserve near Kaitaia – a ghost town that hasn't been occupied since the 19th century.
A visit to Waipoua Forest near Hokianga, home to the world's tallest kauri tree – known as Tane Mahuta (God of the Forest), it is over one thousand years old.
**YOU SHOULD KNOW:**
The Stone Store in Kerikeri is the oldest European building in New Zealand, dating back to 1836.

# Whanganui River Journey

Here's a novelty – a walk that's undertaken by canoe. That's because the Whanganui River Journey is officially classified as a 'Great Walk', underlining its status as one of New Zealand's great outdoor adventure trips. The mighty Whanganui River is situated in the southwestern part of the North Island, winding down in pristine splendour from the volcanic plateau near Mount Tongariro to the Tasman Sea.

The upper reaches run through dense rainforest. In the middle reaches its rocky banks are crowded by broadleaf woodland that forms the heart of Whanganui National Park, before it passes through rolling farmland on the last stretch to the sea. The whole area is rich in Maori tradition and from the 1890s to the 1950s a riverboat service used to support Europeans who had settled along the banks.

The 145-km (90-mi) canoe trip from Taumarunui to Pipiriki is well served with huts and camping grounds, allowing for leisurely paddling that gives ample time to enjoy the awe-inspiring river and its dramatic surroundings. The landscape is young in geological terms, formed a million years ago of soft sandstone and mudstone (*papa*) from the seabed and since eroded into dramatic ridges, deep gorges, sheer cliffs and plunging waterfalls. Broadleaf forest has evolved, and distinctive tree ferns cling to steep riverbanks.

The canoeing is easy – but exciting. There are numerous rapids along the way, but these are never more demanding than Level II, making for an exhilarating passage without much risk of dangerous capsize. The whole journey is special, but the three-day section from Whakahoro through the National Park to Pipiriki is wilderness canoeing at its best, traversing tranquil stretches and rushing water, through deep gorges and past towering bluffs where the local population of feral goats often stand to look down on passing canoes.

**HOW:**
By canoe
**WHEN TO GO:**
Any time (but New Zealand weather can change rapidly and be wet and/or cold in any season).
**TIME IT TAKES:**
Around five days of gentle paddling.
**HIGHLIGHTS:**
Meeting indigenous Tieke people beside the river at Tieka Kainga (if they're there!) and taking part in a traditional *powhiri* (Maori welcoming ceremony).
A side trip up the Mangapurua Gorge to see the haunting 'Bridge to Nowhere' – built in 1935 to open up the Mangapurua Valley to settlers, abandoned when the attempt failed.
Shooting the long Paparoa Rapid just before journey's end at Pipiriki.
**YOU SHOULD KNOW:**
Don't expect the journey to be all peace and quiet – you are likely to encounter an occasional jet ski speeding along the river.

*Canoeing on the Whanganui River*

*Lake Waikaremoana*

# Lake Waikaremoana

**HOW:**
On foot
**WHEN TO GO:**
September to June
**TIME IT TAKES:**
Three to four days
**HIGHLIGHTS:**
The view from the top of towering
Panekire Bluff at the southern end of
Lake Waikaremoana.
A side trip up to Korokoro Falls – a
sight that is well worth the 30-
minute walk.
The distinctive night calls of the
protected – and slowly recovering –
brown kiwi population of the Park.
A drive up from Aniwaniwa to nearby
Lake Waikareiti after completing the
Great Walk.
**YOU SHOULD KNOW:**
The deer, pigs and possums found in
the Te Urewera National Park are
quarry species, so hikers should keep
a weather eye open for hunters.

A natural gem in the North Island's East Coast/Hawke's Bay Region is the remote and rugged Te Urewera National Park, which preserves some of the country's most magnificent scenery. Tucked away in the southwestern corner of the Park is the Lake Waikaremoana Great Walk – one of the nationally designated 'Great Walks' managed by the Department of Conservation, indicating that they are New Zealand's finest tramping tracks.

This 46-km (29-mi) hike loosely follows the lakeshore after which it is named, offering superb lake views when it strays from the water. The going is fairly easy and the Great Walk isn't that long, but the idea is to take it easy, stopping overnight and enjoying recreational opportunities such as swimming and fishing offered by Lake Waikaremoana as you go. There are five huts and campsites and prior booking is mandatory throughout the year – even in winter this is a popular trek, though the Great Walk is occasionally closed as a result of heavy snowfall that brings down overloaded tree branches to block the track.

Most hikers drive in to Aniwaniwa on the gravel-surfaced State Highway 38 that links the East Coast with Central North Island. From there, there are well-signed roads to both walk entrances, though most prefer to park securely at Aniwaniwa and take one of the regular shuttle buses or water taxis that service each end of the walk. They will also return hikers to their vehicles after completing the Great Walk.

It's possible to travel either way between Hopuruahine Suspension Bridge (north) and Onepoto (south). The route passes through a variety of terrain with varied vegetation, from the beech forest of Panekire Bluff to mixed broadleaf woodland, dense rainforest and open grassland. All harbour abundant birdlife, adding a colourful dimension to this unforgettable walk through varied and always stunning scenery.

# The Southern Scenic Route

This expedition in the South Island has a new boast – at last it's all on paved roads. But that doesn't mean travelling on tarmac all the way, as many essential sights and experiences involve exploring old-style New Zealand 'gravel tops'. Either way, the effort's worthwhile – the natural beauty of this wonderful country never ceases to amaze, but nowhere is it more impressive than along the aptly-named Southern Scenic Route.

The U-shaped journey takes you from Te Anau to Dunedin, skirting Fiordland National Park (part of the Te Wahipounamu World Heritage Site) and passing through Manapouri and Tuatapere to the coast at Te Waewae Bay, where the road swings east to Orepuki, Colac Bay and Riverton before turning south into Invercargill. Heading east again, the Route goes through Fortescue into the rugged Catlins, a sparsely populated area that contains New Zealand's southernmost tip, Slope Point. The next ports of call are Owaka and Balclutha. Here 4x4-drivers can take a detour along rough roads through Kaitangata, though the official course is along State Highway 1 to Milton and Lake Waihola. From there, the last leg crosses the Otago Coast Forest to Taieri Mouth before continuing through Brighton and Green Island to Dunedin.

The Southern Scenic Route extends to 440 km (273 mi)...and what kilometres! They connect a stunning combination of features found nowhere else in the country – rolling pastures, jagged mountains, lakes, native forest, bush rolling down to the water's edge, breathtaking ocean views, solitude and empty sandy beaches, spectacular fiords, bays and inlets, colourful fishing villages and Victorian towns. It all adds up to a scenic wonderland, but that's not all – quite apart from fabulous scenery, there are a host of interesting features and places to explore along the way, in an area famed for 'southern hospitality'.

**HOW:**
By car or 4x4
**WHEN TO GO:**
September through to May for the best weather.
**TIME IT TAKES:**
Although the Route can be driven non-stop in just ten hours, that's a criminal waste of opportunity – allow at least three days (five would be better).
**HIGHLIGHTS:**
Lake Te Anou – New Zealand's second-largest lake, mostly within the setting of Fiordland National Park.
Milford Sound – one of the natural wonders of the world.
A side trip from Invercargill to beguiling Stewart Island – a National Park where it's still possible to see kiwis in their natural habitat.
Purakaunui Falls near Owaka – a splendid multi-tiered display of cascading white water that is one of the best cataracts in New Zealand.
**YOU SHOULD KNOW:**
There are proposals to extend the Southern Scenic Route from Dunedin through Waitati to Oamaru.

*Milford Sound – one of the natural wonders of the world*

# The Classic New Zealand Wine Trail

**HOW:**
By car

**WHEN TO GO:**
Any time of year (the grape harvest takes place in March and April).

**TIME IT TAKES:**
A non-stop nine hours, or up to five leisurely days (stopping at Hastings, Martinborough, Wellington and Picton).

**HIGHLIGHTS:**
Pukaha Mount Bruce Wildlife Centre in Wairarapa – see many of New Zealand's most endangered wildlife species up close.
At least a day spent exploring the shops, restaurants and cultural delights of Wellington.

There's no respect left in the world when it comes to viticulture, as upstart newcomers come up with fine wines to compete with the great vintages produced by long-established European vineyards... and New Zealand's wine growers are high on the list of challengers. Anyone who doubts that merely has to drive the East Coast's well-signposted Classic New Zealand Wine Trail, choosing to stop at any number of wineries that welcome visitors with open arms (and opened bottles!), or finding organized collective tastings that offer the opportunity to sample wines from many different growers at the same time in the same place.

The Trail starts in Napier on the North Island and continues via Hastings, Waipukurau, Norsewood, Dannevirke, Woodville, Pahiatua, Eketahuna, Masterton and Martinborough to Wellington.

From there, the Cook Strait is crossed by ferry to Picton on the South Island, before the Trail goes on to end at Blenheim.

This 485-km (300-mi) road trip passes through 3 major wine-growing areas and five regions – Hawkes Bay, Tararua, Wairarapa, Wellington and Marlborough – that together offer the bonus of some great scenery. And many dozens of the vineyards to be visited along the way not only offer fine wines, but also excellent meals to go with them, so this can definitely be considered a self-indulgent gourmet experience.

The start of the Wine Trail takes in the Hawkes Bay wine-growing area, the heart of New Zealand's red wine country. Next comes Martinborough, the country's first great stronghold of the Pinot Noir grape. Then it's on to the sunny skies of Marlborough, where the claim to fame is undoubtedly superb Sauvignon Blanc that proves the point that – sometimes – the New World's winemakers can match or even exceed anything the Old World can put in a wine bottle. Bottoms up!

The 150-minute ferry crossing of the dramatic Cook Strait (if the weather's fine and the sea calm!).
A coastal side trip along the winding Queen Charlotte Drive from Picton to Havelock – it's like cruising the spectacular Marlborough Sounds without a boat!
**YOU SHOULD KNOW:**
Serious gastro tourists should know that there's more – specifically the Northland Food and Wine Trail, through New Zealand's fastest-growing wine region in the subtropical north.

*Black Bridge Vineyard near Hawkes Bay*

# Tararua Mountains Southern Crossing

The North Island has a mountainous spine that stretches from the East Cape to Wellington, parallel to the sea. The southernmost part is formed by the Tararua Range, spanning 80 km (50 mi) from Palmerston North to the Hutt Valley, which runs down to Wellington Harbour.

Within sight of Wellington is one of the country's best-known hiking routes – or tramping tracks, as New Zealanders prefer to say. The rugged Southern Crossing goes over the bare peaks of the southern Tararuas from Otaki Forks (reached by single-track unmade road – drive with care!), past Mount Hector and on to Kaitoke. It is no picnic stroll – New Zealand's unpredictable weather presents an ever-present and often-realized threat and there have been several fatalities over the years. But this is a challenge that will be relished – and met – by the well-prepared and experienced hiker, who will be rewarded with sensational panoramic views of mountains and sea.

There are huts along the route, providing both accommodation and bad-weather shelter. But there is only one hut – Kime Hut – on the exposed tops between the bush lines above Field and Alpha Huts, the latter pair being the usual places to overnight during the Crossing (nights one and two respectively). The climb to Field Hut is relatively short, so some hikers continue and stay at Kime Hut on their first night, though this is technically a bad-weather refuge. But the standard approach on Day One is a three-hour walk up to Field Hut, just below the bush-line, followed by a truly awe-inspiring eight-hour tramp along the tops to Alpha Hut on Day Two, with the Crossing being completed by a less dramatic eight-hour exit via the Marchant Ridge on Day Three.

A winter Southern Crossing in good snow conditions is one of the most exhilarating hikes in New Zealand (alpine equipment and crampons essential!).

*The Tararua Mountains*

**HOW:**
On foot
**WHEN TO GO:**
Any time (June to August for the possibility of a snow crossing).
**TIME IT TAKES:**
Three days
**HIGHLIGHTS:**
A magnificent panoramic view from Field Peak near Kime Hut – west to Otaki, north along the Tararua Range, east to Mount Hector and south to the Hutt Valley and Wellington.
The undulating ridge route over the humps and bumps of the aptly named Beehives.
A dramatically steep path down from Alpha Hut into the scarily named Hell's Gate.
A short side trip after fording the Tauherenikau River to see Cone Hut – one of the best examples of bush carpentry in New Zealand.
**YOU SHOULD KNOW:**
Kime Hut is named in memory of E.J. Kime, who lost his life attempting the Southern Crossing.

# Punakaiki Horseback Ride

Between the towns of Westport and Greymouth on the South Island's West Coast is Paparoa National Park, alongside State Highway 6. This is a land of extraordinary coastline, lush coastal forests, canyons and limestone cliffs, caves and underground streams.

One of the most notable features is the famous Pancake Rocks and accompanying blowholes of Dolomite Point near the small settlement of Punakaiki. The most invigorating way of appreciating these amazing natural phenomena is to see them from horseback after a ride through the heart of the scenic Punakaiki Valley. The local stables offers a variety of custom rides to suit individual requirements, but also run a popular standard short excursion that gives a wonderful flavour of Paparoa National Park's unique attractions. The horses are steady and it is possible to enjoy the trek without having previous riding experience (elementary tuition given).

It begins with an atmospheric ride into the Punakaiki Valley, fording the river and passing through native bush to view huge limestone bluffs topped with temperate rainforest. Abundant birdlife is a feature of the Park, and birds seem less cautious when the watchers are on horseback. Species to look out for are white-breasted native kereru (pigeons), the bright pukeko, inquisitive weka, paradise duck, spur-winged plover and harrier hawk.

There will be a short rest stop at a bush hut on the river flats, before returning to the coast and riding along Punakaiki Beach, with horses strolling through the seething white water at the water's edge. The climax of the ride is simply sitting and marvelling as the powerful sea crashes into the Pancake Rocks and erupts upwards through the blowholes. This expanse of water-sculpted grey rock resembles endless stacks of pancakes forming a fabulous tableau – can't be eaten, but never forgotten!

*A blowhole at Punakaiki*

**HOW:**
On horseback
**WHEN TO GO:**
Any time of year (just be sure to pick a fine day!)
**TIME IT TAKES:**
The standard ride takes around 2.5 hours.
**HIGHLIGHTS:**
Getting to (and going on from) Punakaiki along one of the most spectacular coastal highways in New Zealand, between the sea and Southern Alps.
The fascinating surge pool at Dolomite Point – known as the Devil's Cauldron, it can have a mesmeric effect.
With luck – spotting a pod of Hector's Dolphins disporting themselves just off Pancake Rocks.
**YOU SHOULD KNOW:**
The three blowholes at Dolomite Point put on their best show when there is a strong southwesterly swell at high tide.

# Abel Tasman Coast Track

**HOW:**
On foot
**WHEN TO GO:**
Any time of year.
**TIME IT TAKES:**
Total tramping time is around 17 hours, which most people spread over three to five days.
**HIGHLIGHTS:**
Crossing the dramatic 47-m (155-ft) suspension bridge across the Falls River.
A three-hour return side trip from Torrent Bay up to the Cascade Falls and main Falls River Falls (guess how the river got its name).
Strolling up the stony streambed from Torrent Bay Estuary to Cleopatra's Pool, a crystal clear wading pool beneath a rocky cascade.
A short diversion from the Coast Track near Mutton Point to Separation Point, where fur seals breed.
**YOU SHOULD KNOW:**
The National Park is named after Abel Tasman, the 17th-century Dutchman who in the 1640s was the first European navigator to reach New Zealand – whereupon Maori warriors killed four of his men.

*The Coast Track in Abel Tasman National Park*

The Abel Tasman National Park on the north shores of the South Island is in the Golden Bay area. It contains one of the country's 'Great Walks' – the Abel Tasman Coast Track. This 51-km (32-mi) hike is officially described as an 'easy tramping track', but the usual proviso about going equipped to deal with the weather's notorious mood swings holds good.

The Coast Track runs from Marahau to Wainui through wild and stunning coastal scenery, of which New Zealand has an almost indecent abundance. It crosses numerous watercourses and estuaries along the way. Rivers and streams are bridged, but some estuaries can only be crossed for an hour or two either side of low tide, and both bridges and estuaries can become impassable after heavy rain.

As the name suggests, the Coastal Track follows the sea, though often detouring inland to cross saddles that separate bays, sometimes losing sight of the sea altogether in dense forest. However, most climbs are rewarded with sensational sea and coastal views from those hard-earned vantage points. Down at sea level, there are many interesting coves to be found and estuaries to be explored, so it's best to proceed at a leisurely pace, planning an itinerary that involves overnight stops at the campsites and/or huts to be found at regular intervals (camp passes required).

The route goes from Marahau to Apple Tree Bay, Yellow Point, Torrent Bay, Anchorage Bay (hut and campsite), Bark Bay (hut and campsite), Tonga Quarry, Onetahuti Bay, Awaroa Inlet (hut and campsite), Waiharakeke Bay, Goat Bay, Skinner Point, Totaranui (major campsite complex), Anapai Bay, Mutton Cove, Whariwharangi Bay (campsite and hut – a restored farmstead) and finally on to Wanui Inlet, where transport out is available from the car park. Enjoy (and that's a promise)!

# Fiordland Long Distance Walk

In the southwestern corner of the South Island lies the country's largest National Park. Fiordland protects coastal landscape that typifies New Zealand's natural splendour. It is a wonderland of mountains, glaciers, beech forests and waterfalls that tumble into the sea – and of course the sculpted fiords that give the Park its name. It's possible to enjoy various outdoor recreational activities in Fiordland, but the best way to see the very best of the scenery is to undertake the 55-km (34-mi) waterside hike along the Milford Track from Glade Wharf to Sandfly Point (a permit is required from the visitor centre in Te Anau).

However, those experienced and super-fit individuals who look for a seriously demanding physical challenge will head straight for the Hollyford Track. They know they've got it right when they see the sign at the start of this 112-km (70-mi) return trip from the route's dead end at the sea. It reads: *'Warning: The Pyke Valley is a difficult track. It is subject to flooding and is suitable for fit, experienced trampers'*. Add to that the need to backpack camping equipment, survival gear and enough food rations for two weeks (just in case!) and the size of the task becomes apparent. After the Alabaster Hut on Lake Alabaster, this becomes a wilderness trip par excellence, travelling through wild, untamed landscape and meeting like-minded hikers along the way.

For utterly determined and super-fit adventurers who prefer not to retrace their steps and can take the pain, there is an additional 60-km (37-mi) route from the end of the Hollyford Track that returns to Alabaster Hut. The isolated and testing Pyke Route is badly marked, has only two huts and can be very dangerous if it rains hard. It's the ultimate test!

*Stunning scenery in
Fiordland National Park*

**HOW:**
On foot
**WHEN TO GO:**
September to May (winter is best avoided).
**TIME IT TAKES:**
Around six days for the Hollyford Track – add an optimistic three days for the Pyke Loop.
**HIGHLIGHTS:**
Good company and tall tramping tales when over-nighting in one of the Trail's remote but welcoming huts.
The view of Mount Madeline reflected in the lake from Alabaster Hut at sunset.
Reaching the end of the Hollyford Track at beautiful Martins Bay with its glorious beach.
A hot shower after finally returning to civilization – tired but satisfied after completing this epic hike.
**YOU SHOULD KNOW:**
Pack plenty of insect repellent – sandflies are a persistent nuisance all the way along the Hollyford Track.

*The Canterbury Plains below Mount Hutt*

# The TranzAlpine Train

**HOW:**
By train
**WHEN TO GO:**
Any time of year
**TIME IT TAKES:**
4.5 hours
**HIGHLIGHTS:**
Riding a while in the open-sided viewing carriage that really lets you feel close to – and photograph – the beautiful surroundings.
Crossing the soaring Staircase Viaduct that is a dizzying 73 m (240 ft) above the River Waimakariri.
A delicious Devonshire cream tea from the onboard café bar during the journey.
Passing the old Brunner Mine near Greymouth, site of New Zealand's worst mining disaster in 1896 – spot the old suspension bridge across the River Waimakariri to the industrial area.
**YOU SHOULD KNOW:**
It doesn't have to end at Greymouth – a Scenic Rail Pass gives access to the entire Trans Scenic network on both islands and allows independent travellers to do their own thing at their own pace.

Yes, there are indeed trains in New Zealand – and given the country's outstanding natural attributes it is hardly surprising that one of the world's great scenic railway journeys may be found here. The sleek blue TranzAlpine runs for a distance of 224 km (140 mi) right across the South Island, westwards from Christchurch on the east coast to the small town of Greymouth (and vice versa). It runs once a day, starting at 08.15, and goes through sixteen tunnels and crosses five viaducts along the way, adding to the drama of a splendid journey.

Christchurch is the South Island's largest city, offering the cosmopolitan delights of urban living. However, the comfortable and relaxing TranzAlpine with its panoramic picture windows quickly leaves all that behind. Industrial outskirts and suburbs vanish and the lush pastures and farmland of the fertile Canterbury Plains start to slide by as the train hurries towards the distant mountains.

Before long, it leaves populated parts altogether – reaching the foothills and starting the long climb through the valleys and plunging gorges of the rushing Waimakiriri River. It then continues into the Southern Alps, crossing girder bridges and going through short tunnels amidst fabulous scenery. After crossing a grassy plateau dotted with hills the TranzAlpine stops at Arthurs Pass Station, with its backdrop of misty mountains, before going through the 8.6-km (5.3–mi) Otira Tunnel and starting the descent through a deep valley, criss-crossing the Grey River and passing waterfalls and lush beech rainforest before arriving at the old-fashioned wooden station at Greymouth, gateway to Punakaiki and the rugged splendours of the west coast.

Those who don't want to go on to explore by bus or hire car can actually return to Christchurch on the TranzAlpine that same day, after an hour's stopover in Greymouth.

# Haleakala Highway

Aloha – welcome to Maui, 'The Magic Isle'! And of course there's one journey you must take – the scenic drive from Kahului along the Haleakala Highway to the top of the massive shield volcano that forms more than three-quarters of the island's mass. The road is a modern two-lane highway, but it twists and turns alarmingly on the way to the 3,055-m (10,023-ft) summit with many blind bends, and is frequently close to sheer drops. To add to the risks, wildlife and cattle often stray onto the road, especially at night.

But the effort is well rewarded – there are great views over the island and surrounding sea during the drive and the sight that awaits at the summit is awesome – a vast crater that is around 11.25 km (7 mi) long, 3.2 km (2 mi) across and 800 m (2,600 ft) deep, with steep walls and a scattering of volcanic cones around the barren interior.

Actually, despite every appearance to the contrary, the summit crater of Haleakala is not volcanic in origin. It was formed when the walls of two erosional valleys merged at the volcano's summit and is technically a depression rather than a crater, but the distinction is too fine for all but vulcanologists, so crater it shall be. The volcano is active, but has not erupted since the 1600s and is considered dormant, soon to become extinct.

Haleakala National Park surrounds the crater, much of it is wilderness. Rainforest cloaks the windward slopes of the mountain, though the dry forest that once covered the leeward side has been drastically reduced. The Park contains Kipahula Valley, one of the most complete rainforest ecosystems in Hawaii. Visitors should look out for the rare silversword plant that only grows here, a strange member of the sunflower family.

**HOW:**
By car
**WHEN TO GO:**
Any time of year
**TIME IT TAKES:**
Up to three hours to drive the Highway, depending on traffic – allow a full day to include some exploration.
**HIGHLIGHTS:**
Getting to the summit at dawn to view one of the best sunrises you'll ever see.
The fabulous view into the crater from the Kalahaku Overview below the summit.
Science City at the summit – an astrophysical complex that takes advantage of the clear, dry atmosphere and absence of serious light pollution that makes this the perfect location for ground-based telescopes.
A strenuous 15-minute hike to the top of nearby Pa Ka'oao (White Hill) for a sensational panorama.
**YOU SHOULD KNOW:**
Thrill seekers travel to the top by bus before shooting back down the mountain at high speed on a rented bicycle.

*The volcano in Haleakala National Park*

# Exploring Viti Levu

*The traditional village of Navala*

Fiji's principal island of Viti Levu, the Pacific's third largest, contains most of the Republic's population. The majority live in the towns and villages that ring the coastline, as the centre of the island is forested and largely undeveloped. Main economic activities are sugar cane production, cattle ranching, gold mining and tourism – with holidaymakers attracted by resorts along the Coral Coast in the southwest and in the locally named 'Burning West'. These offer classic Pacific ingredients of offshore islands, white sand, reefs, emerald lagoons and palm trees. But there's more to Viti Levu than that, and those who stick to the beach are missing a great opportunity to explore a fascinating island.

Viti Levu is divided by a mountain range that makes it an island of two halves – with heavy rainfall and lush green vegetation on windward slopes to the east and drier brown landscape to the west. Most visitors who do explore Viti Levu hire a car and take the paved coast road that circumnavigates the island, with side-trips down tempting tracks. The working north coast has few tourist facilities and spectacular scenery whilst the soggy east coast is characterized by extensive mangrove swamps.

For adventurous souls who like to experience the culture of the places they visit, Viti Levu's busy Sunbeam Bus network offers endless possibilities. Express buses connect the major centres and stopping buses serve most villages. It's a great way of meeting the friendly locals and seeing the 'real' Fiji – a world away from the tourist resorts. One of the most interesting journeys is through the undeveloped interior from Nausori in the southeastern corner of the island through the highlands via Vunidawa up to Tavua on the north coast, crossing Viti Levu's mountainous spine and skirting the country's highest mountain – Mount Tomanivi (formerly Mount Victoria).

# Mount Koghi Rainforest Trek

*A hiker walks through the rainforest of Mount Koghi.*

'New Caledonia – now where exactly is that?' is a common reaction when this French overseas territory is mentioned, because the scenic island chain deep in the South Pacific is something of a secret in tourist terms. It is certainly less well known than destinations like French Polynesia or Fiji, though it has all the qualifications of a Pacific paradise – offshore coral islands, blue lagoons and white-sand beaches. To that may be added a certain *je ne sais quoi* – that indefinable element of stylish living that nobody does quite so well as the French.

The island of Grand Terre is at the centre of New Caledonian life, and the capital of Nouméa has a refined ambiance with fine colonial architecture, tree-lined squares, open-air cafés, casinos, boutique shopping and fine dining the norm. But wait! There is another Grand Terre – dismissed as *la brousse* ('The Bush') by sophisticated townies.

Much of the eastern end of the island is undeveloped and remains the domain of the indigenous Kanak people. This is a land of rainforest and fabulous scenery that includes imposing landscapes, bare mountains, unusual rock formations and dramatic cliffs that plunge into the sea. Every visitor to this magical island should venture into the ancient rainforest, which has survived untouched for millions of years – ever since New Caledonia was part of the lost continent of Gondwana.

Just 20 km (12 mi) from Nouméa is one of the most accessible yet rewarding options – a trek through the rainforest of Mount Koghi with its towering trees and lush foliage, alive with tropical birds. There are a number of recognized hikes of various lengths on offer, with or without guides. When the chosen trek is over, relax at the Mount Koghi station and enjoy the splendid views down over the spectacular Dumbéa Valley, Nouméa and the lagoon.

**HOW:**
On foot
**WHEN TO GO:**
Any time of year
**TIME IT TAKES:**
Allow one day for the longest marked rainforest trek at Mount Koghi.
**HIGHLIGHTS:**
Spotting a cagou – the white flightless bird with a large crest and strange barking call that is a national symbol of New Caledonia.
A guided botanical tour from Mount Koghi station for insight into the unique local flora.
The Museum of New Caledonia in Nouméa, for an overview of the ethnology of these fascinating islands – includes a magnificent collection of Melanesian artefacts.
**YOU SHOULD KNOW:**
The New Caledonia Lagoon on the west coast is the world's largest, encircled by a 1,600-km (1,000-mi) reef that is second only to Australia's Great Barrier Reef in length.

# Rapa Nui Tour

**HOW:**
By 4x4
**WHEN TO GO:**
Any time of year
**TIME IT TAKES:**
Two days to explore the island.
**HIGHLIGHTS:**
Two Windows Cave – accessed through a narrow passage that opens out into a cavern with two tunnel-like openings that run out to the cliff face above the sea.
Relaxing on Anakena Beach with its white sand and warm turquoise – plus the Ahu Nau Nau with its seven *moai*.
Ahu Tongariki, where 15 *moai* stand in line on their platform looking out to sea – the only ones to do so.
**YOU SHOULD KNOW:**
Countless horses roam unchecked all over the island – there are nearly as many horses as people!

There can be few more recognizable images in the world than the mysterious stone heads and torsos on Chile's overseas territory of Easter Island, carved by the Rapa nui people. These monumental statues are *moai* some of which are 10m (33 ft) tall. This remote Polynesian outpost is in the southeastern Pacific Ocean and it's one of the world's most isolated inhabited islands, so relatively few people have seen those famous stones at first hand.

Most of the island – a UNESCO World Heritage Site – is protected within the Rapa Nui National Park. There are unresolved arguments concerning the origins of the islanders and the history of the iconic *moai* – it is agreed that they were produced by a Stone Age culture, painstakingly carved with basalt chisels.

After flying in to the grandly named Mataveri International Airport, it is possible to rent a 4x4 and make a comprehensive tour of Rapa Nui. This small island was deforested long before the first

Europeans visited in the 18th century and is now mainly open grassland, but there is much to see. There is a single circular road from the only settlement, Hanga Roa in the southwest of the island, but there are also many dirt roads that allow a complete tour.

It is impossible not to be deeply moved by the sense of timeless history in this extraordinary place. Most of the *moai* are located around the outside of the island, looking inwards, many of them set on beautifully constructed *ahus* (ceremonial platforms), but hundreds at various stages of construction remain where they were abandoned in the quarry at Rano Raraku. There are also caves such as Ana Tai Tangata with red-and-white bird paintings. And it's all set in an atmospheric landscape dominated by three volcanic peaks.

# The Kokoda Track

*One of the trail porters on the
Kokoda Track*

There's a little spat regarding the most famous hike in Papua New Guinea (PNG) – should it be called the Kokoda Track or the Kokoda Trail? Also in the mix are historic names such as 'The Buna Road' and 'The Overland Mail Route'. But whatever the name, the trek's the same – a demanding slog that runs in a straight line across isolated country for 60 km (37 mi). But don't assume that's just a long day's walk – the Track crosses terrain that can only be accessed on foot, demanding serious physical effort.

This single-file walking route runs from Ower's Corner in PNG's Central Province, 50 km (31 mi) east of capital Port Moresby, to Kokoda Village in Oro Province. The Track passes through rugged mountainous country of rainforest, fern jungles and streams tumbling into steep valleys, reaching the lung-testing height of 2,200 m (7,220 ft) as it skirts around the peak of Mount Bellamy. It can be hiked either way, with general agreement that Kokoda to Ower's Corner is the slightly easier direction. This is definitely the way to go for those who want a guide or porter, as there are plenty of experienced locals to choose from in Kokoda. There are rest houses along the route, some in villages and others at traditional staging points.

From Kokoda, the Track passes a number of unspoiled villages on the way to Ower's Corner – Kovolo, Hoi, Isurava, Alolo, Kagi, Efogi Creek, Menari and Naoro. Despite hostile terrain, burning days, freezing nights, intense humidity, capricious tropical rainfall and the ever-present risk of contracting endemic diseases such as malaria, the Track is a popular trekking challenge – especially for Australians. In 1942 Australian troops inflicted World War II's first military defeat on Japanese land forces along the Kokoda Track, which now has iconic status for Australians.

# Aranui Cargo Boat

There's romance in the idea of island hopping in the Pacific aboard a freighter – especially when the journey begins in Tahiti and continues through the remote and unspoiled Marquesas, French Polynesia's most spectacular island group. And that's precisely what's on offer each time the sleek white Aranui 3 sails.

Actually, the 'Freighter to Paradise' offers rather more than the usual basic amenities – she's anything but any old freighter. Although Aranui 3 is a cargo ship, she also carries up to 200 passengers who are accommodated in air-conditioned cabins. There's also a pool, bar, dining salon and small theatre complete with resident lecturer to add culture to the proceedings, so this splendid adventure might be described as slumming it French style.

Better still, creature comforts are supplemented by the extraordinary thrill of a working boat being welcomed by excited islanders everywhere she calls – her regular visit is a highlight of life in the remote villages she serves. The route encompasses two ports of call in the Tuamotu Islands and fourteen on the six inhabited Marquesas, following this course – Tahiti, Fakarava, Ua Pou, Nuku Hiva, Hiva Oa, Fatu Hiva, Hiva Oa again, Tahuata, Ua Huka, Nuku Hiva again, Ua Pou again, Rangiroa and back to Tahiti.

As the ship can only dock at a limited number of places, cargo is mostly landed by barge, while passengers take the whaleboat to put in shore time. Despite the heat and humidity, the Marquesas are magical – with jagged coastlines and soaring volcanic peaks shrouded in mist, black sand beaches and emerald lagoons, coconut groves and lush forests, bougainvillea and frangipani. And luckily the locals no longer practise cannibalism, but are incredibly friendly. The phrase 'journey of a lifetime' is often used and not always warranted, but in the case of this unique cruise it certainly seems justified.

**HOW:**
By boat
**WHEN TO GO:**
Any time – Aranui 3 sails every third week, all year round.
**TIME IT TAKES:**
The round trip takes two weeks.
**HIGHLIGHTS:**
Hearing the Aranui 3's enthusiastic 6-piece crew band in action in the top deck bar on a sultry night, with Polynesian rhythms adding immeasurably to the atmosphere.
On Hiva Oa – visiting Paul Gauguin's grave and the House of Pleasure where he spent his last years.
On Nuku Hiva – the beautiful Notre Dame Cathedral in Taiohae Village, capital of the Marquesas.
A yummy Marquesan beach feast – roast suckling pig, *poisson cru*, curried goat, breadfruit poi, taro, guava, banana *po'e*, as well as coconut, in all its shapes and forms.
**YOU SHOULD KNOW:**
For those who feel freighter trips shouldn't be too comfortable (or expensive), there are two 12-bunk dormitories near the engine room!

*Sailing close to Fatu Hiva.*

# Cruising through the Antarctic

Increasing affluence and awareness of global warming have led to the introduction – and considerable popularity – of cruises to the sixth continent and the world's last pristine wilderness. The Antarctic is undoubtedly suffering as the world warms and the great ice shelves start to disintegrate. So it may be a case of 'catch it while you can', but Antarctica remains an awe-inspiring destination.

Those who make this journey join the relatively tiny number of people who have ever visited this very special place, and are rewarded by a land of icebergs and soaring snow-covered peaks that rise from the sea, glaciers and ice shelves – a hostile land that nonetheless nurtures abundant wildlife that includes penguin colonies, giant albatrosses, six species of seals and different whales. And – perhaps best of all – no humans to spoil it!

Antarctic ships, mostly small by cruise standards, are designed to withstand severe conditions. Usually there are no more than a hundred

passengers (fewer for unusual trips). A wide variety of cruises is offered, allowing considerable personal choice for those lucky enough to be able to afford this unique (and expensive) journey. The grandest is a complete 9,650-km (6,000-mi) journey around the continent, from Argentina to New Zealand, but there are many less ambitious options, all fascinating in their own way.

Most of these specialist voyages commence in Argentina, with passengers flying in to Buenos Aires before transferring to the port of Ushuaia and joining the ship. From there, most cruises take in additional sights on the way to the Antarctic, such as Cape Horn, South Georgia, the Falkland Islands and South Shetland Islands. But the main attraction is always Antarctica, and almost all the visitors actually get to step ashore and gain first-hand experience of the white wonderland that is this magical continent first hand.

*Norwegian ships MS* Nordnorge *and MS* Nordkapp *in Paradise Bay*

**543**

# PICTURE CREDITS

4Corners Images Limited/SIME/Belenos PS 189; /SIME/Spila Riccardo 257

Alamy//H. Abernathy/ClassicStock 52; /Peter Adams Photography 313; /AEP 309; /Amanda Ahn/dbimages 437; /Mark Alberhasky 414; /Walter G. Allgöwer/imagebroker 398; /AndyLim.com 488; /Roger Antrobus 314; /Arco Images GmbH 186 inset 1, 199, 327; /Arco Images/K Loos 247; /Jon Arnold Images Ltd. 7 picture 6, 190, 261, 356, 372, 455 top, 459, 473; /Atmotu Images 485; /Auscape International Pty Ltd 515; /Stefan Auth/imagebroker 413; /AWPhoto 510; /Bill Bachman 503, 513; /Andrew Bain 475, 508; /David Ball 357; /Romain Bayle 20; /Julia Bayne/Robert Harding Picture Library Ltd. 182; /Jason Baxter 506; /Banana Pancake 527; /Suzy Bennett 2 left, 10 inset 1, 114, 416; /Best View Stock 449; /Patricia Berwick/Grapheast 6 picture 4, 400 inset 3, 423; /Walter Bibikow/Jon Arnold Images Ltd. 35, 490; /Romero Blanco 471; /Tibor Bognar 385, 428, 457; /Peter Bowater 322; /Richard Bradley 489; /Bill Byrne/Natural Section/Design Pics Inc. 39; /Frank Blackburn 223; /blickwinkel/McPHOTO/ZAD 161, 162, 174; /G P Bowater 469; /Paul Carstairs 388; /Cephas Picture Library 286; /Nicolas Chan 505; /David Cherepuschak 84; /Carolyn Clarke 8 centre left; /Gary Cook 135, 156; /Alan Copson/Jon Arnold Images Ltd. 474; /Steve Corner/Gallo Images 144; /Dennis Cox 400 inset 2, 442; /Allan Cummins 376 inset 1, 378; /Shaun Cunningham 55; /Sue Cunningham Photographic 7 picture 5, 113; /John Daniels 504; /Sigrid Dauth Stock Photography 339; /Steve Davey Photography 183; /Cameron Davidson 44; /Michael DeFreitas North America 29; /Danita Delimont 56; /Daniel Dempster Photography 62; /Deborah Dennis 154; /Adam Deschamps 145; /Deryck A Dillon 483; /Cora Edmonds/Danita Delimont 468; /Jeffery Drewitz/Cephas Picture Library 497; /Kevin Ebi 73; /Chad Ehlers 203; /Emil Enchev 365; /Javier Etcheverry 128; /eye35.com 296; /Peter Fakler 514; /Michele Falzone 478; /FAN travelstock 305; /Jose Pedro Fernandes 293; /Pavel Filatov 404; /Peter Erik Forsberg 353; /David R. Frazier Photolibrary, Inc. 22; /David Forster 270; /Danielle Gali/Jon Arnold Images Ltd. 9 bottom left; /Bertrand Gardel/Hemis.fr 28, 376 inset 2, 380; /Leslie Garland Picture Library 215; /Lyndon Giffard 517; /Gunter Gollnick/imagebroker 409; /Neil Grant 432; /Franck Guiziou/hemis.fr 429; /Darrell Gulin/Danita Delimont 111; /David W. Hamilton 9 top; /Nic Hamilton 528; /Robert Harding Picture Library Ltd. 226, 281, 292, 300, 361, 410; /Chris Harris/All Canada Photos 14; /Martin Harris 6 picture 5, 430; /Terry Harris Just Greece Photo Library 370; /Martin Harvey 146; /Jim Havey 31; /Gavin Hellier 358; /Gavin Hellier/Robert Harding Picture Library Ltd. 9 centre left above, 407, 408; /Hemis 204, 304, 349; /Brendan Hoffman 399; /Per-Andre Hoffman/LOOK Die Bildagentur der Fotografen GmbH 108; /Zach Holmes 68; /Horizon International Images Limited 530; /Peter Horree 254; /Friedrich von Horsten/Images of Africa Photobank 148; /ICSDB 288; /imagebroker 326, 334, 337, 340, 341; /imagebroker/Kurt Mobus 336; /Image Plan/Corbis Premium RF 461; /ImagesEurope 267; /Images&Stories 6 picture 2, 139 inset 1, 172, 376 inset 3, 382, 386; /ImageState 324; /IML Image Group Ltd. 366, 369, 371; /Ingolf Pompe 19 320; /INTERFOTO Pressebildagentur 76; /International Photobank 312; /Jirirezac.com 295; /Karl Johaentges/LOOK Die Bildagentur der Fotografen GmbH 446, 502; /JTB Photo Communications, Inc. 463, 464; /Jupiterimages/Agence Images 186, 276; /Michael Juno 287; /Bjanka Kadic 106; /Wolfgang Kaehler 5 picture 5, 78, 332, 405; /Bob Kavanagh 481; /Dorothy Keeler 74; /Paul Kingsley 171; /Christian Kober 484; /Art Kowalsky 479; /Hideo Kurihara 462; /Kuttig - Travel 115; /T. Lehne/Lotuseaters 451; /Gareth Leung 16; /Yadid Levy 441; /Barry Lewis 494 inset 3, 537; /Yan Liao 3 centre, 445; /Henrik Lindvall 200; /Eddie Linssen 338; /LOOK Die Bildagentur der Fotografen GmbH 288, 283, 308; /Sabine Lubenow/FAN Travelstock 329; /David Lyons 240; /Ciaran MacKechnie/Aliki Image Library 98; /Tom Mackie 222; /Jef Maion/Nomad's Land - www.maion.com 193, 205, 297; /Lois Mason 72; /Iain Masterton 406; /Pavlos Mastiki/Travel Ink 131, PCL 263, 375, 531; /Buddy Mays 7 picture 4, 11 inset 1, 65; /Neil McAllister 438; /Ross McArthur 436; /Gareth McCormack 10, 130, 248; /Roberto Meazza/IML Image Group 373; /mediacolor's 6 picture 6, 316, 318, 384; /Melba Photo Agency 289; /Mimotito/Digital Vision 51; /Brad Mitchell 53; /nagelestock.com 9 centre left below, 325, 343, 401 inset 1, 444;/Darren Niche Images 491; /David Noble Photography 265; /David Noton Photography 30, 125; /Kai-Uwe Och 198; /Ian Paterson 519; /David Pearson 400 inset 1, 434; /Doug Pearson/Jon Arnold Images Ltd. 8 top; /Bruce Percy 5 picture 1, 494, 496; /Brad Perks Lightscapes 6 picture 1, 36; /Photo Japan 458; /Photolibrary 501; /Picture Contact 291; /Javier Pierini/Photodisc 133; /Pies Specifics 118; /Nicholas Pitt 5 picture 2, 495 inset 1, 507; /Pixonnet.com 195; /Porky Pies Photography 121; /Tony Pleavin 54; /Robert Preston Photography 397; /Jürgen Priewe 450;/Neville Prosser 516; /R A Rayworth 367; /Dave Reede/All Canada Photos 18; /Magdalena Rehova 236; /Philippe Renault/Hemis.fr 21; /Bertrand Rieger/hemis.fr 401 inset 2, 493; /David Robertson 333; /Nigel Roberson 225 top; /Pep Roig 107; /Grant Rooney 427; /Galen Rowell/Mountain Light 123, 424; /Sybil Sassoon/Robert Harding Picture Library Ltd. 425; /George and Monserrate Schwartz 66; /Ian Shaw 348; /Sherab 431; /Juan Silva/Jupiter Images/Brand X 456; /Gordon Sinclair 81; /Skakanka 420; /Don Smith 526; /Don Smith/Robert Harding Picture Library Ltd. 7 picture 1, 419, 522; /Duncan Soar 470; /Joe Sohm/VisionsofAmerica/Digital Vision 37; /Joseph Sohm/Visions of America, LLC 69; /SPP Images 492; /Dave Stamboulis 418; /Will Steeley 122; /Nico Stengert/imagebroker 126; /James Sturcke 127; /Keren Su/China Span 5 picture 3, 448, 452; /Uliana Switucha 209; /tbkmedia.de 331, 352; /Tom Till 253; /Peter Titmuss 268; /Kubes Tomas/Isifa Image Service s.r.o. 173; /tompiodesign.com 354; /Peter Treanor 476; /Richard W Turner 482; /Tom Uhlman 43; /Upperhall Ltd./Robert Harding Picture Library Ltd. 422; /David Wall 494 inset 1, 494

inset 2, 500, 509, 512, 518, 524, 529; /Tony Waltham/Robert Harding Picture Library Ltd. 415, 532; /Richard Wareham Fotografie 206; /Richard Wareham/Sylvia Cordaiy Photo Library Ltd. 158; /Karl Weatherly/Digital Vision 34; /Maximilian Weinzierl 421; /Nigel Westwood 235; /Nik Wheeler 480; /Casey Williams 67; /Pete M. Wilson 110, 112; /Jochem Wijnands/Picture Contact 487; /Hans Winke 5 picture 4, 355; /Julian Worker/World Religions Photo Library 395; /WorldFoto 447; /Worldwide Picture Library 262; /Ron Yue 443, 465; /Ariadne Van Zandbergen 175; /Christian Ziegler/Danita Delimont 90; /Marek Zuk 351

Jon Arnold Images 310

Britain on View/Joe Cornish 186 inset 3, 216; /David Sellman 218

Camden Lock Market 227

John Carter 294

Corbis/Peter Adams 266; 377 inset 1, 391; /Peter Adams/JAI 186 inset 2, 350;
/Peter Adams/zefa 225 bottom, 279; /O. Alamany & E. Vicens 290; /Arctic-Images 188; /Atlantide Phototravel 251, 259, 307, 393; /Dave Bartruff 377 inset 2, 396; /Tom Bean 38; /Remi Benali 169; /Niall Benvie 17; /Walter Bibikow/JAI 179, 196; /Jonathan Blair 298; /Christophe Boisvieux 178, 411; /Demetrio Carrasco/JAI 344; /Laurie Chamberlain 8 bottom; /Dean Conger 409; /Diane Cook & Len Jenshel 10 inset 2, 96; /Gary Cook/Robert Harding World Imagery 244; /Ashley Cooper 258; /Alan Copson/JAI 280; /Rob Cousins/Robert Harding World Imagery 224; /Richard Cummins 10 inset 3, 32; /Fridmar Damm/zefa 2 Centre, 328; /Daniel J. Cox 11 inset 2, 27; /Creasource 237; /Derek Croucher 231; /Fred Derwal/Hemis 439; /epa 208; /Michele Falzone/JAI 392, 472; /Natalie Fobes 15; /Frare/Davis Photography/Brand X 85; /Franz-Marc Frei 255; /Colin Garratt/Milepost 92 ? 233; /Walter Geiersperger 330, 342, 346; /Roland Gerth/zefa 321; /Franz Gingele/Handout/epa 538; /Philippe Giraud/Goodlook Pictures 94; /Franck Guziou/Hemis 165, 264; /Blaine Harrington III 124, 374; /Martin Harvey 77, 129, 155; /Jason Hawkes 234; /Gavin Hellier/JAI 323, 359; /Gavin Hellier/Robert Harding World Imagery 284, 368; /Hemis 269, 271, 275; /Jon Hicks 9 centre, 48; /Dave G. Houser 71, 119; /Rob Howard 168; /George H. H. Huey 49, 59; /The Irish Image Collection 241, 242, 243, 246; /David Kadlubowski 50; /Wolfgang Kaehler 136, 212; /Catherine Karnow 363; /Mark Karrass 61; /Layne Kennedy 40; /Richard Klune 228, 272; /Bob Krist 6 picture 3, 82, 116, 412; /Frans Lanting 87; /Danny Lehman 89; /Michael S. Lewis 23; /Gunter Marx Photography 12; /Tim McGuire 302; /MedioImages 191; /Wolfgang Meier/zefa 194; /Gideon Mendel for The Global Fund 138 inset 2, 157; /John Miller/Robert Harding World Imagery 260; /Christopher Morris 19; /David Muench 79; /Francesc Muntada 277; /Amos Nachoum 95; /Mike Nelson/epa 184; /Kazuyoshi Nomachi 109; /Richard T. Nowitz 33; /Pat O'Hara 387; /Charles O'Rear 137, 466; /Douglas Pearson 278, 306, 315; /Sergio Pitamitz 159; /Sergio Pitamitz/zefa 371; /Bryan Pickering/Eye Ubiquitous 319; /Jose Fuste Raga 7 picture 2, 99, 282, 454, 523; /Jose Fuste Raga/zefa 303; /Bertrand Rieger 192; /Galen Rowell 93; /Martin Ruetschi/Keystone 317; /Anders Ryman 197; /Bob Sacha 97; /Chico Sánchez/epa 103; /Skyscan 229, 232; /Paul A. Souders 7 picture 3, 24, 26, 139 inset 2, 160; /Kevin Schafer 86; /Alan Schein Photography 47; /Gregor M. Schmid 187 inset 2, 210; /Michael T. Sedam 41; /Paule Seux/Hemis 180; /Frédéric Soltan/Sygma 435; /Jon Sparks 394; /Hubert Stadler 117; /George Steinmetz 390; /Michael St. Maur Sheil 256; /Hans Strand 202; /Keren Su 252; /Emilio Suetone/Hemis 289; /Tim Tadder 299; /Tim Thompson 250; /Ivan Vdovin/JAI 213; /Pablo Corral Vega 104; /Ron Watts 64; /Tony Wilson-Bligh/Papilio 152; /Tim Wimborne/Reuters 499; /Winfried Wisniewski/zefa 150; /Adam Woolfitt 364; /Alison Wright 455 bottom, 495 inset 2, 534; /Pawel Wysocki/Hemis 335; /Michael S. Yamashita 389; /Bo Zaunders 45, 46; /Jim Zuckerman 301;

Crazy Horse Memorial Foundation 57

Halim Diker/Images&Stories 381

Renate Eichert 402

Eye Ubiquitous/Bryan Pickering/Hutchison 274; /Paul Thompson 520

Getty Images/AFP 143; /Jerry Alexander 214; /Michael Busselle 60; /Dennie Cody 70; /Connie Coleman 91; /Jason Edwards 440; /David Evans/National Geographic 101, 102; /Pio Figueiroa 134; /Tim Fitzharris 63; /Michael & Patricia Fogden 138, 151; /Stuart D Franklin 3 right, 147; /Amanda Friedman 80; /Gallo Images-Lanz von Horsten 141; /Hans-Georg Gaul 142; /Gavin Hellier 170; /Paul Joynson Hicks 164; /Simeone Huber 2, 177; /Juan Mabromata/AFP 132; /Emil von Maltitz 149; /Hiroyuki Matsumoto 9 bottom right; /Natphotos 153; /Daniele Pellegrini 181; /Robert Postma 3; /Jim Richardson 219; /Whit Richardson 58; /Ellen Rooney 166; /Paul A. Zahl/National Geographic 92; /Ariadne Van Zandbergen 138 inset 3, 163

Joshua Gitlitz 129

Hedgehog House/Colin Monteath 400, 417; Andy Reisinger 521

Wendy Carlson 249

Phil Lawson 167

Jan Mariën 88

Municipality of Korsholm 207

National Geographic Society Image Collection/Otis Imboden 83

Noumea Discovery 533

James R. Page 75

Lonely Planet Images/Sune Wendelboe 176; /Woods Wheatcroft 105

Panos/Tim Dirven 362

Photolibrary Wales/Martin Barlow 221

Pictures of Britain/Dorothy Burrows 217; /Gary Hutchings 230; /John Tremaine 187 inset 1, 220;

Still Pictures/ullstein - CARO/Riedmiller 426

Alwyn Thomson 360

Travel Ink/Robin McKelvie 498

Peter Trubshaw 536

Eiki Yasuda/eyawlk60 460

(England/Scotland-UK)
- ☐ 'Lost City' (Peru) see Cuzco to Machu Picchu; Inca Trail
- ☐ Lost World of Huanchaca and the Caparú Plateau (Bolivia)
- ☐ Lötschberg (Switzerland)
- ☐ Lower Manhattan (USA)
- ☐ Lucerne to Flüelen (Switzerland)
- ☐ Luxembourg City Walk (Luxembourg)
- ☐ Lycian Way (Turkey)
- ☐ Lyse Road (Norway)

- ☐ Maclehose Trail (Hong Kong-China)
- ☐ Madrid to Barcelona (Spain)
- ☐ Maeklong Railway – Bangkok to Samut Songkhram (Thailand)
- ☐ Manali to Leh (India)
- ☐ Mani Peninsula (Greece)
- ☐ Mantario Trail (Canada)
- ☐ Mariel to Valle de Vinales (Cuba)
- ☐ Marrakech Express (Morocco)
- ☐ Mason-Dixon Trail (USA)
- ☐ Matheran Hill Railway (India)
- ☐ Matilda Highway (Australia)
- ☐ Mekong River Voyage – Huay Xai to Luang Prabang (Laos)
- ☐ Middle Rhine Valley (Germany)
- ☐ Minnesota State Highway 61 (USA)
- ☐ Mississippi Riverboat Cruise (USA)
- ☐ Mole National Park Safari (Ghana)
- ☐ Mombasa to Zanzibar Cruise (Kenya)
- ☐ Monasteries Hike (Armenia)
- ☐ Monteverde Cloud Forest (Costa Rica)
- ☐ Montserrat Rack Railway (Spain)
- ☐ Mount Cameroon Trek (Cameroon)
- ☐ Mount Elgon & Sasa River Trail (Uganda)
- ☐ Mount Kailash Kora (Tibet)
- ☐ Mount Kilamanjaro (Tanzania)
- ☐ Mount Kinabalu Trek (Malaysia)
- ☐ Mount Koghi Rainforest Trek (New Caledonia)
- ☐ Mount Sinai (Egypt) see Follow the Footsteps of Moses up Mount Sinai
- ☐ Mount Washington Cog Railway (USA)
- ☐ Mountain Pine Ridge Forest Reserve (Belize)
- ☐ Mountains of Majorca (Spain)
- ☐ Mozart Cycle Path (Austria)

- ☐ Nahanni River on a Raft (Canada)
- ☐ Namib Desert (Namibia)
- ☐ Ned Kelly Trail (Australia)
- ☐ Nestos Valley (Greece)
- ☐ Ngong Ping 360 (China)
- ☐ Ngorongoro Crater Highlands Trek (Tanzania)

- ☐ Nile River (Egypt) see Up the Nile
- ☐ Nilgiri Mountain Railway (India)
- ☐ Normandy Beaches (France)
- ☐ Norsjö Cable-Way (Sweden)
- ☐ North Cascades Scenic Highway (USA)
- ☐ North Holland's Historic Triangle (The Netherlands)
- ☐ North Mayo Drive (Eire)
- ☐ North Yorkshire Moors Railway (England-UK)
- ☐ Northern Loop (Argentina)
- ☐ Nxai Pan Old Cattle Trek (Botswana)

- ☐ Oases of the Great Sand Sea (Egypt)
- ☐ Oaxaca City to Puerto Angel (Mexico)
- ☐ Offa's Dyke Path (England/Wales-UK)
- ☐ Okavanga Delta (Botswana)
- ☐ Old King's Highway (USA) see Cape Cod Scenic Route 6A
- ☐ Old Spanish Trail (USA)
- ☐ Oregon Coast Trail (OCT-USA)
- ☐ Orient Express see Venice Simplon-Orient-Express
- ☐ Orkhon Valley (Mongolia)
- ☐ Osaka to Hiroshima (Japan) see Shinkansen
- ☐ Over the Öresund Bridge (Denmark)
- ☐ Overland Mail Route (Papua New Guinea) see Kokoda Track

- ☐ Pacific Crest Trail (USA)
- ☐ Paddle Steamer on the Murray River (Australia)
- ☐ Padjelanta Trail (Sweden)
- ☐ Palace on Wheels (India)
- ☐ Pamir Highway (Tajikistan)
- ☐ Panama Canal and Lake Gutan (Panama)
- ☐ Pan-American Highway (USA)
- ☐ Pantanal Fazendas (Brazil)
- ☐ Paris (France)
- ☐ Patras to Messolonghi (Greece)
- ☐ 'Pearl of the Tien Shan Mountains' (Kyrgyzstan) see Lake Issyk-Kul Trek
- ☐ Pearl River Twilight Cruise (China)
- ☐ Pearl Road (Japan)
- ☐ Peddlar's Way & Norfolk Coast Path ('England-UK)
- ☐ Pembrokeshire Coast Path (Wales-UK)
- ☐ Penang Ferry (Malaysia)
- ☐ Peneda-Gerês National Park (Portugal)
- ☐ Perfume River Dragon Boat Trip (Vietnam)
- ☐ Perth to Adelaide Road Trip (Australia)
- ☐ Peter Norbeck Scenic Byway (USA)
- ☐ Petra Monastery Hike (Yemen)
- ☐ Pico Duarte (Dominican Republic)
- ☐ Pinnacle's Desert Walk (Australia)
- ☐ 'Pinochet's Folly' (Chile) see Carretera Austral
- ☐ Piraeus to Santorini Ferry (Greece)
- ☐ Port Phillip Bay (Australia)

- ☐ Post Boat Route across the Kvarken (Finland)
- ☐ Poznan to Warsaw Scenic Road (Poland)
- ☐ Prespa Lakes from Kastoria (Greece)
- ☐ P'tit Train du Nord (Canada)
- ☐ Puerto Princesa Subterranean River Trip (Philippines)
- ☐ Punakaiki Horseback Ride (New Zealand)
- ☐ Purnululu National Park (Australia)
- ☐ Puszta (Hungary) see Hortobagy Great Plains
- ☐ Pyrenean Haute Route (France)

- ☐ Raft to Omo River (Ethiopia)
- ☐ Rafting down the Drava River (Slovenia)
- ☐ Rafting Nine Bends River (China)
- ☐ Rafting the Upano River (Ecuador)
- ☐ Railway Trail (Bermuda)
- ☐ Rapa Nui Tour (Easter Island)
- ☐ Rapids of the Noguera Pallaresa River (Spain)
- ☐ Rasende Roland (Germany)
- ☐ Raumabanen Railway (Norway)
- ☐ Rennsteig Trail (Germany)
- ☐ Revolutionary Trail in the Sierra Maestra (Cuba)
- ☐ Rhône Cruise (France)
- ☐ Rice Terrace Hike (Philippines)
- ☐ Ridgeway National Trail (England-UK)
- ☐ Rift Road Trip (Morocco)
- ☐ Rim of the World Drive (USA)
- ☐ Ring of Kerry (Eire)
- ☐ Rio Grande (USA)
- ☐ Rio Sonora (Mexico)
- ☐ Rio Usumacinta (Mexico)
- ☐ River Charente Cruise (France)
- ☐ River Dnieper to the Black Sea (Ukraine)
- ☐ River Lena Cruise (Russian Federation)
- ☐ Riviera Corniches (France)
- ☐ Riviera Day Train (Italy)
- ☐ The Road (Saba)
- ☐ Robben Island Ferry (South Africa)
- ☐ Rogue River Trail (USA)
- ☐ 'Romantic Route' (Brazil) see Rota Romantica
- ☐ Romantic Road (Germany)
- ☐ Romantic Road (Japan)
- ☐ Rome to Catania (Italy)
- ☐ Roof of the World Express (Tibet)
- ☐ Roosevelt Island Tramway (USA)
- ☐ Roraima Tepui Trek (Venezuela)
- ☐ Rota Romantica (Brazil)
- ☐ Route 66 (USA) see Historic Route 66
- ☐ Route Napoléon (France)
- ☐ Route National (France) see Route Napoléon
- ☐ Route of Emperors and Kings (Germany)
- ☐ Royal Road of the Interior (El Camino Real de Tierra Adentro) (USA) see El Camino Real Historic Trail
- ☐ Rub'al Khali – The Empty Quarter (Oman)